A Guide to the Leading Reporting Platform

Applied Microsoft SQL Server 2008 Reporting Services

Teo Lachev

Prologika Press

Applied Microsoft SQL Server 2008 Reporting Services

Published by:
Prologika Press
info@prologika.com
http://www.prologika.com

Printed in the United States of America

ISBN 13, print edition	978-0-9766353-1-4
ISBN 10, print edition	0-9766353-1-3
First printing	2008

Author	*Teo Lachev*
Technical editor	*Heidi Steen*
Copyeditor	*Deborah Dinzes*
Technical reviewers	*Alexzander Nepomnjashiy*
	Andy Potter
Cover design	*Zamir Creations*

The manuscript of this book was prepared using Microsoft Word 2007. Screenshots were captured using TechSmith SnagIt 8.2. The video demos were captured using TechSmith Camtasia Studio 5.1. Diagrams were produced with Microsoft Visio 2007.

contents

preface

Reporting Services is cool! "What's so cool about a technology so mundane?" you may ask. To me, the most exciting part about Reporting Services is that it can bring dormant data back to life easily. To this extent, you can think of Reporting Services as the magic wand on the book front cover. With a few flicks (OK, mouse clicks), you can turn raw data into a cool report that conveys an important message. Another aspect I like about Reporting Services is its flexible and open architecture which helped me implement solutions where other "mature" reporting tools fell short.

I have to admit I've always been fascinated with technologies that facilitate data management and analytics. When I studied database systems in my university years, data could fit on a 360K floppy diskette, so it wasn't that difficult to make sense of it. Today, it's not uncommon for organizations to accumulate gigabytes, if not terabytes, of data. So, the real issue becomes not capturing the data but presenting it efficiently in a format that is easy to digest.

This is where Microsoft Reporting Services and the Microsoft Business Intelligence Platform could help. By letting you organize your data assets and build an efficient reporting layer on top of them, they help you to get *out* what was put *in*. As a result, you spend less time searching for information and have more time to act upon it and make decisions.

Over the past four years, I've worked with Reporting Services extensively and designed business intelligence solutions that used Reporting Services in one form or another. I've been also heavily involved in helping the technical communities to get up to speed with this technology through discussion lists, events, training classes, and publications. It was evident that there are a myriad of ways in which report authors, database administrators, and developers are using Reporting Services. Many of you are eager to push this technology to its limits and customize it to your needs.

I decided to write this book to share with you the knowledge I harvested from my work with Reporting Services and help you use it efficiently. As its name suggests, the main objective of *Applied Microsoft SQL Server 2008 Reporting Services* is to teach you the practical skills you need to implement Reporting Services-centric business intelligence solutions. I worked closely with the Reporting Services team to provide an authoritative yet independent view of the technology. OK, I'll admit my little claim to fame… I secretly hope that I contributed at least a tiny bit to what is now Reporting Services.

Although this book is designed as a comprehensive guide to Reporting Services, it is likely that you may have questions that go beyond what the book covers. As with my previous books, I am committed to help my readers with book-related questions via the book discussion list on my personal web site www.prologika.com.

In archeology, the Rosetta Stone was the key that solved the mysteries of Egyptian hieroglyphics. I hope that Reporting Services, code-named Rosetta, will give you the tool you need to unlock the secret of data and unleash the power hidden within. Happy reporting!

Teo Lachev
Atlanta, GA

acknowledgements

Writing this book has been a lot of fun and a lot of work. It would not have been a reality without the help of many people to whom I am thankful. First and foremost, I would like to thank my family for their ongoing support. They had to tolerate my long absence and put up with more than they had to. To my family I owe my greatest thanks.

Here is how my 5-year old son, Martin, and 8-year old daughter, Maya, portray their absent father during his book writing project. I can assure you that I wasn't smiling all the time...

I've been privileged to enjoy close relationships with the Reporting Services team for the past five years. If it wasn't for their support, this book wouldn't have been a reality. Not only did they not mind my constant pestering but were even more eager to help me understand the "dark side" of Reporting Services! Special thanks to Alex Gorev, Brian Hartman, Brian Welcker, Chris Baldwin, Prash Shirolkar, and Robert Bruckner for reviewing selected parts of the book and ensuring that it is as technically accurate as possible.

Writing a technical book while the product is still in development is like trying to hit a moving target because the technology is constantly evolving. Kudos to my technical reviewer, Alexzander Nepomnjashiy (Alex), for meticulously reviewing the manuscript consistency and code accuracy. As with my previous book, Alex helped me tremendously in transitioning the book from the early builds of Reporting Services to its final release. Thanks to Andy Potter from Solid Quality Mentors for reviewing chapter 17 "Integrating with SharePoint".

Many thanks to my fellow Reporting Services MVP, Bruce Loehle-Conger, for reading the book manuscript and providing valuable feedback and encouragement. Bruce helped me improve the book quality by sharing his extensive experience and suggestions for improvement.

Thanks to my editor, Heidi Steen, from the SQL Server User Education team for not losing faith that my incoherent readings could turn into something readable. Thank you for taking an extra mile and going beyond just checking the grammar. Your commitment and work was outstanding! My copyeditor, Deborah Dinzes, did a great job in polishing the manuscript. Thank you for delivering the final edit on time despite the brutal schedule!

Finally, thank *you* for purchasing this book! I sincerely hope that you will find it as enjoyable to read as it has been for me to write!

about the book

The book doesn't assume any prior experience with Microsoft Reporting Services. It is designed as an easy-to-follow guide for navigating safely the most intricate aspects of the technology.

Part 1, *Introduction*, provides a panoramic overview of Microsoft SQL Server 2008 Reporting Services. Chapter1, *Introducing Reporting Services*, discusses the Reporting Services feature set and how it fits into the Microsoft Business Intelligence Platform. Chapter 2, *Installing Reporting Services*, explains how to install and upgrade Reporting Services from previous releases.

Part 2, *The Report Designer*, teaches report authors how to design reports with Report Designer, which is Microsoft's premium report authoring tool. Chapter 3, *Report Design Fundamentals*, introduces you to the report design tools and walks you through the steps of designing basic reports. In chapter 4, *Designing Data Access*, you'll learn different ways to integrate Reporting Services with a variety of data sources. Chapter 5, *Designing Tablix Reports*, shows you how to leverage the innovative Tablix region to author tabular, crosstab, and free-form reports. In chapter 6, *Designing for Data Visualization*, you'll be introduced to the new charting enhancements that can help you jazz up your reports with charts and gauges. Chapter 7, *Advanced Report Designer*, demonstrates how you can enhance your reports with custom code and provides practical solutions to common design challenges.

Part 3, *The Report Builder*, shows you how to empower business users to create their own reports. Chapter 8 gives you the necessary technical background to build Report Builder models that abstract data sources. In chapter 9, *Authoring Ad Hoc Reports*, you'll use Report Builder client to author simple reports from these models. Chapter 10, *Previewing Report Builder 2.0*, provides a preview of the next-generation designer for ad hoc reporting.

Part 4, *Management*, teaches report administrators the ropes of managing the report server. Chapter 11, *Management Fundamentals*, introduces you to common management tasks, including managing and securing the report catalog. Chapter 12, *Managing Report Execution and Subscriptions*, shows you how to optimize report execution and deliver reports via subscriptions. In chapter 13, *Advanced Report Management*, you'll learn how to program management tasks and monitor the report server.

Part 5, *Integration*, shows developers how to integrate Reporting Services with external applications. Chapter 14, *Integration Fundamentals*, explains the two options for integrating Reporting Services—URL access and Web service. Chapter 15, *Reporting for .NET Clients*, provides code examples for report-enabling Windows Forms and web-based applications. Chapter 16, *Integrating with Analysis Services*, shows you how to implement OLAP reports. In chapter 17, *Integrating with SharePoint*, you'll learn how to integrate Reporting Services with SharePoint to build dashboard pages and report portals.

Part 6, *Extensibility*, teaches developers how to extend Reporting Services to meet more advanced reporting requirements. In chapter 18, *Extending Data Access*, you'll implement a custom data extension to bind reports to application datasets. Chapter 19, *Customizing Security*, shows you how to replace the default Windows-based security with custom solution for authenticating and authorizing users. Chapter 20, *Extending Report Delivery*, demonstrates extending the report server to deliver reports to a Web service. In chapter 21, *Building Custom Report Items*, you'll implement a custom progress tracker report item. Finally, chapter 22, *Customizing Report Definitions*, shows you how to change the report definition at run time.

source code

Table 1 lists the software requirements to run all the code samples included in the book.

Table 1 Software requirements for working with the book source code

Software	Purpose
SQL Server 2008 Developer or Enterprise Edition	Both editions are feature-complete. The only difference is that the Developer Edition is not licensed for production deployments.
Microsoft Visual Studio 2008	To work with the code samples in chapters 7, 13, 14, 15, 18, 19, 20, 21, and 22.
Microsoft SharePoint 3.0	To implement SharePoint integration in chapter 17.
Microsoft Excel 2007	To browse the Adventure Works cube in chapter 16.
Microsoft Silverlight 2.0 Beta 1 and Expression Blend 2.5	To work with the Silverlight Reporter demo in chapter 15.

The code samples can be downloaded from the book web page at *http://prologika.com/Books/-0976635313/Book.aspx*. After downloading the zip file, extract it to any folder on your hard drive and you'll see a folder for each chapter that contains the source code for that chapter.

NOTE The data source settings of the sample reports in this book assume that all SQL Server 2008 services are installed on the default instance (MSSQLSERVER) on your local computer. If your setup is different, such as you installed SQL Server or a named instance, you need to update all data sources to reflect your specific connection details.

Installing the AdventureWorks databases

The book sample reports use the AdventureWorks2008 and AdventureWorksDW2008 databases, which are available on codeplex.com. After installing SQL Server 2008 (see chapter 2), download and install the AdventureWorks databases as follows:

1. Open the Sample Databases for Microsoft SQL Server 2008 webpage (http://tinyurl.com/5j25lx).
2. Click the appropriate installer link to download and install the AdventureWorks2008 database for the targeted hardware platform. For example, to install the 32-bit version of the AdventureWorks2008 database, click SQL2008.AdventureWorks_OLTP_DB_v2008.x86.msi.By default, the setup program installs the database backup file (AdventureWorks2008.BAK) in \Program Files\Microsoft SQL Server\100\Tools\Samples\AdventureWorks 2008 OLTP\.
3. On the Microsoft SQL Server Product Samples Database webpage for SQL Server 2008, click the appropriate installer link to download and install the AdventureWorksDW2008 database based on the targeted hardware platform. For example, to install the 32-bit version of AdventureWorksDW2008, click the SQL2008.AdventureWorks_DW_BI_v2008.x86.msi link. By default, the setup program installs the database backup file (AdventureWorksDW2008.BAK) in the \Program Files\Microsoft SQL Server\100\Tools\Samples\AdventureWorks 2008 Data Warehouse folder.
4. Open the SQL Server 2008 Database Product Samples webpage (http://www.codeplex.com/-MSFTDBProdSamples). Scroll down to the bottom of the page and you will see Details links

next the AdventureWorks2008 and AdventureWorksDW2008 databases. Follow the instructions in the Details page for each database to restore the database backup file.

The Report Builder chapters (8 and 9) use the SQL Server 2005 AdventureWorks database, which you can install as follows:

5. Go to the SQL Server 2005 SP2a webpage (http://tinyurl.com/2xzkf)7and click the AdventureWorksDB.msi link to install the AdventureWorks database.
6. Open SQL Server Management Studio and connect to your SQL Server instance.
7. In Object Explorer, expand the Databases folder. You should see AdventureWorks, AdventureWorks2008 and AdventureWorksDW2008 databases, as shown below:

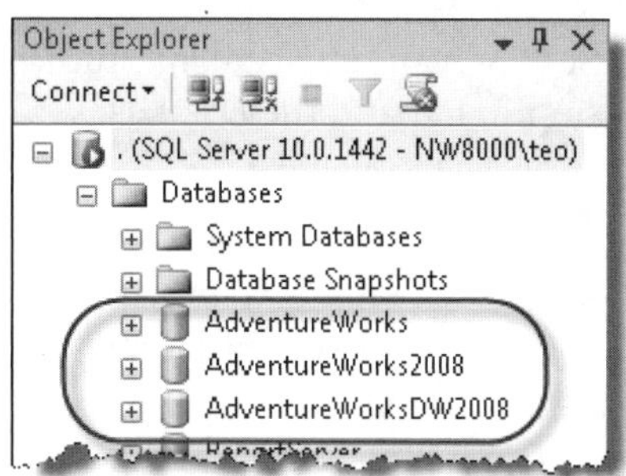

SQL Server Management Studio shows the SQL Server databases you need to run the report samples.

Installing the AdventureWorks reports

Several report management practices reference the Adventure Works sample reports provided by Microsoft. Follow these steps to install these reports:

1. Navigate to the AdventureWorks Sample Reports folder in the book source code and double-click the AdventureWorks Sample Reports.sln solution file to open it in the SQL Server 2008 Business Intelligence Studio.
2. In Solution Explorer, right-click the AdventureWorks Sample Reports project node and click Properties.
3. In the Property Pages dialog box, verify that the default TargetServerURL setting (http://localhost/reportserver) matches your Report Server Web service URL. If you are not sure what the Report Server Web service URL is, open Reporting Services Configuration Manager from the Microsoft SQL Server 2008 ⇨ Configuration Tools program group and click the Web Service URL tab. Update the TargetServerURL setting if needed.
4. Close the Property Pages dialog box. In the Solution Explorer, right-click the AdventureWorks Sample Reports project node and click Deploy to deploy the reports to the report server.

NOTE Microsoft is working on an updated version of the AdventureWorks Sample Reports that use the AdventureWorks2008 database. The updated samples will be available for download on http://www.codeplex.com/-MSFTRSProdSamples. The updated reports should be able to run side by side with the sample reports included in the book source code. If you decide to use the SQL Server 2008 samples, you may find that the practice steps differ somewhat from your setup. For example, the data source name will be AdventureWorks2008 instead of AdventureWorks. To avoid this, use the AdventureWorks Sample Reports project included in the book source code.

Installing the AdventureWorks cube

Several report samples integrate with the Adventure Works Analysis Services cube. Follow these steps to install the cube:

1. When you install the AdventureWorksDW2008 database, the setup program installs the cube source code in the \Program Files\Microsoft SQL Server\100\Tools\Samples\AdventureWorks 2008 Analysis Services Project\ folder. Below this folder, you will find Standard and Enterprise folders. Use the appropriate folder depending on the SQL Server 2008 edition you have.
2. Open the Adventure Works solution (Adventure Works.sln) in Business Intelligence Development Studio. In the Solution Explorer, right-click the project node and choose Properties.
3. In the Property Pages dialog box, click the Deployment tab. In the Server field, enter the Analysis Services instance to which the project will be deployed, such as *localhost*, if you have installed Analysis Services on the default instance on your local server. Click OK.
4. In Solution Explorer, right-click the project node and click Deploy to deploy the project.
5. To verify that the Adventure Works cube is operational, open SQL Server Management Studio and connect to the Analysis Services instance you specified in step 3. Expand the Databases folder. You should see the Adventure Works DW **2008** Analysis Services database.

About the video demos

Report authoring is UI-intensive. I captured video demos to help you stay on track when a picture is worth more than a thousand words. The video demos are bonus material to the book. The play symbol (▶) next to a section title indicates that there is a video demo for this section. Video demos are provided for a subset of the report authoring practices and are not intended to exactly match the practice steps included in the book.

The book web page (*http://prologika.com/Books/0976635313/Book.aspx*) provides a link to the video demos, which you can view online.

Reporting errors

This book has no bugs! We both know that this statement is overambitious to say the least. Please submit bug reports to the book discussion list on www.prologika.com. Confirmed bugs and inaccuracies will be published in the book errata document. A link to the errata document is provided in the book web page.

about the author

Teo Lachev is a developer, author, and mentor who has been working with Reporting Services since its early beta days. He currently works as a technical architect for a leading financial institution where he designs and implements Business Intelligence solutions for the banking industry. Teo has been a Microsoft SQL Server MVP since 2004 for his contribution to the technical community. Teo is also a Microsoft Certified Solution Developer (MCSD) and Microsoft Certified Trainer (MCT). He is the author of *Applied Microsoft Analysis Services 2005*.

Your purchase of *Applied Microsoft SQL Server 2008 Reporting Services* includes free access to a web forum sponsored by the author, where you can make comments about the book, ask book-related technical questions, and receive help from the author and the community. The author is not committed to a specific amount of participation or successful resolution of the questions posted and his participation remains entirely voluntary. You can subscribe to the forum from the author's personal website *www.prologika.com*.

Introduction

If you are new to Reporting Services, welcome! This part of the book provides the essential fundamentals to introduce you to Reporting Services and help you understand its capabilities and features. Veteran Reporting Services users should benefit from it too as it discusses important enhancements in the product architecture and how to upgrade from previous versions.

Now in its third release, Reporting Services has evolved into a mature and versatile reporting tool. Organizations can leverage Reporting Services and the Microsoft Business Intelligence Platform to implement a variety of reporting solutions, including enterprise reporting, Internet reporting, ad hoc reporting, and embedding reports in custom applications.

Reporting Services 2008 brings important tool and architectural changes. Microsoft has redesigned Report Designer to make it more powerful and intuitive. A brand new tablix region was introduced to help you create flexible tabular, crosstab, and free-form reports. The chart region has undergone a complete overhaul to add more features and chart types. The textbox report item has been extended to support multiple bands of text and rich formatting. On the architecture side of things, Reporting Services is no longer dependent on IIS. Microsoft has redesigned the report processing and rendering engine to make Reporting Services more scalable and feature-rich.

Reporting Services 2008 ships as a feature component of SQL Server 2008. Chapter 2 provides the necessary background to help you perform a new installation of Reporting Services or upgrade from previous releases.

Chapter 1

Introducing Reporting Services

I like to think about reporting as the last and most important stage of the long and arduous process for collecting, storing, transforming, and manipulating data. It is the presentation layer business users rely on to quickly make sense of the mountains of data that piles up every day. If you think of reporting like I do, then you can probably agree that a report is much more than a pretty face to data. Reports play a critical role in helping a company understand its customers, markets, and performance.

Now in its third major release, Microsoft SQL Server 2008 Reporting Services has evolved into a sophisticated reporting platform that gives information workers a powerful means to present and analyze data consistently, quickly, and reliably. Reporting Services is the "magic wand" you need to turn enterprise data into meaningful reports that can be shared easily with co-workers, customers, and partners.

This chapter gives you a panoramic view of Microsoft SQL Server 2008 Reporting Services. I'll start by introducing you to this tool and explaining how it fits into the Microsoft Business Intelligence stack. Then, I'll take you on a tour of the Reporting Services features and tools. I'll help you understand the product architecture and programming interfaces so that you have the necessary technical background to tackle the more advanced features later on in this book. Finally, I'll walk you through a hands-on lab that will demonstrate how you can use Reporting Services to author, manage, and deliver reports.

1.1 Understanding Reporting Services

The processes of collecting and analyzing information assets to derive knowledge from data are typically referred to as business intelligence, or BI for short. Simply put, Reporting Services can be viewed as a business intelligence tool for authoring, managing, and delivering reports.

DEFINITION Reporting Services is a server-based reporting platform for the creation, management, and delivery of standard and ad hoc reports. Reporting Services ships as a component of SQL Server.

There are several terms in this definition that may be unfamiliar to readers who are new to Reporting Services, so let's take a closer look at each part of the definition. First, Reporting Services is server-based. This means that you install Reporting Services on a dedicated server which handles report requests from clients. A client can be an end user using a browser to view a report or an application that requests reports from the server.

Reporting Services is also a platform, which means you can build custom solutions, applications, and extensions on top of a programmatic layer. All of the tools and applications that

Reporting Services provides out of the box are created using public APIs that are available to anyone. Reporting Services includes tools to let developers, power users, and business users author reports. Deployed reports can be centrally managed on the server. Finally, end users can view the reports on demand or via subscriptions.

1.1.1 Understanding Reporting Services Reports

Now, let's clarify what a Reporting Services report really is. At this point, you might be thinking, "Come on, everybody knows what a report is." Indeed, reports are so common that Wikipedia doesn't even include a definition of a software report. However, not all reports are equal, so it makes sense to clarify this term right from the start.

What is a Reporting Services report?
Here is my unassuming definition of a Reporting Services report.

DEFINITION A Reporting Services report is a predefined, read-only, system-generated view of data which is human readable and addresses a specific data analytics need.

What a mouthful of a definition! Let's parse it one bit at the time. First, Reporting Services reports have a predefined schema. What I mean by this is that the report presentation is always bound to the report definition that the author has designed. True, some export formats (HTML for instance) support interactive features, such as drilling through a field to jump to another report, conditional visibility to expand hidden sections, interactive sorting, and so on. However, for the most part, the report presentation is fixed. To modify it, you need to open the report in design mode, make the required layout changes, and re-deploy the report.

Reporting Services reports contain read-only data. This means that Reporting Services doesn't natively support writing back to the database to update the underlying data. For example, after reviewing a report and realizing that a sales figure is wrong, you cannot update it directly from within the report.

Reporting Services reports are system-generated. When you request a report, Reporting Services extracts data from the data source, combines data with the report layout, and renders the report. Unlike Excel, it is almost never possible to reference arbitrary cells in a Reporting Services report. For example, you cannot reference the grand total amount in one section from another section in the report. This is because in Reporting Services the "cells" on the report are not known at design time. Remember this when you are asked to convert an Excel report to Reporting Services. This may not be easy because these two tools are vastly different.

Finally, Reporting Services reports must be human readable and address a specific data analytics need. For example, a business analyst may need to analyze how product sales change over time. To meet this requirement, the report author can design a standard report that extracts data from the sales system and presents it in a human readable form, such as in a table or a chart.

1.1.2 Why Use Reporting Services?

Reporting Services can help you implement a wide variety of reporting scenarios. For example, Reporting Services can address two of the most pervasive reporting needs in every organization: standard reporting and ad hoc reporting.

Standard reporting

A standard report is a predefined (canned) report whose layout is not meant to be changed by end users. Sales by Product marketing reports and Balance Sheet financial reports are good examples of standard reports. Standard reports can be rather sophisticated. For instance, the Adventure Works Sales report (see Figure 1.1) features a standard report that has multiple table and chart sections.

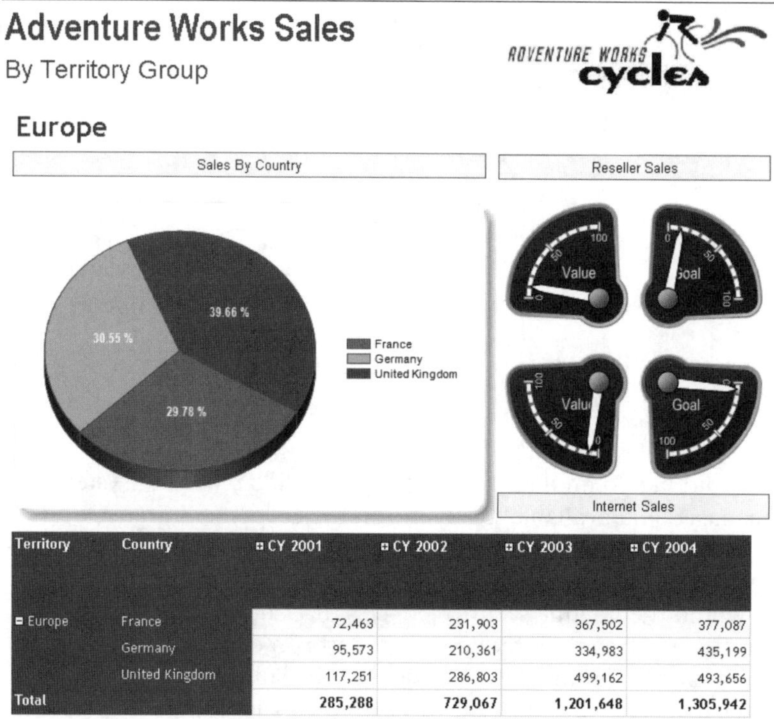

Territory	Country	CY 2001	CY 2002	CY 2003	CY 2004
Europe	France	72,463	231,903	367,502	377,087
	Germany	95,573	210,361	334,983	435,199
	United Kingdom	117,251	286,803	499,162	493,656
Total		**285,288**	**729,067**	**1,201,648**	**1,305,942**

Figure 1.1 Reporting Services reports can display multiple sections side by side and each section can be bound to a different dataset.

Standard reports are usually authored by developers and power users who are familiar with the database schema and know how to create queries and expressions. Standard reports are usually deployed to a web portal, such as a SharePoint portal, or ship with custom applications.

Ad hoc reporting

Ad hoc reporting empowers business users to create their own reports. Since standard reports take significant time and effort to produce, many organizations are looking for ways to let end users create specific, customized reports.

Reporting Services provides ad hoc reporting features that address the business reporting needs of less technically savvy users. End users can build simple reports without prior knowledge of the underlying database schema or query language. For example, Figure 1.2 shows a crosstab report which I authored quickly using the Report Builder 1.0 component of Reporting Services.

This report shows the sales order data broken down by product category on rows and by years on columns. In comparison with standard reports, ad hoc reports typically have simpler report layouts. End users would typically author such reports for private use, although Reporting Services lets users share reports if needed.

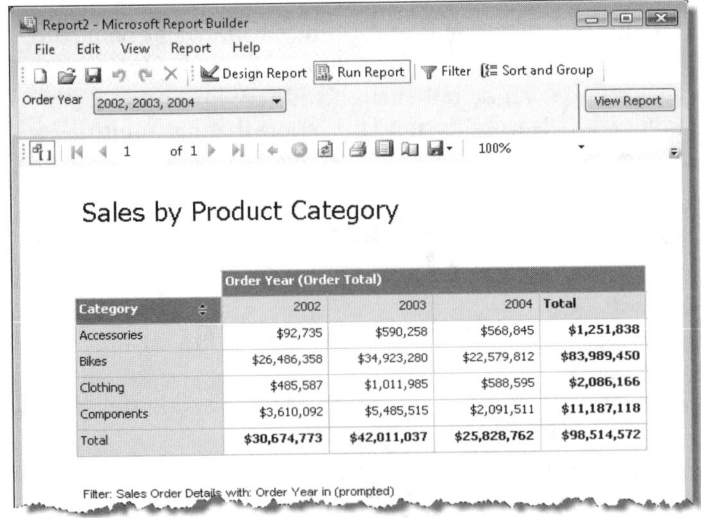

	Order Year (Order Total)			
Category	2002	2003	2004	Total
Accessories	$92,735	$590,258	$568,845	**$1,251,838**
Bikes	$26,486,358	$34,923,280	$22,579,812	**$83,989,450**
Clothing	$485,587	$1,011,985	$588,595	**$2,086,166**
Components	$3,610,092	$5,485,515	$2,091,511	**$11,187,118**
Total	**$30,674,773**	**$42,011,037**	**$25,828,762**	**$98,514,572**

Figure 1.2 Business users can create ad hoc reports that address their specific data analytics needs.

Besides standard and ad hoc reporting, Reporting Services can help you implement other reporting solutions. Let's mention some of the most popular ones.

Enterprise reporting

Suppose that your company would like to implement an enterprise-wide reporting system where reports are centrally managed and available to anyone on the corporate intranet who is authorized to view them. Because Reporting Services is a server-based platform, report authors can deploy reports to a designated report server.

The report administrator would then define security policies that enforce restricted access to these reports as needed. Authorized users can request the reports on demand, analyze their data, and make decisions. Users can also automate report delivery by subscribing to reports on a schedule. For example, a sales manager can subscribe to a Monthly Sales report to receive it on a monthly basis via e-mail. When the schedule event occurs, Reporting Services processes and e-mails the report to the sales manager.

Digital dashboards and portals

Many organizations build digital dashboards and web-based portals to gauge business performance and let users collaborate online. Information workers can use Microsoft Windows SharePoint Services or Microsoft Office SharePoint Server to assemble such solutions by creating personalized dashboard pages consisting of web parts.

Suppose that your organization would like to deploy strategic reports to the corporate SharePoint-based portal. You can configure Reporting Services to integrate seamlessly with SharePoint. From an end-user perspective, reports appear just like any other documents deployed to the portal. For example, users can upload a report, check the report in or out, version reports, change report parameters and execution properties, and so on. Users can click a report to view the report on demand.

With a few clicks, you can assemble a SharePoint dashboard page with multiple report views. For example, Figure 1.3 shows a dashboard page that displays two reports side-by-side. The left report shows the company sales as a chart. The right report shows the value of the Product Gross Profit Margin KPI. Dashboard pages are very powerful as they help the executive management team quickly understand the company business by just glancing at the page.

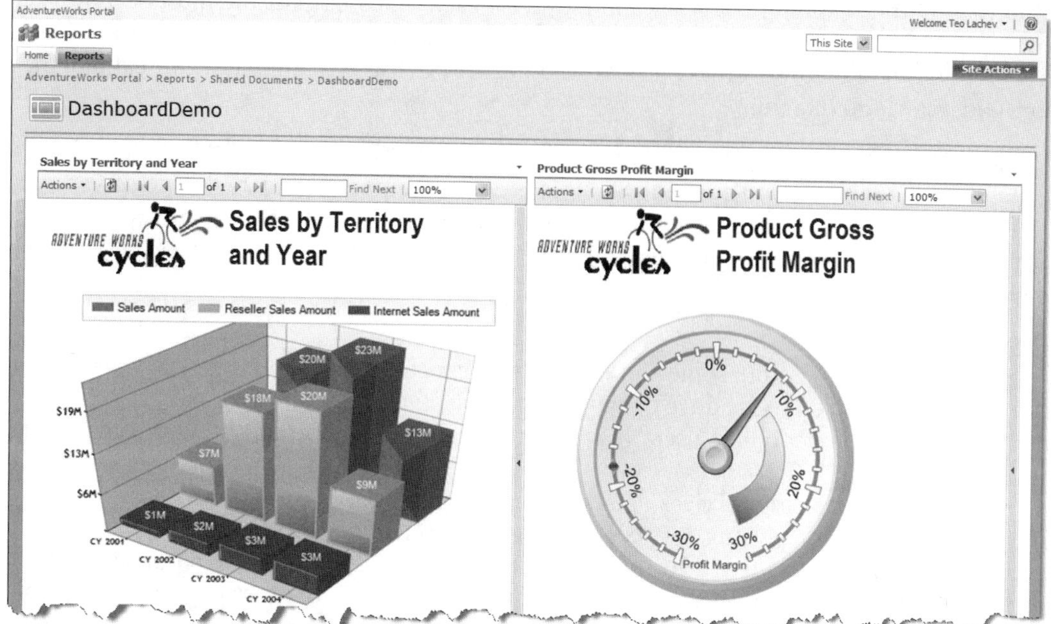

Figure 1.3 A dashboard page can help the executive management quickly understand the company business.

Web-based reporting

In keeping with the fast pace of the Internet age, everyone wants to have up-to-date information by accessing the latest data in real time over the web. Reporting Services reports are web-enabled by default. Consequently, end users can view a report by requesting its URL in the browser.

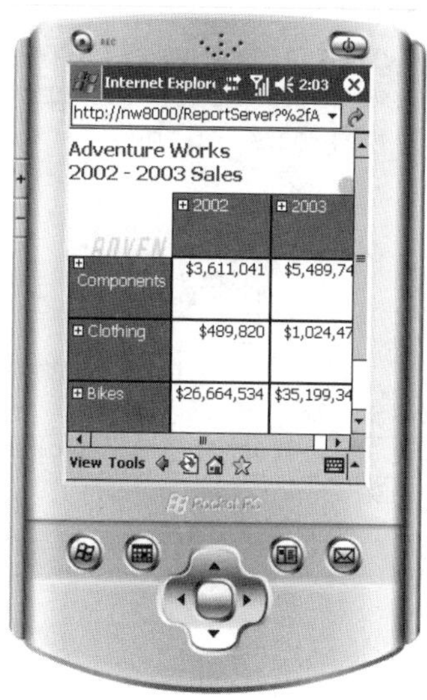

Figure 1.4 Reporting Services reports are web-enabled and can be accessed by any web-capable device, including compact devices, such as Pocket PC.

Suppose that Bob, a Vice President of Sales in your company, is frequently on the road and would like to access the latest sales report from his Pocket PC device. Bob can add the report

URL to the Internet Explorer Favorites and request it each time he needs the most current version of the report. Figure 1.4 shows the Company Sales report (one of the Reporting Services sample reports) rendered with the Visual Studio Pocket PC 2003 SE Emulator. In real life, the report URL may look like this:

```
http://reports.adventure- works.com/ReportServer?/Sales Reports/Company Sales&rc:Toolbar=false&rc:Zoom=Page Width
```

The above URL assumes that Reporting Services is deployed on the company's web server and it is configured for Internet access. Since compact devices have small screens, the report URL instructs Reporting Services to hide the standard report toolbar and fits the report to the page width.

Embedded reporting

Almost all applications require some sort of reporting capability. For example, you may have a desktop application used to produce operational reports. Or, your company may need to enhance its web portal to let online users view reports, such as a report that shows the customer order history.

Thanks to the Reporting Services open programming interfaces, any web-based application can integrate with Reporting Services irrespective of the targeted programming language and operating system. As noted, a custom application can simply request the report by URL. Alternatively, developers can use the Report Server Web service if more programmatic control is needed. Furthermore, adding reporting features to .NET applications is even easier because Microsoft has provided ReportViewer Windows Forms and Web server controls in Visual Studio.

1.1.3 A Short History of Reporting Services

Reporting Services has a short but eventful history. Figure 1.5 tracks in chronological order the major events that have shaped Reporting Services. The black milestones represent the reporting technologies that Microsoft acquired to enhance Reporting Services.

Initial development began in 2000. Realizing the need for a modern reporting tool, Microsoft quietly formed a team of about 30 members to work on the first release of Reporting Services. Almost eight years later, the team has grown to more than 100 members and the product is widely used as a business reporting solution.

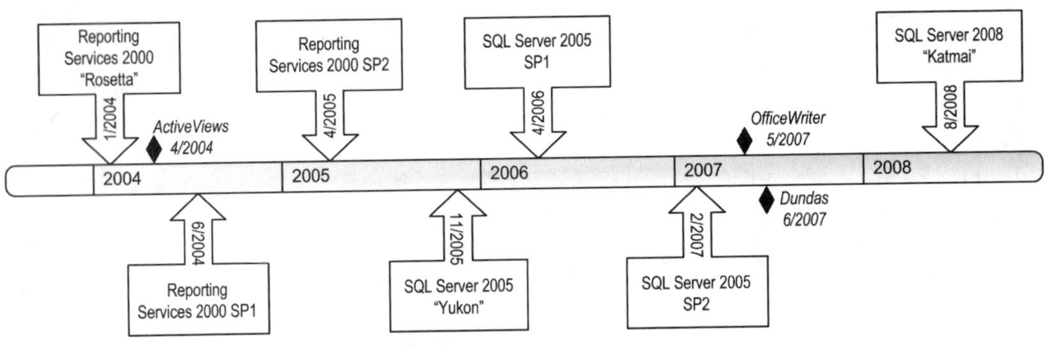

Figure 1.5 The Reporting Services history at a glance.

Reporting Services 2000

Originally, Microsoft was planning to include Reporting Services as a release feature of SQL Server 2005. However, due to popular demand, Reporting Services 2000 (code-named Rosetta) shipped as a post-release add-on to SQL Server 2000 and it was officially named SQL Server 2000 Reporting Services.

The product made quick inroads in the business intelligence market and enjoyed wide adoption and acceptance. However, Reporting Services 2000 was more developer-oriented and didn't include ad hoc reporting capabilities to let business users author their own reports. In April 2004, Microsoft acquired a privately-owned company called ActiveViews whose ad hoc reporting technology later became the bedrock of Report Builder 1.0 technology.

In June 2004, Microsoft released Reporting Services 2000 Service Pack 1, which included feature and performance improvements, such as the ability to reference external images and data caching in report preview mode. Reporting Services 2000 Service Pack 2 followed in April 2005, and brought Report Explorer and Report Viewer SharePoint 2.0 web parts, as well as an ActiveX print control that provided a rich client-side printing experience.

SQL Server 2005

The second major release of Reporting Services was bundled with SQL Server 2005 (code name "Yukon") and it was released in November 2005. It delivered two major enhancements. Report Builder 1.0 empowered business users to author ad hoc reports from pre-defined models. Microsoft Visual Studio 2005, which launched at the same time as SQL Server 2005, introduced the ReportViewer controls to help developers report-enable .NET applications.

SQL Server 2005 Service Pack 1, which followed a few months later, was primarily a maintenance release. SQL Server 2005 Service Pack 2, however, brought in major architectural enhancements. Realizing the growing popularity of SharePoint-based solutions, Microsoft extended Reporting Services to support deep integration with Windows SharePoint Services 3.0 and Microsoft Office SharePoint Server 2007.

In May 2007, Microsoft acquired the OfficeWriter technology from SoftArtisans to let users embed reports inside Microsoft Office 2007 documents. Unfortunately, this feature didn't make the SQL Server 2008 timeframe and it is slated for a future release. Shortly after, Microsoft acquired the Dundas data visualization technology, which provides the basis for new data visualization features in SQL Server 2008. As a result, SQL Server 2008 Reporting Services supercharged its graphical presentation capabilities with full-featured charts and gauge controls.

Microsoft unveiled SQL Server 2008 in August 2008. This third major release of Reporting Services includes several important enhancements which I will discuss next.

1.1.4 What's New in Reporting Services 2008

Due to time constraints, Microsoft couldn't deliver all of the originally planned improvements in Reporting Services 2008. Nevertheless, the enhancements that did make it should warrant your interest. A list of the most important enhancements in SQL Server 2008 Reporting Services is in order. Don't worry if some of the technical terms are not immediately clear. I will explain them in detail later on in this chapter.

Tablix data region

Reporting Services 2008 introduces a new report control called Tablix. I dare to predict that many organizations will upgrade to Reporting Services 2008 just to get this control. Tablix lets you author versatile table-style reports with multiple row groups and column groups. Tablix brings in features that were either not supported or difficult to implement in previous releases.

ADVENTURE WORKS cycles

Product Sales By Year and Territory

	By Year				By Territory		
	⊟ 2002				⊟ North America		
	Q2	Q3	Q4	Total	Canada	Central	Northeas
Accessories	$11,639	$45,335	$31,877	**$88,851**	$21,489	$8,318	$8
Helmets	$11,639	$33,853	$24,871	**$70,363**	$16,710	$6,468	$6
Locks		$6,325	$3,780	**$10,105**	$2,708	$1,155	$1
Pumps		$5,157	$3,226	**$8,383**	$2,071	$696	
Bikes	$5,895,800	$8,072,160	$7,027,269	**$20,995,229**	$3,620,955	$1,814,952	$1,728
Mountain Bikes	$2,416,837	$3,141,467	$2,837,647	**$8,395,951**	$1,390,647	$743,403	$56
Road Bikes	$3,478,964	$4,930,693	$4,189,622	**$12,599,278**	$2,230,308	$1,071,548	$1,160
Clothing	$20,310	$265,585	$192,213	**$478,108**	$113,960	$43,860	$48
Bib-Shorts		$66,860	$35,323	**$102,183**	$25,458	$9,233	$1
Caps	$1,479	$3,991	$3,076	**$8,545**	$2,111	$773	$
Gloves		$52,537	$38,360	**$90,897**	$19,498	$8,698	$9
Jerseys	$16,931	$48,902	$35,495	**$101,328**	$25,055	$10,049	$9
Shorts		$26,207	$23,177	**$49,384**	$11,886	$3,347	$4

Figure 1.6 The Tablix data region supports stepped layout and side-by-side dynamic column groups.

The Product Sales By Year and Territory report shown in Figure 1.6 demonstrates some of these features. The report has two dynamic column groups that provide a cross-tab view of sales by year and territory. The row groups are nested within a single column. By contrast, Reporting Services 2005 supported only cross-tab reports with row groups that occupied separate columns. More importantly, row and column groups can now have independent totals. If you were frustrated by the cross-tab limitations in the previous releases, you will undoubtedly appreciate the simplicity and flexibility of the Tablix data region. No more green triangles and InScope hacks in cross-tab reports!

NOTE In previous releases, the Report Designer would display a green triangle in the right top corner of a total field in a cross-tab (matrix) report. Many developers, including myself, were frustrated because cross-tab totals supported minimal customization through the InScope function and were limited to the Sum aggregation function only. With the Tablix data region these limitations simply disappear.

End-user design enhancements

In this release, Microsoft took a step back and reflected on how to improve the report authoring experience. Consequently, Microsoft built a new designer layout surface that simplifies the report authoring process. Novice users will especially benefit from the new design enhancements, some of which are illustrated in Figure 1.7. This figure shows the report designer that is included in the SQL Server Business Intelligence Development Studio, which comes with SQL Server 2008.

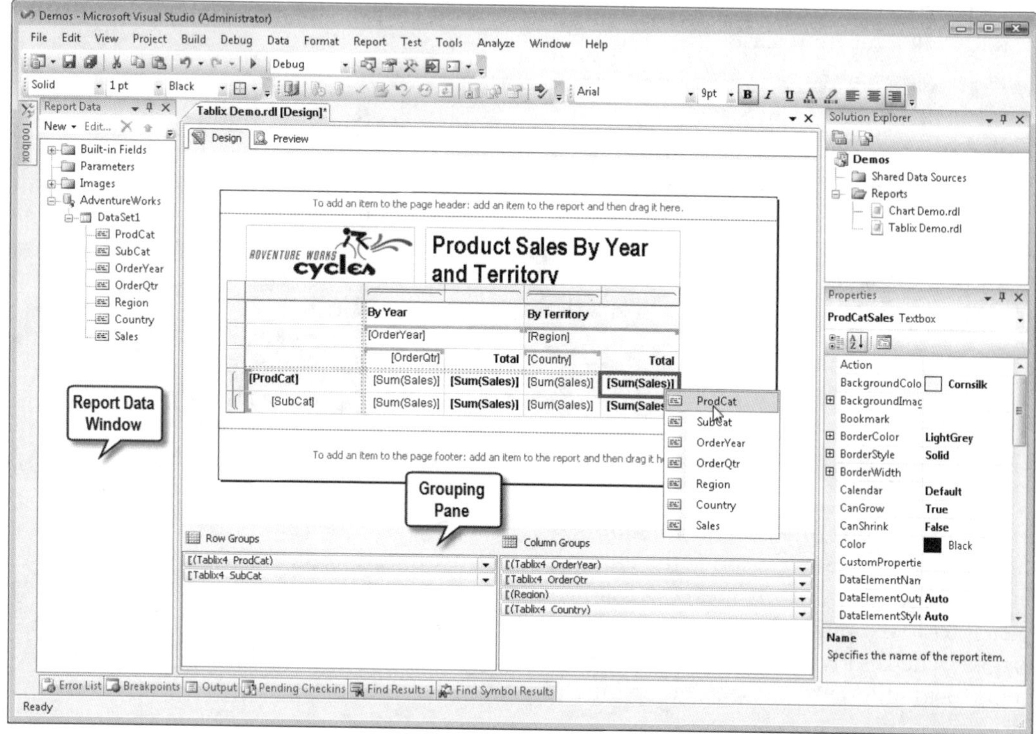

Figure 1.7 End-user improvements in the BIDS Report Designer facilitate report authoring.

Report items, such as built-in fields, report parameters, images, data sources, and datasets, are now conveniently located in a single place—the Report Data window. You can create row and column groups easily, thanks to the Grouping pane. For example, glancing at the report shown in Figure 1.7, you can immediately see that the report has two row groups that group data by product category and subcategory. Creating a new group is a matter of dragging a field from the Report Data pane and dropping it on the appropriate group pane.

Improved data visualization

The data visualization technology that Microsoft acquired from Dundas Software has been used to overhaul the charting capabilities. The scaled-down Dundas chart component that was included in the previous releases was upgraded to the full-featured Dundas chart. As a result, report authors can now implement charting features that were not possible before.

Figure 1.8 demonstrates some of the new charting capabilities. This column chart has two axes that show Sales and Profit. Profit is plotted on the secondary axis that is shown on the right of the chart. Previous releases didn't support a secondary chart axis. In addition, the Sales axis has a scale break to prevent the Bikes sales from eclipsing the sales for other categories. The chart component is interactive at design time (not shown). For example, you can reposition the chart legend by dragging it to a new location. Or, you can select an axis to set its properties.

Another addition to the Reporting Services toolset is the Dundas Gauge component used for displaying gauge indicators, such as circular gauges, linear gauges, angular gauges, and thermometer gauges. Other Dundas controls, such as the Dundas Map and Dundas Calendar, will be added in a future release.

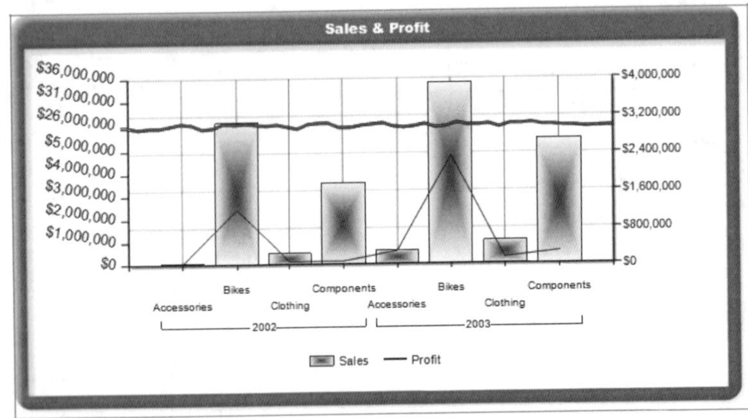

Figure 1.8 The Reporting Services 2008 chart component adds many desirable features, such as secondary axes and axis breaks.

Enhancements for text and rich formatting

Another big leap in report design is the enhanced textbox report item. Previously, if you wanted to mix static and dynamic expression-based text, you either needed multiple textboxes or a Visual Basic expression to concatenate strings together. The first approach led to textbox "explosion". The disadvantage of the second approach was that you couldn't format string fragments inside the same textbox independently.

Sales Order

Order #: [SalesOrderNumber]

Figure 1.9 The textbox report item now supports multiple bands of text and each band can be formatted independently.

In Reporting Services 2008, the textbox report item has been redesigned to support multiple bands of text. Take a look at Figure 1.9, which shows a report title of a Sales Order report. In the past, you would need two textboxes (or three if you wanted different formatting for the sales order number). You may be surprised to find that the entire title is implemented as a single textbox with two paragraphs!

The second paragraph combines static text (Order #:) with dynamic text ([SalesOrderNumber]), which defines a placeholder for a dataset field value. Each element can have its own format settings. Thanks to these enhancements, you'll find that by moving to Reporting Services 2008, you need fewer textboxes and you need to write fewer expressions that concatenate text. Moreover, the new textbox lets you implement report solutions, such as mail merge, that were difficult or impossible to implement with previous releases.

Many report authors will appreciate that the textbox report item now supports a subset of HTML tags for formatting the text content. You can import static HTML text or bind the textbox to a dataset field. For instance, if the dataset field includes HTML tags, such as <b>SO50750</b>, you can configure the textbox to interpret these tags and display the sales order number in bold.

Robust report platform

To improve product manageability and deployment, Microsoft also removed the dependency on Internet Information Services (IIS) and implemented a new hosting model that I will discuss in more detail in section 1.3. This was done for three main reasons:

- Easier configuration—IIS is used by many applications, some of which conflict with Reporting Services. For example, the default SharePoint setup is known to take over the IIS default web site and thus leave Reporting Services non-functional. By removing the IIS dependency, Microsoft isolated Reporting Services from other web applications.
- Better resource management—Reporting Services 2008 has a new on-demand processing model to ensure that report executions will not run out of memory. When it is under memory stress, Reporting Services pages and releases allocated memory to disk. This feature would have been very difficult to implement using the IIS hosting model. In addition, eliminating the IIS dependency made possible consolidating the former IIS-dependent Web service and Windows service into one Windows service.
- Simplified deployment and adoption—Many organizations have strict policies for installing IIS. Windows Vista and Windows Server 2008 aggravated the situation even further by locking down many of the IIS features that Reporting Services required.

What does removing the dependency on IIS mean to you? Simply put, it means you don't have to install IIS just to get Reporting Services running. Even if IIS didn't cause you any problems in the past, removing the IIS dependency is one less thing to worry about.

Enterprise scale reporting engine

Processing and rendering inefficiencies in previous releases of Reporting Services were causing scalability issues with large reports. To a large extent, this was because reports were memory-bound and the report server would load the entire report in-memory. To improve scalability, Microsoft completely redesigned the report processing engine. As a result, large reports load incrementally, which means they consume much less memory and may execute faster. I will discuss the new report processing architecture in more detail later on in this chapter.

On the report rendering side, the rendering extensions that are used to export reports have been rewritten to ensure consistent layout and repagination. The CSV renderer has been redesigned to provide Excel and CSV-compliant modes. The Excel renderer has been enhanced to support nested report sections and subreports. Many scalability and performance improvements have been implemented, such as improving the time to render the first page of the report and to provide constant page-to-page response times.

1.1.5 Reporting Services and the Microsoft Business Intelligence Platform

Reporting Services is not the only business intelligence product that Microsoft provides. It is an integral part of the Microsoft Business Intelligence Platform that was initiated in early 2004 with the powerful promise to "bring BI to the masses".

DEFINITION The Microsoft Business Intelligence Platform is a multi-product offering that addresses the most pressing data analytics and management needs that many organizations encounter every day.

Figure 1.10 clarifies the building blocks of the Microsoft Business Intelligence Platform and how Reporting Services fits in. Microsoft SQL Server forms the foundation of the Microsoft Business Intelligence Platform. It includes four services that I like to think of as four pillars of the platform: Database Engine, Reporting Services, Integration Services, and Analysis Services. This is a great value proposition since a single SQL Server license covers all services installed on the box.

Database Engine

The Database Engine is the core service for storing, processing, and securing data. You can use the Database Engine to create relational databases for online transaction processing (OLTP) or online analytical processing (OLAP) data. While discussing all enhancements of the Database Engine in SQL Server 2008 is outside the scope of this book, I'd like to mention a couple that may be applicable to your Reporting Services and BI projects.

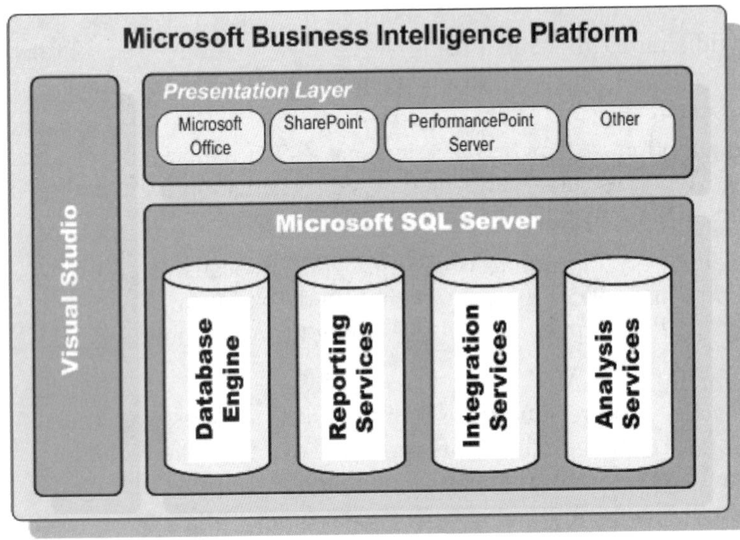

Figure 1.10 The Microsoft Business Intelligence Platform provides valuable services and tools that address various data analytics and management needs.

Data compression

New row and page compression formats were implemented to provide efficient storage for fixed and variable length columns. This can be useful when optimizing data storage of large databases. The row compression format reduces the storage space of fixed length types, such as integer, money and datetime, as well as NULL. Page compression reduces duplicate values in a page by storing the most common duplicate column values.

Change Data Capture

Another interesting new feature is Change Data Capture (CDC). CDC is designed to capture insert, update, and delete activity on a SQL table and place the changed data into a separate relational table. It uses an asynchronous capture mechanism that reads the transaction logs and populates the table with the row data that has changed. ETL processes can leverage CDC to quickly resolve data changes.

Integration Services

Today's enterprise IT shop is often required to maintain an assortment of data sources and technologies. These include desktop databases, legacy mainframe systems (that no one dares to touch), relational database management systems (RDBMS), and so on. For example, order tracking data could reside in a SQL Server database, HR data could be stored in an Oracle database, and manufacturing data could be located in a mainframe database. Integrating disparate and heterogeneous data sources presents a major challenge for many organizations.

Integration Services helps you address this challenge. It is typically used for Extracting, Transforming, and Loading (ETL) processes for data integration. For example, you can build an Integration Services data flow pipeline which extracts data from the source systems, cleanses it, and loads it to your company data warehouse. New features in the 2008 release include enhanced performance for lookup transformations, new ADO.NET source and destination components, and a new script environment that integrates with the Microsoft Visual Studio Tools for Applications (VSTA) and lets you use Visual Basic.NET or C# for writing scripts.

From a Reporting Services perspective, you can use an Integration Services package as a data source to a report. When the report is run, it executes the package that retrieves its data, and presents the data in the layout you defined. By using a package as a data source, you can manipulate the data before it is displayed in the report. For example, your package can apply data mining rules to the raw data to return a list of potential buyers.

Analysis Services

Analysis Services is a multidimensional database which is optimized for fast querying and reporting. It provides OLAP and data mining services. Organizations typically use Analysis Services for trend and historical reporting. For example, you can build an Analysis Services cube that helps business users analyze numeric data (*measures*) from different perspectives (*dimensions*).

You can integrate Reporting Services with Analysis Services to build synergetic business intelligence solutions. For example, you can use an Analysis Services cube as a data source for standard and ad hoc reports. You can also implement reports that leverage the Analysis Services data mining capabilities to display prediction results, such as forecasted sales.

I covered Analysis Services 2005 in detail in my book Applied Microsoft Analysis Services 2005 (see the Resources section at the end of the chapter). Most of what I wrote in that book still applies to the SQL Server 2008 release of Analysis Services. The newest release of Analysis Services introduces incremental changes, such as faster query performance and a better design and manageability experience.

There are other SQL Server components that you may find more or less relevant to your business intelligence projects. These may include Replication Services to clone data and Service Broker to raise event notifications. Notification Services is no longer included as a component of SQL Server 2008. However, Reporting Services and Service Broker cover some of the functionality formerly provided by Notification Services. The long term direction is to incorporate the Notification Services functionality into Reporting Services.

The Presentation Layer

Data by itself is useless if there is no way to make it available to the people who need it. Besides disseminating data via Reporting Services reports, the Microsoft Business Intelligence platform supports other data presentation channels, such as Microsoft Office, Microsoft SharePoint Products and Technologies, Microsoft PerformancePoint Server and third-party applications.

Microsoft Office

Microsoft significantly broadened the business intelligence features in the Microsoft Office 2007 suite of products. Microsoft positioned the ubiquitous Microsoft Excel as a premium client for Analysis Services. For example, business users can use Excel to connect to a cube and build interactive PivotTable reports that let the user slice the cube data. With a few mouse clicks, the user can change the report and view data from different angles.

SharePoint Products and Technologies
As noted, organizations can use SharePoint to build business intelligence portals and dashboards that contain Reporting Services reports and Excel reports connected to Analysis Services cubes. The Excel Services components of Microsoft Office SharePoint Server lets you deploy and process Excel spreadsheets on the server and view them via a web browser or download them to the desktop.

PerformancePoint Server
Microsoft unveiled PerformancePoint Server in 2007. As its name suggests, an organization can use this product to monitor, analyze, and plan its performance. The monitoring component, which builds upon the former Microsoft Business Scorecard Manager (BSM), provides KPI and scorecard capabilities. For example, you can assemble a scorecard that displays key performance indicators defined in an Analysis Services cube.

The ProClarity technology, which Microsoft acquired in 2006, provides guided and contextual analysis by letting users slice and dice Analysis Services multidimensional data to gain further understanding about the performance metrics. Finally, the planning component, formerly known as Biz#, incorporates planning and budgeting capabilities. For example, a business analyst can use the planning component to set up a workflow for submission and approval of the company's budget for next year.

Other applications
Reporting Services provides open programming interfaces that developers can utilize to extend its features and report-enable custom applications. This book includes several chapters that demonstrate how you can leverage this open architecture to extend Reporting Services to meet more advanced requirements and integrate it with custom applications.

Visual Studio
Finally, developers can use Visual Studio to work with Business Intelligence projects. If you don't have the full-blown version of Visual Studio (or you are not willing to purchase a license), the SQL Server 2008 setup program gives you an option to install a scaled-down version of Visual Studio called Business Intelligence Development Studio (BIDS).

BIDS supports only business intelligence projects, such as Analysis Services, Reporting Services, and Integration Services projects. It gives you the power of the Visual Studio Integrated Development Environment at no additional cost. However, if you have the full-blown Visual Studio installed, the SQL Server setup program integrates the BI project templates in your current Visual Studio installation. Consequently, developers can use Visual Studio to work with solutions that include both code projects and BI projects.

NOTE Unfortunately, BIDS 2008 supports only SQL Server 2008 BI projects. If you target SQL Server 2005, you need to keep BIDS 2005 around as well. Similarly, you will need to remove your SQL Server 2005 BI projects from Visual Studio 2008 solutions because they will get upgraded to the SQL Server 2008 format and you will no longer be able to deploy to SQL Server 2005.

Now that we have reviewed the components of the Microsoft BI Platform, let's turn our attention back to Reporting Services.

1.2 Overview of Reporting Services

By now, you should have a good understanding of what Reporting Services can do and how it fits into the rest of the Microsoft Business Intelligence stack. Let's now discuss the Reporting Services major components and how they can help you handle the report lifecycle.

1.2.1 Understanding the Reporting Services Components

Let's start by a high-level overview of the Reporting Services components and understand how custom tools fit into the overall design. As veteran Reporting Services users will quickly notice, the Reporting Services component architecture remains unchanged from the previous release. Figure 1.11 shows the Reporting Services logical architecture.

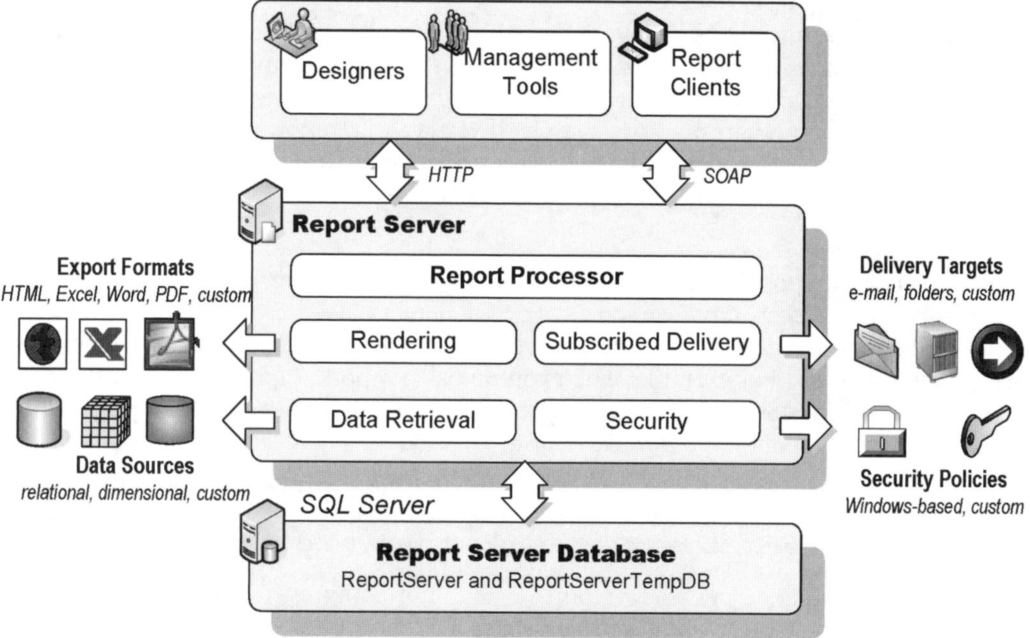

Figure 1.11 This diagram shows the major Reporting Services components.

Report Server

At the heart of the Reporting Services architecture is the report server, a web-based middle-tier layer that receives incoming report requests and generates reports. The diagram shows a simplified logical view of the report server. In section 1.3, I will expand on it and show you how the report server is physically implemented.

To facilitate integration with external client applications, the report server provides two communication interfaces: URL access and a Web service (not shown on the diagram). Consequently, both off-the-shelf and custom tools can communicate with the report server via HTTP or SOAP. The Report Processor component of the report server is responsible for processing the reports at run time. When a report is requested, the Report Processor extracts the report data, combines data with the report layout, and renders the report in the requested export format.

One of my favorite Reporting Services features is its modularized and extensible architecture. Each of the services listed outside the report server box in Figure 1.11 is performed by specialized modules called *extensions*. When the standard extensions are not enough, developers can extend Reporting Services capabilities by plugging in custom extensions. For example, out of the box, reports can draw data from popular databases like SQL Server, Oracle, Analysis Services, and other OLE DB-compatible data sources. But what if the data is not stored in a database, or is stored in an application dataset or XML file? In this case, a developer can write a custom data extension to retrieve data from virtually any data source.

Similarly, users can export reports to several popular formats, such as Microsoft Excel, Microsoft Word, Adobe Acrobat PDF, HTML, CSV, and image formats. If the built-in export formats are not enough, vendors can write custom rendering extensions to export reports to other formats.

By default, the report server is configured for Windows security. This means that it authenticates and authorizes the user based on the user's Windows identity. However, when Windows security is not an option, a developer can plug in a custom security extension that uses a different security mechanism. For example, if you want to report-enable an Internet-facing application, you can create and deploy a custom security extension to use Forms Authentication for user authentication and authorization.

Report Server Database

In Reporting Services, report definitions and properties are saved in the report server database. The report server database is implemented as two SQL Server databases that get installed when you configure the report server. The ReportServer database stores the report definitions and management settings. For example, when you upload a report, Reporting Services saves its definition in the ReportServer database. The second database, ReportServerTempDB, stores temporary information about the report execution.

DEFINITION The report server database is a logical term for two physical databases: ReportServer and ReportServerTempDB. The ReportServer database hosts the report catalog. The ReportServerTempDB stores temporary data. I will use the terms *report server database* and *report catalog* interchangeably throughout this book.

It is important to note that no persistent report-related information is stored in the file system. Consequently, a web farm of report servers can share the report catalog by connecting to the same report server database. By default, if you are installing a report server in the default configuration, the SQL Server setup program installs the report server database on the same computer as the report server. However, if needed, you can host the report server database on another SQL Server 2005 or 2008 server.

Introducing deployment modes

Reporting Services supports two deployment modes.

- Native mode (default)—The report server as a stand-alone application server that provides all processing and management capability exclusively through Reporting Services components.
- SharePoint mode—The report server is integrated with Windows SharePoint Services or Microsoft Office SharePoint Server. Report viewing and management happens inside the SharePoint portal.

The two deployment modes are mutually exclusive but you can switch the deployment mode at any time by reconfiguring the server with the caveat that you'll need to redeploy your report definitions and management settings.

Understanding the report lifecycle

The term "report lifecycle" refers to the range of events or activities that pertain to a report, starting with how it is created. The term provides a useful context for discussing the Reporting Services tools. As Figure 1.12, the report lifecycle spans report authoring, management, and delivery stages.

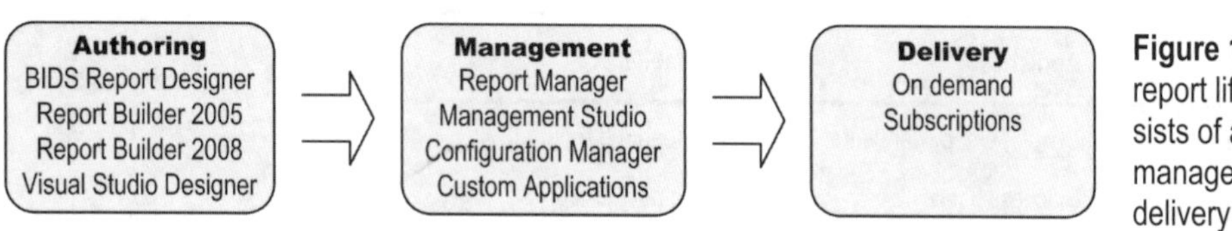

Figure 1.12 The report lifecycle consists of authoring, management, and delivery stages.

In the report authoring stage, the report author lays out the report using one of the Microsoft-provided report designers. For example, you can use the report designer included in the Business Intelligence Development Studio to author a standard report.

Once the report is ready, the report author can upload the report to the server so it is available to end users. In the management stage, the administrator configures the deployed reports and the report environment. For example, the administrator can use Report Manager to organize reports in folders and set up security policies to let users view those reports.

Once the report is configured, it can be viewed by end users or custom applications. Report clients can request reports on demand, such as by typing the report URL address. Alternatively, users can subscribe to reports on a schedule. When a schedule event is received, the report server processes the report and sends it to the recipients via a desired delivery channel, such as e-mail.

1.2.2 Report Authoring

The Reporting Services story sometimes reminds me about the servant who had many masters. It seems that every application out there, including those provided by Microsoft and custom applications built by third parties, wants to integrate with Reporting Services. Examples of Microsoft applications that leverage Reporting Services in one form or another include SQL Server Management Studio, Microsoft Operations Manager, PerformancePoint, Microsoft Dynamics CRM, Visual Studio, and so on. This range of clients creates a demand for flexible report authoring, management, and delivery features.

About Report Definition Language

Reporting Services reports are described in an open XML-based schema, called Report Definition Language (RDL).

DEFINITION Report Definition Language (RDL) is an XML-based schema for defining reports. RDL is an open standard proposed by Microsoft to promote interoperability of commercial reporting products.

Microsoft off-the-shelf and third-party report designers that target Reporting Services produce report definition files as described in RDL. The Reporting Services 2008 RDL specification can be downloaded from the Microsoft web site (see Resources).

Introducing report designers

A report designer is a tool that the report author uses to define report data and layout at design time. Since the technical skills of the report authors may vary greatly, it is not easy to build a single report designer that satisfies all report authoring needs. You probably will be surprised to learn that Microsoft provides three report designers and soon will add a fourth designer to let you author Reporting Services reports. Table 1.1 lists these report designers and explains their target audience and capabilities.

Table 1.1 Microsoft provides four report designers

Designer	Audience	Capabilities
BIDS Report Designer	Developers, power users	Full-featured reports
Report Builder 1.0	Business users	Basic ad hoc reports
Report Builder 2.0	Power users	Full-featured reports outside Visual Studio
Visual Studio Report Designer	Developers	RDL 2005-compatible local reports

It is important to note that all report designers produce Report Definition Language (RDL). Some of the tools support a subset of RDL, losing some report functionality but gaining an easier to use design tool. The first three designers are components of Reporting Services. The last one, Visual Studio Report Designer, ships with Visual Studio.

BIDS Report Designer

This is the original report designer and it is included in the Microsoft Business Intelligence Development Studio (see again Figure 1.7). In this release, Microsoft revamped the layout surface of the BIDS Report Designer so it becomes more intuitive to both experienced and novice report authors. Welcome end-user enhancements, such as the Report Data window, snap-to lines, zooming, the grouping pane, and improved dialogs, debuted in this release.

The BIDS Report Designer supports all report authoring features. Since BIDS is a scaled-down version of Visual Studio, the BIDS Report Designer targets mainly developers who are familiar with the Visual Studio IDE.

Report Builder 1.0

As noted, SQL Server 2005 introduced Report Builder 1.0 to let business users author simple template-based ad hoc reports. In marked contrast with the other report authoring tools, Report Builder 1.0 shields the end user from the technicalities of the underlying database and query syntax by way of a predefined model. Report Builder 1.0 auto-generates the query at run time using a predefined model that abstracts the data source. Report Builder 1.0 remains unchanged from the 2005 release of Reporting Services.

Report Builder 2.0

Microsoft will soon release a new report designer for standard and ad hoc reporting outside the Visual Studio environment. Similar to the BIDS Report Designer, Report Builder 2.0 will provide the full spectrum of report authoring features. This designer features the Microsoft Office 2007 ribbon interface, as shown in Figure 1.13. In this case, I've open the Product Sales by Year and Territory report (see again Figure 1.6) in Report Builder 2.0 to demonstrate that you can use Report Designer and Report Builder 2.0 interchangeably.

Unfortunately, due to time constraints, Microsoft couldn't ship the Report Builder 2.0 in the box with the rest of Reporting Services 2008. However, when Report Builder 2.0 does ship, power users should definitely consider using it for full-featured standard and ad hoc reporting. I'll preview the pre-released version of Report Builder 2.0 in chapter 10.

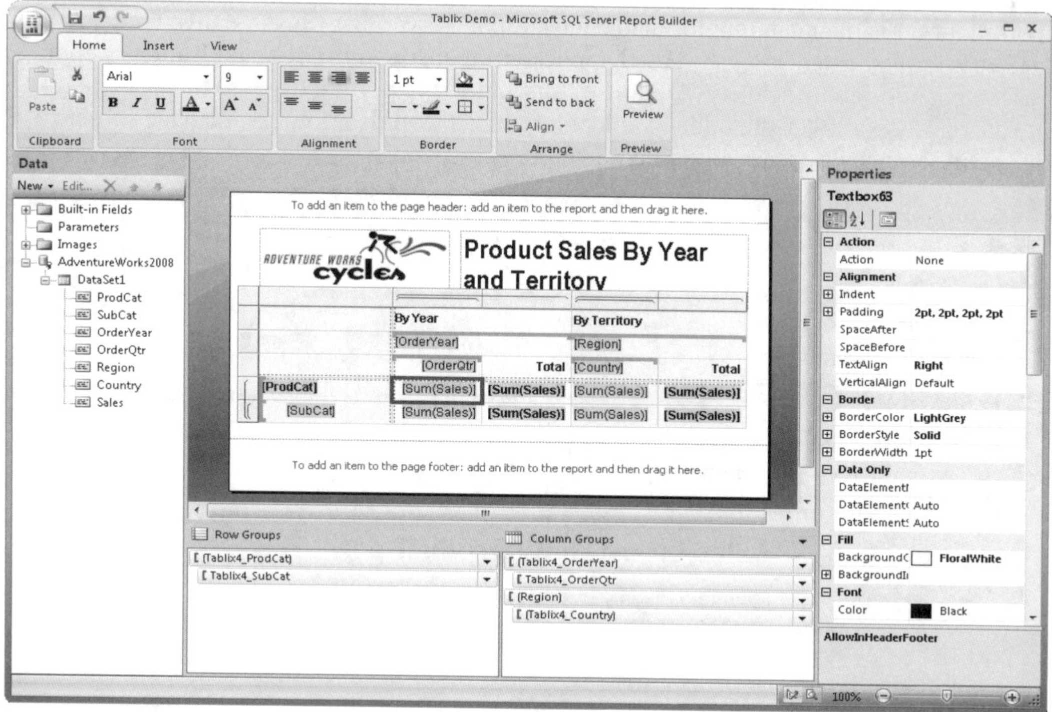

Figure 1.13 Report Builder 2.0 supports all report authoring features.

Visual Studio Report Designer

To let .NET developers include basic report functionality without all the bells and whistles of the report server, Microsoft bundled a scaled-down report designer with Visual Studio 2005 and 2008 to use with the redistributable Report Viewer controls that also ship in Visual Studio. I will call this designer the Visual Studio Report Designer. As it stands, the Visual Studio Report Designer remains unchanged from its Visual Studio 2005 release.

1.2.3 Report Management

In a typical enterprise environment there are usually three different groups of users who get involved in the different phases of the report lifecycle. Report authors focus on report design and programming. Administrators are concerned with managing the report server. End users run reports. Reporting Services provides several tools for addressing various management tasks, but the ones you will use the most are Report Manager, SQL Server Management Studio, and the Reporting Services Configuration Manager.

You can use Report Manager to carry out day-to-day management activities, such as uploading content and setting up security policies. SQL Server Management Studio lets you manage system properties, enable features, and set up the shared schedules and role definitions that you want to roll out on your server. You can use the Reporting Services Configuration Manager to manage the Reporting Services configuration properties, such as the connection string to the report server database.

Introducing Report Manager

Report Manager is the main tool for managing a report server that runs in native mode. Report Manager is implemented as a web-based application that supports two main features: report management and report delivery. Administrators can use Report Manager to manage the report catalog, such as to create folders, upload reports, set up data sources, manage subscriptions, define security policies, and schedule report processing.

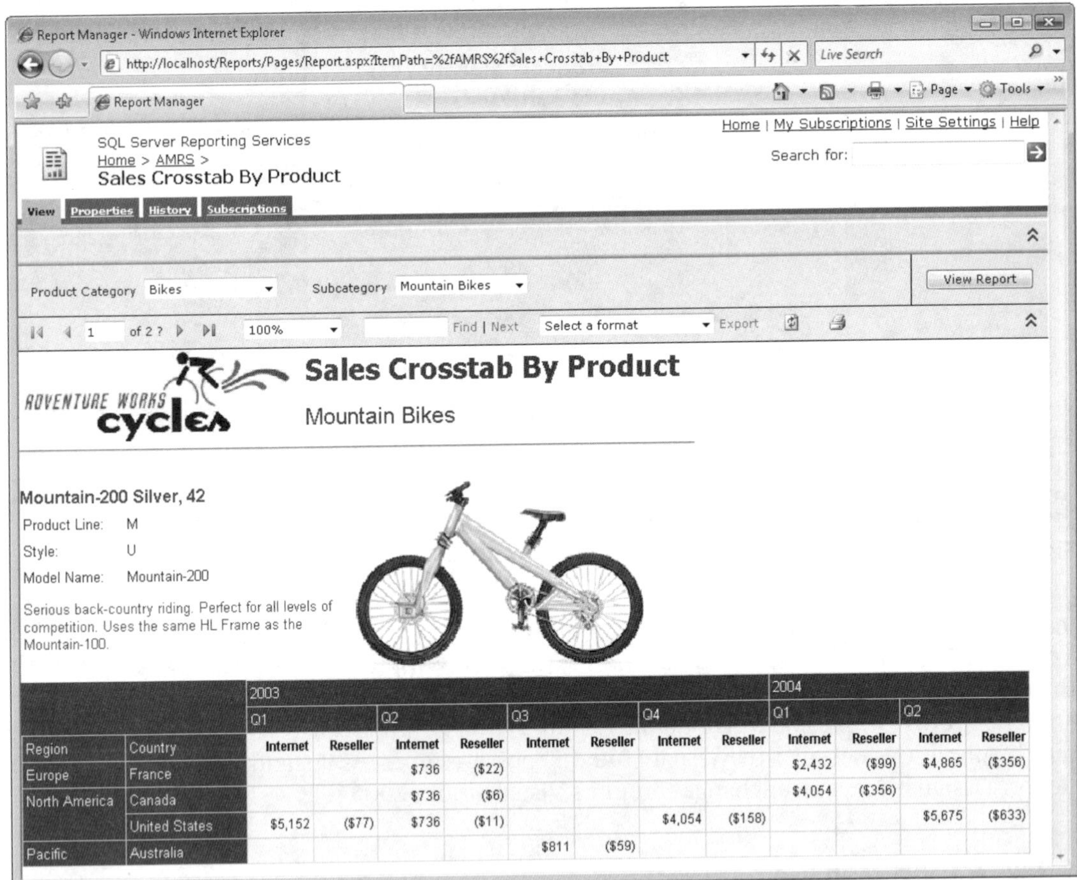

Figure 1.14 You can use Report Manager for report management and delivery.

Organizations can also leverage Report Manager as a reporting tool for viewing reports on demand. For example, Figure 1.14 shows the Sales Crosstab by Product report displayed in HTML format inside Report Manager. The HTML Viewer control, which the Report Manager uses for rendering the report, includes a handy toolbar that provides the user with easy access to common reporting functions. For instance, the end user can expand the Export drop-down list to export the report in one of the supported export formats, such as Excel.

Introducing SharePoint management

As noted, a report server can be configured for SharePoint integration mode. In this scenario, SharePoint supersedes Report Manager. In SharePoint integration mode, the administrator can perform all management activities inside the SharePoint portal.

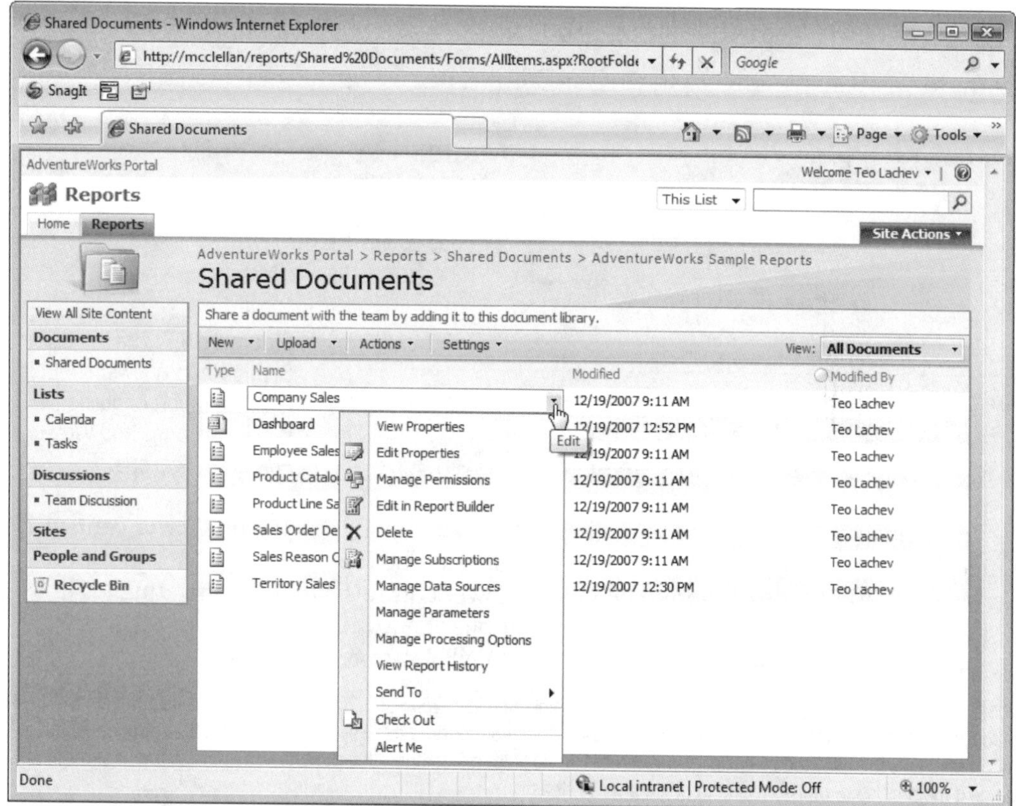

Figure 1.15 In SharePoint integration mode, you can use the SharePoint portal for all management tasks.

For example, as Figure 1.15 shows, Reporting Services reports appear just like other documents uploaded to a SharePoint library. You can click on the report name to view the report. You can expand the report drop-down list to manage various report settings.

1.2.4 Report Delivery

Reporting Services supports flexible report delivery options. Users can request reports on demand or via subscriptions. On-demand report delivery is the most common option. In this case, the user explicitly requests the report that he or she wants to view. Users can also subscribe to reports that they want to see on a regular basis.

Introducing on-demand report delivery

In the simplest scenario, a user can request a report on demand by clicking on the report link. You can make report links available in the Report Manager Home page or in folders. In more complex programmatic scenarios, developers can use the Report Server Web service to enable on demand reporting in custom applications. Thanks to the excellent Visual Studio Report-

Viewer controls, integrating .NET Windows Forms and Web Forms applications with Reporting Services is easy. This is because these controls shield developers from Report Server Web service technicalities.

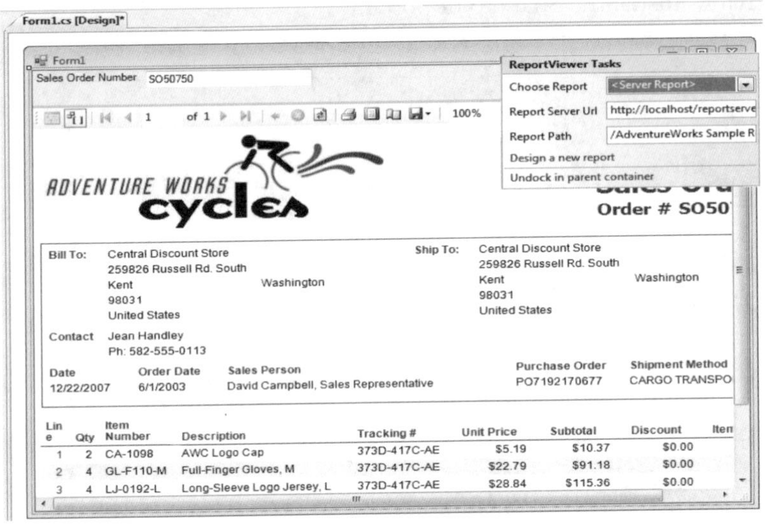

Figure 1.16 The Visual Studio ReportViewer controls facilitate report-enabling .NET Windows Forms and Web Forms applications.

Figure 1.16 demonstrates how you can configure the Window Forms ReportViewer control at design time. You can use the control Task Panel to specify the report server URL and report path. Besides rendering server reports, the ReportViewer controls support generating local reports. In this scenario, the custom application supplies data and parameters to the report. For example, a custom application can bind an ADO.NET dataset to the report.

NOTE The ReportViewer controls support both Reporting Services 2005 and 2008 for viewing published reports. Unfortunately, the release version of SQL Server 2008 does not upgrade the ReportViewer controls to support RDL 2008 definitions in local mode. Similar to the Visual Studio Report Designer, the plans are to upgrade the controls in the next major release of Visual Studio or via a web release.

What if your application is not written in .NET or you cannot use the ReportViewer controls? Rest assured, any Web-service capable client can integrate with the Report Server Web service. Here is what it takes to generate the Company Sales report (see again Figure 1.4) using C#.

```
ReportExecutionService rs = new ReportExecutionService();
rs.Credentials = System.Net.CredentialCache.DefaultCredentials;
rs.Url = "http://myserver/reportserver/ReportExecution2005.asmx";

// Render arguments
byte[] result = null;
string reportPath = "/AdventureWorks Sample Reports/Company Sales";
string format = "PDF";
DataSourceCredentials[] credentials = null;
string showHideToggle, encoding, mimeType, extension, devInfo, historyID = null;
Warning[] warnings = null;
ParameterValue[] reportHistoryParameters = null;
string[] streamIDs = null;
result = rs.Render2(format, devInfo, PageCountMode.Estimate, out extension, out encoding,
          out mimeType, out warnings, out streamIDs);
```

This C# code calls down to the Report Server Web service to export the report in Adobe PDF format. In this case, the Company Sales report doesn't take report parameters. Besides declaring the method arguments, rendering the actual report is accomplished with a single Web me-

thod call. Since the report server renders the report definition as a byte array, additional code is needed to present the report in human-readable format or save it to disk.

Introducing subscribed report delivery

End users can also subscribe to reports to receive them automatically. When the subscription is triggered, the report server generates the report and delivers it to the recipients who subscribed to the report. Reporting Services subscriptions let you meet various requirements for automating report distribution. For example, a sales manager can subscribe to a sales summary report to receive it at the end of each month. Or, an e-commerce organization can automatically send a notification report to a customer when the order status has changed.

Reporting Services supports two subscription types: standard subscriptions and data-driven subscriptions. Standard subscriptions are created and managed by individual users. For example, an end user can set up a standard subscription to receive an updated report every month. Data-driven subscriptions are on a different plane altogether. This powerful feature is used to deliver a report to a dynamic list of destinations with customized content for each destination. For example, imagine a web application that collects from the user his or her preferences for report delivery, export format, parameters, and so on. The application would save this information in a user profile table. Then, the administrator would set up a data-driven subscription that queries the user profile table for subscription data, generates the reports, and sends them to each recipient.

Out of the box, Reporting Services can deliver reports via e-mail, save them as files in Windows folders, or deliver them to SharePoint document libraries (if the report server is configured in SharePoint integration mode). Developers can extend the Reporting Services delivering capabilities by plugging in custom delivery extensions to send a report to other destinations, such as a Web service or a printer.

Now that I have introduced you to the Reporting Services components and its logical architecture, let's drill down to the Reporting Services physical architecture to understand the new Reporting Services hosting model.

1.3 The Reporting Services Architecture

Although Reporting Services hasn't changed its logical architecture from the previous release, the removal of the IIS dependency has brought radical changes to the Reporting Services physical architecture. Working with Reporting Services requires a solid grasp of the new changes. The next section discusses the new Reporting Services hosting model.

1.3.1 Understanding the Report Server Hosting Model

Previous releases of Reporting Services were hosted in IIS. IIS handled HTTP requests and provided network interfaces, authentication, and other services. Now that Reporting Services 2008 is no longer dependent on IIS, it has a new hosting model and new components that replace the "lost" IIS features. Figure 1.17 shows the Reporting Services 2008 architecture.

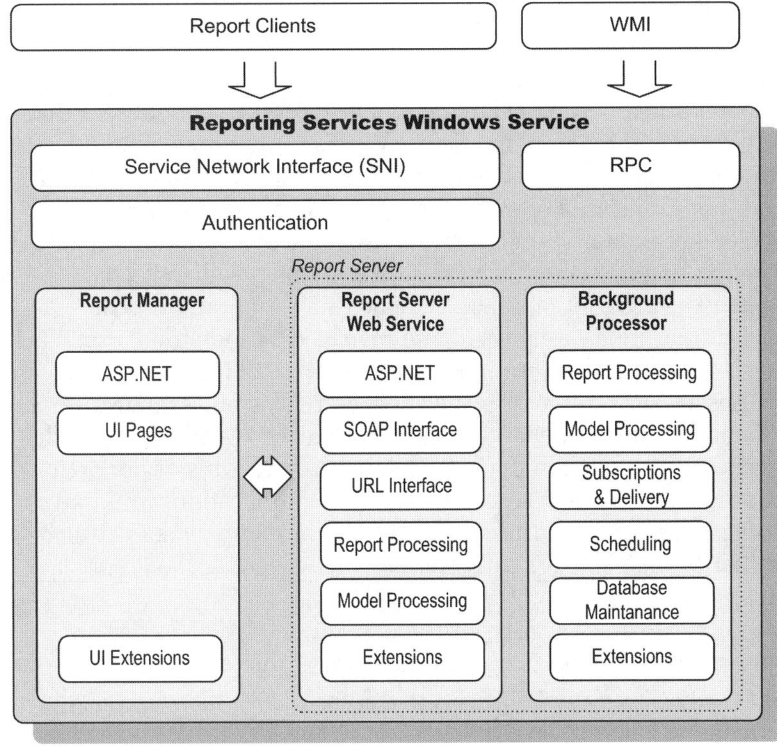

Figure 1.17 The Reporting Services Service hosts the three report server applications: Report Manager, Report Server Web Service, and Background Processor.

Understanding the Reporting Services Windows Service

The server components of Reporting Services 2008 are hosted in a single Windows service process. This is similar to the service model of Analysis Services and Integration Services. You can see the Reporting Services Windows service in the Windows Services console application, as follows:

1. Open the Windows Control Panel and double-click Administrative Tools to go the Administrative Tools program group.
2. Double-click Services to open the Services console application.
3. Scroll down the services list until you locate the SQL Server Reporting Services Windows service.

The Reporting Services Windows service is implemented almost entirely in managed .NET code.

Understanding network interfaces

With previous releases of Reporting Services, IIS was responsible for handling client requests. Now that Reporting Services has parted ways with IIS, it implements its own network interface. Specifically, Reporting Services includes service network interfaces (SNI) that monitors incoming requests from HTTP.SYS.

NOTE HTTP.SYS is a kernel-mode HTTP driver that listens for requests and routes them to the appropriate requests queue. HTTP.SYS was introduced in Windows Server 2003 to improve the performance of IIS 6.0. Windows XP Service Pack 2 and Windows Vista include HTTP.SYS as well. For more information about HTTP.SYS, read the Web and Application Server Infrastructure - Performance and Scalability paper (see Resources). To learn how .NET applications can host HTTP.SYS outside IIS, read the "Run ASMX Without IIS" article by Aaron Skonnard (see the Resources section).

As part of configuring Reporting Services, you must specify the URL addresses (HTTP endpoints) of the report server and Report Manager. Interestingly, in Windows Vista and Windows Server 2003 or above, you can have multiple applications listening on the same port. Consequently, Reporting Services and IIS can run side by side and they can both listen on port 80. In fact, when SQL Server detects these operating systems, it defaults the report server and Report Manager URLs to use port 80.

The default report server URL is *http://<servername>/ReportServer* and the default Report Manager URL is *http://<servername>/Reports*. However, IIS 5.0 in Windows XP doesn't use HTTP.SYS and cannot share the same port with Reporting Services. This is why the SQL Server setup program uses port 8080 for the HTTP endpoints on Windows XP, such as *http://<servername>:8080/ReportServer*.

The Reporting Services team had to implement additional features that were previously provided by IIS, such as user authentication. As it turned out, SQL Server already provided the same services so Reporting Services 2008 "borrowed" some of the SQL Server internal components. Specifically, Reporting Services uses SQL OS, SQL CLR, and SQL Network Interface. However, this doesn't mean that you must install the SQL Server 2008 relational engine to get the shared components. Reporting Services includes these components internally.

In summary, Reporting Services 2008 preserved most of the IIS settings, such as host headers, multiple ports, SSL certificates, NTLM, Kerberos, Negotiate, and Basic authentication. The only IIS features that didn't get migrated from IIS are support for ISAPI applications and some authentication options, including Anonymous Authentication, Digest Authentication, and Client Certificates. These authentication options are not supported in Reporting Services 2008.

1.3.2 Understanding the Reporting Services Applications

The Reporting Services Windows service hosts three server applications: Report Manager, Report Server Web service, and Background Processor. Behind the scenes, the service creates three .NET application domains to host these applications.

NOTE In .NET, application domains are typically used to isolate running applications. A single Windows process can host several application domains. Application domains are created and manipulated by run-time hosts, such as the ASP.NET runtime or a .NET executable.

The Report Manager and Report Server Web service domains are ASP.NET domains. Consequently, they are managed by the ASP.NET runtime with the exception that the Reporting Services Windows service manages the memory settings and process health of all applications as a whole. For example, both the Report Manager and Report Server Web service applications have web.config configuration files that contain ASP.NET-specific configuration settings.

Report Manager

As I explained, Report Manager is an ASP.NET web application that provides report management and viewing capabilities for a Reporting Services instance configured in native mode. You can view Report Manager as a client application that integrates with the report server.

Report Manager provides a number of ASP.NET pages which are installed by default in the \Program Files\Microsoft SQL Server\MSRS10.MSSQLSERVER\Reporting Services\ReportManager folder. Thanks to the consolidated hosting model, the configuration settings of Report Manager and the Report Server Web service are stored in a single configuration file (rsreportserver.config).

Report Manager can accommodate some UI extensions. Specifically, if you develop a custom delivery extension, you can configure the Report Manager to host its web control so the user can configure the extension when setting up a subscription.

Report Server Web Service

The Report Server Web service handles on-demand report processing. For example, when you request a report by typing its URL in the browser, the Report Server Web service receives the request, processes the report, and returns the exported report to the client. To facilitate integration with different types of report clients, the Report Server Web service provides URL and SOAP integration options. The URL interface handles HTTP GET requests, such as http://<servername>/ReportServer?/AdventureWorks Sample Reports/Company Sales.

The Report Server Web service is the primary programmatic interface for custom applications that integrate with Reporting Services. The Report Server Web service provides four Web service endpoints that expose the Reporting Services feature set to external clients. ReportService2005.asmx is the management endpoint for a Reporting Services instance configured for native mode. ReportService2006.asmx is the management endpoint for a Reporting Services instance running in SharePoint mode. Developers can utilize the ReportExecution2005.asmx endpoint for report rendering and execution. Finally, the ReportServiceAuthentication.asmx endpoint is provided to authenticate users against a report server in SharePoint integration mode when SharePoint is configured for Forms Authentication

In comparison with the previous release, Reporting Services 2008 doesn't introduce new Web service endpoints. The Reporting Services 2000 endpoint (ReportService.asmx) is no longer supported and you need to upgrade legacy applications that use it to the new endpoints.

Background Processor

The Background Processor application is responsible for handling all tasks that run in an unattended mode. For example, when a subscription event is received, the Background Processor handles the subscription and distributes the report to its final destination. The Background Processor is what the Reporting Services Windows service was in previous releases.

Similar to the Report Server Web service, the Background Processor is responsible for processing reports. However, the Background Processor doesn't communicate with the Report Server Web service. Instead, both applications make in-process internal calls to the Report Processor. To make things simpler, I will use the term *report server* from now on as a unifying logical name that includes both the Report Server Web service and the Background Processor.

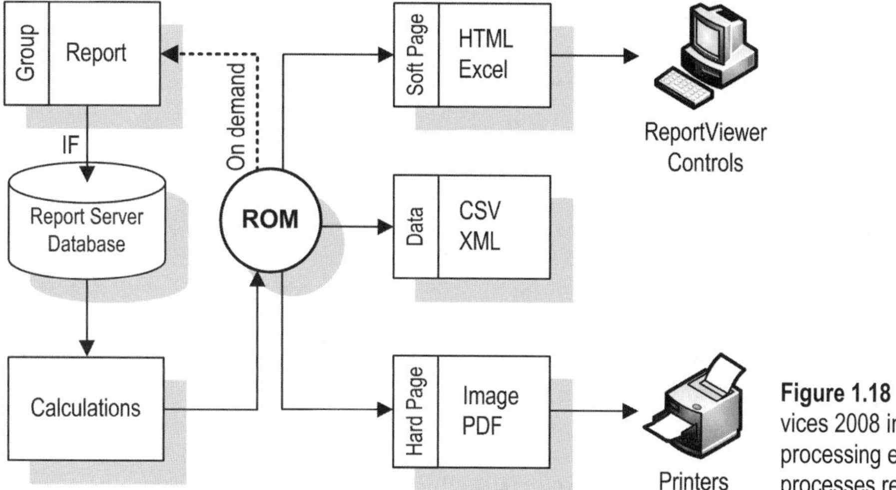

Figure 1.18 Reporting Services 2008 includes a new processing engine that processes reports on demand.

1.3.3 Understanding Report Processing

A significant effort has been made to improve Reporting Services scalability and performance. In previous releases, reports were memory-bound, which means that the memory usage consumed by the report was proportional to the report size. Consequently, large reports were known to cause out-of-memory exceptions. This was particularly problematic when exporting reports to Adobe Acrobat PDF and Microsoft Excel.

How report processing works

To address scalability issues with large reports, Microsoft redesigned the report processing engine in Reporting Services 2008. Specifically, the new Report Processor doesn't store the entire report presentation in memory but processes the report on demand, as Figure 1.18 shows.

When the Report Processor handles a new report request, it extracts the report data, merges the data into the report layout, and produces the report intermediate format. Then, the Report Processor saves the raw report in the report server database. However, unlike the old processing engine, which processed the report as a snapshot, the Report Processor precomputes and stores only certain report invariants, such as grouping, sorting, filtering, and aggregates.

During the report rendering phase, the Report Processor constructs a Rendering Object Model (ROM) object and forwards it to the rendering extension. Textbox values and calculations are calculated on-demand every time the containing page is rendered. This significantly reduces the in-memory presentation of the report.

Just how much memory does the new processing engine save? I tested print preview with an existing 1,270-page report processed by SQL Server 2005 and 2008 versions of Reporting Services and I listed the results in Table 1.2.

Table 1.2 The new report engine should produce significant memory savings

Version	Metrics	Time (sec)	Memory (MB)
SQL Server 2005	TFP	262	240
	TLP	610	312
SQL Server 2008	TFP	218	95
	TLP	430	95

The TFP metric stands for Time to First Page and measures the number of seconds it took the report server to render the first page in print preview mode. TLP (Time to Last Page) measures the number of seconds required to repaginate the entire report and render the last page. I used the Windows Task Manager on the server to track the memory utilization of the Reporting Services process. The result was remarkable. Thanks to the new processing improvements, Reporting Services 2008 consumed about 70% less memory.

Understanding rendering changes

Microsoft also redesigned the rendering extensions to improve further report processing. Previously, rendering was performed entirely on the server and the report clients, such as the ReportViewer and printer controls, were implemented as "thin" clients. They didn't do much processing since they were responsible only for presenting the rendered report to the user. In Reporting Services 2008, the rendering work can be distributed between the server and the clients.

A new RPL (Report Page Layout) renderer was introduced to generate a streamable output format, which is an independent representation of report layout and data. For example, the ReportViewer Web server control included in Report Manager uses this renderer and performs the final stage of report rendering on the client by translating RPL to HTML. The RPL format also lays the foundation for increased interactivity within the ReportViewer controls in future releases.

Another change that took place was unifying the page repagination logic across all renderers. In the past, users complained about getting incorrect page counts when previewing reports in different export formats. Reporting Services 2008 brings consistency to layout and repagination.

1.4 Applied Reporting Services

The short hands-on lab that follows will give you a taste of the report lifecycle and the Microsoft Business Intelligence Platform. Before we start, let's introduce an imaginary company called Adventure Works Cycles. Adventure Works Cycles is a large, multinational manufacturing company. It manufactures and sells bicycles to individuals and resellers in the North American, European and Asian commercial markets.

1.4.1 Introducing Adventure Works Sales Reporting System

The Adventure Works management has decided to implement a BI reporting solution to get more insight into company performance. And, as you probably guessed, Adventure Works has hired you to lead the design and implementation of the Adventure Works Intelligent Reporter—the next generation reporting solution for standard and ad hoc reporting.

Analyzing the current system

Adventure Works has already made a significant effort to implement data logistics processes that facilitate reporting, as shown in Figure 1.19.

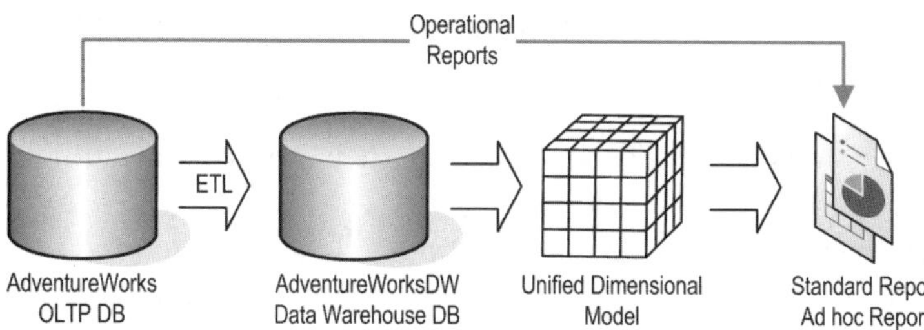

Figure 1.19 The Adventure Works reporting system.

Sales representatives use an intranet application to capture orders placed through the resale channel. Individual customers purchase Adventure Works products online through the Adventure Works web site. In both cases, the sales ordering data is captured in a SQL Server 2008 OLTP database called AdventureWorks2008.

NOTE The AdventureWorks2008 database simulates an OLTP sales order database, while AdventureWorksDW2008 imitates a data warehouse database. Once you download and install the databases (see the book front matter for instructions), you'll find Visio database schema diagrams in the installation folders. As you can see by browsing its seventy tables, the AdventureWorks2008 database is inherently more complex than FoodMart or other SQL Server sample databases that you may have encountered in the past.

Adventure Works has also built a data warehouse that archives the sales data. Integration Services data flow tasks periodically extract, transform, and load the data in the data warehouse database, which is physically implemented as a SQL Server 2008 AdventureWorksDW2008 database. Adventure Works has implemented an Analysis Services Unified Dimensional Model (UDM) layer on top of the data warehouse database for historical and trend reporting. This layer is realized as the Adventure Works multidimensional cube.

There are several advantages in using a cube as a data source for reports. First, performance will be greatly improved because Analysis Services is designed to store and query data efficiently. Second, useful business calculations, such as KPIs, can be easily implemented in the cube. Besides OLAP capabilities, Analysis Services also offers data mining features that can help users discover hidden data patterns, such as which products customers tend to buy together, who are the most likely buyers for a given product, sales forecasting, and more. Finally, in addition to Reporting Services, many other Microsoft and third-party software products can integrate with Analysis Services. Examples include Microsoft Excel for historical and trend reporting, PerformancePoint for monitoring KPIs and deconstructing data, Dundas charts for presenting OLAP data graphically, and so on.

However, given that most reporting solutions retrieve source data from relational databases, I will use Analysis Services sparingly in this book. That said, I strongly encourage you to consider Analysis Services for your real world solutions, especially when you need to address historical and trend reporting requirements.

Understanding reporting challenges

Currently, the Adventure Works reporting processes are subject to several deficiencies, including:

- Inability to share and disseminate reports—Reports are embedded in business applications and not easily accessible. At the same time, there is a need to publish strategic reports to the company's intranet where they can be viewed by authorized users.
- Assorted reporting technologies and tools—Information workers use a variety of reporting tools to produce reports. The Adventure Works management is looking for ways to reduce the Total Cost of Ownership for supporting and licensing these tools and standardize on a single reporting platform.
- Inadequate reporting experience—Business users complain that they cannot easily author ad hoc reports and share these reports with other users.
- Difficult integration with custom applications—Developers find it challenging to report-enable custom applications.
- Inadequate integration with SharePoint—Adventure Works is building a SharePoint portal and is looking for ways to let users run reports within the portal.

To address the current report deficiencies, you've decided to use Reporting Services 2008 as a one-stop reporting platform for addressing these report authoring, management, and delivery needs. Specifically, you will use Reporting Services to author operational reports from the AdventureWorks2008 database, standard reports from the AdventureWorksDW2008 database, and historical and trend reports from the Adventure Works cube. Business users will leverage the Reporting Services Report Builder technology to create their own ad hoc reports.

1.4.2 Your First Report ▶

In this practice, you will use Reporting Services to author, publish, and view a report. The Sales by Country report retrieves source data from the Adventure Works cube and displays it in a chart format. This practice walks you through the following tasks:

- Authoring a chart report
- Using Report Manager to manage the report
- Requesting the report on demand

Complete the instructions in the book front matter to install the Adventure Works cube before starting the practice. Figure 1.20 illustrates the finished report. This is a chart report that shows the Adventure Works Internet and reseller sales broken down by product category for a given sales territory that the user can enter as a report parameter.

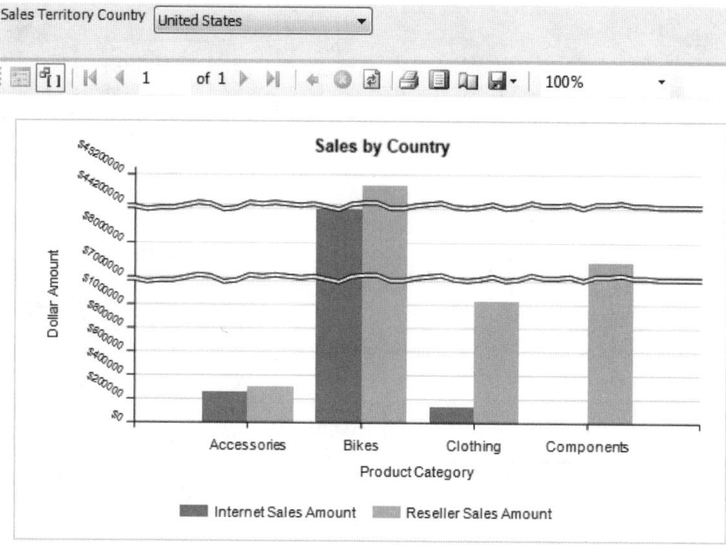

Figure 1.20 The Sales by Country report shows the Adventure Works sales data in a chart format.

Report authoring

You will use Report Designer included in Business Intelligence Development Studio to author and test the report.

Creating a project

Start by creating a Report Server project in Business Intelligence Development Studio.

1. Open Business Intelligence Development Studio from the Microsoft SQL Server 2008 program group.
2. Click File ⇨ New ⇨ Project menu to create a new Report Server project. A Report Server project contains data source and report definitions that you can work with and deploy together.
3. In the New Project dialog box, select the Report Server Project template. Name the project *Reports*, choose a location for the new project and click OK. BIDS creates a Report Server project and project folders in the Solution Explorer pane.
4. In the Solution Explorer pane, right-click on the Reports project node and choose Add ⇨ New Item.
5. In the Add New Item dialog box, click the Report template. Name the report *Sales by Country* and click OK.

BIDS adds the Sales by Country.rdl report definition and opens it in the Report Designer, as shown in Figure 1.21. The Report Designer includes Design and Preview tabs. The Design tab lets you lay out the report by dragging items from the Toolbox and dropping them to the report body. You can use the Preview tab to test the report and see how the data looks in the layout you defined.

Creating a data source

As a first step for authoring a report, you need to create a data source. A data source represents a connection to a database.

6. In the Report Data window, expand the New menu drop-down, and click Data Source.

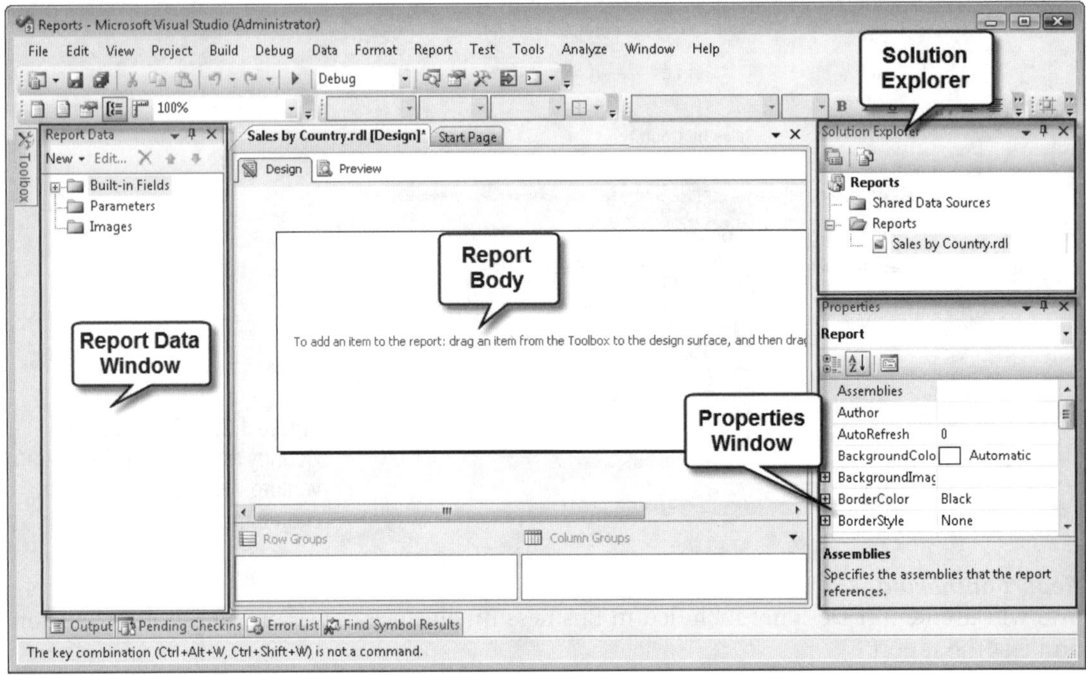

Figure 1.21 The BIDS Report Designer is hosted inside the Visual Studio IDE.

7. In the Data Source Properties dialog box, rename the data source to *AdventureWorksAS2008*.
8. Expand the Type drop-down list and select the Microsoft SQL Server Analysis Services data provider used to connect to Analysis Services cubes.
9. Click the Edit button to configure the data source.

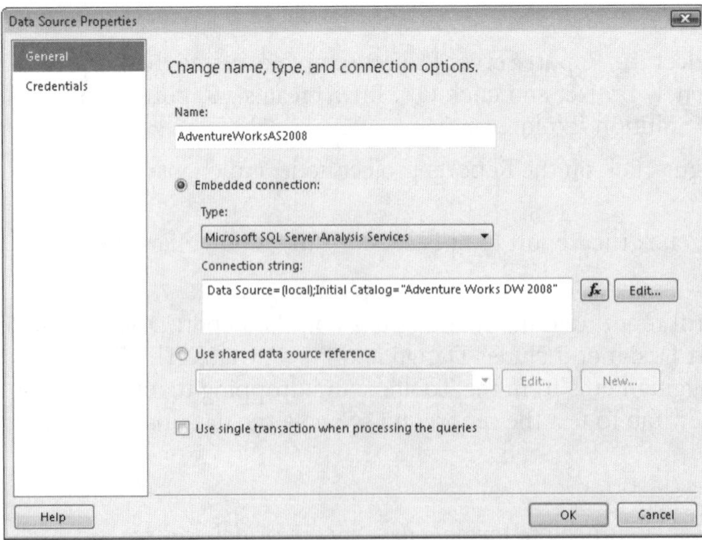

Figure 1.22 The Data Source Properties lets you configure a connection to a data source.

10. In the Connection Properties dialog, enter *(local)* for the server name to connect to your local Analysis Services instance. Expand the Select or Enter a Database Name drop-down list and

select the Adventure Works DW Analysis Services database. Report Designer generates the following connection string (see Figure 1.22):

```
Data Source=(local);Initial Catalog="Adventure Works DW 2008"
```

11. Click OK.

Report Designer adds the AdventureWorksAS2008 data source to the Report Data window.

Generating the report query

Next, you'll set up a report dataset. A report dataset represents the report data. It includes a query that retrieves data from the data source.

12. In the Report Data window, right-click the AdventureWorksAS2008 data source and click Add Dataset.
13. In the Dataset Properties dialog box that follows, click the Query Designer button. Because you've selected an Analysis Services data source, Report Designer opens the MDX Query Designer. This is one of the built-in query designers that ship with Reporting Services. The MDX Query Designer features a graphical interface that auto-generates the query as you drag and drop metadata objects.
14. In the Metadata pane, expand the Sales Territory dimension. Drag the Sales Territory Country attribute and drop it on the Data pane, as shown in Figure 1.23.

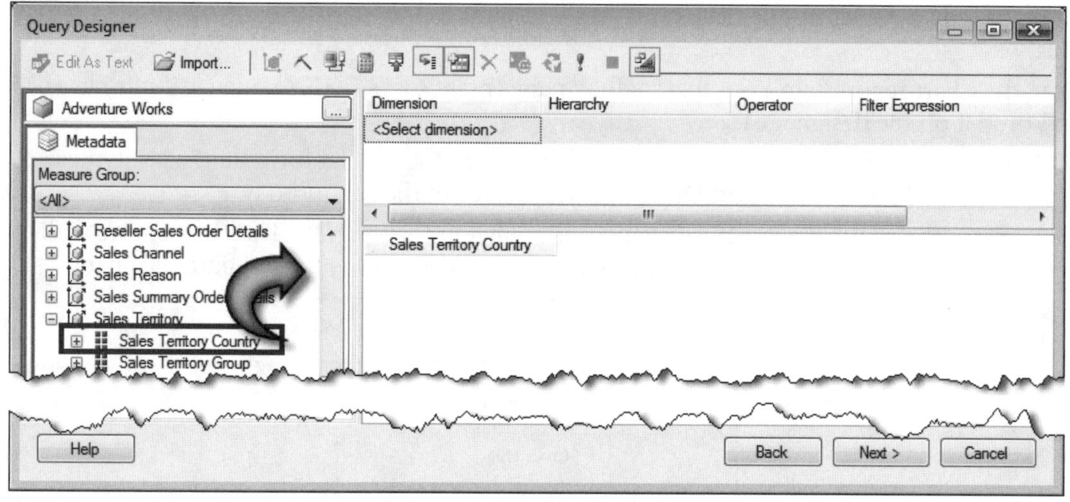

Figure 1.23 The MDX Query Designer lets you drag and drop cube metadata and preview query results.

15. Expand the Product dimension. Drag the Category attribute and drop it next to Sales Territory Country in the Data pane.
16. Scroll to the top of the Metadata pane. Expand the Measures folder and the Internet Sales measure group under it. Drag the Internet Sales Amount measure next to Category in the Data pane. The MDX Query Designer executes the query and shows the results in the Data Pane.
17. Expand the Reseller Sales measures group. Drag the Reseller Sales Amount measure and drop it next to Internet Sales Amount.
18. To filter by territory, drag again the Sales Territory Country attribute of the Sales Territory dimension from the Metadata pane to the Dimension column in the Filter pane.

19. Expand the Filter Expression drop-down list and select United States so the report shows data for United States by default.
20. In the Filter pane, check the Parameters checkbox to create a report-level parameter, as shown in Figure 1.24.

Dimension	Hierarchy	Operator	Filter Expression	Parameters
Sales Territory	Sales Territory Country	Equal	{ United States }	☑
<Select dimension>				

Sales Territory Country	Category	Internet Sales Amount	Reseller Sales Amount
United States	Accessories	256422.07	303515.2279
United States	Bikes	8999859.5308	44832751.7288
United States	Clothing	133507.91	1037436.9473
United States	Components	(null)	7434097.3062

Figure 1.24 Use the Select the Data Source dialog to configure a database connection.

21. Click OK to close the MDX Query Designer. Back to the Dataset Properties dialog box, click OK to close the dialog box and return to Report Designer.

Report Designer adds the DataSet1 dataset to the Report Data window (press Ctrl+Alt+D to open it the Report Data window is closed).

Configuring the chart report

Now that you have set up the data structures you want to use, you are ready to design the report.

22. Drag the Chart report item from the Toolbox pane (press Ctrl+Alt+X to open it if it is closed) and drop it on the design area.
23. In the Select the Chart Type dialog box that follows, leave the default Column chart type selected, and click OK. The Report Designer adds a chart to the report body.
24. Click inside the chart to put it in edit mode, as shown in Figure 1.25. The chart shows additional areas (called adorner frames) that let you drop dataset fields to configure the chart.

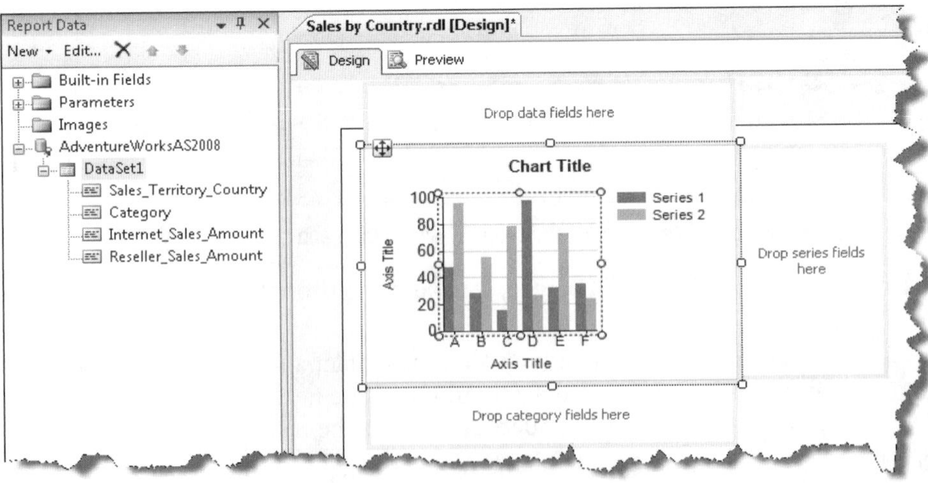

Figure 1.25 You can configure the chart by dragging and dropping dataset fields.

25. If the Report Data window is not shown, press Ctrl-Alt-D to open it.

The Report Data window contains various objects that are useful at design time, such as parameters, data sources, and datasets. For example, it includes the AdventureWorksAS2008 data source that you've just created. If you expand the AdventureWorksAS2008 data source, you'll see the DataSet1 dataset you created in the MDX Query Designer.

26. Expand the DataSet1 node. Drag the Category field and drop it on the Drop Categories Fields Here chart area to group the chart data by this field.
27. Drag the Internet_Sales_Amount field and drop it on the Drop Data Fields Here area.
28. Drag the Reseller_Sales_Amount field and drop it on the Drop Data Fields Here area.
29. Click the report body outside the chart and enlarge the chart by dragging its bottom right corner, such as to a width of 6" and height of 3.5". You can right-click on an empty area outside the report body and select View ⇨ Ruler to show a ruler that can help you size the chart.

One of my favorite features of the Reporting Services 2008 chart item is that you can configure it interactively. This saves you time because the chart item is very complex and has many properties.

30. Click the chart and click the chart title to select it. Click the title one more time to put it in edit mode. Change the title to *Sales by Country*.
31. Click the chart legend to put it edit mode. Chart legends can be moved to different locations. The contents of the legend will adjust to fit the available space. Click the resize handle and drag the chart legend below the chart to free up more horizontal space for the chart data.
32. Preview the report by clicking the Preview tab.

Notice that Bikes sales far exceed the other categories. You can enable scale breaks to prevent very high values from eclipsing low values.

33. Click the Design tab to go back to design mode.
34. Right-click the numbers in the vertical axis and choose Axis Properties (see Figure 1.26).

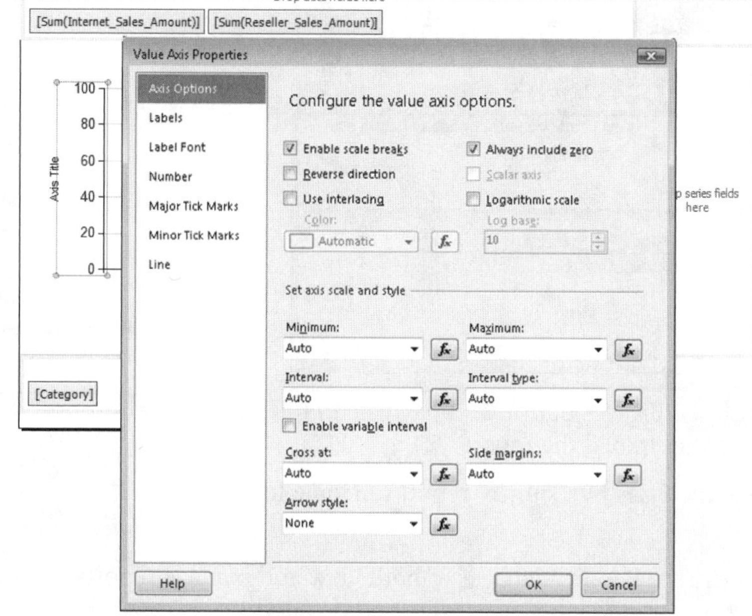

Figure 1.26 Use the Value Axis Properties dialog box to configure the chart axis.

35. In the Value Axis Properties dialog box, check the Enable Scale Breaks property.
36. Select the Labels page and clear the Labels Can be Offset property.
37. Click the Number page and format the axis labels as currency without decimal places. Click OK.
38. Rename the vertical axis title in place to *Dollar Amount* and the horizontal axis title to *Product Category*.
39. Preview the report. It should now look like the one shown in Figure 1.20.
40. Click the Save All toolbar button to save your changes.
41. Right-click the Sales by Country.rdl report definition in the Solution Explorer and click View Code. Notice that the report is described in XML-based report definition language (RDL).

You will probably never have to view or edit the RDL directly, but if you are curious about the underlying definition, the View Code command provides an easy way to look under the hood.

Report management

Once you are done authoring a report, you can deploy it to the server to share it with other users. Recall that Report Manager is a web application provided by Microsoft for managing and viewing reports. You can deploy the report directly from BIDS by configuring the report properties and choosing Build ⇨ Deploy. However, to demonstrate report management features, let's use Report Manager to upload the Sales by Country report to your local report server.

1. In Internet Explorer, type the Report Manager URL, such as http://localhost/reports or http://localhost:8080/reports (Windows XP).
2. In the Report Manager Home page, click the Upload File button, as shown in Figure 1.27. It's okay if your Home page has different items or folders.

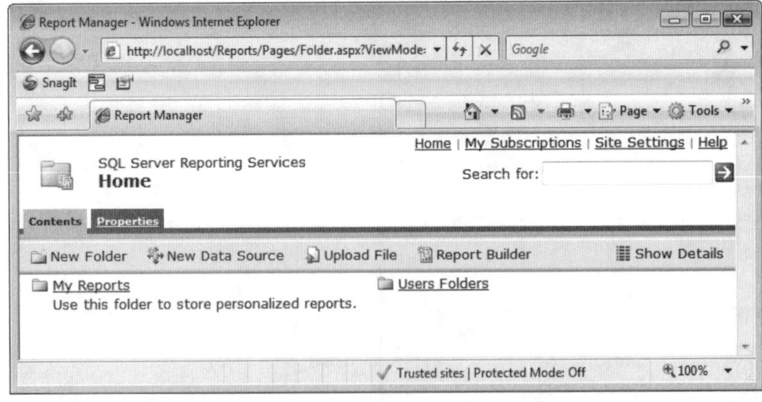

Figure 1.27 Use the Report Manger to manage the report catalog and view reports.

3. In the Upload File page, click the Browse button and navigate to the Sales by Country.rdl report definition file. Click OK to upload the report.

The Report Manager uploads the Sales by Country report to Home folder.

Viewing the report

As noted, organizations can use the Report Manager to both view and manage reports. In the next few steps, you will see how easy it is to view a report on demand.

1. Click the Sales by Country report link to view the report.

   The Report Manager renders the report on the screen. It includes a report toolbar at the top of the report. This toolbar is on by default. You can use it to navigate pages, search for text in the report, or export it to a different format.
2. Optionally, try out a few report features, such as changing the report parameters, exporting the report, printing it, and so on.

This practice demonstrated how you can use the Reporting Services tools to execute the report lifecycle, which consists of report authoring, management, and delivery stages.

1.5 Summary

This chapter has been a whirlwind tour of Reporting Services and its features. By now, you should view Reporting Services 2008 as a sophisticated server-based reporting platform that meets a variety of reporting requirements. You've learned about the history of Reporting Services and the new features in the 2008 release. You've also seen how Reporting Services fits into the Microsoft Business Intelligence initiative.

In this chapter, we took a close look at the Reporting Services logical architecture and the report lifecycle, which consists of report authoring, management, and delivery stages. You learned how the tools support each stage of the lifecycle. During the report authoring stage, you use one of the Microsoft built-in report designers to lay out the report. In the management stage, you upload the report to the server and use Report Manager to configure report settings. You also learned that Report Manager supports the delivery stage by servicing on demand requests for viewing a report and creating subscriptions for automatic, scheduled delivery.

We also discussed the Reporting Services physical architecture and how the new hosting model provides native support for ASP.NET and HTTP.SYS without IIS. We also learned how the new processing engine improves Reporting Services performance. Finally, you completed a practice that demonstrated how to use the Report Designer to author a chart report from an Analysis Services cube and Report Manager to upload and view the report.

Having laid the foundation, we are ready to put our knowledge to use. Let's continue our journey by learning more about how to install, configure, and upgrade Reporting Services.

1.6 Resources

Applied Microsoft Analysis Services 2005 by Teo Lachev
(http://www.prologika.com/Books/0976635305/Book.aspx).

Report Definition Language Specification
(http://www.microsoft.com/sql/technologies/reporting/rdlspec.mspx).

Web and Application Server Infrastructure—Performance and Scalability
(http://tinyurl.com/3oqj4)—Learn how HTTP.SYS improves the IIS performance.

Run ASMX Without IIS by Aaron Skonnard
(http://tinyurl.com/64lrqg)—Learn how to host ASP.NET outside IIS.

Chapter 2

Installing Reporting Services

Reporting Services 2008 ships as a feature component of SQL Server 2008. The SQL Server 2008 setup program makes it simple to perform a new installation or upgrade an existing installation. However, before you insert the setup disk, it makes sense to take the "think before you leap" approach and spend some time planning your deployment.

I will start this chapter by providing the necessary background to help you plan your Reporting Services deployment. Next, I'll walk you through the steps to perform a new installation of Reporting Services. If you have a previous version of Reporting Services, I'll show you how to upgrade to the 2008 release. Finally, I'll discuss additional post-deployment setup steps to finalize a Reporting Services installation.

2.1 Planning for a Reporting Services Installation

Recall from the previous chapter that Reporting Services is a server-based platform. While it's fine to install the SQL Server Database Engine and Reporting Services together on the same computer for development or evaluation purposes, you will probably want to do some thorough planning if you are installing Reporting Services in a production environment.

2.1.1 Planning Hardware and Software

To plan successfully your Reporting Services deployment, you will need to know about the Reporting Services editions, hardware and software requirements, operational and scalability constraints, and integration scenarios. Let's start by reviewing the Reporting Services editions and licensing requirements.

Understanding editions and licensing

As with its predecessors, Reporting Services 2008 follows the SQL Server pricing and licensing model. To address different user needs, Reporting Services is available in the three core SQL Server 2008 editions (Enterprise, Developer, and Standard,) and three specialized editions (Workgroup, Web, and Express Advanced), as shown in Table 2.1. Reporting Services is not available with the SQL Server 2008 Compact and Express editions. For more information about how Reporting Services editions compare, read the document Features Supported by the Editions of SQL Server 2008 (see Resources section).

Table 2.1 **Reporting Services is available in six editions**

Edition	Choose when
Enterprise	You need all Reporting Services features and your solution must be highly scalable.
Developer	You design and develop full-featured Reporting Services solutions on your local development machine. As with the Enterprise Edition, the Developer Edition supports all features but it is not licensed for production use.
Standard	You plan to install Reporting Services on a single server with moderate report loads. The Standard edition doesn't support data-driven subscriptions or the infinite drillthrough feature of Report Builder 1.0.
Workgroup	You want to distribute Reporting Services as a part of your solution that targets desktop deployments and you need more features than the Express Advanced edition provides.
Web	You are a web hosting provider and you want to offer low cost, highly scalable hosting for your clients.
Express Advanced	You need the most lightweight Reporting Services edition at no cost. The Express Advanced edition is free to download, free to redistribute, and free to embed.

The Reporting Services licensing model is simple. Basically, you can think of each of the SQL Server feature components as SQL Server. Therefore, you need a SQL Server license on the machine where Reporting Services is installed. For example, suppose your operational requirements call for installing Reporting Services on a separate server from your database server. In this case, you will need two SQL Server licenses: one for the Reporting Services installation and another one for the SQL Server Database Engine. What if you decide to use SQL Server 2005 to host your data and the report catalog but you want to use Reporting Services 2008? Again, you need separate SQL Server 2005 and SQL Server 2008 licenses.

As far as pricing, Microsoft didn't change the pricing model of SQL Server 2008 from the previous release. The pricing details are available on the SQL Server 2008 home page (http://www.microsoft.com/sqlserver/2008).

Hardware and software recommendations

The minimum hardware and software requirements for installing SQL Server 2008 are documented in SQL Server 2008 Books Online (see Resources). Table 2.2 lists two example hardware and software recommendations for local and production server installations respectively. Use the Development column when planning to install Reporting Services locally on your machine for design and development.

Table 2.2 **Recommended local and server configurations**

Configuration	Development	Server
OS	Windows XP with Service Pack 2 or Windows Vista	Windows Server2003 Standard or Enterprise Edition
SQL Server 2008	Developer Edition	Standard or Enterprise Edition
Example configuration	Dell Precision 490	Dell PowerEdge 2900
RAM	2 GB	8GB
CPU	1 Dual-Core Xeon Processor	2 Quad-Core x64 Intel Xeon Processors

Since deployment topologies and reporting loads may vary greatly between organizations, choosing a server configuration is a function of many variables. As a guideline, the Server column lists a real-life server configuration for a solution that served the reporting needs of about one hundred deployed users. This was a single-server deployment model, where the SQL Server Database Engine, Reporting Services, Analysis Services, Integration Services and SharePoint were installed on the same server.

One thing to note when planning the server configuration is that Reporting Services is a very processor-intensive application so the more CPU power you can afford, the better. This is especially true if Reporting Services shares the box with the other SQL Server services, such as the SQL Server Database Engine or Analysis Services.

Planning an integration mode

Reporting Services supports native and SharePoint integration modes. These two modes are mutually exclusive. If you don't plan to deploy reports to a SharePoint portal, configure Reporting Services for native mode in the default configuration. In this case, the report server will be configured as a stand-alone application server that provides all processing and management functionality through the Reporting Services components. For example, in native mode, you use the built-in Report Manager application to manage the report catalog.

If you need to integrate Reporting Services with Windows SharePoint Services or Microsoft Office SharePoint Server, choose SharePoint integration mode. In this case, report viewing and management happens inside the SharePoint portal. This integration mode is discussed in more details in chapter 17.

While you can use the Reporting Services Configuration Manager to switch between the two integration modes later on, I recommend you make a decision upfront because the two report catalog types are not compatible. For example, you cannot switch from a native mode to a SharePoint mode and use the same report catalog. Instead, you have to create a new report server database for a report server that runs in SharePoint integration mode. Needless to say, you will need to redeploy the report content. Reporting Services doesn't provide a way to move content between the different catalog types.

2.1.2 Planning a Deployment Topology

When you plan hardware and software requirements, you need to consider your deployment topology. For example, you need to decide whether to install all SQL Server components on a single server or spread them on multiple servers. SQL Server 2008 supports flexible deployment scenarios that let you achieve a compromise between cost and performance.

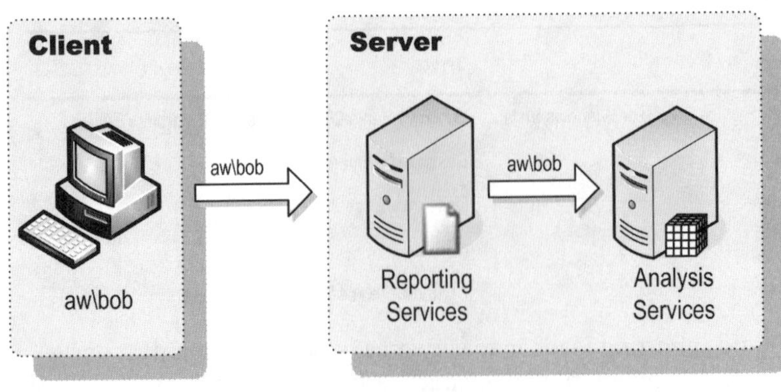

Figure 2.1 With single-server deployment, all SQL Server services are installed on the same machine.

Single-server deployment

The single-server deployment is easy because you install all required services on the same server, as you would on your development machine. Suppose that your reports retrieve source data from an Analysis Services cube. As Figure 2.1 shows, in this deployment mode, you would install Reporting Services and Analysis Services on the same server. If the cube retrieves source data from a SQL Server database, you would install the SQL Server relational engine and possibly Integration Services on that server as well. Since all SQL Server installed services on the same box are covered by the same SQL Server license, this configuration is also cost-effective.

Security is simpler on a single-server deployment too. Suppose that you need to flow the user Windows identity from the client all the way to the database server that is configured for Windows Integrated security. With single-server deployments, there is only one hop (from the client to the server). This is something the Windows NTLM authentication protocol is designed to handle, so impersonating the user succeeds. For example, if Bob logs on to his machine as aw\bob and requests a report, the report server will see the request coming under Bob's identity. Since the report server is configured to impersonate the user, the report server can pass Bob's identity successfully to the database server on the same machine.

Because of its simplicity and cost benefits, you should consider a single-server deployment wherever possible. Independent software vendors (ISVs) and small to mid-size deployments will undoubtedly benefit from single-server deployments.

Multi-server deployment

Operational and performance requirements may outgrow a single-server deployment. For example, you may already have a dedicated OLAP server that hosts an Analysis Services cube and the administrator may be unwilling to let you install Reporting Services on the same server.

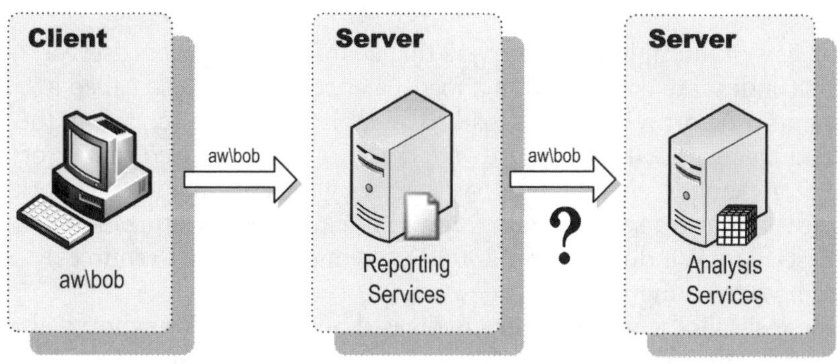

Figure 2.2 Multi-server deployments present security challenges because NTLM doesn't support delegation.

Security gets trickier with the multi-server deployment mode because Windows doesn't support user delegation by default. As Figure 2.2 shows, the first hop is the same as with a single-server deployment because the report server sees the report request coming from Bob. However, to pass Bob's identity to another server, you need more than impersonation. You need the report server to delegate Bob's request so the call to Analysis Services happens as if Bob queried the cube directly. However, since the report server doesn't have the Bob's password, it cannot delegate the call and the request fails. The issue manifests itself with a rather obscure error message when viewing a report:

```
Cannot create a connection to data source '<data source name>'. (rsErrorOpeningConnection)
```

The solution to this predicament is to use Kerberos security (with delegation enabled). In fact, by default, the report server is configured to use Windows Negotiation which attempts Kerberos first and falls back on NTLM if the client doesn't support Kerberos. However, Kerberos necessitates additional steps for configuring the report server to delegate the call. These steps will require some assistance from your Active Directory administrator since you will need domain administrator rights to make changes to the Active Directory. The Troubleshooting Kerberos Delegation paper (see Resource) is a great read to get you started with configuring and troubleshooting the Kerberos security.

Of course, if the data source uses standard security (stored user name and password), you don't need to worry about delegation and Kerberos. However, when standard security is used, the data source will not be able to differentiate users.

Scale-out deployment

As your BI solution gathers momentum, it will attract more users and you may reach the limits of scaling up a single server. Or, your operational requirements may call for a fault-tolerant reporting system. To meet these requirements, consider scaling out the report server, as shown in Figure 2.3.

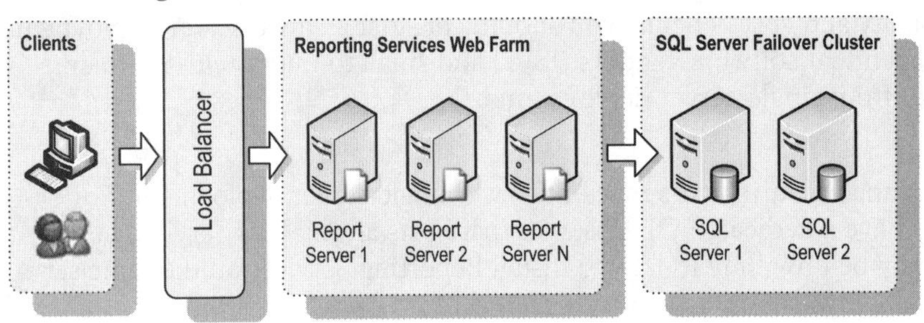

Figure 2.3 You can scale out Reporting Services to meet scalability or fault tolerance requirements.

A scale-out deployment consists of multiple report servers that share the same report server database. The report servers (nodes) are configured in a load-balanced cluster, also called a *web farm*. When a user submits a report request, the load balancer redirects the request to the least-utilized server. The load balancer could be a hardware device, such as a Cisco router, or it could be software-based. For example, Windows Server operating systems include Network Load Balancing (NLB) services that use a software algorithm to track the server utilization and redirect the incoming requests. The Windows Server 2003 Deployment Kit (see Resources) provides information about how to configure NLB.

The report server database should be installed on a dedicated SQL Server. You should also plan a SQL Server failover cluster to make the report server database fault-tolerant. Scale-out deployment is supported in SQL Server Enterprise edition only and requires manual setup for Reporting Services (Install, but Don't Configure the Report Server setup option). Once the setup has completed, you need to use the Reporting Services Configuration Manager to create the report server database and join the report servers to the web farm.

Instance deployment

SQL Server has been supporting multiple instances on the same machine since version 2000. An instance is a named SQL Server installation consisting of one or more SQL Server services that listen on the same port. The SQL Server Browser service listens for incoming requests and redirects them to the appropriate instance.

For example, as Figure 2.4 shows, you may have an application that uses SQL Server 2005 and you may be unwilling to upgrade it to SQL Server 2008. At the same time, you may need to install SQL Server 2008 on the same box for a new project. Or, you may want to use the same test server to test different versions of SQL Server. You can meet such deployment requirements by having SQL Server 2005 and 2008 running side-by-side by installing them on separate instances.

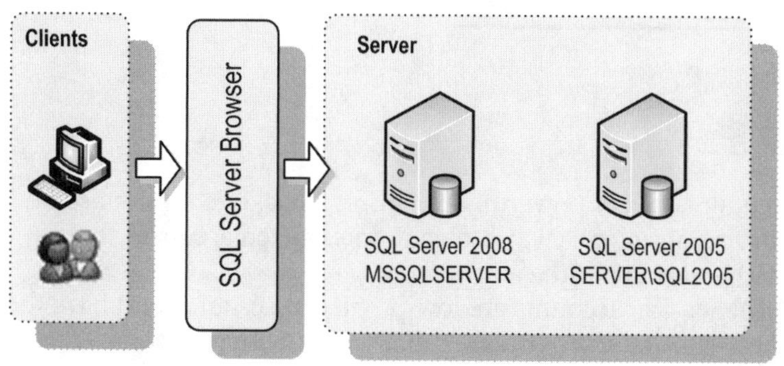

Figure 2.4 You can install multiple SQL Server instances on the same server.

If you don't have existing SQL Server installations, you can install SQL Server on the default instance whose pre-defined name is MSSQLSERVER. Consequently, you can connect to any of the services on the default instance by just using the server name or IP address. If the setup program detects any existing SQL Server instances, it will let you upgrade these instances or install SQL Server 2008 as a separate named instance. To connect to a named instance, append a backslash to the server name. For example, if the server name is MILLENNIA and the instance name is SQL2008, you can connect to any of the services of the SQL2008 instance by entering MILLENNIA\SQL2008.

TIP You can use the Services console application in Administrator Tools to identify the installed SQL Server services and instances. For example, SQL Server Reporting Services (MSSQLSERVER) means that the server is running Reporting Services that is installed as the default instance. Integration Services is not instance-aware and doesn't support multiple instances.

You can mix services and instances. Suppose that the server is running only Reporting Services 2000. You can install SQL Server 2008 Database Engine as the default instance and install Reporting Services 2008 as a named instance.

You should try to minimize the number of instances installed on the server for cost and performance reasons. Each new instance requires a separate SQL Server license (unless it is a SQL Server Express edition) and the instances will be competing for server resources. For example, if you are installing Windows SharePoint Services on a server which already has SQL Server 2008 installed, run the SharePoint setup in advanced mode so you could connect to the existing SQL Server 2008 instance instead of creating a new SQL Server Express instance .

2.1.3 Planning Service Accounts

Before running the setup program, you need to decide what Windows accounts Reporting Services and the other installed SQL Server services will run under. The SQL Server setup program lets you configure the service accounts independently for each service. You can choose a built-in system account or a custom account, such as a domain or local account.

Understanding system accounts

Windows includes system accounts that you can use for startup accounts for the SQL Server services. These system accounts are listed in Table 2.3.

Table 2.3 Built-in system accounts

Account	Privilege Level	Network Credentials
NT AUTHORITY\System	High	✓
NT AUTHORITY\Network Service	Low	✓
NT AUTHORITY\Local Service	Low	

The NT AUTHORITY\System account is a very powerful account. If a hacker compromises a service running under the System account, the hacker can gain unrestricted access to the machine. Therefore, you should use this account with caution.

The Network Service and Local Service accounts are low privileged accounts and have the same rights as the members of the Windows User group. Similar to the System account, the Network Service account can access network resources under the computer's domain account. For example, let's say you configure Reporting Services on a server called MILLENNIA in the adventure-works domain to run under the Network Service. If custom code in a report tries to access a network resource, such as file, located on server B, the request will go out under adventure-works\MILLENNIA$. If MILLENNIA isn't in a domain, no network credentials will be assigned to it and the call will fail.

The Local Service account is that most restricted because it doesn't have rights to access network resources. In other words, it is limited to accessing resources on the local machine only. The SQL Server 2008 setup program doesn't include the Local Service account in the pre-populated drop-down list of system accounts, so if you want to use it, you have to enter it in manually.

Understanding custom accounts

You can choose to run a service under a custom account to further isolate its surface area. For example, suppose that both ASP.NET and Reporting Services run under the Network Service account. If a hacker gains access to a web application, the attacker will get permissions to access the report server database. Another scenario that may favor a custom account is when a service needs to access a network resource under a designated domain account. For example, Analysis Services lets you synchronize databases between servers. However, the service account of the target server (the one that needs to be updated) must have administrator access to the source database. If the Analysis Services service runs under a domain account, you can grant this account the required permissions to the source server.

In the case of Reporting Services, there are limited scenarios where a custom account could be useful. One of them could be when a report custom code needs to access a network resource. For example, custom code may need to open a connection to an Analysis Services cube that requires a designated Windows account. Another scenario is SharePoint integration mode where the report server and the SharePoint databases are on one machine and the SharePoint Web application is on another machine. In this case, SharePoint will block any application that runs under a local machine account from accessing its remote databases. To work around this, you would have to configure the report server to run as a domain user account.

In general, you should avoid running the Reporting Services under a domain account for reasons that are not immediately obvious. First, built-in machine accounts, such as Network Service, have predefined Service Principal Names (SPN) in the Windows Active Directory. These predefined SPNs are used to identify services on computers in the network. In contrast with built-in machine accounts, a domain account may not have a registered Service Principal Name (SPN) in the Windows Active Directory for a particular service. As a result, under Negotiated Kerberos authentication, the service will be unknown in the Active Directory database and no tickets will be granted to access it.

Consequently, due to the authentication failure, the report server will keep on prompting you for Windows credentials even if you supply correct credentials when you connect to the server. As a work-around, you can disable Windows Negotiate by disabling it in the report server configuration file (rsreportserver.config), as follows:

```
<Authentication>
  <AuthenticationTypes>
    <!--RSWindowsNegotiate/ -- >
    <RSWindowsNTLM/>
  </AuthenticationTypes>
</Authentication>
```

If you need to use Kerberos, such as to delegate user credentials to a database server, the network administrator can register an SPN for the domain account in the Active Directory by executing the following two commands:

```
setspn - A HTTP/<servername> <domain \account>
setspn -A HTTP/<FQDN> <domain\  account>
```

This will work as long as Reporting Services is the only service on the box that uses HTTP. As Microsoft Knowledge Base Article 871179 explains, an SPN for a service can only be associated with one account. This means that if you have IIS running on the box, all applications that are hosted by IIS (and consequently run in the HTTP service) must also run under the domain user identity you established for HTTP service on your computer. If you do not use the same account, accessing a web application hosted by IIS will now prompt for credentials and then fail the connection. As noted, built-in accounts don't have this issue because they have SPNs registered in the directory already.

In summary, when choosing an account for Reporting Services, I recommend you stick to the built-in accounts, such as Network Service. You can always change the account later on if needed.

2.2 Performing a New Installation

Now that you have planned your Reporting Services deployment, you are ready to start the setup process. The instructions that follow demonstrate a "happy" installation path that assumes that you are installing the server components on a clean machine. For the purposes of this practice, I'll demonstrate installing SQL Server Developer Edition on Windows Vista.

2.2.1 Performing Initial Setup Steps

Launch the SQL Server setup program by inserting the first SQL Server 2008 setup CD. The SQL Server setup program should start momentarily. If Autoplay doesn't work, run the setup manually by double-clicking setup.exe found in the root folder on the first CD. If not installed, the setup program will prompt you to install .NET Framework 3.5 with Service Pack 1 and Windows Installer version 4.5. Once these prerequisites are installed, the setup program opens the SQL Server Installation Center.

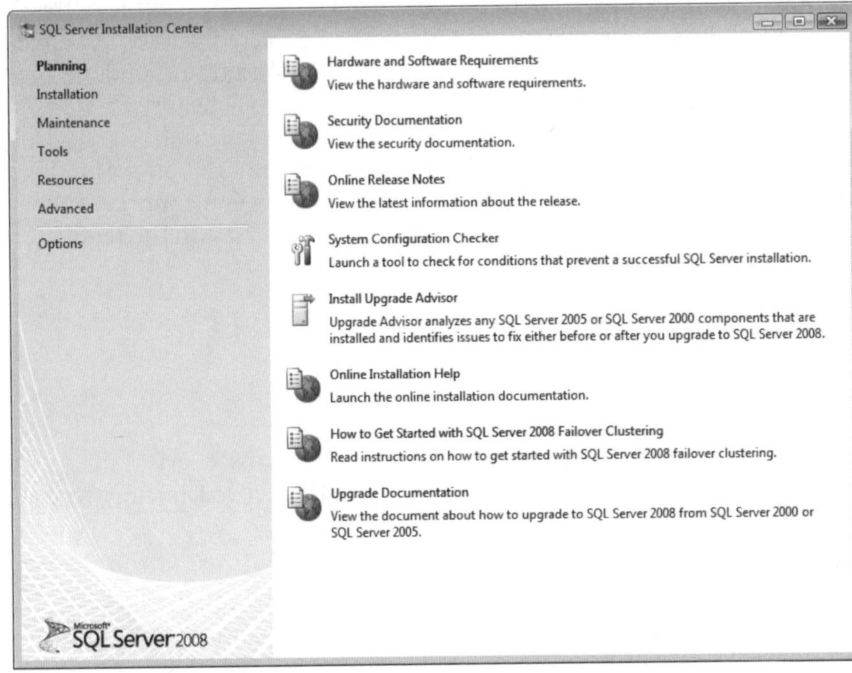

Figure 2.5 The Planning page lets you prepare for the installation.

The SQL Server Installation Center is a central point for planning, installing, and upgrading SQL Server. The left menu includes links that organize features into logical pages. Use the resources in the Planning page (see Figure 2.5) to plan your new installation or upgrade. The Installation page lets you perform the actual deployment. Use the Maintenance page to upgrade your SQL Server edition, repair an existing instance, or remove a node from a cluster.

The Tools page includes links to several utilities, such as a utility that checks your configuration for a set of conditions that may prevent a successful installation. The Resources page provides links to useful resources, including the Books Online and the SQL Server 2008 samples. The Advanced page lets you perform advanced installation tasks, such as adding a node to a SQL Server cluster. Finally, you can use the Options page to specify the processor type, such as x86 or x64, and the installation media root directory.

Please feel free to explore the wealth of resources available in the SQL Server Installation Center. Once you are ready to proceed with the deployment, click the Installation link to open the Installation page, which is shown in Figure 2.6. You can use the Installation page to perform various installation tasks, such as performing a new installation, upgrading an existing installation, or adding new features to an existing SQL Server 2008 installation.

The setup program executes the Setup Support Rules step that checks certain rules which may prevent installing the SQL Server setup files, such as minimum operating system version check, local administrator rights, restart required, and so on.

1. Assuming all rules have checked successfully, click OK.
2. In the Setup Support Files dialog box, click the Install button to install the components by the setup wizard.

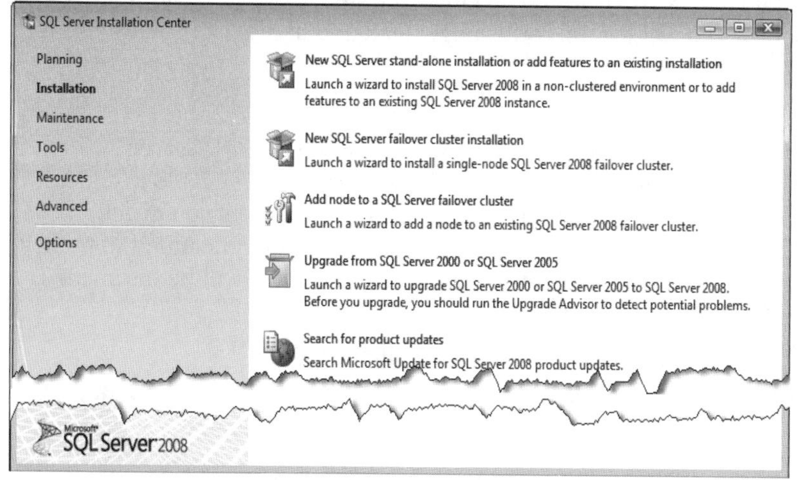

Figure 2.6 Use the Installation page to carry out installation tasks, such as installing a new instance or upgrading an existing instance.

2.2.2 Installing a New SQL Server Installation

The setup wizard installs a new installation in several steps. First, the wizard performs a system configuration check to ensure that the target machine meets the hardware and software requirements. If a requirement fails the check, setup cannot continue. For example, if SQL Server 7.0 is installed, the wizard will flag the Unsupported SQL Server Products requirement as Failed and disable the Next button.

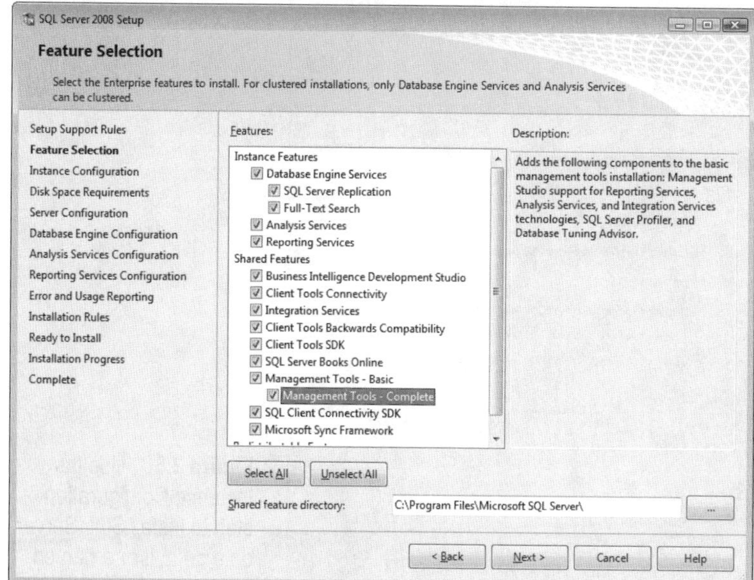

Figure 2.7 The Feature Selection step lets you select instance-specific and shared features.

If you have an existing SQL Server instance installed, the setup wizard will show the Installation Type page to let you choose between performing an existing installation or adding features to an existing named instance. If you have an existing instance, such as SQL Server 2005 on the default instance, and you want to install SQL Server 2008 side by side, leave the New

Installation option selected and click Next. In the Product Key step, enter your product key or choose to evaluate SQL Server. In the License Terms page, read and accept the license terms and click Next.

Selecting features

The Feature Selection step, which is shown in Figure 2.7, lets you select SQL Server 2008 instance-specific and shared features that will be shared among all SQL Server 2008 instances. You can highlight a feature to see its description in the Description pane. As you check instance features, additional steps required to configure the selected feature are added to the left pane. You can also overwrite the component directory where the features will be installed. The default path is C:\Program Files\Microsoft SQL Server\.

1. Assuming a full installation, click the Select All button and click Next.

   The wizard advances to the Instance Configuration step.

Configuring the instance

In the Instance Configuration step (see Figure 2.8), the wizard discovers any existing SQL Server instances and shows them in the Installed Instances grid. At this point, you need to decide whether to install SQL Server on the default or a named instance. You can use the Default instance option only if no previous SQL Server installations exist on the machine. Otherwise, you need to specify a named instance by selecting the Named Instance option.

As a part of configuring a named instance, you need to specify the instance name which clients will use to connect to the instance. For example, if you name the instance SQL2008 and the server name is MILLENNIA, the clients will connect to the instance as MILLENNIA\SQL2008.

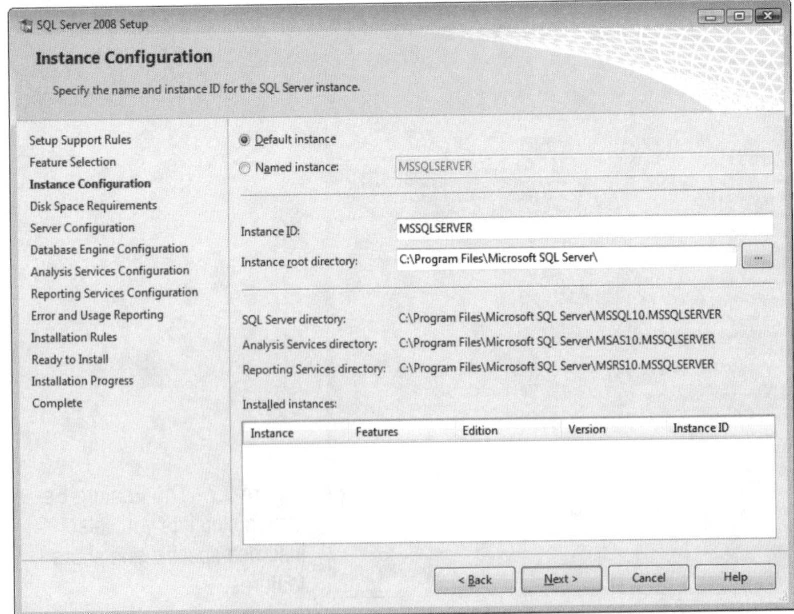

Figure 2.8 Use the Instance Configuration step to install SQL Server on a default or a named instance.

You must also specify an instance identifier. The setup program uses this identifier to define the installation paths. The predefined identifier for the default instance is MSSQLSERVER. Consequently, the Reporting Services installation directory will be C:\Program Files\Microsoft

SQL Server\MSRS10.MSSQLSERVER. For a named instance, the default instance identifier is the same as the instance name.

1. Accept the default values unless you have a good reason to change them and click Next.
2. In the Disk Space Requirements step, the wizard calculates the disk space required by the selected options. Click Next.

Configuring service accounts

The Server Configuration step lets you specify the service accounts. The SQL Server Browser and SQL Server Integration Services are pre-configured to run under system accounts and cannot be changed. You can configure the service accounts for the rest of the services independently or use one account for all services. You can use system or custom accounts. If you are unsure what accounts to select, consider configuring all services to run under the Network Service system account and changing the accounts later on if needed.

1. Click the Use the Same Account for All SQL Server Services button.
2. In the dialog box that follows, expand the Account Name drop-down list and select *NT AUTHORITY\NETWORK SERVICE*, as shown in Figure 2.9. Click OK.

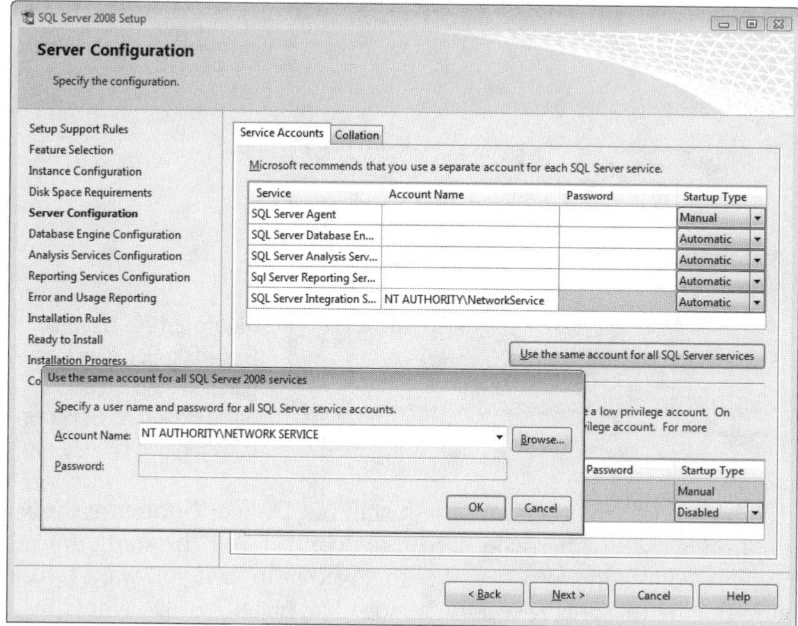

Figure 2.9 Use the Server Configuration step to set up the service accounts.

The wizard configures the rest of the services to run under the Network Service account. You can use the Server Configuration step to specify the service startup type. For example, if you are not planning to use SQL Server Analysis Services immediately, set its startup type to Manual or Disabled to conserve system resources. The Collation type lets you specify the collation type for the SQL Server Database Engine and Analysis Services.

The next two steps, Database Engine Configuration and Analysis Services Configuration, let you configure these services if you have selected them in the Feature Selection page. For example, you can use the Database Engine Configuration step to specify the authentication option for connecting to the SQL Server Database Engine service, such as Windows authentication only or a mixed mode. Both steps require you specify an existing Windows user as an administrator. You can press the Add Current User button to add yourself as an administrator.

NOTE Because the AdventureWorks2008 database demonstrates the filestream feature (new with SQL Server 2008). I recommend you enable filestream during setup. To do so, in the Database Engine Configuration step, click the FILE-STREAM tab, check the two Enable Filestream options, and accept the default share name.

Configuring Reporting Services

The Reporting Services Configuration page, which is shown in Figure 2.10, lets you configure the report server integration mode. Choose the Install the Native Mode Default Configuration option to let the wizard create a report server database configured for native mode. Choose the Install the SharePoint Mode Default Configuration option only if you plan to integrate Reporting Services with SharePoint (requires server operating system, such as Windows Server 2003). Note that you will need to perform additional steps after setup is finished to finalize the integration with SharePoint.

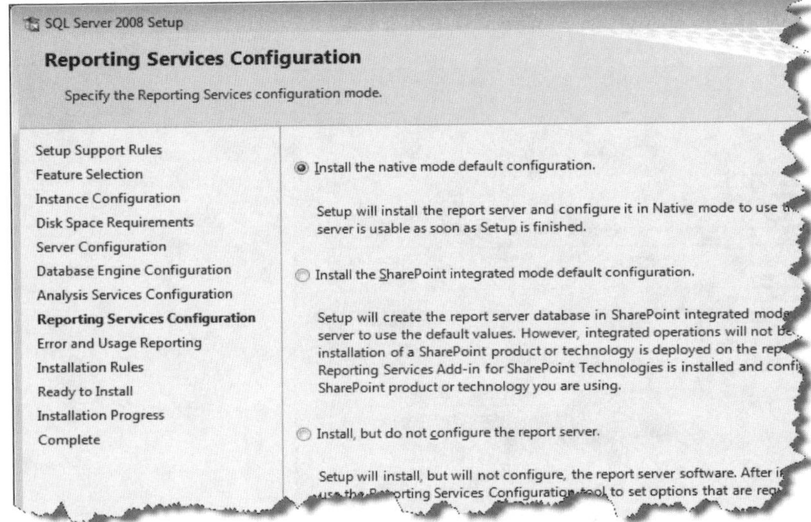

Figure 2.10 Use the Reporting Services Configuration step to specify basic Reporting Services configuration options.

If you don't want to initialize the report server, choose the Install but Do Not Configure the Report Server option. This option is useful when you need more control over the configuration process, such as when you need to add a report server to a web farm or if you want to use a remote SQL Server Database Engine to host the report catalog. The Install but Do Not Configure the Report Server option will be the only available option if you didn't select the SQL Server 2008 Database Engine Services in the Feature Selection page. This is because the setup performs the first two options by installing the report database on the local default SQL Server instance. Assuming native mode, leave the first option selected and click Next.

Performing the remaining setup steps

The Error and Usage Reporting step lets you send error information and anonymous usage data to Microsoft. Microsoft captures and analyzes this data on a regular basis. Consider leaving the two options selected to help Microsoft improve SQL Server. The Ready to Install step gives you a last chance to review the setup tasks. The Installation Progress step performs the actual installation. Finally, the Complete steps informs you about the setup status and suggests further steps if needed. It also includes a link to the SQL Server setup log so you could inspect it in case you encounter a setup error. The default SQL Server setup log folder is \Program Files\Microsoft SQL Server\100\Setup Bootstrap\Log.

2.3 Upgrading Reporting Services

If you are using a previous release of Reporting Services, you can upgrade to Reporting Services 2008 to take advantage of the new features. Of course, one option is not to upgrade at all but to run versions side by side on separate instances. With this approach, you can keep legacy reporting solutions intact and use Reporting Services 2008 for new projects. On the downside, you will need a separate SQL Server license for each instance.

If you decided to upgrade, the SQL Server setup program can upgrade an existing Reporting Services 2000 or 2005 installation. In addition to the information I provide in this section, I recommend you review the Upgrading Reporting Services topic in the product documentation. For the purposes of this practice, I'll demonstrate upgrading from SQL Server 2005 running on Windows Server 2003.

2.3.1 Planning the Upgrade Process

As noted in chapter 1, the Reporting Services architecture and processing engine have changed significantly in this version. Therefore, when planning your upgrade, you need to understand what exactly will be upgraded. Microsoft has done a great job maintaining backward compatibility wherever possible, but there are a few breaking changes that prevent some upgrade paths.

Understanding upgrade scenarios

Reporting Services can be used in a variety of integration scenarios. Table 2.4 lists the most common scenarios and the support statement for each scenario.

Table 2.4 Upgrade scenarios

Scenario	Support Statement
Report server database hosted in SQL Server 2005	Supported
Report server database hosted in SQL Server 2000	Not supported
RDL 2000 and 2005	Can publish but cannot edit in the new designers
SharePoint Integration in 2005 Service Pack 2	Supported
SharePoint version 2 web parts	Supported
Applications built for version 2005	Supported
Applications built for version 2000	The 2000 endpoint (ReportService.asmx) is not supported; URL access will work
Visual Studio 2005 ReportViewer Controls	Supported
Custom report items	RDL 2005 reports will work. RDL 2008 reports require upgrading custom report items
Custom rendering extensions	Need to be rewritten

Let's explain briefly each upgrade scenario. Hosting the report server database in a SQL Server 2005 database is supported, but you cannot use SQL Server 2000 to host the report server database. Consequently, you need to have at least SQL Server 2005 Database Engine to host the report server database.

You can publish legacy report definitions to the report server and although they will run, they will not get upgraded. In other words, whatever you publish is what you will get back. This is because the report server processes 2005 report definitions with the 2005 processing engine. For example, if you upload a 2005 report definition that contains a table or matrix, the definition won't be upgraded automatically to the new tablix data region. Backward compatibility support extends to tools. Specifically, legacy reporting clients will not be affected if you upgrade Reporting Services to version 2008 because they can publish and read the legacy report definitions that run on the 2008 report server.

One catch to all this great backward compatibility support is that you won't be able to edit the legacy report definitions in the BIDS 2008 Report Designer and Report Builder 2.0. These tools support RDL 2008 only and will ask you to upgrade your report definitions. This is a one-way conversion and you won't be able to downgrade your reports to previous versions of RDL. What this means to you is that you have to keep BIDS 2005 around if you need to publish to SQL Server 2005 Reporting Services.

If you have a Report Server 2005 integrated with SharePoint, it will be upgraded in-place. However, the setup program doesn't include the 2008 version of the Reporting Services for SharePoint add-in. Therefore, as a post-installation step, you must download the 2008 version of the Reporting Services for SharePoint add-in and install it. Detailed installation steps are provided in chapter 17. You don't need to remove the 2005 version of the add-in because the setup program for the 2008 version of the add-in will upgrade the old version in place. You can continue using the Report Explorer and Report Viewer SharePoint web parts which were included in the release version of Reporting Services 2005.

Custom applications that target Reporting Services 2005 will continue to work unaffected. Custom applications that integrate with the Reporting Services 2000 Web Service endpoint will not work since this endpoint is not supported. Custom .NET applications that use the Visual Studio 2005 ReportViewer controls will not be affected when you upgrade to Reporting Services 2008.

If you use custom report items, RDL 2005 reports will continue to work unaffected through backward compatibility interfaces. For example, you can still deploy and run RDL 2005 reports that include the Dundas Chart for Reporting Services 2005, which is implemented as a custom report item. You can use BIDS 2005 to edit these reports as before. If you upgrade the report definitions to RDL 2008, legacy custom report items won't work. If you have the code, you can upgrade custom report items by referencing the new interfaces, which I'll discuss in chapter 21. Due to major changes in the report processing and rendering architecture, custom rendering extensions need to be rewritten.

Upgrading the report server

SQL Server setup will only upgrade from the latest service pack of a major release. This means that if you are upgrading Reporting Services 2000 or 2005, you must have the latest SQL Server service pack applied.

When upgrading an existing Reporting Services installation, the SQL Server setup will upgrade its settings and copy configuration state from IIS. Unsupported scenarios, such as hosting the report server database in SQL Server 2000, will block the upgrade process. Therefore, it is important to install and run the SQL Server Upgrade Advisor to discover incompatible scenarios and plan your upgrade process accordingly. For example, as a result of the major changes to the Report Processor, custom rendering extensions need to be updated to work with the new rendering object model. The SQL Server Upgrade Advisor will detect and flag such scenarios.

The setup program will update the report server database automatically. The report content, such as reports, snapshots, and security settings, will be preserved. The setup program will register new URL endpoints for the report server and Report Manager but it will not delete the old IIS virtual folders. If you don't need the IIS virtual folders, you have to manually delete them. Metadata and security policies are upgraded on first use of the report server database. Old snapshots are still rendered with the old processing engine, which includes a Rendering Object Model (ROM) "shim" that translates the old ROM structures on-the-fly to the new Reporting Services 2008 tablix structures.

Upgrading report definitions

Published reports will be upgraded automatically by the SQL Server setup program. As noted, you can still publish legacy report definitions to the report server and they won't get upgraded. If you open reports RDL 2000 or 2005 report definitions in the BIDS Report Designer or Report Builder 2.0, they will be upgraded to RDL 2008. However, this is a one-way process and you won't be able to save reports back to RDL 2000 or 2005 formats.

2.3.2 Working with the SQL Server 2008 Upgrade Advisor

Before upgrading Reporting Services, consider running the SQL Server 2008 Upgrade Advisor to estimate the upgrade effort. The SQL Server 2008 Upgrade Advisor analyzes SQL Server 2000 and 2005 installations in preparation for upgrading to SQL Server 2005 and warns of potential problems. The Upgrade Advisor can be used to analyze all SQL Server services. However, for the purposes of our demo, we will focus on Reporting Services only.

Running the Upgrade Advisor

Follow these steps to install and run the SQL Server 2008 Upgrade Advisor:

1. Install the SQL Server 2008 Upgrade Advisor from the Planning page of the SQL Server Installation Center (see again Figure 2.5).
2. Launch Upgrade Advisor from the Microsoft SQL Server 2008 program group.
3. In the Welcome page, click the Launch Upgrade Advisor Analysis Wizard link on the welcome screen to start the Upgrade Advisor Analysis Wizard. Click Next to advance to the SQL Server Components step.
4. In the Server name textbox, enter the name of the server which hosts the Reporting Services installation and select Reporting Services in the Components list. Click Next.
5. In the Reporting Services Parameters step, select the Reporting Services instance you want to analyze or leave the MSSQLSERVER instance pre-selected if Reporting Services is installed on the default instance.
6. In the Confirm Upgrade Advisor Settings step, note the folder where the report will be generated. Upgrade Advisor saves the results as an XML report. Each wizard run will overwrite an existing issues report that was created for the report server you selected. The default report path is \Documents and Settings\<user>\My Documents\SQL Server 2008 Upgrade Advisor Reports\<servername>. Click Run to advance to the Upgrade Advisor Progress step.

7. The Upgrade Advisor analyzes the Reporting Services instance by evaluating a set of rules, as shown in Figure 2.11. If any issues are detected, Upgrade Advisor displays a warning message.

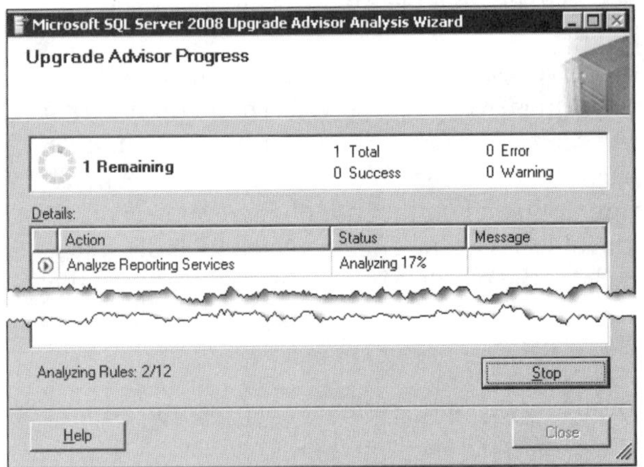

Figure 2.11 The SQL Server 2008 Upgrade Advisor evaluates several rules to identify potential issues that may impact the upgrade process.

8. Click the Launch Report button the view the generated report.

Analyzing the upgrade report

The Upgrade Advisor report (see Figure 2.12) displays deprecated features and other issues that may impact the upgrade process. The When to Fix column tells you when the issue needs to be addressed, such before or after the upgrade. In this case, the Upgrade Advisor has discovered three critical issues and one warning.

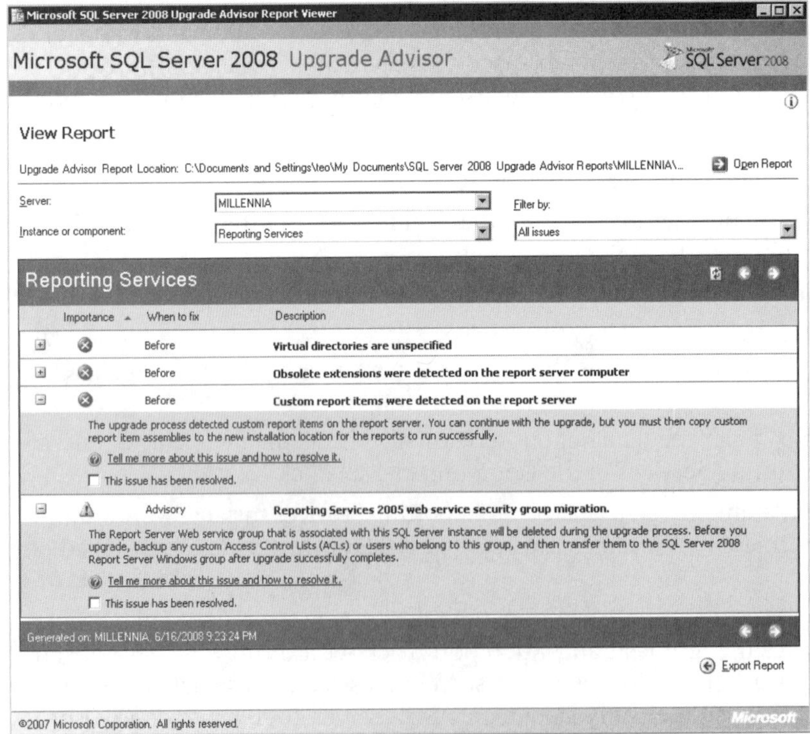

Figure 2.12 The Upgrade Advisor report shows issues that may impact upgrading from previous versions.

1. Expand the Custom Report Items Were Detected on the Report Server issue.
2. Click the Tell Me More link below to obtain more information.

   The Upgrade Advisor navigates to the corresponding help topic, which explains that custom report items that were created for previous releases of SQL Server Reporting Services are not compatible with SQL Server 2008 Reporting Services. Farther down, the help topic provides a corrective action which in this case requires revisions to the custom assembly code and re-compilation.

TIP If upgrading a custom report item is not a near-term option, one workaround in this case is deploying the RDL 2005 version of the report after the upgrade to render the SQL Server 2005 custom report item through compatible interfaces.

As the help explains, the upgrade can continue and both issues can be addressed after the upgrade. The reason why the report (When To Fix column) suggests we fix the issues before the upgrade process is that they may impact existing functionality. For example, a report that uses an incompatible custom report item will be upgraded to RDL 2008 but the custom report item will no longer work.

2.3.3 Upgrading a Reporting Services Installation

Once you understand the upgrade effort, it's time to perform the actual upgrade steps. Let's go through a hands-on lab that demonstrates upgrading an existing Reporting Services 2005 installation.

Selecting an instance to upgrade

The initial steps of the upgrade process are identical to installing a new instance.

1. In SQL Server Installation Center, click the Installation link.
2. In the Installation page (see Figure 2.6), click the Upgrade from SQL Server 2000 or SQL Server 2005 link. The setup program executes the Setup Support Rules step.
3. Go through the Product Key, License Terms, and Setup Support Files steps to start the setup wizard.

   As when performing a new installation, the Select Instance step detects existing SQL Server 2000 and 2005 installations. It gives you an option to upgrade a selected instance or only the shared components, such as the SQL Server Client components or SQL Server Integration Services. You can upgrade only one instance at a time.
4. Expand the Upgrade Selected Instance drop-down list and select the instance you want to upgrade. For example, if SQL Server 2005 is installed on the default instance MSSQLSERVER, selected this instance and click Next.

Checking upgrade rules

The Select Features step lets you select which SQL Server services and shared features you want to upgrade.

1. By default, all SQL Server services and features installed on the box will be upgraded. Click Next.

2. In the Instance Configuration page, the Default Instance and Named Instance options will be disabled because you've already selected which instance will be upgraded. The only change you can make to this page is to modify the instance identifier if you want to change the installation folders.
3. In the Reporting Services Authentication step, specify an authentication mode which the setup program will use to connect to the report server database. The default Windows Authentication model uses your credentials to connect to SQL Server. Alternatively, you can use standard authentication and enter the credentials of a SQL Server login that has rights to connect to the report server database.
4. The Upgrade Rules Check step applies several rules to verify the readiness of the upgrade process. It flags each rule with one of three status codes: Pass, Warning, or Failed. You can click on the status link to obtain more information about the rule status. Failed rules will block the upgrade process and need to be addressed. But you've already run the SQL Server 2008 Upgrade Advisor and addressed critical issues, haven't you?

Once you pass the Upgrade Rules Check step, you have a green light to upgrade. The Ready to Upgrade step gives you a summary of what will be upgraded. The Installation Progress step performs the actual upgrade. Finally, the Complete step informs you about the setup status and suggests further steps if needed.

2.4 Performing Initial Configuration

As you've seen, the SQL Server setup program doesn't offer much control over the Reporting Services configuration. Therefore, after the setup is done, you may need to perform several post-deployment steps to finalize the Reporting Services configuration, such as to configure the report server connections or throttle memory utilization.

2.4.1 Testing the Reporting Services Installation

If the setup program completes successfully and you haven't performed a files-only installation (Install, but do not Configure the Report Server option in the Reporting Services Configuration page), your Reporting Services installation should be operational.

Verifying that the report server is operational

As a first post-deployment step, verify that the report server and Report Manager are operational by requesting their URLs in the browser. Recall that the setup program will configure the report server URLs to use port 80 when Reporting Services is installed on Windows Vista and Windows Server 2003 or above. With Windows XP, port 8080 will be used to avoid conflicts with IIS. To isolate authentication issues, I recommend you perform the following steps as a local administrator on the box where you installed Reporting Services.

NOTE Administrator permissions are not automatically available to local administrators if you are using the User Account Control (UAC) feature of Windows Vista or Windows Server 2008. Follow the steps in the "How to: Configure a Report Server for Local Administration on Windows Vista and Windows Server 2008" topic (see Resources) to grant yourself of another user administrator rights to Reporting Services.

1. On the machine where you install SQL Server 2008, open Internet Explorer and type the Report Server Web Service URL, such as http://<machine>/ReportServer or

http://localhost/ReportServer. You can obtain this URL from the Web Service URL tab in the Reporting Services Configuration Manager.

After a certain period of inactivity required for initializing the report server applications, you should see the report server main page. In the case of a new installation, the page should resemble the one shown in Figure 2.13 (the Reporting Services version may vary).

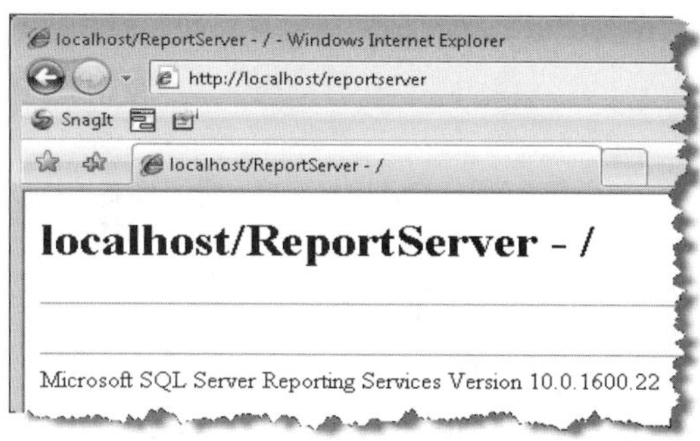

Figure 2.13 Request the Web Service URL to verify that the report server is operational.

If you have upgraded Reporting Services, the report server page should show folder links to let you navigate the report catalog.

2. The next step is to verify that Report Manager is operational. In Internet Explorer, request the Report Manager URL, such as http://<servername>/reports. If all is well, you should see the Report Manager main page.

   Don't panic if the report server or Report Manager pages display error messages. A few basic troubleshooting steps may help you address some of these issues.

3. Open the Services console application and verify whether the SQL Server Reporting Services service is running. Verify that the Database Engine instance used to host the report catalog is running as well.
4. Check for any error messages in the Application log in the Windows Event Viewer.
5. Inspect the report server trace log file in \Program Files\Microsoft SQL Server\MSRS10.MSSQLSERVER\Reporting Services\LogFiles. Search for any error messages that may indicate what went wrong.
6. Open the Reporting Services Configuration Manager found in the Microsoft SQL Server 2008 ⇨ Configuration Tools program group and check for any error conditions.

Verifying Windows authentication

The setup program configures a new Reporting Services installation for Windows security. As a next step for verifying the health of the report server I recommend you access the Report Manager from a remote computer. If all is well, you should see the Report Manager home page. The most common issue with remote access is confronting the notorious Windows credential dialog, as shown in Figure 2.14.

There could be 1,001 reasons for Windows authentication to fail between the browser and the server and none of them have to do with Reporting Services per se. However, here are a few tips that may help you get rid of the dialog box.

1. Use the name of the server in the Report Manager URL, such as http://millennia/reports, so Internet Explorer applies the Local Intranet security settings when connecting to the server. If

you use the server IP address or Fully Qualified Domain Name (FQDN), such as millennia.prologika.com, the browser will apply the Internet security settings which may cause the credentials dialog box to pop up.

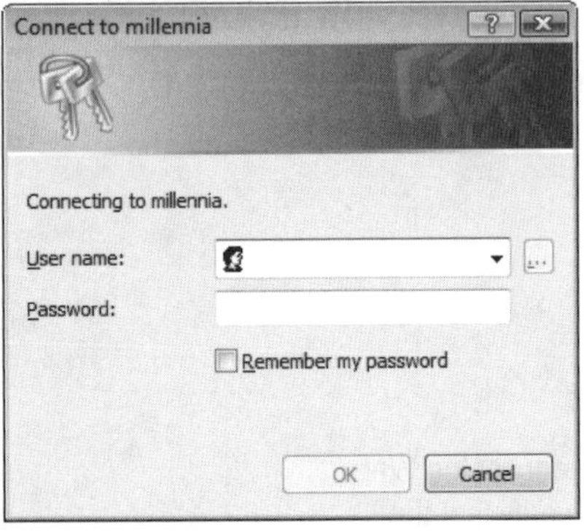

Figure 2.14 You shouldn't see this dialog box if Windows Authentication is working properly with intranet deployments.

2. On the report server computer, open port 80 in Windows Firewall. If you applied the latest service packs or are running one of the newer Windows operating systems, port 80 is closed by default. Open Control Panel and then click Windows Firewall. On the Exceptions tab, enter TCP80 for the name and 80 for the port. Click OK to save your changes.
3. Open the browser Internet Options dialog (Tools ⇨ Internet Options) and flip to the Advanced tab. Make sure that the Enable Integrated Windows Authentication option under the Security section is checked.
4. For some obscure reason which probably has to do with security, if your machine isn't in a domain and Reporting Services is installed locally, Internet Explorer will prompt for credentials with Windows Vista. To get rid of the prompt, in Internet Options, select the Local Intranet zone in the Security tab, and click the Sites button. Deselect the Automatically Detect Intranet Network checkbox and check the three checkboxes below it, as shown in Figure 2.15. Restart the browser.

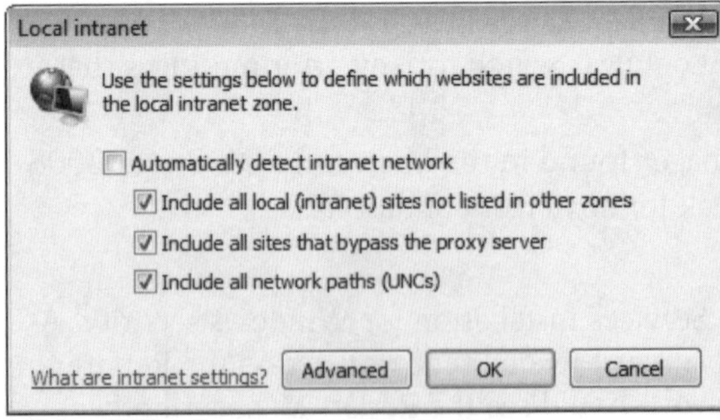

Figure 2.15 Configure the Local Intranet settings to suppress the credentials dialog with Windows Vista.

5. Finally, the Windows Negotiate protocol may be failing. To force the report server to use NTLM, remove the RSWindowsNegotiate element from the report server configuration file (rsreportserver.config), as I mentioned in section 2.1.3.

Lukasz Pawlowski, a Program Manager on the Reporting Services team, has written an excellent blog (see Resources) that provides additional solutions for solving login issues.

2.4.2 Configuring Reporting Services URLs

Recall that Reporting Services 2008 has a new hosting model that is not dependent on IIS. The SQL Server setup program defines report server and Report Manager URLs based on the underlying operating system. Use the Report Manager URL to access the Report Manager application. All client applications, including Report Manager, use the report server URL to integrate with the report server.

The default URLs will probably meet the needs of most deployment scenarios, but sometimes they may not be enough. For example, firewall restrictions may force you to use a specific port. Or, you may need to configure the report server to use SSL if it will be accessed through an Internet-facing web server. To address such advanced deployment scenarios, you need to know how to configure the Reporting Services URLs.

About URL registration and reservation

Recall that the Reporting Services Windows service hosts three Reporting Services applications: Report Manager, Report Server Web service, and Background Processor. Behind the scenes, the Reporting Services Windows service uses HTTP.SYS, a kernel-mode Windows device driver, to listen for network requests and route them to the appropriate request queue. To do this work, HTTP.SYS maintains a URL reservation and registration system for the HTTP endpoints that are accessed on the local computer.

URL *reservation* is a process by which an application stores a URL endpoint in HTTP.SYS. An application can reserve more than one URL endpoint with HTTP.SYS. For example, besides the default Report Manager endpoint (http://<servername>/Reports) that lets you access the Report Manager on the corporate intranet, you may also need to register an external URL endpoint, such as https://reports.adventure-works.com, to make Report Manager accessible to Internet users. HTTP.SYS ensures that multiple URL endpoints are unique and non-conflicting. Report server keeps a copy of its URL reservations in the report server configuration file (rsreportserver.config).

URL *registration* refers to creating the HTTP endpoint for a previously reserved URL when the URL is requested. URL registration happens at run time. For example, when the Reporting Services Windows service starts, it reads the endpoints from the report server configuration file (rsreportserver.config). Then, it creates a queue and registers the endpoints with HTTP.SYS. As incoming requests to the report server arrive, HTTP.SYS receives and dispatches them to the queue. Reporting Services unregisters its endpoints when you stop the Reporting Services Windows service.

Understanding the URL reservation syntax

An HTTP.SYS URL endpoint has the following syntax:

```
scheme://host:port/VirtualDirectory
```

The scheme must be either *http* or *https*, all in lower case. The host could be a machine name, fully qualified domain name (FQDN), an IPv4 or IPv6 literal string, or a wildcard. Unlike the scheme, the host is case-insensitive.

NOTE If you have installed Reporting Services on a named instance, the default Report Manager and report server URLs will include the instance name. For example, if the named instance is SQL2008, the server name is MYSERVER and the port is 80, the default report server URL would be http://MYSERVER_SQL2008:80/ReportServer. If you don't know how the server is configured, you can obtain the URLs from the Reporting Services Configuration Manager.

The port is a decimal numeric string that does not start with zero and that represents a valid TCP port number from 1 to 65,535, such as 8080. Although HTTP.SYS doesn't mandate a virtual directory, Reporting Services requires you to specify report server and Report Manager virtual directories. Similar to IIS virtual directories, an HTTP.SYS virtual directory indicates a subtree within the machine's namespace. It must always starts with a forward slash, such as /ReportServer.

The virtual directories are simplified in Reporting Services 2008. For example, in IIS, a virtual directory has many settings. By contrast, a Reporting Services 2008 virtual directory is just a name. Only one virtual directory is allowed for the Report Server Web service and Report Manager applications. For flexibility, HTTP.SYS supports four different host categories which are listed in Table 2.5.

Table 2.5 HTTP.SYS supports four host categories

Category	Description	Example
Strong wildcard (All Assigned)	It matches all possible host names. Use when you need to avoid specifying a long list of hosts and/or IP Addresses. This is the default host category.	http://+:80/ReportServer/
Explicit	The host name is a machine name, FQDN, or IP address. Use an explicit host when the incoming requests need to be matched directly against the host name in the HTTP headers.	http://millennia/ReportServer
IP-bound weak wildcard	This wildcard is implied when the host element is an IP address. It could be IPv4 literal string, such 192.168.0.0, or IPv6 literal string, such as [::1] or [6FFE:FFFF::6ECB:0101].	http://192.168.100.1/ReportServer
Weak wildcard (All Unassigned)	When an asterisk (*) appears as the host element. A wild card serves as a catch-all bucket. It matches any host name associated with the specified scheme, port and virtual directory that has not already been handled by other categories.	http://*:80/ReportServer

HTTP.SYS routes HTTP requests in the order listed in the table. For example, a strong wildcard match supersedes a weak wildcard match. Suppose that you run both IIS and Reporting Services on Windows Server or Vista operating systems. They both listen on port 80 and they both have a virtual directory called Reports. Which one will win when the user submits an HTTP request, such as http://<servername>/Reports? The answer is easy once you know that IIS makes weak reservations while Reporting Services make strong reservations by default. The request will be routed to Reporting Services.

Changing the report server port

You can use the Reporting Services Configuration Manager to configure the Report Server Web service and Report Manager endpoints. Let's say you have Reporting Services running on Windows Server 2003 and you need to configure the Report Server Web service endpoint to listen on port 8081 instead of the default port 80.

1. Open Reporting Services Configuration Manager from the Microsoft SQL Server 2008 ⇨ Configuration Tools.
2. Connect to the server and Reporting Services instance you want to manage.
3. Select the Web Service URL page.

Observe that the virtual directory is ReportServer, the IP Address drop-down list is set to All Assigned (Recommended), and the TCP port is 80 (8080 on Windows XP). As a result, the actual Report Server Web Service URL reservation is http://+:80/ReportServer using a strong wildcard.

4. Expand the IP Address drop-down list and note it contains a pre-defined list of alternative choices, such as the IP addresses assigned to the machine.
5. In the TCP Port field, enter *8081*. Note that the Report Services Configuration Manager updates the URL link accordingly. Click Apply.

   The Reporting Services Configuration Manager removes the old http://+80 endpoint and reserves the http://+8081 endpoint, as shown in Figure 2.16.

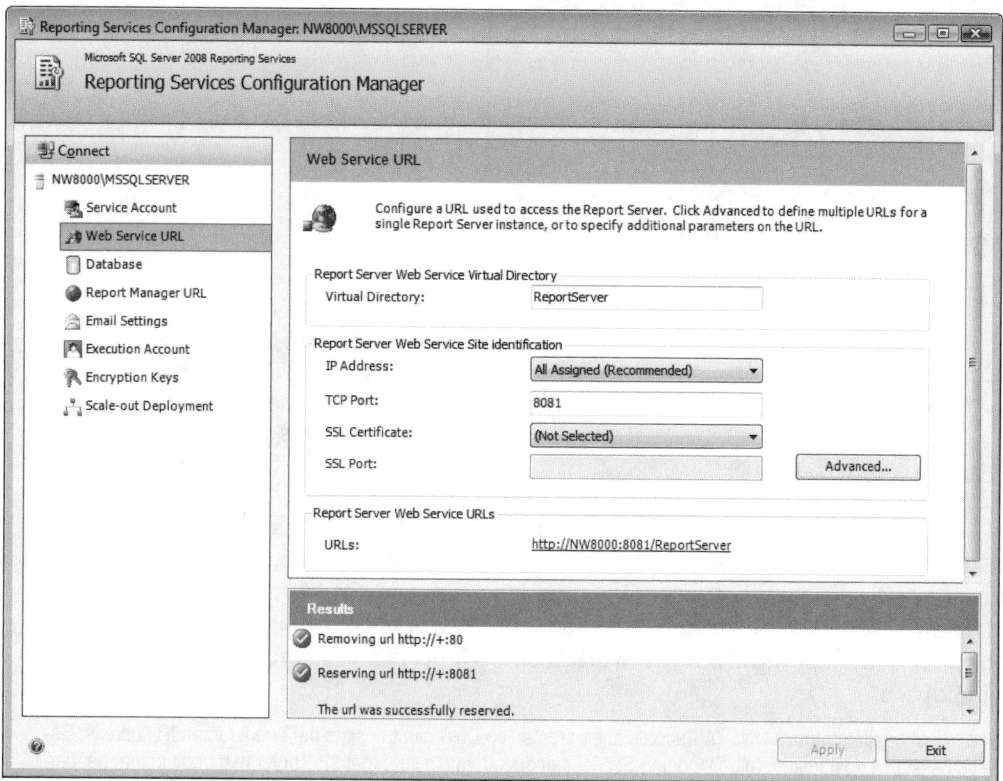

Figure 2.16 Use the Reporting Services Configuration Manager to configure the report server and Report Manager URLs.

6. Click the URL link to open the report server page and test the changes.
7. Select the Report Manager URL page. Note that you can change the Report Manager endpoint by clicking the Advanced button. Click the Report Manager URL link to test that the Report Manager works with the new Report Server Web service endpoint.

Advanced URL endpoint configuration

You can use the advanced settings if you need more control over the endpoint registration process, such as to specify host headers and multiple endpoints.

1. Select the Web Service URL page and click the Advanced button to open the Advanced Multiple Web Site Configuration dialog box, which is shown in Figure 2.17. Note that you can

assign more than one HTTP or SSL endpoint by clicking the Add button. You can edit an existing endpoint reservation by clicking the Edit button.

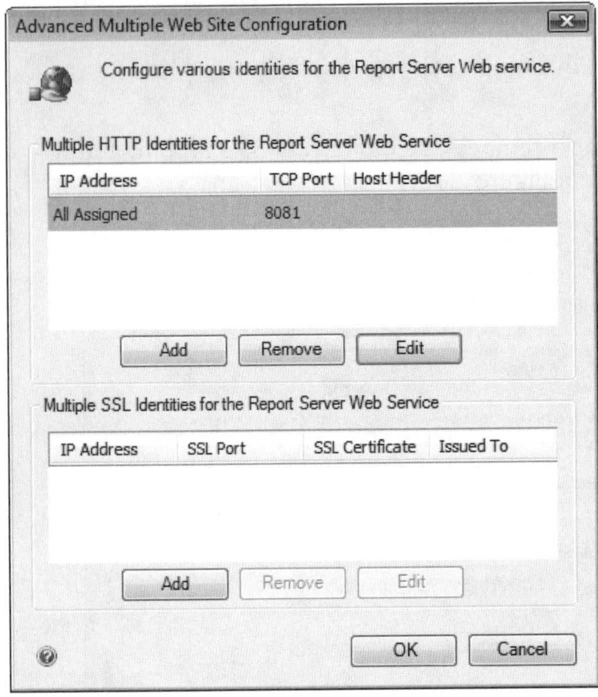

Figure 2.17 Use the Advanced Multiple Web Site Configuration dialog box if you need to assign multiple endpoints, or work with host headers and SSL certificates.

Network administrators use host headers to run several sites on a single box. For example, suppose that the Adventure Works Internet web portal is hosted in IIS and responds to www.adventure-works.com. You want web users to access Report Manager as reports.adventure-works.com instead of www.adventure-works.com/reports. To accomplish this, you can specify reports.adventure-works.com as a header when you register the Report Manager endpoint.

NOTE Host headers require DNS (A) records to be created so DNS can translate the header to an IP address. Before you assign a host header to a Reporting Services endpoint, make sure that the server responds to that header.

Let's use the advanced settings to "undo" our port change.

2. Click the Remove button to remove the 8081 item.
3. Click the Add button. In the Add a Report Server HTTP URL dialog box that follows, set the TCP Port to 80 (or 8080 on Windows XP) and click OK.
4. Go back to the Advanced Multiple Web Site Configuration dialog box and click OK.

Configuring SSL certificates

Suppose that you want to set up Report Manager for Internet access. To protect sensitive information, you want to configure the Report Manager for SSL by installing a server certificate and binding the certificate to the Report Manager endpoint, as follows:

1. Obtain a server certificate from a trusted certificate-issuing authority, such as Verisign, and install the certificate on the server.

TIP For testing purposes, you can use the Certificate Creation Tool (makecert.exe) which comes with Visual Studio and Windows Platform SDK to create a test certificate. For example, I used the following command to create a test certificate for a machine name NW8000 and install it in the My store:
makecert -r -pe -n "CN=NW8000" -b 01/01/2000 -e 01/01/2015 -eku 1.3.6.1.5.5.7.3.1 -ss "My" -sr localMachine -sky exchange -sp "Microsoft RSA SChannel Cryptographic Provider" -sy 12

Next, check the issued certificate by following these steps.

2. In Windows, click Start ⇨ Run. Enter *mmc* and click Enter.
3. In the Microsoft Management Console, click File ⇨ Add/Remove Snap-in.
4. In the next dialog, click the Certificates snap-in and click the Add button. Click OK.
5. In the Certificates Snap-in dialog, select the Computer Account and click Finish.
6. Expand the Console Root root node ⇨ Personal and click Certificates.

   Reporting Services can use any of the listed certificates where the Intended Purposes list contains Server Authentication. Note the Issued To column. This is what you need to provide in the URL when connecting to the server. For example, if the certificate is issued to server.adventure-works.com, then trying to connect to the server using http://localhost/ will fail. In addition, ensure the certificate is issued by a certificate authority recognized by your domain controller. Self-signed certificates do not work. Once you ensure that the certificate is installed, you can proceed with configuring the Report Manager URL.
7. Open the Reporting Services Configuration Manager and connect to the server.
8. Select the Report Manager URL page and click the Advanced button.
9. In the Advanced Multiple Web Site Configuration dialog box, click the Add button below the Multiple SSL Identities pane.

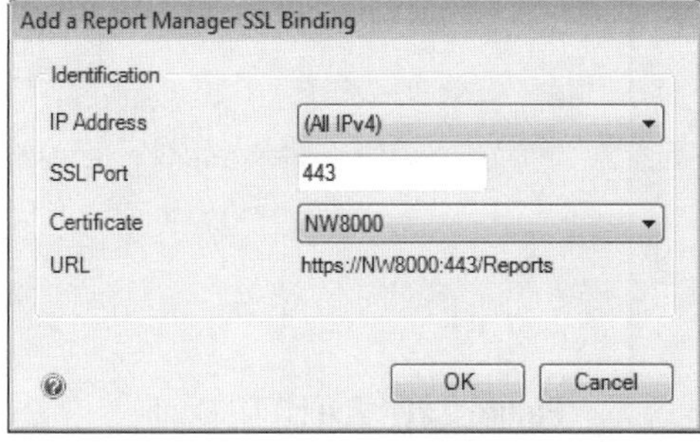

Figure 2.18 You can configure the Reporting Services URLs to use SSL.

10. In the Add a Report Server SSL Binding dialog, expand the Certificate drop-down list and select the server certificate, as shown in Figure 2.18.
11. Click OK to return to the Advanced Multiple Web Site Configuration dialog box, which should look like the one shown in Figure 2.19.
12. Optionally, remove the port 80 binding if you want Report Manager to respond to https only.
13. Click OK to register the new endpoint. Test the changes by clicking the Report Manager URL, which should be https://<servername>:443/Reports.
14. Consider increasing the security level of the Web service connections. You can do so by opening the report server configuration file (rsreportserver.config) and manually changing the SecureConnectionLevel setting to 2 or 3.

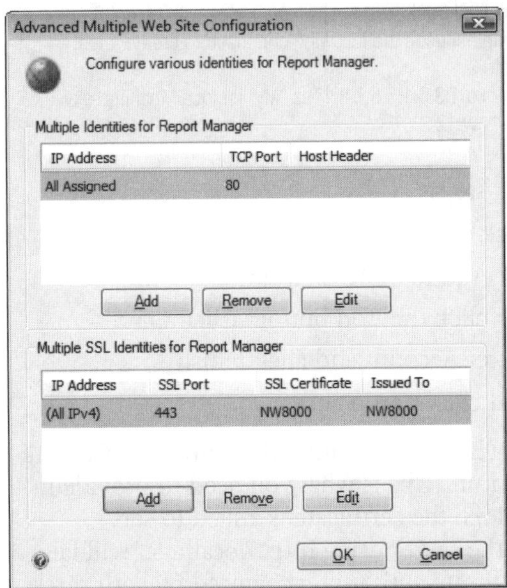

Figure 2.19 With this configuration, Report Manager will respond to http and https protocols.

If you want to disable SSL, set SecureConnectionLevel to 0. For more information about the SecureConnectionLevel setting, refer to the Using Secure Web Service Methods topic in Books Online (see Resources for a link).

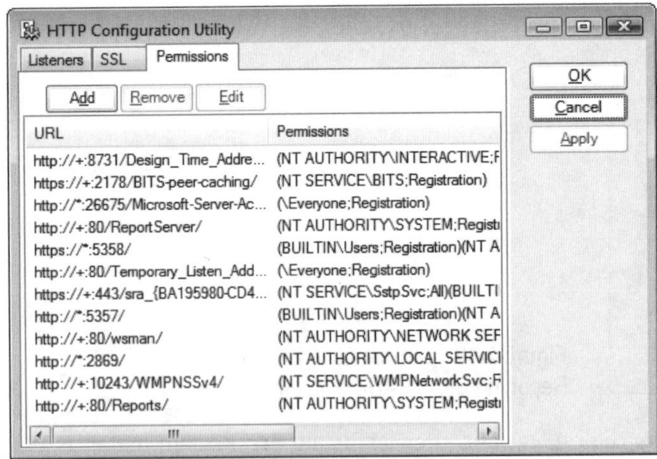

Figure 2.20 The HTTP Configuration Utility lets you manage the HTTP.SYS endpoints.

Troubleshooting URL configuration

Sometimes, the Reporting Services endpoints in the report server configuration file may get out of sync with the HTTP.SYS endpoints. Consequently, you may be able to register an endpoint although the Reporting Services Configuration Manager doesn't show that endpoint. To fix this issue, you can call the HTTP APIs or use the httpcfg.exe utility, which is included in the Windows Server 2003 support tools, but none of them is easy to use. Instead, consider the excellent Steve Johnson's HTTP Configuration Utility (see Resources), which provides a graphical interface that wraps the HTTP configuration APIs. For example, as Figure 2.20 shows, the Permissions tab lets you view the registered endpoints.

While you should never add or edit Reporting Services endpoints outside the Reporting Services Configuration Manager, you can use the HTTP Configuration Manager to view what's registered and delete "orphan" endpoints. To delete an endpoint, simple select it, click the Remove button and then the Apply button. You can use this utility to see the SSL bindings that the Reporting Services Configuration Manager has created when you configure an endpoint to use SSL.

2.4.3 Performing Additional Configuration Steps

Depending on your operational and reporting requirements, you may need to perform a few more configuration steps before you declare that you are "done" deploying Reporting Services. Let's go through some of these post-deployment steps.

Backing up the encryption keys

The report server uses machine-specific symmetric encryption keys to encrypt sensitive information, such as connection and subscription credentials. I highly recommend you back up the encryption keys as soon as possible on a new deployment. You will need the backup in case you have to re-initialize the server, such as when you re-install the server or when you migrate the report catalog from one machine to another. If you don't have a backup, your only choice to initialize the server is to delete the encryption keys. To back up the encryption keys:

1. In the Reporting Services Configuration Manager, select the Encryption Keys tab, and click the Backup button.
2. In the Backup Encryption Key dialog box that follows, specify a file location and a password to protect the file from unauthorized access, and click OK.

If you need to re-initialize the server later on, use the Restore button to restore the encryption keys. You will know that this moment has arrived when you access the Report Server report page and get the following error:

```
The report server cannot decrypt the symmetric key used to access sensitive or encrypted data in a report server database. You must either restore a backup key or delete all encrypted content and then restart the service.
```

If you don't have a backup or forgot the password, you have no other option but to delete the encrypted content by clicking the Delete button. Consequently, you must re-configure the connection credentials in all data sources.

Configuring server security

By default, the report server authenticates and authorizes users using Windows security. Specifically, the report server accepts requests that specify Negotiate and NTLM authentication, as you can see by inspecting the Authentication element in the report server configuration file (rsreportserver.config).

```
<Authentication>
    <AuthenticationTypes>
        <RSWindowsNegotiate/>
        <RSWindowsNTLM/>
    </AuthenticationTypes>
    <EnableAuthPersistence>true</EnableAuthPersistence>
</Authentication>
```

This matches the IIS authentication behavior when IIS is configured for Windows security. To use Windows integrated security, the interactive user must have a valid Windows local or domain user account or be a member of a Windows local or domain group account.

In most cases, the default settings will work just fine. If needed, you can overwrite the default Windows security configuration or configure the server for Basic Authentication. For more details, refer to the How to: Configure Windows Authentication in Reporting Services topic in Books Online (see Resources). When Windows security is not an option, you can replace it with custom security, which is also known as Forms Authentication, as I'll demonstrate in chapter 19.

NOTE In this release, Reporting Services doesn't support Anonymous authentication. This was a conscious decision to discourage users from using Anonymous access and making the server vulnerable to security attacks. If you must support anonymous users, consider implementing a custom security extension (discussed in chapter 19) and configuring the report server for custom security that grants minimum rights to your users.

Configuring the unattended execution account

By default, Reporting Services carries out unattended operations, such as subscribed delivery, under the Reporting Services service account which you configure when you install SQL Server. If your reports will use images from external sources, such as a file server that doesn't allow anonymous access, or data sources that don't require credentials, you need to configure a special unattended execution account so the network call succeeds. The report server uses this account to impersonate calls that fetch external images and connect to the data sources with no credentials. To configure the unattended execution account:

1. In the Reporting Services Configuration Manager, select the Execution Account tab.
2. Enter the credentials of a Windows domain account (domain\login) that has permissions to connect to the external service.

What's not so obvious is that once you specify an unattended execution account, Reporting Services will always use it, even if reports are requested on demand. Therefore, you must keep the credentials (user name and password) of the unattended execution account current. Failure to do so will result in the following error when you attempt to run a report:

```
Logon failed (rsLogonFailed) Logon failure: unknown user name or bad password.
```

Configuring scale-out deployment

Recall that Reporting Services lets you scale out your reporting solution by clustering multiple report servers. With scale-out deployment all nodes in the cluster point to the same report server database.

Configuring report server cluster

Follow these steps to configure scale-out deployment:

1. Configure a load-balanced cluster of Windows servers. You can use a software-based load balancer, such as the Windows NLB Services, or a hardware-based device. Record the virtual address of the NLB cluster.
2. On each node, install Reporting Services with the Install but Do Not Configure the Report Server option. This is done to avoid creating node-specific report server databases.
3. Use the Reporting Services Configuration Manager on one of the nodes to create a report server database on a remote SQL Server 2005 or 2008 instance.

4. Use the Reporting Services Configuration Manager (Database tab) on the other nodes to connect them to the report server database you created in the previous step.
5. In the Reporting Services Configuration Manager, connect to the first node and click the Scale-out Deployment tab.

   You should see as many entries as the number of the cluster nodes. The first node should have a "Joined" status. The other nodes should be "Waiting to join". In Figure 2.21, NW8000 is the first report server node. NOR15279 was configured to use the shared report server database but has not been added yet to the report server cluster.

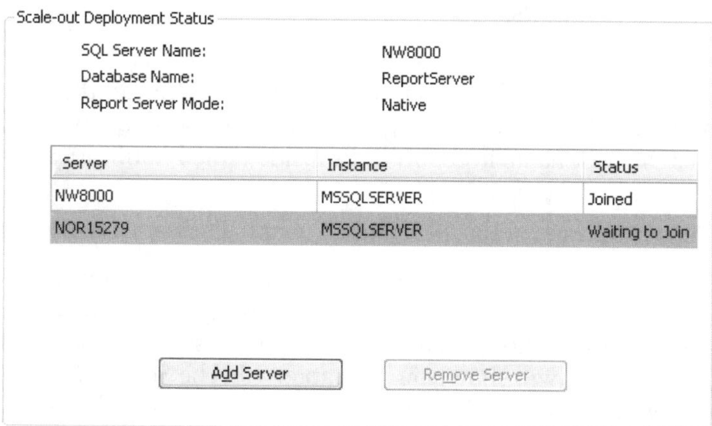

Figure 2.21 Use the Reporting Services Configuration Manager to join nodes to the report server cluster.

6. Select each of the Waiting to Join nodes and click the Add Server button.
7. Restart each of the report server nodes that you added. You can use the Reporting Services Configuration Manager to connect to and restart Report Services on each node.
8. Configure ViewState validation on each node to use the same machine key.

NOTE The ASP.NET ViewState validation is tied to each server by default because it uses a machine-specific validation key. As a result, you will get the error "The viewstate is invalid for this page and might be corrupted" when a Report Manager posts back to a different server. To address this issue, overwrite the machineKey element in the Report Manager web.config file for each node to use the same machineKey. You can use the handy MachineKey Generator Tool (see Resources) to generate a machine key.

Configuring virtual address

Next, you need to change the URL endpoints of the Report Server Web Service and Report Manager to use the virtual name or virtual IP address of the NLB cluster. Use the Reporting Services Configuration Manager to connect to each of the nodes and perform the following steps:

9. Click the Web Service URL tab and click Advanced.
10. In the Advanced Multiple Web Site Configuration dialog box, click Add.
11. In the Add a Report Server HTTP URL dialog box, click Host Header Name.
12. Enter the virtual server name of the NLB cluster. If you do not have a virtual server name, you can use the virtual server IP address instead.
13. Back to the Reporting Services Configuration Manager main page, click the Report Manager URL and repeat steps 10-12.

Verifying Report Server access

Finally, verify that you can access the report server cluster and all nodes are operational.

14. Access the report server cluster by the virtual address of the NLB cluster, such as http:// MyVirtualServerName/reportserver.
15. Examine the report server trace log files on each node or the ExecutionLogStorage table in the report server database (InstanceName column) to verify that each node processes report requests.

    If requests do not reach the report server instances, check the rsreportserver.config file on the node to verify the virtual server address as follows:
16. Open the rsreportserver.config file in a text editor.
17. Find ReportServerUrl and UrlRoot settings. They should specify the virtual address of the NLB cluster. The Report Manager uses the ReportServerUrl setting to connect to a remote report server. The UrlRoot setting specifies the host name in report links inside e-mail notifications sent via subscriptions.
18. If these settings don't specify the virtual address of the NLB cluster, manually change them.

Looking at the rest of the options in the Reporting Services Configuration Manager, you will see the Email Settings tab which you use to you configure the e-mail subscription delivery. We will cover report server e-mail configuration in more details in chapter 12. Use the Database tab to manage the report server database, as I will show you in chapter 13. The Service Account tab lets you change the Windows account the Reporting Services runs under. This is discussed in more detail in chapter 11.

Configuring Reporting Services features

Consider disabling the Reporting Services features you don't need to reduce the attack surface of a production server and conserve resources. For example, if you need only Report Manager on an Internet-facing server, disable the Report Server Web service on the Internet-facing server. By default, all features are turned on. Boolean configuration settings in the report server configuration file let you turn off Report Manager, the Report Server Web service, and some features of the Background Processor.

Table 2.6 Configuration settings for turning features off

Setting	Description
IsReportManagerEnabled	Controls the availability of the Report Manager. When set to False, Reporting Services returns 503 HTTP Status "Service Unavailable" when the user attempts to access Report Manager.
IsWebServiceEnabled	Controls the availability of the Report Server Web Service. When set to False, Reporting Services returns 503 HTTP Status "Service Unavailable" when the user attempts to access the Report Server Web service.
IsSchedulingService	Specifies whether the report server dedicates a management thread to synchronize the schedules in the report server database with the SQL Server Agent schedules.
IsNotificationService	Specifies whether the report server dedicates a thread to poll the notification table in the report server database to check for pending notifications. Setting this setting to False disables all scheduled activities, such as subscriptions and snapshot refreshes.
IsEventService	Specifies whether the report server processes events in the event queue (Event table).

The last three options control features of the Background Processor application. You cannot turn the Background Processor completely off because it provides database maintenance functionality that is required for server operations.

Configuring Internet deployment

Internet reporting presents additional deployment challenges, first and foremost being security. Suppose you need to report-enable an Internet-facing application. In general, I recommend against letting web users directly access the report server and request reports by URL. Instead, consider the deployment model shown in Figure 2.22.

NOTE Regardless of the exact topology chosen, viewing reports with sensitive data over the Internet will require transport layer security, such as Secure Socket Layer (SSL).

Externals users access a web server behind a firewall that lets only HTTP traffic pass through. To view reports, users can use Report Manager, which is installed on the Internet-facing server. Alternatively, if you need to report-enable an existing application or you need to validate the report request, such as to ensure that the report parameters are valid, a custom web application can be used for report viewing. In both cases, the report is rendered in the Visual Studio ReportViewer Web server control.

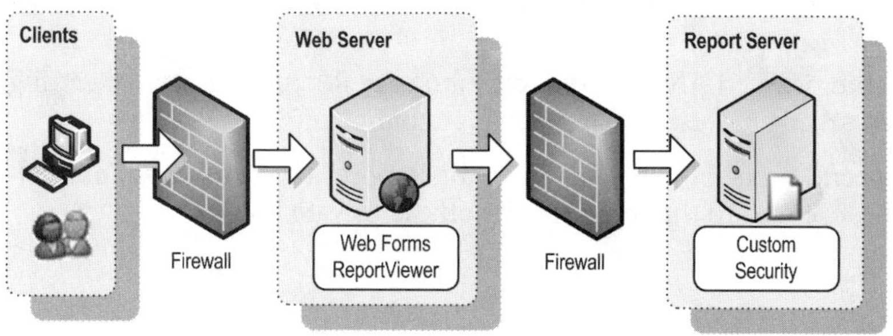

Figure 2.22 A recommended deployment model for report-enabling Internet applications.

The ReportViewer control generates the report on the server by calling down to the Report Server Web service. Note that in this scenario the report server is on the private LAN. On the downside, some report features will not work when the report server is not directly accessible, including report drillthrough links, report links in e-mail subscriptions, and Report Builder. If these features are a must, you need to install the report server on an Internet-facing server, such as your front-end web server. The following configuration steps assume that the Report Manager will be used for report viewing and the report server is installed on a private LAN.

1. Install Reporting Services on both servers. On the Internet-facing server, install Reporting Services with the Install but Do Not Configure the Report Server option because you don't need a functional report server on that box.
2. After the setup is done, open Reporting Services Configuration Manager and configure the Report Manager URL for SSL, as explained in section 2.4.2. Initialize the Report Manager URL by clicking the Apply button.
3. Although the report server database on the Internet-facing server is not configured and the report server is non-operational, I recommend that you explicitly disable the Report Server Web service on the Internet-facing server. To do so, open the report server configuration file (rsreportserver.config) and set the IsWebServiceEnabled setting to False.
4. In the report server configuration file, locate the ReportServerUrl element and point it to the URL of the remote report server instance. The Report Manager needs this setting to connect to a remote report server.

```
<ReportServerUrl> http://myserver/reportserver</ReportServerUrl>
```

5. Since you running the Report Manager on a separate machine then the report server, in the Report Manager web.config file, enable the defaultProxy element, such as:

```
<system.net>
  <defaultProxy enabled="true" />
</system.net>
```

   For more information about the defaultProxy setting, see <defaultProxy> Element (Network Settings) in the Resources section.

6. Restart the Reporting Services Windows service.
7. Since Windows Security is rarely practical with web users, consider implementing a custom security extension and configure the report server for custom security. I will discuss the implementation details in chapter 19. Alternatively, if the report server doesn't need to discriminate users and the custom web application is taking care of authenticating and authorizing report requests, grant the web application account minimum rights to the report catalog, such rights to view reports only. Then, all requests to the report server will go under this trusted account.
8. On the report server box in the private LAN, consider disabling the Report Manager by setting the IsReportManagerEnabled setting to false in rsreportserver.config.

   After completing these steps, end users will be able to use the Report Manager on the Internet-facing server to view reports deployed to the report server on the private LAN.

2.5 Summary

This chapter gave you the necessary background to install and upgrade Reporting Services. Reporting Services supports flexible deployments scenarios. Take some time to plan your Reporting Services installation before you start the SQL Server setup program. Decide upon a deployment topology for your reporting solution, such as a single-server or multiple-server deployment, scale-out deployment, instance deployment, or Internet deployment.

You can install Reporting Services on the default or a named instance. Choose the latter option if you need to run Reporting Services side by side with a previous version. By default, the setup program configures the report server for native mode but it also supports SharePoint integration mode and files-only installation mode. The files-only installation option gives you complete control over the installation and initialization process. The SQL Server setup program supports upgrading previous versions of Reporting Services. Make sure you understand what will be upgraded and what scenarios are not supported. Use the SQL Server 2008 Upgrade Advisor to plan your upgrade.

Once the setup is done, test the server to make sure it is operational. Use the Reporting Services Configuration Manager to finalize the installation, such as to configure the Web service and Report Manager URLs, back up encryption keys, and configure scale-out deployment. Set configuration settings in the report server configuration file to turn features off.

By now, your Reporting Services installation should be operational and you are ready to author reports.

2.6 Resources

SQL Server 2008 Features Comparison
(http://tinyurl.com/4uqqux)—Compare SQL Server 2008 editions.

Hardware and Software Requirements for Installing SQL Server 2008
(http://tinyurl.com/2vg5qd)—Documents the minimum hardware and software requirements for installing SQL Server 2008.

Troubleshooting Kerberos Delegation
(http://tinyurl.com/5bskv)—This whitepaper explains how to troubleshoot and configure Kerberos authentication.

<defaultProxy> Element (Network Settings)
(http://tinyurl.com/37nzz6)—Explains how to use the defaultProxy setting to configure the HTTP proxy server.

Windows Server 2003 Deployment Kit: Planning Server Deployments
(http://tinyurl.com/2pmjk5)—This book provides comprehensive information about planning Windows Server 2003 installations. Chapters 8 and 9 discuss Network Load Balancing.

How to: Configure a Report Server for Local Administration on Windows Vista and Windows Server 2008
(http://tinyurl.com/6rhlpz)—Lists the steps to configure administrator access.

Planning for Scalability and Performance with Reporting Services
(http://tinyurl.com/2upc5j)—This paper provides information about the scalability characteristics of different Reporting Services implementation architectures.

SQL Server 2008 Books Online
(http://tinyurl.com/2sug4d)—The SQL Server 2008 documentation.

Using Secure Web Service Methods
(http://tinyurl.com/5ryatw)—Explains how to use the SecureConnectionLevel setting in rsreportserver.config.

Solving the Reporting Services Login Issue by Lukasz Pawlowsky
(http://tinyurl.com/4ve5uc)—Explains how to troubleshoot login issues.

HTTP Configuration Utility by Steve Johnson
(http://tinyurl.com/2te4vd)—Lets you view and manage the HTTP.SYS endpoints.

Machine Key Generator Tool
(http://tinyurl.com/2laxcg)—Generates random keys for validation and encryption/decryption of the view state.

How to: Configure Windows Authentication in Reporting Services
(http://tinyurl.com/392gu3)—Explains how Reporting Services Windows authentication works and how to configure it.

PART 2

The Report Designer

As a report author, you can use Reporting Services to design professional-looking standard and ad hoc reports. While Reporting Services provides several designers, Report Designer will be the tool of choice for developers and power users. It supports all report authoring features and is hosted inside the Visual Studio integrated development environment.

The best way to learn report design is by practicing it. The exercises included in this book walk you through the steps of creating different types of reports, including tabular, crosstab, and free-form reports. Working with data is a fundamental skill that every report author needs to master. You'll learn different ways to integrate your reports with a variety of data sources, including relational and multidimensional databases, Web services, and more. You'll also understand how to parameterize reports to filter data at the data source and the report server.

One of the most exciting new features in this release of Reporting Services is the versatile tablix region which unites the former table, matrix, and list controls and removes many limitations that were pestering report authors in the past. As a report author, you'll be glad to know that Reporting Services 2008 has supercharged its data visualization capabilities with an upgraded chart region and a brand new gauge region. You'll also witness how the enhanced textbox report item can help you simplify the report layout and help you add rich formatting features to your reports.

Every tool has its design limitations and Report Designer is no exception. Complex business needs may surpass Report Designer capabilities and present unique challenges that require more advanced design skills. However, you can supercharge your reports with custom code that is embedded in the report definitions or located in external assemblies. By integrating your reports with custom code, you can meet more advanced report requirements that transcend the Report Designer limitations.

Chapter 3

Report Design Fundamentals

Recall from chapter 1 that the report lifecycle consists of authoring, management, and delivery phases. In the authoring phase, you create a report definition that serves as the blueprint of a report. To facilitate this process, Microsoft provides four report designers to address different report authoring needs and technical skills. Although different in functionality, all tools transform your design choices into a report definition based on the Report Definition Language (RDL).

In this chapter, I will introduce you to report authoring with Reporting Services 2008. I will start by suggesting a methodology for planning the design process and providing guidelines for choosing a report authoring tool. Next, I will introduce you to report server projects and the Business Intelligence Development Studio (BIDS) environment. The rest of the chapter will be spent walking you through the steps of authoring a basic table report using the BIDS Report Designer. This chapter concludes with a demonstration of two other report authoring options supported by BIDS: the Report Wizard and importing reports from Microsoft Access.

3.1 Designing for Report Design

Anyone who has delivered a finished report without first going through a solid design process knows that there is an unhappy ending to that story almost every time. Almost immediately, the hapless report author is flooded with requests for modifications and additional reports.

As with any project, the report authoring process can benefit from planning and design stages. In this section, I will present a methodology that has proved useful in my real-life projects. Irrespective of whether you use this or another methodology, the important thing is to have a guided process and to spend time planning your solution before jumping into construction.

3.1.1 Understanding the Report Authoring Cycle

The report authoring process can be described as four-stage cycle that consists of envisioning, design, construction, and testing phases, as shown in Figure 3.1. Large report solutions may benefit from breaking the authoring process into more manageable steps or iterations to deliver value to business users as quickly as possible. Let's discuss each stage in more detail.

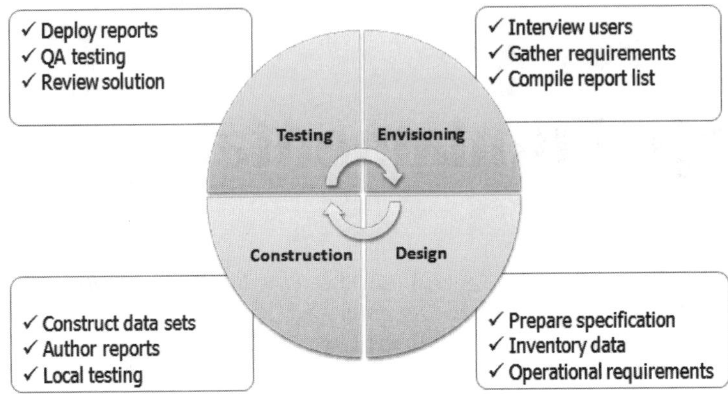

Figure 3.1 The report authoring cycle consists of envisioning, design, construction, and testing phases.

Envisioning stage

The report design is led by user requirements. Therefore, your first task during the envisioning stage is to identify who will use your reports. Knowing your user not only ensures wide acceptance of the reporting solution, but helps you plan report security later on.

Next, interview users to assess their reporting needs. Ask design questions to understand what standard reports are expected, the level of data summarization (such as monthly, annual, detail-level), and the IT skills of the users. Create a target list of candidate reports and assign an importance factor on a scale from one to ten. If you end up with a long list, explore the option of letting business users create reports in an ad-hoc tool such as Report Builder. Prepare a high-level reporting requirement specification, similar to the one shown in Table 3.1.

Table 3.1 Sample reporting requirements

User group	Report	Interactivity	Delivery	Importance
Executives	Chart report showing the Adventure Works sales for the current month	None	E-mail subscription	10
Executives	Sales Summary cross-tab report showing the Adventure Works sales by year	None	On-demand	10
Marketing Managers	Top 100 Internet Products that shows the top 100 products sold via direct sales	None	On-demand	9
Internet Sales Department	Customer Orders that lists the customer's order history	Drill-down to the customer order	On-demand	8

Prioritize the targeted report list by importance and negotiate a cutoff list of 10-15 of the most strategic standard reports for the first iteration.

Design stage

During the design stage, you prepare a detailed report specification for each report you need to create. The report specification should include a report mock-up and a mapping between the report items and data. To help you understand what a report specification might look like, I included a sample report specification for the Product Sales by Category report (Product Sales by Category.xlsx) in the source code for this chapter. In the lessons that follow, you will implement a report that matches this specification.

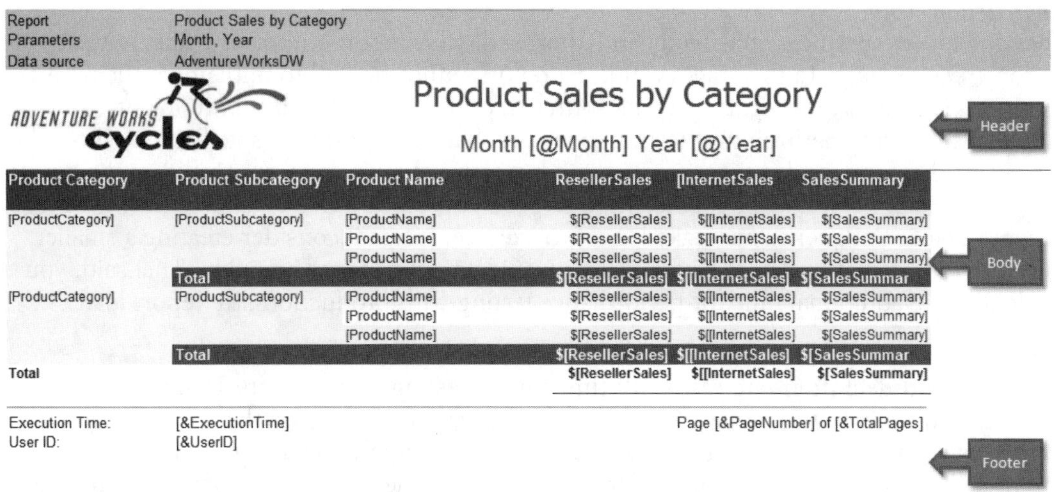

Figure 3.2 You can use Microsoft Excel to construct the report mock-up.

The Product Sales by Category report takes two parameters, Month and Year, and shows the reseller and Internet sales grouped by product category. The report specification uses Report Designer placeholders to denote calculated fields, as shown Table 3.2.

Table 3.2 Mock-up placeholders

Token	Description	Example
[]	Dataset field	[ResellerSales]
@	Report parameter	[@Month]
&	Built-in field	[&PageNumber]

You can come up with placeholders for other features, such as to denote drillable fields and navigation actions. The sample report specification also includes a Data Inventory worksheet that shows the mapping between the report fields and data, as shown in Figure 3.3.

Report Field	Source Column	Table	Comments
ProductCategory	EnglishProductCategoryName	DimProductCategory	Group By
ProductSubcategory	EnglishProductSubcategoryName	DimProductSubcategory	Group By
ProductName	EnglishProductName	DimProduct	Group By
ResellerSales	SalesAmount	FactResellerSales	SUM
InternetSales	SalesAmount	FactResellerSales	SUM
SalesSummary	N/A	N/A	ResellerSales+InternetSales

Figure 3.3 The report specification should include a mapping between report fields and data.

In the sample specification, the ProductCategory report field maps to the EnglishProductCategoryName column in the DimProductCategory table. The Comments column denotes how the field will be aggregated or calculated if it is not present in the data source. When you create a report specification, be sure to include operational requirements, such as who will be authorized to view the report, how report data will be secured, and the expected report performance.

Construction stage

When the report specification is ready and approved, your report authoring cycle moves to the construction stage. In this stage, you use a report authoring tool to implement the report definition. This involves preparing a data source, report dataset(s), and report layout.

You also need to perform unit testing to ensure that the report meets its functional requirements. I recommend you prepare a small but representative dataset to validate the report results. For example, it may be inefficient to target a large cube as a data source during development because the queries may take longer to execute. Instead, consider creating a smaller cube with representative data. This will let you validate report results quickly. That said, you should allocate additional time for performance testing with production-size report loads.

Testing stage

Once the report definitions are ready, it's time for the testing stage to start. Deploy your reports to a dedicated testing server. Conduct usability tests to make sure the reports align with the user expectations. Perform quality assurance test to verify the accuracy of the report results. Finally, assess the solution to understand if it meets the user expectations and provides value to the business. If it doesn't, return to the design stage before you continue with the next iteration.

3.1.2 Understanding Report Designers

Recall from chapter 1 that Microsoft provides four report designers that address different report authoring needs. In this section, I will compare their features and discuss how to choose a report designer based on the user type and reporting task at hand.

Comparing report designers

Table 3.3 shows the high-level differences among the report designers.

Table 3.3 High-level feature comparison of the Microsoft-provided report designers

Feature	BIDS Report Designer	Report Builder 2.0	Report Builder 1.0	Visual Studio 2008 Report Designer
Visual Studio integration (source code control, projects, debugging)	✓			✓
Full RDL 2008 support	✓	✓		
Built-in connection and query designers for data retrieval	✓	✓		
Local report processing				✓
Doesn't require Visual Studio		✓	Client only	
Report models as data sources	✓	✓	✓	
Require Report Builder model			✓	
System-generated drillthrough			✓	
Auto-generated queries			✓	

All report designers are implemented as rich, Windows Forms clients that are installed on the user's machine. Currently, Microsoft doesn't provide a thin, Web-based design tool. Having so many designers is a little confusing, so let's take a close look at each one of them.

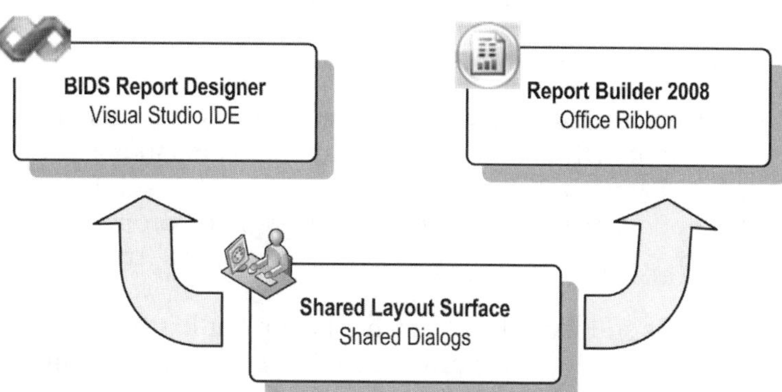

Figure 3.4 The BIDS Report Designer and Report Builder 2.0 provide full RDL 2008 support and share the same layout surface.

The BIDS Report Designer

This designer supports all report authoring features and is hosted inside the Visual Studio integrated development environment (IDE). Since BIDS is a scaled-down version of Visual Studio, the BIDS Report Designer mainly targets developers who are familiar with the Visual Studio IDE. It's important to note that the BIDS Report Designer and Report Builder 2.0 share the same layout surface, as shown in Figure 3.4.

NOTE The layout surface is the WYSIWYG (What-You-See-Is-What-You-Get) design area to which you add report items, such tables and charts, to define the report layout at design time. Currently, developers cannot embed the shared layout surface in custom applications. Microsoft hints that a future release may enable this integration scenario.

Since the property dialog boxes are included in the layout surface, the BIDS Report Designer and Report Builder 2.0 share them as well. For the most part, the only implementation difference between the two designers is the hosting environment. The BIDS Report Designer is hosted in the Visual Studio shell and supports developer-oriented features, such as debugging, source control, and projects. By contrast, Report Builder 2.0 is designed as a stand-alone Windows Forms application that doesn't use the graphical environment of Visual Studio.

The BIDS Report Designer will be *the* Report Designer that I will use for most of the report authoring demos in this book. For the sake of brevity, I will drop the "BIDS" portion of its name and refer to this designer as simply *Report Designer*.

Report Builder 2.0

Similar to Report Designer, Report Builder 2.0 supports the full spectrum of report authoring features. Unlike Report Designer, Report Builder 2.0 lets the report author work with one report at a time. Although dubbed Report Builder 2.0, this designer has very little in common with the Report Builder you may be familiar with in SQL Server 2005 Reporting Services. For example, Report Builder 2.0 connects directly to the data source and doesn't require a semantic model. That said, both Report Builder 2.0 and Report Designer support Report Builder 1.0 report models as data sources.

Report Builder 2.0 is still under development but Microsoft has provided a preview version available via web download from the Microsoft SQL Server 2008 Feature Pack page. Irrespective of the Report Builder 2.0 release status, you should definitely consider using it for standard and ad hoc reporting outside the Visual Studio IDE. Note that Report Builder 2.0 raises the bar for required technical skills because the user must now know how to work with data sources and lay out the report. In a long run, however, Report Builder 2.0 is expected to add more end-user oriented features and supersede Report Builder 1.0. I will preview Report Builder 2.0 in chapter 10.

Report Builder 1.0

SQL Server 2005 introduced the Report Builder tool to let non-technical users author simple ad hoc reports. Unfortunately, while very user-friendly, Report Builder has limitations that can be difficult if not impossible to work around. For example, it provides only a subset of the report authoring features. It doesn't support free-form layout, expression-based properties, or side-by-side report regions. In addition, it supports only SQL Server, Oracle, and Analysis Services data sources.

In SQL Server 2008, Report Builder is still part of the designer lineup but has been renamed to Report Builder 1.0. Although it was not enhanced in SQL Server 2008, it remains in the box because it is a viable option for creating simple ad hoc reports. As such, I will cover it in chapters 8 and 9. If you use it, be aware that Report Builder 1.0 has been deprecated in favor of Report Builder 2.0, which delivers both ease-of-use and powerful reporting features previously found only in the BIDS Report Designer.

Visual Studio Report Designer

If you have Visual Studio 2008 and you install the SQL Server client components, you will get the BI project templates in your existing Visual Studio installation. This lets you use Visual Studio to work with both code projects and business intelligence projects that target SQL Server 2008. But what if you don't use SQL Server 2008 and still want to report-enable your .NET applications? For example, suppose you want to include some operational reports that display data from application datasets in a custom Windows Forms application.

The Visual Studio Report Designer is provided so that you can build reports that run in the Visual Studio ReportViewer controls. This designer doesn't support working with data sources and report preview. It lets you lay out a report from a pre-defined application dataset schema. At run time, the application must pass the report parameters and data to the report.

As it stands, the Visual Studio Report Designer remains unchanged from its Visual Studio 2005 release. It does not support the RDL 2008 schema and it doesn't use the new layout surface. The plans are to upgrade this designer with new features and support for RDL schema in the next major Visual Studio release or in a web release after SQL 2008 ships.

If you also happen to have BIDS and you are not using the ReportViewer controls, you should use BIDS to create any reports that you intend to run on a report server. I will discuss the Visual Studio Report Designer in chapter 15, where I will show you how to report-enable custom .NET applications.

Choosing a report designer

Although four report authoring tools may seem overwhelming, choosing a report designer for the reporting task at hand is not difficult. If you are a developer who lives and breathes in Visual Studio, the BIDS Report Designer should be your report authoring tool of choice. If you are power user and prefer a full-featured report designer outside Visual Studio, choose Report Builder 2.0. In fact, since BIDS Report Designer and Report Builder 2.0 fully support RDL 2008, you can use them interchangeably.

If you are a non-technical user and you need a simple ad-hoc report authoring tool that doesn't assume knowledge of the database schema and query syntax, evaluate Report Builder 1.0. If you find it too limiting, "upgrade" to Report Builder 2.0 or Report Designer.

NOTE One ad-hoc reporting scenario that may favor Report Builder 2.0 instead of Report Builder 1.0 even with non-technical users is sourcing data from an Analysis Services cube. Report Builder 2.0 with Analysis Services gives end users the best of both worlds–full support of RDL 2008 and an intuitive end-user model. The graphical MDX Query Designer can auto-generate MDX queries for simple reports by providing drag-and-drop support.

Finally, the Visual Studio Report Designer lets developers design and distribute reports with custom .NET applications without requiring SQL Server.

3.2 Working with Report Server Projects

As I explained earlier, I will use the BIDS Report Designer predominantly for the report authoring demos. Since Report Designer is hosted in the SQL Server 2008 Business Intelligence Development Studio, you need to have a good grasp of the BIDS environment before you can start using Report Designer. You cannot use earlier versions of BIDS to run the Reporting Services 2008 Report Designer, nor can you use BIDS 2008 to author older report definitions.

3.2.1 Business Intelligence Development Studio vs. Visual Studio

Business Intelligence Development Studio is a subset of Microsoft Visual Studio 2008. As its name suggests, it supports project types that are specific to SQL Server business intelligence, such as Reporting Services, Analysis Services, and Integration Services projects. Note that these project types are part of BIDS and not Visual Studio. If you have installed Visual Studio 2008 only, you will find that the BI-related project types are missing. During the SQL Server 2008 setup, you must install BIDS to integrate the BI project types into the Visual Studio 2008 IDE. Once you've installed the SQL Server client components, you can use BIDS and Visual Studio interchangeably to work with BI projects.

Another important point to remember is that you don't require full-blown Visual Studio if you work with business intelligence projects only. BIDS is designed exactly for this task with no additional cost besides a SQL Server license. However, if you require code projects, for example to extend reports with Visual Basic or C# custom code, then you'll probably need Visual Studio (or another developer tool) because BIDS alone doesn't support code projects.

3.2.2 Performing Project Tasks

As a prerequisite for authoring reports with Report Designer, you must create a Report Server project. The Report Server project type supplies templates for creating definitions of data sources and reports. It also includes a variety of designers, tools, and wizards to work with these definitions. You can add several BI projects to a Visual Studio solution. For example, you can add an Analysis Services project and Reporting Services project to the same solution and then work with them in a single instance of BIDS or Visual Studio.

Next, let's practice a few common tasks that will help you get familiar with BIDS and Report Server projects. If you have both BIDS and Visual Studio 2008, you can use either one to complete the practices that follow.

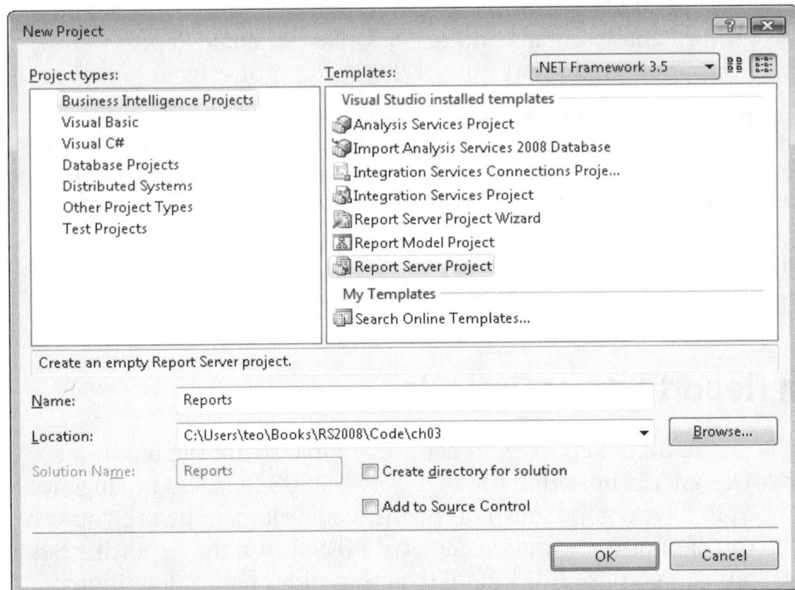

Figure 3.5 Select the Report Server Project template to author reports with the Report Designer.

Creating a Report Server project

Follow these steps to create a new Report Server project in BIDS:

1. Open SQL Server Business Intelligence Development Studio from the Microsoft SQL Server 2008 program group.
2. Click File ➪ New ➪ Project to open the New Project dialog box, shown in Figure 3.5. In my case, the Project Types list includes code project types, such as Visual Basic and C# project types because I have installed Visual Studio 2008.
3. Click the Business Intelligence Projects project type and note that the Templates pane lists BI-related project types.

   The Analysis Services Project templates let you create Analysis Services database definitions. The Integration Services Project templates include the necessary objects for creating Integration Services packages. The Report Server Project Wizard project creates a Report Server project but runs the Report Wizard to help you auto-generate the report definition. The Report Model Project template lets you design Report Builder 1.0 report models. The Report Server Project template includes Report Designer.
4. Let's ignore the Report Wizard for now. Select the Report Server Project template.
5. Enter *Reports* as the name of the project.
6. In the Location field, enter the folder path where the project will be created and click OK to create the project.

Understanding Report Server projects

BIDS creates an empty report server project, as shown in Figure 3.6. The Solution Explorer window shows a Reports project node, followed by Shared Data Sources and Reports folders. You can use the Shared Data Sources folder to add data source definitions that are shared among the reports in the same project. Don't worry if the concept of shared data sources is not immediately clear. It will all make sense in the next chapter.

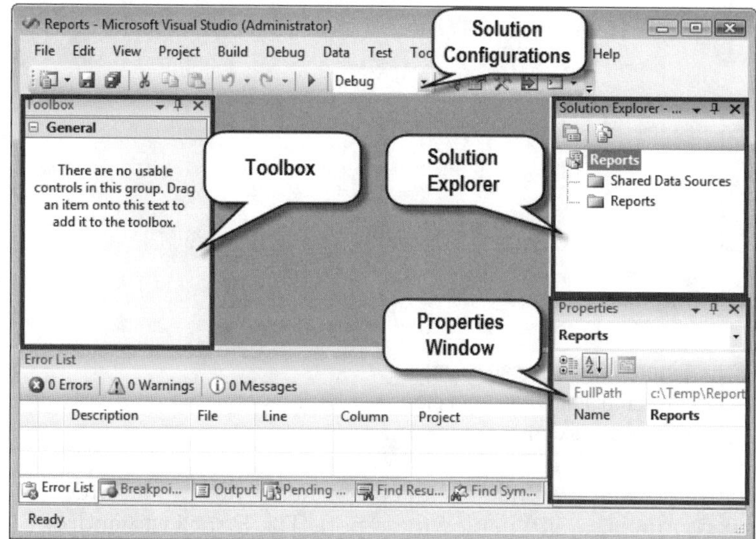

Figure 3.6 The Report Server Project template integrates with the Visual Studio integrated development environment.

As I noted in chapter 1, reports are described in an XML-based grammar called Report Definition Language (RDL). The Reports folder contains the report definition (*.rdl) files, as well as other report content, such as images.

NOTE BIDS doesn't let you create nested folders under the Reports folder although the report server supports a hierarchical folder structure and nested folders in the report catalog. If you need to organize the report content in nested folders, consider splitting the project into multiple projects (one per folder). Alternatively, you can deploy all reports to a single folder and use the Report Manager to move report content to subfolders.

You can select an object in the Solution Explorer to view and change its properties in the Visual Studio Properties window. Changed property values are shown in bold. If you open a report definition in the Report Designer, the Toolbox pane (press Ctrl+Alt+X if the Toolbox isn't visible) will list report items that you can drag to the layout surface to define the report layout.

When you create a new project, BIDS generates a solution file (*.sln) in the project folder. The Solution Explorer doesn't show the solution file if the solution contains a single project. You can add a new project to the solution by clicking File ⇨ Add ⇨ New Project or add an existing project by clicking File ⇨ Add ⇨ Existing Project.

Understanding project tasks

You can right-click a node in the Solution Explorer (or use the Visual Studio menu bar) to carry out related tasks.

1. In the Solution Explorer, right-click the Reports project node.

The context menu displays project-related tasks, as shown in Figure 3.7. Let's quickly review the most common tasks. The Build task lets you verify the report definitions. Building a project or a report doesn't result in a binary. Instead, when you build a report project, BIDS validates the report definition and shows inconsistencies in the Error List pane. For example, if you misspell a report parameter in a field expression and build the project, the following error will be shown in the Error List window.

```
[rsParameterReference] The Value expression for the textbox '<name> ' refers to a non- existing report parameter '<parametername> '
```

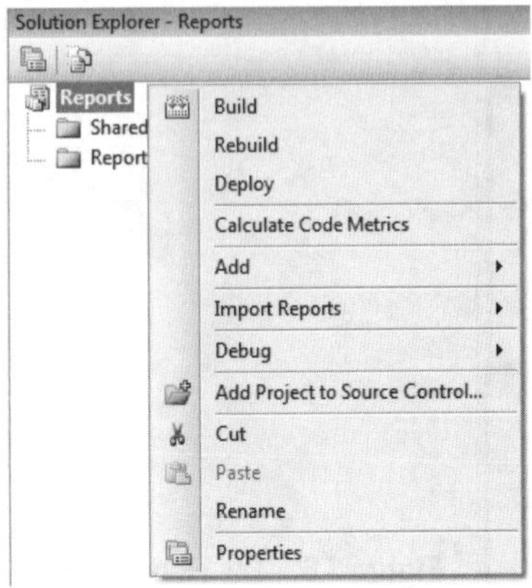

Figure 3.7 You can initiate project-related tasks from the project context menu.

You can explicitly build the report by using the Build menu command or you can let BIDS build the report implicitly when you preview and deploy the report. The Error List window shows errors, warnings, and informational messages that result from the build process. You must correct errors to successfully preview and deploy a report. You can quickly select the offending item by double-clicking the error text.

TIP Another way of locating report items on a busy report is by expanding the item drop-down list in the Properties window, type the first letter on the item's name, and click the item. The Report Designer will select the item on the report canvas. As a best practice, I recommend that you assign meaningful names to report items that you need to reference in expressions and property settings, such as for sorting and hidden visibility.

The Deploy task lets you publish the project files to the server. During deployment, BIDS displays the deployment progress in the Output window. The Add task lets you add new or existing report files to the project. You can use the Import Reports task (only available if Microsoft Access is installed locally) to import Access reports, as I'll discuss in section 3.4.2.

As one of the first tasks after creating a new project, I add the project to source control, such as Visual SourceSafe or Team Foundation Server, by using the Add Project to Source Control menu. This lets you maintain version control of the report definition files and allows multiple developers to work on the same project without overwriting each other changes.

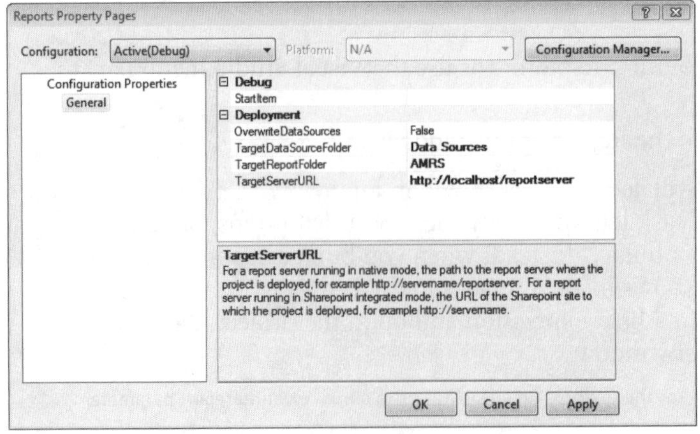

Figure 3.8 The project properties specify settings for deploying reports to the server.

Understanding project properties

Recall that if you want to make the report publicly available, you need to deploy the report to the report server. As a prerequisite for deploying reports successfully from BIDS, you need to set the project properties.

1. Right-click the project node in the Solution Explorer and click Properties to open the project Property Pages dialog box (see Figure 3.8).

   Table 3.4 explains the project properties.

Table 3.4 Project properties

Setting	Description	Default Value
StartItem	Specifies which report will be previewed when you debug the project (F5).	Empty
OverwriteDataSources	When set to True, overwrites the shared data source definitions on the server.	False
TargetDataSourceFolder	Specifies the server folder the project data source definitions will be deployed to.	Data Sources
TargetReportFolder	Specifies the server folder the project report definitions will be deployed to.	Reports
TargetServerURL	Indicates the Web Service URL.	Empty

Let's assume that you need to deploy the project to your local report server for local testing.

2. Change the TargetReportFolder setting to *AMRS*.
3. In TargetServerURL, enter *http://localhost/reportserver* (Vista or Windows Server 2003) or *http://localhost:8080/reportserver* (Windows XP).

   As a result, when you deploy the project, shared data sources will be deployed to the Data Sources folder and the report definitions will be deployed to the AMRS folder. If the AMRS folder doesn't exist, the report server will create it.

Understanding project configurations

A project configuration is a saved set of project properties. If you expand the Configuration drop-down list, you will see that BIDS has three predefined project configurations: Debug, DebugLocal, and Release. Project configurations simplify deployment. For example, during development, you will probably deploy and test reports to your local server by using the settings of the Debug or DebugLocal configurations. When local testing is complete, you can deploy the project to the production server by choosing the Release configuration.

Each configuration maintains an independent set of project properties. Unfortunately, unlike Analysis Services and Integration Services projects, Report Server projects don't support configuration-specific connection strings for shared data sources. Consequently, you may need to update the data source connection strings when you switch configurations.

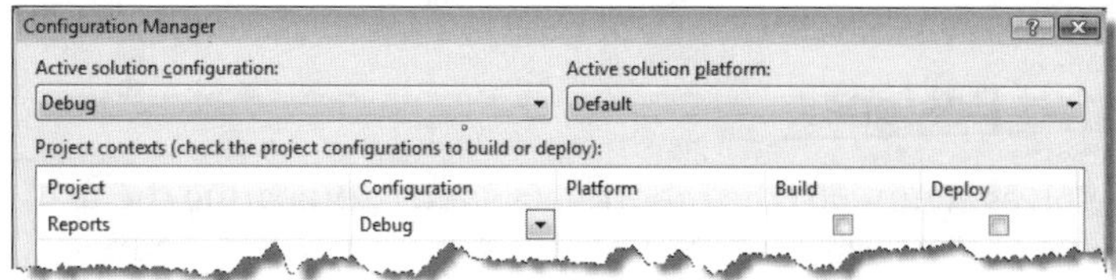

Figure 3.9 Use the Configuration Manager to work with project configurations.

1. In the project Property Pages, click the Configuration Manager button to open the Configuration Manager (see Figure 3.9).

The default active configuration is Debug. The Build and Deploy settings specify what happens when you debug (F5) the project. For example, if you check both settings and debug the project, BIDS will build and deploy the project. If you have a solution that includes multiple projects, it may be time consuming to re-deploy them each time. Instead, you may decide to clear the Build and Deploy checkboxes for the projects that you are not planning to change often. You can build and deploy them manually when needed.

You can create additional configurations, such as QA for deploying to a QA server, as follows:

2. Expand the Active Solution Configuration drop-down list and choose <New...>.
3. In the New Solution Configuration dialog box that follows, name your new configuration. You can select a configuration in the Copy Settings From drop-down list if you want to copy the settings from an existing configuration. Leave the Create New Project Configurations checkbox checked to create project configurations for each project in the solution.
4. In the Property Pages dialog box, enter the deployment settings for the new configuration.

To switch to the active configuration, expand the Solutions Configuration drop-down list (see again Figure 3.6) and click the new configuration.

TIP Project configurations come handy when you need an easy way to automate report deployment, such as with MSBuild. For example, the following command deploys the solution using the settings in the QA configuration.

```
C:\>devenv "C:\Books\RS2008\Code\ch03\Reports\Reports.sln" /deploy QA
```

This is especially useful when automating deployment to SharePoint because you need to change the report definitions to use absolute paths to external resources, such as shared data sources. Instead of writing write custom code to automate deployment, consider BIDS command-line deployment with project configurations.

3.3 Authoring a Basic Report

Now that you have a good grasp of Report Server projects and the BIDS IDE, let's go through the steps of creating the Product Sales by Category report (see Figure 3.2) to gain further understanding of the report authoring process. This report demonstrates:

- Creating a shared data source
- Defining a report dataset
- Working with query and report parameters
- Authoring a tabular report
- Working with report groups
- Implementing basic expressions

3.3.1 Getting Started in Report Designer

In a nutshell, authoring a report involves setting up the report data source, preparing the report dataset(s), and laying out the report. Let's start by creating a new report and examining the report in the Report Designer. This will help you understand the elements of a report and the Report Designer environment.

Creating a report

Start by creating a new project in BIDS by following these steps:

1. In the Solution Explorer, right-click the project node and choose Add ➪ New Item. Alternatively, you can right-click the Reports folder and choose Add ➪ New Item.
2. In the Add New Item dialog box that follows, select the Report template.

> **TIP** The Report Designer loads the templates from the \Program Files\Microsoft Visual Studio 9.0\Common7\IDE\PrivateAssemblies\ProjectItems\ReportProject folder. You can add your own report definitions to that folder to implement "standard" templates for jump-starting the report authoring process.

3. In the Name field, enter *Product Sales by Category.rdl* and click OK.

BIDS creates a new report definition and opens it in the Report Designer.

Understanding the Report Designer

Report Designer is a collection of graphical query and design tools that are hosted in the Business Intelligence Development Studio environment. When you open a report, the Report Designer (Figure 3.10) displays the report in design mode (the Design tab is active).

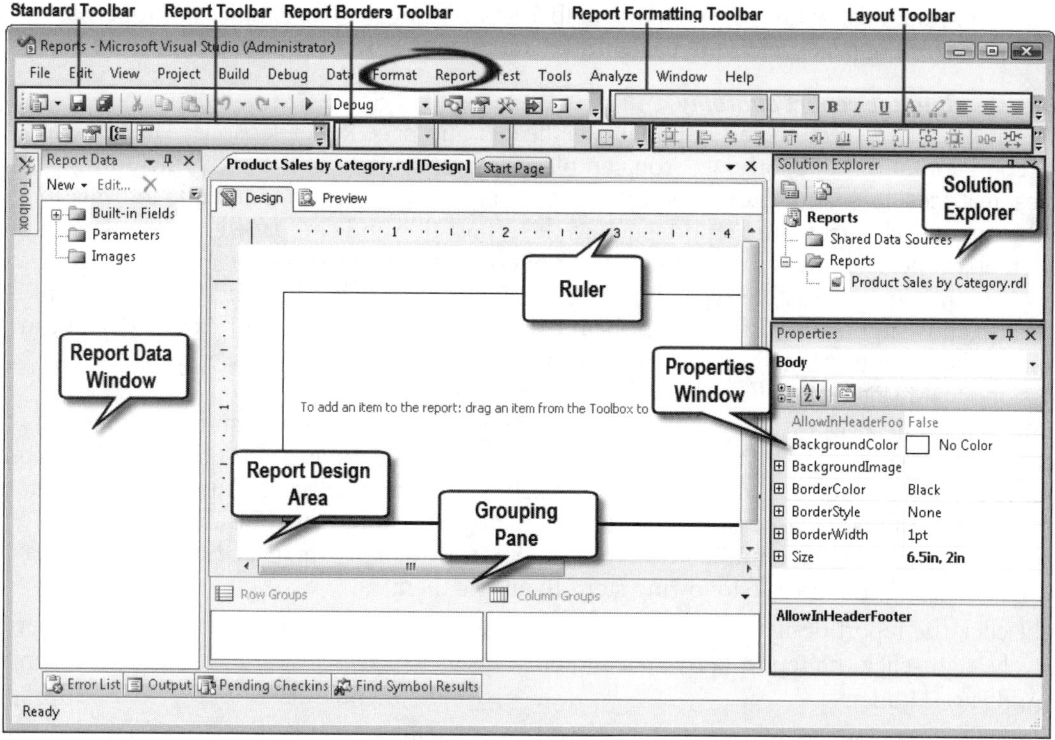

Figure 3.10 The Report Designer is a collection of graphical query and design tools that are hosted in BIDS.

The Preview tab lets you test the report. The report design area that surrounds the report body represents the report itself. For example, when you right-click the report design area, Report Designer shows a context menu to let you access the report properties and show/hide the report ruler and the Grouping pane. The same options are available when you click the Reports main menu, which is available only in design mode.

If the report has groups, the Grouping pane shows the row and column groups defined on the report. The Report Data window (press Ctrl+Alt+D if the window isn't visible) contains data objects that can be dragged on the report. As you progress through the report authoring process, the Report Designer adds additional objects, such as data sources and datasets, to the Report Data window. The Toolbox window (inactive on Figure 3.10) contains report items that you drag on the design area to lay out the report.

NOTE Readers who have experience with previous releases of Report Designer have probably noticed that the Data tab is now gone. It has been superseded with the Report Data window that now consolidates all data-related objects, including report parameters, which are no longer accessible in the Report menu.

The Standard toolbar lets you carry out common tasks, such as saving report definitions or copying and pasting report items. You should build a habit of saving the report you are working on frequently, as the Report Designer holds layout changes in memory. Use the Layout toolbar to perform various common layout tasks in design mode, such as aligning objects. Report Designer adds additional toolbars and menus to BIDS. The Report Borders toolbar lets you define borders around report objects. Use the Report Formatting toolbar to format text, such as to set the font and color. The functionality of the last three toolbars is also available from the Format main menu. The Report toolbar lets you toggle the visibility of Properties window, Grouping page, ruler, the page header and footer.

Understanding the report anatomy

A report has a body section and optional page header and page footer sections. The body of the report contains the report data. You can place any report item in the body, including tables, matrices, lists, and charts. You can use the page header section to include information on the top of each page of the report, such as the report title and company logo. Similarly, the page footer repeats information on the bottom of each page, such as the page number. You can place only images, textboxes, and lines report items in page headers and footers. This release also adds support for field references in page headers and footers. For example, you can add a textbox that displays the overall reseller sales from the Products dataset using the expression =SUM (Fields!ResellerSales.Value, "Products").

In Reporting Services, a report doesn't have designated report header and report footer sections. However, you can use the report body to achieve the same effect. For example, if you want to show the report title only on the first page of the report, place the title text box at the top of the report body before the report data. Similarly, place static text inside the body section after the report data to implement a report footer. By default, the page header and footer sections are disabled. Use the following steps to enable them:

1. Right-click the report design area and click Add Page Header to enable the page header. Alternatively, right-click the report body area and click Insert ⇨ Page Header or click Report menu ⇨ Add Page Header.
2. Right-click the report design area and click Add Page Footer to enable the page footer.

The Report Designer adds empty page header and footer sections to the report.

Setting up the page properties

Assuming United States regional settings, by default a new report has a portrait layout with width of 8.5" and height of 11". Most real-live reports will probably need more horizontal space. To configure the Product Sales by Category report for landscape orientation:

1. Right-click the report design area and click Report Properties.

   The Report Properties dialog box opens, as shown in Figure 3.11. This is one of the shared dialogs that come with the designer layout surface and are shared by both Report Designer and Report Builder 2.0. All shared dialogs have consistent look and feel. The settings are organized logically in tabs listed in the left pane. The actual settings are shown in the right pane.

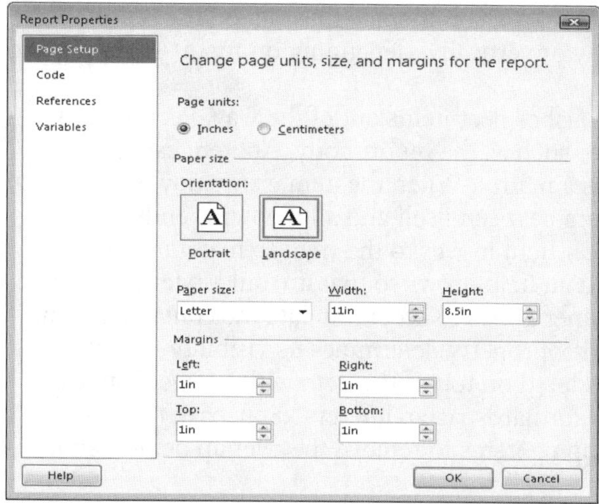

Figure 3.11 Use the Report Properties dialog box to set up the page size, orientation, and margins.

   The Page Setup tab of the Report Properties dialog box lets you configure the page properties, including the page units, page size, and margins.

2. Click the Landscape orientation.
3. Set all page margins to one inch and click OK.

Alternatively, you can click the design area outside the report and use the Properties window to set the PageSize and Margins properties. The page size affects how the report paginates when exported with hard-page renderers, such as PDF and Image.

About report pagination

Pagination refers to the number of pages within a report and how report items are arranged on these pages. When the report is processed, the Report Processor prepares a Rendering Object Model that combines report data and report layout, and forwards this object to the rendering extension (renderer) associated with the export format the user has selected. The renderer determines how much data fits on each page by evaluating the size of the report items on the report and the size of the report body.

Once you set up the page size, you can set the maximum width of the report body to accommodate as much content horizontally as possible. You can use the following formula to determine the maximum body width.

```
Body Width <= Page Width - (Left Margin + Right Margin)
```

When determining the body width, you should account for extra space with cross-tab reports because they expand horizontally. If the body width exceeds the page width and margins, the renderer will flow the report content to the next page, which may result in blank pages. Applying the above formula, we determine that the maximum body width of the Product Sales by Category report is nine inches.

1. Click the body section.
2. In the Properties window, expand the Size property and set the Width property to 9 inches (9in). Alternatively, you can resize the body section interactively by dragging its right border.

About item positioning and sizing

The height of the body section set at design time does *not* affect the physical page height. This is because the renderer expands the report body to accommodate the data on the report. The items in a report may grow either horizontally or vertically, depending on report grouping and content size

When an item grows, such as a table, it pushes peer items out of the way. Peer items are those items within the same parent container, such as the report body. An item can grow down, such as a table, or to the right, such as a matrix. When the item grows down, each peer item below it moves down to maintain spacing between itself and all the items ending above it. When the item grows to the right, each peer item moves to the right to maintain spacing between itself and the items to the left of it. If an item grows so that it would extend beyond the bounds of the containing item, the container grows to accommodate the contained item.

If an item overlaps another item, its ZIndex property determines its visibility. The item with the higher ZIndex value wins and is rendered on top of the item with a lower ZIndex value. Overlapping items are supported only for hard-page renderers. Soft-page renderers (HTML, Word, Excel) will reposition overlapping items to remove the overlap before rendering.

About logical page breaks

The report author can control where a vertical page break will occur by setting page breaks before or after various report elements, including group, rectangle, list, table, matrix, and chart. For example, you can set a logical page break on the product category group to generate a new page each time the product category changes. Logical page breaks are honored in all export formats except XML and CSV because these two formats export data only.

Reporting Services does not have a page break report item that you can drag to the page to specify the exact location where a page break will be generated. Instead, you can use the page break properties of the report items. For example, you can configure a rectangle item to generate a page break after the rectangle. Unfortunately, Reporting Services doesn't support conditional page breaks that cause a new page to occur based on changes in the data (for example, when the product category changes from Accessories to Bikes). Conditional page breaks are long due on the Reporting Services wish list but didn't make it to SQL Server 2008.

NOTE There is one enhancement in Reporting Services 2008 with regard to conditional visibility and logical page breaks. In previous releases, if a page break was defined on an object with conditional visibility, such as a report group whose Hidden value uses an expression to show/hide the group conditionally, the page break would never occur, even if the object was visible. In version 2008, the page break will occur if the object is visible.

3.3.2 Working with Data ▶

Most reports query and display data residing in a database. Next, you will set up a data source to connect to the AdventureWorksDW2008 database and a report dataset that represents the report data.

Creating a shared data source

A data source represents a connection to a database. A report can reference a report-specific (private) data source or a shared data source. The hands-on lab in chapter 1 demonstrated how to work with a report-specific data source. As its name suggests, a shared data source can be shared among reports. This simplifies data source management because once the administrator updates the data source definition all reports that use the shared data source will pick up the changes. Let's set up a shared data source that represents a connection to the AdventureWorksDW2008 SQL Server database.

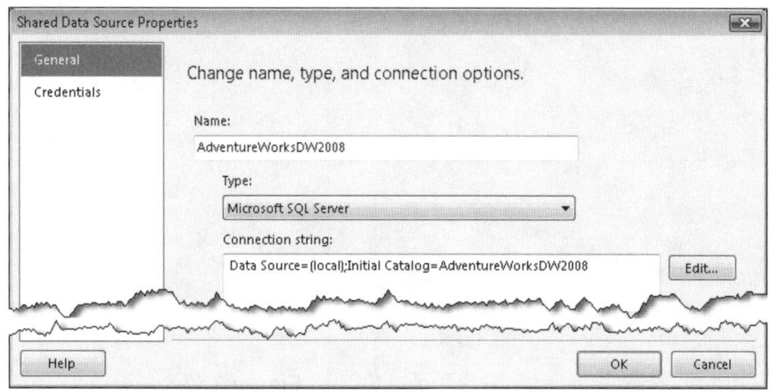

Figure 3.12 Set up a shared data source that can be referenced by all reports in the project.

1. In the Solution Explorer, right-click the Shared Data Sources folder and click Add New Data Source.
2. In the Shared Data Source Properties dialog box that follows, enter *AdventureWorksDW2008* as a data source name.
3. Expand the Type drop-down list and select the Microsoft SQL Server data provider because AdventureWorksDW2008 is a SQL Server database.
4. Assuming you want to connect to your local SQL Server default instance, enter the following connection string in the text box below the Type drop-down, as shown in Figure 3.12:

   ```
   Data Source=(local);Initial Catalog=AdventureWorksDW2008
   ```

   Alternatively, instead of typing the connection string, click the Edit button and use the Connection Properties dialog to specify the connection details.
5. Click the Credentials tab and verify that the Use Windows Authentication (Integrated Security) option is selected. Consequently, the report will connect to the data source using your Windows credentials.

   Don't worry for now about the rest of data source options. I will explain them in detail in the next chapter.
6. Click OK to create the data source.

   The AdventureWorksDW2008.rds data source definition is added to the Shared Data Sources folder in the Solution Explorer. Next, we need to associate the AdventureWorksDW2008 data source with the Product Sales by Category report by creating a data source reference that is saved inside the report definition. Although in this exercise the data source and the reference have identical name (AventureWorksDW2008), this is not a requirement.
7. With the Product Sales by Category report open in design mode, expand the New drop-down menu in the Report Data window and click Data Source.

8. In the Data Source Properties dialog box that follows, name the data source *Adventure-WorksDW2008*.
9. Click the Use Shared Data Source Reference radio button. Expand the drop-down list below and select AdventureWorksDW2008, as shown in Figure 3.13.

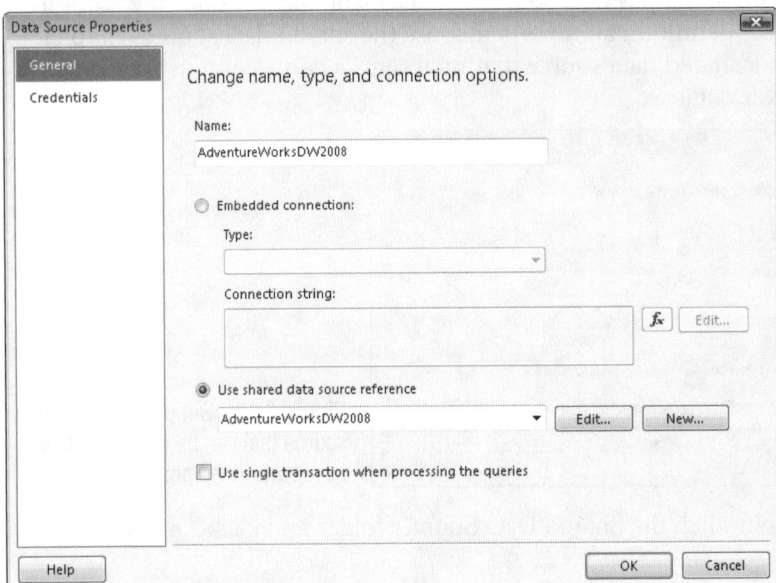

Figure 3.13 Set up a shared data source that can be referenced by all reports in the project.

Notice that you can use the Data Source Properties dialog to set up a report-specific (embedded) connection, which gets saved in the report, or create a new shared data source definition if it doesn't already exist in the project. Report-specific and shared data sources are discussed in more detail in chapter 4.

Creating a dataset

A dataset represents the report data. At design time, you use a query designer to define the dataset definition, which consists of the query statement, dataset fields and other properties. At run time, the report server executes the query to fetch the data.

1. In the Report Data window, right-click the AdventureWorksDW2008 data source reference and click Add Dataset. Another way to add a dataset is to expand the New menu in the Report Data window, choose Dataset and use the Dataset Properties dialog and to create a new data source or reference an existing data source that has been added to the Report Data window.

   The Report Designer opens the generic query designer, which is the default query building tool for supported relational data sources such as Microsoft SQL Server and Oracle, and when you use OLE DB, XML Web Services, and ODBC data providers. The generic query designer doesn't validate the query syntax in any way. Instead, it passes whatever you type directly to the data source.

2. Click the Import button and navigate to the Products.sql file that is included in the Queries folder with the chapter's source code. This query sums the SalesAmount field from the FactInternetSales and FactInternetSales fact tables and groups the results by the product category, subcategory, and product.
3. Click the Exclamation Point button to execute the query and see the results (see Figure 3.14).

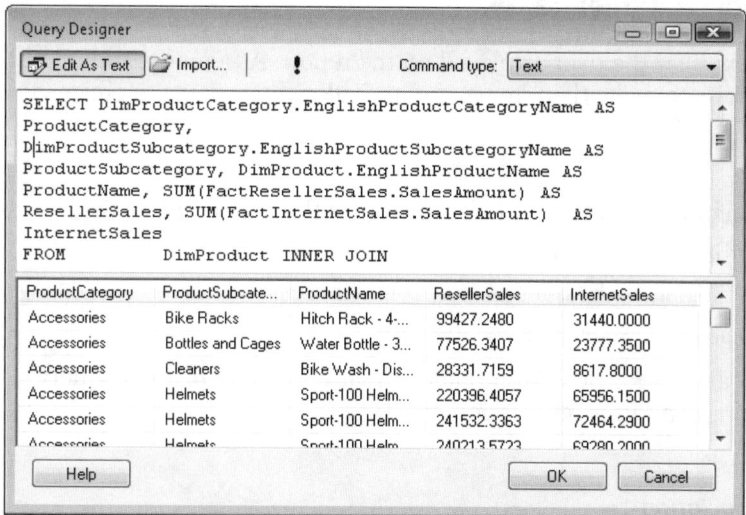

Figure 3.14 The generic query designer is the default query building tool for supported relational data sources.

If you prefer to work with a graphical query tool to author SQL queries, toggle the Edit As Text button. This launches the graphical query designer. This query designer may look familiar to you as it is bundled with several Microsoft products and other SQL Server components. It provides a visual design environment for selecting tables and columns and builds joins and the query for you automatically when you select which columns to use.

4. Click OK to go back to the Dataset Properties window. Click OK to return to Report Designer.

   The Report Designer creates a DataSet1 dataset and adds it under the AdventureWorksDW2008 data source in the Report Data window. The Report Data window shows the dataset fields below the dataset node.

5. In the Report Data window, double-click the DataSet1 node (or right-click and click Dataset Properties). Alternatively, select DataSet1 and click the Edit button. The Edit button is context-aware and displays the appropriate property window depending on the selected object.

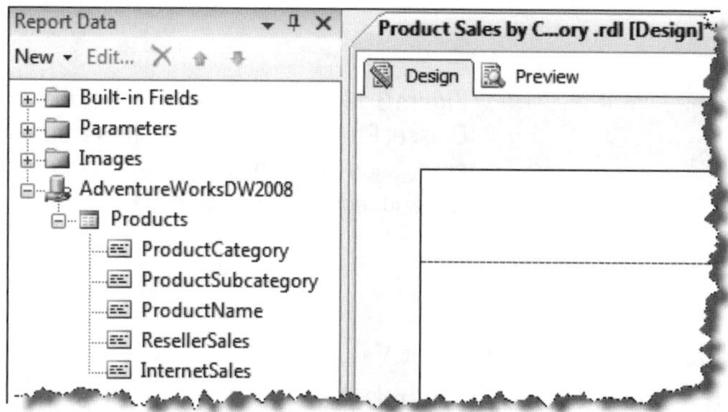

Figure 3.15 The Report Data window shows the Products dataset under the AdventureWorksDW2008 data source.

6. In the Dataset Properties window, rename the dataset to *Products* and click OK.

   At this point, your Report Data window should look like the one shown in Figure 3.15.

3.3.3 Working with Report Parameters ▶

Report parameters lets end users filter the data displayed on the report. As a report author, you can parameterize your reports to make them more useful. Follow these steps to create Month and Year parameters.

Creating query parameters

The easiest way to implement report parameters is to parameterize the dataset query first.

1. In the Report Data window, right-click the Products dataset and click Query.
2. Add the following WHERE clause before the query GROUP BY clause.

```
WHERE D.MonthNumberOfYear = @Month AND D.CalendarYear = @Year
```

   Here, D is an alias to the DimDate table. The @Month and @Year placeholders define query parameters to filter data by month and year respectively.

3. Click OK.

Understanding parameter association

As soon as you click OK, several things happen. First, the Report Designer creates Month and Year query-level parameters. Next, the Report Designer creates Month and Year report-level parameters and adds them to the Parameters node in the Report Data window. Finally, the Report Designer associates the report-level parameters with the query-level parameters. Let's take a look at these changes.

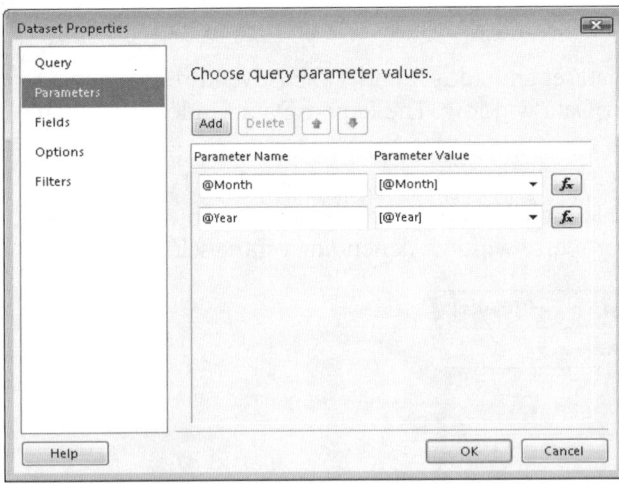

Figure 3.16 The Parameters tab of the Dataset Properties dialog box shows the association between query-level parameters and report-level parameters.

1. In the Report Data window, expand the Parameters node.
2. Double-click the Month report-level parameter.
3. In the Report Parameter Properties dialog box, click the Default Values tab.
4. Click the Specify Values option. Click the Add button and enter *1* to default the Month parameter to January. Click OK.
5. Repeat the last three steps to default the Year parameter to *2004*.
6. Back to the Report Data window, double-click the Products dataset.
7. In the Dataset Properties dialog box, click the Parameters tab, as shown in Figure 3.16.

The Parameter Name column lists the query-level parameters. The Parameter Value column lets you define what values will be passed to these parameters. Click the *fx* button next to the @Month parameter. Note that the [@Month] placeholder represents the following expression:

```
=Parameters!Month.Value
```

The Parameters keyword references the standard Reporting Services Parameters collection that represents the report-level parameters. Consequently, at run time, the report server will pass the value of the Month report-level parameter to the Month query-level parameter. Once the parameters are in place, you are ready to lay out the report by adding report items to the report body. Before doing so, let's gain some understanding about what report items are available with Reporting Services.

3.3.4 Understanding Report Items

Now that you've defined report data, you are ready to lay out the report. Before doing so, however, let me explain a few more report design concepts that will introduce you to report items, expressions, and functions.

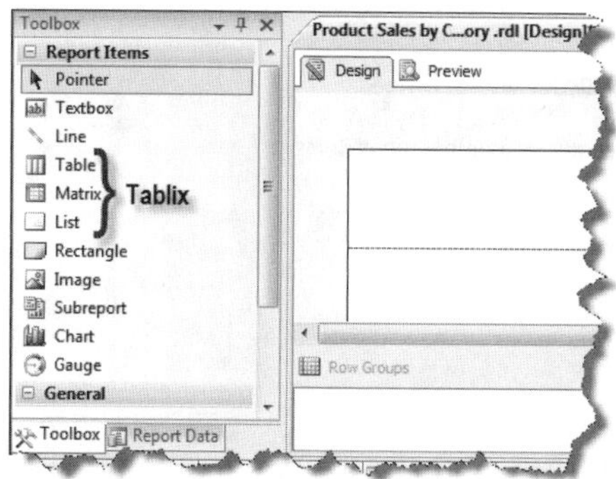

Figure 3.17 You lay out by adding report items and data regions to the report.

You can define the report appearance by dragging report items from the Toolbox window, shown in Figure 3.17, and dropping them on the report. With Reporting Services, you can place report items anywhere on a report. You are not limited to "bands" of data that you may be accustomed to with other reporting tools, such as Microsoft Access. This gives you great flexibility to define the report's appearance. For example, you can have table and chart sections side-by-side. Report items can be classified as regular report items and data regions, as shown in Table 3.5.

Report items

Reports items are simple controls that you can use to define the layout for data and graphical elements. The one that you will use the most is the *textbox* report item. Textboxes are building blocks of reports. A textbox can contain static text, such as "Product Sales by Category", or dynamic expression-based text that the report server resolves at run time. Textboxes can be used as stand-alone report items, such as to display a report title, but they are most useful when used inside a data region, such as inside a table region, where they display the values of the dataset fields.

The *line* report item is used purely for decorative purposes, such as to emphasize the beginning of a new section. A line cannot be associated with data. The *rectangle* report item can be used for decorative purposes to show a border around a group of items, but it can also contain other items. For example, you can create free-form reports by placing textboxes arbitrarily inside a rectangle.

TIP You can also use a rectangle item to keep items together. Let's say you want a table report to grow to fill the blank space below it rather than preserving the blank space. You can group the tablix data region with the blank space below it in a rectangle. Since growth only pushes peer items out of the way, the table in the rectangle has no items to push down below it, so it will consume the blank space until it fills the rectangle.

The *image* report item displays image data. You can display embedded and external images, as well as images stored in a database, by setting the Source property of the image report item. An embedded image is saved in base64 format inside the report definition. An external image located outside Reporting Services can be referenced by its URL. You can also configure the image report item to render binary image data returned in the report dataset.

Table 3.5 Report Designer includes regular report items and data regions.

Type	Item	Description
Report Items	Textbox	Displays static or dynamic text.
	Line	Draws a line, such as to separate the report body from the page footer.
	Rectangle	Can be used in two ways: as a graphical element and as a container for other report items.
	Image	Displays binary image data in a report.
	Subreport	Renders another report in the parent report
Data Regions	Table	Displays data in a tabular format
	Matrix	Displays data in a crosstab format
	List	Displays data in a free-form layout
	Chart	Displays graphical representation of the data as a chart
	Gauge	Displays graphical representation of the data as a gauge

The *subreport* report item defines a placeholder that references another report. Although subreports are popular with other reporting tools, with Reporting Services you should consider using separate data regions instead of subreports for performance reasons. This is because subreports must be processed separately, which is less efficient than processing data regions. This is not to say that subreports are not useful. One common scenario where subreports can help is implementing a master report which packages existing reports. Another scenario where you should consider subreports is when you need to correlate two datasets, such as to display multiple orders with order header and order details sections.

Data regions

Besides regular report items, Reporting Services supports more sophisticated report controls called *data regions*. While they present information in different ways, all data regions except gauge, which is a one-dimensional data region, act as repeaters of data. When bound to a dataset, they iterate through the dataset rows and expand to render the field values.

The *table* data region displays data in a two-dimensional tabular format that has dynamic rows and fixed columns. The *matrix* data region generates a crosstab format that has dynamic rows and columns. The *list* data region lets you position report items in arbitrary locations for implementing free-form reports. The *chart* region displays data in a chart format, such as a line chart. The *gauge* data region helps end users visualize a value by presenting it as an indicator, such as a thermometer.

Internally, the table, matrix, and list regions are represented by the tablix data region, as you can see by examining the report source code. The Toolbox pane "splits" the tablix region into three regions to help you define a starting point for your report. For example, if you drop the table region, tablix will assume a fixed-column format and won't include a pre-defined column group for dynamic columns. However, regardless of which of the three regions you use, you can always "morph" the tablix region to another layout. For example, you can start with a table format but decide later that you need a crosstab format. Instead of deleting the table region and starting from scratch with the matrix region, you can simply add dynamic groups to the existing report.

NOTE What's the etymology of the word "tablix"? According to Microsoft, Tablix = Table + Matrix. However, this definition ignores the list region which is also represented by tablix. So, my tablix etymology is Tablix = **Tab**le + **Li**st + Matri**x**.

A report can have any number of data regions placed side-by-side on the report, and each of them can be bound to a different dataset. For example, you can place a chart and table region side by side. The chart region can display the company sales per territory in chart format, while the table region can provide a breakdown by product and territory. You can also nest data regions. For example, you can nest a gauge region inside a table region to display indicators for each row or group.

When the Microsoft-provided report items and data regions are not enough, developers can implement custom report items that render data as raster images. Chapter 21 includes an example of a custom report item that displays a field value as a progress bar.

3.3.5 Understanding Expressions

Expressions are code snippets written in Visual Basic.NET compatible syntax that you can use to dynamically change the content and appearance of a report. An example of a common expression is *=Sum(Fields!SalesAmount.Value)* which sums the values of the SalesAmount field in a report group or the report grand total line. Expressions let you supercharge your reports in flexible and powerful ways.

For example, suppose that you need to conditionally hide a report column. You can enter an expression in the column's Hidden property that evaluates a parameter value or a dataset field to hide the column if needed. You won't go very far with Reporting Services if you don't have a solid grasp of expressions, so let's discuss them in more detail.

Understanding expression types

We can classify expressions in two types based on the complexity of the expression code:

- Simple—A simple expression is a single reference to an item in a built-in collection. Don't worry if you don't understand the concept of collections yet. I will explain collections in section 3.3.6. For example, the following expression references the value of the Month parameter:

```
=Parameters!Month.Value
```

- Complex—Any expression that is not is a single reference. For example, the following expression calculates the discounted sales amount:

```
=Fields!SalesAmount.Value * Fields!Discount.Value
```

Authoring expressions

An expression must begin with an equal sign (=). This tells the report server to evaluate the text that follows as an expression instead of as static text. After the equal sign, the expression text can include field identifiers, constants, functions, and operators. For example, the expression *=Fields!SalesAmount.Value* returns the value of the SalesAmount dataset field. You can use Visual Basic.NET to create more complicated expressions.

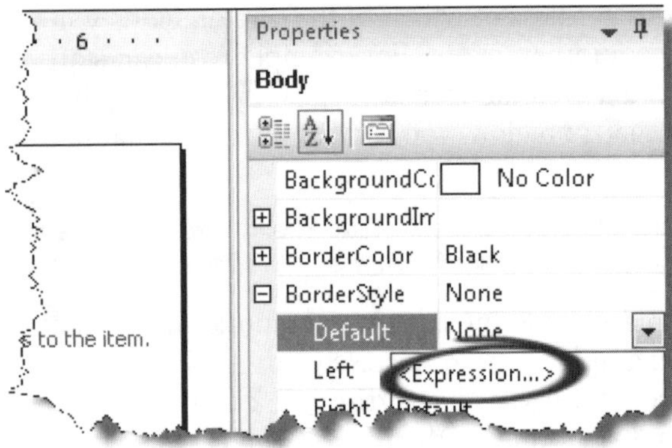

Figure 3.18 Expand the property drop-down list to check if the property can be expression-based.

Most report item properties can be expression-based and there is an easy way to verify this.

1. Click the report body section of the Product Sales by Category.
2. In the Properties window, expand the BorderStyle ⇨ Default property, as shown in Figure 3.18.

   Notice that the first item in the drop-down list is <Expression…>, which means you can use an expression to dynamically control the property value. For example, the expression can check the value of a report parameter and change the border style accordingly.
3. Now, expand the BackgroundImage property, which you can use to set up a background image for the report body.
4. Expand the Source drop-down list and note that the <Expression…> item is missing. Therefore, you cannot use an expression to change the image Source property dynamically.

   Another example of properties that cannot be expression-based is the size-related properties (height and width) of the report and report items. This is because Reporting Services doesn't currently support variable sizing.

   You can type the report expression text manually in the Properties window and the standard dialog boxes, or you can use the Expression dialog box. You will probably find the first method handy when you want to quickly change the expression text or enter simple expressions. For example, you can click inside a text box and directly type a field expression to bind the textbox to a dataset field, such as =Fields!Sales.Value. Alternatively, you can use the Expression dialog box, which is especially useful for more complicated expressions as it offers IntelliSense support and color-coding.
5. Expand the BorderStyle ⇨ Default property and click the <Expression…> item.

The Report Designer launches the Expression dialog box. You can enter the expression text in the Set Expression field. The panes below the expression pane can help you author the expression. For example, if the report item is data-bound, you can click the Fields item in the Category pane and drag a field from the Items pane.

6. In the Expression dialog box, enter *=Iif(*

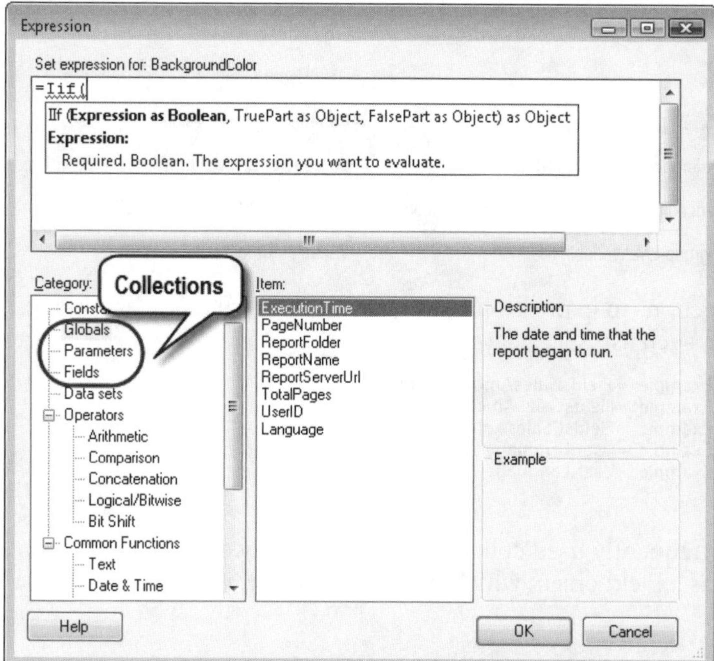

Figure 3.19 The Expression dialog box provides IntelliSense support for authoring expressions.

IIF is a Visual Basic function that evaluates a condition and returns one of two values depending on whether the condition evaluates to true or not. The moment you type the left parenthesis, Report Designer opens an IntelliSense help that shows the IIF syntax to help you author the expression, as shown in Figure 3.19.

NOTE Since expressions use Visual Basic.NET, the expression text is not case-sensitive. However, names of data objects, such fields and datasets, and parameters are case-sensitive.

You may wonder about the purpose of the category items shown in the Category pane. The Constants category provides a list of constant values that are relevant to a given property, such as a list of standard colors if a color-related property is selected in the Properties window. The Operators lets you access the Reporting Services operators. The Common Functions category organizes the functions supported by Reporting Services into categories. You can drag an item from the Item pane and drop it in the expression pane to insert the item in the cursor position.

3.3.6 Understanding Collections

Reporting Services supports eight read-only global collections that you can reference in expressions. Table 3.6 explains these collections and provides expression examples of how to use them.

Table 3.6 **Reporting Services provides seven global collections.**

Collection	Description	Expression Example
Fields	Represents a collection of Field objects that map to dataset field.	=Fields!SalesAmount.Value
ReportItems	Represents a collection of textbox report items within the report.	=ReportItems!Title.Value
Globals	Contains built-in global fields.	=Globals!PageNumber
User	Includes user-related fields	=User!UserID
Parameters	Represents the report parameters	=Parameters!Month.Value
DataSources	Represents the data sources referenced by the report.	=DataSources!AdventureWorksDW2008.Type
DataSets	Represents the datasets referenced from the body of a report definition.	=DataSets!Products.CommandText
Variables	Provides access to report and group-level variables	=Variables!Rate.Value

You can reference the global collections in expressions using any of the Visual Basic supported syntaxes for accessing collections, such as:

```
Collection!ObjectName.Property         Example: =Fields!SalesAmount.Value
Collection!ObjectName("Property")      Example: =Fields!SalesAmount(" Value")
Collection("ObjectName").Property      Example: =Fields("SalesAmount").Value
Collection.Member                      Example: =User.Language
Collection("Member")                   Example: =User.Language
```

Fields collection

The Fields collection is the most frequently used collection as it lets you access dataset fields. Each dataset field is represented as a Field object which has Value and IsMissing properties, as shown in Table 3.7.

Table 3.7 **The properties of the Field object**

Property	Description
Value	Returns the field value
IsMissing	Indicates if the underlying field is missing from the dataset

The Value property returns the field value from the underlying dataset in its native type. The IsMissing property lets you check if the dataset includes a given field. Let's say you have a stored procedure that returns different columns based on an input parameter. If you want to hide a table column that references a field that may be missing, you can use the following expression for the column's Hidden property:

```
=Fields!ProductSubcategory.IsMissing
```

If the data providers support extended properties, you can use the Field object extended properties, such as Color. For example, the Microsoft Analysis Services data provider supports extended properties, as I'll demonstrate in chapter 16

ReportItems collection

The ReportItems collection references all textboxes in the report. Each item has a single Value property. For example, let's say the report has two textboxes: a Sales textbox that displays a sales value and a hidden Status text box that contains a static string "Goal exceeded". The following expression for the Hidden property of the Status text box makes it visible if the Sales textbox exceeds 100,000.

```
=ReportItems!Sales.Value<=100000
```

Note that each item in the ReportItems collection is represented as an internal object, which preserves the data type of the field so that you don't have to convert it. Of course, assuming that the underlying field name of the Sales textbox is Sales, you can rewrite the expression to use the Fields collection:

```
=Fields!Sales.Value<=100000
```

If you need to access the textbox itself in one of its properties, you can use Me.Value or just Value. For example, if you want to change the foreground color of the Sales text box to red if it exceeds 100,000, you can plug in the following expression in its Color property.

```
=Iif (Me.Value <= 100000, "Black", "Red")
```

Globals collection

The Globals collection contains commonly used built-in variables, as shown in Table 3.8.

Table 3.8 The members of the Globals collection

Member	Description	Data Type
ExecutionTime	The date and time the report began to run.	DateTime
PageNumber	The current page number. Can be used only in a page header and footer.	Integer
ReportFolder	The full path to the report excluding the report server URL	String
ReportName	The report name.	String
ReportServerUrl	The Web service URL.	String
TotalPages	The total number of pages. Can be used only in a page header and footer.	Integer

User collection

The User collection includes UserID and Language members, as shown in Table 3.9.

Table 3.9 The members of the User collection

Member	Description	Example
UserID	Returns the user identity.	adventure-works\bob
Language	Returns the user's locale identifier.	en-US

If the report server uses Windows authentication (default), UserID returns the Windows logon in the format domain\logon. If the report server is configured for custom security, UserID returns the user name that was passed to the custom security extension. The UserID member is typically used to enforce row-level security, such as to pass the user identity to the data source for restricted data shown on the report.

For the report author's convenience, the members of the Globals and User collections are exposed under the Built-in Fields node in the Report Data window and Globals category in the Expression dialog.

Parameters collection

The Parameters collection gives you access to the report parameters. Each parameter object has the properties shown in Table 3.10.

Table 3.10 The Parameter properties

Property	Description
Value	Returns the parameter value.
Label	Returns the user-friendly label.
IsMutliValue	Returns True if the parameter is a multivalued parameter.
Count	Returns the number of parameter values.

When you define a parameter, you can specify a value and optionally a label. For example, you can map a database key column to the Value property so you can pass it to the report query and a user-friendly description column to the Label property. In the absence of a label, the Label property returns the parameter value. The last two properties, IsMultiValue and Count, are useful with multivalued parameters.

DataSources collection

This collection represents the data sources referenced by the report. Each data source object has the properties shown in Table 3.11.

Table 3.11 The data source properties

Property	Description	Example
DataSourceReference	The path to the data source.	/Data Sources/AdventureWorksDW2008
Type	The type of the data provider.	SQL

DataSets collection

The DataSets collection represents the datasets defined in the report. Each dataset object has the properties shown in Table 3.12.

Table 3.12 The dataset properties

Property	Description
CommandText	Returns the dataset query text verbatim.
RewrittenCommandText	For data providers that implement the IDbCommandRewriter interface (as Report Model data sources do), returns the expanded command text with parameter placeholders replaced with actual parameter values.

Variables collection

Reporting Services 2008 introduces variables to store values for time-dependent calculations, such as currency rates or time stamps that don't change between page refreshes. I discuss variables in more detail in chapter 7.

3.3.7 Understanding Functions

Reporting Services lets you reference built-in and external functions in expressions. Built-in functions let you perform common computations tasks, such as aggregating data. External functions allow you to extend your reports with .NET or custom code.

Built-in functions

Table 3.13 lists some of the most common built-in functions.

Table 3.13 Common Reporting Services built-in functions

Category	Function	Description
Aggregates	Sum	Returns a sum of field values.
	Avg	Returns the average of all non-null field values.
	Count	Returns a count of all non-null field values.
	CountDistinct	Returns a count of all non-null distinct field values.
	Min	Returns the minimum value from all non-null field values.
	Max	Returns the maximum value from all non-null field values.
Running Values	RowNumber	Returns a running count of the number of rows.
	RunningValue	Calculates a running aggregate, such as running sum.
Row Counts	CountRows	Counts the rows in the specified scope, such as a row group.
Dataset Navigation	First	Returns the fist value in a set of data.
	Last	Returns the last value in set of data.
	Previous	Returns the value or the specified aggregate value for the previous instance of an item.

Consult with the Using Built-in Report and Aggregate Functions in Expressions topic in Books Online (see Resources) for a full list of the built-in functions.

External functions

Besides the Reporting Services built-in functions, your expressions can reference external functions, such as .NET functions or custom functions you or someone else wrote. In order to evaluate expressions, the Report Processor generates and compiles code during publishing. The resulting expression host assembly pre-references two standard .NET assemblies, Microsoft.VisualBasic.dll and mscorlib.dll. It imports the following namespaces so you can readily reference their types and functions in expressions without having to specify the namespace.

- Microsoft.VisualBasic—This namespace lets you access many of the common Visual Basic runtime functions. For example, you can use the Format function to format dates and numbers. The Visual Basic Run-Time Library Members (see Resources) provides a full list of the Visual Basic run-time functions.
- System.Convert—Allows you to perform runtime conversion between types, for example, from string to double using System.Convert.ToDouble.
- System.Math—Provides constants and static methods for trigonometric, logarithmic, and other common mathematical functions, such as Abs, Ceiling, Floor, Sqrt, and so on.

To reference the rest of the System namespaces, you need to specify the fully qualified class name, including the namespace. For example, if you need to use a collection of the type ArrayList in an expression, you have to use its fully qualified name, System.Collections.ArrayList. You can also reference functions in custom code, as I will discuss in chapter 7.

Understanding expression context and scope

Each expression is associated with context and scope. The expression context is the consecutive order in which the expression is evaluated. When the server processes a report, it starts with the dataset itself and sequentially processes nested sets of data, such as data regions and groups, all the way down to detail rows. For example, examining the Product Sales by Category report (see again Figure 3.2) shows how the server evaluates the context of the Internet Sales field expression in the detail rows. The server applies filter and sort expressions (if any) to the Products dataset, followed by filter and sort expressions at the table region level, followed by filter and sort expression at the product category and subcategory groups, followed by filtering and sorting at the details group level.

The expression scope represents the set of data that is used to evaluate the expression. If you examine the syntax of the built-in functions, you will notice that most of them take an optional scope argument. If the scope is omitted, the expression is evaluated in the default scope, which is determined by the expression context. For example, the default scope of a Sum function in the product subcategory group totals is the product category group because this is the innermost group in which the function is evaluated.

Some functions (RowNumber, RunningValue, Previous), support specifying a null scope (Nothing in Visual Basic), such as RowNumber(Nothing). When the expression scope is set to Nothing, the expression is evaluated in the outermost context, usually the report dataset.

Scopes can be nested. Nested scopes are evaluated in the order Dataset ⇨ Data region ⇨ Row and column groups ⇨ Nested data regions ⇨ Row and column groups for nested data regions. Built-in functions can reference containing (outer) scopes. For example, to calculate the contribution of the product Internet sales to its subcategory you can use the expression =Sum(Field!InternetSales.Value, "ProductSubcategory"). This expression returns the subcategory total assuming that the name of the subcategory group is ProductSubcategory.

You cannot reference inner scopes. What will happen if you try to obtain a subcategory total in the product category group? Since a product category may have many children (subcategories), the server has no way of telling which subcategory subtotal you need. Subsequently, you will get the following error when you build the report at design time:

```
The Value expression for the textbox 'name' has a scope parameter that is not valid for an aggregate function. The scope parameter must be set to a string constant that is equal to either the name of a containing group, the name of a containing data region, or the name of a data set.
```

Don't worry if the scope discussion sounds mind-boggling. The tablix region provides visual clues to help you understand the expression scope at design time. You can also use the InScope built-in function to check the expression scope when the report is run.

3.3.8 The Anatomy of a Textbox

Now that you've been introduced to report items and expressions, let's learn more about the textbox report item, which is the control that you'll use most when authoring text-based reports. Veteran Reporting Services users will find that the textbox report item has undergone a complete overhaul in Reporting Services 2008 to support mixed formatting and multiple bands of text. Understanding these important changes will help you optimize the report layout and minimize the use of expressions.

Understanding textbox elements

In the previous releases, the textbox report item didn't support mixed formatting. Consequently, you can only format the textbox content in its entirety. If you wanted a text fragment to have different format styles, such as to format a text fragment in bold, you had no other choice but to use another textbox. Because of the textbox formatting limitations, it wasn't possible to display text with mixed formatting or implement mail merge reports.

This has changed in Reporting Services 2008, wherein the textbox is a constituent control with multiple bands of text that can be formatted independently. Specifically, a textbox consists of paragraphs and each paragraph is composed of string fragments called *textruns* (TextRun RDL element). An analogy to Microsoft Word can help you understand this better. If you think of a textbox as a Microsoft Word document, then textbox paragraphs correspond to Word paragraphs and textruns are the spans of contiguous like-formatted substrings in a paragraph. The Textbox Anatomy report (see Figure 3.20) that is included in the source code for this chapter is meant to help you understand these textbox elements.

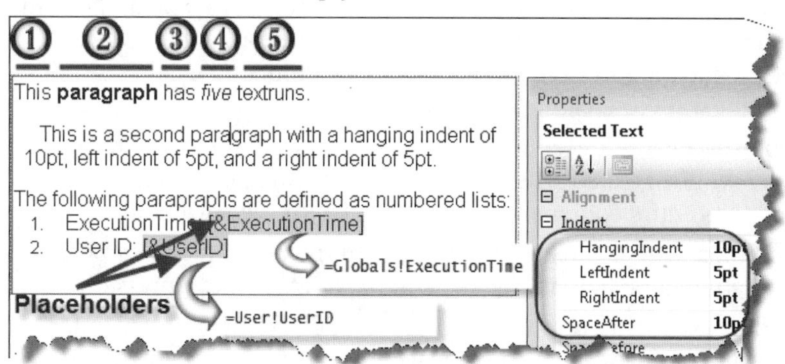

Figure 3.20 A textbox consists of paragraphs and each paragraph is a collection of sequential textruns.

I used one textbox to display the entire report content. By default, when you add a textbox to a report or when you upgrade a legacy report definition, a textbox has a single paragraph with a single textrun. The moment you change the formatting styles of a string fragment (even a single letter), Report Designer breaks down the paragraph into textruns. Thus, the first paragraph on the report has five textruns whose spans are indicated by the numbers above them.

Understanding textbox editing

Report Designer supports natively editing the textbox elements in place. Similar to Microsoft Word, if the textbox is in edit mode (double-click the textbox) and you press the Enter key, Report Designer creates a new paragraph. However, if you press Shift+Enter, it will create a newline at your current position in the textrun instead of creating a next textrun or paragraph. In the latter case, the textrun text will just flow to the new line.

The analogy with Microsoft Word can be extended even further. Similar to Word, textbox paragraphs can be indented. For example, the second paragraph has a hanging indent (HangingIndent property), as well as a left indent (LeftIndent property) and a right indent (RightIndent property) defined. You can define spacing between paragraphs by setting the SpaceAfter and SpaceBefore properties. Paragraph numbers and bullets are supported too. For example, I formatted the last two paragraphs as numeric lists by changing their ListLevel and ListStyle properties.

Report Designer lets you apply format settings down to the inner textbox elements. For example, if you select the entire textbox and set its font to bold, all paragraphs and textruns will be formatted in bold. Consequently, you can apply common format setting at a higher level. Again, this behavior is similar to Microsoft Word.

NOTE Strictly speaking, there is no style inheritance in RDL. For example, the FontFamily style element exists only at the textrun level. If you select the textbox and set its font, it does not set the font on the textbox itself. Rather, it sets it for all textruns in the textbox. The editing experience allows users the benefit of not thinking about that particular detail.

Understanding placeholders

As noted in section 3.3.4, the textbox report item can display dynamic expression-based text. In the past, if you wanted to mix static text with expressions, you either had to use separate textboxes (if you wanted to apply different format settings) or a Visual Basic.NET expression that concatenates the static and dynamic text if they have the same format settings. In this release, static and dynamic text can coexist just fine within a *single* textbox. This eliminates the need to use separate textboxes or use expressions that concatenate static and dynamic text.

When a simple or complex expression is defined inside a text box, the resulting UI representation of this expression is known as a *placeholder*. For example, the last two paragraphs in Figure 3.20 include placeholders. The [&ExecutionTime] placeholder represents the expression =Globals!ExecutionTime, while the [&UserID] placeholder symbolizes the expression =User!UserID. There are different ways to create a placeholder:

- Drag a field from the Report Data window and drop it into the textbox. If the textbox is in edit mode, the placeholder will be created where the mouse cursor is positioned. If the textbox is not in edit mode, its entire content will be replaced with the placeholder.
- Right-click inside the textbox and click Create Placeholder. In the Placeholder Properties dialog box that follows, use the Value field in the General tab to enter the expression.
- Enter the actual placeholder text enclosed in square brackets. For example, if you enter [Name], Report Designer will automatically create a placeholder with the expression =Fields!Name.Value.
- In an empty textbox, type in the expression text prefixed with an equal sign (=).

Understanding placeholder syntax

Placeholder labels improve the visual experience at design time and let the user see enough information to understand the content of a textbox. The placeholder label is a special token that the Report Designer displays at design time in lieu of the actual placeholder expression. Table 3.14 lists examples of placeholder labels and their corresponding expressions.

Table 3.14 Examples of placeholders used to display simple and complex expressions

Collection	Placeholder	Actual Expression
Fields	[SalesAmount]	=Fields!SalesAmount.Value
	[SUM(Sales)]	=Sum(Fields!Sales.Value)
Parameters	[@Month]	=Parameters!Month.Value
Built-in fields	[&ReportName]	=Globals!ReportName
Complex expression	<<Expr>>	=Iif (Me.Value <= 100000, "Black", "Red")

The last example deserves more attention. For textboxes with just one textrun, the Value property will return the value as the appropriate data type. For textboxes with multiple textruns, it will return a string of the concatenated values. You can see the actual expression text by right-clicking the placeholder and clicking Expression, by pointing the mouse cursor to the placeholder when the textbox is in edit mode (a tooltip will pop up), or by inspecting the text box Value property.

TIP You can enter the placeholder label directly in the textbox. For example, if you enter [SalesAmount] in a textbox, Report Designer will set the textbox Value to the expression =Fields!SalesAmount.Value. If you want to display square brackets as literal strings, prefix them with a backslash, such as \[Name\].

You can define your own placeholder labels using the Label property in the General tab of the Placeholder Properties dialog box. This will be the text that is shown at design time for the placeholder.

I hope by now you've started to appreciate the enhancements to the textbox report item. But that's not all. The textbox item is also capable of interpreting rich formatting styles, such as HTML markup. However, to keep us on track, let's postpone these features to chapter 7.

3.3.9 Designing the Report Layout ▶

Now that you have been introduced to the report design fundamentals, you are ready to finalize the Product Sales by Category report. Let's leverage some of the new textbox features to implement the page header.

Implementing the page header

The page header includes a report title, subtitle, and the Adventure Works logo. We will implement these elements in this order.

1. If it is not active, activate the Toolbox window (press Ctrl+Alt+X or click the Toolbox tab). Drag a Textbox report item and drop it on the page header section.
1. Double-click the textbox to enter edit mode, and type *Product Sales by Category*.
2. Press Esc to select the entire textbox. With the textbox selected, use the Properties window to configure its properties as follows (only changed properties are shown).

Property	Value	Alternative Way
Color	DarkSlateBlue	Click Foreground color toolbar button in the Report Formatting toolbar.
Font:FontFamily	Tahoma	Use the Font Name drop-down in the Report Formatting toolbar to select font.
Font:FontSize	24pt	Enter the value in the Font Size drop-down in the Report Formatting toolbar.
Location:Left	2.88542in	Drag the report item to a location or click the Center Horizontally toolbar button.
Location:Top	0.10764in	
Name	Title	
Size:Width	5.60083in	Resize the control on the design surface by dragging its resize handles.
Size:Height	0.53819in	
TextAlign	Center	Click the Center button in the Report Formatting toolbar.

As you get used to the Report Designer, you might find that you favor the techniques in the Alternative Way column because they save time.

Implementing the report subtitle

Since the report subtitle requires an expression and different formatting, your first impulse might be to add a new textbox. This will work but requires an expression to concatenate static and dynamic text, such as this:

```
=String.Format("Month {0} Year {1}", Parameters!Month.Value, Parameters!Year.Value)
```

This expression uses the .NET String.Format function to replace the format placeholders enclosed in curly brackets with a comma-delimited list of values. Novice users will probably struggle with this expression. However, thanks to the textbox enhancements in this release, you can use one textbox and eliminate expressions whatsoever, as follows:

2. Increase the textbox height to 0.92". Double-click the textbox to enter edit mode. Position the mouse cursor after the title text and press Enter to add a new paragraph.
3. Move the mouse pointer to the new paragraph and change the font to Arial, 16pt. Change the SpaceBefore property to 6pt.
4. In the new paragraph, enter *Month* and a space.
5. With the textbox still in edit mode, drag the Month parameter from the Report Data pane and drop it after "Month ", as shown in Figure 3.21.

Figure 3.21 Create a placeholder by dragging a field from the Report Data pane.

6. With the mouse cursor after Month [@Month], type *Year* and a space.
7. Drag the Year parameter after " Year ". The entire subtitle expression should now be:

```
Month [@Month] Year [@Year]
```

This expression uses two placeholders for the Month and Year parameters.

8. With the textbox in edit mode, double-click the [@Month] placeholder to open the Placeholder properties dialog box, which is shown in Figure 3.22.

As noted, you can enter a custom label in the Label field if you prefer a different placeholder label then the default ([@Month]) to show up at design time. You can use the Number, Alignment, and Font tabs to format the placeholder text if you need different formatting than the containing paragraph.

9. Save the report definition.
10. Optionally, inspect the report definition source. In the Solution Explorer, right-click Product Sales by Category.rdl and click View Source

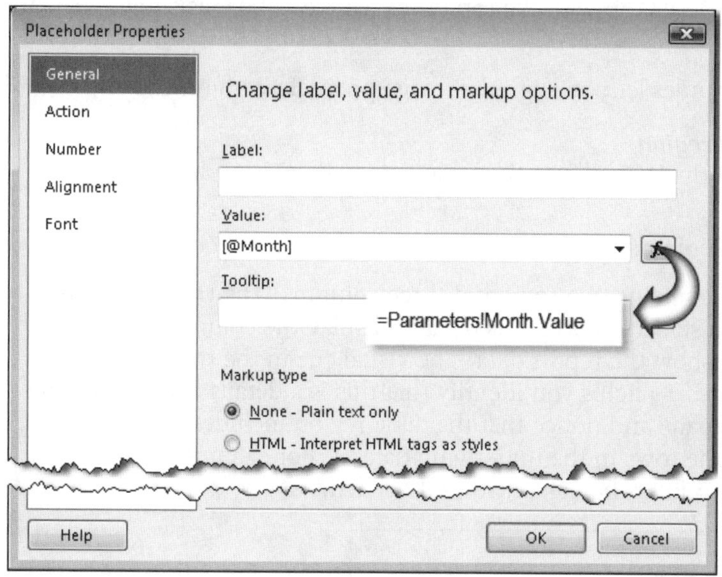

Figure 3.22 Use the Placeholder Properties dialog box to format the placeholder text.

Notice that the Title textbox has two paragraphs and the second paragraphs has two placeholders. To accommodate the placeholders, Report Designer has split the second paragraph into four textruns, as you would notice by examining the report definition source.

Displaying the company logo

The image report item is frequently used to show a company logo on the report.

1. Drag the Image report item from the Toolbox window to the page header to the left of the report title.
2. In the Image Properties dialog box that follows (General tab), change the image name to *Logo*.
3. Click the Import button. Navigate to the Reports folder in the chapter source code, select the AWC.jpg image, and click Open. This embeds the image binary data in the report definition.
4. Select the Size tab and change the Display option to Fit To Size, so the image fits its dimensions. Click OK.
5. Resize the image to a width of 2.75in and a height of 0.92375in.

If the image overlaps the textboxes, select both textboxes by holding the Shift key, and press the right arrow key to move them to the right (or drag them). You can also select adjacent items by clicking an empty area in the report section and dragging the mouse cursor to "lasso" the items.

Figure 3.23 Snap lines help you align items as you drag them around the design surface.

6. Select the image and drag it to align its top with the top of the Title text box, as shown in Figure 3.23.

   As you drag the image, blue snap lines let you align the image precisely with other items.

Getting started in the table data region

Next, we will tackle the report body. We will use the table data region to implement the report body.

1. Drag the Table region from the Toolbox window and drop it on the report body section.

   The predefined table data region contains two rows and three columns. The Header row is grayed out to denote that this is a static row which is used to display the column headers. The Data row expands at run time to show the report data. The visual cue in the row selector of the second row (three stacked lines ≡) helps you identify that this is a details row (see Figure 3.24). Examine the Row Groups pane and notice that the table region includes a details group (Details). This group represents the rows in the underlying dataset. For example, you can use the details group to sort, group, or filter the dataset rows if needed.

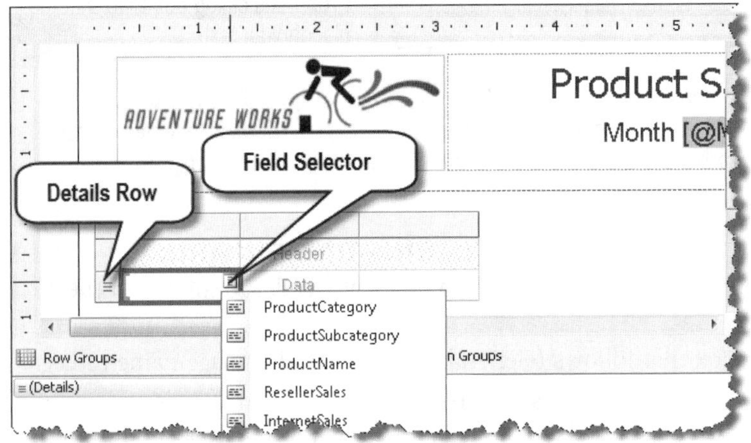

Figure 3.24 Tablix visual cues help you identify the tablix elements and group membership.

Next, you'll bind the dataset fields to the details cells to implement the Reseller Sales and Internet Sales columns. You can do so by dragging dataset fields from the Report Data window to the details cells inside the tablix region. Or, you can point the mouse pointer to a details cell, click the Field Selector drop-down list, and select a dataset field.

2. Use the Field Selector to bind the details cell in the first column to the ResellerSales field.

   The Report Designer shows the [ResellerSales] placeholder in the details cell and sets the column header text to Reseller Sales. Let's take a moment to review what changes Report Designer has made to the table region behind the scenes. You need to select the table region to access its properties. There are several ways to select a report item. First, you can click its outline. A selected region shows a resize handle in its upper left corner, which you can drag to move the region to another location. If you select a cell inside the region, press Esc to change the selection to its containing region. You can also use the drop-down list in the Property window to select the region by name. Finally, you can lasso a region by dragging the mouse cursor to enclose it and select it.

3. Select the table region.

The moment you bind a cell to a dataset field, Report Designer binds the containing region to that dataset. Examine the Properties window and notice that the DataSetName property is set to the Products dataset.

NOTE A data region can be bound to one dataset only. However, expressions can use aggregated values from another dataset that isn't bound to the data region. For example, assuming you have a Customers dataset, the expression =Sum(Field!Field1.Value, "Customers") will return the grand total value of Field1 which you can use in a data region bound to the Products dataset.

4. Use the Field Selector to bind the details cell in the second column to the InternetSales field.
5. The third column (Sales Amount) is a calculated column that sums the reseller sales and Internet sales. In the column header of the third column, enter *Sales Summary*.
6. Right-click the details cell, click Expression, and enter the following expression in the Edit Expression dialog box.

```
=Fields!InternetSales.Value+Fields!ResellerSales.Value
```

Previewing the report

During the report design process, you will find yourself switching often to the Preview tab to quickly test the report. Although the Product Sales by Category report is far from complete, let's preview it by clicking on the Preview tab. The Report Designer preview mode connects to the data source, retrieves data, and processes the report locally via internal interfaces. Consequently, you can author and test reports completely outside the report server.

Report queries may take long time to execute. However, Report Designer preview can help you here in that it caches the report data locally in a <reportname>.data file to speed up the report processing. As long as you don't make changes to the report datasets, report preview uses the cached data. Click the Refresh button to execute the dataset query if you want to see the most recent data. If you want to turn caching completely off, change the CacheDataForPreview setting to False in the Report Designer configuration file (\Program Files\Microsoft Visual Studio 9.0\Common7\IDE\PrivateAssemblies\RSReportDesigner.config).

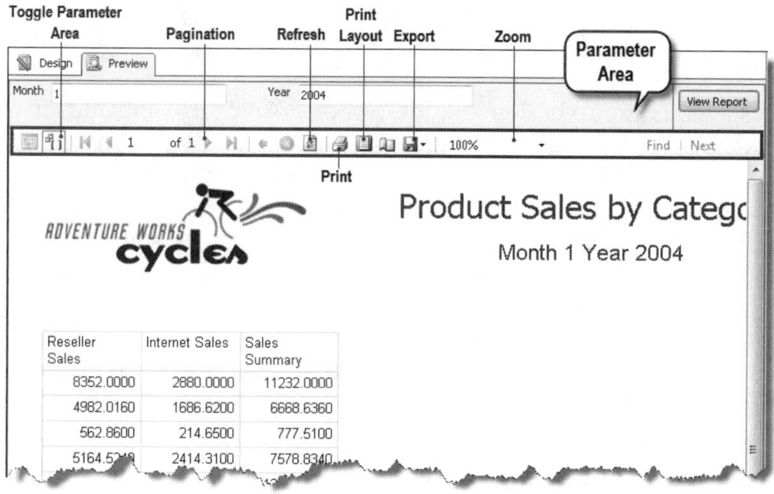

Figure 3.25 In preview mode, the Report Designer generates a toolbar to let you perform common report operations.

As Figure 3.25 shows, the table report has three columns and as many rows as the number of the rows in the dataset. Report Designer generates a handy toolbar to let you perform common functions, such as exporting the report to any of the supported export formats. If you want to see what the report looks like when printed, click the Print Layout button. The toolbar includes a parameter area which you can use to change the parameters. Click View Report to render the report with the new parameter values. Notice that in preview mode, the Report Data window is disabled because you cannot make changes to the report layout.

Defining row groups

Next, you'll define row groups to group data by product category, subcategory, and product.

1. Switch to design mode by clicking the Design tab.
2. Drag the ProductCategory field from the Products dataset (Report Data window) and drop it before the Details row group in the Row Groups pane.

   Several things happen at this point. The Report Designer creates a new ProductCategory row group and adds it to the Row Groups pane, as shown in Figure 3.26. If you double-click the ProductCategory group in the Row Groups pane to open the Group Properties dialog box (General tab), you will see that Report Designer has set the group expression to the [Product-Category] placeholder. This placeholder represents the ProductCategory dataset field and it's equivalent to the expression =Fields!ProductCategory.Value.

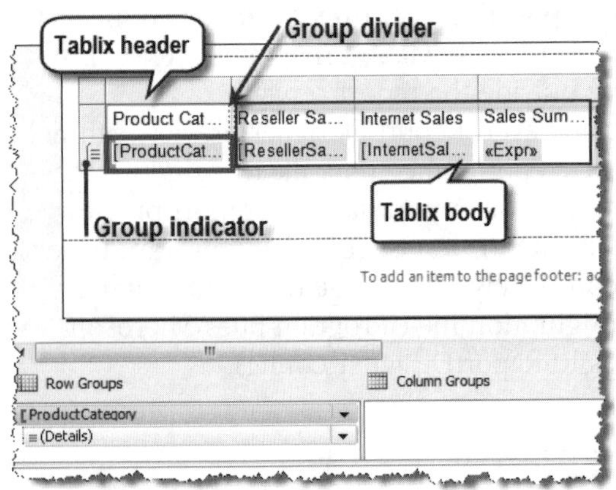

Figure 3.26 When you drop a field on the Row Groups pane, the Report Designer creates a new row group and adds a table group header to the table region.

   Report Designer also generates a tablix group header column (Product Category) and adds it to the table. Tablix group headers are a new feature of Reporting Services 2008. A tablix group header spans over its content, including inner groups and subtotals. If you have used previous releases of Reporting Services, you would find tablix group headers similar to matrix headers. Or, if you are familiar with Office Web Components or Excel PivotTable reports, you can think of tablix group headers as row groups that the PivotTable control creates to group data on rows.

   Tablix shows visual cues to provide information about row and column groups. The double dashed line is a group divider that separates the tablix body from tablix group headers. The group indicator (left parenthesis) in the row selector shows the rows that the group spans. This becomes more useful as you add group subtotals.

3. Preview the report to understand tablix group headers. Note that the Product Category header spans details rows. Switch back to design mode.
4. Drag the ProductSubcategory field from the Products dataset (Report Data window) and drop it between the ProductCategory group and the Details row group in the Row Groups pane.

Alternatively, you can create a new row group by dropping a field on the tablix region to the left of the group divider line or between tablix group headers. As you hover on the tablix region, a blue guideline is shown to give you a visual cue where you can drop the field. If you drag the field over the group divider and you move the cursor slightly to the left towards the row group area, the blue line will change to a right square bracket (]). This indicates that a new row group will be created. If you move the mouse cursor towards the tablix body, a left square bracket ([) will be shown to indicate that the field will be added to the details row in the tablix body area.

5. Drag the ProductName field and drop it between the ProductSubcategory row group and Details row group.

   The Rows Groups pane should now contain ProductCategory, ProductSubcategory, ProductName, and Details groups in this order. If the group order doesn't match, you can relocate a group by dragging it to the correct position in the Row Groups pane.

6. To generate a page break after each product group, double-click the ProductCategory group in the Row Groups pane (or right-click it and click Group Properties).

7. In the Tablix Group Properties dialog box, click the Page Breaks tab and check Between Each Instance of a Group.

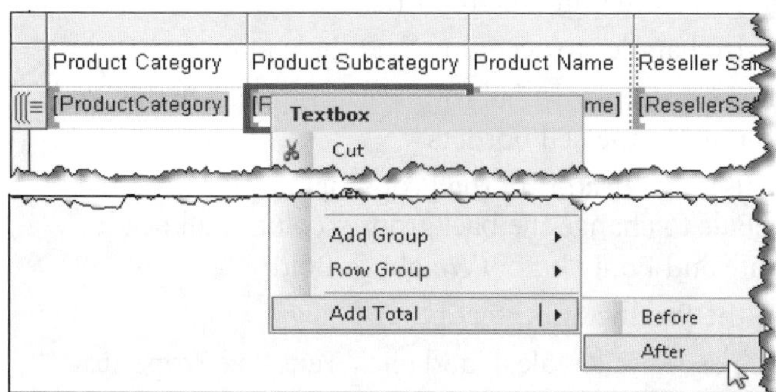

Figure 3.27 To add a group total, right-click the group cell and click Add Total.

Adding group subtotals

The Product Sales by Group report totals data at the subcategory level and has a grand total footer.

1. Right-click the ProductSubcategory cell in the details row and click Add Total ⇨ After, as shown in Figure 3.27.

   The Report Designer adds a total row that sums the numeric columns (Internet Sales and Reseller Sales).

2. Right-click the ProductCategory cell in the details row and click Add Total ⇨ After.

   The Report Designer adds a total line after the ProductCategory group. Since ProductCategory is the outermost group, its total acts as a report grand total line.

3. Preview the report to test the row groups. Note that the Sales Summary column doesn't have totals.

4. Back to design mode, enter the following expression in the total rows of the Sales Summary column.

```
=Sum(Fields!ResellerSales.Value+Fields!InternetSales.Value)
```

The aggregate functions are not limited to a single field only. In this case, Sum aggregates over an expression.

5. Click the total cell of the product subcategory group, as shown in Figure 3.28.

   Tablix shows visual cues to help you understand which group the cell belongs to and its expression scope. The active group indicator (highlighted in orange) shows the innermost group. In this case, the innermost group is ProductCategory. Therefore, the expression scope is the ProductCategory group. Inactive group indicators mark the tablix groups.

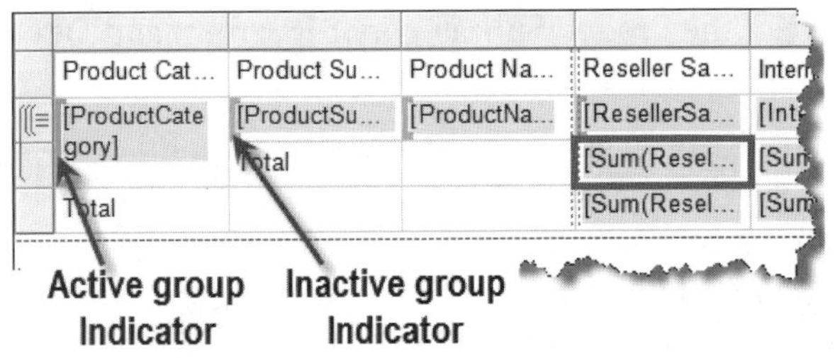

Figure 3.28 Tablix visual cues help you understand the expression scope and group membership.

Formatting the report

Next, let's improve the report appearance by formatting the report:

1. Resize the columns by dragging their resize handles to accommodate the content.
2. Select all tablix cells by dragging the mouse cursor down all row selectors. Change the BorderStyle ⇨ Default property to None to remove the cell borders.
3. Select the tablix header row by clicking its row selector. In the Properties window, set the BackgroundColor property to *DarkSlateBlue* to change the background color of all header cells. Change the Color property to White and Font ⇨ FontWeight to Bold.
4. Repeat the last step to format all cells in the ProductSubcategory total row.
5. Right-click one of the numeric cells, such as [ResellerSales], and click Text Box Properties.
6. In the Textbox Properties dialog box, click the Number tab. Format the textbox as currency with zero decimal places and a thousand separator. Click OK.
7. In the Properties window, copy the Format setting of the textbox, which should be '$'#,0;('$'#,0) (assuming United States regional settings).
8. Select all numeric cells (hold Shift for extended selection). Paste the format setting in the Format property to format all numeric cells this way.
9. Select the Reseller Sales, Internet Sales, and Sales Summary details cells of the last row and change their BorderStyle ⇨ Bottom property to Solid and BorderWidth ⇨ Bottom property to 2pt in the Properties window. This adds a single underline below the grand total numeric columns.
10. Select all cells in the last row by clicking its row selector and change their Font ⇨ FontStyle property to Bold.
11. Select the ProductCategory group cell and change its BackgroundColor to AliceBlue and Font ⇨ FontStyle to Bold.
12. Select the ProductSubcategory group cell and change its BackgroundColor to AliceBlue.
13. Select the last three columns by holding Shift and clicking the column headers and click the Align Right button in the Report Formatting toolbar to right-align their content.

14. To alternate the background color of the details cells (green bar effect), select the Product Name, Reseller Sales, Internet Sales, and Sales Summary cells in the details row and enter the following expression in the BackgroundColor property.

```
=Iif(RowNumber("ProductCategory") Mod 2, "AliceBlue", "White")
```

The Iif function uses the RowNumber function to change the color of even rows to AliceBlue and odd rows to White.

Implementing the page footer

Finally, it's time to implement the page footer. All it takes is two textboxes and a line item.

1. In the Toolbox window, click the Line report item. Click inside the page footer area and drag a line horizontally.
2. In the Toolbox window, click the Pointer item. Select the line and change its LineColor property to DarkSlateBlue.
3. Drag a Textbox report item to the page footer and enter the following text in it:

```
Execution Time:    [&ExecutionTime] ↵
User:              [&UserID]
```

Make sure to press the Enter key after the first line to start a new paragraph. You can press the Tab key or add spaces to left align the placeholders.

4. Drop a new textbox for the page number and align it with the right edge of the page footer.

TIP You can copy report items by using the familiar shortcut keys. For example, you can select one or more textboxes, press Ctrl-C to copy and Ctrl-V to paste them. Then, drag the new items to the desired location.

5. Enter the following expression in its Value property:

```
Page [&PageNumber] of [&TotalPages]
```

6. Select the two textboxes in the page footer and change their font size to 9pt.

That's it. If you preview the report at this point, it should match its specification.

3.4 Auto-generating Report Definitions

To get you started quickly with the report authoring process, BIDS supports two options for auto-generating report definitions. The Report Wizard walks you through a series of steps and generates table and matrix (crosstab) reports. If you have existing Microsoft Access reports, BIDS can import and convert them to Reporting Services reports.

3.4.1 Using the Report Wizard ▶

Report Wizard is a report authoring tool that guides you through the process of creating a report. You can use the Report Wizard to quickly generate table and matrix reports using predefined report templates. Let's use the Report Wizard to author the report shown in Figure 3.29. This is a cross-tab report that shows the product sales on rows and years on columns, grouped by sales territory on pages. The report also lets the user drill down the row groups to see more data on the report.

Product Sales by Territory

Australia

		2003		2004	
		Reseller Sales	Internet Sales	Reseller Sales	Internet Sales
⊟ Accessories	⊞ Bike Racks			2088.0000	600.0000
	⊞ Bottles and Cages	511.9740	194.6100	377.2440	179.6400
	⊞ Cleaners			267.1200	95.4000
	⊞ Helmets	5584.4040	1364.6100	1952.4420	769.7800
	⊞ Tires and Tubes			8.2440	4.5800
⊞ Bikes		47567.6860	24991.4700	88985.8020	76865.5400
⊞ Clothing		3520.5160	1220.6800	2915.5410	1064.0700

Figure 3.29 The Product Sales by Territory cross-tab report is auto-generated by the Report Wizard.

Running the Report Wizard

Auto-generating the Product Sales by Territory report with the Report Wizard takes a few mouse clicks.

1. In the Solution Explorer pane, right-click on the Reports project node and click Add New Report. This starts the Report Wizard and shows the Welcome to the Report Wizard page. Click Next.
2. In the Select the Data Source step, leave the AdventureWorksDW2008 data source pre-selected and click Next.
3. In the Design the Query step, copy and paste the ReportWizard.sql query included in the book source code. This query is similar to the one used by the Product Sales by Category report but groups data by sales territory and year. Click Next.
4. In the Select the Report Type step, select the Matrix type to create a cross-tab report.

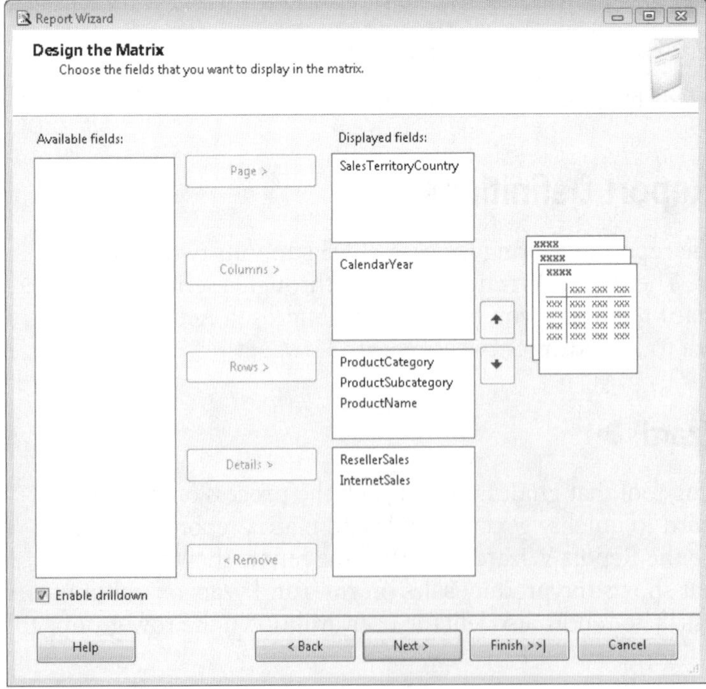

Figure 3.30 The Design the Matrix step lets you define the report groups and details.

The Design the Matrix step lets you specify how the report will group data. The Available Fields list shows the dataset fields.

5. Select the SalesTerritoryCategory in the Available Fields list and click the Page button to group by territory and generate a page break when the territory changes.
6. Select the CalendarYear field and click the Columns button to group data by years on columns.
7. Hold the Ctrl key and select ProductCategory, ProductSubcategory, and ProductName fields. Click the Rows button to group data by these fields on rows, as shown in Figure 3.30.
8. Select the ResellerSales and InternetSales fields and click the Details button to show these fields as report details.
9. Check the Enable Drilldown checkbox to let the user drill down the report interactively.
10. In the Choose the Matrix Style step, click the Corporate style.

> **TIP** You can alter existing style templates or add new ones by editing the StyleTemplates.xml file in the \Program Files\Microsoft Visual Studio 9.0\Common7\IDE\PrivateAssemblies\Business Intelligence Wizards\Reports\Styles\<lang> folder. You need to make this change on the client machine where BIDS is installed.

11. In the Completing the Wizard step, name the report *Product Sales by Territory* and click Finish.

The Report Wizard generates the report definition and opens it in Report Designer.

Understanding the generated report

Let's take a moment to understand the wizard's changes.

1. Click on Reseller Sales details cell, as shown in Figure 3.31.

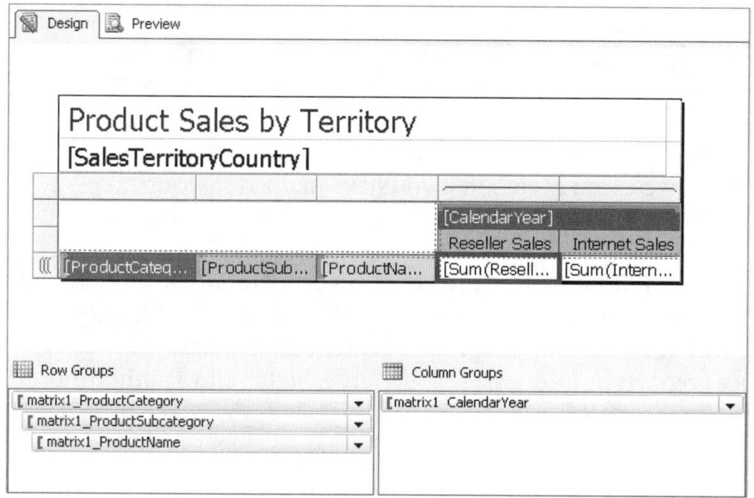

Figure 3.31 The Product Sales by Territory cross-tab report uses the matrix data region and a dynamic column group.

Note that the tablix region has three row groups and one column group. The column group is what defines the cross-tab behavior. At run time, the report server groups the report data on year and rotates the years from rows to columns. Notice also that the matrix region is nested inside a list region. The list region is nothing more than a tablix with a single cell. The cell has a rectangle that contains the second tablix region. In our case, the list region has a single row group that groups the report data by sales territory.

TIP Selecting the containing item with nested report items can be tricky. To quickly find the item's parent, select the item and press Esc. Each time you press Esc, the Report Designer selects the parent of the currently selected item, all the way up to the report body.

2. Double-click the ProductSubcategory row group in the Row Groups pane.
3. In the Group Properties dialog box, click the Visibility tab.

Note that when the report is initially run, the ProductSubcategory group will be hidden but the user can toggle its visibility by the ProductCategory textbox. Consequently, when the user clicks the plus sign on the left of the Product Category group, the matrix will expand to show the product subcategory data. This lets the user drill down the report data to see more details.

3.4.2 Importing Reports from Microsoft Access

If you have existing Microsoft Access reports, you can migrate them to Reporting Services. Reporting Services supports importing reports from a local installation of Microsoft Access 2002 and above. Microsoft Access is the only database format that is supported for import operations by Reporting Services.

NOTE Although somewhat outdated, Microsoft has published a Migrating from Business Objects Crystal Reports to SQL Server 2005 Reporting Services guide (see Resources) to help you manually upgrade Crystal reports. In addition, a few Microsoft partners offer migrating Crystal reports to Reporting Services reports as a service. See http://www.microsoft.com/sql/technologies/reporting/partners/crystal-migration.mspx.

About importing from Microsoft Access

Because there is not an exact match between Access and Reporting Services features, you can expect to lose some functionality when you import an Access report to a report server. For a full list of the supported Access features, please consult the Importing Reports from Access topic in Books Online (see Resources). The most noticeable unsupported Access feature, which will probably cause some grief, is custom modules and events. Since Reporting Services currently doesn't support events, any custom events that you have defined in your Access report will be lost. As a workaround, consider replacing Access code-behind modules with custom code and expressions.

The import process does the bare minimum to convert the report definitions. Basic reports will probably convert successfully. More complex reports are likely to lose some functionality during the report process. You shouldn't consider the imported reports as a best practice of how to author Reporting Services report. In most cases, you will be better off to author the Reporting Services counterparts from scratch.

Importing the Northwind reports

To demonstrate how this report authoring option works, let's import reports from the Northwind sample database that comes with the Microsoft Access samples. BIDS doesn't let you pick individual reports to import. Instead, it imports all reports in the Access database.

1. In the Solution Explorer, right-click the Reports folder and click Import Reports ⇨ Microsoft Access.
2. In the File Open dialog that follows, specify the path to the Northwind database and click OK.

BIDS imports each report and adds the report definition to the Reports folder.

3. Double-click the Invoice.rdl file to open it in the Report Designer, as shown in Figure 3.32.

The Reporting Services equivalent has a free-form layout. If you click on any field in the report body, you will notice that report sections are enclosed in rectangles. All sections are nested in a list region.

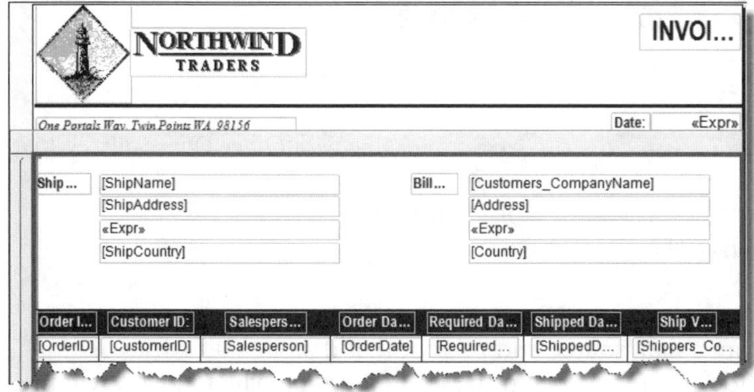

Figure 3.32 Imported from Access reports use the list data region and have free-form layout.

3.5 Summary

If a journey starts with a single step, you travelled far in this chapter! You learned about the report authoring process and its envisioning, design, construction, and testing stages. You also learned about the Microsoft-provided report authoring tools and how to select a tool given the reporting task at hand.

By now, you should have a good understanding of the report anatomy and report items. Authoring a report involves setting up a data source, a dataset, and laying out the report by using the report items and regions. You went through a "click-intensive" exercise to put things together by creating a basic tabular report with the Report Designer. You also practiced auto-generating reports with the Report Wizard and importing existing Microsoft Access reports.

In the next chapter, you continue mastering the design process by learning how to work with report data.

3.6 Resources

Using Built-in Report and Aggregate Functions in Expressions (http://tinyurl.com/2jv56c)—Lists the Reporting Services built-in functions.

Visual Basic Run-Time Library Members (http://tinyurl.com/2pkwo4)—Lists the functions in the Visual Basic Run-Time Library which you can use in expressions.

Migrating from Business Objects reports to SQL Server 2005 Reporting Services (http://tinyurl.com/396eya)—Explains how to manually upgrade Crystal Reports to Reporting Services.

Importing Reports From Access (http://tinyurl.com/5ocokn)—Explains what features are supported when importing reports from Microsoft Access.

Chapter 4

Designing Data Access

Most reports retrieve raw data from a data source and present that data in a user-friendly format. As such, the process of authoring a report begins with defining the data that you will use. With Reporting Services, a data definition includes specifying a data source and configuring a query. You can then use report items and data regions to map the data to a report layout.

This chapter starts by discussing the Reporting Services data access architecture. You will learn different ways to connect to a data source. Most of the chapter will focus on showing you how to work with data that you retrieve from a SQL Server relational database. As you'll see, Reporting Services provides many ways to filter report data and implement parameterized reports. I'll also show you how to integrate your reports with other types of data sources, including OLE DB data sources, XML Web services, SQL Server Integration Services packages, and .NET Framework data providers.

4.1 Understanding Data Access

Nowadays, data can be found in a variety of data sources that range from relational and OLAP databases to XML files and spreadsheets. Proliferation of data sources and database standards present unique challenges because each one has different requirements for securing, connecting, and querying data. Building reports that use a variety of data sources has been traditionally difficult even with the most popular reporting tools. One of the most prominent strengths of Reporting Services is that it helps you meet this challenge head on. It can draw data from virtually any data source, and even combine data from multiple data sources on the same report.

4.1.1 Understanding Data Architecture

To meet demanding data integration needs, Reporting Services provides a flexible and extensible data architecture whose major components are shown in Figure 4.1. The diagram depicts the flow of data from the data source to the report.

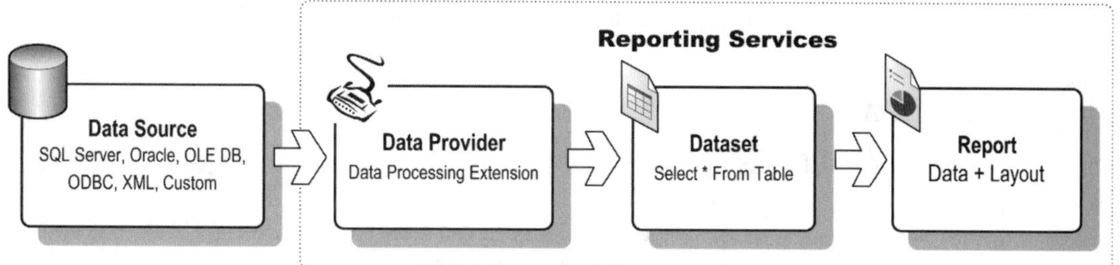

Figure 4.1 The major Reporting Services data components are the data source, data provider and dataset.

Data sources

As the term is commonly used, a data source can be defined as an external repository from which data originates. Familiar examples of data sources that are in wide-spread use include relational databases, cubes, ODBC or OLE DB-compliant databases, Web services, and so on. In Reporting Services parlance, a data source is a definition of a data connection. In this chapter, I will use the term "data source" to refer to both physical data sources and connections.

Data providers

A data provider (also called a data processing extension or DPE), is a .NET component that is designed to retrieve data from a specific type of data source and provide extra functionality that supports report design and report processing. The data provider sends the report query to the data source, retrieves data, and exposes the data as a Reporting Services dataset.

Reporting Services includes built-in data providers that support relational databases, multidimensional databases, report models, and XML-based data. In addition, you can extend the Reporting Services data capabilities by plugging in custom data providers that you or someone else wrote.

NOTE Perhaps, you've heard about the Microsoft ADO.NET Entity Framework, which is designed to abstract the database schema, and you may wonder if you can use it with reports. As it stands, Reporting Services doesn't natively support the Entity Framework. One workaround is to implement a custom data processing extension that loads your entity model and returns the data via the data extension interfaces.

Datasets

At design time, a dataset definition contains query information that is used by the report. Specifically, it contains a reference to a data source, the query, any query parameters, and additional information, such as collating and filtering options. At run time, the data provider executes the query and returns a two-dimensional dataset object with rows and columns. The report processor combines the dataset with the report layout to produce the raw report.

The way you specify the dataset query depends on the type of the data source. For example, if you target a relational database, you would use a SQL query or a stored procedure. If the report draws data from an Analysis Services cube, you would use a multidimensional (MDX) query.

Reports can have multiple datasets and each dataset can reference a different data source. Suppose that you need a report with a chart showing the Adventure Works company performance data that originates in an Analysis Services cube, followed by a table showing more detailed operational data that is kept in a SQL Server relational database. To implement this report, you need two data sources and two datasets, as shown in Figure 4.2. You can bind the chart region to the first dataset, and the table region to the second.

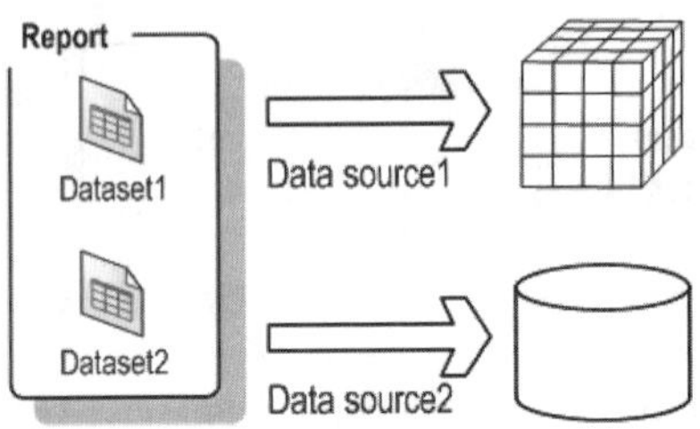

Figure 4.2 A report can reference more than one data source and have multiple datasets.

4.1.2 Understanding Data Providers

As noted, a data provider is a bridge between the report and the data source. A data provider is responsible for connecting Reporting Services to a data source, executing commands, and returning the results as a Reporting Services dataset. Reporting Services provides several built-in data providers to access the most popular data sources, as shown in Table 4.1.

Table 4.1 The Reporting Services built-in data providers

Provider	Data Source	Underlying .NET Data Provider
Microsoft SQL Server	SQL Server 7.0 or later	System.Data.SqlClient
OLE DB	OLE DB-compatible data sources	System.Data.OledbClient
Microsoft SQL Server Analysis Services	SQL Server Analysis Services 2000 or later	ADOMD.NET
Oracle	Oracle 8.1.7 or later	System.Data.OracleClient
ODBC	ODBC-compatible data sources	System.Data.OdbcClient
XML	XML documents	N/A
Report Server Model	Report Builder 1.0 models	N/A
SAP NetWeaver BI	SAP BW 3.5	N/A
Hyperion Essbase	Hyperion System 9 BI+ Analytic Provider Services 9.3	N/A
SSIS	SQL Server Integration Services 2005 or later	N/A
Teradata	Teradata data warehouses	.NET Data Provider from Teradata

Let's briefly discuss the built-in data providers in the order listed in the table.

Microsoft SQL Server

The Microsoft SQL Server data provider wraps the System.Data.SqlClient .NET data provider that you may have used in custom .NET applications to connect to SQL Server. As you saw in the previous chapter, the Report Designer providers a graphical query designer when you target the Microsoft SQL Server provider. This graphical query designer analyzes the query, and sometimes rewrites it by replacing parameter placeholders with actual parameter values. You can use the generic query designer if you want to control the exact query sent to the data source. Most of the report samples in this book use the Microsoft SQL Server data provider.

OLE DB

OLE DB is a generic data provider that lets you access OLE DB-compliant data sources. In the process of configuring this generic provider, you must select a data source-specific OLE DB provider. Supported data sources are SQL Server 7.0 and later, Analysis Services 2000 and later, and Oracle 8 and later.

Microsoft SQL Server Analysis Services

If you did the hands-on lab in chapter 1 that walks you through creating a chart report that retrieves source data from the Adventure Works cube, you are already familiar with the built-in Microsoft SQL Server Analysis Services data provider. This provider wraps the ADOMD.NET programming library to communicate with Analysis Services 2000 or later.

The Analysis Services provider supports several features that would otherwise require significant implementation effort on your part, including support for defining parameterized queries, server aggregates, and extended properties. Report Designer includes graphical tools to facilitate authoring multidimensional and data mining queries.

Oracle

The Oracle data provider extends the .NET System.Data.OracleClient provider, which you may have used in custom applications that connect to Oracle databases. As a prerequisite for using this provider, you must install the Oracle client tools. The provider supports named parameters. Multivalued parameters are supported with Oracle 9 or later. You can retrieve data from stored procedures with multiple input parameters, but the stored procedure must return only one output cursor.

ODBC

This is another generic data provider that lets you access ODBC-compliant data sources via the .NET System.Data.OdbcClient provider.

XML

The XML data provider debuted in Reporting Services 2005. It lets you query XML data returned from URL-addressable resources, such as Web services, or embedded XML document inside the dataset query. This provider supports a proprietary syntax for navigating XML. It remains unchanged from the previous release.

Report Server model

Recall from chapter 3 that Report Builder 1.0 lets business users author basic ad hoc reports from a predefined report model. The report server uses the report model to auto-generate queries to an underlying data source, which could be a SQL Server, Oracle, or Analysis Services database. You can use the Report Server Model data provider in Report Designer to author reports from Report Builder 1.0 models. A graphical query designer is provided to let you author queries by dragging and dropping model entities.

Other providers

The SAP NetWeaver BI provider lets you integrate reports with SAP NetWeaver Business Intelligence (SAP BW). Microsoft has also provided a query designer for SAP NetWeaver Business Intelligence. For more information about using the SAP NetWeaver BI provider, read the Using SQL Server 2005 Reporting Services with SAP NetWeaver Business Intelligence paper (see Resources).

Hyperion Essbase is a multidimensional database very similar to Analysis Services. The Using SQL Server 2005 Reporting Services with Hyperion Essbase paper explains how to leverage the Hyperion Essbase provider to integrate Reporting Services with Hyperion Essbase.

Although not officially supported and disabled by default, the SSIS data provider allows you to retrieve data from a SQL Server Integration Services package. For example, you may need to extract data from a flat file and transform that data before it's used in the report.

Finally, the Teradata provider (new with Reporting Services 2008), enables you query Teradata databases. This provider extends the .NET Data Provider for Teradata from Teradata, which must be installed before you can query data.

4.2 Connecting to Data

As a first step of authoring a data-driven report, you need to set up a data source. A data source contains the definition of a data source connection. The definition can be shared among several reports or stored inside the report.

4.2.1 Working with Shared Data Sources

As its name suggests, a shared data source can be shared among multiple reports. If you use the BIDS Report Designer, a shared data source can be referenced by any report in the Report Server project. Once you deploy a shared data source to the server, any published report can reference it. A report that uses a shared data source stores only a reference to the data source definition.

```
<Report>
 <DataSources>
  <DataSource Name="AdventureWorksDW2008">
   <DataSourceReference>AdventureWorksDW2008</DataSourceReference>
   <rd:DataSourceID>fef5e490- dea9-4933- 8fda-e38ef757dd4d</rd:DataSourceID>
  </DataSource>
```

In this example, the report definition references the AdventureWorksDW2008 shared data source. The actual data source definition is saved in a separate (.rds) file that contains the name of the data source and other connection-specific information, such as the connection string. The data source identifier is used only at design time by Report Designer; hence the rd namespace. When you publish the data source, reports reference it by its path in the report catalog.

Advantages of shared data sources

You should consider configuring and using a shared data source whenever possible for several reasons. First, a shared data source centralizes connection information. If you need to change the connection string or credentials, you can do so in one place and all dependent reports will pick up the new settings. Second, a shared data source is a securable item. The report administrator can define security policies that control who is authorized to change the connection information. Finally, because all reports use the same connection string, a shared data source can minimize the number of open connections to a database that supports connection pooling.

NOTE Database connections are expensive resources. Many data providers, such as the Microsoft SQL Server provider, perform connection pooling behind the scenes to minimize the number of open database connections. When a connection is closed, it is returned to the pool. When the application needs to connect to the database again, the provider checks the pool for available connections. If it finds one, it uses that connection; otherwise it creates a new one. However, in order for connection pooling to work, all connections must have identical connection string settings.

Creating a shared data source

You can create shared data sources in BIDS and Report Manager. Next, I will walk you through the steps for setting up a shared data source to the AdventureWorksDW2008 database.

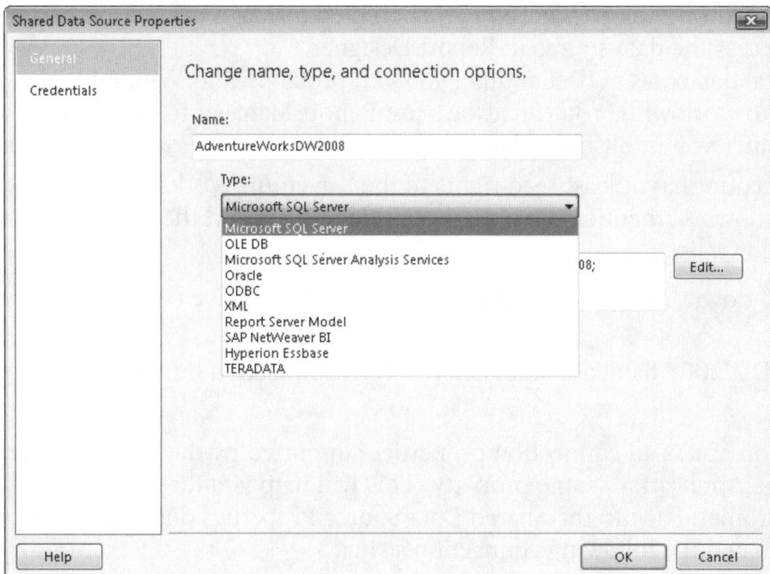

Figure 4.3 The Type drop-down list in the Shared Data Source Properties dialog box lists the Reporting Services built-in data providers.

1. In BIDS, create a new Report Server project.
2. Right-click the Shared Data Sources folder and choose Add New Data Source to open the Shared Data Source Properties dialog box.

   Observe that the Microsoft SQL Server data provider is pre-selected by default.
3. In the Shared Data Source Properties dialog box (see Figure 4.3), enter *Adventure-WorksDW2008* in the Name field. Choosing a descriptive name is important because reports reference the data source by its name.
4. Expand the Type drop-down list. Notice that it shows all data providers except the SSIS data provider, which is disabled by default.
5. While you can enter the connection string manually in the field below the Type drop-down list, you can let the Connection Properties dialog box auto-generate the connection string for you. With the Microsoft SQL Server provider selected, click Edit to open the Connection Properties dialog box.
6. Enter *(local)* in the Server Name field. If you want to connect to another server, you can click the Refresh button or expand the server drop-down list to find all SQL Server instances on your LAN, but this may take a while. To avoid delay, type the server name directly.

TIP What's the difference among (local), locahost, and "." when connecting to a local SQL Server anyway? Because Reporting Services use .NET data providers, all of the three settings are equivalent. The client will connect with different protocols depending upon the server configuration. It will first attempt shared memory, then TCP/IP, and then named pipe. For other providers, such as Microsoft OLE DB Provider for SQL Server, the last two settings are protocol dependent. To avoid confusion, I would recommend you stick with (local). The only exception would be if you want to control the TCP/IP address of the server in the Hosts configuration file. In this case, use localhost since it is a socket-based construct.

The Connection Properties dialog box provides a subset of the authentication modes supported by Reporting Services. Specifically, if the data source supports Windows integrated security, you can select the Use Windows Authentication option. Alternatively, you can use standard security by selecting the Use SQL Server Authentication options and entering login credentials. This option lets you save the password in an encrypted format so you don't have to retype it each time you access the data source in Report Designer.

When working with local databases at design time, you will probably find Windows authentication more practical to work with. You can always use Report Manager to re-configure the data source credentials after you publish the data source to the server.

7. Assuming your Windows account has at least read rights to the AdventureWorksDW2008 database, leave the Use Windows Authentication option selected and expand the Select or Enter a Database Name drop-down list.

   After a short delay, the drop-down list shows all databases for which you have connection rights.

8. Select the AdventureWorksDW2008 database and click the Test Connection button to test the connection. Click OK.

   The Advanced button lets you access all connection properties supported by the provider. For example, you can change the Application Name property. This will help you identify the connection in the SQL Server Profiler. Back to the Shared Data Source Properties dialog box, notice that BIDS has now generated the following connection string:

```
Data Source=(local);Initial Catalog=Adven tureWorksDW2008
```

Understanding authentication options

The Credentials tab, which Figure 4.4 shows, provides more authentication options than what you see in Connection Properties. Let's go over each one.

Use Windows Authentication (integrated security)

The connection will be established under the identity of the interactive user. At design time, the interactive user is you. When you deploy the report to the server, the interactive user will be the user requesting the report. For example, if Bob logs in to the adventure-works domain as adventure-works\bob, the database will attempt to authenticate him with his Windows login credentials.

As a prerequisite for using Windows authentication, the database administrator must set up database logins for all report users and grant these logins at least read access to the data. Alternatively, account management can be simplified and made less granular by grouping users in Windows groups, such as Report Users, and granting rights to the groups instead.

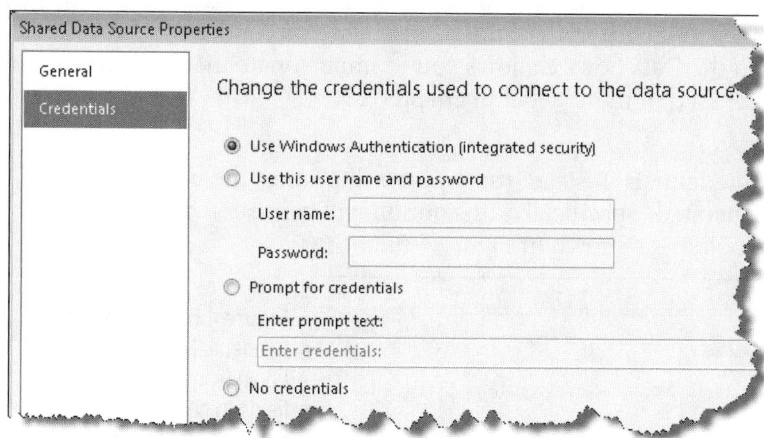

Figure 4.4 Reporting Services supports flexible database authentication options.

Windows authentication is inherently more secure than standard authentication because Windows maintains the password, not you. In addition, this authentication method lets you flow the user identity to the database and implement schema and data security policies. For example, a stored procedure can query a policy table and return only the rows that the user is authorized to see.

On the downside, report caching and subscriptions (discussed in chapter 12) don't support Windows authentication. In addition, this authentication method may also present deployment challenges. For example, if the report server and database servers are on different machines and you need to pass the user's Windows credentials to the database server, you will need to configure Kerberos to avoid the "double hop" issue which I discussed in more detail in chapter 2.

In addition, Windows authentication may prevent connection pooling, which can impact performance when the server is under heavy report loads. Since the connection string for each user will be different (via different Windows logins), the connections will not be pooled. More accurately, you will end up with as many connection pools as the number of users requesting the report.

Use This User Name and Password

This authentication method, which is also referred to as "stored credentials," requires that you specify a single set of user credentials that are used every time the report is requested. When you publish the data source definition, the report server encrypts and stores the credentials with a machine-specific encryption key. As a security best practice, I'd recommend you use a login that has minimum rights to the database. For example, if you target SQL Server, consider assigning the login to the db_datareader role which grants read-only rights.

Standard security is a wide-spread security authentication mode because it is supported by all commercial RDBMS. This option works with report caching and subscriptions. Moreover, because all users connect with the same connection string, stored credentials improve performance because the server pools connections if the data source supports connection pooling. On the downside, the data source won't be able to differentiate the users.

Once you deploy the data source definition to the server and open its properties in Report Manager, you will notice that this authentication option is called Credentials Stored Securely In the report server. More importantly, it supports two additional settings that are not available in BIDS. The Use As Windows Credentials When Connecting To the Data Source lets you use a Windows login with standard security. The Impersonate The Authenticated User After a Connection Has Been Made To the Data Source allows you to impersonate the database connection. These settings are discussed in more detail in chapter 11.

Prompt for Credentials

This option doesn't store any credentials. Instead, the report will prompt the user to enter credentials before the report is generated. Specifically, this option will generate Login Name and Password fields in the report toolbar, as shown in Figure 4.5.

Figure 4.5 The Prompt for Credentials option generates Login Name and Password fields to collect credentials before the report is run.

This option should be used with caution because it may present a security vulnerability as a hacker may intercept the user credentials on their way to the server. One scenario where this option could be useful is a distributed deployment where the report server and the data source are installed on different machines, and enabling Kerberos is not an option. In this case, the Prompt for Credentials option lets you work around the "double hop" limitation and pass the user credentials to the data source.

No Credentials

You may come across a data source that doesn't require authentication. For example, in chapter 18, you will implement a custom data provider that lets you create reports from ADO.NET datasets that do not require authentication. Another scenario where the No Credentials option might be useful is when the credentials are embedded in the connection string. Finally, you can consider this option with a subreport that uses the credentials of the parent report to connect to its data source.

When a data source uses the No Credentials authentication option, the report server uses a special unattended execution account to impersonate the call to the data source. Chapter 2 explained how to configure the unattended execution account.

Deploying shared data sources

You can publish definitions of shared data sources to the server as a part of deploying the project from BIDS, or individually by right-clicking the data source and choosing Deploy. If the data source doesn't exist on the server, the deployment process will create it. If the data source uses stored credentials, the credentials are not transferred to the deployed data source. After deploying the data source, you need to use Report Manager to open the data source and set the credentials.

The OverwriteDataSources project property setting determines what happens if the data source already exists on the server. If OverwriteDataSources is False (default), subsequent deployments will not overwrite that data source. The premise here is that the administrator may have changed the data source definition of the published data source. If you want to overwrite the published data source each time the project is published, change OverwriteDataSources to True.

4.2.2 Working with Report-Specific Data Sources

A report-specific (or private) data source is available only in the report in which it is defined. For example, the sample report you authored in chapter 1 uses a report-specific data source definition whose report definition is shown below.

```
<Report>
 <DataSources>
  <DataSource Name="DataSource1">
    <ConnectionProperties>
    <DataProvider>OLEDB - MD</DataProvider>
    <ConnectString> Data Source=(local);Initial Catalog="Adventure Works DW"</ConnectString>
    <IntegratedSecurity>true</IntegratedSecurity>
    </ConnectionProperties>
    <rd:DataSourceID>6abc2688 -c82c-413a-  a41b- 43ce6d9dc1e0</rd:DataSourceID>
  </DataSource>
```

As you can see, the definition of a report–specific data source is embedded in the containing report and becomes part of the report itself. Consequently, the data source can be shared by multiple datasets within the report, but not among other reports on the server.

TIP You can start with a report-specific data source and convert it to a shared data source later on if needed. To do so, right-click the data source reference in the Report Data window and click Convert to Shared Data Source.

Advantages of report-specific data sources

Report-specific data sources may simplify deployment because you can distribute both the report layout and connection information in one file. For example, a third-party vendor may choose to encapsulate the database connection information in the RDL file to simplify the process of distributing the report to its customers.

More importantly, only report-specific data sources can have expression-based connection strings. The reason for this limitation is that when the report server evaluates expressions, it generates and compiles an expression host assembly during report publishing. Expressions used in report-specific data sources become part of the expression host assembly and are evaluated like other expressions. By contrast, there is no equivalent compiled code for shared data sources.

On the downside, you cannot use a query designer to test dataset queries with expression-based connections. To make designing the report easier, you can initially set up the data source to use a regular connection string, allowing you to build the dataset using the query designers. After the report layout is finalized, change the connection string to use the expression. Let's go through a couple of examples that demonstrate how expression-based connection strings can be useful.

Constructing a connection string from a parameter

Suppose you are implementing a reporting solution for multiple companies and all companies share the same report definitions. For performance and security reasons, you decide to host the data for each company in a separate database and possibly on a separate server. At run time, the user passes the company database name as a parameter to the report. The report dynamically constructs the connection string and connects to the appropriate database.

The Connection From Parameters report (shown in Figure 4.6) demonstrates this scenario. It uses a report-specific data source with an expression-based connection string that depends on the Company parameter. To implement this report, start by creating a report-specific data source.

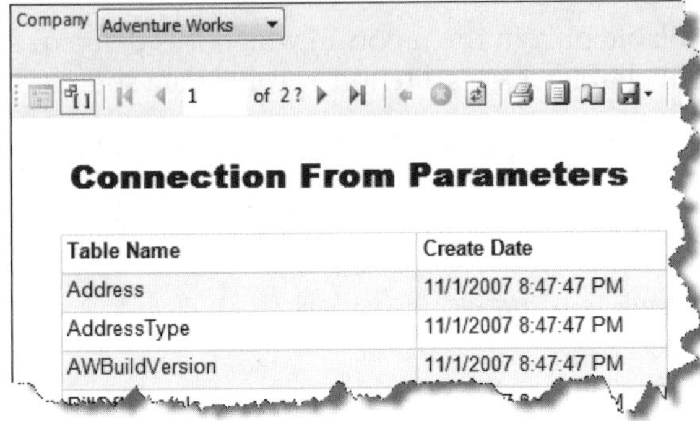

Figure 4.6 This report demonstrates constructing the data source connection string from a parameter.

1. In BIDS, create a new report and name it Connection From Parameters. Open the report in design mode.
2. In the Report Data window, expand the New drop-down button and click Data Source to set up a new data source reference.
3. In the Data Source Properties dialog box, leave the Embedded Connection option selected and click the Edit button to connect to the AdventureWorksDW2008 database. Click OK.
4. In the Report Data window, click New ⇨Dataset. In the Dataset Properties dialog box, rename the dataset to *Main* and click the Query Designer button.
5. In the generic query designer, enter the following query statement.

```
select name, crdate from sysobjects where xtype = 'U' order by name
```

   This statement returns the names of all tables in the database and their creation dates.
6. In the Report Data window, click New ⇨ Parameter (or right-click Parameters and click Create Parameter).
7. In the General tab of the Report Parameter Properties dialog box, name the parameter *Company*.
8. Click the Available Values tab. Select the Specify Values option to define static available values.
9. Click Add to define a new available value with a label of *Adventure Works* and a value of *AdventureWorks2008*.
10. Click Add to define a second new available value with a label of *Prologika* and a value of *AdventureWorksDW2008*.

    As you've probably guessed, the Value property of the Company parameter specifies which target database to connect to when the report is run.
11. Drag a table region from the Toolbox window to the report area and configure it to show the Name and Crdate dataset fields.
12. Preview the report to test the changes. It should show the names of all tables in the AdventureWorksDW2008 database.
13. Back to design mode, double-click the DataSource1 data source in the Report Data window. Replace the connection string with the following expression:

```
=String.Format("Data Source=(local);Initial Catalog={0}",Parameters!Company.Value)
```

When you run the report, the Initial Catalog connection string setting will be set to the value of the Company parameter.

14. In the Report Data window, right-click the Main dataset and click Query. Notice that Report Designer shows an error message:

```
An error occurred while connection to "DataSource1". Only the text-based query designer will be available. Connection string expressions cannot be evaluated at design time. You must preview or deploy the report to verify the connection.
```

Although you can edit the query text, you cannot use the query designers to execute queries with test expression-based data sources.

15. Click OK to close error dialog. Report Designer opens the generic query designer, which you can use to change the query text if needed. Click OK to close the query designer. Another error message is shown:

```
Could not update a list of fields for the query. Verify that you can connect to the data source and that your query syntax is correct.
```

Again, Report Designer shows this message because the query designer is not capable of executing queries that use expression-based connections. Click OK.

16. Preview the report.

When you select Adventure Works, the report should show the table names in the AdventureWorks2008 database. When you select Prologika, the report should show the table names in the AdventureWorksDW2008 database.

NOTE In real life, security requirements may disallow users from choosing a company they are not authorized to access. If you report-enable a custom application, the application can validate security policies and load the Company parameter with the authorized companies only. Alternatively, you can pass the user identity to the database and populate the parameter available values from a query, as I will demonstrate in section 4.4.3.

Constructing a connection string from a configuration setting

An expression-based connection doesn't have to reference parameters. Instead, its expression can call custom code that returns the connection string. The Connection From Configuration Settings report demonstrates how to read a connection string from the report server web.config file. Recall that the application domain of the Report Server Web service is hosted by ASP.NET. Consequently, although not officially supported, you can add application settings to the report server web.config file and read them when the report is run.

1. Open the report server web.config file (located at Program Files\Microsoft SQL Server\MSRS10.MSSQLSERVER\Reporting Services\ReportServer\web.config) and add the following application setting before the </configuration> element:

```
<appSettings>
 <add key="connectionString" value="server=(local);database=AdventureWorksDW2008;Integra ted Security=SSPI"/>
</appSettings>
</configuration>
```

2. Save the file.
3. Open the Connection From Configuration Settings report and double-click DataSource1 in the Report Data window.
4. Click the *fx* button next to the connection string field and notice that the data source uses the following expression:

```
=Code.ConnectionString
```

5. Open the Report Properties dialog and click the References tab. Notice that the report has a reference to the .NET System.Configuration assembly. This assembly defines the ConfigurationManager class that lets you access configuration settings.
6. Click the Code tab. It shows the code of the ConnectionString property:

```
Const CONNECTION_STRING As String = "Data Source=(local);Initial C atalog=AdventureWorks2008;
Integrated Security=SSPI"

Public ReadOnly Property ConnectionString() As String
   Get
     Dim conn As String=System.Configuration.ConfigurationManager.AppSettings("connectionString")
     If String.IsNullOrEmpty(conn) Then
         conn = CONNECTION_STRING
     End If
       Return conn
   End Get
End Property
```

The code attempts to read the connectionString setting from the configuration file. This will succeed if the report is deployed to the server. However, when you preview the report in BIDS, the Report Designer won't be able to find the setting. In this case, the code falls back on a static connection string so you could test the report at design time.

4.2.3 Using Transactions

Reporting Services doesn't start processing the report until all queries are executed and data is returned. Because data retrieval, report processing, and rendering are sequential stages, the user cannot see a partial report until after the queries are finished executing. By default, the report server will execute all report queries in parallel unless the queries are interdependent, such as queries that return available values for cascading parameters. However, in some cases, you may need to force the report queries to execute sequentially. For example, suppose that you need to execute a statement to prepare the report data before showing it on the report. This is a sequential flow that requires a specific query order.

You can execute queries sequentially in the order they appear in the report definition by enabling the Use single transaction when processing the queries property on the Data Source Properties dialog box. This option is only available for data source references in the Report Data window.

Working with data source advanced properties

The Transaction report included in the book source code demonstrates this approach. It has two datasets. Dataset1 has the following command text:

```
CREATE TABLE #MyTempTable (Result INT PRIMARY KEY)
INSERT INTO #MyTempTable VALUES (1)
```

The first command creates a local (connection-specific) temporary table in the AdventureWorksDW2008 database. The second statement inserts a value in the temporary table. Because the .NET SqlClient provider doesn't let you execute multiple statements by default, you will get the following error when you attempt to preview the report:

```
Failed to roll back transaction for data source 'AdventureWorksDW2008'. There is already an open DataReader associated
with this Command which must be closed first.
```

As a workaround, enable the MultipleActiveResultSets advanced connection property, as follows:

1. In the Report Data window, double-click the AdventureWorksDW2008 data source.
2. In the Data Source Properties dialog box, click Edit to open the Connection Properties dialog box, and click the Advanced button.
3. In the Advanced section, change the MultipleActiveResultSets property to True and click OK. The resulting connection string (see Figure 4.7) should now be:

```
Data Source=(local);Initial Catalog=AdventureWork sDW2008;MultipleActiveResultSets= True
```

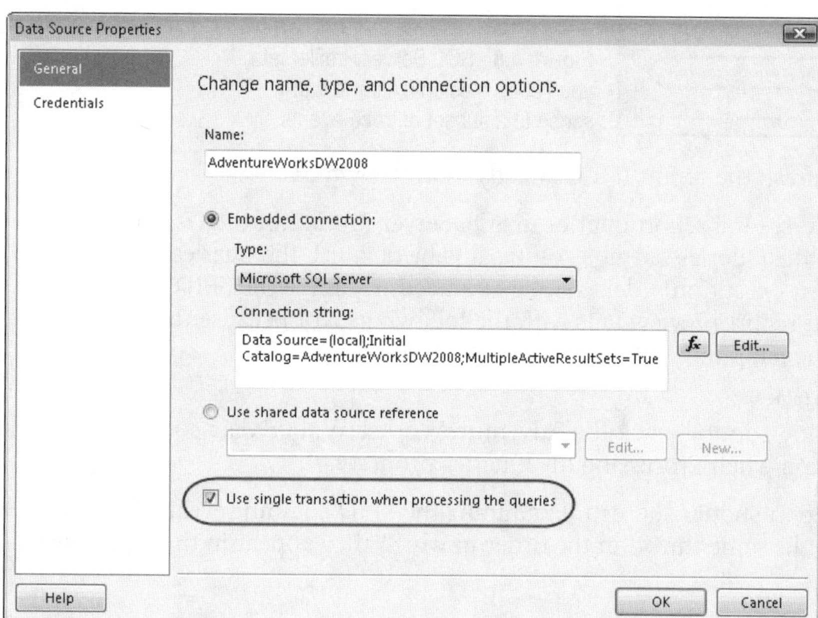

Figure 4.7 Check the Use Single Transaction when Processing the Queries property to force queries to execute sequentially.

Understanding query execution

The second dataset, DataSet1, reads from the temporary table and displays the results on the report. You can use SQL Server Profiler to understand how the report executes the dataset queries.

1. Open SQL Server Profiler from the Microsoft SQL Server 2008 ⇨ Performance Tools program group.
2. Click File ⇨ New Trace or press Ctrl+N to start a new trace.
3. In the Connect to Server dialog box, connect to your database server.
4. In the Trace Properties dialog box that follows, click the Events Selection tab, and click the Column Filters button.

   SQL Server Profiler lets you filter trace events. To eliminate "noise", let's set up a column filter that shows the trace events associated with your connection.

5. In the Edit Filter dialog box, set up a filter on the NTUserName, as shown in Figure 4.8. Check the Exclude Rows that Do not Contain Values checkbox and click OK to return to the Trace Properties dialog box. Click Run to start the trace.

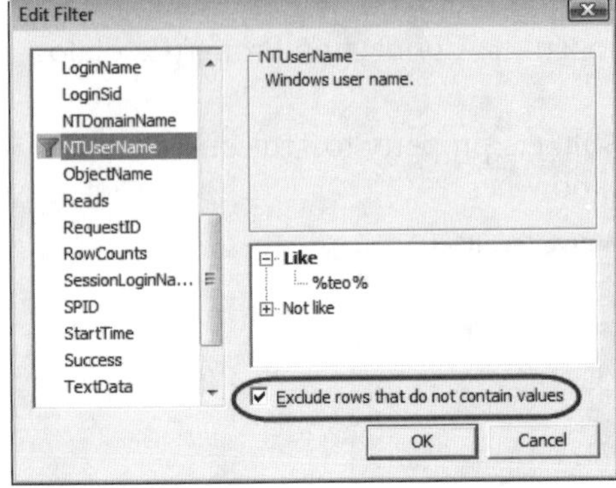

Figure 4.8 SQL Server Profiler lets you set up a column filter to subscribe to a subset of trace events.

6. Preview the report or refresh the report if it is already in preview mode.

   At this point, you should see the report queries in SQL Server Profiler. If the Use Single Transaction when Processing the Queries setting is off (as it is by default), the queries execute on separate threads and their execution order is not guaranteed. Examine the SPID column to confirm this. Notice that report preview fails with the following error because the SELECT statement fails to find the temporary table.

   ```
   Invalid object name '#MyTempTable'
   ```

7. In the Report Data window, double-click the AdventureWorksDW2008 data source and check the Use Single Transaction when Processing the Queries property.

   Now, previewing the report should succeed. Examining the SPID column reveals that queries execute sequentially on the same thread in the order in which they appear in the report definition.

Working with temporary tables

Here are some additional tips for working with stored procedures that use temporary tables:

1. If the field list is not showing up, click on the Refresh Fields button in the Dataset Properties (Query tab).
2. Do not use SET NOCOUNT ON in your stored procedure.
3. Do not explicitly drop the temporary tables. Let the temporary tables just fall out of scope. SQL Server will properly dispose of them when they are no longer needed.
4. Have your last statement be a SELECT statement.
5. If you still cannot retrieve the dataset fields, add SET FMTONLY OFF to the stored procedure.

   You need SET FMTONLY OFF when you create a temporary table in your stored procedure that is then filled with data from another stored procedure.

4.3 Working with Datasets

A report dataset is a contract between a data source and a report that uses data from that data source. Specifically, a dataset definition includes a reference to the data source used by the dataset, a command text that the report server sends to the data source at run time to extract data, a list of fields that the query returns, and additional settings, such as query parameters.

4.3.1 Understanding the Dataset Definition

A dataset can reference a single data source and a single query. A partial definition of the Products dataset that you defined in the preceding chapter for the Product Sales by Category report illustrates how a dataset appears in the report definition.

```
<DataSet Name="Products">
  <Fields>
    <Field Name="ProductCategory">
      <DataField>ProductCategory</DataField>
      <rd:TypeName>System.String</rd:TypeName>
    </Field>
    <Field Name="ProductSubcategory">
      <DataField>ProductSubcategory</DataField>
      <rd:TypeName>System.String</rd:TypeName>
    </Field>
    <!-- More dataset fields -- >
  <Query>
      <DataSourceName>AdventureWorksDW2008</DataSourceName>
      <CommandText>SELECT DimProductCategory.EnglishProductCategoryName AS ProductCategory, . . .
      </CommandText>
      <QueryParameters>
            <QueryParameter Name="@Month"><Value>=Parameters!Month.Value</Value>   </QueryParameter>
            <QueryParameter Name="@Year"><Value>=Parameters!Year.Value</Value></QueryParameter>
      </QueryParameters>
  </Query>
</DataSet>
```

The Products dataset references the AdventureWorksDW2008 data source. The CommandText query statement specifies the dataset query. The QueryParameters element defines the query parameters. The Fields element enumerates the dataset fields and data types. Each field has a Name property which is used by the report and a DataField property that maps the field to the underlying column in the query results. Next, let's go through a few exercises to practice working with datasets.

4.3.2 Using the Generic Query Designer

In this practice, you'll recreate the datasets for the Sales Order report (see Figure 4.9), which is included in the book source code. The order header section of the report is implemented with a list region (bound to a SalesOrder dataset), while the order item section uses a table region (bound to a SalesOrderDetail dataset).

Creating a dataset

The Sales Order Start report provides the starting point for this practice. It includes the report layout, but it doesn't contain the report datasets. To prevent build errors, I excluded the Sales Order Start report from the Reports project. Start by including the report definition file in the project.

1. In Solution Explorer, right-click the Reports folder and click Add ⇨ Existing Item. In the Add Existing Item dialog box that follows, select the Sales Order Start report and click Add.
2. In Solution Explorer, double-click the Sales Order Start report to open it in Report Designer.

Next, you'll create the SalesOrder dataset for the order header section. In the Report Data window, note that the report has a reference to the AdventureWorks2008 data source. The AdventureWorks2008 data source is a shared data source in the project that connects to the AdventureWorks2008 database.

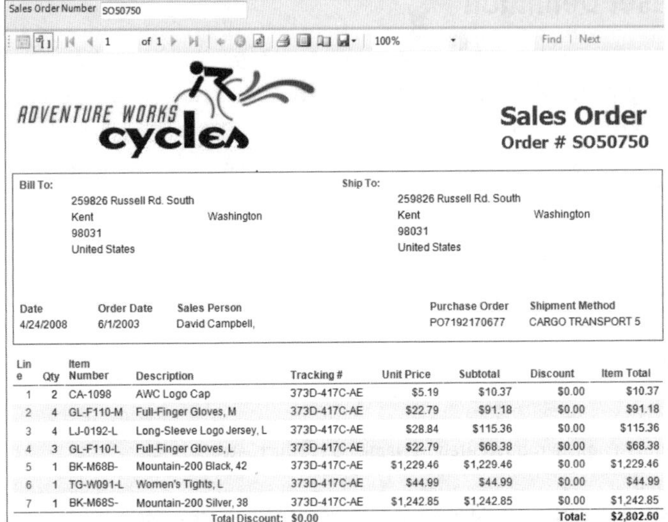

Sales Order Number SO50750

ADVENTURE WORKS cycles

Sales Order
Order # SO50750

Bill To:
259826 Russell Rd. South
Kent Washington
98031
United States

Ship To:
259826 Russell Rd. South
Kent Washington
98031
United States

Date	Order Date	Sales Person	Purchase Order	Shipment Method
4/24/2008	6/1/2003	David Campbell,	PO7192170677	CARGO TRANSPORT 5

Line	Qty	Item Number	Description	Tracking #	Unit Price	Subtotal	Discount	Item Total
1	2	CA-1098	AWC Logo Cap	373D-417C-AE	$5.19	$10.37	$0.00	$10.37
2	4	GL-F110-M	Full-Finger Gloves, M	373D-417C-AE	$22.79	$91.18	$0.00	$91.18
3	4	LJ-0192-L	Long-Sleeve Logo Jersey, L	373D-417C-AE	$28.84	$115.36	$0.00	$115.36
4	3	GL-F110-L	Full-Finger Gloves, L	373D-417C-AE	$22.79	$68.38	$0.00	$68.38
5	1	BK-M68B-	Mountain-200 Black, 42	373D-417C-AE	$1,229.46	$1,229.46	$0.00	$1,229.46
6	1	TG-W091-L	Women's Tights, L	373D-417C-AE	$44.99	$44.99	$0.00	$44.99
7	1	BK-M68S-	Mountain-200 Silver, 38	373D-417C-AE	$1,242.85	$1,242.85	$0.00	$1,242.85
			Total Discount:	$0.00			Total:	$2,802.60

Figure 4.9 The Sales Order report uses two datasets; the SalesOrder dataset supplies data for the order header, while the SalesOrderDetail dataset provides data for the order items.

3. In the Report Data window, click New ⇨ Dataset to open the Dataset Properties dialog box. Alternatively, to associate the new dataset with a data source reference, right-click the AdventureWorks2008 data source in the Report Data window, and click Add Dataset.

NOTE Configuring the data source and dataset as separate steps before laying out the report is my preferred way of authoring a report, which you don't have to follow. For example, you can start by dropping a data region, such as a table or a chart. If the report doesn't have a data source reference, Report Designer will open a wizard-like version of the Data Source Properties dialog box that will let you set up a data source and a dataset. If the report has a data source reference but doesn't have a dataset, adding a data region will open the Dataset Properties dialog. Regardless of the approach chosen, you must have a dataset in place for a functional data region.

4. In the Query tab (see Figure 4.10), rename the dataset to *SalesOrder*.

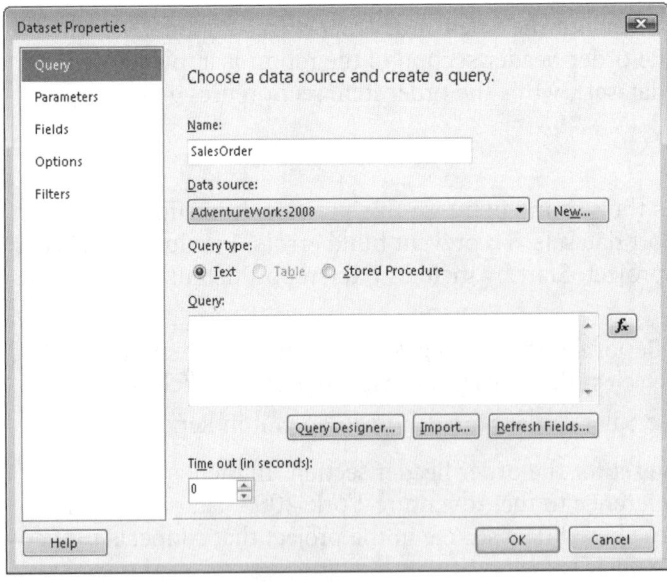

Figure 4.10 Use the Query tab of the Dataset Properties dialog box to establish a data source reference and set up the dataset query.

You can author three types of queries. Use the Text query type to create free-form command text. Use the Table query type to retrieve all data from a single database table (note that this query type is not supported by the .NET SqlClient provider). Use the Stored Procedures query type to specify a stored procedure that retrieves the data you want to use. You can also specify a query timeout to cancel a long running query. By default, the query will not time out.

You can click the Import button to import the query from a file or another report definition. Alternatively, you can initiate the import action within the query designer, as you will do next. Finally, you can refresh the dataset fields by clicking the Refresh Fields button. When you do this, Report Designer executes the query and updates the dataset fields based on the columns returned by the query.

5. Click the Query Designer button.

Report Designer opens the generic query designer, which is the default query designer for relational data sources.

Importing queries

The generic query designer is the default query building tool for most supported relational data sources. It doesn't validate the query syntax during query design. In other words, it passes the query verbatim to the data source. You will use the generic query designer to execute stored procedures, work with the XML data provider, and author complex queries that are not supported in the graphical query designer. For your convenience, all query designers support importing external query statements. Let's demonstrate this feature.

1. Click the Import toolbar button. Notice that the file dialog box defaults to *.sql and *.rdl files.
2. Navigate to the SalesOrder.sql file, which is included in the Queries folder with the source code for this chapter, and click Open.

NOTE If you import datasets from a report definition file, Report Designer will open an Import Query dialog to let you preview the dataset or pick a dataset if the source report includes multiple datasets. You can import only one dataset at the time.

The generic query designer loads the query text, as shown in Figure 4.11. If you scroll down the query text, you will see that it defines a @SalesOrderNumber query parameter.

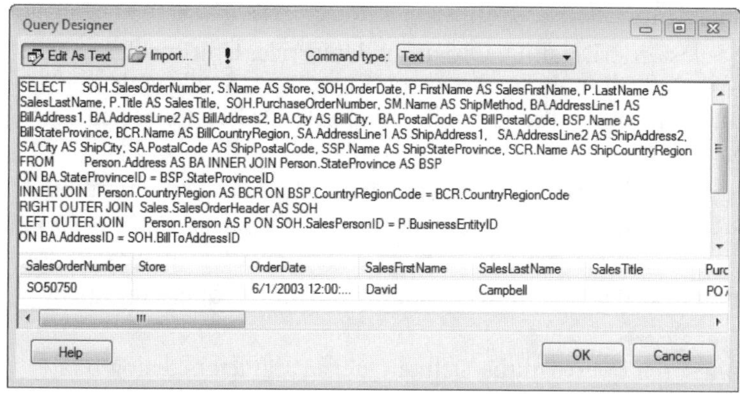

Figure 4.11 Use the generic query designer to execute pass-through queries.

3. Click the Run toolbar button to test the query. In the Define Query Parameters dialog box that follows, enter *SO50750* as a parameter value for the SalesOrderNumber parameter and click OK.

4. Click OK to return to the Dataset Properties dialog box and OK again to return to Report Designer.

   The Report Data window shows the SalesOrder dataset. Since the dataset query contains a query parameter, Report Designer has generated a SalesOrderNumber report parameter, which you can find under the Parameters node.

4.3.3 Using the Graphical Query Designer

The graphical query designer is a query building tool used in several Microsoft products. It provides a visual design environment that auto-generates the query as you pick columns. This makes it appealing to novice users who are not familiar with the Transact-SQL syntax. The graphical query designer always validates the query syntax but it doesn't support all Transact-SQL features. For example, it doesn't support executing multiple SQL statements or representing graphically UNION queries.

Auto-generating queries
Let's use the graphical query designer to author the query for the SalesOrderDetail dataset. The source code includes the SalesOrderDetail query (SalesOrderDetail.sql). You can import it in the graphical query designer in case you want to skip the next steps.

1. In the Report Data window, right-click the AdventureWorks2008 data source and click Add Dataset.
2. In the Dataset Properties window, rename the dataset to *SalesOrderDetail,* and click the Query Designer button.
3. In the generic query designer, toggle the Edit As Text button to switch to the generic query designer.

   The graphical query designer connects to the data source and retrieves the database schema.
4. Right-click the diagram (topmost) pane and click Add Table. In the Add Table dialog box, select the SalesOrderHeader, SalesOrderDetail, and Product tables, and click OK.

   The graphical query designer detects the referential integrity constraints among the tables and auto-generates a SELECT statement.
5. In the diagram pane, check the SalesOrderDetailID, OrderQty, UnitPrice, UnitPriceDiscount, CarrierTrackingNumber, and SalesOrderID columns from the SalesOrderDetails table, the ProductNumber and Name columns from the Product table, and SalesOrderNumber column from the SalesOrderHeader table.
6. In the Grid pane, uncheck the Output checkbox next to the SalesOrderNumber column because we don't need it in the query results. In the Filter column, enter *@SalesOrderNumber* to parameterize the query.
7. Change the Sort Type of the SalesOrderID column to Ascending to sort the query results by this column.
8. Click the Run toolbar button to test the query. In the Define Query Parameters dialog box, enter *SO50750* for a value of the SalesOrderNumber parameter.
9. Click OK to return to the Dataset Properties dialog box and OK again to return to Report Designer.

Implementing a dataset calculated field

A dataset calculated field is an expression-based field that the report author adds to the dataset definition. You can implement calculated fields at the query, dataset, and report levels.

- Query calculated field—Consider a query-level calculated field when you want to add a calculated column to the query results using the syntax of the underlying data source.
- Dataset calculated field—You can extend the dataset definition with calculated fields. Consider this approach when you want to reuse the same calculation more than once on the report, and defining a calculated query field is not an option.
- Report calculated field—You can also add a calculated column to a data region by using a field expression, as demonstrated in chapter 3.

Dataset calculated fields use the same expression syntax as fields on the report. They can call external code if more complex expressions are needed to derive the field value. However, calculated fields cannot use aggregate functions, which means you cannot sum values of other fields in the dataset. Let's implement a LineTotal dataset calculated field that represents the order item total.

1. In the Report Data window, double-click the SalesOrderDetail dataset.
2. In the Dataset Properties dialog box, click the Fields tab.

   The Fields tab lets you work with the dataset fields. The Field Name column shows the field name that is used on the report. The Field Source column shows the name of the underlying column to which the field is bound. To rename a field, change the Field Name column. If the name of the underlying column has changed, use this tab to re-bind the field by changing the Field Source column. To rearrange a field, click the up or down arrow. Changing the field position is for your convenience only and has no effect on exiting reports.
3. Click the Add button and click Calculated Field, as shown in Figure 4.12. A shortcut for combing the last three steps is to right-click the dataset in the Report Data window and click Add Calculated Field.

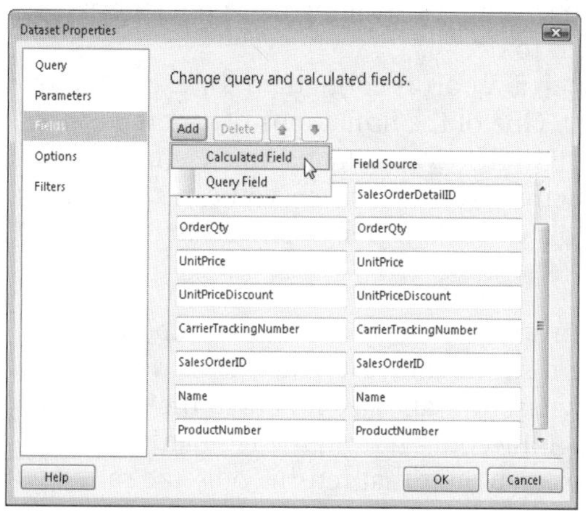

Figure 4.12 Use the Fields tab to rename fields, change field bindings, and add calculated fields.

4. Enter *LineTotal* as a field name and click the *fx* button to open the Expression dialog box.
5. Enter the following expression:

```
=Iif(Fields!UnitPrice.Value is Nothing, 0, (Fields!UnitPrice.Value *
(1.0- Fields!UnitPriceDiscount.Value))*Fields!OrderQty.Value)
```

You can check for null values in the query results by using the Visual Basic Nothing keyword. The Iif operator checks whether the UnitPrice is null and returns zero if this is the case. Otherwise, it computes the order item total by multiplying the field value, the order quantity, and the discount percentage.

6. Click OK to close the Expression dialog box and OK again to close the Dataset Properties dialog box.

Report Designer adds the LineTotal field to the SalesOrderDetail definition in the Report Data window. At this point, you should be able to preview the report successfully.

4.3.4 Filtering Datasets

While we are on the Dataset Properties tab, let's demonstrate another dataset feature. Suppose that you cannot parameterize the dataset query to restrict data at the data source. For example, the database administrator may have created a stored procedure that returns all sales orders but doesn't accept any parameters. At the same time, you need to filter the data on the report to show only the orders submitted by the employee viewing the report.

Another scenario where filters could be useful is when you have multiple data regions, such as tables, matrices, and charts, bound to the same dataset. In this case, filters let you restrict data on a per-region basis without affecting the data displayed in the other regions.

Understanding dataset filters

The Filters tab in the Dataset Properties dialog box lets you define filter conditions to restrict the dataset results. Similar to a SQL WHERE clause, a dataset filter limits the data by applying criteria that excludes rows. Unlike a WHERE clause, however, the filter is applied *after* data has been retrieved from the data source. For example, if there are one million sales orders in the AdventureWorks2008 database, the dataset will contain one million records before the filter is applied. Therefore, you should use dataset filters with caution since they may impact performance. You should always try to perform as much data manipulation as possible at the database level. This includes filtering, grouping, and sorting. Performing these operations quickly and efficiently is what databases are designed to do.

Report caching can also benefit from filters. When a report is configured for execution or snapshot caching, its results are shared among users. One of the limitations of report caching is that for security reasons you cannot pass the User!UserID to a query parameter (for example, to return only the data that applies to the interactive user). However, you can set up a dataset filter whose expression uses User!UserID. This scenario is demonstrated in chapter 12.

Implementing a dataset filter

The Sales Order with Filter report shows you how to apply a dataset filter. This report is a simplified version of the Sales Order report because it shows only the order header section. I removed the WHERE clause from SalesOrder query to return all sales orders in the AdventureWorks2008 database. In addition, I added the LoginID column from the HumanResources.Employee table to the query results. Let's set up a filter that returns only the sales orders where the employee's login matches the login of the interactive user.

1. Double-click the SalesOrder dataset. In the Dataset Properties dialog box, click the Filters tab.
2. Click Add to create a new filter.
3. Expand the Expression drop-down list and select the LoginID field, as shown in Figure 4.13.

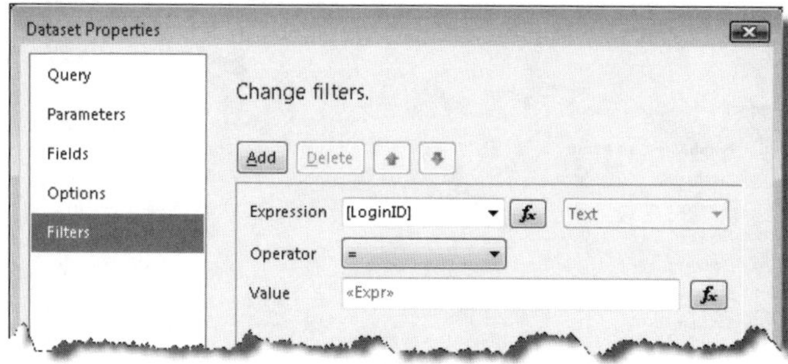

Figure 4.13 You can set up one or more dataset filters to exclude rows after the query is executed.

Although we won't be using this feature in this exercise, notice that you can create a filter that is based on an expression, such as the expression [LastName] & ' ' & [FullName] to filter on the employee full name

4. Expand the Operator drop-down list and notice that Reporting Services supports common filter operators, such as Equal, Like, Less Than, Greater Than, Top, Bottom, Between, and so on. Leave the Equal (=) operator pre-selected.
5. In the Value field, enter *=User!UserID*. Make sure to append the equal sign in front since this is an expression. If you omit the equal sign, the filter won't work.

What you've accomplished is setting up a filter that returns only dataset rows where the LoginID column matches the Windows logon of the interactive user (assuming the report server is configured for Windows security). Of course, when you run the report, no data will be shown. This is because your Windows logon won't match any of the logins in the HumanResources.Employee table. To see data on the report, you can replace one of the Adventure Works logins with your login in the format domain\username. Alternatively, you can use a static filter expression by replacing the Value expression in the filter with a valid Adventure Works login, such as ="adventure-works\tsvi0".

4.3.5 Working with Stored Procedures

Database developers and administrators favor stored procedures because they centralize security, administration, and maintenance of common routines, and improve performance. SQL Server supports Transact-SQL stored procedures and, since version 2005, CLR stored procedures that are written in .NET code. You can call both types of stored procedures from a report.

NOTE If a stored procedure returns multiple rowsets (executes multiple SELECT statements), only the first rowset is processed by the report. If you need all results, consider implementing a wrapper stored procedure that merges the multiple rowsets in a temporary table and returns all rows with one SELECT statement.

Using T-SQL stored procedures

The TSQL Stored Procedure report, which Figure 4.14 shows, demonstrates these features:

- Using Transact-SQL stored procedures in dataset queries.
- Hiding duplicate rows in a table region.
- Displaying a custom message if the query returns no data.

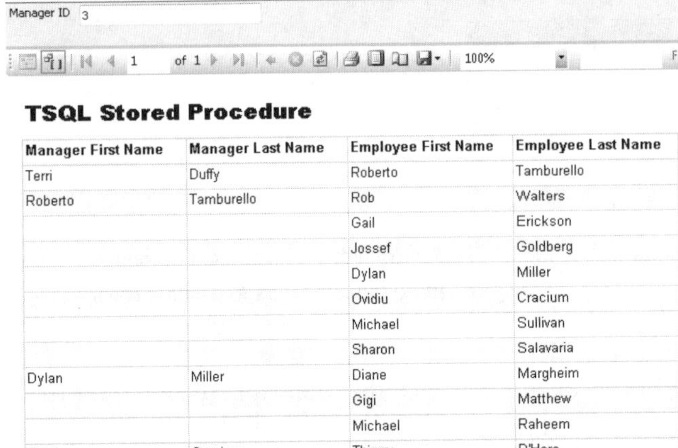

Manager ID 3

TSQL Stored Procedure

Manager First Name	Manager Last Name	Employee First Name	Employee Last Name
Terri	Duffy	Roberto	Tamburello
Roberto	Tamburello	Rob	Walters
		Gail	Erickson
		Jossef	Goldberg
		Dylan	Miller
		Ovidiu	Cracium
		Michael	Sullivan
		Sharon	Salavaria
Dylan	Miller	Diane	Margheim
		Gigi	Matthew
		Michael	Raheem
Ovidiu	Cracium	Thierry	D'Hers
		Janice	Galvin

Figure 4.14 This report uses a Transact-SQL stored procedure to show the employees that report directly or indirectly to a given manager.

The report uses the uspGetManagerEmployees stored procedure that is included in the AdventureWorks2008 database. This stored procedure takes a manager identifier as an input parameter and uses a recursive query to return employees who directly or indirectly report to this manager.

1. In the Report Data window, right-click the AdventureWorks2008 data source and click Add Dataset.

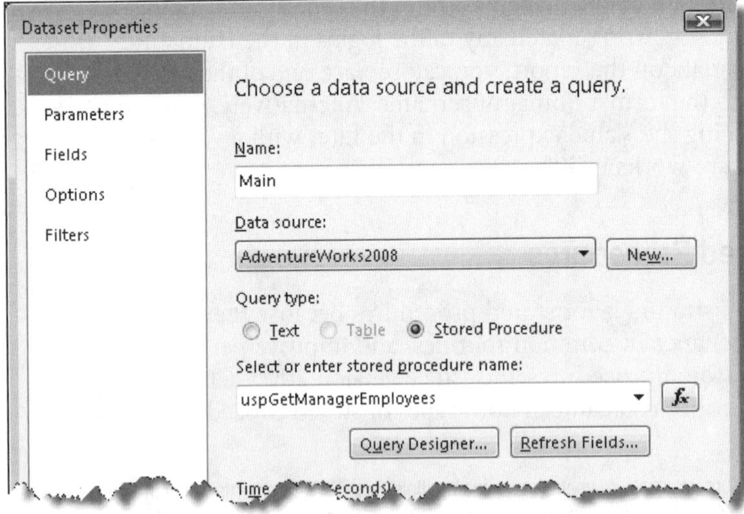

Figure 4.15 Change the Query Type option to Stored Procedure to see a list of all user-defined functions and stored procedures in the database.

2. In the Dataset Properties (Query tab), name the dataset *Main*.
3. Select the Stored Procedure query type.

   You can enter the stored procedure name or select the stored procedure from the drop-down list, which shows all user-defined functions and stored procedures in the database. CLR stored procedures are excluded from the list.

4. Expand the Select or Enter Stored Procedure Name drop-down list and select the uspGetManagerEmployees stored procedure, as shown in Figure 4.15.

5. Optionally, to test the stored procedure, click the Query Designer button. In the generic query designer, click the Run toolbar button. In the Define Query Parameters dialog box, enter 3 as a value for the @BusinessEntityID parameter.

   Click OK to close the Dataset Properties dialog. Report Designer executes the stored procedure and shows the dataset fields of the Main dataset in the Report Data window.

6. Back to Report Designer, drag a table region to the report area and add a fourth column to it by right-clicking on the third column and clicking Insert Column ⇨ Right.
7. Bind the detail cells to the Manager First Name, Manager Last Name, First Name, and Last Name fields.

   Preview the report and notice that the manager's first and last names are duplicated for each of his subordinates. To fix this, you can create a row group to group by manager. Alternatively, you can simply hide the duplicated values. Let's demonstrate the latter approach.

8. Select the ManagerFirstName and ManagerLastName details cells. In the Properties window, expand the HideDuplicates property and set it to Main, which is the name of the dataset.

   You can display a custom message when the data region has no data.

9. Select the table region and enter *No Employees Found* in its NoRowsMessage property. Preview the report with for BusinessEntityID of 3 and 0 to test the changes.

Using CLR stored procedures

A CLR stored procedure is a SQL Server stored procedure written in .NET code. Consider CLR stored procedures when you need complex programming logic to prepare report data at the data source level. For example, you may need to merge data from many SELECT statements and evaluate complex business rules that require .NET code. To avoid "chatty" network round trips, you can package the .NET code as a CLR stored procedure. You need Visual Studio 2005 or later to implement SQL Server projects and CLR stored procedures.

REAL LIFE One of my real-life projects involved implementing an ad hoc reporting tool to let business users auto-generate reports. The business user would specify what columns and level of detail the user wanted to see on the report. The ad hoc reporting tool would serialize the report definition and forward it to a custom data gatherer module that would analyze the report object and generate the data. We implemented the data gatherer as a CLR stored procedure.

The book source code includes a CLR project. It includes a simple GetOrders CLR stored procedure whose code is shown below.

```
[Microsoft.SqlServer.Server.SqlProcedure]
public static void GetOrders (DateTime date) {
      using (SqlConnection conn = new SqlConnection("context connection=true")) {
      conn.Open();
      SqlCommand cmd = new SqlCommand("select * from Sales.SalesOrderHeader
                where OrderDate=@OrderDate", conn);
      cmd.Parameters.Add(new SqlParameter("@OrderDate", date));
      SqlContext.Pipe.ExecuteAndSend(cmd);
   }
}
```

GetOrders returns all customer orders for a given date that is passed as an input argument. It opens a context connection to the database to which it is deployed. Then, it prepares a SqlCommand object to retrieve all sales orders whose order date matches the input date. Finally, it uses the SqlContext object to execute the command and pipe back the results to the report. To deploy GetOrders to SQL Server, complete the following steps:

1. In SQL Server Management Studio, connect to the AdventureWorks2008 database. Enable the AdventureWorks2008 database for CLR integration by executing the following statements:

```
sp_configure 'clr enabled', 1
GO
RECONFIGURE
GO
```

2. In the project properties of the CLR project, verify that the connection string in the Database tab points to the AdventureWorks2008 database.
3. In the Solution Explorer, right-click the project node and click Deploy.

Order Date 7/1/2004

CRL Stored Procedure

Order Number	Status	Tax Amt	Freight	SubTotal
SO74148	5	2.7992	0.8748	34.99
SO74149	5	2.1824	0.6820	27.28

Figure 4.16 This report retrieves data from a CRL stored procedure.

The CLR Stored Procedure report, shown in Figure 4.16, demonstrates how a dataset query can invoke a CLR stored procedure. As it stands, the .NET SqlClient data provider treats CLR stored procedures differently than regular stored procedures. Consequently, CLR stored procedures won't show up on the Stored Procedure drop-down list in the Dataset Properties dialog box. Instead, you need to execute them as text.

4. Create a new dataset and open the generic query designer.
5. Enter the following command text:

```
EXEC dbo.GetOrders @OrderDate
```

6. Click the Run Query button and enter *7/4/2004* as a parameter value.

The report also demonstrates how to work with date parameters. If you double-click the OrderDate parameter in the Report Data window to open its properties, you will see that its type is set to Date/Time. Consequently, Reporting Services displays a calendar control in the report toolbar to help the user select a date.

NOTE My Implementing Smart Reports with the Microsoft Business Intelligence Platform article (see Resources) demonstrates another scenario that benefits from CLR stored procedures. The Sales Forecast report featured in the article calls a CLR stored procedure that leverages the Analysis Services data mining capabilities to generate forecasted data.

Working with expression-based queries

An expression-based query uses a Reporting Services expression to generate the command text. For example, suppose that you want to extend the CLR Stored Procedure report to let the user pick a date within the last ten years of the current date.

One way to implement this is to define available values for the OrderDate parameter that returns dates for the past ten years. If the user doesn't pick a valid date, the report won't run. Another approach could be to use an expression-based query text, as the Dynamic Query report demonstrates. This approach is more flexible because it lets you change the query statement at run time.

```
=String.Format ("EXEC dbo.GetOrders '{0}'", Iif (Parameters!OrderDate.Value>DateTime.Now.AddYears( -10),
Parameters!OrderDate.Value, DateTime.MinValue))
```

This query executes the same GetOrders CLR Stored procedure but changes its argument at run time. If the user has entered an invalid date, the query executes but returns no data. The Iif expression checks if the selected date by the user (Parameters!OrderDate.Value) is within ten years of the current selection. If this is the case, the user date is passed to GetOrders. Otherwise, the report passes the minimum date of the .NET DateTime date type. This results in no rows.

TIP When working with dates, you can use both the Visual Basic date-related functions, such as Today, DateAdd, Year, and the members of the .NET DateTime structure, such as Now, AddYears, and so on.

None of the query designers support expression-based queries, which is why the Report Data Query menu is disabled when you right-click a dataset that uses an expression-based query. This means that you cannot auto-generate the dataset fields. To work around this limitation, I recommend you use the following procedure to work with expression-based queries:

1. Use the generic query designer or graphical query designer to test a regular query that returns the same dataset schema. Alternatively, you can add the dataset fields manually using the Fields tab of the Dataset Properties.
2. In the Dataset Properties dialog box (Query tab), click the *fx* button next to the query text to change the query text to an expression. Once this is done, you will no longer be able to use any of the query designers to work with the query.

Given that Reporting Services expressions can call custom code, using expression-based queries offers a lot of flexibility. This flexibility comes with a cost. If you use them, you need to be aware that expression-based queries are susceptible to SQL injection attacks. SQL injection happens when some (malicious) SQL code is appended to a legitimate SQL statement contained within the report query. For example, if a report uses a free-form expression-based statement, a hacker could pass another SQL statement to a string report parameter, such as a data modification statement, to change, append or delete data. You should never trust report parameters! Consider restricting string parameters by providing available values. For added security, use stored procedures and validate input parameters.

Now that you've seen how to work with dataset queries, let's make them more flexible by using parameters.

4.4 Working with Report Parameters

Most real-life reports use parameters to restrict the data on a report, connect related reports together, and vary report presentation. For example, the Product Sales by Category report you authored in chapter 3 includes month and year report parameters to let the user filter data. Reporting Services supports flexible parameter options to help you address more advanced reporting needs.

4.4.1 Understanding Report Parameters

Recall that Reporting Services is a server-based platform. Report definitions are published to the server so they can be shared by all authorized users. From an end user perspective, a published report is like a black box that takes report parameters as input and returns the exported report, as shown in Figure 4.17. The only option available to end users for personalizing the report content and appearance is via report parameters.

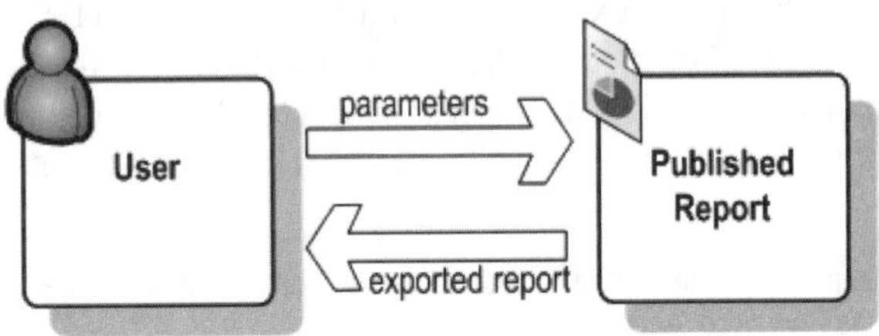

Figure 4.17 End users can pass parameters to the report to control the report data and presentation.

Common ways to use parameters

Here are some common reporting needs where parameters can help:

- Filter data at the data source—You can pass a parameter value to a dataset query to restrict the data returned by the query.
- Implement row-level security—A sensitive report can pass the user identity as a query parameter, so the data source returns only the rows the user is authorized to see.
- Set up cascading parameters—A parameter can control the possible values of another report parameter.
- Control report appearance—You can write expressions that change the report appearance, such as hiding a table column, based on a parameter value.

Reporting Services supports two parameter types: query parameters and report parameters.

Understanding query parameters

Report Designer creates a query parameter when you use a variable (placeholder) inside the query statement. For example, the following query includes a @OrderDate variable:

```
select * from Sales.SalesOrderHeader where OrderDate = @OrderDate
```

The syntax of the query variable depends on the type of the data provider. With the SQL .NET provider, you use named parameters, such as @OrderDate. With the Oracle data extension, you use named parameters prefixed with a colon, such as :OrderDate. The OLE DB provider doesn't support named parameters, but you can use the question mark (?) to denote query variables.

A query parameter is private to the containing dataset. You cannot access query parameters in expressions because they are not added to the Parameters collection. Similarly, you cannot manage the query parameters of a published report because they are not available in the management tools, such as Report Manager. Instead, to change query parameters, you need to open the report definition in Report Designer and use the Parameters tab in the Dataset Properties dialog box to view and change the query parameters.

Understanding report parameters

While query parameters are private to the dataset, report parameters are public. They appear in the report toolbar to let report users set their values. Report Designer generates report parameters automatically from query parameters. For example, when Report Designer encounters the @OrderDate placeholder in the dataset query, it performs the following actions:

1. It creates a @OrderDate query parameter.

2. It creates an OrderDate report parameter.
3. It links the query parameter to the report parameter so the value of the report parameter is passed on to the query when the report is run.

If necessary, you can break the association between query and report parameters. Suppose you need to pass the user identity (User!UserID) to the data source to return only rows the user is authorized to see. In this case, you don't need a report parameter because you can obtain the user identify from User!UserID. To disassociate parameters, set the value of the query parameter to User!UserID and delete the auto-generated report parameter.

The reverse is true as well. You can have a report parameter that is not used in a query. For example, you may need a report parameter solely to control the appearance of the report or to define a filter expression that is applied to the dataset results.

When setting up a report parameter, you define the parameter type, which could be one of the following types: Boolean, Date/Time, Integer, Float, and Text. In the report toolbar, the parameter is displayed in a textbox for string, integer, or float types. For Date/Time, a calendar control is used. A radio button is used for a Boolean type.

You can reference the Parameters global collection to use report parameters in expressions. You can manage report parameters of a deployed report in Report Manager (native mode) or SharePoint (SharePoint integration mode).

4.4.2 Designing a Parameterized Report

Next, let's go through the steps of implementing a Sales Orders by Date report that demonstrates various parameter options. Figure 4.18 shows the finished report. The user can use the calendar control to pick a date (by default, the last date with sales orders is used). When the Date parameter is changed, the report refreshes and updates the Sales Order Number parameter to show only the orders submitted for this date. The user can select multiple order numbers to view multiple sales orders on the report.

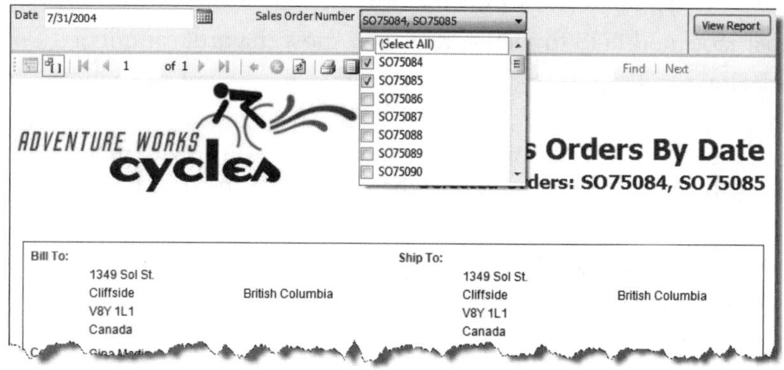

Figure 4.18 The Sales Orders by Date report lets the user select multiple orders for a given date.

Preparing the startup report

The Sales Order report, on which Sales Orders by Date is based on, is designed to display a single order. It used two datasets (SalesOrder dataset for the header section and SalesOrderDetail dataset for the detail section) and two side-by-side data regions (a list region for the header section and a table region for the detail section).

As it stands, Reporting Services doesn't let you join datasets at the report level. Consequently, you cannot relate the SalesOrder and SalesOrderDetail datasets to preserve the one-to-many relationship between order headers and order details across multiple orders. Instead, consider the following workarounds:

- Single query—The report can have a single SELECT statement that combines the master and detail rows. You can define appropriate groups in the data regions to create the master and details sections.
- Subreport—You can use a subreport for the detail section.
- Custom data extension—You can write a custom data processing extension that merges the datasets and returns a single dataset.

For the purpose of this demo, I chose the first approach to implement the Sales Orders by Date Start report, which you can use as a starting point for implementing the Sales Orders by Date report. The changes I've made to the Sales Orders by Date Start are as follows:

1. I merged the SalesOrderDetail dataset into the SalesOrder dataset and removed the WHERE clause.
2. In the Report Data window, I deleted the SalesOrderNumber report parameter.
3. I bound the OrderDetail table region to the SalesOrder dataset by changing its DataSetName property.
4. I nested the OrderDetail table region inside the OrderHeader list region. I accomplished this by dragging the table region inside the list region. Alternatively, cut the table region (Ctrl+X), select the list region, and paste the table region (Ctrl+V) inside the list region.
5. I changed the Details group of the OrderHeader list region. In the Row Groups pane, I double-clicked the OrderHeader_Details_Group group. In the Group Properties dialog box, I clicked Add to create a new group and selected [SalesOrderNumber] as a field to group on.

   Because of these changes, the list region starts a new group for each new order and propagates the group scope to the nested table region to show only the order items for this order.
6. I added a Sales Order Number label and field to the list region to show the order number.
7. I moved the Adventure Works logo and report title outside the list region to create a report header.
8. I changed the second paragraph of the Title textbox to "Selected Orders: ". You will modify the expression later on to show the sales order numbers of the orders that the user has selected.

   To avoid performance degradation, the SalesOrder dataset query includes a TOP 50 clause that returns only the first 50 sales orders in the Adventure Works database.

Creating a query parameter

Next, you will create a SalesOrderQuery parameter to filter the data returned by the report. Make the following changes to the Sales Order by Date Start report.

1. In the Report Data window, right-click the SalesOrder dataset and click Query to open it in the generic query designer (or the graphical query designer).
2. Append the following WHERE clause at the end of the SELECT statement:

```
WHERE SOH.SalesOrderID = @SalesOrderNumber
```

Since we target SQL Server, I used a named parameter in the query. Because we filter data on the primary key (SalesOrderID), the query will execute efficiently.

3. Execute the query. Enter *50750* as a value of the SalesOrderNumber query parameter. The query results should display all order items for order 50750.
4. Click OK to close the query designer.

Report Designer auto-generates a SalesOrderNumber report parameter and adds it to the Parameters node in the Report Data window.

5. Double-click the Sales Order dataset to open the Dataset Properties window.
6. Click the Parameters tab.

Note that Report Designer has generated a @SalesOrderNumber query parameter and set its value to [@SalesOrderHeader]. If you click the *fx* button next to the parameter, you will see that the [@SalesOrderHeader] token is a substitute for =Parameters!SalesOrderNumber.Value.

7. Preview the report. Note that the report now takes a Sales Order Number parameter.
8. In the Define Query Parameters dialog box, enter *50750* as a parameter value and click View Report.

The report should display a single order. This is because when the report is generated, the value of the report parameter is passed to the query parameter.

Understanding the parameter general properties

Let's take a moment to understand how the SalesOrderParameter is configured.

1. In the Report Data window, double-click the SalesOrderNumber parameter. Alternatively, you can right-click the SalesOrderNumber parameter and click Parameter Properties.

The Report Parameter Properties dialog box (see Figure 4.19) that follows lets you manage report parameters. Use the General tab to specify the parameter prompt text, data type, and visibility. The Prompt field specifies the parameter field label that will be displayed in the toolbar when the user views the report. By default, the report parameter will be visible to end users. Select the Hidden option to exclude the parameter from the report toolbar.

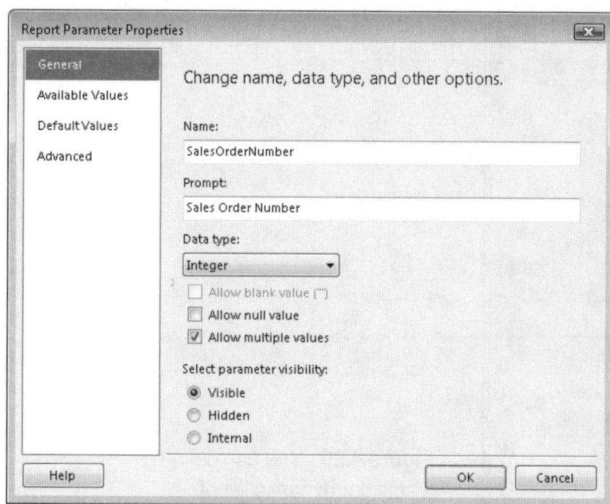

Figure 4.19 You can use the General tab of the Report Parameter Properties dialog box to specify the parameter prompt text, data type, and visibility.

A hidden parameter can still be set from another source, such as a report URL.This could be useful when you need to specify a report parameter as part of configuring a subscription to a parameterized report. You can also use a hidden parameter to pass some system settings to a report. For example, if you are report-enabling a custom application, you might want to pass some settings to a Settings report parameter. Since these settings are not meant to be accessed by end users, you can hide the Settings parameter from the user without hiding them from your application.

By contrast, an internal parameter can be modified only by the report author or administrator, and not by the user. You can think of an internal parameter as a private constant that is available internally, such as in report expressions, but not to external clients. For example, if you need to version report definitions, you can implement an internal parameter to store the report version. Each time a new report definition is deployed, the report administrator can use Report Manager to change the value of the internal parameter. Selecting the Internal option disables the Prompt field because the parameter is not available to end users.

I will cover the Available Values and Default Values tabs in the next sections. You can use the Advanced tab to overwrite the Reporting Services default auto-detection behavior for discovering whether the parameter are used in a query. This could be useful with execution snapshots and is explained in more detail in chapter 12.

Implementing available values

As it stands, the Sales Orders by Date report requires the user to enter the sales order number. Let's make it more user-friendly by letting the user pick the number from a drop-down list. To do so, we can set up available values for the parameter. You can define a static parameter value by entering a label and a value for each item, or you can reference a query that returns a dynamic list. Let's use the latter approach.

1. Create a new OrderNumbers dataset that uses the following query statement:

```
SELECT DISTINCT    SalesOrderID, SalesOrderNumber
FROM               Sales.SalesOrderHeader
ORDER BY           SalesOrderNumber
```

This query returns all distinct sales orders from the Sales.SalesOrderHeader table.

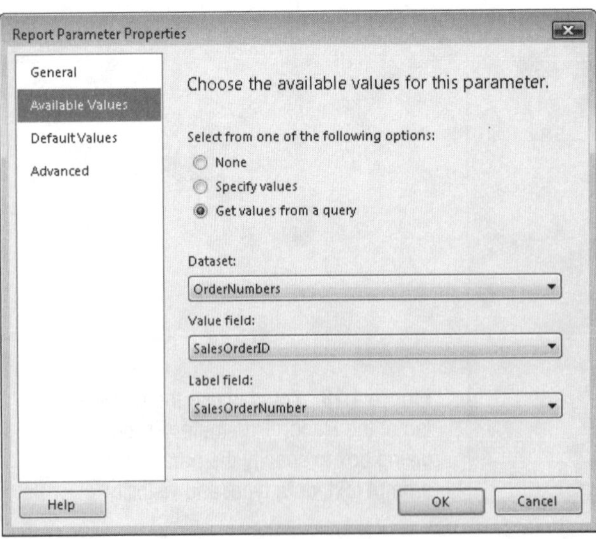

Figure 4.20 You can define a static or dynamic list of available parameter values.

2. In the Report Parameter Properties dialog box, click the Available Values tab.
3. Click the Get Values from a Query option, as shown in Figure 4.20.
4. Expand the Dataset drop-down list and select the OrderNumbers dataset.

   As I mentioned earlier, a report parameter can have a label and a value. The parameter label is what gets displayed to the user. The parameter value is typically used for internal purposes, such as passing the key of the selected item to the main dataset query. If you don't define a parameter label, the parameter value will be displayed to the user.
5. Expand the Value Field drop-down list and select the SalesOrderID field.
6. Expand the Label Field drop-down list and select the SalesOrderNumber field. Click OK.
7. Preview the report.

   Notice that the Sales Order Number parameter is now a drop-down list. However, it presents a long list of available values and the user cannot locate an order number easily. In the next exercise, you will implement a Date report parameter and configure the Sales Order Number as a cascading parameter.

Implementing cascading parameters

A cascading parameter is a report parameter that depends on another parameter. Cascading parameters are typically used to limit the number of available parameter values based on the selected value of another parameter.

NOTE Sometimes, the "cascade" effect is a side effect of using a complex RDL expression as parameter default/valid values or labels. Reporting Services may not be able to fully parse all RDL expressions (due to custom code, assemblies, Visual Basic run-time functions). In that case, it assumes it is a complex expression that references previous parameters and you get the cascade effect.

1. In the Report Data window, right-click Parameters and click Add Parameter.
2. In the Report Parameters dialog box, enter *Date* for both the parameter name and prompt, and change the parameter date type to Date/Time.

   We don't need to link the Date parameter to the SalesOrder dataset because we don't need to pass it to the query.
3. Preview the report and notice that the Date parameter appears after the Sales Order Number parameter.
4. In the Report Data window, select the Date parameter and click the Move Up toolbar button to move it before the Sales Order Number parameter.
5. Preview the report to test the changes. Notice that although you can change the date, the Sales Order Number parameter doesn't refresh to show only the orders for the selected date.
6. In the Report Data window, right-click the OrderNumbers dataset and click Query.
7. Change the OrderNumbers query as follows and click OK.

```
SELECT DISTINCT   SalesOrderID, SalesOrderNumber
FROM              Sales.SalesOrderHeader
WHERE             OrderDate = @Date
ORDER BY          SalesOrderNumber
```

   This query returns only sales orders whose order date matches the Date parameter. Since the Date report parameter already exists, Report Designer doesn't create a new parameter but links the @Date query parameter to the existing Date report parameter.

8. Preview the report. Enter *7/4/2004* in the Date parameter or use the calendar control to pick a date. If you entered the date manually, press the Tab key to let Report Designer refresh the report.

   The report refreshes and the Sales Order Number parameter now contains only those orders whose order date is 7/4/2007. This is because the Sales Order Number parameter depends on the Date parameter.

Setting up a default parameter value

If the parameter doesn't have a default value and Allow Null Values is off, Reporting Services will prompt the user to specify a parameter value to view the report. However, if the parameter has a default value, Reporting Services will proceed with the report generation. Suppose that users would like the Date parameter to default to the last date for which there is an order. To accomplish this, set up a default value for the Date parameter, as follows:

1. Create a new LatestDate dataset which uses the following query:

```
select max(OrderDate) as OrderDate from Sales.SalesOrderHeader
```

   This query selects the latest order date from the Sales.SalesOrderHeader table.

2. Open the properties of the Date parameter and click the Default Values tab, as shown in Figure 4.21.

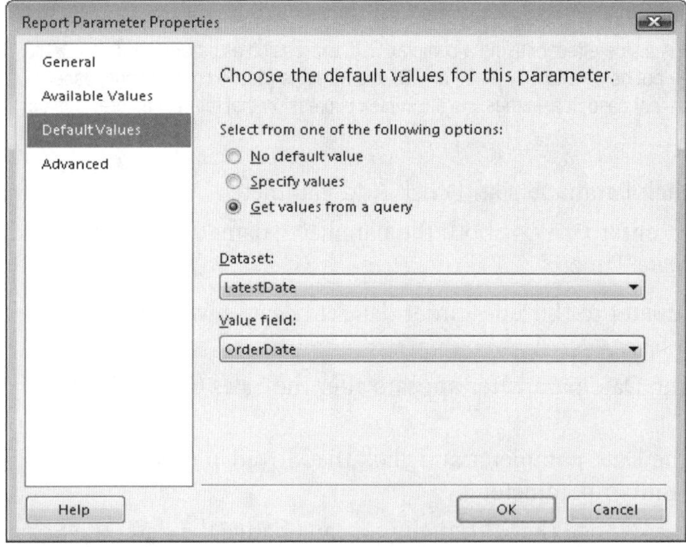

Figure 4.21 You can define an explicit or data-driven default parameter value.

   The Specify Values option lets you enter a static or expression-based default value. For example, to default the Date parameter to the current date, enter =Today(). The Get Values From a Query option lets you reference a dataset that returns the default value.

3. Click the Get Values From a Query option.
4. Expand the Dataset drop-down list and select the LatestDate dataset.
5. Expand the Value field and select the OrderDate field.
6. Preview the report.

   The Date parameter should now default to 7/31/2004 because this is the latest order date.

Configuring multivalued parameters

To let the user select multiple orders, we need to configure the SalesOrderNumber parameter as a multivalued parameter.

1. In the Report Data window, double-click the SalesOrderNumber parameter.
2. In the General tab, click the Allow Multiple Values checkbox.

When a report parameter is configured as a multivalued parameter, Reporting Services automatically generates a comma-delimited string of the selected parameter values and passes the string to the query parameter. To support multivalued parameters, we will need to change the WHERE clause of the SalesOrder dataset.

3. Right-click the SalesOrder dataset and click Edit Query. Change the query WHERE clause, as follows:

```
WHERE SOH.SalesOrderID IN (@SalesOrderNumber)
```

Make sure to include the parenthesis surrounding the @SalesOrderNumber. The parentheses enclose the list of individual values selected by the user. For example, if the user selects orders 50750 and 50751, this is how Reporting Services rewrites the query:

```
WHERE SOH.SalesOrderID IN (50750, 50751)
```

Reporting Services automatically handles the parameter data type by surrounding each value with single quotes if the parameter data type is Text. In addition, Reporting Services appends a Select All parameter value to the drop-down list to let the user select or unselect all values.

NOTE The Select All feature may produce an inefficient query with a large parameter list because it may result in a huge IN clause. To make things worse, there is no way to remove Select All. Realizing the performance issues surrounding Select All, Microsoft turned off this feature in SQL Server 2005 Service Pack 1 but brought it back in Service Pack 2 due to the popular demand. Brian Welcker, a former Group Program Manager for Reporting Services, covered the Select All story well in his blog (see Resources).

Reporting Services supports several functions and properties to use multivalued parameters in expressions.

Table 4.2 Expression examples with multivalued parameters

Function	Example	Description
IsMultiValue property	=Parameters!SalesOrderNumber.IsMultiValue	Returns True if the parameter is a multivalued parameter.
Count property	=Parameters!SalesOrderNumber.Count	Returns the number of the selected parameter values.
Value(n) property	=Parameters!SalesOrderNumber(0)	Returns the first selected parameter value.
Split function	=Split("50750, 50751", ",")	Creates an array of parameter values. Use the Split function to set default values of a multivalued parameter.
Join function	=Join(Parameters!SalesOrderNumber.Label, ", ")	Generates a string by concatenating the selected values using the specified delimiter.

Let's use the Join function to show the selected order numbers on the report.

4. Double-click the Title textbox to put in edit mode.
5. Position the mouse pointer after the end of the second paragraph after "Selected Orders:". Right-click and click Create Placeholder.

6. In the Placeholder Properties dialog box (General tab), enter the following expression in the Value field. Click OK.

```
=Join(Parameters!SalesOrderNumber.Label, ", ")
```

This Join function obtains the selected parameter values and concatenates their labels by using a comma as a delimiter.

TIP You cannot reference the Select All parameter value. At the same time, you may need to default a multivalued parameter to Select All. Assuming you use a query for the available values, you can use the same query for the parameter default value. This works because setting Select All is the same as selecting all available values.

4.4.3 Securing Reports with Parameters

As I've mentioned before, you should never trust report parameters with sensitive reports. Even if you report-enable a custom application that validates the parameters, a hacker can easily intercept the parameter values and request the report by URL passing the same parameters. Next, I will present two techniques that show you how to use parameters with sensitive reports. To learn these techniques, we'll use the Sales Orders Restricted report. This report is based on the Sales Orders by Date report, but includes modifications that restrict access so that a user can view only his or her sales orders.

Restricting parameter values

The first technique leverages the parameter available values list. If the user passes a parameter value that doesn't have a match in the parameter valid values list, no data will be shown on the report. Let's change the Sales Orders by Date report to show only the sales orders associated with the user in the Sales Order Number parameter.

1. We don't need the Date parameter anymore. In the Report Data window, delete the LatestDate dataset and the Date report parameter.
2. Change the query of the OrderNumbers dataset, as follows:

```
SELECT DISTINCT    SOH.SalesOrderID, SOH.SalesOrderNumber
FROM               Sales.SalesOrderHeader AS SOH
INNER JOIN         HumanResources.Employee AS E ON SOH.SalesPersonID = E.BusinessEntityID
WHERE              E.LoginID = @UserID
ORDER BY           SOH.SalesOrderNumber
```

This query joins the SalesOrderHeader table and the Employee table and returns the sales orders where the employee's login matches the @UserID query parameter.

3. In the Report Data window, delete the UserID report parameter that Report Designer autogenerated when it detected the query changes.
4. Double-click the OrderNumbers dataset and click the Parameters tab.
5. Change the Parameter Value column of the @UserID query parameter to the =User!UserID expression.
6. To test the report, in SQL Server Management Studio, open the HumanResources.Employee table and update the LoginID column of the employee with BusinessEntityID of 283 (adventure-works\david8) to your Windows login in the format domain\login.
7. Preview the Sales Orders Restricted report and notice that the Sales Order Number parameter shows only the orders associated with this employee.

8. Deploy the report to the server.
9. Open Internet Explorer and request the report by URL, such as:

   ```
   http://localhost/ReportServer?/AMRS/Sales Orders Restricted&SalesOrderNumber=50750
   ```

   Notice that the report renders successfully because you (as employee 283) are associated with this sales order.
10. Next, submit a report request for a sales order which is not associated with employee 283, such as:

    ```
    http://localhost/ReportServer?/AMRS/Sales Orders Restricted&SalesOrderNumber=5075 1
    ```

    Notice that the report shows no data. To view the report, the user must choose a parameter value that is valid for him or her.

Implementing row-level data security
Many organizations implement home-grown security solutions to enforce security policies at the data source and return only data that the user is authorized to see. To implement row-level data security, a report can pass the user identity to the data source.

1. Change the WHERE clause of the SalesOrder dataset, as follows:

   ```
   WHERE (SOH.SalesOrderID IN (@SalesOrderNumber)) AND (E.LoginID = @UserID)
   ```
2. Delete the UserID report parameter that Report Designer auto-generates.
3. In the Report Data window, double-click the SalesOrder dataset and click the Parameters tab.
4. Change the Parameter Value column of the @UserID query parameter to the =User!UserID expression.

   At run time, the server passes the user identity to the @UserID query parameter, which in turn is passed to the data source. The resulting dataset contains only the sales orders associated with the employee.

4.5 Working with Other Data Sources

Besides SQL Server, Reporting Services includes data providers for other popular data sources. In this next section, I will demonstrate how you can integrate your reports with OLEDB-compatible data sources, XML data, Integration Services packages, and standard .NET providers.

4.5.1 Using Microsoft Access Databases

Microsoft Access is a popular desktop RDBMS and you may need to produce reports from it. The Northwind Orders report, shown in Figure 4.22, demonstrates how you can build a Reporting Services report from data in a Microsoft Access database. It is similar to the Sales Orders by Date report but displays sales order data from the Northwind sample database.

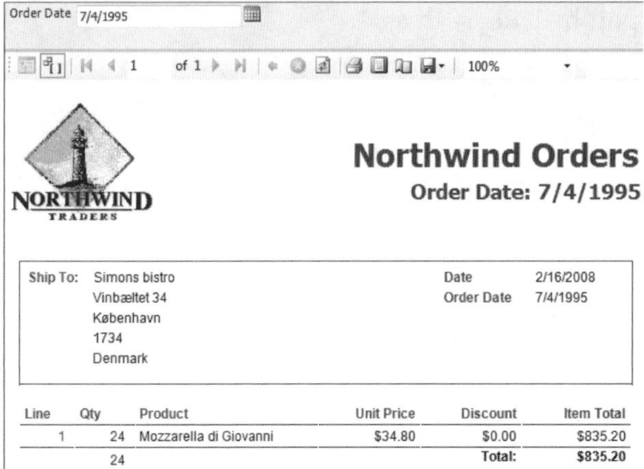

Figure 4.22 This report retrieves data from the Microsoft Access Northwind database.

Connecting to Microsoft Access

You can connect to Microsoft Access by using the Microsoft Jet OLE DB provider.

1. Create a new report and click the link in the report body to set up a data source.
2. In the Data Source Properties dialog box, select the OLE DB data provider and click Edit.
3. In the Connection Properties dialog box, select the Microsoft Jet 4.0 OLE DB Provider, as shown in Figure 4.23.

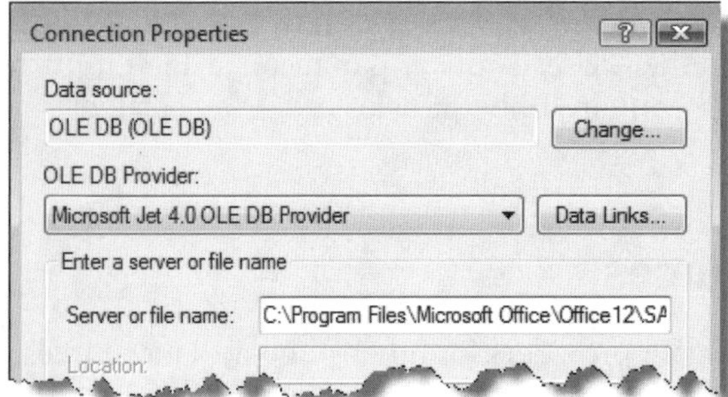

Figure 4.23 Use the Microsoft Jet OLE DB provider to connect to a Microsoft Access database.

4. In the Source or file name, enter the path to the Northwind database. By default, the path is \Program Files\Microsoft Office\Office12\SAMPLES\Nwind.mdb.
5. Click Test Connection to test the database connection and click OK.

Querying data

You can use either the generic or graphical query designers with Microsoft Access databases. Because you are using the OLE DB data provider, you need to denote query parameters with question marks.

1. In the generic query designer, add Order Detail, Orders, Customers, Employees, and Products tables.
2. Select the following columns: Orders.OrderID, Orders.OrderDate, Orders.RequiredDate, Orders.ShippedDate, Orders.ShipName, Orders.ShipAddress, Orders.ShipCity, Orders.ShipRegion, Orders.ShipCountry, Orders.ShipPostalCode, Orders.Freight, [Order

Details].UnitPrice, [Order Details].Quantity, [Order Details].Discount, Products.ProductName.

3. In the Filter Column of the graphical query designer, enter *?* in the OrderDate row. Click OK.

   Report Designer creates a new Parameter1 report parameter.

4. Rename the Parameter1 parameter to *OrderDate* and change its type to Date/Time.
5. In the dataset properties, link the Parameter1 query parameter to the OrderDate report parameter.

   Once the dataset is in place, you can lay out the report as usual.

4.5.2 Working with XML Data

XML is omnipresent nowadays. Web services communicate using XML messages that follow the SOAP protocol. Organizations exchange information described in XML. Because XML is so widely used, chances are you may need to author reports from XML documents. Reporting Services includes an XML data provider to help you access XML data sources and Web services from a report.

Understanding the XML data provider

Extensible Markup Language (XML) is designed to represent structured hierarchical data. The XML data provider lets you navigate the document structure and return a "flattened" two-dimensional dataset that Reporting Services reports can use. The XML data provider debuted in Reporting Services 2005 and remains unchanged in 2008. It supports three types of XML data sources:

- Web service—The XML provider can query Web services and parse the SOAP payloads.
- URL-based resources—The XML provider can connect to a URL-based resource, such as a web page, and parse the XML document that is returned.
- Embedded XML—You can embed the XML content inside the query statement. While embedding static XML inside the query may not seem very useful, recall that dataset queries can be expression-based and obtain the query statement from elsewhere. For example, the query expression may call custom code that returns an XML fragment. The query can shred the XML fragment and expose it as a two-dimensional dataset.

The XML data provider supports a proprietary XPath-like syntax for navigating the XML document, which is explained in Books Online (XML Query Syntax for Specifying XML Report Data topic) and in the Using XML and Web Service Data Sources paper by Jonathan Heide. Next, I will show you how to use the XML data provider to build reports that retrieve data from Web services. You will need Visual Studio 2008 to work with the solution.

Understanding the Customers Web service

The book source includes a Visual Studio solution (XML Provider.sln) that consists of a Report Server project (Reports) and an ASP.NET project. To simplify configuring the Web service, the ASP.NET project is configured to use the ASP.NET development server that listens on a static port 1966. It includes a Web service (Customers.asmx) that defines a single GetOrders web method.

```
[WebMethod]
public CustomerOrders.SalesOrderHeaderDataTable GetOrders(int customerID)
{
      CustomerOrdersTableAdapters.SalesOrderHeaderTableAdapter adapter =
      new CustomerOrdersTableAdapters.SalesOrderHeaderTableAdapter();
      CustomerOrders.SalesOrderHeaderDataTable orders = adapter.GetData(customerID);
      return orders;
}
```

This method returns a typed ADO.NET dataset whose schema is defined in the CustomerOrders.xsd file.

1. Double-click the CustomerOrders.xsd file to open it in the Visual Studio Dataset Designer.
2. Right-click the SalesOrderHeader dataset and click Configure. Notice that the dataset connects to the AdventureWorks2008 database and uses the following query to extract sales order data:

```
SELECT    CustomerID, OrderDate, SalesOrderNumber, SubTotal, TaxAmt, Freight, TotalDue
FROM      Sales.SalesOrderHeader
WHERE     (CustomerID = @CustomerID)
```

The GetOrders method accepts a customer identifier. The web method calls the GetData method of the table adapter to execute the query and return the dataset.

```
  <?xml version="1.0" encoding="utf-8" ?>
- <soap:Envelope xmlns:soap="http://schemas.xmlsoap.org/soap/envelope/" xmlns:xsi="http://www.w3.org/2001/XMLSchema-
    instance" xmlns:xsd="http://www.w3.org/2001/XMLSchema">
  - <soap:Body>
    - <GetOrdersResponse xmlns="http://tempuri.org/">
      - <GetOrdersResult>
        + <xs:schema id="NewDataSet" xmlns="" xmlns:xs="http://www.w3.org/2001/XMLSchema"
            xmlns:msdata="urn:schemas-microsoft-com:xml-msdata">
        - <diffgr:diffgram xmlns:msdata="urn:schemas-microsoft-com:xml-msdata" xmlns:diffgr="urn:schemas-microsoft-
            com:xml-diffgram-v1">
          - <DocumentElement xmlns="">
            - <SalesOrderHeader diffgr:id="SalesOrderHeader1" msdata:rowOrder="0">
                <CustomerID>676</CustomerID>
                <OrderDate>2001-07-01T00:00:00-04:00</OrderDate>
                <SalesOrderNumber>SO43659</SalesOrderNumber>
                <SubTotal>24643.9362</SubTotal>
                <TaxAmt>1971.5149</TaxAmt>
                <Freight>616.0984</Freight>
                <TotalDue>27231.5495</TotalDue>
              </SalesOrderHeader>
            - <SalesOrderHeader diffgr:id="SalesOrderHeader2" msdata:rowOrder="1">
```


Figure 4.24 This screenshot shows a sample SOAP payload from the GetOrders method.

Figure 4.24 shows an example of the SOAP response obtained by calling the GetOrders web method. The actual order data is found under the SalesOrderHeader element whose path is GetOrdersResponse/GetOrdersResult/diffgram/DocumentElement/SalesOrderHeader.

3. In Solution Explorer, right-click Customers.asmx and click View in Browser to start the ASP.NET development server. The Windows taskbar should show a new icon that says ASP.NET Development Server – Port 1966.

Using the XML data provider

Let's author a report that uses the built-in XML data provider to invoke the GetOrders web method. The report will display the sales orders submitted by a given customer. The XML Data Provider report included in the Reports project represents the finished report.

1. Create a new report. In the Report Data window, expand the New button and click Data Source to set up a data source reference.
2. In the Data Source Properties window, name the data source *Customers*.
3. Expand the Type drop-down list and click XML. Enter the following connection string:

```
http://localhost:1966/Web/Customers.asmx
```

This connection string specifies the URL address of the Customers.asmx Web service.

4. Click the Credentials tab and verify that the Use Windows Authentication option is selected. If the Web service is configured for Anonymous access, you can use the No Credentials option.
5. In the Report Data window, create a new dataset that references the Customers data source. Name the dataset *SalesOrder*.

   When you target the XML data provider, you must use the generic query designer to set up the report dataset.
6. Enter the following query statement:

```
<Query>
<Method Namespace="http://tempuri.org/" Name="GetOrders">
  <Parameters>
    <Parameter Name="customerID">
      <DefaultValue>1</DefaultValue>
    </Parameter>
  </Parameters>
</Method>
<SoapAction>http://tempuri.org/GetOrders</SoapAction>
<ElementPath IgnoreNamespaces="true">
     GetOrdersResponse/GetOrdersResult/diffgram/DocumentElement/SalesOrderHeader
</ElementPath>
</Query>
```

   The Method element specifies the name of the web method. The Parameters element enumerates the arguments of the web method. Embedding parameters in the query statement simplifies design-time testing. Alternatively, you can specify the query parameters in the Dataset Properties window, similar to how you define parameters when using the SQL Server data provider. Note that the parameter name is case-sensitive and must exactly match the name of the web method argument, which is customerID in our case.

   The SOAP request specification requires a SoapAction element that spells out the web method namespace and name. The element path specifies the XML path to the XML element you need to query. To facilitate XML navigation, the provider lets you omit the XML namespaces by including an IgnoreNamespaces="true" attribute in ElementPath.
7. In the Report Data window, double-click the CustomerID parameter. In the Parameters tab of the Dataset Properties window, verify that the CustomerID query parameter is linked to the CustomerID report parameter.
8. Execute the query in the generic query designer. If all is well, you should see four rows that represent the sales orders submitted by this customer.

   Now that the dataset is done, you can proceed with laying out the report.

4.5.3 Retrieving Data from Integration Services

Suppose that you need to transform data before it's shown on the report. Some common examples include cleansing the data, adding additional columns, or pre-aggregating the results. SQL Server Integration Services (SSIS) is designed to handle such data transformation processes. Reporting Services includes an experimental (yes, this means unsupported) data provider that lets you use an Integration Services package as a data source.

The SSIS Demo solution demonstrates how you can use Reporting Services with Integration Services. The SSIS demo report executes the CalculatedColumns.dtsx and displays the results.

Enabling the SQL Server Integration Services (SSIS) data provider
As I mentioned earlier, the SSIS data provider is disabled by default. To enable it, complete the following steps.

1. Open the RSReportDesigner.config file from the \Program Files\Microsoft Visual Studio 9.0\Common7\IDE\PrivateAssemblies folder.
2. In the Data section, locate the SSIS extension and remove the <! - - and - - > enclosing characters to uncomment the entire line.
3. In the Designer section, locate the SSIS extension and remove the <! - - and - - > enclosing characters to uncomment the entire line.
4. If BIDS is open, restart it to reflect the configuration changes.

To publish reports that use the SSIS provider, you need to enable this provider on the report server.

5. Open the RSReportServer.config file from the \Program Files\Microsoft SQL Server\MSRS10.MSSQLSERVER\Reporting Services\ReportServer folder.
6. In the <DATA> section, locate the SSIS extension and remove the <! - - and - - > enclosing characters to uncomment the entire line.

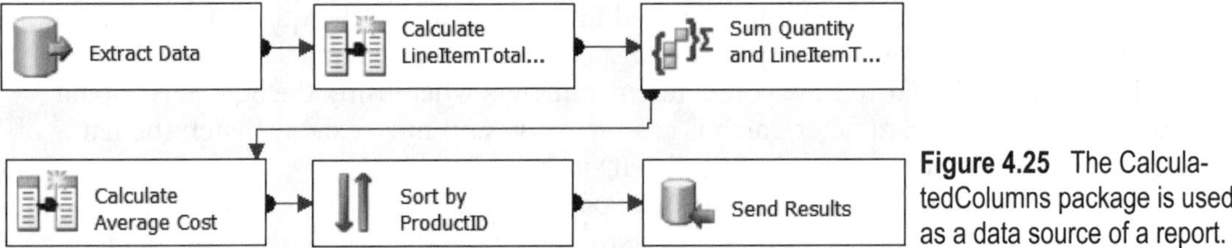

Figure 4.25 The CalculatedColumns package is used as a data source of a report.

About the CalculatedColumns package
The CalculatedColumns package (see Figure 4.25) is one of the Integration Services samples (see the Resources section for a download link) that come with SQL Server. The CalculatedColumns sample package extracts data from the Production.TransactionHistoryArchive table in the AdventureWorks2008 database and performs a series of data transformations, such as adding additional columns, aggregating data values, and sorting data.

To use a package as a data source for a report, the package must send results to a DataReader destination task. This requires that you make the following changes to the original package. The updated version of the package is included in the book source code.

1. In the Control Flow tab, delete the File System task (Copy File).
2. In the Data Flow tab, delete the Flat File Destination task (Load Data) and replace it with a DataReader Destination Task (Send Results).
3. Double-click Send Results. In the Advanced Editor dialog box, click the Input Columns tab, and check all columns.

As a result of these changes, the package sends the results to a data reader instead of a flat file.

Working with the SSIS data provider
Once the package is in place, you can use the SSIS data provider with a report, as the SSIS demo report demonstrates.

1. When setting up the report data source, choose the SSIS data provider.
2. Enter the following connection string:

```
-f " <path> \CalculatedColumns.dtsx"
```

Replace <path> with the path to the CalculatedColumns.dtsx file.

TIP You can use an expression-based connection string to pass a report parameter to a package variable. For example, to pass the value of the MyParameter report parameter to a MyVariable package variable, use the following expression-based connection string: ="/f c:\package.dtsx /Set \Package.Variables[MyVariable];" & Parameters!MyParameter.Value

3. Create a new dataset. Use the generic query designer to set up the data source query.
4. Enter the name of the DataReader Destination task, *Send Results* in our case, as query text.
5. Click the Exclamation button to execute the page and view results.

4.5.4 Using a .NET Framework Data Provider

A .NET Framework data provider is a component available from Microsoft or third-party vendors that implements the .NET System.Data interfaces and lets you retrieve data from a specific type of data source. Consider using a .NET data provider to extend the Reporting Services data architecture when no standard data providers meet your requirements.

NOTE In most cases, NET Framework providers will not support the full report design functionality in BIDS. If this hinders your ability to create the reports you want, consider implementing a custom data processing extension that wraps the .NET Framework provider.

About the DotNetDataProviderTemplate data provider

To demonstrate how you can integrate a .NET Framework provider in your reports, I will use the DotNetDataProviderTemplate data provider, which is one of the samples included with the .NET Framework (see the Sample .NET Framework Data Provider link in the Resources section). The book source code includes a DotNetDataProviderTemplate solution that contains the source code and a report to test it. You will need Visual Studio 2008 to work with the solution.

The Visual Studio documentation describes the source code in detail, so I'll just mention the interesting classes. The TemplateConnection class represents a data connection. For example, you can pass the connection string to the ConnectionString property. The TemplateCommand object represents a command object that executes a command statement and returns a data reader object back to the caller. The TemplateParameterCollection class represents the collection of parameters passed to the command object.

The SampleDb class simulates a data source that stores customer and order information. It returns a dataset consisting of five rows and three columns (id, name, and orderid).

Deploying the DotNetDataProviderTemplate data provider

Before using a .NET Framework data provider, you must deploy and register it with Report Designer and report server. Configuring the extension involves modifying several configuration files. For your convenience, I included my version of the affected configuration files in the Config folder, but do not just replace your configuration files with mine. Instead, use them as a reference to make changes to the files in your installation.

Deploying to Report Designer

To register the DotNetDataProviderTemplate provider with Report Designer, complete the following steps.

1. Copy the provider binaries, DotNetDataProviderTemplate.dll and DotNetDataProviderTemplate.pdb, to the Report Designer folder.

   The BIDS Report Designer default folder is \Program Files\Microsoft Visual Studio 9.0\Common7\IDE\PrivateAssemblies.

   TIP To automate the deployment from Visual Studio, I've created a post-build script (see the Build Events tab on the project properties of the DotNetDataProviderTemplate project) that copies the binaries to the BIDS Report Designer folder and report server bin folder when you build the project.

2. In the same folder, open the rsreportdesigner.config file and locate the <Data> element.
3. Add the following line after the last <Extension> element in the <Data> section:

```
<Extension Name="DotNetDataProvider" Type="DotNetDataProviderTemplate.TemplateConnecti on,
DotNetDataProviderTemplate"/>
```

4. Add the following line after the last <Extension> element in the <Designers> section:

```
<Extension Name="DotNetDataProvider" Type="Microsoft.ReportingServices.QueryDesigners.GenericQueryDesigner,
Microsoft.ReportingServices.QueryDesigners"/>
```

5. Next, you need to elevate code access security for the DotNetDataProviderTemplate assembly. In the same folder, open the RSPreviewPolicy.config file.
6. Scroll to the end of the file and add the following CodeGroup element after the last code group element:

```
<CodeGroup class="UnionCodeGroup" version="1" Name="DotNetProvider"
    Description="Code group for the Microsoft DotNet Data Provider" PermissionSetName="FullTrust">
  <IMembershipCondition class="UrlMembershipCondition" version="1"
   Url="C:\Program Files\Microsoft Visual Studio 9.0\Common7\IDE\PrivateAssemblies\
      DotNetDataProviderTemplate.dll" />
</CodeGroup>
```

7. If the Visual Studio IDE is open, close and reopen it to reflect the configuration changes.

   At this point, the Report Designer configuration is complete. You should be able to create a data source using the DotNetDataProvider data provider.

Deploying to Report Server

To configure the DotNetDataProviderTemplate provider on the report server, complete the following steps.

8. Copy the extension binaries, DotNetDataProviderTemplate.dll and DotNetDataProviderTemplate.pdb, to the report server binary folder \Program Files\Microsoft SQL Server\MSRS10.MSSQLSERVER\Reporting Services\ReportServer\bin.
9. Open the rsreportserver.config file from the \Program Files\Microsoft SQL Server\MSRS10.-MSSQLSERVER\Reporting Services\ReportServer folder.
10. Locate the <Data> element and register the provider just as you did with the Report Designer configuration file.
11. To grant the code the necessary security permissions, open the rssrvpolicy.config in the same folder and add the following code group after the last code group element, as follows:

```
<CodeGroup class="UnionCodeGroup" version="1" Name="CustomDataExtensionCodeGroup"
  Description="Code group for .NET Framework data provider" PermissionSetName="FullTrust">
    <IMe mbershipCondition class="UrlMembershipCondition" version="1"
      Url=" C:\Program Files\Microsoft SQL Server\MSRS10.MSSQLSERVER\Reporting
          Services\ReportServer\bin\DotNetDataProviderTemplate.dll "/>
</CodeGroup>
```

After these steps are complete, you should be able to successfully define a server report that uses the .NET Framework data provider. The next section will walk you through the process.

Working with the DotNetDataProviderTemplate data provider

Once the provider is deployed and registered, you can author reports that use it. The TestDataProvider report, which is included in the Reports project, demonstrates how to use the DotNetDataProviderTemplate provider with a report.

1. When setting up the report data source, select DotNetDataProvider in the Type drop-down list in the Data Source Properties dialog box.

   Because the DotNetDataProvider does not establish a physical database connection, the connection string is ignored, so you can leave this field blank or press the space bar to add an empty space in place of a value.

2. In the generic query designer, enter the following query statement:

   ```
   select * from customers
   ```

3. Execute the query.

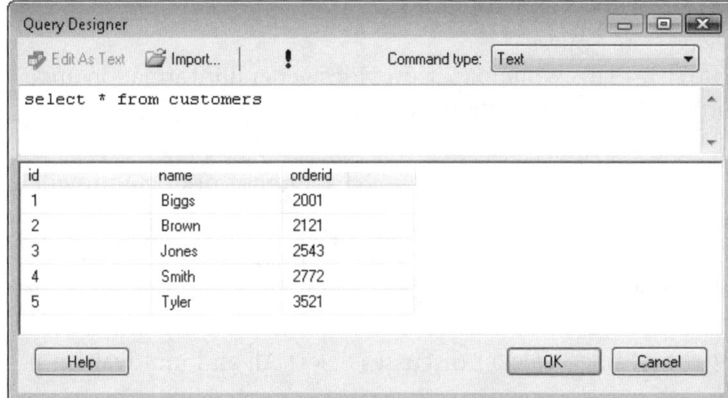

Figure 4.26 Use the generic query designer to test DotNetDataProvider.

The resulting dataset should consist of five rows and three columns, as shown in Figure 4.26.

4.6 Summary

Reporting Services has a flexible and extensible data architecture that allows you to connect to a variety of data sources. It comes with several built-in data providers so that you can easily access popular data sources.

To define data source connections, you can specify either shared or report-specific data sources. Shared data sources are easier to manage because you can centralize connection information in a single definition. Private or report-specific data sources are embedded in the report definition. Report-specific data sources can be expression-based and may simplify report deployment.

A dataset defines the query or command text that retrieves data used in the report. Dataset filters allow you to select a subset of the result set that was returned to the report. Query parameters filter data at the data source. A query parameter is typically linked to a report parameter. A parameter can have default and available values. Use a cascading parameter when the parameter available values are dependent on another parameter. Multivalued parameters let the user specify multiple values for a single parameter.

The OLE DB provider is a generic provider that lets you access OLE DB-compatible data sources. Use the XML data provider to integrate reports with Web services and report off XML data. If report data requires transformation, consider the SSIS provider and an Integration Services package as a source of report data. .NET Framework data providers from Microsoft and third-party vendors let you access specific data sources that don't have corresponding Reporting Services built-in data providers.

4.7 Resources

Using SQL Server 2005 Reporting Services with SAP NetWeaver Business Intelligence (http://tinyurl.com/34s4zz)—Discusses the integration of SAP NetWeaver Business Intelligence (BI) with Reporting Services.

Using SQL Server 2005 Reporting Services with Hyperion Essbase (http://tinyurl.com/2pzchy)—Discusses the integration of Hyperion Essbase with SQL Server 2005 Reporting Services Service Pack.

Using XML and Web Service Data Sources (http://tinyurl.com/2w9o7h)—This white paper provides general information and tips for designing reports with the XML data provider.

Sample .NET Framework Data Provider (http://tinyurl.com/33rkrb)—Learn how to create a .NET Framework data provider.

Implementing Smart Reports with the Microsoft Business Intelligence Platform (http://tinyurl.com/232vb2)—Demonstrates how you can integrate CLR stored procedures with data mining to generate forecasted data.

Select All in Service Pack 1 (http://tinyurl.com/2v4tru)—Brian Welcker discusses Select All and multivalued parameters.

SQL Server Samples (http://tinyurl.com/6b9bev)—Install the SQL Server samples to obtain the CalculatedColumns samples.

Chapter 5

Designing Tablix Reports

By now, you should feel comfortable authoring basic reports with Report Designer. Recall from chapter 3 that Reporting Services 2008 introduces a flexible tablix data region that lets you author tabular, crosstab, and freeform reports. As is often the case, flexibility and complexity go hand in hand. Tablix is a very versatile control but you need to know it well if you want to get the most out of it. In this chapter, you will kick it up a notch and "graduate" to the next level of report design where you will learn how to author more complex reports that use the tablix data region.

Because the report design process is very interactive, the best way to present this chapter is by example. Each report type explanation includes an exercise that shows you how to create a specific report. By the time we finish this chapter, you will have created tabular reports with stepped layout and row groups, crosstab reports with dynamic and static groups, freeform reports, and subreports. Along the way, I will show you how to jazz up your reports with interactive features, such as drilldown, drillthrough, interactive sorting, document maps, and more.

5.1 Designing Tabular Reports

Tabular reports are very common. The report output is organized in multiple rows and fixed (static) columns. By contrast, crosstab reports define dynamic columns that expand to accommodate data, such as to show the data broken down by years on columns. Typically, tabular reports include row groups that group report data and subtotal lines that sum the values in a column. The report may also have a report footer to show the grand totals. In Reporting Services, you can implement tabular reports by using the table region. The table region is a preconfigured tablix with fixed columns.

5.1.1 The Anatomy of a Table Region

Before delving into the implementation details, let's take a moment to understand the anatomy of a Reporting Services table report. Figure 5.1 shows the Product Sales Stepped report, which is the first report you will author in this chapter. This figure illustrates the main components of a typical table report and how they relate to the table region.

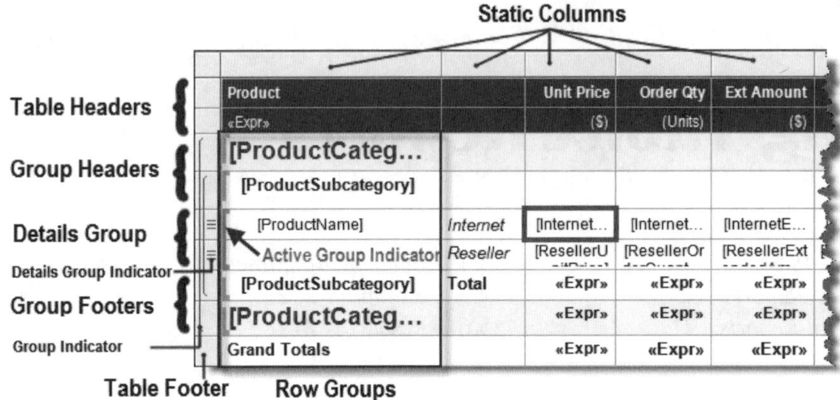

Figure 5.1 A table report typically includes static columns and multiple rows with row groups.

Row groups

Table reports typically aggregate and group data into row groups. For example, the Product Sales Stepped report groups data at product category and subcategory levels. The ProductCategory group displays the product category in the group header and the subtotals in the group footer.

The table region has a pre-defined details group that represents detail data. Detail data correspond to the rows of the dataset to which the table region is bound. Detail data is essentially what you see in the query designer Results pane when you run a dataset query. The details group comes in handy when you need to process detail rows before they are shown on the report. For example, suppose that the report dataset contains fine-grained information, such as order transactions. If you want to group report data by product but you cannot do so in the report query, you can use the details group to group and sort the details. Detail rows that are associated with the details group are symbolized as three stacked lines ≡ in the narrow row selector area.

Each group can have an arbitrary number of rows in its group headers and footers. The details group of the Product Sales Stepped report, for example, contains two rows. The first row displays Internet sales, while the second row displays reseller sales. Notice that the row group header (in this case, ProductName) is placed alongside the first detail row.

Tablix provides visual cues to help identify the cell scope and group membership. Glancing at the screenshot, we can deduce that the first group that the selected cell (InternetUnitPrice) is associated with is the details group because the active group indicator (colored in orange) shows the innermost group to which the currently selected cell belongs. The group indicators that are shown as lines that span row selectors indicate that this cell also belongs to the ProductSubcategory and ProductCategory row groups. Therefore, this cell will be repeated within each instance of these groups.

Static columns

A table report contains static columns that are always present at run time. As it stands, Reporting Services doesn't let the user add or remove tablix columns dynamically at run time. However, you can use expressions to control column visibility and you can hide columns based on certain conditions. For example, if the user picks January as the current period, you can hide a Year-To-Date column on the report.

You can select all cells within a column by clicking on the column selector. This is convenient if you want to change their format settings in one step. For example, to change the format of all cells in the Unit Price column, click the Unit Price column selector and change the Format property in the Properties window.

Table headers

A table header is a static row that appears at the beginning of the report. The Product Sales Stepped report has two table header rows with dark blue background color. You would typically use a table header to define column labels that display static or expression-based text. Most of the column captions show static text, such as Product, Unit Price, and so on. The first cell on the second header row contains an expression that displays the count of all products shown on the report.

5.1.2 Designing a Stepped Report ▶

To hone your tablix skills, you will now create a stepped report called Product Sales Stepped. You may have authored tabular reports that display each row group in a separate column. This usually results in wide reports that exceed the page width. In contrast, a stepped report displays nested detail or row groups in the same column, as shown in Figure 5.2.

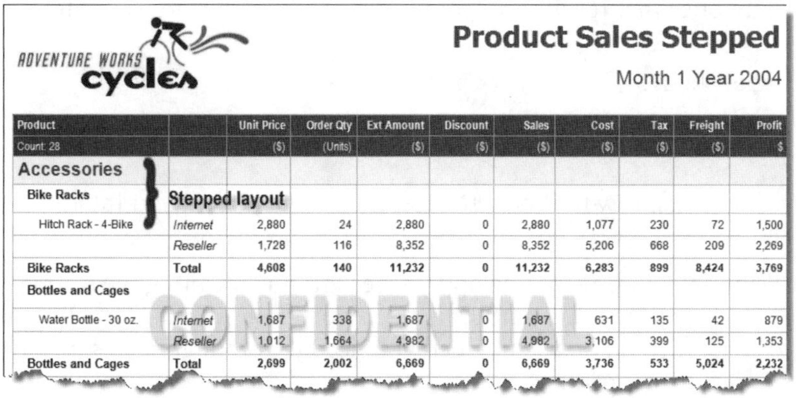

Product		Unit Price	Order Qty	Ext Amount	Discount	Sales	Cost	Tax	Freight	Profit
Count: 28		($)	(Units)	($)	($)	($)	($)	($)	($)	$
Accessories										
Bike Racks										
Hitch Rack - 4-Bike	*Internet*	2,880	24	2,880	0	2,880	1,077	230	72	1,500
	Reseller	1,728	116	8,352	0	8,352	5,206	668	209	2,269
Bike Racks	**Total**	**4,608**	**140**	**11,232**	**0**	**11,232**	**6,283**	**899**	**8,424**	**3,769**
Bottles and Cages										
Water Bottle - 30 oz.	*Internet*	1,687	338	1,687	0	1,687	631	135	42	879
	Reseller	1,012	1,664	4,982	0	4,982	3,106	399	125	1,353
Bottles and Cages	**Total**	**2,699**	**2,002**	**6,669**	**0**	**6,669**	**3,736**	**533**	**5,024**	**2,232**

Figure 5.2 A stepped report has indented groups in the same column.

Besides having a stepped layout, the Product Sales Stepped report also demonstrates the following features:

- Dataset calculated fields
- Expressions in column header cells
- Grouped and sorted report data
- Repeated table headers
- Pagination at the group level
- External images and background image for the report body

Understanding tablix group header limitations

Recall from chapter 3 that Report Designer automatically creates a row group when you drag a field into the Row Groups pane. In addition, Report Designer auto-generates a column (tablix group header) for each row group so that you can label it. Tablix group headers are useful because they reduce the height of the report since the group headers of all row groups occupy the same row. Tablix group headers also simplify how you define group subtotals. To add a group subtotal, you can simply right-click the group header and click Add Total.

Although tablix group headers have unquestionable value, they can sometimes get in the way. Suppose your objective is to minimize report width by placing rows groups in a single column, such as stacking the ProductCategory, ProductSubcategory, and Product columns within one column. To implement this, you would need to reverse the default layout that tablix creates so you can get groups to share columns instead of rows. Another scenario when tablix group headers may get in the way is when you need a separate header row for a group. Fortunately, tablix group headers are entirely optional. On the downside, authoring more advanced layouts require additional steps to manually configure the row groups.

Creating the basic tabular report

When tablix group headers are not desirable, you can re-configure tablix to have a more traditional layout with designated group header and footer rows. The Product Sales Stepped Start report provides the starting point for this practice. It contains datasets, but no layout. Complete the following steps to design a stepped layout:

1. In the Report Data window, double-click the Products dataset to open its properties. In the Fields tab, notice that the InternetProfit and ResellerProfit fields are defined as calculated fields.
2. Preview the query results and notice that results are grouped by product category, subcategory, and product.
3. Add a tablix region to the report body.

   Since the dataset query already groups data by product, you don't need to define a Product row group.
4. Bind the three cells in the tablix detail row to ProductName, InternetUnitPrice, and InternetOrderQuantity fields.

   To demonstrate the tablix flexibility, I'll present two approaches for implementing the stepped layout. The first approach is easier but assumes authoring the report from scratch. The second approach requires more steps but it could be useful when you need to reconfigure existing reports with tablix group headers to stepped layout.

Implementing stepped layout (option 1)

This approach explores the tablix capability to add parent groups, as follows:

1. In the Row Groups pane, right-click the Details group and click Add Group ⇨ Parent Group.
2. In the Table Group dialog box that follows (see Figure 5.3), expand the Group By drop-down list and select [ProductSubcategory]. Check the Add Group Header and Add Group Footer checkboxes and click OK.

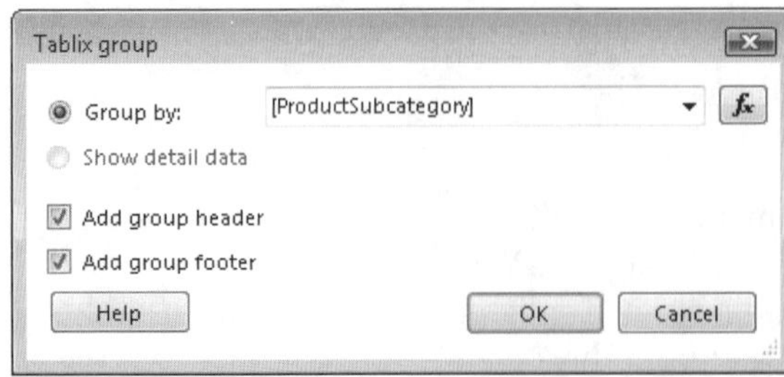

Figure 5.3 Use the tablix parent group support to add a row group that groups data on the ProductSubcategory field.

Report Designer adds a new row group (Group1) to the Row Groups pane and creates a tablix group header, as shown in Figure 5.4. Notice that the detail cells are within the scope of both Group1 and Details groups. However, the ProductSubcategory cell is within the scope of Group1 only because the Group1 indicator (spanning line) extends to ProductSubcategory.

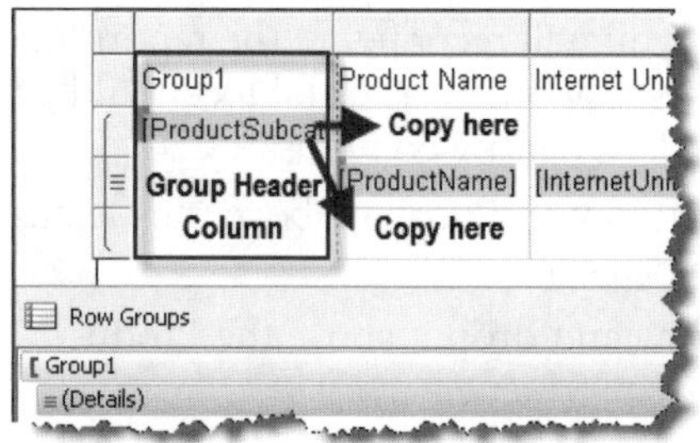

Figure 5.4 The ProductSubcategory tablix group header is not needed with stepped layout.

The ProductSubcategory tablix group header column is not needed. What you need to implement the stepped layout is only the row group itself and its header and footer rows.

3. Copy the ProductSubcategory cell from the Group1 column and paste it in the empty cell above the ProductName cell. This configures the group header of the product subcategory group. Paste the ProductSubcategory cell one more time in the cell below ProductName to configure the group footer.
4. Right-click any cell in the Group1 column and click Delete Columns.
5. In the Row Groups, double-click the Group1 group. In the Group Properties dialog box, rename the group to *ProductSubcategory*.

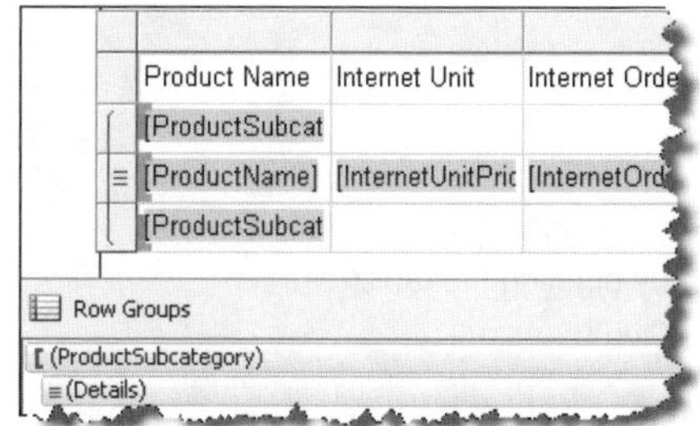

Figure 5.5 The ProductSubcategory group and ProductName group share the same column.

Compare your report layout with the one shown in Figure 5.5. Notice that the ProductSubcategory and ProductName groups share the same column.

6. In the Row Groups pane, right-click the ProductSubcategory group and click Add Group ➪ Parent Group.
7. Follow similar steps to configure the ProductCategory group.

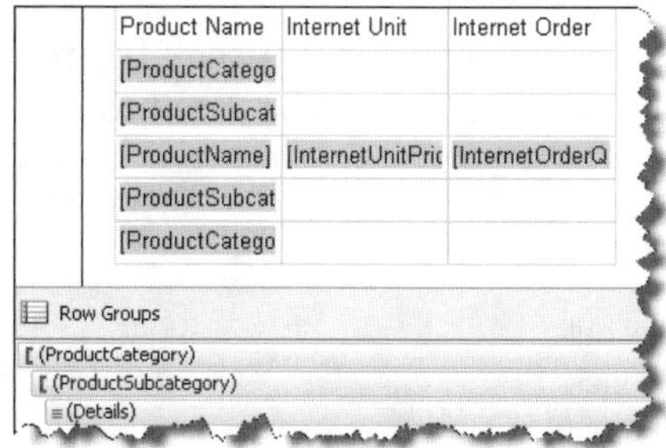

Figure 5.6 All groups are stacked in the same column.

Compare your report layout with Figure 5.6.

Implementing stepped layout (option 2)

While we have a few more steps to go, let's now demonstrate another approach for stacking columns. First, you'll create ProductCategory and ProductSubcategory row groups to simulate an existing report with tablix header group columns. Next, you will reconfigure the report for stepped layout. The starting point is the same as with the first approach. Your tablix should have only ProductName, InternetUnitPrice, and InternetOrderQuantity columns.

1. Drag the ProductSubcategory field from the Report Data window and drop it above the Details row group in the Row Groups pane to group by product subcategory.
2. Drag the ProductCategory field from the Report Data window and drop it above the Product-Subcategory row group in the Row Groups pane to group by product category.
3. The last two steps add two new columns to the left of the table to accommodate the Product Category and Product Subcategory tablix group headers.
4. Preview the report and notice that the report includes Product Category and Product Subcategory header columns and that they span the detail rows.

Let's now configure the stepped layout.

5. Click the Design tab to go back to design mode. Select the first two tablix columns (Product Category and Product Subcategory) by holding the Ctrl key and clicking on the column headers, as Figure 5.7 shows.

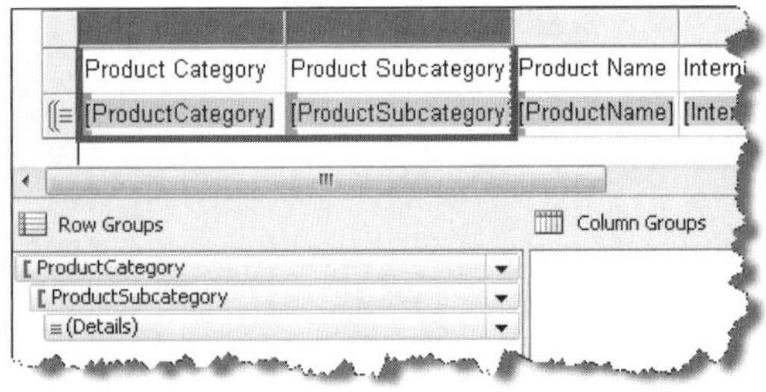

Figure 5.7 Start designing the stepped report by deleting the tablix group header columns.

6. Right-click any of the selected column headers and click Delete Columns to remove the Product Category and Product Subcategory columns.
7. This step is important. Report Designer shows a prompt asking if you want to delete the columns and associated group or the columns only. Choose Delete Columns Only and click OK.

Examine the Row Groups pane. Notice that although you've deleted the Product Category and Product Subcategory columns, tablix has preserved the row groups. This is important because you need the row groups to define the stacked layout.

8. Select the detail row by clicking its row selector. Right-click the row selector and click Insert Row ⇨ Outside Group – Above. Alternatively, you can right-click any cell in the detail row and click Insert Row ⇨ Outside Group – Above.

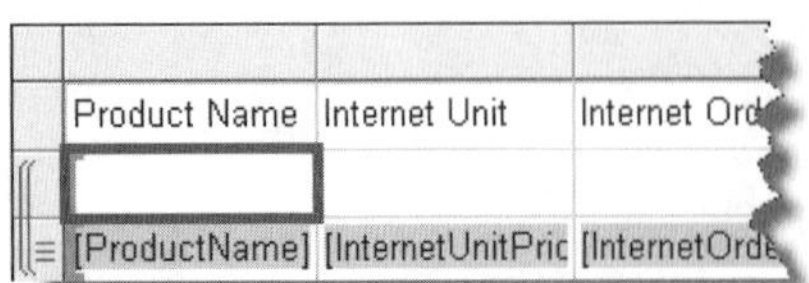

Figure 5.8 Inserting a row outside the selected group scopes the new row to the parent group.

At this point, your report layout should look like the one shown in Figure 5.8. You will use the empty cell above the ProductName detail cell, which is selected in Figure 5.8, for the ProductSubcategory group header. This works because this cell is associated with the ProductCategory and ProductSubcategory groups, as the group indicators (spanning lines) show. The first spanning line represents the ProductCategory group, while the second represents the ProductSubcategory group.

9. Bind the selected cell to the ProductSubcategory field by clicking its field selector and clicking ProductSubcategory.
10. Right-click the same cell and click Insert Row ⇨ Outside Group – Above. All cells in the new row are in the ProductCategory scope. Only the first group indicator should extend to the new row because you need the new row to be associated with the ProductCategory group.
11. Bind the first cell of the new row to ProductCategory.
12. Compare your report layout to Figure 5.9.

Product Name	Internet Unit	Internet Order
[ProductCatego		
[ProductSubcat		
[ProductName]	[InternetUnitPric	[InternetOrderQ

Figure 5.9 The stepped row group headers share the same column.

Next, follow similar steps to add group footers below the detail row.

13. Right-click the detail row and click Insert Row ⇨ Outside Group – Below. The new row represents the ProductSubcategory group footer. Bind its first cell to ProductSubcategory.
14. Right-click the ProductSubcategory row and click Insert Row ⇨ Outside Group – Below. The new row represents the ProductCategory group footer. Bind the first cell to ProductCategory.

At this point, the report layout should match Figure 5.6. The next two steps indent the ProductCategory and ProductSubcategory cells to achieve the desired stepped layout.

15. Select the ProductSubcategory cell and change its Padding ⇨ Left to 10pt. Select the ProductName cell and change its Padding ⇨ Left to 20pt.
16. Indent ProductSubcategory footer cell with 10 pt and the ProductCategory footer cell at 2 pt.

Working with the Details group

While you can display all numeric columns side by side, this will result in a very wide report. Instead, consider arranging them in two detail rows to minimize the report width. The first row will show the Internet-related fields, while the second row will show the reseller fields.

1. Right-click the detail row and click Insert Row ⇨ Inside Group – Below.
2. The new row shares the same group (Details) with the original detail row.
3. Right-click the Internet Unit Price column and click Insert Column ⇨ Left.
4. In the first detail cell of the new column enter *Internet*. In the cell below it, enter *Reseller*.
5. To set up a report footer, right-click the last row (ProductCategory) and click Insert Row ⇨ Outside Group – Below. Enter *Grand Totals* in the first cell of the new row. This row is outside of the row groups and it represents the report footer that will show a single row of grand totals for the entire report.

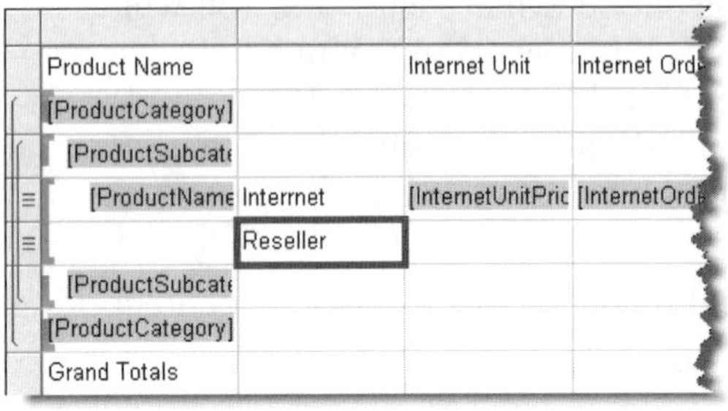

Product Name		Internet Unit	Internet Ord
[ProductCategory]			
[ProductSubcat			
[ProductName	Interrnet	[InternetUnitPric	[InternetOrd
	Reseller		
[ProductSubcat			
[ProductCategory]			
Grand Totals			

Figure 5.10 You can have an arbitrary number of rows in group headers and footers. The second detail row displays reseller sales.

At this point, your report layout should match the one shown in Figure 5.10. Notice that Internet and Reseller rows are detail rows that are associated with the Details group as the active group indicator shows. Later, we'll bind the cells from the second row to the Reseller-related fields.

Working with table headers and totals

As it stands, the table region has a single header row that contains the column captions. Suppose you need to display additional information below the first row. For example, you may to show the currency symbol under the column caption. Let's add a second table header row to address this requirement.

> **TIP** Instead of adding a new header row, you can add a new paragraph (press Enter) to each header textbox. Or, you can press Shift+Enter to force the text to flow to the next line. However, a separate header row is preferable in this case as it facilitates formatting the cells in that row. For example, you can click the row selector to select all cells and apply the same formatting style in the Properties window.

1. Right-click the table header row and click Insert Row ⇨ Below.
2. In the first cell of the new row, enter *Count:* and add a space.
3. With the mouse cursor at the end of "Count: ", right-click and click Create Placeholder.
4. In the Placeholder Properties dialog box, enter the following expression in the Value property:

   ```
   = CountRows("Products")
   ```

   This expression uses the Reporting Services CountRows function to return the number of products in the Products dataset. The entire textbox text should now read "Count: <<Expr>>" without the quotes.
5. Right-click the right-most table column and click Insert Column ⇨ Right to add a new column. Repeat this step six more times to create enough columns for all numeric fields that we want to display on the report.
6. Bind Internet-related numeric fields to the cells in the Internet row. Bind reseller-related numeric fields to cells in the Reseller row.
7. Rename the Internet Unit Price and Internet Order Quantity column headers to *Unit Price* and *Order Qty*. Enter column captions for the remaining columns in the first table header row. Enter *($)* in the second header row for all currency fields and *(Units)* for the Order Qty column.
8. Add aggregate expressions in the ProductSubcategory, ProductCategory, and Grand Totals rows for each numeric column to sum the Internet and reseller fields in that column. For example, use the following aggregate expression for the Unit Price column:

   ```
   =Sum(Fields!InternetUnitPrice.Value +  Fields!ResellerUnitPrice.Value)
   ```

This function sums the InternetUnitPrice and ResellerUnitPrice fields horizontally and aggregates the result vertically for all rows in the group. Alternatively, you could use the expression:

```
=Sum(Fields!InternetUnitPrice.Value) + Sum( Fields!ResellerUnitPrice.Value)
```

This expression aggregates the fields vertically and then sums the two values.

Formatting the report

Let's spend some time polishing the report layout:

1. Hold the Ctrl key and select the two table header rows. This selects all cells within the row so that you can apply format settings in one step.
2. In the Properties window, change the BackgroundColor property to DarkSlateBlue and Color to White.
3. Select the first table header row only and change the font style of all cells to Bold.
4. Select the ProductCategory group header and change its background color to WhiteSmoke.
5. Click the first cell in this row and change its foreground color to DarkSlateBlue, font size to 14pt, and font style to Bold. Apply the same format settings to the ProductCategory group footer row.
6. Select the ProductSubcategory group header and footer rows and change the font size to 9 pt and font style to Bold.
7. Select the table footer row and change the font size to 10 pt and font style to Bold.
8. Select all rows and set BorderColor to DarkGray and BorderStyle to Solid to make the borders visible.
9. Right-click any numeric cell inside the Unit Price column and click Textbox Properties. Click the Number tab and format the textbox as Number, 0 decimal places, Use 1000 Separator, and (12,345) sample format for negative numbers. Click OK and inspect the Format property of the textbox in the Properties window. The format setting should be #,0;(#,0).
10. Select all numeric columns (except Order Qty) by dragging the mouse cursor. In the Properties window, change their Format property to *#,0;(#,0)*. Alternatively, use the Text Box Properties dialog box (Number tab) to format the cells as numbers with no decimal places and a thousand separator.

    The textbox CanGrow property determines what happens when report content exceeds its width. If CanGrow is True (default setting), the textbox content wraps vertically and continues on a new line to accommodate its content. If CanGrow is False, the user can see only the content that fits the textbox width as though the text is truncated. The textbox width cannot expand dynamically. However, because tablix supports merging cells horizontally and vertically within the same group, we can use a different technique to increase the field's width without wrapping. Let's give the ProductCategory cells more space to the right by merging cells:

11. In the ProductCategory group header, select the ProductCategory cell and the adjacent cell to the right. Right-click the selection and click Merge Cells.
12. Repeat the last step to merge the ProductCategory cell in the group footer with the next cell.

    If you want to split a merged cell, right-click the cell and click Split Cells.

Sorting data

Reporting Services doesn't sort data by default. If a tablix region has groups, Reporting Services groups the underlying data by adding qualifying rows for each group instance in the order they appear in the dataset. However, when you define a new group, Report Designer configures this group to sort data by its grouping field. You can overwrite this behavior if needed.

1. In the Report Data window, double-click the Products dataset. Preview the query results and observe that data is not sorted and that the first row is associated with the Clothing category.

> **TIP** You should delegate as much processing to the database server as possible, such as grouping, sorting, and filtering. This is what database servers are designed to do. Consider report sorting only when doing so at the data source level is not an option or when you need more flexibility, such as implementing dynamic sorting based on a parameter value.

2. Preview the report and notice that the first group is Accessories.
3. To understand why data is sorted this way, double-click the ProductCategory group in the Row Groups pane.

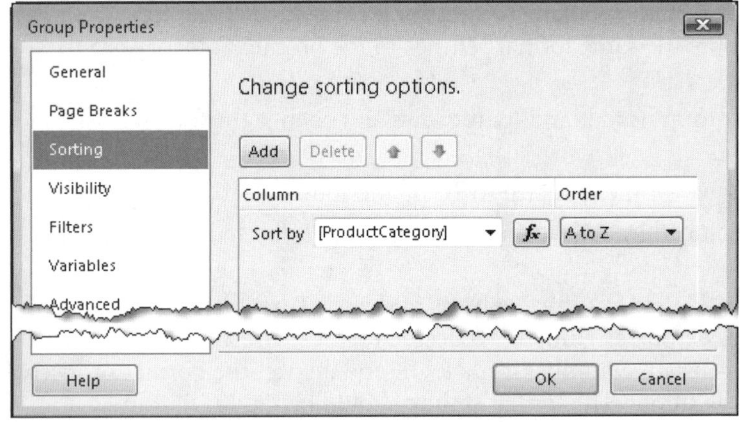

Figure 5.11 Use the Tablix Group Properties dialog box to access the group sorting options.

4. In the Group Properties dialog box, click the Sorting tab, as shown in Figure 5.11.

   As noted, Report Designer pre-configures each group to sort data in ascending order by the grouping field. Click OK.

5. Double-click the ProductSubcategory group. In the Group Properties dialog box, notice that its sorts its data by ProductSubcategory. Consequently, Reporting Services will sort the report data by product category first. Within each instance of the product category group, data will be sorted by product subcategory. Suppose that you want to sort the details row within each subcategory instance in descending order by profit.
6. In the Row Groups pane, double-click the Details group. In the Group Properties dialog box, click the Sorting tab. Notice that detail data is not sorted.
7. Click the Add button and enter the following expression in the Sort By drop-down:

```
=Fields!InternetProfit.Value + Fields!ResellerProfit.Value
```

8. Change the Order column to Z to A and click OK. Preview the report.

   The report is now sorted by product category in ascending order. Product subcategory sections within each product category are also sorted in ascending order. Within each subcategory, individual products are sorted by their overall profit in descending order.

Working with external images

As noted in chapter 3, you can use external images on your reports. Similar to a shared data source, external images can be centrally managed and shared across reports. Suppose you want to add a background image to the report body to inform the user that this report is confidential. In addition, suppose that you want all reports to reflect the changes when the image has been updated. This can be accomplished by referencing the external image. Start by adding the image file to the Report Server project:

1. In Solution Explorer, right-click the project node, and click Add ⇨ Existing Item.
2. In the Add Existing Item dialog box, change the file filter to All Files (*.*). Navigate to the Reports folder in the chapter source code and double-click the Confidential.jpg image to add it to the project.
3. In the design area, click the report body section. Alternatively, expand the drop-down in the Properties window and select the Body item.
4. In the Properties window, expand the BackgroundImage section.
5. Change BackgroundImage ⇨ Source to External.
6. Enter Confidential.jpg in the BackgroundImage ⇨ Value property.
7. Preview the report. The report should now show "Confidential" in the report body. If parts of the image don't show, make sure that the BackgroundColor property of the overlapping cells is set to Transparent.

Any external images that you use in a report will eventually need to be published to the report server so it's available when the user requests the deployed report. When you do publish the item, you might want to hide the image item from general view or move it into a folder that contains other hidden items. You will need to modify role assignments to hide an image or a folder by revoking the end users Browser rights to the image or its containing folder.

5.1.3 Working with Advanced Grouping Options

Although not immediately obvious, the tablix region supports additional grouping options to support more advanced layout requirements, such as configuring tablix to repeat table header rows. Before showing you how to work with the advanced grouping options, let's learn more about the structure of the tablix data region.

Understanding static and dynamic members

We'll use the collective term tablix *member* to refer to a tablix row or a column. A tablix member can be either static or dynamic. Simply put, a static member (or simply *static*) corresponds to a row in a tablix region when it's shown in design mode. Similarly, a static column corresponds to a tablix column. Dynamic members (*dynamics*) represent row groups and column groups respectively. By default, the Grouping pane doesn't show static members.

1. Expand the down arrow indicator located in the right-most corner of the Grouping pane.
2. Click Advanced Mode.

Advanced mode (see Figure 5.12) is a skeletal view of a tablix that describes all of its parts as either static or dynamic members. Dynamic members are named and correspond to the row or column groups you define. Static members are indicated as (Static), and you get to deduce how it relates to a tablix item by where it appears in the tablix hierarchy.

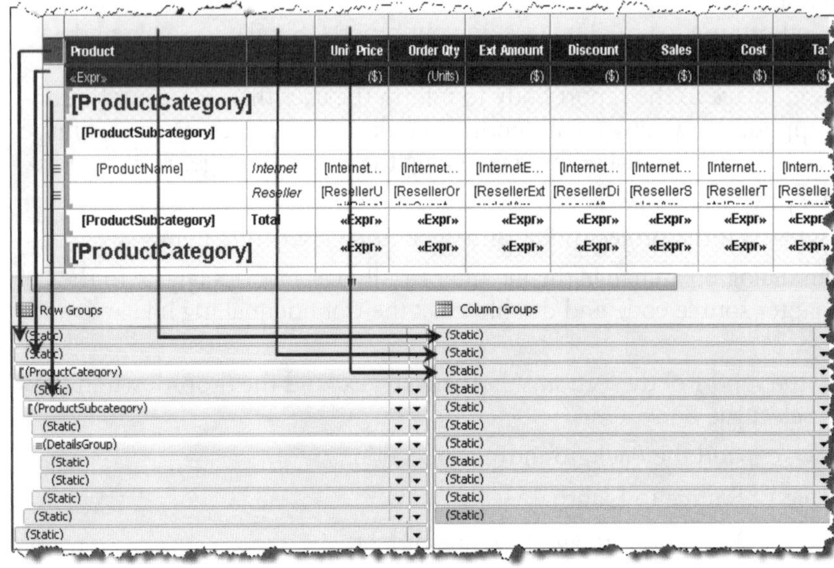

Figure 5.12 Turn on the Advanced Mode of the Grouping pane to see tablix static members.

Figure 5.12 shows the relationship between the first three rows and columns to tablix members. Examining the tree view of the tablix members in the Row Groups pane, we can make the following conclusions. The table region starts with two statics that represent the table header rows. Next, we have a ProductCategory dynamic member. Recall that any row group creates a dynamic member.

The static below the ProductCategory is intended because it belongs to the ProductCategory dynamic. Therefore, it represents the ProductCategory group header. Similarly, the static below ProductSubcategory represents the ProductSubcategory group header, while the two statics below the Details group are the two detail rows. The statics below them represent the group footers. The Column Groups pane has eleven static members because our tablix has that many columns.

TIP As a first step of troubleshooting issues with tablix, I'd recommend you examine the Grouping pane in advanced mode. Specifically, make sure that you don't have more statics than tablix rows. As it stands, Report Designer doesn't let you delete static members. This leaves you with no other choice but to recreate the table report if you detect structural inconsistencies.

Repeating row and column headers

Let's now discuss the practical implications of the advanced mode. The Product Sales Stepped report has many columns and is several pages long. Without repeating column headers on each page, it may be difficult for the user to keep track of which data is in each column as he or she pages through the report. Fortunately, you can configure tablix to repeat table header rows on new pages.

1. In the Row Groups pane, click the first static member and change its RepeatOnNewPage property to True, as shown in Figure 5.13. KeepWithGroup should be set to After.
2. Select the second static row and change RepeatOnNewPage to True.

The result of these changes is table header rows repeating on each new page. When KeepWithGroup is set to After, the static row will repeat on a new page if an instance of the next dynamic group (ProductCategory in our case) spills over onto the next page. If I want to repeat the ProductCategory footer on a new page as well, I could select the last static row and change its RepeatOnNewPage to True and KeepWithGroup to Before.

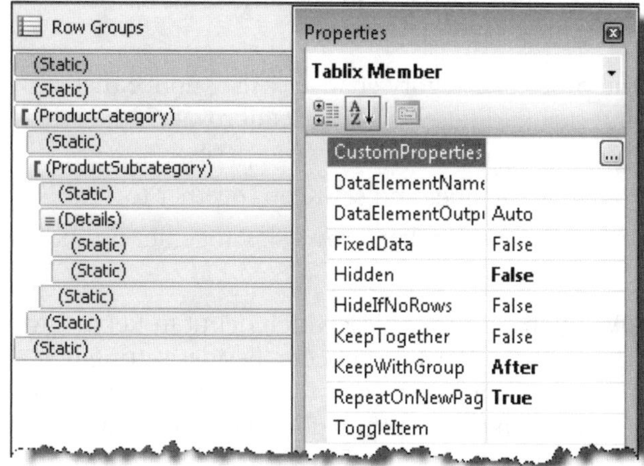

Figure 5.13 Set RepeatOnNewPage to True and KeepWithGroup to After to repeat table header rows on new pages.

3. Preview the report in Print Layout mode. The tablix header rows should now repeat on each page.

While we are on the subject repeating headers, let's clear a potential source of confusion. Select the tablix region and examine its properties in the Properties window (or right-click a tablix row and click Tablix Properties). In the General property group, you'll find RepeatColumnHeaders and RepeatRowHeaders properties. These properties apply only to reports that have row header and column header areas. The report has these areas if there is a double dashed line that separates groups from the tablix body. Going back to Figure 3.26 in chapter 3 could be useful to understand this. The Product Sales Stepped report doesn't have a row group area because we removed the auto-generated tablix headers. It doesn't have a column header area either because only crosstab reports have a column header area. Therefore, find RepeatColumnHeaders and RepeatRowHeaders don't apply to the Product Sales Stepped report.

If your report has these areas, RepeatRowHeaders will make row headers repeat when the tablix is *horizontally* paginated. Assuming that your tablix exceeds the page width and you export to a hard-page renderer (PDF, Image, Print), when RepeatRowHeaders is set to True, you'll see the tablix group headers repeated on the next page. With crosstab reports, RepeatColumnHeaders will repeat the column headers vertically. During design time, preview the report in Print Layout mode to test the effect of these properties. If the report doesn't have row header and column header areas, you can still repeat rows by setting the RepeatOnNewPage property.

Controlling pagination

Recall from chapter 3 that the report author can define logical page breaks to control how the report paginates. Let's set up a logical page break to force a new page when the product category changes:

1. In the Row Groups pane, click the ProductCategory member to select it.
2. In the Properties window, expand the Group section and change the PageBreak property to Between.

Alternatively, to define a group page break, double-click the ProductCategory group in the Row Groups pane. In the Group Properties dialog box, click the Page Breaks tab and check the Between Each Instance of a Group checkbox.

3. Preview the report in Print Layout mode (click the Preview tab and click the Print Layout toolbar button) to see how the report paginates.

   Notice that a page break occurs each time the product category changes. Also, notice that a page break sometimes occurs between the Internet and Reseller's two detail rows. Suppose that you want to keep the detail rows together so they don't split between pages.

4. In the Row Groups pane, click the Details dynamic member and set KeepTogether to True.
5. Preview the report and notice that the Internet and Reseller detail rows stay together on the same page.

   As you can see, the KeepTogether and KeepWithGroup properties, which debut in Reporting Services 2008, give you more control over the report pagination process. Besides setting it at a group level, you can also turn on KeepTogether for data regions and rectangles if you want to keep their content together on a single page. During report repagination, the renderer will move the item to the next page so it stays in one piece if possible. The downside is that your report may contain gaps.

   It's also worth pointing out that Reporting Services does not support fitting a report to size. By that, I mean there is no auto-adjustment to font size or row spacing that prints a larger report onto a fixed number of pages. As a workaround, consider exporting the report to Excel and using the Excel fit-to-page setup capabilities.

6. Preview the report and enter *2008* for the year parameter.

   You will notice immediately that the report contains no data. It displays the two table header rows and the table footer row. Other static members are not shown because there aren't any instances of product category data for 2008. For reports that contain fixed headers and footers but no data, you can improve overall appearance by removing the table footer when it is not needed. Let's do this now.

7. In the Row Groups pane, click the last static member and change its HideIfNoRows property to True.
8. Preview the report for year 2008 and notice that the table footer is not shown.

5.1.4 Implementing a Balance Sheet Report

Standard financial reports, such as Balance Sheet, Income Statement, Statement of Condition, and so on, are other examples of tabular reports. The Balance Sheet report (see Figure 5.14) shows the current amount and the year-to-date amount of assets and liabilities accounts. The % Total column is calculated by dividing the Amount value by the YTD value. The report demonstrates the following design features:

- Expression-based group subtotals
- Grouping at detail level
- Conditional column visibility

The report accepts Organization, Fiscal Year and Current Period parameters.

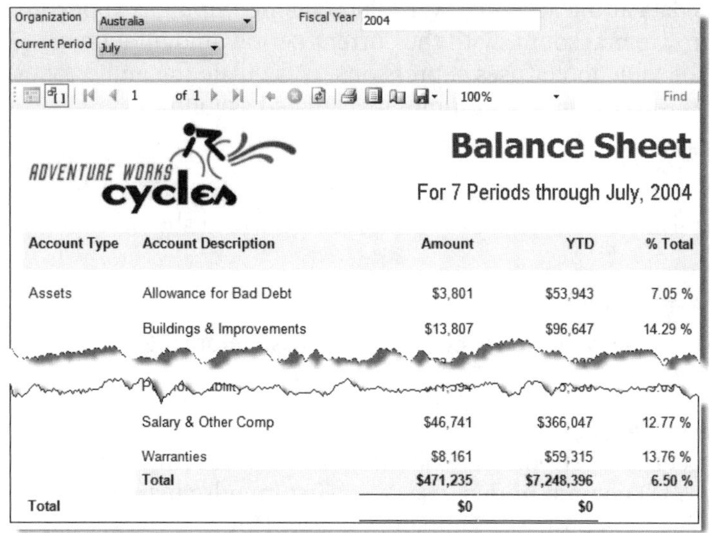

Figure 5.14 The Balance Sheet report demonstrates expression-based groups and conditional column visibility.

Preparing the report dataset

Financial and accounting reports are based on a chart of accounts, which is a listing of all general ledger accounts organized in categories, such as assets, liabilities, equities, and so on. What makes financial reports interesting from a report design standpoint is the way data aggregates. For example, asset accounts add up to the report total, while liability accounts subtract. Since assets and liabilities must balance, the Balance Sheet report grand total should produce zero. The DimAccount table in the AdventureWorks2008 database demonstrates a chart of accounts.

OrganizationKey	OrganizationName	AccountType	Accou...	Sign	CurrentAmount	YTDAmount
13	Australia	Assets	Trade R...	1	0	394308.6
13	Australia	Assets	Trade R...	1	0	490891.1
13	Australia	Assets	Trade R...	1	0	399498.17
13	Australia	Liabilities	Accoun...	-1	0	64400.7
13	Australia	Liabilities	Accoun...	-1	0	56579.5

Figure 5.15 The Balance Sheet report demonstrates expression-based groups and conditional column visibility.

Implementing the group aggregates on the report necessitates some data preparation. Specifically, the report query introduces a Sign column that has a value of 1 for asset accounts and -1 for liability accounts, as shown in Figure 5.15. To produce the year-to-date totals, the query returns data for all months in the selected year. Conditional logic zeros out the CurrentAmount column for all periods that don't match the current period. This technique is discussed in more detail in the Cross-Tab Reports article (see Resources).

TIP If you target Analysis Services, the server can aggregate the chart of accounts for you automatically. The DimAccount dimension table provides the necessary row and column structures. It includes an Operator column that defines how the account aggregates, including an addition operator (+) for adding a value to the parent and a subtraction operator (-) if the account needs to be subtracted from the parent value. The UnaryOperatorColumn property of the Accounts parent-child hierarchy (Account dimension in UDM) is mapped to the Operator column. At run time, the server examines the UnaryOperatorColumn property and aggregates data accordingly.

Implementing report groups

The tablix details group aggregates data at the account level. After detail grouping is applied, the resulting dataset contains one row per account, with the current period amount and an aggregated year-to-date amount. The table footer uses expressions to calculate the grand totals. For example, the grand total of the CurrentAmount column is calculated as follows:

```
=Sum(Fields!CurrentAmount.Value * Fields!Sign.Value)
```

As a result, asset accounts add to the grand total, while liability accounts subtract. Bear in mind that this expression is not equivalent to the following expression, which should never be used:

~~=Sum(Fields!CurrentAmount.Value) * Sum(Fields!Sign.Value)~~

The expression above is incorrect because we need to sign the value first before adding it to the aggregated total.

Implementing conditional column visibility

When the user selects January as a current period, the Amount and YTD values are the same. Suppose that you want to hide the YTD column in this case. Your first impulse may be to select the YTD column and set up an expression-based Hidden property. However, recall that when you click the column selector, you are actually selecting all cells in the column. Consequently, when the Hidden expression resolves to True, it will hide all cells inside the column but the column will still occupy a space on the report. Instead, follow these steps to conditionally hide the entire column.

1. Switch the Grouping pane to advanced mode.
2. In the Column Groups pane, select the static member that represents the desired column.

   In our case, the Column Groups pane shows two static members because we have two columns that are not tablix headers. You need to select the second item because that is the one that represents the YTD column.
3. Set the Hidden property of the second (Static) item to the following expression:

   ```
   =Parameters!CurPeriod.Value=1
   ```

   When the value of the CurPeriod parameter is 1 (January), the expression evaluates to True and the column is hidden. The difference between hiding all cells in the column and hiding the (Static) column is that in the latter case the column space is reclaimed. For example, if the (Static) column for YTD is hidden, the % Total column moves to the left to take over the space of the YTD column.

NOTE If your customization requirements go beyond what expressions and conditional visibility can deliver, consider implementing a report definition customization extension. As its name suggest, this extensibility mechanism lets you customize the entire report definition at run time, including adding or removing report regions, columns, etc., based on the report parameter values and user identity. I cover report definition customization extension in chapter 22.

5.2 Designing Crosstab Reports

Another common report layout is a crosstab, also known as a pivot. A crosstab report has dynamic columns that expand to accommodate data. Behind the scenes, a crosstab report rotates (pivots) data from dataset rows to columns. For example, if the dataset groups data by product category and year, a crosstab might show data broken down by product category on rows and time on columns.

5.2.1 The Anatomy of the Matrix Region

You can implement crosstab reports with a matrix region, whose main elements are shown in Figure 5.16. The report illustrated in this figure is the Product Sales Crosstab report, which you will author in the next practice. This report demonstrates:

- Nested dynamic groups
- Inner static groups
- Calculating growth with the Previous function
- Adjacent dynamic groups
- Repeating matrix headers and conditional formatting

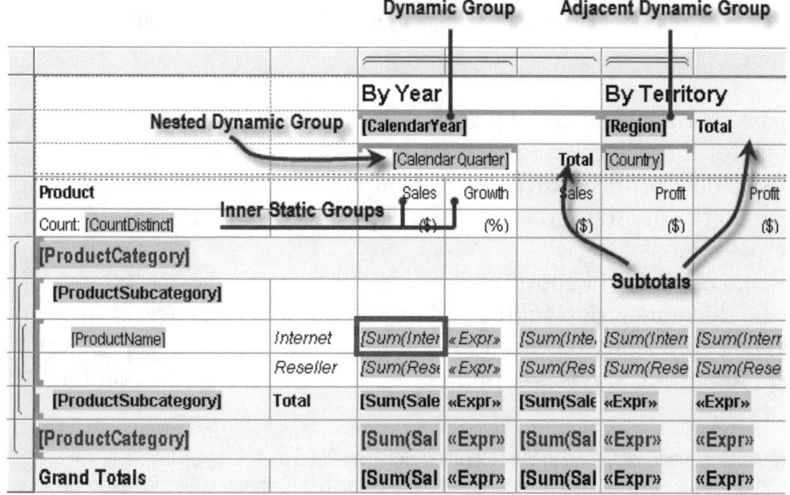

Figure 5.16 The matrix region supports dynamic and static groups to let you implement crosstab reports.

Dynamic groups

Similar to dynamic row groups, dynamic column groups expand at run time to show the underlying data. The Product Sales Crosstab report includes CalendarYear, CalendarQuarter, Region, and Country dynamic groups. Dynamic column groups give the matrix region the crosstab look. For example, when you run the report, Reporting Services groups data by year and shows the years on columns.

Dynamic groups can be nested. The CalendarQuarter dynamic group is nested inside the CalendarYear dynamic group. In Reporting Services parlance, the CalendarQuarter group is a child group whose parent group is CalendarYear. Similarly, the Country group is a child group of the Region group. Consequently, the report shows data broken down by years and quarters, as well as regions and countries, as shown in Figure 5.17.

Adjacent columns

You can have adjacent dynamic columns that are parallel to each other. For example, the Region group is parallel with the CalendarYear group. Consequently, the matrix region produces two column group sections side by side that show data by year and region. If the Region group was nested inside the CalendarYear group, the report would show results broken by years followed by regions that have data for the parent year. However, when the columns are adjacent, they are independent of each other.

		By Year					By Territory						
		2004					Europe			North America		Pacific	Total
			1		2	Total	France	Germany	United Kingdom	Canada	United States	Australia	
Product		Sales	Growth	Sales	Growth	Sales	Profit	Profit	Profit	Profit	Profit	Profit	Profit
Count: 65		($)	(%)	($)	(%)	($)	($)	($)	($)	($)	($)	($)	($)
Mountain Bikes	**Total**	**406,937**		**476,699**	**15 %**	**883,636**	**8,368**	**3,761**	**5,767**	**3,698**	**61,396**	**3,096**	**86,086**
Road Bikes													
Road-350-W Yellow, 42	*Internet*	*3,402*		*17,010*	*80 %*	*20,412*	*880*		*880*		*3,519*		*5,279*
	Reseller	*6,124*		*20,412*	*70 %*	*26,535*	*(338)*		*(1,014)*		*(3,043)*		*(4,396)*
Road-750 Black, 58	*Internet*	*1,620*		*1,080*	*-50 %*	*2,700*	*279*	*140*			*279*		*698*
	Reseller	*1,944*		*648*	*-200 %*	*2,592*	*(107)*	*(107)*			*(215)*		*(429)*

Figure 5.17 The Product Sales Crosstab cross-tab report shows data by time and territory on columns.

Subtotals

Subtotals let you aggregate data across instances of a group. For example, the Product Sales Crosstab report has a subtotal for the CalendarQuarter dynamic group and a subtotal for the Region group. There isn't a subtotal for the Growth static group because it cannot be meaningfully aggregated by summing up the quarter growth values. The report also includes a Region subtotal that sums profit across regions.

Unlike matrices in previous releases of Reporting Services, the new matrix (tablix) gives you complete control over the dynamic group subtotals. You can use whatever aggregate functions (Sum, Avg, and so on) or expressions you need in subtotals. This is a huge step forward from previous releases where Reporting Services supported only limited customization for subtotals via the InScope function.

REAL LIFE Matrix subtotal limitations made us abandon the Reporting Services 2005 matrix region in one of my projects where we had to report-enable a custom financial application. The report requirements called for expression-based aggregates to produce matrix subtotals. It quickly became obvious that this level of customization surpassed the matrix capabilities. The only workaround we found was generating a table report with static columns programmatically. Since tablix group subtotals are now in par with row group subtotals, this predicament simply disappears with tablix.

About the Product Sales Crosstab Start report

Next, I'll walk you through the steps of implementing the Product Sales Crosstab report. The Product Sales Crosstab Start report represents the starting point for this practice. This report is similar to the Product Sales Stepped report, with the following significant changes:

1. The Products dataset now groups by Region and Country. To simplify calculating the group subtotals, I added a Sales Amount calculated field to the Products dataset that has the following expression:

```
=Fields!InternetSalesAmount.Value+Fields!ResellerSalesAmount.Value
```

2. Next I changed the query WHERE clause to:

```
WHERE T.CalendarYear IN (@Year))
```

3. I deleted the Month parameter, and then configured the Year parameter as a multivalued parameter.
4. I deleted all static numeric columns with the exception of Sales.
5. I used the following group expression for the Details group:

   ```
   =Fields!ProductName.Value
   ```

   This was needed to aggregate data by product.
6. I changed the expression in the first cell of the second table header to:

   ```
   Count: =CountDistinct(Fields!ProductName.Value)
   ```

   Because the grouping of the dataset changed, the previous expression, which used the CountRows function to count the dataset rows, was no longer accurate. To get the correct count, I used the CountDistinct function to count the distinct products. I labeled the expression placeholder with a CountDistinct custom label.

5.2.2 Working with Dynamic Column Groups ▶

Start by adding two dynamic column groups to group data by calendar year and quarter. Recall that we removed the tablix group headers when we designed the stepped report. In this exercise, we add them back. The tablix groups are needed because they allow us to place the dynamic column groups alongside the static columns. If you do not create the tablix group first, adding a dynamic column group will enclose all static columns, which is not what you are after.

Create a dynamic group

Follow these steps to create a dynamic column group that groups data by calendar year:

1. Right-click any cell in the Sales column and click Add Group ⇨ Parent Group.
2. In the Tablix Group dialog box that follows, expand the Group By drop-down list and select [CalendarYear] to bind the group to the CalendarYear field. Click OK.

   Report Designer adds a Group1 group to the Column Groups pane and adds a new row for the dynamic group in tablix, as shown in Figure 5.18. A double dotted line separates the group area from the other rows. All cells in the Sales column are in the scope of the new column group. Consequently, they will be repeated for each year as the column group expands at run time.

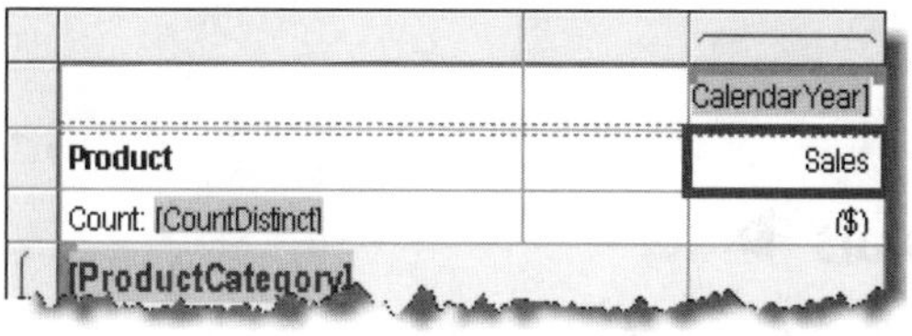

Figure 5.18 A dynamic column group pivots the report results.

3. In the Grouping pane (advanced mode), double-click the Group1 member in the Column Groups pane. Alternatively, to access the group properties, right-click the Group1 member and click Group Properties.
4. In the Group Properties dialog box (General tab), rename the group to *CalendarYear*.
5. Click the Sorting tab. Verify that the group will sort data by the CalendarYear field. Click OK.

6. In the tablix region, right-click the CalendarYear cell and click Expression. Note that the group uses the following expression for the column header:

```
=Fields!CalendarYear.Value
```

You can change this expression if needed. For example, if you want to prefix each year with "CY", you can enter:

```
CY [CalendarYear]
```

This works because the [CalendarYear] placeholder is a substitute for the expression =Fields!CalendarYear.Value.

7. Preview the report.

Notice that the CalendarYear group pivots the report data by years 2003 and 2004, which are the default values of the Year parameter.

8. Click the CalendarYear cell and use the Properties window to change its Font ⇨ FontStyle to Bold and Font ⇨ Font Family to Arial Narrow.

Creating a child group

You can add an arbitrary number of child groups to see additional level of detail in the crosstab report. In the following steps, you will add a child group to the CalendarYear group to pivot data by quarter:

1. Right-click the CalendarYear cell and click Add Group ⇨ Child Group. Alternatively, you can right-click the CalendarYear member in the Column Groups pane and click Add Group ⇨ Child Group.
2. In the Tablix Group dialog box, expand the Group By drop-down list and click [Calendar-Quarter] to bind the new group to the CalendarQuarter field. Click OK.

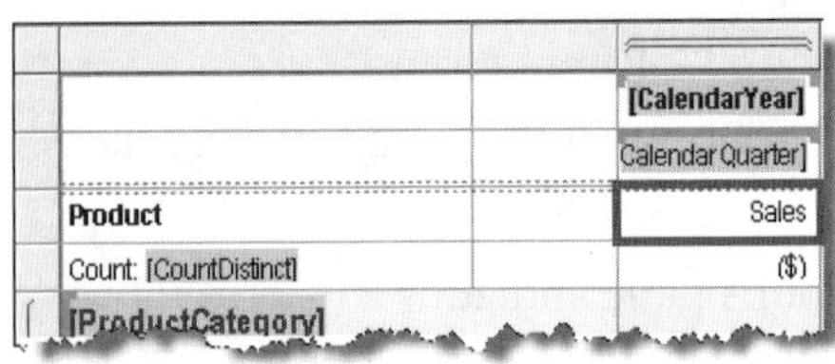

Figure 5.19 The Product Sales Crosstab pivots first by year and then by the quarter child group.

3. Double-click the Group1 group in the Column Groups pane. In Group Properties, rename the group to *CalendarQuarter*. Click OK. Your report layout should match Figure 5.19.
4. Preview the report.

The report should now pivot by year and quarter.

5.2.3 Working with Static Groups and Totals ▶

A dynamic group can have an arbitrary number of inner static groups. As it stands, the Product Sales Crosstab report has a single static group (Sales). It is not uncommon for a crosstab report to pivot on several numeric columns.

Adding a static group

Suppose that report users have requested a new column that shows the growth in sales from the previous quarter side by side with the Sales column.

1. Click any cell in the Sales column. Observe that tablix shows an orange active group indicator above the CalendarQuarter dynamic group so the innermost group is CalendarQuarter.
2. Right-click the CalendarQuarter cell and click Insert Column ⇨ Inside Group – Right.

   A new column is added to the tablix region. The CalendarQuarter group spans the Sales column and the new column. Consequently, both columns will pivot on quarter.

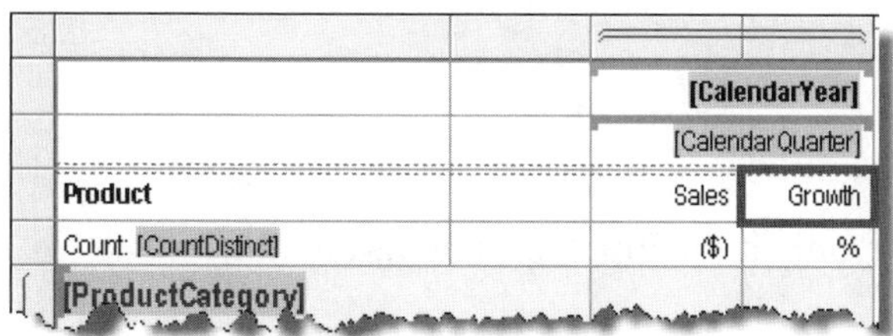

Figure 5.20 You can have more than one static column associated with a dynamic column.

3. Enter *Growth* as a column header in the first static row and *(%)* in the second static row, as shown in Figure 5.20.

   If you preview the report at this point, the report should repeat an empty Growth column for each quarter alongside the Sales column.

Defining growth expression

Next, you need to define expression-based totals to calculate the sales growth from the previous quarter:

1. Right-click the intersecting cell of the Growth column and the Product Name row with Internet sales, and click Expression.
2. In the Expression dialog box, enter the following expression:

```
=(Sum(Fields!InternetSalesAmount.Value)-Previous(Sum(Fields!InternetSalesAmount.Value),"CalendarQuarter"))/
Sum(Fields!InternetSalesAmount.Value)
```

   The first operand returns the aggregated sales value for the current quarter. The second operand used the Previous function to return the sales for the previous quarter. Because referencing a previous or parallel time period is a common reporting requirement, Reporting Services 2008 has extended the Previous function to take scope as an argument. Because the scope is set to the CalendarQuarter group, the Previous function returns the aggregated value from the previous quarter. If you want to reference the parallel quarter for last year, set the scope to "CalendarYear" instead.
3. Preview the report.

   Although the expression is working, there are many cells with NaN and #Error values. The NaN values result from 0/0 or Null/Null operations, which occur because we are missing some quarterly sales data. The #Error values are caused by run-time errors. In our case, we get #Error values when there are results for the previous quarter, but not for the current quarter. This results in a division by zero error. To fix these issues, we need to check the expression operands. In our first attempt, we could try the Iif() function. Unfortunately, this function executes both the true and false parts of the expression, so using it to avoid division by zero is not so simple.

TIP If you want to use the Iif() function to check for Null or Zero conditions, you can nest two Iif functions so both the true and false parts execute successfully, such as =IIF(Field!B.Value=0, 0,Field!A.Value / IIF(Field!B.Value =0, 1,Field!B.Value)).

Instead, we will use a simple embedded function to check the expression arguments:

4. Right-click the report design area outside the report body, and click Report Properties.
5. In the Report Properties dialog box, click the Code tab, and enter the following function:

```
Public Function GetGrowth(ByVal CurrentValue, ByVal PreviousValue) As Object
   If IsNothing(PreviousValue) OR IsNothing(CurrentValue) Then
      Return Nothing
   Else if PreviousValue = 0 OR CurrentValue = 0 Then
      Return Nothing
   Else
      Return (CurrentValue - PreviousValue) / CurrentValue
   End If
End Function
```

This function performs the growth calculation only if the input arguments are not zero or Null.

6. Right-click the intersecting cell of the Growth column and Internet row, and change its expression to:

```
=Code.GetGrowth(Sum(Fields!InternetSalesAmount.Value),
Previous(Sum(Fields!InternetSalesAmount.Value), "CalendarQuarter"))
```

Don't worry if you don't understand the Code keyword. For now, simply note that it allows us to execute custom functions. We'll cover the Code keyword in more detail in chapter 7.

7. Right-click the intersecting cell of the Growth column and Reseller row, and enter the following expression:

```
=Code.GetGrowth(Sum(Fields!ResellerSalesAmount.Value),
Previous(Sum(Fields!ResellerSalesAmount.Value), "CalendarQuarter"))
```

8. Enter the following expression in the ProductSubcategory and ProductCategory group footers, as well as in the table footer subtotals in the Growth column:

```
=Code.GetGrowth(Sum(Fields!SalesAmount.Value),
Previous(Sum(Fields!SalesAmount.Value), "CalendarQuarter"))
```

9. Format the Growth cells as percentages with no decimals (P0 format setting).
10. To show the negative growth numbers in red, use the following expression for the Color property for the Growth cells in the detail rows:

```
=Iif(Me.Value < 0, "Red", "Black")
```

Now that you have defined the groups, you are ready to add dynamic group totals that show subtotals for each product category and subcategory.

Adding dynamic group totals

Similar to row groups, dynamic groups can have subtotals. Let's add a subtotal to the CalendarQuarter group to show the total sales amount:

1. Right-click the CalendarQuarter cell in the tablix region and click Add Total. By default, the tablix adds the subtotal after the group.

   Report Designer adds two tablix group header columns because the CalendarQuarter group spans two columns. The new columns are pre-populated with subtotal expressions from the Sales and Growth columns.

2. We don't need a subtotal for the Growth column because its values cannot be meaningfully aggregated. Right-click the column header of the second column and click Delete Columns.

Note that you have the same control over column group subtotals as over row group subtotals. For example, you can use the Sum aggregate function in one group footer to roll up data and the Avg function in another to calculate averages. This was very difficult to implement with the Reporting Services 2005 matrix data region.

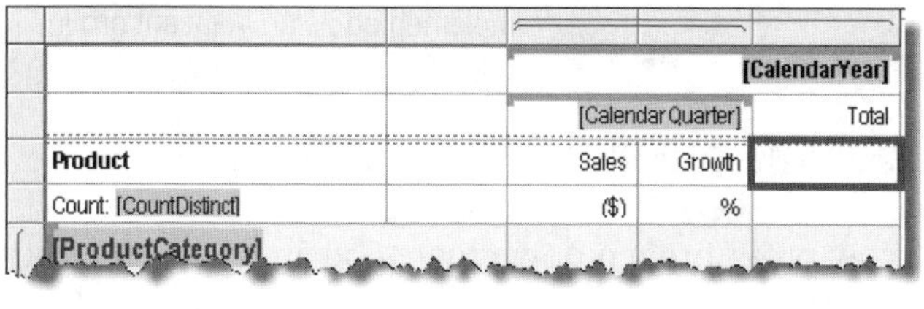

Figure 5.21 Unlike previous releases, Reporting Services 2008 gives you complete control over dynamic group subtotals.

3. Click a cell in the CalendarYear column and note that its scope is the CalendarYear group, as shown in Figure 5.21.
4. Preview the report.

The Subtotals values are produced by summing the values for all quarters within the year. If you want the report to show a grand total column for all years, you could add a total for the CalendarYear group (right-click CalendarYear and click Add Total).

I'd like to mention one cautionary note about subtotals and semi-additive measures. Although you can use any aggregate function, remember that the subtotals are produced over all *detail* values. For example, if you replace the Sum function with Avg, you will find that a quarter subtotal is *not* the average of the individual quarter sales. For example, the ProductSubcategory subtotal is under the dynamic scope of the ProductSubcategory and the CalendarYear groups. If you check all the detail rows that go into that particular product subcategory and year, you will see that average subtotal is actually the correct average value of the detail rows.

TIP What's really needed to produce average subtotals over displayed values is an expression like Avg(Sum(Fields!Sales.Value)). However, Reporting Services doesn't currently support aggregates over aggregates. Instead, you can produce simple averages by summing the sales and dividing by the number of quarters, such as by using the following expression =Sum(Fields!Sales.Value) /CountDistinct (Fields!CalendarQuarter.Value, "CalendarYear"). Since the CountDistinct function is scoped for the CalendarYear group, it returns the number of quarters in each group instance.

5.2.4 Implementing Adjacent Groups ▶

The matrix data region doesn't limit you to one parent dynamic group on columns. You can add adjacent groups to implement side-by-side crosstab sections. For example, the first section can show sales by time while the second section can show profit by territory.

Adding adjacent groups

Suppose that you want to add another section that shows the sales profit by territory. You can address this requirement by implementing an adjacent group to the CalendarYear group:

1. Right-click the CalendarYear cell in tablix and click Add Group ⇨ Adjacent Right. Alternatively, to add an adjacent group, right-click the CalendarYear member in the Column Groups pane, and click Add Group ⇨ Adjacent After.
2. In the Tablix Group dialog box, bind the new group to the [Region] field. Click OK.
3. Rename the new group to *Region*.

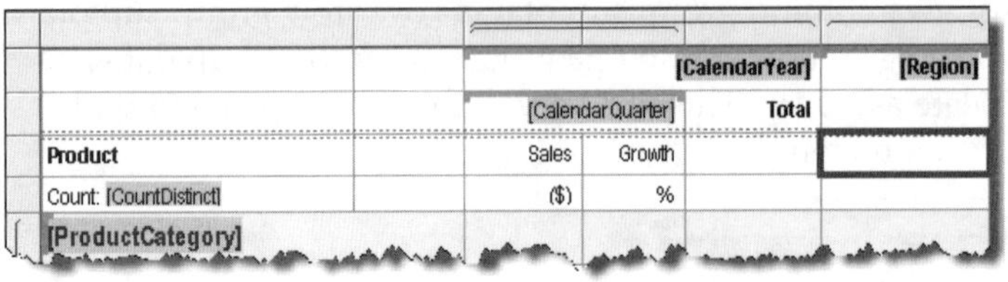

Figure 5.22 The Region group is implemented as an adjacent group to the CalendarYear group.

Report Designer adds the Region group next to the CalendarYear group, as shown in Figure 5.22. Adjacent groups need not be balanced. In other words, they don't need to have the same number of child groups. In our case, to show profit broken down by region and country, you need to add a child group to the Region group.

4. Right-click the Region cell in the tablix and click Add Group ⇨ Child Group. Alternatively, right-click the Region member in the Column Groups pane and click Add Group ⇨ Child Group.
5. In the Tablix Group dialog box, bind the group to the [Country] field. Click OK. Rename the new group to *Country*.

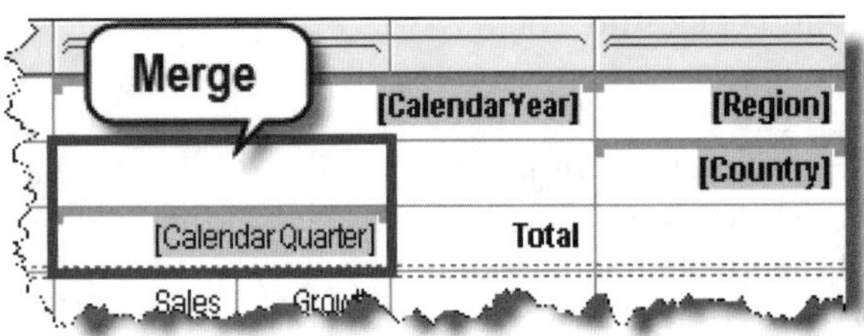

Figure 5.23 You can eliminate extra rows by merging cells and deleting the unwanted rows.

At this point, Report Designer creates somewhat of a mess which I affectionately call *messlix*. It adds a new row to accommodate the Country group (see Figure 5.23) while it should have reused the existing row of the CalendarQuarter group. Fear not, however, as you can fix this easily.

6. Select the CalendarQuarter cell and the one above it. Right-click the selection and click Merge Cells.
7. Copy the Total cell to the cell above it.
8. Right click the third row where the original Total cell is located, and click Delete Rows.

The end result is that CalendarQuarter, Total, and Country cells are on the same row.

9. Enter the following expression in the intersecting cell of the detail row for Internet sales and Country column:

```
=Sum(Fields!InternetProfit.Value)
```

10. Enter the following expression in the intersecting cell of the detail row for Reseller sales and Country column:

```
=Sum(Fields!ResellerProfit.Value)
```

11. Enter the following expression in ProductSubcategory, ProductCategory, and the table footer:

```
=Sum(Fields!InternetProfit.Value + Fields!ResellerProfit.Value)
```

12. Format all numeric cells in the Country column as #,0;(#,0).
13. To include a grand total, right-click the Region cell and click Add Total.

14. To add a static row for the section headers, right-click the CalendarYear cell, and click Insert Row ⇨ Outside Group – Above.
15. In the merged cell above the CalendarYear cell, enter *By Time*.
16. Select the two cells above the Region column and its subtotal column. Right-click the selection and click Merge Cells. In the merged cell, enter *By Territory*.

Use your artistic skills to format the report as needed.

Implementing repeating matrix headers

Preview the Product Sales Crosstab report and notice that it is three pages long. However, the headers of the dynamic groups appear only on the first page. Consequently, it may difficult for end users to guess where a crosstab section starts and ends. Fortunately, adding repeated matrix headers only takes a mouse click with reports that have column group area.

1. Select the tablix region.
2. In the Properties window, set RepeatColumnHeaders to True.
3. Preview the report.

Notice that the column headers repeat on new pages.

TIP You can easily invert a crosstab report to show row headers on the right followed by columns on the left by changing the tablix LayoutDirection property to RTL (right-to-left). If you want the column header text to be written vertically, change the WritingMode of the textbox to Vertical. Unfortunately, Reporting Services doesn't support full text rotation so you are stuck with top to bottom, right to left rotation.

5.3 Designing Freeform Reports

As its name suggests, a freeform report layout arranges report items arbitrarily on a page. Consider a freeform report layout when you find a tabular layout too restrictive. For example, an order header section might not be easily arranged in columns, or you might want to show text information vertically with an image on the side. While you may be able to implement such requirements by merging cells, this approach doesn't give you complete control over the item positioning. Besides, you can merge tablix cells only if they share the same group. Instead, when the report layout is not strictly tabular, consider the list data region, which lets you position items wherever you want to.

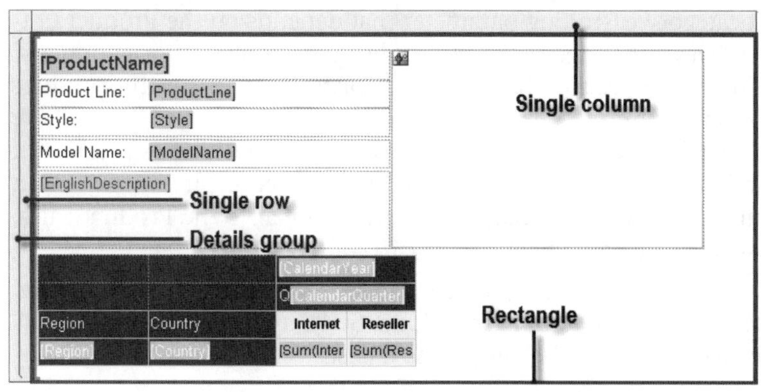

Figure 5.24 The list data region is a tablix with a single row, a single column, and an embedded rectangle.

5.3.1 The Anatomy of the List Region

The list region lets you implement freeform reports. As Figure 5.24 illustrates, the list region is nothing more than a tablix with a single cell. The report illustrated in this figure is the Sales Crosstab by Product report which you will author in the next practice. This report demonstrates:

- Freeform report design
- Nested data regions
- Database images

Rectangle
The list region cell includes a rectangle report item. The rectangle is what lets you place items anywhere on the report. You can place any number of report items in the rectangle, including textboxes, images, and nested data regions. For example, the list in the Sales Crosstab by Product report includes several textboxes for displaying product information, an image item that displays the product image, and a matrix data region that shows a crosstab report with product sales by territory and time.

Details grouping
Similar to the table region, the list region includes a pre-defined Details group, which does not have a grouping expression. You can use this group to sort or group the data before it's fed to the list. If no grouping expression is defined, the Details group represents a row in the underlying dataset. Consequently, at run time Reporting Services will generate the list for each row. If there is a grouping expression defined, the list will be repeated for each group instance.

The context of the Details group is passed to nested regions. To display the sales for the current product in the matrix, we need to group the list on products. This will cause the list to pass only the dataset rows associated with the current product to the nested matrix. If you don't define a grouping expression in the list Details group, you will get the following error when you run the report:

```
[rsInvalidDetailDataGrouping] The tablix 'Table' has a detail member with inner members. Detail members can only contain static inner members.
```

About the Sales Crosstab by Product Start report
Now that you have an understanding of how list regions work, let's walk through the steps of implementing the Sales Crosstab by Product report, shown in Figure 5.25. It has a Product Category parameter, and a Subcategory cascading parameter that depends on the Product Category parameter. When the user views the report, the report displays product information arranged in a freeform format. The matrix section that follows displays the sales for this product by territories on rows and time on columns.

The Sales Crosstab by Product Start report represents the starting point for this practice. It contains the datasets and the minimal layout you will use to build the report. If you have been stepping through all of the demos, you will find that this report is similar to the Product Sales Crosstab report with the following significant changes:

1. In the Sales Crosstab by Product Start report, the Products dataset includes the following new columns from the DimProduct table: LargePhoto, ProductLine, Style, and ModelName. Because the report has a Subcategory parameter, I changed the dataset WHERE clause to:

```
WHERE (P.ProductSubcategoryKey = @ProductSubcategory)
```

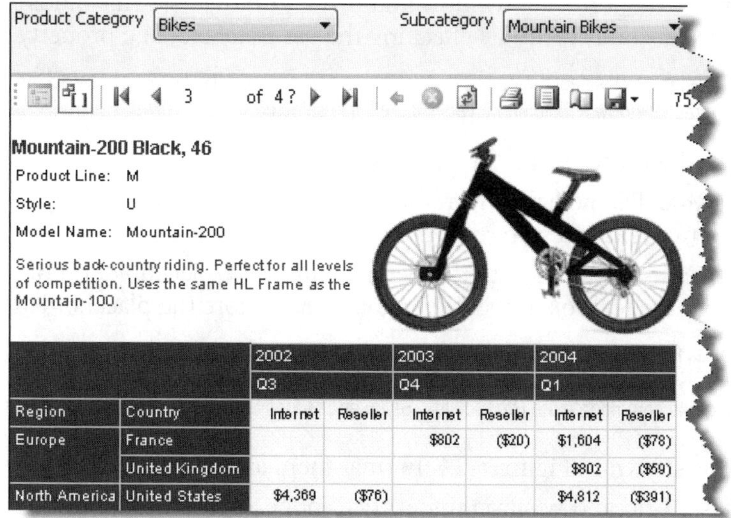

		2002		2003		2004	
		Q3		Q4		Q1	
Region	Country	Internet	Reseller	Internet	Reseller	Internet	Reseller
Europe	France			$802	($20)	$1,604	($78)
	United Kingdom					$802	($59)
North America	United States	$4,369	($76)			$4,812	($391)

Figure 5.25 The Sales Crosstab by Product report generates a crosstab section for each product.

2. I created ProductCategory and ProductSubcategory datasets for the available values of the report parameters.
3. I created ProductCategory and ProductSubcategory parameters. I configured the ProductSubcategory parameter as a cascading parameter that depends on the ProductCategory parameter.
4. I added a matrix region to the report.
5. I added the InternetProfit and ResellerProfit columns side by side in the tablix body.
6. I used tablix group headers for the row groups. I implemented them by adding the Region and Country columns to the Row Groups pane. This created two dynamic row groups that group report data by region and country.
7. I added the CalendarYear and CalendarQuarter columns to the Column Groups pane to create two dynamic column groups that group report data by year and quarter. I also changed the CalendarQuarter column header to show the quarter prefixed with "Q", such as Q1, Q2, and so on. To do so, I configured the CalendarQuarter cell with two textruns, as follows:

```
Q[CalendarQuarter]
```

8. Finally, I added a row outside the Region group for the column headers for the two static columns. I entered *Internet* and *Reseller* as column captions.

5.3.2 Designing a Freeform Layout ▶

Now that we understand what is in the Sales Crosstab by Product Start report, let's get to work on configuring the list region. This involves designing the freeform section of the report that shows the product details and nesting the matrix region inside the list.

Working with the List region

Start by adding the list region to the report:

1. In the Toolbox, double-click the List item to add an empty list region to the report.
2. Resize the list region 6" wide and 3" tall.

3. Drag the ProductName field from the Report Data window and drop it on the list. This binds the list to the Products dataset, as you could verify by checking the list DataSetName property.

   TIP If you click inside the list, Report Designer will select the embedded rectangle and not the list. Click Esc to select the list. The drop-down selector of the Properties window should show Tablix if the list is selected.

   Next, you will add report items to the list to define the report layout:

4. Drag the ProductLine, Style, and ModelName fields from the Report Data window and drop them on the list. This will create three textboxes nested inside the list.
5. Double-click each of these textboxes and type in a static label in front of the placeholder. For example, double click the Product Line textbox and enter *Product Line:* before the placeholder.

   TIP There aren't any guidelines as far as how much content you should fit into a single "rich" textbox. If the field positioning doesn't vary too much, you could try consolidating the content into fewer textboxes. For example, instead of three textboxes, you can use a single textbox to accommodate the ProductLine, Style, and ModelName fields.

6. Arrange the textboxes vertically, as shown in Figure 5.24. Format them as needed.
7. Drag the EnglishDescription dataset field and position under the Model Name textbox.
8. Select the matrix and drag it inside the list. Position it below the textboxes.

   The next two steps are required when nesting regions inside the list.

9. Click the list region to select it. In the Row Groups pane, double-click the Details group.
10. In the Group Properties dialog box (General tab), click Add and group on [ProductName].
11. Click the Page Breaks tab and check Between Each Instance of a Group. As a result, the list will display each product on a new page.
12. Preview the report.

    The list should repeat for each product. The matrix should show the sales for the product displayed in the list.

Working with database images

If the database contains images, you can use the Image report item to display these images on the report. The LargePhoto column in the DimProduct table stores the product image. To use an image on the report, do the following:

1. Drag the Image item from the Toolbox and drop it inside the list.
2. In the Image Properties dialog box (General tab), expand the Select the Image Source drop-down list and select Database.
3. Expand the Use This Field drop-down list and select [LargePhoto] to bind the image to the LargePhoto dataset field.
4. Expand Use this MIME Type and select image/jpeg.
5. Click the Size tab. Select Fit To Size display option to size the image proportionally within the bounds of the image report item. Click OK.
6. Resize the image as needed.
7. Preview the report.

   The report should show the product image if it is available. Products that don't have images should show No Image Available.

5.3.3 Working with Subreports

The Sales Orders by Date report, which I discussed in chapter 4, demonstrates another example of a freeform report layout. It uses a list region for the order header section and a nested table region for the order details. As I mentioned in that chapter, Reporting Services doesn't let you join datasets on the report. To work around this limitation, the Sales Orders by Date report used a single query to return the order header and order details rows. Another workaround, which I will demonstrate next, is to use a subreport for the order details.

Understanding subreports

A subreport is a report that is embedded inside another report. You can use any report as a subreport. The master (parent) report can include more than one subreport. Both the master report and a subreport have separate report definitions, which are usually stored together in the same folder when the reports are deployed. The master report can pass parameters to the subreport to get related data. Subreports are useful in the following scenarios:

- When your report has multiple sections with one-to-many relationship, such as order header-to-order items, as I will demonstrate shortly.
- When you need to reuse a subreport in multiple parent reports. For example, you may need to show a summary section in multiple reports. You can refactor this section as a stand-alone report to simplify overall maintenance.
- When you want to group several smaller reports into a single larger report. Suppose that you want to create a shareholder report by assembling several existing report definitions into a single report package. You can accomplish this by creating a master report consisting of subreport items that reference the financial reports you want to include.

Subreports are subject to certain limitations. First of all, subreports cannot pass information back to the master report. You can only have a one-way data exchange from the master to the subreport by passing report parameters. Second, subreport page headers and footers are ignored when the master report is rendered. Third, you cannot execute subreports conditionally. For example, you cannot disable an order details subreport if the parent query indicates that there are no orders for a given date. In other words, the subreport and its queries are always executed.

Finally, the master report cannot have a mixed page layouts that include both landscape and portrait orientations. If one of the subreports has a landscape page layout, you must set the master to accommodate the widest subreport (landscape in this case). The page layout of the master page ultimately determines the page layout of all the subreports. The Sales Order Header report demonstrates working with subreports. It produces the same output as the Sales Orders by Date, but it references the Sales Order Items subreport to produce the order details section.

Implementing subreports

Start by creating the Sales Order Items subreport:

1. Create a new report and name it *Sales Order Items*.
2. Open the chapter 4 Reports project in BIDS. Open the Sales Orders by Date report in Report Designer.
3. Select the OrderDetail table region and copy it (Ctrl+C).
4. Paste the OrderDetail table region in the body section of the Sales Order Items report.

5. Create a data source reference to the AdventureWorks2008 database.
6. Create a SalesOrderDetail dataset. Import the query statement from the SalesOrderDetail.sql file, which is included with the book source code.
7. Examine the Parameters node in the Report Data window. It should contain a SalesOrderNumber report parameter.
8. Optionally, set the default value of the SalesOrderNumber parameter to 50750, so you don't have to enter an order number each time you preview the report while testing it.

Implementing the master report

Follow the next set of steps to author the master report:

1. Copy the Sales Orders by Date report definition from the chapter 4 Reports project and include it in the chapter 5 Reports project. Rename the report to *Sales Order Header*.
2. Open the Sales Order dataset in design mode and add the SalesOrderID column from the SalesOrderHeader table in the Products dataset query.
3. Remove the SalesOrderDetail table from the query statement. You don't need this table because the subreport will handle the order details.
4. Remove the Top 50 clause from the query.
5. In the report design area, select the OrderDetail table region and delete it.
6. Drag the Subreport item from the Toolbar and drop it inside the list region in the same place where the OrderDetail table was. The subreport item must be nested inside the list region.
7. Click the subreport item and change its Name property in the Properties window to *OrderItems*.
8. Right-click the subreport item and click Subreport Properties.
9. In the Subreport Properties dialog box (General tab), expand Use this Report as a Subreport drop-down list and select Sales Order Items.

The Sales Order Items report accepts the sales order number as a parameter called SalesOrderNumber. To show data about the same order in both reports, you need to configure the master report to pass the sales order number to the subreport. This process is similar to configuring query parameters.

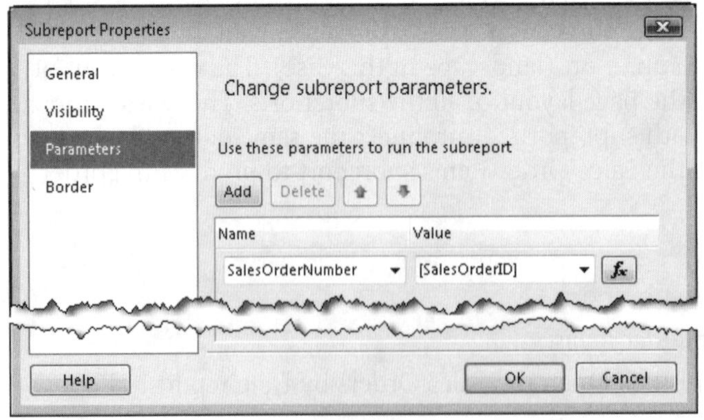

Figure 5.26 The Sales Order Header report passes the SalesOrderID field to the SalesOrderNumber parameter of the Sales Order Items subreport.

10. Click the Parameters tab and click the Add button to define a new parameter.
11. Expand the Name drop-down and click the SalesOrderNumber parameter.

12. Expand the Value drop-down list and click [SalesOrderID], as shown on Figure 5.26.

As a result of these changes, the list region will repeat the SalesOrderItems subreport for each sales order. The list will pass the value of the SalesOrderID field to the SalesOrderNumber parameter of the subreport. At this point, previewing the Sales Order Header report should work. The rendered report should look the same as the Sales Orders by Date report. If for some reason the subreport fails, you'll see the following error in its location on the master report:

```
Error: Subreport could not be shown.
```

Unfortunately, the error message doesn't give any indication about what went wrong with the subreport. To troubleshoot the subreport execution, try previewing the subreport as a standalone report.

5.3.4 Implementing Multicolumn Reports

A multicolumn report has a newspaper-like layout where data flows down multiple adjacent columns. When the server processes a multicolumn report, it creates a series of very narrow pages that are rendered on the same physical page, giving the appearance of multiple columns. Consequently, if you set up a logical page break, such as between group instances, the report will flow to the next column. The multicolumn report layout is subject to the following limitations:

- The layout applies to the entire report—For instance, the report cannot start with a multicolumn layout and change to a tabular layout. Put another way, you set the multi-column layout at the report level and not at the data region level.
- For master report and subreport combinations, the column layout must be the same across the entire set of reports. Subreports inherit the column settings from the parent. If the subreport is configured for a multicolumn layout but the parent is not, the subreport will ignore the multicolumn layout.

Inventory by Category
21-Jun-2008

SubCategory: Bike Racks

Product Name	Quantity
Hitch Rack - 4-Bike	1
Number of products:	0

SubCategory: Bike Stands

Product Name	Quantity
All-Purpose Bike Stand	2

SubCategory: Fenders

Product Name	Quantity
Fender Set - Mountain	7
Number of products:	108

SubCategory: Helmets

Product Name	Quantity
Sport-100 Helmet, Black	8
Sport-100 Helmet, Blue	9
Sport-100 Helmet, Red	10
Number of products:	828

SubCategory: Hydration Packs

SubCategory: Locks

Product Name	Quantity
Cable Lock	15
Number of products:	252

SubCategory: Panniers

Product Name	Quantity
Touring-Panniers, Large	16
Number of products:	72

SubCategory: Pumps

Product Name	Quantity

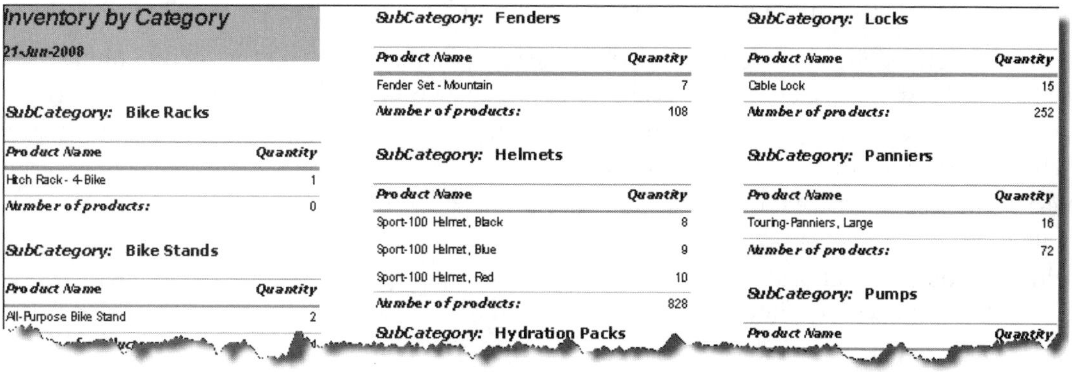

Figure 5.27 The Inventory by Category report has three columns to conserve horizontal space.

The Inventory by Category report, which Figure 5.27 shows, features a multicolumn report layout. It shows the product inventory counts grouped by product subcategory for the current date.

Determining the column width

When working with multiple columns, you need to make sure that the page width can accommodate all columns. You can use the following formula to calculate the column width:

```
column width <= (page width -  (left margin + right margin) - (number of columns – 1)
* column spacing) / number of columns
```

For example, the Inventory by Category report has three columns with a half-inch gap between columns. Assuming a landscape page layout with 0.5" left and right margins, the column width will be:

```
(11" – (0.5"+0.5") – (3 – 1) * 0.5") / 3 = 3"
```

This will result in a column width that is 3" or less.

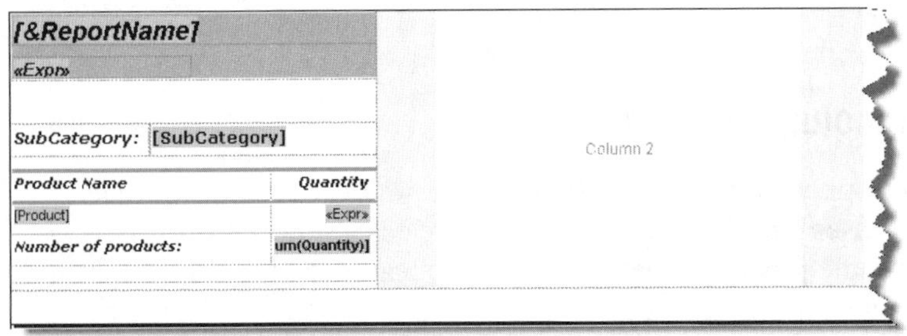

Figure 5.28 Report Designer divides the report body into column sections.

Designing the multicolumn layout

Once you have determined the column width, setting up the report layout is straightforward:

1. In Report Designer, click outside the report body. In the Properties window, set Columns ➪ Columns property to 3 and Columns ➪ ColumnSpacing property to 0.5in.
2. Set Margins ➪ Top to 1in, Margins ➪ Bottom to 1in, Margins ➪ Left to 0.5in, and Margins ➪ Right to 0.5 in.
3. Set PageSize ➪ Width to 11in and PageSize ➪ Height to 9in.
4. Click the report body area and set its Size ➪ Width to 3in.

   Report Designer divides the report body in three sections that represent the report columns, as shown in Figure 5.28. Only the first column (Column 1) is accessible.
5. Drop a list region. Group the list region by [SubCategory]. Add a textbox and bind it to [SubCategory] to show the product subcategory.
6. Nest a table region inside the list. Bind the first detail cell to [Product] and the second to [Quantity].
7. Add a row outside and below the detail group in the table region and enter the following expression in the Quantity column:

```
=Sum(Fields!Quantity.Value)
```

8. Preview the report.

> **TIP** You can limit the number of rows displayed by using the Ceiling function. For example, to break on 20 rows, use the following expression in the list details group =Ceiling(RowNumber(Nothing)/20) and set it to page break between group instances. The RowNumber () function returns the positional number of the current dataset row. The System.Math.Ceiling function returns the smallest number that is not less than the argument. Thus, the group expression returns 1 for the first 20 rows, 2 for the second 20 rows, and so on. This makes the group break on each batch of 20 rows.

5.4 Implementing Interactive Reports

Your report can go beyond the dull presentation of static data. Reporting Services supports a variety of interactive features that let the user interact with the report. Consider adding interactivity to your reports to improve the user experience and make your report more intuitive.

5.4.1 Understanding Report Interactivity

You have already witnessed the most popular interactive feature—report parameters. The user can pass parameter values to the report to customize the report data and layout. Besides parameterized reports, you can extend your reports with other features that allow for interaction at run time.

Toggled visibility

Each report item has a set of properties that determine item visibility. You can use these properties to hide items on a report, conditionally hide data based on other data in the report, or provide a toggle switch so that the user can expand or collapse a report section. For example, you can use toggled visibility to implement report drilldown. When the report opens initially, report groups are hidden to reduce the data shown on the report. If the user wants to see more data, he or she can expand a group to the see the next level of detail. Toggled visibility can be set on any element but it is most commonly used to control visibility of groups, rows, and columns.

Hyperlink actions

Hyperlink actions are links that the user can click to navigate to other resources, such as an external web page. Reporting Services supports three link types:

- A bookmark link provides a link to a bookmark, or anchor, within the current report. For example, similar to HTML pages, the user can click a link to jump to another location in the report.
- A drillthrough link lets the user navigate to another report. For example, the user may start with a summary report and click on a link to see a more detailed report, such as the orders submitted by a customer on a given date.
- A URL link provides a link to an external web page. For example, a URL link can redirect the user to a web page that lets the user update the data shown on the report.

Actions can be applied at textbox, paragraph, and textrun levels. Higher-level actions overwrite lower-level actions. For example, if you have an URL action defined for the textbox and another action defined for a textrun, only the textbox action will be available to the end user.

Document map

Think of a document map as a table of contents in a book that helps the user navigate through long reports. A document map summarizes report content into a hierarchical set of links. When the user clicks a link, focus is immediately set to the corresponding location in the report.

Interactive sorting

This feature lets the user customize the way the data is sorted on the report. When enabled on a textbox, interactive sorting displays a sort indicator inside the textbox. The user can click the sort indicator to sort the report data. Each time the sort indicator is clicked, interactive sorting toggles between ascending and descending order.

Understanding rendering support

Not all of the report renderers support the full range of interactive features. Table 5.1 helps you determine whether the interactive feature is supported in specific renderers.

Table 5.1 Rendering support for interactive features

Feature	HTML	GDI	Excel	Word	PDF	MHTML
Toggled visibility	✓	✓	✓			
Navigation actions	✓	✓	✓	✓	✓	✓
Interactive sorting	✓	✓				
Document map	✓	✓	✓	✓	✓	

In case it's not immediately obvious, the GDI renderer is used by the Windows Forms ReportViewer control. Other output formats that don't support interactivity in any way are not included in the table. Specifically, interactive features are not available with data renderers (XML and CSV) or the Image renderer, which exports reports to binary images, such as TIFF or GIF.

5.4.2 Implementing Toggled Visibility

Toggled visibility is typically used to reduce the perceived complexity of a complex report. In this next section, I'll discuss two reports that demonstrate toggled visibility. Since you are already familiar with the tablix region, I won't do too much hand-holding in this section but I will give you the necessary background to understand the final solution.

Hiding rows and columns

The Toggled Visibility report builds upon the Product Sales by Category report that you authored in chapter 3. However, the similarity ends once you begin adding interactive features. In the Toggled Visibility report, only a subset of the report data is shown when the report is initially run. Specifically, the Discount column appears only when it is greater than zero, and the product subcategory and detail rows appear only if certain conditions are met.

1. Open the Toggled Visibility report in Report Designer. Right-click the column selector of the Discount column and click Column Visibility (see Figure 5.29).
2. Notice that the Discount column uses the following expression that controls its visibility:

```
=(Fields!InternetDiscountAmount.Value+Fields!ResellerDiscountAmount.Value)=0
```

   Consequently, the column will be shown only on those pages where there is at least one row with a discount value greater than zero. The user can click the plus indicator of the Product cell (the leftmost cell in the table region) to see the Discount column if needed.
3. Right-click the ProductSubcategory row and click Row Visibility. Notice that this row uses the following expression that controls its visibility:

```
=Sum(Fields!InternetSalesAmount.Value+Fields!ResellerSalesAmount.Value) < 100000
```

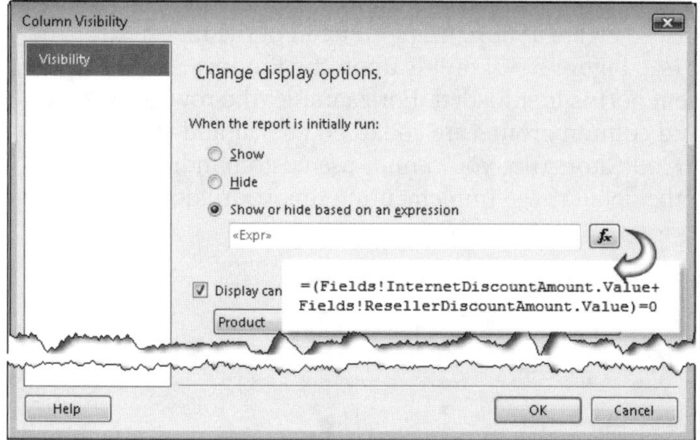

Figure 5.29 The Discount column is hidden when the discount value is zero but can be toggled by the Product item.

4. Check the Display can be Toggled by This Report Item checkbox and select the Category item.

   As a result, this row will be hidden if the total sales amount for the current group instance is less than 100,000.

5. Right-click the Internet detail row and click Row Visibility.

   Note that the row is hidden if Internet sales are less than 100,000, but can be toggled when the user expands the Category field. A similar expression is defined to control the visibility of the Reseller row.

6. Preview the report.

   The report displays a summarized view that shows only the subtotal rows for the product subcategories in the Accessories category.

7. Click the plus sign of the Accessories category to see all rows.
8. Click the plus sign of the Product cell to see the Discount column.

   The report expands vertically to show more rows and horizontally to show the Discount column. Optionally, export the report to Excel and observe that the exported report supports row toggled visibility via Excel collapsible outlines. However, toggled column visibility is not supported.

Implementing drilldown

Besides rows and columns, you can set toggled visibility on report groups. This lets you implement a drilldown effect that you may be familiar with if you have worked with OLAP browsers, such as Excel PivotTable reports. Similar to OLAP drilldown, the user can expand rows and columns to see more data on the report.

However, there is one important difference. Unlike OLAP browsers that generate queries and fetch data with each drilldown action, the report server always retrieves all data at once and caches the data in the report database. This is standard behavior for all report execution, including processing of a drillthrough report. Interestingly, the report server doesn't send the entire report to the client. As the user drills down data, subsequent requests are made to the server to render the report in chunks. Therefore, although report drilldown doesn't optimize data retrieval, it may reduce the report processing and rendering time with large reports because report sections are generated on demand.

The Product Sales Crosstab report, which you authored in this chapter, could be overwhelming for the end user to analyze. To create a more usable version of the report, the Product Sales Crosstab Drilldown report (see Figure 5.30) builds upon the Product Sales Crosstab, but displays summary data when the report is first loaded. For example, the row groups are collapsed at the subcategory level, and column groups are collapsed at year and territory levels. The user can click the plus sign indicators (no, you cannot use custom indicators) to expand the collapsed sections and see the detail rows. Implementing report drilldown takes just a few mouse clicks.

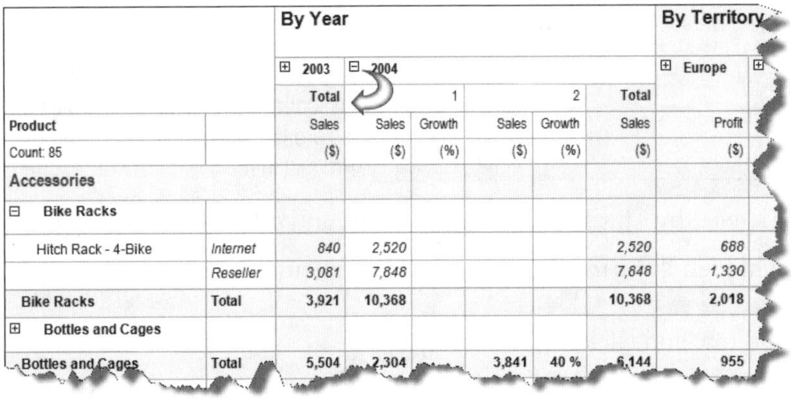

		By Year						By Territory
		⊞ 2003	⊟ 2004					⊞ Europe
		Total		1		2	Total	
Product		Sales	Sales	Growth	Sales	Growth	Sales	Profit
Count: 85		($)	($)	(%)	($)	(%)	($)	($)
Accessories								
⊟ Bike Racks								
Hitch Rack - 4-Bike	Internet	840	2,520				2,520	688
	Reseller	3,081	7,848				7,848	1,330
Bike Racks	Total	3,921	10,368				10,368	2,018
⊞ Bottles and Cages								
Bottles and Cages	Total	5,504	2,304		3,841	40 %	6,144	955

Figure 5.30 The Product Sales Crosstab Drilldown report shows summary data when the report is first loaded and shows detail rows when the user expands a section.

1. Start by assigning meaningful names to the textboxes that will toggle the group visibility so you can locate them easily. For example, rename the first cell in the product category group header to *ProductCategory*, the first cell in the product subcategory group header to *ProductSubcategory*, and so on.
2. In the Row Groups pane, double-click the Details group.
3. In the Group Properties dialog box, click the Visibility tab.
4. Set the When the Report is Initially Run section to Hide.
5. Check the Display Can be Toggled by This Report Item. Expand the drop-down list below and select the ProductSubcategory textbox.
6. Follow similar steps to configure the visibility for the CalendarQuarter group to be toggled by the CalendarYear textbox and the Country group to be toggled by the Region textbox.
7. Preview the report and verify that the report shows summary information. Click the plus sign indicator of the collapsed section to test the drilldown feature.

TIP If drilldown doesn't work or it doesn't hide all rows within the group, switch the Groupings pane to advanced mode and verify that you don't have an extra static member in the group.

5.4.3 Implementing Hyperlink Actions

As noted earlier, you can add bookmark, drillthrough, and URL actions to your reports to let the user navigate within the report and away from the report to view external resources. Examples that demonstrate these three action types are covered next.

Bookmark actions

The Product Sales Crosstab report, which you implemented in this chapter, lets the user analyze Internet and reseller sales by the product natural hierarchy (category, subcategory, and product), time, and territory. Suppose a business analyst would prefer a quick way to jump to the bikes product category. This is where a bookmark action can help.

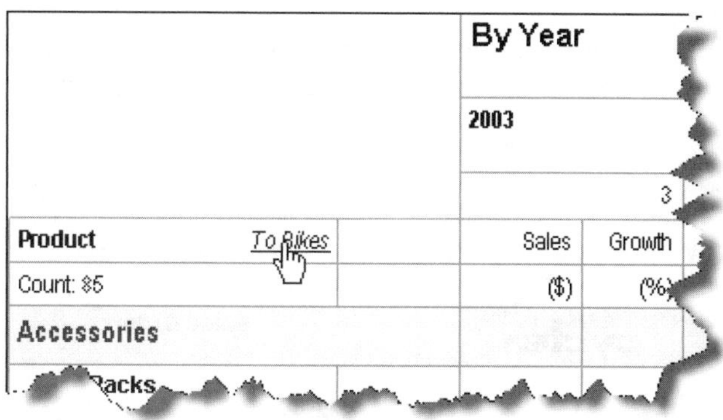

Figure 5.31 The user can click the link to jump to the Bikes section on the report.

The Bookmark Action report (see Figure 5.31) extends the Product Sales Crosstab report with a bookmark action. When the user clicks the To Bikes link, the user navigates to the Bikes product category instance on the report even if this instance is located on a different page. Start implementing the bookmark action by defining a bookmark identifier that serves as the action target. The bookmark identifier could be data-driven or static text. In our case, we want the user to jump to the Bikes product category. Since this product instance is not known at design time, we need a data-driven bookmark identifier. Complete the following steps to implement a bookmark action:

1. Open the Product Sales Crosstab report.
2. Click the ProductCategory textbox. This is the first cell in the ProductCategory group header.
3. In the Properties window, enter the following expression in the Bookmark property:

```
=Fields!ProductCategory.Value
```

As a result of this change, when the report is rendered, the bookmark identifier will match the group header (that is, it will be Accessories, Bikes, or Clothes). Next, you need to implement the actual bookmark link. This will require adding a new textrun inside the Product textbox.

1. Double-click the Product textbox to enter edit mode.
2. Position the cursor after "Product" and type "To Bikes".
3. Select the "To Bikes" text, right-click the selection and click Text Properties.
4. In the Text Properties dialog box, select the Action tab.
5. Click the Go to Bookmark option and enter Bikes in the Select Bookmark drop-down below.
6. Select the Font tab and change the textrun font style to bold, italic, with Underline effect and Blue color. Click OK.
7. With the textbox still in edit mode, move the cursor after "Product" and add spaces to move "To Bikes" to the right.
8. Preview the report to the test the bookmark action.

Clicking the To Bikes link should take you to the Bikes product group instance.

Drillthrough actions

The Product Sales Crosstab Drilldown report, which you implemented in this chapter, presents a cross-tab view of sales data aggregated at the product level. Suppose that the end user would like to see the detail data behind a cell. You can implement a drillthrough action that lets the user jump to another report and pass the current context to the drillthrough report so it can show more detailed information.

The Drillthrough Action report, shown in Figure 5.32, extends the Product Sales Crosstab Drilldown report to let the user drill down on Internet sales to see the sales orders that contribute to the clicked cell on the parent report.

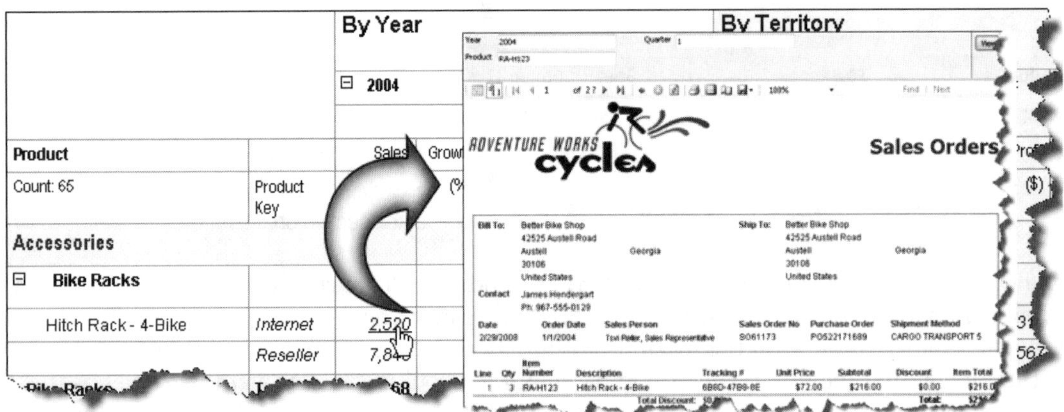

Figure 5.32 A drillthrough action lets the user navigate to another report.

To reduce the data shown on the drillthrough report, the drillthrough action is available only at product and quarter levels and on non-empty Internet cells. Clickable cells are underlined on the report. When the user clicks a cell, the drillthrough action launches the Sales Orders report. This report is very similar to the Sales Orders by Date report you authored in chapter 4. The only difference is that the Sales Orders takes year, quarter, and product number as parameters. The Drillthrough Action report passes these values to the drillthrough Sales Order report.

1. Open the Product Sales Crosstab Drilldown report in Report Designer
2. Right-click the intersecting cell (named InternetSales) of the CalendarQuarter column group and ProductName row group and click Text Box Properties.
3. In the Text Box Properties dialog box (Action tab), select the Go to Report option, as shown in Figure 5.33.

If you want the drillthrough action to be always available, expand the Select a Report drop-down list and select a drillthrough report from the list of reports in the project. Since we want to narrow the scope of the drillthrough action, we need to define an expression that limits the action scope:

4. Click the *fx* button next to the Select a Report From the List field and enter the following expression:

```
=Iif(InScope("CalendarQuarter") and Sum(Fields!Intern etSalesAmount.Value)>0, "Sales Orders", Nothing)
```

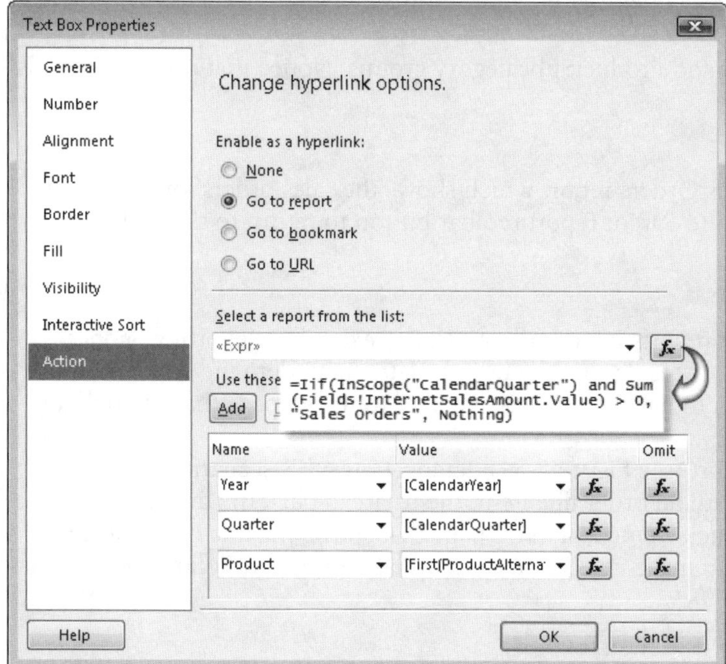

Figure 5.33 Configure a drillthrough action that launches another report by configuring the report name and parameters.

The Iif function uses the InScope function to check if the cell is inside the CalendarGroup scope and if the aggregated Internet sales amount is greater than zero. If this is the case, the expression returns *Sales Orders*, which is the name of the drillthrough report. Otherwise, the expression returns Nothing, so the cell is not clickable.

5. Click the Add button to define a parameter that will be passed to the drillthrough report.

   Because the name of the drillthrough report is expression-based, expanding the Name drop-down doesn't show the parameters of the Sales Orders report. You will need to enter them manually.

6. In the Name column, enter *Year*. Expand the Value drop-down list and select [CalendarYear] to bind the Year parameter of the drillthrough report to the CalendarYear field.
7. Add a Quarter parameter and bind it to [CalendarQuarter].
8. Add a Product parameter and bind it to =First(Fields!ProductAlternateKey.Value). You need to use the First aggregate function because the cell contains an aggregated value.

   If you check the Omit checkbox of a parameter, the parameter will be ignored. This could be useful if the parameter has a default value that you don't want to overwrite. This Omit checkbox is always disabled. To omit the parameter, click the *fx* button next to the checkbox and enter True as the expression text.

9. To underline cells conditionally, select the Font tab, and enter the following expression in the Effects drop-down list:

```
=Iif( InScope("CalendarQuarter") and Sum(Fields!InternetSalesAmount.Value)> 0, "Underline", "Default")
```

   This expression evaluates the same condition as the drillthrough action. If the condition is true, the cell will be underlined. Click OK to close the Text Box Properties dialog.

10. Preview the report. Because the CalendarQuarter and ProductName groups are collapsed by default, you cannot drill through any cell.
11. Expand the CalendarYear group and ProductSubcategory groups. Notice that non-empty cells are now clickable.
12. Click any of the clickable cells.

    You will be navigated to the Sales Orders report which shows the sales orders for the current selection. You can click the Back to Parent report toolbar button to return to the Drillthrough Action report.

URL actions

URL actions let you extend your reports in versatile ways. For example, Reporting Services doesn't support data writeback (that is, letting the user update the underlying data). However, you can implement a URL action to navigate the user to a custom web page that can update the report data.

The Sales Order Header report (see Figure 5.34) demonstrates this scenario. If the user discovers data inconsistencies with an order line item, the user can click the line number. The URL action launches the Writeback Demo ASP.NET page that shows the line item information. The user can use the page to make corrections and update the order. Follow these steps to add a URL action:

1. Open the Sales Order Items report in design mode.
2. Right-click the first cell in the tablix detail row, which is named LineNumber, and click Textbox Properties.
3. In the Textbox Properties dialog box, click the Action tab, and select the Go to URL option.
4. Click the *fx* button next to the Select URL drop-down, and enter the following expression:

```
=String.Format("http://localhost:1966/Web/Writeback.aspx?SO={0}&LN={1}",
Fields!SalesOrderID.Value, Fields!SalesOrderDetailID.Value)
```

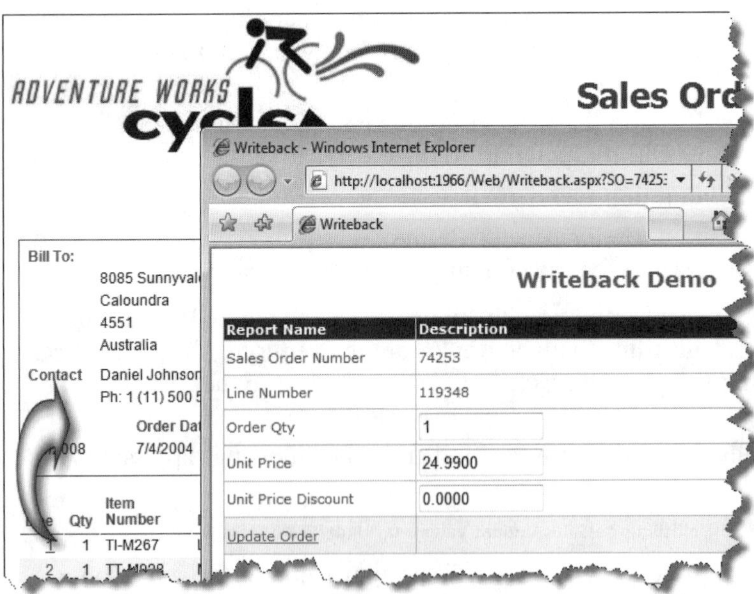

Figure 5.34 The Sales Order Header report uses a URL action to let the user update the order line item.

This expression constructs the URL address of the writeback page (Writeback.aspx). This page is included in the Web project inside the chapter 5 solution. The project uses the local ASP.NET Development Server, which is configured to listen on port 1966. Assuming that the user clicks on a line number with SalesOrderID of 50750 and SalesOrderDetailID of 35137, the resulting URL link will be:

```
http://localhost:1966/Web/Writeback.aspx?SO=50750&LN=35137
```

Writeback.aspx parses the query parameters and queries the AdventureWorks2008 database to display the line item details. The user can make corrections as needed. To avoid making changes to the AdventureWorks2008 sample database, the Update Order link doesn't actually write back the changes, but enhancing the page to support that action is straightforward:

5. In Solution Explorer, right-click the Writeback.aspx page and click View in Browser to start the ASP.NET Development Server. An icon that says ASP.NET Development Server – Port 1966 should appear in the Windows taskbar.
6. Preview the Sales Order Header report for Date 7/4/2004 and Sales Order Number SO74253.
7. Hover on the line number of any line number and notice that the mouse cursor changes to a hand cursor to indicate that the cell is clickable. Click the line number.

The writeback page should pop up and should show the line order details.

> **TIP** You can use JavaScript if you need more control over the URL link, such as to size the window. For example, the following link opens the page in a new window and sizes the window to 740 pixels wide and 400 pixels tall.
> =String.Format("javascript:void window.open ('http://localhost:1966/web/writeback.aspx?SO={0}&LN={1}', '_blank', 'resizeable=1, toobar=0,status=0,menu=0,top=20,left=20,width=740,height=400')", Fields!SalesOrderID.Value,Fields!SalesOrderDetailID.Value)
>
> Note that JavaScript links don't work in report preview with Report Designer. To test the link you need to deploy and run the report on the server.

5.4.4 Implementing Interactive Sorting

Users frequently request the ability to sort report data interactively. One approach is to use a report parameter and an expression-based sort order. The downside is that this approach won't work if you require more advanced sorting capability, such as sorting by multiple columns, sorting within groups, and so on. Fortunately, Reporting Services supports very powerful interactive sorting capabilities, as demonstrated by the Interactive Features report (see Figure 5.35). This report extends the Product Sales Stepped report by adding different ways to sort report data.

Sorting groups

Suppose that the user would like to sort the product category group alphabetically in ascending or descending order by clicking its column header:

1. Right-click the first cell in the first header row (Products) and click Text Box Properties.
2. In the Text Box Properties dialog box, select the Interactive Sort tab.

This tab lets you configure the interactive sort scope and which field or expression the sort will be based on.

3. Turn on the Enable Interactive Sort on This Text Box checkbox.

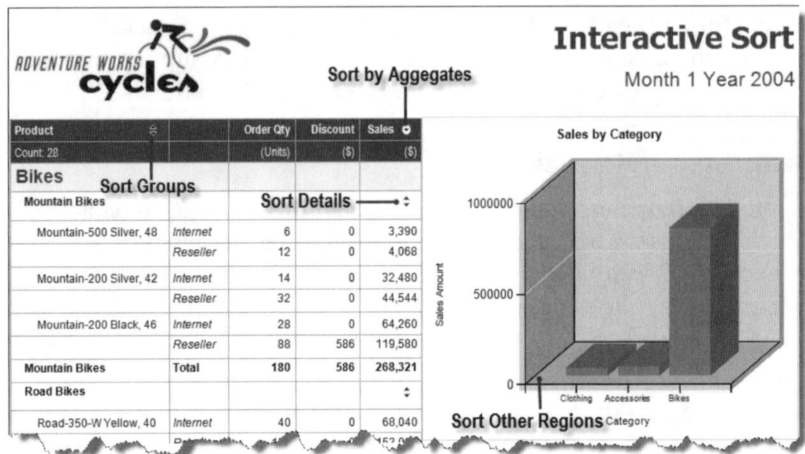

Figure 5.35 This report demonstrates different ways to sort report data interactively.

4. Click the Groups option and select the ProductCategory group in the drop-down list below.
5. Expand the Sort By drop-down list and select the [ProductCategory] field, as shown in Figure 5.36.

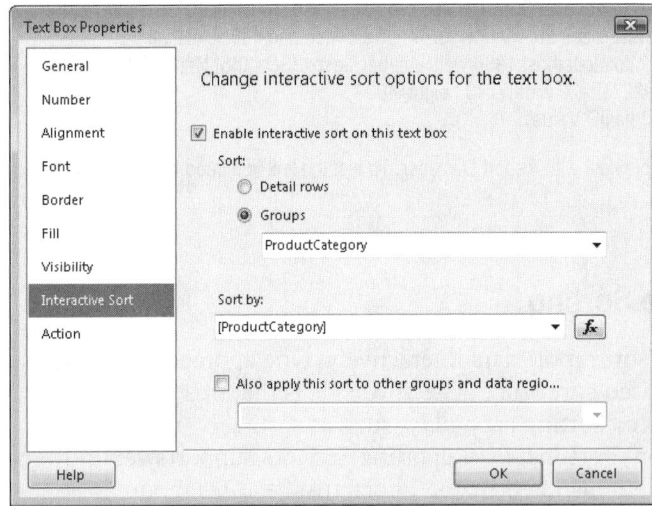

Figure 5.36 This interactive sort configuration enabled interactive sort on the Product-Category group.

6. Preview the report.

Notice that a sorting indicator is added to the column header. By default, this indicator has up and down arrows to indicate that the group is not sorted interactively (dataset or group sorting orders are still applied). You can click the indicator to sort data. Each time you click it, interactive sorting toggles between ascending and descending order.

NOTE Reporting Services doesn't support pre-selecting the interactive sort order at design time. For example, you cannot set the interactive sort order to descending. By default, interactive sort is not applied and data won't be sorted unless it is pre-sorted in the report query or groups.

7. Click the sort indicator. Notice that the product category group is sorted alphabetically in ascending order: Accessories, Bikes, and Clothes.

8. Click the sort indicator again to toggle the sort order. Notice that now the Clothes category is on top because the group is sorted in descending order by the ProductCategory field.

Sorting by aggregates

Suppose you want to sort on aggregated values or any other field that gets its value through an expression. To do this, you can implement expression-based interactive sorting:

1. Right-click the Sales column header, click Text Box Properties, and select the Interactive Sort tab.
2. Turn on the Enable Interactive Sort on This Text Box checkbox.
3. Click the Groups option and select the ProductCategory group in the drop-down list below.
4. Click the *fx* button next to the Sort By drop-down and enter the following expression:

```
=Sum(Fields!SalesAmount.Value)
```

   This expression sorts the product category group by the aggregated Sales Amount.

5. Preview the report and click the sort indicator in the Sales column header to sort the product group in ascending order. This should show the Clothing group on top because it has the least sales.
6. Click the sort indicator again to sort the product group in descending order.

   Notice that Bikes appears on top now because this product group has made the most sales.

Sorting within groups

Suppose that you want to sort the detail rows by sales amount within each instance of the group:

1. Right-click the last cell in the ProductSubcategory group header whose textbox is named SortDetails and click Text Box Properties. Select the Interactive Sort tab in the Text Box Properties dialog box.
2. Turn on the Enable Interactive Sort on This Text Box checkbox.
3. Select the Detail Rows sort option.
4. Expand the Sort By drop-down list and select [SalesAmount].
5. Preview the report and click the new sort indicator to sort the detail rows within each instance of the product subcategory group, as shown in Figure 5.37. Because SalesAmount is a dataset calculated field that sums InternetSalesAmount and ResellerSalesAmount, the group is sorted by the combined sales in ascending order.

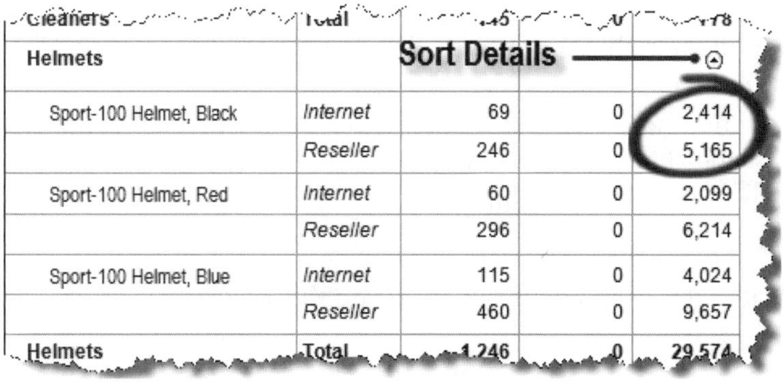

Helmets				Sort Details
Sport-100 Helmet, Black	*Internet*	69	0	2,414
	Reseller	246	0	5,165
Sport-100 Helmet, Red	*Internet*	60	0	2,099
	Reseller	296	0	6,214
Sport-100 Helmet, Blue	*Internet*	115	0	4,024
	Reseller	460	0	9,657
Helmets	Total	1,246	0	29,574

Figure 5.37 Clicking the sort indicator sorts on the SalesAmount, which is a calculated field that sums InternetSalesAmount and ResellerSalesAmount.

Sorting other regions

Suppose that you have a chart region side-by-side with the table region and you want to sort the chart interactively as you sort the table:

1. Drop a chart region next to the table region and accept the default chart type (Column).
2. Drop the ProductCategory field in the Drop Category Fields Here area of the chart and SalesAmount in the Drop Data Fields Here area.
3. Preview the report and notice that interactive sorting of the table region doesn't affect the chart.
4. In the Interactive Sort tab of the Products cell, check the Also Apply This Sort checkbox.
5. In the drop-down below it, enter *Products*.

   Products is the name of the dataset that the table and chart regions are bound to. When you sort the product category interactively, the sort order will be applied to the Products dataset. As a result, all regions that are bound to the Products dataset will pick up the sort order.
6. Optionally, apply the same changes to the Sales column header cell.
7. Preview the report and click the sort indicator in the Products cell.

   Note that data in both the table and chart regions are sorted in the same way. Specifically, if the product group is sorted in ascending order, both regions show Accessories, Bikes, and Clothing product categories in this order.

Configuring fixed headers

You can configure table row and column headers to remain visible when the user scrolls through the report. This could be useful with long or wide reports when you need to keep specific rows and columns visible. Report fixed headers are analogous to the frozen rows and columns used in Excel. How are report fixed headers different from repeating headers that we looked at in section 5.2.3? Unlike repeating headers, which repeat on each new page when the report is rendered and printed, fixed headers are only active when the user interacts with the report and scrolls off the header area. As a user-oriented feature, fixed headers don't affect the printed page.

Suppose that you want to keep the two header rows and the first column in the Interactive Features report always visible. If the report has row area and group area (there is a double dashed line separating the tablix body from the groups), you can configure fixed headers by turning on FixedRowHeaders and FixedColumnHeaders options in the tablix properties. The Interactive Features report doesn't have row and group areas but you can configure fixed headers as follows:

1. Expand the down arrow indicator in the right top corner of the Grouping pane and click Advanced Mode.
2. In the Row Groups pane, click the first static member, which represents the first table header row. In the Properties window, change FixedData to True.
3. Repeat the last step to configure the second static member.
4. Preview the report and scroll down the page.

   As you scroll down, the table header rows should remain visible on the top of the page, as shown in Figure 5.38.

5. Since the Interactive Features report is not very wide, you may need to resize the BIDS window so that a horizontal scroll bar appears. Alternatively, you could reduce the InteractiveSize ⇨ Width property to decrease the page width of the interactive page.

Product		Order Qty	Discount	Sales
Count: 28		(Units)	($)	($)
Mountain-500 Silver, 48	Internet	6	0	3,390
	Reseller	12	0	4,068
Mountain-200 Silver, 42	Internet	14	0	32,480
	Reseller	32	0	44,544

Scroll down

Figure 5.38 Fixed headers are always shown on the page as the user scrolls down the page.

6. Preview the report and scroll to the right.

The row headers under the Product column should remain visible as you scroll down.

5.4.5 Implementing a Document Map

End users may find it difficult to navigate through a large report to find the right information. If you are producing a report that contains data about hundreds of individual products, you can quickly appreciate how navigating such a report might be problematic. In the absence of navigational links, a user has no choice but to page through the report or search text to locate a specific product. This is where a document map can help.

Understanding document maps

The Interactive Features report implements a document map, which is shown in Figure 5.39. Each node in the tree represents an instance of a row group. Because the ProductCategory, ProductSubcategory, and ProductName rows groups are nested, the map links are organized in a tree structure based on the inner and outer groups.

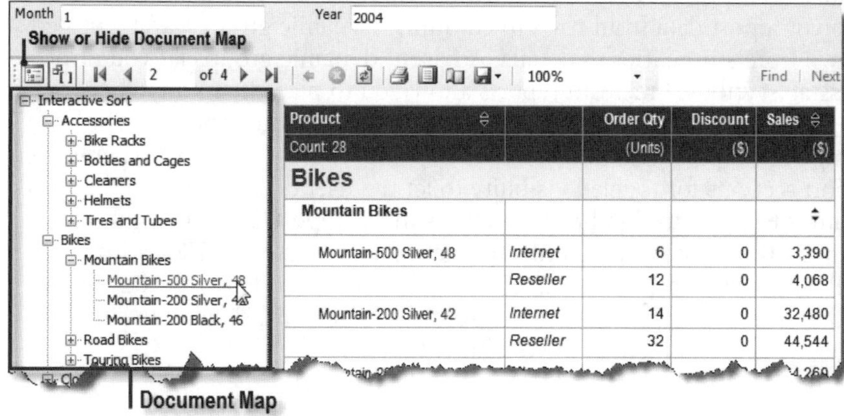

Figure 5.39 A document map can simplify navigation through large reports.

The end user can click a link to jump to a particular part of the report. For example, if the user wants to see the sales for the Mountain-500 Silver bike, the user can expand the Bikes and Mountain Bikes sections, and click the Mountain-500 Silver link. The user can hide the document map by clicking the Show or Hide Document Map.

Implementing document maps

Implementing a document map is remarkably simple. Follow these steps to extend the Interactive Features report with a document map that shows a link of each instance of the row groups on the report:

1. In the Row Groups pane, double-click the ProductCategory group.
2. In the Group Properties dialog box (General tab), expand the Document Map drop-down list and select the [ProductCategory] field.

   The Document Map setting lets you specify the link label, which can be expression-based. For example, the following expression marks product groups that exceed 100,000 of sales by adding an exclamation point after the group name:

```
=Iif(Sum(Fields!SalesAmount.Value)>100000, Fields!ProductCategory.Value & " !", Fields!ProductCategory.Value)
```

   With the exception of link text, you do not have control over the document map appearance. Specifically, you cannot change font style, color, or add custom graphics to the map.

3. Repeat the last two steps to bind the Document Map property for the ProductSubcategory and ProductName groups to the [ProductSubcategory] and [ProductName] fields, respectively.
4. Preview the report.

   Notice that the report has a document map whose nodes are clickable.

5.5 Summary

Tablix is a versatile control that lets you implement reports with tabular, crosstab, and freeform layouts. By default, tablix generates tablix group headers for each row group. Tablix headers simplify working with totals but may get in the way when you need more control over the report layout. In such cases, re-configure tablix by adding rows and groups as needed.

Crosstab reports pivot report data from rows to columns. Dynamic groups can be nested to let the user drill down from summaries to details. Adjacent dynamic groups let you implement side-by-side crosstab sections. Freeform reports allow you to place items anywhere on the report, such as to group reports on pages or implement multi-column reports.

Consider enhancing your report with interactive features to improve the user experience. You can configure report sections for toggled visibility to let the user drill down into the data. Add bookmark hyperlinks to jump to significant locations in the report. Implement drill-through links that launch other reports. URL links navigate the user to other URL-addressable resources, such as ASP.NET web pages. You can let the user sort report data interactively on details, across and within groups, by aggregates, and across data regions. Finally, to simplify navigating large reports, consider implementing document maps.

5.6 Resources

Cross-tab Reports
(http://tinyurl.com/32kaw4)—Learn how to create T-SQL queries that pivot data.

Chapter 6

Designing for Data Visualization

Sometimes a picture is worth more than a thousand words. This is especially true when presenting data on reports. Decisions makers love charts and graphs! Offer them text-based and graphical versions of the same report and they will undoubtedly prefer the latter. That's because conveying information graphically can help users analyze large volumes of data and spot trends that are not easily discernable when that same information is presented as text.

In this release, Reporting Services supercharges its data visualization capabilities with an upgraded chart region and a brand new gauge region. In this chapter, I will show you how to author feature-rich and visually appealing charts that can help users quickly grasp the meaning of data. You will also learn how to leverage the gauge region to present Key Performance Indicators (KPIs) and other numeric data.

6.1 Designing Chart Reports

A chart report presents data in a visual format. A chart is a drawing that displays relative sizes of numerical quantities. It often conveys information more effectively than can tabular or crosstab views of data. Business users who typically benefit the most from chart reports are decision makers, such as executives, managers, and marketers. Charts help such users get "a big picture" of the company business. For example, board reports and dashboard reports usually include charts to help business users quickly answer the most important question "How are we doing?"

6.1.1 Understanding the Chart Region

Reporting Services has been supporting charts since its first release. In Reporting Services 2008, charting really comes of age. The upgraded chart region brings new chart types and features that were either previously not supported or required significant implementation effort. At the same time, the new chart region is as easy to use as the chart controls included in Microsoft Excel and Access.

About Reporting Services charting

The older version of the Reporting Services chart was based on Dundas Charts, developed by Dundas Software (see Resources). Report authors could easily add charting capabilities to reports by binding the chart region to a dataset, just as they would do with tables and matrices.

The original chart region, however, had its own limitations which was a major factor in putting chart enhancements at on the top of the wish list for this release.

Meanwhile, Dundas enhanced its Chart for Reporting Services component and made it available as a commercial product. In June 2007, Microsoft acquired the Dundas data visualization technology, including the Dundas chart, gauge, map, and calendar controls. Due to time constraints, only the first two components are included in the release version of SQL Server 2008. The map and calendar controls are slated for a future release of SQL Server.

The upgraded chart region brings welcome features, such as multiple axes, scale breaks, custom palettes, and new chart types, including polar, radar, funnel, and pyramid chart types. One of my favorite features is the ability to configure the chart interactively at design time by selecting a chart element and accessing its properties. Another design-oriented feature is updating the design-time chart image before the property value is committed so you can immediately see the effect of the change. No more guessing which knob to turn on or having to undo wrong settings!

NOTE Interactive features that facilitate chart configuration are available only at design time. When the user exports the report, the chart gets rendered as a static image and the end user cannot access the chart properties to reconfigure the chart. At run time, the chart supports only limited interactivity via actions, such as letting the user drill through to another report to see more details.

Upgrading from previous chart controls

The SQL Server 2008 setup program will automatically upgrade deployed reports with RDL 2005 charts to the new chart control. Report Designer will prompt you to upgrade RDL 2005 report definitions to RDL 2008 the first time you open them. If for some reason you prefer to work with RDL 2005 charts, you can continue using the BIDS 2005 Report Designer and deploy to Reporting Services 2008. Recall from chapter 2 that you can deploy RDL 2005 report definitions to a report server running Reporting Services 2008.

If you purchased the Chart for Reporting Services component from Dundas and used it in your reports, you will be glad to know that Reporting Services supports a partial upgrade path from the Dundas Chart to the new native chart region in Reporting Services 2008. Custom code-based features are not supported and will not upgrade, including code-behind events, such as PostInitialize, CustomizeChart, annotations, and custom legends.

At design time, you can upgrade to the native chart region by opening the report definition in Report Designer. Report Designer will analyze the Dundas chart for the unsupported features. If none found, it will silently upgrade; otherwise a dialog box will be displayed with options. Once you confirm the upgrade prompt, the Dundas chart control will be upgraded to the native chart region. This is a one-way conversion process and you cannot downgrade back to the Dundas chart control. In any case, before the upgrade, a backup file will be created.

If you prefer to continue using the Dundas chart control, you must leave your reports in RDL 2005 format and use BIDS 2005 to edit your reports. Since Dundas Chart is designed as a custom report item, legacy report definitions will continue to work via the backward compatibility interfaces on the server.

NOTE Dundas is currently working on the 2008 version of Dundas Chart. Customers will be able to upgrade from the 2005 version to 2008. As before, the 2008 control is implemented as a Reporting Services custom report item.

When you upgrade a report server, the upgrade process will detect whether published reports that contain Dundas charts can be upgraded. As long as charts contain only supported features, Reporting Services will upgrade the chart in the report in place. Report definitions that use custom chart code will not get upgraded to RDL 2008 and will continue to reference the Dundas chart control.

How to choose a chart type
Reporting Services supports many chart types, so it's important to select the most appropriate chart type for the task at hand. Table 6.1 can help you select the right chart based on the report data.

Table 6.1 How to choose a chart type

Chart Type		Linear Data	Ratio Data	Multivalued Data
Column		✓		
Line		✓		
Shape			✓	
Bar		✓		
Area		✓		
Range		✓		✓
Scatter		✓	✓	
Polar		✓		✓

Analyzing linear data, such as sales over time, is a very common requirement. Hence, it is supported by many charts, including column, line, bar, area, range, and scatter charts. Visualizing data as a proportion of a whole, such as plotting the contribution of individual regions to overall sales, is best achieved with shape charts, such as pie charts, as well as scatter and polar charts.

A range chart can display a set of data points that are each defined by multiple values. For example, a stock chart, which is one of the supported range charts, is designed for financial or scientific data that uses up to four values per data point.

6.1.2 The Anatomy of a Chart Region

The chart region is packed with features and it may take some time for novice users to get used to it. It is composed of various elements, such as series, axes, legends, and so on. Figure 6.1 illustrates the main elements of a chart. The sample chart is included in the Sales by Region report that you will author in the next practice.

To understand how the chart region works, it makes sense to compare it to the matrix region you are already familiar with. When you configure the chart at design time, you specify category groups, series groups, and values by adding dataset fields to the Drop Category Fields Here, Drop Series Fields Here, and Drop Data Fields Here areas (shown in Figure 6.2).

Chart groups and values

A category group is equivalent to a matrix dynamic column group, as it lets you group data by a dataset field or expression. A chart can have multiple category groups. For instance, the Reseller Sales chart groups by both year and quarter.

A series group is a grouping of related data and it is similar to a matrix row group. The Reseller Sales chart has a single series group that groups on territory. Because Adventure Works sells in three territories (Europe, North America, and Pacific), each series group has three members.

Chart values are equivalent to matrix static column groups. For example, the Internet Sales/Orders chart has Sales and Orders chart values which are plotted on the left and right axes respectively.

Finally, you can think of a chart data point as a matrix cell. Each data point must belong to a chart series. The chart type determines how data points will be plotted. A column chart displays data points as bars, while a line chart displays them plotted as a line.

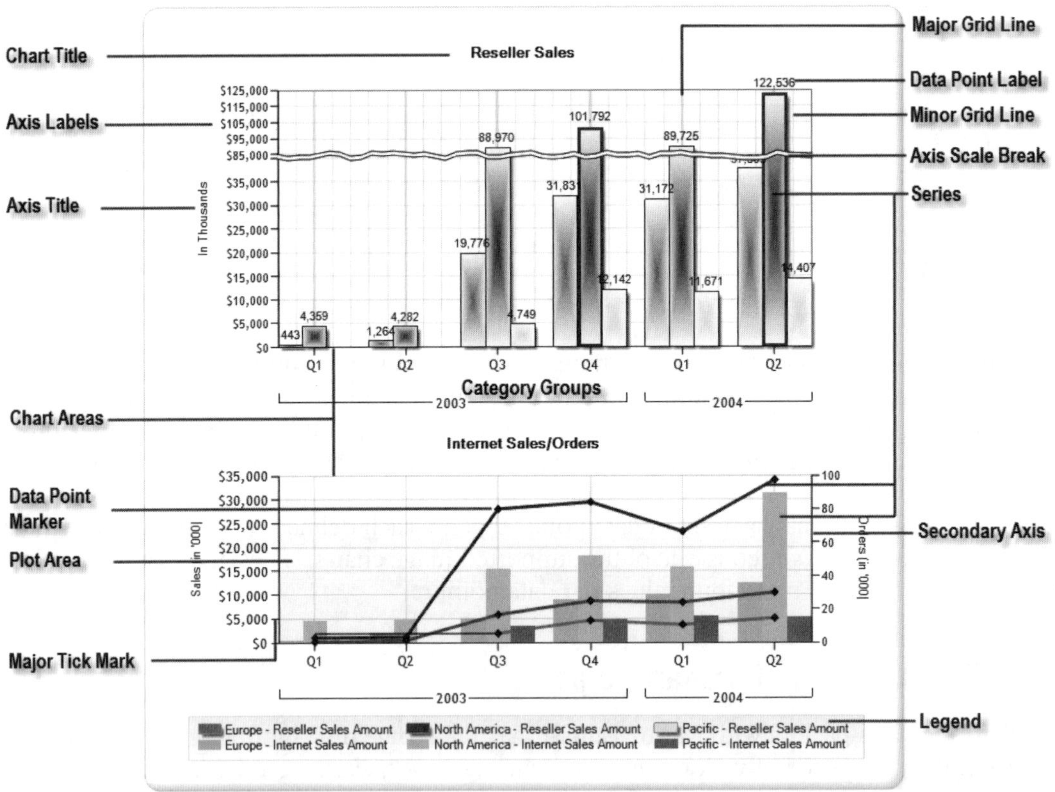

Figure 6.1 This chart data region is a complex control which consists of many elements.

Chart areas

A chart area is a rectangular area that contains chart elements, such as series, labels, axes, grid lines, and so on. A chart region includes one or more chart areas. For instance, the chart shown in Figure 6.1 has Reseller Sales and Internet Sales/Orders chart areas. All areas are bound to the same dataset but they can have different chart types. The Reseller Sales chart area displays only the Sales series, while the Internet Sales/Orders chart area displays Sales and Order Quantity series. The Internet Sales/Orders chart is a hybrid chart that shows the Sales series as a column chart and the Order Quantity series as a line chart.

Axes

The chart area of most chart types, such as column and line charts, has an x-axis and a y-axis. An axis can have an axis title that describes what's plotted on the axis. Chart values are shown along the value axis (y-axis in Figure 6.1). Of course, this will only work if the underlying dataset fields are numeric. An axis usually has axis labels.

In auto-scale mode, the minimum value of the y-axis corresponds to the lowest chart value ($443,000 in the Reseller Sales chart). Similarly, the maximum value is set to the highest chart value ($122,536,000). The chart region can automatically infer the axis intervals based on the minimum and maximum chart values. However, you can overwrite the interval size if needed. For example, you can set the chart y-axis Interval property to 10 to set the interval size to $10 assuming the y-axis plots a currency amount. By default, the chart displays labels for each interval. The chart region also supports minor intervals that divide the major intervals into equal segments.

The values on the category axis (x-axis in Figure 6.1) are derived from the category values, such Q1 for the first quarter. The major intervals are set for each category value. There are four minor intervals within each major interval. You can optionally turn on the chart major and minor grid lines to display lines for major and minor intervals respectively. You can also enable major and minor horizontal and vertical tick marks, which usually occur in conjunction with major and minor grid lines. For example, in Figure 6.1, major tick marks show for each quarter.

Sometimes, high y-axis values may eclipse the rest of the values and skew your chart, crowding relevant data into an area too small to see. To remedy this problem, you can configure the y-axis to show a scale break. At run time, the chart automatically generates a y-axis scale break when it detects an outlier value. For example, reseller sales for North America far exceed the sales for the other territories. In the absence of scale breaks, the sales for other territories would be barely discernable. The y-axis break at around 85 million prevents this from happening. You can enable data point labels to show the data point values as text or markers to emphasize data points.

If you need to display chart values that are measured in different units on the same chart area, plotting them on the same axis may not make sense. However, the chart region supports primary and secondary axes to support data series on additional axes. For example, the sales values in Internet Sales/Orders chart area are plotted on the primary value axis on the left, while the order quantity shows along the secondary value axis on the right.

Legends

A chart can have one or more legends that describe the series plotted on the chart. You can configure which series is displayed in a legend. For example, I chose not to display the order quantity axis in the chart legend. You can customize the legend format settings and its position, such as whether it is inside or outside the chart area.

6.1.3 Designing a Column Chart ▶

Consider a column chart when you need to graphically summarize and display the differences between groups of data, or identify outliers. Next, I will walk you through the steps of implementing the Sales by Region report. I'll start with the Reseller Sales column chart. The Sales By Region Start report provides the starting point for this practice. The Sales By Region report demonstrates a cornucopia of chart features, including:

- Working with column and line charts
- Working with multiple chart areas
- Configuring scale breaks and secondary axis
- Using expressions to highlight data points

Before starting the practice, I highly recommend you review Robert Bruckner's excellent Get More Out of SQL Server Reporting Services Charts article (see Resources). Although originally written for Reporting Services 2005, most of the information presented there is still applicable as it explains how the chart region works.

Getting started with the chart region

Start by adding a chart region to the report and choosing a chart type:

1. Open the Sales by Region Start report.
2. Drag the chart data region from the Toolbox and drop it on the report body.

   Report Designer pops up a Select Chart Type dialog box that shows the supported charts. The charts are organized into the same chart types that appear in Table 6.1. Each chart type supports additional variations. For example, the column chart type has several variations, including stacked column, 100% stacked column, and 3D effect variations.

3. Accept the default Column chart, which is a plain variation of the column chart type. Click OK. Report Designer adds a column chart with a title of Chart Title.
4. Click different elements of the chart, such as the chart title, chart area, and legend.

   Note that clicking a chart element selects the element and shows its properties in the Properties window. The Properties window exposes the full set of the element properties. A subset of the most common properties are exposed in property dialog boxes that you can access by right-clicking the element and clicking the appropriate context menu.

5. Resize the chart to a height of 3.5" and a width of 7.5".
6. Right-click an empty space on the chart area and click Chart Properties.
7. In the Chart Properties dialog box, select the Border tab, and select a Raised border type. Click OK.
8. Click the chart title to select it. Double-click the title and rename it in place to *Reseller Sales*.

Configuring chart groups and values

Next, you will configure the chart data.

1. Double-click an empty space on the chart area to put the chart in edit mode.

   When the chart is in edit mode, additional areas, called adorner windows, surround the chart, as shown in Figure 6.2. You can click the field selectors in these areas to configure the chart data. Alternatively, you can drag dataset fields from the Report Data window.

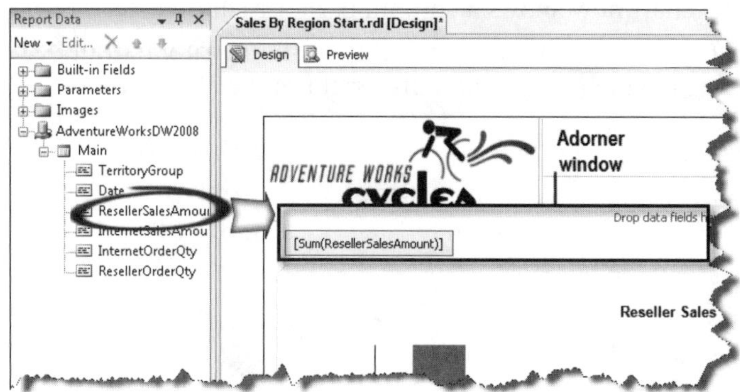

Figure 6.2 You can bind the chart categories, series, and values by dragging dataset fields and dropping them in the chart areas.

2. Drag the ResellerSalesAmount field and drop it on the Drop Data Fields Here area to create a new chart series.

   Because the chart displays summary information, it uses the Sum function by default to aggregate the data field.

3. Right-click the [Sum(ResellerSalesAmount)] field and click Series Properties. In the Series Properties dialog box (Series Data), click the *fx* button next to the Value field.

   Notice that [Sum(ResellerSalesAmount)] is a substitute for the expression =Sum(Fields!ResellerSalesAmount.Value). Click OK. Next, you will configure the chart category groups. Our chart will group values by year and quarter.

4. Drag the Date field on the Drop Category Fields Here area. Right-click the Date field and click Category Group Properties.

5. In the Category Group Properties dialog box (General tab), enter the following expression in both Label and Group On fields to group data by years:

   ```
   =Year(Fields!Date.Value)
   ```

6. Preview the report.

   The chart shows two column bars. The y-axis plots the sales amount and has major gridlines and tick marks for every interval of 50 million. The x-axis shows years 2003 and 2004 which are the default values of the Calendar Year multivalued parameter.

7. Drop the Date field again next to the existing Date field in the Drop Category Fields Here area to create a nested category group for quarters.

8. Right-click the Date field and click Category Group Properties. In the Category Group Properties window, set the Label property (General tab) to the following expression:

   ```
   =String.Format("Q{0}", DatePart(DateInterval.Quarter, Fields!Date.Value))
   ```

   At run time, the String.Format function replaces the {0} placeholder with the quarter number. Consequently, the labels will show more descriptive quarter names, such as Q1, Q2, and so on.

9. Bind the Group On setting of the group to the following expression:

   ```
   =DatePart (DateInterval.Quarter, Fields!Date.Value)
   ```

10. Select the Sorting tab and add a new sorting option to sort by the [Date] field in ascending order.

11. Preview the report and notice that the chart now shows a column bar for each quarter.
12. To show sales broken down by territory, we need a series group. Drag the TerritoryGroup field on the Drop Series Fields Here area, which is located on the right of the chart when the chart is in edit mode.

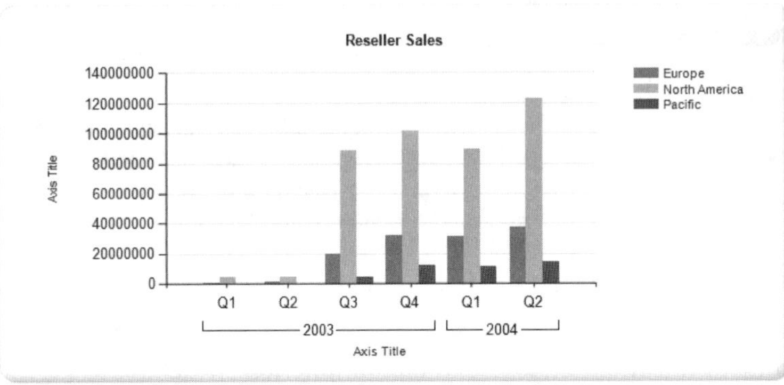

Figure 6.3 The chart shows sales amount broken down by years and quarters, and grouped by territory.

13. Preview the report and compare the output with the one shown in Figure 6.3.

    Notice that the North America sales eclipse the sales of other regions because they are much higher.

Formatting the y-axis

Let's spend some time formatting the chart to improve its visual appearance:

1. Right-click the y-axis label area and click Axis Properties.
2. In the Axis Options tab, check the Enable Scale Breaks option to let the chart automatically break the y-axis.

   As noted, the chart automatically determines the axis scale, minimum value, maximum value, and intervals. You can change the settings in the Set Axis Scale and Style section to overwrite the automatic behavior if needed. For example, if you want all labels to be visible, set the Interval property to 1. Keep in mind that it may cause some labels to overlap.
3. Select the Labels tab. Clear the Labels Can be Offset and Labels Can be Rotated checkboxes. Set the Font Can be Decreased To slider to 7pt.

   Note that as you change the settings, the changes are applied to the design-time chart image in real time so that you can immediately see the effects of your changes.
4. Select the Label Font tab and change the font to Trebuchet MS, 7pt.
5. Select the Label Format tab and format the labels as currency, no decimal places, with a thousands separator. Check the Show Values In checkbox to show values in thousands.

   You can use the Major Tick Marks and Minor Tick Marks tabs to configure the major and minor tick marks respectively, such as to enable minor tick marks (not shown by default). The Line tab lets you format the y-axis line (for example, to change its color or border width if needed).
6. Click OK to return to the design area. Double-click the Axis Title and rename it to *In Thousands.*
7. Preview the chart and notice that the chart generates a scale break at around $85 million.

TIP Not all element properties are exposed in the property dialog boxes. For example, the chart supports a ScaleBreakStyle property that is not available in the Axis Properties dialog box. Select the element and use the Properties window to access all properties.

8. In the chart area, click any of the horizontal major gridlines (the ones that have tick marks in the y-axis). In the Properties window, change LineColor to *#32418cf0* and LineStyle to Solid.

Formatting the x-axis

Follow similar steps to format the X-axis:

1. Right-click the x-axis and click Axis Properties.

   In the Axis Options tab, note that the Scalar Option is not enabled. The x-axis has two modes. In category mode (default), the category group expression determines the individual category values. The chart shows labels for the individual category values. In scalar mode, which is only applicable to DateTime and numeric group values, the chart scales the x-axis based on the minimum and maximum group values. The Scale Modes report, which is included in the Report project, demonstrates the difference between category and scalar modes. If you prefer working in a chart scalar mode, turn the Scalar Option on.
2. Uncheck the Always Include Zero option. Set the Side Margins option to Disabled to avoid gaps between the chart series and sides. Click OK.
3. To turn the major gridlines on, right-click the x-axis and click Show Major Gridlines.
4. In the chart area, click on any of the vertical major gridlines (the ones that have tick marks in the x-axis). In the Properties window, change the LineColor to *#32418cf0*, LineStyle to Solid, and LineWidth to 2pt.
5. To turn the minor gridlines on, right-click the x-axis and click Show Minor Gridlines
6. In the chart area, click any of the vertical minor gridlines (the ones between the major gridlines). In the Properties window, change the LineColor to *#32418cf0* and LineStyle to Solid.

Formatting the chart area

Follow these steps to format the chart area:

1. Click the empty space inside the chart. In the Properties window, click the ellipsis (…) button inside the ChartAreas property.
2. In the ChartAreas Collection Editor, rename the chart area to *ResellerSales*. Change its BorderColor property to *#418cf0* and BorderStyle to Solid. Click OK.

Formatting the chart series

You can apply global format settings to chart series.

1. Right-click any of the column bars in the chart and click Series Properties.
2. Select the Markers tab. To turn the data point markers on, expand the Marker Style drop-down list and select Diamond. Set the marker color and border color to Black.
3. Select the Fill tab. Set the Fill Style to Gradient and Gradient Style to Center.

   Suppose that you want to highlight data points based on some condition. For example, let's say you want to change the border color to Red and the border width to 2pt for all data points that exceed 100 million.

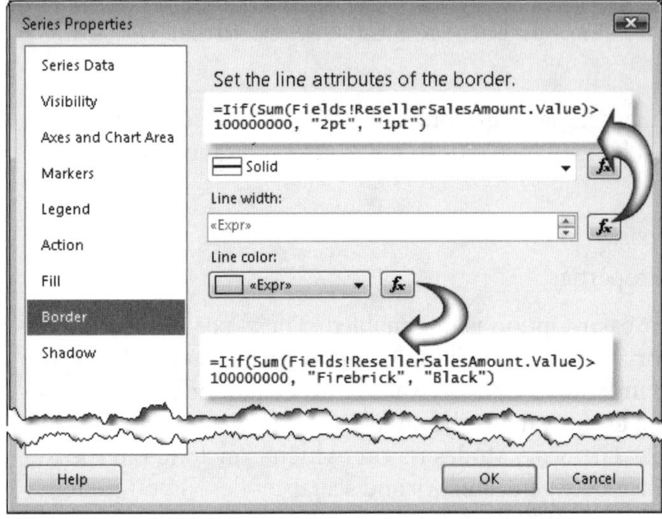

Figure 6.4 Data points can have expression-based properties to highlight interesting values.

4. Select the Border tab (see Figure 6.4). Enter the following expression in the Line Width property:

```
= Iif(Sum(Fields!ResellerSalesAmount.Value)>100000000, "2pt", "1pt")
```

This expression sets the border width to 2pt if the data point value is greater than 100 million.

5. Enter the following expression in the Line Color property:

```
= Iif(Sum(Fields!ResellerSalesAmount.Value)>100000000, "Firebrick", "Black")
```

This expression checks if the data point aggregated value is greater than 100 million. If this is the case, the border color will be set to Firebrick.

6. Change the Line Style setting to Solid.
7. Select the Shadow tab. Change the shadow offset to 2pt. Click OK to close the dialog box.
8. Right-click any of the column bars in the chart and click Show Data Labels.
9. Right-click any of the data labels and click Series Label Properties. In the Font tab, change the font size to 8pt.
10. In the Number tab, format the series labels as numbers, with a thousands separator, and no decimal places. Check the Show Values In checkbox to show values in thousands. Click OK.

TIP You can use chart keywords for the label text. The Label Data drop-down list in the General tab of the Series Label Properties dialog box lists the available keywords. The keywords are replaced with the actual values at run time. For example, you can select the #PERCENT keyword if you want the label to show the percentage contribution of data points to the series total. You can also combine keywords. For example, #PERCENT of #TOTAL{C0} shows the percentage contribution of the data point and the overall total formatted as currency with no decimal places. Don't precede the expression with an equal sign because Reporting Services will attempt to parse it, at which point it will fail because chart keywords cannot be used in expressions.

11. In the chart area, click any of the bars to select the series.

In the Properties window, note that the Type property shows the chart variation, which in this case is Column, Plain. You can click the … button inside the Type property to change the chart type if needed.

12. In the Properties window, expand the Label category. Set Label ⇨ Position to Top.
13. Enter the following expression in the Tooltip property:

```
=Fields!TerritoryGroup.Value
```

When the user hovers on a column bar, the chart will display the name of the associated territory group.

Configuring the legend

By default, the chart legend is positioned to the right of the chart and takes up some of the chart width. Let's position the legend below the chart to free up more space on the right:

1. Click the legend to select it.
2. Drag its resize handler to move the legend below the chart. Report Designer highlights areas where the legend can be positioned.
3. Right-click the legend and click Legend Properties.
4. Select the Font tab and change the legend font to Microsoft Sans Serif, 8pt.
5. Select the Fill tab and change the Fill Style to Gradient. Click the *fx* button next to the first gradient color, and enter *#e6f2fc*. Set the Gradient Style to Top Bottom.
6. Select the Border tab. Change Line Style to Solid and Line Color to *#e6f2fc*. Click OK.
7. In the Properties window, change EquallySpacedItems to True to space the items equally in the legend. Change TextWrapThreshold to 50 to truncate legend labels if they exceed 50 characters.

If you preview the report at this point, your chart should look like the Reseller Sales chart area shown in Figure 6.1.

6.1.4 Designing a Line Chart ▶

Next, you'll implement the Internet Sales/Orders chart area. It's designed as a hybrid chart that shows Internet sales amount as a column chart and Internet order quantity as a line chart. The sales amount is plotted on the primary axis (left y-axis), while the order quantity is shown along the secondary axis.

Adding a chart area

A chart can have more than one chart areas. The first chart area, which the chart automatically creates, is the primary chart area. All chart areas share the same dataset, category groups, and series groups. You decide which series is shown on which chart area.

1. Select the chart and set its height to 7.5" to free up space for the second chart area.
2. Right-click an empty space on the chart and click Add New Chart Area.
3. In the Properties window, rename the chart area to *InternetSales*.
4. Set the BackgroundGradientEndColor property to LemonChiffon and BackgroundGradientType to TopBottom to give the plot area a gradient background effect.
5. Drag the InternetOrderQty field from the Report Data window and drop it next to the ResellerSalesAmount field in the Drop Data Fields Here area.
6. Drag the InternetSalesAmount field from the Report Data window and drop it next to the InternetOrderQty field in the Drop Data Fields Here area.

Configuring the chart series

By default, the chart plots the series on the primary chart area (ResellerSales). Follow these steps to reconfigure the new series to be shown on the InternetSales chart area:

1. Right-click the [Sum(InternetSalesAmount)] field in the Drop Data Fields Here area and click Series Properties.

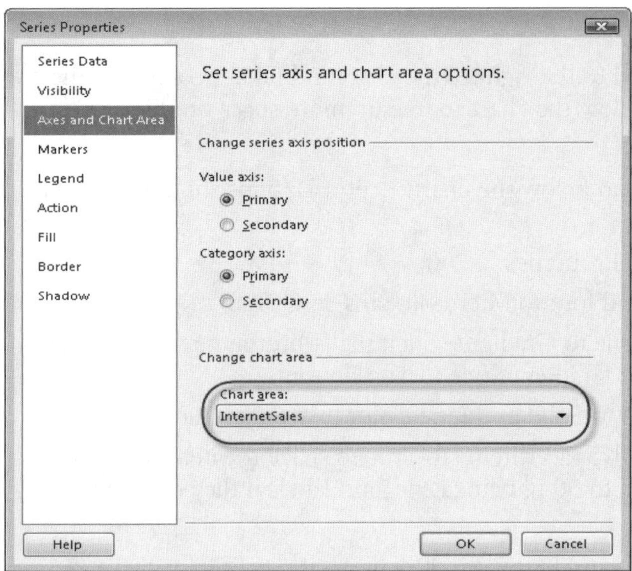

Figure 6.5 Use the Series Properties dialog box to assign a series to a chart area.

2. In the Series Properties dialog box, select the Axes and Chart Area tab, as shown in Figure 6.5.
3. Expand the Chart Area drop-down list and select InternetSales. The chart region shows the InternetSalesAmount series on the InternetSales chart area. Click OK.
4. Right-click the [Sum(InternetOrderQty)] field in the Drop Data Fields Here area and click Series Properties.
5. In the Axes and Chart Area tab, configure the series to be plotted on the InternetSales chart area too.

   Internet sales and order quantity are measured in different units and you may not want them to share the same axis. Let's configure the InternetOrderQty values to be plotted on a secondary axis:
6. In the Axes and Chart Area tab, set the Value Axis setting to Secondary.

   Suppose you don't want to display the InternetOrderQty series in the chart legend. Let's remove it now:
7. In the Legend tab, check the Do Not Show This Series In a Legend checkbox. Click OK.
8. In the design area, right-click an empty space in the chart and click Add New Title.
9. Rename the new title in place to *Internet Sales/Orders*.
10. Drag the title above the InternetSales chart area. As you drag the title, the chart shows a blue rectangle to indicate areas when you can drop the title.
11. Right-click the primary (left) y-axis and click Axis Properties. In the Axis Options tab, turn off Enable Scale Breaks if checked.

Working with a line chart

As it stands, the InternetSales chart area shows both series as column charts. Suppose you want to show the order quantity as a line chart:

1. Right-click the [Sum(InternetOrderQty)] field in the Drop Data Fields Here area and click Change Chart Type.
2. In the Select Chart Type dialog box, click the Line tab and leave the default variation selected. Click OK.

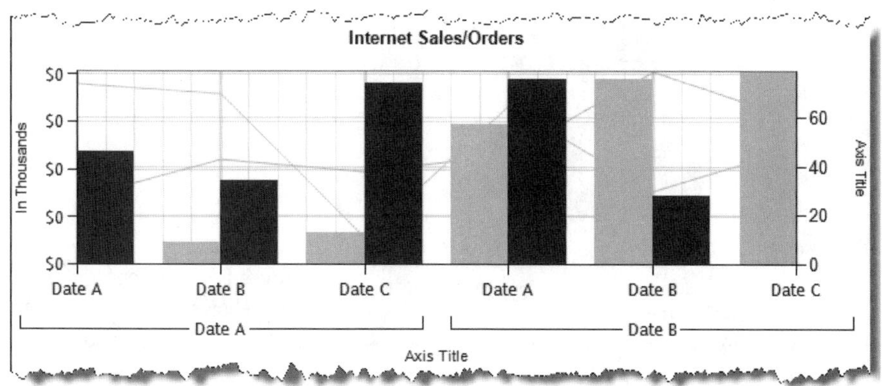

Figure 6.6 You can select different chart types for the chart series.

The InternetOrderQty series is now plotted as a line chart, as shown in Figure 6.6. Note that the line chart is behind the column chart. That's because the order in which the fields appear in the Drop Data Fields Here panes is significant. Because the InternetOrderQty field appears in front of the InternetSalesAmount field, its series is plotted first on the chart area.

3. In the Drop Data Fields Here pane, drag the [Sum(InternetOrderQty)] field after the [Sum(InternetSalesAmount)] field.

   Now the line chart appears in front of the column chart.

4. In the Drop Data Fields Here pane, click the [Sum(InternetOrderQty)] to select it.
5. In the Properties window, change the BorderWidth property to 2pt to make the line ticker. Alternatively, you can right-click [Sum(InternetOrderQty)] and click Series Properties to use the Series Properties dialog to make the changes.
6. In the Properties window, change Marker ⇨ Color property to Black, Marker ⇨ MarkerType to Diamond, and Marker ⇨ Size to 6pt.

   The InternetOrderQty line chart shows markers for each data point.

7. Format the chart as you did for the Reseller Sales chart, including renaming the axis titles, formatting the axis labels, and so on.

   At this point, your chart report should look like the one shown in Figure 6.1.

6.2 Working with Chart Types

The chart region lets you do much more than plain column and line charts. Next, I'll present additional chart types that demonstrate more chart capabilities. For the sake of brevity, I'll highlight the most important implementation steps that are relevant to each chart type.

6.2.1 Histogram Charts

A histogram chart is a type of a column chart that summarizes and displays the distribution of data. The chart region constructs a histogram by segmenting the range of data into equal sized bins, also known as segments, groups, or classes. The y-axis is labeled Frequency and shows the number of data points in each bin. The x-axis shows the range of values for each bin.

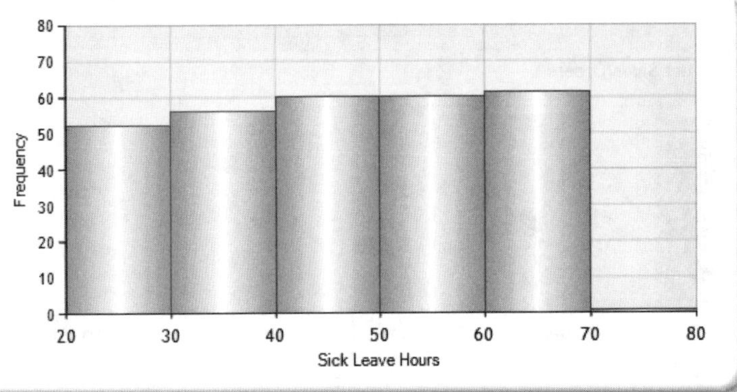

Figure 6.7 This histogram chart shows the distribution of employee sick leave hours.

Understanding the Histogram Chart report

Figure 6.7 shows the Histogram Chart report. The chart shows the distribution of employee sick leave hours. The data ranges from 20 to 80 sick leave hours. I configured the chart to divide this range into bins of 10 hours which are shown on the x-axis. The y-axis shows the frequency, which in our case is the number of employees. It ranges from 0 to 80 employees.

Analyzing the chart, we can deduce that for the most part the data distribution is relatively even. There about 60 employees who have taken between 60 and 70 sick leave hours. There is one outlier bin for an employee who has taken 70-80 hours.

NOTE Before alarming the Human Resources department about the excessive number of sick leave hours, note that the report queries table HumanResources.Employee, which is not time-dependent. Most likely, this table captures the overall employee's sick leave hours to date.

Implementing a histogram chart

If you compare a histogram and a column chart side by side, you can see they both have vertical columns, but the histogram has fewer of them. You implement a histogram chart in the same way you implement a column chart, with the exception that the category group would group on each dataset row. In our case, the category group (EmployeeID) groups on each employee. Of course, if you render the column chart without configuring it in histogram mode, it will be hardly readable because it will plot as many columns as the number of employees. Fortunately, turning the column chart into a histogram is a matter of changing a single property:

1. Click the SickLeaveHours series to select it.
2. In the Properties window, change CustomAttributes ⇨ ShowColumnAs to Histogram.

There are additional custom properties you can set to configure the histogram. For example, I changed CustomAttributes ⇨ HistogramSegmentIntervalWidth to *10* to configure the bin size.

6.2.2 Pareto Charts

Vilfredo Pareto was an economist who is credited with establishing what is now widely known as the Pareto Principle, or 80/20 law. This law states that, for many events, 80% of the effects come from 20% of the causes. A Pareto chart summarizes and displays the relative importance of the differences between groups of data.

Understanding the Pareto Chart report

Pareto charts distinguish the "vital few" from the "useful many." A Pareto chart is a column chart that sorts columns in descending order so that the largest group contributors appear first. A line chart shows the running total of the chart values as each one is measured. The right y-axis displays the cumulative percentage, which always ranges from 0 to 100%.

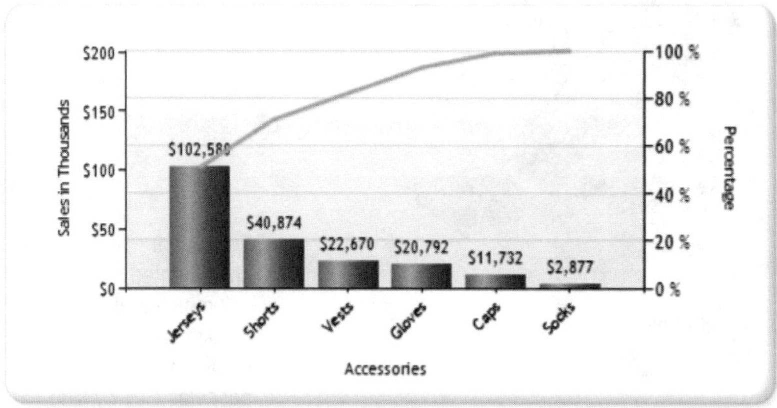

Figure 6.8 A Pareto chart shows the cumulative percentage of the chart value.

The Pareto Chart report (see Figure 6.8) demonstrates a Pareto chart showing the accessory sales for a given year. The Jerseys category has sold the most (about $100,000), followed by Shorts, and so on. Analyzing the line chart, we can deduce that the combined sales of Jerseys and Shorts have contributed to about 80% of the overall sales. The results deviate somewhat from the Pareto rule, as they yield an 80/30 distribution (two categories out of six produce 80% of sales), but for our purposes it is close enough.

Implementing a Pareto chart

Start implementing the Pareto chart as a column chart that has data fields, category fields, and series fields. The Pareto Chart report groups by product category and uses the aggregated sales amount for the chart series. Similar to histogram charts, configuring a Pareto chart requires changing the ShowColumnAs property:

1. Click the Sales series to select it.
2. In the Properties window, change CustomAttributes ⇨ ShowColumnAs to Pareto.
3. Adjust the series BorderWidth property to make the line chart more visible. In Figure 6.8, the border width is set to 2pt.

As a result of these changes, the chart will auto-generate the y-axis and the line that shows the running total.

6.2.3 Three-Dimensional Column Charts

Almost every chart type comes in a 3D version. The 3D versions are eye-catching but they may be somewhat difficult to analyze. In addition, 3D charts don't support all of the features of their two-dimensional counterparts. For example, scale breaks don't work with 3D. For these reasons, I recommend you use 3D effects sparingly.

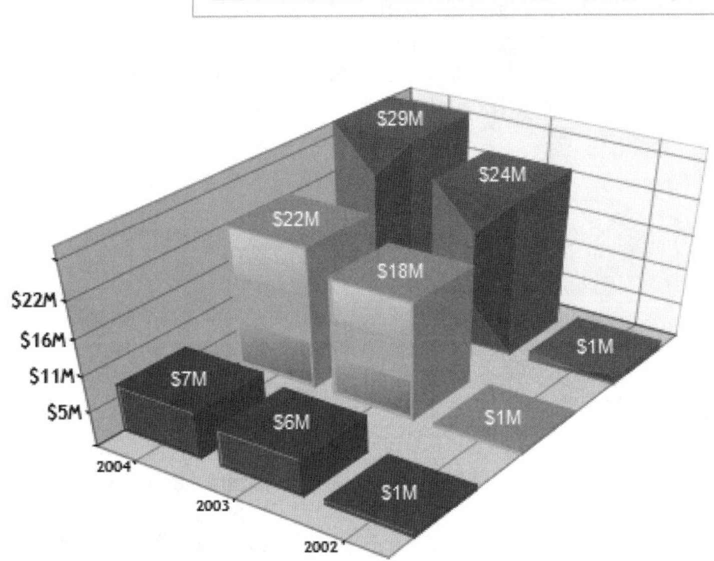

Figure 6.9 This chart is implemented as a 3D column chart that shows the Adventure Works gross, reseller, and Internet sales side by side.

The 3D Column Chart report, shown in Figure 6.9, demonstrates the following features:

- 3D column chart with custom drawing styles
- Series custom intervals and custom positioning
- Drillthrough actions

The report shows the Adventure Works gross sales, reseller sales, and Internet sales by year on the x-axis and sales amount on y-axis. The user can filter the report data by the Country report parameter (not shown on Figure 6.9).

Working with 3D effects

Follow these steps to configure a 3D column chart:

1. Add a chart data region . In the Select Type Chart dialog box, select 3D Column chart.

> **TIP** The 3D column chart is a pre-configured template for creating a new column chart with 3D effects. If you have an existing 2D column chart, you can configure it as a 3D chart by right-clicking on the chart and clicking 3D Effects.

2. Bind the chart to CalendarYear as a category field, and then SalesAmount, InternetSalesAmount, ResellerSalesAmount as data fields. In the CalendarYear group properties, sort by the CalendarYear field in descending order.
3. In the Chart Area Properties dialog box (3D tab), specify the 3D settings listed in Table 6.2.

Table 6.2 3D settings for the chart in the 3D Column Chart report

Property	Setting	Property	Setting
Enable 3D	✓	Projection Mode	Perspective
Enable Series Clustering	✓	Perspective	7
Rotation	35	Wall Thickness	7
Inclination	35	Depth Ratio	100
Projection Mode	Perspective	Gap Depth	100

Configuring the chart area

A 3D chart needs more real estate than its 2D counterpart. You can overwrite the default chart area settings and specify custom plot and position settings. The CustomInnerPlotPosition settings define the plot area on which the chart area will be drawn as a percentage of the entire chart area. The CustomPosition property defines the custom positioning of the chart area.

1. Select the chart area by clicking one of its walls. The Properties window should show ChartAreal selected.
2. In the Properties window, specify the following settings:

Table 6.3 Additional chart area settings that define custom positioning and formatting

Property	Setting	Property	Setting	Property	Setting
CustomInnerPlotPosition ⇨ Enabled	True	CustomPosition ⇨ Enabled	True	BorderColor	#40404040
CustomInnerPlotPosition ⇨ Height	97	CustomPosition ⇨ Height	100	BorderStyle	Solid
CustomInnerPlotPosition ⇨ Left	0	CustomPosition ⇨ Left	0	BackgroundColor	OldLace
CustomInnerPlotPosition ⇨ Top	0	CustomPosition ⇨ Top	0	Area3DStyle ⇨ Shading	Simple
CustomInnerPlotPosition ⇨ Width	100	CustomPosition ⇨ Width	0		

Configuring the chart series

The chart region supports custom drawing styles to enhance the 3D effects of the chart series:

1. Select the InternetSalesAmount series by clicking the [Sum(InternetSalesAmount)] field in the Drop Data Fields Here area or by clicking one of the column bars of the InternetSalesAmount series in the chart.
2. In the Properties window, change Custom Attributes ⇨ DrawingStyle ⇨ Emboss.
3. Select the ResellerSalesAmount series and change its drawing style to LightToDark.
4. Select the SalesAmount series and change its drawing style to Wedge.
5. Preview the report.

   Notice that the y-axis labels are rather congested. However, you can use expressions to set the label intervals.

6. Click the y-axis to select it. Enter the following expression in the chart axis Interval property:

```
=SUM(Fields!SalesAmount.Value)/10
```

This expression divides the y-axis into ten intervals based on the overall sales amount.

7. Set the Margin property for both axes to False to remove the side margins.

Configuring series drillthrough

As with tablix reports, you can add navigation features to your charts. Suppose that the user would like to drill through a column bar of the Sales Amount series to see the monthly sales. You can meet this requirement by configuring a drillthrough action for the SalesAmount series:

1. Add an action to the series. For example, if you were adding drillthrough to show a level of details behind the Sales Amount series, you would open the SalesAmount series properties and select the Action tab, as shown in Figure 6.10.

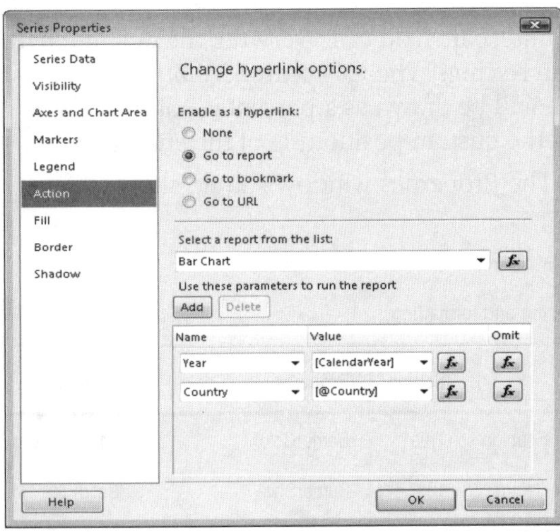

Figure 6.10 Use the Series Properties to configure a navigation action for the entire series.

2. Select the Go To Report option and select the drillthrough report to navigate to. In our case, I selected the Bar Chart report, which I'll discuss in the next section.
3. Add parameters to pass to the drillthrough report, (for example, Year and Country parameters). Map the Year parameter to CalendarYear field (enter *[CalendarYear]*) and Country parameter to the County report-level parameter (enter *[@Country]*).
4. Preview the report and click any of the column bars in the SalesAmount series.

Reporting Services launches the Bar Chart report, which I'll discuss next.

6.2.4 Bar Charts

A bar chart is closely related to a column chart. The difference is that this chart type displays a series as a set of horizontal bars. In fact, the bar chart is the only chart type that displays data horizontally by inverting the axes, so the x-axis shows the chart values and the y-axis shows the category values. Bar charts are typically used to compare individual items, as they place more emphasis on comparing values and less emphasis on time. Time is usually projected on the y-axis. Because a bar chart inverts the axes, you cannot combine it with another chart type.

The bar chart has several variations. A stacked bar chart displays multiple series stacked vertically. The percent stacked bar chart shows multiple series stacked vertically to fit 100% of the chart area. The 3D clustered variation shows individual series in separate rows on a 3D chart. Finally, the 3D cylinder chart shapes the bars as cylinders with 3D effects.

Understanding the Bar Chart report

The Bar Chart report (see Figure 6.11) compares the Internet sales and resale sales side-by-side for a given year. This report is designed as a drillthrough report from the 3D Column Chart report and it accepts the year and country as input parameters.

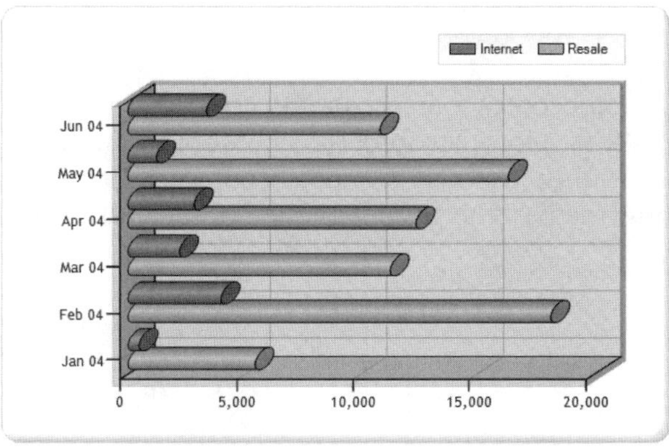

Figure 6.11 This bar chart compares the Internet and resale sales by month.

The y-axis shows the months with sales for the selected year. The x-axis plots the sales amount. Glancing at the chart, we can see that resale sales outperform Internet Sales by far.

Implementing a bar chart

Follow these steps to implement the bar chart report:

1. Drop a chart region and select 3-D Clustered Horizontal Cylinder chart type, which is the last chart type in the Bar section on the Select Chart Type dialog box.
2. Drop the Date field in the Drop Category Fields Here area.
3. Drop the InternetSalesAmount and ResellerSalesAmount fields in the Drop Data Field Here area.
4. Delete the chart title and axis labels. Change the legend's Position property to TopRight.
5. Click the y-axis to set its LabelsFormat property to *MMM yy*. Click the x-axis and set its LabelsFormat property to *#,0,;(#,0,)*.
6. Select either of the two series and open its Properties window. Notice that the series CustomAttributes ⇨ DrawingStyle property is set to Cylinder. You can change the drawing style for each series to increase its visual impact.
7. Click the InternetSalesAmount series. In the Properties window, change the LegendText property to *Internet* and BorderColor property to Black.
8. Click the ResellerSalesAmount sales series. In the Properties window, change the LegendText property to *Resale* and BorderColor property to Black.

Bar charts are effective for comparing data among a relatively small number of groups. If more than three series are present on the chart, consider using a stacked bar. To convert the bar chart to a stacked bar, right-click the chart area and choose any of the stacked bar charts, such as 3-D Stacked Bar or 3-D Stacked Bar 100% if you want to see the series contribution as a percentage.

6.2.5 Shape Charts

A shape chart displays values as percentages of a whole. Categories are represented by individual segments of the shape. The size of the segment is determined by its contribution. This makes a shape chart useful for proportional comparison between category values. Shape charts have no axes. Share chart variations include pie, doughnut, funnel, and pyramid charts. All shape charts display each group as a separate slice on the chart. Funnel and pyramid charts order categories from largest to smallest.

Understanding the Pie Chart report

The Pie Chart report, shown in Figure 6.12, demonstrates a shape chart that shows the Adventure Works sales by product category. The chart plots data for a single year or multiple years depending on the selected values in the Year multivalued parameter (not shown in Figure 6.12). I configured the series labels to show the percentage contribution of each category to the overall sales.

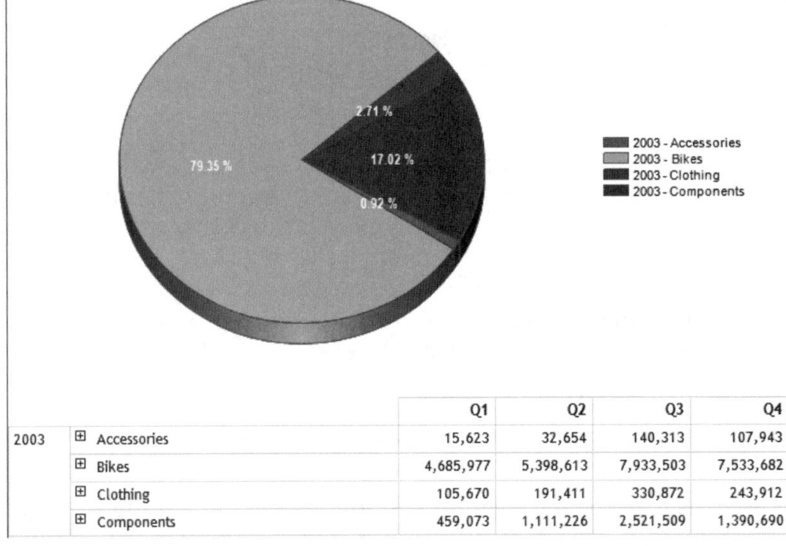

		Q1	Q2	Q3	Q4
2003	⊞ Accessories	15,623	32,654	140,313	107,943
	⊞ Bikes	4,685,977	5,398,613	7,933,503	7,533,682
	⊞ Clothing	105,670	191,411	330,872	243,912
	⊞ Components	459,073	1,111,226	2,521,509	1,390,690

Figure 6.12 This pie chart shows the Adventure Works sales by category and year.

As it stands, the chart region doesn't natively support a data table that shows the underlying chart data in a tabular format. However, you can implement a data table by placing a table or a matrix side-by-side with the chart region. The matrix below the chart region demonstrates this approach. The pie chart presents the summarized report data. To see more details, the user can analyze the crosstab report and drill down to products and quarters.

Implementing a pie chart

Follow these steps to implement the Pie Chart report:

1. Drop a chart region and select the 3-D Pie chart variation in the Shape tab of the Select Chart Type dialog box. Change the chart name to *SalesChart*.
2. Add the CalendarYear and Category fields to the Drop Category Fields Here area to define the category groups. Consequently, the chart will show as many slices as the number of categories with sales in the selected year(s).

3. Right-click the CalendarYear group field and choose Category Group Properties. In the Sorting tab, click the Add button and set up a new sorting option to sort the group by [CalendarYear]. Repeat this step to sort the Category group by [Category].
4. Add the SalesAmount field to the Drop Data Fields Here area to set up the chart series.
5. By default, a pie chart doesn't show data labels. Right-click the chart pie area and click Show Data Labels.
6. Right-click the data labels and click Series Label Properties. Format the labels as needed.

   To create the labels for each slice, you can use an expression that calculates the slice contribution of each slice as a percentage of all sales. You need to define the expression at the data point level instead of the series level because the expression requires the data point value.
7. Select the chart area. In the Properties window, enter the following expression in the Label ⇨ Label property:

   ```
   =Sum(Fields!SalesAmount.Value)/Sum(Fields!SalesAmount.Value, "SalesChart")
   ```

   This expression divides the data point value by the overall sales. The second Sum function calculates the overall sales value by using the name of the chart as the expression scope.
8. When prompted, confirm to change the Label ⇨ UseValueAsLabel property to False.
9. Set Label ⇨ Format to P2 to format the label as a percentage with two decimals. Set the Label ⇨ Color property to White.
10. Preview the report.

Working with custom pie attributes

A pie chart supports custom attributes that define the chart appearance and behavior. For example, if the chart doesn't have 3D effects (in the Chart Area properties, uncheck Enable 3D), you can set CustomAttributes ⇨ PieDrawingStyle to SoftEdge or Concave to change the visual appearance of the chart. While a pie chart is a very effective data visualization tool, it may become crowded as the number of category values increase. Suppose that you want to consolidate into a single slice all of the small slices that together contribute to 10% of overall sales. You can do this by configuring the chart to collect slices:

1. Click the [Sum(SalesAmount)] field in the Drop Data Fields Here area to select the chart series.
2. Change CustomAttributes ⇨ CollectedStyle to SingleSlice.
3. Change CustomAttributes ⇨ CollectedThreshold to 10.
4. Change CustomAttributes ⇨ CollectedThresholdUsePercent to True.
5. If you want to pull the collected slice slightly away from the chart, set CustomAttributes ⇨ CollectedSliceExploded to True.

   There are additional properties applicable to the collected slice, such as whether to show it in the legend, what its legend text will be, and so on. If you prefer to show the data labels outside the chart, do the following:
6. Set CustomAttributes ⇨ PieLabelStyle to Outside.

   You can also use the CustomAttributes ⇨ MinimumRelativePieSize series property if you want to adjust the pie size as a percentage of the chart area size.

Implementing a data table

The matrix below the chart shows the chart data in a tabular format. It lets the user drill down to the product level on rows and quarters on columns. One interesting implementation detail is that the pie chart supports a bookmark navigation action that lets the user click a slice and jump to its details in the crosstab report.

1. Click the … button inside the Action property and set up a bookmark navigation action for drilling through to a bookmark using the following expression:

```
=String.Format("{0}{1}", Fields!CalendarYear.Value, Fields!Category.Value)
```

At run time, this expression returns a combination of the year and the product category associated with the clicked slice, such as 2004Accessories.

2. In the tablix region, click the Category cell and note that its Bookmark property uses the same expression to define the bookmark target.
3. Preview the report and select years 2003 and 2004 in the Year parameter.
4. Expand year 2003 in the matrix report. Expand the Accessories and Bikes categories to see data broken down by product.
5. In the pie chart, click the 2004 Accessories slice.

The report jumps to the 2004 Accessories row in the matrix region. The navigation action lets the user quickly navigate to the details of the selected slice.

6.2.6 Area Charts

Similar to a line chart, an area chart displays a series as a set of points connected by a line with the exception that all of the area below the line is filled in. The line chart and area chart are the only chart types that display data contiguously. Consequently, the area chart is commonly used to represent data that occurs over a continuous period of time.

The area chart has three variations. The smooth area chart type connects the data points by a smooth line which makes it more suitable to identify trends instead of actual values. The stacked area chart type displays multiple areas stacked vertically. This could be useful when you need to analyze more than two series and you want to prevent overlapping series that obscure data values. The percent stacked area chart type shows the multiple series stacked vertically that taken together fit the entire chart area.

Understanding the Area Chart report

The Area Chart report (see Figure 6.13) shows the Adventure Works reseller sales for a given year. The user can select which sales territories to see on the report. Each territory is plotted as a separate chart series. In Figure 6.13, the chart has two series because I selected the North America and Pacific values of the Territory parameter (not shown in the screenshot).

This report also demonstrates handling missing data. The chart supports a set of properties that control the appearance of empty points. For example, the Pacific region has missing data for the first four months of 2003. There is a value for May 2003, followed by missing data for June 2003. I configured the chart to show a red cross when data is missing. Besides showing the empty points as zero, the chart lets you average them across the data points that contain non-zero values.

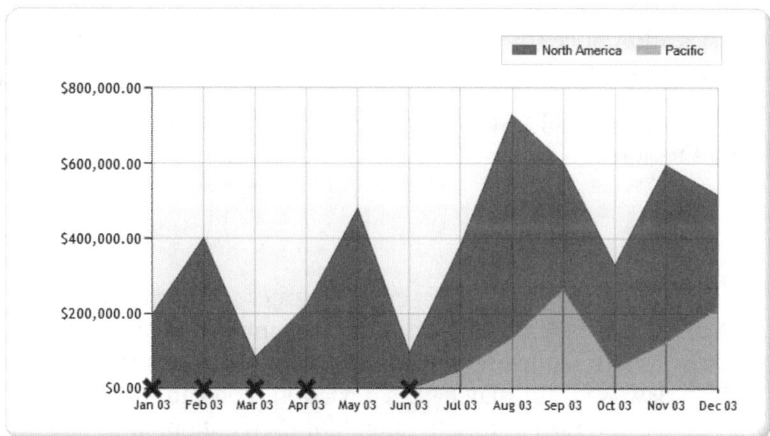

Figure 6.13 This area chart shows sales by region over time and displays markers for missing values.

Implementing the Area Chart report

Implementing the area chart report is straightforward.

1. Choose the Area chart type when configuring a new chart region.
2. In the Chart Properties dialog box (General page), choose the Semi Transparent color palette to let the overlapping series show through.
3. Drag the ResellerSalesAmount to the Drop Data Fields Here area, Date to the Drop the Category Fields Here area, and TerritoryGroup to the Drop Series Fields Here area.
4. Click any of the series in the chart area. In the Property window, set the Interval to *1* to show major tick marks and labels for every month.

Handling missing data

Empty data points are points that have NULL values or don't have values at all. For example, the Pacific territory has no data recorded prior to May 2003 and NULL for June 2003.The chart lets you control how missing data will be presented to the end user.

1. Select any of the series in the chart area. In the Properties window, expand the CustomAttributes category.

   Note that CustomAttributes ⇨ EmptyPointValue is set by default to Average. Consequently, the chart will average empty points across the data points that do contain data.

2. Assuming you want to show empty points as zeros, change CustomAttributes ⇨ EmptyPointValue to Zero.

   You can customize the empty point appearance to inform the user that there is missing data.

3. In the Properties window, set EmptyPoint ⇨ BorderColor to Gray to show a line for the missing points.
4. Set EmptyPoint ⇨ Marker ⇨ Color to Red, EmptyPoint ⇨ Marker ⇨ MarkerType to Cross, and EmptyPoint ⇨ Marker ⇨ Size to 15pt.
5. Preview the report and check Select All in the Territory multivalued parameter.

   Note that as the number of series increase, the chart becomes difficult to read because series overlap each other.

6. In design mode, right-click the chart and change its type to Stacked Area.
7. Preview the report for all territories and notice that the chart is more readable because the three areas are stacked on top of each other.

   The band of each series shows the proportional contribution of the series. The area height shows the cumulative value for all regions.

6.2.7 Range Charts

Some measures, such as weather temperatures, stock data, currency rates, and error margins, are best analyzed within a range of values. A weather forecast predicts minimum and maximum values for the next day. A stock has open, close, low and high values. A currency rate has start and end values for a given day. An error may have a deviation. You can use a range chart to display data points by plotting several Y values (a range) for each data point.

The plain range chart lets you define a range consisting of two values. A stock chart is designed for financial or scientific data that uses up to four values per data point, such as high, low, open and close values. The candlestick chart is similar to a stock chart but displays boxes to show the range between the open and close values. Error bar charts are used to display statistical information about the data, using three Y values for each data point (center or average point value, lower error value, and upper error value). Finally, the boxplot chart type shows a box symbol that summarizes the distribution of the data within one or more datasets.

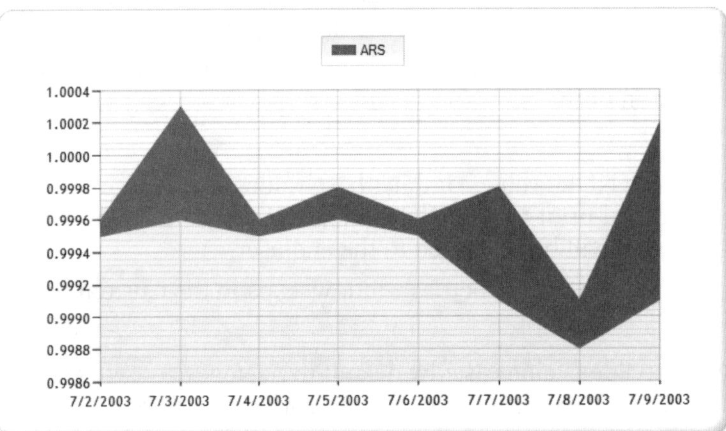

Figure 6.14 This range chart shows the fluctuations of a currency rate over a given period where each data point has a starting and closing daily rate.

Understanding the Range Chart report

The Range Chart report (see Figure 6.14) illustrates an example of a range chart. The chart shows the currency rate for a given currency over a user-specified time period. The currency rates are retrieved from the CurrencyRate table in the AdventureWorksDW2008 database. In the example, the chart shows the rate history of the Argentine Peso (ARS) currency for the period from 7/2/2003 to 7/9/2003. Each data point has a start and end rate values that were recorded for that day.

Although the range chart can handle multiple categories, the report is designed to show a single currency. This is because the currency rates vary greatly between different currencies. If multiple currencies are selected, their plotted ranges would be very narrow. This defeats the purpose of having a range chart as the resulting graph would look more like a line chart. If your real-life data points are within comparable ranges, consider plotting multiple categories on the same chart.

Implementing a range chart

Start implementing a range chart by preparing a dataset that includes a range of values of each data point. Recall that we need at least two values for each data point.

CurrencyRate...	FromCurrency...	ToCurrencyCo...	StartRate	EndRate
7/1/2003 12:00:...	USD	ARS	0.9996	1.0001
7/2/2003 12:00:...	USD	ARS	0.9995	0.9996
7/3/2003 12:00:...	USD	ARS	0.9996	1.0003
7/4/2003 12:00:...	USD	ARS	0.9995	0.9996

Figure 6.15 The dataset includes start and end rate values for each currency per day.

The report dataset, shown in Figure 6.15, returns the historical currency rate for each day in the selected period. Each row has a start and end rate.

1. Add a chart to the report. In the Select Chart Type dialog box, select the first chart variation in the Range section.
2. Drag the CurrencyRateDate field to the Drop the Category Fields Here area. Drag the ToCurrencyCode field to the Drop Series Fields Here area.
3. Drag the EndRate to the Drop Data Fields Here area to define the series high values.

   Note that an additional Low field is displayed next to the EndRate field to remind you that you need to supply another field for the low range value.
4. Drag the StartRate to the Low field inside the Drop Data Fields Here area.
5. Select the chart series. In the Properties window, expand the DataPoint ⇨ Values property group.

   Observe that the DataPoint ⇨ Values ⇨ High property is set to =Sum(Fields!EndRate.Value) and the DataPoint ⇨ Values ⇨ Low property is set to =Sum(Fields!StartRate.Value). This is all you need to configure a plain range chart. Other variations of the range chart may require configuring additional range properties. For example, if you work with a stock chart, you may need to also configure DataPoint ⇨ Values ⇨ Start and DataPoint ⇨ Values ⇨ End properties.

6.2.8 Scatter Charts

Scatter charts reveal relationships or associations between two variables. For example, you may find a correlation between reseller size and sales. You can use a scatter chart to show the reseller sales along the y-axis and the reseller size, such as the number of employees, along the x-axis. The resulting chart can help you understand if the two variables are related and, if so, how (for example, whether they have a linear relationship). Scatter charts are commonly used for displaying and comparing numeric values, including scientific, statistical, and engineering data.

The scatter chart type has the following variations. The bubble chart replaces data points with bubbles of different size. The second Y value is used to control the size of the bubble. Although the chart is called "bubble" it also can display different shapes, such as square, diamond, or triangle. The 3-D bubble chart variation displays the chart in 3D.

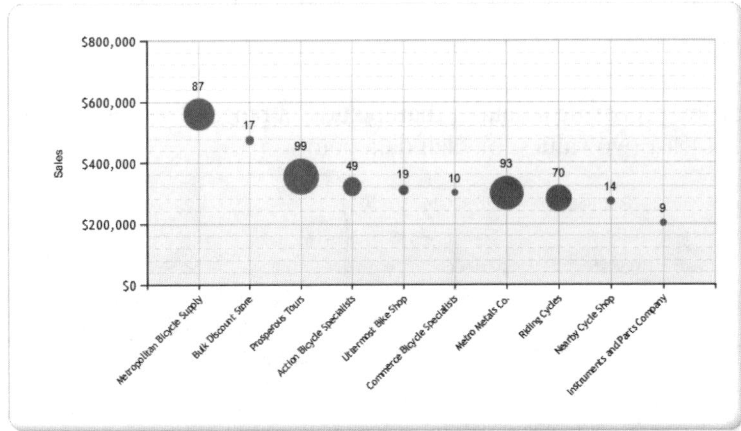

Figure 6.16 This bubble chart shows a correlation between the reseller's sales and size.

Understanding the Bubble Chart report

The Bubble Chart report, shown in Figure 6.16, demonstrates the bubble chart variation of the scattered chart type. It helps you analyze the correlation between reseller size and sales. The chart shows a subset of the Adventure Works resellers with their names plotted on the x-axis and sales on the y-axis. The size of the bubble represents the reseller size in number of employees. The label above the bubble shows the number of employees for that reseller.

The report supports Country and Top Count parameters (not shown in Figure 6.16). The Country parameter, whose default value is United Kingdom, lets you filter resellers by territory. Use the Top Count parameter to specify how many resellers you want to see on the report. The default value of the Top Count parameter is 10. Subsequently, the report shows the top 10 resellers with the most sales.

Glancing at the chart, we can deduce that in the case of the Adventure Works data, there isn't a strong correlation between reseller size and sales. For example, the second UK reseller with the most sales has only 17 employees. When you hover on top of a bubble, a tooltip pops up that shows the reseller sales amount.

Implementing the Bubble Chart report

A bubble chart requires two numeric values for each data point. As with a linear chart, the first numeric value defines the y-axis position of the bubble. The second numeric value controls the size of the bubble.

1. In the Select Chart Type dialog box, select the Bubble variation of the Scatter chart type.
2. Drag the Reseller Name field to the Drag Category Fields Here area.
3. Drag the Sales field to the Drop Data Fields Here area.

   Note that the chart shows an empty Size field next to the Sales field in the Drop Data Fields Here area.

4. Drag the NumberEmployees field to the Size field in the Drop Data Fields Here area.
5. Click the chart series. In the Properties window, expand the DataPoint ⇨ Values property.

   Note that the DataPoint ⇨ Values ⇨ Size property, which controls the bubble size, is set to =Sum(Fields!NumberEmployees.Value). The DataPoint ⇨ Values ⇨ Y property, which controls the y-axis position of the bubble, is bound to Sum(Fields!Sales.Value).

6. You can change the plotted shape as needed. Set the Marker ➪ MarkerType property to Circle.

7. To show the number of employees, set the Label ➪ Label property to the following expression:

```
=Sum(Fields!NumberEmployees.Value)
```

8. When prompted, confirm to set the Label ➪ UseValueAsLabel to False. Set Label ➪ Visible to True.

9. Set the Tooltip property to =Sum(Fields!Sales.Value) to show the reseller sales as a tooltip.

6.2.9 Polar Charts

Polar charts are most commonly used to graph polar data, where each data point is determined by an angle and a distance. A polar chart plots the data points by category on a 360-degree circle by default and can be changed by setting the X-axis Maximum property to a different degree, such as 180. Its chart area is a circular graph on which data points are plotted at a distance from the center point. The farther the point is from the center, the greater its value.

The radar chart is a variation of the polar chart type. Unlike a polar chart, a radar chart doesn't display data in terms of polar coordinates. It is similar to a pie chart, except that the category values are at an equal angle and extend from the center of the circle. Consider a polar chart when you need to compare multiple data series and you need clear and concise presentations of data. The polar chart type also supports a 3D Radar variation.

Understanding the Radar Chart report

The Radar Chart report, shown in Figure 6.17, illustrates the radar chart variation of the polar chart type. It shows the Adventure Works reseller sales for a given year by reseller type. The y-axis shows the sales amount in thousands. Polar charts don't plot data points on the x-axis. However, the x-axis still exists to shows the category values (months in this case).

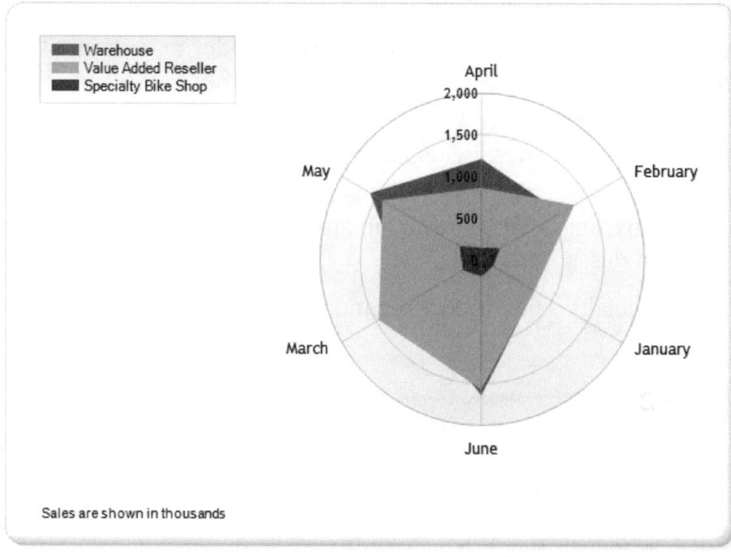

Figure 6.17 This radar chart shows how the warehouse, value-added, and specialty reseller sales compare.

Analyzing the chart, we can determine that in April, warehouse resellers have generated about $1,250,000, while value-added resellers have sold about $800,000. Reseller sales are lowest in January and highest in May and June. The sales of specialty bike shops, which are plotted in red, are much lower than the other two reseller types. This report also demonstrates working with custom color palettes and ordering series.

Implementing the Radar Chart report

To implement a radar chart, start with the datasets and basic chart configuration steps you know so well, and then add the following steps:

1. In the Select Chart Type dialog box, choose the Radar variation of the Polar chart type.
2. Drag the Sales field to the Drop Data Fields Here area, Month field to the Drop Category Fields Here area, and ResellerType field to the Drop Series Fields Here area.
3. Preview the report and note that the Specialty Bike Shop series is not visible because it is obscured by the other two series.

There are several ways to work around this issue. To start with, instead of plotting data points as areas, you can plot them as lines or markers. The radar chart supports customization via a set of attributes which you can find under the series CustomAttributes property group. For example, change CustomAttributes ⇨ RadarDrawingStyle from Area to Marker if you want to see the data series plotted as markers. You can also configure the chart to use a custom color palette if you need more control over the series colors.

4. Select the chart. In the Properties window, click the ... button inside the CustomPaletteColors and notice that I have defined a custom palette of three colors (LightGrey, MistyRose, and LemonChiffon).
5. With the chart selected, expand its Palette property and change it to Custom.

Previewing the report should now show each area colored in one of the custom colors.

NOTE When you define a custom color palette, make sure to add as many colors as the maximum number of series you expect. If you have fewer colors than series, the chart will start reusing the same colors.

If changing the chart plot style and using custom colors doesn't help, consider re-ordering the chart series. In our case, we need to plot the specialty sales on top of the other two series. To do so, we need to sort the chart series in descending order on sales.

6. Right-click the ResellerType field in the Drop Series Fields Here area and click Series Group Properties.
7. In the Series Group Properties dialog box, select the Sorting tab and add a new sort expression that sorts the series on the Sales field in descending order.

Preview the report and note that the specialty sales appear behind the other two chart series.

6.3 Designing Gauge Reports

The gauge is a one-dimensional data region that displays a single value from a report dataset. Gauges are commonly used because they are very easy to read. They put data into the context by visually defining what the good, medium, and bad values represent. For example, you can use the gauge region to implement a dashboard page that shows the company performance as a set of Key Performance Indicators (KPIs). Another popular use for the gauge region is to place it inside a containing region, such as table or matrix, to visualize the tablix cells as repeating gauges.

6.3.1 Understanding the Gauge Region

The gauge region debuts in this release of Reporting Services and is based on the Dundas data visualization technology. Reporting Services supports radial (circular) and linear gauges. Similar to the chart region, each gauge type comes with several variations for different styles.

Understanding gauge types

Radial and linear gauges are very similar and contain the same elements, including back frames, pointers, scales, and ranges. At the same time, there are some differences. Radial gauges have a pivot point around which the pointer(s) rotate. The pivot point is set by default to a coordinate of (50, 50) which corresponds to the center of the gauge. Radial gauges support marker, bar, and needle pointers. Circular scales have a start angle, a sweep angle, and radius.

Linear gauges display the value as a portion of the scale. They can have a horizontal or vertical orientation. A linear gauge can have bar or marker pointers. The needle pointer is not available with linear gauges. Linear scales have a start margin and an end margin.

Upgrading from Dundas gauge

Similar to upgrading from Dundas Chart, Reporting Services supports a partial upgrade path from the Dundas Gauge for Reporting Services. As it stands, Reporting Services doesn't support numeric and state indicators, nor does it support Dundas custom code.

At design time, you can upgrade to the native gauge region by opening the report definition in Report Designer. This is a one-way conversion process and you cannot downgrade back to the Dundas gauge control. Unsupported features are removed on upgrade. For example, if the Dundas gauge has a child numeric gauge, the numeric gauge will be removed from the upgraded report.

If you already have and prefer the Dundas Gauge control, you can continue using BIDS 2005 to edit your reports. You can deploy legacy report definitions to a report server running Reporting Services 2008. When you upgrade a report server, the upgrade process will detect whether deployed reports with Dundas gauges can be upgraded with no loss in functionality. If this is the case, it will upgrade them in place. Report definitions that use unsupported Dundas features will not get upgraded, but users can continue running these reports unaffected.

Understanding the gauge anatomy

The gauge region contains several elements, which are shown in Figure 6.18. The gauge scale displays a range of possible values, such as from -30% to +30%. A scale has a minimum value and a maximum value. It can also have major and minor tick marks. Similar to charts, the scale is divided into intervals which can be auto-generated or set by the report author.

A gauge can have one or more pointers that indicate values on the scale. The gauge region supports needle (radial gauges only), marker, bar, and thermometer (linear gauges only) pointer styles. Ranges can be used to highlight a range of values. The sample gauge shown in Figure 6.18 uses a green range to highlight business over-performance. A range has a start value and start width, as well as an end value and an end width.

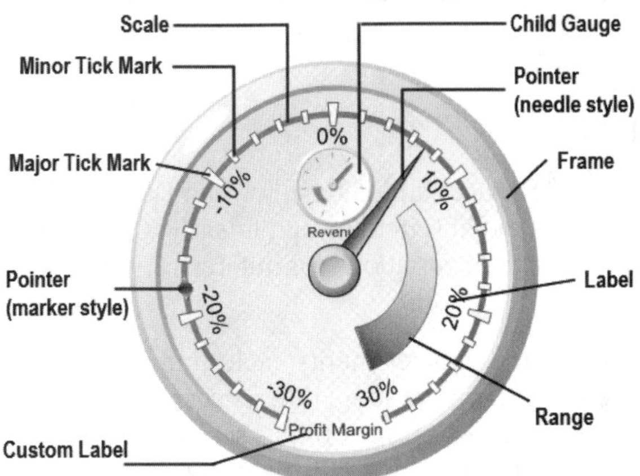

Figure 6.18 This diagram illustrates the elements of the gauge region.

A gauge can include nested child gauges (sub-gauges). For example, the main gauge can show a Profit Margin KPI while a child gauge can display the Revenue KPI. You position the child gauge by specifying its coordinates within the window of the parent gauge. Besides scale labels, you can add custom labels to display textual information anywhere on the gauge. If the Microsoft-provided visual styles are not enough, custom images can be used. For example, you can use a custom image for the pointer shape.

6.3.2 Implementing a Radial Gauge ▶

Next, I will walk you through the process of implementing the radial gauge shown in Figure 6.18. The Radial Gauge report represents the finished solution. It retrieves the properties of the Product Gross Profit Margin and Revenue KPIs that are defined in the Adventure Works Analysis Services cube and displays them in a radial gauge. The report demonstrates the following features:

- Querying Analysis Services KPIs
- Configuring marker and needle pointers
- Implementing ranges and custom labels
- Working with child gauges

Use the Radial Gauge Start report as a starting point for this practice.

Retrieving the report data

As noted, gauges are typically used to display KPIs. As a multi-dimensional database, Analysis Services is well suited for defining and calculating KPIs. In fact, an Analysis Services KPI is nothing more than an MDX calculated member with additional properties, such as Value, Goal, Status, and Trend. You use MDX expressions to define how these properties are calculated at run time. As with other measures, Analysis Services automatically computes the KPI properties as the user slices the data.

To facilitate querying the KPI objects, Analysis Services provides four MDX functions: KPIValue, KPIGoal, KPIStatus, and KPITrend, which you can use in the report query to retrieve the KPI properties and display them on the report. The abbreviated MDX query of the Radial Gauge report is as follows:

```
SELECT NON EMPTY { KPIStatus("Revenue"), KPIValue("Revenue"), KPITrend("Revenue"), KPIGoal("Revenue"), KPIGoal("Product
Gross Profit Margin"), KPIValue("Product Gross Profit Margin"), KPITrend("Product Gross Profit Margin"), KPIStatus("Product
Gross Profit Margin")}
ON COLUMNS
FROM ( SELECT ( STRTOSET(@SalesTerritorySalesTerritoryCountry, CONSTRAINED) ) ON COLUMNS
FROM [Adventure Works])
```

This query slices the results by country, which the user can then pass as a report parameter. The query returns a single row that includes the status, value, goal, and trend properties of the Revenue and Product Gross Profit Margin KPIs.

Getting started with the gauge region

Once the dataset is in place, you are ready to configure the gauge region:

1. Drop the gauge region on the report. In the Select Gauge Type dialog box that follows, leave the default Radial gauge type selected, and click OK.
2. Resize the gauge to a width of 4.2 inches and a height of 3.6 inches.

   The gauge region supports various frame styles and properties that control the visual appearance of the gauge.

3. Double-click the gauge to put it in edit mode and click its frame. The Property window should have RadialGauge1 item selected.

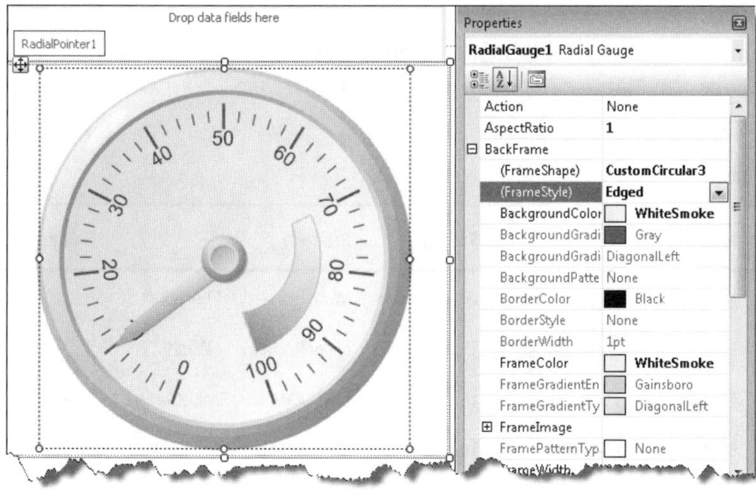

Figure 6.19 The gauge region supports various frame styles and properties to change the visual appearance of the gauge.

4. In the Properties window, expand the BackFrame ⇨ FrameShape property and select the CustomCircular3 frame shape, as shown in Figure 6.19.

Configuring the pointer

Recall that the gauge region is a one-dimensional data region and can display a single value. In our case, the gauge pointer will point to the value of the Product Gross Profit Margin KPI.

1. Drag the Product_Gross_Profit_Margin_Value field from the Report Data window and drop it on the RadialPointer1 placeholder in the Bind Gauge Values to Data Fields Here area.

   This binds the pointer to the aggregated KPI value. By default, the gauge uses the Sum aggregated function. You can change the aggregated function in the pointer properties, which you can access by right-clicking the Product_Gross_Profit_Margin_Value field and clicking Pointer properties. Alternatively, you can select the pointer and change the properties in the Properties window. The Value property group gives you access to the pointer data properties.

2. Click the [Sum(Product_Gross_Profit_Margin_Value)] field in the Bind Gauge Values to Data Fields Here area.

   Note that selecting the field selects the gauge pointer. You can also click the pointer directly in the gauge frame to access the pointer properties.

3. Change the pointer visual appearance by setting the properties shown in Table 6.4.

Table 6.4 Pointer properties for the radial gauge

Property	Setting	Property	Setting	Property	Setting
BorderStyle	Solid	FillGradientType	LeftRight	NeedleStyle	Triangular
FillGradientEndColor	Red	Name	ProfitMargin		

Configuring the scale

If you preview the report at this point, you'll find that the pointer points to zero. This is because by default the gauge scale ranges from 0 to 100. To get the pointer to "move", you need to calibrate the scale:

1. Click the gauge scale to select it. The Properties window should show Gauge Scale as the name of the selected item. Change the Name property to *ProfitMarginScale*.
2. Configure the scale properties, as shown in Table 6.5.

Table 6.5 Scale properties for the radial gauge

Property	Setting	Property	Setting	Property	Setting
(MaximumValue)	0.3	MajorTickMarks⇨FillColor	WhiteSmoke	MinorTickMarks⇨Length	8
(MinimumValue)	-0.3	MajorTickMarks⇨EnableGradient	True	MinorTickMarks⇨Width	4
Interval	0.1	MajorTickMarks⇨Length	15	MinorTickMarks⇨EnableGradient	True
LabelStyle⇨FormatString	0%	MajorTickMarks⇨Shape	Trapezoid	MinorTickMarks⇨FillColor	WhiteSmoke
MajorTickMarks⇨BorderStyle	Solid	MajorTickMarks⇨Width	7	Width	4

Besides changing the scale visual appearance, these settings configure the scale range from -30% (MinimumValue) and 30% (MaximumValue). The scale interval is set to 10%.

Configuring the range

Let's implement a range to indicate when the Profit_Margin KPI exceeds expectations. For demonstration purposes, the lower value of the range will be defined as 80% of the KPI goal value, while the upper value will be set to the maximum scale value of 30%. The default radial gauge variation already includes a range which we will reuse. However, the process of calibrating the scale caused the range to "disappear". Follow these steps to configure the range:

1. Click the scale to select it. Click the ellipsis (...) button in the Ranges property. In the RadialRange Collection Editor, notice that there is a default range.
2. Configure the range properties, as shown in Table 6.5.

Table 6.6 Range properties for the radial gauge

Property	Setting	Property	Setting
BorderColor	Gray	StartValue	=.8 * Fields!Product_Gross_Profit_Margin_Goal.Value
FillGradientEndColor	ForestGreen	EndValue	0.3
		Name	ProfitMarginRange

The gauge can have multiple ranges if needed. If you want to add more ranges to your gauge, such as to indicate under-performance, right-click the gauge and click Add Range.

Implementing a marker pointer

Besides needle-style pointers, the radial gauge supports marker and bar pointers. You can use such pointers to indicate significant values on the scale. Next, you will implement a marker pointer to indicate the lower boundary of under-performance. For demonstration purposes, the lower boundary will be calculated as 150% less the profit margin goal value.

1. Right-click the gauge or its scale and click Add Pointer. The gauge region adds a new needle-style pointer.
2. Select the new pointer by clicking it and configure it as follows:

Table 6.7 Properties for the maker pointer

Property	Setting	Property	Setting
(Type)	Marker	Name	ProfitMarginMarker
FillGradientType	VerticalCenter	Placement	Cross
MarkerStyle	Diamond	Value	=-1.5 * Sum(Fields!Product_Gross_Profit_Margin_Goal.Value)
MarkerLength	10		

Implementing a child gauge

You can implement a combination gauge by nesting gauges inside each other. Follow these steps to add a child gauge to show the value of the Revenue KPI:

1. Right-click the radial gauge and click Add Gauge ⇨ Child.
2. In the Select Gauge Type dialog, leave the default radial gauge variation selected and click OK.

   You can position the child gauge anywhere within the frame of the main parent gauge by setting its Top and Left properties.

3. Select the child gauge and set its Top property to 20, Left property to 40, and Width property to 20.

   Because the gauge's AspectRatio is set to 1, you don't need to set its Height property as the gauge frame will be automatically resized to a circle.

4. Drag the Revenue_Value field from the Report Data window and drop it on the new field placeholder in the Bind Gauge Values to Data Fields Here area.
5. Follow similar steps as the ones you did when configuring the parent gauge to set up the range, scale, and pointer properties of the child gauge.

Implementing a custom label

You can add custom labels to display text inside the range. Similar to textbox report items, custom labels can show static text or can be expression-based.

1. Right-click the gauge and click Add Label. Change the Name property to *ProfitMarginLabel*.
2. Click the new label to select and configure it, as shown in Table 6.8.

Table 6.8 Properties for the Profit Margin custom label

Property	Setting	Property	Setting	Property	Setting
Height	6	Text	Profit Margin	Width	25
Left	38.5	Top	85		

Follow similar steps to implement a custom label with static text "Revenue" below the child gauge.

6.3.3 Implementing a Linear Gauge

Besides radial gauges, Reporting Services supports linear gauges, such as gauges that simulate equipment monitors and thermometers. The Linear Gauge report, shown in Figure 6.20, demonstrates the following features:

- Implementing a thermometer-style linear gauge
- Working with data groups

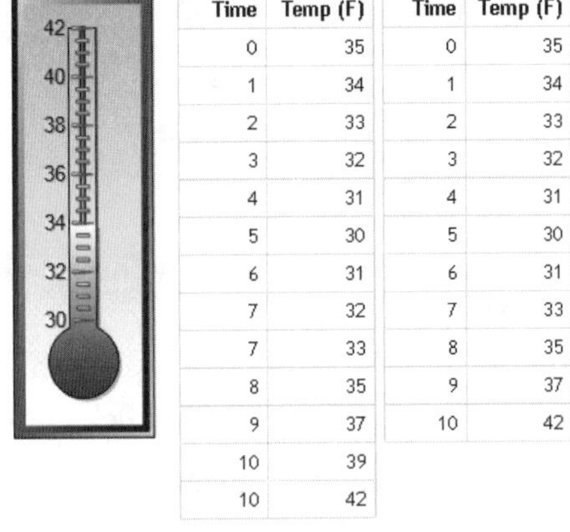

Time	Temp (F)
0	35
1	34
2	33
3	32
4	31
5	30
6	31
7	32
7	33
8	35
9	37
10	39
10	42

Time	Temp (F)
0	35
1	34
2	33
3	32
4	31
5	30
6	31
7	33
8	35
9	37
10	42

Figure 6.20 The Linear Gauge report demonstrates implementing linear gauges with data groups.

Understanding data groups

As noted, the gauge region is a one-dimensional control that can display a single value. This is okay when the dataset returns a single row. But what if you need the pointer value to be calculated over a dataset? For example, you may need to calculate the average temperature over a dataset that contains the temperature measurements per hour. This is where data groups come in.

The gauge region supports statistical formulas that are available only if they are applied to multiple values. In the absence of data groups, the gauge uses only the first value from a multi-row dataset. For example, if you bind the gauge pointer to the temperature column of the dataset shown on the left, it will point to 35 because this is the temperature value stored in the first row.

However, if you group the dataset, then you can use aggregate formulas to derive the value. You can group the dataset using any of the Reporting Services aggregate functions, such as First, Last, Min, Max, Sum, Avg, and expressions. Examining the dataset on the left, you can see that some hours, such as the hours 7 and 10, have multiple temperatures recorded. Let's say you want use only the last temperature value if multiple measurements exist. In this case, you can group on Time and use the Last aggregate function to pre-aggregate data before it's made available to the gauge. Consequently, the input dataset will look like the one on the right.

Once the input values are correct, you can use one of the supported aggregate functions to derive the pointer value. For example, you can use the Average function if you want the pointer to point to the average temperature calculated over the entire input dataset. In Figure 6.20, the gauge points to 34 because this is the average temperature calculated over the dataset on the right.

Implementing the linear gauge report

Follow these steps to implement the Linear Gauge report:

1. In the Select Gauge Type dialog box, select Thermometer variation of the Linear gauge type.
2. Right-click the gauge and click Add Data Group.
3. In the Gauge Panel Group Properties dialog box that follows, add a new group expression that groups on the Time field.
4. Drag the Temperature field from the Report Data window and drop it on the Bind Gauge Values to Data Fields Here area to bind this field to the pointer.

   By default, the gauge aggregates the data values using the Sum aggregate function.
5. Right-click the [Sum(Temperature)] field and click Pointer Properties. Alternatively, you can select the pointer and work directly with the properties of the Value property group in the Properties window.
6. In the Linear Pointer Properties dialog box, change the Value expression (Pointer Options tab) to the following expression and click OK:

   ```
   =Last(Fields!Temperature.Value)
   ```
7. With the pointer selected, expand the Value ⇨ Formula property group in the Properties window and select the Average formula.
8. Click the gauge scale to select it.
9. In the Properties window, change the (MaximumValue) ⇨ Formula property to Max.
10. In the Properties window, change the (MinimumValue) ⇨ Formula property to Min.
11. Preview the report.

    The scale minimum value should be set to 30, which is the minimum value in the input dataset, and the maximum value should be set to 42, which is the maximum value in the input dataset. The gauge pointer should point to 34, which is the average value calculated over all values of the input dataset.

6.3.4 Combining Charts and Gauges

Recall from the previous chapter that you can nest data regions. Placing a chart or a gauge inside another region, such as a list, allows you to pass the grouping context to their values. Consequently, you can implement reports that repeat graphs for all group instances of the outer region.

Understanding nested charts and gauges

The Nested Regions report, shown in Figure 6.21, demonstrates how nested regions can be used to repeat charts and gauges. The report pages on territory group. For each territory, the matrix, chart, and gauge regions show data for the current territory. The report draws data from the Adventure Works Analysis Services cube. The pie chart displays the contribution of each country to the overall gross profit for this territory. The Reseller Sales radial gauges show the value and goal properties of the Channel Revenue KPI. Similarly, the Internet Sales gauges display the value and goal properties of the Internet Revenue KPI.

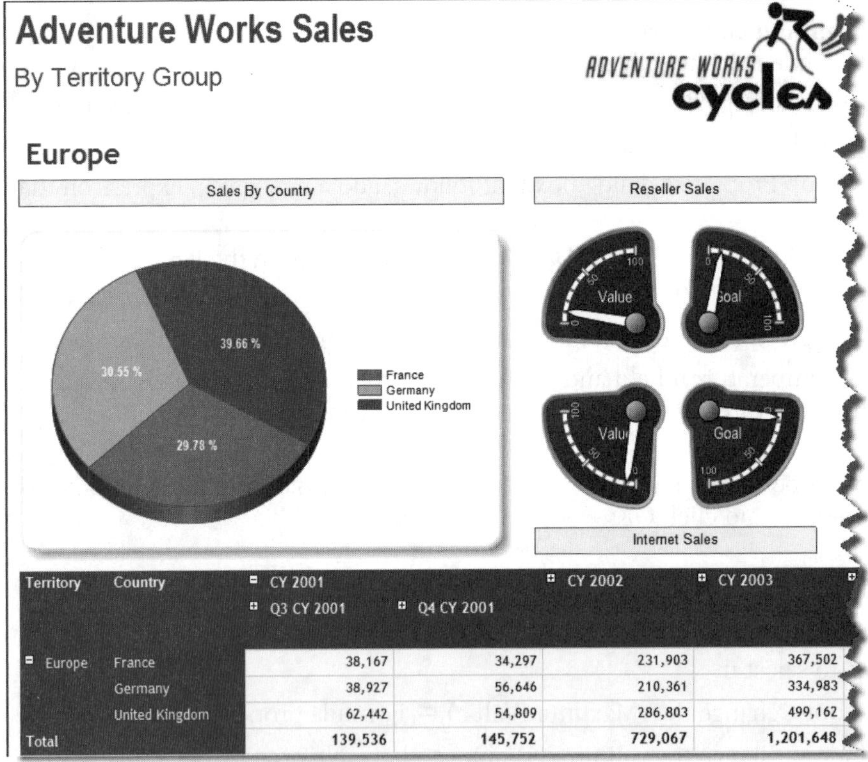

Figure 6.21 This report repeats the chart, gauges, and matrix for each territory.

The matrix region shows gross profit broken down by territory on rows, and time on columns. The user can drill down to see more details, such as from year to quarter to month.

Implementing nested charts and gauges

Here are some implementation highlights to help you understand how the Nested Regions report works. The report uses a list region as an outermost container. The Details group of the list region groups on territory. Consequently, the list will repeat its content for each territory.

The chart region groups on country. Because the list passes the current territory group to the chart, only the countries that are associated with that territory are made available to the chart. Each of the radial gauges binds its pointer value to the corresponding KPI property. Again, the report passes current context to the gauges, so they will display the KPIs for the current territory only. One Analysis Services-specific detail is that the pointer Value property uses the Aggregate function instead of Sum to retrieve the aggregated values directly from the cube. The Aggregate function is discussed in more detail in chapter 16.

Finally, the matrix region serves as a data table that provides an additional level of detail. Because the matrix region is nested inside the list region, it inherits the scope of the list region. Consequently, its data is constrained by the current territory.

6.3.5 Implementing Sparklines

Edward Tufte, a professor emeritus of statistics, information design, interface design and political economy at Yale University, proposed the term sparkline for "small, high resolution graphics embedded in a context of words, numbers, images". Instead of full-blown charts and gauges that are designed to visualize more information, sparklines are intended to be concise and easy to understand graphs that appear inline with other data presentation controls, such as textboxes and images.

Understanding the Sparklines report

You can nest the chart and gauge data regions inside other regions to implement sparklines in reports to help end users visualize report data, as the Sparklines report (see Figure 6.22) demonstrates.

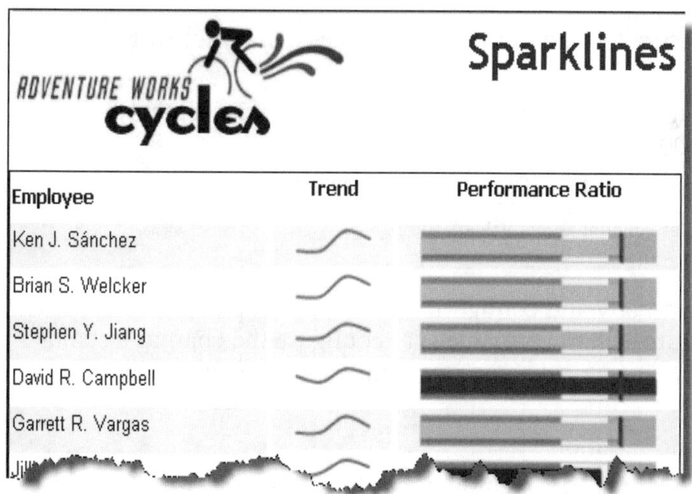

Figure 6.22 This report includes sparklines that help the user visualize contextual information.

This report shows the sales performance of the Adventure Works employees in a graphical format. The YTD Trend column uses a line chart that plots the employee's sales history. The Performance Ratio column leverages a linear gauge. The gauge deserves more attention because it illustrates several aspects of the employee's performance. Figure 6.23 shows the elements of the Performance Ratio gauge.

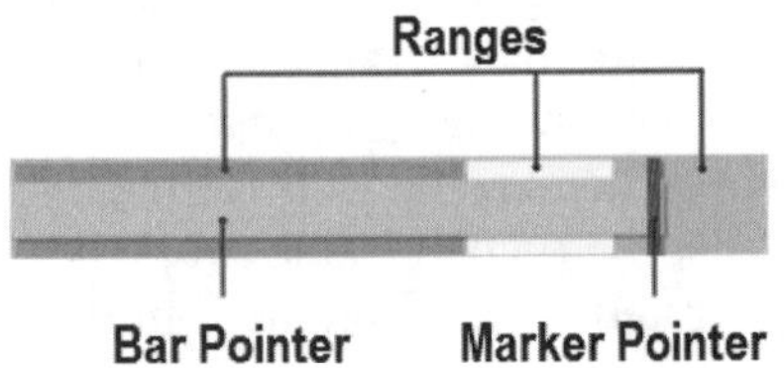

Figure 6.23 The Performance Ratio uses a linear gauge to track the employee performance.

The gauge includes three ranges to show underperformance (red), acceptable performance (yellow), and good performance (green). The bar pointer tracks the performance ratio calculated as the employee's actual sales divided by the employee's sales quota. (Actual Sales/Sales Quota). The FillColor property of the bar pointer uses an expression that changes the pointer color to red (underperformance), yellow (acceptable performance), and green (good performance) based on the value of the PerformanceRatio field. The second marker pointer marks a threshold of 85% to emphasize exceptional performance.

Setting up the report data

The Sparklines report draws data from the Adventure Works cube. Follow these steps to set up the report dataset:

1. In the MDX Query Designer connected to the Adventure Works cube, expand the Date dimension and the Calendar display folder. Drag the Calendar Quarter of Year attribute to the Query Results pane.
2. Drag the Employees hierarchy of the Employee dimension to the Query Results pane.
3. Expand the Measure folder and the Sales Targets display folder. Drag the Sales Amount Quota measure to the Query Results pane.
4. Drag the Reseller Sales Amount measure located in the Reseller Sales display folder to the Query Results pane.
5. To parameterize the report year, drag the Calendar Year attribute of the Date dimension to Filter pane and set it to default to 2003.
6. Finally, add a calculated field to the dataset based on the following expression:

```
=Fields!Reseller_Sales_Amount.Value/Fields!Sales_Amount_Quota.Value * 100
```

Setting up the chart sparkline

Next, use a table region for the report body and configure the details group to group on each employee. The easiest way to configure a chart sparkline is to configure the chart as a standalone region outside the table region. Once ready, you can easily move the chart inside the table cell.

1. Select a line chart with a Smooth Line variation.
2. Delete all chart elements except the chart series, including the chart legend, axis title, and axes.
3. Drag the Calendar_Quarter_of_Year data set field to the Drop Category Fields Here area to group the chart data by quarter.
4. Drag the Reseller_Sales_Amount dataset field to the Drop Data Fields Here area to set up the chart series.
5. Click the chart series to select it and set its BorderWidth to 1.5pt to make the line thicker.

6. Cut the chart and paste it inside the Trend detail cell.

Setting up the gauge sparkline

Next, set up the Performance Ratio sparkline. As with the chart sparkline, it's more convenient to configure the gauge outside the table.

1. Use a linear gauge with a Bullet Graph variation, which is preconfigured with two linear pointers and three ranges.
2. Double-click the gauge to put it in edit mode and bind the first linear pointer to the PerformanceRatio field by dragging the PerformanceRatio field and dropping it onto the LinearPointer1 area. Table 6.9 lists the property changes of the gauge control.

Table 6.9 Configuration settings of the Performance Ratio gauge

Property	Setting	Property	Setting
AspectRatio	Auto	BackFrame ⇨(FrameStyle)	Edged
BackFrame ⇨(FrameShape)	AutoShape	BackFrame ⇨(GradientType)	None

3. Click the linear scale to select and change its settings, as shown in Table 6.10.

Table 6.10 Configuration settings of the linear scale

Property	Setting	Property	Setting
(MaximumValue)	100	MajorTickMark ⇨ Hidden	True
(MinimumValue)	0	MinorTickMark ⇨ Hidden	True
LabelStyle ⇨ Hidden	True		

4. Configure the gauge ranges. Table 6.11 lists the settings you need to make to the first range (underperformance).

Table 6.11 Configuration settings of the first range

Property	Setting	Property	Setting
BorderColor	Silver	FillColor	Salmon
EndValue	60	StartValue	0
EndWidth	70	StartWidth	70

5. Click the bar pointer and configure it as a progress indicator (see Table 6.12).

Table 6.12 Configuration settings of the bar pointer

Property	Setting	Property	Setting
FillColor	=Switch(Fields!PerformanceRatio.Value<80,"Red", Fields!PerformanceRatio.Value<=90 ,"Gold", Fields!PerformanceRatio.Value>90,"Green")	Value	=Fields!PerformanceRatio.Value
FillGradientType	None	Width	40

6. Click the second marker pointer and configure it as a fixed marker (see Table 6.13).

Table 6.13 Configuration settings of the marker pointer

Property	Setting	Property	Setting
FillColor	DimGray	Value	85
FillGradientType	None	Width	10
MarkerLength	70		

7. Cut (Ctrl+X) and paste (Ctrl+V) the gauge inside the Performance Ratio detail cell.

6.4 Summary

In this chapter, you learned how to add data visualization features to your reports. Charts are a powerful way to present aggregated values. Reporting Services supports several chart types for different types of data and presentation formats. Column, line, bar, area, range, and scatter chart types are best suited for analyzing linear data, such as sales over time. Consider shape, scatter, and polar charts to plot ratio data, such as a pie chart that displays the contributions of individual regions relative to the entire country. Range charts let you display multivalued data, such as currency rates, temperatures, and stock data.

The gauge is a one-dimensional data region that displays a single value from a report dataset. Radial gauges have a pivot point, around which the pointer(s) rotate. Linear gauges display the value as a portion of the scale. The gauges support aggregate and statistical functions that can calculate the pointer value over a dataset.

Charts and gauges can be nested inside table, matrix, and list regions. This lets you implement reports with repeating charts and gauges that inherit the current context of the containing region. You can also configure chart and gauges as basic controls and nest them inside other data regions to implement sparklines.

6.5 Resources

Dundas Chart for Reporting Services (http://tinyurl.com/2am5yf)—The Dundas chart on which the Reporting Services 2008 chart is built on.

Get More Out of SQL Server Reporting Services Charts article by Robert Bruckner (http://tinyurl.com/2hjndd)—A great resource for understanding how the chart region works.

Chapter 7

Advanced Report Design

As you would probably agree, Reporting Services certainly makes it easy to design versatile reports, ranging from simple tabular reports to multi-section reports with interactive features. However, every tool has its design limitations and Report Designer is no exception. Complex business needs may surpass Report Designer capabilities and present unique challenges that require more advanced design skills.

This chapter consolidates advanced techniques and guidelines for report authoring that can help you tackle the last mile of report design. It starts by showing you how the enhanced textbox report item can help you display rich formatting and author mail merge reports. You will also learn how to configure and customize the report renderers for exporting reports. Next, it teaches you how to supercharge report capabilities with custom code. Finally, the chapter presents common report challenges and solutions, some of which have been harvested from my real-life work with the product and interaction with the technical community.

By now you should be familiar with Report Designer so I'm not going to do much hand-holding in this chapter. Instead, I'll provide enough information to explain the solution but I won't provide step-by-step instructions about how to implement the entire report.

7.1 Designing For Rich Formatting

In chapter 3, you witnessed some of the new enhancements to the textbox report item. Recall that the Reporting Services textbox is a composite control that can contain multiple bands of text. Each band forms a paragraph and each paragraph consist of contiguous string fragments (textruns) that can be formatted independently. You can inject dynamic text in the textbox content by defining expression-based placeholders. Let's now bring the textbox to next level and expand more on its formatting capabilities.

7.1.1 Understanding Rich Formatting

When you use Report Designer to format textboxes, paragraphs, and textruns, Report Designer uses native format elements that conform to the RDL schema. For example, if you change the font style of the word Hello to bold, Report Designer emits the following RDL fragment:

```
<TextRun><Value>Hello</Value><Style> <FontWeight>Bold</FontWeight> </Style></TextRun>
```

The same thing happens when you copy text from Microsoft Word and paste it inside the textbox. Report Designer automatically translates the Word format styles to native format styles. Besides native formatting, the textbox item is capable of supporting rich formatting.

Understanding the supported grammar

The term *rich formatting* here means that the textbox supports a subset of HTML markup tags and a few Cascading Style Sheet (CSS) attributes that lets you display text formatted this way. It shouldn't be confused with Rich Text Format (RTF), which is a free document file format developed by Microsoft. As it stands, the textbox report item doesn't support RTF.

TIP If you need to display RTF on your reports, consider a third-party .NET component that translates RTF to HTML or create your own module that replaces RTF format settings with HTML markup tags. This works because your reports can call external code that accepts the RTF text and returns the converted HTML text.

Table 7.1 shows a complete list of the formatting codes supported by the textbox report item.

Table 7.1 The textbox item supports the following rich formatting grammar

HTML Tag	Description	CSS Attribute	Description
<A HREF>	Hyperlink	text-align, text-indent	Paragraph formatting
<FONT>	Font	font-family, font-size, font-weight	Font formatting
<H{n}>, <DIV>, <SPAN>,<P>, , <DIV>, <LI>, <HN>, <BLOCKQUOTE>	Header and block elements	padding, padding-bottom, padding-top, padding-right, padding-left	Text padding
<B>, <I>, <U>, <S>, <EM>, <STRONG>, <STRIKE>	Text format	color	Text color
<OL>, <UL>, <LI>, <DD>, <DT>	Lists		

The textbox item ignores attributes it doesn't understand. When configuring HTML formatting, make sure that the text is well-formed. A well-formed HTML conforms to XML constraints, such as each element bust have a closing element. The <b>**Hello**</b> HTML fragment is well-formed because the <b> element has a closing </b> element. Visual Studio produces well-formed HTML when you design HTML and ASP pages.

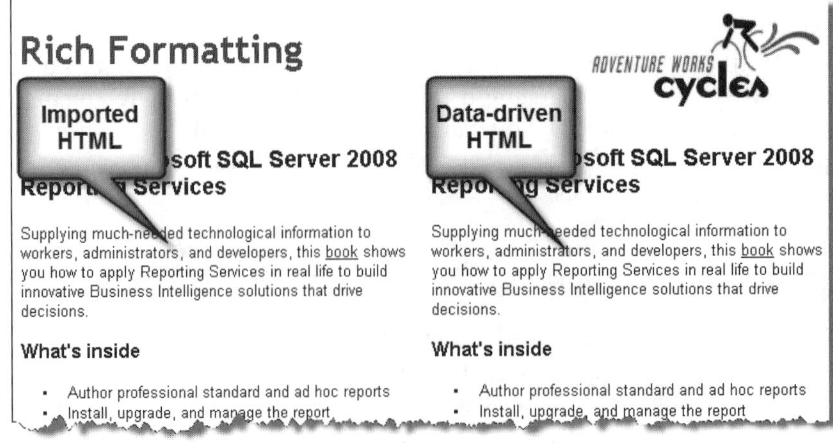

Figure 7.1 This report demonstrates the textbox rich formatting capabilities to display HTML.

Working with rich formatting
The Rich Formatting report, shown in Figure 7.1, demonstrates the rich formatting capabilities of the textbox report item. This report uses two textboxes to display text formatted with HTML markup. The textbox on the left shows static HTML, which I copied and pasted from an existing HTML page. The second textbox is bound to a dataset field that contains the same HTML text. Follow these steps to implement the report:

1. Add two textboxes to the report.
2. Copy the content of the HTML.html page (included in the chapter source code) from the <h3> element to the </ul> element.
3. Double-click the left textbox to put it in edit mode and paste the HTML content inside the textbox.

   When working with HTML-formatted text, you need to tell Reporting Services that the textbox text contains HTML markup. Otherwise, Reporting Services will display the HTML tags literally.

4. With the textbox in edit mode, press Ctrl+A to select the entire content.
5. Right-click the selection and click Text Properties.
6. In the Text Properties dialog box that follows (General tab), select the HTML – Interpret HTML Tags as Styles option.

   As it stands, the Adventure Works sample databases don't include HTML-formatted content that I could use for the data-driven example. Consequently, I had to change the query to return literal markup code. Follow these steps to implement the data-driven textbox:

7. Drag the AMRS field from the Report Data window and drop it on the textbox.
8. Double-click the textbox to enter edit mode and press Ctrl+A to select the expression placeholder.
9. Enable HTML formatting in the Text Properties dialog.

   If only a fragment of the content is formatted in HTML, you can select it and enable HTML formatting for this fragment only. That's because similar to native formatting styles, HTML formatting can be applied at textbox, paragraph, and textruns levels.

7.1.2 Implementing Mail Merge Reports

The rich format advancements in this release of Reporting Services enable report solutions that were difficult or impossible to implement before. One of these scenarios is mail merge. In the context of reporting, mail merge produces multiple report sections from a single template by merging static and dynamic data that comes from a data source. Mail merge is typically used to personalize the report content. For example, a company may want to send letters to its customers. The letter format and content is the same. However, to reuse the same template, placeholders can be defined to specify the recipient's name, address, and so on. These placeholders can be placed anywhere in the report layout.

About the Mail Merge report
The Mail Merge report (see Figure 7.2) demonstrates how the textbox report item can help you implement mail merge reports. This report produces business letters to Adventure Works

customers to inform them about the status of their orders. The letter content is the same—what changes are the recipient and order details. The fields that change are implemented as data-driven placeholders (highlighted in the screenshot).

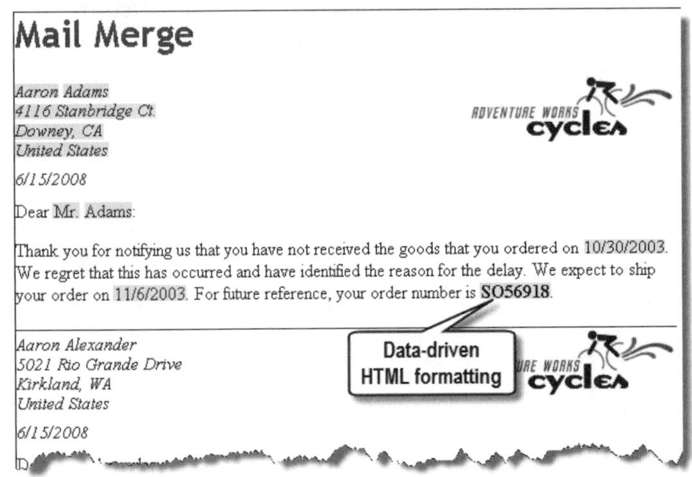

Figure 7.2 This report merges static layout and content with dynamic text coming from the data source.

At run time, the report retrieves the customer dataset. For each customer, it produces a separate letter and merges the static content with the dataset fields. One thing to notice is that the order number comes from the database formatted with HTML tags, such as <b>SO56918</b>. When laying out the report, I configured its placeholder to support HTML format styles.

Implementing the report

Follow these high-level steps to design the Mail Merge report:

1. Use a table region for the report body. Configure the table region with two detail rows and two columns.
2. Merge the cells in the second detail row.

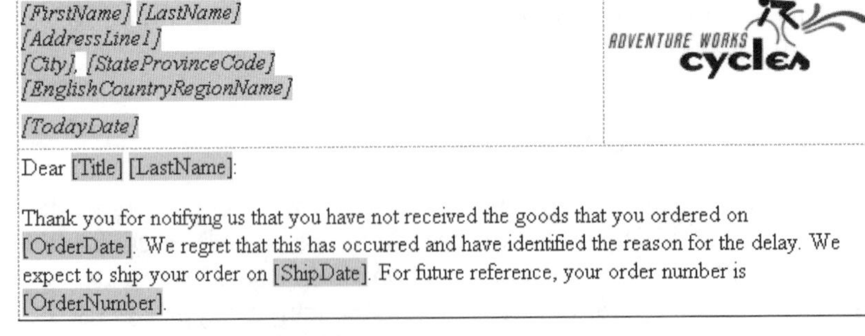

Figure 7.3 The tablix region repeats the report content for each customer.

3. Use the first cell of the first detail row to show the customer's address and today's date. Implement the customer address section by dragging the corresponding fields from the Report Data window and dropping them side by side or in new paragraphs.
4. Configure the TodayDate placeholder to use the expression =Today() and format it as a short date. Use the Placeholder Properties dialog box to define a TodayDate custom label.
5. Use the second cell of the first detail row to display the Adventure Works logo.

6. The second row displays the letter content. Add placeholders that display the original order date, ship date, and order number dataset fields.
7. Since the OrderNumber dataset field contains HTML formatting, configure the [OrderNumber] to support HTML format styles. To do so, double-click the [OrderNumber] placeholder to open the Placeholder Properties dialog box. In the General tab, change the markup type option to HTML-Interpret HTML Tags as Styles.

   If the OrderNumber field didn't contain HTML markup tags but you want it to stand out, you could simply select the [OrderNumber] placeholder and use the Report Designer format capabilities to change its format styles.

7.2 Designing For Report Output

As you know by now, an out-of-the-box Reporting Services installation lets you export reports in several export formats, including HTML, Excel, comma-separated values (CSV), XML, Image, PDF, and Word. Each export format is handled by a special rendering extension, also called a *renderer*. Let's learn more about the Microsoft-provided renderers and understand how they affect report pagination and design.

7.2.1 Understanding Report Renderers

In terms of pagination, the renderers can be classified as hard page-break, soft page-break, and pure data renderers. Table 7.2 highlights the pagination differences among the standard renderers.

Table 7.2 Reporting Services supports data, soft page-break, and hard page-break renderers

Renderer	Page Breaks	Pagination
CSV	N/A (data only)	N/A
Excel	Logical page breaks	N/A
GDI (Windows Forms ReportViewer)	Soft	InteractiveSize
HTML (Web Server ReportViewer)	Soft	InteractiveSize
Image	Hard	Page size
PDF	Hard	Page size
Print (EMF)	Hard	Page size
Word	Logical page breaks	Page size
XML	N/A (data only)	N/A

Hard page-breaks renderers

Hard page-break renderers (Image, Acrobat (PDF), and Print) are optimized for print output where pages have the same size. Their pagination story is simple because they respect the page size precisely during repagination and generate *physical* page breaks horizontally and vertically based on the page size set at design time.

You can preview the report in print layout mode to see how a hart page-break renderer will paginate the report. In Report Designer, to do this click the Preview tab to preview the report and click the Print Layout toolbar button.

Soft page-breaks renderers

Soft page-break renderers, such as HTML and GDI (used by the Windows Forms ReportViewer control), are optimized for a screen-based experience where pages can have variable length. When the report is exported with one of these renderers, the report server doesn't paginate the entire report at once. Instead, it returns the first page to the user as soon it is rendered. Page navigation and repagination, such as when the report is printed or previewed in Print Layout mode, are executed as background tasks.

The soft page renderers use the report's InteractiveSize property (click the report design area and locate the InteractiveSize property in the Properties window) to determine the page size of the rendered report. By default, InteractiveSize matches the page size. However, you can set the report interactive size independently of the page size. This could be useful, for example, if you prefer to show more data on the screen than on the printed page. In this case, you can set the report interactive size to be larger than the page size.

For on-screen report viewing, page breaks that are based on InteractiveSize are called *soft* page breaks. Soft page breaks are on by default to prevent large reports from rendering as one very long HTML page. By using soft page breaks, you avoid performance problems that result from trying to load a very large report in the browser window. If you don't need them, you can disable soft page breaks by setting the InteractiveSize Height property to zero.

You can use Report Preview (Preview tab) to see how a soft page-break renderer will paginate the report. The previewed report will be paginated based on the report InteractiveSize Height property, which could be different than the page size. The InteractiveSize Width is ignored as soft-page break based renderers don't perform horizontal pagination.

Data renderers

XML and CSV renderers are pure data renderers because they export only the report data and not the layout. These renderers don't paginate the exported report. Therefore, the page size and InteractiveSize properties have no effect on the XML and CSV renderers. In this release, the CSV renderer has been significantly changed and it's now a "pure" data renderer, while in previous releases it produced a mix between data and some layout rendering.

Using logical page breaks to improve performance

Recall from chapter 3 that you can define logical page breaks at the beginning or end of data regions and rectangle items. Logical page breaks are honored by all renderers except the data renderers. You can also define a logical page break before the first instance of a group, between the group instances, and after the last group instance.

In general, logical page breaks improve rendering performance because end users can view the first page while the rest of the report is being rendered as a background task. To enhance report performance, the report server automatically generates a soft page break after the first page when paginating reports exported to HTML. As a result, the first page of a report loads fast even with large reports.

If a report has a page header/footer and references the current page number and the total page count, the entire report will be paginated first to obtain the total page count. However, still the report server will render only the first page when the report is exported with a soft-page renderer.

Configuring renderers

The renderers are registered in the Report Designer configuration file (rsreportdesigner.config) and report server configuration file (rsreportserver.config) so that they are available at design time and run time. Suppose you want to prevent end users from exporting to a given format. To hide a renderer from end users, set its Visible property to False, such as:

```
<Extension Name="CSV" Type="Microsoft.ReportingServices.Rendering.DataRenderer.CsvReport,
   Microsoft.ReportingServices.DataRendering" Visible="False">
```

If you make this change to rsreportdesigner.config, the CSV renderer will not show in the Report Designer toolbar but it will show in Report Manager. Making this change to rsreportserver.config excludes the renderer from Report Manager and when the report is requested by URL. Hiding a renderer doesn't disable it. For example, you can still use a hidden renderer with URL access or in subscriptions. If you want to disable the renderer completely, comment or remove the entire Extension element.

To change the displayed name of the renderer, use the OverrideNames element. The following configuration overwrites the display name of the CSV renderer from CSV (comma delimited) to Comma-separated Value:

```
<Extension Name="CSV" Type="Microsoft.ReportingServices.Rendering.DataRenderer.CsvReport,
  Microsoft.ReportingServices.DataRendering">
      <OverrideNames>
           <Name Language="en -US">Comma-  separated Value</Name>
      </OverrideNames>
</Extension>
```

Because display names are localized, you need to specify a separate Name element for each language identifier. You can also have different configuration settings for the same renderer. Suppose you want to have two CSV configurations side-by-side that specify a comma delimiter and a tab delimiter:

```
<Extension Name="CSV Comma" Type="Microsoft.ReportingServices.Rendering.DataRenderer.CsvReport,
   Microsoft.ReportingServices.DataRendering">
           <OverrideNames>
                      <Name Language="en - US">CSV (comma delimiter)</Name >
           </OverrideNames>
</Extension>

<Extension Name="CSV Tab" Type="Microsoft.ReportingServices.Rendering.DataRenderer.CsvReport,
    Microsoft.ReportingServices.DataRendering">
           <OverrideNames>
                      <Name Language="en - US">CSV (tab delimiter)</Name>
           </Ove rrideNames>
           <Configuration>
              <DeviceInfo>
                      <FieldDelimiter xml:space="preserve">      </FieldDelimiter>
                      <UseFormattedValues>False</UseFormattedValues>
                      <NoHeader>True</NoHeader>
              </DeviceInfo>
           </Configuration>
</Extension>
```

This requires two configuration sections. Notice that the Name attribute for each configuration must be different. Figure 7.4 shows how these two configurations appear in the HTML Viewer.

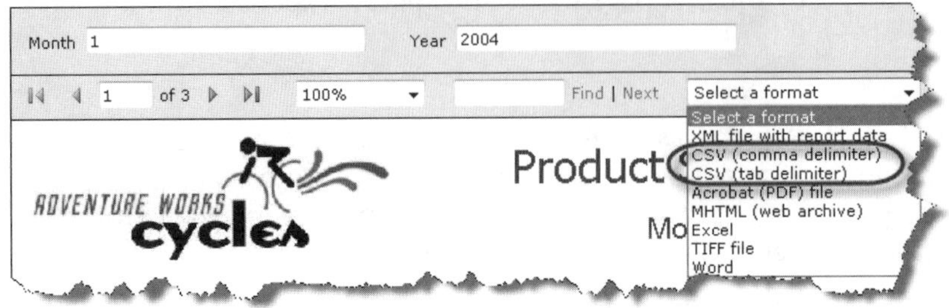

Figure 7.4 You can have multiple configurations for the same renderer.

Each renderer supports various device information settings that can be used to customize the exported report. For example, in the CSV (tab delimiter) configuration above, I used FieldDelimiter, UseFormattedValues and NoHeader device information settings that are specific to the CSV renderer. For a full list of the supported device information settings, see the Reporting Services Device Information Settings topic in the SQL Server Books Online (see Resources).

Specifying device configuration settings in rsreportserver.config affects all exported reports. Alternatively, you can apply device information settings per report by appending them to the report URL link, as I'll demonstrate in chapter 14.

7.2.2 Working with Report Renderers

Now that you know about the different types of report renderers and how to configure them, let's review some important renderer-specific considerations that will help you understand how the choice of a renderer affects the report output.

Exporting to CSV

The Comma-Separated Values (CSV) renderer is a pure data renderer that exports only the report data. Note that only textbox report items export their content to CSV. You cannot export the content of chart and gauge regions to CSV. Exporting to CSV can be useful when you need to feed report data into another application.

In this release, the CSV renderer supports two output formats: Excel mode and Compliant mode. Excel mode is the default mode, and it is optimized for loading the exported file in Microsoft Excel. This is especially useful when you export large reports to Excel but you need only the report data. In this case, you may get better performance by exporting the report first to CSV and opening the CSV file in Excel. The compliant mode is optimized for third-party applications that require strict adherence to the CSV specification in RFC 4180.

NOTE Opening CSV exported files in Excel was problematic with previous releases of Reporting Services. This was because the CSV renderer would default to Unicode encoding which Excel didn't handle very well. Consequently, Excel showed the entire report in a single column. To address this issue, Reporting Services 2008 introduces an Excel mode (ExcelMode device setting) that defaults to UTF-8 encoding. However, it appears that Excel still has some issues understanding delimited files with formatted values. Instead of opening the file directly in Excel, I recommend that you use Excel's Text Import Wizard to bring the file into Excel.

The CSV renderer supports device information settings that control the output, including the field delimiter, field qualifier, record delimiter, and header rows. The default field delimiter is a comma (,) but you can override it by using the FieldDelimiter device setting, as the CSV (tab delimiter) configuration demonstrated. In this example, I had to use the xml:space="preserve" attribute (new to Reporting Services 2008) to denote the actual tab space that follows. I pressed the Tab key to create the whitespace for the tab character.

Besides using the ExcelMode setting, another workaround for opening CSV files in Excel is to configure the CSV renderer to export to ASCII instead of Unicode, as follows:

```
<Extension Name="CSV" Type="Microsoft.ReportingServices .Rendering.CsvRenderer.CsvReport,
   Microsoft.ReportingServices.CsvRendering">
   <Configuration>
      <DeviceInfo>
            <Encoding>ASCII</Encoding>
            </DeviceInfo>
   </Configuration>
</Extension>
```

When the report is exported as ASCII, Excel will load the exported report in separate columns instead of placing the entire contents of the report in a single column.

Exporting to Excel

Reporting Services supports rendering reports for Microsoft Excel 2000 and later. The Excel renderer doesn't support page size. When exporting to Excel, define logical page breaks to break the report into multiple worksheets. Each page in the report caused by a logical page break becomes an Excel worksheet. As it stands, Reporting Services does not support specifying worksheet names and there is no workaround.

Charts are rendered as pictures, not as Excel charts. Subreports are rendered as rectangles in the current report on the same worksheet as the parent report. The Excel renderer is designed to preserve the report layout as much as possible. Spaces between items result in narrow "filler" columns in Excel. To avoid these columns, change the report definition so that stacked report items are aligned on both sides. For example, align the report title with a tablix column to avoid a filler column between these items.

In Reporting Services 2008, the Excel renderer was enhanced to support nested regions and nested subreports. In this release, the Excel renderer exports only values and not formulas. In previous releases, certain formulas were exported, such as formulas that used the ReportItems collection.

One interesting Excel-specific device information setting is SimplePageHeaders. When SimplePageHeaders is False (default setting), the page headers are rendered in the first row in the Excel worksheet. If you set SimplePageHeaders to True, the report server generates the page headers and footers as Excel headers and footers. Since the Excel headers and footers are very basic, this may result in some fidelity loss, such not honoring the textbox padding settings.

Exporting to HTML

The HTML renderer, which Report Manager uses by default when you view a report, generates HTML 4.0 that is compatible with Microsoft Internet Explorer 5.5 and later, Mozilla Firefox 1.5 and later, and Safari with some restrictions documented in Books Online. Although most report features are supported on these browsers, you should test your reports on targeted browsers to ensure it renders appropriately. When displayed on the client, an HTML report uses browser-specific settings, such as font substitutions. If you want to precisely control the layout of the report on all clients used to view the report, consider using the image renderer.

The HTML renderer generates HTML tables to preserve report layout. It doesn't support overlapping items. This can result in layout changes as the report is displayed. To keep items together on a page, consider enclosing them with a rectangle.

One interesting option supported by the HTML renderer is auto-refreshing reports. For example, you can author a company stock performance report that automatically refreshes itself on a set schedule to get the latest stock value. You can set up the report to automatically refresh itself at a certain interval by using the AutoRefresh report-level property. Behind the scenes, this property emits a meta browser tag, such as <META HTTP-EQUIV="Refresh" CONTENT="5">, if you set the AutoRefresh to 5 seconds.

Exporting to MHTML

The MHTML (MIME Encapsulation of Aggregate HTML Documents) format encapsulates the report and its images in a single file. This eliminates a round-trip to the report server to fetch the report images when you export reports to HTML.

Since MHTML is based on MIME, rendering reports in MHTML format is generally the best export option when you need to push the report to users via e-mail subscriptions, as I'll discuss in chapter 12. MHTML is especially suited for e-mail delivery because it is more compact compared to PDF and TIFF.

Exporting to Image

The Image renderer exports reports as image files. It can generate files in any format supported by GDI+, including BMP, EMF, GIF, JPEG, and PNG. You can use the OutputFormat device information setting to specify the image format. If OutputFormat is omitted, TIFF is assumed. The following example configures the image renderer to export reports as BMP images.

```
<Extension Name="IMAGE" Type=" Microsoft.ReportingServices.Rendering.ImageRenderer.ImageRenderer,
Microsoft.ReportingServices.ImageRendering">
      <OverrideNames>
            <Name Language="en - US">BMP File</Name>
      </OverrideNames>
      <Configuration>
         <DeviceInfo>
            <OutputFormat>BMP</OutputFormat>
         </DeviceInfo>
      </Configuration>
</Extension>
```

Consider the image renderer when you want the exported report to look the same on every client. The image renderer supports page height, page width, and margins.

Exporting to PDF

The portable document format (PDF) renderer creates reports that can be viewed with Adobe Acrobat readers. Similar to the image renderer, you might consider the PDF renderer when you need to produce a client-independent report layout. The renderer creates PDF 1.3, which is compatible with Adobe Reader 4.0 and later. The PDF renderer doesn't embed fonts. Therefore, be sure to install the fonts used in the report on the client computer.

For example, if you use the MingLiu font to display Chinese characters, you will find that exporting the report to Excel or Image will show the text correctly but exporting to PDF will not show the Chinese characters if the user doesn't have the MingLiu font installed. This is because when the report is displayed, Adobe Reader will substitute MingLiu with another font that may not support Chinese characters.

Exporting to Word

The Word renderer has been added to Reporting Services to support exporting reports as Microsoft Word binary documents that are supported by Microsoft Word 2000 and above. Similar to the Excel renderer, it generates tables to enclose sets of items and exports charts as pictures. The Word renderer doesn't support interactive features. As such, the device information settings for Microsoft Word are used to control how interactive features are converted when the report is exported to Word.

One such setting is ExpandToggles, which controls the toggled state of the drilldown sections. When ExpandToggles is False (default setting), a report with drilldown features will be exported with all sections collapsed and you won't be able to expand the sections in Microsoft Word. However, setting ExpandToggles to True will expand the drilldown sections.

By default, URL navigation links are included in an export to Word. If you want URLs in a report to appear in a Word document, change the OmitHyperlinks setting to False. To do the same for drillthrough links, set OmitDrillthroughs to False.

Exporting to XML

Extensible Markup Language (XML) facilitates data exchange between heterogeneous platforms, particularly via the Internet. The XML renderer lets you export report data as an XML document. This can be useful if you need to integrate Reporting Services with other applications or external partners. For example, a vendor could request an inventory report in XML to determine the current inventory levels. The report could be processed later by a BizTalk workflow that extracts the product information and sends it to manufacturing.

You can also pair the XML renderer with a custom Extensible Stylesheet Language Transformations (XSLT) file to produce a human-readable layout not already supported by the Microsoft-provided renderers. For example, you may need complete control over the HTML representation of the report. One option is to write a custom rendering extension, but this entails significant implementation effort. The other option is to design an XSL transformation that transforms report data into the desired HTML format.

The XML renderer can export the contents of textboxes, rectangles, and data regions, including charts and gauges. XML elements and attributes are rendered in the order in which they appear in the report definition. The XML renderer provides limited customization over the XML output via the DataElementName, DataElementOutput (applicable for CSV rendering as well), and DataElementStyle properties. Use the DataElementName property if you want to overwrite the name of an XML element. The DataElementOutput property lets you configure whether an element and its child elements should be exported. The DataElementStyle property controls whether an item is exported as an XML node or an attribute. By default, textboxes are exported as attributes.

Designing for XML Output

The Product Sales by Category report demonstrates exporting to XML. The exported report is saved in the ProductSales.xml file. I followed these steps to prepare the Product Sales by Category for export to XML:

1. Open the Product Sales by Category report in Report Designer and select the report by clicking the design area outside the report body.
2. Change the DataElementName property to *ProductSales* to define the name of the root node, as shown in Figure 7.5.
3. Enter *http://www.prologika.com* in the DataSchema property. This defines the XML document namespace. If the DataSchema property is not specified, the XML renderer will auto-generate the namespace based on the report name, but this makes it difficult to reference XML elements in an XSL transformation. To avoid this, define a namespace explicitly.

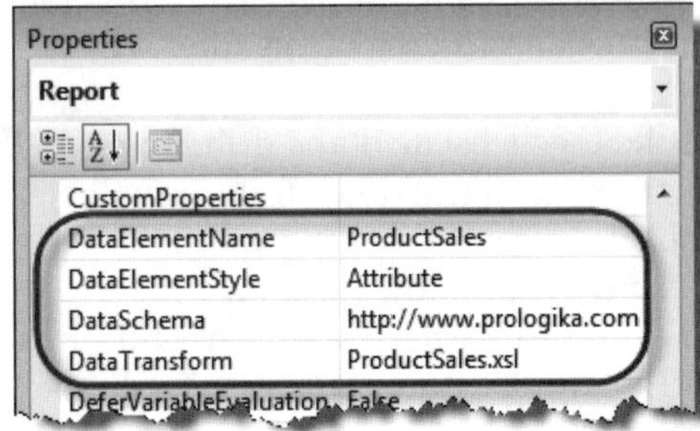

Figure 7.5 You can fine-tune the XML output by setting the DataElementName, DataElementStyle, and DataElementOutput properties.

4. Enter *ProductSales.xsl* in the DataTransform property to specify the XSLT file that will be used to transform the XML output to HTML.
5. Rename all significant textboxes inside the tablix region, such as renaming Textbox14 to *txtResellerSales*. Assigning meaningful names to report items makes it easier to reference them when navigating the XML document.
6. Select the header row and change the DataElementOutput property to NoOutput. Consequently, the header textboxes won't be exported to XML.

   As a result of these changes, the XML renderer produces the following raw XML if the DataTransform report-level property is empty. For the sake of brevity, only the first product node is shown.

```
<?xml version="1.0" encoding="utf - 8"?>
<ProductSales xsi:schemaLocation="http://www.prologika.com
http://reportserver/?%2fProduct+Sales+by+Category&amp;rs%3aFormat=XML&amp;rc%3aSchema=True" Name="Product
Sales by Category" xmlns:xsi="http://www.w3.org/2001/XMLSchema-instance" xmlns="http://www.prologika.com">
<Tablix1>
      <ProductCategory_Collection>
            <ProductCategory txtProductCategory="Accessories">
                <ProductSubcategory_Collection>
                        <ProductSubcategory txtProductSubcategory="Bike Racks">
                            <ProductName_Collection>
                                <ProductName txtProductName="Hitch Rack  - 4- Bike">
                                    <DetailsGroup_Collection>
                                     <DetailsGroup       txtResellerSales="8352.0000"
                                                         txtInternetSales="2880.0000"
                                                         txtSalesSummary="11232.0000" />
                                     </DetailsGroup_Collection>
                              </ProductName>
                            </ProductName_Collection>
                        </ProductSubcategory>
```

From here, this document can be handed out to any XML-capable application, such as BizTalk, to automate processes or facilitate application integration scenarios.

Product Sales

Product	Reseller Sales	Internet Sales	Sales Summary
Hitch Rack - 4-Bike	8352.0000	2880.0000	11232.0000
Water Bottle - 30 oz.	4982.0160	1686.6200	6668.6360
Bike Wash - Dissolver	562.8600	214.6500	777.5100
Sport-100 Helmet, Black	5164.5240	2414.3100	7578.8340
Sport-100 Helmet, Blue	9657.2400	4023.8500	13681.0900

Figure 7.6 You can use an XSL transformation to convert the raw XML output to a human-readable format.

Applying XSL Transformation

Suppose that you want the XML renderer to produce a human-readable report by transforming the raw XML output to the HTML format shown in Figure 7.6. The ProductSales.xsl XSLT file demonstrates how this could be done.

```
<xsl:stylesheet version="1.0" xmlns:xsl="http://www.w3.org/1999/XSL/Transform"
   xmlns:msxsl="urn:schemas-microsoft-com:xslt" exclude-result-prefixes="xmlns msxsl n1"
      xmlns:n1="http://www.prologika.com">
      <xsl:output method="html" indent="yes" omit-xml-declaration="yes"/>
      <xsl:template match="/">
       <html>
           <body>
           <h2>Product Sales</h2>
             <table border="1">
             <tr bgcolor="#9acd32">
               <th>Product</th><th>Reseller Sales</th><th>Internet Sales</th><th>Sales Summary</th        >
             </tr>
             <xsl:for-each select="//ProductName">
                 <tr>
                        <td><xsl:value-of select="./@txtProductName"/></td>
                        <td><xsl:value-of select="DetailsGroup_Collection/DetailsGroup/@txtResellerSales"/></td>
                        <td>< xsl:value-of select="DetailsGroup_Collection/DetailsGroup/@txtInternetSales"/></td>
                         <td><xsl:value-of select="DetailsGroup_Collection/DetailsGroup/@txtSalesSummary"/></td>
                 </tr>
             </xsl:for-each>
            </table>
           </body>
       </html>
      </xsl:template>
</xsl:stylesheet>
```

Similar to an ASP.NET page, this transformation includes HTML intermixed with code that outputs the report data at run time. The for-each select command selects all ProductName elements. The XSLT processor loops through each element and uses the xsl:value-of select command to output the values of the txtProductName, txtResellerSales, txtInternetSales, and txtSalesSummary XML attributes.

TIP You can use the Visual Studio XML support to test the XSLT file. Open the ProductSales.xsl in Visual Studio 2008 and click XML ⇨ Show XSLT Output or click XML ⇨ Debug XSLT if you want to step through it. You can use ProductSales.xml, which was produced by exporting the Product Sales by Category report to XML without XSLT, as an input XML file.

Once you set the DataTransform report property to ProductSales.xsl and deploy the report, end users will get the HTML report when they export Product Sales by Category to XML. To let the XML renderer know that the report content is HTML, append the MIMEType and FileExtension device information settings to the report URL, as follows:

```
http://<servername>/ reportserver?/AMRS/Product Sales by Category&rs:Command=Render
&rs:Format=XML&rc:MIMEType=text/html&rc:FileExtension=htm
```

If you want all reports to share the same XML export settings, configure the appropriate device settings for the XML renderer in rsreportserver.config.

7.3 Extending Reports with Custom Code

Recall that most of the report item properties can be expression-based. You can enhance your report with inline expressions, such as to hide a tablix column conditionally. Sometimes, expressions and built-in functions may not be enough to satisfy more demanding requirements. For example, Reporting Services doesn't provide a native function to calculate the median value over a dataset. However, you can extend your reports with custom code that goes beyond what inline expressions and built-in functions have to offer.

7.3.1 Understanding Custom Code

Reporting Services is designed as a flexible and extensible platform. Report expressions can call custom code that you or someone else wrote. This gives you a tremendous power over report data and appearance. As a seasoned report designer, you must learn how to work with custom code so that you can build your reports exactly as you envision them to be. In doing so, you might just find yourself having fewer occasions to say "Reporting Services can't do this."

Comparing Custom Code Options

You can extend reports with custom code in two ways: by embedding code within a report or by invoking methods located in an external .NET assembly. Table 7.3 shows how these two options compare.

Table 7.3 Comparing embedded and external code options

Criteria	Embedded Code	External Code
Code location	Inside report definition	In an external assembly
Programming language	Visual Basic.NET only	Any .NET language
Scope	Report	Can be shared by multiple reports
Developer tools	None	Visual Studio, third-party
Deployment effort	Deployed with report	Additional deployment steps required
Typical usage	Simple functions	More complex programming logic

Let's look at both options in more detail.

Understanding embedded code

As its name suggests, embedded code becomes part of the report definition. Specifically, when you add embedded code to the report, Report Designer inserts a Code element inside the report definition. Embedded code lets you implement report-specific functions that are available only to the containing report. Embedded code can be useful when you need to simplify report deployment by distributing the code together with the report.

On the flip side, embedded code is limited to using only Visual Basic.NET as a programming language. The Report Properties dialog box includes a Code tab that lets you enter the custom code, but it doesn't provide syntax checking, IntelliSense, or debugging features. Consequently, syntax errors cannot be discovered at design time and may take a few trial-and-error cycles to fix. As a workaround, consider testing the code outside Report Designer, such as by creating a Visual Studio console application. When the code is tested, copy and paste it inside the Code tab. Consider embedded code when you need to implement simple report-specific functions that you can distribute together with the report.

Understanding external code

External code is located in one or more external assemblies. A report can directly call only .NET managed code. If you need to call native code, create a .NET "wrapper" assembly that the report can call. External code is more flexible for several reasons. To start with, external code can be referenced by multiple reports. This lets you implement a library of common functions that can be reused across reports. You are not limited to Visual Basic as a programming language. Instead, you can use your favorite .NET language to write external code.

Since Business Intelligence Development Studio doesn't support code projects, you must use another development tool to write and test your code. For example, you can use the powerful Visual Studio IDE to implement and debug an external C# assembly. Once the assembly is ready, you can reference it in the report. External code requires additional steps to deploy and secure the external assemblies.

REAL LIFE I don't recall a project that didn't require some custom code to extend reports. I almost never use embedded code because it cannot be easily tested and cannot be shared across reports. Instead, I add a Class Library project to the Visual Studio solution as one of the first steps after creating a Report Server project. I use external code to implement a library of common functions that I can reuse in multiple reports in the same Report Server project.

7.3.2 Working with Embedded Code

The book source code includes two sample reports that demonstrate working with embedded code. The Calculate Median report utilizes an embedded function to calculate a median value over a dataset. The Pie Chart with Custom Color report shows how to assign custom colors to a chart series.

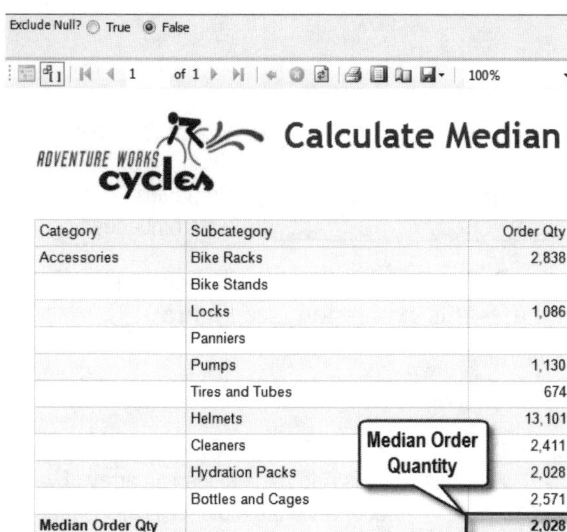

Category	Subcategory	Order Qty
Accessories	Bike Racks	2,838
	Bike Stands	
	Locks	1,086
	Panniers	
	Pumps	1,130
	Tires and Tubes	674
	Helmets	13,101
	Cleaners	2,411
	Hydration Packs	2,028
	Bottles and Cages	2,571
Median Order Qty		**2,028**

Figure 7.7 This report uses embedded code to calculate the median order quantity over a set of ten product subcategories.

Calculating a median value

As it stands, Reporting Services doesn't provide a function that calculates a median value from a set of values. However, embedded code lets us overcome this limitation. Consider the following set of values:

```
10, 2, 15, 5, 7, 3, 17
```

To find the median value, we first need to sort the set:

2, 3, 5, 7, 10, 15, 17

The number in the middle (7) is the median value of this set. The Calculate Median report (see Figure 7.7) includes embedded code that calculates the median order quantity over ten product subcategories. The user can exclude the NULL values from the calculation by setting the ExcludeNull parameter to True.

Here is how this report works:

1. Open the Calculate Median report in Report Designer and select Report ➪ Report Properties menu.
2. Click the Code tab and notice that it contains embedded code, as shown in Figure 7.8.

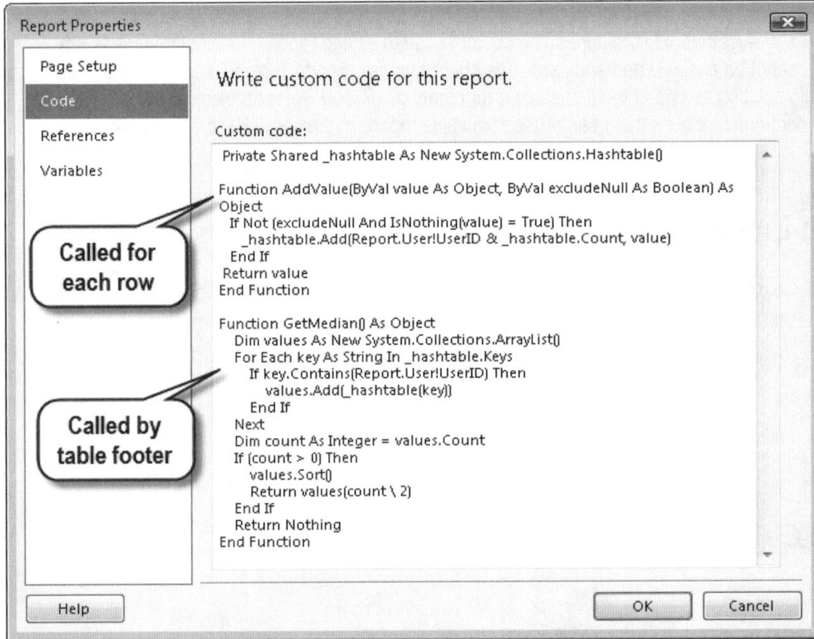

Figure 7.8 Use the Code tab of the Report Properties dialog box to write embedded code.

3. Close the Report Properties dialog. Right-click the Order Qty detail cell and click Expression. Notice that the Value of the Order Qty detail cell uses this expression (see Figure 7.9):

```
=Code.AddValue(Fields!Order Qty.Value, Parameters!ExcludeNull.Value)
```

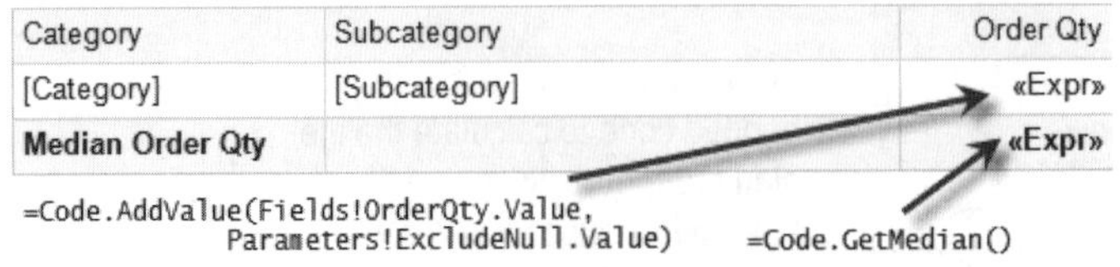

Figure 7.9 The Order Qty detail cell calls AddValue to load an array of values, while the footer cell calls GetMedian to obtain the median value.

The footer cell that displays the median value uses the following expression:

```
=Code.GetMedian()
```

At run time, when Reporting Services processes the tablix region, it calls the AddValue embedded function as many times as the number of the tablix detail rows. Each function call adds the order quantity value of the current row to a static (Shared in Visual Basic) Hashtable object. The end result is that by the time the tablix details are processed, the hash table will contain all order quantity values. The AddValue function returns the same value that is passed to it so the detail cell can display it.

Moving to Reporting Services 2008, you need to use static variables to maintain state between page requests. If you use an instance variable, you'll find that the report works fine if it has only one page. However, as a result of the new on-demand report processing model, instance variables do not live across multiple requests, such as when the user requests the first page, and then navigates to the next page. Consequently, if your table spans multiple pages, the instance variable will not hold all values.

Working with static variables presents a challenge though because they are shared among concurrent users for the lifetime of the report execution. This is why I use a unique key, composed from the user login and the count of items in the hash table, when adding values to the Hashtable object. With the exception of the Globals and User collections, which can be accessed using a special Report keyword (Report.User!UserID), custom code cannot access the rest of the Reporting Services global collections directly. To make the rest of the collections available to custom code, you need to pass them as arguments to the methods.

The footer cell calls the GetMedian function to display the median value. GetMedian loads an array with all values that belong to the same user, sorts the array, and returns the middle value.

NOTE In Reporting Services 2008, expressions in textboxes are no longer calculated in a predefined order. The Calculate Median report works because it retrieves the calculated value in the table footer. However, it won't work if you attempt to display the median value in the table header because most rendering extensions will ask for the value of the table header cells first before going further down in the page. One workaround, which is demonstrated by the Calculate Median Value with Variable report, is to define a group variable at the innermost grouping level (Details group in this case). Report variables are discussed in section 7.4.1.

Implementing a pie chart with custom colors

By default, the chart region automatically selects colors from the specified palette. If specific colors are desired, you can configure the chart to use a custom palette, which I demonstrated in chapter 6. Suppose you need more control over the color selection. For instance, you may want to plot the series data in red, if they exceed a given value. Embedded code lets you implement this requirement.

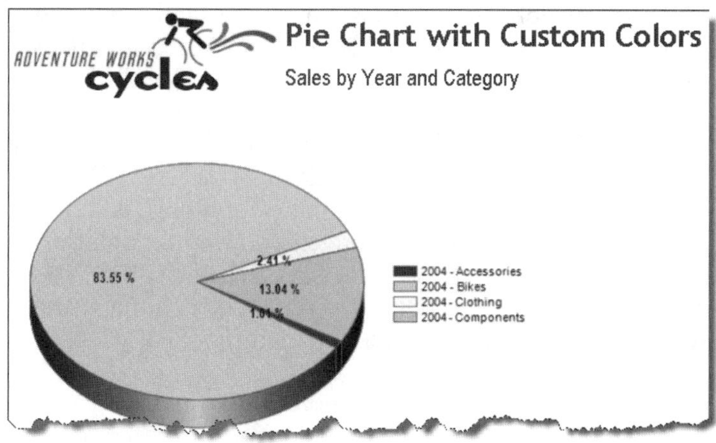

Figure 7.10 This report uses embedded code to select specific custom colors for the chart series.

The Pie Chart with Custom Colors report (Figure 7.10) builds upon the Pie Chart report from chapter 6. The difference is that the chart calls a GetColor embedded function that returns a custom color for each chart series. The original implementation for using custom chart colors was presented in the article "Get More out of SQL Server Reporting Services Charts" by Robert Bruckner (listed in chapter 6 Resources section).

```
Private colorPalette As String()
Private count As Integer = 0
Private mapping As New System.Collections.Hashtable()

Public Function GetColor(ByVal groupingValue As String, ByVal seriesValue as Double) As String
  If mapping.ContainsKey(groupingValue) Then
      Return mapping(groupingValue)
  End If

  Dim c As String = colorPalette(count Mod colorPalette.Length)
  count = count + 1
  mapping.Add(groupingValue, c)
  If seriesValue < 200000 Then
      return "Red"
  Else
      Return c
  End if
End Function
Protected Overrides Sub OnInit()
  colorPalette = new String() {"MistyRose", "LightGreen", "LemonChiffon", "LightSteelBlue",
          "LightCoral", "LimeGreen", "Gold", "DodgerBlue"}
End Sub
```

Custom code can override a special OnInit method to perform initialization tasks. The report overrides the OnInit method to initialize the colorPalette string as an array with custom colors.

TIP The OnInit method can access the Globals and User collections to obtain the user identity (User!UserID) and load user-specific custom colors for each report user. To use the Globals and User collections, you need to prefix them with the Reports object reference, such as Reports.User!UserID. The rest of the global collections (Parameters, ReportItems, Fields, etc.) are not available to custom code.

The chart series Color property uses the following expression:

```
=Code.GetColor(String.Format("{0}~{1}", Fields!CalendarYear.Value, Fields!Category.Value),
Sum(Fields!SalesAmount.Value))
```

The chart plots a series for each year and product category. This expression constructs a series group identifier by concatenating the Year and Category values. It passes the identifier and the series value as arguments to the GetColor function. GetColor maintains a hashtable collection for all chart series. If the series group color has already been added to the collection, GetColor returns the color. Otherwise, GetColor assigns the next color to the series group and adds it to the collection.

The net result is that colors are assigned consecutively in the order that the chart series are plotted on the chart and appear in the legend. For example, since the 2004-Accessories series is the first series plotted on the chart, it will be assigned the first color (MistyRose). Bikes will be plotted in LightGreen, and so on. As you can see, this function lets you vary the color of each series. If the collection has fewer colors than series, GetValue starts reusing colors.

GetColor demonstrates evaluating business rules to control the series color. If the series value is less than 200,000, GetColor overwrites the custom color and returns "Red". Consequently, the corresponding pie will be plotted in red.

7.3.3 Working with External Code

The second option for extending reports with custom code is to integrate them with external .NET assemblies. This lets you use any .NET programming language and write code a whole lot easier by leveraging the powerful Visual Studio IDE instead of the Code tab.

To demonstrate working with external code, I'll borrow a real-life scenario. In one of my projects, we had to implement custom formatting to get the right look for a report-enabled desktop application. For this particular report, the report dataset could return columns with mixed data types. For example, the dataset rows might contain currency and percentage values in the same column.

A special column in the dataset was used to indicate the data type of each field. At run time, the application would pass the user culture (obtained from the user's regional settings) as a report parameter. Custom code in an external assembly would evaluate the user culture and the field type and return the field format string that was correct for that culture.

ADVENTURE WORKS cycles

Custom Formatting

Row	Col 2	Col 3	Col 4
Row1	1,000.11	10.50 %	1/1/2008
Row2	15.00 %	-3,445.	#,##0.00 %;-#,##0.00%
Row3	10/1/2008	5,431.34	-5.60%

Figure 7.11 This report integrates with external code to return custom format strings.

The Custom Formatting report demonstrates this approach. As Figure 7.11 shows, the last three columns in the tablix report contain heterogeneous data types. Yet, the report formats the report data correctly based on the field type.

Understanding the Custom Formatting report

In the real-life project, we used a SQL Server CLR stored procedure to prepare the report dataset. For the sake of simplicity, I embedded a static rowset in the report, as shown in Figure 7.12.

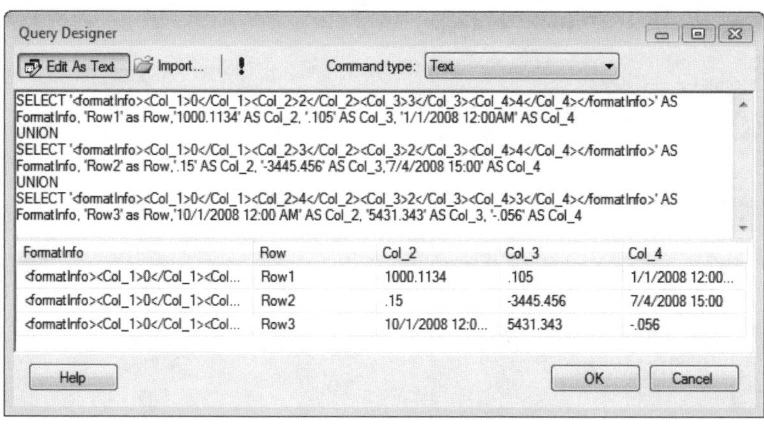

Figure 7.12 The FormatInfo column in the dataset indicates the field data type for all columns that have custom format strings.

The FormatInfo column contains an XML fragment that indicates the data type for all columns that require custom format strings. An example of a sample formatInfo fragment follows:

```
<formatInfo>
    <Col_1>1</Col_1> <!— Number-- >
    <Col_2>2</Col_2> <! -- Currency-- >
    <Col_3>3</Col_3> <! -- Percentage-- >
    <Col_4>4</Col_4> <! -- Date-- >
</formatInfo>
```

The data type is indicated as an integer value which corresponds to an enumeration defined in the custom code. Thus, 1 indicates that the field in Col_1 column should be formatted as a general number, 2 indicates that the Col_2 field should be formatted as currency, and so on. As noted, in the real project, the custom application passes the serialized user culture to the Settings report parameter. For the sake of simplicity, I set up a default value for the Settings parameter that contains my regional setting culture. I used the following code to serialize the culture:

```
CultureInfo ci = System.Threading.Thread.CurrentThread.CurrentUICulture;
string cis = Shared.Util.StringFromObject(ci);
```

The StringFromObject helper method (not shown), which is included in the Util class, serializes the CultureInfo class using the .NET binary formatter and encodes the result as a base64 string.

Referencing external code

Similar to working with code projects, you need to set up a reference to the external assembly before you can call it.

1. Open the Custom Formatting report in Report Designer.
2. In the Report Properties dialog box, click the References tab, as shown in Figure 7.13.

The Add button brings up the familiar Add Reference dialog box that lets you set up a reference to a private or shared assembly. A shared assembly can be referenced by multiple applications but it has to be deployed to the .NET Global Assembly Cache (GAC). Private assemblies need to be deployed to the Report Designer folder for design-time testing and the report server bin folder when the report is deployed to the report server. In my case, I referenced the Prologika.Reporting.Extensibility assembly as a private assembly from the \Program Files\Microsoft Visual Studio 9.0\Common7\IDE\PrivateAssemblies folder.

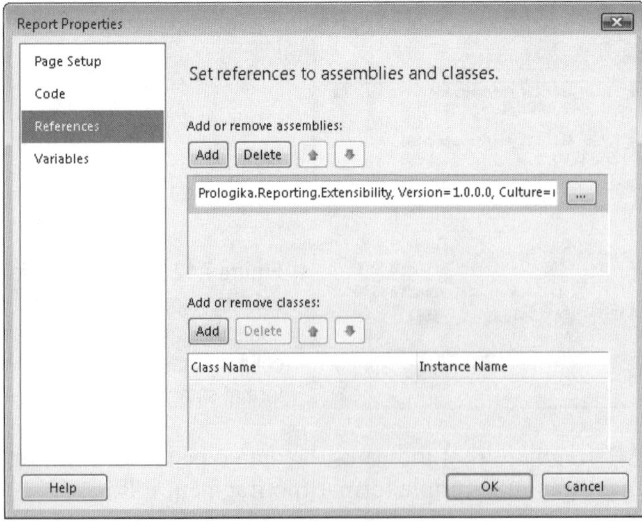

Figure 7.13 Before using external code, you must create an assembly reference.

If you'll be calling only static (or *Shared* as it's known in Visual Basic documentation) methods in the external assembly, setting up an assembly reference is all that's needed. That's because static methods don't require an object instance and can be invoked by using the fully qualified class name using this syntax:

```
<Namespace>.<ClassName>.<Method> (argument1, argument2, ..., argumentN)
```

For example, you can call the GetCustomFormat static method as follows:

```
=Prologika.Reporting.Extensibility.Util.GetCustomFormat
(Parameters!Settings.Value, Fields!FormatInfo.Value, "Col_2", False)
```

Static methods are useful for implementing helpful routines by passing all required data as arguments to the method. They are also more efficient because no overhead is required to construct and maintain an object instance.

WARNING Static variables are not private to a report user so sensitive user-specific data should not be kept in a static variable. In addition, static class variables are subject to multithreading concurrency issues. To avoid these issues, design your static methods as stateless methods that accept all required data as input arguments. As noted in section 7.3.2, however, one scenario that requires static variables in this release is maintaining state between page requests.

By contrast, instance methods require an object instance and are object-specific. This involves setting up an instance name in the References tab. For example, suppose that you want to call an instance method called Foo in the Util class.

3. Click the Add button in the Add or Remote Classes section.
4. In the Class Name column, enter *Prologika.Reporting.Extensibility.Util,* which is the fully qualified class name.
5. In the Instance Name column, enter an instance name that will be used to call the instance methods, such as *m_Util*.

Once this is done, you are ready to call the Foo method in report expressions. When doing so, you need to use the Code keyword followed by the instance name and method name:

```
Code.m_Util.Foo(argument1, argument2, ..., argumentN)
```

When calling instance methods, you need to set up as many instance names as the number of the classes in the external assembly you need to access. Again, in our case, I don't need to set up an instance name because I call static methods only.

Implementing custom formatting

Once you have set up a reference to the external assembly, you are ready to call its methods. The detail cells in the tablix region use an expression to derive the format string. For example, the Format property of the Col_1 detail cell uses the following expression:

```
=Prologika.Reporting.Extensibility.Util.GetCustomFormat
(Parameters!Settings.Value, Fields!FormatInfo.Value, "Col_2", False)
```

This expression calls the GetCustomFormat static method in the Util class. It passes the user culture (Parameters!Settings.Value), the formatInfo fragment, the field name, and a Boolean value that indicates whether the format string should include a currency symbol.

```
public static string GetCustomFormat (string paramSettings, string formatInfo,
   string columnID, bool currencySymbol){
   string setting = GetSetting(formatInfo, columnID);
   if (String.IsNullOrEmpty(setting)) return null;
   FormatTypeEnum settingType = (FormatTypeEnum)Enum.Parse(typeof(FormatTypeEnum), setting);
```

```
    switch (settingType)    {
        case FormatTypeEnum.None             : return null;
        case FormatTypeEnum.Number           : return GetNumberFormat(paramSettings);
        case FormatTypeEnum.Currency         : return GetCurrencyFormat(paramSettings, currencySymbol);
        case FormatTypeEnum.Percentage       : return GetPercentFormat(paramSettings);
        case FormatTypeEnum.Date             : return GetDateFormat(paramSettings);
    }
    return null;
}
public static string GetNumberFormat(string settings) {
    string format = null;
    string cultureInfo = GetSetting(settings, SETTING_CULTURE_INFO);
    if (cultureInfo == null) return null;
    CultureInfo ci = DeserializeCulture (cultureInfo);
    string pf = GetGenericNumberFormatString(ci, true);
    string nf = GetGenericNumberFormatString(ci, false);
    format = pf + ";" + nf;
    string decimalPlacesExpanded = GetDecimalPlaces(ci, FormatTypeEnum.Number);
    format = format.Replace("n", "#" + ci.NumberFormat.NumberGroupSeparator + "##0" +    decimalPlacesExpanded);
    return format;
}
```

To determine if there is a format string associated with the column, GetCustomFormat calls the GetSetting helper method (not shown) and passes the formatInfo fragment and the column identifier. GetSetting loads the formatInfo XML fragment in an XmlDocument object and returns the value for the specified node.

If formatInfo includes the field, GetCustomFormat casts the field type to the FormatTypeEnum enumeration. Then, GetCustomFormat calls the associated helper method to derive the format string based on the field type, such as GetNumberFormat for numbers, GetCurrencyFormat for currencies, and so on. Let's take a closer look at one of these helper methods: GetNumberFormat.

GetNumberFormat calls the GetSetting helper method to obtain the user culture, which is passed to the Settings report parameter. It calls the DeserializeCulture helper method to deserialize the CultureInfo object from the base64-encode string. Next, it calls GetGenericNumberFormatString to derive the format strings for positive and negative numbers based on the user's culture.

For example, if the user regional settings indicate a thousand separator and parentheses for negative numbers, the format string would be #,##0;(#,##0). GetNumberFormat invokes the GetDecimalPlaces helper method to obtain the decimal portion of the format string. Finally, GetNumberFormat constructs the complete format string. For example, if the users' regional settings indicate two decimal places, the format string would be #,##0.00;(#,##0.00).

Deploying external assemblies

External assemblies must be deployed to Report Designer and report server so they are accessible at both design time and run time.

1. Copy the Prologika.Reporting.Extensibility.dll and Prologika.Reporting.Extensibility.pdb binaries to the Report Designer folder whose default location is \Program Files\Microsoft Visual Studio 9.0\Common7\IDE\PrivateAssemblies.
2. Copy the Prologika.Reporting.Extensibility.dll and Prologika.Reporting.Extensibility.pdb binaries to the report server binary folder whose default location is \Program Files\Microsoft SQL Server\MSRS10.MSSQLSERVER\Reporting Services\ReportServer\bin.

To facilitate design-time deployment, I've defined a post-build event for the Reporting.Extensibility project which automatically copies the binaries to Report Designer and report server after a successful build. To see this event, right-click the Reporting.Extensibility project in Solution Explorer and click Properties. In the Project Properties dialog box, click the Build Events tab. Notice that the Post-build Event Command Line field includes the following commands:

```
copy $(TargetName).* "$(DevEnvDir)PrivateAssemblies\"
copy $(TargetName).* "C:\Program Files\Microsoft SQL Server\MSRS10.MSSQLSERVER\Reporting
Services\ReportServer\bin\"
```

Be careful when using a post-build event to deploy to the report server because each build will effectively restart the report server. The report server monitors its folders for file change notifications and restarts itself under certain conditions, such as after detecting changes to its web.config file or binary folder. To avoid unnecessary restarts, manually deploy external code to the report server.

7.3.4 Securing Custom Code

As long as custom code performs simple tasks, such as arithmetic and string operations, you don't need to worry about securing it. However, chances are that your custom code may need elevated privileges to access protected resources, such opening files and connecting to databases. This requires that you understand and adjust the .NET Code Access Security policies to give your custom code rights to execute successfully.

Understanding code access security

Reporting Services leverages the Code Access Security (CAS) infrastructure baked into the .NET Framework to sandbox custom code execution and to prevent malicious code from performing unauthorized actions. Discussing CAS in detail is outside the scope of this book. The first two links in the Resources section should help you acquire the necessary background knowledge in case you want to learn more about CAS after reading this section.

In a nutshell, when the .NET Framework common language runtime (CLR) loads an assembly, it obtains an *evidence* for the assembly so it can identify which *code group* the assembly belongs to. Evidence is known information about the assembly, such as the assembly location, publisher, strong name, and so on.

Code groups associate a piece of evidence with a named permission set to define a CAS security policy. The .NET Framework includes several pre-defined code groups, such as My Computer which includes all code originating on the local computer. Administrators can use the .NET Framework Configuration tool to create custom code groups and permission sets. For example, assuming that the Prologika.Reporting.Extensibility assembly requires permissions to open connections to a SQL Server database, you can set up a custom permission set that grants it a SqlClient permission. Then, you can define a custom code group for Prologika.Reporting.Extensibility located in the report server bin folder (evidence) and associate the code group with the custom permission set.

To simplify management, .NET applications can use configuration files that specify CAS security policies. For example, Reporting Services and SharePoint use configuration files to control what CAS permissions are assigned to custom code.

How Reporting Services use code access security

Reporting Services evaluates CAS both at design time and run time. Report Designer Reporting Services uses security configuration files that define default CAS policies. Table 7.4 lists these files, their default location and purpose.

Table 7.4 Reporting Services supports several security configuration files

Component	Security File	Default Path	Purpose
Report Server	rssrvpolicy.config	\Program Files\Microsoft SQL Server\MSRS10.MSSQLSERVER\Reporting Services\ReportServer	The report server CAS configuration file. Affects run-time custom code execution.
Report Manager	rsmgrpolicy.config	\Program Files\Microsoft SQL Server\MSRS10.MSSQLSERVER\Reporting Services\ReportManager	The Report Manager CAS configuration file. Affects custom code that extends Report Manager, such as UI for custom delivery extensions.
Report Designer	rspreviewpolicy.config	\Program Files\Microsoft Visual Studio 9.0\Common7\IDE\PrivateAssemblies	The Report Designer CAS configuration file. Affects custom code at design time.

Follow these steps to understand how Reporting Services CAS security works and determine the default CAS permissions Report Designer grants to custom code (the report server defines the same permissions in rssrvpolicy.config):

1. Open the Report Designer configuration file (RSReportDesigner.config) which is located by default in \Program Files\Microsoft Visual Studio 9.0\Common7\IDE\PrivateAssemblies.
2. Locate the policyLevel element.

```
<Add Key="PolicyLevel" Value="rspreviewpolicy.config" />
```

The securityPolicy element points to the rspreviewpolicy.config that defines the CAS policies.

3. Open the rspreviewpolicy.config in your favorite text editor.
4. Locate the Report_Expressions_Default_Permissions code group.

```
<CodeGroup
     class="UnionCodeGroup" version="1" Permission SetName="Execution"
     Name="Report_Expressions_Default_Permissions"
     Description="This code group grants default permissions for code in report expressions and Code element. ">
     <IMembershipCondition class="StrongNameMembershipCondition" version="1" Publ icKeyBlob="..." />
</CodeGroup>
```

As you can see, the Reporting Services default security policy grants Execution permissions to custom expression and embedded code. The Execution permission allows code to access only the CPU. Similarly, the next CodeGroup element below the Report_Expressions_Default_-Permissions element grants external custom code that originates on the local computer (MyComputer zone) Execution permissions as well.

5. Preview the Custom Formatting report in Report Designer.

Although the report appears to execute successfully, the custom formatting code doesn't work because the report content is not formatted. What's going on? If you examine the Visual Studio Output window, you will see that the Format expressions have generated the following exception:

```
[rsRuntimeErrorInExpression] The Format expression for the textbox '<textbox> ' contains an error: Request for the permission of type 'System.Security.Permissions.SecurityPermission, mscorlib, Version=2.0.0.0, Culture=neutral, PublicKeyToken=b77a5c561934e089' failed.
```

NOTE If a textbox calls custom code and the code fails, the textbox will display #Error. Expressions in other textbox properties don't provide visual indicators that the custom code has generated an exception. If you suspect that custom code doesn't work as expected, inspect the Output window for error messages or debug the external code.

Unfortunately, the error messages in the Output window don't tell you exactly what caused the external code to fail. However, if you debug the code using the techniques I'll present in section 7.3.5, you'll discover that the code fails when it tries to deserialize the user culture in the StringToObject method.

```
BinaryFormatter formatter = new BinaryFormatter();
thisDeserializedObject = formatter.Deserialize(ms);  ' SecurityPermission exception here!!!
```

Why does the Deserialize method fail? Given the error text and what I said about the default Reporting Services security policies, you can conclude that the external code doesn't have the required permissions to call this method. Let's find what permissions the Deserialize method requires to execute successfully.

6. Place the cursor on Deserialize and press F1 to open the Visual Studio Help.
7. In the help topic for Deserialize, scroll all the way down to the Permissions section.

Note that the method requires SecurityPermission, which is not included in the Execution permission set. There are two approaches to grant the code the required rights. The first approach is easy but less secure because it grants the custom assembly full rights. The second approach grants the assembly the minimum rights to execute successfully but requires additional steps to configure the security policies.

Elevating custom code rights the easy way

The easy way to elevate the custom code permissions is to configure the assembly as fully trusted by following these steps:

1. Make a backup of the rspreviewpolicy.config and rssrvpolicy.config files.
2. Open the rspreviewpolicy.config file and add a new CodeGroup that grants the assembly FullTrust permissions.

```
<CodeGroup class="UnionCodeGroup" version="1" Name="SecurityExtensionCodeGroup"
    Description="Code group for the RsViewer library" PermissionSetName="FullTrust">
    <IMembershipCondition class="UrlMembershipCondition" version=" 1"
    Url="C:\ Program Files\Microsoft Visual Studio 9.0\Common7\IDE\PrivateAssemblies\Prologika.↵
        Reporting.Extensibility.dll" />
</CodeGroup>
```

The Url element specifies the full path to the assembly. When deploying the assembly to the report server, you need a similar CodeGroup element to the rssrvpolicy.config file.

```
<CodeGroup class="UnionCodeGroup" version="1" Name="SecurityExtensionCodeGroup"
    Description="Code group for the RsViewer library" PermissionSetName="FullTrust">
    <IMembershipCondition class="U rlMembershipCondition" version="1" Url="C: \Program Files\Microsoft SQL
Server\MSRS10.MSSQLSERVER\Reporting Services\ReportServer\bin\Prologika.Reporting.Extensibility.dll" />
</CodeGroup>
```

Notice that the CodeGroup element in rssrvpolicy.config references the assembly in the report server binary folder. For your convenience, I included my configuration files in the Config folder in the book source code. Do not replace your files with mine! Use the files for reference only.

Suppose that you have granted the assembly FullTrust rights. What will happen if malicious code executes the assembly? It can get access to all authorized resources that the assembly can access. To avoid this, when evaluating the CAS security policy, CLR walks up the call stack to check if all direct and indirect callers have rights to perform a privileged operation in the custom code. If the callers don't have the required rights, CAS will fail the attempted action even if the custom assembly is authorized to execute.

In our case, report expressions call the custom code. At run time, the report server compiles all report expression in a special expression host assembly and assigns this assembly to the Report_Expressions_Default_Permissions code group. You can elevate the CAS rights of this code group to FullTrust but this presents a security risk because all expressions in all reports will be fully trusted. Instead, you can tell CRL to stop the stack walk by asserting the required permission in the external assembly.

```
private static CultureInfo DeserializeCulture(string culture) {
   try {
      SecurityPermission sp = new SecurityPermission(PermissionState.Unrestricted);
      sp.Assert();      // stop the stack walk
   }
   catch (System.Exception ex) { throw ex; }
   CultureInfo ci = (Cultur eInfo)StringToObject(culture); // call privileged operation
   return ci;
}
```

The report should now work both in Report Designer and Report Manager. If the assembly is opening a connection to SQL Server, you must assert SqlClientPermission.

```
System.Data.SqlClient.SqlClientPermission sp = new SqlClientPermission
(System.Security.Permissions.PermissionState.Unrestricted);
sp.Assert();
```

If the assembly is reading from a file, you must assert FileIOPermission.

```
FileIOPermission sp = new FileIOPermission(FileIOPermissionAccess.Read, "C:\TestFile");
sp.Assert();
```

If the assembly is calling a Web service, you must assert WebPermission and EnvironmentPermission rights, as I'll demonstrate in section 7.4.1. If the custom code is performing other operations, check the .NET documentation to determine what permissions you need to assert.

Elevating custom code rights the recommended way

The recommended way to configure CAS security is to grant the assembly the minimum rights to execute successfully. This requires creating a new permission set. The easiest way to create a permission set is to use the Microsoft .NET Framework 2.0 Configuration tool.

1. In the Windows Control Panel, double-click Administrative Tools.
2. In the Administrative Tools window, double-click Microsoft .NET Framework 2.0 Configuration.
3. In the left pane of the .NET Configuration 2.0 window, expand Runtime Security Policy.
4. Under Runtime Security Policy, expand Machine. Right-click the Permission Sets node under Machine and click New.
5. In the Create Permission Set dialog box, enter *PrologikaPermissionSet* in the Name field and click Next.

   Recall that the Prologika.Reporting.Extensibility assembly requires the SecurityPermission rights to run.

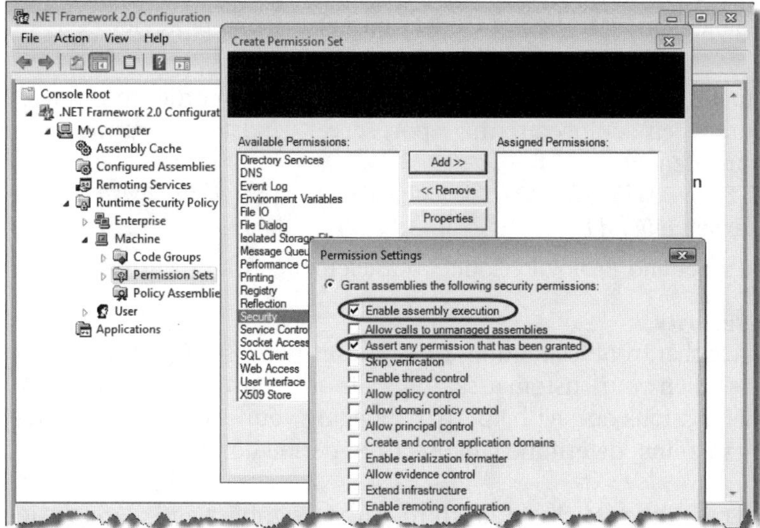

Figure 7.14 Use the .NET Framework 2.0 Configuration tool to create custom permissions sets and code groups.

6. Click the Security permission (see Figure 7.14) and click the Add button.
7. In the Permission Settings dialog box, check Enable Assembly Execution and Assert Any Permission That Has Been Granted checkboxes and click OK.
8. If your code needs additional permissions, repeat the last two steps to add the permissions. Click Finish when you are done.

   Next, you'll create a custom CodeGroup that references the PrologikaPermissionSet.

9. In the .NET Configuration 2.0 window, expand Code Groups under Machine.
10. Under Code Groups, right-click All_Code, and then click New.
11. On the Create Code Group page, enter *PrologikaCodeGroup* in the Name field, and then click Next.
12. Expand the Choose the Condition Type For This Code Group drop-down list and select URL.
13. In the URL field, enter the full path to your assembly, such as C:\Program Files\Microsoft Visual Studio 9.0\Common7\IDE\PrivateAssemblies\Prologika.Reporting.Extensibility.dll if you are deploying the assembly to Report Designer, and click Next.
14. Expand the Use Existing Permission Set drop-down list and select PrologikaPermissionSet and click Next and then Finish.

    The Microsoft .NET Framework 2.0 Configuration tool writes the changes to the .NET machine-wide security.config file.

15. In your favorite text editor, open security.config from the C:\Windows\Microsoft.NET\Framework\v2.0.50727\CONFIG folder.
16. Copy the PrologikaPermissionSet element.

```
<PermissionSet class="NamedPermissionSet" version="1" Name="PrologikaPermissionSet">
      <IPermission class="SecurityPermis sion" version="1" Flags="Assertion, Execution"/>
</PermissionSet>
```

17. Open rspreviewpolicy.config and paste the PrologikaPermissionSet element in the NamedPermissionSets element after the last PermissionSet element.

18. In security.config, copy the PrologikaCodeGroup element.
19. Paste the PrologikaCodeGroup element after the last CodeGroup element in rspreviewpolicy.config.
20. Repeat the last three steps to make the same changes to rssrvpolicy.config in order to configure the custom code to execute when deployed to the report server. Update the assembly URL in the PrologikaCodeGroup element to *C:\Program Files\Microsoft SQL Server\MSRS10.MSSQLSERVER\Reporting Services\Report Server\bin\Prologika.Reporting.Extensibility.dll*.
21. Remove the PrologikaPermissionSet and PrologikaCodeGroup elements from security.config.

Troubleshooting code access security

I know from personal experience that troubleshooting CAS issues is not easy. This is especially true with chained calls, such as when your custom assembly calls other assemblies. If giving your custom code FullTrust permissions doesn't help, try debugging your code to find where it fails. Once you identify the exact line, determine what security permission it requires by examining the error message.

However, when your code calls other Microsoft or third-party assemblies and CAS fails in these assemblies, debugging the code may not be an option. To the best of my knowledge, there is no tool that can help you troubleshoot CAS issues in this scenario. When nothing else helps, consider elevating the permissions of the report expressions to FullTrust.

```
<CodeGroup
      class="UnionCodeGroup" version="1" PermissionSetName=" FullTrust"
      Name="Report_Expressions_Default_Permissions"
      Description="This code group grants default permissions for code in report
      expressions and Code element. ">
     <IMembershipCondition class="StrongNameMembershipCondition" version="1" PublicKeyBlob="... " />
</CodeGroup>
```

Without underestimating the importance of securing custom code, I personally believe that report authors need not become CAS experts just to get a piece of code working. I hope a future release of Reporting Services simplifies custom code security. One way this could work is to follow the approach used by SQL Server and Analysis Services to secure .NET code by assigning the assembly one of three permission sets: Safe (only internal computation and local data access are allowed), External Access (can access external system resources such as files, networks, environmental variables, and the registry), and Unrestricted (all bets are off). If you agree, log this wish on connect.microsoft.com.

7.3.5 Debugging Custom Code

Apart from testing the code in a separate code project, such as a console or Windows Forms application, there aren't any options for debugging embedded code. In section 7.1.5, we explore the techniques that you can use to test your code before adding it to a report. Once the code is tested, copy and paste the code into the Code tab of the Report Properties dialog box. Before doing so, make sure that the embedded code uses fully qualified object names, such as System.Collections.ArrayList, because embedded code cannot import namespaces.

Using report preview

There are several options to debug external code. The easiest option is to use stand-alone preview (F5), as follows:

1. Add Reporting.Extensibility and the Reports project to the same Visual Studio solution.
2. Build and then deploy the custom code assembly that you want to test to C:\Program Files\Microsoft Visual Studio 9.0\Common7\IDE\PrivateAssemblies. Consider setting up a post-build event to automate deployment.
3. In Solution Explorer, right-click the Reports project and click Set as Startup Project.
4. In Solution Explorer, right-click the Reports project and click Properties.
5. In the Reports Property Pages dialog box, expand the StartItem drop-down list and select the report that uses the external code (Custom Formatting.rdl in our case). Click OK.
6. Put breakpoints in the custom code as needed and press F5.

   Visual Studio will open the report in a special viewer called Report Host (RSReportHost.exe). When you preview the report, Visual Studio will load and execute the custom code and your breakpoints will be hit.

TIP What happens when you press F5 depends on the Configuration Manager settings. If the Build and Deploy options are checked, Visual Studio will build and deploy all reports in the project. As this may take considerable time, consider turning off these options to start your debugging session faster.

Start Report Designer as an external program

The problem with stand-alone preview is that the moment the report calls the assembly, the Visual Studio IDE loads and locks the assembly. Consequently, you won't be able to redeploy an updated version of the assembly unless you restart the Visual Studio IDE. As you can image, this could be irritating during early stages of development. In addition, if your code project is in the Visual Studio 2005 format, you won't be able to add both projects to the same solution because they have incompatible project formats. Therefore, I recommend that you debug custom code by starting Report Designer as external program.

1. Open your code project in Visual Studio. If the Report Server project is part of the same solution, right-click the project node and click Remove to remove it from the solution.
2. In the Project Properties dialog box of the code project, select the Debug tab.
3. In the Start Action section, select Start External Program and enter C:\Program Files\Microsoft Visual Studio 9.0\Common7\IDE\devenv.exe.
4. In the Command Line Arguments field, enter the full path to the report project enclosed in quotes, such as "C:\Users\teo\Books\RS2008\Code\ch07\Reports\Reports.rptproj".
5. Put breakpoints in the custom code as needed and press F5.

   This will open another instance of the Visual Studio IDE with your Report Server project. When you preview a report that uses custom code, your breakpoints should be hit. When you stop the debugging session, the second Visual Studio instance will be terminated as well, so you can make changes and rebuild the custom code if needed.

Attaching to the report server process

To debug custom code at run time under the report server, attach to the Reporting Services service, as follows:

1. Deploy the latest custom code and reports to the report server.
2. Open the code project in Visual Studio.
3. Click the Debug ⇨ Attach to Process menu.

4. In the Attach to Process dialog box, check the Show Processes From All Users and Show Processes In All Sessions checkboxes.
5. In the Available Processes grid, select ReportingServicesService.exe and click the Attach button.
6. Open Report Manager and run the report or request the report by URL.

Once the report invokes the custom code, breakpoints will be hit and you will be able to step through the code. Once you are done debugging, click Debug ⇨ Detach All to detach the debug session from the report server.

TIP To facilitate troubleshooting custom code execution at run time without debugging it, consider implementing tracing, such as invoking System.Diagnostics.Trace.WriteLine to output exception details. This approach will let you attach a trace listener, such as the SysInternals DebugView tool, and watch the trace output real time.

7.4 Report Design Challenges and Solutions

As I've worked with Reporting Services, I've discovered interesting approaches for solving various design challenges. I'd like to wrap up the report authoring part of this book by presenting solutions and tips I've accumulated through my real life projects and interaction with the technical community. I hope that by the end of this section, you will have at least one "a-ha" moment that leads you to say one less time "Reporting Services can't do that".

7.4.1 Working with Variables

As chapter 1 explained, the Reporting Services 2008 processing engine was redesigned to perform on-demand report processing with better scalability. As a result, textbox values are calculated on-demand every time the containing page is rendered. On-demand report processing may have important ramifications on data latency and performance.

The dataset-bound textboxes are not affected much by the new processing model. This is because the underlying data is cached for the duration of the execution session. Consequently, values of dataset-bound textboxes won't change between page refreshes, such as when the user pages to another page and then back again to the same page.

But what about textboxes that call custom code? As it turns out, the new processing engine will execute the custom code each time the page is rendered. This may or may not be what you want. If you need up-to-date information, the new behavior will be welcome. However, there will be cases when you need the custom code to execute only once (for example, when custom code takes a very long time to execute and you want to cache the result, or when you don't want the report results to change when the user scrolls to the next page). How do you solve these requirements? Enter variables–a new feature in Reporting Services 2008.

Understanding variables

Variables provide a mechanism for guaranteeing one-time evaluation semantics for an expression. Think of Reporting Services variables as a read-only variable in .NET programming languages. A variable is a named reference to data stored in memory. Reporting Services variables are not typed and can store any of the object types supported by RDL, such as string, int, float, double, or byte array.

The DeferVariableEvaluation report-level property controls when variables will be evaluated. When set to False (default value), variables will be evaluated at the beginning of report processing. By setting it to True, you are telling the report server that the variables are not required to be pre-evaluated and should be evaluated on-demand based on usage. In this case, Reporting Services does not guarantee a particular point in time when a variable value will be evaluated. It just guarantees that it will be evaluated before its first usage in the report and once it is evaluated, it won't be re-evaluated.

As it stands, the report server doesn't take full advantage of deferred evaluation. One scenario that may give you deferred evaluation is when a report contains multiple data regions, but you only view the first page. In this case, data regions with group variables that are not on the first page might not get immediately evaluated. Another deferred evaluation scenario is when a report contains multiple subreports. Report variables on the subreports may not be evaluated if you don't view the page with the contents of the subreport.

Just like code variables, Reporting Services variables have a scope. Specifically, variables can be scoped at a report or a group level. A report variable is evaluated once for the lifetime of the report and it's available for any expression in the report. A group variable is evaluated each time the group value changes. You can define a group variable on a parent group and refer to its value from a nested child group. You can access the variable value by using the Variables collection.

Variables are subject to certain limitations. Once initialized by Reporting Services, a variable is read-only and cannot be used to cache results from other expressions, such as to maintain state. You cannot use a variable inside an aggregate function or a calculated dataset field. For example, the following expression results in an error because it includes a variable in the Sum aggregated function:

```
=Sum(Fields!SalesAmount.Value * Variables!Rate.Value)
```

If the field is additive, you can rewrite the expression as follows:

```
=Sum(Fields!SalesAmount.Value) * Variables!Rate.Value
```

About the Daily Sales in USD report

So far, we've been blissfully unaware that Adventure Works sales are captured in local currencies. Suppose that you need to produce a report that converts the local currency values to United States dollars. Let's assume that Adventure Works has already built a Web service that returns the currency conversion rate for a given date and currency. The report needs to call the Web service to obtain the currency rate in order to calculate sales in USD.

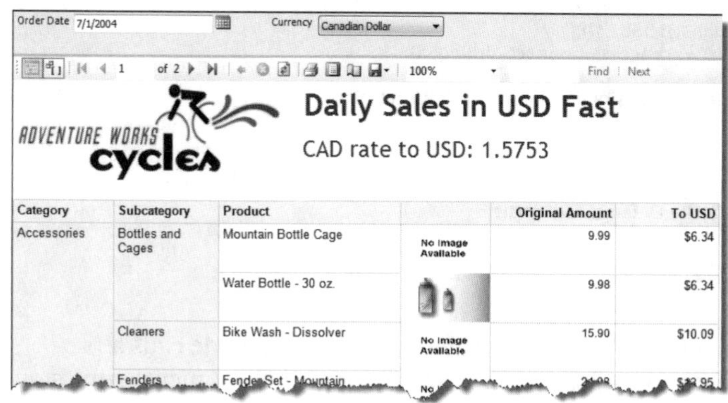

Figure 7.15 This report uses a report variable to cache the currency conversion rate.

The book source code includes two reports, Daily Sales in USD Slow and Daily Sales in USD Fast, which demonstrate this scenario. The user can select a date by setting the Order Date field. The Currency parameter is configured as a cascading parameter that shows only the currencies used on that date.

The Daily Sales in USD Slow report doesn't use variables and executes much slower because it calls the Web service for each expression that needs the currency rate. By contrast, the Daily Sales in USD Fast report (see Figure 7.15) calls the Web service once to obtain the currency rate and caches that rate in a report variable. Instead of calling the Web service, the report expressions use the cached rate. This improves the report performance significantly.

Implementing the Web service

I implemented a simple Web service to return the currency conversion rate. To avoid dependency on IIS, the AdventureWorksServices Web service project uses the ASP.NET development server. The Web service is implemented in the Services.asmx file.

```
[WebMethod]
public decimal GetRate(DateTime date, string currency) {
   decimal rate = 0;
   string sql = "SELECT [AverageRate] FROM [Sales].[CurrencyRate] WHERE CurrencyRateDate = @Date
                            AND ToCurrencyCode = @Currency";
   using (SqlConnection conn = new SqlConnection(connectString)) {
      SqlCommand cmd = new SqlCommand(sql, conn);
      cmd.Parameters.Add("@Date", SqlDbType.DateTime);
      cmd.Parameters.Add("@Currency", SqlDbType.NChar, 3);
      cmd.Parameters["@Date"].Value = date;
      cmd.Parameters["@Currency"].Value = currency;
      conn.Open();
      rate = (Decimal)cmd.ExecuteScalar();
   }
   return rate;
}
```

The GetRate web method accepts the date and currency code as input arguments. It establishes a connection to the AdventureWorks2008 database and queries the CurrencyRate table to return the currency conversion rate.

Implementing the custom code

I extended the Reporting.Extensibility assembly with a GetRate method that wraps the call to the Web service.

```
public static decimal GetRate(DateTime date, string currency) {
   decimal rate = 0;
   Trace.WriteLine("GetRate called...");
   PermissionSet ps = new PermissionSet(PermissionState.None);
   Regex urlRegEx = new Regex(@"http://localhost:1966/.*");
   WebPermission wp = new WebPermission(NetworkAccess.Connect, urlRegEx);
   ps.AddPermission(wp);
   EnvironmentPermission ep = new EnvironmentPermission(PermissionState.Unrestricted);
   ps.AddPermission(ep);
   ps.Assert();

   AW.Service proxy = new Service();
   proxy.Credentials = System.Net.CredentialCache.DefaultCredentials;
   rate = proxy.GetRate(date, currency);
   System.Threading.Thread.Sleep(500);
   return rate;
}
```

As you know by now, you must obey the CAS security rules when custom code calls a protected resource. Invoking a web method requires WebPermission and EnvironmentPermission rights. GetRate starts by constructing a PermissionSet object that includes these two permissions. The WebPermission uses a regular expression to grant rights to all URLs that include localhost:1966 (the ASP.NET development server is configured to listen on port 1966). Once the permission set is constructed, GetRate asserts it to stop the stack walk.

Then, GetRate invokes the Web service. I introduced an artificial delay of 500 milliseconds to simulate a long running custom method. This will help you understand performance benefits of using a report variable. You can use the SysInternals DebugView tool to watch the trace output from the GetRate method. Before testing the code changes, make sure to deploy and secure the Reporting.Extensibility assembly as discussed in section 7.3.4.

The Daily Sales in USD Slow report

The Daily Sales in USD Slow doesn't use variables. Instead, the To USD column uses the following expression to calculate the USD sales.

```
=Fields!Sales.Value/P rologika.Reporting.Extensibility.Services.GetRate
(Parameters!OrderDate.Value, Parameters!Currency.Value)
```

Similar expressions are used to calculate the report totals and show the rate in the report title. At run time, the Daily Sales in USD Slow report makes a total of 42 calls to the Web service. On my laptop, the report takes some 20 seconds to execute. Notice that when you page, the report makes more calls to GetRate because each page is rendered on demand. Another indication of the on-demand processing mechanism is the Date field in the page footer. If you navigate to the second report page and go back to the first page, the Date field changes. This is because it uses the Now() function to display the current date and this expression is executed each time the page is rendered.

The Daily Sales in USD Fast report

Follow these steps to implement a report variable for caching the currency conversion rate.

1. In the Report Properties dialog box, select the Variables tab.
2. Click the Add button to create a new variable. Name the variable *Rate* and use the following expression for the value:

   ```
   =Prologika.Reporting.Extensibility.Services.GetRate (Parameters!OrderDate.Value, Parameters!Currency.Value)
   ```

3. Change all rate-dependent expressions to use the Rate variable instead of calling custom code.

   For example, change the expression of the detail cell of the To USD column as follows:

   ```
   =Fields!Sales.Value/Variables!Rate.Value
   ```

4. Preview the report.

The report makes a single call to the GetRate method and it takes only a few seconds to execute! Paging through the report is very fast and it doesn't result in additional method invocations. That's because the report expressions reuse the currency rate cached in the Rate report variable.

7.4.2 Working with External Images

Recall that the image report item can render images that are embedded in the report, stored in the database, or located outside Reporting Services. So far, the report samples have used the first two image types. Next, I'll discuss two reports that demonstrate how to integrate your reports with external images. The first report displays images by URL, while the second gets the binary image from a Web service.

Requesting images via URL

The External Images via URL report, shown in Figure 7.16, displays a list of Adventure Works customers and their addresses. It shows an image map for each customer by requesting the map via URL. To the best of my knowledge, only the Google Static Maps service supports rendering maps as static images. I used the Google Static Map Wizard (see Resources) to generate the map URL. For example, this is what the map URL for Jon Yang looks like:

```
http://maps.google.com/staticmap?center=47.579322,-122.383278
&markers=47.579322,-122.383278,red&zoom=13&size=300x200&key= MAPS_API_KEY
```

NOTE You must get a MAPS API key and replace the MAPS_API_KEY token in the map URL to render the maps successfully. You can obtain a free API key from the Static Map Wizard page.

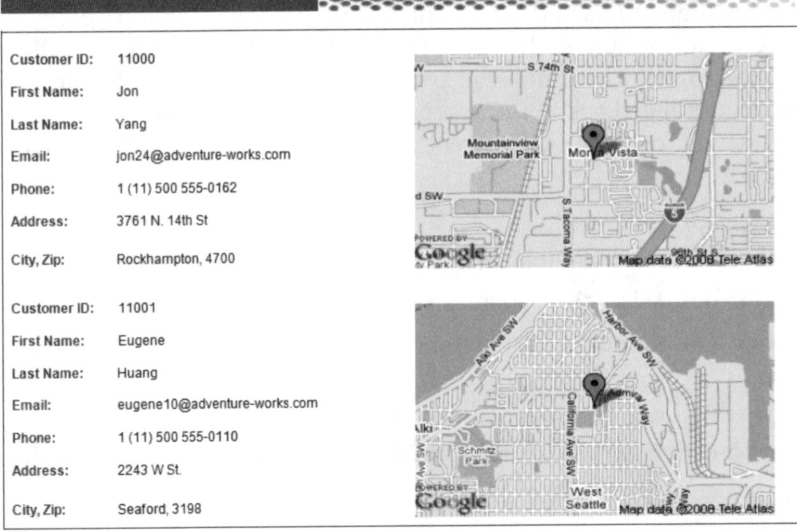

Figure 7.16 This report shows external images by URL.

Once you have the image URL, configuring the report to display the image is straightforward:

1. Add an image report item to the list region.
2. Set its MIMEType property to image/gif because Google Static Maps returns the image in GIF format.
3. Set the image Source property to External.
4. Set the image Value property to the image URL. In my case, I set the Value property to =Fields!MapURL.Value because the MapURL dataset field provides the image URL.

If the external images are located on a separate server and the service is not configured for anonymous access, the image request will fail. As I discussed in chapter 2, you must configure the Reporting Services unattended execution account to impersonate the call by specifying the Windows credentials of an account that has read access to the external image files. You can configure the image Action property to make the image clickable and let the user navigate to another URL resource or report.

5. Click the ellipsis (...) button inside the image Action property.
6. In the Image Properties dialog, select the Action tab and click the Go to URL option.
7. Enter the following expression in the Select URL field:

```
="http://localhost:1966/AdventureWorksServices/images/" & Fields!CustomerID.Value & ".gif"
```

This expression constructs an URL address to the image located in the images folder of the AdventureWorksServices ASP.NET project. As a result, when the user clicks the image, the image will be displayed in a separate browser instance.

Requesting images via Web service

Sometimes, the external images may not be directly accessible by URL. For example, once I had to design a report that would show scanned images of customer checks. To obtain the images, the report had to integrate with a Web service that would take a customer identifier and return the image in a binary format. The External Images via Web Service report demonstrates how this could be implemented. It builds upon the External Images via URL report but obtains the external image via custom code that calls a Web service. The GetMap web method in the AdventureWorksServices project fulfills the role of the Web service.

```
[WebMethod]
public byte[] GetMap(int customerID) {
   string imagePath = "";
   imagePath = String.Format(@"{0}\{1}.gif", Server.MapPath("images"), customerID);

   if (File.Exists(imagePath))
      return FileAsBytes(imagePath);
   else
      return new byte[] { };
}
```

For the sake of simplicity, GetMap loads the map image from the file system and returns it as a byte array. I also added a wrapper GetMap method in the Services class in the Reporting.Extensibility project.

```
[PermissionSet(SecurityAction.Assert, Unrestricted = true)]
public static byte[] GetMap(int customerID) {
   AW.Service proxy = new Service();
   proxy.Credentials = System.Net.CredentialCache.DefaultCredentials;
   return proxy.GetMap(customerID);
}
```

Recall that calling Web services requires elevated CAS permissions. The GetMap helper method demonstrates a declarative way for asserting permissions by decorating the method with a PermissionSet attribute instead of doing so programmatically. In this case the PermissionSet attribute doesn't enumerate the required permissions (WebPermission and EnvironmentPermission). Instead, it instructs CLR to assert all permissions granted to this assembly. Since the custom assembly is granted FullTrust, the net result is that CLR will fully trust the method callers. Of course, this is less secure than asserting only the permissions you need, so use this approach with caution. Once the custom code is in place, follow these steps to configure the image report item to call it:

1. Set the image Source property to Database.
2. Set the image Value property to an expression that calls the custom code:

```
=Prologika.Reporting.Extensibility.Services.GetMap(Fields!ContactID.Value)
```

This expression calls the GetMap helper method in the Prologika.Reporting.Extensibility assembly, which in turns calls the GetMap web method.

7.4.3 Passing Multivalued Parameters to Stored Procedures

Recall from chapter 4 that Reporting Services supports multivalued parameters to let the end user select multiple parameter values. When designing the report query, you must append an IN operator to the query WHERE clause of the SELECT statement to filter on multiple values. This works fine with freeform SQL statements. But what if you need to pass multiple values to a stored procedure? Prior to SQL Server 2008, you had to resort to parsing the comma-delimited string inside the stored procedure to extract the parameter values. Needless to say, this approach is difficult to implement and debug.

Table-valued parameters, a new feature in SQL Server 2008, changes all that. They provide a built-in mechanism to send multiple rows of data as a single parameter to a stored procedure. The Area Chart with Table Type report demonstrates how you can leverage table-valued parameters to send a multivalued parameter to a stored procedure. This report builds upon the Area Chart report you implemented in chapter 6 except that it uses a stored procedure instead of a freeform SQL statement for data retrieval.

Working with table-valued parameters

The Area Chart with Table Type has CalendarYear and Territory parameters. The Territory parameter is configured as a multivalued parameter. As a prerequisite for passing its values to a table-valued parameter of a stored procedure, you need to define a user-defined table type in the AdventureWorksDW2008 database. Execute the TVP.sql script included in the Queries folder of the source code of this chapter to create the user-defined table type and the stored procedure.

```
CREATE TYPE [dbo].[TerritoryType] AS TABLE (
	[TerritoryKey] [int] NOT NULL,
	[TerritoryName] [nvarchar](50) NOT NULL
)
CREATE PROCEDURE [dbo].[uspGetSalesByTerritory] (
	@CalendarYear int,
	@Territory TerritoryType READONLY
)
AS
BEGIN
	SET NOCOUNT ON;
	SELECT ST.SalesTerritoryGroup AS TerritoryGroup, D.FullDateAlternateKey AS [Date],
	SUM(FRS.SalesAmount) AS ResellerSalesAmount
	FROM DimDate AS D INNER JOIN
	FactResellerSales AS FRS ON D.DateKey = FRS.OrderDateKey INNER JOIN
	DimSalesTerritory AS ST ON FRS.SalesTerritoryKey = ST.SalesTerritoryKey INNER JOIN
	@Territory AS T ON ST.SalesTerritoryKey = T.TerritoryKey
	WHERE (D.CalendarYear = @CalendarYear)
	GROUP BY ST.SalesTerritoryGroup, D.FullDateAlternateKey
END
```

Let's take a moment to explain the script. The CREATE TYPE statement creates the user-defined table type. The TerritoryType table defines two columns. The TerritoryKey column will store the territory identifier. The TerritoryName column is for the territory name. Strictly speaking, the TerritoryName column is not needed but included for reference only.

The CREATE PROCEDURE statement creates the uspGetSalesByTerritory stored procedure, which takes @CalendarYear and @TerritoryType as arguments. I copied the SELECT statement from the original Area Chart report. The only change I've made is to join the DimSalesTerritory table to the @TerritoryType to filter on territory.

Designing the report query

Once the stored procedure is in place, you can design a report query to use it. As it stands, Reporting Services doesn't support table-valued parameters natively. However, you can use an expression-based query which generates statements to load the stored procedure parameters and execute the stored procedure. Here is what the statements look like if the user selects year 2004 for the year and North America and Pacific for the territories:

```
DECLARE @CalendarYear int = 2004
DECLARE @Territory TerritoryType
insert into @Territory values (1, 'North America')
insert into @Territory values (9, 'Pacific')
EXECUTE [dbo].[uspGetSalesByTerritory] @CalendarYear,@Territory
```

Given this syntax, I added the following GetQuery method to the Util class in the Reporting.Extensibility project:

```
public static string GetQuery(int calendarYear, object[] values, string[] labels) {
   StringBuilder sb = new StringBuilder();
   sb.AppendLine(String.Format("DECLARE @CalendarYear int = {0}", calendarYear ));
   sb.AppendLine("DECLARE @Territory TerritoryType");

   for (int i = 0; i<values.Length; i++)
   {
      sb.AppendLine(String.Format("insert into @Territory values ({0}, '{1}')",  values[i], labels[i]));
   }
   sb.AppendLine("EXECUTE [dbo].[uspGetSalesByTerritory] @CalendarYear,@Territory");
   return sb.ToString();
}
```

Next, I changed the report dataset to use the following expression-based query:

```
=Prologika.Reporting.Extensibility.Util.GetQuery
(Parameters!CalendarYear.Value, Parameters!Territory.Value, Parameters!Territory.Label)
```

At run time, this expression calls the GetQuery method and passes the parameter values. The selected values of the Territory parameter will be passed as an object array while the labels will be passed as a string array. GetQuery uses a StringBuilder object to construct the required Transact-SQL statements. First, it declares the CalendarYear parameter. Next, it loops through the values of the Territory parameter and generates Ttansact-SQL code to insert the selected territories into the TerritoryType TVP. Finally, it appends a statement to execute the stored procedure and pass the parameters. Since the GetQuery method performs string manipulation only, the default CAS Execution permission is sufficient for the GetQuery method to execute successfully.

7.4.4 Localizing Reports

If you've ever had to design applications for international users, you know that localizing the user interface is not easy. Not only do you need to translate data and captions (labels, buttons, entity names, etc.), but you must also handle currency conversion, text orientation, extra space requirements for the translated captions, and so on. The bad news is that you face the same challenges when localizing your reports. The good news is that Reporting Services provides some features to help you in this endeavor. To use these features effectively, you must understand how Reporting Services localizes resources.

Understanding report localization

Reporting Services evaluates the report server language, browser language, and the report language to determine how to localize the report content and tools, such as the Report Manager and HTML Viewer. Table 7.5 shows which resources are affected by each language.

Table 7.5 How Reporting Services chooses a language resource

Language	Localized resources
Report Server language	Report formatting when culture-neutral format settings are used. Report server messages (errors, warnings, and informational messages). Other static resources, such as role names, folder names for My Reports and Users folders.
Browser language	Report Manager HTML Viewer
Report language	Overwrites the report server language when culture-neutral format settings are used.

The SQL Server setup program sets the default report server language when it creates the report server database by evaluating the operating system language and SQL Server language. If they match exactly, the setup program uses this language. If there is a close match, for example when the OS language is English (UK) but the SQL Server language is English (US), the OS language will be used. In cases where there isn't a close match, the report server language will be set to English (US).

The report server language is used to format report content that uses culture-neutral format strings, such as "C2" for formatting numbers as currencies with two decimal places. However, you can overwrite the report server language per report and even per textbox by setting the Language property. The order of precedence is Report Server Language ⇨ Report Language ⇨ Textbox Language. For example, if the report server language is English (US), and you set the report Language property to English (UK), all report content that uses culture-neutral format strings will be formatted using the English (UK) resources locale.

If you set the Language property of a textbox to German (Germany), the textbox content will be formatted using the German (DE) locale. In addition to the Language property, the textbox report items also support NumeralLanguage and NumeralVariant to support culture-specific numerals, such as formatting numbers in Arabic and Indian locales.

Finally, the browser language (if the report is displayed in the browser) is used to localize the Report Manager user interface and the captions of the HTML Viewer toolbar. By default, the browser language matches the OS language. However, you can specify another language by using the browser settings.

NOTE If you are upgrading from Reporting Services 2000, you should know that there is a behavior change in Reporting Services 2005 and later. If you do not set the report language, the report server language determines the formats that are used. In Reporting Services 2000 however, if you do not set a language, the browser language will be used by default.

Using culture-neutral format settings

In a multilingual environment, the report server, browser, and report language settings may combine in such a way that multiple languages are displayed to a user within the same report. The Localized Demo report, shown in Figure 7.17, is meant to help you understand how these settings affect report presentation.

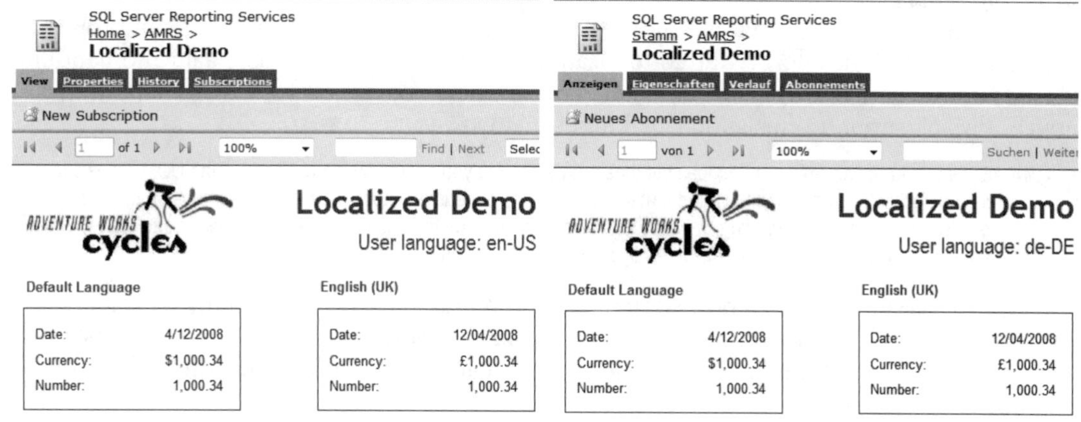

Figure 7.17 The Localized Demo report demonstrates how the report server language, browser language, and report language affect the report localization.

The Report Manager screenshot on the left shows the Localized Report requested when the browser language is set to English (US). The report content in the Default Language section uses culture-neutral format settings for the textbox Format properties, such as "d" for a short date, "C2" for currencies with two decimal places, and "N2" for numbers with two decimal places. The English (UK) section displays the same numbers but the Language property of each textbox is set to English (UK). This demonstrates that setting the textbox Language property overwrites the report server language. Now, let's change the browser language to German to simulate a German user.

1. In Internet Explorer, click Tools ➪ Internet Options and click the Languages button.
2. In the Language Preference dialog box, click the Add button and add the German (Germany) [de-DE] language.
3. Press F5 to refresh the report.

As the screenshot on the right in Figure 7.17 shows, the Report Manager and HTML Viewer captions are now localized in German. That's because these tools use the browser language to select a resource locale. However, the content Language section is still formatted in English (US) because the report server language is used to format report content. What if you want the browser language to take precedence over the report server language? You can do so by using an expression-based report (or textbox) Language property.

4. Open the Localize Demo report in Report Designer and set the report Language property to the following expression:

```
= User!Language
```

The User!Language returns the current thread language. When the report is requested by URL, User!Language returns the browser language. The net result of the above expression is that the report language will be set to German.

5. Deploy the report to Report Manager and refresh it in the browser.

Notice that the Default Language section is now formatted in German locale.

Localizing report data

As you've seen, Reporting Services simplifies how you format dates and numbers, but this is only a small part of the effort required to localize reports. Translating report data and handling currency conversion is by far more difficult. This is where you are on your own. Reporting Services doesn't support translation capabilities in any way.

NOTE If you target an Analysis Services cube as a data source, you should take advantage of the UDM Translations feature that facilitates translating the cube metadata (cube and dimension captions) and data (dimension member names). You can integrate Reporting Services with Analysis Services to bring the translated captions into the report. I demonstrate this approach in chapter 16. Analysis Services also can handle currency conversion.

One approach to localize the report content is to store the translated data in the data source. This is the approach that the Product Catalog Localized report (see Figure 7.18) demonstrates. This report builds upon the Product Catalog report that ships with the AdventureWorks sample reports.

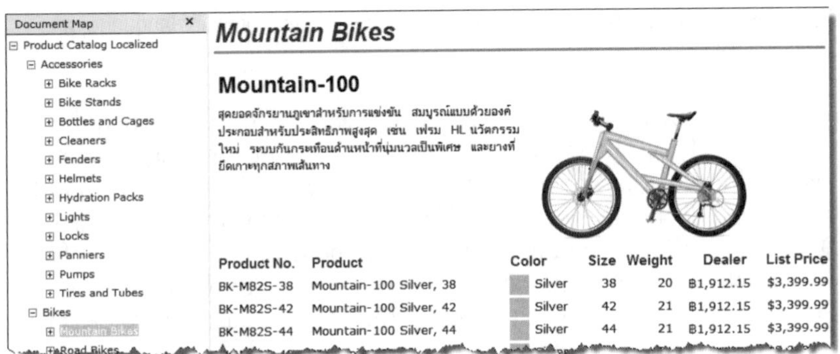

Figure 7.18 The Product Catalog Localized report shows the translated product descriptions based on the browser language.

The AdventureWorks2008 database includes Production.ProductModelProductDescriptionCulture and Culture tables to demonstrate localizing the product descriptions in several languages. To retrieve the translated product description, I changed the report query to pass the user language to the @Language query parameter. The Culture table uses two-letter culture identifiers, such as "en" for English and "fr" for French. However, User!Language returns the full language code, such as "fr-FR". The Language query parameter uses the following expression to get the two-letter identifier:

```
=Code.GetTwoLetterISOLanguageName(User!Language)
```

The GetTwoLetterISOLanguageName function embedded in the report.

```
Function GetTwoLetterISOLanguageName (LocaleID as String) as String
   Dim ci As New System.Globalization.CultureInfo(LocaleID, False)
   return ci.TwoLetterISOLanguageName
End Function
```

I've also made the following localization-related changes to the report.

1. Set the report Language property to =User!Language to overwrite the report server language.
2. Changed the Language property of the List Price textbox to en-US to show the amount formatted as United States Dollars. If I had not done so, the List Price field would have been formatted based on the browser language.

I also provided another simple function inside the report embedded code, GetLanguageNativeName, to display the language name on the first page of the report. To test the report:

3. Deploy the report to Report Manager.
4. Set the browser language to Thai (Thailand) and request the Product Catalog Localized report. Notice that the product description appears in Thai.

7.4.5 Generating RDL Programmatically

As useful as the Microsoft-provided report designers are, they may not be able to meet all report authoring requirements. Advanced report authoring needs may force you to take the road less travelled and generate the report definitions programmatically. For example, you may need to gather some input from the user and generate the report definition in accordance with user preferences.

NOTE In one of my projects, we had to integrate a Windows Forms financial application with Reporting Services 2005. To facilitate the process of authoring reports, we had to provide a report wizard to walk the user through the steps of creating a report. Unfortunately, all Microsoft-provided report designers are implemented as monolithic stand-alone applications and are not embeddable. Consequently, we had to implement a custom wizard. We created a report object model to facilitate working with RDL. A sample that demonstrates this approach is provided on my website (see Resources). Implementing a custom RDL object model took significant development effort. Moving to Reporting Services 2008, consider the Microsoft-provided RDLOM if you need to generate RDL programmatically.

Understanding the RDL Object Model

In general, there are two approaches for generating reports programmatically:

- XML APIs—You can use your favorite XML APIs (such as XmlDocument) and change RDL directly. However, this approach requires navigating RDL elements by using XPATH expressions and can quickly lead to code that is difficult to debug and maintain.
- RDL Object Model—Alternatively, you can work with an object model that abstracts RDL. This lets you interact with RDL in an object-oriented way.

In Reporting Services 2008, Microsoft provides an unsupported RDL object model (RDLOM). This model is implemented in the Microsoft.ReportingServices.RdlObjectModel.dll assembly, which is located in the report server bin folder (C:\Program Files\Microsoft SQL Server\MSRS10.MSSQLSERVER\Reporting Services\ReportServer\bin\). RDLOM is used internally by Reporting Services and it is not officially supported in this release. Therefore, use RDLOM at your own risk.

Keep the following considerations in mind about RDLOM. RDLOM only checks for syntactic correctness to ensure that the report definition conforms to the RDL specification. It doesn't validate whether the report definition is semantically correct. It doesn't execute the validation rules Report Designer performs when you build a report.

There isn't a way to customize the process of serializing or deserializing the report definition. However, most report elements support custom properties (CustomProperties property), which you can use to save custom settings. You need to write helper methods if you want to extend the object model, such as to add a new constructor to the Field object which takes the field name and data field.

```
Field (string name, string dataField) {
   this.Name = name;
   this.DataField = dataField;
}
```

Since the RDLOM source code is not provided, your only option is to create a wrapper class with the methods you need, such as Util.CreateField(string, string) as a shortcut to construct a field. RDLOM supports RDL 2008 only. It includes methods to upgrade RDL 2000 and 2005 formats. Specifically, it includes the Microsoft.ReportingServices.ReportProcessing.RDL-Upgrader.UpgradeToCurrent method that you can use to upgrade RDL 2000 or 2005 to RDL 2008.

Generating a report definition

The RDLOM console application included in the source code for this chapter (Ch07 Visual Studio Solution) demonstrates using RDLOM to generate a simple tablix report programmatically. The bulk of the code is located in the GenerateTablixReport method, whose partial code is provided below.

```
static void GenerateTablixReport() {
   RdlSerializer serializer = new RdlSerializer();
   TablixMember member;
   TablixColumn column;
   TablixRow row;
   Field f;

   Report report = new Report();
   // Report- level properties
   report.Language = "en - US";
   report.Width = new ReportSize(6.5);
   report.Author = "Teo Lachev";
   report.Page.LeftMargin = report.Page.TopMargin = report.Page.RightMargin =
   report.Page.BottomMargin = new ReportSize(.5);
   // Data source
   DataSource dataSource = new DataSource();
   dataSource.Name = "AdventureWorks 2008";
   dataSource.ConnectionProperties = new ConnectionProperties();
   dataSource.ConnectionProperties.ConnectString = "data source=localhost;  initial catalog=AdventureWorks2008;";
   dataSource.ConnectionProperties.DataProvider = "SQL";
   dataSource.ConnectionProperties.IntegratedSecurity = true;
   report.DataSources.Add(dataSource);
   // Generate the report body
   . . .
   // serialize to disk
   using (FileStream os = new FileStream(ReportPath, FileMode.Create))
   {
      serializer.Serialize(os, report);
   }
```

Use the RDLOM RdlSerializer object to serialize or deserialize a report definition to and from a stream. The code instantiates the Report object. It sets the report-level properties, creates a report-specific data source to the AdventureWorks2008 database, constructs a report dataset, and generates a table report. Finally, GenerateTablixReport writes the report (TablixDemo.rdl) to the application startup folder. To test the report, open and preview it in Report Designer. As you can see, RDLOM makes RDL programming much easier because you work with objects and not XML APIs.

7.5 Summary

In this chapter, you've learned how to use the textbox built-in formatting capabilities to display rich text and implement mail merge reports. You've also learned how to configure the Microsoft-provided rendering extensions and export reports to XML. Custom code and some out-of-the-box thinking lets you extend your reports in versatile ways. Use embedded code to implement simple utility functions that you can write in Visual Basic and distribute with the report. Consider external code to encapsulate more complex programming logic. Reporting Services leverages the .NET Code Access Security infrastructure to prevent malicious code from performing unauthorized actions. As a best practice, grant custom code the minimum CAS permissions to execute successfully.

The second part of this chapter demonstrated how you can use custom code to solve interesting challenges. Use variables to cache the results of executing custom methods and improve report performance. I also showed you how you can leverage custom code to work with external images and pass multivalued parameters to stored procedures. Finally, I presented approaches for localizing reports and generating report definitions programmatically.

Report Designer is a great tool for authoring standard reports but it may require more in-depth design knowledge for working with data and RDL. Let's see how Report Builder can help a business user author reports outside the Visual Studio IDE.

7.6 Resources

The Security Infrastructure of the CLR Provides Evidence, Policy, Permissions, and Enforcement Services
(http://tinyurl.com/6s8nla)—Introduces you to code access security.

Security in .NET: Enforce Code Access Rights with the Common Language Runtime
(http://tinyurl.com/6co92b)—Keith Brown discusses the CAS internals.

Reporting Services Device Information Settings
(http://tinyurl.com/23xery)—Explains the device information settings supported by the Reporting Services renderers.

Google Static Map Wizard
(http://tinyurl.com/24ftct)—Lets you generate a map URL to embed a map as an image in your reports.

Prologika Report Object Model
(http://tinyurl.com/24ftct)—A partially-implemented RDL 2005 object model that demonstrates how you can develop your own object models to abstract RDL.

PART 3

The Report Builder

Report Builder empowers business users to design their own reports. Reporting Services 2008 includes two flavors of the Report Builder technology. Report Builder 1.0, which remains unchanged from the previous release, allows less technically-savvy users author simple ad hoc reports from pre-defined models. Report Builder 2.0 is a standalone report designer tool that supports full-featured reports but requires more advanced technical skills.

As a prerequisite for building a Report Builder 1.0-based solution, you need to implement a report model and deploy the model to the server. The report model shields end users from the technicalities of the underlying relational and dimensional data sources by presenting the data source schema in the form of entities, attributes, and roles. The report model is capable of auto-generating the native queries when the user runs the report.

Once the report model is in place, end users can author reports from it with the Report Builder 1.0 client. The purpose of the Report Builder 1.0 client is to support end users who want to create simple ad hoc reports, but without the learning curve that comes with adopting new business tools. To reduce the learning curve, the Report Builder 1.0 client uses more built-in features such as templates and gives up some of the more powerful features that you find in the BIDS Report Designer and Report Builder 2.0.

To let end users access all report authoring features, Microsoft will introduce a stand-alone report designer called Report Builder 2.0. To help you evaluate Report Builder 2.0 for ad hoc reporting, the book includes several practices that introduce you to the pre-release version of this technology and walk you through the steps of authoring reports from relational and multidimensional data sources.

Chapter 8

Building Report Models

It often seems that as soon the developer is done with a report, the business user wants to change it. For this reason, ad hoc reporting (which is all about empowering business users to author their own reports) is the Holy Grail of many reporting solutions. In Reporting Services, ad hoc reporting is supported through Report Builder.

Recall from chapter 1 that Reporting Services 2008 includes two flavors of the Report Builder technology. Report Builder 1.0, which remains unchanged from the previous release, lets less technically-savvy users author simple ad hoc reports from pre-defined models. Report Builder 2.0 is a standalone report designer tool that supports full-featured reports but requires more advanced technical skills, such as knowing how to create database queries and work with report regions. We will preview Report Builder 2.0 in chapter 10.

Report Builder 1.0 is the subject of this chapter and chapter 9. In this chapter, I will lay out the ground work required to implement a Report Builder 1.0 solution. The main focus will be the Report Model component of the Report Builder 1.0. As an exercise, you will implement two report models on top of the Adventure Works relational database and cube. In the next chapter, you will use these models to author several ad hoc reports.

8.1 Understanding Report Builder 1.0

Report Builder 1.0 was first introduced in the 2005 release of Reporting Services after Microsoft acquired ActiveViews, a privately held company based in Provo, Utah. Report Builder 1.0 is included in the Enterprise, Developer, Evaluation, Standard, and Workgroup editions of SQL Server and is free of charge to SQL Server licensed users. In this section, we'll take a close look at the Report Builder 1.0 architecture and understand its components.

DEFINITION Report Builder 1.0 is a report authoring and processing tool for end-user reporting. It uses report models for data sources and lets you save reports directly to a report server or as report definition (.rdl) files on your computer. Report Builder 1.0 is a unifying name of the Reporting Services ad hoc reporting feature set that includes Model Designer, report model, Report Builder 1.0 client, and the semantic query engine.

8.1.1 The Report Builder Architecture

To support ad hoc reporting, Reporting Services architecture includes several components shown in bold type in Figure 8.1. Recall that at the heart of the Reporting Services architecture is the report server, a Web-based middle-tier layer that receives incoming report requests, generates, renders, and delivers reports. Here's a brief description of the ad hoc reporting components.

Report models

As I mentioned earlier, the Report Builder 1.0 target audience is non-technical business users who need not be familiar with the technical aspects of the database schema to generate ad hoc reports. The report model provides a metadata layer that enriches the data source schema and exposes it to the end user as related entities, attributes, and roles. The term *metadata* here means that the report model doesn't store any data; it simply describes data. Sometimes, you may hear business users refer to the report model or its equivalents as a *data dictionary*. The Report Builder 1.0 client uses the model as input during the report authoring phase.

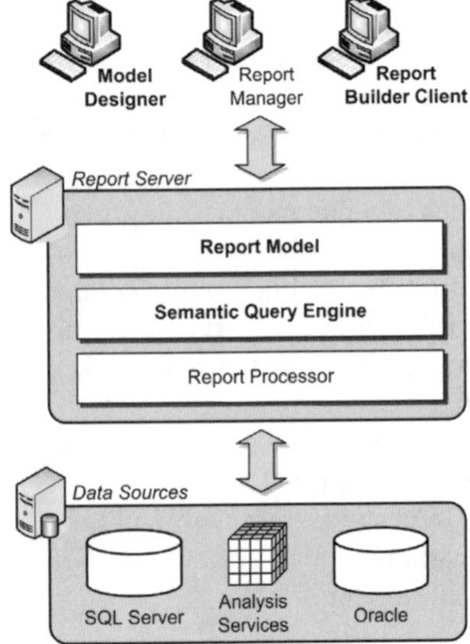

Figure 8.1 This high-level diagram shows how the Report Builder 1.0 components fit into the overall Reporting Services architecture. The Report Builder 1.0 components are the Model Designer, Report Builder client, Report Model, and Semantic Query Engine.

Working with a report model eliminates the need to join tables because the table relationships are defined in the model. For example, if a user wants to create a report that shows sales by territory and product, he or she can simply drag the territory attribute onto the report canvas. If there is a role (relationship) defined in the model between the Territory and Product entities, the Report Builder 1.0 client will discover this relationship and let the user select attributes from the Product entity. We will discuss the report model internals in section 8.1.2.

The Model Designer

You use the Model Designer, included in the Business Intelligence Development Studio (BIDS), to create the report models. Creating report models involves defining report model items, such as entities, attributes, and roles. As you can imagine, creating a report model from scratch can be tedious. Fortunately, Microsoft has provided a handy Report Model Wizard that can automatically generate the raw model with a few simple clicks.

However, the wizard doesn't produce an optimized model that is ready for production. For example, the Report Model Wizard applies system-generated names to report elements, and it doesn't detect inheritance relationships. As a modeler, you will probably need to take one or more passes through the model to refine the names and relationships. Once the model is ready, you can publish it to the report server to make it available for ad hoc reporting.

Report Builder 1.0 Client

The Report Builder 1.0 client is the design tool that the end users will interact with to author ad hoc reports. It is implemented as a Windows Forms application that users download and install from a report server and run on their local computer. End users will undoubtedly find the Report Builder 1.0 client interface intuitive because it has a look and feel similar to Microsoft Office products. Authoring a simple ad hoc report in the Report Builder 1.0 client is a matter of dragging and dropping fields to the WYSIWYG (**W**hat **Y**ou **S**ee Is **W**hat **Y**ou **G**et) report canvas.

Once the report is ready, the user can upload it to the report server to share it with other users. From there, the Report Builder 1.0 report can be managed, secured, and delivered just like a report produced in Report Designer. This is because the reports you create in both Report Designer and Report Builder 1.0 are described in the same report definition language (RDL). We will discuss the Report Builder 1.0 client in more details in chapter 9.

Semantic Query engine

In contrast with reports that you create in Report Designer, the reports that you create in the Report Builder 1.0 client do not store the actual query that will be sent to the data source. Instead, the report definition includes a *semantic* query that describes the model items and filters used on the report. When the report server starts processing the report, it extracts the report query. If the query is a semantic query, the report server forwards it to the Semantic Query Engine. The Semantic Query Engine translates the semantic query to a native query, using the syntax of the underlying data source. As it stands, Report Builder 1.0 includes query translators for four data sources—SQL Server 2000 or later, SQL Server Analysis Services 2005 or later, and Oracle 9.2.0.3 or later. No extensibility mechanism is currently provided for plugging in third-party or custom query translators.

A unique Report Builder 1.0 feature is infinite drillthrough, also known as *clickthrough*, that lets the end user click an item on the report to see the details behind it. For example, if the user requests a report that shows sales by employee, the user can click on a sales number to see the individual orders that contribute to that number. The Semantic Query Engine handles drillthrough report requests and generates drillthrough reports on the fly.

8.1.2 Understanding Report Models

The main characteristic of the report model is that it is designed with the user (not system) in mind. As Figure 8.2 shows, you can visualize the report model as three layers—data source, data source view, and semantic model—stacked on top of each other. Interestingly, you will find similar models in Analysis Services and Integration Services. The difference is in the top layer. In Analysis Services 2005, the top layer is the dimensional model, while in the Integration Services it is the control flow. Although the models share similarities, they are not interchangeable. You cannot publish an Analysis Services model to a report server and expect to build ad hoc reports with it.

What you can share across the various models are data sources and data source views. This is because both data sources and data source views have the same construction across the three project types in BIDS. The data source provides connection information for accessing the underlying data source. A data source view (DSV) is a metadata layer that describes the database schema.

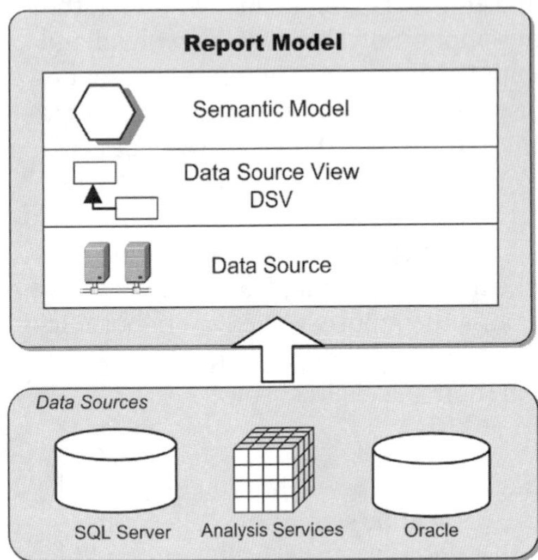

Figure 8.2 The report model serves as a bridge between the end users and the data. It consists of Data Source, Data Source View, and Semantic Model layers.

A DSV lets you change and extend the database schema without affecting the underlying data source. For example, suppose that you need to build a report model on top of a vendor's database. Furthermore, suppose that security or licensing restrictions prevent you from making changes to the database schema. With a DSV, this predicament simply disappears. You can add any required tables to the DSV designer to get the additional data structures you need, but without modifying the schema of the vendor database. For example, you can define table relations and primary keys, or create virtual tables (similar to SQL views) in the form of *named queries*. You can also define calculated columns in the form of *named calculations*.

NOTE Although DSV supports multiple data sources, a DSV inside a Report Model project can only use a single data source. Trying to define an entity from a secondary data source results in a build error: "The Table property of the Entity "EntityName" refers to the Table "TableName", which is not in the primary data source". You can get around this limitation by configuring the secondary data source as a linked server to your SQL Server instance or by using an OPENROWSET named query.

The semantic model is the layer that the user interacts with. If you are familiar with the Object Role Modeling (ORM) methodology (see Resources), you will undoubtedly discover many similarities between the two. Similar to the report definition language (RDL) that describes Reporting Services reports, the semantic model uses an XML-based grammar called Semantic Model Definition Language (SMDL).

A semantic model includes the following items:

Entities

An entity is a named collection of attributes, roles, folders, and filters. In the most common case, an entity maps to a DSV table or named query. For example, an Employee entity maps to an Employee table. Sometimes, however, an entity may derive from another entity and inherit its attributes. Suppose you have SalesPerson and Employee tables. Since a sales person *is* an employee, you can configure the SalesPerson entity to derive from the Employee entity. As a result, the end user doesn't have to navigate from the SalesPerson entity to the Employee entity to see the employee-related attributes.

Attributes

An attribute typically represents a table column. For example, the Name column in the Employee table maps to a Name attribute in the Employee entity. However, attributes can also be expression-based. For example, you can create an attribute that maps to a LineTotal expression used to calculate the order line total for a given unit price, quantity and discount:

```
LineTotal = (OrderQuantity * UnitPrice) * (1 - UnitPriceDiscount)
```

Roles

A role defines an entity relationship. An example of entity relationships are "a customer has orders" or "an order header has order items". You can define different role cardinalities between entities, such as one-to-one or one-to-many. From an end-user perspective, roles define the navigational paths for entity selection. For example, given a one-to-many relationship between Customer and Orders, a user can view multiple orders for a single customer. Without roles, there is no navigation path. For example, suppose that the Customer and Vendor entities are not related via a role. When the user selects an attribute from the Customer entity, the Report Builder 1.0 client won't let the user add vendor-specific attributes.

Folders

Folders are a purely metadata construct that have no counterpart in a database schema. You use folders to group related fields together to make your model more user-friendly. For example, if a Customer entity has many fields, you might group the demographics-related fields into a Demographics folder, contact-related fields into a Contact folder, and so on.

Filters

You can set up an entity filter to limit the data that the end user can see on the report. Filters are typically used for row-level security. For example, suppose that security requirements dictate that a sales person sees only his data. You can set up a filter on the Sales Person entity that returns a single row from the underlying table whose LoginID column matches the user login name.

8.1.3 Comparing Report Models and UDM

The Report Builder 1.0 model is not Microsoft's first attempt at providing a user-oriented model to facilitate reporting. Analysis Services introduced the Unified Dimensional Model (UDM) in SQL Server 2005. Readers who are familiar with UDM may wonder how report models compare with UDM and when to choose one over the other.

After all, there are many similarities between the two model types. Both models are designed to provide an intuitive user experience and interactive reporting. Both eliminate the need to join entities due to how they store entity relationships. Architecturally, both models include data source and data source view layers. Finally, both belong to components of SQL Server that share the same licensing model. At the same time, there are profound differences.

Understanding model differences

Table 8.1 outlines the differences between Report Model and UDM. Perhaps the most important difference is that a report model is biased towards relational data sources that support well normalized schemas, such as those used in OLTP databases. In contrast, UDM favors dimensional modeling where additional work may be needed to organize data in a set of dimension and fact tables.

Table 8.1 Report Model vs. Unified Dimensional Model

Criteria	Report Model	Unified Dimensional Model
Database schema	Relational	Dimensional
Data volumes	Small to medium	Large
Data sources	SQL Server, Oracle, Analysis Services	All OLE DB and .NET-compliant data sources
Hierarchies	Attribute	Attribute, user-defined, parent-child
End-user features	Perspectives	Perspectives, translations, KPIs, Actions
Security	Model, attribute, and row-level	Dimension, dimension data, and cell security
Query language	Semantic Query	MDX
Programmability	Basic proprietary language and functions	MDX
Extensibility	No	Yes
Reporting tools	Report Builder 1.0 Client, Report Designer	Report Designer, Report Builder 1.0 Client, Excel, ProClarity, third-party

Now, don't jump to hasty conclusions that report models are easier to build because they don't require schema changes. The primary goal of dimensional modeling is to optimize the database schema for reporting purposes. Therefore, irrespective of the model technology, end users will certainly benefit from simplifying large and complex schemas by denormalizing them in accordance to dimensional modeling best practices. Simple schemas reduce the guesswork required to find which table stores the data that is needed for the report. Assuming that data is already stored in a dimensional database, the effort needed to implement both models should be about the same.

NOTE To get a better idea of the differences between relational and dimensional modeling, take a look at the AdventureWorks and AdventureWorksDW sample databases. Note that the AdventureWorks database schema is highly normalized and has some 70 tables. In comparison, the AdventureWorksDW schema is denormalized to a much smaller set of dimension and fact tables and it is more suitable for reporting purposes.

In terms of performance, UDM is generally better. Analysis Services is designed to scale well with large reporting loads, such as trend reports that aggregate historical data. For example, UDM can handle queries from pre-aggregated data summaries called aggregations. Besides better performance, UDM is a more mature and richer model. In contrast, report models do not provide equivalents of the following UDM features: data hierarchies (parent-child, user-defined, ragged), KPIs, a flexible and proactive security model, currency conversion, data mining, or data and metadata localization. Finally, there are many reporting tools that can source data from Analysis Services cubes, while the report models are supported only by the Report Builder 1.0 client and Report Designer.

When to choose a report model

Given these observations, I suggest that you consider a Report Builder 1.0 model when the following conditions are true:

- Relational data source—a semantic model used with the Report Builder 1.0 client is a good choice when end users are producing ad hoc reports straight from relational sources. Report Builder 1.0 is deeply rooted in relational reporting and handles well normalized database schemas. That said, be careful with highly normalized schemas because they may be counter-intuitive to end users. The more entities the model has, the more confusing it will be to navigate through the model.

- Small to medium-size data loads—In general, the more data the report aggregates, the slower report models and Report Builder 1.0 reports perform. For example, a Sales by Year trend report that aggregates all sales data would take much longer to execute than a Sales Order report that shows the details for a single order. When in doubt as to whether Report Builder 1.0 can handle your data volumes, quickly auto-generate a report model on top of your database and test a few reports that aggregate data. Increase the query time at least twice to account for multi-user report loads. If the report performance is not adequate, you don't have much choice as far as Report Builder 1.0 is concerned. It virtually impossible to optimize the database design given that semantic queries will differ greatly from one report to another. Moreover, you can't tune semantic queries because they are auto-generated.

TIP When facing performance issues with large data volumes, your best bet may be replacing relational reporting and report models with dimensional reporting and Analysis Services. Unfortunately, this may require replacing the Report Builder 1.0 client as well because its Analysis Services support is limited. Instead, consider Report Builder 2.0, which features a drag-and-drop MDX Query Designer.

- Simple ad hoc reporting needs—Don't expect more from Report Builder 1.0 than what an ad hoc reporting tool can reasonably deliver. More advanced data analytics requirements, such as interactive reporting, hierarchies, and KPIs, go beyond the Report Builder 1.0 capabilities. You will need UDM if you have advanced requirements.

In summary, choose the right tool for the job. Consider Report Builder 1.0 for simple ad hoc reporting from small to medium-size relational databases. Consider UDM when data loads and report requirements surpass the capabilities of Report Builder 1.0.

Here is a good business scenario for using the Report Builder 1.0, which I "borrowed" from real life. We have a SQL Server 2000 database with sales data. The database has about twenty tables with the largest table containing about two hundred thousand records. In this scenario, our sales people were looking for ways to produce their own reports with minimum impact on the IT staff. Enter Report Builder 1.0. We auto-generated a semantic model on top of the sales database. We trained the business users how to maintain the model and produce reports so they could take ownership over not only the reports, but the model as well. The end users loved the solution and it took us only a few hours to set it up! Now that you have a good high-level overview of Report Builder 1.0 and when to use it, it's time to walk through the implementation steps.

8.2 Implementing Report Models

Recall that as a prerequisite for building ad hoc reports, you need to build a report model that provides a business-oriented metadata layer on top of the data source. Suppose the Adventure Works management has decided to empower its sales force with an ad hoc reporting solution. This solution would allow the sales people to author simple table, matrix, and chart reports without requiring any technical knowledge of the data source schema or a query language. As it stands, the AdventureWorks database captures three-years worth of sales data with a few hundred thousand rows in the largest table.

Another project is under way to build an OLAP solution, but it will take a few months to complete. Meanwhile, you need to implement a more light-weight solution to address the immediate ad hoc reporting needs of the sales force. While gathering operational requirements, you determine that there are seventeen sales people. Each sales person will author and run no more than fifty reports per day. You conclude that ad hoc reporting straight from the AdventureWorks database will not impact the performance of the OLTP sales system. You decide to implement an ad hoc solution that leverages Report Builder 1.0.

8.2.1 Working with Data

Recall a report model consists of data source, data source view, and semantic layers. To build the entire model, implement each layer in this order starting with the data source.

NOTE The report model you will build next uses the SQL Server 2005 AdventureWorks (not AdventureWorks**2008**) database. The book front matter (Source Code section) includes instructions for downloading and installing the AdventureWorks database.

Creating a Report Model project

As a first step for implementing a report model, create a Report Model project in BIDS. Follow these steps to create an Adventure Works Report Model project:

1. Start SQL Server Business Intelligence Development Studio from the Microsoft SQL Server 2008 program group. Choose File ⇨ New Project or press Ctrl+Shft+N.
2. In the New Project dialog box that follows, make sure that the Business Intelligence Projects node is selected in the Project Types pane. In the Templates pane, select the Report Model Project template.
3. Enter *Adventure Works Report Model* as a name of the project and a project location. Click OK to create the project.

BIDS creates an empty Report Model project. The Solution Explorer window shows three folders—Data Sources, Data Source Views, and Report Models—that correspond to the ad hoc model layers presented in Figure 8.2.

Creating a data source

A data source provides connection information for accessing the database. At design time, Report Builder 1.0 uses the data source to retrieve the database metadata and data statistics. Once the report model is deployed on a production server, Report Builder 1.0 uses the data source to send report queries and retrieve data. Follow these steps to define a data source that points to the AdventureWorks database:

1. In the BIDS Solution Explorer, right-click on the Data Sources folder and choose Add New Data Source. This starts the Data Source Wizard.
2. In the Select How to Define the Connection step, click New to define a new connection.

In the Connection Manager dialog box that follows (see Figure 8.3), make sure that the SQLClient Data Provider is pre-selected in the Provider drop-down. Since the report server is implemented in .NET managed code, the SqlClient provider gives you the best performance when connecting to SQL Server-based data sources.

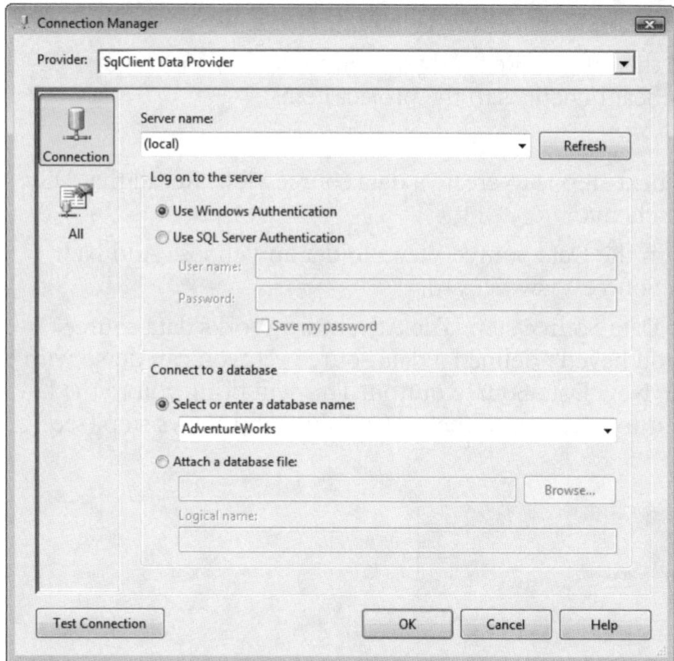

Figure 8.3 Use the Connection Manager to set up and edit the data source definition.

3. Expand the Provider drop-down and note that it has only two .NET data providers: SQLClient Data Provider to connect to SQL Server and OracleClient Data Provider to connect to Oracle. The Analysis Services data provider is not listed. That's because an Analysis Services based report model cannot be generated from scratch but must be auto-generated in the Report Manager (or SharePoint).
4. Enter the name of the SQL Server instance that hosts the AdventureWorks database. To connect to your local server, enter *(local)*. To connect to a SQL Server named instance, use the ServerName\InstanceName syntax.
5. Leave the Use Windows Authentication option selected if you want the SQL Server to authenticate users with Windows integrated security. Choose the Use SQL Server Authentication option if you prefer standard authentication and enter the user name and password.

NOTE Windows Integrated security is recommended for several reasons. First, it is more secure since the connection string doesn't store the password. Second, users maintain their passwords, not you. Finally, Windows Integrated security lets you define row-level security based on the Windows identity of the interactive user. As a prerequisite for the user to authenticate successfully to SQL Server with Windows Integrated security, you need to create SQL Server logins for each user or Windows group(s) the user belong to and grant the logins at least read-only access to the database.

6. Expand the Select or Enter a Database Name drop-down and select the AdventureWorks database.
7. Click the Test Connection button to verify that you can connect to the database. If all is well, click OK to return to the Data Source Wizard.
8. Click Next to advance to the Completing the Wizard step and accept *Adventure Works* as a data source name. Click Finish to create the Adventure Works data source. If you need to change the data source definition later on, in the Solution Explorer, expand the Data Sources

folder, double-click on the Adventure Works.ds item to open the Data Source Designer dialog box, and click Edit to open the Connection Manager dialog box.

9. Click the Save toolbar button to save the project. Remind yourself to do this on a regular basis, such as after you have made significant changes to the project items.

Creating a data source view

Once the data source is in place, the next step is to create a data source view. Recall that DSV abstracts the underlying data source schema.

1. In the Solution Explorer, right-click on the Data Source Views folder and choose Add New Data Source View to launch the Data Source View Wizard.
2. Click Next to advance to the Select a Data Source step. The Adventure Works data source should be pre-selected. Note that if you haven't defined a data source yet, you can do so without leaving the wizard by clicking the New Data Source button. This will bring you to the familiar Data Source Wizard. Click Next to move on to the Select Tables and Views step (see Figure 8.4).

Figure 8.4 Use the Select Table and Views step to select the tables and views that will be included in the data source view.

The Data Source View Wizard retrieves a list of the tables and views in the AdventureWorks database. For the sake of simplicity, our reporting model will be limited to a few tables only. These tables will let end users browse sales order data by the most significant business perspectives—Sales Person, Sales Territory, Product, Customer, and Store.

3. Double-click the Name column header of the Available Objects grid to sort the schema objects alphabetically. Select the Employee (HumanResources), Contact (Person), Product (Production), ProductSubcategory (Production), Customer (Sales), SalesOrderDetail (Sales), SalesOrderHeader (Sales), SalesPerson (Sales), SalesTerritory (Sales), and Store (Sales) tables. You can hold the Ctrl key for selecting multiple items or the Shift key for extended selection.
4. Click the > button to add these tables to the Included Objects pane. You can double-click the object name to include the object.

5. You can use the Add Related Tables button to add all related tables to a selected table in the Included Objects pane. Select the ProductSubcategory (Production) table and click the Add Related Tables button. The ProductCategory (Production) table is added to the list. Click Next.

6. In the Completing the Wizard step, accept the default name for the data source view—Adventure Works—and click Finish. The Data Source Wizard generates the Adventure Works data source view and adds its definition to the Data Source Views folder in Solution Explorer.

   Let's take a look at the Adventure Works data source view and make some changes to it.

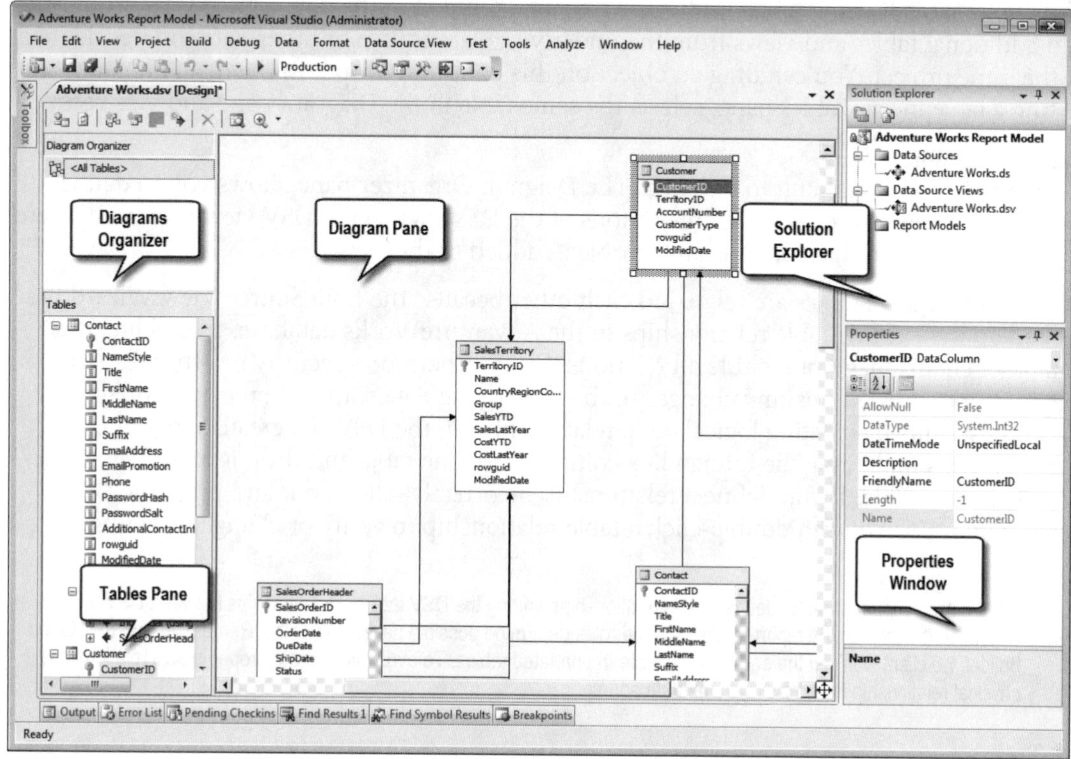

Figure 8.5 The Adventure Works data source view loaded in the Data Source View Designer.

Understanding the Data Source View Designer

Recall that you can use a data source view to augment the database schema (such as adding logical relationships, logical primary keys, named calculations, and named queries) without affecting the underlying data source.

1. Double-click on Adventure Works.dsv in the Solution Explorer to open in the Data Source View Designer (see Figure 8.5).

2. Expand the Zoom toolbar button and select To Fit to fit the data source view diagram in the Diagram Pane.

   The DSV Designer is divided into three panes to show you different views of the data source schema.

Diagram pane

The Diagram pane shows the data source schema of the selected tables (views) and their relations. By default, the DSV Designer will analyze the table schema and join the tables based on the referential integrity relationships defined in the database schema. If you wish, you can use the NameMatchingCriteria property in the Properties window to change this behavior, such as joining two tables that have keys with the same name. You can right-click on an object to see a context menu with relevant commands. For example, if you want to see the table data, right-click on a table and select Explore Data.

Tables pane

The Tables pane lists the tables and views that are included in the data source view. You can add additional tables and views from the underlying data source or other data sources defined in the same project. You can drag an object off this pane and drop it in the diagram pane. Selecting a table in the Tables pane, selects the same table in the Diagram pane and vice versa.

Diagram Organizer pane

A large DSV can be difficult to navigate. The Diagram Organizer pane allows you to define logical views that comprise different sections of the DSV. When the DSV view is created, there is only one diagram that contains all the objects added to the view.

Observe that the all tables are related to each other because the Data Source View Wizard has picked up the existing table relationships in the AdventureWorks database. In real life, the database schema may not include all relationships. Furthermore, security or other restrictions may prevent you from making changes to the underlying data source. You can work around these constraints by creating logical table relationships in the DSV. To create a logical table relationship, simple drag the foreign key column from one table and drop it onto the primary key of another table. If you define a relationship incorrectly, click on it and press the Delete key to remove it. You can double-click a table relationship to verify or change its configuration.

NOTE It is very important to define proper relationships among the DSV tables. Relationships between DSV tables determine the roles in the report model, and the roles determine possible navigation paths. Remember that the Report Builder 1.0 client won't let the end user navigate to unrelated tables. To avoid this, create proper logical relationships if physical relationships are missing in the data source.

Working with named queries

Sometimes, you may need to use a query to filter a table or combine columns from two or more tables in the DSV. If you have rights to create objects in the database, I recommend you define a SQL view for performance and security reasons. However, if security or other limitations prevent you from changing the database schema, you can create a named query—the DSV equivalent of a SQL View. For example, suppose that you need the employees' manager name in the Employee table.

1. In the Data Source View Designer, right-click on the Employee table and choose Replace Table ➪ With New Named Query.
2. In the SQL pane of the Create Named Query dialog (see Figure 8.6), enter the following SELECT statement, which you can find in the Employee.sql file in the source code:

```
SELECT E.EmployeeID, E.NationalIDNumber, E.ContactID, E.LoginID, E.ManagerID, E.Title, E.BirthDate,
    E.MaritalStatus, E.Gender, E.HireDate, E.SalariedFlag, E.VacationHours, E.SickLeaveHours,
    E.CurrentFlag, E.rowguid, E.ModifiedDate, C.FirstName + ' ' + C.LastName AS ManagerName
FROM  HumanResources.Employee AS E LEFT OUTER JOIN Person.Contact AS C ON E.ContactID=C.ContactID
```

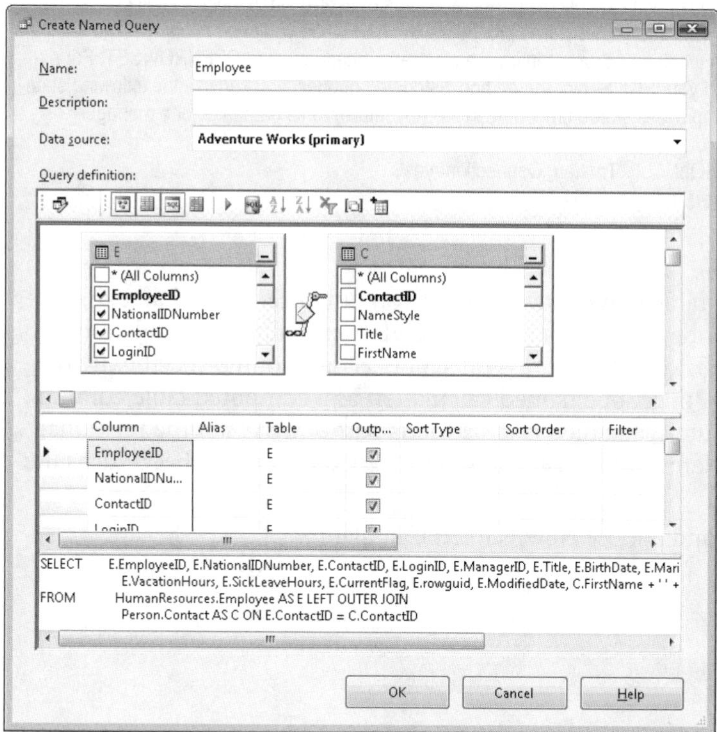

Figure 8.6 Use a named query to create a DSV table based on a SQL SELECT statement.

3. Click the Run button (green triangle icon) to execute and test the statement. Click OK to return to the DSV Designer.

Note that the Employee table has a different icon that indicates that the Employee item is now a named query. Right-click on the table and choose Edit Named Query if you want to change the query later on.

Named queries are also useful when you need to retrieve data from another data source. As I mentioned in section 8.1.2, Report Builder 1.0 doesn't natively support multiple data sources. There are two workarounds and both require SQL Server. From a performance standpoint, the recommended approach is to configure the other data source as a linked server to your SQL Server instance. Once you set up the linked server, you can create a view in the SQL Server database that queries that server. Another option is to implement a named query that sends an ad hoc distributed query to the other data source. For example, suppose that the Employee data is kept in a database hosted by an Oracle server. You can use the following named query to retrieve the employee data:

```
SELECT * FROM OPENROWSET ('MSDAORA', 'server';'user';'pwd', 'select * from Employee')
```

I included the SQL Server equivalent of the above statement in the OpenRowset.sql file. Sometimes, the DSV Designer is unable to determine a column that is a good primary key candidate for a named query. You won't be able to bind an entity to a table if the table doesn't have a primary key defined. However, you can create a logical primary key on a column that uniquely identifies each row. To do so, in the DSV Designer right-click the column and choose Set Logical Primary Key. Primary keys can be easily identified by their special key icon. You can have composite primary keys that span more than one column.

TIP Report Builder 1.0 doesn't officially support executing stored procedures or user-defined functions in DSV. At the same time, you may need to base a named query on a stored procedure, such as when you need to apply some rules that filter the records that are returned. As a workaround, you can invoke a stored procedure using OPENROWSET. For example, assuming that you have enabled your SQL Server for ad hoc distributed queries, you can use the following statement to execute the uspGetManagerEmployees stored procedure in the AdventureWorks database for a manager identifier of 16:

```
SELECT a.* FROM OPENROWSET('SQLNCLI', 'Trusted_Connection=yes',
'[AdventureWorks].[dbo].uspGetManagerEmployees 16') AS a
```

Working with named calculations

You don't have to convert a DSV table to a named query if you only need to add an expression-based column. Instead, consider creating a named calculation. A named calculation is a column that is based on an expression. The expression syntax is data source-specific. If you have experience with SQL Server, think of a named calculation as a computed table column. However, unlike a computed column, a named calculation is part of DSV, not the relational table definition. Let's add a FullName named calculation to the Contact table that returns the contact full name.

1. Right-click on the Contact table and choose New Named Calculation.
2. In the Create Named Calculation dialog box (see Figure 8.7), enter FullName in the Column Name field.

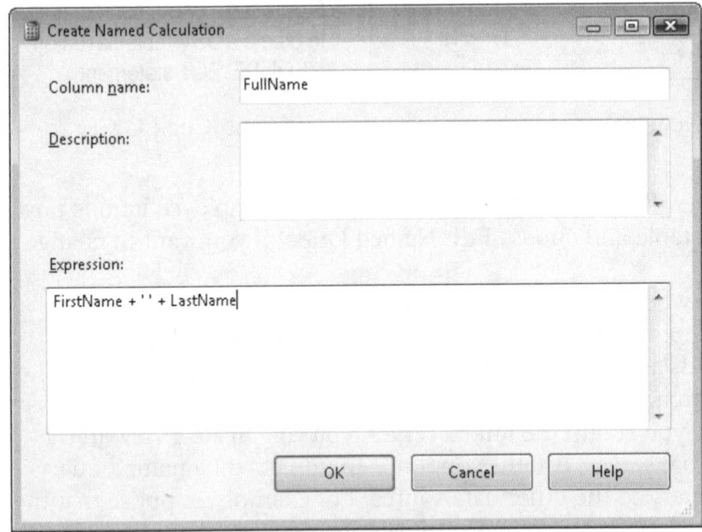

Figure 8.7 Create a named calculation to add an expression-based column to a DSV table.

3. Enter the following expression in the Expression field:

```
FirstName + ' ' + LastName
```

4. Click OK to create the FullName named calculation and return to the DSV Designer. A new named calculation column with a special icon will be added to the Contact table.
5. Right-click on the Contact table and choose Explore Data. Scroll all the way to the right in the Explore Contact Table grid to see the data in the FullName column.

A named calculation can span tables. Suppose that you need to add the product subcategory name from the ProductSubcategory table to the Product table. Define a new named calculation in the Product table that uses the following statement:

```
(SELECT Name as Subcategory
FROM Production.ProductSubcategory
WHERE ProductSubcategoryID=Production.Product.ProductSubcategoryID)
```

Working with diagrams

Your DSVs may contain many tables. Similar to SQL Server diagrams, you can create DSV diagrams to organize tables in logical subject areas. By default, the DSV Designer creates a diagram named <All Tables> that includes all tables in the DSV. Let's create a diagram that shows only the tables related to the SalesOrderDetail table.

1. Right-click on the <All Tables> item in the Diagram Organizer pane and choose New Diagram.
2. Rename the diagram in-place to *Sales Order*.
3. Drag the SalesOrderDetail table from the Tables pane to the designer canvas.
4. Right-click on the SalesOrderDetail table on the designer canvas and choose Show Related Tables. The DSV Designer adds the Sales Order Header and Product tables.

Dealing with schema changes

Changes made to the underlying data source schema are not automatically reflected in the DSV. To update the view, you need to refresh it by either clicking on the Refresh toolbar button or selecting the Refresh command from the Data Source View menu. The refresh process compares the view schema with the underlying data source schema. If changes are detected, the view is updated and you are presented with a helpful report of the changes made. You cannot pick individual objects to refresh. This may look like a limitation, but in the vast majority of cases you would typically want to get all schema changes at the same time. This way, you don't leave the view in an inconsistent state that might break the report model.

TIP When the DSV is first created, the table columns are ordered in the same way as in the underlying data source table. When you refresh your DSV, new columns that are discovered are added at the end of the table. At this point, the order of columns may be out of sync with the database. If you want to order DSV columns in a specific way, e.g. sort them alphabetically, you can do so in the DSV source file. To do so, in the Solution Explorer window, right-click on DSV and choose View Code. Then, search for table name and reorder the columns as desired.

Changes to the underlying DSV are not automatically propagated up to the semantic model. For example, if a column is renamed in the DSV, the name of the corresponding attribute doesn't change. Moreover, the attribute binding will not change and you will get an error when you try to build the model. Similarly, changes made to DSV schema are never propagated down to the data source. In other words, DSV only reads from and never writes to the data source. Refreshing a data source view updates only the tables and views included in the DSV. If you want to add a new object, such as a table or a view, you need to do so manually, as I will demonstrate in section 8.3.3.

8.2.2 Generating the Raw Model

Having implemented the Adventure Works DSV, we are ready to tackle the last layer of the Report Builder 1.0 report model—the semantic model. Recall that the semantic model represents the business-oriented view of the model—that is the layer that the end users will interact with. To jump-start the model generation, the Reporting Services team has provided (you guessed it) a handy Report Model Wizard.

TIP You can use the Report Manager to auto-generate a default report model without the wizard by clicking the Generate Model button in the data source properties page. Behind the scenes, the Report Manager invokes the ReportingService2005.GenerateModel method. First, this method generates a DSV that includes all tables in the data source. Next, GenerateModel creates a default model and embeds the DSV in the model. This is exactly what the Report Model Wizard does except that you get more control over the generation process, such as specifying a subset of rules to be applied.

Running the Report Model Wizard

Generating the Adventure Works semantic model with the Report Model Wizard takes just a few clicks.

1. In the Solution Explorer, right-click on the Report Models folder and choose Add New Report Model to launch the Report Model Wizard.
2. In the Select Data Source View step, Adventure Works.dsv should be pre-selected in the Available Data Source Views pane. Click Next to advance to the Select Report Model Generation Rules step (Figure 8.8).

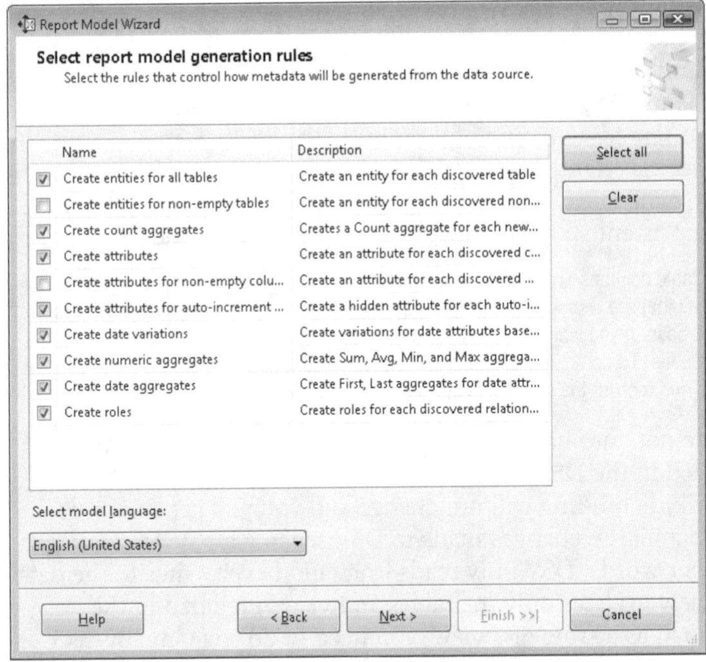

Figure 8.8 The Report Model Wizard applies various rules that control the generation of the semantic model.

The Report Model Wizard generates the raw model in two passes and each pass applies generation rules. In the first pass, the Report Wizard discovers and creates entities and attributes. Optionally, it can create various expression-based attributes. For example, when you select the Create Count Aggregates rule, the Report Model Wizard generates count aggregates, such as # of Orders. Similarly, if you check the Create Numeric Aggregates rule, the wizard creates the aggregate attribute on numeric fields such as sum, avg, min and max.

The second pass refines the model. For example, during the second pass the Report Model Wizard might assign appropriate attribute formats, such as currency, dates, and so on. The generation rules are described in more detail in the Select Report Model Generation Rules topic in SQL Server Books Online (see Resources). I recommend that you keep the default selections to save time. You can always delete the changes later on if you decide that you don't need them. The Model Language drop-down list lets you choose a default culture for formatting date and numbers. You can overwrite it later by changing the DataCulture attribute property.

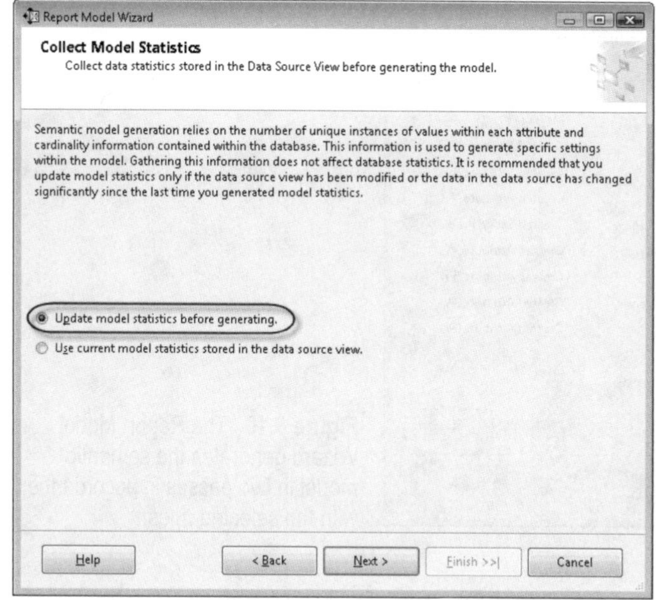

Figure 8.9 The Report Model Wizard needs the model statistics to default data cardinality and instance selection properties.

In the Collect Model Statistics step (Figure 8.9), the Report Model Wizard offers to gather model statistics by examining the database schema and sampling data. It uses the statistics to discover data cardinality and uniqueness. For example, model statistics help the wizard detect one-to-one or one-to-many relationships between entities and to detect a default value for the attribute instance selection, such as a drop-down or list.

The wizard stores the model statistics in the data source view. Because gathering data statistics is time-consuming for large databases, consider accepting the default Update Model Statistics option only when generating a new model. Consider using the Use Current Model Statistics option only if you later regenerate all or part of the model and the data hasn't changed significantly in the database.

3. Accept the Update Model Statistics Before Generating option and click Next.
4. In the Completing the Wizard step (see Figure 8.10), accept Adventure Works as the default name for the model and click Run. Choose descriptive names for your models. This is important because the name you provide determines how end users will identify the model in the Report Builder 1.0 client.

Once the Adventure Works model is generated, the wizard loads it in the Model Designer.

5. Click Finish to close the wizard. If the Adventure Works DSV is open in the DSV Designer, BIDS prompts you to reload the DSV since the wizard has updated it with the model statistics.

Note that a new file, AdventureWorks.smdl, has been added to the Report Models folder in the Solution Explorer. If you need to rename the model later on, double-click its name or right-click and choose Rename.

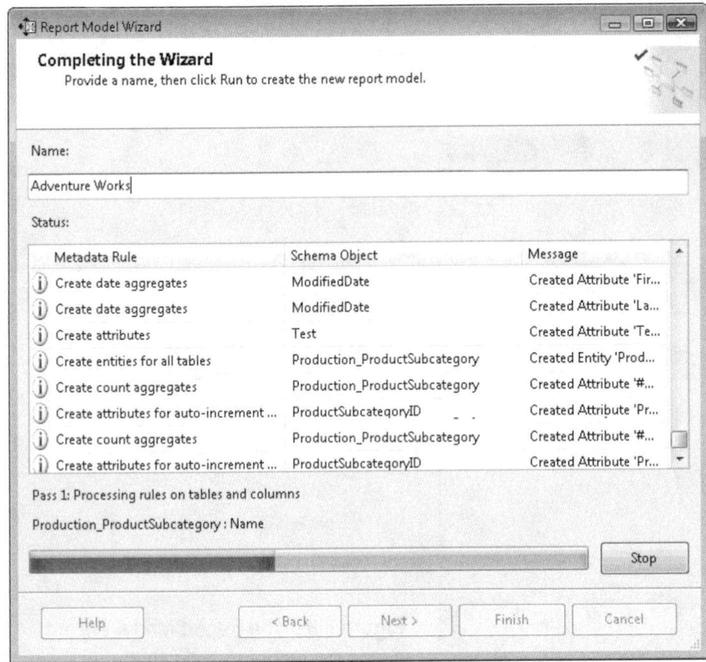

Figure 8.10 The Report Model Wizard generates the semantic model in two passes in accordance with the selected rules.

Exploring the Adventure Works model

Figure 8.11 shows the raw Adventure Works model that the wizard has created. Looking at the left pane, you see that the Report Model Wizard has generated an entity for each DVS table, such as Contact, Customer, and so on. When you select an entity, the Model Designer displays its fields in the right pane. Note that the Report Model Wizard has automatically generated user-friendly names for entities and fields by separating the words in the underlying column names with a space, such as Sales Order instead of SalesOrder.

You can easily deduce the field type by examining its icon. Text-based attributes are prefixed with **a**. For example, in the Sales Order Detail entity, Carrier Tracking Number is a text-based attribute. In comparison, numeric and expression-based attributes are prefixed with #. For example, the Order Qty field of the Sales Order Detail entity is a numeric attribute. To tell expressions apart from numeric attributes, examine the Expression property in the Properties pane. If the Expression property contains a value, the attribute is an expression.

Because the Create Numeric Aggregates rule is selected by default, the wizard has generated Sum, Avg, Min, and Max aggregate expressions for each numeric attribute. For example, the wizard has generated a Total Unit Price expression that uses the formula SUM(Unit Price), as you can see by clicking the ellipsis (…) button in the Expression property. In addition, the wizard has set the Total Unit Price VariationOf property to point to the Unit Price attribute. Numeric aggregates are very useful because they tell Report Builder 1.0 how to aggregate data. For example, if the end user authors a report that includes the Product and Total Unit Price attributes, Report Builder 1.0 will sum up the Total Unit Price at the product level.

If an attribute has numeric aggregates, you can specify a default numeric aggregate that Report Builder 1.0 will use to aggregate data when the attribute is requested on the report. By default, the Report Model Wizard sets the Total numeric aggregate as a default aggregate since

SUM is the most common aggregate function. For example, if you inspect the DefaultAggregateAttribute property of the Unit Price attribute, you will notice that it is set to Total Unit Price.

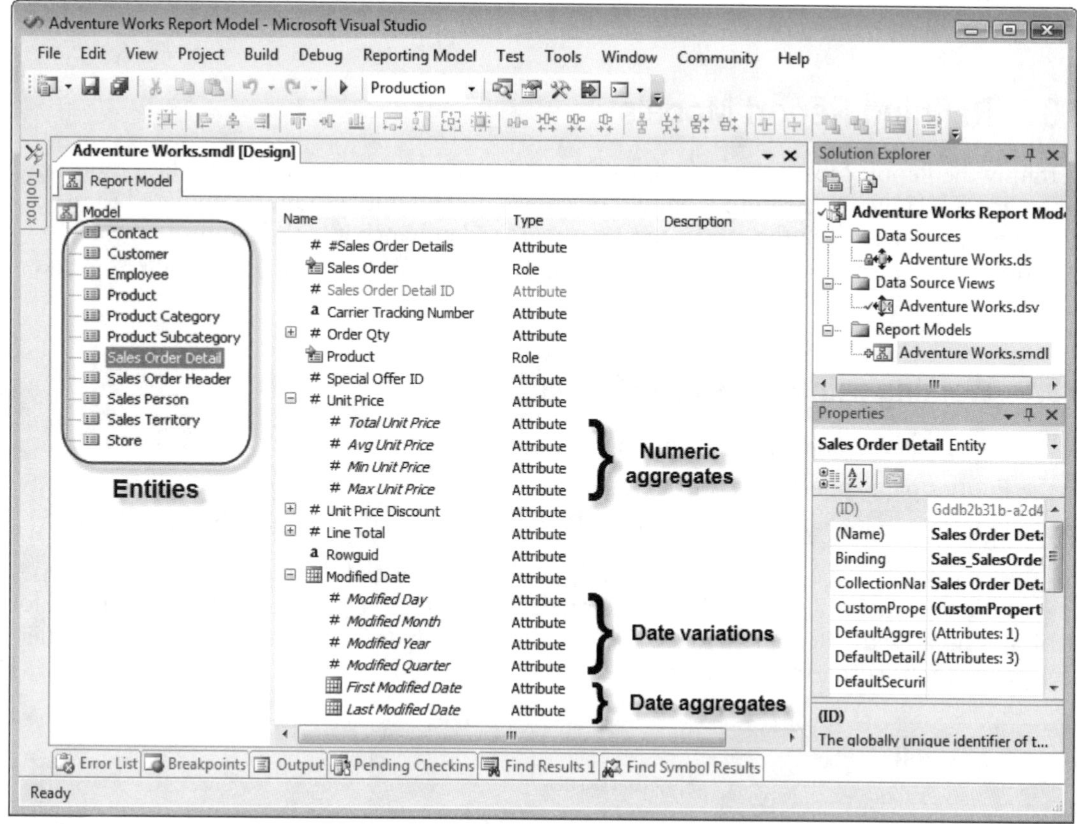

Figure 8.11 The Report Model Wizard generates an entity for each DSV table and an attribute for each column.

Similarly, since the Create Date Variations rule was pre-selected, the wizard has generated date variations for date columns, such as Day, Month, Year, and so on. For example, the Modified Date attribute includes Modified Day, Modified Month, and so on. Date variations make it easier to define useful report filters. For example, a filter that specifies Modified Year = 2004 will return sales orders for year 2004 only. The Create Date Aggregates rule (selected by default) also generates date aggregates. Examples include First Modified Date with an expression of Min(Modified Date) and Last Modified Date with an expression of Max(Modified Date). Because I accepted the default Create Count Aggregates rule, the Report Model Wizard has also generated expressions that use the Count aggregate function, such as #Contacts in the Contact entity. Reports can use these expressions to count records (for example, showing the number of contacts per customer).

By examining the right pane, you can also see the roles defined for the selected entity. For example, the Sales Order Detail entity has Sales Order and Product roles because the SalesOrderDetail table is related to the SalesOrderHeader and Product tables. If the role's icon shows a single rectangle, the cardinality between the two entities is One. For instance, a sales order detail can be associated with a single product. If the icon shows multiple rectangles, the cardinality is Many, such as a customer who has many orders.

The Report Model Wizard doesn't generate folders and filters. If needed, you can manually define these fields when you refine the model.

8.3 Refining Report Models

Certainly the Report Model Wizard goes a long way to jump-start the implementation of the report model. However, its output should be considered an initial draft. Be prepared to make additional passes through the model to fine-tune it and enhance it with features that the wizard doesn't support. Let's visit each item in the Adventure Works model and make some additional changes.

8.3.1 Working with Entities and Fields

Let's start by entering a helpful description for the model.

1. In the Entities pane, select the root Model node.
2. In the Properties pane, enter *The Adventure Works Report Model* in the Description property.

For the sake of brevity, I won't specify descriptions for the rest of the model items although you should consider doing so with real-life models. Having descriptions is especially useful for attributes because the Report Builder 1.0 client displays the descriptions as tooltips when the user points the mouse to the item.

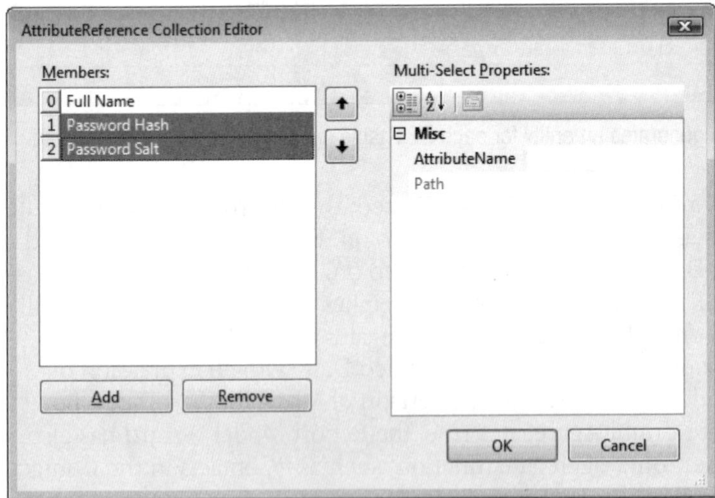

Figure 8.12 Use the AttributeReference Collection Editor to specify one or more default attributes.

Contact entity

In the Adventure Works model, the Contact entity represents a person's contact details, such as first name, last name, email address, and so on. The Report Builder 1.0 client uses the entity's DefaultDetailAttributes collection to auto-select which fields show up on the report when the user drags and drops the entity itself. In addition, Report Builder 1.0 uses this collection when it auto-generates a drillthrough multi-instance report, such as showing a list of the individual sales order items when the user clicks on an aggregated Line Total number. I suggest you keep the DefaultDetailAttributes list short by choosing a limited number of useful attributes that the user may want to see by default.

1. In Model Designer, select the Contact entity and click the … button inside the DefaultDetail-Attributes property in the Properties pane.

   This opens the AttributeReference Collection Editor dialog box, as shown in Figure 8.12. Note that the wizard has identified Full Name, Password Hash, and Password Salt as default attributes. You definitely don't want the last two as default attributes so let's replace them with the Email Address attribute.

2. Select the Password Hash and Password Salt attributes and click the Remove button.
3. Press the Add button to open the Default Detail Attributes dialog, as shown in Figure 8.13.

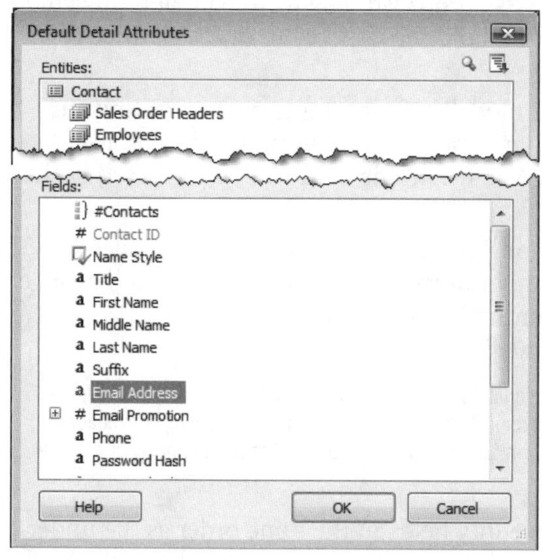

Figure 8.13 Keep the Default-DetailAttributes list short to include just a few useful attributes.

4. Select the Email Address attribute and click OK. Click OK again to return to the Model Designer.

Report Builder 1.0 doesn't provide a way to set a default value for an attribute. To workaround this, consider the filtering options available in the Report Builder 1.0 client (for example, relative dates). Adding a filtering option might be useful if you want a report parameter to default to a certain value, such as the last month with data.

Another important entity property is IdentifyingAttributes. When I first encountered the IdentifyingAttributes property, I thought that the model used this property to *select* unique entity instances. For example, readers familiar with Analysis Services know that the Key-Columns attribute property in UDM tells the server how to determine unique attribute members when it builds the attribute hierarchy. This is not the case with Report Builder 1.0 since it doesn't create any hierarchies or store data. Instead, IdentifyingAttributes is simply a user-oriented property. The Report Builder 1.0 client uses it to help the end user identify an instance of the entity. For example, if the end user looks up a particular customer by an account number, you may want to set the IdentifyingAttributes property of the Customer entity to the Account Number attribute.

The Report Model Wizard employs certain heuristic rules to select the identifying attributes, which might cause it to select a column other than the one used as all or part of the table primary key. For instance, the presence of the word Name in the column name and near 100% uniqueness of the data in that column is often sufficient to select that column as the identifying attribute instead of the primary key. The wizard doesn't favor primary keys because they are usually system-generated and are not meant to be seen by end users. As a guideline, you should have only one attribute as an identifying attribute. The noticeable exception is if the entity contains a long list of items, such as cities, where the user might need to identify a single item by two or more columns, such as City and State.

5. Click the … button inside the IdentifyingAttributes property of the Contact entity. Note that the wizard has decided to use the Full Name attribute as an identifying attribute. We will accept the wizard's choice. Click OK.
6. In the Contact entity in the Model Designer, the Password Hash, Password Salt, and Rowguid attributes are not meaningful to end users. Press and hold the Ctrl key to select all three of them and press Delete to remove them.
7. The Modified Date attribute may be useful for the modeler (for example, when creating an expression that returns the recently added customers), but it is not useful for the end user. Select it and change its Hidden property to True. As a result, the field will be preserved in the model but won't be visible to users.
8. The Sales Order Headers role represents the relationship between the Contact and SalesOrderHeader table in DSV. To make its name more intuitive to end users, select it and change its Name property to *Sales Orders*. Note that its cardinality is set correctly to OptionalMany because a person may have none, one, or many orders.

TIP Use a plural case when naming roles with a Many or OptionalMany cardinality (Sales Orders, Employees). Use a single case when naming roles with a One or Optional One cardinality (Customer, Product). This naming convention can help the end user understand whether the report will break down further in the case of the "Many" cardinality or if only a single value will be returned.

By default, the Report Model Wizard arranges the entity fields in the same order as the underlying columns in the DSV table. The Report Builder 1.0 client preserves this order in the Fields pane. Unfortunately, neither the Model Designer nor the Report Builder 1.0 client supports an easy way to change the sort order of the metadata items. However, you can rearrange fields in the Report Model Designer by dragging them to the desired location.

9. To show the Full Name attribute after the Last Name attribute, drag the Full Name attribute below the Last Name attribute. Alternatively, right-click on the Full Name attribute and choose Move Up or Move Down context menus. To move several attributes, select them by holding the Ctrl key and drag them to a new position.

Customer entity

There are more than 19,000 customers in the Sales.Customer table in the AdventureWorks database. Generating a report for all customers may take a very long time. You can force the end user to specify a filter when a field from a large entity is used on the report. To do this, make the following changes to the Customer entity.

1. Select the Customer entity in the Entities pane and make sure its InstanceSelection property is set to MandatoryFilter.

2. You can tell Report Builder 1.0 how to display attribute values when the user sets up a filter on that attribute. The Customer Type attribute has only a couple of values: S for Store and I for Individual. Verify that its ValueSelection property is set to Dropdown.
3. Remove the Modified Date attribute from the DefaultDetailAttributes collection.
4. Delete the Rowguid attribute.
5. Set the Hidden property of the Modified Date attribute to True.
6. Rename the Sales Order Headers role to *Sales Orders*.

Employee entity

Adventure Works has less than 300 employees and business users would typically select a single employee when authoring employee-related reports.

1. In the Entities pane, select the Employee entity and change its InstanceSelection property to Dropdown. As a result, when the end user filters the Employee entity Report Builder 1.0 will present a drop-down list from which the user can pick a single employee.
2. Remove all attributes from the IdentifyingAttributes and DefaultDetailAttributes collections of the Employee entity and add the National ID Number attribute only.
3. Verify that the ValueSelection property of the Gender and Marital Status attributes is set to Dropdown.
4. Set the Hidden property of the Login ID and Modified Date attributes to True.
5. Delete the Rowguid attribute.

Product entity

The Product entity has many attributes. Let's organize some of them in logical folders so the end user can find them easily.

1. In the Entities pane, select the Product entity.
2. Right-click on an empty space in the Attributes pane and chose New Folder. A NewFolder field is added to the Product entity.
3. Rename the NewFolder folder in-place to *Manufacturing*.
4. Press and hold the Ctrl key and select the Make Flag, Finished Goods Flag, Safety Stock Level, Reorder Point, Size, Weight, Days to Manufacture, Size Unit Measure Code, and Weight Unit Measure Code attributes. Drag the selected attributes and drop them on the Manufacturing folder.
5. Create a new folder called *Dates*. Select the Sell Start Date, Sell End Date, and Discontinued Date attributes and move them to the Dates folder.
6. Delete the Product Model ID and Rowguid attributes. Hide the Modified Date attribute.
7. Make sure that the ValueSelection property of the Color, Product Line, Class, and Style attributes is set to Dropdown so Report Builder 1.0 client shows drop-downs when filtering on these attributes.
8. Set the Format property of the Standard Cost and List Price attributes, and their variations, such as Total Standard Cost, Avg Standard Cost, and so on, to C2 to format them as currency with two decimal places.

Product Category and Product Subcategories entities

Make the following changes to Product Category and Product Subcategory entities.

1. Make sure that the entity InstanceSelection property is set to Dropdown.
2. Make sure that the ValueSelection property of the Name field is set to Dropdown.
3. Change the DefaultDetailAttributes collection to include the Name attribute only.
4. Delete the Rowguid attribute and hide the ModifiedDate attribute.

Sales Order Detail entity

The Sales Order Detail entity represents a sales order line item.

1. Rename the Sales Order Detail entity to *Sales Order Item* and #Sales Order Details attribute to *#Order Items*.
2. Rename the Sales Order Detail ID attribute to *Line Item* and set its Hidden property to *False* to make this attribute visible to end users.
3. The IdentifyingAtributes collection of this entity should consist of the order number and line item number since this combination uniquely identifies a line number. Click the ... button inside the IdentifyingAttributes property. In the AttributeReferenceCollection dialog box, remove all fields.
4. Press the Add button to open the Identifying Attributes dialog box.

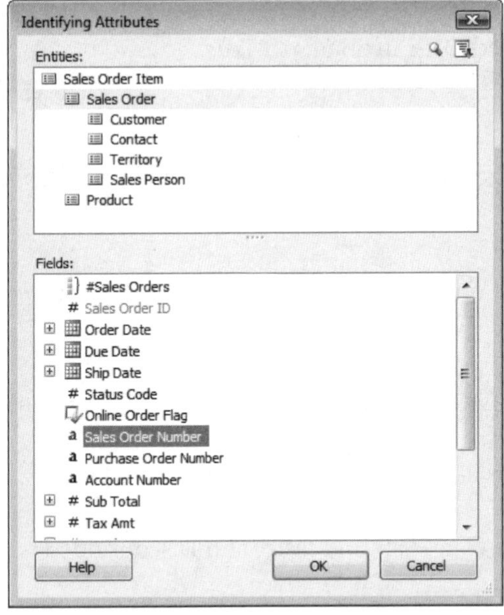

Figure 8.14 The Sales Order Item IdentifyingAttributes collection includes the Sales Order Number attribute from the Sales Order entity.

5. Click on the Sales Order entity and select the Sales Order Number attribute, as shown in Figure 8.14. Click OK.
6. Add the Line Item attribute from the Sales Order Item entity to the IdentifyingAttributes collection.
7. Configure the DefaultDetailAttributes collection to include the Line Number, Career Tracking Number, Order Qty, and Line Total fields.

An entity can have default aggregate attributes, which are useful for drillthrough reports. When a user clicks a drillthrough report, the resulting report contains all of the default detail attributes for the entity and the default aggregate attributes for all the entities that have a many-to-one relationship to the entity. For example, if the user clicks on a sales order number to see a single-instance drillthrough report, the report will show all non-hidden fields of the Sales Order entity, plus the default aggregate attributes of the Sales Order Item entity. This is because Sales Order has a one-to-many relationship with Sales Order Item.

8. Suppose that the user would like to see the total sales amount and order quantity on a drill-through report. Click the ... button inside the DefaultAggregateAttributes property. In the Default Aggregate Attributes dialog box, expand the Order Qty node, select the Total Order Qty aggregate and click OK. Repeat the last step to add the Total Line Total aggregate of the Line Total attribute.
9. Make sure that the InstanceSelection property of the Sales Order Item entity is set to MandatoryFilter. This forces the user to filter the entity if it is used on the report.
10. Delete the Special Offer ID and Rowguid attributes.
11. Set the Hidden property of Modified Date to True.
12. Select the Unit Price, Unit Price Discount, Line Total attributes and all of their aggregate variations and set the Format property to *C2* to format them as currency with two decimal places.

Sales Order Header entity

Make the following changes to the Sales Order Header entity.

1. Rename the Sales Order Header entity to Sales Order and #Sales Order Headers attribute to *#Sales Orders*.
2. Make sure that the InstanceSelection entity property is set to MandatoryFilter.
3. Delete the Revision Number, Rowguid, Bill To Address ID, Ship To Address ID, Ship Method ID, Credit Card ID, and Currency Rate ID attributes.
4. Set the Hidden property of the Modified Date attribute to True.

If you explore the data in the SalesOrderHeader table you will notice that the Status column contains integer values. This is why the Report Model Wizard generated aggregate variations of the Status attribute and formatted the Status attribute as a general number. However, the Status field could be more useful to end users if it did not have aggregate variations and showed the status name instead of a numeric value. Let's define an expression that will translate the numeric status codes to human-readable names.

5. Rename the Status attribute to *Status Code*. Delete its aggregate variations: Total Status, Avg Status, Min Status and Max Status.
6. Set the Hidden attribute of the Status Code attribute to True to make it unavailable to end users.
7. Right-click on an empty space inside the Attributes pane and choose New Expression to open the Define Formula dialog box.
8. Click the Functions tab, as shown in Figure 8.15. Note that Report Builder 1.0 supports many functions that you can use in expressions. The Switch function, found in the Conditional section, evaluates a list of expressions and returns the value associated with the first condition that returns True.

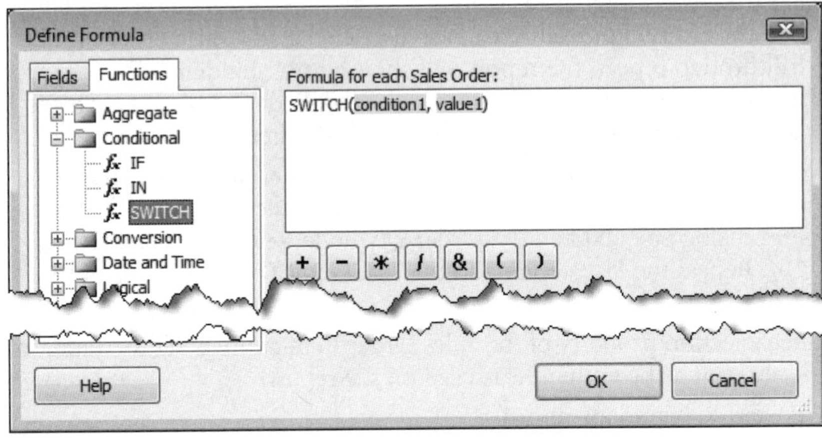

Figure 8.15 Report Builder 1.0 supports many functions that you can use in your expressions.

9. Expand the Conditional node and double-click the Switch function. This generates the following line in the Formula textbox:

```
Switch(condition1, value1)
```

The condition1 and value1 arguments are highlighted in yellow to let you know that you need to replace them with fields or functions.

10. Switch to the Fields tab.

NOTE If you need to use a field in a formula you cannot just type in the field name because Report Builder 1.0 won't be able to create a field reference. Instead, you need to use the Fields tab and either drag the field or double-click on it.

11. Click the condition1 argument to select it.

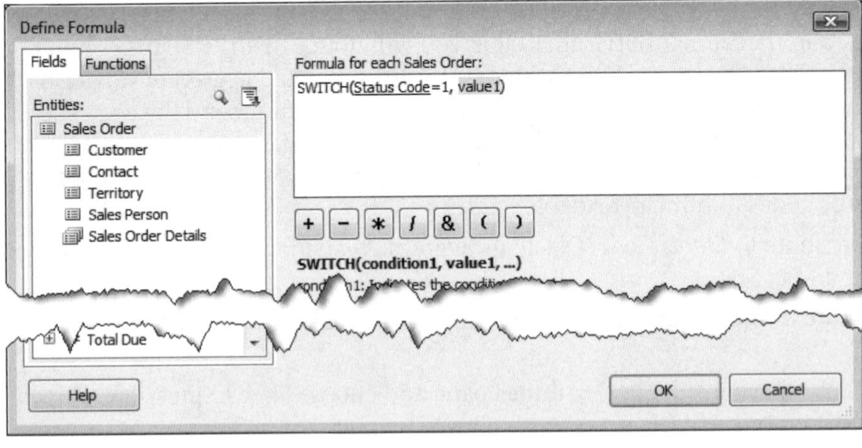

Figure 8.16 Use the Fields tab if you need to insert a field reference in the formula.

12. Double-click the Status Code to replace the condition1 argument with the Status Code field.
13. Place the mouse cursor after Status Code in the formula and type *=1*, as shown in Figure 8.16. The formula text changes to the following expression:

```
SWITCH(Status Code=1, value1)
```

14. If the status code is 1, we want our expression to return "New" as the order status. Click the value1 argument to select it and type *"New"*. The formula is now SWITCH(Status Code=1, "New").
15. Enter comma after "New" and repeat the last three steps four more times to define the following formula:

```
SWITCH(Status Code=1, "New", Status Code=2, "Cancelled", Status Code=3 , "Backordered",
Status Code=4, "Onhold", Status Code=5 , "Shipped")
```

16. Click OK to close the Define Formula dialog box. Rename the NewExpression expression you've just created to *Status*.
17. Change the Nullable property of the Status expression to True and the ValueSelection property to Dropdown.

Sales Person entity

The Sales Person entity represents the Adventure Works employees who are sales people. For now, we will make just a few changes. Later on, we will make more changes in section 8.3.2.

1. Select the Sales Person entity and make sure its InstanceSelection property is set to Dropdown.
2. Delete the Rowguid attribute.
3. Change the Hidden property of the Modified Date attribute to True.
4. Rename the Sales Order Headers role to *Sales Orders*.

Sales Territory entity

Adventure Works sells products both in the USA and internationally. The Sales Territory entity defines a common geographical hierarchy where sales territories are organized by continents (groups), countries, and regions. Unfortunately, Report Builder 1.0 doesn't support multi-level and parent-child hierarchies so we won't be able to define any. However, you can arrange attributes in an order that best approximates a parent-child hierarchy.

1. Make sure that the InstanceSelection of the Sales Territory entity is set to Dropdown.
2. Rename the Name attribute to *Region* and Country Region Code attribute to *Country*.
3. Select the Sales Territory entity and configure the DefaultDetailAtributes collection to include only the Region, Country, and Group attributes. Rearrange the attributes into the the order Group, Country, and Region so the user can see them ordered this way when they drag and Sales Territory Entity on the report. Click OK.
4. Select the Region, Country, and Group attributes and change their ValueSelection to Dropdown.
5. Delete the Rowguid attribute and change the Hidden property of the Modified Date attribute to True.
6. Remove the Modified Date field from the DefaultDetailAttributes collection of the Sales Territory entity.
7. Rename the Sales Order Headers role to *Sales Orders* to make its name more intuitive to the user.

Store entity

Besides direct sales over the Internet to individuals, Adventure Works sells to resellers. The Store entity represents a reseller.

1. Because the Demographics attribute is XML-based, it can't be shown as-is to end users. Select the Demographics attribute and delete it. Delete also the Rowguid attribute.
2. Set the Hidden property of the Modified Date attribute to True.
3. Remove the Modified Date field from the DefaultDetailAttributes collection of the Store entity.

As you have seen, refining a Report Builder 1.0 model requires a fair amount of routine and repetitive work. Let's now leverage a few advanced modeling techniques to enhance the Adventure Works model.

Verifying the model

When you build a Report Model project, Report Builder 1.0 verifies the model consistency against a set of pre-defined validation rules. Report Builder 1.0 flags all discovered violations as errors in the Visual Studio Error List pane. I recommend you build the model on a regular basis to catch and correct errors as early as possible during the design cycle.

1. In the Solution Explorer pane, right-click on the Adventure Works Report Model project and click Build or click Build ⇨Build Adventure Works Report Model from the main menu.
2. Examine the Error List pane.

There shouldn't be any errors listed.

8.3.2 Advanced Report Modeling

Report Builder 1.0 supports additional features to help you meet more advanced business requirements and make your models more intuitive to end users. These features include entity inheritance, role expansion, lookup entities, advanced expressions, and perspectives.

Entity inheritance

Report Builder 1.0 is typically used for ad hoc reporting against relational data sources. Relational databases are typically heavily normalized to operate at peak performance and store data efficiently. Unfortunately, normalized database schemas are not so suitable for ad hoc reporting. Consequently, business users may get lost trying to find the entity they need. Report Builder roles can certainly help by guiding the users to related entities, but many models can also benefit from denormalization techniques that reduce the perceived schema complexity.

The first technique for report model denormalization is entity inheritance. Consider this technique when one entity derives from another entity; that is, when one entity *is* another entity. For example, in the Adventure Works model, a sales person is an employee. It is likely that the end users would prefer to see the employee-related attributes when they browse the Sales Person entity instead of having to navigate to the Employee entity. Assuming that a foreign key relationship already exists between the two entities, you can implement entity inheritance easily by setting the Inheritance property of the derived entity.

1. In the Entities pane, select the Sales Person entity.
2. Expand the Inheritance property.
3. Expand the InheritsFrom drop-down list and select the Employee entity.
4. Expand the Binding drop-down list and select the FK_SalesPerson_Employee_SalesPersonID relationship, as shown in Figure 8.17.

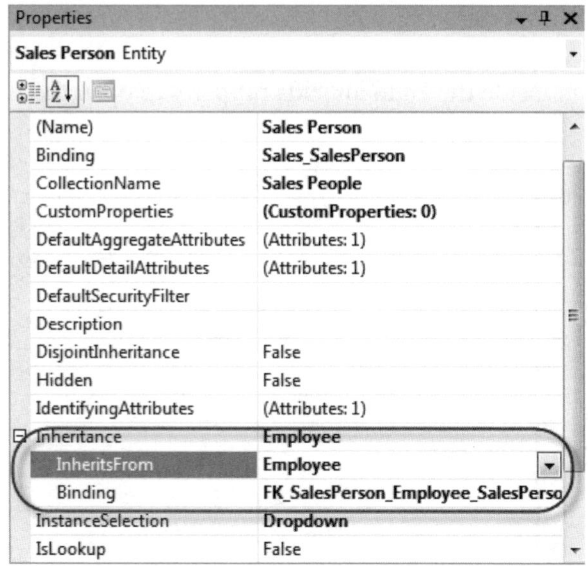

Figure 8.17 Set up the Inheritance property of the Sales Person entity to configure it to inherit from the Employee entity.

5. Select the Employee entity in the Entities pane and delete the Sales Person role. Report Builder 1.0 also deletes the Sales Person role in the Sales Person entity and removes the Manager Name attribute from the IdenfyingAttributes collection of the Sales Person entity.
6. In the Entities pane, select the Sales Person entity and click the … button inside the IdentifyingAttributes property and remove all attributes from the IdenfyingAttributes collection.
7. Click the Add button. Notice that the Fields pane of the Identifying Attributes dialog now lists both Sales Person and Employee attributes and roles because the Sales Person entity inherits from the Employee entity.
8. Select the National ID Number attribute and click OK to return to the AttributeReference Collection Editor and then click OK again to return to the Model Designer.
9. Remove all attributes from the DefaultDetailAttributes collection of the Sales Person entity. Add the National ID Number, First Name, Last Name attributes to it.
10. Build the project again. Report Builder 1.0 shouldn't report any errors.

Configuring an entity for inheritance will not break existing reports that use that entity. However, removing entity inheritance is a braking change.

Role expansion

Sometimes, you may have an entity whose attributes logically belong to another entity. For example, the Contact entity represents the employee's contact details that logically should be a part of the Employee entity. However, to optimize storage, the database schema designer has decided to refactor the contact-related columns from several tables, such as Employee, Individual, Vendor, and so on, into a separate Contact table. From a reporting perspective, the end user would rather see the Contact fields inside the Employee entity. In other words, we need to expand the Employee entity to include the Contact fields.

1. In the Entities pane, select the Employee entity.
2. Select the Contact role and change its ExpandInline property to True.

Since a role expansion unites two entities, you may want to hide the roles of the referenced entity (in this case, Contact) to prevent duplicating roles and self-references (where Employee references itself).

3. Select the Contact role and click the … button inside the HiddenFields property to open the Hidden Fields dialog box.

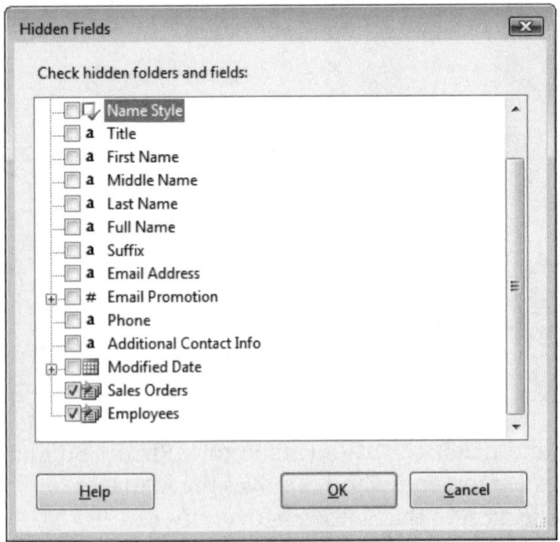

Figure 8.18 Consider hiding the roles of the expanded entity to prevent duplicating roles.

4. Check the Sales Orders and Employees roles to select them, as shown in Figure 8.18. Click OK.
5. Since we are merging the Contact fields into the Employee entity, consider also hiding the entire Contact entity so it doesn't confuse end users. In the Entities pane, select the Contact entity and set its Hidden property to True. The Contact entity name should now appear grayed out in the Entities pane.

Changing the value of the ExpandInline property will not break existing reports.

Lookup entities

The third and last denormalization technique is defining lookup entities. As its name suggests, use this technique when you have entities based on narrow lookup tables in the database. For example, the Adventure Works model includes a Product Subcategory and Product Category entities that have a single useful attribute Name. The end users would probably appreciate "promoting" the product category and subcategory to the Product entity to minimize entity navigation.

In general, it is useful to define an entity as a lookup entity when you want to flatten out a hierarchical (snowflake) database schema. When Report Builder 1.0 encounters a role whose related entity is a lookup entity, it displays the identifying attribute of that entity as if it were an attribute on the current entity. A lookup entity must have only one identifying attribute.

1. In the Entities pane, select the Product Subcategory entity and change its IsLookup property to True.
2. In the Entities pane, select the Product entity and note that the Model Designer displays the Product Subcategory role as an attribute although its type is Role.

The role's ContextualName property defines the name of the lookup entity. The default value for the ContextualName property is Role. This means that the lookup entity name will match the role name. If you change the ContextualName property to Merge, the name of the lookup entity will be a combination of the role name and the name of the identifying attribute, such as Product Category Name.

You can promote a lookup entity via another lookup entity. For example, you can promote the Name identifying attribute of the Product Category entity all the way to the Product entity via the Product Subcategory entity.

3. In the Entities pane, select the Product Category entity and change its IsLookup property to True.
4. In the Entities pane, select the Product Subcategory entity. Select its Product Category role and change its PromoteLookup property to True.

Changes to PromoteLookup, IsLookup, and ContextualName are non-breaking changes to existing reports.

Creating perspectives

Denormalization techniques can go a long way towards making your model simpler and more intuitive to end users, but they may not be enough. Consider implementing perspectives if you want to further reduce the perceived complexity of large models. A perspective is a logical subset of the model that contains selected entities and fields. Perspectives cannot be used as a security mechanism. You cannot restrict access to items included in the perspective. Follow these steps to create Internet Sales and Reseller Sales perspectives in the Adventure Works report model.

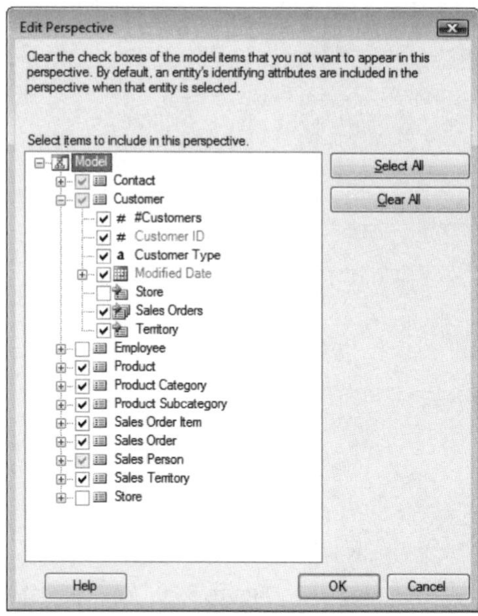

Figure 8.19 Create model perspectives to implement logical subsets of the model.

1. In the Entities pane, right-click on the root Model node and choose New ⇨ Perspective to open the Edit Perspective dialog box, as shown in Figure 8.19.
2. By default, a perspective includes all items. Exclude the Employee and Store entities from the new perspective by clearing their checkboxes because they are not applicable to Internet sales.

3. Expand the Customer entity and observe that the Model Designer has removed the Store role. This is because excluding an entity removes all roles to that entity.
4. Click OK to return to the Model Designer and rename the NewPerspective item to Internet Sales.

Follow similar steps to create a Resellers Sales perspective that excludes the Customer entity.

> **TIP** Although unsupported, you can force the end user to select a perspective by defining a model-level custom property called MustUsePerspective. To do so, select the Model node in the Entities pane and click the ellipsis (...) button inside the CustomProperties. Then, click the Add button and set up a new custom property MustUsePerspectives with a Boolean data type and namespace http://schemas.microsoft.com/sqlserver/2004/11/semanticquerydesign. Deploy the model. When the end user launches the Report Builder 1.0 client, the root model will be disabled forcing the user to choose a perspective.

Authoring advanced expressions

Sometimes, report requirements call for more advanced calculated fields that span entities. While the end user can author expression-based fields at the report level, I recommend you define frequently used business calculations as expressions in the model. Besides helping the end user, model-level expressions are preferred because they are defined and maintained in one place—the model. For example, if you need to change an expression formula later on, you can simply update the expression in the model. All reports that include the expression will automatically pick up the new formula.

Suppose that security requirements dictate that the Adventure Works sales managers are denied access to customer orders. Instead, they can only see the total order amount for all shipped orders to a given customer. You can fulfill this requirement by creating an opaque expression for Total Order Amount as follows:

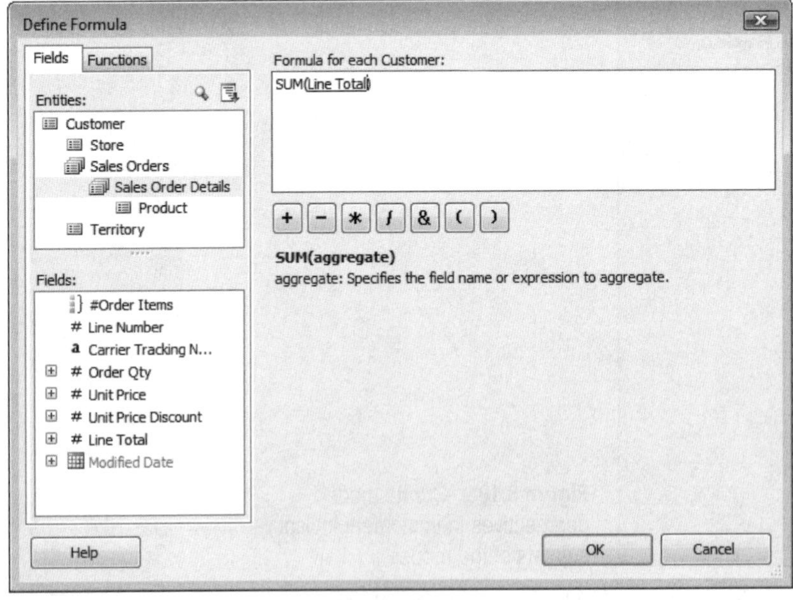

Figure 8.20 You can define formulas that span entities.

1. Right-click the Customer entity and choose New ⇨ Expression to open the Define Formula dialog box.

2. Click the Functions tab and double-click the SUM function found under the Aggregate node in the tree.
3. Click the Field tab. In the Formula pane, click the aggregate argument of the SUM formula.
4. In the Entities pane, click the Sales Orders role, and then the Sales Order Details role.
5. In the Fields pane, double-click the Line Total field to replace the formula argument, as shown in Figure 8.20.

   To apply the formula to shipped orders only, we need to define a filter for the formula as follows.

6. Double-click the Line Total argument inside the SUM formula to see the expanded formula, as shown in Figure 8.21.

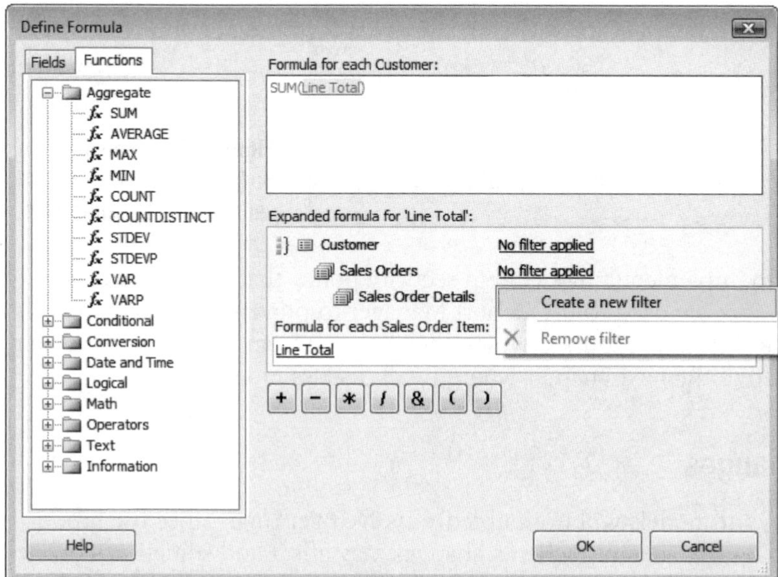

Figure 8.21 Create a filter to select a subset of the entity rows.

7. The Expanded Formula pane lets you define filters for each entity related to the root entity. Click the No Filter Applied link next to the Sales Orders entity and choose Create a New Filter to open the Filter Data dialog box, as shown in Figure 8.22.

   The Filter Data dialog box lets you create sophisticated filters that can have multiple conditions and filter on multiple entities. Since the Report Builder 1.0 client uses the same dialog box to let users filter report data, I will defer discussing the Filter Data dialog in more details to chapter 9.

8. In the Filter Data dialog box, double-click the Status field to add it to the right pane.
9. Expand the Status drop-down list and choose Shipped. Incidentally, all Adventure Works sales orders have a Shipped status, which is why the drop-down list has a single item.
10. Enter *Shipped Orders* for a filter name and click OK to return to the Define Formula dialog box. Click OK to return to the Model Designer.
11. Rename the new expression to Total Order Amount and format it as currency.
12. Make sure that the Nullable property of Total Order Amount is set to True.

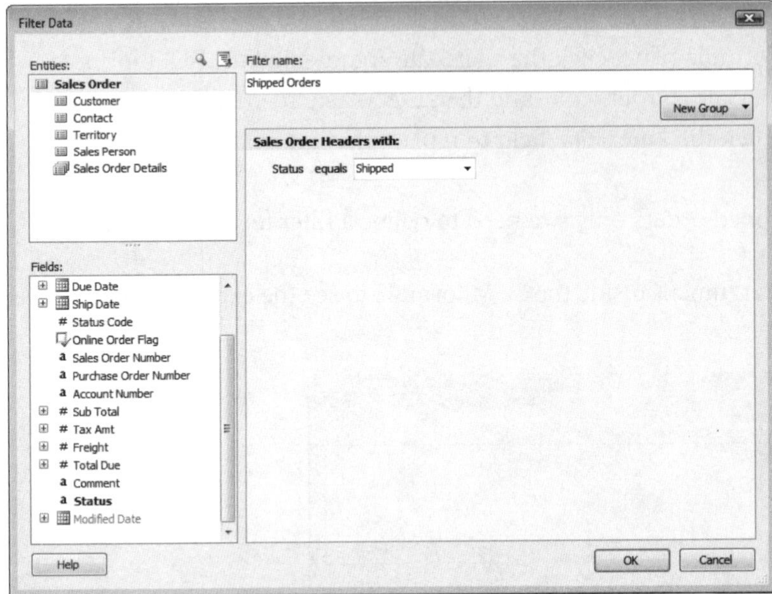

Figure 8.22 Report Builder 1.0 supports advanced filtering capabilities.

The only remaining step is to implement a model item security policy that restricts access to the Sales Order entity. To do so, we need to use Report Manager to prevent the Adventure Works sales manager (or the Windows group to which they belong) from reading Sales Order data. I will postpone this step to the next chapter where I will discuss model security.

8.3.3 Dealing with Changes

Change is a part of life and your models will undoubtedly evolve over time. Since the report model is a layer above the database schema, schema changes may affect and sometimes break the report model. Report Builder 1.0 doesn't support any built-in mechanism to detect schema changes and adjust the underlying model. It will not drop attributes that are bound to deleted columns, nor will it notify you if a data type has changed or a new column is added. In other words, all schema changes must be resolved manually. As a report modeler, you need to learn how to deal with schema changes, such as adding new tables, changing column names, and deleting columns.

Adding new entities

As it stands, the Customer entity is not very useful as it includes only Customer Type and Account Number customer-related attributes. That's because its base table, Sales.Customer, stores both individual customers and resellers. Specifics about the individual customer are stored in the Sales.Individual table, while the reseller-specific details are in the Store table. We already have the Store entity included in the model. Let's see what it takes to enhance the Adventure Works model to handle individual customers.

1. In the Solution Explorer, double-click the Adventure Works.dsv file to open in the DSV Designer.

2. In the DSV Designer, click the Add/Remove Objects toolbar button to open the Add/Remove Tables dialog box, which is similar to the Data Source View Wizard's Select Tables and Views dialog box (see again Figure 8.4).
3. In the Available Objects pane, select the Individual (Sales) table and press the > button to add the table to the Included Objects pane. Click OK to add the table to the Adventure Works DSV.
4. Open the Adventure Works model in the Model Designer.
5. In the Entities pane, right-click on the Model node and choose New ⇨ Entity.
6. Rename the NewEntity entity you just created to *Individual*.
7. To associate the Individual entity with a DSV table, select it in the Entities pane and click the ellipsis (...) button inside the Binding property to open the Entity Binding dialog box, as shown in Figure 8.23.

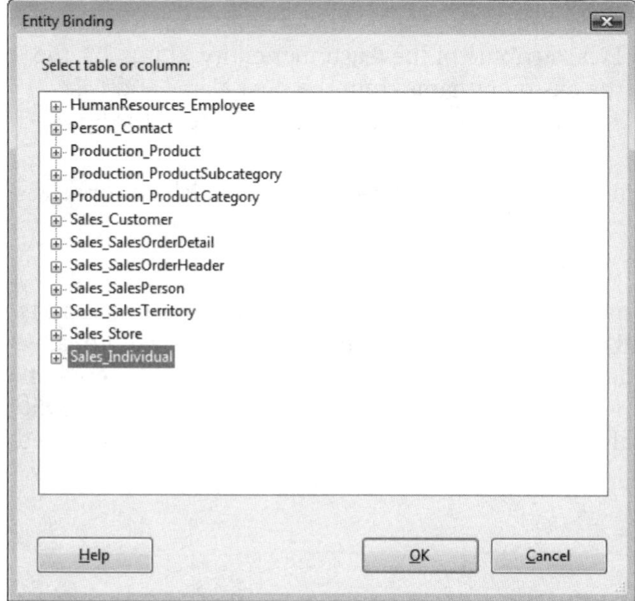

Figure 8.23 Use the Entity Binding dialog box to bind an entity manually to a data source table.

8. Select the Sales_Individual table in the Entity Binding dialog box and click OK.
9. You could manually add the entity fields but this is time-consuming. Instead, let's auto-generate its fields. Right-click on the Individual entity and choose Autogenerate. Confirm the warning message that follows.
10. The familiar Report Model Wizard starts. In the Selected Item Autogeneration confirm that only the Individual entity is listed.
11. Accept the defaults in the Select Report Mode Generation Rules step.
12. In the Collect Model Statistics step, select the Use Current Model Statistics setting to save time.
13. In the Completing the Wizard step, click Run to auto-generate the Individual entity. Notice that once the process completes, the following error message is shown in the Status field:

```
The Entity 'Individual' doesn't have any IdentifyingAttributes.
```

14. This error is generated because the Report Model Wizard was unable to locate an identifying attribute for the Individual entity and the IdentifyingAttributes collection empty. Go back to the Model Designer and add the Account Number field from the Customer Entity to the IdentifyingAttributes collection of the Individual entity.
15. Similar to the Employee entity, select the Contact role of the Individual and set its ExpandInline property to True to expand the role.
16. In the Entities pane, select the Customer entity. Observe that the Report Model Wizard has added a new role, Individual. This is because the Report Model Wizard has detected the relationship between the Customer and Individual tables.
17. Since both the Individual and Store entities are customers, set their Inheritance property to inherit from the Customer entity.
18. Let's add a new expression field to the Customer entity for the customer name based on the following formula:

    ```
    IF(Customer Type="I", First Name & " " & Last Name, Name)
    ```

    The IF operator evaluates the Customer Type attribute of the Customer entity. If it is "I", the customer is an individual and we derive the customer name from the First Name and Last Name attributes of the Individual entity. Otherwise, we use the Name attribute of the Store entity.
19. Finally, rename the new expression to Customer Name and make sure its Nullable property is True.

Breaking vs. non-breaking changes

Report Builder 1.0 can accommodate some schema changes without breaking existing reports. For example, moving model items in and out of display folders and perspectives will not affect existing reports. Changing expression formulas, bindings, or definitions of named queries and named calculations in the DSV are non-breaking changes too, although they may produce different report results. In general, all model changes will be non-breaking except the ones listed in Table 8.2.

Table 8.2 Report Model Breaking Changes

Item Type	Change
Entity	Model identifier (ID) and Inheritance properties
Attribute	ID, DataType, IsAggregate properties, and entity membership
Role	ID and Cardinality properties, entity membership, related role and its cardinality and entity membership

The Report Builder 1.0 client detects breaking changes when loading an existing report and displays an error message. The Semantic Engine detects breaking changes at run time and returns an error message when previewing the report in the Report Builder 1.0 client or when viewing the report on demand. An end user can fix a breaking change by opening the report in design mode and making the necessary change, such as removing a column bound to a field that has been deleted from the model.

TIP If you want to deprecate a field, consider setting its Hidden property to True instead of deleting it. Hiding a field is a non-breaking change that will not affect existing reports.

8.3.4 Deploying Report Models

Now that the Adventure Works model is ready, let's deploy it to the server to make it available for end-user reporting.

1. In the Solution Explorer, right-click on the Adventure Works Report Model project node and choose Build to verify the model. If the Model Designer displays any error messages, review them and correct the errors.
2. In the Solution Explorer, right-click on the Adventure Works Report Model project node and choose Properties to open the familiar Property Pages dialog, as shown in Figure 8.24.

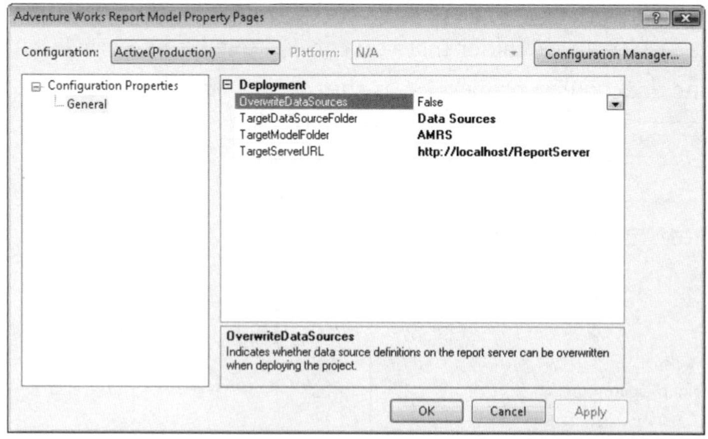

Figure 8.24 Before deploying the report model, review and change the project deployment settings.

3. Change the TargetModelFolder setting to *AMRS* to deploy the model to the AMRS folder.
4. Verify that the TargetServerURL setting points to an existing report server instance. You can verify the URL by opening a browser window and enter the URL you plan to use. If it resolves to the report server endpoint, you have a valid URL. Click OK to close the dialog.
5. In the Solution Explorer, right-click on the Adventure Works Report Model project node and choose Deploy to start the deployment process.

The Visual Studio Output window shows the deployment progress. If all is well, you will see the following message:

```
========== Deploy: 1 succeeded, 0 failed, 0 skipped ==========
```

You have successfully implemented and deployed the Adventure Works Report Model project!

8.4 Working with Analysis Services Models

Recall that one of the data sources supported by Report Builder 1.0 is Analysis Services. This integration scenario is discussed in detail in the whitepaper "Building Ad-hoc Reporting Solutions with SQL Server 2005 Report Builder and Analysis Services OLAP" (see Resources). I don't have much more to add except to share some real-life experience and provide a few guidelines. Let's first see what it takes to generate a Report Builder 1.0 model on top of a cube.

8.4.1 Generating Report Models from Analysis Services

When you use Analysis Services, you need to auto-generate the report model. The steps for auto-generating models from all supported data sources are identical.

Auto-generating a model

Follow these steps to auto-generate a semantic model from the AdventureWorksAS2008 data source:

1. Open the Report Manager application by pointing your Internet browser to the Report Manager URL, such as http://localhost/reports.
2. Navigate to the folder that has a data source pointing to the Adventure Works 2008 cube. If you have deployed the demo report you authored in chapter 1, you should have an AdventureWorksAS2008 data source in the Data Sources folder that you can use for this exercise.
3. Click on the data source to go to the data source properties, as shown in Figure 8.25.

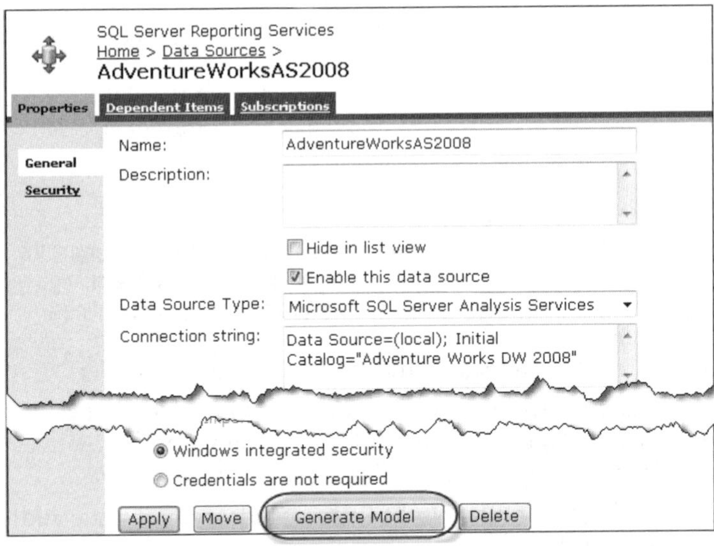

Figure 8.25 Click the Generate Model button to auto-generate a model from an Analysis Services data source.

4. In the screen that follows, enter Adventure Works UDM as the model name.
5. Click the Change Location button to navigate to the AMRS folder to which you've been deploying the sample reports and click OK.

Editing the auto-generated model

Just because the report model is auto-generated doesn't mean that you cannot open it and make changes to it in the Model Designer. Be warned though that if you subsequently auto-generate the model again, your changes will be lost.

1. In the Report Manager, navigate to the AMRS folder the model was generated.
2. Click the Adventure Works UDM link to go to its property page, as shown in Figure 8.26.
3. Click the Edit link and save the model as a file locally.

Once you save the model definition, you can add it to the Adventure Works Report Model project and make changes to it. When you are done, go back to the model property page in the Report Manager and click the Update link to upload the model definition.

Modified Date: 11/7/2007 4:45 PM
Modified By: NW8000\teo
Creation Date: 11/7/2007 4:45 PM
Created By: NW8000\teo

Properties

Name: Adventure Works UDM

Description:

Hide in list view

Model definition

Edit Update

Apply Delete Move Regenerate Model

Figure 8.26 Click the Edit link to save the model definition as a file or the Update link to update the model from a file.

8.4.2 Understanding Analysis Services Limitations

As you've seen, auto-generating a model from an Analysis Services data source is simple. Figure 8.27 shows what happens when you do this. Auto-generating a model from SSAS means wrapping UDM with a Report Builder 1.0 semantic layer—the top layer in the Report Builder Report Model stack. This is needed because the Report Builder 1.0 client only understands SMDL. When the report is run, the Semantic Engine interprets the semantic query and translates it to an MDX query. So far so good, or is it?

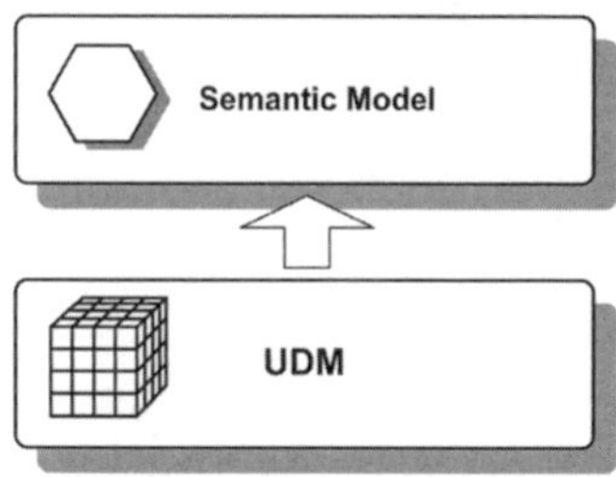

Figure 8.27 When you auto-generate a report model from an Analysis Services data source, Report Builder 1.0 adds a semantic model on top of UDM.

Unfortunately, as it turns out, mixing a relational model to a dimensional model produces a model which is neither dimensional nor relational. The problem is that when used with Analysis Services data sources, the semantic model wrapper gets in the way. First, it strips UDM from features it doesn't support, such as parent-child dimensions, user-defined hierarchies, multi-grain relationships, and so on. For more information about these limitations, read KB Article 899825 and the whitepaper I've just mentioned.

Second, the Semantic Model doesn't translate the UDM metadata to an entity-based model very well. Mapping UDM relationships to roles is especially problematic. For example, unlike traditional OLAP browsers, which expose UDM metadata as a static list of dimensions and measures, the Report Builder 1.0 client collapses the entity tree as soon as you add a dimension attribute or measure to the report. As a result, selecting dimensions and measures may require several hops through the intervening roles. Not only does this confuse the user, but it also results in various issues when filtering a report that spans multiple measure groups. The

MDX query translator is another sore spot. Issues range from queries that produce wrong results to inefficient queries that take hours to execute.

REAL LIFE I wrestled the Report Builder-SSAS 2005 integration beast long and hard. One of the deficiencies that caused the most grief was the inefficient queries that the MDX Query Translator produces when the user filters on measures, such as show me all customers with sales greater than $1,000. Such reports would take hours to execute with a medium-size cube. When I looked at the generated query, I was appalled to find out that it cross-joins all dimensions in the query subselect filter! This resulted in enormous amount of subcube requests by the SSAS query engine. It turned out later that the performance improvements in SSAS 2008 reduced the query time to about a minute, so SSAS 2005 was partly to blame for the poor query performance.

In summary, consider using semantic models and the Report Builder 1.0 client only with simple and relatively small cubes. If the cube has multiple measure groups, consider using the Report Builder 1.0 if the users will report on a single measure group at a time. Avoid Report Builder 1.0 if cross-measure group reporting is a requirement.

8.5 Summary

Report Builder 1.0 is an ad hoc reporting tool that targets business users. Before end users can use Report Builder 1.0 to author reports, you need to build or auto-generate a report model. A report model consists of data source, data source view, and semantic model layers. Use the Report Model Wizard to generate the raw model. Refine the model by reviewing and making changes to each entity and its fields.

Leverage denormalization techniques, such as entity inheritance, role expansion, and lookup entities, to make your models more intuitive to end users. Define expressions that represent useful business calculations. Consider display folders and perspectives to reduce the perceived complexity of the model. Learn how to evolve your model in time to reflect schema changes. Evaluate your reporting requirements carefully and know when to use Report Builder 1.0.

8.6 Resources

Select Report Model Generation Rules
(http://tinyurl.com/5qu3fy)—Explains the rules that the Report Model Wizard applies to generate the metadata from the data source.

Bob Meyers Blog
(http://blogs.msdn.com/bobmeyers/)—Tips and tricks from the Report Builder mastermind.

Object Role Modeling: An Overview
(http://tinyurl.com/2smdhn)—This paper discusses the Object Role Modeling (ORM), a fact-oriented method for performing information analysis at the conceptual level.

Building Ad-hoc Reporting Solutions with SQL Server 2005 Report Builder and Analysis Services OLAP whitepaper by Tian Ying He and Carolyn Chao
(http://tinyurl.com/273qzh)— This paper discusses how to integrate Report Builder and Microsoft SQL Server 2005 Analysis Services UDM.

Chapter 9

Authoring Ad Hoc Reports

In the previous chapter, we covered how to create and deploy report models. In this chapter, we build on those skills by learning how to build ad hoc reports from these models. The Report Builder 1.0 client is the premium tool for authoring reports that are based on a Report Builder 1.0 report model. In this chapter, you will learn how to create table, matrix, and chart ad hoc reporting views from the models you implemented in the previous chapter.

After walking through the steps required to author basic reports, this chapter teaches you how to get the most from Report Builder 1.0 by covering advanced filtering, custom drill-through reports, and how to use a report model as a data source for Report Designer reports. Finally, you will polish your report management skills by understanding how to secure report models.

9.1 Understanding Report Builder 1.0 Client

When the Report Builder 1.0 client was first introduced in SQL Server 2005, it had a well-defined target audience—business users. In comparison, Microsoft envisioned the Report Designer as the tool of choice for developers and power users. As it turned out, there is no clear-cut dividing line between these two user groups when it comes to report authoring. Developers would appreciate a more user-friendly interface that simplifies some of the groundwork required for laying out a report, and business users would welcome the ability to create more complex ad hoc reports outside of the Visual Studio environment.

In the long run, Report Builder 2.0, which I'll preview in chapter 10, is well positioned to satisfy the requirements of both audiences. As it stands, however, Report Builder 2.0 leans more towards the "developer" side and requires a report author to have a solid understanding of the report authoring process even for creating simple ad hoc reports. Getting beyond these barriers is where the Report Builder 1.0 client can help.

9.1.1 Understanding Features

The purpose of the Report Builder 1.0 client is to support end users who want to create simple ad hoc reports, but without the learning curve that comes with adopting new business tools. The intended audience for the Report Builder 1.0 client is a less technically savvy user who is willing to trade advanced reporting features for the ability to produce simple reports quickly. To keep the learning curve small, the Report Builder 1.0 client uses more built-in features such as templates and gives up some of the more powerful features that you find in the BIDS Report Designer and Report Builder 2.0. For example, the Report Builder 1.0 client doesn't support side-by-side or nested regions, list regions, page header and footers, page numbers, and expression-based properties.

Understanding the user interface

End users will undoubtedly find the Report Builder 1.0 client interface (see Figure 9.1) intuitive as it has a look and feel that is similar to Office products. For example, like PowerPoint, Report Builder 1.0 client includes several panes and a work area for assembling items that you drag and drop to the design surface. Report Builder 1.0 includes the Explorer pane used for working with model metadata, an Entities pane that contains model items, and a Fields pane that displays the fields that belong to the entity you select.

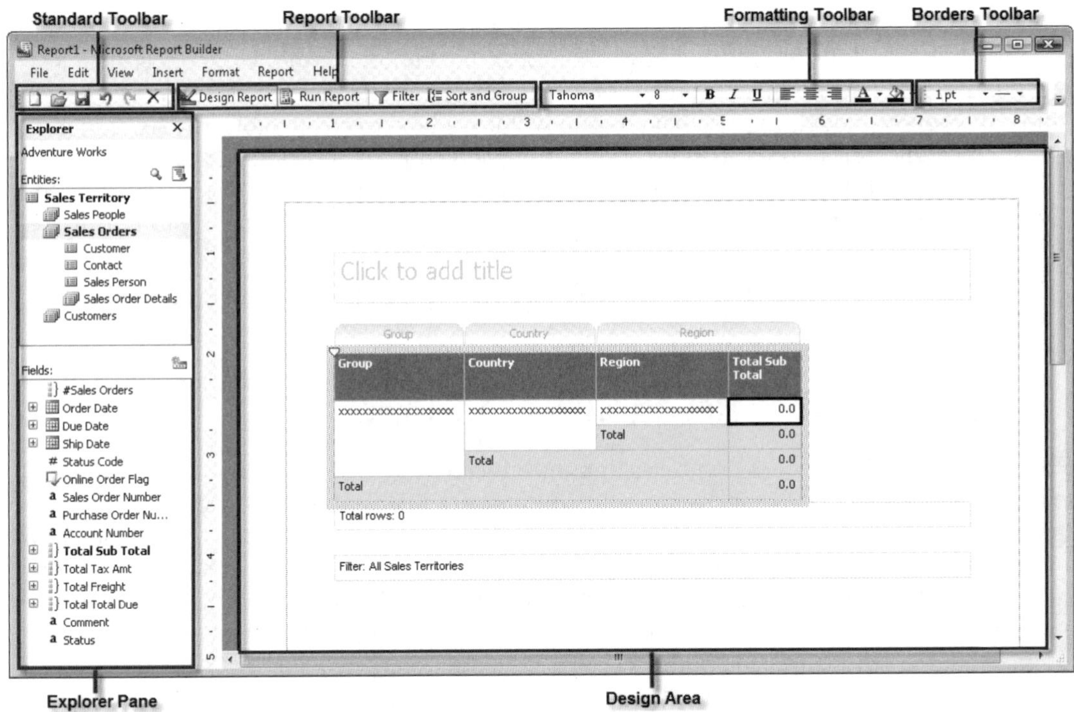

Figure 9.1 The Report Builder 1.0 client features an intuitive PowerPoint-like user interface.

Authoring a simple ad hoc report is a matter of dragging fields to the WYSIWYG (What You See Is What You Get) design area. The Report Builder 1.0 client supports previewing, printing, exporting, and publishing reports to the report server. The user can preview a report by pressing the Run Report button on the report toolbar. While in report preview mode, the user can export a report to any of the supported export formats. Finally, the File menu lets you publish the report definition to the server or save it to disk.

When the user runs the report, the Report Builder 1.0 client uploads the report definition to the server on the fly by invoking the ReportExecutionService.LoadReportDefinition API followed by a call to the ReportExecutionService.Render API. Therefore, a Report Builder 1.0 report is always processed and rendered on the server.

When to use Report Builder 1.0 client

So, when would you use the Report Builder 1.0 client as an end-user reporting tool? My short answer is when you cannot use the forthcoming Report Builder 2.0. That said, considering that in a long run Report Builder 2.0 will probably become the Microsoft premium tool for both standard and ad hoc reporting outside Visual Studio, my advice will be to evaluate it first and offer the Report Builder 1.0 client only if Report Builder 2.0 doesn't fit the bill. Specifically, I suggest you consider the Report Builder 1.0 client when the following conditions are true:

- Report Builder 2.0 is not an option—Less technically savvy users may find Report Builder 2.0 too complex and intimidating. For example, end users may not be willing to tinker with parameters and query statements. Or, they may not have the patience to learn how table groups work.
- The Report Builder Model meets your requirements—Please review chapter 8 for considerations about when to use Report Builder 1.0 models. Again, the Report Builder 1.0 client requires a Report Builder model as a data source.
- Simple ad hoc reports—The Report Builder 1.0 client is a great tool for producing quick and easy reports. More involved reports will require "graduating" to Report Builder 2.0 and more advanced report authoring skills.

Now that you know when to use the Report Builder 1.0 client, let's see how you can deploy it to end users.

9.1.2 Deploying Report Builder 1.0 Client

When Report Builder 1.0 was still on the drawing board, the Reporting Services team debated how to implement the Report Builder 1.0 client—as a thin web-based client or a rich Windows Forms client. Finally, they settled on an approach that combines the best of both worlds. To provide rich reporting experience, the Report Builder 1.0 client is implemented as a .NET Windows Form application. To simplify setup, the Report Builder 1.0 client uses .NET ClickOnce technology for downloading and installing it on demand when a user requests its URL.

About ClickOnce

The ClickOnce technology is baked into the .NET Framework. It lets developers create self-updating Windows-based applications that can be installed and upgraded automatically. The binaries of the ClickOnce-enabled application reside on the server, along with the application and deployment manifest files that describe the deployment. For example, by default, the SQL Server 2008 setup installs the Report Builder 1.0 client assemblies in the \Program Files\Microsoft SQL Server\MSRS10.MSSQLSERVER\Reporting Services\ReportServer\ReportBuilder folder. With ClickOnce, the end user doesn't launch the application directly, such as by double-clicking on the Report Builder 1.0 client executable. Instead, similar to opening web-based applications, the end user requests a URL to the application manifest file that resides on the server. The .NET Framework runtime on the client machine recognizes the file extension and performs the initial ClickOnce deployment of the application by downloading and executing the application on the user's desktop.

If the application binaries are updated on the server, ClickOnce detects the new version when the user requests the application URL, downloads the new bits, and upgrades the client copy automatically. No more building and shipping setup programs and patches to the end user! If you want to learn more about ClickOnce, Duncan McCenzie's article "Introducing

Client Application Deployment with ClickOnce" (see Resources) is a great start. Here is what happens when the user starts the Report Builder 1.0 client.

- The user opens the Report Manager and clicks on the Report Builder button or directly requests the Report Builder 1.0 client URL— http://<server>/ReportServer/ReportBuilder/-ReportBuilder.application.

NOTE The above URL launches the Report Builder 1.0 client in full trust but under the permissions granted to the end user. If the user has local administrator rights, the Report Builder 1.0 client will run with unrestricted access. As a precautionary measure, ClickOnce will show a security prompt so the user can approve the application startup. In this release, the Report Builder 1.0 client always runs in full trust.

- The SQL Server Report Builder 1.0 client requires the .NET Framework to be installed on the user machine. If the .NET Framework is not installed, ClickOnce prompts the user to download and install it. If the user clicks Yes, ClickOnce installs the .NET Framework.
- ClickOnce verifies whether the Report Builder 1.0 client is already installed and its version matches the server version. If Report Builder 1.0 client is not installed, ClickOnce downloads and installs the Report Builder 1.0 client binaries in the ClickOnce local download cache—\Users\<user>\AppData\Local\Apps\2.0\ Data (Vista) or \Documents and Settings\<USER>\Local Settings\Apps\2.0\Data (Windows XP). In case of a version mismatch, ClickOnce replaces the older version with the version used by the report server.
- ClickOnce launches the Report Builder 1.0 client from the ClickOnce download cache, using the credentials of the interactive user.

Understanding Report Builder 1.0 client parameters

When I first saw the Report Builder 1.0 client, I immediately tried to find a way to embed its designer in a custom application so end users could design custom reports without leaving the application. Unfortunately, this is not possible. The Report Builder 1.0 client is designed as a monolithic Windows Forms application and it cannot be extended or programmatically controlled. It provides only a limited startup control by supporting the input parameters listed in Table 9.1.

Table 9.1 Report Builder 1.0 Client command-line parameters

Parameter	Description	Example
<reportpath>	Loads an existing report	http://<servername>/reportserver/reportbuilder/reportbuilder.application?/AMRS/<reportname>
model=<modelpath>	Loads a model	http://<servername>/reportserver/reportbuilder/reportbuilder.application?model=/AMRS/Adventure Works
perspective=<perspectiveID>	Loads a model perspective	http://<servername>/reportserver/reportbuilder/reportbuilder.application?model=/AMRS/Adventure Works&perspective=G801c203b-57ad-4126-a4bb-0626f5042664

Note the perspective parameter takes the perspective identifier and not the perspective name as a parameter. To get the perspective identifier, in the Model Designer, select the perspective and copy the (ID) property in the Properties window.

TIP Although unsupported, once initially installed, the Report Builder 1.0 client can be launched locally from the ClickOnce download cache, as follows: Reportbuilder.exe /s=http://<servername>/reportserver.The /s parameter specifies the report server URL.

9.2 Designing Ad Hoc Reports

Thanks to Report Builder's intuitive interface, authoring an ad hoc report is simple as long as the user is familiar with the model metadata. Therefore, make sure to document the report model and walk users through it before they start using the Report Builder 1.0 client. Doing so will minimize the trial-and-error routine that end users will be subjected to if they don't understand which entities and fields to use. Let's go through the steps required to author table, matrix, and chart reports.

9.2.1 Authoring Table Reports

Suppose you are a sales manager at Adventure Works. You need a report that shows the performance of each sales person for a given year broken down by sales territory. You will use the Report Builder 1.0 client to create the Sales by Employee table report which is shown in Figure 9.2.

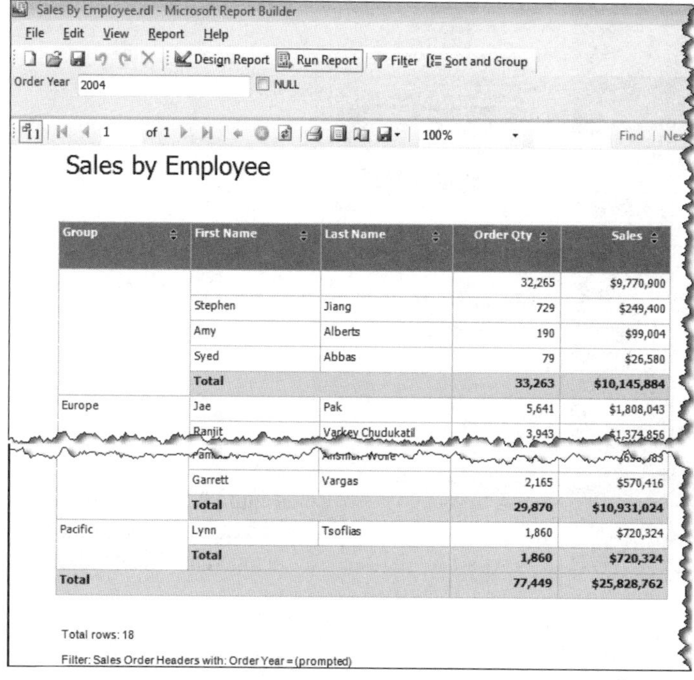

Figure 9.2 The Sales By Employee report shows sales by employee and territory for a given year.

This report demonstrates:

- Authoring ad hoc table reports
- Entity and value groups
- Entity navigation
- Sorting and filtering
- Prompted parameters

Choosing a report model

Follow these steps to launch the Report Builder 1.0 client and select a model:

1. Open Report Manager and click the Report Builder button or type in the Report Builder URL directly in the browser. If you don't see the button, verify you have a system user role assignment that includes the Execute report definitions task. The ClickOnce deployment technology verifies if the Report Builder 1.0 client is installed locally and downloads it if needed. Next, ClickOnce launches the Report Builder 1.0 client.
2. The Report Builder 1.0 client queries the server and loads all available report models in the Select a Source of Data for Your Report list in the Getting Started pane, as shown in Figure 9.3. Check the Show Path checkbox to show the full report catalog path to the folder where the model is deployed. This will help you identify a model in case the list shows models with the same name.

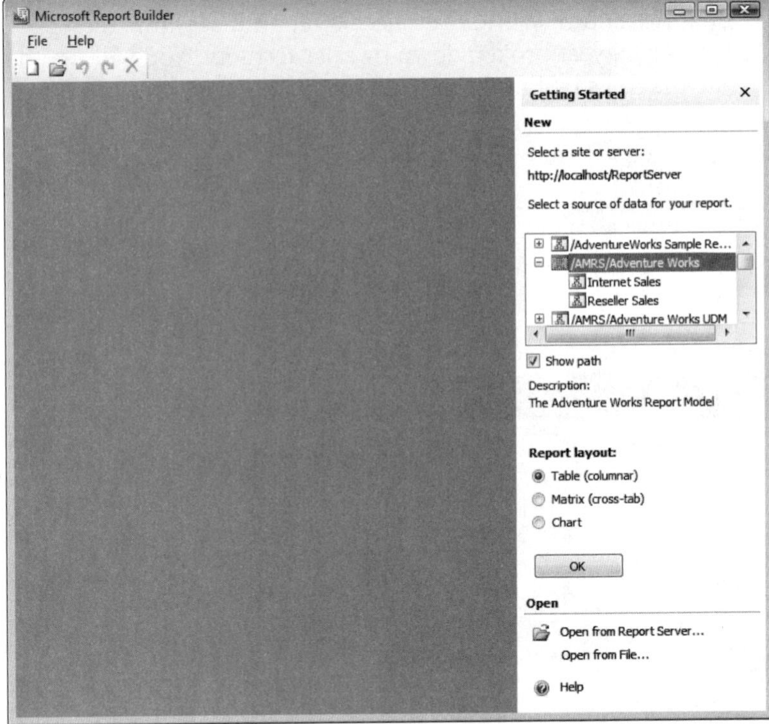

Figure 9.3 Use the Getting Started pane to choose a report model and layout.

3. Select the /AMRS/Adventure Works model you created in the previous chapter. Observe that the model perspectives are shown below the model. The end user can select a perspective if they prefer to work with a subset of the model. The Open section includes links that let you open an existing report definition from the report server or a physical file.

   The Report Builder 1.0 client supports three predefined report layouts: Table (columnar), Matrix (cross-tab), and Chart. The Report Builder 1.0 client includes report templates for each layout type. Once the Report Builder 1.0 client generates the report template, you cannot change its layout. In addition, you can have only one report layout (region) on the report because the Report Builder 1.0 client doesn't support side-by-side regions.
4. Leave the Table (columnar) option selected and click OK.

The Report Builder 1.0 client downloads the Adventure Works report model by calling the GetUserModel API and shows its metadata in the Explorer pane. The metadata should look familiar to you because it contains the entities and fields you created in the preceding chapter. The Explorer pane supports a few more features you may find useful. The Search button lets you search a model item and quickly navigate to it. When you click the Advanced Mode button, the Report Builder 1.0 client displays additional items that are not normally shown, including reverse roles, lookup entities, and indirect inheritance roles.

- A reverse role is a role that points back to the same entity. For example, in advanced mode, the Report Builder 1.0 client will show below the Customer entity the Sales Orders role that points back to the Customer entity.
- Recall from the previous chapter that a lookup entity corresponds to a "lookup" table. By default, the Report Builder 1.0 client doesn't show lookup entities. However, in advanced mode, lookup entities, such as Product Category and Product Subcategories, are shown in the Entities pane.
- Indirect inheritance roles points to entities that inherit from the direct ancestors of the selected entity but are not a direct ancestor of the current entity. For example, although the Store and Individual entities do not have role relationships with each other, they are indirectly related because they both inherit from the Customer entity. As a result, in advanced mode, the user will see an "As Individual" role below the Store entity that lets the user navigate to the Individual-related fields.

Understanding entity and value groups

To lay out a report, you can drag both entities and fields to the design area. However, the type of the item you select determines how data will be grouped on the report. An entity group groups the report data for each instance of the entity. By contrast, if you select an individual field, the Report Builder 1.0 client creates a *value* group for each distinct value of that field. Don't worry if this is not immediately clear, as the examples that follow will clarify the difference between entity and value groups.

1. Select the Sales Person entity in the Entities pane. Observe that due to its inheritance relationship to the Employee entity, the Fields entity shows both the Sales Person and Employee fields. Select the First Name field and drag it to the table region in the design area.
2. Do the same with the Last Name field. Note that the Report Builder 1.0 client changes the field font of these fields to bold in the Fields pane to indicate that they are used on the report.

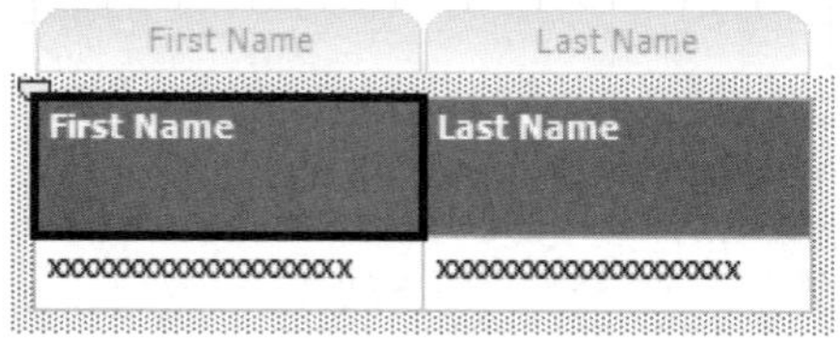

Figure 9.4 Adding an individual field to the design area creates a value group.

At this point, your report layout should match the one shown in Figure 9.4. The blue text boxes that show the field names represent report column headers. The text boxes with white background below them represent the field values. The default field width is determined by the Width property of the field in the model.

3. Click on any of fields inside the table region.

The Report Builder 1.0 client displays tabs above each field. A tab represents a report group. As it stands, the report will group data first on the employee's First Name and then on the employee's Last Name. However, what we want is to group data by each employee and not by the individual fields. To do so, we need an entity group instead of value groups.

4. Select the Edit ⇨ Undo menu (Ctrl-Z) to clear the design area. Alternatively, right-click the First Name tab and choose Delete, then do the same with the Last Name field.
5. Select the Sales Person *entity* in the Entities pane and drag it to the table region or just double-click on Sales Person.

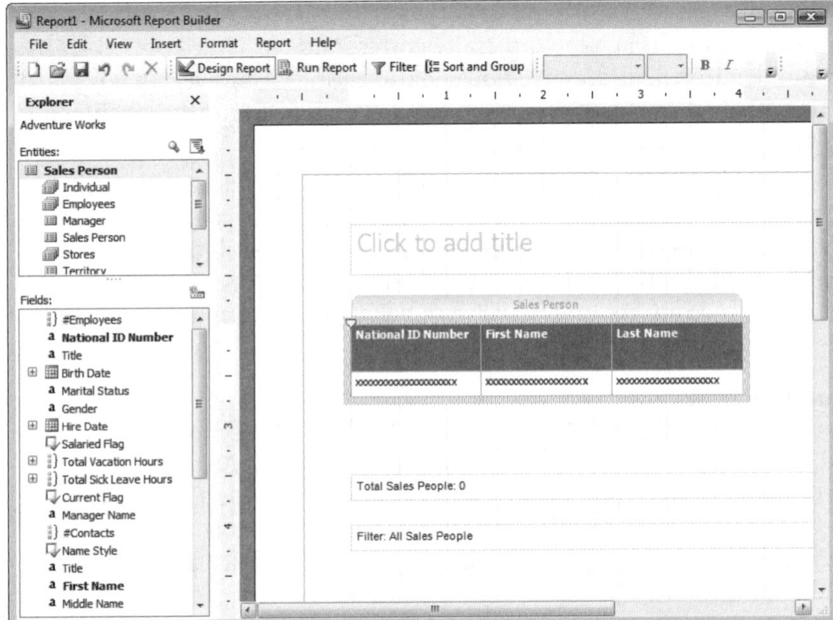

Figure 9.5 Drag an entity to table region to create an entity group.

Notice that the Report Builder 1.0 client adds the National ID Number, First Name, and Last Name fields (see Figure 9.5) on the report because they are included in the entity's DefaultDetailAttributes collection. More importantly, note that the all fields share the same Sales Person tab. As a result, the Report Builder 1.0 client will group report data per sales person.

6. We don't need the National ID Number field on the report. Right-click on the National ID Number column header and choose Delete.

NOTE In case you wonder what the little triangle glyph on the left corner of the table region does, it is a fixed column marker. You can drag it between any two columns of a table report. The column marker is useful when if you have more columns than what will fit on a page, and you want to "lock" the columns that are on the left to keep them from scrolling off the page while you are looking at data in the other columns. If you want to test this feature, resize your columns so that they exceed the page width and run the report.

If you want to add more fields from the Sales Person entity on the report, drag them onto the table region or double-click each field. If you want to add more than one field at the same time, select the fields in the Fields pane while holding the Ctrl key (or Shift key for extended selection), and drag them to the table region.

Understanding entity navigation

When you add the first field to the report, the Report Builder 1.0 client promotes its entity to a primary (root) report entity. Because we added fields from Sales Person, the Sales Person entity becomes the primary entity. In other words, the Sales Person entity becomes the focus of the report. As a result, the Report Builder 1.0 client collapses the Entities list and makes the Sales Person entity the top node in the entity tree (see again Figure 9.5). In addition, the Report Builder 1.0 client displays only those entities to which the Sales Entity is related via roles in the model.

This feature may take you by surprise, especially if you have experience with OLAP browsers whose metadata list is always static. So, what's going on here? Recall that the Report Builder 1.0 client assumes no knowledge of the underlying database schema. If the entity list is static, there is nothing stopping the user from using unrelated entities on the report. Readers familiar with SQL know that querying two unrelated tables results in a Cartesian join that returns all the rows in the two tables where each row in the first table is paired with all rows in the second table. To avoid this, the Report Builder 1.0 client guides the user to select related entities only. For example, glancing at the Entities pane, we can see that the Sales Person entity is related to the Individual, Manager, Store, and other entities.

1. Since our report requires grouping sales people by territory, select the Territory role below the Sales Person entity. The Fields pane shows the fields of the Territory entity.
2. Drag the Group field of the Territory entity and drop it before the First Name column on the report. As you drag it, the Report Builder 1.0 client will show a blue vertical line between columns to indicate that you can drop the field there.

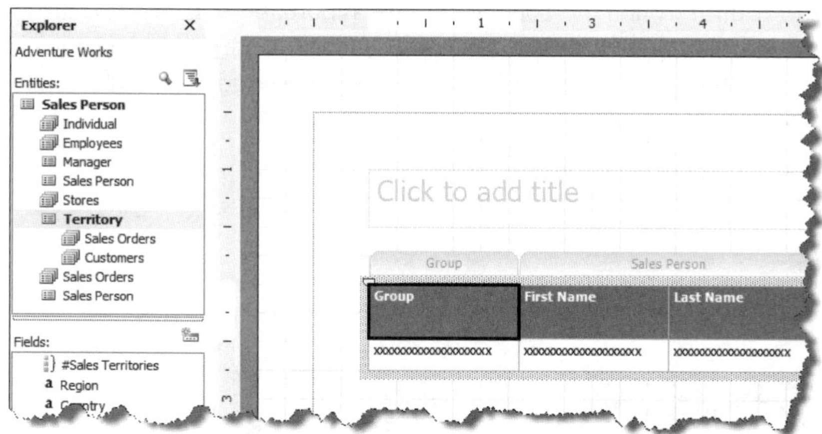

Figure 9.6 Adding the Group field of the Territory entity results in a new value group.

3. Select any field on the report. Note that the Report Builder 1.0 client has created a value group for the Group entity, as shown in Figure 9.6. As a result, the report will group data first by territory and then by sales person.

Next, we need the order quantity field of the Sales Order Item entity. This is where things get interesting. We need to use the Sales Orders role to get to the Sales Order Item entity. But should we select the Sales Orders role of the Sales Person entity or should we select the one below the Territory entity? As it turns out, each choice produces very different results. If we choose the Sales Orders role of the Sales Person entity we will get the sales orders that are associated with a given sales person; that is sales orders submitted by that sales person. That's because we follow the direct relationship between the SalesPerson and SalesOrderHeader table in the AdventureWorks database. In this respect, the Sales Person's roles represent more than related entities. They point to specific entity instances that are associated with the root entity.

By contrast, if we choose the Sales Order role of the Territory entity, we follow the SalesPerson ⇨ Territory ⇨ Sales Orders navigational path in the model. The business question we're asking is "Show me all sales orders that have the same territory as the territory for which a given sales person is responsible." Note that in this case the report may return orders that are not directly associated with the sales person. For example, if Jae Pack is responsible for sales in Europe, we will get not only his orders but also those orders by other sales people who oversee Europe, as well as orders from Europe that are not associated with any sales person. In our case, to get the total order quantity by sales person, we need to go via the Sales Person's Sales Orders role.

4. Select the Sales Orders role of the Sales Person entity and then select the Sales Order Details role below it to get to the Sales Order Item fields.
5. Note that there isn't an Order Qty field in the Fields pane. Instead, there is a Total Order Qty field. Total Order Qty appears because it is set up as a default aggregate of the Order Qty field in the model. As a result, using Total Order Qty on the report will sum the order quantity for each report group. Drag the Total Order Qty field and drop it next to the Last Name column in the design area.
6. Rename the Total Order Qty text in the column header in-place to *Order Qty*. Position the mouse cursor on the right border of the Order Qty column so it turns into a resize cursor, and drag the border to increase the column width a bit.
7. Repeat the last two steps to add the Total Line Total field to the report and rename it to *Sales*.
8. Add a title. The Report Builder templates include pre-defined text boxes for the report title, number of rows returned, and the report filter. Click inside the Click to Add Title text box and enter *Sales by Employee*.

At this point, you report layout should look like the one shown in Figure 9.7.

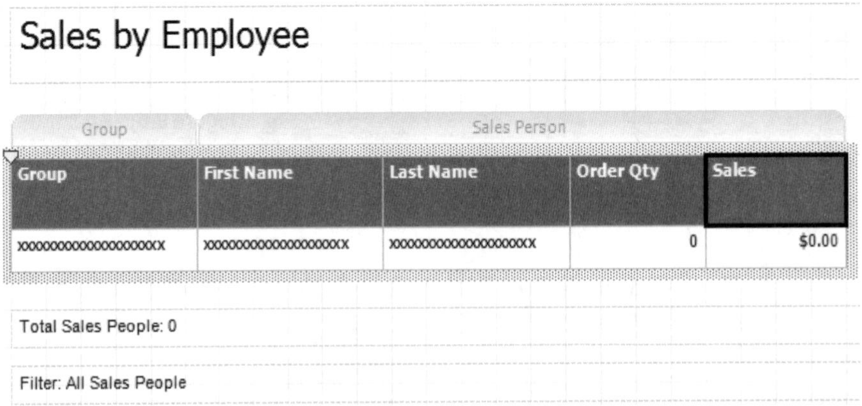

Sales by Employee

Group	First Name	Last Name	Order Qty	Sales
xxxxxxxxxxxxxxxxxxxx	xxxxxxxxxxxxxxxxxxxx	xxxxxxxxxxxxxxxxxxxx	0	$0.00

Total Sales People: 0

Filter: All Sales People

Figure 9.7 The Sales by Employee report in design mode after adding the Order Qty and Sales columns.

Defining group totals and sorting

Let's preview the report to test it:

1. Click the Run Report button. Behind the scenes, the Report Builder 1.0 client invokes the ReportExecutionService.LoadReportDefinition API to upload the report definition to the server on the fly. Next, it calls the ReportExecutionService.Render API to render the ad hoc report.

   Similar to running a report in the Report Manager, the Report Builder 1.0 client generates a standard report toolbar. The standard toolbar lets you page through the report, print, zoom, search, and export the report to any of the predefined export formats. Since this toolbar is identical to the Report Designer toolbar, I will let you explore it on your own.
2. Note that the report doesn't have group totals and it is not sorted in a descending order by the Sales field. Click the Design Report button to go back to design mode. Click on any field on the report to show the report group tabs.
3. Right-click on the Group tab and select the Show Group Subtotals option. Note that a total line is added to the report for the Group field.
4. Right-click on the Sales Person tab and select the Show Group Subtotals option to add a group total for the Sales Person group.
5. Run the report. To change the report sorting order, click the Sort and Group button, which is available in both design and preview modes.
6. In the Sort dialog box, note that you can define three-levels of sorting for each report group. Select the Sales Person entity. Expand the first Sort By drop-down list and select Sales, as shown in Figure 9.8.

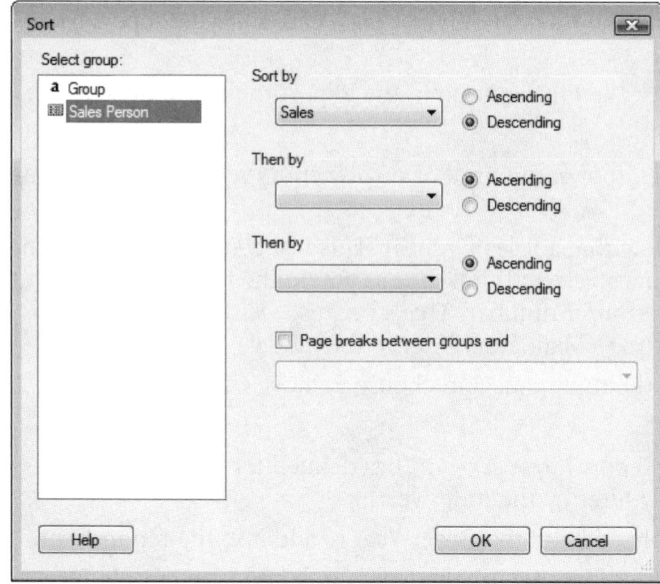

Figure 9.8 Use the Sort dialog box to sort the report in descending order by Sales.

7. Run the report to test the changes.

   The Report Builder 1.0 client also supports interactive sorting at run time. Each column header has an up-down indicator that lets the user sort the report in ascending or descending order within the containing group. Interactive sorting can be disabled by selecting the Report ⇨ Report Properties menu and turning off the Allow Users to Sort the Report Data When They View It checkbox.

Formatting fields

Note that the Order Qty field doesn't have a thousands separator and the Sales field has two decimal places.

1. In design mode, hold the Shift key to select the three fields below the Order Qty column header.
2. Right-click on the selection and choose Format.
3. In the Number tab of the Format dialog box, select the format 1234.56. Change the Decimal Places up-down field to 0 and check the Use 1000 Separator checkbox. Click OK.

> **TIP** You can define custom format settings. To do so, select the Custom Format option and enter the custom format string, such as $#,##0.00;($#,##0.00);Zero. For more information about the .NET rules for custom format strings, see the Custom Numeric Format Strings and Custom DateTime Format Strings topics in the Format Types section of the Visual Studio.NET documentation (see Resources).

4. Select the three fields below the Sales column and format them as currency with no decimal places.
5. Select all fields in the Sales Person's Total line and click the B button in the Formatting toolbar to format them in a bold font style. Repeat the same for the Group's Total line.
6. Select the Order Qty and Sales column headers and click the Right Justify button in the Formatting toolbar to align them on the right.

Filtering reports

As it stands, the Sales by Employee report shows data for all years. Let's filter the report by year.

1. In either design or preview modes, click the Filter button in the Report toolbar to open the familiar Filter Data dialog box.

   The end user can filter the report on the root entity itself or on any entity related to the primary report entity.

2. Double-click the Sales Order entity. Note that a Sales Order In This List condition is added to the right pane. Clicking on the (No Values Selected) link brings you to the Filter List dialog that lets you find a sales order by a sales order number. That's because we set the InstanceSelection property of the Sales Order entity to MandatoryFilter in the model.
3. Right-click on the Sales Order item in the right pane and choose Remove Condition to clear the filter.

   Thanks to the date variations that the Report Model Wizard has defined for us when we created the model, we can conveniently filter by the order year.

4. Expand the Order Date field and double-click on the Order Year to add it to the report filter.
5. By default, the filter condition is *Equals*. Right-click on the *Equals* link and note that the Report Builder 1.0 client supports other common filter criteria, such as Greater Than, Less Than, and so on.

> **NOTE** The In a List condition is very useful since it shows a multivalued list of the field's distinct values if the field's ValueSelection is set to Dropdown. However, since we left the Order Year ValueSelection property set to its default value of None, selecting this option doesn't show a populated list. Instead, if you need to filter on multiple values, you must enter the values manually. You can press Enter to go to the next line to enter the next value.

6. To use a default value of 2004, which is the last year with data in the AdventureWorks database, enter *2004* in the text box next to the Equals link. If you run the report at this time, it will show data for the year 2004 only. Users cannot overwrite the year at run time.
7. To promote the Order Year to a prompted parameter, right-click on Order Year and choose the Prompt context menu. A green question mark appears to the left of Order Year to denote that the filter is now a report parameter, as shown in Figure 9.9.

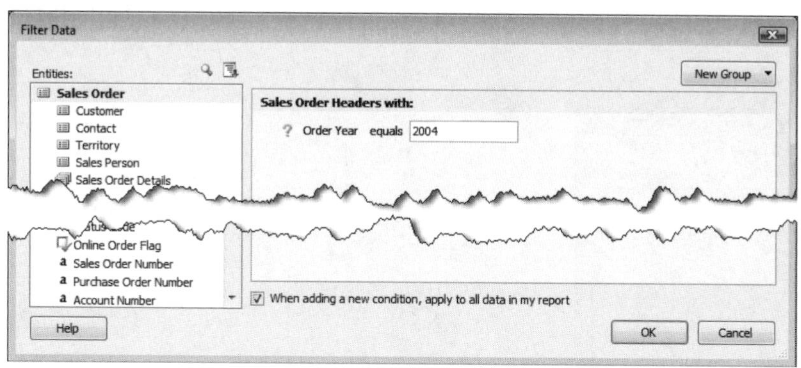

Figure 9.9 Define an Order Year prompt parameter that filters the report by year.

8. Click OK to return to the report. Note that the Filter text box below the table region shows a restatement of the report filter: Sales Order Headers with: Order Year = (prompted). If you run the report now it should look similar to the one shown in Figure 9.2.

You can reposition the report items by dragging them to a new location. When you do this, the Report Builder 1.0 client snaps the item to the design area grid. You can change the grid settings in the report properties (File ⇨ Page Setup menu).

Generating drillthrough reports

As noted before, a unique Report Builder 1.0 feature is generating drillthrough reports on the fly.

1. Run the Sales by Employee report.
2. Hover on top of any of the Order Qty or Sales numbers. Note that the mouse cursor changes to a hand cursor to indicate the item is clickable.
3. Click on a number. Because you clicked on an aggregated value, Report Builder 1.0 generates a multi-instance drillthrough report that shows the individual sales order items contributing to that value. The report shows only the Line Number, Career Tracking Number, Order Qty, and Line Total fields of the Sales Order Item entity because its DefaultDetailAttributes collection includes these fields.
4. Click any of the carrier tracking numbers in the drillthrough report. Since you clicked on a single instance of the Sales Order Item entity, Report Builder 1.0 generates a single-instance report. Unlike a multi-instance report, which shows only the fields in the DefaultDetailAttributes collection, a single-instance report includes all non-hidden fields of the target entity.
5. Hover on top of any of the Line Number fields. Note the cursor doesn't change and you cannot drill through the line number. That's because the EnableDrillthrough property of the Line Number field is set to False in the model. Changing EnableDrillthrough to True will make the field clickable.
6. Click the back arrow on the report toolbar to go back to the main report.

As long as the EnableDrillthrough field property is set to True and there is a navigational path in the model, the end user can generate single and multi-instance drillthrough reports by drilling through the field and navigating to another entity. This feature is called *infinite drillthrough*.

Saving reports

The Report Builder 1.0 client lets you save the report to the report catalog or a physical file.

1. Select File ⇨ Save menu. Alternatively, click the Save toolbar button or press Ctrl-S. Since the report hasn't been saved yet, the Report Builder 1.0 client displays the Save As Report dialog box, as shown in Figure 9.10.

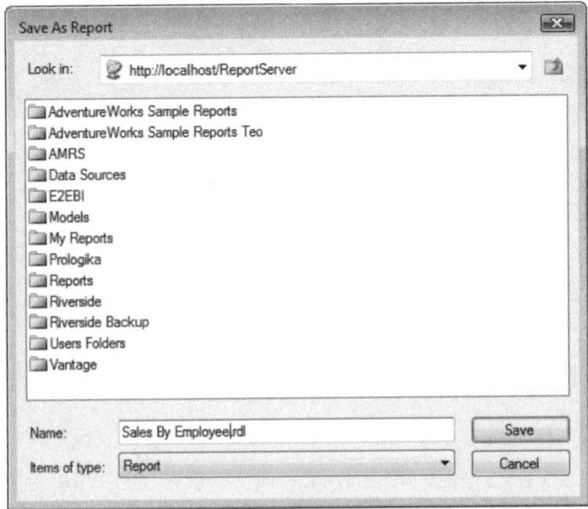

Figure 9.10 You can publish the finished report to the server to share it with other users.

By default, the Report Builder 1.0 client lets you save the report to the report server where you launched the Report Builder 1.0 client from. You can choose a different server by changing the Look In drop-down list. The Report Builder 1.0 client shows only the folders to which you have write permissions.

2. Assuming that My Reports is enabled in the Report Manager Site Settings, double-click the My Reports folder. This will save the report to your private My Reports folder. If you want to share the reports with other users, save the report to a shared folder. You can open a report that was saved to the report catalog, by selecting the File ⇨ Open menu or pressing Ctrl-O.
3. Enter Sales By Employee.rdl in the Name field and click Save.
4. To save the report to disk, select File ⇨ Save to File menu. To open the report definition file later on, choose File ⇨ Open from File menu.

9.2.2 Authoring Matrix Reports

Recall from chapter 3 that a matrix (crosstab) report is a table report with dynamic columns. At run time, the report expands horizontally to accommodate the actual data. Let's author a matrix report that displays sales by territory on rows and years on columns. Figure 9.11 shows the Sales by Territory report that demonstrates the following features:

- Value groups
- Images
- Relative date parameters

- Multivalued parameters

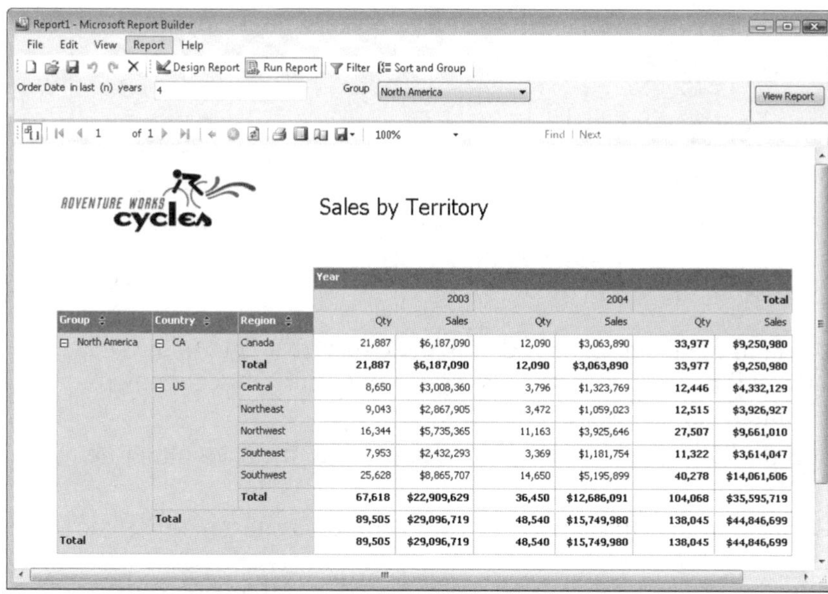

Group	Country	Region	2003 Qty	2003 Sales	2004 Qty	2004 Sales	Total Qty	Total Sales
North America	CA	Canada	21,887	$6,187,090	12,090	$3,063,890	33,977	$9,250,980
		Total	21,887	$6,187,090	12,090	$3,063,890	33,977	$9,250,980
	US	Central	8,650	$3,008,360	3,796	$1,323,769	12,446	$4,332,129
		Northeast	9,043	$2,867,905	3,472	$1,059,023	12,515	$3,926,927
		Northwest	16,344	$5,735,365	11,163	$3,925,646	27,507	$9,661,010
		Southeast	7,953	$2,432,293	3,369	$1,181,754	11,322	$3,614,047
		Southwest	25,628	$8,865,707	14,650	$5,195,899	40,278	$14,061,606
		Total	67,618	$22,909,629	36,450	$12,686,091	104,068	$35,595,719
	Total		89,505	$29,096,719	48,540	$15,749,980	138,045	$44,846,699
Total			89,505	$29,096,719	48,540	$15,749,980	138,045	$44,846,699

Figure 9.11 The Sales by Territory report demonstrates matrix reports.

Designing the Sales by Territory report

Follow these steps to create a matrix report.

1. Launch the Report Builder 1.0 client. In the Getting Started pane, select the Adventure Works model and choose the Matrix (cross-tab) report layout. Click OK.
2. The Report Builder 1.0 client loads the Adventure Works model and adds an empty matrix region to the design area, as shown in Figure 9.12.

Figure 9.12 The Report Builder default matrix template.

Recall that dragging the Sales Territory entity to the report creates an entity group that has a grand total for the entire group. Since our report includes group totals at territory group, country, and region levels, we need value groups for each of these fields.

3. Select the Sales Territory entity in the Entities pane and drag its Group field to the Drag and Drop Row Groups area of the matrix region. This creates a value group for the Group field.
4. Drag the Country attribute and drop it to the right of the Group field on the report.
5. Drag the Region attribute and drop it to the right of the Country field on the report. Rename the Region column caption to *Region*.

At this point, your report layout should look like the one shown in Figure 9.13. Each of the three fields should have a tab and total line.

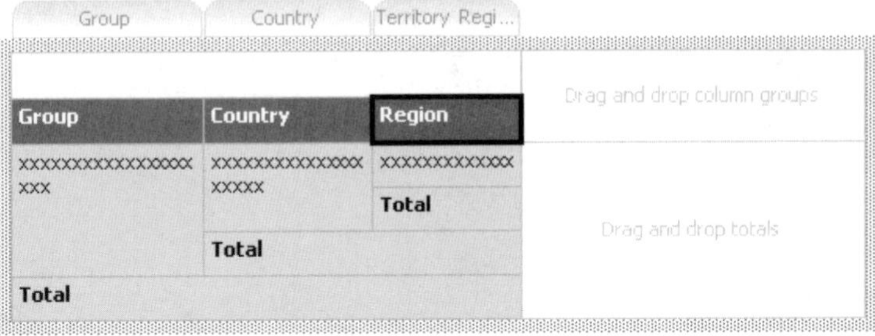

Figure 9.13 The Group, Country, and Region fields form value row groups.

6. In the Entities pane, select the Sales Orders role of the Sales Territory entity to navigate to the Sales Order entity.
7. Expand the Order Date field in the Fields pane and drag the Order Year field to the Drag and Drop Column Groups area of the matrix region. This creates an Order Year column group. Rename the Order Year column caption in-place to *Year*.
8. In the Entities pane, select the Sales Order Details role to navigate to the Sales Order Item entity.
9. Drag and Total Order Qty field to the Drag and Drop Totals area to create a matrix static group.
10. Click any of the Total cells to show the Total Order Qty tab, as shown in Figure 9.14.

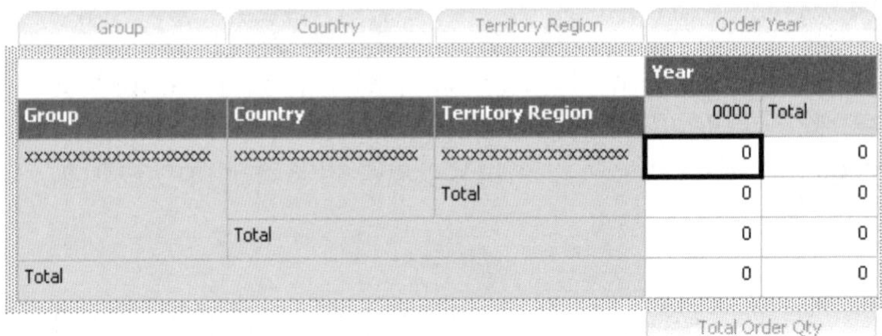

Figure 9.14 Click a total cell in the matrix report to show the group tab.

11. Drag the Total Line Total field and drop it on the Total Order Qty tab to create a second matrix static group.
12. Rename the Total Order Qty caption in-place to *Order Qty* and Total Line Total to *Sales*.
13. Right-align all column captions below the Year column by selecting them and clicking the Right Justify button on the Standard toolbar.
14. Format the total cells below the Total column header as bold.
15. Format the cells in the two Order Qty columns as a general number with a thousands separator and no decimal places.
16. Format the cells in the two Sales columns as currency with no decimal places.
17. Since a matrix report expands horizontally and needs more horizontal space, change the page layout to landscape from the File ⇨ Page Setup main menu.

At this point, you can run the report to verify that its layout matches the one in Figure 9.11.

Working with images

If needed, you can add images such as company logos to your ad hoc reports.

1. Click inside the Click To Add Title text box and enter Sales by Territory as a report title. Select the report title and move it to the right.
2. Select Insert ⇨ Picture main menu and navigate to the ch09 folder. Select the awc.jpg image and click Open.
3. Resize the image and move it to the desired location on the report.

You can also use commands on the Insert menu to add text boxes with static text.

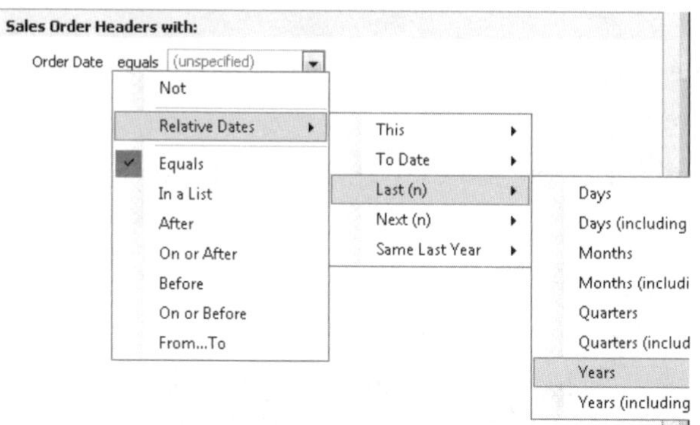

Figure 9.15 The Report Builder 1.0 client supports relative date filters.

Implementing relative date parameters

As it stands, our matrix report aggregates all data. Let's define a parameter to let the user filter the report by a relative date, such as the last five years.

1. Click the Filter button to open the Filter Data dialog box.
2. Ensure that the Sales Order entity is selected in the Entities pane. Relative dates work only with the date fields in the model and not with their date variations. Double-click the Order Date field to add it to the right filter pane.

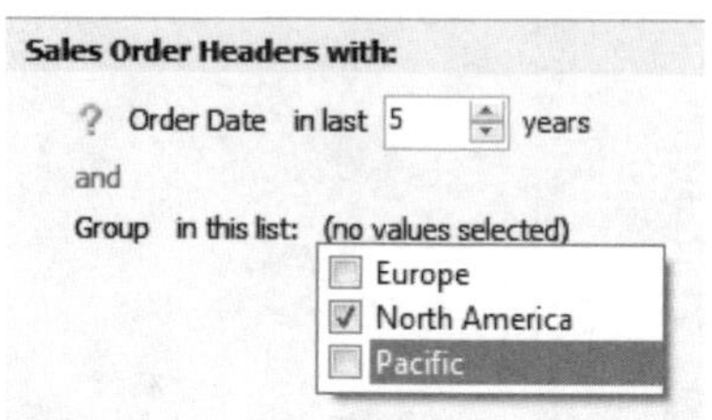

Figure 9.16 When you change the filter condition to In This List, the Report Builder 1.0 client creates a multivalued parameter.

3. Right-click on the *Equals* condition and select Relative Dates ⇨ Last(n) ⇨ Years context menu, as shown in Figure 9.16. The filter conditions changes to I*n* Last.
4. Default the filter to five years because the last year with data in the AdventureWorks database is 2004.
5. Make the Order Date parameter a prompt parameter by right-clicking on Order Date and choosing Prompt.

Implementing multivalued parameters

The final change that you will make to the Sales by Territory report is defining a multivalued parameter to filter the report data by one or more territories.

1. With the Filter Date dialog open, select the Territory role to navigate to the Sales Territory entity and double-click on the Group field to add it to the filter area.

Because you set the ValueSelection property of the Group field to Dropdown, the Report Builder 1.0 client shows a drop-down list next to the Equals condition. As a result, you can select a single territory group only. If you select the In This List filter condition, the Report Builder 1.0 client creates a multivalued parameter. The Report Builder 1.0 client populates the list with the distinct field values.

2. Right-click on the Equals filter condition and replace it with the In a List condition. Click the (on values selected) link and notice that the Report Builder 1.0 client presents a multivalued list.
3. Check North America to set the default value in the filter to this territory.
4. Set up the Group parameter as a prompt parameter.

Run the report to test your changes. Optionally, save the report to the report catalog or as a file.

9.2.3 Designing Chart Reports

The Report Builder 1.0 client also supports simple chart reports based on the Reporting Services 2005 chart region. Suppose that you need to create a line chart report that shows sales by territory and time, similar to the Sales by Territory Chart report shown in Figure 9.17. This report displays the order sales amount on the y-axis and sales regions grouped by a territory group on the x-axis. As the legend shows, the four chart lines represent sales for years 2001, 2002, 2003, and 2004.

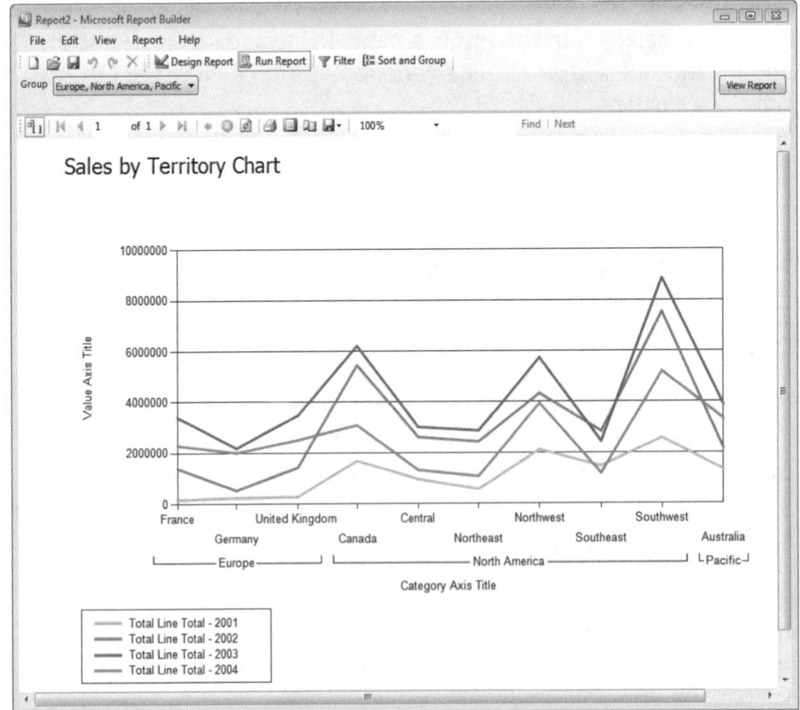

Figure 9.17 The Sales by Territory Chart report shows territory group and region on the category axis, order year on the series axis, and order sales amount on the value axis.

Designing the Sales by Territory Chart report

Follow these steps to create the report:

1. Assuming the Report Builder 1.0 client is open, click the New toolbar button to create a new report. Make sure the Adventure Works model is selected in the Getting Started pane.
2. Select the Chart report layout and click OK. The Report Builder 1.0 client adds an empty chart region to the design area.
3. Click the chart region. The Report Builder 1.0 client shows adornment areas around the chart region (see Figure 9.18) where you can drop fields to bind the chart to data.

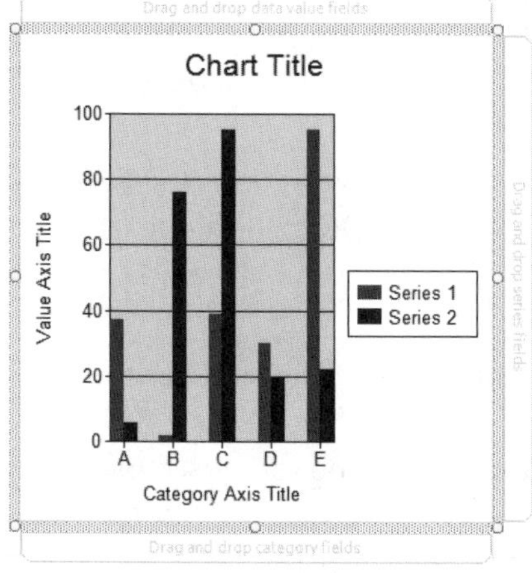

Figure 9.18 The chart region has adornment areas where the user can drop data value, category and series fields.

4. Select the Group and Region fields of the Sales Territory entity and drop them on the Drag and Drop Category Fields adornment area.
5. In the Entities pane, select the Sales Orders role to navigate to the Sales Order entity.
6. In the Fields pane, expand the Order Date field and drag Order Year to the Drag and Drop Series Fields adornment area.

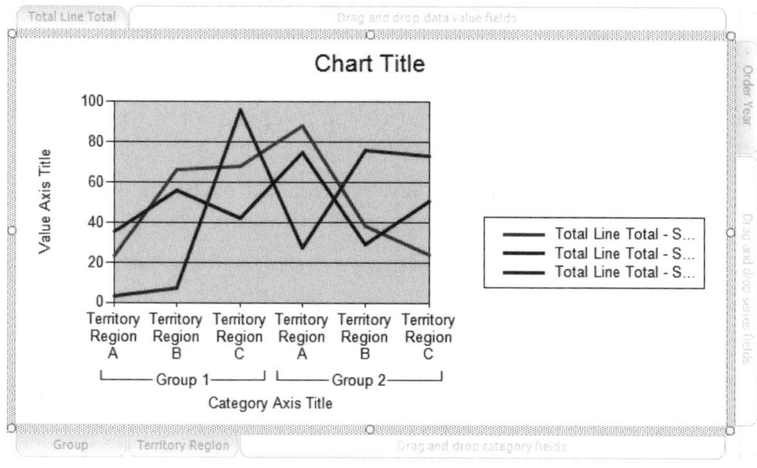

Figure 9.19 The Sales by Territory chart report has a category axis, data value axis, series axis, and a legend.

7. In the Entities pane, select the Sales Order Details role to navigate to the Sales Order Item entity.
8. Drag the Total Line Total field to the Drag and Drop Data Value Fields adornment area.

9. Right-click on the chart area and select Chart Type ➪ Line ➪ Simple Line from the context menu to change the chart type to a line chart. Compare your report to the one shown in Figure 9.19.
10. Preview the report to test it.

Refining the report
As it stands, the report is somewhat crowded. Let's make a few changes to improve its appearance.

1. Go back to design mode, right-click on the chart, and choose Chart Options.
2. In the Chart Options dialog, on the Chart Type tab, change the Palette property to Pastel.
3. Click the Format Plot Area button. In the Format dialog box, switch to the Fill tab and change the fill color to White. Click OK to return to the Chart Options tab.
4. In the Titles tab, clear the Chart Title text box to remove the chart title to free up more space.
5. In the Legend tab, change the Position property to Bottom Left. Click OK to close the Chart Options dialog box.
6. Enter *Sales by Territory Chart* as a report title.
7. Change the page layout to Landscape and enlarge the chart both horizontally and vertically by dragging its border handles.
8. Optionally, click the Filter button and create a Group prompt filter as you did in section 9.2.2.

Run the report now and compare its output to the one shown in Figure 9.17.

9.2.4 Authoring OLAP Reports

In chapter 8, you auto-generated the Adventure Works UDM model from the Adventure Works cube. Let's author a matrix report that uses this model. Although very basic, the Reseller Sales by Product Category report (see Figure 9.20) demonstrates some of the pros and cons for integrating Report Builder 1.0 with Analysis Services, which I discussed in chapter 8.

Implementing the report
The Reseller Sales by Product Category report is very similar to the Sales by Territory report both in terms of layout and implementation, so I will gloss over its implementation steps.

1. Assuming the Report Builder 1.0 client is open, click the New toolbar button to create a new report.
2. When you use an Analysis Services cube-based report model, you must choose a perspective. Select the Adventure Works perspective of the Adventure Works UDM model.
3. Select the Matrix layout and click OK to create the report template.

Although the Entities pane lists more entities than the Adventure Works model, you should be able to recognize many of them.

4. Select the Product entity. Drag the Category field and drop it on the Drag and Drop Row Groups area of the matrix region. Drag the Subcategory field and drop it next to the Category column on the report.

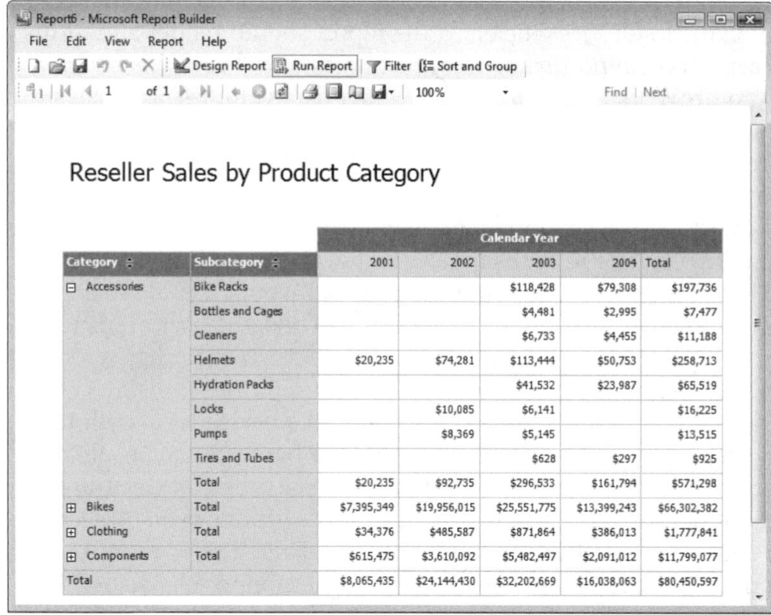

Report6 - Microsoft Report Builder
File Edit View Report Help
Design Report
Run Report
Filter
Sort and Group
1 of 1
100%
Find | Next
Reseller Sales by Product Category
Calendar Year
Category
Subcategory
2001
2002
2003
2004
Total
Accessories
Bike Racks
$118,428
$79,308
$197,736
Bottles and Cages
$4,481
$2,995
$7,477
Cleaners
$6,733
$4,455
$11,188
Helmets
$20,235
$74,281
$113,444
$50,753
$258,713
Hydration Packs
$41,532
$23,987
$65,519
Locks
$10,085
$6,141
$16,225
Pumps
$8,369
$5,145
$13,515
Tires and Tubes
$628
$297
$925
Total
$20,235
$92,735
$296,533
$161,794
$571,298
Bikes
Total
$7,395,349
$19,956,015
$25,551,775
$13,399,243
$66,302,382
Clothing
Total
$34,376
$485,587
$871,864
$386,013
$1,777,841
Components
Total
$615,475
$3,610,092
$5,482,497
$2,091,012
$11,799,077
Total
$8,065,435
$24,144,430
$32,202,669
$16,038,063
$80,450,597

Figure 9.20 The Reseller Sales by Product Category report uses an Analysis Services 2005 cube as a data source.

As soon as you drag the first field, the Report Builder 1.0 client collapses the Entities pane to show only those roles directly related to the Product dimension in the cube. This behavior is very different from OLAP browsers, such as Microsoft Excel, which display a static list. Although very helpful with relational data sources, the Report Builder 1.0 entity navigation is confusing with cubes and can quickly get us into trouble, as you will see in a moment.

5. Expand the Reseller Sales Order Details to navigate to the Reseller Sales measure group.
6. Drag the Reseller Sales Amount field to the Drag and Drop Totals area. Rename its column header to *Sales*.
7. Select the Date role below Reseller Sales Order Details and then select the Calendar folder. Drag the Calendar Year field to the Drag and Drop Column Groups matrix area. Rename the column header to Calendar Year.
8. Enter Reseller Sales by Product Category as a report title and compare your report with the one shown in Figure 9.21.

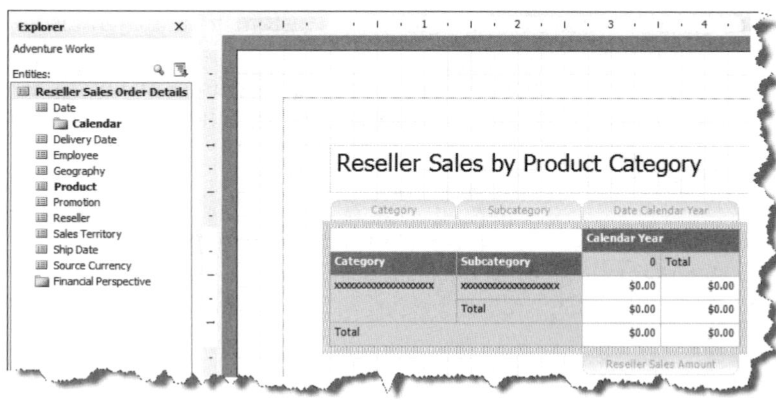

Figure 9.21 The Reseller Sales by Product Category report in the works.

So far, so good. If you run the report at this point, it should look similar to the one shown in Figure 9.20. More importantly, due to OLAP's efficiency, the report should render almost instantaneously. The improvement in the report response time may not be that obvious with a modest database such as AdventureWorks. However, given larger data volumes, an Analysis Services UDM model will outperform a report model that queries a relational database containing the same data. Performance is the most important reason for choosing Analysis Services and its Unified Dimensional Model.

Now, the bad news. Cubes typically have more than one measure group. For example, the Adventure Works cube has Internet Sales and Reseller Sales measure groups. Both measures groups join the Product and Date dimensions. Suppose the end user would like to see the Internet Sales side-by-side with the reseller sales on this report. To do this, the user needs to navigate to the Internet Sales entity. Unfortunately, the Report Builder 1.0 client has set the Reseller Sales Order Details as a root entity.

So, we embark on a quest to find Reseller Sales. Even if you find a navigational path that leads to it, setting up a filter, such as a date filter, will result in an unhappy outcome, also known as a run time exception. That's because Report Builder 1.0 treats the cube measure groups as separate entities and it doesn't recognize that both measure groups need be sliced by the same filter. There are, of course, other rifts waiting for you ahead, such as poor performance with larger cubes. By now, you probably appreciate my suggestion to re-consider the Report Builder 1.0-Analysis Services integration scenario.

9.3 Advanced Ad Hoc Reporting

Now that I've covered the basic features of the Report Builder 1.0 client, let me kick it up a notch and demonstrate some of its more advanced features. In this section, you will learn how to implement more complex filters and formulas, custom drillthrough reports, and how to use a Report Builder model as a data source for a Report Designer report.

9.3.1 Working with Filters and Formulas

One of my favorite Report Builder 1.0 client features is its advanced filtering capabilities. Suppose that the Adventure Works sales department is planning a mailing campaign to promote a new bike to targeted customers. They have requested a report that lists individuals who have purchased a mountain bike in 2003 or a road bike in 2004, have spent more than a user-specified value on bike products, and live in a given territory. The Customer Campaign List report (see Figure 9.22) fulfills this requirement.

The report lets the user filter customers by one or more countries. The user can enter the targeted total order amount as a report parameter. In this case, the report will return customers whose order amount exceeded $8,000.

Implementing the basic report

The steps required to lay out the Customer Campaign List should be familiar to you by now.

1. Launch the Report Builder 1.0 client and choose the Adventure Works report model and a table report layout.

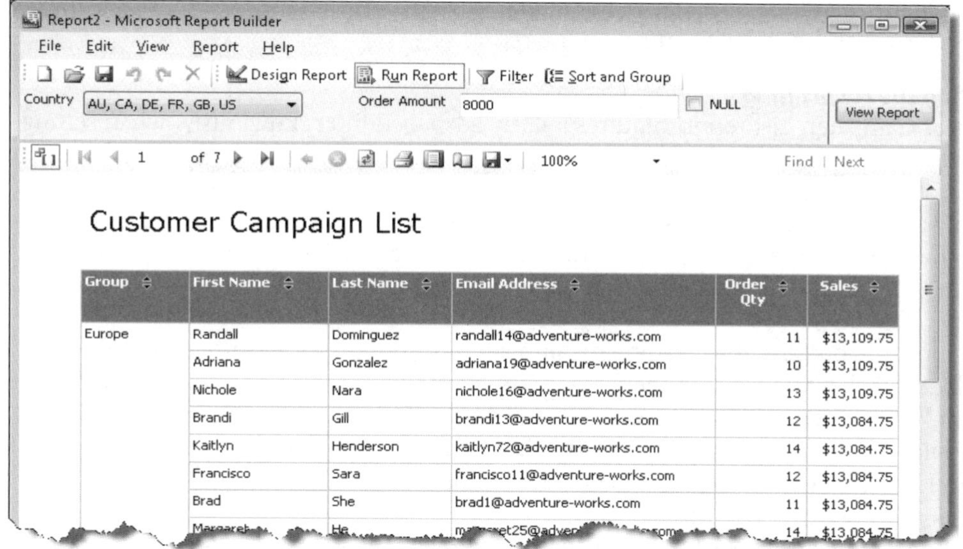

Figure 9.22 This report shows individual customers who have purchased a mountain bike in 2003 or a road bike in 2004 and whose order amount exceeds a given value

2. Drag the Customer entity from the Entities pane and drop it on the table region.
3. Remove the Customer Type field but leave the Account Number field to preserve the entity group.
4. Add the First Name, Last Name, and Email Address fields from the Customer entity.
5. Remove the Account Number column from the report.
6. In the Entities pane, select the Sales Orders role and then the Sales Order Details role to navigate to the Sales Order Item entity.
7. Add the Total Order Qty and Total Line Total fields to the report. Rename their column captions to Order Qty and Sales respectively.
8. In the Entities pane, select the Territory role to navigate to the Sales Territory entity and add the Group field on the report before the First Name column. This creates a new value group that groups customers by territory.
9. Format the report as needed. At this point your report layout should match the one shown in Figure 9.23.

Group	Customer				
Group	First Name	Last Name	Email Address	Order Qty	Sales
xxxxxxxxxxxx xxxxxxx	xxxxxxxxxxxxxx	xxxxxxxxxxxxxx	xxxxxxxxxxxxxxxxxxx	0	$0.00
	Total			0	$0.00
Total				0	$0.00

Figure 9.23 The Customer Campaign List report groups customers by territory group.

10. Enter *Customer Campaign List* as a report title in the Click to Add Title text box.
11. Attempt to run the report. The Report Builder 1.0 client displays an error message: "A filter must be specified." That's because the report uses the Customer entity whose InstanceSelec-

tion property is set to MandatoryFilter in the model. This means that the user must set up a filter on the Customer Entity before running the report.

Implementing the report filter

The Customer Campaign List report requires a fairly advanced filter. Previously, when setting up report filters we didn't pay much attention to a little but rather important (and verbose) checkbox located at the bottom of the Filter Data dialog box called When Adding a New Condition, Apply to All Data in My Report checkbox. When left to its default checked status, it propagates the report filter from the root entity to entities that are in one-to-many relationships with the root entity. In other words, it applies the filter not only to the report rows, but the totals as well.

For example, if you filter the Customer Campaign List to return sales orders for 2004, the Report Builder 1.0 client will switch the primary report entity to the Sales Order entity. Subsequently, only customers with orders in 2004 will be displayed and the Sales column will display the total sales amount for these orders. This is most likely what the user would expect anyway and it is consistent with the filtering behavior of other reporting tools, such as Excel pivot reports.

If you uncheck the checkbox before setting up the filter, the Report Builder 1.0 client will attempt to preserve the totals and apply the filter conditions to the report rows only. Assuming the same scenario, this means that the Customer entity will remain the primary entity and a filter group Any Orders with Order Year = 2004 will be created instead. As before, only customers with sales orders in 2004 will be returned. However, the sales amount will not be affected by the filter as it will show the cumulative totals for all orders submitted by the customer, not only the 2004 orders. So, clearing the checkbox lets you separate the report row filter from the filter used for the report totals.

1. Click the Filter button to open the Filter Data dialog box.
2. This is the most important step. Clear the When Adding a New Condition checkbox.
3. In the Entities pane, select the Territory role and double-click the Country field to add it to the filter. Change its filter condition to In a List and pre-select all countries. Make the Country filter a prompted parameter.
4. In the Entities pane, click the root Customer entity. Double-click the Customer Type field to add it to the filter. Expand the drop-down list and select the "I" item to filter only individual customers.
5. In the Entities pane, select the Sales Orders role. In the Fields pane, expand Order Date and double-click the Order Year date variation field.

   Since the Customer entity has a one-to-many cardinality to the Sales Order entity, Report Builder 1.0 client creates a new Any Of filter group.
6. Enter *2003* in the Order Year text box.
7. In the Entities pane, select the Sales Order Details role below the Sales Order entity and then the Product role below Sales Order Details to get to the Product entity.
8. Drag the Product Subcategory Name field inside the Any Sales Orders group and set the default to Mountain Bikes.

   Compare your filter with the one shown in Figure 9.24. Click the Any Sales Orders With link and observe that the Report Builder 1.0 client supports also All Sales Orders With, No Sales

Orders With, and Not All Sales Orders With group types. You can also manually create a filter group by using the New Group button.

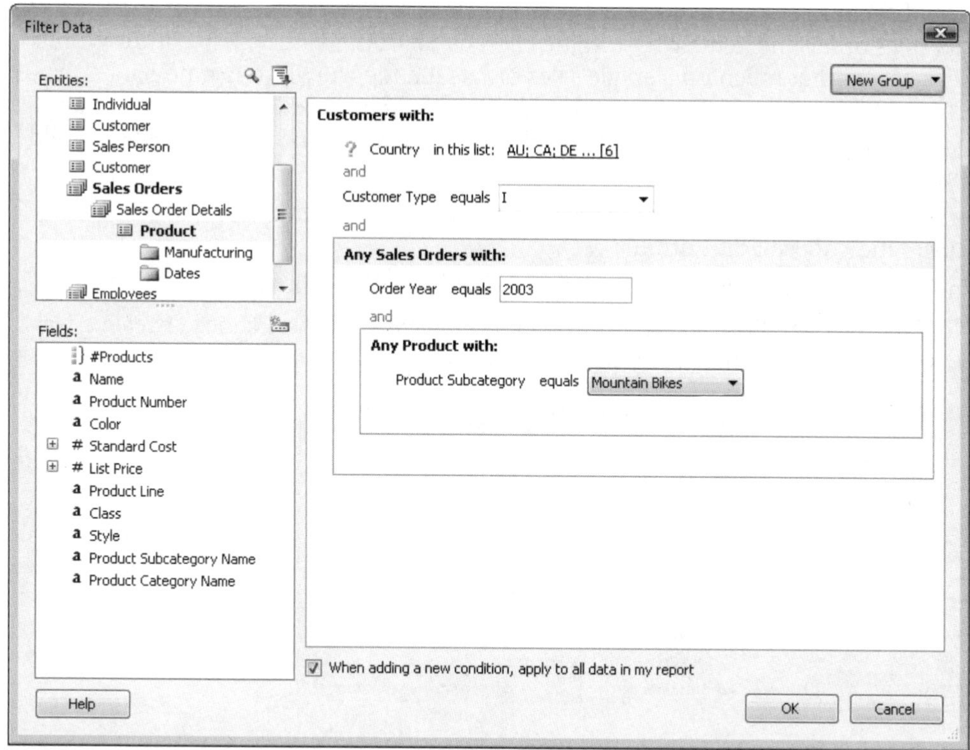

Figure 9.24 If the When Adding a New Condition checkbox is unchecked, the Report Builder 1.0 client will create an Any Of group that doesn't affect the report totals.

9. Expand the New Group drop-down list and select Any Of to create a new Any of group.
10. Drag the Order Year date variation of the Order Date field inside the new group and set it to *2004*.
11. Drag and Product Subcategory Name field of the Product entity inside the new group and set it to Road Bikes.
12. Click the *and* filter condition between the two Any Of groups and change it to an *or* condition. Click OK to return to close the Filter Data dialog.

What you've accomplished up to this point is to create a filter that selects all individual customers in all countries who have placed Mountain Bikes orders in 2003 or Road Bikes orders in 2004. The filter text box should show the following filter restatement:

```
Filter: Customers with: All of (Country in (prompted), Customer Type = "I",
Any of (Any Sales Orders with All of (Order Year = 2003,
Any Product with Product Subcategory = Mountain Bikes),
Any Sales Orders with All of (Order Year = 2004, Any Product with Product Subcategory = Road Bikes)))
```

Filtering on totals

Recall that our report needs to filter on totals to return only customers with bike sales exceeding a given amount. You may think you can use the Filter Dialog again to filter on the sales order total but this won't work. If the When Adding a New Condition checkbox is selected, attempting to filter on Sales Order Details will change the primary entity to the Sales Order Item. As a result, Report Builder 1.0 will apply the filter to the individual sales orders.

Assuming that the user enters 8,000 as the parameter value, the Report Builder 1.0 will attempt to find sales order line items whose value exceeds $8,000. Since no Adventure Works customers have spent that much on a single sales order, the report will return no data. Turning off the When Adding a New Condition checkbox won't help either because it won't apply the filter to the report totals. What we really need is a way to apply the filter to the Sales field on the report.

1. In the report design area, right-click on the Sales field that is immediately below the Sales column header, and choose Edit Formula.
2. In the Define Formula dialog box, double-click the Total Line Total field.
3. Click the No Filter Applied link next to the Sales Order Details role and choose Create a New Filter, as Figure 9.25 shows. This opens an empty Filter Data dialog box.

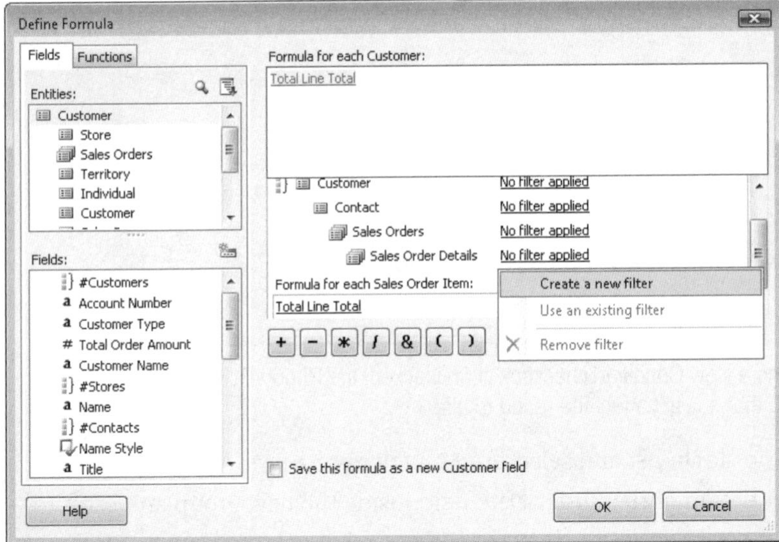

Figure 9.25 Create a field-level filter to select customers with sales exceeding a given value.

4. In the Filter Data dialog box, select the Product role and double-click the Product Category Name field to add it to the report.
5. Set the Product Category Name drop-down list to Bikes and click OK to close the Filter Data dialog box (see Figure 9.26). This filters the Sales field to include only orders for products in the Bikes category.
6. Check the Save This Formula as a New Customer Field checkbox and click OK.
7. When prompted, enter Order Amount as the field name.
8. Back to the design area, select the Customer entity in the Entities Pane and note that the Report Builder 1.0 client has added the Order Amount field to the Fields list.
9. Click the Filter button to open the main filter.
10. Double-click the Order Amount field of the Customer entity to create a new *and* group.
11. Change the Order Amount filter condition to Greater Than and default it to 8000. Configure the Order Amount filter as a prompt and click OK.

12. Press the Sort and Group button. Select the Group item in the Select Group pane and define an ascending sort order on it. Check the Page Break Between Groups checkbox to start a new page when the territory group changes.

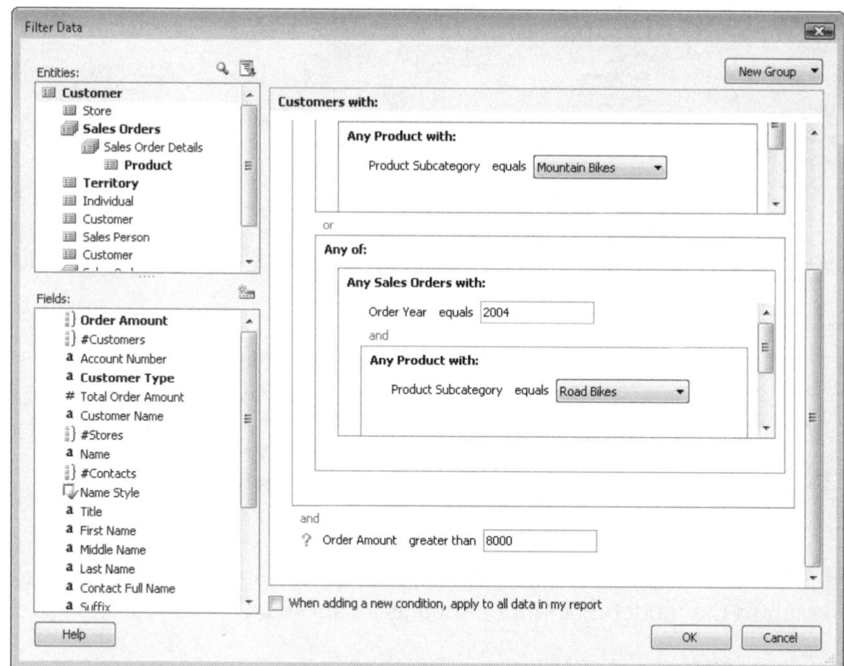

Figure 9.26 Use the Order Amount field to filter the customer totals.

13. Select the Customer group and sort it by Sales in descending order.

If you now run the report, the report should return only customers whose bike orders have exceeded $8,000.

9.3.2 Working with Report Model Data Sources

As I mentioned earlier, you can use Report Designer to build reports that use a report model as a data source. If end users demand sophisticated ad hoc reports that surpass the capabilities of the Report Builder 1.0 client, consider using the Report Designer to produce reports from an existing report model. This approach combines the best of both worlds—an intuitive Report Builder model and a feature-rich report authoring tool— but it requires more advanced report authoring skills.

For example, the Sales Order report shown in Figure 9.27 looks almost the same as the Sales Order report discussed in chapter 4. The difference is that this report uses our Adventure Works report model as a data source. Let me walk you through its high-level implementation steps.

Defining a report model data source

Start by creating a data source in Report Designer that points to the report model.

1. Start the BIDS Report Designer and open a new report.
2. Create an Adventure Works Model data source as follows:

- Type: Report Server Model
- Connection string: Server=http://<servername>/reportserver; datasource=/amrs/adventure works
- Credentials: Use Windows Authentication (integrated security)

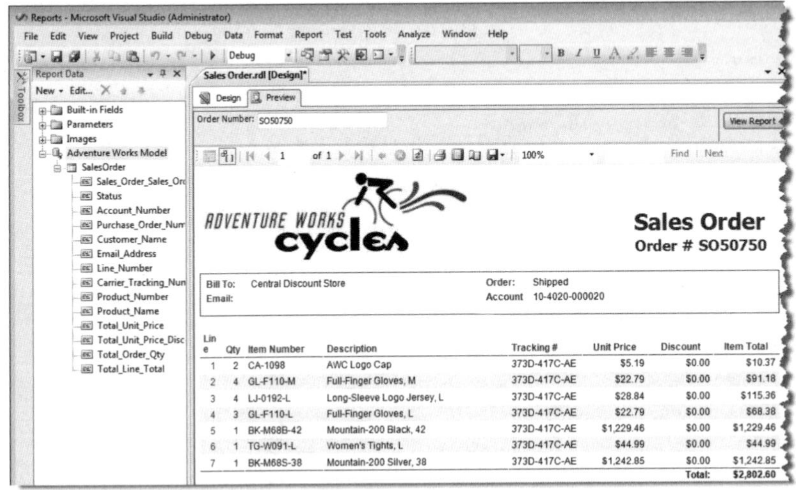

Figure 9.27 When the Report Builder 1.0 client is not enough, you can use the Report Designer to author reports from a Report Builder model.

When using the Report Server Model data provider, the connection string includes the report server URL and the full path to the model that will be used as a data source.

Defining a report model data source

Start by creating a data source in Report Designer that points to the report model.

1. Start the BIDS Report Designer and open a new report.
2. Create an Adventure Works Model data source as follows:
   - Type: Report Server Model
   - Connection string: Server=http://<servername>/reportserver; datasource=/amrs/adventure works
   - Credentials: Use Windows Authentication (integrated security)

When using the Report Server Model data provider, the connection string includes the report server URL and the full path to the model that will be used as a data source.

Creating the report dataset

The Report Designer includes a graphical Report Model Query Designer that lets you create the semantic query by dragging and dropping fields.

1. Create a new dataset that uses the Adventure Works Model data source.
2. If the Report Designer loads the query in the Generic Query Designer, toggle the Generic Query Designer toolbar button to switch to the Report Model Query Designer, which is shown in Figure 9.28.

Similar to the Report Builder 1.0 client, the Report Model Query Designer loads the model metadata in the Entities and Fields panes. Creating the report model dataset is a matter of dragging fields from the Fields pane and dropping them on the Drag and Drop Column Fields area.

3. In the Entities pane, select Sales Order and then drag the Sales Order Number, Purchase Order Number, Account Number, and Status fields from Fields to the Drag and Drop Column Fields area.

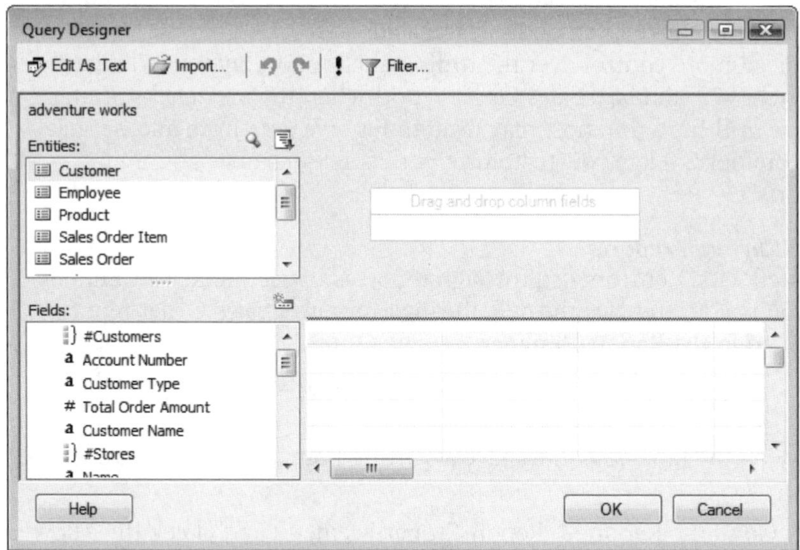

Figure 9.28 The Report Model Query Designer auto-generates the semantic query as the user drags and drops model items.

4. In the Entities pane, select Sales Order Item and then drag the Line Number, Career Tracking Number, Total Order Qty, Total Unit Price, Total Unit Price Discount, and Total Line Total fields to the column fields area.
5. Select the Customer entity and then drag the Customer Name and Email Address fields.
6. Select the Product entity and drag Product Number and Name fields.
7. Click the Generic Query Designer to see the semantic query generated as a result of the dragging and dropping fields.

If you execute the query at this point, it will fetch all sales orders and their associated line items. This is a lot of data so let's filter the query to return a single order only.

8. Click the Filter button to open the Filter Data dialog box. Double-click the Sales Order Number field of the Sales Order entity to create a filter condition. Optionally, default the Sales Order Number to a given order number, such as SO50750, and configure it as a prompted parameter. Click OK.
9. In the Report Data window, expand the Parameters node and notice that the Report Model Query Designer has defined a Sales_Order_Sales_Order_Number report-level parameter to let the user enter the sales order number at runtime.
10. Click the exclamation toolbar button to execute the query and see the results.
11. Click the Refresh Fields toolbar button to update the dataset field definition.

Once the report dataset is in place, authoring a report that uses it should be familiar to you.

9.3.3 Implementing Custom Drillthrough Reports

Recall that the Report Builder 1.0 client generates drillthrough reports when the user clicks on a field whose EnableDrillthrough property is set to True. Specifically, Report Builder 1.0 generates a single-instance drillthrough report that shows all non-hidden entity fields when the clicked item represents a single instance. It generates a multi-instance report that includes all default detail attributes when the clicked item is an aggregated value.

Sometimes, you may need more control over the drillthrough report layout and data. For example, you may need to show a standard Sales Order report when the user clicks on the sales order number. Or, the drillthrough report may need to retrieve data from another database. Fortunately, Report Builder 1.0 lets you customize both single-instance and multi-instance drillthrough reports.

Implementing custom drillthrough reports

The easiest way to get started with a custom drillthrough report is to use the Report Builder 1.0 client. Suppose that you need to replace the default single-instance Sales Order report with a report that you created in the Report Designer.

1. Launch the Report Builder 1.0 client and choose the Adventure Works model and a table report layout.
2. Drag the Sales Order entity on the table region to have a starting point for the drillthrough report.
3. This is the important step. Go to the Report ⇨ Report Properties menu and check the Allow Users to Drill to This Report From Other Reports option.

   When you do this, the Report Builder 1.0 client creates two report-level parameters: DrillthroughSourceQuery and DrillthroughContext. When the user initiates the drillthrough action, the Report Builder 1.0 client passes the semantic query to the first parameter and the user selection to the second. A drillthrough report must have both these parameters.
4. Click File ⇨ Save to File menu and save the report definition to disk. Open the report definition in Notepad and copy the entire <DataSources> element because you will need to change the report data source in the BIDS Report Designer.
5. Open the report in Report Designer and change the report data source to point to your report model, as demonstrated in section 9.3.2.
6. Use the Report Model Query Designer to add additional entities as needed and test the query. When doing so, make sure that the Sales Order entity remains the primary entity (the top entity in the Entities list). Report Builder 1.0 will throw a run time exception if the primary entity in a single-instance drillthrough report is different than the clicked entity.
7. Lay out the report as needed. Once you're done, save the report to disk. Open its definition in Notepad and restore the <DataSources> element.
8. Use the Report Manager to upload the report to the AMRS folder. For your convenience, I have included the finished report, Sales Order Drillthrough, in the source code for this chapter.

Configuring drillthrough reports

Once the drillthrough report is deployed, you have to associate it with the appropriate entity in the model. Follow these steps to associate the Sales Order Drillthrough report with the Sales Order entity.

1. In Report Manager, navigate to the AMRS folder and click the Adventure Works model.
2. In the model properties page, select the Clickthrough link.
3. In the model entity list, select the Sales Order entity, as shown in Figure 9.29.
4. Click the Browse button next to the Single Instance Report text box and navigate to the Sales Order Drillthrough report. Click Apply.

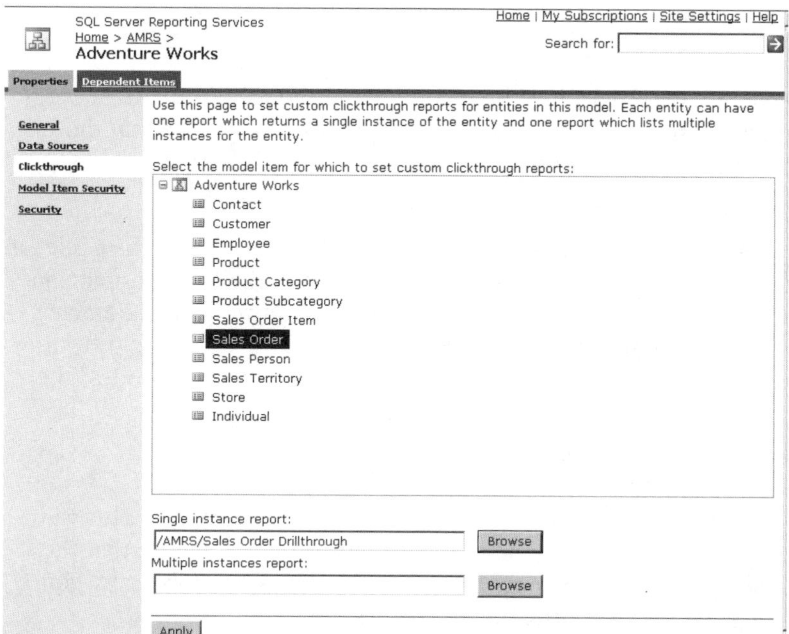

Figure 9.29 Use Report Manager to associate the custom drillthrough report with the entity.

5. Close the Report Builder 1.0 client if it is open. Start Report Builder 1.0 client and open the Adventure Works model.
6. Author an ad hoc report that uses fields from the Sales Order entity or open the Sales Order Drillthrough Test report that I provided.
7. Click on a field that drills through to more data. When you click on a field, you should see the Sales Order report instead of a default drillthrough report.

Authoring external drillthrough reports

The Sales Order Drillthrough report retrieves data from the Adventure Works model. But what if you want the drillthrough report to show data from an external database, such as the AdventureWorks relational database? Although not officially supported, it is possible to parse the DrillthroughContext parameter and extract the identifier of the clicked item. You can then use this identifier as a query parameter. The Sales Order Drillthrough Action report demonstrates this approach. I used the word "action" in the report name because external drillthrough reports resemble UDM report actions.

> **SLEAZY HACK** The DrillthroughContext parameter and the modeling interfaces used by the Sales Order Drillthrough Action report were not intended to be public and may change in a future release. Use them at your own risk.

As I mentioned, a drillthrough report must have DrillthroughSourceQuery and Drillthrough-Context parameters. An external drillthrough report can obtain the identifier of the clicked item from the DrillthroughContext parameter. Here is what the DrillthroughContext parameter may look like when the user clicks on a Sales Order field:

```
<DrillthroughContext xmlns="http://schemas.microsoft.com/sqlserver/2004/10/semanticmodeling">
    <SelectedItems>
        <SelectedItemName>Sales Order Number</SelectedItemName>
    </SelectedItems>
    <GroupingValues>
        <GroupingValue Name="Sales Order">AKQhAQA=</GroupingValue>
    </GroupingValues>
</DrillthroughContext>
```

So, the Report Builder 1.0 client base64-encodes the identifier and writes it to the Grouping-Value element. If you examine Parameters tab of both report queries you will see that the value of the @SalesOrderNumber parameter uses the following expression:

```
="SO" + Code.GetSetting(Parameters!DrillthroughContext.Value, "// GroupingValue[@Name='Sales Order']")
```

The GetSetting helper function is embedded in the report. You can access it from the Code tab on the Report Properties dialog box. GetSetting loads the XML value of the DrillthroughContext parameter into an XmlDocument object and navigates to the GroupingValue parameter. Unfortunately, getting the identifier requires a bit more work than simply decoding it from base64 because the semantic engine stores it in an internal format. GetSetting "decodes" the identifier as follows:

```
Return Microsoft.ReportingServices.Modeling.EntityKey.FromBase64String(node.InnerText).
ToKeyParts(new Type() {Type.GetType("System.Int32")},Nothing) (0)
```

This line returns the primary key of the clicked Sales Order instance as an integer. This value is passed to the report query which retrieves the details of a single order. Note also that the report references System.Xml and Microsoft.ReportingServices.Modeling assemblies by going to the Report Properties dialog box and selecting the References tab.

9.3.4 Capturing Native Queries

Sometimes, when troubleshooting an ad hoc report, you may want to see the native query that the semantic engine sends to the data source. There are two ways to do this. The first approach captures the native queries in the report server log file and works with all supported data sources. The second approach applies only to SQL Server and Analysis Services data sources.

Using the report server log file

By default, the report server doesn't log semantic queries so you need to increase the trace level as follows:

1. Open the Reporting Services Windows service configuration file (ReportingServicesService.exe.config) located by default in the \Program Files\Microsoft SQL Server\MSRS10.MSSQLSERVER\Reporting Services\ReportServer\bin folder.
2. Locate the RStrace section and change the Components setting as shown below:

```
<RStrace>
  <add name="FileName" value="ReportServer_" />
  ...
  <add name="Components" value="all,RunningJobs:3,SemanticQueryEngine:4,SemanticModelGenerator:2" />
</RStrace>
```

You don't need to restart the Report Server Windows service because the server will recycle the Reporting Services application after detecting changes to its config files.

3. Run the report in the Report Builder 1.0 client. To get the latest trace output, you may need to restart the Report Server Windows service to flush the trace log.
4. Go to the \Program Files\Microsoft SQL Server\MSRS10.MSSQLSERVER\Reporting Services\LogFiles and open the latest log file whose name will be ReportServer__<date stamp>.log and search for SELECT to locate the native query.

Using the SQL Server Profiler

If your Report Builder model uses SQL Server or Analysis Services as data sources, you can use the SQL Server Profiler to watch the Report Builder real-time queries.

1. Start the SQL Server Profiler from the Performance Tools group inside the Microsoft SQL Server 2008 program group.
2. Create a new SQL Server or Analysis Services trace.

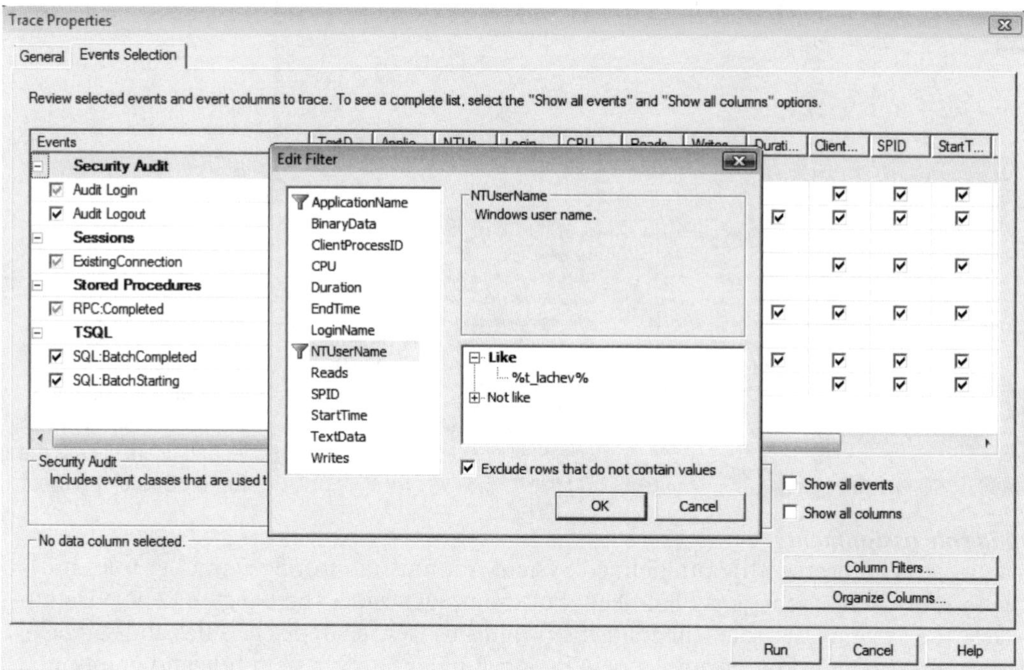

Figure 9.30 Use the SQL Server Profiler to capture Report Builder native queries submitted by a given user.

To minimize the number of trace events captured, consider setting up a column filter. For example, to watch only queries submitted by a user whose Windows login is t_lachev, set up a wildcard column filter on the NTUserName column, as shown in Figure 9.30. Once you run the report, you should see the native query text in the TextData column.

9.4 Securing Report Builder Models

An important management task is securing user access to the model. Reporting Services supports setting up security polices at different levels. The administrator must grant end users permission to download the Report Builder 1.0 client and run ad hoc reports. Published ad hoc reports can be secured in the same way as any other report server item. With report models, however, you can work with more granular security policies. You can leverage model-level security to restrict access to model entities and fields. Finally, you can implement data security in the model to filter data returned on the report based on the user identity.

9.4.1 Granting Report Builder Access

By default, only members of the System Administrator and System User report server roles can author ad hoc reports. This means that out of the box, only Windows local administrators will be able to use the Report Builder 1.0 client. Others users won't see the Report Builder button when they open the Report Manager. They need Execute Report Definition rights to be able to use the Report Builder 1.0 client.

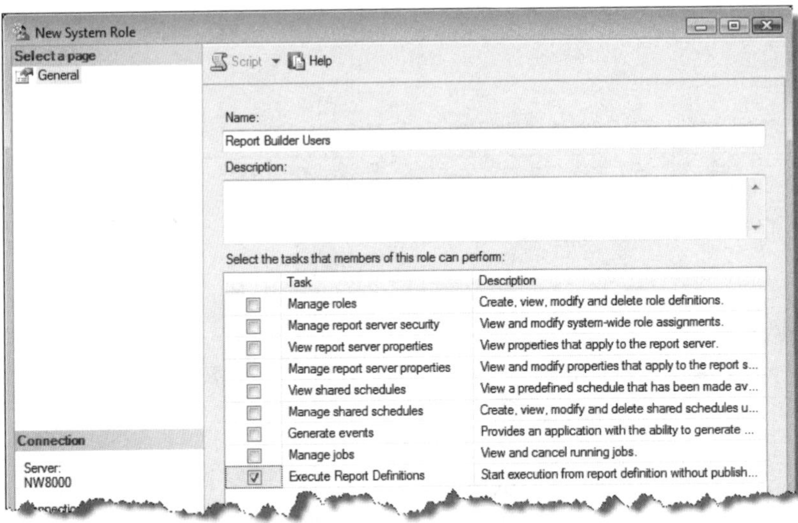

Figure 9.31 Create a new system role that includes the Execute Report Definitions task to let end users access the Report Builder 1.0 client.

Defining role assignments

You can assign end users to the pre-defined System Administrator or System User roles but they will get extra rights they may not need. For example, besides the Execute Report Definitions task, the System User role will grant them rights to view shared schedules and server properties. Instead, consider creating a new Report Builder Users system role and granting users rights to execute report definitions only, as follows:

1. Open SQL Server Management Studio (SSMS). In the Object Explorer pane, expand the Connect drop-down list and choose Reporting Services. Connect to the report server instance you want to manage.
2. Expand the Security folder and then System Roles folder.
3. Right-click on the Security folder node and choose New System Role.

4. In the New System Role dialog box, name the role *Report Builder Users* and select the Execute Report Definitions task, as shown in Figure 9.31. Click OK to create the Report Builder Users system role.

   Once the role is in place, you can open Report Manager and assign the Windows users or/and groups to the role.

5. Open the Report Manager application and click on the Site Settings link in the upper right corner.
6. On the Site Settings page, click the Security link.
7. Click the New Role Assignment button.

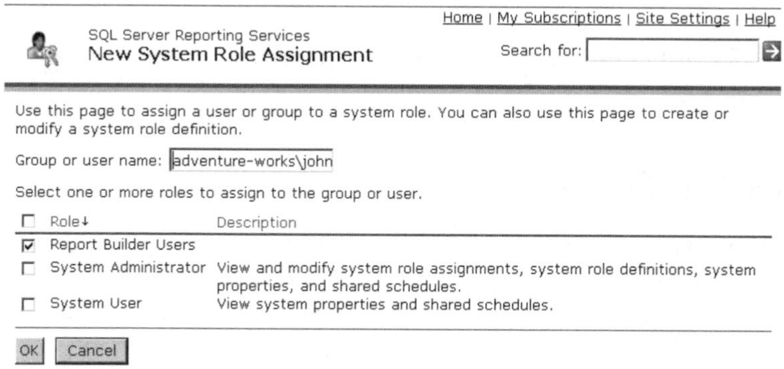

Figure 9.32 Define a new role assignment to grant rights to Windows users and groups to access Report Builder 1.0.

8. In the New System Role Assignment page (Figure 9.32), enter the name of the Windows user or group in the format <domain>\<login> (or <machine>\<login> for local users and groups).
9. Check the Report Builder Users role and click OK to create the role assignment.

   You need to repeat the last three steps for each user and group that will access the Report Builder. For easier maintenance, consider assigning all users to a domain or local Windows group and create a single role assignment for that group only.

   You may need also to grant end users rights to the report catalog. For example, you need to grant at least Browser rights to the Home folder if users will start the Report Builder 1.0 client by clicking the Report Builder button. Content Manager rights will be needed if you want to let them publish ad hoc reports to the server. Therefore, you need to define an item-level role assignment. The easiest way is to do this at the Home folder level because it propagates down the folder namespace.

10. Click the Home link to go to the Home folder and select the Properties tab to access the Security settings.
11. Click the New Role Assignment button and create role assignments for each Windows user or group. SSRS includes a predefined role called Report Builder that grants the permissions end users need to view folders, reports, and models but it doesn't let them publish reports. Select this role and click OK. If you want to let the Report Builder users save reports, consider assigning them to the predefined Publisher role.

Controlling server-wide Report Builder access

There are two server settings, EnableLoadReportDefinition and EnableReportDesignClientDownload, which control the Report Builder 1.0 availability for all users.

1. In Management Studio, right-click on the Reporting Services server node in the Object Explorer and choose Properties.
2. Select the Advanced page and note the Security section in the properties grid.

By default, both settings are enabled. The EnableLoadReportDefinition property is only applicable for a report server running in a SharePoint integration mode. When set to False, EnableLoadReportDefinition prevent the end users from previewing reports in the Report Builder 1.0 client although they can author reports. The EnableLoadReportDefinitions setting is also available on the Security page in the server properties (Enabled ad hoc report executions checkbox). If the EnableReportDesignClientDownload setting is False, the end users won't be able to download the Report Builder 1.0 client and the Report Builder button won't show in the Report Manager.

Once you publish the report model and grant access to the Report Builder 1.0 client, end users can start using it to author reports.

9.4.2 Implementing Model Item Security

Model item security lets you provide restricted access to entities, attributes, and roles in the model to Windows users and groups. For example, you can use model item security to let only members of the Human Resources department access the Employee entity or specific fields in it. In this respect, you will find model item security similar to database schema security which protects database tables and columns.

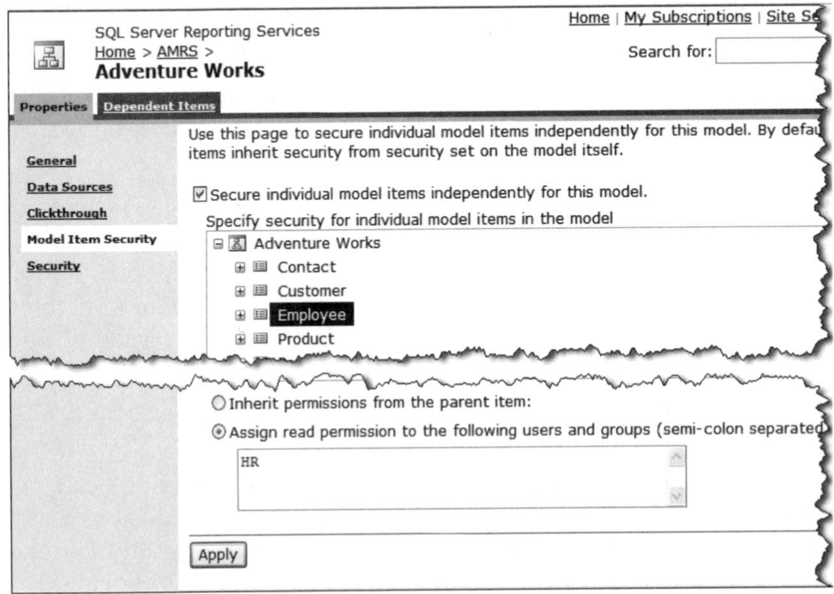

Figure 9.33 You can use model item security to grant access to specific entities or fields in the model.

You can set up model item security by going to the model Properties page in the Report Manager, as shown in Figure 9.33. The Security link lets you secure the model as a whole. For example, you can use the Security link to grant Content Manager rights to the user who will administer the model. Follow these steps to implement model item security that lets only users of the HR Windows group access the Employee entity.

3. In Report Manager, navigate to the AMRS folder and click the Adventure Works model link.
4. In the model properties page, click the Model Item Security link.
5. By default, users who can browse the model have unrestricted access to the model content. Check the Secure Individual Model Items Independently For This Model checkbox. This reverses the default security policy by requiring each user to have model item permissions before they can access model content.
6. Select the root Adventure Works node, which represents the entire model. Enter a semi-colon separated list of all Windows users and/or groups that will use the model in the Assign Read Permissions text box. Click Apply.
7. Select the Employee entity. By default, model items inherit their permissions from their parent. Therefore, the Windows users and groups you entered in the previous steps will have access to the entire model. Clear the Inherit Permissions From the Parent Item checkbox to break the inheritance chain.
8. Enter a semi-colon separated list of the Windows users and groups that will be able to access the Employee entity. For example, assuming that the HR Windows group includes users from the Human Resources department, enter HR and click Apply.

When the Report Builder 1.0 client downloads the model, the report server evaluates the model item security polices and returns only those items that the end user is authorized to see. If the user is not authorized to see an item, the item simply doesn't exist for that end user. As a result of the above steps, only members of the HR group will see the Employee entity.

9.4.3 Implementing Data Security

Finally, the most granular security model is data security. By default, if the user can access an entity, the user can view all rows of that entity. Suppose that you want to implement a security policy that lets a sales person view his orders only. This is where data security can help. You implement data security by setting up security filters that limit the data returned based on the user identity.

With the default Windows authentication, the user identity is the user Windows login. If custom security is used, the user identify will be the user name that your application passes to the LogonUser API. In order for data security to work, your database needs to store the user identity. For example, in the AdventureWorks database, the user identity is stored in the LoginID column in the HumanResources.Employee table.

Setting up a security filter

1. Open the Adventure Works model in Model Designer and select the Sales Person entity. Since the Sales Person entity derives from the Employee entity, it inherits the fields of the Employee entity.
2. Right-click on the Sales Person entity and choose New ⇨ Filter.
3. In the Filter Data dialog box that follows, double-click the Login ID field to create a new filter condition.
4. Right-click the Login ID field in the filter condition and choose Edit As Formula.

The Define Formula dialog box that follows shows the following formula text:

```
Login ID = EMPTY
```

5. Select the Functions tab. Double-click on the EMPTY word to select it.
6. Expand the Information section of the Functions tab and double-click the GETUSERID function.
7. Click OK to dismiss the Define Formula dialog box and return to the Filter Data dialog box, as shown in Figure 9.34.

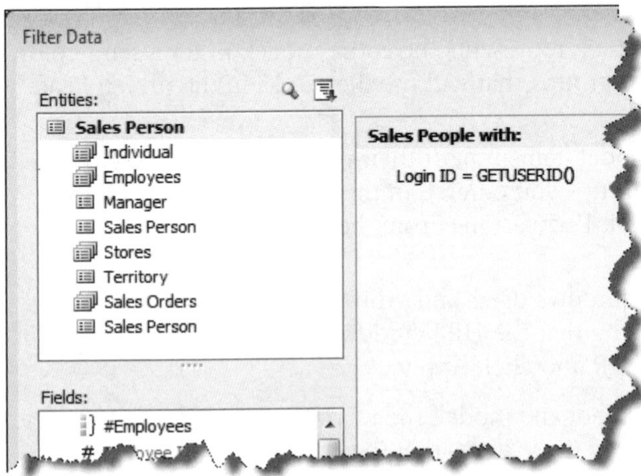

Figure 9.34 Implement data security by creating a security filter that passes the user identify to the database.

8. Click OK to close the Filter Data dialog box.
9. Rename the NewFilter attribute to *Security Filter* and set its Hidden property to True so the end users cannot see this attribute.
10. This is the most important step. Click the ellipsis (…) button inside the SecurityFilters property of the Sales Person entity. In the AttributeReference Collection Editor dialog box, add the Security Filter attribute and click OK.
11. Deploy the model to the server.

> **TIP** In real life, you will probably need to let power users or administrators see all rows. To meet this requirement, create a new filter but leave the filter dialog empty. This works because an empty filter doesn't filter anything.

You've now set up a security filter which limits the Sales Order entity to return only rows where the Login ID column matches the user login id.

Testing the security filter

Let's use the Report Builder 1.0 client to test the filter.

1. Launch the Report Builder 1.0 client and select the Adventure Works model. Choose a table layout.
2. Drag the Sales Person entity to the table region and run the report. Note that the report returns no rows because your Windows login doesn't match any of the Adventure Works logins.
3. In the SQL Server Management Studio, connect to the relational engine and open table Sales.SalesPerson. Note that the SalesPersonID column of the first row is 269.
4. Open table HumanResoures.Employee and locate the record with EmployeeID=269.
5. Copy the value in the LoginID column (adventure-works\stephen0) and replace it with your Windows login in the format domain\loginid or computername\loginid if you computer doesn't belong to a domain.

6. Refresh the report. Now, the report should return a single row showing Stephen Jiang.

   If you run the SQL Profiler and inspect the native query behind the report you will see that it has the following WHERE clause:

```
WHERE [HumanResources_Employee].[LoginID] = '<login>'
```

   If you don't see the WHERE clause make sure that the Sales Person's SecurityFilters property includes the Security Filter attribute.

9.5 Summary

The main advantage of the Report Builder 1.0 client as an ad hoc reporting tool is that it is designed with business users in mind. Its intuitive user interface helps users to get started quickly with authoring reports without requiring them to be familiar with the underlying database schema or query syntax.

The Report Builder 1.0 client supports three pre-defined report templates. Use the Table report template to author reports that display data in a tabular form. Choose the Matrix report template to author crosstab reports. Choose the Chart report template to present the report data in a chart. The Report Builder 1.0 client supports powerful filtering capabilities. You can construct entity filters that limit the rows returned in an entity and value filters that limit the rows contributing to an aggregated value.

Power users can produce ad hoc reports from a report model in the Report Designer. You can plug in single-instance and multi-instance custom drillthrough reports. When troubleshooting report execution, you can capture native queries in the report log or SQL Server Profiler. Reporting Services supports a comprehensive security model that lets you secure both model items and data.

Report Builder 1.0 has not been enhanced in Reporting Services 2008. Report Builder 2.0, which I'll discuss next, is designed to replace the Report Builder 1.0 technology in a long run.

9.6 Resources

Introducing Client Application Deployment with "ClickOnce" by Duncan Mackenzie (http://tinyurl.com/my7p4)— Introduces you to the click-once technology.

Formatting Types (http://tinyurl.com/nf6fs)—Learn how to create custom numeric and date format strings.

Chapter 10

Previewing Report Builder 2.0

As you've seen in the preceding two chapters, non-technical users can leverage the Report Builder 1.0 technology to author ad hoc reports from SQL Server, Oracle, and Analysis Services data sources. However, Report Builder 1.0 supports only a subset of the RDL features and supports simple template-based reports. Moreover, before end users can start building reports, an IT professional must pre-configure a report model as an underlying data source for the reports.

To let end users access all report authoring features and the full range of supported data sources, Microsoft has completely redesigned Report Builder in Reporting Services 2008. Due to time constraints, Report Builder 2.0 doesn't ship with SQL Server 2008, but will instead be available as a separate download in the SQL Server 2008 timeframe. In this chapter, I'll introduce you to the pre-release version of Report Builder 2.0 technology. The bulk of the chapter covers tutorials that walk you through the steps of authoring an OLAP report and a relational report. These practices should give you a taste of how Report Builder 2.0 changes the authoring experience relative to its predecessor.

The usual disclaimer for pre-release technology applies to this chapter. The pre-release version of Report Builder 2.0 is subject to change until the product finally ships. The features and user interface described in this chapter may vary in the final release.

10.1 Understanding Report Builder 2.0

Reporting Services has evolved based on the feedback Microsoft gets from customers. Part of this evolution includes improving the user experience in the area of report design. When it was first introduced in Reporting Services 2005, Report Builder 1.0 promised to empower non-technical business users by giving them the ability to author their own reports. While business users rejoiced over the user-friendly Report Builder client, more advanced users found it too limiting. The key request from customers using Report Builder was to enhance it to support the full spectrum of RDL features, including multiple data regions, expression-based styles, and support for more data sources besides SQL Server, Analysis Services and Oracle.

The Reporting Services product group went back to the drawing board and realized that by combining the design foundation of the BIDS Report Designer and the Office user experience, they could move Report Builder in a direction that that would meet their customer's requirements. BIDS Report Designer provided a baseline of the functionality that customers wanted to see in all of their report authoring tools. To use its features in Report Builder 2.0, the team re-factored the Report Designer layout surface as a shared component. The outcome of that effort is that the application environment and steps for setting up data and creating the report layout is virtually identical in both BIDS Report Designer and the next generation Report Builder 2.0.

As a result, Report Builder 2.0 "inherits" full access to all RDL features and supported data sources. To ensure that less technically savvy users wouldn't be left behind, Microsoft simplified the user interface and packaged Report Builder 2.0 in an Office 2007-like authoring environment. Microsoft is currently working on enhancing Report Builder with other features to make it even easier for business users to create reports.

DEFINITION Report Builder 2.0 is a report designer for authoring full-featured ad hoc reports outside the Visual Studio environment. Report Builder 2.0 is the successor of Report Builder 1.0, which was introduced in SQL Server 2005 and is still available in SQL Server 2008.

10.1.1 Introducing Report Builder 2.0 Environment

Business users will undoubtedly find the Report Builder 2.0 client interface (see Figure 10.1) familiar by virtue of its Microsoft Office 2007 Ribbon interface. The blue background gradient gave Report Builder 2.0 the code name "Blue", which is still affectionately used internally by Microsoft.

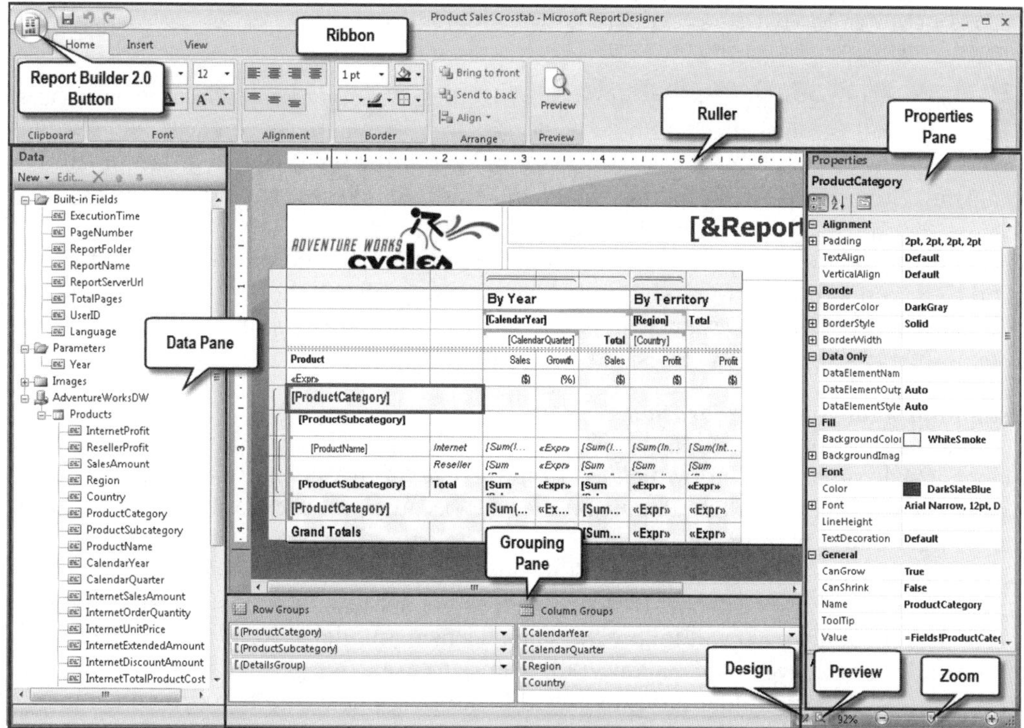

Figure 10.1 Report Builder 2.0 features the familiar Office 2007 ribbon interface.

Understanding the Report Builder 2.0 Ribbon Interface

Since you are already familiar with Report Designer, you will undoubtedly notice similarities between the Report Designer and Report Builder 2.0 environments. They both include the same Report Data pane (called Data pane in Report Builder 2.0), Group pane, Properties pane, dialogs, and design surface. Again, this is because behind the scenes both designers share the same design surface. For the most part, the only difference between the two designers is the hosting environment. The BIDS Report Designer is hosted in the Visual Studio shell and supports developer-oriented features, such as debugging, source control, and projects. By contrast, Report Builder 2.0 runs outside the Visual Studio IDE and lets you work on only one report at a time.

The Ribbon interface helps you quickly find the commands that you need to complete a task. The tasks are organized in logical groups called *tabs* (Home, Insert, View tabs). The toolbar buttons in each tab are organized in groups, such as Font and Alignment groups. As with other Microsoft Office 2007 products, the Report Builder 2.0 Button lets you initiate common actions, including creating a new report, saving a report to disk, and publishing a report to the report server.

The Home tab is a collection of commonly used commands, including those that you use to control the appearance of items within your report. You can use the Home tab to access the Windows clipboard for copying and pasting, change the textbox font, preview the report, and so on.

DEFINITION Unlike Report Designer, which supports only client-side report preview, the release version of Report Builder 2.0 is expected to support both client-side and server-side preview modes. Previewing reports on the server could be useful when the report references external resources, such as shared data sources, subreports, and external images. Currently, only client preview is available.

The Insert tab substitutes the Visual Studio toolbar for Report Server projects. It lets you insert report items, as well as a page header and page footer. The View tab lets you switch between design and preview modes, as well as to toggle elements of the shared layout surface, including Data pane, Grouping pane, Properties pane, and ruler. All of these should be familiar to you because they are available in the BIDS Report Designer.

Besides using the Ribbon, you can also switch between design and preview modes by clicking the corresponding button in the status bar. Pressing F5 is a shortcut for previewing a report. Finally, unlike Report Designer, Report Builder 2.0 supports zooming. The zoom slider in the status area lets you zoom the design surface in and out.

Understanding setup and configuration

Report Builder 2.0 is not included in the SQL Server 2008 setup. Instead, Microsoft provides a stand-alone installer that can be downloaded from the latest SQL Server 2008 Feature Pack web page. This simplifies installing Report Builder 2.0 because end users don't need to run the SQL Server 2008 setup program just to author reports. At the time of this writing, the latest SQL Server 2008 Feature Pack is Microsoft SQL Server 2008 Feature Pack RC0 (see Resources for a link). The RC0 release of Report Builder 2.0 does not specify the licensing details. More than likely, Report Builder 2.0 will follow the same licensing model as Report Builder 1.0 and require the end user to have a SQL Server 2008 license to use it.

When it ships, Report Builder 2.0 is expected to support ClickOnce deployment similar to Report Builder 1.0. The administrator will be able to configure which Report Builder version the user can launch by specifying the URL to the ClickOnce *.application file. In SQL Server Management Studio, this can be done by setting the ReportBuilderLaunchURL setting in the

Server Properties (Advanced tab). In Report Manager, you can configure the Report Builder version URL in the Site Settings page.

The web download installs Report Builder 2.0 in the \Program Files\Microsoft SQL Server\100\Tools\Reporting Services\Report Builder 2.0\ folder. End-user help is included in the download as a Microsoft Compiled HTML (.chm) file that gets installed in the same folder. Similar to the BIDS Report Designer, Report Builder 2.0 uses configuration files for feature customization and security. The ReportDesigner.config file lets you customize the available rendering and data extensions. The rspreviewpolicy.config configuration file is for setting up Code Access Security (CAS) policies if the report uses external custom code. For example, if your report calls an external assembly, you need to grant that assembly the appropriate rights by registering it in rspreviewpolicy.config. This is identical to configuring custom code in Report Designer.

Report Builder 2.0 is dependent on .NET Framework 3.5, which the user must install first. The Feature Pack resource page provides a link to the .NET Framework 3.5 redistributable package.

10.1.2 Understanding Report Builder 2.0 Features

When Report Builder 1.0 was first introduced in SQL Server 2005, it had a well-defined target audience—business users. In comparison, Microsoft envisioned the Report Designer as the tool of choice for developers and power users. As it turned out, there is no clear-cut dividing line between these two user groups when it comes to report authoring. The ambitious goal of Report Builder 2.0 is to unite the best from both worlds. It gives you full-featured access to RDL without requiring Visual Studio.

Comparing Report Builder 1.0 and Report Builder 2.0

Now that you've been introduced to Report Builder 2.0 at a high level, you may wonder how it measures up against its predecessor, Report Builder 1.0, and which one to choose for your reporting needs. Table 10.1 outlines the significant differences between the two tools.

Table 10.1 Report Builder 1.0 vs. Report Builder 2.0

Criteria	Report Builder 1.0	Report Builder 2.0
Target audience	Business users	Power users, bisiness users
Report layout	Basic template-based layout	Full RDL support
RDL support	RDL 2005	RDL 2008
Report model	Required	Not required but supported as a data source
Queries	Auto-generated	Native language of the target data source
Data sources	SQL Server, Oracle, Analysis Services	Any data source
Extensibility	Not extensible	Can be extended with custom code

The intended audience for Report Builder 1.0 is a less technically savvy user who is willing to trade advanced reporting features for the ability to produce simple reports quickly. By contrast, Report Builder 2.0 assumes that the user understands the database schema and knows how to write queries. To keep the learning curve small, Report Builder 1.0 uses more built-in features such as templates and gives up some of the more powerful features that you find in Report Builder 2.0.

Features that you won't find in Report Builder 1.0 include side-by-side or nested regions, list regions, page headers and footers, page numbers, and expression-based properties. By contrast, Report Builder 2.0 fully supports RDL 2008 and an open design experience (no templates). Report Builder 1.0 has not been enhanced in this release and supports only RDL 2005. It cannot open a report produced with Report Builder 2.0 or BIDS Report Designer. However, Report Builder 2.0 can open Report Builder 1.0 reports by upgrading them to RDL 2008.

Report Builder 1.0 requires a report model that abstracts the data source. When the user runs the report, the model auto-generates the native query. You can build models on top of SQL Server, Oracle and Analysis Services data sources. By contrast, Report Builder 2.0 connects directly to the database. It supports any data source, including Report Builder models. However, with Report Builder 2.0, the report author must provide the report query written in the syntax supported by the data source. When not using a Reporting Builder entity model as a data source, Report Builder 2.0 doesn't auto-generate queries at run time but instead provides graphical query designers that facilitate creating and testing the queries at design time.

Finally, while reports produced by Report Builder 2.0 can be extended with custom code and third-party components, Report Builder 1.0 reports are not extensible. For example, you cannot plug in a custom function library in Report Builder 1.0. As you can see, apart from its name, Report Builder 2.0 has very little in common with its predecessor. In fact, Report Builder 2.0 is much closer to Report Designer because both share the same design foundation.

When to use Report Builder 2.0

I have to admit that I am excited about Report Builder 2.0 and the direction Microsoft is taking with the report design tools. I believe that in the long run Report Builder 2.0 will blur the difference between standard and ad hoc reporting and satisfy the requirements of both technical and non-technical users. As it stands, however, the pre-release version of Report Builder 2.0 leans more towards the "professional" side. Consequently, the end user must have a solid understanding of the report authoring process even for creating simple ad hoc reports.

It's unfortunate that as they stand, none of the four Microsoft-provided report designers is currently capable of targeting equally well both developers and business users. Don't despair though! While waiting for Report Builder 2.0 to evolve to a point where it can satisfy the needs of both audiences, consider turning lemons into lemonade by offering several design choices to your users. Table 10.2 shows report design tool positioning based on report author expertise for a BI project that involves standard and ad hoc reporting from an Analysis Services cube.

Table 10.2 Positioning the Microsoft report design tools as clients of Analysis Services

Reporting Tool	User Audience	Reporting Needs
Excel 2007	Executive managers	Historical and trend reporting
Report Builder 1.0	Non-technical users	Simple ad hoc reports
Report Designer	Developers, power users	Full-featured standard reports
Report Builder 2.0 (when available)	Power users, non-technical users	Full-featured ad hoc and standard reports

Executive management is typically interested in the "big picture" of the company business. The most effective channels for delivering this information are digital dashboards and canned reports, especially chart reports. Should executive managers be willing to author reports, Excel is probably your best choice for OLAP historical and trend reporting.

Less technically savvy users may find Report Designer too complex and intimidating. For example, end users may not be willing to tinker with report parameters and query statements or may not have the necessary knowledge to do so. When the Report Designer features exceed user skills, consider using Report Builder 1.0.

The BIDS Report Designer remains the premium report authoring tool for developers. Despite its tight integration with Visual Studio, the Report Designer end-user enhancements may make it a good choice for power users who are not willing to compromise report authoring features for simplicity.

Definitely evaluate Report Builder 2.0 for full-featured standard and ad hoc reporting outside the Visual Studio IDE. Power users and users who already know BIDS Report Designer will easily adapt to the new tool. Although it shows great promise, it remains to be seen how well the release version will support non-technical users.

Now that you've been introduced to Report Builder 2.0, let's take it for a ride and author a few reports. In the first practice, you will author a chart report from an Analysis Services cube. In the second practice, you'll design a chart report that retrieves data from a relational database. If you've read through the Report Designer chapters (chapters 3-7), you may find these practices somewhat redundant because Report Builder 2.0 is functionally almost identical to Report Designer. However, I advise you not to skip them. If nothing else, you'll at least be able to evaluate the Report Builder 2.0 user interface and its ad hoc reporting environment. Who knows, you may even find a nugget of report authoring treasure left uncovered in the preceding chapters.

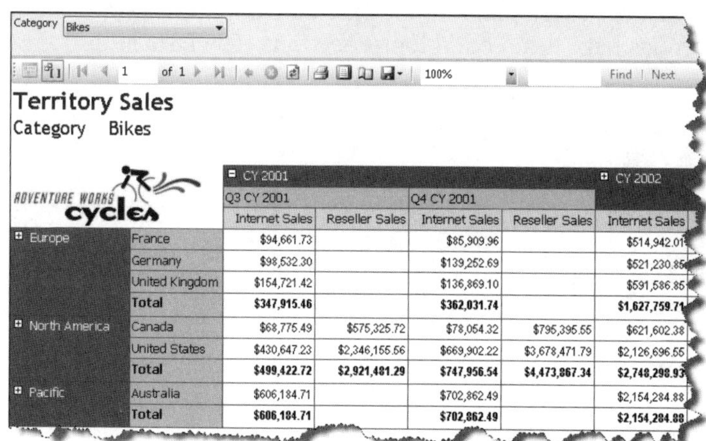

		CY 2001				CY 2002
		Q3 CY 2001		Q4 CY 2001		
		Internet Sales	Reseller Sales	Internet Sales	Reseller Sales	Internet Sales
Europe	France	$94,661.73		$85,909.96		$514,942.01
	Germany	$98,532.30		$139,252.69		$521,230.85
	United Kingdom	$154,721.42		$136,869.10		$591,586.85
	Total	**$347,915.46**		**$362,031.74**		**$1,627,759.71**
North America	Canada	$68,775.49	$575,325.72	$78,054.32	$795,395.55	$621,602.38
	United States	$430,647.23	$2,346,155.56	$669,902.22	$3,678,471.79	$2,126,696.55
	Total	**$499,422.72**	**$2,921,481.29**	**$747,956.54**	**$4,473,867.34**	**$2,748,298.93**
Pacific	Australia	$606,184.71		$702,862.49		$2,154,284.88
	Total	**$606,184.71**		**$702,862.49**		**$2,154,284.88**

Figure 10.2 The Territory Sales report draws data from the Adventure Works cube.

10.2 Authoring an OLAP Report

Multidimensional OLAP cubes are well suited for ad hoc reporting. This is because they present data schema in a set of intuitive dimensions and measures the business users can quickly relate to. Moreover, the relationships are built into the cube so the user doesn't need to know how to navigate the data source schema and join tables. Let's wear a business user's hat and use Report Builder 2.0 to author a crosstab report from the Adventure Works Analysis Services cube.

The Territory Sales report (see Figure 10.2) shows Internet and reseller sales by territory on rows and time on columns. The user can filter report data by selecting one or more product categories in the Category parameter. The report demonstrates the following report authoring features:

- Using the MDX Query Designer to auto-generate MDX queries and report parameters
- Authoring a crosstab report
- Implementing drilldown interactive features to see more data on the report
- Sorting the report interactively

Before jumping to the report implementation details, let's make sure we've configured Report Builder 2.0 so that it works the way we expect it to.

10.2.1 Getting Started with Report Builder 2.0

One of the first steps in working with Report Builder is to configure the design environment and the report page.

Configuring the design environment

The setup program installs the Report Builder 2.0 executable and its help in the Microsoft SQL Server 2008 Report Builder program group.

1. Click Start ⇨ All Programs ⇨ Microsoft SQL Server 2008 Report Builder ⇨ Report Builder 2.0.

   Report Builder 2.0 opens to the Home tab, with a blank report named Untitled shown in the layout surface. By default, the report has page header and footer sections. The Data and Groupings panes are visible.

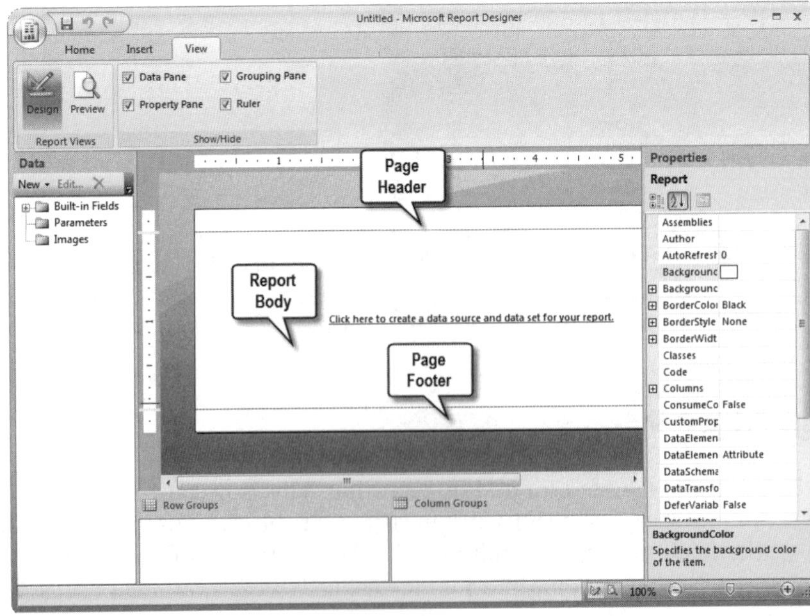

Figure 10.3 A new report includes a page header, report body, and page footer section.

2. Click the View tab and check the Property Pane and Ruler options.

   This shows the Data pane, Property pane, Grouping pane, and ruler, as Figure 10.3 shows. A new report has a page header, report body, and page footer sections. The Property pane is analogous to the Visual Studio Properties window and gives you access to the properties of the selected item in the design surface. The ruler is useful to help you size and position report items. Alternatively, you can activate these features by right-clicking the layout surface outside the white report area and clicking the View menu.

3. The Territory Sales report doesn't require page header and footer sections. To turn them off, click the Insert tab. Expand the Header button in the Header & Footer group and click Remove Header. Alternatively, right-click the layout surface outside the report area and click Remove Page Header.

4. Repeat the last step to remove the page footer.

   If you decide later that you need page header and/or footer sections, you can re-enable them by reversing the last two steps.

Configuring the report page

Another common start-up task is setting up the report page. Since crosstab reports tend to be quite wide, let's change the page layout to Landscape.

1. Right-click an empty area outside the report body and click Report Properties.
2. In the Report Properties dialog box (Page Setup tab), select the Landscape orientation.
3. Set all margins to one inch.

   If you have completed the Report Designer practices, you'll undoubtedly find the Report Properties dialog boxes familiar. Again, this is because both Report Designer and Report Builder 2.0 share the same layout surface and windows. This brings consistency and allows you to access the same features in both designers. For example, you can use the same Code, References, and Variables tabs to add custom code to advanced reports, as previously discussed in chapter 7. Spend some time getting familiar with the Report Builder 2.0 environment. Make sure to check out the zoom slider in the status bar area to zoom the surface area in and out.

10.2.2 Configuring the Report Data

The report authoring process should be familiar to you by now. It involves setting up the report data, creating the layout, and testing the report. In the steps that follow, we'll configure the report data. If you have already gone through the Report Designer part of this book, you will find that the steps are identical.

Setting up the report data source

The Territory Sales report draws data from the Adventure Works cube. Start by configuring a data source that points to the Adventure Works DW 2008 Analysis Services database.

1. In the Data pane, expand the New button and click New Data Source.

   Report Builder 2.0 shows the familiar Data Source Properties dialog box. This is one of the common dialogs included in the shared layout surface component that both Report Designer and Report Builder 2.0 share. You can use it to either create a report-specific data source whose definition gets embedded in the report, or reference an existing data source definition on the server (shared data source). Chapter 4 explains the two data source types in detail. For the purposes of this practice, you will create a report-specific data source.

NOTE The final release of Report Builder 2.0 will let the end user reference shared data sources whose definitions are deployed to the report catalog. This feature doesn't work with the RC0 build.

2. In the Data Source Properties dialog box, rename the data source to *AdventureWorksAS2008*.
3. To configure a report-specific data source, expand the Type drop-down list and select Microsoft SQL Server Analysis Services.
4. In the Connection String field, enter the following connection string:

```
Data Source=(local);Initial Catalog="Adventure Works DW 2008"
```

Alternatively, you can click the Edit button and use the Connection Properties dialog box to configure the connection string. This will also let you test the connection.

5. Click OK.

Report Builder 2.0 adds the AdventureWorksAS2008 data source to the Data pane.

Setting up the report dataset

Once the data source is in place, it's time to configure the report dataset.

1. In the Data pane, right-click the AdventureWorksAS2008 data source and click Add Dataset.
2. In the Dataset Properties dialog box that follows, click the Query Designer button.

Because you used an Analysis Services database as a data source, Report Builder 2.0 launches the MDX Query Designer. This is the same query designer you used when you authored the Product Sales by Category chart report in chapter 1. Recall that this query designer is capable of auto-generating MDX queries as you drag entities from the Metadata pane and drop them in the Query Results pane. Consequently, business users can author basic reports without having to know MDX.

3. In the Metadata pane, expand the Measures folder and the Internet Sales folder under it. Drag the Internet Sales Amount measure from the Metadata pane to the Query Results pane.

The MDX Query Designer auto-generates an MDX Query that requests the grand total Internet Sales amount across all dimensions. You can toggle the Design Mode toolbar button to see the actual MDX query statement.

4. In the Metadata pane, expand the Measures folder and the Reseller Sales folder under it. Drag the Reseller Sales Amount measure from the Metadata pane to the Query Results pane.
5. To slice the measures by territory, in the Metadata pane, expand the Sales Territory dimension. Drag the Sales Territory hierarchy to the Query Results pane.

The Sales Territory hierarchy lets users browse data by the Group ⇨ Country ⇨ Region navigational path. However, our report only needs to show data broken down by territory groups and countries. In the next step, we'll remove Region from the navigational path.

6. In the Query Results pane, click a cell inside the Region column and click the Delete toolbar button to remove the Region column. Alternatively, you can remove a column by dragging the column header away from the Query Results pane.

At this point, the Territory Sales report shows data broken down by years and quarters.

7. In the Metadata pane, expand the Date dimension and the Calendar folder under it. Drag the Date.Calendar hierarchy to the Query results pane and drop it after the Country column.
8. Since the report needs to show data at the quarter level, remove the Month and Date columns from the Query Results pane. Remove also the Calendar Semester column.

   Let's define a report parameter to filter the report data by product category. Because the MDX Query Designer is capable of auto-generating the report parameters, we can do this with just a few mouse clicks.
9. In the Metadata pane, expand the Product dimension. Drag the Category attribute to the Filter pane.
10. To set the Bikes category as the default value for the parameter, click the Filter pane, expand the drop-down list in the Filter Expression column and check the Bikes category.
11. Check the Parameters checkbox in the last column.

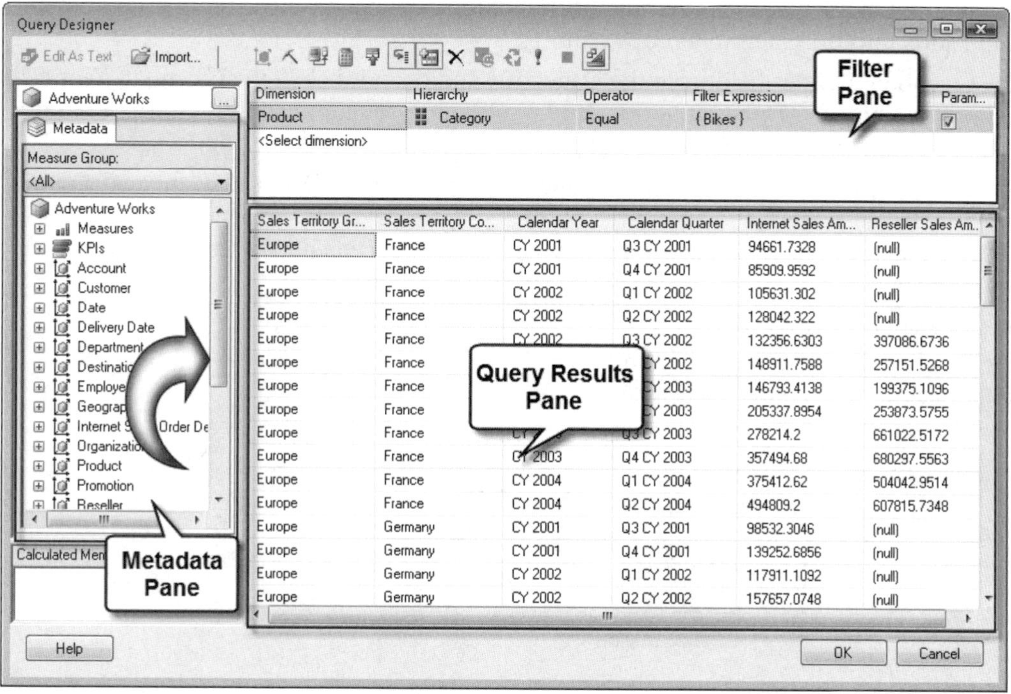

Figure 10.4 Use the MDX Query Designer drag and drop support to set up data for basic OLAP reports.

Compare your dataset configuration with the one shown in Figure 10.4. Click OK to create the dataset. Report Builder 2.0 adds the DataSet1 dataset under the AdventureWorksAS2008 data source in the Data pane.

10.2.3 Designing the Report

With the dataset in place, you can proceed with laying out the report. This involves using tablix to configure the raw report, refining the report appearance, and testing the report. Next, I'll walk you through a "click-intensive" process to get this done.

Working with the matrix region

Recall from the Report Designer chapters that this release of Reporting Services introduces a versatile tablix control that powers the table, matrix, and list data regions. For example, the matrix region is really a tablix that is pre-configured for a crosstab report layout.

1. Click the Insert tab and click the Matrix button to add an empty matrix region to the design surface.
2. To set up the matrix rows, drag the Group field from the Data pane and drop it in the Rows cell of the matrix region. Report Builder 2.0 creates a Group row group and adds it to the Row Groups pane.
3. Drag the Country field from the Data pane and drop it to the right of the Group cell in the matrix region. This creates a new Country group shows it in the Row Groups pane below the Group row group.
4. To set up the matrix columns, drag the Calendar_Year field from the Data pane and drop it in the Columns cell of the matrix region. Report Builder 2.0 creates a Calendar_Year column group and adds it to the Column Groups pane.
5. Drag the Calendar_Quarter field from the Data pane and drop it below the Calendar_Year cell in the matrix region. This creates a new Calendar_Quarter group and shows it in the Column Groups pane below the Calendar_Year group.
6. Drag the Internet Sales field from the Data pane and drop it in the Data cell of the matrix region. By default, matrix uses the Sum function to aggregate data. This explains the [Sum(Internet_Sales_Amount)] placeholder, which is a concise version of the following expression:

```
=Sum(Fields!Internet_Sales_Amo unt.Value)
```

7. Drag the Reseller_Sales_Amount field from the Data pane and drop it to the right of the [Sum(Internet_Sales_Amount)] cell.

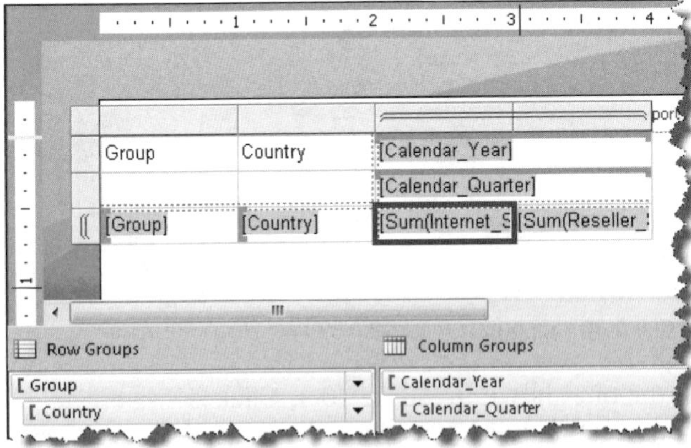

Figure 10.5 This figure shows the structure of the Territory Sales report.

Compare your report layout with the one shown in Figure 10.5. The [Sum(Internet_Sales_Amount)] and [Sum(Reseller_Sales_Amount)] fields should be located inside the double-dotted line in the matrix region because they are detail cells. Clicking on either one of these cells should show an orange active group selector above the Calendar_Quarter cell and to the left of the Country cell. This means that the innermost group on which the matrix region will group data is the Country group on rows and Calendar_Quarter group on columns. If your results don't match Figure 10.5, press Ctrl+Z (or the Undo button in the Report Builder 2.0 title bar) to undo your changes and repeat the previous steps.

8. Press F5 (or click the Run the Report button in the status bar or the View tab ⇨ Preview button) to preview the report.

   Report Builder 2.0 connects to the cube, executes the query, retrieves the results and generates the report on the client. Although plain looking, the report should have a crosstab appearance with years and quarters on columns and territory groups and countries on rows.

9. Click the Report Builder 2.0 Button and click Save to save a working copy of the report on your hard drive. Choose a file location and name the report *Territory Sales*.

Formatting the report

Let's polish the report's appearance by making format and layout changes, implementing drilldown features, adding a company logo, and adding a report title.

1. Click the matrix outer border to select the matrix. Alternatively, click a matrix cell and press Esc. Use the Properties pane to make the following changes:

Property	Value	Property	Value
BorderColor ⇨Default	DimGray	Location ⇨ Left	0
BorderStyle ⇨Default	Solid	Location ⇨ Top	0.83in
RepeatColumnHeaders	True	Size ⇨ Width	4.29167in
RepeatRowHeaders	True	Size ⇨ Height	1.09in

2. Click the Calendar_Year cell to select it and make these changes:

Property	Value	Property	Value
BackgroundColor	#60759b	Font ⇨ Family	Tahoma
Font ⇨ Color	White	Font ⇨ Size	10pt

3. Repeat the last step for the Group cell.

4. Format the Calendar_Quarter, Country, Internet Sales, and Reseller Sales cells, as follows:

Property	Value	Property	Value
BackgroundColor	LightSteelBlue	Font ⇨ Size	10pt
Font ⇨ Family	Tahoma		

5. Rename the Internet Sales Amount column header to *Internet Sales* and Reseller Sales Amount header to *Reseller Sales*.

6. To create a subtotal by territory group, right-click the [Country] cell and click Add Total.

7. Select the four numeric cells (with text [Sum(Internet_Sales_Amount)] by holding Shift and clicking each one of them. Format these cells as follows:

Property	Value	Property	Value
Font ⇨ Family	Arial Narrow	Font ⇨ Size	10pt
Format	C		

8. Click the row selector of the last row to select all cells in this row and click the Bold button in the Font group (Home tab) to change their font to bold.

Implementing a company logo

Let's add the Adventure Works company logo inside the matrix corner.

1. Select the four empty cells in the matrix corner. Right-click the selection and click Merge Cells to merge them into a single cell.
2. Click the matrix corner cell to select it. Make sure you are not in edit mode (the mouse cursor shouldn't be blinking inside the cell).
3. Select the Report Builder Insert tab and click the Image button.
4. In the Image Properties dialog box (General tab), click the Import button and navigate to the Reports folder in the chapter 10 source code. Select the AWC.jpg image and click Open.
5. Back to the Image Properties dialog box, select the Size tab and click the Fit Proportional display option. Click OK.

   Report Builder 2.0 saves the image inside the report and shows it in the matrix corner.

Implementing drilldown

Next, you'll implement conditional visibility to hide the quarter data when the report is initially rendered, but show them when you drill down from a given year.

1. Click the Calendar_Year cell to select it and change its Name property in the Properties pane to *txtYear*. Assigning meaningful names to textboxes is helpful when you need to reference them, such as when configuring conditional visibility.
2. In the Column Groups pane, double-click the Calendar_Quarter group. In the Group Properties dialog box that follows, click the Visibility tab.
3. Click the Hide option in the When the Report is Initially Run group.
4. Check the Display Can be Toggled by This Report Item checkbox. Expand the drop-down list below and select txtYear.

   Preview the report. Notice that the report no longer shows quarter-level data. However, you can click the plus sign for any given year to drill down to quarterly data.

Implementing the report title

A single textbox is sufficient to implement both the report title and subtitle.

1. Click the report body outside the matrix region.
2. In the Insert tab, click the Text Box button to add a new textbox report item.
3. Double-click the textbox to enter edit mode. Enter *Territory Sales*.
4. Press Esc to select the textbox. Click the Home tab and use the buttons in the Font and Alignment groups to change the textbox font to Trebuchet MS, 18pt, Bold and alignment to Left. In the Properties pane, change the textbox Color property to *#1c3a70*.
5. Resize the textbox to a width of 4 inches and a height of 0.64 inches.

We will reuse the same textbox to implement the report subtitle.

6. Click inside the textbox to enter edit mode and place the cursor after "Territory Sales". Press Enter to start a new paragraph.
7. Type *Category* and add a space.
8. Drag the ProductCategory parameter and drop it after "Category ", as shown in Figure 10.6.

   Report Builder 2.0 displays the [@ProductCategory] placeholder in place of the parameter. This placeholder is replacement of the expression =Parameters!ProductCategory.Value
9. Select the entire subtitle and change its font to Trebuchet MS, 14pt, Normal.

   If you preview the report at this point, it will show #Error in place of the parameter. This is because the ProductCategory parameter is a multi-valued parameter and its Value property returns an array of the selected parameter values.

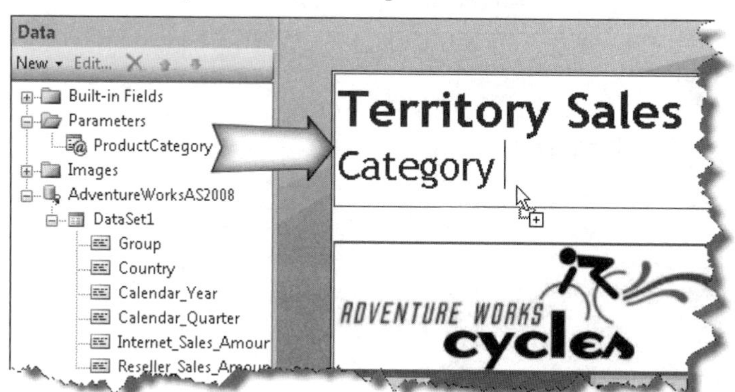

Figure 10.6 Drag the ProductCategory parameter to add it to the report subtitle.

10. With the textbox in edit mode, right-click the @ProductCategory placeholder and click Expression.
11. In the Expression dialog box that follows, replace the entire expression text with:

    ```
    =Join(Parameters!ProductCategory.Label, ",")
    ```

    This expression concatenates all selected categories in the Category parameter and returns them as a comma-delimited string. If you preview the report, its layout should match the one shown in Figure 10.2.

Publishing the report

Now that the report is ready, let's publish it to the report server to share it with other users. Because Report Builder 2.0 produces RDL 2008, you can deploy reports only to a SQL Server 2008 report server.

1. Click the Report Builder 2.0 Button and click Save to save a local copy of the report.
2. To publish the report to the server, click the Report Builder 2.0 Button and click Publish ⇨ Settings.
3. In the Deployment Settings dialog box, verify the Report Server URL and Report Folder settings and change them if needed. You must have Content Manager rights to publish reports. Click OK.
4. Click the Report Builder 2.0 Button and click Publish ⇨ Deploy. Accept the Deployment Settings dialog box and click OK to publish the report to the server.

5. Open Report Manager and navigate to the folder you specified in the deployment settings.
6. Click the Territory Sales report to preview it.

If other users have Browser rights, they can use Report Manager to navigate and view the Territory Sales report.

10.3 Authoring a Relational Report

Next, I'll walk you through the steps of implementing a relational report with Report Builder 2.0. The term *relational* means that the report will retrieve source data from the AdventureWorksDW2008 SQL Server database as opposed to an OLAP cube. Top N/Bottom N filtering is a common ad hoc reporting requirement that is easy to implement with Transact-SQL. Figure 10.7 shows the Top Customers report that you will author in this practice.

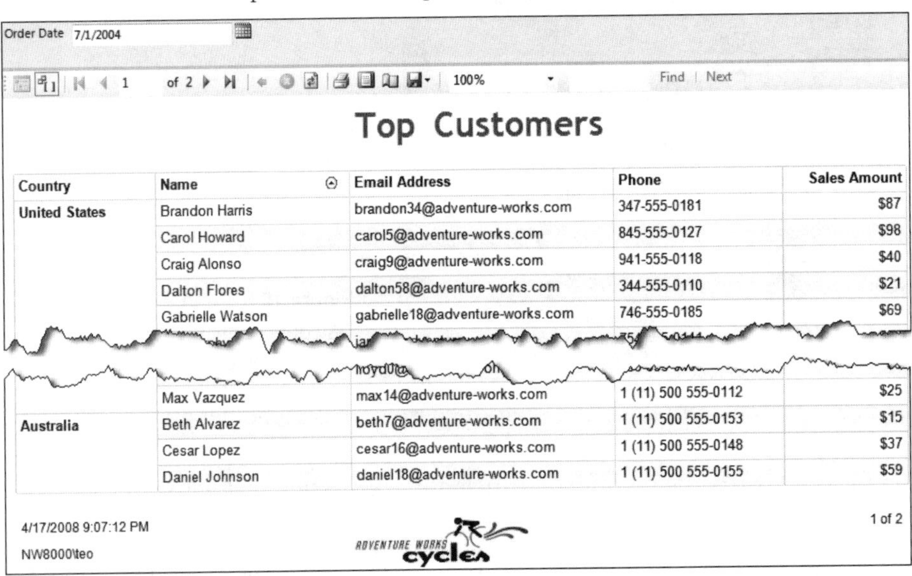

Country	Name	Email Address	Phone	Sales Amount
United States	Brandon Harris	brandon34@adventure-works.com	347-555-0181	$87
	Carol Howard	carol5@adventure-works.com	845-555-0127	$98
	Craig Alonso	craig9@adventure-works.com	941-555-0118	$40
	Dalton Flores	dalton58@adventure-works.com	344-555-0110	$21
	Gabrielle Watson	gabrielle18@adventure-works.com	746-555-0185	$69
	Max Vazquez	max14@adventure-works.com	1 (11) 500 555-0112	$25
Australia	Beth Alvarez	beth7@adventure-works.com	1 (11) 500 555-0153	$15
	Cesar Lopez	cesar16@adventure-works.com	1 (11) 500 555-0148	$37
	Daniel Johnson	daniel18@adventure-works.com	1 (11) 500 555-0155	$59

Figure 10.7 The Top Customers report shows the top customers for a given date grouped by country and sorted by sales in descending order.

In addition to showing you how to get the top customers, the report also demonstrates the following features:

- Using the graphical query designer
- Authoring a table report with the tablix region
- Implementing a "green bar" report with alternating row shading
- Sorting the report interactively
- Implementing a page footer

The user can use the Order Date parameter to pick a date and click the View Report button to run the report. The report query retrieves the top 100 customers for the given date based on their total order amount. The report groups the customers by country and shows the customer details and the total sales amount for each customer. The page footer shows the report execution time, the name of the user who requested the report, and the page number.

10.3.1 Configuring the Report Data

As you know by now, you start the report by preparing the report data. This involves setting up a connection to the data source and configuring the report dataset.

Creating a new report

Before you set up the data source, follow these quick steps to create a new report in Report Builder 2.0 and configure the report design environment:

1. Launch Report Builder 2.0 from the Microsoft SQL Server 2008 Report Builder program group.
2. Click the View menu and turn on all options in the Show/Hide group pane.
3. Click the Insert menu. Expand the Header drop-down menu in the Headers and Footers section and click Remove Header to remove the page header section.
4. Click the Report Builder 2.0 Button ⇨ Save As to save the report to your hard drive. Name the report Top Customers.

Setting up the report data source

The Top Customers report draws data from the AdventureWorksDW2008 database. Let's set up a report-specific data source that points to this database.

1. In the Data pane, expand the New drop-down list and click Data Source.
2. In the Data Source Properties dialog box, change the data source name to AdventureWorksDW2008. Leave the Type drop-down list set to the Microsoft SQL Server data provider.
3. Click the Edit button.
4. In the Connection Properties dialog box, specify the connection details to the AdventureWorksDW2008 database. Click OK to return to the Data Source Properties dialog box.
5. In the Data Source Properties dialog box, select the Credentials tab and verify that the Use Windows Authentication option is pre-selected. Consequently, the database server will authenticate you based on your Windows identity.

   If you prefer to use standard security, select the Use This User Name and Password option, and enter credentials of a SQL Server login that has read rights to the AdventureWorksDW2008 database.
6. Click OK. The AdventureWorksDW2008 data source is added to the Date pane.

Setting up the report dataset

Once the data source is in place, you are ready to set up the report dataset.

1. In the Data pane, right-click the AdventureWorksDW2008 data source and click Add Dataset.
2. In the Dataset Properties dialog box, name the dataset *Customers* and click the Query Designer button.

   Microsoft has provided two query designers for authoring SQL queries. Use the generic query designer to send a pass-through query to SQL Server without validating its syntax. When connecting to SQL Server, you can use also the graphical query designer. The graphical query designer can auto-generate the query for you. If you click the Edit As Text button in the Query Designer, Report Builder 2.0 switches to the generic query designer.
3. If the Edit As Text button is not selected, click it to switch to the generic query designer.

4. Type the following query. Alternatively, you can switch to the graphical query designer and author the query interactively. Or, to save time, click the Import button to import the query from the Customers.sql file located in the Queries folder of the book source code for this chapter.

```
SELECT TOP (100)
          DimGeography.EnglishCountryRegionName, DimCustomer.FirstName, DimCustomer.LastName,
          DimCustomer.EmailAddress, DimCustomer.Phone, SUM(FactInternetSales.SalesAmount)
          AS SalesAmount
FROM      DimCustomer INNER JOIN
          FactInternetSales ON DimCustomer.CustomerKey = FactInternetSales.CustomerKey INNER JOIN
          DimDate ON FactInternetSales.OrderDateKey = DimDate.DateKey INNER JOIN
          DimGeography ON DimCustomer.GeographyKey = DimGeography.GeographyKey
WHERE     (DimDate.FullDateAlternateKey = @OrderDate)
GROUP BY DimGeography.EnglishCountryRegionName, DimCustomer.FirstName, DimCustomer.LastName,
          DimCustomer.EmailAddress, DimCustomer.Phone
ORDER BY SalesAmount DESC
```

   This query groups the customers by country and sorts them by sales in descending order. It uses a TOP 100 clause to return the top 100 customers. It also defines a @OrderDate query parameter to parameterize the query by date.

5. Click the Run button to execute the query. In the Define Query Parameters dialog box, enter a valid Adventure Works order date, such as 7/1/2004 (recall that the Adventure-WorksDW2008 database stores data for the 2001-2004 time range).
6. Click OK.

   Report Builder 2.0 adds the dataset definition under the AdventureWorksDW2008 data source and adds an OrderDate parameter under the Parameters node. Our report will need to display the full name of the employee. However, as currently defined, the query returns the employee's first and last name as independent fields. You can use an expression in the tablix field to concatenate them together, but you'll need to repeat the expression when you configure the interactive sort on the Name column. A better approach is to define a FullName dataset calculated field that defines the expression once.

7. In the Data window, right-click the Customers dataset and click Add Calculated Field.
8. In the Dataset Properties dialog box, enter FullName in the Field Name column and add the following expression in the Field Source column.

```
=Fields!FirstName.Value & " " & Fields!LastName.Value
```

9. Click OK. The FullName field is added to the Customers dataset. Its value will be calculated at run time by concatenating the customer's first and last names.

Configuring a report parameter

Let's make a few changes to finalize the configuration of the OrderDate parameter.

1. In the Data pane, expand the Parameters node and double-click the OrderDate parameter.
2. In the General tab of the Report Parameter Properties dialog box, change the Prompt field to Order Date and the Data Type drop-down list to Date/Time.
3. Next, let's configure the OrderDate parameter to default to the current date. Click the Default Values tab and click the Specify Values option.
4. Click the Add button and click the *fx* button next to the new row.
5. In the Expression dialog, enter the following expression:

```
=Today()
```

This expression uses the Visual Basic Today function which returns the current date.

6. Click OK to close the Expression dialog box and OK one more time to close Report Parameter Properties dialog box. Press F5 to preview the report.

   Notice that you can use the date picker control to select a date. Do you see how the OrderDate parameter shows the current time after the date (for example, 5/19/2008 10:25:30 AM)? If you want just the date, you can modify the expression accordingly.

7. Back to the Default Values tab, change the expression to:

```
=CDate(Today().ToString("d"))
```

   This expression formats the date as a short date and uses the CDate Visual Basic function to cast the resulting string back to a date type.

8. Preview the report.

   Notice that the OrderDate parameter no longer displays the time alongside the date.

10.3.2 Designing the Report Layout

The next step of implementing the report involves designing the report layout. This includes configuring Reporting Services data regions, designing page headers and footers, working with images, and implementing interactive features, such as end-user sorting. During this process, you can use the Report Builder Preview feature to test the report.

Getting started with designing the report

Let's start by setting up the page layout.

1. Right-click the design surface outside the report body and click Report Properties.
2. In the Report Properties dialog box, select the Landscape paper size orientation and click OK.
3. Drag the right border of the report body to resize to a width of 9 inches. Alternatively, click the report body and set its Size ⇨ Width property in the Properties pane to 9 inches.

   Next, let's add a report title.

4. Click the Insert menu and click the Text Box item in the Report Items menu group. Report Builder 2.0 adds a textbox report item to the report body.
5. Configure the textbox properties in the Properties pane, as follows:

Property	Value	Property	Value
Location ⇨Left	2.85"	Color	RoyalBlue
Location ⇨Top	0"	Name	Title
Font ⇨FontFamily	Trebuchet MS	Value	Top Customers
Font ⇨FontSize	24pt	TextAlign	Center
Font ⇨FontWeight	Bold		

TIP Another way of formatting report items besides setting property values in the Properties pane is to use the toolbar buttons in the Home menu. Recall that the Home menu lets you apply font, alignment, border, and position settings.

Working with the table region

The Top Customers report has a tabular layout. You will use the table data region to lay out the body of the report.

1. Click the Insert menu and click the Table button to add a table region to the report body.
2. Drag the table region handle to position the table region below the report title.
3. Report Builder 2.0 has pre-configured the table region with three columns. Excluding the Country column, which groups customers by country, our report needs four columns to display the customer details (see again Figure 10.7).
4. Right-click the last column of the tablix region and click Insert Column ⇨ Right to add a new column to the table region.

Next, you'll bind dataset fields to the detail cells in the tablix region. You can do this by dragging dataset fields from the Data pane to the detail cells or by using the field selector.

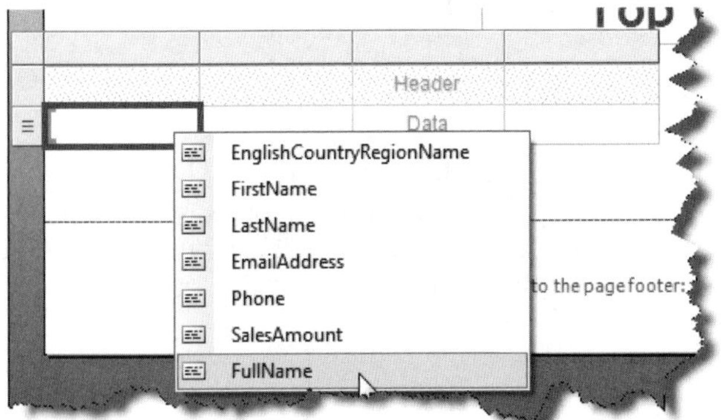

Figure 10.8 Use the field selector to bind a dataset field to a table cell.

5. Position your mouse cursor on top of the first detail cell in the Data row and click the field selector button. Report Builder 2.0 displays the fields of the Customers dataset, as shown in Figure 10.8.
6. Click the FullName field.
7. Repeat the last two steps to bind the other detail cells to EmailAddress, Phone, and SalesAmount fields.
8. Preview the report. Enter *7/1/2004* in the Order Date parameter.

Notice that the report displays all customers who have placed orders on that date, sorted in descending order by sales.

Grouping report data

Next, you'll set up a row group to group the customers by country.

1. If the report is in preview mode, click the Design toolbar button to switch to design mode.
2. Click the table region to select it.

Notice that the Rows Groups pane in the Grouping pane below the report body includes only the Details group. The Details group represents the individual rows of the report dataset. To group report data by country, you need to set up a new row group.

3. Drag the EnglishCountryRegionName field from the Customers dataset in the Data pane and drop it above the Details group in the Row Groups pane, as shown in Figure 10.9.

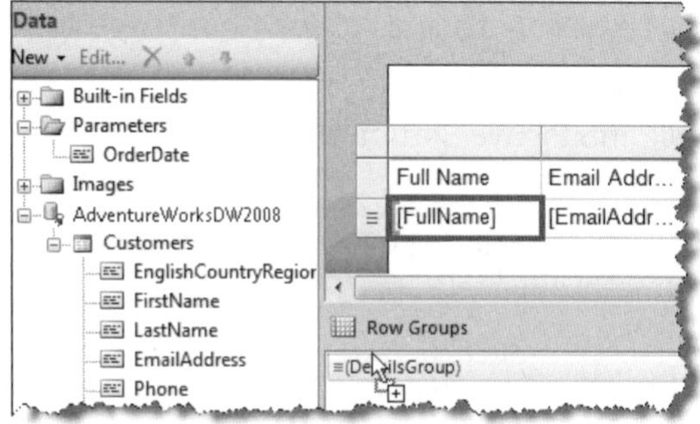

Figure 10.9 Create a new row group by dragging a dataset field and dropping it above the DetailsGroup group in the Rows Groups pane.

Alternatively, you can drop the EnglishCountryRegionName field to the left of the [FullName] cell in the tablix region. In both cases, Report Builder adds a new column to the left of the table region and configures the column as tablix header.

4. To show report grand totals, right-click the EnglishCountryRegionName detail cell and click Add Total. A new row is added to the table region to display the report grand total.

Formatting the report

Let's apply a few format settings to improve the appearance of the report.

1. Select all cells in the first row by clicking the row selector and change their font style to Bold.
2. Rename the header of the first column to *Country*.
3. Click the EnglishCountryRegionName detail cell and change its font style to Bold.
4. Right-click the SalesAmount detail cell and click Text Box Properties.
5. In the Text Box Properties dialog box, select the Number tab. Format the textbox as Currency with zero decimal places and a thousand separator. Repeat the last two steps to format the [Sum(SalesAmount)] textbox.
6. Click the SalesAmount column header to select all cells in this column. In the Home tab, click the Align Text to the Right button in the Alignment group to right-justify the column.
7. Select all cells in the footer row by clicking the row selector and change their font to Bold.
8. To alternate the row background color, press and hold the Shift key and click all detail cells except EnglishCountryRegionName to select them. In the Properties pane, enter the following expression for the BackgroundColor property:

```
=IIF(RowNumber(Nothing) Mod 2 = 0, "White", "Azure")
```

The RowNumber function returns the ordinal row number. Because Nothing is used as an expression scope, the expression operates on the outermost scope, which is the report dataset. The Iif function sets the background color to White for even rows and Azure for odd rows.

9. Click any cell inside the table region and press Esc to select the table region itself.
10. In the Properties pane, expand the NoRowsMessage drop-down list and click Expression.
11. In the Expression dialog box, enter the following text:

```
***No data***<Ctrl><Enter>  ↵
***Select a different date***
```

12. Preview the report. Notice that when the query returns no rows, Report Builder displays the NoRowsMessage text.

Implementing interactive sorting

Follow these steps to let the user sort by customer within each instance of the Country group:

1. Right-click the Name column header cell and click Textbox Properties.
2. In the Text Box Properties dialog box, turn on Enable Interactive Sort on this Text Box.
3. Select the Detail Rows sort option.
4. Expand the Sort By drop-down list and select [FullName]. Preview the report.Notice that there is an up-down sort indicator in the Name column header cell.
5. Click the sort indicator to sort customers within each Country group in ascending order. Each time you click the sort indicator, you toggle the sort order of the customers.

Implementing a page footer

The only remaining task is to add the page footer. Page footers can contain text and images. To demonstrate the use of images, we'll start by adding the Adventure Works company logo.

1. In the Data pane, right-click the Images folder and click Add Image. Alternatively, you can right-click the page footer section and click Insert ⇨ Image. This will bring you to the familiar Image Properties dialog box.
2. In the File Open dialog box that follows, navigate to the chapter 10 Reports folder and select the AWC.jpg image. Click OK.
3. Drag the AWC image from the Images folder to the page footer. Resize the image by dragging its resize handles as needed.
4. Click the image to select it and change its Sizing property to Fit in the Properties pane.

Follow the steps in the Implementing the Report Footer practice in section 3.3.9 (chapter 3) to configure the rest of the report footer.

10.4 Summary

This chapter previewed the pre-release version of Report Builder 2.0, which is one of the Microsoft-provided report design tools. Report Builder 2.0 aims to replace Report Builder 1.0 sometime after the SQL Server 2008 release date. You can use Report Builder 2.0 to author standard and ad hoc reports outside the Visual Studio environment. Remember that Report Builder 2.0 raises the bar on technical skills required to author reports.

Report Builder 2.0 shares components with the BIDS Report Designer, but without the dependency on Visual Studio. It provides full-featured access to RDL and supports the full range of OLAP and relational data sources. The report definitions can be saved to disk or published to the report server.

Recall that the typical report lifecycle includes authoring, management, and delivery phases. This chapter concludes the report authoring part of this book. Next, we'll see how report administrators can manage and secure the report server.

10.5 Resources

Microsoft SQL Server 2008 Feature Pack RC0
(http://tinyurl.com/5h46tn)—Includes a link for downloading Report Builder 2.0.

PART 4

Management

An enterprise-level platform, such as Reporting Services, must be trustworthy. A trustworthy system is easy to manage and support. It is also highly-available and scalable. Finally, it provides the means to protect data assets by enforcing restricted access to authorized users only.

Report Manager is the tool of choice for administrators who manage report servers running in native mode. This web application can be used to perform routine management tasks, such as uploading report content, setting up data sources and report parameters, creating subscriptions, and enforcing restricted access to reports. SQL Server Management Studio can be used to manage server-wide properties and security role definitions. In SharePoint integration mode, SharePoint provides the management framework, and Report Manager is not available.

As a report administrator, you can configure how reports are executed. Typically, end users would prefer to see the latest data on the report. However, if some data latency is acceptable, you can optimize report performance by configuring the report for caching. Besides requesting reports on demand, you can let end users subscribe to reports to receive them automatically on a schedule. As report administrator, you can set up data-driven subscriptions that retrieve dynamic recipient and configuration data from an external database.

Occasionally, Report Manager and SharePoint may not be up to the task to meet more advanced management requirements. When the management tools provided by Microsoft don't meet your needs, you can write custom applications that pick up from where these management tools leave off. These applications can integrate with the Reporting Services API to manage the report server programmatically.

It is unrealistic to expect that your management responsibilities will come to an end once the reports are deployed to the production server. By monitoring the report server and examining its log files and performance counters, you can ensure that it functions correctly at an acceptable performance level.

Chapter 11

Management Fundamentals

In a typical enterprise environment there are usually three different groups of users who get involved in the different phases of the report lifecycle. Report authors focus on report design and programming. Administrators deploy and manage the report server. End users run reports. In this chapter, we will wear the administrator's hat and dive into the mechanics of managing report server content and operations. As we will find, Reporting Services provides not one but several tools and approaches for doing this work.

This chapter starts by providing an overview of the Reporting Services management tools and interfaces. The main focus of this chapter is Report Manager, which is the primary tool for managing content in Reporting Services. I will show you how to leverage Report Manager to perform common administrative tasks, such as managing the folder space and securing report server content and operations.

The exercises in this chapter use the Adventure Works sample reports. If you haven't installed the Adventure Works sample reports yet, follow the instructions in the book front matter to install them.

11.1 Understanding Report Management

As a report server administrator, tasks that you will perform on a routine basis include managing the report server, controlling access to the report catalog, adding or deleting reports, working with report data sources and parameters, automating repetitive tasks, and monitoring the server performance. Reporting Services provides a comprehensive set of management tools and interfaces to help you perform all of the above activities.

11.1.1 Understanding Report Management Tools

While Reporting Services provides several management tools, the ones that you will use the most are Report Manager, SQL Server Management Studio, and Reporting Services Configuration Manager, as shown in Figure 11.1. All Reporting Services management tools use public programming interfaces to integrate with the report server.

Report Manager
Report Manager is the out-of-the box Web front-end tool for managing a report server instance that is configured for native mode. In SharePoint integration mode, SharePoint provides the management functionality via the SharePont Web front end and Report Manager is

not supported. In native mode, you use Report Manager to both view and manage reports. Report Manager supports common management tasks that you are likely to perform on a daily basis, including searching, printing, and viewing reports, managing the report content, defining security policies that determine access to the report server, configuring the report execution and history, and defining report subscription delivery.

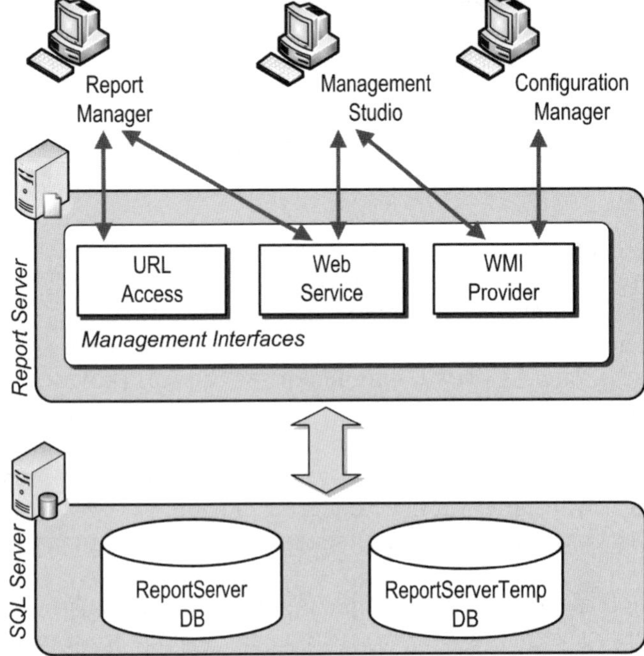

Figure 11.1 Reporting Services provides three main management tools: Report Manager, SQL Server Management Studio, and Reporting Services Configuration Manager.

Report Manager is implemented as an ASP.NET web application that is installed by default in the \Program Files\Microsoft SQL Server\MSRS10.MSSQLSERVER\Reporting Services\ReportManager folder. Regretfully, Microsoft doesn't provide the source code for Report Manager so you are out of luck if you need to make changes to any of its functionality. On a superficial level, Microsoft lets you customize Report Manager's appearance by changing its Cascading Style Sheet (\Program Files\Microsoft SQL Server\MSRS10.MSSQLSERVER\Reporting Services\ReportServer\Styles\ReportingServices.css).

If you need more customization than this and you are really adventurous, you can take the unsupported road and write client-side JavaScript to enhance (hack) the Report Manager. In case you decide to try this approach, I provided a link in the Resources section to a blog that demonstrates how to add a custom logo image.

NOTE In my opinion, the best thing that Microsoft can do to satisfy the barrage of customization needs is to declare Report Manager a "sample" and publish its source code. Not only an open source Report Manager will let developers tailor its functionality but also will serve as a great learning tool for integrating custom applications with Reporting Services. If you agree, log this wish on http://connect.microsoft.com.

Report Manager runs in a browser window. You open Report Manager by entering the Report Manager URL in the address bar. By default, the URL is http://<servername>/reports. You can find the actual URL that is valid for your installation in the Reporting Services Configuration tool (Report Manager URL tab). You can use Report Manager to administer a single report server instance and view reports on demand. Behind the scenes, Report Manager uses the Report Server Web service for all management tasks. Report Manager uses both the Report Server Web service and URL access for on-demand report viewing.

SQL Server Management Studio (SSMS)

SQL Server Management Studio is an integrated environment for managing all components of SQL Server, including Reporting Services. You can find SSMS in the Microsoft SQL Server 2008 program group. In SQL Server 2005, SSMS provided full-featured management access to the report server, including features that Report Manager didn't have, such as scripting management tasks and the ability to set model item security. As it turned out, most administrators (including myself) preferred using Report Manager for a report server running in native mode (or SharePoint for a report server configured for SharePoint integrated mode). Given customer preference and a desire to reduce the overhead of supporting and enhancing several management interfaces, the Reporting Services team decided to streamline the management tool set by eliminating redundant functionality.

In SQL Server 2008, the Reporting Services team scaled down SSMS to support server settings and moved all content management tasks to Report Manager. Specifically, in version 2008, SSMS doesn't provide access to the report content or the folder namespace, so you cannot view, secure, or manage report folders and their content. Furthermore, SSMS discontinued scripting support for report management tasks. What you can do in SSMS is carry out the following system management tasks: connect to one or more report servers running in native or SharePoint mode, set server properties, enable or disable features, view and cancel running jobs, define security roles used on the server, and define server schedules.

In Report Manager, Microsoft removed role and job management features. Report Manager also lost the checkbox for enabling or disabling My Reports and execution logging server properties, but kept schedule management. Personally, I think that these changes make sense. The idea is to rely on the Report Manager for your day-to-day management activities and use SSMS occasionally to manage system settings.

If you enter only the server name (or <server name>\<instance name> with instance deployments) on connect, SSMS uses the report server Windows Management Instrumentation (WMI) provider to connect to the server and retrieve the Report Server Web service URL. Next it uses the Report Server Web service for all tasks. If you directly provide the Report Server Web service URL, sich as http://localhost/reports, then SSMS doesn't use WMI provider. SQL Server 2008 introduced breaking changes to the report server WMI provider as a result of the new hosting model and URL reservation system. Consequently, if you need to use SSMS 2008 to manage SQL Server 2005 report server, specify the Report Server Web service URL instead of the server name to bypass the WMI provider.

NOTE Perhaps, you've heard about the new SSMS management features for the Database Engine in SQL Server 2008, such as Policy Management, Data Collection, and Resource Governor. Unfortunately, Reporting Services doesn't integrate with the SQL Server 2008 management framework in any way. Microsoft realizes the importance of consolidating all services to leverage the management framework and will work toward this goal in a future release.

Reporting Services Configuration Manager

I introduced you to the Reporting Services Configuration Manager in chapter 2 when I showed you how to make URL reservations for the report server and Report Manager. Recall that Reporting Services Configuration Manager is a Windows-based tool for configuring local or remote servers. You can find Reporting Services Configuration Manager in the Microsoft SQL Server 2008 ⇨ Configuration Tools program group. You can use it to perform various configuration tasks, including changing the service account that the report server runs under, managing URL reservations and SSL settings, connecting to or creating a new report server database, specifying the database credentials, configuring e-mail settings for subscription-based report delivery, managing the report server unattended execution account and encryption keys, and configuring scale-out deployment.

Behind the scenes, the Reporting Services Configuration Manager uses the report server WMI provider to read from and write to the report server configuration file. Although the configuration tool should be your first stop to verify server configuration, it shouldn't be treated as a troubleshooting or diagnostic tool. Its main design goal is to accurately present current configuration settings of your report server and allow you to reliably and consistently change these configuration settings based on your needs. It may flag certain conditions as warnings or errors, but it doesn't communicate with the server to verify that it is operational or monitor its health. In addition, the configuration tool doesn't support WMI events, so it cannot notify you when a change takes place.

Other management options

Reporting Services supports additional management tools to support more advanced management scenarios, such as automating report deployment or programmatic management. These tools include:

- Reporting Services Script Host (rs.exe)—Rs.exe is a command-line utility that lets you run a script file to automate management tasks. For example, you can use rs.exe to publish reports to a report server. You use Visual Basic.NET to code the script file. Then, you can pass the script file as an input to the Reporting Services Script utility or schedule it to run unattended. I will demonstrate the Reporting Services Script Host in chapter 13.
- Rskeymgmt Utility—Rskeymgmt is a command-line utility that lets you manage the report server encryption key. For example, suppose that you need to install a report server database from another server. Assuming you have a backup of the encryption keys from the source server, you can prevent losing the encrypted content by restoring the encryption keys on the target server. To do this, execute the following commands in the order shown: rskeymgmt –e, rskeymgmt –r, and then rskeymgmt –a. Alternatively, you can use the Reporting Services Configuration Manager to manage the encryption key since it supports most of the rskeymgmt features.
- Rsconfig Utility—This utility lets you manage the connection string to the report server database. Unless you need a command-line utility, I would recommend you use the graphical interface of the Reporting Services Configuration Manager to configure the report server database.
- Custom Applications—Thanks to the open management APIs, you can write a custom application to manage a report server if you need more features than what Microsoft provides off-the-shelf. The ReportService2005 and ReportService2006 Web service endpoints provide full access to the report server management functionality in native and SharePoint integration modes. To help you get started, Microsoft provides an RS Explorer sample application (see Resources for a link). RS Explorer demonstrates how to develop a .NET Windows application that uses the Report Server Web service to manage the report catalog and view reports.

11.1.2 Understanding the Report Server Service

Besides the brief overview of the report server in chapter 1, we didn't discuss how the server is implemented and how it integrates with the rest of the SQL Server services. Let's fill in this gap now.

How is the Report Server service implemented

As noted in chapter 1, SQL Server 2008 introduced a new hosting model. The report server is a collective name for three applications: Report Manager, Report Server Web service, and Background Processor. From an implementation standpoint, these three applications are hosted in a single process—the Report Server service.

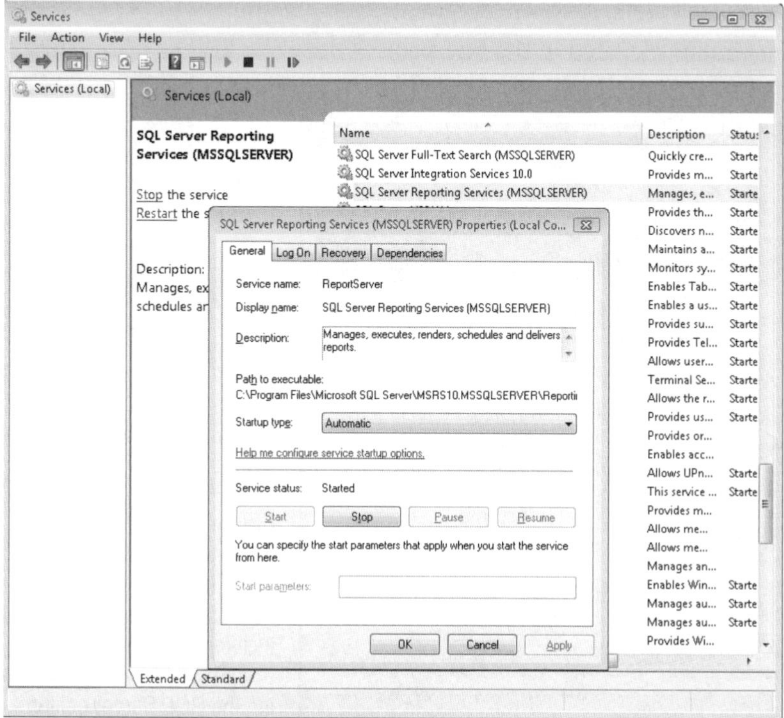

Figure 11.2 The report server is implemented as a Windows service that hosts the Report Server Web service, Background Processor, and Report Manager applications.

The Report Server service is implemented as a Windows service (ReportingServicesService.exe). To see the Report Server service, open the Windows Services applet and locate SQL Server Reporting Services. Double-click it to access its properties, as shown in Figure 11.2. In my case, I have a single Report Server service which is configured to run on the default instance (MSSQLSERVER).

However, if you install multiple instances of SQL Server or run SQL Server 2008 side-by-side with an older version, you may have more than one report server instance. The setup program installs the report server binary folder, whose default location (assuming that all SQL Server components are installed) is \Program Files\Microsoft SQL Server\MSRS10.MSSQLSERVER\Reporting Services\ReportServer\bin folder.

Understanding dependent services

The report server may rely on other SQL Server services to function properly. For example, the SQL Server service must be running if the report server database is located on the same machine as the report server. If you have two or more SQL Server instances on the same machine, you also need to enable the SQL Browser service. This service listens for incoming requests and redirects them to the appropriate server instance.

If you are planning to use subscribed report delivery or would like to automate management tasks, you also need the SQL Server Agent service too. This service allows you to schedule jobs and run them in an unattended mode. If you are using the management sample reports to view report execution log data, you need Integration Services to configure and run the package that extracts log data and copies it to a separate database, as I will demonstrate in the next chapter.

Finally, if your reports retrieve data from Analysis Services cubes hosted on the same machine, the SQL Server Analysis Services service must be running as well. You can manage the startup properties of the SQL Server services from Windows Services applet or the SQL Server Configuration Manager tool, which is located in the Microsoft SQL Server 2008 ➪ Configuration Tools program group.

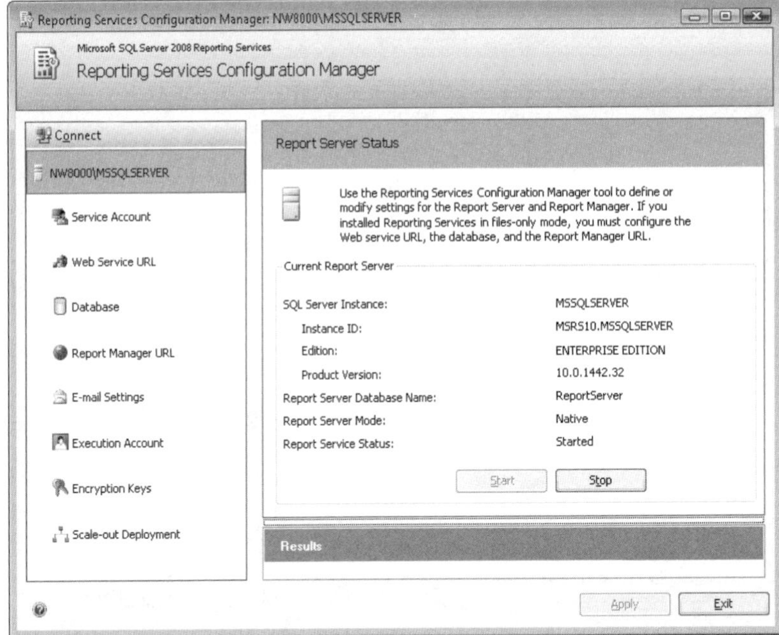

Figure 11.3 You can use Reporting Services Configuration Manager to perform various management tasks, including restarting the Report Server service and viewing the SQL Server edition and version.

11.1.3 Managing the Report Server

As an administrator, you need to know how to manage and troubleshoot the report server. Common report server management tasks include starting and stopping the report server and setting server properties.

Starting and stopping the report server

The Report Server service must be running at all times in order for the report server to be functional. Sometimes, you may need to restart the service, such as when you need to deploy a new version of a custom assembly and the old assembly is locked by the report server. Besides using the Windows Services applet and the SQL Server Configuration Manager, there are other ways to restart the Report Server service. For example, you can use the Reporting Services Configuration Manager.

1. Open the Reporting Services Configuration Manager and connect to the report server.
2. Click the top node in the left pane that represents the report server.

Note that the Current Report Server pane shows the instance details, such as the edition, the version, the integration mode, and server status. For example, looking at Figure 11.3, you can see that I am running SQL Server Enterprise edition and the report server is configured in native (non-SharePoint) mode. You can also start and stop the report server by running the following command-line statements.

```
net stop "SQL Server Reporting Services (MSSQLSERVER)"
net start "SQL Server Reporting Services (MSSQLSERVER)"
```

Replace MSSQLSERVER with the instance name if Reporting Services is not installed on the default instance.

Changing the service account

You define the account that the Report Server service runs under when you install the server, as I demonstrated in chapter 2. Sometimes, you may need to change the service account. Suppose you may have selected the NETWORK SERVICE account at install but have found it to be too restrictive. For example, you may need to report from a data source located on another server, such as an Analysis Services cube, and you want to pass the user credentials to the data source. To avoid the double-hop NTLM limitation, you decide to use Kerberos security and change the Report Server service account to Local System, which is trusted for delegation by default.

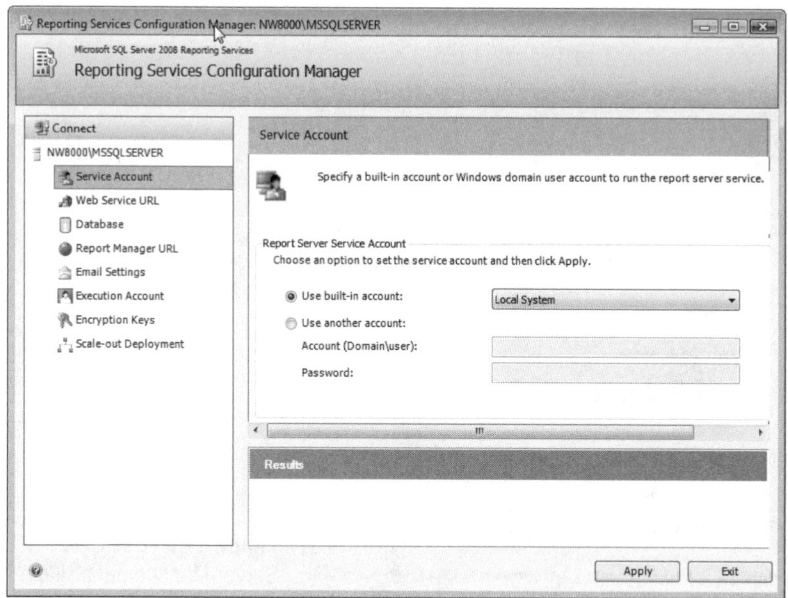

Figure 11.4 Use the Reporting Services Configuration Manager to change the service account.

While you can change the service account in the Windows Services applet, you should use the Reporting Services Configuration Manager for three reasons. First, it adds the new account to the SQLServerReportServerUser Windows group (or $<instance_name>SQLServerReport-

ServerUser with instance deployment), which has the necessary ACL permissions to the report server folders. Second, it grants the account access to the report server database by adding it to the RSExecRole role. Third, it updates the service identity portion of encryption key data, enabling the service to continue to access its copy of the key. To change the service account using the Reporting Services Configuration Manager:

1. Start the Reporting Services Configuration Manager from the Microsoft SQL Server 2008 ⇨ Configuration Tools program group.
2. Select the Service Account page, as shown in Figure 11.4.
3. Select the Use Built-in Account option to choose Local System, Network Service, or Local Service Windows built-in accounts. Or, use the Another Account option if you need another account and enter the account name in the format domain\user (or servername\user for local accounts), and the account password. Click the Apply button.

Before making a selection, you may want to review the considerations for choosing a service account that I discussed in chapter 2.

Managing server properties

The report server supports various system properties that control the server functionality and security. Follow these steps to view and manage the server properties in SQL Server Management Studio.

1. In Object Explorer, expand the Connect drop-down list and choose Reporting Services.
2. In the Connect to Server dialog box, you can enter either the Report Server Web service URL, or URL to the SharePoint Document library in SharePoint mode, or name of the SQL Server instance that hosts the report server. Click Connect
3. In Object Explorer, right-click on the Report Server node and choose Properties to bring up the Server Properties dialog box, as shown in Figure 11.5.

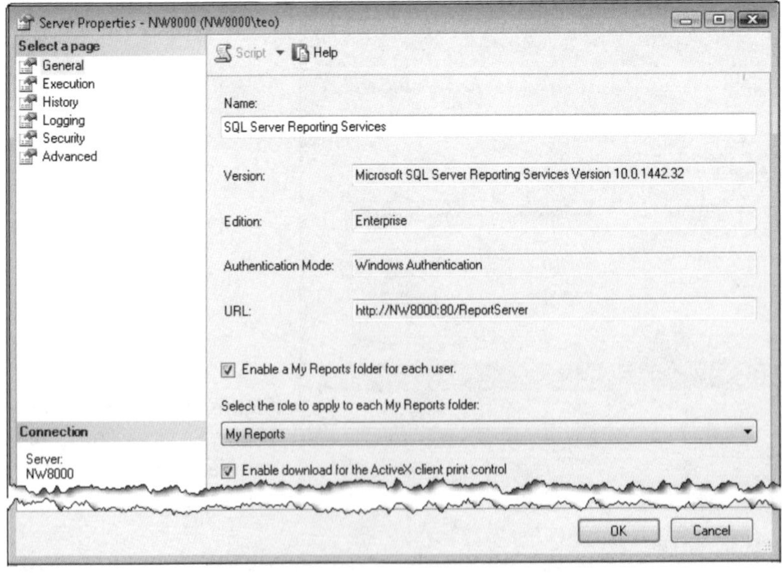

Figure 11.5 Use SQL Server Management Studio to manage the report server properties.

SSMS reads the system properties from table ConfigurationInfo in the ReportServer database and displays them in the Server Properties dialog box. You can overwrite the default settings if needed. For example, the My Reports feature is disabled by default to prevent end users from draining system resources. If you want end users to save reports to their private My Reports folders, you can use the General page to enable the My Reports role, as shown in Figure 11.5. The Advanced page gives you access to all system properties.

NOTE While you can update the system properties directly in the ConfigurationInfo table in the ReportServer database, the recommended and supported way is to use a management tool, such as SSMS, or call the SetProperties API. This will ensure that the property value is evaluated properly and the new value becomes effective immediately.

You can also use Report Manager to manage a subset of the system properties, such as the site name and report execution settings.

4. Open Internet Explorer and navigate to the Report Manager URL, such as http://<servername>/reports.

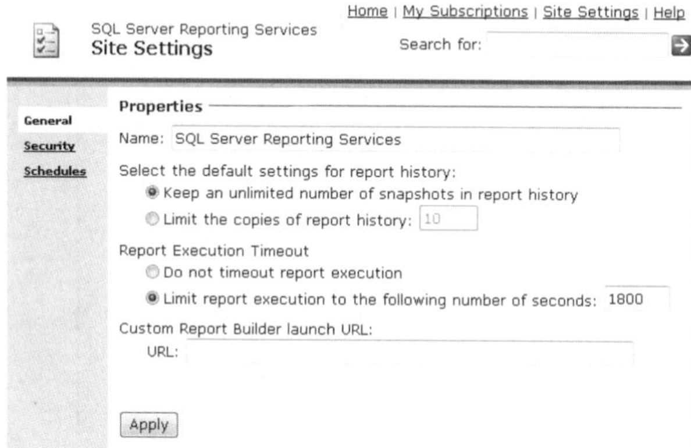

Figure 11.6 The Report Manager Site Settings page gives you access to a subset of the report server system properties.

5. Click the Site Settings menu link on the top right, as shown in Figure 11.6.

If you don't see the Site Settings link, you don't have administrator rights to the report server. By default, only Windows local administrators are granted rights to manage the report server. However, as I mentioned in chapter 2, administrator permissions are not automatically available to local administrators if you are using the User Account Control (UAC) feature of Windows Vista or Windows Server 2008. Use SQL Server Management Studio to create explicit role assignments for your account that grant it System Administrator rights.

The Report Server System Properties topic in the SQL Server Books Online describes the purpose and supported values for all report server system properties. I'll explain many of them on as-needed basis throughout the book.

Managing jobs

Jobs are running processes on the server. User jobs are activities initiated by the user, such as running a report and manually generating a snapshot. System jobs are activities initiated in an unattended mode by the report server, such as scheduled report execution snapshots and data-driven subscriptions. The report server periodically scans the RunningJobs table in the report server database to discover any in-progress jobs.

The RunningRequestsDbCycle setting in the report server configuration file (rsreportserver.config) determines how often the report server polls the database. By default, the report server scans the database every 60 seconds to evaluate running jobs. The RunningRequestsAge setting specifies the interval at which the report server changes the job status from New to Running.

You can use SSMS to view and cancel user jobs and system jobs. The Long Running Report sample report included in the book source code simulates a long running job. The dataset query uses the WAITFOR statement to delay the query execution for one minute:

```
WAITFOR DELAY '00:01:00';
SELECT * FROM HumanResources.Employee;
```

Follow these steps to run the report and monitor the user job in SSMS.

1. Publish the Long Running Report definition to the report server.
2. Use the Report Manager to run the report.
3. In SSMS, connect to the report server.
4. Expand the Jobs folder and double-click the Long Running Report job to view its Properties, as shown in Figure 11.7.

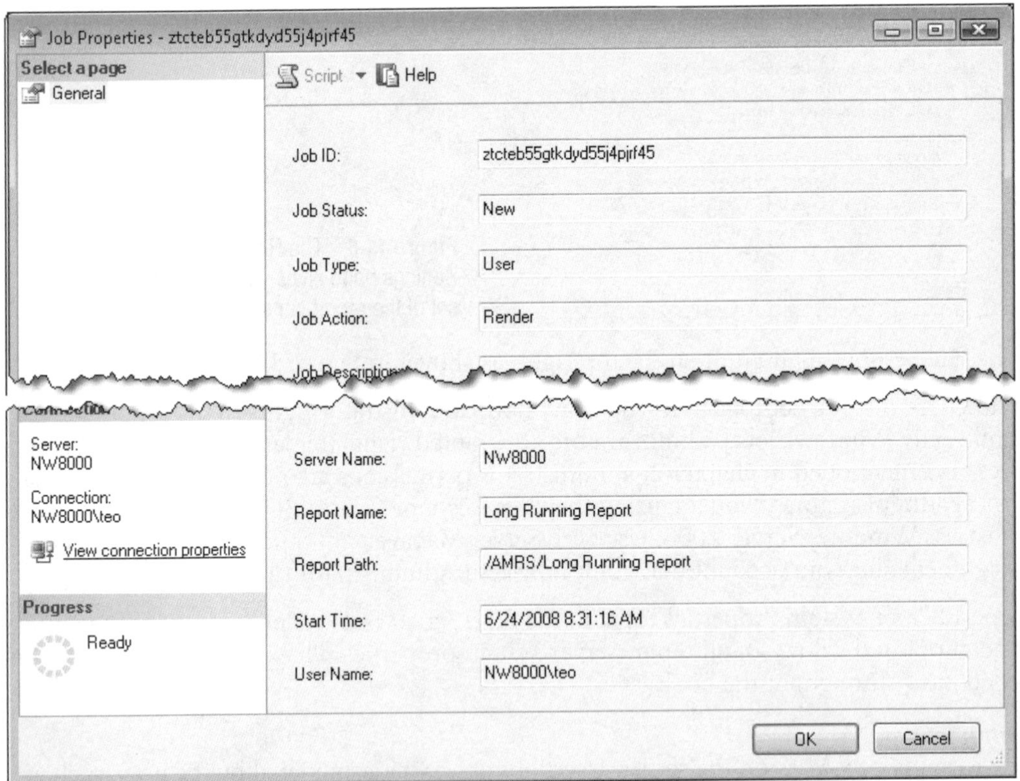

Figure 11.7 Use SSMS to view and cancel running jobs on the server.

The Job Properties dialog box shows that this is a user job as a result of rendering Long Running Report. In case of reports, you can see the report path, the job start time, and user name. You can cancel certain jobs, such as on-demand report delivery, scheduled report execution, and standard subscriptions. To cancel a job, right-click the job and choose Cancel Job(s). You can select and cancel multiple jobs at the same time.

11.2 Managing Report Server Content

Managing content on a report server is an ongoing management task that every administrator needs to master. This includes managing folders, reports, data sources, models, and resources. Note that the terms "server namespace", "folder namespace", and "report server content" are used interchangeably to represent the items stored in the report catalog. As an administrator, you will rely on Report Manager to manage report server content.

11.2.1 Understanding Report Server Content

Similar to the Windows file system, Reporting Services organizes content into hierarchical folders. Unlike Windows, Reporting Services stores the content in the report server database instead of on disk. This is needed to enable scale-out deployment where multiple report servers share the same content.

Understanding content types

Reporting Services supports the following content types: folder, report, data source, model, and resource. Table 8.2 shows the content types, the icons that the Report Manager associates with them, and a brief description for each content type.

Table 11.1 Content types supported by Reporting Services

Content Type	Icon	Description
Folder		A logical container of items
Report		An SSRS report
Data Source		A data source object that represents a connection to a database
Model		A Report Builder model
Resource		Any other item in the report catalog

You are already familiar with the first four content types. The resource content type deserves more attention. A resource represents an external file that is not a report definition, data source definition, or a Report Builder 1.0 model definition. While you can upload any file to the report catalog, it rarely makes sense to do so. Instead, you would upload only files that can be used by reports, including image files for external report images, web pages for report hyperlinks (for example, to display helpful information to the end user), and XSLT files for reports that use XSL transformations when exported to XML. If the MIME type of the resource files is one of the standard MIME types, Report Manager will display a MIME-specific icon for the resource. Otherwise, a generic resource icon, as the one shown in Table 8.2, will be used.

TIP To prevent denial-of-service attacks, ASP.NET limits the maximum file size for uploading files to 4 MB. If you need to upload a report or resource that is bigger than 4 MB, increase the maxRequestLength setting in the web.config.comments file, which is located in the \%systemroot%\ Microsoft.NET\Framework\<version>\CONFIG folder.

Understanding content navigation

As an administrator, you can organize related catalog items in folders. Folders can be nested to an arbitrary nesting level. End users or custom applications can request a catalog item by its path in the report catalog. For example, the path /AdventureWorks Sample Reports/Company Sales points to the Company Sales report inside the AdventureWorks Sample Reports folder. Note that an item path always starts with a forward slash.

Reporting Services supports a My Reports feature to let end user save reports in a private folder for his own use. By default, this feature is turned off to prevent end users from draining the server resources. When you enable My Reports (see again Figure 11.5), users can reference its content by navigating to /My Reports, such as /My Reports/Sales Report. Behind the scenes, the server maps My Reports to /users/<username>/My Reports. If the server is configured for Windows security, the user name will be the user Windows login. If custom security is used, it will be the username argument that the application passes to the LogonUser API.

11.2.2 Managing Folders

Users with Content Manager rights can manage folders and their content. This includes creating new folders, deleting existing folders, and uploading items. Let's use Report Manager to demonstrate folder management.

Navigating content

Navigating report server content with Report Manager is easy.

1. Open the Report Manager application in Internet Explorer by entering the Report Manager URL in the address bar. By default, the URL is http://<servername>/reports.

Report Manager shows the content of the root folder in a list view, as shown in Figure 11.8. For user convenience, Report Manager names the root folder Home. However, when you reference items in the catalog by URL or programmatically, you use a forward slash to represent the root folder. Report Manager provides also a Home link in the main menu, which you can click to get to the root folder from anywhere in the folder namespace.

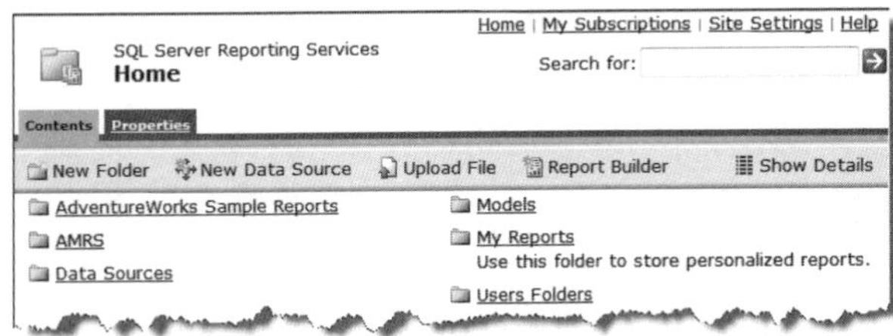

Figure 11.8 The Report Manager displays the content of the root folder.

The default name of the Report Manager application is SQL Server Reporting Services. However, if you want to personalize the site, you can change the site name from the Site Settings page if needed. The New Folder button lets you create a new folder. Use the New Data Source button to create a new data source. Use the Upload File button to upload report content. If Report Builder 1.0 is enabled on the server, you can click the Report Builder button to launch the Report Builder 1.0 client.

2. Suppose you want to quickly find all sales-related reports. In the Search For field, enter *sales* and click the green arrow button. Report Manager searches the report catalog and shows you a list of reports whose name contains the criteria. Click the Home menu link to go back to the Home folder.

3. Right-click on the AdventureWorks Sample Reports folder and choose Properties. The Address (URL) property shows the following link:

http://localhost/Reports/Pages/Folder.aspx?ItemPath=%2fAdventureWorks+Sample+Reports&ViewMode=List

The Report Manager knows that the content type of AdventureWorks Sample Reports is a folder and will navigate to the Folder.aspx page to display the folder properties when you click on the link. The ItemPath parameter shows the URL-escaped path to the item in the report catalog.

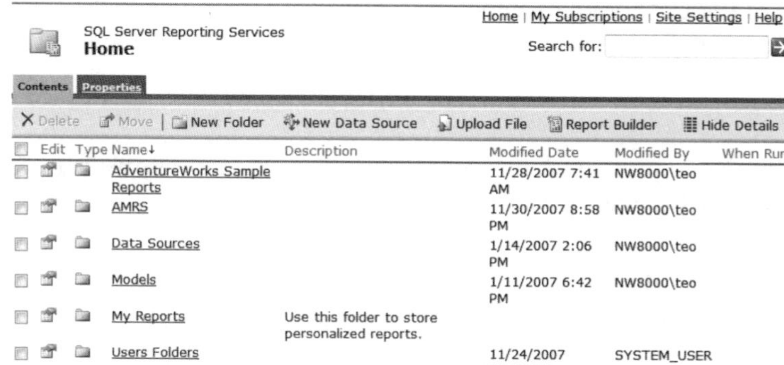

Figure 11.9 Use the Show Details mode to see the details of the items in the folder and conveniently delete items.

4. Click the Show Details button. The Report Manager shows the folder details, such as when the folder was last modified and who modified it. The Show Details mode also lets you select and delete multiple catalog items. Clicking the Hide Details mode button will get you back to the list view. I typically use the Show Details mode when I want to go directly to the report properties page and bypass viewing the report, since clicking a report link runs the report.
5. Click the Data Sources folder to see its content. If you wonder how the Data Sources folder got created, the TargetDataSourceFolder project property of all Report Server demo projects is set to Data Sources. As a result, when you deploy the project in BIDS, BIDS creates the Data Sources folder and uploads the project shared data sources to it.

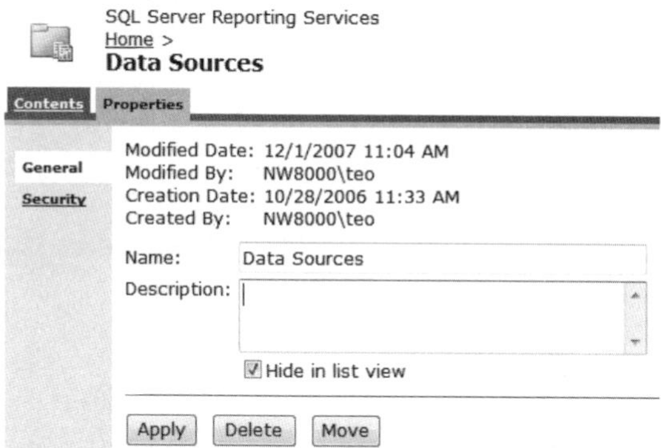

Figure 11.10 Use the folder's Properties page to rename the folder, enter a folder description, and exclude the folder from the list view.

6. Select the Properties tab to access the folder properties of the Data Sources folder, as shown in Figure 11.10. The Properties page lets you rename a folder and enter a folder description. You can use the Properties page to delete a folder or move it to a new location in the report catalog.
7. You can hide a catalog item to exclude it from the list view of its containing folder. Suppose that you want to exclude the Data Sources folder from the folder list to reduce clutter. Select the Properties tab of the Data Sources folder and check the Hide in List View checkbox. Click the Apply button and then click the Home menu link on the top right.

Observe that the Data Sources folder is no longer shown in the Home folder content. However, clicking the Show Details button will show the Data Sources folder. Hiding items in the list view is not a security measure; it is only meant to reduce the perceived complexity of busy folders. You need to set up role-based security policies if you want to prevent users from seeing and accessing folders and their content.

8. Go back to the Properties page of the Data Sources folder and clear the Hide in List View checkbox to restore the original view. Click the Apply button and then click the Home menu link to go back to the Home folder.

Creating new folders

Suppose that you cannot use BIDS to deploy the Adventure Works sample reports. Instead, let's use Report Manager to create the AdventureWorks Sample Reports folder and upload manually report definitions to it.

1. Navigate to the Home folder and click the Show Details button.
2. Select the checkbox of the AdventureWorks Sample Reports folder to select it and click the Delete button. Confirm the action to delete the item. Report Manager deletes the AdventureWorks Sample Reports folder and its content.
3. Click the New Folder button. In the New Folder page, enter *AdventureWorks Sample Reports* as a folder name and click OK.

   The Report Manager creates the AdventureWorks Sample Reports folder. Report Manager shows a green glyph that says !NEW next to the report name to indicate that this is new content.

Uploading content

Let's now upload the Adventure Works sample reports to the new folder.

1. Click the AdventureWorks Sample Reports link to go to the Contents page of the folder.
2. Click the Upload File button.

Figure 11.11 Use the Upload File page to upload folder content.

3. In the Upload File page (see Figure 11.11), click the Browse button and navigate to the AdventureWorks Sample Reports folder in the book source code.
4. Unfortunately, Report Manager doesn't let you upload multiple items at the same time, so we need to upload the Adventure Works reports one at a time. Select the Company Sales.rdl report definition file and click OK to go back to the Upload File page. Click OK to upload the Company Sales report.

 **NOTE** The server always stores the original RDL file that you publish. If you edit properties or parameter values in Report Manager, your changes are not applied to the RDL that was uploaded to the report server.

5. Repeat the last three steps to upload the rest of the reports (*.rdl files) to the AdventureWorks Sample Reports folder.

   Do not upload the AdventureWorks.rds and AdventureWorksAS.rds data source definition files because they should already exist in the Data Sources folder. In the next exercise, you will set up the Company Sales sample report to reference the existing data source definitions in the Data Sources folder. For now, this means that you won't be able to run the reports you've uploaded just yet.

11.2.3 Managing Data Sources

Recall that Reporting Services supports report-specific and shared data sources. A report-specific data source is embedded in the report definition and cannot be shared among reports. By contrast, a shared data source can be centrally managed and can be referenced by multiple reports. The AdventureWorks sample reports use two shared data sources: *AdventureWorks*, which represents the AdventureWorks relational database, and *AdventureWorksAS* which points to the Adventure Works DW Analysis Services database.

Understanding broken data source references

As a best practice, I'd recommend you store all data source definitions in a separate folder. This will let you define security policies that prevent end users from accessing that folder and viewing the data source definitions. This doesn't prevent users from running reports that reference these data sources because rights to view reports imply rights to use the report data sources.

1. Navigate to the AdventureWorks Sales Report folder and attempt to run the Company Sales report. Note that Report Manager displays the following error message:

   ```
   The report server cannot process the report. The data source connection information has been deleted.
   (rsInvalidDataSourceReference)
   ```

   That's because the Company Sales report is no longer associated with a valid data source. Unfortunately, the error message doesn't include the name of the data source that the report was associated with at design time, but you can get that information from the report definition.

2. Select the Properties tab of the Company Sales report, and then click the Edit button to view the report definition. Locate the DataSources element toward the top of the report definition and note the DataSourceReference element below it.

   ```
   <DataSourceReference>AdventureWorks</DataSourceReference>
   ```

   This means that the report author referenced the AdventureWorks shared data source at design time.

Understanding data source properties

Let's verify that the Adventure Works data sources exist and view their definitions.

1. Click the Home link to go to the Home folder and then click the Data Sources folder.
2. Click the AdventureWorks data source to view its properties, as shown in Figure 11.12.

Many of the data source properties should look familiar to you, as I discussed them in chapter 4. For example, the General tab lets you manage to the data source type, connection string, and credentials. However, Report Manager adds a few more properties that deserve further explanation. To start with, Report Manager lets you disable a data source by clearing the Enable the Data Source checkbox. Disabling a data source could be useful to quickly prevent processing all reports, report models, and data-driven subscriptions that use that data source.

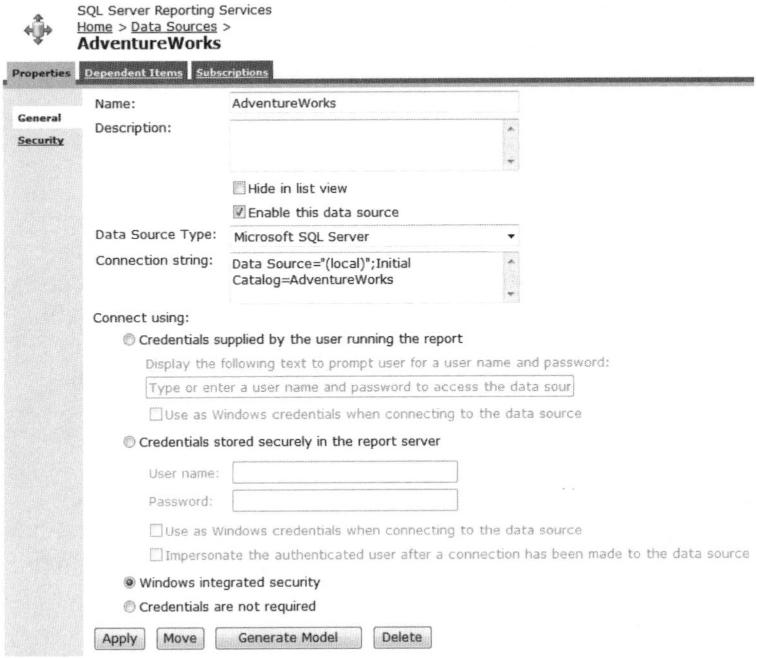

SQL Server Reporting Services
Home > Data Sources >
AdventureWorks

Properties | Dependent Items | Subscriptions

General
Security

Name: AdventureWorks
Description:
Hide in list view
Enable this data source
Data Source Type: Microsoft SQL Server
Connection string: Data Source="(local)";Initial Catalog=AdventureWorks
Connect using:
Credentials supplied by the user running the report
Display the following text to prompt user for a user name and password:
Type or enter a user name and password to access the data sour
Use as Windows credentials when connecting to the data source
Credentials stored securely in the report server
User name:
Password:
Use as Windows credentials when connecting to the data source
Impersonate the authenticated user after a connection has been made to the data source
Windows integrated security
Credentials are not required
Apply | Move | Generate Model | Delete

Figure 11.12 Use the Data Source General tab to manage the data source connections string and credentials.

Report Manager also gives you more control over stored credentials; that is, the Credential Stored Securely in the Report Server option. First, you can tell the server to use the stored credentials as Windows credentials by checking the Use as Windows Credentials option. This could be useful for data sources that support only Windows integrated security. For example, you may have an Analysis Services database on another server. If the server that hosts Reporting Services is not configured for Kerberos delegation, the connection to Analysis Services will fail because Windows will not pass credentials a second time. Passing credentials to a second computer is known as a "double-hop" connection and NTLM doesn't support it.

However, if you don't need to pass the user identity all the way to Analysis Services, you can store and use the credentials of a trusted account that has access to the cube. As a result, all requests to the cube database will go under that trusted account. This could be useful to get a report running as quickly as possible, such as for demo or testing purposes. Make sure that if you store credentials, the account you specify has Log On Locally permissions on the report server computer.

The Impersonate the Authenticated User option only works for logins with administrator rights and database servers that support user impersonation. In the case of SQL Server, this option executes the SETUSER system function to impersonate the database connection. For example, imagine that you log in to Windows as adventure-works\bob. The report administrator has chosen the Credentials Stored Securely option and has entered the credentials of an account that belongs to the sysadmin SQL Server role. When you run the report, behind the scenes the report server will send the SETUSER adventure-works\bob command to the SQL Server to impersonate Bob. The net result is the same as if Windows Integrated security was used because the report connects to the database under Bob's identity. The difference is that the server uses the stored credentials to establish the initial connection.

Viewing dependent items

A shared data source can be used by many items in the report catalog. You may want to know which items will be affected by changes to the data source definition. To view the dependent items, do the following:

1. Open the data source properties.
2. Select the Dependent Items tab.

   The Dependent Items page will show all reports and models that reference the data source. You can click the Show Details button if you want to delete or move the dependent items.

3. Select the Subscriptions tab if you want to view the data-driven subscriptions that depend on the data source.

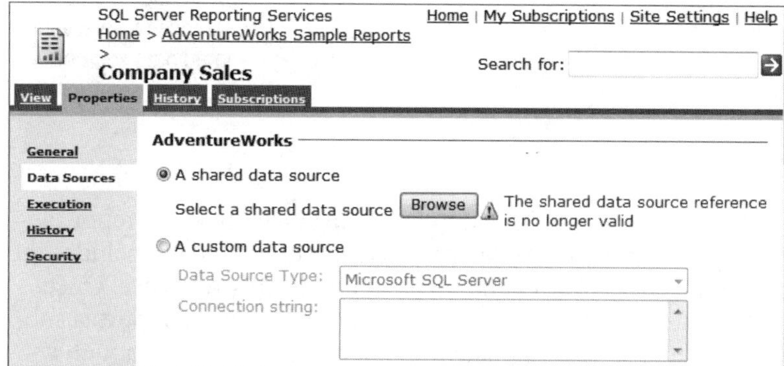

Figure 11.13 A common reason for non-operational reports is a broken data source reference.

Fixing broken data source references

Back to the problem at hand. Let's make the Adventure Works sample reports operational by fixing the data source references.

1. Navigate to the AdventureWorks Samples Reports and click the Show Details button.
2. Click the Properties button located in front of the Company Sales report to open its properties and click the Data Source link.
3. Report Manager detects the invalid data source reference and displays an error message, as shown in Figure 11.13.
4. Click the Browse button to open the Browse Folders page, as shown Figure 11.14.
5. Expand the Data Sources folder. Don't be surprised if your list of data sources differs from mine.
6. Select the AdventureWorks data source and click OK to return to the Company Sales report. Click the Apply button to apply the changes to the report.
7. Select the View tab to test the report and make sure it runs successfully.

8. Repeat steps 2-6 to associate the rest of the reports with the AdventureWorks data source, except for the Sales Reason Comparison report. Since this report uses the Adventure Works DW cube database, associate it with the AdventureWorksAS data source.

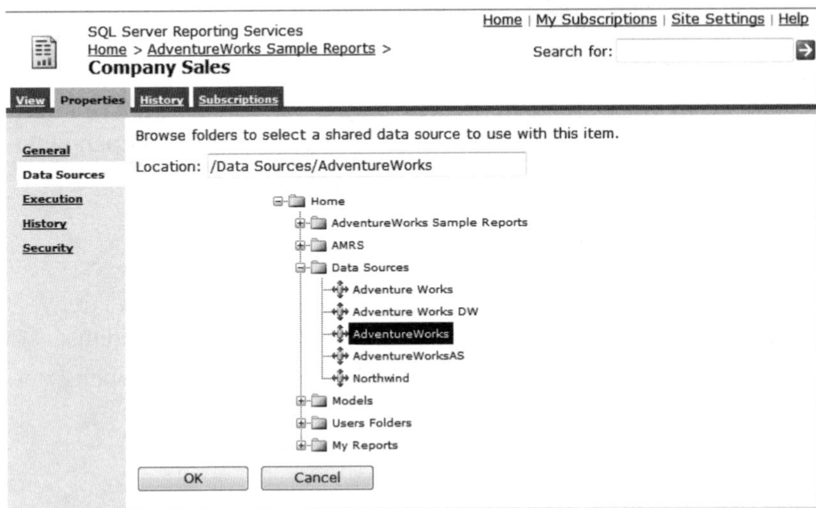

Figure 11.14 Fix a broken data source reference by selecting a shared data source.

11.2.4 Managing Reports

When you publish a report, the report server extracts the report metadata from the report definition and saves the metadata in the report server database. The report metadata includes the report name, description, data source information, and certain parameters properties. Once the report is published, the report metadata takes on a life of its own. When the report is subsequently re-published, the report server doesn't update the report metadata even though it may have changed. This behavior is sure to take report authors by surprise, but it is by design. The Reporting Services team decided to favor the report administrator so design-time changes don't wipe out the changes made by the administrator.

Viewing reports

Before I show you how you can manage the report content, let me point out that organizations can use the Report Manager not only for report management but also for viewing reports in the default HTML format. Let's demonstrate this feature.

1. Navigate to the AdventureWorks Sample Reports folder and click the Product Line Sales report link.
2. The report server renders the report in HTML. The Report Manager displays the report in the HTML Viewer, as shown in Figure 11.15.

Behind the scenes, the HTML Viewer uses the ReportViewer Web server control to display reports that are requested by a user. The ReportViewer control includes a handy toolbar that lets the user perform common report tasks with a click of a button. If the report has parameters, the toolbar includes a parameter area. For example, the Product Line Sales report takes four parameters. The end user can enter the parameters that he or she wants to use, and click the View Report button to regenerate the report with those values.

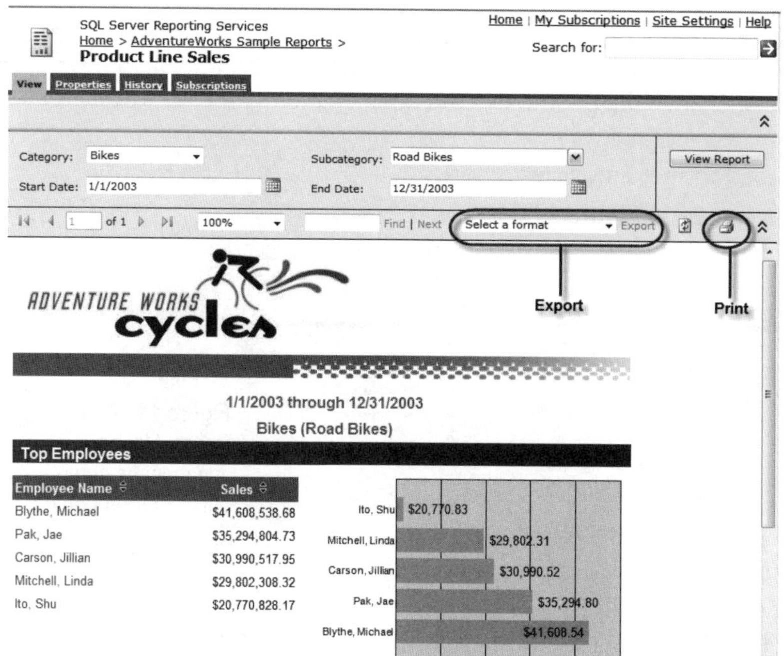

Figure 11.15 The Report Manager uses the Web-Forms ReportViewer control for report delivery.

From a management standpoint, you can control the availability of export formats (renderers) and the print functionality. Chapter 7 demonstrated how you can customize the renderer configuration to hide or disable an export option. Although you can use the browser printing functionality to print a report, the Print button on the report toolbar provides a better printing experience. It lets you preview and control the report layout and margins before printing the report. Behind the scenes, the Print functionality is provided by an ActiveX control that gets downloaded and installed on first use.

NOTE You cannot add custom functionality to the report toolbar of the HTML Viewer. However, you can change its appearance via a Cascading Style Sheet (.css) file. The HTML Viewer CSS file is HtmlViewer.css and it is installed by default in the \Program Files\Microsoft SQL Server\MSRS10.MSSQLSERVER\Reporting Services\ReportServer\Styles folder. I'll show you an example of customizing the HTML Viewer with CSS styles in chapter 14.

You can disable the ActiveX control download by connecting to the report server in SQL Server Management Studio and setting the EnableClientPrinting server property (Advanced tab) to False. If printing is problematic, it could be because the user has the old version of the control. The user can re-install the ActiveX control as follows:

3. Assuming Internet Explorer, go to Tools ⇨ Manage Add-ons ⇨ Enable or Disable Add-ons menu.
4. Expand the Show drop-down list and select the Downloaded ActiveX Controls item.
5. Select the RSClientPrint Class and press the Delete button to delete it.

The next time you click the Print button, the browser will download and install the latest version of the ActiveX control from the server.

Managing report parameters

Report Manager gives you access to the report parameters that the report author created for the report. You can change the parameter visibility, prompt string, and default values. You can't add or delete parameters, change the parameter data type, or modify the Multivalued and Available Values properties.

1. Select the Properties tab of the Product Line Sales report.
2. Click the Parameters link, as shown in Figure 11.16.

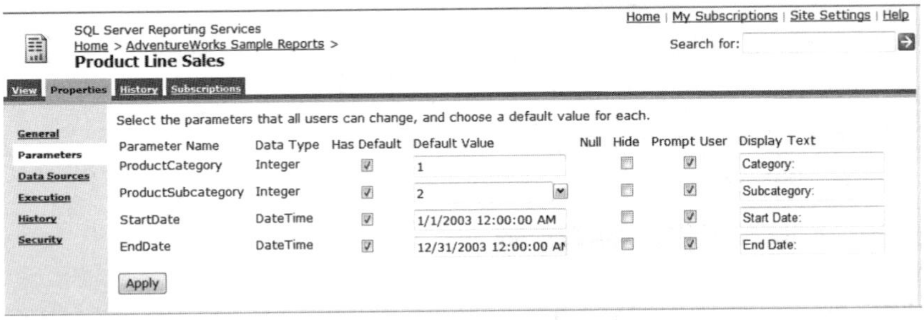

Figure 11.16 The Report Manager lets you manage some parameter properties.

As I noted, once the report is published, the report parameters can be managed independently from the report definition. Once you begin modifying parameter properties on a published report, be aware that subsequently changing them in Report Designer and republishing the report definition does not overwrite the parameter values that you set in Report Manager. If this is not the desired behavior, you can delete the report and re-publish it again.

If you want to assign a default value to a parameter, check the Has Default checkbox and enter the default value. You can't modify the parameter default value if it is query-based. The Hide and Prompt User checkboxes are exclusive options. Hiding a parameter doesn't show the parameter to the user. However, the user or client application can still set the parameter in the report URL or programmatically. If you uncheck the Prompt User checkbox and leave the Display Text property blank, the parameter will not be displayed and the default parameter value will be used when the user runs the report. If you leave the prompt blank and the parameter doesn't have a default value, the report cannot run and the report server returns the following error:

```
Parameter validation failed. It is not possible to provide valid values for all parameters. (rsParameterError)
```

Report Manager does not validate parameter values. You must know which values are valid for your report. Because you cannot customize the Report Manager functionality, you cannot implement custom validation rules either.

Working with linked reports

A linked report is a "smart" shortcut that provides a level of indirection to an existing report that runs on a native (non-SharePoint integrated) report server. A linked report can have its own execution, history, and security settings. More importantly, a linked report can have parameter settings, including default values, visibility, and prompt text, that are different from the existing report upon which it is based. However, you can't add parameters to a linked report nor can you change their valid values list. Another important aspect of linked reports is that the report server automatically updates the link when the location of the original report changes. The ability to independently move the linked and original report enables some interesting deployment scenarios.

In one of my real-life projects, I used linked reports to implement master reports. A custom application would let the user define a master report that contains an arbitrary number of subreports. The catch was that the user could move a subreport to another location. If the subreport points to a regular report, changing the report location would invalidate the master report. Using linked reports gave us a way to work around this limitation. Let's take a closer look at the solution.

1. In Report Manager, navigate to the AdventureWorks Sample Reports folder and click the Upload File button.
2. In the Upload File page, browse to the Report Package with Subreports.rdl file in the source code for this chapter. Name the new report *Report Package* and click OK.

   The Report Package with Subreports report contains two subreports that point to the Company Sales and Product Line Sales reports.
3. View the Report Package report. It should run successfully.
4. Now, let's change the location of the Company Sales report. Go to the Properties page of the Company Sales report and click the Move button. Choose the Home folder and click OK to move the Company Sales report to the root folder.
5. View the Report Package report again and note that the Company Sales report is not shown. Instead, the following error message is displayed:

```
Error: Subreport could not be shown.
```

6. Move the Company Sales report back to the AdventureWorks Sample Reports folder.
7. Go to the Company Sales report General Properties page and click the Create Linked Report button, as shown in Figure 11.17. Name the linked report *Company Sales Linked*.

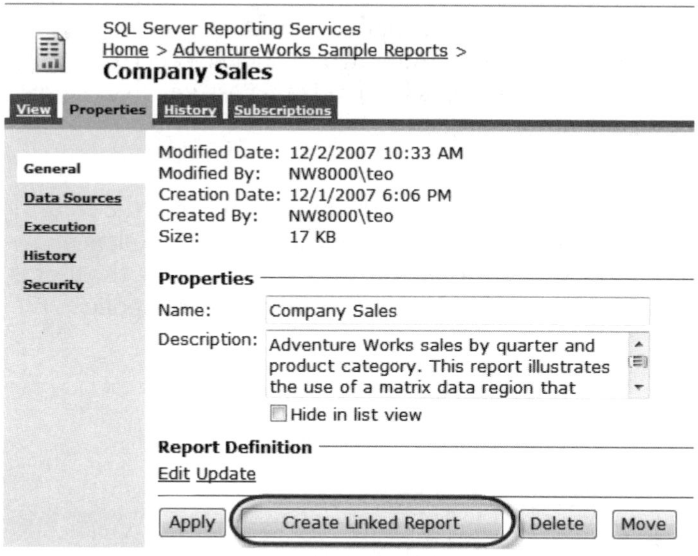

Figure 11.17 Create a linked report that updates its link automatically as the location of the target report changes.

8. Open the Properties page of the Report Package report and click the Update button to update its report definition from the Report Package with Linked Reports.rdl file that uses the Company Sales Linked report.
9. View the Report Package report to verify that it runs successfully.

10. Move the Company Sales report to the Home folder again. View the Report Package report. It should run successfully this time.

The master report runs successfully because it uses a linked report that actively tracks the location of the report to which it is linked. You can even delete the Company Sales report and republish it without affecting the master report. As long as the report link points to an existing report, the linked report will work fine.

11.3 Managing Security

One important task that every report administrator needs to master is managing security. You won't get very far with a report server deployment if you don't have a good grasp of its security model. Out of the box, only local Windows administrators have access to the report server. As a report administrator, you are responsible for defining security policies that grant end users selective rights to the report server.

Because the Reporting Services security model is layered on top of Windows, understanding security is not easy and explaining this topic in detail is beyond the scope of this book. Therefore, I will assume that you have a basic knowledge of how Windows authentication and authorization work. The Microsoft MSDN Security Center (see Resources) is a great place to start if you want to get up to speed with Windows security.

11.3.1 Understanding Report Server Security

By default, the report server is configured for Windows authentication. This works well with intranet deployments and Active Directory but it may not be practical for Internet-facing reporting solutions. When Windows authentication is not an option, you can replace it with custom security, which I will demonstrate in chapter 19. Although the underlying concepts for default and custom security are the same, the exercises in this chapter assume that the report server is configured for Windows authentication.

Understanding role-based security model

You will probably find the Reporting Services role-based security model similar to the security models of other Microsoft or home-grown solutions you have come across. The implementation details are report server-specific but the basic ideas are the same. In a nutshell, the user is authenticated based on the user identity, and authorized according to the security policies the administrator has set up.

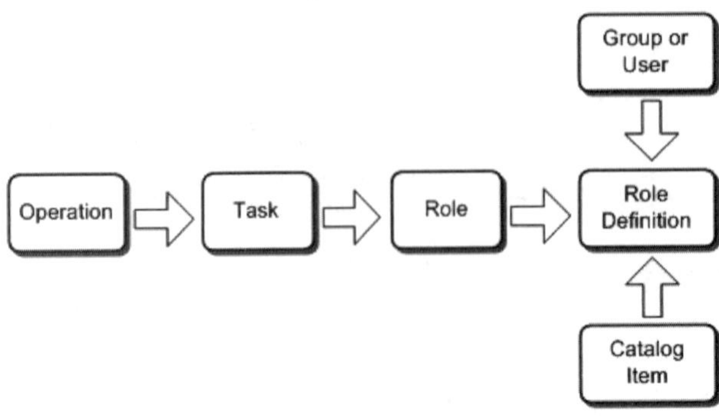

Figure 11.18 Reporting Services has a role-based security model where the user is authenticated based on the user identity and authorized according to the security policies the administrator has set up.

Figure 11.18 shows the components of the report server security model. The server enforces restricted access to the report catalog through *role assignments*. A role assignment specifies what rights a user or group has to a given catalog item.

Operations

Operations define the most granular permissions. There are system-level and item-level operations. The system-level operations give rights to system tasks. For example, CatalogOperation.CreateRoles is a system level operation that grants the user rights to create roles. Item-level operations control access to items in the report catalog. For example, FolderOperation.UpdateProperties is an item-level operation that grants the user rights to update the folder properties. Reporting Services has many predefined operations but you cannot view or customize them in Report Manager. Only developers who write custom security extensions have programmatic control over operations.

Tasks

To reduce the management effort, Reporting Services groups related operations into tasks. Similar to operations, there are system-level and item-level tasks. An example of a system-level task is Manage Roles, which includes all operations required to manage roles, such as CatalogOperation.CreateRoles, CatalogOperation.DeleteRoles, CatalogOperation.ReadRoleProperties. Similarly, Manage Folders is an item-level task that includes all item-level operations needed to create, delete, and update catalog folders. Reporting Services comes with twenty-five predefined tasks. Similar to operations, you cannot change these tasks and you cannot create new tasks.

Roles

A role definition is a named collection of tasks that are used together. Reporting Services provides several pre-defined system and item-level roles, as shown in Table 11.2.

Table 11.2 The default system and item-level roles

Role Type	Role	Purpose
System	System Administrators	Enable system-wide features and security, create role definitions, and manage jobs.
System	System Users	View report server properties and shared schedules. Can execute report definitions, such as when previewing a Report Builder 1.0 report.
Item-level	Browser	Navigate folders and view reports.
Item-level	Content Manager	Manage report catalog, set security, and view items.
Item-level	Publisher	Publish items to the report catalog.
Item-level	My Reports	Publish reports to and manage the My Reports folder.
Item-level	Report Builder	View and edit report definitions in Report Builder1.0 client.

System-level roles authorize access at the site level. Item-level roles provide access to report server items and operations that affect those items. They are defined on the root node (Home) and all items throughout the report catalog. Item and system-level roles are mutually exclusive but are used together to authorize user access to report server content and operations. The administrator can customize the default roles or create new ones if needed. Reporting Services roles are additive, which means that the user is granted the union of the permitted tasks of the roles that the user is assigned to.

Understanding role assignments

The administrator controls access to the report catalog by defining role assignments. A role assignment is a combination of a securable item, a user principal, and one or more role(s). In Reporting Services, securable items are folders, reports, report models, resources, and shared data sources. With the default Windows security model, a user principal can be an individual Windows user or a group.

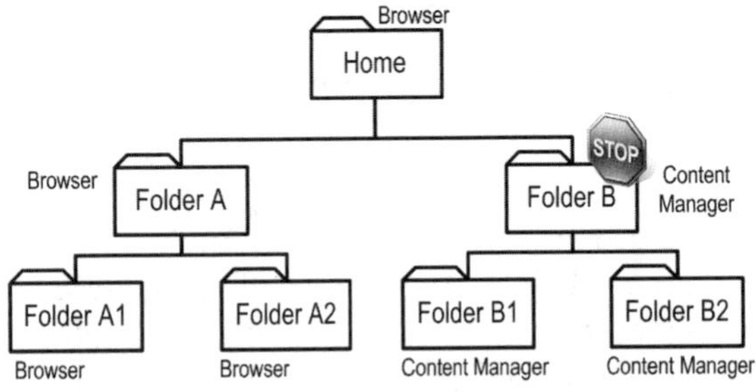

Figure 11.19 Role assignments are inherited from a parent but permission inheritance can be broken at any level.

Similar to Windows ACL permissions, role assignments are inherited from the parent folder. In the example shown in Figure 11.19, the user has Browser rights to the Home folder. Thanks to security inheritance, you don't need to define explicit role assignments for the folders below the Home folder and their content. That's because the report server will automatically propagate the Browser rights down the folder hierarchy. However, you can break the security inheritance at any level or securable item. For example, assuming that the user needs to have Content Manager rights for Folder B, you can break the security inheritance in folder B and define a role assignment that grants the user Content Manager rights for that folder. The new rights will flow down to the folder descendants until the inheritance chain is severed again. The administrator can always restore security inheritance at any level to inherit from parent.

To simplify security management, I suggest you stick with security inheritance as much as possible. I recommend enforcing the minimum set of permissions at the top Home folder, such as granting users Browser rights. Then, expand the user rights down the folder namespace on as-needed basis. It is important to point out that if the user doesn't have rights to view a given item, the user won't be able to see that item. That's because, behind the scenes, when the user browses the report catalog, Report Manager calls the ListChildren API. ListChildren excludes items that the user is not authorized to see. Consequently, make sure to grant the user at least Browser rights to folders above the user's working folder so the user can navigate the folder hierarchy and get to the folder in the Report Manager or custom applications.

11.3.2 Granting Administrator Access

Now that you have a good understanding of how Reporting Services security works, let's apply it in practice. One of your first tasks after installing Reporting Services may be granting another user rights to manage the report server. The SQL Server 2008 setup program grants local Windows administrators System Administrator rights and Content Manager rights for the Home folder. This explains why members of the Windows local Administrators group have unrestricted rights to the report server. Let's say you want to grant another user, who is not a local Windows administrator, rights to manage the report server. This will require granting the user System Administrator and Content Manager rights.

Reviewing role definitions

Let's use SQL Server Management Studio to review the definitions of the System Administrator and Content Manager roles.

1. Open SSMS and connect to the report server instance you need to manage.
2. Expand the Security folder, as shown in Figure 11.20. Note that the item-level roles are listed under the Roles folder, while the system-level roles are found under the System Roles folder.

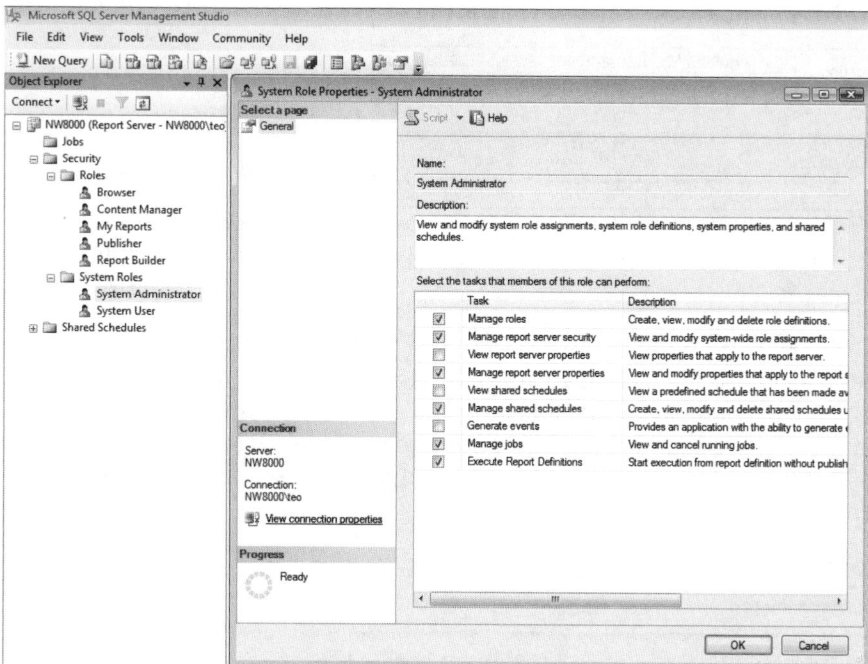

Figure 11.20 Use SSMS to review role definitions and create new roles.

3. Double-click the System Administrator role to view its definition.

   The selected tasks in the System Role Properties dialog box are the tasks that the role provides. You can change the role definition by adding additional tasks or remove tasks. You can create a custom system or item-level role by right-clicking on the System Roles or Roles folder and choosing New System Role or New Role respectively.

4. Double-click on the Content Manager item-level role to review its definition. Notice that the Content Manager role grants the user rights to perform catalog management and report viewing tasks.

Granting system administrator rights

Next, we will use the Report Manager to create role assignments for granting the user unrestricted rights to the report server. It is important to point out that although you are using Report Manager to create role assignments, you are actually securing the report server and not Report Manager. To understand this, recall that the Report Manager is just a front end to the report server

1. Open the Computer Management console from the Administrative Tools program group and create a new Windows user, as follows:
   - User name—Bob
   - Password—P@ssw0rd
   - Uncheck User Must Change Password at Next Logon and check Password Never Expires options.
2. Open Report Manager and click the Site Settings menu link.
3. Click the Security link to review the system-level role definitions, as shown in Figure 11.21. As noted, the SQL Server 2008 setup program assigns the local Windows administrators group to the System Administrators role. This explains the single system role definition.

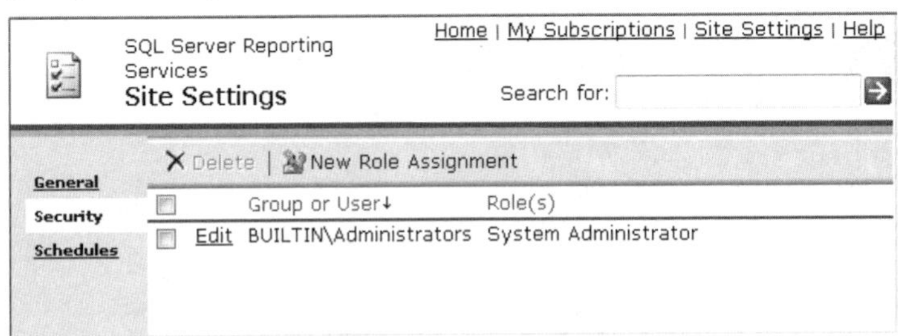

Figure 11.21 Use the Site Settings Security page to grant the user system rights.

4. Click the New Role Assignment button to open the New System Role Assignment page.
5. In the Group or User Name field, enter *Bob*, as shown in Figure 11.22. To use a domain user or group, prefix the principal name with the domain name, such as adventure-works\Bob for a single user or adventure-works\Sales Managers for a Windows domain group. In our case, because Bob is a local Windows user account that you created on your computer, the correct format is <machinename>\Bob or just Bob.

Home | My Subscriptions | Site Settings | Help
SQL Server Reporting Services
New System Role Assignment
Search for:
Use this page to assign a user or group to a system role. You can also use this page to create or modify a system role definition.
Group or user name: Bob
Select one or more roles to assign to the group or user.
Role / Description
System Administrator — View and modify system role assignments, system role definitions, system properties, and shared schedules.
System User — View system properties and shared schedules.
OK Cancel

Figure 11.22 Use the New System Role Assignment page to grant the user System Administrator rights.

6. Select the System Administrator role and click OK.

   At this point, Bob is set up as a system administrator and he can perform all tasks included in the System Administrator role.

Granting Content Manager rights

The System Administrator role lets the user manage the report server site but it doesn't give the user rights to manage the report catalog, such as rights to create new folders, upload content, and assign item-level role definitions. To delegate catalog management rights to Bob, create a new role definition that grants him Content Manager rights for the Home folder.

1. In the Report Manager, click the Home menu link to navigate to the Home folder and select the Properties tab.
2. Click the Security link to view the role definitions for the Home folder. By default, only the Windows local administrators have Content Manager rights.
3. Click the New Role Assignment button to open the New Role Assignment page and assign Bob to the Content Manager role.

Because permissions are inherited throughout the folder namespace, Bob has Content Manager rights to the entire report catalog.

11.3.3 Granting User Access

By default, end users don't have access to the report server so they won't be able to browse the report catalog and run reports. As an administrator, you need to create role assignments that grant the users the permissions they need without compromising security.

Granting Browser rights

In the following exercise, you will set up a new Windows user and grant the user rights to browse the report catalog.

1. Open the Computer Management console from the Administrative Tools program group and create a new Windows user, as follows:
   - User name—Alice
   - Password—P@ssw0rd
   - Uncheck User Must Change Password At Next Logon and check Password Never Expires options.
2. Run the Report Manager under the Alice's identity.

   TIP In Windows XP and Windows Server 2003, the easiest way to run Internet Explorer as another user is to right-click on the Internet Explorer, choose Run As, and enter the user credentials. For some obscure reason that probably has to do with security, in Vista you can use Run As only if you log in to Windows as a non-administrator. While there is a runas command-line utility, it doesn't work for Internet Explorer. This means you will need to log off and log on as the new user or use the Switch User feature.

3. Note that the Report Manager Home page is blank. That's because Alice is not assigned to any role.
4. Open Report Manager as an administrator. Select the Properties tab to access the Security page.
5. Create a new role assignment that grants Alice Browser rights to the folder.
6. Go back to the user instance of the Internet Explorer, and press F5 to refresh the page.

Notice that now Alice can browse the report catalog and run reports.

Revoking folder access

As you know by now, role assignments are inherited from the parent folder. If this is not desired, consider breaking the security inheritance by granting different rights on specified folders or items. For example, you may not want users to read data source definitions. Alice cannot view the data source definitions in the Data Sources folder because the Browser role doesn't include the View Data Sources task. However, Bob can because the Content Manager role includes this task. Let's say you want to revoke Bob's rights to the Data Sources folder.

1. Log in the Report Manager as an administrator and navigate to the Data Sources folder, as shown in Figure 11.23.

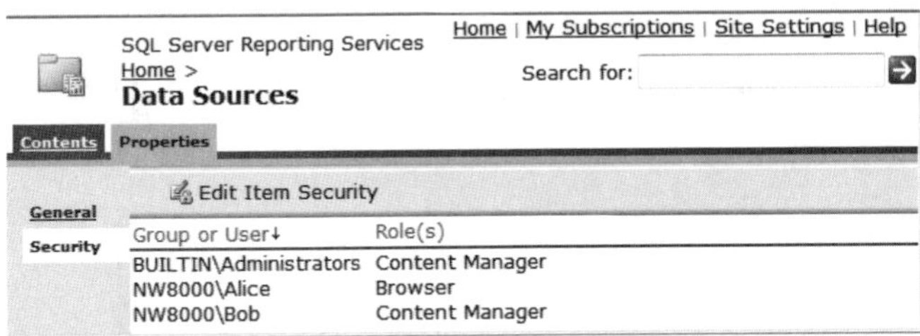

Figure 11.23 As a best practice, consider revoking end user access to the Data Sources folder.

2. Click the Edit Item Security button. Report Manager displays the following prompt.

Item security is inherited from a parent item. Do you want to apply security settings for this item that are different from those of the Home parent item?

3. Click OK to break the security inheritance chain.

   Report Manager copies the role assignments of the Home folder to the Data Sources folder. In addition, Report Manager adds a Revert to Parent Security button to let you restore security inheritance from the parent item later on.

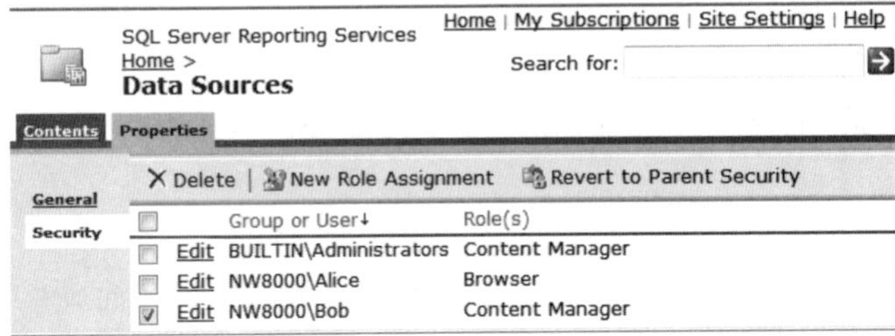

Figure 11.24 The Revert to Parent Security button lets you restore security inheritance.

4. Select Bob's role assignment, as shown in Figure 11.24, and press the Delete button to revoke Bob all rights to the Data Sources folder.
5. Log in to the Report Manager as Bob and notice that you cannot see the Data Sources folder.

   If the user is not authorized to view an item, the report server excludes the item as though it doesn't exist for that user. Again, note that Bob will be able to run reports that use the data sources in the Data Sources folders because rights to run a report imply rights to use the report data sources.

11.3.4 Viewing Security Policies

Using Report Manager to review the security policies requires navigating the folder namespace and manually checking the security page of each folder and item. This may get difficult if you have many nested folders. To avoid this, I authored a report that retrieves information about all of the security policies defined for a given catalog item.

Understanding the Get Policies report

Figure 11.25 shows the Get Policies report, which is loaded in the BIDS Report Designer. The report has a single parameter (Item), which accepts the full path to the catalog item, such as the /AMRS folder. When you run the report, the report calls down to the Report Server Web service to obtain the security policies for that item. The Inherit From Parent field indicates whether the item inherits security from parent. The table section enumerates the role assignments for that item. For each role assignment, the report shows the principal name and the role definition that is assigned to that principal.

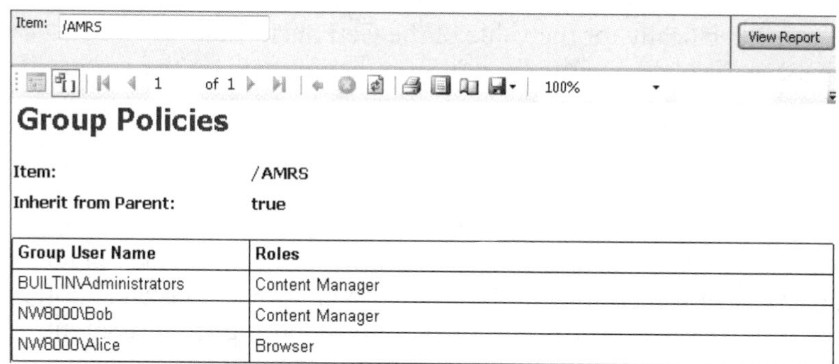

Group User Name	Roles
BUILTIN\Administrators	Content Manager
NW8000\Bob	Content Manager
NW8000\Alice	Browser

Figure 11.25 The Get Policies report lets you review the security policies defined for any catalog item.

Implementing the report

Thanks to the Reporting Services XML data provider, implementing the Get Policies report is easy. Recall that the XML data provider lets you query XML documents that are returned from URL-based sources, such as a Web service. The report has two datasets that reference the same report-level data source. The data source uses the XML data provider to connect to the ReportService2005 service, as follows:

```
http://localhost/reportserver/ReportService2005.asmx
```

Both datasets have an Item query-level parameter that obtains its value from the report-level Item parameter. The first dataset (Main) has the following query:

```
<Query>
<Method Namespace="http://schemas.microsoft.com/sqlserver/2005/06/30/reporting/reportingservices"
Name="GetPolicies"/>
</Query>
```

This query invokes the GetPolicies web method to retrieve the role assignments. Here is a sample XML payload that GetPolices returns.

```
<GetPoliciesResponse xmlns=" . . .">
    <Policies>
        <Policy>
                <GroupUserName>BUILTIN \Administrators</GroupUserName>
                <Roles>
                        <Role>
                                <Name>Content Manager</Name>
                        </Role>
                </Roles>
        </Policy>
        <Policy>
        . . .
        </Policy>
    </Policies>
    <InheritParent>false</InheritParent>
</GetPoliciesResponse>
```

The Main dataset query returns the principal name from the GroupUserName node and role name from the Name node. Getting the InheritParent node text is a somewhat trickier. The returned XML payload includes the InheritParent element, which is at the same level as the Policies element because it applies to the item itself. However, the XML data provider cannot navigate parallel nodes. That's why I defined a second dataset which uses the following query:

```
<Query>
  <Method Namespace=". . ." Name="GetPolicies"/>
  <ElementPath IgnoreNamespaces="true">GetPoliciesResponse/InheritParent</ElementPath>
</Query>
```

The ElementPath statement asks specifically for the value of the GetPoliciesResponse/InheritParent node that gets displayed in the Inherit From Parent field on the report.

11.4 Summary

In this chapter you have learned how to manage the report server environment. You can use SQL Server Management Studio to manage server properties, features, and roles. Most of the time, you will rely on Report Manager to perform routine content management tasks. Reporting Services supports folders, reports, data sources, resources, and report models as content types. You can use Report Manager to upload content and organize content items in a hierarchical folder namespace.

Out of the box, the report server is configured for Windows security and only local Windows administrators have access to the report server. As an administrator, you can set up system and item-level role assignments to grant end users selective rights to perform report server operations. Simplify security management by configuring catalog items to inherit security polices from their parent.

11.5 Resources

RSExplorer Sample Application
(http://tinyurl.com/24avoe)—The RSExplorer sample application demonstrates how you can write a custom .NET application for report viewing and management.

Add a logo to the Report Manager blog by Jon Gallaway
(http://tinyurl.com/y3776w)—Demonstrates how to add a custom logo to the Report Manager Web interface using client-side JavaSript.

The Microsoft MSDN Security Center
(http://msdn.microsoft.com/security)—Tons of excellent information, including entire books to help you secure your applications.

Chapter 12

Managing Report Execution and Subscriptions

Reporting Services can deliver reports on demand and via subscriptions. With on-demand delivery, the report server immediately processes the request and streams the rendered report to the client. With subscription delivery, a predefined subscription specifies when the report is run, where it is delivered, and in what format. Individual users or report administrators can create subscriptions that determine report delivery.

As a report administrator, you can configure how an on-demand report is executed. Typically, end users would prefer to see the latest data on the report. However, if some data latency is acceptable, you can optimize report performance by configuring the report for caching. You can also save permanent report snapshots for auditing and archiving purposes.

I will start this chapter by explaining the report execution options. Then, I will show you how to use Report Manager to configure those options. Next, I will introduce you to subscription-based report delivery and walk you through the steps to set up a standard subscription. Finally, you will learn how to work with data-driven subscriptions that retrieve dynamic subscription data from an external database.

12.1 Managing Report Execution

Before you set report execution properties, it helps to know how reports are generated. The report server generates a report in three phases. First, the report server retrieves data for all datasets defined in the report. Second, the report server processes the report by combining the report data and report layout into an internal report object (raw report) and expression code, and saves the report object in the report catalog. Finally, the report server renders the report in the requested export format and streams the report to the user. The report execution options let you control the lifetime of the cached report execution so new report requests can reuse the raw report instead of generating the report anew.

12.1.1 Understanding Report Execution Options

The report server supports three mutually exclusive execution options to help you achieve a reasonable compromise between data latency, data consistency, and performance. Table 12.1 summarizes these options, their scope, duration, and purpose.

Table 12.1 Reporting Services supports several execution options

Execution Option	Scope	Duration	Purpose
Execution session	Single user	10 min by default	Ensures data consistency with interactive report features and report paging
Cache snapshot	Multiple users	Absolute expiration or schedule	Caches a report instance for each parameter combination
Execution Snapshot	Multiple users	Potentially indefinite	Saves a single instance of a processed report for auditing or archiving purposes

Before we go any further, I want to quickly point out that all report execution options store a cached copy of the report in the report server database. Contrary to what you may imagine when you hear the term "cache", report execution caching is not a memory-based cache. Storing the raw report in the report server database instead of in memory leaves more system resources available for report processing.

12.1.2 Managing Execution Sessions

A report server creates and retains an execution session for every instance of a report that is processed. The sessions are created because the client may benefit from it later on. For example, as the user pages through a report in Report Manager, the HTML Viewer submits a request to the server each time the user moves to a new page. User interaction with the report, such as drilldown and interactive sorting, also require round trips to the server.

If the report is not cached, the report server has no other choice but to re-process the report again. Not only will this be detrimental to report performance but may also lead to inconsistent data. For example, suppose that the end user looks at the report grand total and then navigates to another page. If the server queries the data source again, and the data changed since the user last looked at it, the user will see different results. Another scenario that produces an unhappy outcome is when you export a report and realize that the exported version has different data.

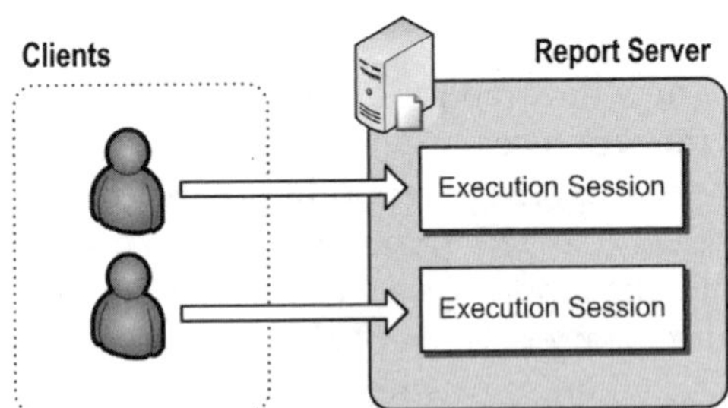

Figure 12.1 The report server uses execution sessions to correlate users with cached report instances.

Understanding execution sessions

The report server uses execution sessions mainly for data consistency between server round trips. An execution session is a cached per-client instance of a report. In this respect, execution sessions are somewhat similar to ASP.NET user sessions that you may be familiar with. As Figure 12.1 shows, when a new report request arrives, the report server caches a new copy of the raw report in the report server temporary database (ReportServerTempDB). Next, the report server sends a session identifier back to the client to correlate the execution session with that client. Note that I said *client* not user. That's because the user may open several instances of the client application, such as Internet Explorer. If the client doesn't pass back the session identifier, the report server considers this a new report execution even through it belongs to the same user.

An execution session maintains information about the details of the requested report, such as the interaction state, parameter state, and so on. The report server always creates execution sessions for new report executions. Although you cannot turn off execution session caching completely, you can, as an administrator, control the session expiration interval and how the session identifier is transmitted between the client and the server.

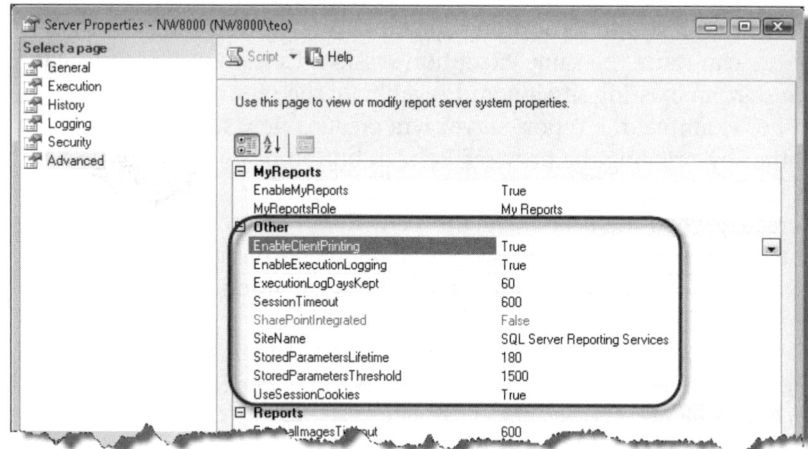

Figure 12.2 As an administrator, you can manage the execution session timeout and how the session identifier will be transmitted.

Managing session timeout

You can configure how long an execution session is retained before it times out. To view and change the execution session timeout, use SQL Server Management Studio (SSMS) as follows:

1. Open SSMS and connect to the report server.
2. Right-click the server node in Object Explorer and select Properties.
3. In the Server Properties dialog box, select the Advanced page, as shown in Figure 12.2.

The default session timeout is 600 seconds and it applies to all report executions. The report server uses a sliding expiration policy to renew the session timeout. In other words, if the same client requests the session before it times out, the report server extends the session timeout. If no new requests reference the execution session, the session eventually times out. The report server periodically polls the report server database and purges expired sessions.

TIP You can call the GetExecutionInfo API to keep the session from expiring and reset its expiration clock. However, you don't have to do this with custom applications that use the ReportViewer controls because they call GetExecutionInfo to ping the server periodically in order to keep sessions alive.

If you want the report server to expire execution sessions faster, decrease the SessionTimeout property value. However, don't set it too low because the user will get an rsExecutionNotFound exception if the session expires before the next report interaction occurs. The minimum session timeout duration is 10 seconds. While SSMS will let you set a session timeout less than 10 seconds, the report server will revert to 600 seconds.

Managing session identifier

By default, the report server issues a web cookie to correlate the client with the execution session. If security or other policies prevent using cookies, you can configure the report server to use cookieless execution sessions by setting the UseSessionCookies server property (Advanced tab) to False. In this case, instead of sending a cookie, the report server adds the session identifier to the report URL address. This is known as *URL munging*.

NOTE Instead of working with cookies, Reporting Services clients can use other mechanisms to store the session identifier between requests. For example, the ReportViewer Web server control (discussed in chapter 15) saves the session identifier in the page view state and never uses cookies.

In general, only report actions that result in a round trip, such as interactive actions, image requests, and page navigation, can reuse the same execution session. Certain user actions can cause the report server to restart an existing session and regenerate the report even if the session identifier is the same. For example, the report server will create a new session when the user refreshes the report either by pressing the browser Refresh button or by clicking the Refresh button on the report toolbar.

A new session is also created when the user clicks the View Report button on the Report Viewer toolbar. When the report server restarts the session, it generates the report from scratch and replaces the existing cached copy with the new report execution, but keeps the same session identifier.

URL access supports session management. If you know the session identifier, which you can obtain from the session cookie, you can associate a report to reuse an existing session by using the SessionID command, such as:

```
http://<servername>/ReportServer?/AdventureWorks Sample Reports/Company Sales ↵
&rs:SessionID=52v13e55bfox0zisan0rsqjy
```

You can clear the existing session to force a report run on a new session by appending the ClearSession command to the report URL. For example, the following link forces the Company Sales report to execute on a new session:

```
http://<servername>/ReportServer?/AdventureWorks Sample Reports/Company Sales&rs:ClearSession=True
```

The Report Server Web service also supports managing execution sessions programmatically by calling the Report Server Web service APIs, as I'll demonstrate in chapter 14.

12.1.3 Managing Cache Snapshots

The report server creates a report execution session for each user requesting that report. However, you could let users share a report execution. For example, suppose that the report query is very slow. If certain data latency is acceptable, you can configure the report as a cache snapshot to share it among multiple users when they request the report on demand.

Understanding cache snapshots

A cache snapshot is a saved report execution that can be shared among users. You can use cache snapshots to optimize report server performance and reduce the number of times a report is generated. Figure 12.3 shows what happens when users request a report that is configured as a cache snapshot. In this scenario, the report takes two parameters. When the first user requests the report, the report server generates the report. Similar to execution session caching, the report server saves the raw report in the ReportServerTempDB database.

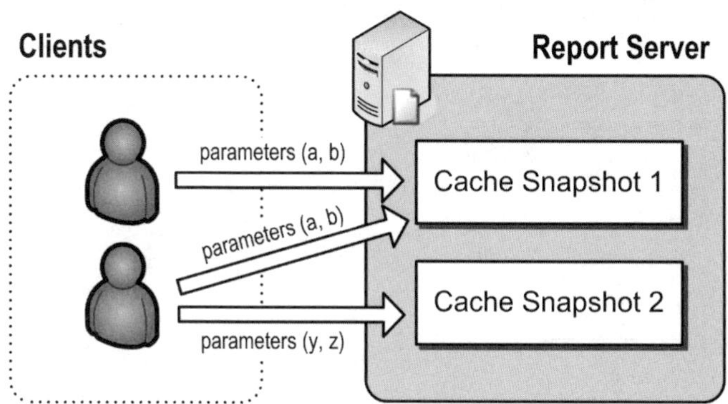

Figure 12.3 Users share the cache snapshots if they pass the same parameters.

Unlike execution session caching, however, the report server creates a new cache snapshot for each parameter combination and maintains a cache index based on the parameter values. Assuming that the first user passes parameter values *a* and *b*, the first snapshot will be associated with these parameters. If the second user requests the report with the same parameter values, the report server satisfies the request from the existing cache snapshot. However, if the parameter values are not same, the report server generates a new snapshot instance.

As a part of configuring a cache snapshot, you specify how the report server will invalidate and purge the snapshot. You have two options. One option is to specify an explicit time interval after which the cache snapshot is deleted. With this option, the report server does not extend the expiration period when new requests are received for the same report. The second option is to clear the snapshot on a report specific or a shared schedule.

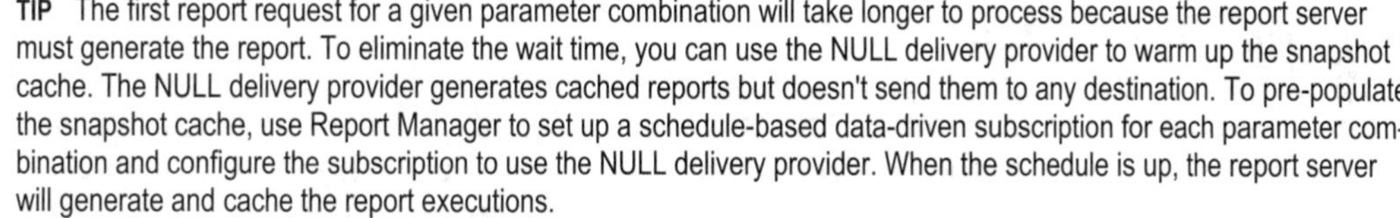

TIP The first report request for a given parameter combination will take longer to process because the report server must generate the report. To eliminate the wait time, you can use the NULL delivery provider to warm up the snapshot cache. The NULL delivery provider generates cached reports but doesn't send them to any destination. To pre-populate the snapshot cache, use Report Manager to set up a schedule-based data-driven subscription for each parameter combination and configure the subscription to use the NULL delivery provider. When the schedule is up, the report server will generate and cache the report executions.

You can also clear the cache snapshot programmatically by calling the FlushCache API. A cache snapshot is dependent on the report definition. If you change and deploy the report definition, the report server will invalidate the snapshot.

Understanding cache snapshot limitations

Suppose that you need to implement row-level security in the report. To do this, you decide to pass the user identity (User!UserID) to the data source to get only those records associated with that user. Will this work if the report is cached? The answer is no. If you use User!UserID in the query, a less privileged user might get access to data that he is not authorized to see. Therefore, while you can use User!UserID to display the user identity on the report, the report server will not allow you to cache a report that passes User!UserID to a query parameter. For the same security reasons, the report data source cannot use Windows Integrated security. Instead, the data source must use stored credentials.

If you need to filter data per user, you can set up a dataset filter to filter the report data while the report is generated. For example, suppose that the query returns a dataset that contains the sales for all employees based on the employee's Windows login. You can set up a dataset filter to show only the records where the employee matches User!UserID. In this scenario, the cache snapshot will contain all data. The report server will apply the dataset filter at run time.

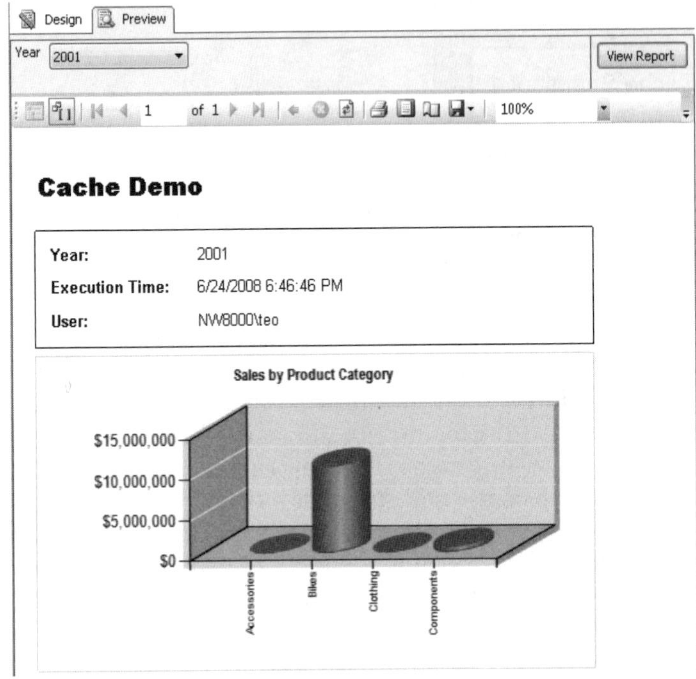

Figure 12.4 Use the Cache Demo report to understand how cache snapshots work.

Working with cache snapshots

Let's use the Cache Demo report to demonstrate how cache snapshots work. You can find the Cache Demo report in the source code for this chapter. Figure 12.4 shows what the report looks like when previewed in the Report Designer. The chart region shows the Adventure Works sales by product category. It accepts a Year report parameter to filter the report data by year. The report displays the parameter value, execution time (Globals!ExecutionTime), and the identity of the interactive user (User!UserID) in the rectangle above the chart.

Configuring the Cache Snapshot

Follow these steps to configure the Cache Demo report as a cache snapshot.

1. Deploy the report to the report server. The following steps assume that you have deployed the report to the AMRS folder.
2. Open Report Manager and go to the report properties page. Click the Execution link to access the report execution properties.

   To configure the Cache Demo report as a cache snapshot, select one of the two Cache a Temporary Copy of the Report options in the Always Run This Report in the Most Recent Data section. To invalidate the report after a fixed time period, select the Expire Copy of Report after a Number of Minutes option. By default, the report server will invalidate the snapshot in 30 minutes. Or, to invalidate the report on a set schedule, select the Expire Copy of Report on the Following Schedule option.
3. Select the Expire Copy of the Report after a Number of Minutes option and enter 5 minutes. Click Apply.

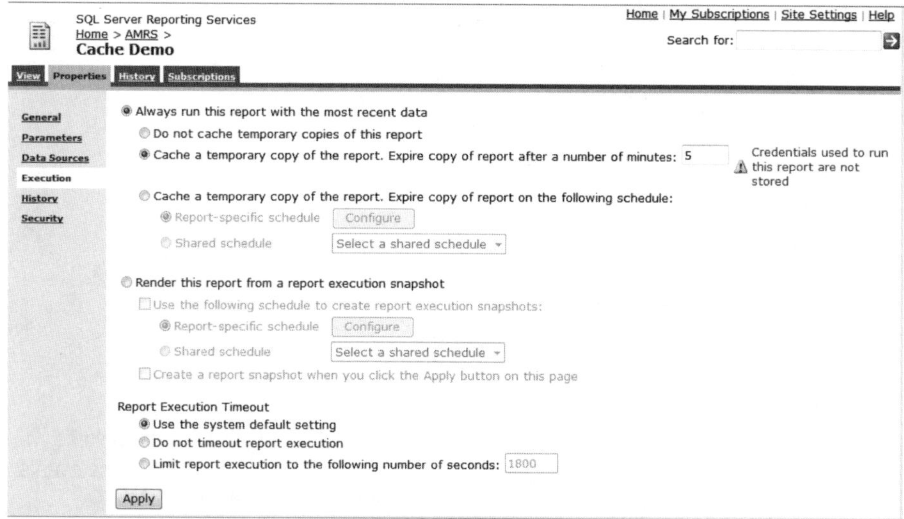

Figure 12.5 Select the Cache a Temporary Copy of the Report options to configure a report as a cache snapshot.

Observe that the Report Manager displays the following error message (see Figure 12.5):

```
Credentials used to run this report are not stored
```

That's because the report's data source uses Windows Integrated security but cache snapshots don't support this option.

4. Click the Data Sources link and select the Credentials Stored Securely in the Report Server option. Enter credentials (user name and password) of a SQL Server login that has read permissions to the AdventureWorks2008 database and click Apply.
5. Back on the Execution page, click Apply to configure the report for a cache snapshot execution.

Configuring the SQL Server Profiler

You can use the SQL Server Profiler to see when the report server generates the report by tracing the queries Server sends to the AdventureWorks2008 database.

6. Start the SQL Server Profiler which you can find in the SQL Server 2008 ⇨ Performance Tools program group.
7. Click the New Trace toolbar button and connect to SQL Server.
8. When using the SQL Server Profiler, it is useful to filter out the trace events you don't want to see by setting up a column filter. In the Events Selection page of the Trace Properties dialog box, select the Show All Columns checkbox and click the Column Filters button.
9. In the Edit Filter dialog box, select DatabaseName.
10. Expand the Like node in the right pane and enter *AdventureWorks2008* to see the trace events for the AdventureWorks2008 database only, as shown in Figure 12.6.
11. Select the Exclude Rows That Do Not Contain Values checkbox and click OK to return to the Trace Properties dialog.
12. Click the Run button to run the trace.

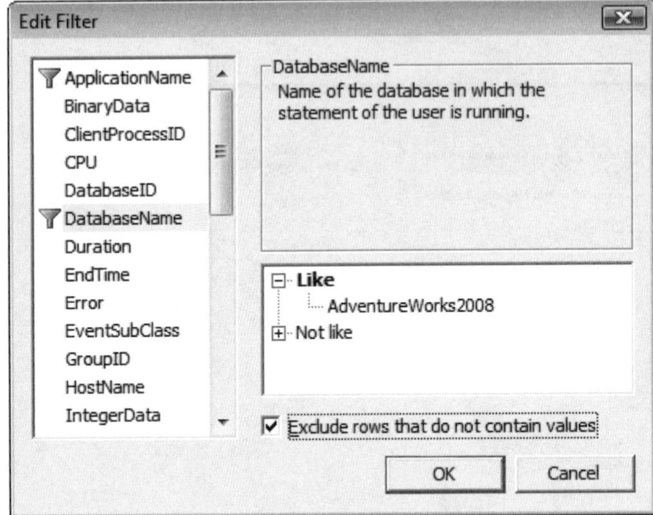

Figure 12.6 Use a DatabaseName column filter to see only the trace events for the AdventureWorks database.

Testing the Cache Snapshot

Let's use the Bob and Alice Windows accounts that you set up in chapter 10 to test the cache snapshot.

13. Log in as Bob and use Report Manager to run the report for year 2001.
14. Switch to the SQL Server Profiler and notice that the report server executes the report dataset query. This means that the report server has generated the report from scratch.
15. Log in as Alice and run the report for year 2001 again. This time, you shouldn't see a query statement in the SQL Server Profiler. This is because the report server has detected that the report request uses the same parameter value. Consequently, the report server satisfied the request from the cache snapshot.
16. Using either Bob's or Alice's browser instance, run the report for year 2002. The SQL Profiler should show a new query statement. This is because the report server was unable to find a cache snapshot for the new parameter value and has generated a new report.
17. Wait for five minutes and run the report for year 2001 or 2002. Note that the SQL Profiler shows a query statement. The report server has invalidated the snapshot because you set it to expire in five minutes. Consequently, the report server generated the report and cached the report.

Optionally, configure the report to expire on a report-specific or shared schedule by using the Expire Copy of Report on the Following Schedule option.

12.1.4 Managing Execution Snapshots

Recall that cache snapshots are generated and managed internally by the report server. They are cached temporarily and then deleted, which means they cannot be saved in history or referenced by the user. For example, a user cannot request a cache snapshot that was generated a week ago. At the same time, you may need to keep a report execution for auditing and archiving purposes. This is where execution snapshots could help.

REAL LIFE Execution snapshots proved very useful in one of my projects where we report-enabled a Windows Forms application. Since the reports could take a substantial time to execute, we didn't want to block the user while waiting for the report. Instead, when the user requested a report, the application would forward the report to a custom job service that would generate an execution snapshot asynchronously and save it in the report history. Then, the job service would send a notification to the user that would include the history identifier. The end user could click on the notification link to display the execution snapshot at the user's convenience.

Understanding execution snapshots

An execution snapshot is a *single* instance of a report execution that is saved in the report server database. Similar to cache snapshots, execution snapshots improve report performance because all report requests are served from a cached report copy as shown in Figure 12.7. Unlike cache snapshots, however, the report server keeps a single cached report for the default values of the report parameters. When users request a report that is configured as an execution snapshot, they get the same data because they cannot vary the report parameters.

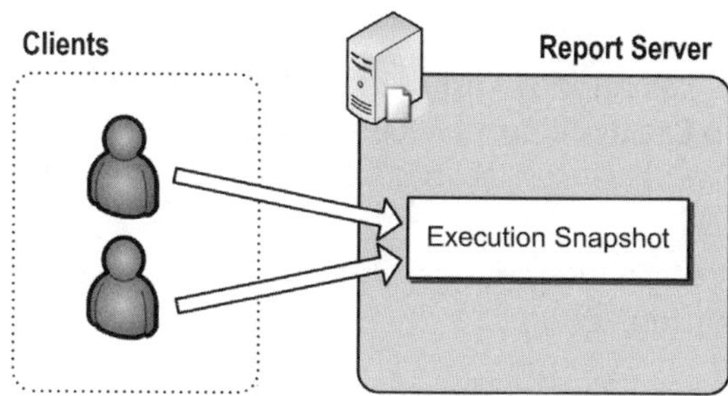

Figure 12.7 When a report is cached as an execution snapshot, all requests use the same cached copy.

Execution snapshots can be created on a schedule. For example, the administrator can schedule a monthly performance report to be generated every month. You can also explicitly generate an execution snapshot in Report Manager or programmatically by calling the UpdateReportExecutionSnapshot API. The report server stores the execution snapshot in table SnapshotData in the ReportServer database and replaces it when the execution snapshot is refreshed. Once created, the execution snapshot doesn't depend on the report definition. Consequently, the report author can publish a new version of the report definition without affecting the execution snapshot.

Understanding execution snapshot limitations

Similar to cache snapshots, the report query cannot be user-specific; that is, a query parameter cannot reference user-specific information, such as User!UserID. The report data source must be configured for stored credentials. Unlike cache snapshots, where the user can pass parameters at run time, all report parameters must have default values before the execution snapshot is generated.

If you generate execution snapshots programmatically, setting the default values prior to snapshot generation requires a somewhat awkward two-step approach. First, you need to update the parameter default values by invoking the SetReportParameters API. Second, you need to follow up with a call to the UpdateReportExecutionSnapshot API to generate the actual snapshot by passing the report path. Hopefully, a future release will enhance the UpdateReportExecutionSnapshot API to let developers pass the report parameters and generate the snapshot in one step.

When the report is rendered, all report parameters and disabled and the end user cannot change the report parameters. Again, that is because the execution snapshot is generated once, and all requests use the same cached instance. To use new parameter values, use Report Manager to change the default values of the report parameters and regenerate the snapshot.

TIP You may have report parameters that are not linked to query parameters and exist solely for controlling the report appearance. For example, the parameter may be used in conditional sorting or visibility expressions. By default, all parameters are disabled when the report is configured for execution snapshot caching. However, you can tell Reporting Services to enable a parameter if it is used in expressions only. To do so, open the report in Report Designer and double-click the report parameter. In the Report Parameter Properties dialog box (Advanced tab), click Never Refresh, and re-deploy the report.

Working with execution snapshots

Follow these steps to configure the Cache Demo report for execution snapshot caching.

1. In the Execution report properties, select the Render This Report from a Report Execution Snapshot option.

   As noted, you can let the report server process the execution snapshot in unattended mode. To do so, check the Use the Following Schedule to Create Report Execution Snapshots checkbox to schedule the snapshot generation on a report-specific or shared schedule. You can also generate the snapshot immediately.

2. To generate the snapshot immediately, select the Create a Report Snapshot when You Click the Apply Button checkbox and press the Apply button.

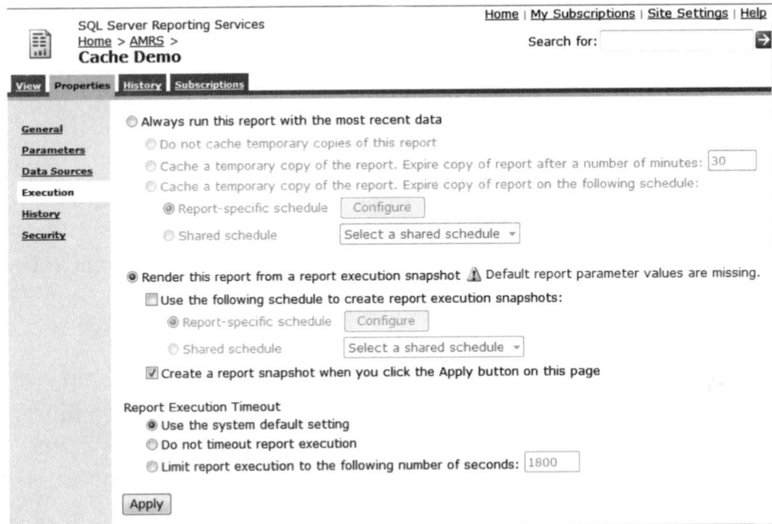

Figure 12.8 You must provide default report parameters before generating a report execution snapshot.

   Report Manager fails the snapshot generation and displays the following error message (see Figure 12.8):

   ```
   Default report parameter values are missing.
   ```

   This is because the Year report parameter doesn't have a default value.

3. Click the Parameters link to access the report parameters. Check the Has Default checkbox of the Year parameter and sets its default value to *2001*.

4. Return to the Execution properties page and configure the report for execution snapshot caching, as shown in Figure 12.8, and then click the Apply button. This time, Report Manager should be able to generate the execution snapshot successfully.
5. Select the View tab to view the report.

   If use the SQL Server Profiler, you shouldn't see the report query. The report server satisfies the report request from the cached copy. Note the Year parameter is disabled in the report toolbar of the HTML Viewer. This is because the user cannot pass parameter values at run time with execution snapshots.

Managing history snapshots

By default, the report server keeps only one execution snapshot per report and replaces it each time you refresh the snapshot. However, if needed, you can keep multiple snapshot executions by enabling snapshot history. Snapshot history is useful for archiving and auditing purposes.

1. In the Properties page of the Cache Demo report, select the History page.

   The Allow Report History to be Created Manually option is selected by default. As a result, the Report Manager displays a New Snapshot button in the History tab to let you manually save an execution snapshot in the history. You can also automate the process of archiving snapshots. For example, if you want the report server to keep the latest execution snapshot at month end, you can create a report-specific or shared schedule that tells the report server to add snapshot to report history on the last day of every month.

   You can also specify a snapshot retention policy. The Use Default Setting option uses the value that is set on the Site Settings page. By default, the server retains an unlimited number of snapshots in report history. Or, you can limit the number of snapshots and let the server invalidate and delete old snapshots when that number is exceeded.

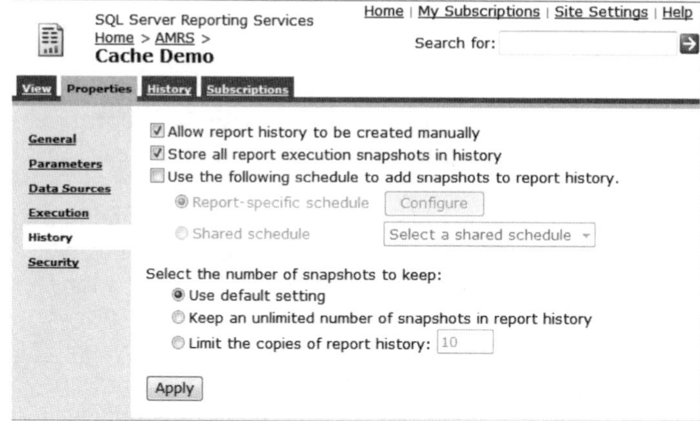

Figure 12.9 Use the report History page to enable the execution snapshot history.

2. Select the Store All Report Execution Snapshot in History checkbox, as shown in Figure 12.9. When this option is enabled, the report server will copy the snapshot to history each time the execution snapshot is refreshed. Click the Apply button to save your changes.
3. Select the Execution link to access the report execution properties.
4. Select the Create a Report Snapshot When You Click the Apply Button on This Page checkbox and then click Apply to create a new execution snapshot.

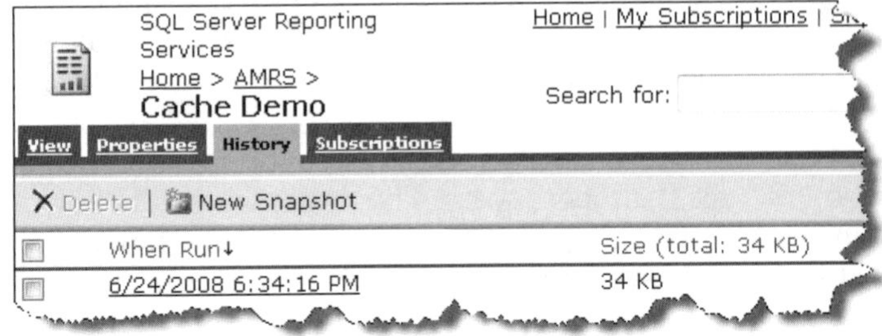

Figure 12.10 Use the History tab to view and delete the history snapshots.

5. Select the History tab (not the History page), as shown in Figure 12.10.

   Observe that the report server has added the new execution snapshot in the history. The History tab shows the snapshot creation date and its size in kilobytes.

6. To view history snapshot, click the snapshot hyperlink.

   The report server associates a history snapshot with a history identifier, which has a YYYY-MM-DDTHH:MM:SS format. This format is based on the International Organization for Standardization (ISO) 8601 standard. You can obtain this identifier by viewing the hyperlink properties. The client can request the snapshot later by passing the history identifier to the report server. For example, the following URL requests the history snapshot of the Cache Demo report shown in Figure 12.10:

```
http://<servername>/ReportServer?/AMRS/Cache Demo&rs:Snapshot= 2008-06-24T22:34:16
```

   History snapshots are preserved when you change report execution options. For example, you can configure the report for live execution without affecting the snapshot history. As with execution snapshots, any changes you make to the report defintion have no effect on existing history snapshots.

12.1.5 Managing Report Execution Timeouts

The Execution page lets you specify a report execution timeout for processing the report (see again Figure 12.8). Notice that the Use Default Setting option is pre-selected. This means that the report will use the system-wide execution timeout setting which the administrator can set in the Report Manager Site Settings page or in SQL Server Management Studio. By default, the report server times out after processing the report in 1,800 seconds (30 minutes). You can override the report execution timeout on a per report basis. For example, if you have a long running report, select the Do Not Timeout Report Execution option.

A report can time out for various reasons. First, the report author can specify a query timeout property for the report dataset. The default query timeout setting is 0, which means that the report query will not timeout. Second, the entire report may be set to time out. As noted, if you accept the default settings, the report server will time out the report in 30 minutes. When the report timeout is up, the report server simply terminates the process.

The ASP.NET runtime has an executionTimeout property that indicates the maximum number of seconds a request is allowed to execute before being automatically shut down by ASP.NET. Reporting Services overwrites this setting in the report server web.config file and sets it to 9,000 seconds.

```
<http Runtime executionTimeout="9000" />
```

Finally, if you use a custom application to view reports, the web service call may time out. The default Timeout property of a Web service proxy is -1, which means that .NET will not time out the call. However, the developer may have overwritten the property. This may cause the Web service to time out when the application requests the report.

12.2 Managing Subscriptions

Besides on-demand report delivery where the user actively requests the report, the report server can deliver reports via subscriptions. Subscriptions let you automate the process of generating and distributing reports. For example, suppose that the Sales department wants to receive an updated sales report every month. To meet this requirement, you can set up an e-mail subscription that sends the report via e-mail on a schedule.

Reporting Services subscriptions let you meet various requirements for automating report distribution. For example, a bank can let its customers subscribe to a statement report and receive it on a regular basis. An e-commerce organization can automatically send a notification report to a customer when the order status has changed. A report administrator can schedule the report server to process a large report overnight and save it on a file share. I am sure you can expand on this list and add more scenarios that address your specific needs for subscription delivery.

12.2.1 Understanding Subscriptions

A Reporting Services subscription is a standing request to the report server to process a report in an unattended mode, such as on a schedule, and then deliver it to one or more subscribers. We can break down the subscription delivery process into two phases. During the definition phase, the client creates the subscription and saves it to the report catalog. The subscription specifies how, when, and where the report will be delivered. The processing phase starts when the subscription event fires. When the report server receives the event, it generates and delivers the report.

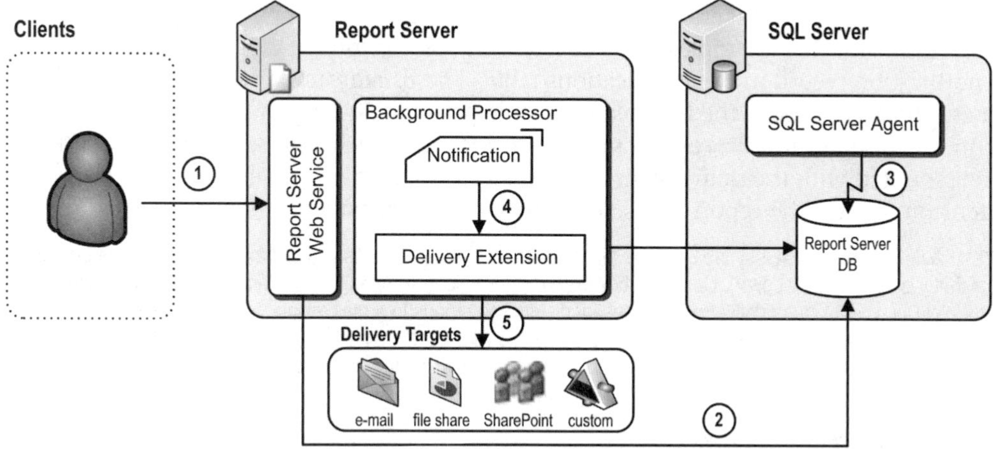

Figure 12.11 With subscription-based report delivery, the report server generates the report in an unattended mode and sends it to the delivery target.

Understanding subscription events

Figure 12.11 shows the subscription process. In step 1, the user creates the subscription for a given report. The easiest way to accomplish this is to use Report Manager. Alternatively, a custom application can invoke the Report Server Web service to create the subscription programmatically. As part of setting up the subscription, the user chooses a delivery method, such as e-mail delivery. Out of the box, Reporting Services supports e-mail delivery, shared folders delivery, and delivery to SharePoint document libraries (if the report server is configured for SharePoint integration mode). Note that developers can extend the report server delivery architecture by plugging in custom delivery extensions, as I will demonstrate in chapter 20.

In addition, the user specifies the event that will trigger subscription processing. By default, the report server supports two event types: time events and snapshot refreshes. When the standard events are not enough, developers can generate events programmatically to trigger subscriptions by calling the FireEvent API. For example, a custom application can post an event when the orders status has changed to trigger a subscription that sends a report to users who subscribed to the report. I will show you how to use the FireEvent API in chapter 13.

The report server triggers a time event based on the schedule information provided in the subscription. A user can specify a report-specific schedule or a shared schedule. If the subscribed report is configured as an execution snapshot, the user can configure the subscription to execute when the snapshot is refreshed. In step 2, the report server saves the subscription definition in the report server database (in the Subscriptions table) and creates a job that SQL Server Agent service will use to create the event. This concludes the subscription definition phase.

Step 3 marks the beginning of subscription processing. In step 3, the SQL Server Agent service runs the job that was created for the schedule event. The report server posts a notification record in the Event table in the report server database. Recall that the Background Processor is one of the three applications hosted in the Reporting Services service and it is responsible for executing tasks in an unattended mode. The Background Processor polls the Event table on a regular basis to check for new events. By default, the report server polls the Event table every 10 seconds. You can customize the polling interval by changing the PollingInterval setting in the report server configuration file (rsreportserver.config).

When the Background Processor discovers a new event, it retrieves the event information and handles the event. For example, with time-based subscriptions, the Background Processor inserts a notification record in the Notifications table. The Background Processor has another management thread that polls the Notifications table periodically. When it discovers a new notification, the Background Processor creates a notification object and sends it to the delivery extension associated with the delivery method (as shown in step 4). Finally, in step 5, the delivery extension renders the report and sends it to the delivery target.

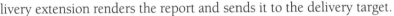

NOTE A delivery extension is a .NET module that receives server notifications and distributes reports to the delivery target that it is designed to support. Out of the box, Reporting Services includes E-Mail, Windows File Share, and SharePoint Document Library delivery extensions for distributing reports to e-mail recipients, shared folders, and SharePoint document libraries respectively. As noted in section 12.1.3, there is also a NULL Delivery Provider extension that does not actually deliver reports, but is instead used to warm up the snapshot cache.

Understanding subscription types

Reporting Services supports two subscription types: standard subscriptions and data-driven subscriptions. Standard subscriptions are created and managed by individual users. For example, an end user can set up a standard subscription to deliver reports in a specific output format to his or her mailbox. To set up a standard subscription, the user must have Manage Individual Subscriptions rights. Standard subscriptions are available in the Standard and Enterprise editions of SQL Server.

The data-driven subscriptions are a very powerful feature of Reporting Services. You can use them to deliver a report to a dynamic list of recipients to destinations with customized content for each delivery. You can specify data-driven subscriptions in Report Manager, a SharePoint site, or create a custom application used to collect information used in a data-driven subscription. For example, imagine a web application that lets end users personalize report delivery by specifying a delivery method, output format, report parameters, and so on. The application could collect user preferences and save them in the user profile table. Then, the administrator can set up a data-driven subscription that applies the user preferences when the subscription is processed.

When the report server executes a data-driven subscription, it queries an external database to retrieve a list of recipients and other subscription settings. The report server generates a report for each recipient based on the user preferences and delivers the report to the target destination. To set up a data-driven subscription, the user must have Manage All Subscription rights, which the Content Manager role includes by default. Data-driven subscriptions are available in the Enterprise edition of SQL Server only.

Understanding subscription limitations

Since the report server runs subscriptions in unattended mode, the reports have the same limitations as execution snapshots. If the report is parameterized, you must assign default values to all parameters when you set up a standard subscription. A data-driven subscription can have static parameter values or dynamic parameters whose values are retrieved from the database and passed to the report at run time. Reports that you subscribe to cannot use Windows Integrated security to connect to the data source. Instead, the report data source must use stored credentials.

TIP If the live report must use Windows Integrated security, such as when connecting to an Analysis Services cube, consider creating a separate copy of the report for subscription purposes. The data source of the second report can store the credentials of a trusted Windows account.

Again, similar to execution snapshots, standard subscriptions can display user-specific information by referencing the User collection, such as the user identity (User!UserID) and the user language identifier (User!Language). When used with standard subscriptions, the User collection returns information about the subscription owner; that is, the user who set up the standard subscription. Furthermore, standard subscriptions can also pass the user-specific information to the report query, such as to return only the sales orders associated with the subscription owner. Data-driven subscriptions cannot reference the User collection at all.

Now that you have a good understanding of how subscriptions work, let's set a few of them up.

12.2.2 Managing Standard Subscriptions

Suppose that you are a sales manager at Adventure Works and you want yourself and your team to receive a sales report at the beginning of each month via e-mail. In the first exercise, you will set up a standard e-mail subscription that sends the Cache Demo report to selected recipients.

Configuring the report server for e-mail delivery

By default, the report server is not configured for e-mail delivery. Consequently, the E-Mail delivery extension won't show up when you set up a subscription in Report Manager. As a prerequisite for configuring e-mail subscriptions, you need to set up the report server for e-mail delivery. This may require some cooperation from your mail server administrator. To start with, you can use the Reporting Services Configuration Manager to specify the sender address and SMTP server.

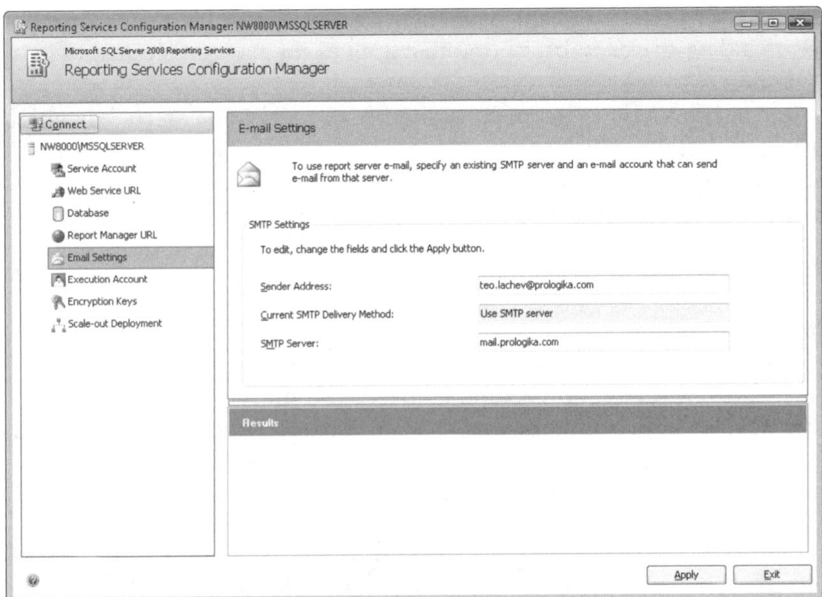

Figure 12.12 Use the Reporting Services Configuration Manager to configure the sender address and SMTP server for e-mail delivery.

Configuring basic e-mail settings

Follow these steps to configure Reporting Services for e-mail delivery:

1. Open the Reporting Services Configuration Manager from Microsoft SQL Server 2008 ⇨ Configuration Tools program group and connect to the report server.
2. Select the E-mail Settings page, as shown in Figure 12.12.
3. In the Sender Address field, enter the e-mail address of an account that has permissions to send e-mail from the SMTP server.

   The Reporting Services Configuration Manager supports only e-mail delivery through an SMTP server. If you don't have network access to the SMTP server, you can edit the report server configuration file (RSReportServer.config) to specify a pickup directory for the outgoing e-mail by changing the SMTPServerPickupDirectory setting.
4. In the SMTP Server field, type the name of the SMTP server and click Apply.

   The report server configuration file has additional e-mail settings that you may need to change to finalize e-mail delivery configuration based on your specific setup. This may require configuring default host settings and allowing other recipients to receive reports by e-mail.

TIP If you use an Exchange Server for e-mail delivery, you can find its SMTP server name from the account settings in Microsoft Outlook. In Outlook 2007, go to the Tools ⇨ Account Settings menu, select the Microsoft Exchange account in the E-mail Accounts dialog box, and click the Change button to get to the Microsoft Exchange Settings page. If you use the Windows SMTP service, clicking the Change button will open the Internet E-Mail Settings page and the SMTP server name can be found in the Outgoing Mail Server (SMTP) field. Alternatively, you can right-click on a message in your Outlook Inbox and choose Message Options to see the Internet Headers of the message. Typically, the SMTP server name is the host name found in the first Received From line.

Configuring default host settings

If the user doesn't have Manage All Subscriptions rights, the user can only set up a self-addressed e-mail subscription. Consequently, the To field in the Report Delivery Options page is read-only and will be set to the Windows login of the interactive user. Note that if you have an SMTP server that is part of a different domain from the domain the user belongs to, the report delivery will fail when the SMTP server tries to deliver the report to that user.

To verify how the user is set up, look up the user account in the Outlook address book, go to the account properties, and select the E-mail Addresses tab. If the domain name doesn't match the user's domain, add the user's domain name in the DefaultHostName setting. For example, if the SMTP server sends email to users in mail.com instead of prologika.com, change the DefaultHostSetting as follows:

```
<DefaultHostName> mail.com</DefaultHostName>
```

At run time, the report server will append the default host name to the user domain account. So, if the user Windows login is t_lachev, the resulting e-mail address will be t_lachev@mail.com. If you want to allow a user who has only Manage Individual Subscriptions rights to enter other recipient addresses in the subscriptions that he or she owns, change the SendEmailToUserAlias setting to False.

Sending to other recipients

If the user has Manage All Subscriptions rights (or Manage Individual Subscriptions rights and SendEmailToUserAlias setting is set to True), the user can enter a semi-colon separated list of e-mail addresses to send the report to multiple recipients. By default, the report server will send e-mail to any external domain. You can use the PermittedHosts setting to restrict the domains the report server will send e-mails to.

E-mail delivery to external domains will fail if the report server doesn't have relay rights to the SMTP server. To avoid this, the network administrator needs to add the report server TCP/IP address to the computers that are permitted to relay. For example, to let the report server relay a request to a Windows 2003 SMTP server, open the SMTP service properties, select the Access tab, and click the Relay button in the Relay Restrictions section. In the Relay Restrictions dialog box, click the Add button to add the report server TCP/IP address to the list of the allowed computers to relay through the SMTP server.

For more information about the rest of the e-mail delivery settings, read the Configuring a report server for E-Mail Delivery topic in the SQL Server 2008 Books Online (see Resources).

Creating a shared schedule

Similar to cache snapshots, you can schedule the subscription to run on a report-specific or shared schedule. A shared schedule is preferred because you can manage it independently of the items that use it, such as subscriptions and snapshots. Similar to shared data sources, shared schedules let you reduce the management effort required to schedule multiple activities. Once you change a shared schedule, all dependent items will pick up the new shared schedule properties. You can also pause and resume shared schedules, as well as expire them on a fixed date. You can create a shared schedule in the Report Manager Site Settings page or in SQL Server Management Studio. Both settings require that the SQL Server Agent service is running.

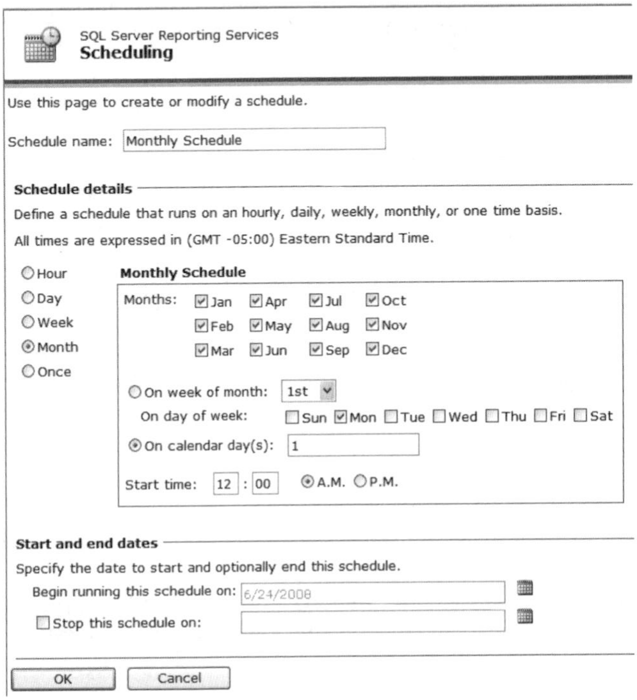

SQL Server Reporting Services
Scheduling

Use this page to create or modify a schedule.

Schedule name: Monthly Schedule

Schedule details

Define a schedule that runs on an hourly, daily, weekly, monthly, or one time basis.

All times are expressed in (GMT -05:00) Eastern Standard Time.

○ Hour ○ Day ○ Week ⦿ Month ○ Once

Monthly Schedule

Months: ☑ Jan ☑ Apr ☑ Jul ☑ Oct ☑ Feb ☑ May ☑ Aug ☑ Nov ☑ Mar ☑ Jun ☑ Sep ☑ Dec

○ On week of month: 1st

On day of week: ☐ Sun ☑ Mon ☐ Tue ☐ Wed ☐ Thu ☐ Fri ☐ Sat

⦿ On calendar day(s): 1

Start time: 12 : 00 ⦿ A.M. ○ P.M.

Start and end dates

Specify the date to start and optionally end this schedule.

Begin running this schedule on: 6/24/2008

☐ Stop this schedule on:

OK Cancel

Figure 12.13 You can use Report Manager to create a shared schedule for running multiple processes at the same time.

Let's use Report Manager to create a shared schedule that will run the e-mail subscription on the first day of every month.

1. In Report Manager, click the Site Settings menu link and then click the Schedules link.
2. Click the New Schedule button to open the Scheduling page, as shown in Figure 12.13.
3. Enter *Monthly Schedule* as a schedule name.
4. Since we want the schedule to run every month, select the Month interval.
5. In the Monthly Schedule section, select the On Calendar Day(s) option and enter *1* to start the schedule on the first day every month.
6. Set the schedule to start at midnight by setting the Start Time to 12:00 A.M.
7. Click the OK button to create the schedule.

Back on the Schedule tab, note that Report Manager has added the Monthly Schedule and has set the next run date to the first day of the next month. Also, note that you can select the schedule to delete, pause, or resume it.

Setting up a standard e-mail subscription

Now that you have completed all prerequisites, let's use Report Manager to set up the Cache Demo report for subscription delivery via e-mail. Start by configuring the Cache Demo report to execute with the most recent data. Later, we will re-configure the report for execution snapshot caching to see how this affects the subscription options.

1. In Report Manager, open the Execution properties of the Cache Demo report and select the Always Run This Report with the Most Recent Data execution option. Make sure that the Do Not Cache Temporary Copies of This Report option is preselected.
2. Select the Subscriptions tab and click the New Subscription button to open the Subscription page, as shown in Figure 12.14.

Figure 12.14 The E-Mail delivery extension lets you send a report to one or more recipient on a schedule that you define.

The E-Mail delivery extension should be preselected in the Delivered By drop-down list. If it doesn't show up, the report server is not configured for e-mail delivery. Figure 12.14 shows the subscription page you will see if you have Manage All Subscriptions rights, which the Content Manager role includes by default. If you have only Manage Individual Subscriptions rights, the Cc, Bcc and Reply to fields will not be shown. As noted, if SendEmailToUserAlias is False (default setting), the To field will default to your Windows login and it will be read-only.

3. Enter your e-mail address in the To field. Optionally, if your account has rights to relay to the mail server, add additional e-mail addresses separated by semi-colons.

You can use the subject field to define the e-mail subject. Reporting Services supports two predefined variables which you can use in the e-mail subject. The report server replaces their values at run time. The @ReportName variable returns the name of the report. The @ExecutionTime variable returns the execution time of the report. Unfortunately, you cannot define additional variables.

4. Suppose that you want to deliver the report in Adobe Acrobat PDF format. Expand the Render Format drop-down list and select Acrobat (PDF) File.

If the Include Report checkbox is selected, the report server will include a report copy in the e-mail. The render format determines if the report will be sent as an attachment or embedded in the e-mail body. For example, if you select the MHTML render format, the report will be embedded in the e-mail body. All other render formats will send the report as an attachment.

This is because the EmbeddedRenderFormats setting in the report server configuration file includes only the MHTML render format.

Including a large report in the e-mail message may be impractical. In this case, you can consider disabling the Include Report setting. If the Include Link checkbox is selected, the report server will add a URL link to the server report. The report link is also useful if you want the user to render the report with the most recent data.

NOTE The report link will not work if you deliver reports to external recipients and the report server is not Internet-facing. The UrlRoot setting in the report server configuration file defines the server name in the report link.

The Priority drop-down list lets you specify the e-mail priority status. For example, if you choose high priority, Microsoft Outlook will show an exclamation sign in the Importance field.

5. In the Subscription Processing Options section, select the On a Shared Schedule option and select the Monthly Schedule.

   Alternatively, if you want to test the subscription quickly, select the When the Scheduled Report Run Is Complete option, click the Select Schedule button, and set up a report-specific schedule to run the subscription a few minutes later from the current time.

6. As I explained earlier, when a report is parameterized, you need to specify default values for all parameters. Expand the Year drop-down list and choose 2004 to filter the report data for year 2004.
7. Click the OK button to create the subscription and return to the Subscriptions tab, as shown in Figure 12.15.

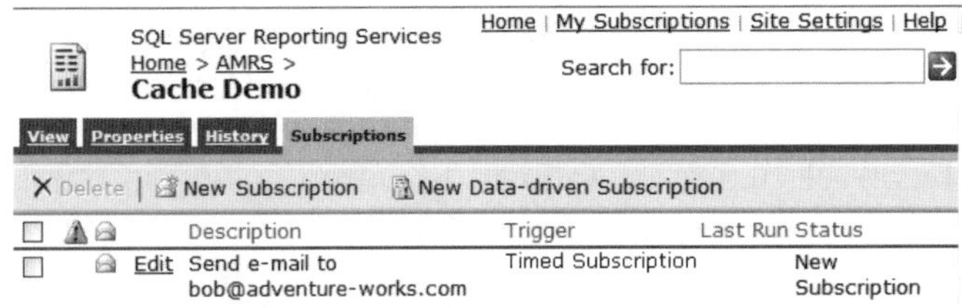

Figure 12.15 Use the Subscriptions tab to monitor the subscription status.

Observe that Report Manager has added a new TimedSubscription e-mail subscription. When the schedule is up, the report server will process the subscription and deliver the report to the e-mail recipient(s) you specify. If the e-mail delivery fails, the Status column in the Subscriptions page will show the error message. However, note that the report server doesn't verify the status of the e-mail delivery in any way. As far as the report server is concerned, the execution of the subscription and delivery task is successful as long as the e-mail is relayed successfully to the mail server. Therefore, you need to work together with the mail server administrator to make sure that the report has indeed been delivered successfully to all recipients. You can see all subscriptions that you own by clicking the My Subscriptions menu link.

Triggering a subscription on snapshot refresh

If the report is configured as an execution snapshot, you can trigger the subscription to execute when the snapshot is refreshed.

1. Open the Execution page of the Cache Demo report and configure the report to run as an execution snapshot.
2. Select the Subscriptions tab and click the Edit link to go to the subscription properties.

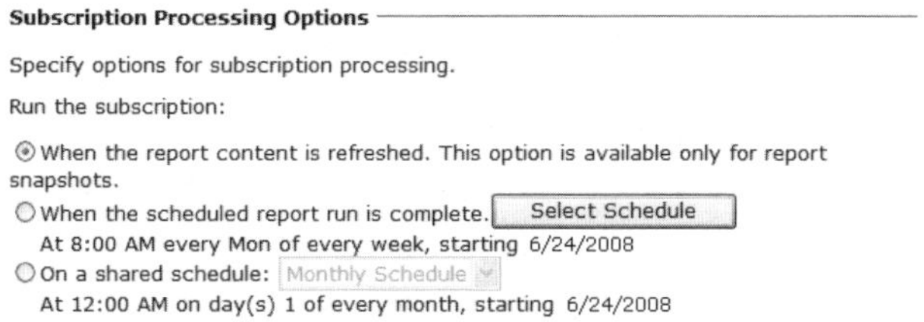

Subscription Processing Options

Specify options for subscription processing.

Run the subscription:

When the report content is refreshed. This option is available only for report snapshots.

When the scheduled report run is complete. Select Schedule

At 8:00 AM every Mon of every week, starting 6/24/2008

On a shared schedule: Monthly Schedule

At 12:00 AM on day(s) 1 of every month, starting 6/24/2008

Figure 12.16 You can trigger a subscription when the execution snapshot is refreshed.

Notice that the Subscription Processing Options section now includes a new When the Report Content Is Refreshed option, as shown in Figure 12.16.

3. Select this option and click OK to update the subscription and return to the Subscription tab.

   Note that the Trigger column in the Subscriptions tab now shows SnapshotUpdated to indicate that the subscription will be initiated when the report snapshot is refreshed.

4. Go back to the Execution page of the Cache Demo report, select the Create a Report Snapshot When You Click the Apply Button checkbox, and click Apply.

   The report server will refresh the snapshot and execute the subscription.

Configuring the Windows file share extension

Configuring the Windows File Share extension is very similar to the E-Mail delivery extension so I will just point out the differences. Figure 12.17 shows the Report Delivery Options section when you select the Windows File Share delivery method. In the File Name, enter the name of the output file. By default, the file will have same name as the report. When the Add a File Extension When the File Is Created option is selected, the report server will add a file extension based on the render format chosen, such as Cache Demo.pdf if you select the Acrobat (PDF) format.

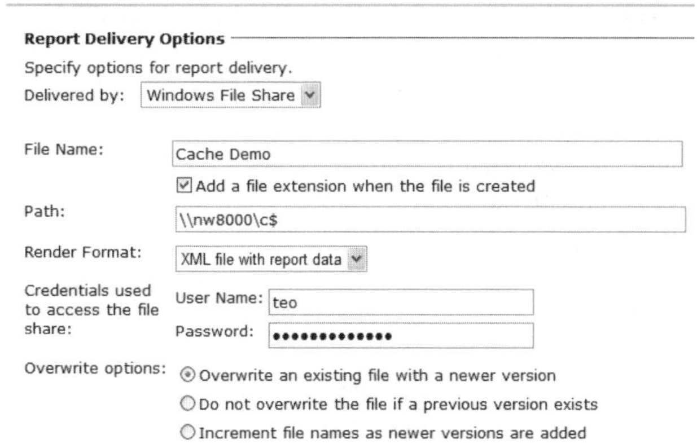

Report Delivery Options

Specify options for report delivery.

Delivered by: Windows File Share

File Name: Cache Demo

Add a file extension when the file is created

Path: \\nw8000\c$

Render Format: XML file with report data

Credentials used to access the file share: User Name: teo Password: •••••••••••••

Overwrite options: Overwrite an existing file with a newer version

Do not overwrite the file if a previous version exists

Increment file names as newer versions are added

Figure 12.17 The Windows File Share delivery extension lets you distribute a subscribed report to a Windows folder.

Use the Path field to enter the folder path in the Uniform Naming Convention (UNC) format, such as \\ComputerName\FileShareName. Use the credentials fields to specify the user name and password of a Windows account that has write permissions to the folder. The Overwrite options are self-explanatory.

Configuring the SharePoint document library extension

When the report server is configured for SharePoint integration, the subscribed report can be delivered to a SharePoint document library, as follows:

1. In SharePoint, navigate to the report and expand the report drop-down list.
2. Click Manage Subscriptions.
3. In the Manage Subscriptions page, click the Add Subscription button.
4. In the Subscription Properties page, expand the Delivery Extension drop-down list and select SharePoint Document Library, as shown in Figure 12.18.

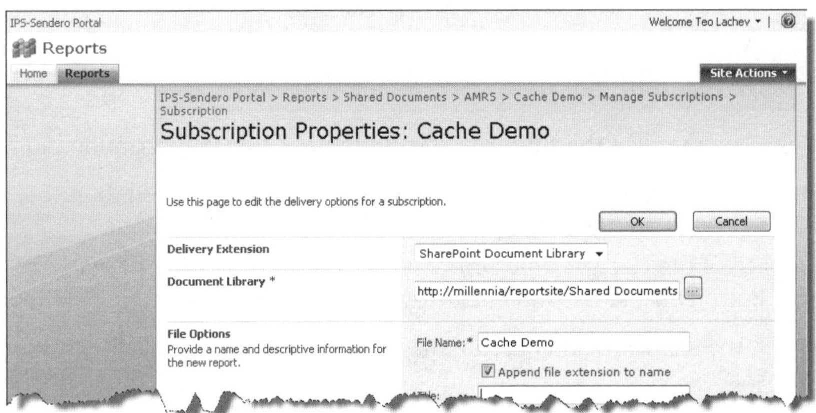

Figure 12.18 Use the SharePoint Document Library extension to deliver a report to a SharePoint document library.

5. In the Document Library field, enter the document library URL where the subscribed report will be delivered to, such as http://millennia/reportsite/Shared Documents, or click the … button to navigate the SharePoint namespace.

12.2.3 Managing Data-Driven Subscriptions

Sometimes you need more flexibility than a standard subscription can offer. For example, suppose that you want to build a web page that lets an Adventure Works customer subscribe to a Customer Order History report that shows all orders that the customer has placed to date. As part of the subscription process, the customer can personalize the subscription settings by specifying which render format, e-mail subject line, and other options to use. You can meet such requirements by setting up a data-driven subscription.

Customer Order History

Product #	Product Name	Order Qty	Unit Price	Discount	Total
⊟ Order: SO43860	8/1/2001				**$10,993.39**
BK-R50R-62	Road-650 Red, 62	2	$419.46	0.00 %	$838.92
BK-R50B-52	Road-650 Black, 52	1	$419.46	0.00 %	$419.46
BK-R68R-44	Road-450 Red, 44	1	$874.79	0.00 %	$874.79
⊞ Order: SO44501	11/1/2001				**$19,669.41**
⊞ Order: SO45283	2/1/2002				**$28,395.22**
⊞ Order: SO46042	5/1/2002				**$26,119.06**

Figure 12.19 The Customer Order History report shows all orders for a given customer.

Understanding the Customer Order History report

The data-driven subscription that you will create in this exercise uses the Customer Order History report which is shown in Figure 12.19. The report accepts a CustomerID hidden parameter to let the data-driven subscription pass the customer identifier at run time. The report retrieves all sales orders for that customer and displays them in the table region. The user can toggle the order header band to see the order details. The Customer Order History report is included in the source code that accompanies this chapter.

1. Deploy the report to the AMRS folder on the server.
2. Open Report Manager and go to the Properties page of the Customer Order History report.
3. Since subscriptions cannot use Windows Integrated security to connect to the data source, configure the report data source for stored credentials.
4. Select the Subscriptions tab and click the New Data-driven Subscription button.

NOTE If you don't see the New Data-driven Subscription button, you either don't have Manage All Subscription rights or you are not running a Developer or Enterprise edition of SQL Server 2008. If there is an exclamation icon next to the button, click the button to see the error message. Reasons for error conditions with data-driven subscriptions include referencing the User collection on the report or using a data source configured for Windows Integrated security.

If all is well, Report Manager will start the Data-driven Subscription Wizard.

Configuring the subscription basic settings

In step 1 of the wizard, you specify basic settings of the data-driven subscription, including its description, delivery method, and whether it will use a report-specific or a shared data source.

1. In the Description field, enter *Customer Order History*.
2. Expand the Specify How Recipients are Notified drop-down list and select E-mail.
3. Similar to reports, data-driven subscriptions can use private or shared data sources to connect to the recipient store. Assuming you have deployed a shared data source that connects to the AdventureWorks2008 database, select the Specify a Shared Data Source option, as shown in Figure 12.20, and click Next.

Figure 12.20 The Customer Order History subscription delivers reports via e-mail.

Configuring the data source

In step 2 of the wizard, you need to configure the subscription data source. If you chose the Specify for This Subscription Only option in step 1, this step lets configure the data source details, including the connection string and credentials. Since you chose the Specify a Shared

Data Source option in the first step, you need to select an existing shared data source in the report catalog.

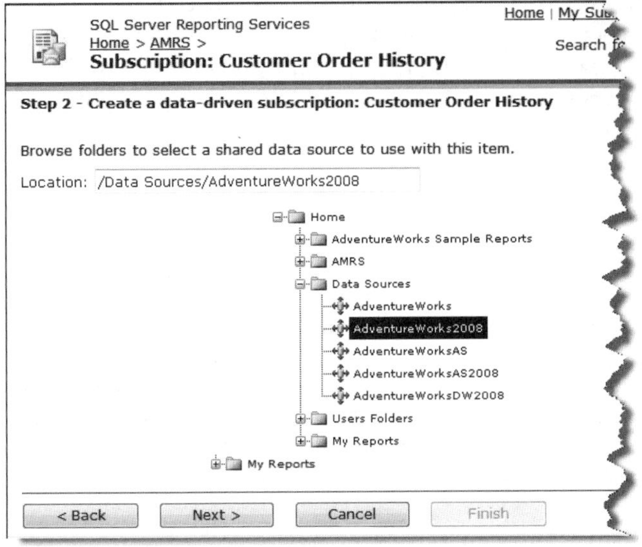

Figure 12.21 The Customer Order History uses the AdventureWorks shared data source.

1. Expand the Data Sources folder.
2. Select the AdventureWorks2008 data source, as shown in Figure 12.21, and click Next. If you don't see the AdventureWorks 2008 data source, deploy any of the Report Server projects included in the book source code that include it, such as the Reports project in chapter 4. Alternatively, in Report Manager navigate to the Data Sources folder, click New Data Source button, and set up a data source that connects to the AdventureWorks2008 database.

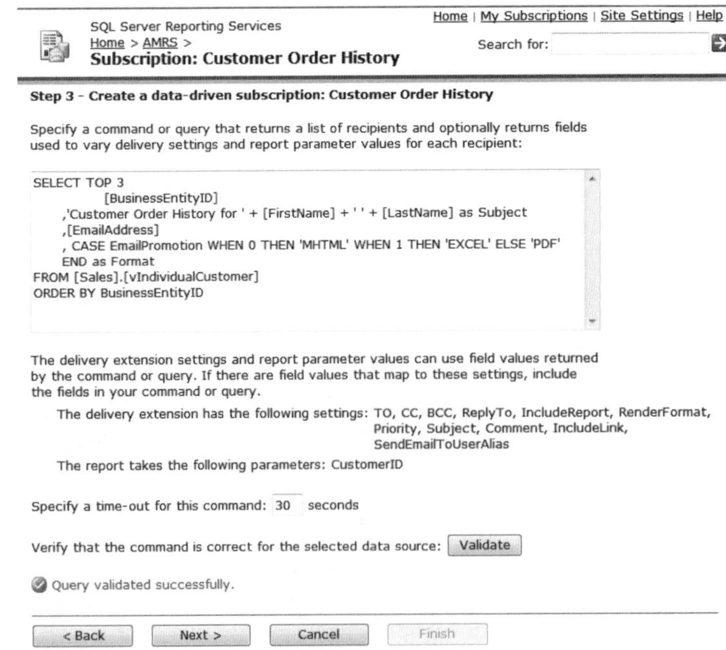

Figure 12.22 Enter a command that returns the list of recipients from the data source.

Configuring the recipient query

In step 3, you need to enter a command that the report server will execute at run time to retrieve the recipient list from the data source. The command must adhere to the syntax of the underlying data source. The command could be a SQL SELECT statement or a stored procedure call, such as:

```
EXEC uspGetRecipients parameter1, parameter2, ... parameterN
```

1. For the purposes of this demo, enter the following SQL SELECT statement (Figure 12.22), which you can find in the Customer Order History.sql file in the source code.

```
SELECT TOP 3  [BusinessEntityID]
              , 'Customer Order History for ' + [FirstName] + ' ' + [LastName] as Subject
              ,[EmailAddress]
              ,CASE EmailPromotion WHEN 0 THEN 'MHTML' WHEN 1 THEN 'EXCEL' ELSE 'PDF'  END as Format
FROM          [AdventureWorks2008].[Sales].[vIndividualCustomer]
ORDER BY      BusinessEntityID
```

This statement returns the results shown in Figure 12.23.

	BusinessEntityID	Subject	EmailAddress	Format
1	1699	Customer Order History for David Robinett	david22@adventure-works.com	EXCEL
2	1700	Customer Order History for Rebecca Robins...	rebecca3@adventure-works.com	MHTML
3	1701	Customer Order History for Dorothy Robinson	dorothy3@adventure-works.com	PDF

Figure 12.23 The recipient list for the Customer Order History subscription.

When the subscription is triggered, the report server executes the statement and obtains the recipient list. Then, the report server loops through the list and generates a report for each recipient. Report Manager shows you which settings and report parameters can be data-driven. In the next step, you will bind some of these settings to columns of the recipient rowset. We will pass the business entity identifier to the CustomerID parameter of the Customer Order History report. We will use the Subject column for the e-mail subject. The E-Mail delivery extension will use the EmailAddress column to send the report to the recipient e-mail address.

Instead of changing the AdventureWorks2008 database schema to accommodate a customer-specific Format setting, I used the EmailPromotion column in the vIndividualCustomer view and I "translated" it to an export format. Again, for demo purposes, the query returns only the first three Adventure Works customers. In real life, a custom application will most likely be used to collect the user preferences and store them in the database. The Step 3 page lets you specify a command timeout. By default, the command will time out in 30 seconds. You can also validate the command for syntax errors.

2. Click the Validate button to validate the command syntax. If Report Manager validates the command successfully, it will display a Query Validated Successfully message (see again Figure 12.22).

The validation logic checks whether the query is syntactically correct by parsing and sending the query to the data source. It doesn't validate the recipient list in any way.

Configuring the extension settings

Unlike standard subscriptions, which can have only static settings, data-driven subscriptions are more flexible because they support static and data-driven settings. Step 4 of the Data-driven Subscription Wizard lets you configure settings of the e-mail delivery extension. Report Manager retrieves the schema of the recipient query and lets you bind settings to the rowset columns.

1. Select the Get the Value from the Database option for the To field and bind it to the EmailAddress column, as shown in Figure 12.24.
2. Bind the Render Format to the Format column and the Subject field to the Subject column.

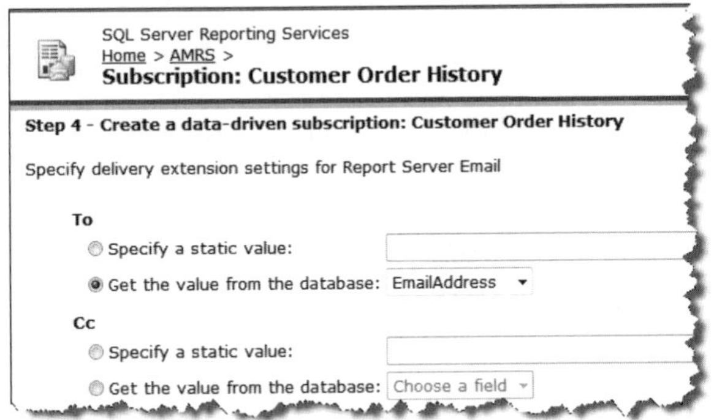

Figure 12.24 You can specify static and data-driven extension settings.

Leave the rest of the settings to their default values.

Configuring the report parameters

If the report is parameterized, you can use step 5 to assign a static parameter value or bind the parameters to columns in the recipient dataset. We need to use the latter option for the CustomerID report parameter.

1. Select the Get the Value from the Dataset option.
2. Expand the drop-down list and select the BusinessEntityID column, as shown in Figure 12.25.

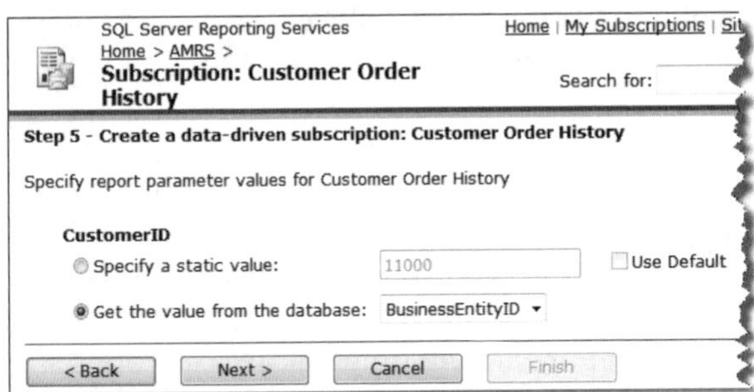

Figure 12.25 Configuring a report parameter as a data-driven parameter.

Configuring the subscription processing

Use the last step of the wizard to configure the subscription trigger. As Figure 12.26 shows, you have three options. If the report is configured for execution snapshot caching, you can select the When the Report Data is Updated on the report server option to run the subscription when the report snapshot is refreshed.

Choose the On a Schedule Created for this Subscription option to trigger the subscription execution on a subscription-specific schedule. You can use this option to test the subscription quickly by scheduling it to execute a few minutes ahead of the current time. Selecting this option introduces a new step in the wizard's flow that lets you configure the schedule details. Finally, if you have a shared schedule, you can configure the subscription to use it, by following these steps.

1. Select the On a Shared Schedule option.
2. Expand the drop-down list and select the Monthly Schedule item.

As a result, the Customer Order History subscription will be run at 12 A.M. on the first day of each month.

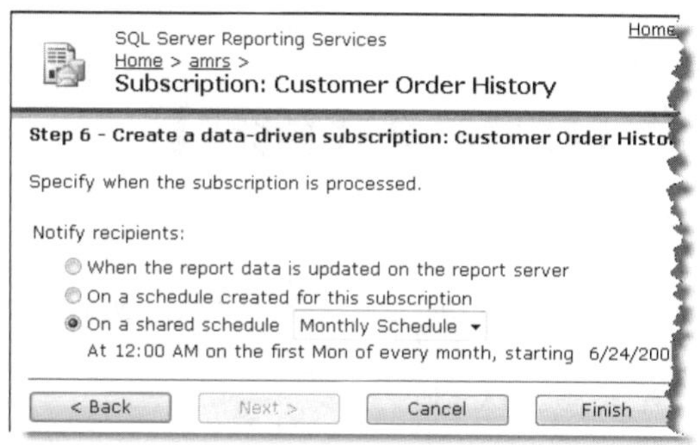

Figure 12.26 You can configure the subscription to run on a schedule or when the execution snapshot is refreshed.

3. Click the Finish button. Report Manager saves the subscription definition and adds it to the My Subscriptions page, as Figure 12.27 shows.

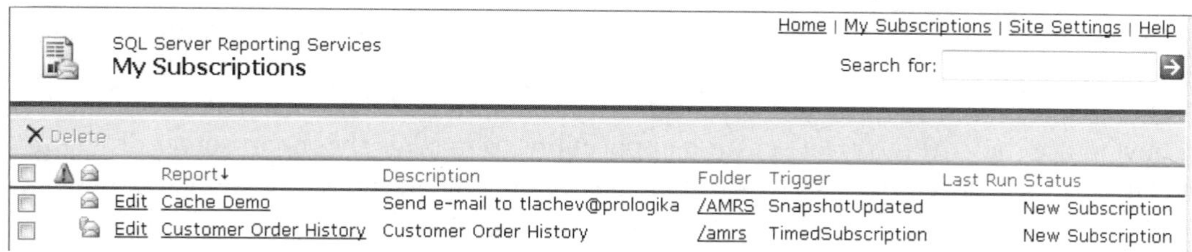

Figure 12.27 Use the My Subscriptions page to view and manage your subscriptions.

You can determine the subscription type from its icon. Data-driven subscriptions have a database symbol next to the envelope icon. Similar to standard subscriptions, Report Manager will update the subscription status to reflect the status of the last subscription execution.

12.3 Summary

In this chapter, you've learned how to manage report and subscription processing. Reporting Services supports three execution options. First, you configure the report to execute with the most recent data where the report server creates a user-specific execution session for each request. Second, cache snapshots let users share a single report execution within a predefined period of time. Third, execution snapshots store a permanent copy of the report in the report server database for report archiving or auditing purposes.

Besides on-demand delivery, Reporting Services supports subscription and delivery. Out of the box, Reporting Services can deliver reports to e-mail recipients, network folders, and SharePoint document libraries. Users can create standard subscriptions to distribute reports to static e-mail addresses or Windows folders. Data-driven subscriptions let you personalize subscribed delivery by using dynamic delivery settings and report parameters.

12.4 Resources

Configuring a Report Server for E-Mail Delivery (http://tinyurl.com/26g9cw)—Explains the Report Server e-mail settings.

Chapter 13

Advanced Report Management

By now, you should have a solid grasp of how to manage the report server environment. As you've seen, Report Manager is a great tool for carrying out day-to-day management activities. Occasionally, Report Manager may not be up to the task. When Report Manager does not meet your needs, you can write custom applications that pick up from where Report Manager leaves off.

This chapter starts by introducing you to the report server management API. I will show you how to use these API to create custom applications to manage the report server programmatically. You will also learn how to script and automate management tasks. Finally, this chapter teaches you how to monitor report execution and server performance, and how to manage the report server database.

13.1 Programming Report Management

As I noted in chapter 11, Report Manager is just a presentation layer on top of the report server management interface. As you interact with Report Manager, the application calls down to the Report Server Web service to handle all management actions. For example, when you use Report Manager to create a new folder, Report Manager calls the CreateFolder method on the Report Server Web service. If Report Manager does not support a management action that you require, you can write your own administration utilities that call the same APIs to manage the report server programmatically.

13.1.1 Understanding the Management API

Recall from chapter 1 that the report server provides four Web service endpoints: ReportExecution2005.asmx, ReportService2005.asmx, ReportService2006.asmx, and ReportServiceAuthentication.asmx (internally used in SharePoint integration mode only). The ReportExecution2005 Web service endpoint handles report rendering and viewing.

The ReportService2005.asmx and ReportService2006.asmx represent the management API. Note that these are the same endpoints found in Reporting Services 2005. Reporting Services 2008 doesn't introduce new endpoints. It only adds a few new Web methods to support new features, such as estimated pages versus actual pagination modes. The Microsoft SQL Server 2000 Reporting Services endpoint (ReportService.asmx) is no longer supported.

Understanding the management endpoints

The ReportService2005 endpoint provides the management API for a report server that is running in native mode. If the report server is configured for SharePoint integration mode, use the ReportService2006 endpoint instead. Make sure to target the ReportService2006 endpoint that is located in the _vti_bin folder of the SharePoint site (for example, http://<ServerName>/<SiteName>/_vti_bin/ReportServer/ReportService2006.asmx?wsdl). Avoid the ReportService2006 endpoint in the report server bin folder because the SharePoint site may have more recent versions of report content.

Choosing the right management endpoint is important because the ReportService2005 and ReportService2006 endpoints are mutually exclusive. If the report server is configured for SharePoint integration mode, calling the ReportService2005 API will return an rsOperationNotSupportedNativeMode error. Vice versa, if the report server is configured for native mode, the ReportService2006 APIs will return an rsOperationNotSupportedNativeMode error. This chapter assumes that the report server is running in native mode and that you are using the ReportService2005 endpoint. The ReportService2006 endpoint provides almost identical features. If you are using the ReportService2006 endpoint, you should still be able to benefit from the information presented in this chapter.

Understanding the management methods

The ReportService2005 management endpoint includes more than one hundred Web methods. To see all of them, request the ReportService2005 WSDL contract by typing the following URL in Internet Explorer:

```
http://<ServerName>/ReportServer/ReportService2005.as mx?wsdl
```

Table 13.1 organizes the management APIs in categories, describes each category, and lists some of the most common methods in each one.

Table 13.1 The report server supports many management APIs

Category	Purpose	Method examples
Content	Manage the report catalog	CreateFolder, GetReportDefinition, MoveItem, CreateReport
Data Sources	Manage data source connections and credentials	CreateDataSource, EnableDataSource
Linked reports	Manage linked reports	CreateLinkedReport, GetReportLink
Report parameters	Set and retrieve report parameters	GetReportParameters, SetReportParameters
Report History	Create and manage	CreateReportHistorySnapshot, SetReportHistoryOptions
Scheduling	Create and manage shared schedules	CreateSchedule, SetScheduleProperties
Security	Handles report server security	CreateRole, GetPolicies, GetPermissions
Subscriptions	Manages subscribed delivery	CreateSubscription, CreateDataDrivenSubscription

For a full list of the report server management APIs, please see the Report Server Web Service Methods topic in SQL Server 2008 Books Online.

13.1.2 Tracing Web Methods

Given the sheer number of Web methods available, you might find yourself asking which web method should I choose for the management task at hand and how should I call it? In fact, this is one of the most frequently asked questions on the Reporting Services public forum. At the same time, it is likely that Report Manager or Management Studio already supports some aspect of the management feature you want to implement.

Wouldn't it be nice to be able to peek under the hood and see what APIs Report Manager calls? This is exactly what my RsRequestViewer sample was designed to handle. RsRequestViewer intercepts the server calls and outputs them to a trace listener. It helps you see the APIs that Report Manager invokes and what arguments it passes to each interface. Armed with this information, you can easily reproduce the same feature in your custom management application.

Understanding RsRequestViewer

I implemented the RSRequestViewer sample as an ASP.NET HTTP module. An HTTP module is a .NET assembly that is called on every request to an ASP.NET application. Once installed, RSRequestViewer intercepts the incoming traffic to the report server and outputs it to a trace listener, such as the SysInternal DebugView tool.

```
public class RsHttpModule : IHttpModule
{
    public delegate void MyEventHandler(Object s, EventArgs e);

    public void Init(HttpApplication app) {
        app.BeginRequest += new EventHandler(this.OnBeginRequest);
    }
    public void Dispose() { }
    public void OnBeginRequest(object obj, EventArgs ea) {
        bool soapRequest = false;
        Stream stream = null;
        HttpApplication app = (HttpApplication)obj;
        HttpContext ctx = app.Context;
        soapRequest = (ctx.Request.Headers["SOAPAction"] != null);
        if (!soapRequest)
        {   // URL request
            Trace.WriteLine(String.Format("RsHttpModule - URL request: {0}",
            ctx.Request.Url));
        }
        else
        {   // SOAP request
            stream = ctx.Request.InputStream;
            byte[] requestBody = new byte[stream.Length];
            stream.Read(requestBody, 0, requestBody.Length);
            ctx.Request.InputStream.Position = 0;
            string request = System.Text.ASCIIEncoding.ASCII.GetString(requestBody);
            Trace.WriteLine(String.Format("RsHttpModule -  SOAP request: {0} from {1}",
                ctx.Request.Headers["SOAPAction"], ctx.Request.Url));
            Trace.WriteLine("RsHttpModule -  SOAP payload: " + request);
        }
    }
}
```

Quickly walking through the code, the RsHttpModule registers a BeginRequest callback in the Init method. ASP.NET invokes the OnBeginRequest callback each time a new URL or SOAP request is submitted to the report server. First, OnBeginRequest inspects the request headers to determine the request type. If this is a URL request, the code outputs the URL. Otherwise, in the case of a SOAP call, OnBeginRequest gets the name of the web method from the SOAPAction header. Next, OnBeginRequest outputs the request payload so you can see what parameters are passed to the method. All RSRequestViewer trace messages are prefixed with *RsHttpModule* so you can easily tell them apart when you watch the trace output.

Installing RSRequestViewer

Installing RsRequestViewer is a simple three-step process.

1. Copy the RsRequestViewer.dll and RsRequestViewer.pdb files to the report server binary folder. The default report server binary folder is Program Files\Microsoft SQL Server\MSRS10.-MSSQLSERVER\Reporting Services\ReportServer\bin.
2. Open the report server web.config file in your favorite editor and add RsRequestViewer to the list of the registered HTTP modules, as follows.

```
<httpModules>
  <clear />
  <add name="RsHttpModule" type="RsRequestViewer.RsHttpModule, RsRequestViewer"/>
  <add name="OutputCache" type="System.Web.Caching.OutputCacheModule"/>
  . . .
</httpModules>
```

3. Open the report server policy file (rssrvpolicy.config) and register the RsHttpModule module by adding the following XML fragment after the last CodeGroup element.

```
<CodeGroup class="UnionCodeGroup" version="1" Name="SecurityExtensionCodeGroup"
    Description="Code group for the RsRequestViewer HTTP Module"
    PermissionSetName="FullTrust">
  <IMembershipCondition class="UrlMembershipCondition" version="1"
    Url="C:\Program Files\Microsoft SQL Server\MSRS10.MSSQLSERVER\
       Reporting Services\ReportServer\bin\RsRequestViewer.dll"/>
</CodeGroup>
```

At this point, RsRequestViewer is registered with the report server and you can start using it.

Using RSRequestViewer

Suppose you want to write a management utility to programmatically generate an execution snapshot, add it to the report history, and obtain the history identifier. As you've seen in the previous chapter, execution snapshot caching requires that all report parameters have default values. Therefore, if you want to generate an execution snapshot with new parameter values, you need to set the default values before generating the snapshot. Suppose you don't know which management API updates parameter default values, but you do know that Report Manager lets you manage report parameters. Let's see if RsRequestViewer can help.

1. Download and install the Microsoft DebugView utility. See the Resources section for a download link.
2. Run DebugView. To see only the RsRequestViewer trace, click the Filter toolbar button and set up a filter that includes only the RsRequestViewer messages. For example, enter *RsHttpModule** to watch only trace messages that start with *RsHttpModule*.
3. Open Report Manager and go to the parameter properties page of the Cache Demo report.

   As you interact with Report Manager, you should see many calls to the report server. You can click the Clear toolbar button to clear the trace or toggle the Capture button to pause and resume the trace.
4. Click the Clear toolbar button (or press Ctrl-X) to clear the trace.
5. Go back to the parameter properties page in Report Manager. If the Has Default checkbox of the Year parameter is not checked, check it and set the parameter default value to 2001. Click the Apply button.

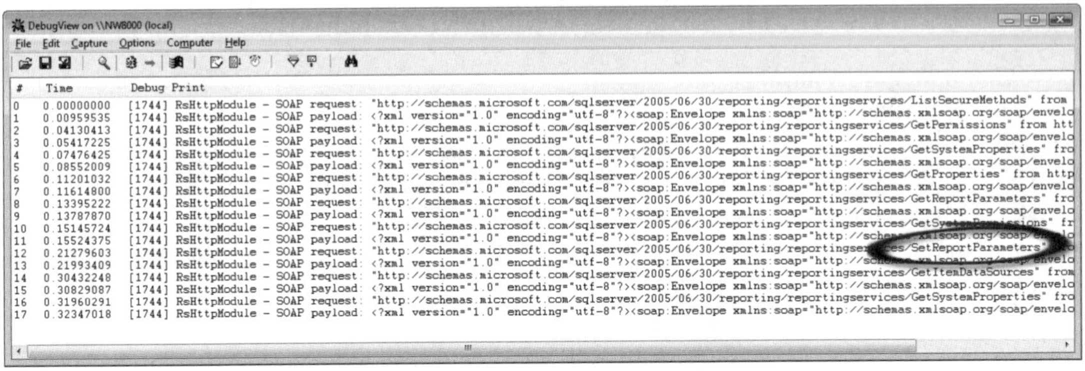

Figure 13.1 Use the Microsoft DebugView to watch the RsRequestView output.

At this point, DebugView should intercept a few method calls, such as ListSecureMethods, GetPermissions, and so on, as shown in Figure 13.1. Because you are updating the report content, you deduce that you need a Set method. Further down the list you see a SetReportParameters method that looks promising. If you hover on the line below it, you will see the method arguments.

6. Select the line below the SetReportParameters call and press Ctrl-C to copy its content to the clipboard.
7. Open Notepad and press Ctrl-V to paste the content.

You should see the following trace message.

[1744] RsHttpModule - SOAP payload: <?xml version="1.0" encoding="utf - 8"?><soap:Envelope xmlns:soap="http://schemas.xmlsoap.org/soap/envelope/" xmlns:xsi="http://www.w3.org/2001/XMLSchema - instance" xmlns:xsd="http://www.w3.org/2001/XMLSchema"><soap:Body><SetReportParameters xmlns="http://schemas.microsoft.com/sqlserver/2005/06/30/reporting/reportingservices"><Report>/AMRS/Cache Demo</Report><Parameters /></SetReportParameters></soap:Body></soap:Envelope>

You can see the arguments passed to the call toward the end of the trace message. Notice that SetReportParameters takes two arguments. The Report argument takes the report path (in this case, the path is /AMRS/Cache Demo). However, the Parameters argument is a complex structure and its content doesn't show up in DebugView. So how will you find out how to set it?

8. Open SQL Server 2008 Books Online, switch to the Index tab, and enter SetReportParameters. You should see the SetReportParameters method in the list.
9. Double-click on the SetReportParameters method to see its signature and definition of the Parameters argument.

The Parameters argument takes an array of ReportParameters objects. Oftentimes, the documentation also includes a code sample in both C# and Visual Basic.NET that demonstrates how to call the method. Follow similar steps to understand the APIs that Report Manager invokes when generating an execution snapshot and a history snapshot.

13.1.3 Programming Management Tasks

Empowered by what you have learned from the RsRequestViewer sample, you are well positioned to tackle writing custom code to manage the report server. Included in the chapter's source code, you'll find a GenerateExecutionSnapshot C# console application that provides an example for generating a report execution snapshot programmatically.

The 2.0 version of the GenerateExecutionSnapshot sample is based on the .NET Framework 2.0 and uses a web reference technique to generate a web proxy. The 3.5 version is based on the .NET Framework 3.5 and uses the Windows Communication Foundation (WCF) to integrate with the Report Server Web service. First, I will walk you through the implementation steps of the 2.0 version. Then, I'll point out the differences when WCF is used.

Generating a Web service proxy

A Web service proxy lifts some of the complexity of communicating with a Web service. Follow these steps to use Visual Studio 2008 to create a C# Console Application project and generate a proxy for the ReportService2005 endpoint.

1. Open Visual Studio 2008 and select the File ⇨ New ⇨ Project menu to create a new project.
2. In the New Project dialog box that follows, expand the .NET Framework drop-down in the upper right corner and select .NET Framework 2.0 to target this version.
3. In the Project Types pane, select the Visual C# project type and choose the Console Application template in the Templates pane.
4. Name the project GenerateExecutionSnapshot. Choose a location for the project and click OK to generate the project.

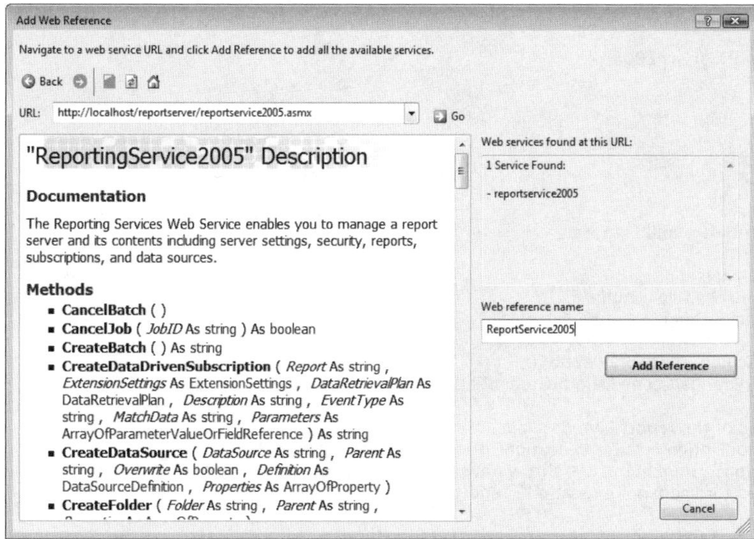

Figure 13.2 Add a web reference to the ReportService2005 endpoint to generate a Web service proxy.

5. In the Solution Explorer pane, right-click on the GenerateExecutionSnapshot project node and select the Add Web Reference context menu.
6. In the Add Web Reference dialog box that follows (see Figure 13.2), enter the URL address of the ReportService2005 endpoint, such as http://localhost/ReportServer/ReportService2005.asmx if Reporting Services is installed locally. Click the Go button to retrieve the Web service description.
7. In the Web Reference Name field, enter *ReportService2005* and click the Add Reference button to generate the Web service proxy.

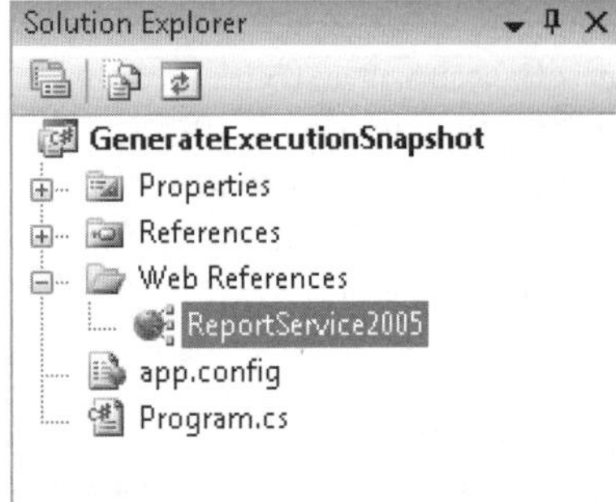

Figure 13.3 The ReportService2005 web reference is added to the Web References folder.

Visual Studio creates a new Web References folder and adds to it the ReportService2005 web reference, as shown in Figure 13.3. You can click the Show All Files toolbar button in the Solution Explorer pane to see all source files that Visual Studio has generated. The Reference.cs source file contains the actual proxy definition.

Generating the execution snapshot

Now, let me walk you through the code to generate a report execution snapshot and save it in the snapshot history.

```
using System;
using System.Collections.Generic;
using System.Text;
using GenerateExecutionSnapshot.ReportService2005;
namespace GenerateExecutionSnapshot {
   class Program    {
      static void Main(string[] args)
      {
         bool forRendering = false;
         string historyID = null;
         ParameterValue[] values = null;
         DataSourceCredentials[] credentials = null;
         Warning[] warnings = null;
         bool keepExecutionShapshots = false;
         ScheduleDefinitionOrReference schedule = null;
         string reportPath = "/AMRS/Cache Demo";

         ReportingService2005 rs = new ReportingService2005();
         rs.Credentials = System.Net.CredentialCache.DefaultCredentials;

         // Check the execution options of the report (live or snapshot)
         ExecutionSettingEnum executionOption = rs.GetExecutionOptions(reportPath, out schedule);
         if (executionOption == ExecutionSettingEnum.Live) throw new ApplicationException
            (The report is not configured for snapshot execution", reportPath));

         ReportParameter[] parameters = rs.GetReportParameters(reportPath, historyID,
                              forRendering, values, credentials);
         parameters[0].DefaultValues[0] = "2002";

         // All parameters have to be assigned default values before snapshot is generated
         rs.SetReportParameters(reportPath, parameters);
         // Create the report snapshot
         rs.UpdateReportExecutionSnapshot(reportPath);
         // Check if the report is configured to keep snapshots in history
         bool result = rs.GetReportHistoryOptions(reportPath, out keepExecutionShapshots, out schedule);

         if (keepExecutionShapshots)
         {
            // history is automatically created, get the list of history runs
            ReportHistorySnapshot[] history = rs.ListReportHistory(reportPath);
            // Need to sort by date since history runs may not be chronologically sorted
```

```
            Array.Sort(history, CompareReportHistoryByDate);
            historyID = history[history.Length - 1].HistoryID; // get the last history run
        }
        else
        {
            // explicitly create history snapshot
            historyID = rs.CreateReportHistorySnapshot(reportPath, out warnings);
        }
    }
    private static int CompareReportHistoryByDate(ReportHistorySnapshot x, ReportHistorySnapshot y)
    {
        return x.CreationDate < y.CreationDate ? -1 : 1;
    }
}
```

To start with, note that the code adds a reference to the web reference namespace (GenerateExecutionSnapshot.ReportService2005) to bring it in scope. The code instantiates an instance of the ReportService2005 proxy and sets its Credentials property to System.Net.CredentialCache.DefaultCredentials. As a result, all calls to the Web service will execute under the identity of the interactive user (this is you). This is important because by default, .NET will not impersonate the call. If you don't overwrite the Credentials property, the calls will go under a Windows NULL session and will be rejected by IIS with a 401 Unauthorized error.

Next, the code calls the GetExecutionOptions API to check the report execution settings of the Cache Demo report. If the report is configured as a live report (that is, it runs with the most recent data), an execution snapshot cannot be generated and the code throws an exception. Otherwise, the code calls the GetReportParameters API to obtain the definition of the report parameters. As noted, all parameters must have default values before the snapshot is generated. Assuming that we want the snapshot to show the 2002 sales data, we set the value of the first (and only) parameter to 2002 and call SetReportParameters to update the Year report parameter.

Next, we generate the actual snapshot by calling the UpdateReportExecutionSnapshot API. This is equivalent to selecting the Create a Report Snapshot When You Click the Apply Button on This Page option in the Execution page in Report Manager. At this point, the snapshot is generated and all requests to the Cache Demo report will be served by the cached instance. If we want to add the snapshot to report history and get the history identifier, we have a bit more work to do. First, the code determines how the report history is configured by invoking the GetReportHistoryOptions API.

If the Cache Demo report is configured to automatically add new snapshot instance to the report history each time the execution snapshot is refreshed (this is the Store All Report Execution Snapshots in History option on the History Page), the code retrieves the history list by calling the ListReportHistory API. Since the list is not sorted in chronological order, the code sorts the list and obtains the history identifier of the last history snapshot.

If report history for the Cache Demo report is not configured to automatically store new versions of the snapshot as they are generated, the code adds a one-time execution snapshot to report history by calling the CreateReportHistorySnapshot API. This is the same as manually adding a snapshot to report history. In Report Manager, this is done by clicking the New Snapshot button on the History page.

Using Windows Communication Foundation

Let's now move on to the world of the Windows Communication Foundation (WCF). Previously codenamed Indigo, WCF debuted in .NET Framework 3.0. It is a communication subsystem that enables applications to communicate with each other in flexible ways. If you tell Visual Studio to target the 3.5 version of the .NET Framework when you create a new project, it will default to using WCF for communicating with Web services. Be prepared for some surprises. The WCF programming model is considerably different than the web reference approach that you may already be familiar with.

The first difference is that the Add Web Reference dialog box is now called Add Service Reference to denote the fact that WCF supports more than just Web services. You will use the Add Service Reference dialog box to establish a reference to the ReportService2005 endpoint and generate a proxy.

TIP If your project already targets the .NET Framework 3.5, you can still create 2.0-style proxies. To do so, in the Add Service Reference dialog box, click the Advanced button. In the Service Reference Settings dialog box that follows, click the Add Web Service Reference button to open the familiar Add Web Reference dialog box.

What's more interesting is that WCF generates somewhat different method signatures. For example, you will find that all methods return a ServerInfoHeader object (although Books Online states otherwise). In WCF, the documented return values become out parameters that you need to pass on the call.

```
ExecutionSettingEnum executionOption;
ReportingService2005SoapClient rs = new ReportingService2005SoapClient();
rs.ClientCredentials.Windows.AllowedImpersonationLevel =
System.Security.Principal.TokenImpersonationLevel.Impersonation;
ServerInfoHeader header = rs.GetExecutionOptions(reportPath, out executionOption, out schedule);
```

For example, Books Online tells you that the GetExecutionOptions API should return an ExecutionSettingEnum value that indicates how the report is configured for execution. This is what you will get in the .NET 2.0 world. However, the WCF programming model makes the return value an out parameter.

Another difference is in how WCF impersonates the call and passes the user credentials to the service. In 2.0, you can simply set the proxy's Credentials property to System.Net.CredentialCache.DefaultCredentials. With WCF, the easiest way I've found to accomplish the same thing is to change the service declaration in the application configuration file (yes, we now have a declarative model), as follows:

```
<security mode=" TransportCredentialOnly">
   <transport clientCredentialType=" Ntlm" proxyCredentialType="None" realm="" />
   <message clientCredentialType="UserName" algorithmSuite="Default" />
</security>
```

In addition, WCF will not let the client impersonate the user unless you make your intention explicit. This is why the code sets the AllowedImpersonationLevel of the proxy's ClientCredentials property to TokenImpersonationLevel.Impersonation.

In summary, unless you absolutely need WCF, I'd suggest you stick to the .NET 2.0 programming style for invoking the Report Server Web service because it's simpler and well documented. For this reason, all my Web service demos target .NET 2.0 excluding the GenerateExecutionSnapshot demo in this chapter and the SilverlightReporter demo in chapter 15.

Batching methods

Sometimes, you may need to perform several update commands to the report catalog in a single atomic operation. That is, the entire operation should succeed only if all commands execute successfully. If any of the commands fail, the operation *must* roll back. Similar to database transactions that you may already be familiar with, Reporting Services lets you group multiple Web method calls in a single batch. For example, suppose you want to execute the tasks of updating the report parameters and generating a report execution snapshot in the GenerateExecutionSnapshot demo as an atomic transaction.

```
BatchHeader batchHeader = new BatchHeader();
batchHeader.BatchID = rs.CreateBatch();              // start a new batch
rs.BatchHeaderValue = batchHeader;
rs.SetReportParameters(reportPath, parameters);
rs.UpdateReportExecutionSnapshot(reportPath);       // create the report snapshot
rs.ExecuteBatch();                                  // commit the batch
rs.BatchHeaderValue = null;
```

Creating a batch requires several steps. First, you create a BatchHeader object. Next, you call the CreateBatch API to obtain a batch identifier. Then, you invoke the management APIs that write to the report catalog. In our case, the code calls SetReportParameters to update the report parameters, followed by UpdateReportExecutionSnapshot to refresh the report snapshot. Finally, you commit the changes by invoking the ExecuteBatch API.

Again, similar to database transactions, you can nest batches. Although resembling database transactions, Reporting Services batches are implemented differently. First, the report server doesn't lock any objects when CreateBatch is called. This is because SOAP is a stateless protocol. Instead, the report server simply accumulates the method calls in the report catalog (table Batch) for later execution. Therefore, the catalog changes are not immediately made as you call the management APIs.

When you invoke the ExecuteBatch API, the report server starts a database transaction and performs the updates inside the transaction. If all methods succeed, the report server commits the database transaction. If ExecuteBatch is not called within a certain period, the report server expires and deletes the batch. This is equivalent to cancelling the batch with the CancelBatch API.

A batch is cancelled automatically in case of an error. If you decide that you want to discard the batch programmatically, you can call the CancelBatch API. After you execute or cancel the batch, you need to clear out the batch header by setting proxy's BatchHeaderValue to null. Otherwise the proxy will continue to send the header and you will still be operating under a batch.

Because of the way they are implemented, batches have several limitations. First, batches only support write operations. For example, you cannot call GetReportParameter API within a batch. If read operations were allowed, they would return results for the original state of the catalog and the changes made by the write commands would not be reflected. Second, write methods that return results are permitted but their results are discarded. For example, you can call the CreateReportHistorySnapshot API within a batch but you won't be able to get back the history identifier. Finally, batches are not supported in SharePoint integration mode.

13.1.4 Scripting Management Tasks

Administrators love scripts! As a report server administrator, you can write scripts to automate mundane management tasks. For example, you can write a script to automate the process of publishing reports to a report server instance. A Reporting Services script is a file written in Visual Basic.NET and that has an .rss file extension. You can execute scripts from the command line or schedule them for an unattended execution.

Understanding the Script Host

Reporting Services include a Script Host utility (rs.exe) which can run script files. The Script Host (rs.exe) is a command line utility that supports various switches. Table 13.2 shows the three most popular switches.

Table 13.2 Script Host command line switches

Category	Purpose	Example
-i (required)	Specifies the script file to execute	-i FireEvent.rss
-s (required)	Specifies the report server URL	-s http://localhost/ReportServer
-v	Defines a global variable	-v reportPath="/AMRS/Cache Demo"

The Script Host includes a predefined global variable called rs to let you communicate with the Report Server Web service without having to create a Web service proxy. Unfortunately, the Script Host doesn't support SharePoint integration mode and custom security. These integration scenarios require custom management utilities. Chapter 17 includes such a utility for uploading report definitions to a report server configured in SharePoint integration mode.

Implementing the script code

The Reporting Services samples include several scripts for automating common management tasks, such as publishing reports, changing system properties, cancelling jobs, and setting up security policies. Let's add to these by creating a FireEvent.rss script that lets you trigger a subscription on demand. This could be useful to test a subscription quickly because you don't have to run the subscription on a schedule.

TIP Another quick way to test subscriptions is to manually run the scheduled job in SSMS. It fires the event right away, irrespective of the schedule.

The Script Host can run script files but it doesn't let you debug them. Therefore, the easiest way to implement a Reporting Services script is to create a Visual Studio VB.NET project. Once you test the code, you can easily convert it to a script file. The FireEvent VB.NET console application lets you step through the code in Visual Studio.

```
Module Module1
   Dim rs = New ReportingService2005()
   Sub Main()
      rs.Credentials = System.Net.CredentialCache.DefaultCredentials
      FireEvent("/AMRS/Cache Demo")
   End Sub
   Private Sub FireEvent(ByVal reportPath As String)
      Try
         Console.WriteLine("Getting subscriptions...")
         Dim subs As Subscription() = rs.ListSubscriptions(reportPath, Nothing)
         If subs IsNot Nothing Then
            ' Fire the first subscription in the list
            Console.WriteLine("Firing event...")
            rs.FireEvent("TimedSubscription", subs(0).SubscriptionID)
            Console.WriteLine("Event fired successfully")
         End If
      Catch ex As Exception
         Console.WriteLine(ex.ToString())
      End Try

   End Sub
End Module
```

NOTE The user must have Generate Events system rights to invoke the FireEvent API successfully. However the System User and System Administrator roles don't include these rights by default. If you are a System Administrator, you can grant yourself permissions to call FireEvent by going to the SQL Server Management Studio, double-clicking the System Administrator role to open its properties, and selecting the Generate Events task.

The Main function is the entry point of the application. It sets the proxy credentials to DefaultCredentials to pass the user credentials to the server with each call. Next, it calls the FireEvent helper method and passes the report path. Excluding the error handling and tracing code, the FireEvent method calls the ListSubscriptions API to obtain the subscriptions associated with the Cache Demo reports. Next, it calls the FireEvent API to trigger the first subscription by passing the subscription identifier. In the previous chapter, I explained that the report server supports TimedSubscription and SnapshotUpdated event types. However, because the SnapshotUpdated event is an internal event type, the FireEvent can only raise TimedSubscription events.

Once the report server picks up the event, it will trigger the first subscription associated with the Cache Demo report. To make sure that the FireEvent call has succeeded, open the Subscription tab of the Cache Demo report in Report Manager. The Last Run column should show the time the FireEvent was called.

Working with script files

Converting the FireEvent sample to a script file requires only a couple of changes. First, as mentioned earlier, there is no need to instantiate the proxy because the rs global variable fulfills exactly this purpose. Second, instead of using a static folder path, the code gets the path from a reportPath global variable that you pass to the script. I provided a FireEvent.bat file that demonstrates how to invoke the FireEvent.rss script file. It includes the following command line:

```
rs -i FireEvent.rss -s http://localhost/reportserver -v reportPath="/AMRS/Cache Demo"
```

This command invokes the RS Script Host and passes the FireEvent.rss script file to it. The -s switch tells the Script Host to target the local report server. The -v switch passes the path to the Cache Demo report to the reportPath global variable.

TIP If you need to migrate the report content from one server to another, consider the excellent Report Scripter utility by Jasper Smith (see Resources). The Report Scripter automatically generates scripts to load reports, data sources definitions, resources, linked reports and folders with all their associated properties.

13.1.5 Using the WMI Provider

As useful as it is, Report Manager is limited in that it only lets you manage a single report server instance at a time. Chances are that in real life you may need to manage several report servers. For example, you may have a testing server for QA testing and a production server that hosts the production reports. As you know by now, you can use SQL Server Management Studio and the Reporting Services Configuration Manager to manage any report server on your network.

Behind the scenes, these management tools use the Reporting Services Windows Management Instrumentation (WMI) provider. You can use the WMI provider to write your own management utilities too. For example, you could write a custom management application based on the WMI provider to discover which machines in the network are running the Report Server Web service.

Understanding the Reporting Services WMI provider

The Reporting Services WMI provider is essentially an API layer on top of the report server configuration data. Consequently, the WMI provider works even if the Reporting Services service is not running. This is because the WMI provider doesn't communicate with the report server. Instead, it directly accesses configuration data for your report server installation.

The Reporting Services WMI provider gets installed by the SQL Server 2008 setup program. Developers can write custom code that uses the WMI provider to programmatically access the configuration settings of local and remote installations. Since Reporting Services 2008 now keeps both Report Manager and report server configuration settings in a single report server configuration file, programming the WMI provider got easier in this release. The Reporting Services 2005 WMI provider includes two configuration classes:

- MSReportServer_Instance—This class provides instance discovery features and basic information required for a client to connect to an installed report server, such as obtaining the report server URLs.
- MSReportServer_ConfigurationSetting—This class abstracts the configuration settings stored in the report server configuration file (rsreportserver.config).

.NET developers can use the classes in the System.Management assembly to access the WMI provider. One cautionary note is that WMI relies on the Windows DCOM infrastructure. Therefore, if you don't have administrator access to the remote server, the WMI provider may fail with remote configuration tasks. Review the Configuring a Report Server for Remote Administration topic in Books Online (see Resources) for instructions on how to configure the WMI provider for remote access.

Working with the WMI provider

My RSWMI console utility demonstrates how you can integrate .NET applications with the WMI provider to manage report server instances. You can start RSWMI from the command line using the following syntax:

```
rswmi <servername> <instancename>
```

Both arguments are optional. If they are omitted, RSWMI assumes that you are targeting the local server (localhost) using the default SQL Server instance name (MSSQLSERVER). The RSWMI reads and displays report server configuration properties in the Windows command prompt. A partial output obtained by running RSWMI on my laptop follows:

```
C:\>rswmi localhost
Instance Info ...
EditionID: 1804890536
EditionName: ENTERPRISE EDITION
InstanceID: MSRS10.MSSQLSERVER
InstanceName: MSSQLSERVER
IsSharePointIntegrated: False
Version: 10.0.1442.32
ReportServerWebService: http://NW8000:80/ReportServer
ReportManager: http://NW8000:80/Reports
Admin settings ...
Instance MSSQLSERVER
Property Name: ConnectionPoolSize     Value: 100
Property Name: DatabaseLogonTimeout     Value: -1
. . .
```

First, RSWMI generates an Instance Info section that outputs information obtained from the MSReportServer_Instance class. Next, it outputs the properties of the MSReportServer_ConfigurationSetting class (Admin Settings section). The most interesting properties in the first section are the SQL Server 2008 edition, the instance name, and whether the server is configured for SharePoint integration mode. In addition, RSWMI displays the report server and Report Manager URLs. The GetReportServerUrl method is responsible for generating the Instance Info section.

```
internal static void GetReportServerUrl(string machineName, string instanceName) {
   string reportServerVirtualDirectory = String.Empty;
   string fullWmiNamespace = string.Format(_wmiNamespace, machineName, instanceName);
   ManagementScope scope = null;
   ConnectionOptions connOptions = new ConnectionOptions();
   //Get management scope
   scope = new ManagementScope(fullWmiNamespace, connOptions);
   scope.Connect();
   //Get WMI class
   ManagementPath path = new ManagementPath("MSReportServer_Instance");
   ObjectGetOptions options = new ObjectGetOptions();
   ManagementClass serverClass = new ManagementClass(scope, path, options);

   serverClass.Get();
   if (serverClass == null)
      throw new Exception(string.Format(CultureInfo.InvariantCulture, "No WMI class found."));
   //Get instances
   ManagementObjectCollection instances = serverClass.GetInstances();

   foreach (ManagementObject instance in instances)
   {
      instance.Get();
      foreach(PropertyData p in instance.Properties) Console.WriteLine(p.Name + ": " + p.Value);
      ManagementBaseObject outParams =
         (ManagementBaseObject)instance.InvokeMethod("GetReportServerUrls", null, null);

      string[] appNames = (string[])outParams["ApplicationName"];
      string[] urls = (string[])outParams["URLs"];
      for (int i = 0; i < appNames.Length; i++) Console.WriteLine(appNames[i] + ": " + urls[i]);
   }
}
```

First, RSWMI creates a management scope based on the WMI namespace (such as \\localhost\root\Microsoft\SqlServer\RS_ReportServer\MSSQLSERVER\v10) and connects that scope to the WMI namespace.

TIP The WMI namespace path has changed in this release to include the RS_ prefix. When working with WMI, I found the Microsoft Scriptomatic 2.0 utility (see Resources) very useful to obtain the WMI namespace paths and class names.

Second, RSWMI creates a WMI management path that points to the MSReportServer_Instance class and creates a management object that uses the path. Third, RSWMI calls the Get method to bind to the management object that represents the report server instance. Fourth, the code calls the GetInstances method of the management object to obtain all instances (there should be only one management object for a single report server instance) and displays the instance properties.

Finally, RSWMI gets the URLs for the report server and Report Manager and outputs the URLs to the console. The WMI provider provides a new GetReportServerUrls method that returns the full URL addresses of both Report Server Web service and Report Manager. RSWMI calls this method to output the URL addresses to the console. When testing the RSWMI utility, try stopping the target report server by shutting down the Reporting Services service and running the utility. Although the report server is stopped, the utility should run successfully because it doesn't communicate with the server or any Web service APIs.

13.2 Monitoring Reporting Services

It is unrealistic to expect that your management responsibilities will come to an end once the reports are deployed to the production server. In real life, end users may occasionally report errors or degradation of server performance over time. By monitoring the report server, you can ensure that it functions correctly at an acceptable performance level.

13.2.1 Understanding the Reporting Services Log Files

Reporting Services provides various log files to help you track the health and performance of the server. Table 13.3 shows the log files and their purpose.

Table 13.3 Reporting Services Log Files

Log File	Purpose
Execution Log	Logs report execution data, such as the report export format, parameters, performance data, and so on.
Trace Log	Logs trace output from the report server, including exception information.
HTTP Log	Logs HTTP requests handled by the report server and Report Manager.
Windows Event Log	Logs the report server events, such as error conditions.
Setup log	Contains trace output from the SQL Server 2008 setup program that could help you troubleshoot setup issues. The default location is \Program Files\Microsoft SQL Server\100\Setup Bootstrap\Log.

Let's explore the first three log files in more detail.

13.2.2 Working with the Execution Log

Why is my report so slow? This is another common question on the public discussion list. The execution log should be your first stop for troubleshooting report performance problems. It tracks detailed information about report execution, including who requested the report, the report parameter values, report size, source of the report execution (live, cache, snapshot, or history), and so on. If you have a web farm of report servers, the execution log is shared among all servers.

Configuring the Execution Log

The Execution Log is enabled by default. Follow these steps to manage its settings.

1. In SQL Server Management Studio, connect to the report server instance.
2. In Object Explorer, right-click on the server and choose Properties.

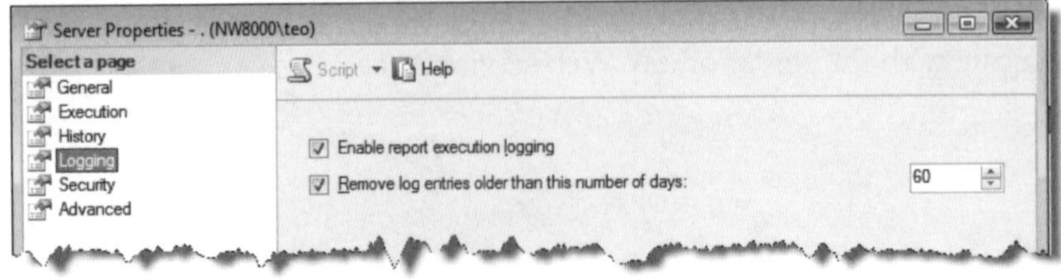

Figure 13.4 Use the Logging property page to manage the Execution Log settings.

3. In the Server Properties dialog box, select the Logging page, as shown in Figure 13.4.

To disable execution logging, clear the Enable Report Execution Logging checkbox. Use the Remove Log Entries Older Than This Number of Days setting to specify a retention policy. By default, the report server will keep the log entries for 60 days. Clear the checkbox if you don't want the report server to expire the execution log.

Viewing the Execution Log

The report server stores the execution log in the ExecutionLogStorage table in the report server database. You can view this table directly, as show in Figure 13.5. Alternatively, you can use the Microsoft-provided ExecutionLog and ExecutionLog2 SQL views that facilitate analyzing the data in the ExecutionLogStorage table, such as converting the report identifier to the report path. From a performance standpoint, the most interesting columns are TimeDataRetrieval, TimeProcessing, and TimeRendering. These columns indicate how much time (in milliseconds) the report server has spent in retrieving the report data, processing the report, and rendering it in the requested export format.

	Format	Parameters	ReportAction	TimeStart	TimeEnd	TimeDataRetrieval	TimeProcessing	TimeRendering	ByteCount	Status	Source	RowCo
1	RPL	DataSource=C:\DatasetSalesOrder.xml|Nothing	1	2007-11-20 13:51:46.917	2007-11-20 13:51:48.157	0	628	0	0	rrRenderingError	1	0
2	RPL	DataSource=C:\DatasetSalesOrder.xml|Nothing	1	2007-11-20 14:00:08.243	2007-11-20 14:01:11.443	0	63069	0	0	rrRenderingError	1	0
3	RPL	DataSource=C:\DatasetSalesOrder.xml|Nothing	1	2007-11-20 14:03:13.860	2007-11-20 14:03:30.013	14358	820	716	[illegible]	rsSuccess	1	100
4	RGDI	DataSource=<EntitySalesOrder xmlns%3D"http://ww...	1	2007-11-20 14:04:40.743	2007-11-20 14:04:41.187	30	16	346	15257	rsSuccess	1	100
5	RPL	DataSource=c:\datasetsalesorder.xml	1	2007-11-20 15:16:00.430	2007-11-20 15:16:00.590	3	20	11	18109	rsSuccess	1	100
6	RPL	ProductCategory=[Product].[Category].%26[1]&Produc...	1	2007-11-20 16:35:04.743	2007-11-20 16:35:05.117	0	228	0	0	rrRenderingError	1	0
7	RPL	ProductCategory=[Product].[Category].%26[1]&Produc...	1	2007-11-20 16:35:26.923	2007-11-20 16:35:27.167	0	69	0	0	rrRenderingError	1	0
8	RPL	ProductCategory=[Product].[Category].%26[1]&Produc...	1	2007-11-20 16:37:38.600	2007-11-20 16:37:38.633	0	10	0	0	rrRenderingError	1	0
9	RPL	ProductCategory=[Product].[Category].%26[1]&Produc...	1	2007-11-20 16:38:09.027	2007-11-20 16:38:09.273	0	98	0	0	rrRenderingError	1	0
10	RPL	ProductCategory=[Product].[Category].%26[4]&Produc...	1	2007-11-20 16:39:36.747	2007-11-20 16:39:36.843	0	50	0	0	rrRenderingError	1	0
11	RPL	ProductCategory=[Product].[Category].[All Products]	1	2007-11-20 16:51:48.847	2007-11-20 16:51:50.330	1119	106	80	12404	rsSuccess	1	21
12	RPL	ProductCategory=[Product].[Category].%26[4]&Produc...	1	2007-11-20 16:52:05.917	2007-11-20 16:52:06.127	0	65	0	0	rrRenderingError	1	0

Figure 13.5 The report server execution log contains a wealth of information about the report execution.

For example, in my case, the report server has spent almost 15 seconds to retrieve the data for the third report shown in Figure 13.5. Therefore, it may be beneficial to optimize the report query to make this report run faster. If the report server was under pressure when working on the report, it may log additional information in the AdditionalInfo column, which is described in XML. For example, it may log how much time was spent paginating the report.

Analyzing the Execution Log

While you can query the ExecutionLogStorage table directly, you may need to join it to other tables to understand its content. This is because the report server database is highly normalized. For example, to see the report path, you need to join the ExecutionLogStorage table to the Catalog table on the ReportID column. In addition, you need to write queries to analyze the execution log, for example, to find the top ten most executed reports. Finally, you should avoid querying the report server database directly as its schema is not guaranteed to be the same from one release to the next and this may degrade the server performance.

To help you analyze the execution log, Microsoft has provided a sample Integration Services package that extracts the raw log data from the ExecutionLogStorage table and loads it into a separate database that is optimized for reporting purposes. Microsoft has also provided a few useful reports that you can run right away or customize to fit your specific needs.

Assuming you have downloaded and installed the Reporting Services samples, you can find the execution log samples in the \Program Files\Microsoft SQL Server\100\Samples\-Reporting Services\Report Samples\Server Management Sample Reports. Follow the instructions in the readme file to configure the package and load the database. Once the database is populated, open the Execution Log Sample Reports project and run the Execution Summary report, which is shown in Figure 13.6.

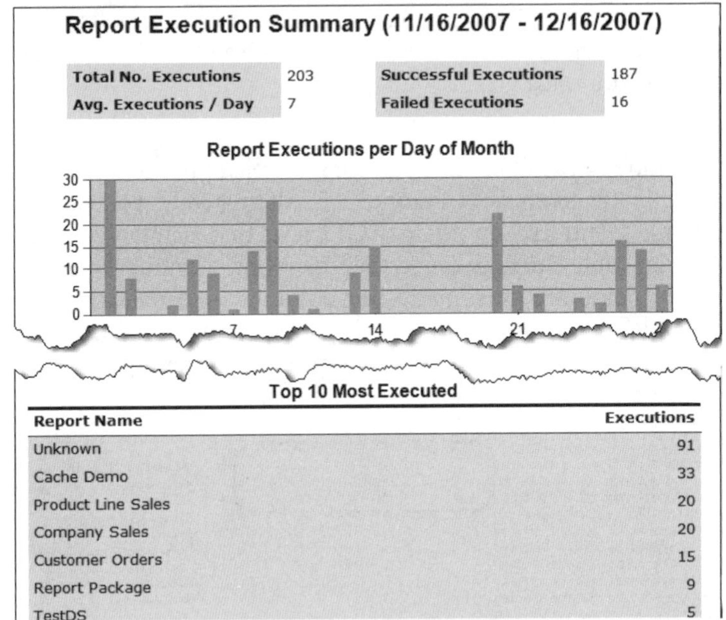

Figure 13.6 The Execution Summary report gives a high-level understanding of the report activity.

The Execution Summary report summarizes the report activity for a given time period. For example, glancing at the Report Execution per Day of Month chart, you can get a high-level understanding about the report loads within the given month. Below the chart reports, you will find sections for the top 10 most executed reports, top 10 longest running reports, top 10 largest reports, and top 10 most active users. Clicking on a report name opens a summary report that shows you detail information about the report, such as number of successful and failed executions and parameter values that were passed to the report.

13.2.3 Working with the Trace Log

As a general best practice for troubleshooting performance problems, I recommend you start with the execution log to find out which reports are failing and when they failed. Then, use the timestamp to find detailed error information in the trace log that indicates the exact cause of the failure. The trace log is a system-wide log that contains detailed information about report server operations, including system information (operating system, version, number of processors, and memory), Reporting Services component and version information, errors, low resource warnings, inbound and outbound SOAP messages, HTTP header, stack trace and debug trace information, report delivery status, recipient, and number of delivery attempts for subscribed delivery.

Configuring the Trace Log file

The trace log supports several configuration settings which you can find in the Reporting Services service configuration file (ReportingServicesService.exe.config). The default location of the Report Server service configuration file is the Program Files\Microsoft SQL Server\MSRS10.MSSQLSERVER\Reporting Services\ReportServer\bin folder.

```
<system.diagnostics>
  <switches>
    <!-- 1 = error, 2 = warning, 3 = info, 4 = verbose -- >
    <add name="DefaultTraceSwitch" value="3" />
  </switches>
</system.diagnostics>
<RStrace>
      <add name="FileName" value="ReportServerService_" />
      <add name="FileSizeLimitMb" value="32" />
      <add name="KeepFilesForDays" value="14" />
      <add name="Prefix" value="tid, time" />
      <add name="TraceListeners" value="file" />
      <add name="TraceFileMode" value="unique" />
      <add name="Components" value="all:3" />
</RStrace>
```

The DefaultTraceSwitch setting controls the level of information that is reported to the ReportServerService trace log. The default setting of 3 logs exceptions, restarts, warnings, and status messages. The maximum level for logging verbose output is 4. Reporting Services creates a new trace log file daily, when the Reporting Services service is restarted, and when the log file exceeds the maximum size (FileSizeLimitMb setting). The KeepFilesForDays setting defines the retention policy of the old trace log files. The FileName and Prefix settings control the name of the log file. You need to restart the Reporting Services service if you have changed any setting.

Viewing the Trace Log file

The report server stores the trace information in ASCII format so you can use any text editor to view its content, such as Notepad.

1. Use Windows Explorer to navigate to the report server LogFiles folder. The default location is \Program Files\Microsoft SQL Server\MSRS10.MSSQLSERVER\Reporting Services\LogFiles.

   Each time, you restart the Reporting Services service, the report server creates a new log file. The default name of the file is ReportServerService__<timestamp>.log.

NOTE The report server may not immediately log messages to the file so you may need to wait for the report server to flush the output buffer. Alternatively, restart the Reporting Services service to force the server to flush the trace.

2. Sort the files by date, and open the most recent log file.

   At the top the file, you will find a header section that displays useful report server installation details, such as SQL Server edition, version, and locale. Assuming you are troubleshooting the server, search for "error" to locate the error messages.

```
ReportingServicesService!ui!f98!12/14/2007-21:08:24:: e ERROR: HTTP status code -- > 200
-------Details--------
System.Web.Services.Protocols.SoapException: System.Web.Services.Protocols.SoapException: The SQL Agent service is not running. This operation requires the SQL Agent service. --- >
Microsoft.ReportingServices.Diagnostics.Utilities.SchedulerNotRespondingException: The SQL Agent service is not running. This operation requires the SQL Agent service.
```

If the report server has logged an error, you will find the error message and the full exception stack. You can help the Microsoft Product Support investigate server issues by sending them the error information from the trace log. If the report server has generated a Dr. Watson minidump file (*.mdmp) in the \Program Files\Microsoft SQL Server\MSRS10.MSSQLSERVER\-Reporting Services\LogFiles folder, you should include this file as well. A Dr. Watson minidump captures stack traces of the server process and could assist Microsoft Product Support to debug the internal state of the server before the crash.

Watching report server trace real time

If you're like me, you'd prefer a faster way to monitor the report server trace file then sifting through large log files. Fortunately, the report server outputs trace messages. This lets you watch the server trace real time by attaching a trace listener, such as the SysInternals DebugView, that I've just demonstrated. For security reasons, the report server doesn't output trace messages. Follow these steps to enable and monitor the trace output.

1. Open the Reporting Services service configuration file (ReportingServicesService.config) whose default location is the \Program Files\Microsoft SQL Server\MSRS10.MSSQLSERVER\Reporting Services\ReportServer\bin folder.
2. In the RStrace section, locate the TraceListeners element and add a debugwindow setting, as follows:

```
<RStrace>
  <add name="TraceListeners" value=" debugwindow, file" />
</RStrac e>
```

3. Restart the Reporting Services service.
4. Start DebugView. Click the Capture menu and make sure that the all capture options are enabled.
5. Initiate a Reporting Services action of interest, such as viewing a report in the Report Manager.

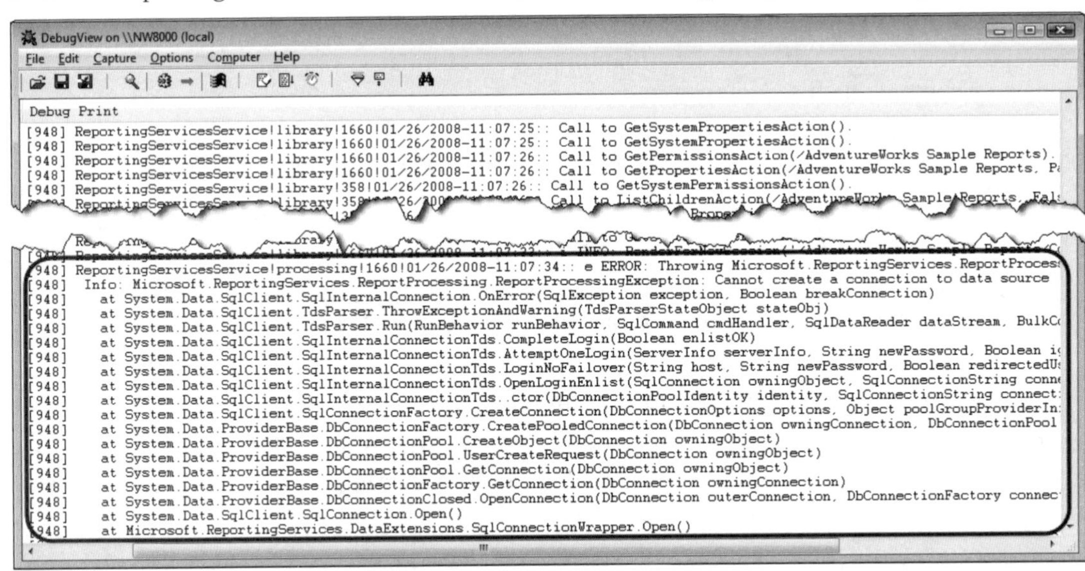

Figure 13.7 Use DebugView to watch the trace log in real time.

The same output that is generated in the trace log file is outputted in DebugView, as shown in Figure 13.7. DebugView lets you search the trace. For example, to find an error condition, search for "error". In this case, the report server has thrown an exception because it wasn't able to open a connection to the data source. You can click the Clear toolbar button (Ctrl+X) to clear the trace output to remove non-significant trace messages before you initiate the action of interest. The Capture button (Ctrl+E) lets you freeze the trace. The Autoscroll buton (Ctrl+A) lets you toggle auto scrolling to the latest message on and off.

13.2.4 Working with the HTTP Log

Now that Reporting Services is no longer dependent on IIS, you cannot use the IIS web log to capture and analyze the HTTP requests to the server. However, Reporting Services supports its own HTTP log file that fulfills the same purpose and has the same format. Among other things, it logs all HTTP requests to the report server, client IP address, and HTTP status.

Enabling the HTTP log

The HTTP log file is not enabled by default. Follow these steps to enable it.

1. Open the ReportingServicesService.exe.config configuration file and add the http:4 setting to the RSTrace section, as follows:

```
<RStrace>
      <add name="FileName"  value="ReportServerService_" />
      <add name="FileSizeLimitMb" value="32" />
      <add name="KeepFilesForDays" value="14" />
      <add name="Prefix" value="tid, time" />
      <add name="TraceListeners" value="debugwindow, file" />
      <add name="TraceFileMode" value="uniqu e" />
   <add name="HTTPLogFileName" value="ReportServerService_HTTP_" />
   <add name="HttpTraceSwitches"  value="date,time,activityid,sourceadtivityid,clientip,username,
      serverip,serverport,host,method,uristem,uriquery,protocolstatus,bytessent,bytesreceived,
      timetaken,protocolversion,useragent,cookiereceived,cookiesent,referrer" />
      <add name="Components" value="all:3, http:4" />
</RStrace>
```

2. Optionally, add the HTTPLogFileName and HttpTraceSwitches settings to specify the file name format and the request fields that will be logged. For more information about the supported fields and other HTTP log settings, read the Report Server HTTP Log topic in Books Online.
3. Save the configuration file and restart the Reporting Services service.
4. Issue an HTTP request to the report server (for example, open a report).
5. The log file is created after the first HTTP request is received. If you don't see the latest requests in the file, you may need to restart the Reporting Services service to flush the log writer.

Each time you restart the service, a new HTTP log file will be created.

Viewing the HTTP log

The report server creates the HTTP log file in the LogFiles folder and logs the HTTP requests as users submit report requests and navigate the report server pages. Here is an extract from my local HTTP log file.

```
#Fields: date time s- activityid c- ip cs- username s- ip s- port s- host cs- method cs- uri- stem cs- uri- query sc- status sc-
bytes cs- bytes time- taken cs- version cs(User-Agent) cs(Cookie) sc(Cookie) cs(Referrer)
12/16/2007 19:08:07 ::1 - ::1 20480 localhost GET /Reports/Reserved.ReportViewerWebControl.axd
?ReportSession=zoayft55j1i2xy451adnfm45&ControlID=182612d5b5ca49afa544c6826066b944&Culture=1033&UICultur
e=9&ReportStack=1&OpType=ReportArea&Controller=ctl139&PageCountMode=Estimate&LinkTarget=_top&&ZoomMode
=Percent&ZoomPct=100&ActionType=Toggle&ActionParam=27iT0R0x0&PageNumber=1 401 -   2669 0 1.1
12/16/2007 19:08:09 ::1 - ::1 20480 localhost GET /ReportServer 401 - 629 10 1.1 localhost - - -
12/16/2007 19:08:10 ::1 - ::1 20480 localhost POST /ReportServer/ReportExecution2005.asmx 401 - 1064 0
```

The report server HTTP log file has the same format as the W3C extended log file in IIS. Therefore, you can use third-party IIS log file viewers to read the report server HTTP log file and analyze the HTTP activity.

13.2.5 Monitoring Server Performance

An important management task is monitoring server utilization of system resources. As an administrator, you can watch resource utilization in real time by monitoring the Reporting Services performance counters. As a part of the setup process, Reporting Services installs various performance counters that cover essential server statistics, including caching, memory utilization, processing, and more.

Understanding Reporting Services performance objects

The SQL Server 2008 setup program installs the following Reporting Services performance objects:

- MSRS 2008 Web Service—This performance objects tracks the utilization and performance of the Report Server Web service application. Recall from chapter 1 that the Report Server Web service application handles interactive report viewing operations.
- MSRS 2008 Windows Service— This performance object tracks the utilization and performance of the Background Processor application, which is responsible for handling all tasks that run in an unattended mode. This performance object includes a collection of counters to track these tasks, including snapshot generation and subscriptions.
- ReportServer:Service—This performance object is new in Reporting Services 2008. It monitors HTTP-related events and memory management. It also provides counters that were included with Internet Information Services (IIS), such as number of active connections, bytes sent and received, total requests, and so on.

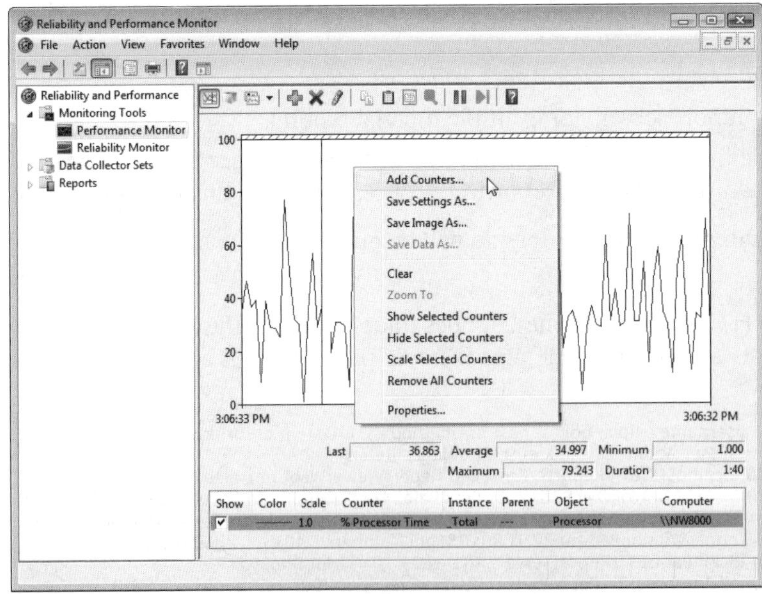

Figure 13.8 Use the Vista Reliability and Performance Monitor to watch the report server utilization in real time.

Configuring performance counters

In Windows Vista, you can use the Reliability and Performance Monitor to monitor the utilization of local or remote servers. In Windows XP and Windows Server 2003, use the Performance tool found in the Administrative Tools program group. The following steps assume Windows Vista operating system.

1. Open Windows Reliability and Performance Monitor from the Administrative Tools program group.
2. Select the Performance Monitor item under the Monitoring Tools section (see Figure 13.8).
3. By default, the Performance Monitor includes only the %Processor Time counter to track the CPU utilization on the local machine. Right-click the graph area and choose Add Counters.
4. In the Add Counters dialog box, enter the server name in the Select Counters from Computer field or leave the default <Local computer> item select to use local performance counters.
5. Scroll down the performance objects list until you find the MSRS 2008 Web Service object, as shown in Figure 13.9.

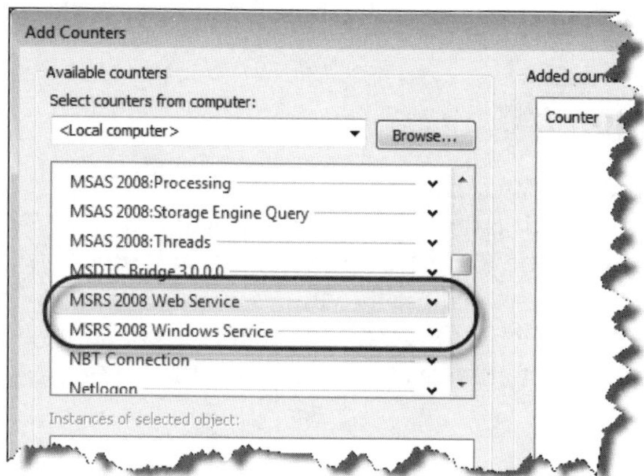

Figure 13.9 Reporting Services includes performance counters to monitor the utilization of the Web service and Windows service.

The Reporting Services performance counters are well explained in the Performance Counters for MSRS Web Service and the Performance Counters for MSRS Windows Service topics in the product documentation, so check Books Online for more information. Suppose you want to watch the total number of on-demand report requests submitted to the server. The following steps will show you how:

6. Click on the down arrow of the MSRS 2008 Web Service performance object to see its collection of counters.
7. Select the Report Requests performance counter.
8. Select the Show Description checkbox at the bottom of the dialog box to see the description of the counter. Note that the Report Requests counter shows the number of active report requests.

   The Instances of Selected Object pane shows all installed instances of Reporting Services. If you have multiple instances, you can select a single instance to track its utilization only. Leave the <All Instances> item selected.
9. Click the Add button to add the counter and press OK to return to the graph.

Monitoring performance counters

To monitor the Report Requests performance counter:

1. Open Report Manager and view some reports.
2. Switch to the Performance console and watch the graph. You should see spikes as the server receives the report requests and processes them.

Performance counters are typically used in stress tests that measure the server throughput and to plan hardware resources that address scalability requirements. This section won't be complete without mentioning two excellent whitepapers (see Resources). Although originally written for Reporting Services 2005, these resources are not outdated. The Planning for Scalability and Performance with Reporting Services whitepaper by John Miller, Anne Janzer, and Brian Welcker shows you how to scale up and out the report server.

The Using Visual Studio 2005 to Perform Load Testing on a SQL Server 2005 Reporting Services Report Server whitepaper by Runying Mao and Heidi Steen teaches you how to use the Visual Studio testing capabilities to stress-test the report server and determine its throughput. In addition, Lukasz Pawlowski, who oversees the Reporting Services management features, provides excellent tips for diagnosing report server issues in his blog (see Resources).

13.3 Configuring Memory Utilization

As a result of monitoring the server, you may find that it consumes too much memory. Or, you may be getting OutOfMemoryException errors with large reports and many users. As I mentioned in chapter 1, one motivation for changing the Reporting Services hosting model is better resource management. Recall also that the primary goal for moving to an on-demand processing model as opposed to an instance-based model is to reduce the memory consumption with large reports. Let's now see what management changes took place in this release to help you manage the server memory.

13.3.1 Understanding Memory Zones

As in the past, by default Reporting Services will use all memory that is available to it as reporting loads increase. However, as a part of configuring a new Reporting Services installation, you can throttle its memory utilization. This is especially important if you run other memory-intensive services on the same box, such as Analysis Services and SQL Server. When you configure the Reporting Services memory utilization, you do so for all Reporting Services applications (Report Manager, Report Server Web service, and Background Processor) as a whole. In other words, you cannot specify memory settings per application.

Table 13.4 The report server memory zones

Memory Zone	Description
Low Memory Pressure	Current requests continue. New requests are accepted. Background processes are given low priority.
Medium Memory Pressure	Current requests continue. New requests might be accepted. Memory allocations are reduced for all of the three Reporting Services applications with relatively larger reductions to background processing.
High Memory Pressure	Current requests are slowed down. New requests are denied (the report server may return HTTP 503 Server Unavailable error). The report server swaps in-memory data to disk.

When there is no memory pressure, each server application requests memory as needed to deliver optimum performance. As the memory pressure builds up, the report server adjusts its memory utilization as described in Table 13.4.

13.3.2 Understanding Memory Configuration Settings

There are four configuration settings that you can specify in the Report Server configuration file (rsreportserver.config) to configure the thresholds for the memory zones. These settings determine how Reporting Services reacts to memory pressure, as shown in Figure 13.10.

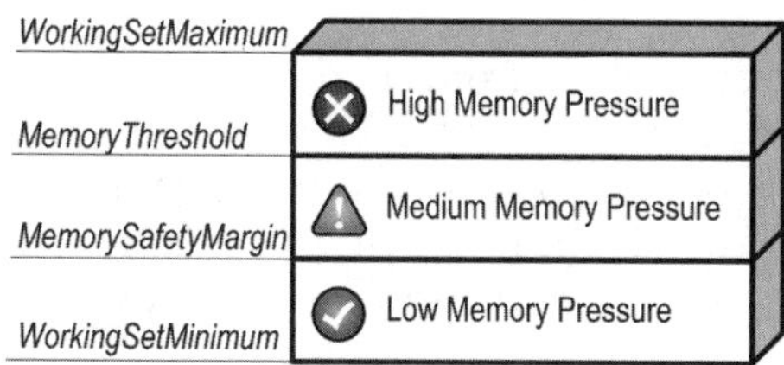

Figure 13.10 Four configuration settings determine how Reporting Services reacts on memory pressure.

Table 13.5 explains the memory settings. The WorkingSetMaximum and WorkingSetMinimum settings are not included by default in the rsreportserver.config but you can add them manually if needed.

Table 13.5 The memory configuration settings

Setting	Description
WorkingSetMaximum (kilobytes)	Specifies the maximum amount of memory that is allocated to Reporting Services in kilobytes. The default value is all available memory. When Reporting Services reaches the WorkingSetMaximum value, it rejects new requests. If existing requests continue to consume additional memory, Reporting Services recycles the application domains.
MemoryThreshold (percentage)	Expressed as a percentage of the WorkingSetMaximum value, MemoryThreshold defines the low boundary of the High Memory Pressure zone. When this value is reached, Reporting Services slows down report processing and re-assigns memory among the three applications. The default value is 90.
MemorySafetyMargin (percentage)	Expressed as a percentage of the WorkingSetMaximum value, MemoryThreshold defines the low boundary of the Medium Memory Pressure zone. It specifies the amount of memory that it is reserved for the rest of the system and cannot be used for reporting operations. The default value is 80.
WorkingSetMinumum (kilobytes)	Specifies the minimum amount of memory which is reserved for Reporting Services. Reporting Services will not release memory below the WorkingSetMinumum threshold. The default value is 60% of WorkingSetMaximum.

Here is a sample section that uses the above settings to configure the Reporting Services memory utilization.

```
<WorkingSetMaximum>2097152</WorkingSetMaximum>
<MemoryThreshold>90</MemoryThreshold>
<MemorySafetyMargin>80</MemorySafetyMargin>
<WorkingSetMinimum>524288</WorkingSetMinimum>
```

This configuration throttles Reporting Services memory utilization to a maximum of 2 GB (WorkingSetMaximum) and minimum of 500 MB (WorkingSetMinimum). The MemoryThreshold and MemorySafetyMargin settings are left to their default values. If you would like to learn more about how Reporting Services allocates memory, read John Gallardo's Memory Management in Reporting Services 2008 blog (see Resources).

TIP If you run SQL Server Database Engine or Analysis Services on the same server as Reporting Services, consider throttling their memory as well. You can configure the SQL Server Database Engine and Analysis Services memory utilization from the server properties (in SSMS, right-click the server and choose Properties). There aren't any memory configuration guidelines because deployment and load scenarios may vary greatly. I recommend you use the Windows Task Manager or Profiler to monitor the server utilization under heavy load and adjust the memory settings as needed.

13.4 Managing the Report Server Database

Recall that the report server stores all report content and metadata in the report server database which consists of the ReportServer and ReportServerTempDB SQL Server databases. Since the report server database is very important, plan to back it up on a regular basis. Sometimes, you may need to replace the report server database.

For example, you may need to install the report server database from another machine to troubleshoot an issue. One way to do so is to replicate the report catalog, such as by using the Report Scripter utility I mentioned in section 13.1.4. A faster approach is to configure the report server to temporarily use a different report catalog. The Reporting Services Configuration Manager includes handy options for quickly connecting to different report catalogs that you want to work with.

13.4.1 Installing the Source Database

Suppose that you have an application that uses Reporting Services 2000 and you need to develop a migration plan for moving a Report Services 2000 installation to the 2008 version. Or, a customer has reported a failed report execution and you need to troubleshoot the issue locally on your development machine. Let's use the Reporting Services Configuration Manager to configure the report server to use the customer's report catalog.

Backing up content

Start by backing up the report server encryption keys and databases.

1. Back up the encryption key on the source server. Since Reporting Services 2000 doesn't have a graphical utility for key management, you need to use the rskeymgmt command-line utility, as follows:

   ```
   rskeymgmt - e - fc:\rskey.snk –p<password>
   ```

   This command will extract the encryption key from the report server database, save it to an rskey.snk file in the root C drive, and protect it with a password that you specify. If the source server is running Reporting Services 2005 or 2008, you can use the Reporting Services Configuration Manager to back up the key. If you don't have access to the source server or you cannot obtain the backup key for security reasons, you can skip this step. However, to activate the server, you will have no other choice but to delete the encrypted content, including connection and subscription credentials.
2. Back up the ReportServer and ReportServerTempDB databases (or detach them) from the source SQL Server.

Creating new databases

Next, create the new report server databases by following these steps:

1. Use the SQL Server Management Studio to create two new databases on the target server and name them ReportServer1 and ReportServer1TempDB.

   Note that we leave the original ReportServer and ReportServerTempDB databases intact so we can revert to the original catalog once we are done testing. Also, note that the new ReportServerTempDB database must follow the <ReportServerDatabaseName>TempDB naming convention. Thus, if you name the new report server database ReportServer1, the temporary database must be named ReportServer1TempDB. This is because the stored procedures in the report catalog use this naming convention to reference the temporary database.

2. Restore the source databases on the target server. Assuming that you want test locally, restore the source databases on your local SQL Server. At this point, you have two ReportServer databases (ReportServer and ReportServer1) and two temporary databases (ReportServerTempDB and ReportServer1TempDB).

   In the next section, you will re-configure the report server to use the ReportServer1 and ReportServer1TempDB databases.

13.4.2 Changing the Report Server Catalog

Each version of Reporting Services has a corresponding version of the report server database. The version is defined as a static number in the report catalog. If you connect to a legacy report server database, the Reporting Services Configuration Manager will automatically upgrade the database. You cannot downgrade a report server database. For example, you cannot configure Reporting Services 2005 to use a 2008 catalog.

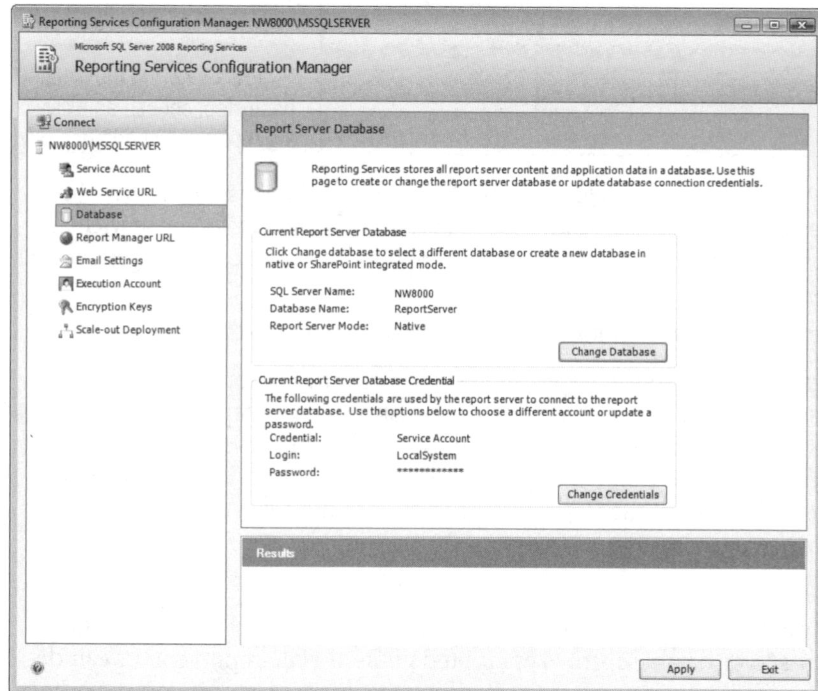

Figure 13.11 Use the Reporting Services Configuration Manager to manage the report server database.

Using the Report Server Database Configuration wizard

The Reporting Services Configuration Manager certainly makes it easier to manage the report server database. The following steps show you how simple it is to select a different database to use with the current report server instance.

1. Open the Reporting Services Configuration Manager and select the Database page, as shown in Figure 13.11.This page lets you change the database or change the credentials to connect to the database.

2. Click the Change Database button to start the Report Server Database Configuration Wizard.
3. The Action step lets you create a new report server database or use an existing one. Choose the Existing Report Server Database option.
4. In the Database Server database, specify the server name that hosts the existing database, such as localhost if this is your computer, and the credentials to connect to the server.
5. In the Database step, expand the Report Server Database drop-down list and select the ReportServer1 database, as shown in Figure 13.12.

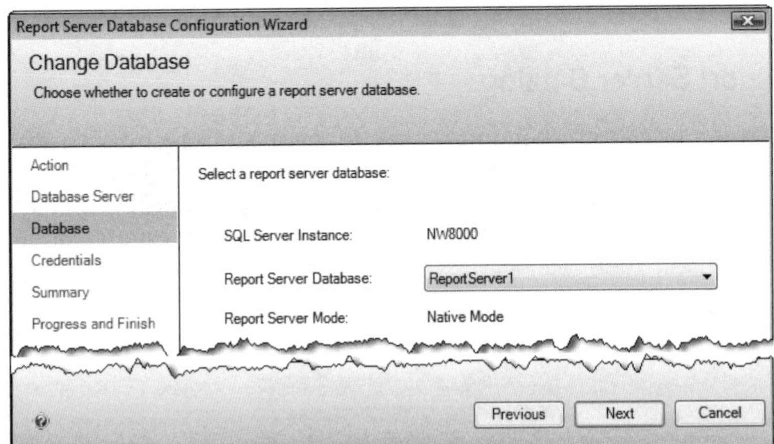

Figure 13.12 In the Database step, choose an existing report server database.

6. In the Credential step, specify the credentials to connect to the new database. Leave the Service Credentials option selected to connect under the identity of the report server service account. The Report Server Database Configuration Wizard will grant the necessary rights to the service account to connect to the database.
7. In the Summary page, review the configuration information and click Next.

In the Progress and Finish page, watch the Reporting Services Configuration Manager configuring the database in several steps. In the Progress and Finish step, the Reporting Services Configuration Manager verifies the database version number and upgrades if needed. It also grants the service account read rights to the database. If all is well, the database will be configured successfully. In case of an error, the Reporting Services Configuration Manager will show the error message next to the configuration step.

Activating the server

You are halfway done. As a last step, you need to activate the server to use the new database. This is because the report server database stores encrypted content. The report server can decrypt this content only if it has the same encryption key as the source server. If you don't have a backup key, you have no other choice but to delete the encrypted content by clicking the Delete button in the Encryption Keys page or executing the following command-line command:

```
RsKeyMgmt.exe -d
```

This will remove any encrypted content, including connection strings, stored credentials, and subscription owner information. Consequently, use the Report Manager to re-configure the data sources and subscriptions to make the reports operational. Assuming you have the encryption key, follow these steps to initialize the server.

1. In Internet Explorer, navigate to http://localhost/ReportServer. You will get the following error:

```
The report server installation is not initialized. (rsReportServerNotActivated)
```

   You will get this error also with other conditions, such as when changing the service account in the Windows Services applet instead of in the Reporting Services Configuration Manager.
2. In the Reporting Services Configuration Manager, select the Encryption Keys page.
3. Click the Restore button and restore the encryption key from the source server.
4. At this point, the report server should be initialized and ready to go.
5. In the Reporting Services Configuration Manager, click the Scale-out Deployment tab. It should list one server only.

   If you see duplicated servers, Reporting Services should still work but you may want to delete the "orphan" instance by selecting the second server and clicking the Remove Server button. If this doesn't work, open the report server configuration file (rsreportserver.config), locate the InstanceID element toward the top of the file, and note its identifier. This is the instance identifier of the initialized instance. Open the Keys table in the report server database and delete the row that has a different installation identifier (InstallationID column).

13.5 Summary

As an administrator, you need to ensure that the server functions correctly and performs optimally. In this chapter, we covered advanced management techniques that will help you meet this goal. When the Microsoft-provided management tools are not enough, you can write your own management application that integrates with the report server management endpoint. I provided a RsRequestViewer utility which will help you to understand which management APIs to call and how to call them.

Consider automating mundane management tasks by creating Reporting Services scripts and execute them with the Reporting Services Script Host. The Reporting Services WMI provider lets you manage the configuration settings of any Reporting Services 2008 installation on the network. Reporting Services provides various options for monitoring the server. Analyze the Execution Log as a first step to troubleshoot performance issues. Inspect the trace log to troubleshoot error conditions. Finally, use the Performance Console to watch the server utilization. Establish a maintenance plan to back up the report server database on a regular basis. Use the Reporting Services Configuration Manager to manage the report server database.

Now that we covered the first two phases of the report lifecycle, report authoring and management, let's see how we can deliver reports to users and custom applications.

13.6 Resources

Microsoft DebugView for Windows
(http://tinyurl.com/yngv5c)—Microsoft DebugView is an application that lets you monitor debug output on your local system.

Reporting Services Scripter
(http://www.sqldbatips.com/showarticle.asp?ID=62)—Reporting Services Scripter is a free tool that lets you script all Microsoft SQL Server Reporting Services catalog items to aid in transferring them from one server to another.

Planning for Scalability and Performance with Reporting Services
(http://tinyurl.com/34fh67)—This paper provides information about the scalability characteristics of different Reporting Services implementation architectures. It also offers guidelines, suggestions, and tips for running your own performance tests with Microsoft SQL Server Reporting Services.

Using Visual Studio 2005 to Perform Load Testing on a SQL Server 2005 Reporting Services Report Server
(http://tinyurl.com/2l5k3q)—This technical article shows you how to use the Microsoft Visual Studio 2005 Team System to stress-test a Microsoft SQL Server 2005 Reporting Services deployment.

How to diagnose issues when running reports in the Report Server?
(http://tinyurl.com/268vr3)— Lukasz Pawlowski provides excellent tips for diagnosing Report Server issues.

How to: Configure a Report Server for Remote Administration
(http://tinyurl.com/4c23rc)— Learn how to enable a remote server for WMI access.

How to: Configure a Report Server for Remote Administration
(http://tinyurl.com/5rwqsq)—Learn how to configure the RSExecRole database role.

Scriptomatic 2.0 Utility
(http://tinyurl.com/3rw63l)—Helps you write WMI scripts.

Memory Management in Reporting Services 2008 by John Gallardo
(http://tinyurl.com/5abcbb)—Explains how memory allocation works.

PART 5

Integration

One of my favorite Reporting Services features is its open and extensible architecture which supports a wide range of integration scenarios. Consequently, developers can report-enable any custom application, irrespective of the programming language used to code the application or the targeted platform on which the application runs.

Reporting Services provides URL access and Web service access options for integrating report clients with the report server. With URL access, report clients request a report by sending its URL address to the server. The Report Server Web service goes beyond report viewing only and provides full-featured programming access to the report server.

If you are a developer tasked with embedding reports in a .NET application, your first stop should be the ReportViewer controls that are bundled with Visual Studio 2008. The ReportViewer Windows Forms control is used to embed reports in .NET Windows Forms application projects. The ReportViewer Web server control is for hosting reports in ASP.NET projects. Both controls support remote and local processing modes that control where the report is processed.

An organization that only occasionally reviews its data through spreadsheets or canned reports is probably missing the strategic value of SQL Server 2008. Once you've successfully mastered the basics of reporting, you may find that it is time to "graduate" to OLAP and Analysis Services. You can integrate Reporting Services with Analysis Services to implement reporting solutions that leverage the best features of these two technologies. Reports can draw data from Analysis Services cubes or data mining models. Reports can also leverage the Analysis Services end-user features, including report actions and translations.

Chances are your company is already using SharePoint to manage documents and collaborate online. Reporting Services supports a deep integration with SharePoint that lets you view and manage reports from a SharePoint site. Microsoft has provided the necessary tools to construct report web parts and implement dashboard pages in Windows SharePoint Services and Microsoft Office SharePoint Server.

Chapter 14

Integration Fundamentals

Reporting is an essential part of every complete software solution. However, report-enabling a custom application can be challenging if your reporting tool has limited integration capabilities and a proprietary architecture. Fortunately, Reporting Services provides open programming interfaces that support a wide range of integration scenarios.

Recall that deployed reports can be delivered on demand or via subscriptions. I covered subscribed report delivery in chapter 12. This chapter discusses how report clients can integrate with Reporting Services to request reports on demand. It starts with a side-by-side comparison of the two integration methods: URL access and Web service. Each approach is explored in detail so that you can learn essential syntax, steps, and when to use each one. Finally, the chapter concludes by walking you through the implementation details of a sample application that demonstrates programming techniques for requesting reports on demand via URL access and the Web service.

14.1 Understanding Reporting Services Integration

Recall from chapter 1 that Reporting Services is a server-based platform for deploying and centrally managing reports on a server. In addition to the report server engine, Reporting Services includes Report Manager—a web-based application for managing and viewing reports. Although Report Manager is adequate for many on-demand reporting scenarios, you may at times find that you need more flexibility than what Report Manager can offer. For example, you may want to let end users export a report to a given format as a one-step operation by clicking a report link. Or, a distributed application may need to generate reports in the middle tier.

Reporting Services was designed from the ground up as a developer platform and can meet a wide range of integration scenarios. However, with flexibility comes the need to make some up-front decisions about report navigation and functionality that the reporting solution must support. Before you can make these decisions, you will need in depth knowledge about the Reporting Services integration options, which I'll discuss next.

14.1.1 Understanding Integration Options

There are two ways to integrate report clients with Reporting Services: URL access and Web service. Figure 14.1 shows how these options fit into the Reporting Services architecture.

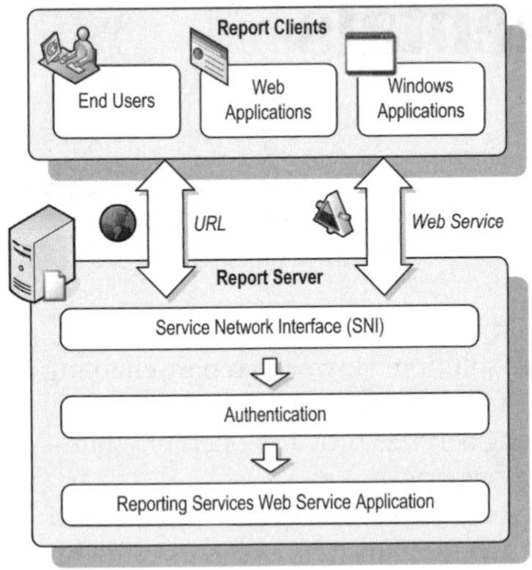

Figure 14.1 Reporting Services supports URL access and Web service integration options.

Regardless of the integration option used, requests are received by the Service Network Interface (SNI) from HTTP.SYS and forwarded to the authentication module to obtain the identity of the user or application that makes the request. The call is then forwarded to the Report Server Web service to process the request.

Introducing URL access

With URL access, report clients (which could be end users or custom applications) request a report by sending its URL address to the server. This is not much different than requesting a web page. The report client can submit the report request via the HTTP GET or HTTP POST protocols. For example, here is how you would request the Product Sales by Category report that you authored in chapter 3 by URL via HTTP GET:

```
http://<servername> /reportserver?/AMRS/Product Sales by Category&Month=1&Year=2004
```

The part of the URL address before the question mark specifies a valid report server Web Service URL, followed by the catalog path of the report and the report parameters.

NOTE Replace <servername> in all URL link examples in this chapter with the machine name of the computer that Reporting Services is installed on, such as *localhost* if Reporting Services is installed locally.

When you submit the above request, the report server redirects you to the HTML Viewer (ReportViewer.aspx page) whose unescaped URL looks like this:

```
http://<servername>/ReportServer /Pages/ReportViewer.aspx?/AMRS/Product Sales by Category&Month=1&Year=2004
```

The server redirects to HTML Viewer when the following conditions are true:

- The specified catalog item is a report or a linked report.
- The report is requested by URL.
- The requested export format is HTML4.0 or unspecified.
- The rc:Toolbar device information setting is True or unspecified.

Behind the scenes, HTML Viewer leverages the ReportViewer Web server control to render the report on the server side. The control includes the standard report toolbar that lets the user perform common report actions, such as printing the report. I'll cover the ReportViewer Web server control in detail in chapter 15. The main advantage of the URL access integration option is its simplicity. However, URL access is limited to report viewing only and doesn't provide management features. This is where the Report Server Web service comes in.

Introducing Web service

Reporting Services provides four Web service endpoints for full-featured programming access to the report server, which are listed in Table 14.1.

Table 14.1 The Report Server Web service endpoints

Endpoint	Default contract address	Purpose
ReportService2005	http://<servername>/reportserver/ ReportService2005.asmx?wsdl	Management API for a report server in native mode
ReportService2006	http://<servername>/<Site Name>/ _vti_bin/ReportServer/ReportService2006.asmx?wsdl	Management API for a report server in SharePoint integration mode
ReportExecution2005	http://<servername>/ReportServer/ ReportExecution2005.asmx?wsdl	Execution API for report rendering and execution
ReportServiceAuthentication	http://<servername>/<Site Name>/_vti_bin/ReportServer-/ReportServiceAuthentication.asmx?wsdl	Authenticating users in SharePoint integration mode

You are already familiar with the management endpoints, as you used them in chapter 13 to program management tasks. The ReportExecution2005 endpoint provides a slew of methods for rendering live reports and handling report interactive features. The ReportServiceAuthentication endpoint applies only to SharePoint integration mode when SharePoint is configured for Forms Authentication. Reporting Services 2008 doesn't introduce version 2008-specific endpoints. It only extends the ReportExecution2005 endpoint with new versions of some methods (e.g.; Render2) to support new report rendering features, such as page estimation versus actual pagination modes. You should use version 2 methods as they are more efficient.

As with any other Web service, the Report Server Web service uses the Simple Object Access Protocol (SOAP) protocol, which is layered on top of HTTP. For example, here is what the raw SOAP request may look like when you invoke the Reporting Services Render API:

```
POST /ReportServer/ReportExecution2005.asmx HTTP/1.1
SOAPAction: "http://schemas.microsoft.com/sqlserver/2005/06/30/reporting/reportingservices/Render"
Host: localhost
Content- Length: 670
<soap:Envelope xmlns:soap="http://schemas.xmlsoap.org/soap/envelope/"
xmlns:xsi="http://www.w3.org/2001/XMLSchema- instance" xmlns:xsd="http://www.w3.org/2001/XMLSchema">
<soap:Header>
<ExecutionHeader xmlns="http://schemas.microsoft.com/sqlserver/2005/06/30/reporting/reportingservices">
     <ExecutionID>ak0ed2iw1pl5jjvoyieap455</ExecutionID>
</ExecutionHeader>
</soap:Header>
 <soa p:Body>
  <Render2 xmlns="http://schemas.microsoft.com/sqlserver/2005/06/30/reporting/reportingservices">
     <Format>HTML4.0</Format>
     <DeviceInfo><DeviceInfo>
     <Toolbar>False</Toolbar>
  </Render>
 </soap:Body>
</soap:Envelope>
```

Fortunately, the .NET Framework abstracts the SOAP technicalities so you don't have to know much about SOAP to program Reporting Services. Thanks to the .NET Web service support, invoking a web method is not much different than invoking a local object.

14.1.2 Choosing an Integration Approach

Choosing between URL access and Web service integration options depend on your functional and operational requirements. In the following section, I'll discuss the pros and cons of each integration option and provide recommendations for when to use each one.

Integration options at a glance

Table 14.2 provides a high-level feature comparison between URL access and the Web service. I'll be quick to point out that.NET developers have a third option (not shown in Table 14.2) for report-enabling .NET custom applications, which is to use the Visual Studio ReportViewer controls (discussed in detail in chapter 15). If you are a .NET developer, you should definitely consider these controls when you need to embed reports in custom applications.

Table 14.2 URL access vs. Web service integration options

Feature	URL Access	Web Service
Features	Report viewing only	Full-featured access
Integration effort	Low	High
Report toolbar	Yes	No
Interactive Features	Yes	No
Object-oriented access	No	Yes
Request generation	Typically client side	Both client and server
Performance	Faster	Slower

In general, deciding between URL access and the Web service is straightforward. If all you need is an easy way to view reports, consider URL access as it requires minimum integration effort. Choose Web service integration when your application requires full-featured access to the report server or when you need to generate reports programmatically.

TIP The URL access and Web service options are not mutually exclusive. For example, a custom application can use the Web service for report navigation and management and URL access for report viewing. The Integration Options demo, which I will discuss in section 14.4.2, demonstrates this integration scenario.

Let's see how integration options stack against each other in more detail.

Evaluating integration options

Examining Table 14.2, we can see that URL access is easier to implement. In the simplest case, the end user can add a report link to the browser favorites list and click the link to request the report on demand. The Web service integration option requires more programming effort to invoke web methods and present the report to the end user.

When you request a report by URL, the report server navigates to the ReportViewer.aspx page. This page generates a handy report toolbar that lets you initiate common reporting actions and set report parameters. By contrast, the report toolbar is not available when you integrate with the Web service. URL access and HTML support all interactive features, such as drilldown, document maps, and navigation links. In comparison, interactive features are not available when programming the Report Server Web service.

NOTE The ReportExecution2005 endpoint does provide methods for report interactivity, such as Sort, ToggleItem, and so on, which were introduced to support the ReportViewer controls. However, these methods require item identifiers which are not available at design time and cannot be obtained programmatically. This makes the interactive methods not very useful to developers who target the Web service for report rendering.

Sometimes, you may need more programming control over how the report request is generated. This is where the Web service scores better. As its name suggests, SOAP lets developers interact with the report server in an object-oriented way. In addition, the report server exposes exceptions as SOAP faults, so developers can handle errors in code. By contrast, URL access embeds the error message in the report.

When the user clicks a report link, the report request originates on the client side of the application and assumes direct access to the report server. This could be an issue in cases where an additional layer, such as a business logic layer, exists between the consumer and the report server. The Web service is more flexible in this case as the custom application can submit both on the client and on the server.

URL access fares better in terms of performance. Rendering a report by calling the Render method of the Web service increases the report payload by 20-30% because the report server serializes the report content as a byte array. Moreover, the client application must hold the entire report payload in memory, which may lead to memory constraints with large reports.

14.2 Working with URL Access

A report client can request a report by its URL address. This makes the URL address option useful when you need to view the report directly (outside any application), or when you need to embed report links inside custom applications. Customizing the report links requires knowledge of the URL syntax, which I'll discuss next.

14.2.1 Understanding URL Syntax

URL access follows the Uniform Resource Identifier (URI) generic syntax:

```
ReportServerWebServiceURL?[/pathinfo][&prefix:param=value]...n]
```

The ReportServerWebServiceURL is a registered Web Service URL address, such as http://localhost/ReportServer. You can obtain it from the Web Service URL tab in the Reporting Services Configuration Manager. Note that you must append a question mark (?) after the Web Service URL. *Pathinfo* specifies the path to the catalog item. The following URL requests the Product Sales by Category report that is deployed to the AMRS folder on the server:

```
http://<servername>/reportserver?/AMRS/Product Sales by Category
```

With the exception of parameter names, the URL syntax is not case-sensitive. You can use all lower case, all upper case, or any combination in between. The parameter names must be specified exactly as they are declared. For example, the following link generates an rsUnknownReportParameter error because it references a month parameter instead of Month:

http://<servername>/reportserver?/AMRS/Product Sales by Category&month=1&Year=2004

Understanding URL parameter syntax

URL access supports various parameters you can use to control report generation, including passing report parameter values or exporting a report in a given format. Similar to handling URL queries, each parameter is prefixed with an ampersand (&) and is specified as a name-value pair. If the parameter prefix is omitted, a report parameter is assumed. For example, the following link passes Month and Year parameters to the Product Sales by Category report:

http://<servername>/ReportServer/Pages/ReportViewe r.aspx?/AMRS/Product Sales by Category&Month=1&Year=2004

If specified, the prefix must be one of the following:

- rs—Use the *rs* prefix to specify a command parameter.
- rc—Use the *rc* prefix to pass a device information settings.
- dsu—Specifies a user name with reports whose data sources are configured to prompt the user for credentials.
- dsp—Specifies a password with reports whose data sources are configured to prompt the user for credentials.

Don't worry if you don't immediately understand the concepts of command and device information settings. I will provide examples in the next sections.

About URL encoding

As you've probably noticed when testing the above links, the browser automatically encodes the link according to URL encoding standards. For example, here is what the URL-encoded link to the Product Sales by Category report looks after the ReportViewer.aspx page redirect:

http://<servername>/ ReportServer/Pages/ReportViewer.aspx?/AMRS/Product%20Sales%20by%20Category

Specifically, space characters are replaced with "%20". A space character in the parameter portion of the URL is replaced with a plus character "+". A semicolon in any portion of the string is replaced with the characters "%3A."

TIP Although both the encoded and decoded links work, sometimes you need a "clean" link, for example when you want to include a URL in documentation or in an email. I've found the URL Escaper utility (see Resources) useful to restore the original link from its decoded counterpart. It can perform bi-directional encoding/decoding.

14.2.2 Requesting Catalog Items

Besides reports, URL access lets you request other catalog items, such as folders, resources, and data sources. The output depends on the type of the catalog item requested. Let's see how we can use URL access to request different types of catalog items, starting with folders.

Requesting folders

When a folder is requested, the report server returns the folder content as a list of hyperlinks. Only catalog items that the interactive user is authorized to browse are included in the list. Besides exploring the report catalog, requesting a folder can be useful for obtaining the URL link to a particular resource. For example, the following URL link displays the content of the AMRS folder, as shown in Figure 14.2:

http://<servername>/ reportserver?/AMRS

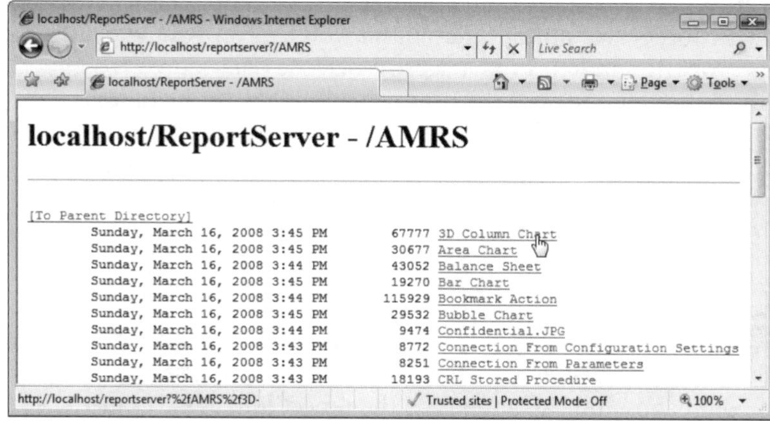

Figure 14.2 When you request a folder, the report server shows the folder content.

Let's say I want to send a user a link to the 3D Column Chart report. I can right-click the report link, click Properties, and copy the URL link from the Properties dialog box. If you don't specify a folder (http://<servername>/reportserver), the report server returns the content of the root (Home) folder. As a first step of troubleshooting a report server, I request this link to make sure that the server is operational.

For faster performance on a folder request, use the ListChildren command. The ListChildren command returns a list of child items, which only occurs if the item type is a folder. If this command is not specified, the report has to infer the resource type. For example, the following link performs better because you tell the server that the AMRS resource is a folder:

```
http://<servername>/ reportserver?/AMRS&rs:Command= ListChildren
```

Requesting resources

Recall that you can upload files such as images, HTML web pages, and XSL Transformation files to the report catalog. When you request resources by URL, the report server displays the resource content. The following URL link shows the Confidential.jpg image in the browser:

```
http://<servername>/ reportserver?/AMRS/Confidential.JPG&rs:Command= GetResourceContents
```

By adding the GetResourceContents command to the URL, you instruct the server to process the requested item as a resource.

Requesting data sources

If the URL link requests a data source, the server returns the data source definition. The following link requests the AdventureWorks2008 data source in the Data Sources folder:

```
http://<servername>/ reportserver?/Data Sources/AdventureWork2008s&rs:Command= GetDataSourceContents
```

The server returns the definition of the AdventureWorks2008 data source:

```
<DataSourceDefinition>
  <Extension>SQL</Extension>
  <ConnectString> Data Source="(local)";Initial Catalog=AdventureWorks 2008;</ConnectString>
  <UseOriginalConnectString>False</UseOriginalConnectString>
  <OriginalConnectStringExpressionBased>False</OriginalConnectStringExpressionBased>
  <CredentialRetrieval>Store< /CredentialRetrieval>
  <WindowsCredentials>False</WindowsCredentials>
  <ImpersonateUser>False</ImpersonateUser>
  <UserName>reader</UserName>
  <Enabled>True</Enabled>
</DataSourceDefinition>
```

In this case, the AdventureWorks2008 data source is configured for standard security (Credentials Stored Securely in the Report Server option). Recall that you can verify how the data source is set up by viewing its properties in Report Manager. When the data source is configured for standard security, the definition includes the user name but it never includes the password. However, if the credentials are embedded in the connection string, the data source definition will show the connection string verbatim. Consequently, a user who has View Data Sources rights (the standard Browser role doesn't include View Data Sources) will be able to see the credentials. For this reason, avoid embedding credentials in the connection string.

14.2.3 Requesting Reports

URL access is most commonly used to request reports that are deployed to the server. Reporting Services supports various commands you can append to the report link to customize the report content and presentation.

Basic report link

The following link requests the Area Chart report without passing report parameters:

http://<servername>/ ReportServer?/AMRS/Area Chart**&rs:Command=Render**

The Render command is optional but recommended for performance reasons because it instructs the report server to process the requested item as a report. If the requested report has parameters, and one or more of those parameters is missing a default value, the HTML Viewer will present a parameter input area so that the user can enter values. Each parameter must be specified before the report is displayed in the viewer. What this means is that the end user must specify the values for all report parameters to view the report. If all parameters have default values, the HTML Viewer shows the report rendered with those default values.

Passing report parameters

You can pass parameter values in the URL link by prefixing each parameter name-value pair with an ampersand (&). The following link requests the Area Chart report for year 2004:

http://<servername>/ ReportServer?/AMRS/Area Chart**&CalendarYear=2004**&rs:Command=Render

Note that you must specify the parameter *name* (CalendarYear) instead of the parameter *prompt* (Calendar Year). Similarly, if the parameter has a value and a label, you must enter the parameter value after the equal sign. In the case of a multivalued parameter, you can pass multiple values by repeating the parameter for each value. The following link requests the Area Chart report for North America and Europe:

http://<servername>/ ReportServer?/AMRS/Area Chart**&CalendarYear=2004&Territory=1&Territory=7** ↵
&rs:Command=Render

You may need to review the report definition of the Area Chart report to understand this link. The Area Chart report defines the Territory parameter as a multivalued parameter that obtains the available values from a query. The parameter value is bound to the SalesTerritoryKey dataset field, while the parameter label is derived from the SalesTerritoryGroup field. Execute the query of the Territory dataset and verify that the SalesTerritoryKey value for North America is 1 and the SalesTerritoryValue for Europe is 7.

To pass a null value for a parameter that is configured to allow null values, add isnull=true to the parameter name, such as CalendarYear:isnull=true. Use a value of 1 or 0 for Boolean parameters. Culture-sensitive report parameters, such as dates, times, and currencies, are interpreted using the browser language. However, you can pass the ParameterLanguage command to force the server to interpret parameters for a given culture. Consider the following link:

```
http://<servername>/ ReportServer?/AMRS/Sales Orders By Date&Date=7/4/2004&SalesOrderNumber=74253
```

If the browser language is English (United States) [en-US], the Date parameter will be interpreted as July 4th, 2004. However, if the browser language is set to German (Germany) [de-DE], the server will interpret the date as April 7th, 2004. In the following link, the Parameter-Language command is used to evaluate the date parameter in the en-US locale independently of the browser language:

```
http://<servername>/ ReportServer?/AMRS/Sales Orders By Date&Date=7/4/2004&SalesOrderNumber=74253 ↵
&rs:ParameterLanguage=en-US
```

Alternatively, you can specify DateTime parameters in the format YYYY-MM-DDTHH:MM:SS, which is based on the International Organization for Standardization (ISO) 8601 standard and it is independent of the browser language:

```
http://<servername>/ReportServer?/AMRS/Sales Orders By Date& Date=2004-07-04&SalesOrderNumber=74253
```

Exporting reports

You may need to export a report to one of the supported formats right away, bypassing the HTML output that is generated by default. You can do so by appending the Format command to the report URL link. For example, this URL exports the Bubble Chart report to PDF:

```
http://<servername>/ ReportServer?/AMRS/Bubble Chart&Country=Germany&TopCount=5 ↵
&rs:Command=Render& rs:Format=PDF
```

The export format that you enter after the Format command must correspond to a name of a registered renderer, as specified under the Render element in the rsreportserver.config file. If the Format command is omitted, the report server assumes HTML4.0. The report server informs the report client about the content type by adding a content-type element to the response header. For example, when the report is requested in PDF, the report server adds an "application/pdf" content type. As a result, the browser will pop up the familiar prompt that asks the user whether to open or save the report as a file.

14.2.4 Working with Device Information Settings

Recall from chapter 7 that each renderer supports various device information settings that can be used to customize the exported report. Besides using them in the rsreporserver.config, you can append one or more device information settings to the report link to tailor the output of a specific report. Remember to denote each setting with the "rc:" prefix. Incorrect device information settings, such as misspelled settings, are ignored by the report server. Renderers ignore settings they don't understand.

Customizing the HTML Viewer

When you request a report in HTML, the report server redirects you to the HTML Viewer page that shows the rendered report. The HTML renderer supports various device information settings that you can use to configure the report toolbar of the HTML Viewer. Suppose you want to hide the report parameters so that the user cannot change them in the HTML Viewer. The following URL requests the Redial Gauge report and uses the Parameters device information setting to hide the parameter prompt area:

http://<servername>/ reportserver?/AMRS/Radial Gauge&rs:Command=Render& **rc:Parameters= False**

If you want to collapse only the parameter area, then use the rs:Parameters=Collapse setting. If you want to hide the entire toolbar, use the Toolbar=False setting:

http://<servername>/ reportserver?/AMRS/Radial Gauge&rs:Command=Render& **rc:Toolbar= False**

It is important to understand what happens when you hide the toolbar (rc:Toolbar=False). In this case, the report request bypasses the HTML Viewer entirely. Your request will be sent directly to the HTML renderer. This means you won't get redirected to the ReportViewer ASPX page and you will see the entire report in one HTML page. It also means that you will get errors rather than prompts for unspecified report parameters (the same behavior as when exporting to other formats). The server will also use cookies (by default) to correlate the client with the execution session for subsequent requests, such as paging, rather than using the page ViewState and URL parameters when the ReportViewer Web server control is used.

The DocMap setting lets you hide the document map in a report that supports this interactive feature:

http://<servername>/ reportserver?/AMRS/Interactive Features&rs:Command=Render **&rc:DocMap= False**

The Zoom device information setting lets you zoom a report as an integer value or a string constant, such as Page Width or Whole Page. The following link zooms out the Interactive Features report to a whole page:

http://<servername>/ reportserver?/AMRS/Interactive Features&rs:Command=Render **&rc:Zoom= Whole Page**

You can also change the appearance of the HTML Viewer with a custom cascading stylesheet (CSS). Let's say you want to make the parameter drop-down list wider to accommodate long parameter values.

1. Copy the HtmlViewer.css file located in the \Program Files\Microsoft SQL Server\MSRS10-.MSSQLSERVER\Reporting Services\ReportServer\Styles folder and save the copy in the same folder. Let's say the name of the new file is MyStylesheet.css.

NOTE The default styles that the HTML Viewer uses are embedded in resource files. Consequently, changes to the original HtmlViewer.css have no effect. The HTMLViewer.css file is for your reference only and includes the styles that the HTML Viewer supports. You must create a new CSS file to apply custom styles.

2. Add the following style to MyStylesheet.css:

```
SELECT
{
   font- size          : 8pt;
   font- family        : Verdana;
   width               : 200px
}
```

To understand what's going on, recall HTML uses a SELECT element to render a drop-down list. This style essentially says "apply these format settings to any SELECT element on the page". Consequently, the width of the parameter drop-down (as well as other drop-down lists, such as Zoom and Format) will be set to 200px.

3. Save MyStylesheet.css.

There are two ways to reference a custom stylesheet. First, you can use the Stylesheet device setting in the report URL to apply the stylesheet on per report basis, such as:

http://<servername>/ reportserver?/AMRS/Interactive Features?**rc:Stylesheet= MyStylesheet**

Or, if you want to apply the custom styles to all reports, add a new HTMLViewerStyleSheet element to the rsreportserver.config file, such as:

```
<Configura tion>
...
  <HTMLViewerStyleSheet>MyStyleSheet</HTMLViewerStyleSheet>
...
</Configuration>
```

Exporting to HTML

Of the remaining device information settings for HTML, the most interesting settings are HTMLFragment and LinkTarget. Use the HTMLFragment setting to strip the HTML and BODY elements from the report page. This setting is more useful when rendering a report programmatically with the Report Server Web service than URL access. Let's suppose you generate a web page on the server side. You want to remove the HTML and BODY elements so that you can embed the report inside a web page that already has HTML and BODY elements. To do so, you can pass HTMLFragment=True to the server when you invoke the Render method. For testing purposes, use the following link to generate the Jump to Bookmark report as an HTML fragment:

```
http://<servername>/ reportserver?/AMRS/Jump to Bookmark&rs:Command=Render ↵
&rc:HTMLFragment= True&rc:Toolbar=False
```

Once the report is generated, right-click the report page in Internet Explorer and click View Source. Notice that the page doesn't have HTML and BODY elements. The HTMLFragment setting is supported also by the MHTML renderer.The LinkTarget setting displays the report in a specific frame on a web page or opens the report in a new browser window. For example, the following hyperlink targets a frame called "main":

```
<a href="http://server/reportserver?/ AMRS/Jump to Bookmark &rs:Command=Render&rc :LinkTarget=main"
target="main">Click here for the Territory Sales Drilldown sample report</a>
```

Pointing the link target to the name of your own frame could be useful if you want the link to always open side-by-side with the report. The LinkTarget device setting doesn't support _parent and _self settings.

Exporting to Excel

The Excel renderer also has device information settings that you can specify. Perhaps the most interesting Excel device information setting is SimplePageHeaders. When SimplePageHeaders is False (default setting), the page headers are rendered in the first row in the Excel worksheet. If you set SimplePageHeaders toTrue, the report server generates the page headers and footers as Excel headers and footers. Since the Excel headers and footers are very basic, this may result in some fidelity loss, such not honoring the textbox padding settings.

1. Export the Product Sales by Category report to Excel using the following link and click the Open button in the File Download dialog box:

```
http://<servername>/ ReportServer?/AMRS/Product Sales by Category&rs:Command=Render ↵
&rs:Format=Excel &rc:SimplePageHeaders= True
```

2. In Excel, open the page header and footer settings. The exact steps depend on which version of Excel you are using. In Excel 2007, click the Page Layout menu. In the Page Setup group, click the Dialog Box Launcher (the downward arrow) next to Page Setup.
3. In the Page Setup dialog box, click the Header/Footer tab and note that the report footer was exported as Excel footer.
4. Print the Excel spreadsheet.

Notice that each report group prints on a separate page and each page has a footer section.

Exporting to Word

Recall that the Word renderer doesn't support interactive features. As such, the device information settings for Microsoft Word are used to control how interactive features are converted when the report is exported to Word. One such setting is ExpandToggles, which controls the toggled state of the drilldown sections. When ExpandToggles is False (default setting), a report with drilldown features will be exported with all sections collapsed and you won't be able to expand the sections in Microsoft Word. However, setting ExpandToggles to True will expand the drilldown sections. The following link exports Product Sales Crosstab Drilldown with expanded sections:

```
http://<servername>/ reportserver?/AMRS/Product Sales Crosstab Drilldown&rs:Command=Render ↵
&rs:Format=WORD &rc:ExpandToggles=True
```

By default, URL navigation links are not included in an export to Word. If you want URLs in a report to appear in a Word document, change OmitHyperlinks setting to False. To do the same for drillthrough links, set OmitDrillthroughs to False.

Exporting to PDF

The PDF renderer supports device information settings that let you control the page layout and the range of the pages exported. Let's say you want to export the Range Chart report to PDF but change the page layout from portrait to landscape. To do so, you can specify the PageWidth and PageHeight settings in the report link:

```
http://<servername>/ reportserver?/AMRS/Range Chart&rs:Command=Render&rs:Format=PDF ↵
&rc:PageWidth=11in&rc:PageHeight=8.5in
```

The page size and margin settings must specify the size in inches.

Exporting to Image

The Image renderer supports several Graphics Device Interface (GDI) output formats, including BMP, EMF, GIF, JPEG, PNG, and TIFF. The OutputFormat device information setting lets you specify the preferred format. If OutputFormat is omitted, TIFF is assumed. The following link exports the Product Sales Crosstab report as a JPEG image:

```
http://<servername>/ reportserver?/AMRS/Product Sales Crosstab&rs:Command=Render ↵
&rs:Format=IMAGE&rc:OutputFormat=JPEG
```

Exporting to CSV

The Comma-Separated Values (CSV) renderer exports only the report data. Note that only textbox report items export their content to CSV. You cannot export the content of chart and gauge regions to CSV. Exporting to CSV can be useful when you need to feed report data into another application. If you export large reports to Excel and you need only the report data, you may get better performance by exporting the report first to CSV and opening the CSV file in Excel.

NOTE Opening CSV exported files in Excel was problematic with previous releases of Reporting Services. This was because the CSV renderer would default to Unicode encoding which Excel didn't handle very well. Consequently, Excel showed the entire content in a single column. To address this issue, Reporting Services 2008 introduces an ExcelMode device setting which is enabled by default. In this release, the CSV renderer defaults to UTF-8 encoding. However, it appears that Excel still has some issues understanding delimited files with formatted values. Instead of opening the file directly in Excel, use Excel's Text Import Wizard to bring the file into Excel.

The CSV renderer supports device information settings that control the output, including the field delimiter, field qualifier, record delimiter, and header rows. The following link exports the Product Sales by Category to CSV. The fields will be delimited with a tab character and format settings will be ignored. Header rows, such as group headers, will not be exported:

```
http://<servername>/ reportserver?/AMRS/Product Sales by Category&rs:Command=Render ↵
&rs:Format=CSV&rc:FieldDelimiter=%09&rc:UseFormattedValues=False&rc:NoHeader=True
```

The default field delimiter is a comma (,). The FieldDelimiter setting lets you specify a delimiter string, which must be URL-encoded. To encode the delimiter, use a percentage sign followed by the ASCII character code, such as %09 for the tab character. The URL Escaper utility I mentioned will encode the value for you automatically.

Exporting to XML

The XML renderer is a pure data renderer that exports only the report data in XML format. In chapter 7, I demonstrated how you can customize the XML output by using XML-specific report item properties and XSL Transformations. The XML renderer supports additional device information settings that let you further customize the XML output, including the XSLT file, format settings, indentation, XSD schema reference, encoding, and the file extension. The following link exports the Product Sales by Category report in XML. The resulting XML document will be indented and it will not contain XSD schema references:

```
http://<servername>/ reportserver?/AMRS/Product Sales by Category&rs:Command=Render ↵
&rs:Format=XML&rc:Indented=True&rc:OmitSchema=True
```

14.3 Working with the Report Server Web Service

Another option to report-enable custom applications is to use the Report Server Web service. Web services let developers use open standards, such as XML, SOAP, WSDL, and UDDI, to integrate Web applications using Internet protocols and connections. The wide-spread adoption of these standards allows you to integrate Reporting Services with many types of report clients and platforms. As long as it is SOAP-aware, any client application can invoke the Report Server Web service. For example, a Java-based application running on UNIX can integrate with the Report Server Web service to generate reports.

14.3.1 Getting Started in Report Server Web service

The Report Server Web service provides full-featured access to report server functionality. Consequently, you can implement complete management and report viewing tools using your favorite programming language. In this next section, I'll walk you through the basic steps required to implement a .NET console application that integrates with the Report Server Web service to generate a report.

BEST PRACTICE In general, you should avoid building additional layers on top of the Web service to simplify integrating custom clients with Reporting Services. The ReportViewer controls, for example, assume direct access to the report server. This forces you to implement a proxy layer if you want to use the ReportViewer controls when the report server is not directly accessible. Furthermore, security gets trickier when another layer is introduced between the client and the report server.

Creating a web reference

While you can work with SOAP messages directly, the .NET Framework can handle the plumbing infrastructure for you. When you add a Web reference in your project, Visual Studio creates a Web service proxy from the Web service contract that is described in Web Services Description Language (WSDL). The proxy represents the remote Web service as though it is a local object to your application. It handles mapping parameters to XML elements, sending the SOAP message over the network, and encapsulating the results as objects.

Recall that the ReportExecution2005 endpoint of the Report Server Web service provides report execution and rendering features. Follow these steps to set up a Web reference to the ReportExecution2005 endpoint:

1. Use Visual Studio to create a new C# Console Application project. In the New Project dialog box, select .NET Framework 2.0 and name the project *WebServiceDemo*. We target .NET Framework 2.0 to work with "classic" web references instead of the Windows Communication Foundation (WCF) service references that .NET Framework 3.5 would generate by default. Chapter 13 explains why web references are preferable.
2. In the Solution Explorer pane, right-click the WebServiceDemo project node and click Add Web Reference.
3. In the Add Web Reference dialog box, enter the URL of the ReportExecution2005 endpoint in the URL field and press Enter. For example, use the following URL to reference the ReportExecution2005 endpoint on a local server configured to listen on port 80 (use localhost:8080 with Windows XP):

   ```
   http://localhost/reportserver/reportexecution2005.asmx?wsdl
   ```

   Visual Studio parses the WSDL of the ReportExecution2005 endpoint and lists the web methods it supports, as shown in Figure 14.3.

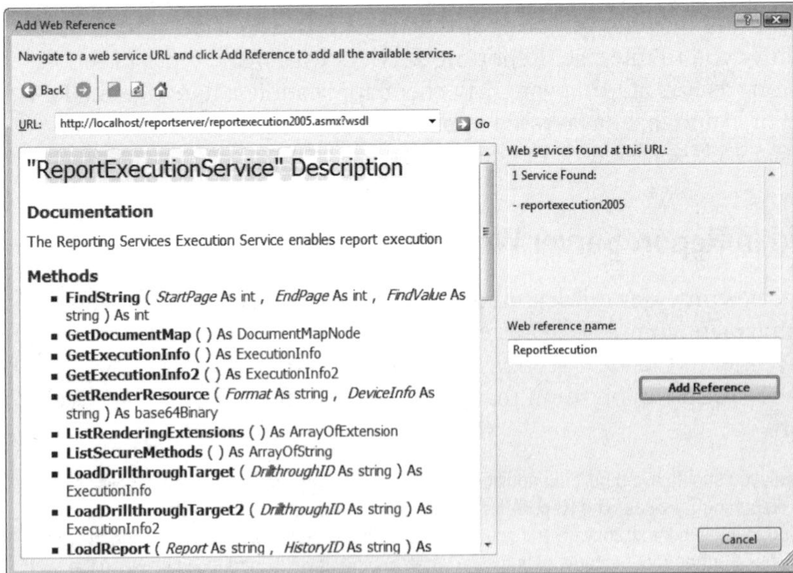

Figure 14.3 Create a Web reference to the ReportExecution2005 endpoint.

4. Enter *ReportExecution* in the Web Reference Name field and click the Add Reference button to create the reference.

Examining the web service reference

Let's take a moment to understand what Visual Studio does behind the scenes when it creates the Web reference. Visual Studio adds references to System.EnterpriseServices, System.Web.Services, and System.Xml assemblies in the References folder and a ReportExecution Web reference to the Web References folder.

1. Click the Show All Files toolbar button in the Solution Explorer pane.
2. Expand the Web References folder and the ReportExecution folder under it.

   Notice that Visual Studio has generated Reference.map and reportexecution2005.wsdl files.

3. Double-click the reportexecution2005.wsdl file and notice that it describes the service definition of the ReportExecution2005 endpoint in XML.
4. Expand the Reference.map folder and double-click the Reference.cs file.

   The Reference.cs file contains the source code of the classes exposed by the ReportExecution2005 endpoint. The ReportExecutionService class represents the proxy for the ReportExection2005 endpoint. The fully qualified name of the ReportExecutionService class is WebServiceDemo.ReportExecution.ReportExecutionService.

5. Select the WebServiceDemo.ReportExecution.ReportExecutionService item in the class drop-down list. Expand the method drop-down list on the right to see the list of methods of the ReportExecution2005 endpoint.

   Now that you've configured the Web service, you are ready to use it to generate reports programmatically.

14.3.2 Rendering Reports

For the purposes of this demo, you will render programmatically the Interactive Features report you authored in chapter 5. This practice demonstrates the following programming tasks:

- Load a report for execution.
- Inspect the report configuration.
- Set report parameters.
- Render a report.
- Save the report payload to disk.

The WebServiceDemo report represents the complete solution for this practice. You'll need Visual Studio 2008 to work with the source code. The code sample uses version 2 methods of the ReportExecution2005 endpoint.

Loading reports for execution

Hypertext Transfer Protocol (HTTP) is a stateless protocol, which means that the Web server discards any client state after it has processed the request. Consequently, the Web server doesn't know whether different requests come from the same client. At the same time, the client may need to execute tasks in succession, such as setting the report parameters, rendering the report, page navigation, and so on. Recall from chapter 12 that the report server maintains execution sessions so it can identify report clients and keep the report execution alive between requests. By default, the server times out the execution session after 10 minutes.

As a first step of rendering a report, you need to load the report for execution by calling the LoadReport2 method. The LoadReport2 method creates an execution session and returns an ExecutionInfo2 object that contains useful configuration information about the report.

1. Add the following namespaces at the top of the Program.cs source file:

```
using System.IO;
using System.Web.Services.Protocols;
using WebServiceDemo.ReportExecution;
```

2. Add the following code to the Main method:

```
string historyID = null;
string reportPath = "/AMRS/Interactive Features";
ReportExecutionService rs = new ReportExecutionService();
rs.Credentials = System.Net.CredentialCache.DefaultCredentials;
rs.Url = "http://localhost/reportserver/ReportExecution2005.asmx";
ExecutionInfo2 execInfo = rs.LoadReport2(reportPath, historyID);
```

The code creates an instance of the ReportExecution proxy class. Next, the code sets the proxy's credentials to System.Net.CredentialCache.DefaultCredentials. Consequently, the call to the report server will go out under the identity of the interactive user. When you add a Web reference to your project, Visual Studio configures the proxy to read the URL address of the endpoint from the application configuration file (app.config). The code demonstrates how you can overwrite the endpoint address as needed by setting the proxy's Url property.

Next, the code invokes the LoadReport2 method and passes the report path. The report server creates an execution session and starts the session expiration clock. The report server returns configuration information about the report, which the code saves in the execInfo object.

Analyzing the report configuration

If you know how the report is configured, you can skip this step and proceed with rendering the report. Otherwise, you can inspect the ExecutionInfo2 object that was returned by the LoadReport2 method. Among other things, it can tell you what parameters the report accepts and give you detailed information for each parameter, such as the parameter name, type, default values, and so on. The WebServiceDemo application traverses the ExecutionInfo2 object and displays some of its properties to the screen for testing purposes:

```
Console.WriteLine("SessionID: {0}", execInfo.ExecutionID);
Console.WriteLine("Credentials Required: {0}", execInfo.CredentialsRequired);
Console.WriteLine("Parameters Required: {0}", execInfo.ParametersRequired);

foreach (ReportParameter p in execInfo.Parameters)
{
   Console.WriteLine("Parameter Name: {0}, Default Value: {1}", p.Name,
      String.Join(",", p.DefaultValues == null ? new string[0] : p.DefaultValue s));
}
```

The code displays the session identifier from execInfo.ExecutionID. Alternatively, you can get the session identifier from the proxy's ExecutionHeaderValue.ExecutionID.

NOTE You don't need to worry about the session identifier if you use the same proxy instance and you work with one report at a time. However, executing LoadReport for another report will overwrite ExecutionHeaderValue.ExecutionID and you will "lose" the session identifier for the first report. Consequently, subsequent Web methods for the first report, such SetReportParameters and Render, will fail with the message "Execution 'sessionID' cannot be found." If you mix report executions, you need to save the session identifier and set the proxy's ExecutionHeaderValue.ExecutionID before you call an execution method.

The CredentialsRequired property will be True if the report data source is configured to prompt the user for credentials. In this case, you need to populate an instance of the Data-SourceCredentials class and call the SetExecutionCredentials method before invoking the Render method. If the report data source is configured for Windows Integrated security or standard security, CredentialsRequired returns False.

The execInfo.ParametersRequired property tells you if you must pass parameter values to the report. If the report has parameters and a parameter doesn't have a default value, this property returns True. The code loops through the Parameters collection and displays the name and default values for each parameter. A multivalued parameter may have several default values. The code concatenates the parameter default values by using the String.Join function so it can display them together. Recall that you cannot pass parameters to a report configured for snapshot caching. The AllowQueryExecution property indicates this state.

Passing the report parameters

The Interactive Features report takes Month and Year parameters. Both of them have default values. Suppose that you want to render the report with different parameter values. You can accomplish this by calling the SetExecutionParameters2 method. This method sets the new temporary parameter values that are used for the current execution. It doesn't permanently change the report parameters. You can use the SetReportParameters2 method of the Report-Service2005 endpoint (or ReportService2006 in SharePoint mode) if you want to update the definition of the report parameters in the report catalog:

```
ParameterValue[] parameters = new ParameterValue[2];
parameters[0] = new ParameterValue();
parameters[0].Name = "Month";
parameters[0].Value = "12";
parameters[1] = new ParameterValue();
parameters[1].Name = "Year";
parameters[1].Value = "2003";
rs.SetExecutionParameters2(parameters, null);
```

Start by defining an array of two ParameterValue objects. Set the Name property to the parameter name and Value property to the parameter value.

NOTE I wish Reporting Services were more consistent with parameter structures. As you can see, the ExecutionInfo object returns an array of ReportParameter objects, while the SetExecutionParameters method takes an array of ParameterValue objects. What's really needed is a single collection of parameter objects that provides helper methods to facilitate working with parameters, such as getting a parameter by name. Handling multivalued parameters presents yet another challenge because you need to expand the array to accommodate the multiple values before you call SetExecutionParameters.

Once the parameter array is ready, call SetExecutionParameters2 to update the parameters for the current report execution. Optionally, you can specify the language in which the parameters will be interpreted as the second argument. This works in the same way as the Parameter-Language URL command I discussed in the section 14.2.3. If the language is null, the server will evaluate the parameter value using the current thread culture (the Accept-Language header on the web request). In a browser, the current thread culture is determined by the browser language. A console application or a rich client can overwrite the culture by adding the Accept-Language header to the HttpWebRequest used by the Web service proxy.

Rendering the report

Once the parameters are set, you are ready to render the report in the desired format. This code fragment demonstrates how to render the Interactive Features report in MHTML:

```
string encoding;
string mimeType;
string extension;
Warning[] warnings = null;
string[] streamIDs = null;
string format = "MHTML";
string devInfo = null;
byte[] result = null;
try
{
   result=rs.Render2(format, devInfo, PageCountMode.Estimate, out extension, out encoding,
        out mimeType,out warnings,out streamIDs);
   execInfo = rs.GetExecutionInfo2();
   Console.WriteLine("Execution date and time: {0}", execInfo.ExecutionDateTime);
}
catch (WebException ex)
{
   Console.WriteLine(ex.Message);
}
Using (FileStream stream = File.Create("report.mhtml", result.Length))
{
   Console.WriteLine("File created.");
   stream.Write(result, 0, result.Length);
   Console.WriteLine("Result written to the file.");
}
```

The Render2 method takes several arguments. The Format argument specifies the export format. You can use the DeviceInfo setting to pass one or more device information settings to the renderer. Use the PageCountMode argument (new with version 2 of the Render method) to instruct the server to return an estimated or actual page count. As you've probably guessed, PageCountMode.Estimate is faster because the server guess-estimates the page count instead of having to paginate the entire report.

Once the Render2 method is executed, it returns the name of the renderer used to process the report in the Extension argument. The MimeType argument indicates the Multipurpose Internet Mail Extensions (MIME) type of the report payload, such as multipart\related if the report is exported in MHTML. The Encoding argument indicates the encoding format that the server used to generate the report, such as ASCII. The Warnings argument may return an array of Warning objects that describe any warnings that occurred during report processing. I'll explain the purpose of the StreamIDs argument in the next section.

Next, the code invokes the GetExecutionInfo2 method to refresh the ExecutionInfo2 object and display the date and time the report was rendered. This step is optional. The Render2 method returns the report payload as a byte array. WebServiceDemo saves the report payload in the application folder (\bin\debug\). You can browse the file with Internet Explorer. If WebServiceDemo executes successfully, you should see the following console output when you run the application (Ctrl+F5):

```
SessionID: <sessionID>
Credentials Required: False
Parameters Required: False
Parameter Name: Month, Default Value: 1
Parameter Name: Year, Default Value: 2004
Execution date and time: <current date and time>
Estimated number of pages: 5
File created.
Result written to the file.
Press any key to continue . . .
```

Any exceptions generated by the report server are exposed as SOAP exceptions. Your try…catch block can catch exceptions of the SoapException type and react accordingly.

14.4 Putting It All Together

URL access and Web service are not mutually exclusive. You can leverage both integration options when you report-enable your custom applications. You can use the Web service SOAP for report navigation and management tasks, and URL access for viewing reports on demand.

The Integration Options demo, shown in Figure 14.4, demonstrates how you can use both integration options together. When you click Get Reports, the application retrieves a list of the reports deployed to the specified folder. Once you pick a report in the Report drop-down list, the application displays the report parameters and their default values in the Parameters grid. These tasks use the Web service. You can specify the export format and the integration method for rending the report. The application supports three programming techniques for rendering reports via URL. The URL Web Browser option uses the Visual Studio WebBrowser control to request the report by URL. The URL Shell option shells the report request to Internet Explorer. Both URL Web Request and URL Shell options request reports by URL.

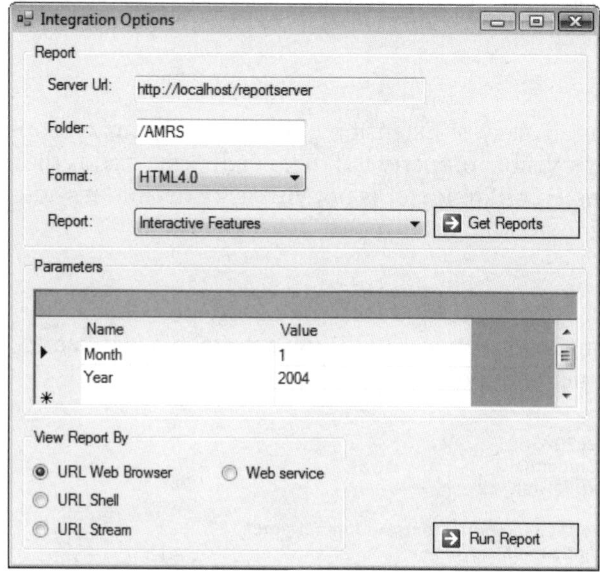

Figure 14.4 The Integration Options sample demonstrates how you can report enable a custom application by using both URL access and the Report Server Web service.

To avoid the SOAP overhead and save memory, the URL Stream option streams the report payload in chunks and save the streams to a file. Finally, the Web service option generates the report by calling the Render Web method and saves the report payload as a file. Both URL Stream and Web Service options shell out to whatever application is associated with the file extension of the saved report, such as Adobe Reader if the report is exported to PDF. More information about each of these view options is presented later in section 14.4.2.

14.4.1 Programming Report Server Web service

The Integration Options sample uses the Report Server Web service for all management tasks, including retrieving the available export formats, obtaining a list of all deployed reports in the specified folder, and getting the report parameters. Before running the sample, right-click the IntegrationOptions project node in Solution Explorer and click Properties to open the project properties. Click the Settings tab and verify that the URLs of the execution and management endpoints match your setup.

Loading the export formats

When the application starts, it calls the LoadFormats method. LoadFormats invokes the ListRenderingExtensions Web method of the ReportExecution2005 endpoint to obtain a list of the registered renderers on the server.

```
private void LoadFormats() {
      ReportExecutionService rs = new ReportExecutionService();
       rs.Credentials = System.Net.CredentialCache.DefaultCredentials;
      Extension[] extensions = null;

      cmbFormat.Items.Clear();
      extensions = rs.ListRenderingExtensions();
      if (extensions != null)
      {
         foreach (Extension extension in extensions)
         {
             if (extension.Visible || extension.Name.StartsWith("HTML4.0")) cmbFormat.Items.Add(extension.Name);
         }
         cmbFormat.Text = "HTML4.0";
      }
}
```

The ListRenderingExtension method returns an array of Extension objects. LoadFormats loops through the list of renderers. If the renderer's Visible property is True, LoadFormats adds the renderer to the drop-down list. Although the HTML renderer is not visible by default, it's added to the list to demonstrate how exporting to HTML affects report images.

Loading the reports

When the user clicks the Get Reports button, the application calls the LoadReports helper method, which uses the management endpoint (ReportServices2005). As a prerequisite, I had to add a project Web reference to the management endpoint.

```
private void LoadReports() {
   RS.ReportingService2005 rs = new RS.ReportingService2005();
   rs.Credentials = System.Net.CredentialCache.DefaultCredentials;
   RS.CatalogItem[] items = rs.ListChildren(txtFolder.Text, false);
   foreach (RS.CatalogItem item in items)
      if (item.Type == ReportService.ItemTypeEnum.Rep ort) cmbReports.Items.Add(item.Name);
   if (cmbReports.Items.Count > 0) cmbReports.SelectedIndex = 0;
}
```

LoadReports calls the ListChidren Web method, which returns a list of all catalog items the user is authorized to view. LoadReports enumerates through the list and adds the item to the cmbReports drop-down list if the item is a report.

Loading the report parameters

When the user selects a report, the application obtains the report parameters by calling the LoadReportParameters helper method.

```
private void LoadReportParameters() {
   ReportExecutionService rs = new ReportExecutionService();
   rs.Credentials = System.Net.CredentialCache.DefaultCredent ials;
   _execInfo = rs.LoadReport2(this.ReportPath, null);
   EntityParameter.ParametersDataTable userParameters = new EntityParameter.ParametersDataTable();
   foreach (ReportParameter p in _execInfo.Parameters)
      userParameters.AddParametersRow(p.Name, String.Join(",", p.DefaultValues));
   grdParams.DataSource = userParameters;
}
```

You can get the report parameters both from the execution and management endpoints. I chose the former because I wanted to cache the ExecutionInfo object so I don't have call LoadReport2 again if the user decides to render the report. Once LoadReportParameters calls LoadReport2, it adds the report parameters to an EntityParameters typed dataset and binds the parameter dataset to the grid control.

Generating reports with the Web service

If the Web Service option is selected, the application generates the report by calling the Render method of the execution endpoint. This is very similar to the WebServiceDemo sample which I discussed previously, so I'll focus only on the new features.

```
private void RunByWS() {
string devInfo = String.Format("<DeviceInfo><StreamRoot>{0}</StreamRoot></DeviceInfo>",    "img");
rs.ExecutionHeaderValue = new ExecutionHeader();
rs.ExecutionHeaderValue.ExecutionID = _execInfo.ExecutionID;
ParameterValue[] parameters = this.GetSoapParameters;
rs.SetExecutionParameters2 (parameters, null);

result = rs.Render2(format, devInfo, PageCountMode.Estimate, out extension, out mimeType,
            out encoding, out warnings, out streamIDs);

if ("ht" == format.Substring(0, 2).ToLower())
   foreach (string streamID in streamIDs)
   {
      byte[] image = rs.RenderStream(format,streamID,null,out optionalString,out optionalString);
      FileStream stream = File.OpenWrite(String.Format("{0}{1}{2}{3}",
         Application.UserAppDataPath, Path.DirectorySeparatorChar, "img", streamID));
      stream.Write(image, 0, image.Length);
      stream.Close();
   }
string filePath = Util.GetFileForReport(reportPath, cmbFormat.Text);
FileStream stream = File.Create(filePath, result.Length);
stream.Write(result, 0, result.Length);
stream.Close();
Process.Start(filePath);
}
```

Recall that the execution methods work within the scope of an execution session. The RunByWS method obtains the ExecutionInfo2 object that was cached in the LoadReportParameters method. Next, RunByWS sets the session identifier by setting the ExecutionHeaderValue.ExecutionID property. Next, the code configures the report parameters by calling the GetSoapParameters property. GetSoapParameters obtains the new parameters values from the grid control. If the user has specified multiple values for a multivalued parameter, GetSoapParameters resizes the ParameterValue array to accommodate the additional values. RunByWS invokes the Render method to generate the report and obtain the report payload as a byte array.

If you are exporting to any format other than HTML, save the report payload to a file and present the report to the end user. Integration Options creates a new file with the appropriate extension and writes the resulting byte array to the file. Finally, it shells out to the external application associated with the file extension.

Rendering image streams

Exporting to HTML requires an extra step because of the way the browser handles images. When processing the report, the report server saves the report images in the execution session. When the rendered report is loaded, the browser spans additional HTTP requests to fetch the images from the server. This works just fine within the lifetime of the current execution session. Once the session expires, however, image URLs won't work anymore and the report won't show the images. This behavior is by design, as rendering to HTML and persisting images out-of-band beyond the session lifetime is not a supported scenario. Now you understand why the HTML renderer is configured as hidden in the rsreportserver.config file.

NOTE In previous releases of Reporting Services, HTML reports generated by calling the Render method wouldn't show external images at all. You either had to use the HTMLFragment device setting or download the image streams. SQL Server 2008 improves upon this by adding the session identifier to the image URL so that the images show up if the execution session is still alive.

Again, this issue is specific to HTML since more "document-centric" renderers, such as MHTML, save images inside the exported report. If you must export to HTML, for example to implement a custom Web-based report viewer control, and you want HTML reports to show images after the execution session has expired, you need to save the images to disk. This requires passing a special StreamRoot device information setting to the Render method.

When the report server processes the report, it will see the StreamRoot setting and will adjust the report image URLs to point to the downloaded image streams. The StreamIDs argument of the Render method returns the stream identifiers of report image items and graphic images (charts, gauges, and custom report items). RunByWS loops through the stream identifiers and calls RenderStream to obtain the image data. Finally, the code saves the image in the user's application data folder. Consequently, instead of pointing to the server, the image URL will reference the local image file similar to the following example:

```
file:///C:/Users/teo/AppData/Roaming/IntegrationOpti ons/IntegrationOptions/1.0.0.0/imge0333b044e8848e2915e90f6
ec9f89e5
```

Since the report images are downloaded as files, the report will show images even after the user session has expired.

14.4.2 Programming URL Access

A custom application can use a variety of techniques to request reports via URL. These techniques range from embedding static URL links in the application presentation layer to streaming reports programmatically. The Integration Options sample demonstrates three ways to render reports programmatically with URL access.

Using the WebBrowser control

Visual Studio includes a WebBrowser control for navigating and displaying Web resources in .NET Windows Forms applications. Thanks to this control, you can easily embed a report in a form. Because the WebBrowser is designed to display Web resources, the application calls the RunByURLWebBrowser method only when the report is exported to HTML. If you select another format, the application shells out to the external application associated with this format by calling the RunByURLShell method.

```
private void RunByURLWebBrowser(){
   ReportBrowser reportBrowser = new ReportBrowser();
   reportBrowser.RenderReport(this.ReportURL);
   reportBrowser.Show();
}
public void RenderReport(string url) {
      Object optional = System.Reflection.Missing.Value;
      txtURL.Text = url.Replace("&", "&&");
      webBrowser.Navigate(url);
}
```

The ReportBrowser form hosts the WebBrowser control. The RunByURLWebBrowser method instantiates the ReportBrowser form. Next, RunByURLWebBrowser obtains the report URL address by calling the ReportURL property and passes it to the RenderReport method of the ReportBrowser form. The ReportBrowser form calls the Navigate method of the WebBrowser control to navigate to the requested report. Consequently, the form shows the familiar HTML Viewer.

Shelling to an external application

Sometimes, you may just need a quick way to show the report programmatically by navigating to the report URL address. You can do this by shelling out the request to the browser, as the RunByURLShell method demonstrates:

```
private void RunByURLShell() { Process.Start("IExplore", this.ReportURL);}
```

Once the code obtains the report URL, it calls the Process.Start method to start Internet Explorer and pass the report URL. The net result is the same as opening Internet Explorer interactively and requesting the report by URL.

Streaming reports

As noted, SOAP facilitates Reporting Services programming but may add some performance overhead. In his Transitioning between SOAP and URL Access blog (see Resources), John Gallardo, a software engineer on the Reporting Services team, demonstrated how you can stream large reports by using the .NET WebRequest and WebResponse objects. The RunByURLStream method builds upon this approach:

```
private void RunByURLStream() {
   string url = this.ReportURL;
   if (cmbFormat.Text.StartsWith("HTML")) url += "&rc:Toolbar=false";
   WebRequest request = WebRequest.Cr eate(url);
   request.UseDefaultCredentials = true;
   string filePath = Util.GetFileForReport(url, cmbFormat.Text);

   using (WebResponse response = request.GetResponse())
   using (Stream readStream = response.GetResponseStream())
   using (FileStream writeStream = new FileStream(filePath, FileMode.Create))
   {
      byte[] readBuffer = new byte[4096];
      int bytesRead = 0;
      while ((bytesRead = readStream.Read(readBuffer, 0, readBuffer.Length)) != 0)
         writeStream.Write(readBuffer, 0, bytesRead);
   }
   Process.Start(filePath);
}
```

RunByURLStream uses the WebRequest object to request the report by URL. Next, the WebResponse object reads the report payload in streams of 4 KB so the application can write them to disk. This avoids loading the entire report into memory. In addition, the SOAP overhead from serializing the report payload into a byte array is eliminated because the report is requested by URL. The ReportViewer controls, which I will discuss in the next chapter, use a similar hybrid approach to render reports. They call down to the Report Server Web service to obtain the report metadata, such the available report parameters. However, the report is rendered by URL.

If you need more programming samples that demonstrate how you can combine URL access with the Web service to provide integrated reporting, take a look at the Microsoft-provided RSExplorer sample. This application is distributed with the Reporting Services 2008 samples, which you can download from www.codeplex.com.

14.5 Summary

Reporting Services provides two communication options for report-enabling external clients. URL access is the fastest and easiest way to request reports but it is limited to report viewing only. The Report Server Web service exposes the entire functionality of the report server but it requires more programming effort.

End users and custom applications can leverage URL access to requests reports with minimum implementation effort. URL access supports various parameters and commands that let you customize report presentation and functionality. The Report Server Web service includes management and execution endpoints. You can program the management endpoint to manage the report catalog. Use the execution endpoint to render reports programmatically.

Having laid out the foundation for integrating custom applications with Reporting Services, let's move on to the next chapter to learn how you can leverage the ReportViewer controls to report-enable .NET clients.

14.6 Resources

URL Escaper
(http://tinyurl.com/25sktr)—Encodes/decodes URL links.

Reporting Services Device Information Settings
(http://tinyurl.com/23xery)—Explains the device information settings supported by the Reporting Services renderers.

Transitioning between SOAP and URL Access
(http://tinyurl.com/33e7wk)—Learn how to stream the report with URL access.

Chapter 15

Reporting For .NET Clients

Recall from chapter 1 that Reporting Services provides URL access and Web service options for integrating custom applications with the report server. Wouldn't it be nice to combine the simplicity of URL access with the power of the Web service to more easily embed reports in your applications? If you are a .NET developer, you are in luck. Visual Studio 2008 includes a set of ReportViewer controls and tools that facilitate report-enabling .NET applications.

This is a code-intensive chapter so be prepared to wear your developer's hat. I'll start by introducing you to the ReportViewer controls. Next, I'll demonstrate how you can leverage the ReportViewer Windows Forms control to render local and remote reports. Then, I'll show you how to accomplish the same tasks using the ReportViewer Web server control. Finally, I'll show you how to report-enable Rich Internet applications that use the Microsoft Silverlight technology. You will need Visual Studio 2008 to work with the source code for this chapter.

15.1 Understanding Embedded Reporting

Embedded reporting is a common requirement for both desktop and web applications. Typically, the application presents a list of reports to the user so the user can pick which one to view. The application then generates the report and displays it in the presentation layer. Depending on how involved your requirements are, your application might also call for validating report parameters, distributing report definitions with the application, and binding reports to application datasets. The ReportViewer controls are designed to handle these tasks.

15.1.1 Understanding the ReportViewer Controls

The first thing you should know about the ReportViewer controls is that there are two of them. The ReportViewer Windows Forms control is used to embed reports in .NET Windows Forms application projects. The ReportViewer Web server control is for hosting reports in ASP.NET projects. Visual Studio determines which version to use based on the type of the application project. For example, if you create a Windows Forms Application project, you get the ReportViewer Windows Forms control automatically.

Understanding the similarities

Although targeting different application types, the ReportViewer controls share the same look and feel and have similar programming interfaces. They are both written in managed code. Common features include the following:

- Report toolbar—Similar to the HTML Viewer, which is based on the ReportViewer Web server control, both controls include a handy report toolbar that provides convenient access to common report operations, including handling report parameters, paging, zooming, searching, printing, and exporting. Unlike the HTML Viewer, the ReportViewer toolbar is customizable. For example, the developer can hide or replace the toolbar with a custom toolbar if needed.
- Report processing modes—Both controls supports remote and local processing modes that control where the report is processed. In remote mode, the ReportViewer controls submit report requests to a report server and display the rendered report. In local mode, ReportViewer processes and renders reports.
- Object model—Both controls provide similar object models that let developers configure the controls through code at run time or by setting the control properties at design time. The controls raise events at different stages of report processing to give the application a chance to execute report pre-processing or post-processing tasks.

Understanding functionality differences

Naturally, there are architectural differences between the two controls that are caused by the application types that each one targets. Table 15.1 shows these differences.

Table 15.1 Functionality differences between Windows Forms and Web Server ReportViewer controls

Feature	ReportViewer Windows Forms	Report Viewer Web Server
Default presentation format	Graphics Device Interface (GDI)	HTML
Deployment	On the client	On the server
Printing	.NET Framework print support	Downloadable ActiveX control
Report processing	Asynchronous	Synchronous or asynchronous

The default presentation format of the ReportViewer Windows Forms control is Graphics Device Interface (GDI). In contrast, the ReportViewer Web server control renders reports to HTML (see Resources for more information about browser support). Client-side deployment requirements are fundamentally different. Whereas the ReportViewer Windows Forms control must be installed on every client that runs the application, the ReportViewer Web server control doesn't require any client installation because the report is processed on the web application server.

Printing through the ReportViewer Windows Forms control is supported through the .NET Framework, while its web counterpart requires downloading the RSClientPrint ActiveX control, which I discussed in chapter 11. Finally, the ReportViewer Windows Forms control always uses a background thread to generate the report, whereas you can configure the Web Server control to process server reports synchronously or asynchronously.

Upgrading from Visual Studio 2005

Veteran Reporting Services users might recall that Microsoft introduced the ReportViewer controls with Reporting Services 2005 and Visual Studio 2005. Because Reporting Services 2008 is backward compatible with Reporting Services 2005, an application can use the Visual Studio 2008 controls to connect to both Reporting Services 2005 and 2008. Visual Studio 2008 brings incremental changes to the ReportViewer controls.

Design-time enhancements

A new Reports Application project template has been added to the Reporting section of Visual Basic and C# projects. This project template gives you a jump start on configuring the ReportViewer controls to render local reports.

On the report authoring side, a new Report Wizard guides report authors through the steps of creating a basic report. After the wizard is finished, you can edit the report by using the Visual Studio Report Designer. The Expression Editor has been extended to support common sample expressions.

Run-time enhancements

The ReportViewer controls now compress reports that are exported to the Adobe PDF format. The ReportViewer Web Server control can now print a report in local processing mode.

Installing ReportViewer controls

Although they're related to Reporting Services, the ReportViewer controls are *not* shipped with either Reporting Services or Business Intelligence Development Studio. Instead, they are bundled with Visual Studio 2008 and documented in the Visual Studio product documentation (see Resources). Therefore, to work with the controls at design time, you need Visual Studio 2008. The viewers are physically implemented in six .NET assemblies, as shown in Table 15.2.

Table 15.2 ReportViewer controls are implemented in five assemblies

Assembly	Description
Microsoft.ReportViewer.WinForms.dll	The Windows Forms control implementation.
Microsoft.ReportViewer.WebForms.dll	The Web Server control implementation.
Microsoft.ReportViewer.Common.dll	Functionality common to both controls.
Microsoft.ReportViewer.ProcessingObjectModel.dll	The processing object model for processing reports.
Microsoft.ReportViewer.Design.dll	Design-time functionality of ReportViewer Windows Forms. Not required at run-time.
Microsoft.ReportViewer.WebDesign.dll	Design-time functionality of ReportViewer Web server. Not required at run-time.

The ReportViewer controls are freely redistributable. To make distribution easier, Microsoft has provided a Microsoft ReportViewer Redistributable 2008 package (see Resources). Remember that the ReportViewer controls have a dependency on .NET Framework 2.0, so prior to deploying your application you will need to install the .NET Framework 2.0 on the client machine if your desktop application uses the Windows Forms control. Similarly, you will need .NET Framework 2.0 on the server if your ASP.NET application uses the Web Server control.

The redistributable package installs the 2008 version of the controls in the Global Assembly Cache (GAC) side-by-side with the 2005 ReportViewer controls. Consequently, applications targeting the older controls will continue to run unaffected. If you wish to upgrade legacy applications to use the Visual Studio 2008 controls, you need to change the assembly references in your project. The version of the Visual Studio 2005 ReportViewer controls is 8.0.0.0, while the version of the Visual Studio 2008 controls is 9.0.0.0.

NOTE The SQL Server 2008 setup program doesn't install new versions of the ReportViewer controls for public use. Consequently, the Visual Studio 2008 ReportViewer controls use the Reporting Services 2005 processing engine and support only the RDL 2005 format in local processing mode. Microsoft is expected to release upgraded versions of the controls in the SQL Server 2008 timeframe. Currently, only the HTML Viewer, which Report Manager and URL access leverage for report viewing, uses the latest version of the ReportViewer Web server control.

15.1.2 Understanding Report Processing Modes

Both ReportViewer controls support remote processing mode and local processing mode for report generation. The processing mode affects the entire report lifecycle so it's important to understand how each mode works. Figure 15.1 illustrates the differences.

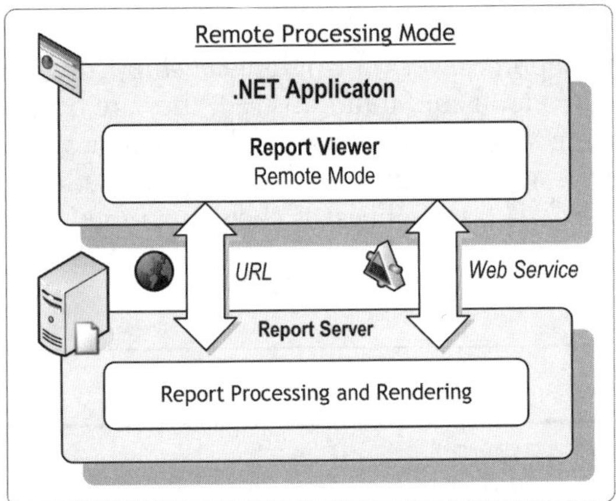

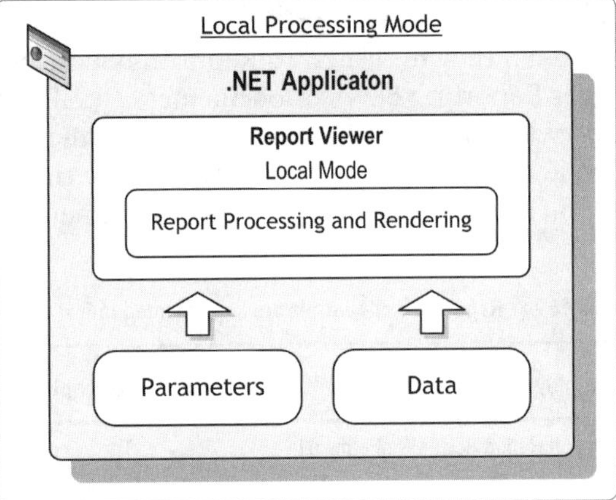

Figure 15.1 The ReportViewer controls support remote and local processing modes.

Remote processing mode

In remote processing mode, the report server processes and exports a report that is requested on demand. This lets you use the familiar report lifecycle for report authoring, management, and delivery. You use the BIDS Report Designer or Report Builder 2.0 to author the report definition. When the report is ready, you deploy the report to the report catalog to make it available to report clients. To embed the report in custom applications, you configure the ReportViewer in remote processing mode and point it to the server report.

In remote processing mode, ReportViewer essentially acts as a presentation layer to the report server. Working in tandem, the report server does the heavy lifting to process and render the report, while the ReportViewer control displays the streamed report in your application. Because the native presentation format of ReportViewer Windows Forms control is GDI, report requests that originate from the control are exported in GDI using the RGDI renderer.

NOTE As noted in chapter 1, Reporting Services 2008 introduces a new RPL renderer capable of producing an output format that is an independent representation of the report layout and data. The next generation of the ReportViewer controls will offload some of the server processing by performing the final stage for converting RPL to their native presentation formats. Currently, only the Reporting Services 2008 ReportViewer Web server control, which is used by the HTML Viewer, utilizes the new RPL format.

Behind the scenes, a ReportViewer that is configured for remote processing uses both URL access and SOAP to integrate with the report server. Specifically, the Report Server Web service is used for management and execution tasks, including retrieving report and parameter metadata, passing parameters, and carrying out user-initiated commands, such as printing and searching. For performance reasons, ReportViewer uses URL access for previewing and rendering reports.

When should you use remote processing mode? Consider using it when your application is hosting reports that are deployed on a report server. One of the benefits of this scenario is that you can centrally manage all of your reports in a single repository—the report catalog. You can leverage all report server features, including scheduling, security, session and snapshot execution, and linked reports.

Local processing mode

In local processing mode, ReportViewer handles report processing and rendering, not the report server. In fact, in this mode, the report server is not used at all. Instead, the application supplies the ReportViewer control with parameters and data (such as an application dataset or a business object). ReportViewer processes the report locally via internal interfaces.

Before you get too excited about not needing a report server (and a SQL Server 2008 license), evaluate both options carefully. Local mode is limited to report processing and rendering. As such, it is hardly a replacement for a full blown report server that provides enterprise reporting features for centralized management, caching, subscription delivery, security, and so on. In addition, in local mode, export formats are limited to PDF and Excel only.

You might be curious about how you would author report definitions if you don't have SQL Server 2008 and the Reporting Services report designers. As it turns out, Microsoft bundled a scaled-down report designer in Visual Studio 2008, which I'll refer to as Visual Studio Report Designer. It is scaled-down because it doesn't support data sources and report preview (recall that the application supplies data to the report). As it stands, this designer is capable of producing RDL 2005 format only, which is the only format supported by ReportViewer in local mode. The unfortunate side effect is that your local reports cannot include any of the Reporting Services 2008 design enhancements, such as tablix, charts, and gauges. Essentially, you are stuck with the Reporting Services 2005 design support until Microsoft updates the Visual Studio 2008 designer.

When should you use local processing mode? Consider using it when simple processing is sufficient for the reports that you distribute with your application, and you do not require the features and components that are part of a SQL Server 2008 installation. You should also consider using it if your report requirements call for implement flexible data binding strategies. For instance, a custom application can retrieve an ADO.NET dataset from the data access layer or a web service, and then bind the dataset to the report. As with previous releases, binding datasets to server reports is not supported and requires a custom data extension, as I demonstrate in chapter 18.

15.2 Reporting for Windows Forms Clients

Now, let's start exploring the ReportViewer controls by starting with ReportViewer Windows Forms. Most of the information presented in this chapter applies to the ReportViewer Web server control. In section 15.3, I'll explain the differences.

Windows Forms applications are often referred to as rich clients to emphasize the fact that they enjoy the full feature set of the operating system on which they run. Yet, providing comprehensive reporting capabilities in these applications traditionally has been difficult. Let's see how ReportViewer Windows Forms control can help.

15.2.1 Getting Started with the ReportViewer Windows Forms Control

The ReportViewer Windows Forms control lets you embed reports in Windows Forms custom applications. It supports a cornucopia of features, including image handling and sessions, report interactive features, printing and print preview, export to multiple formats, integration with report server security, and snapshots. In the next several pages, we'll take a closer look at how to use this control by working through the WinReporter sample shown in Figure 15.2.

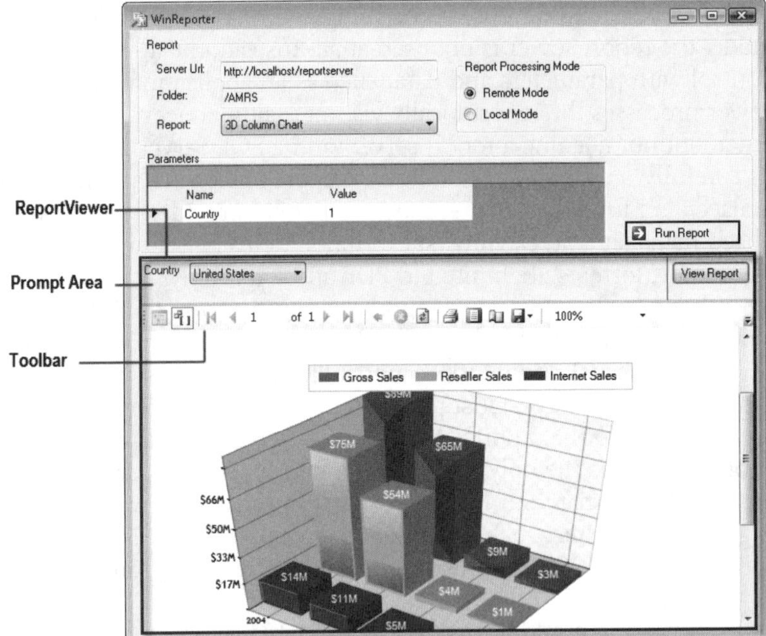

Figure 15.2 The WinReporter sample demonstrates the remote and local processing modes of the ReportViewer Windows Forms control.

Introducing the WinReporter sample

The WinReporter sample that accompanies this chapter demonstrates various features of the ReportViewer Windows Forms control. It builds upon the IntegrationOptions sample I discussed in chapter 14, except that it uses ReportViewer for viewing reports on demand. The source code of WinReporter is included in the WinReporter Visual Studio project (WinReporter.csproj). Before running the sample, right-click the WinReporter project node in Solution Explorer and click Properties to open the project properties. Click the Settings tab and verify that the AdventureWorks 2008ConnnectionString and ReportServerUrl configuration settings match your setup.

WinReporter demonstrates both the remote and local processing modes of ReportViewer by letting the user select one of the Report Processing Mode options. In remote mode, WinReporter connects to the report server to retrieve a list of reports deployed to the specified folder. In local mode, WinReporter loads the list with the names of the report definition files from the local file system.

When you select a report, the application obtains the report parameters from ReportViewer and displays them in the Parameters grid. You can change the parameter values if needed. Click the Run Report button to view the report. In remote mode, ReportViewer passes the parameters to the server report and delegates report processing to the server. In local mode, ReportViewer bypasses the report server. The application supplies the report with both parameters and data. ReportViewer processes and renders the report.

Configuring ReportViewer Windows Forms

Follow these steps to add the ReportViewer Windows Forms control to a form:

1. Start Visual Studio 2008 and create a Windows Forms Application project.
2. Open a form in design mode.
3. Expand the Reporting tab of the Visual Studio toolbox. Double-click the MicrosoftReportViewer control to add it to the form.

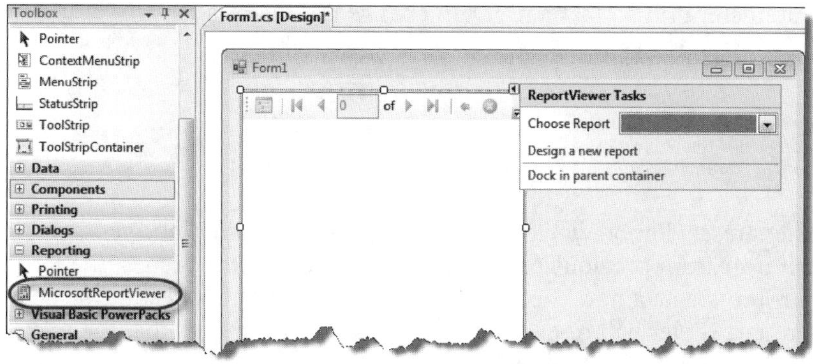

Figure 15.3 You can use the ReportViewer Tasks panel to configure the control at design time.

When you drop the ReportViewer control on the form, Visual Studio adds references to Microsoft.ReportViewer.Common, Microsoft.ReportViewer.WinForms, System.Web, and System.Web.Services assemblies which are used by the control. To avoid fully qualifying ReportViewer objects in code, import the Microsoft.Reporting.Winforms assembly, as follows:

```
using Microsoft.Reporting.WinForms;
```

As with other Windows Forms controls, you can configure the ReportViewer at design time by using its smart tag panel. For example, you can use the smart tags panel to configure ReportViewer to render a specific server or local report. To open the smart tags panel, click the small arrow in the upper right corner of the control, as shown in Figure 15.3. Use the Visual Studio Properties window to access all control properties. For example, you can hide the toolbar by setting the ShowToolBar property in the Properties window.

Alternatively, you can configure ReportViewer programmatically at run time by working with its object model. In remote mode, you interact with the ServerReport object, while in local mode you use the LocalReport object. These objects expose almost identical programming interfaces, so switching from one mode to another is easy.

15.2.2 Working with Remote Processing Mode

Programming for the remote processing mode is simple because the report server performs all of the complex operations of collecting the report data and processing the report. In the simplest case, you only need to point the control to the remote report. More involved scenarios may require an additional effort to handle report parameters and configure security.

Handing report parameters

ReportViewer can handle report parameters for you. When the ShowParameterPrompts property is set to True (this is the default setting), ReportViewer displays parameter placeholders in the toolbar prompt area. This behavior is consistent with rendering reports in Report Manager. Behind the scenes, the ReportViewer invokes the LoadReport method, which returns an ExecutionInfo object describing the report and the report parameters. The ReportViewer uses this information to configure the parameter prompts and display appropriate controls. For example, it displays a calendar control for DateTime parameters and a multi-select list for multi-valued parameters.

If you need more control over the report parameters, you can hide the prompt area and implement your own user interface. WinReporter demonstrates this approach by loading the report parameters in the Parameter grid so that a user can change their values.

```
private ReportParameterInfoCollection LoadRemoteReportParameters()
{
   reportViewer.Reset();
   reportViewer.ProcessingMode = ProcessingMode.Remote;
   reportViewer.ServerReport.ReportPath = this.ReportPath;
   return reportViewer.ServerReport.GetParameters();
}
```

LoadRemoteReportParameters resets ReportViewer to restore the default values and remove any residual state that is left over from previous report executions. Behind the scenes, the Reset method causes the control to create a new execution session even if you request the same report. Consequently, the report server will re-execute the report. It also means that the report parameter values will be reset to their initial defaults.

The code configures ReportViewer for remote processing mode and sets the ReportPath property to the report catalog path. LoadRemoteReportParameters calls ServerReport.GetParameters to obtain the parameter configuration. For the sake of simplicity, WinReporter doesn't validate user input for the report parameters. A more realistic implementation should probably include a custom user interface for presenting parameters and validating them against specific business rules.

Generating reports

When you compare the code required for generating reports with the Report Server Web service against equivalent code for the same operation using the ReportViewer control, you'll undoubtedly appreciate the simplicity that the ReportViewer brings to the table. Requesting a server report takes only a few lines of code.

```
internal void RunRemote() {
  reportViewer.Reset();
  reportViewer.ProcessingMode = ProcessingMode.Remote;
  reportViewer.ServerReport.ReportPath = this.ReportPath;
```

```
  ReportParameter[] parameters = UserParametersToReportParameters();
  reportViewer.ServerReport.SetParameters(parameters);
  reportViewer.RefreshReport();
}
```

The RunRemote method configures ReportViewer for remote processing mode. It calls the UserParametersToReportParameters helper method to convert the user parameters dataset to an array of ReportParameter objects that ReportViewer expects. RunRemote calls ServerReport.SetParameters to configure the report parameters. Behind the scenes, ReportViewer calls the SetExecutionParameters API to set the parameters for the current report execution. Finally, RunRemote calls the ReportViewer RefreshReport method to execute and render the report.

TIP Recall that a report may be configured to keep execution snapshots in history. If you need to request a specific history snapshot, set the ReportViewer.ServerReport.HistoryId property to the history identifier. Recall also that you cannot pass parameters to a report configured for snapshot caching. The ServerReport.IsQueryExecutionAllowed property, which wraps ExecutionInfo.AllowQueryExecution), indicates whether you can pass parameters to the report.

By default, exceptions thrown during report processing are embedded in the ReportViewer report pane. However, you can overwrite this behavior by handling the ReportViewer ReportError event. The Exception property of the ReportErrorEventArgs class provides the error that occurred. Setting the Handled property to True prevents ReportViewer from displaying an error message.

By default, ReportViewer will time out the connection to the report server after ten minutes. If your reports take longer to process, increase the ReportViewer.ServerReport.Timeout property or set it to System.Threading.Timeout.Infinite (-1) to prevent a timeout.

Securing ReportViewer

When you work with remote processing mode, you must ensure that you have permission to access the report catalog. As a prerequisite, use Report Manager to set up role-based policies to grant users permission to the report catalog. To meet a variety of security requirements, ReportViewer support different authentication mechanisms.

Windows Integrated security

Out of the box, the report server is configured for Windows Integrated security. This security mode is your best bet when you have Windows Active Directory in place and requests to the report server go under the domain identity (domain\username) of the interactive user.

You don't have to do anything special to configure the Report Viewer for Windows Integrated security. That's because the ReportViewer automatically passes the user identity to the report server by setting the Credentials property of the web service proxy to CredentialCache.DefaultCredentials.

You can also impersonate a specific Windows user other than the current thread user by setting ReportViewer.ServerReport.ReportServerCredentials.ImpersonationUser. This is useful if you already have the impersonation token. In this case, the call to the server goes under one user, but the rest of the application still runs as the interactive user.

Basic authentication

Sometimes, Windows Integrated security is not an option. For example, a vendor may not be able to control the security infrastructure of its customers. In this case, you can configure the report server to use Basic authentication and authenticate the user with specific credentials to the report server. For example, if the report server doesn't belong to an Active Directory domain, you can create local user accounts for each user on the server and pass the account credentials (username and password) to the report server. This takes one line of code:

```
private void SetBasicSecurity()
{
  reportViewer.ServerReport.ReportServerCredentials.NetworkCredentials= new NetworkCredential("Bob", "P@ssw0rd");
}
```

The code assumes that a local Windows account is created on the report server with a user name of "Bob" and password of "P@ssw0rd ". You must use Report Manager to grant the local account rights to view reports.

Custom security

When security requirements rule out Windows-based security, you can configure the report server for custom security. For example, your security requirements may call for supporting an application-based security model where the end user logs in to the application with credentials kept in a database. I'll explain how custom security works in chapter 19. The simplest (and less secure) approach to integrate ReportViewer with custom security is to pass the user credentials explicitly:

```
private void SetCustomSecurity1()
{
    reportViewer.ServerReport.ReportServerCredentials.SetFormsCredentials(null, "uid", "pwd", null);
}
```

Behind the scenes, ReportViewer will call the LogonUser method and cache the authentication ticket for the lifetime of the ReportViewer control instance. ReportViewer also provides a GetFormsCredentials method if you want to retrieve the cached user credentials later on. However, be aware that GetFormsCredentials doesn't return the authentication ticket. This means you will need to keep the user credentials for as long as the application is running. Because this presents a security risk, I recommend you adopt a slightly more involved approach where the application calls LogonUser and caches the authentication ticket. The SetCustomSecurity2 method demonstrates this approach:

```
private void SetCustomSecurity2() {
  ReportServerProxy rs = new ReportServerProxy();
  rs.LogonUser("uid", "pwd", null);
  // Save the authentication ticket and discard user credentials
  reportViewer.ServerReport.ReportServerCredentials.SetFormsCredentials
  (ReportServerProxy.AuthCookie, null, null, null);
}
```

For example, upon application startup, the application can collect the user login credentials and authenticate the user for report server access by invoking explicitly the LogonUser method. Then, the application can save the ticket and discard the user credentials.

Customizing ReportViewer

Besides parameter handling, the ReportViewer object model exposes several other methods to meet more advanced integration requirements. Such requirements might include changing the default rendering format, adding preview, customizing or replacing the toolbar, or localizing the control into a specific language.

Let's start by looking at how you might set the output format. Suppose that you need to export your report to an image format other than TIFF (the default image format). The ReportViewer toolbar doesn't let you pick a specific image format. However, because the ReportViewer object model supports rendering a report programmatically, you can set the image format by calling the ServerReport.Render method which wraps the Render Web service API.

```
byte[] result=reportViewer.ServerReport.Render("PDF",null,null,out mimeType,out fileExtension);
```

Another interesting pass-through method is LoadReportDefinition. The LoadReportDefinition method lets you render a server report without requiring the report to be uploaded to the report catalog. This lets you to implement report previewing. Suppose that your application creates an ad hoc report definition and you don't want to force the user to upload the report to the server before viewing it. The following code shows you how to let users preview the report on the fly:

```
using (System.IO.MemoryStream stream = new System.IO.MemoryStream()) {
     byte[] reportPayload = GetReportDefinition()  //obtain the report definition from somewhere
     stream.Write(reportPayload, 0, reportPayload.Length);
     stream.Position = 0;
     StreamReader reader = new StreamReader(stream);
     reportViewer.ServerReport.LoadReportDefinition(reader);
}
```

NOTE As a prerequisite for invoking the LoadDefinition method successfully, grant rights to execute the Execute Report Definitions system task by assigning user accounts to the System User system role. Be aware that the ad hoc report is processed in the root (Home) folder of the report catalog. Therefore, you must adjust the location of the resources used by the report (images, data sources, etc.) to be relative to the Home folder so that they are rendered properly.

The GetReportDefinition helper method obtains the report definition, such as by loading it from disk or by calling the ReportService2005.GetReportDefinition API. Next, the code prepares a memory stream and a StreamReader object to read from the stream. Finally, the code calls the ReportViewer LoadReportDefinition method to generate the report on the fly.

You aren't limited to the default ReportViewer toolbar, either. You can customize the toolbar to suit your needs. For example, the toolbar may not blend with your application's user interface or you may just want to have more control over the ReportViewer toolbar features. You can hide the toolbar areas you don't want (or the entire toolbar) and implement your own toolbar. If you do that, you'll need to call the appropriate method of the ReportViewer object model when a user initiates the action. As it stands, ReportViewer controls don't let you customize individual buttons on the toolbar.

Suppose you decide to implement a custom toolbar for searching text within reports. To do so, hide the ReportViewer Find toolbar controls (set ShowFindControls to False) and call the ReportViewer Find method manually:

```
reportViewer.Find(searchString, startPage);
```

The potential for customization goes beyond the control itself to include packaging custom code with the control. You might have noticed that ReportViewer is a standard Windows Forms control and is not sealed (NotInheritable in VB.NET). Therefore, there is nothing stopping you from subclassing it whenever it makes sense to do so (for example, to enforce business rules, set precedence, or establish a security context before the control is instantiated).

REAL LIFE I once had to implement a proprietary security model to impersonate the user and package through ReportViewer. To accomplish this, I created a custom class that inherited from the ReportViewer control and handled the security requirements. Once the control was ready, I compiled it and distributed its binary to the application developers to integrate the control with custom applications.

Localizing ReportViewer

You can also localize the ReportViewer user interface by installing the appropriate ReportViewer language pack. The ReportViewer control includes language packs for eight languages: Chinese-Simplified, Chinese-Traditional, French, German, Italian, Japanese, Korean, and Spanish. Follow these steps to install a language pack:

1. Go to the Microsoft Report Viewer Redistributable 2008 download page (see Resources).
2. Change the Language drop-down list to the desired language.
3. Scroll to the bottom of the page and click the Microsoft Report Viewer Redistributable 2008 Language Pack link to download and install the language pack for the selected language.
4. Run ReportViewerLP.exe.

   You can also get the ReportViewer language pack by downloading it from http://go.microsoft.com/fwlink/?LinkId=98185&clcid=<lcid> where <lcid> is the locale id as a hexadecimal number, for example http://go.microsoft.com/fwlink/?LinkId=98185&lcid=0x40c for French. This is how the ClickOnce ReportViewer package obtains the language pack.

NOTE The languages installed by the SQL Server setup program are not that relevant to the ReportViewer user interface. However, the report server language is relevant for data that comes from the server in server mode. This includes the localized names of rendering extensions on the server as well as error messages from the server.

ReportViewer uses the UI culture of the current thread to locate the language resource file. This happens automatically for the Windows Forms version of ReportViewer. However, ASP.NET does not set automatically the thread culture based on the header information provided by the client. Instead, you must overwrite the thread culture programmatically, as follows:

```
Thread.CurrentThread.CurrentCulture = CultureInfo.CreateSpecificCulture(Request.UserLanguages[0]);
Thread.CurrentThread.CurrentUICulture = CultureInfo.CreateSpecificCulture(Request.UserLanguages[0]);
```

Finally, if you are building a custom application in a language that is not one of the eight languages mentioned above or you need more control over the ReportViewer localization, you can replace the strings in the ReportViewer user interface by implementing the IReportViewerMessages or IReportViewerMessages2 interfaces, as follows:

5. Code a custom class that implements IReportViewerMessages and IReportViewerMessages2 interfaces and provides the localized strings for the languages you need to support.

```
public class ReportViewerCustomMessages : IReportViewerMessages, IReportViewerMessages2
{
   public string BackButtonToolTip {get { return("Add your custom text here."); } }
   public string BackMenuItemText {get { return("Add your custom text here."); }}
. . .
```

6. Set the ReportViewer Messages property to an instance of this class.

```
ReportViewerCustomMessages myMessageClass = new ReportViewerCustomMessages();
reportViewer.Messages = myMessageClass;
```

Due to an unfortunate bug which will be probably fixed in next ReportViewer redistributable, attempting to add these two lines to the Form.Load event will result in a "The source of the report definition has not been specified error" exception. This error occurs because ReportViewer mistakenly tries to get the parameter metadata when it attempts to recalculate the size of the parameters area. If you see this error, you can work around it by adding these lines to the LoadRemoteReportParameters method after setting the report path. For more information about localizing the ReportViewer controls, see the examples in the IReportViewerMessages interface in the Visual Studio Books Online (see Resources).

15.2.3 Working with Local Processing Mode

In local processing mode, the application provides ReportViewer with report parameters and data. WinReporter comes with two sample reports, Customer Orders and Sales Order Detail, which I'll use to demonstrate local processing mode. The Customer Orders report shows the order history for a given customer, as shown in Figure 15.4. You can click the order number to drill through to the Sales Order Detail report that shows the order details. Because the Sales Order Detail report is dependent on the Customer Orders report, the application loads only the Customer Orders report in the Report drop-down list.

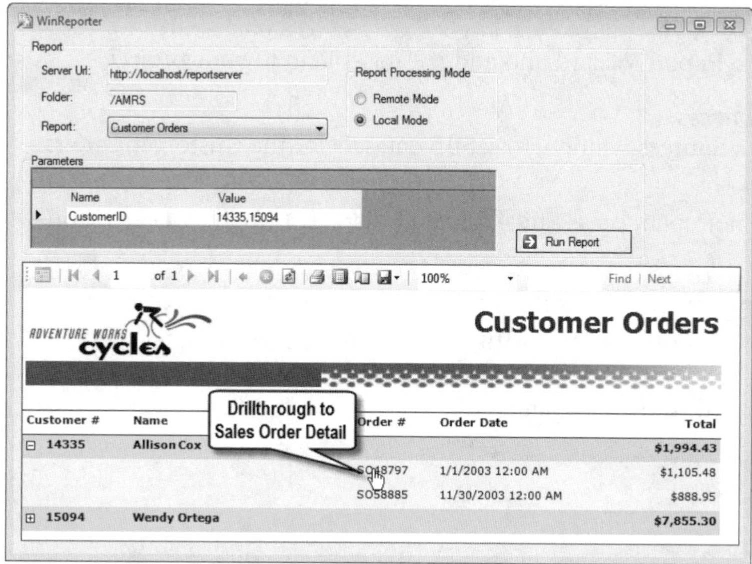

Figure 15.4 In local processing mode, the application provides ReportViewer with report parameters and data.

The customer number is also clickable to demonstrate how the application can handle hyperlink events, for example to let the user update his or her customer data. Configuring local processing mode involves three steps. First, you prepare the report data source. Second, you author the local report definition. The third step involves writing code to program the ReportViewer control to process the local report.

TIP If you have a server report that you need to convert to a local report, you can skip the data source preparation step. That's because your report definition already describes the dataset(s) that will feed the report. The only step remaining is to bind the local report to an application dataset with an identical schema at run time.

Understanding report data sources

In general, ReportViewer supports two types of data sources in local processing mode: a dataset that contains an ADO.NET DataTable object or an enumerable collection of business objects. ReportViewer Windows Forms also supports binding to instances of System.Windows.Forms.BindingSource and to System.Type. Report Viewer Web server supports binding to an instance of System.Web.UI.IDataSource. Visual Studio supports several ways of designing the two data source types (dataset and business objects):

- Data Sources window—Create a new data source using the Visual Studio Data Sources window.

- Report Wizard—Click the Design New Report link in the ReportViewer smart tags panel (see again Figure 15.3). This starts the Report Wizard that walks you through the process of setting up the report data and layout. Visual Studio also launches the Report Wizard right away when you create a new Reports Application project.
- Dataset item—Create a typed dataset by adding a Dataset item to your project.

The first two options support setting up a data source from a database, a Web service, or a business object. Choose the Database data source type to set up a typed dataset from a SQL query or a stored procedure. Choose the Web Service data source type if you use a Web service as a data source. Use the Object data source type if you are planning to bind the local report to a business object. Finally, if you plan to use a typed dataset as a data source for the local report, you can bypass the Report Wizard and add a Dataset item to your project.

Configuring the report data sources

Let's use the Visual Studio Data Sources window to set up datasets for the Customer Orders and Sales Order Details reports.

1. If the Data Sources window is not open, press Shift+Alt+D to display it (or click Data menu ⇨ Show Data Sources).

   The Data Sources window shows all project data sources. If you have set up a Web reference to a Web service, the Data Sources window shows the Web service.

2. In the Data Sources window, click the Add New Data Source toolbar button to launch the Data Source Configuration Wizard, shown in Figure 15.5.

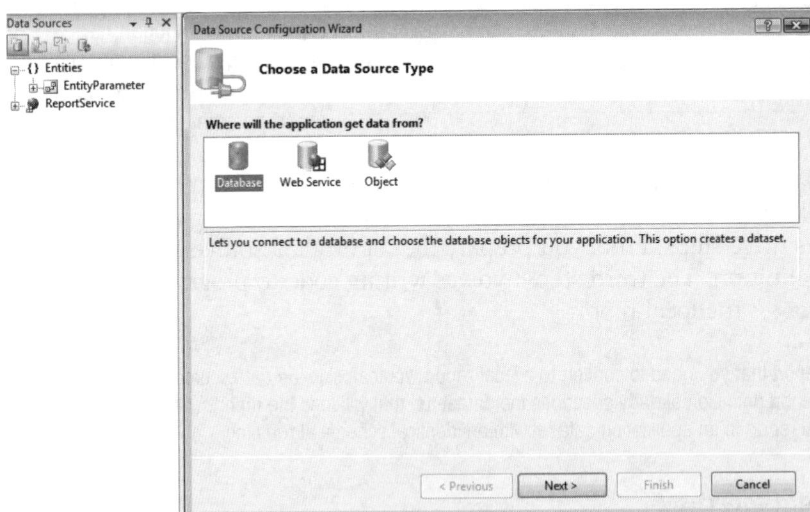

Figure 15.5 Use the Data Source Configuration Wizard to set up a data source for a local report.

   As noted, the wizard gives you three choices for configuring the report data based on how the data will be provided to the dataset.

3. Leave the Database option selected and click Next.
4. In the Choose Your Data Connection step, set a connection to the AdventureWorks2008 database.
5. In the Save the Connection String to the Application Configuration File, check the Yes, Save the Connection As option and enter *AdventureWorksConnectionString* in the field below. This

simplifies connection management because you can update the connection string in the application configuration file (app.config).

6. Unfortunately, the wizard doesn't support free-form SQL statements to define the data source. Consequently, you need to finalize the data source definition after the wizard is done. In the Choose Your Database Objects step, don't select a database object. Enter *CustomerOrders* as a dataset name and click Finish. When prompted, confirm your choice and move on to the next step, providing the SQL statement that selects your data.

Using free-form SQL statements
In the previous steps, Visual Studio created an empty CustomerOrders dataset and added an XSD schema file to the Entities folder in Solution Explorer. You now need to open the dataset in the Dataset Designer to configure it to use a free-form SQL statement that populates the dataset with values.

7. In the Data Source window, right-click the CustomerOrders dataset and click Edit DataSet with Designer.
8. Right-click on the Dataset Designer canvas and choose Add ⇨ TableAdapter. This launches the TableAdapter Configuration Wizard.
9. In the Choose Your Data Connection step, select the connection to the AdventureWorks2008 database
10. In the Save the Connection String to the Application Configuration File step, click Next.
11. In the Choose a Command Type step, leave the Use SQL Statements option selected.
12. In the Enter a SQL Statement step, enter the following SELECT statement, which you can copy from the CustomerOrders.sql file in the book source code:

```
SELECT  SOH.CustomerID, C.FirstName, C.LastName, SOH.SalesOrderNumber, SOH.OrderDate, SOH.TotalDue
FROM    Sales.SalesOrderHeader AS SOH INNER JOIN
        Sales.vIndividualCustomer AS C ON SOH.CustomerID = C.BusinessEntityID
WHERE   (SOH.CustomerID IN (1, 2))
ORDER BY SOH.OrderDate
```

13. In the Choose Methods to Generate step, accept the defaults and click Finish.
14. Go back to the Dataset Designer, and rename DataTable1 in place to *CustomerOrders*.
15. Repeat steps these steps to add two new data sources, SalesOrder and SalesOrderDetail. Their queries are provided in the SalesOrder and SalesOrderDetail files. In the Dataset Designer, rename their tables to *Order* and *OrderDetail* respectively.

Using Objects as Data Sources
If your application uses business objects, you can use an object as a data source. The SalesOrderObject source file in the Entities folder of the WinReporter project defines a SalesOrderObject object that you can use as a data source for a local report. Notice that the source file also includes a SalesOrders object whose GetData method returns a collection of the SalesOrderObject objects. Follow these steps to configure the SalesOrderObject object as a data source:

16. Rebuild your project.
17. Select the Object data source type in the Data Source Configuration Wizard.
18. In the Select the Object You Wish to Bind To step, expand the WinReporter.Entities namespace and select the SalesOrderObject object.

All public properties are exposed as fields in the Data Sources window so you can bind them to report fields. Use the following code to bind a collection of objects to the report at run time:

```
SalesOrders orders = new SalesOrders();
reportViewer.LocalReport.DataSources.Add(new ReportDataSource("SalesOrderObject",orders.GetProducts()));
```

The ObjectDataSource sample available on the ReportViewer site (see Resources) demonstrates a working report that uses an object as a data source.

Authoring local reports

With the report data source in place, you can proceed with authoring the actual report by using the Visual Studio Report Designer. Follow these steps to author a new report:

1. In the Solution Explorer, right-click the WinReporter project node and click Add ⇨ New Item.
2. In the Add New Item dialog box, select the Report template if you want to start with a blank report. Or, select the Report Wizard template to auto-generate a report with the Report Wizard.
3. Once the report definition file is generated, double-click it in the Solution Explorer to open it in the Visual Studio Report Designer.
4. Lay out the report as usual. To bind report items to data, drag fields from the Data Sources window and drop them onto the report.

Understanding Report Definitions

Recall that in local mode, ReportViewer understands RDL 2005 only. You can use the Visual Studio Report Designer to design the report definition of the local report because this designer generates RDL 2005.

You cannot author a report with the BIDS 2008 Report Designer or Report Builder 2.0 and convert it easily to a local report because those tools produce RDL 2008 only. If you have SQL Server 2005, another option is to author and test a report with the full-featured BIDS 2005 Report Designer by connecting to a database. Then, you can convert the report to a local report by following the steps in the Converting RDL and RDLC topic in the Visual Studio Books Online.

NOTE By default, local report definition files have *.rdlc file extensions. To differentiate remote from local reports, the Reporting Services team introduced the .rdlc file extension where "c" stands for client-side processing. While you can use any file extension for local reports, the .rdlc extension is recommended because it is associated with Visual Studio Report Designer. In addition, when you specify a report definition by file name or embedded resource in local mode, the viewer will try to automatically resolve the location of subreports and drillthrough reports by looking for files with the .rdlc extension.

The WinReporter demo uses the CustomerOrders and Sales Order Details reports that are included in the Reports folder. Click on either report definition in Solution Explorer and notice in the Properties window that Build Action is set to None, and Copy to Output Directory is set to Copy if Newer. Consequently, Visual Studio will copy the most recent report definitions to the application build folder when you build the project. When it's time to deploy your application, you can remove the report definition file from the project and let the application setup program copy the report definitions to a known location where ReportViewer can find them. This lets you deploy newer report definitions by simply overwriting the external files.

Sometimes, security requirements may mandate embedding the report definitions in the application executable as resources instead of distributing them as external files. You can accomplish this by setting the Build Action property to Embedded Resource, and setting Copy to Output Director to Do Not Copy. Then, you can use the following code to load an embedded report definition:

```
reportViewer.LocalReport.ReportEmbeddedResource = "WinReporter.Reports.Customer Orders.rdlc";
```

Working with embedded report definitions is trickier with web applications because ReportViewer will try to load the resource from the same assembly that sets the ReportEmbeddedResource property. Behind the scenes, ReportEmbeddedResource attempts to load the resource by calling the .NET Assembly.GetManifestResourceStream method. If the resource file and the code that sets ReportEmbeddedResources end up in different assemblies, the application will fail to load the report definition.

There are two workarounds for this predicament. You can pass a reference to the ReportViewer object to your class library containing the resource files and then have that assembly set the property. Or, you can load the embedded resource manually using Assembly.GetManifestResourceStream and pass the stream to the viewer using LoadReportDefinition. The disadvantage of the latter approach is that drillthrough reports and subreports will not load automatically. This is because ReportViewer has no way of resolving relative paths when the parent report definition is supplied from a stream.

Working with External Images

Handling external images requires some additional steps when working with local reports. This is because ReportViewer won't load the image from the folder where the report is located. As a workaround, you can use the file:// protocol to load external images. You should avoid static image paths for maintenance reasons. Instead, the Customer Orders report contains a simple Visual Basic embedded function that returns the application path:

```
Public Function GetAppPath() As String
    Return System.IO.Directory.GetCurrentDirectory
End Function
```

The Value property of the Adventure Works logo image uses the following function to reference the external AWC.jpg file:

```
=String.Format("file:///{0}\{1}", Code.GetAppPath(), "AWC.jpg")
```

As a result, Reporting Services will load the image from the application startup folder. You won't see the image at design time, but it should appear when the report is run.

Requesting local reports

The final step to implement local report processing requires writing code to program the LocalReport object:

```
internal void RunLocal() {
    reportViewer.Reset();
    reportViewer.ProcessingMode = ProcessingMode.Local;
    reportViewer.LocalReport.ReportPath = this.ReportPath;
    reportViewer.LocalReport.EnableHyperlinks = true;
    reportViewer.LocalReport.EnableExternalImages = true;
    reportViewer.LocalReport.ExecuteReportInCurrentAppDomain(
        System.Reflection.Assembly.GetExecutingAssembly().Evidence);
    ReportParameter[] parameters = this.UserParametersToReportParameters();
    reportViewer.LocalReport.SetParameters(parameters);
    reportViewer.LocalReport.DataSources.Add(GetCustomers(parameters[0])); break;
    reportViewer.RefreshReport();
}
```

The code configures ReportViewer for local processing. Notice that it sets LocalReport.ReportPath to the local report definition file. As a security measure, if the local report uses navigation actions (hyperlinks), you need to explicitly enable hyperlinks (more on this in a moment). Similarly, since the local report loads the AdventureWorks logo as an external image, you need to enable external images. You also need to elevate the CAS permissions of the local report by running the report in the current application domain. This is because the GetAppPath embedded function that is in the Customer Orders report needs FileIOPermission to get the application path where the external image is located.

Recall that the application is responsible for supplying the local report with parameters and data. RunLocal calls the UserParametersToReportParameters helper method, which converts the user-defined parameters in the Parameters grid to an array of ReportParameter objects. Next, the code passes the parameters to the local report.

The code proceeds by calling the GetCustomer helper method to obtain the report data as a ReportDataSource object. The Name property of the ReportDataSource object must match the name of the dataset inside the report definition. The Value property must reference either an ADO.NET DataTable object or a collection of business objects. Finally, the RefreshReport method renders the report locally.

Synchronizing data sources

The definition of the report dataset (<DataSet> element in the report definition file) and the definition of the project data source must match in order for the local report to render successfully. Chances are that you will need to make changes to the project data source at some point. Adding or removing columns in either the dataset or the project data source will require that you update the corresponding data structure. While you can do this manually, Visual Studio provides several options to synchronize the report dataset definition with the Data Source.

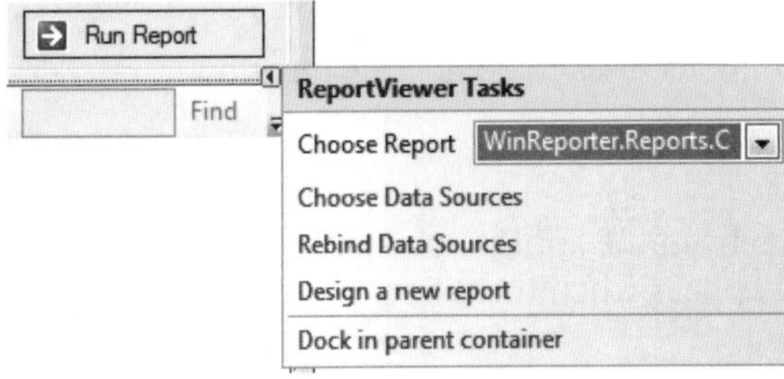

Figure 15.6 Use the smart tags panel to synchronize the dataset of the local report with the report data source.

Suppose you have made changes to the CustomerOrders Data Source and you need to update the Customer Orders report. The following steps show you how to synchronize your changes:

1. Open the Main form in design mode.
2. Click the ReportViewer control to select it and click the side arrow to open the smart tags panel, as shown in Figure 15.6.
3. Expand the Choose Report drop-down list and select WinReporter.Reports.Customer Orders.rdlc.

Use the Choose Data Sources task in the ReportViewer Tasks smart tags panel to bind a data source to a client report definition (.rdlc) file that you converted from a server report definition (.rdl) file. Use the Rebind Data Sources task to synchronize the report definition with the project data source.

Suppose that you have copied local report definition files between projects that have different data sources.

4. Double-click the Customer Orders.rdlc file in the Solution Explorer to open it in design mode.
5. Click Report menu ⇨ Data Sources.

To add a new dataset to the report definition, select the data source and click Add to Report. In most cases, this option is not necessary. Project data sources are added to the report definition automatically when you drag fields to the report layout. To remove an existing dataset reference from the report definition, select the dataset and click Remove.

If you renamed a data source in your project, you can use the Report Data Sources dialog box to update the dataset name in the report definition. Click the Rename button to set the dataset name in overwrite mode, and then type the new name. Click Refresh All to update the report definition file with your changes.

Handling events

ReportViewer supports a number of events that your code can handle at run time. For example, ReportViewer always processes the report request on a background thread to keep the main application thread responsive. If the application needs to be notified when the report is ready, it can handle the RenderingComplete event:

1. Open the Windows Form that hosts the control in design mode, and then click the ReportViewer control to select it.
2. In the Visual Studio Properties window, click the Events toolbar button.
3. Double-click the RenderingComplete event.

Visual Studio generates the following empty event handler:

```
private void reportViewer_RenderingComplete(object sender, RenderingCompleteEventArgs e)
{
}
```

Each event passes additional information pertinent to the event to the second argument. For example, the RenderingCompleteEventArgs argument includes a Warnings object that may contain warnings the server has generated when rendering the report. The second argument for most events supports a Cancel property that you can set to True to cancel the attempted action.

It is important to point out that in remote processing mode, the ReportViewer events are raised by the control, not by the server. Therefore, you cannot use these events to change the report definition. Instead, the ReportViewer raises events when the control state changes, giving your application a chance to do some pre- or post-processing before or after the report is generated.

Although the ReportViewer raises events in both modes, you will probably find events more useful in local mode. That's because in local mode your application must handle additional reporting tasks, such as passing data to a drillthrough report or subreport, and collecting parameters. WinReporter demonstrates how your application can handle two of the most useful events: Drillthrough and Hyperlink events.

Implementing report drillthrough

As with its server counterpart, the Customer Orders local report lets the end user click on an order number to drill through to the Sales Order Detail local report and see the order details.

However, as with any local report, the application must supply the data for the drillthrough report. This happens in the Drillthrough event:

```
private void reportViewer_Drillthrough(object sender, DrillthroughEventArgs e) {
   if (e.Report is ServerReport) return;
   LocalReport localReport = (LocalReport)e.Report;
   OrderTableAdapter orderAdapter = new Entities.SalesOrderTableAdapters.OrderTableAdapter();
   SalesOrder.OrderDataTable orderTable =
            orderAdapter.GetData(localReport.OriginalParametersToDrillthrough[0].Values[0]);
   OrderDetailTableAdapter orderDetailAdapter = new OrderDetailTableAdapter();
   SalesOrderDetail.OrderDetailDataTable orderDetailTable =
            orderDetailAdapter.GetData(localReport.OriginalParametersToDrillthrough[0].Values[0]);
   localReport.DataSources.Add(new ReportDataSource("SalesOrder", orderTable));
   localReport.DataSources.Add(new ReportDataSource("SalesOrderDetail", orderDetailTable));
}
```

ReportViewer passes the drillthrough target report in the DrillthroughEventArgs argument. First, the code checks the report processing mode. If the event was triggered in remote processing mode (that is, e.Report is ServerReport), the code exits because we want to handle only drillthrough events from local reports. The application gets the selected order number from the OriginalParametersToDrillthrough property. Finally, the application binds the report to its data by passing two datasets to the Sales Order Detail report (one for the order header and another for the order details).

TIP Instead of hard coding the dataset name, consider using the LocalReport.GetDataSetNames method. This method returns the names of the datasets defined in the report definition. By not hard coding the dataset names, you avoid a bug if you change a dataset name in the report definition and forget to update the code.

Implementing custom navigation action

What if you need to pass information from the report to the application, such as a customer identifier that a user happened to click on the report? In this scenario, the application intercepts the event and displays a form that can be used to update the customer details. With the updated information in hand, the application would refresh the report to show the changed data. To illustrate this scenario, I used the Hyperlink event. The Customer Orders report defines an expression-based Jump to URL action on the textbox that displays the customer identifier:

```
="customerid:" & Fields!CustomerID.Value
```

Next, handle the ReportViewer Hyperlink event as follows:

```
private void reportViewer_Hyperlink(object sender, HyperlinkEventArgs e) {
   Uri uri = new Uri(e.Hyperlink);
   if (String.Compare(uri.Scheme, "customerid", StringComparison.OrdinalIgnoreCase)==0)
   {
      e.Cancel = true;
            MessageBox.Show(String.Format("Display data for customer: {0}",
                     System.Web.HttpUtility.UrlDecode(uri.AbsolutePath)));
            ((ReportViewer)sender).RefreshReport();
   }
}
```

The HyperlinkEventArgs argument includes the hyperlink target. Assuming that the end user has clicked on customer 14335, the hyperlink will be "customerid:14335". Since there may be other hyperlink events raised by the same report or other reports, the code checks the hyperlink schema, which in this case will return "customerid". Next, it is up to the application to do something with this customer. For demo purposes, the code pops up a message box that displays the customer identifier. Finally, the event handler refreshes the report to show the latest data if the application has changed the underlying data.

15.3 Reporting for Web Clients

Now, let's take a look at the ReportViewer Web server control. A common reporting requirement is to distribute reports over the Web to make data easily accessible to internal users, customers and partners. You can leverage the Visual Studio ReportViewer Web server control to report-enable your intranet, Internet, and extranet applications.

15.3.1 Understanding the ReportViewer Web Server Control

Microsoft has done a great job of unifying the appearance and programming interfaces of the ReportViewer Windows Forms and Web Server controls. Both controls expose the same set of properties to control the processing mode and toolbar. Similar to its Windows Forms counterpart, you can add the ReportViewer Web Server control to a Web form by dragging it from the Reporting section of the Visual Studio Toolbox and dropping it on a web form. Both controls have the same look and feel, support remote and local processing modes, and expose similar object models. Yet, the implementation of the Web server control is very different because of the targeted technology.

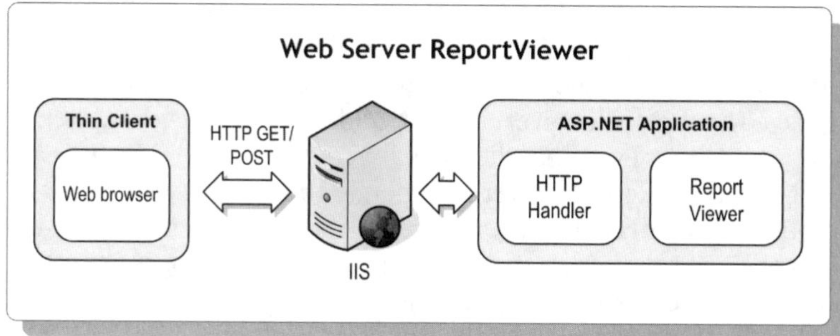

Figure 15.7 In remote mode, the HTTP handler of the ReportViewer Web server control handles images, exporting reports, and keeping report sessions alive.

The ReportViewer Web Server architecture

Because the ReportViewer Web Server control runs in a server application, the Web server control always generates the report on the server side of the web application, as shown in Figure 15.7. The client never accesses the server directly. For the Web Server control, local processing occurs in the context of your server application. As you might expect, remote processing occurs on the report server. Remote report processing follows these steps:

1. Server-side ASP.NET code configures the control to request a server report.
2. The ReportViewer Web server control calls the report server APIs to generate the report in HTML. The report server (not shown in Figure 15.7) processes the report and sends it back to ReportViewer.
3. ReportViewer streams the HTML report to the browser.

Local processing mode follows similar steps with the exception that ReportViewer itself processes the report, not the report server. If you have implemented server-side report generation without ReportViewer, you are aware of the complexities surrounding this integration scenario. For example, extra steps were required to handle report images and correlate report requests with execution sessions. Other features, such as report interaction were simply not available when rendering the report via SOAP. These limitations simply disappear with ReportViewer. How is this possible?

The first time you add ReportViewer to a web form, Visual Studio automatically registers a special ASP.NET HttpHandler (Reserved.ReportViewerWebControl.axd), which you can see by examining the application Web.config file. The ReportViewer HTTP handler is an integral part of the Web ReportViewer control. You cannot remove or unregister it. If the ReportViewer HTTP handler is missing from web.config, you will get the following error:

```
The Report Viewer Web Control HTTP Handler has not been registered in the application's web.config file.
```

The main responsibilities of the HTTP handler include handling images and events, exporting reports to other report formats, and keeping report sessions alive. For example, if a report uses an embedded image, the browser submits an HTTP GET request to the HTTP Handler to fetch the image by URL.

Understanding rendering modes

The ReportViewer Web Server control supports an AsyncRendering property that controls how the report is rendered. If AsyncRendering is True (this is the default setting), ReportViewer generates the report asynchronously. Specifically, ReportViewer injects an IFRAME, which sends an HTTP GET request to the HTTP Handler to generate the report. The net result is that the hosting page can load without being blocked by ReportViewer.

In asynchronous mode (default), ReportViewer toolbar actions, such as page navigation, and report interactive features (drillthrough, bookmarks, and document maps) are forwarded to the HTTP Handler. Assuming that you don't handle events in the page code-behind, these actions don't cause the hosting page to repost. However, if you decide to handle events, then report actions result in a page repost so your event handler gets fired

Setting AsyncRendering to False causes ReportViewer to generate the report synchronously. ReportViewer renders the report as inline HTML with the rest of the page. Consequently, the hosting page is rendered after the report is generated and no progress indicator is shown. Note that document maps are not available when the report is generated synchronously. Interactive features always cause the hosting page to repost to the server.

In both modes, ReportViewer shows a progress indicator while the report is being generated. However, since processing always happens synchronously in local mode, the progress indicator is only visible during the rendering portion of local mode, which tends to be much faster than the data retrieval/processing time so the user may not notice the progress indicator at all.

How ReportViewer handles parameters

You may wonder how ReportViewer Web server handles report parameters and how it passes them to the report server. The control doesn't make any deliberate attempt to hide or obscure parameters. However, the report parameters are not passed on each request to the server, such as when the user pages through the report. That's because the report execution state, including parameter values, is encapsulated in the execution session, whose identifier is sent to the client. This was not the case in Reporting Services 2000, where parameters were sent on each request.

NOTE The ReportViewer Web server doesn't encrypt the report parameters values in any way. It simply base64-encodes their values and adds the parameters to the page viewstate so they get submitted when the page is reposted via HTTP POST. This makes it more difficult, but not impossible, for a hacker to obtain the parameter values. As I discussed in chapter 3, you should never trust report parameters with sensitive reports. Instead, protect report data by other means, such as row-level security.

Customizing ReportViewer Web Server operations

ReportViewer supports a set of configuration settings to customize its operations. You can use these settings to control how ReportViewer connects to the report server, where it will save its temporary streams, and how its viewstate will be handled in a web farm environment.

ReportViewer uses ASP.NET sessions to store certain state between page reposts, including the report server URL, timeout, user credentials, custom cookies, and custom headers. The ASP.NET session state must be enabled for local report processing but it's optional for remote report processing. If you turn ASP.NET sessions off, you must implement IReportServerConnection or IReportServerConnection2 interfaces as described in the MSDN document Web.config Settings for ReportViewer topic (see Resources).

ReportViewer holds temporary streams in memory when calling the RenderReport API, such as when the user previews and exports reports. This could stress server memory if the server is under heavy loads or servicing many users. However, you can configure ReportViewer to save temporary streams to disk by implementing the ITemporaryStorage interface, as I'll demonstrate in the next section.

By default, in remote processing mode, ReportViewer connects to the report server using the credentials of the interactive user. This works best with intranet applications and Windows integrated security. If Windows integrated security is not an option, you can implement the IReportServerCredentials interface and set the ReportViewer.ServerReport.ReportServerCredentials property. Chapter 19 demonstrates how this can be done when the report server is configured for custom security.

ASP.NET encrypts the page view state with a machine-specific encryption key. If your application is running in a web farm environment, all servers must use an identical machine key in the application web.config files to synchronize the ReportViewer view state across servers. For more information, read the MSDN topic MachineKey Element (ASP.NET Settings Schema). Chapter 2 provides a link to a MachineKey Generator Tool that can help you generate the machine key.

15.3.2 Embedding Reports in Web Applications

The WebReporter sample demonstrates how you can leverage the ReportViewer Web server control to embed remote or local reports in ASP.NET applications. The source code can be found in the WebReporter web application project in the book source code. For easier configuration, the project uses the ASP.NET Development Server so you don't have to configure an IIS application.

Introducing the WebReporter sample

Figure 15.8 shows the WebReporter user interface (default.aspx page). As you've probably guessed, WebReporter is an ASP.NET version of the WinReporter sample. When the page is initially requested, it defaults to remote processing mode. This causes WebReporter to connect to the report server and load a list of reports deployed to the specified folder.

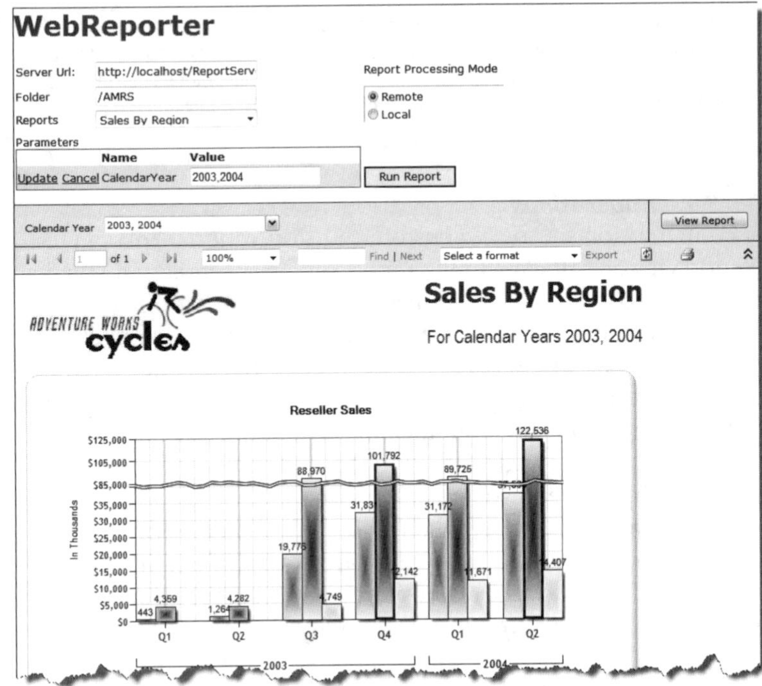

Figure 15.8 The WebReporter sample demonstrates embedding reports in custom web applications by using the ReportViewer in remote and local processing modes.

When you select a report, WebReporter shows the report parameters in the Parameters grid. You can click the Edit link to put the grid in edit mode if you want to change the report parameters. Once you enter the parameter values, you can click the Update link to post the new parameter values to the server. You can click the Run Report button to view the report with the new parameters.WebReporter lets you switch to local processing mode where it uses the Customer Orders report I've already discussed. Irrespective of the chosen processing mode, the ReportViewer Web server control renders the report on the server side of the application.

As its Windows Forms counterpart, the ReportViewer Web server control generates a toolbar. Report printing uses an ActiveX control that is downloaded from the report server and installed on the client the first time you click the Print toolbar button. In contrast with previous releases, report printing is supported in both local and remote processing modes.

Since the ReportViewer Web Server control is very similar to its Windows Forms counterpart, discussing the WebReporter implementation in detail will be redundant. Instead, I'll highlight the most significant differences.

Configuring the ReportViewer Web Server control

To add ReportViewer to a web form, complete the following steps:

1. Open a web form in design mode.
2. In the Visual Studio toolbar, expand the Reporting section and double-click the MicrosoftReportViewer control to add it to the web form.

If the page uses XHTML format, which Visual Studio generates by default, and ReportViewer is configured for asynchronous rendering (AsyncRendering property is True), the control will not resize properly if it uses a relative height, such as 100%. To avoid this, set the control

Height property to a fixed value, such as 600px. Alternatively, use the cascading style sheet (CSS) style to force the HTML elements to maximum height by following these steps:

3. Add the following style to the StyleSheet.css file or embed it inside the hosting page:

```
html, body, form
{
   height: 100%;
}
```

4. Set the ReportViewer Height property to a relative value, such as 100%.

Optionally, you can set additional properties to change the control's appearance. For example, you can change the toolbar appearance by setting the properties under the Appearance category in the Visual Studio Properties window or apply an ASP.NET skin by setting the SkinID property.

Handling report parameters

The bulk of the changes required to implement WebReporter are not related to the control but to porting the user interface to ASP.NET. For example, I had to replace the Windows Forms DataGrid with the ASP.NET GridView control. This required programming the GridView control to support changing the parameter values.

GridView supports data updates best when it is bound to one of the ASP.NET data source controls, such as SQLDataSource. However, in our case WebReporter binds the grid to an application dataset. This involved handling a few GridView events and caching the parameter dataset in the ASP.NET session so it's available between page reposts:

```
protected void grdParams_RowEditing(object sender, GridViewEditEventArgs e) {
   grdParams.EditIndex = e.NewEditIndex;
   BindData();
}
private void BindData() {
   grdParams.DataSource = Session[WebReporter.Util.SESSION_PARAMETERS];
   grdParams.DataBind();
}
protected void grdParams_RowUpdating(object sender, GridViewUpdateEventArgs e) {
   DataTable dt = (DataTable)Session[WebReporter.Util.SESSION_PARAMETERS];
   if (dt == null) return;
   GridViewRow row = grdParams.Rows[e.RowIndex];
   dt.Rows[grdParams.EditIndex]["Value"] = ((TextBox)(row.Cells[2].Controls[0])).Text;
   grdParams.EditIndex = -1;
   BindData();
 }
protected void grdParams_RowCancelingEdit(object sender, GridViewCancelEditEventArgs e) {
   grdParams.EditIndex = -1;
   BindData();
}
```

First, I had to enable the GridView AutoGenerateEditButton property to True so the grid would display the Edit link. When you click the Edit link, GridView raises a RowEditing event on the server and passes the row index of the selected row. This gives you the opportunity to check whether the row should be updateable. In our case, the event confirms the operation by setting the EditIndex property to the row index and rebinding the grid.

When you click the Update link to commit the changes, GridView raises a RowUpdating event to let you validate the new values. WebReporter writes the changes to the cached parameter dataset. Next, WebReporter resets the grid index to -1 to clear the row selection and then rebinds the grid. Finally, when you click the Cancel link to cancel the update operation, GridView calls the RowCancellingEdit event. WebReporter resets the grid index and rebinds the control.

GridView supports different row styles. I changed the BackColor property of the EditRowStyle property to highlight the row being edited. To configure the grid columns, I used the Edit Columns link in the GridView smart tags panel. I added two BoundField columns (Name and Value) and bound them to the Name and Value data fields respectively. I also made other formatting changes, such as setting the column HeaderStyle properties to resize the columns, setting the column text alignment, and so on.

Handling external images

Recall that the Customer Orders report uses an external image for the company logo. I had to change the image Value property to reference the URL address of the external image instead of its physical path, such as http://localhost:1966/Reports/AWC.jpg. This required a change to the GetAppPath embedded function inside the Customer Orders report, as follows:

```
Public Function GetAppPath() As String
      return  String.Format("http://{0}:{1}{2}",
      System.Web.HttpContext.Current.Request.ServerVariables("SERVER_NAME"),
      System.Web.HttpContext.Current.Request.ServerVariables("SERVER_PORT"),
      System.Web.HttpContext.Current.Request.ApplicationPath)
End Function
```

As a prerequisite, I had to reference the System.Web.dll in the Report Properties dialog box. However, because ReportViewer will not run reports that reference external assemblies for security reasons, you must explicitly configure it to trust these assemblies. This required adding the following line to the WebReporter RunLocal method:

```
reportViewer.LocalReport.AddTrustedCodeModuleInCurrentAppDomain(
  "System.Web, Version=2.0.0.0, Culture=neutral,PublicKeyToken=b03f5f7f11d50a3a");
```

The AddTrustedCodeModuleInCurrentAppDomain method adds System.Web to the list of assemblies that are trusted to execute in the current application domain.

Exporting reports

By default, the ReportViewer Web server control will display the standard Internet Explorer download dialog box when the user exports a report. If this is not desirable, you can configure ReportViewer to bypass the confirmation dialog box and render the exported report inline. To demonstrate this feature, I set the ReportViewer ExportContentDisposition property to AlwaysInline.

As a result, when the report is exported, ReportViewer adds a content-disposition:inline header to the response to instruct the browser to render the report inline. Other supported ExportContentDisposition values include AlwaysAttachment, which indicates that content is always presented as an attachment regardless of the export format, and OnlyHTMLInline, which indicates that only HTML-formatted content is presented inline.

Handling events

Suppose you want to handle the report drilldown event in order to evaluate some business rules to determine whether the user can drill down to another report. Follow these steps to create a new page that demonstrates how handling events affect page processing:

1. Add a new Web Form and drag the ReportViewer control to the form. Rename the control to *reportViewer*.
2. Use the ReportViewer smart tags panel to bind it to the Drillthrough Action server report.
3. Put a breakpoint in the Page_Load event. In Solution Explorer, right-click the new Web Form and click Set as Start Page. Press F5 to start the debugger.

4. In the Drillthrough Action report, expand the Bike Racks accessories on rows and year 2003 on columns.
5. Click the Internet Sales hyperlink under quarter 4 and year 2003 to initiate the drillthrough action.

   Notice that Page_Load event is not called because the page doesn't repost. Instead, the ReportViewer HTTP Handler receives and handles the drillthrough event. This is good because it avoids refreshing the entire page with each postback.

NOTE You may have heard of a web development technology called AJAX (Asynchronous JavaScript and XML) for creating interactive web applications. AJAX-enabled pages exchange data with the server behind the scenes so that entire web pages do not have to be reloaded each time there is a need to fetch data from the server. As it stands, the ReportViewer Web server control is not AJAX-capable. Consequently, interactive features and toolbar actions will result in refreshing the entire ReportViewer area. While you might be able to get some simple reports to display in the Visual Studio UpdatePanel AJAX control, most of the supporting javascript will not work. Consequently, most interactive features and toolbar features are likely to be broken, and even the keep-alive pings from the client to keep the execution session open will not execute.

In the steps that follow, let's reconfigure ReportViewer to register a drillthrough event.

6. Open the web form in design mode and click the ReportViewer control.
7. In the Visual Studio Properties Window, click the Events toolbar button.
8. Double-click the Drillthrough event to create an event handler.
9. Change the Drillthrough event handler as follows:

```
protected void reportViewer_Drillthrough(object sender,  DrillthroughEventArgs e) {
   // Evaluate some business rules and cancel report drillhtrough
   e.Cancel = true;
}
```

10. Start the debugger and simulate the drillthrough action again.

Notice that this time the page posts to itself, which means that you can program the drillthrough event. Moreover, once you register a ReportViewer server-side event, the page will continue to repost with each interactive action even if the initiated action doesn't have a registered event handler.

The ReportViewer Web Server control doesn't support a Hyperlink event. The assumption is that most developers will want to navigate the user directly to the link target. For example, if you want to redirect the user to a web page that displays the customer details, you would directly specify the web page URL address in the navigation link. This necessitates a change to the Jump to URL link of the Customer field in the Customer Orders report, as follows:

```
="http://localhost:1966/CustomerDetails.aspx?CustomerID=" & Fields!CustomerID.Value
```

Consequently, when the user clicks the customer identifier, the user is redirected to a CustomerDetails.aspx page (not implemented) for maintaining the customer details.

Implementing temporary stream storage

In remote processing mode, ReportViewer uses URL access for report delivery to avoid holding the entire report in memory by streaming the report in chunks of 80KB. As the number of concurrent report users increases, you may find that the memory required for holding the report streams increases as well. You can minimize the memory utilization by streaming the report streams to disk instead of memory when users export and preview reports:

1. Create a class that implements the ITemporaryStorage interface, as the TemporaryStorage in the WebReporter project demonstrates. This interface defines a single CreateTemporaryStream method that must return a custom stream, such a stream to a disk file:

```
public class TemporaryStorage:ITemporaryStorage {

 public System.IO.Stream CreateTemporaryStream() {
   FileStream stream = null;
   try
   {
      string streamPath = String.Format(@"{0}\ webreporter.tmp",
                        System.Web.HttpContext.Current.Server.MapPath("."));
      stream = new FileStream(streamPath, FileMode.OpenOrCreate);
   }
   catch (System.Exception ex)
   {
      throw ex;
   }
   return stream;
 }
```

   CreateTemporaryStream creates a webreporter.tmp file and returns the file stream.

2. Register the TemporaryStorage class in the web.config file, as follows:

```
<appSettings>
    <add key="ReportViewerTemporaryStorage" value="WebReporter.TemporaryStorage, WebReporter"/>
</appSettings>
```

   The first argument of the value setting specifies the fully qualified class name that implements the ITemporaryStorage interface, while the second specifies the assembly name. When the web application starts, the ReportViewer Http Handler checks the ReportViewerTemporaryStorage element and discovers that ReportViewer is configured to use custom streams. Consequently, streams required to support report export and preview will be saved in the webreporter.tmp file.

3. Grant the ASP.NET process ACL rights to create files in the folder where the stream will be located.
4. Use WebReporter to request a server report in remote processing mode.
5. Preview or export the report.
6. In Windows Explorer, navigate to the WebReporter folder.

   If the size of the response from the server exceeds 80KB, ReportViewer should have created a webreporter.tmp file. ReportViewer overwrites the temporary file with subsequent report requests. It will increase the file size to accommodate more requests if needed. As you would expect, saving report streams to disk will slow down report previewing and exporting, but it will save memory and make the application more scalable when memory utilization is a resource constraint.

15.4 Reporting for Rich Internet Applications

If you've been following the evolution of the user experience (UX), you have undoubtedly heard the latest buzzword – Rich Internet Applications. A Rich Internet Application (RIA) is a hybrid between a traditional desktop application (rich client) and a web application. Similar to a desktop application, a RIA provides a rich presentation layer and eliminates annoying page refreshes. Not unlike traditional web applications, RIAs are easy to install and distribute.

The quest for rich Internet applications is not new. Wrestling its RIA beast for years, Microsoft has delivered a number of development technologies, including Visual Basis Documents, Remote Data Services, XML data islands with XSL Transformations, and remote scripting, but they have failed to receive broad support. The silver lining is the latest .NET based technology called Silverlight.

Since RIAs represent the next generation of web applications, I felt that a sneak preview that demonstrates how you can integrate them with Reporting Services would be useful. In this next section, I'll introduce you to the Silverlight technology and demonstrate a couple of techniques for report-enabling Silverlight applications. The demo is based on Silverlight 2.0 Beta1, which is the most recent Silverlight version at the time of this writing.

15.4.1 Understanding Microsoft Silverlight

Microsoft Silverlight is a cross-browser, cross-platform client technology that lets you implement rich Internet applications. It is cross-browser because Silverlight is compatible with a variety of browsers including Internet Explorer, Firefox, and Safari. It is also a cross-platform technology because it can run on Windows, Macintosh, and Linux (through the Novell Moonlight project).

Silverlight applications are web-based applications that are easy to install and configure. They can provide a rich user experience that goes far beyond the traditional web applications by including features such as animation, vector graphics, and audio-video playback. The best way to appreciate the Silverlight presentation capabilities is to see them in action. Visit the Silverlight official website (www.silverlight.net) to learn more about this technology through videos and tutorials.

Although originally designed to enhance the user web experience, Silverlight can also power your business applications. This approach lets you realize a browser-hosted, cross-platform RIA. Moreover, you can leverage your existing .NET skills to code the presentation layer without being stuck with the limitations of HTML.

About the Silverlight history

As a newcomer, Silverlight has a short history. Microsoft unveiled Silverlight version 1.0 Beta in April 2007 at the MIX07 conference, followed by the release version in September 2007. Silverlight 1.0 consisted of four components, including a core presentation framework (UI core), Input for handling input from devices, Media for playing back media files, and Extensible Application Markup Language (XAML, pronounced zammel) for describing the user interfaces. Besides Silverlight, XAML is also used in Windows Presentation Foundation (WPF) and Windows Workflow Foundation (WF). Developers can programmatically manipulate the user interface by interacting with the browser Document Object Model (DOM) using JavaScript.

Silverlight 2.0 Beta 1, which was previously referred to as version 1.1, was released in March 2008 at the MIX08 conference. It includes two main components: a core presentation framework and .NET Framework for Silverlight. The core presentation framework handles the user interface and user interaction. It includes a set of lightweight controls for user input, digital rights management, data binding, and presentation features, such as vector graphics, text, animation, and images. The .NET Framework for Silverlight is a subset of the .NET Framework 3.0 and provides data integration, extensible Windows controls, networking, base class libraries, and the common language runtime (CLR). What this means to you as a developer is that you can program the user interface using a .NET-compatible language like C# or Visual Basic.NET.

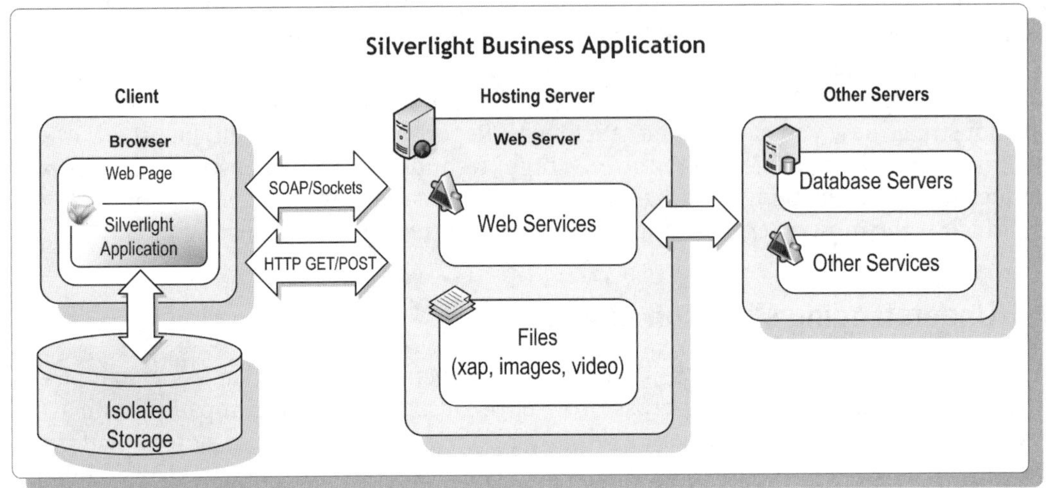

Figure 15.9 A Silverlight application is downloaded and executed in the browser.

Understanding Silverlight applications

Figure 15.9 shows a diagram of what a Silverlight business solution might look like. The Silverlight application, consisting of the XAML markup and code, is compiled into .NET assemblies, which are then compressed into an .xap file. The application is hosted in a web server that supports Silverlight. A hosting page, such as an ASP.NET or HTML page, references a Silverlight browser plug-in. When the user requests the page, the plug-in downloads and decompresses the application .xap file on the client. Additional resources like video and application binaries can be downloaded on demand outside the .xap file.

The presentation code is compiled and executed on the client. The presentation layer can employ several techniques for managing state. Just like a traditional desktop application, the client can maintain state in-memory during the application lifetime because there are no page reposts. You can use the .NET Framework isolated storage to maintain durable state per application and user (for example, storing the user preferences between application restarts). Finally, the application can make service calls to save the data elsewhere to make it available to other users.

Silverlight supports standard protocols to exchange data with Windows Communication Foundation (WCF) services, Plain Old XML (POX) services, and Representational State Transfer (REST) services. A Silverlight application can make secure cross-domain calls. All service calls are asynchronous.

Understanding developer tools

Microsoft has provided several developer tools to help you implement Silverlight solutions. Visual Studio 2008 is the Microsoft premium environment for developing and debugging Silverlight solutions. At the time of this writing, you need to install Microsoft Silverlight Tools Beta 1 for Visual Studio 2008 (see Resources) to integrate Silverlight with Visual Studio 2008. You can optionally use Microsoft Expression Blend to design the presentation layer. The version I used is Expression Blend 2.5 March 2008 Preview (see Resources for a download link). Designer-oriented tools include:

- Expression Designer for graphics
- Expression Blend for composition
- Expression Media for video
- Deep Zoom Composer for implementing image zooming that lets the user explore high resolution images without waiting for huge file downloads.

Now that you have high-level understanding of Silverlight, let me walk you through the process of creating and report-enabling a Silverlight application.

15.4.2 Implementing the User Interface

Implementing a Silverlight application is not much different than implementing a traditional ASP.NET application. It involves creating a project, designing the user interface as a set of pages, and writing code to implement the application presentation and business logic.

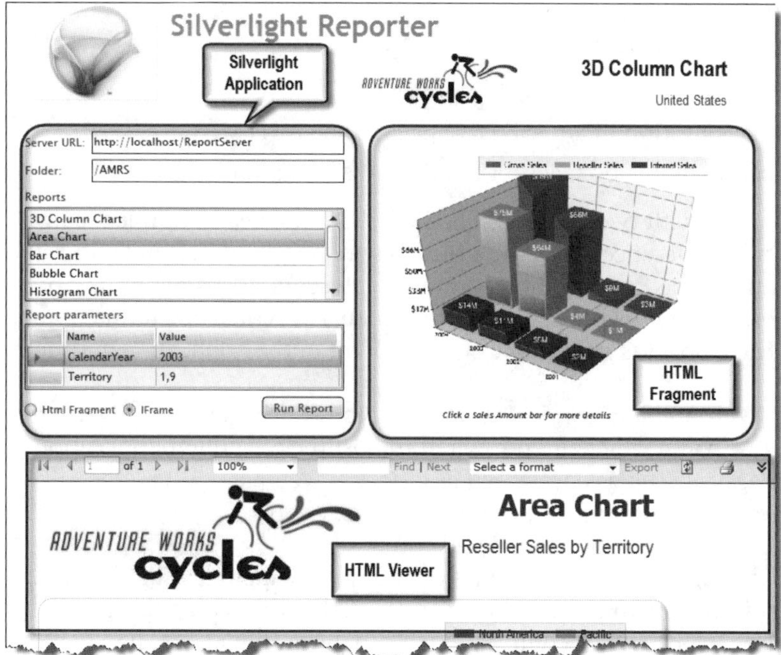

Figure 15.10 The Silverlight Reporter sample demonstrates two approaches for report-enabling Silverlight applications.

Figure 15.10 shows my Silverlight Reporter sample whose implementation details are discussed in the remainder of this section. As you've probably guessed, it is a RIA version of the WebReporter sample except that it doesn't support local report processing. The user can enter the report server URL and the folder path. The application "remembers" these settings between restarts.

Upon startup, the application loads a list of server reports deployed to the specified folder. When the user selects a report, Silverlight Reporter displays the report parameters in the grid below the Reports list. The user can change the parameter values if needed and click the Run Report button to view the report.

As it stands, the ReportViewer controls are not Silverlight-aware so you must use other techniques for integrating Reporting Services with Silverlight. Silverlight Reporter demonstrates two approaches for embedding reports in a Silverlight application:

- HTML Fragment—If the user selects the HTML Fragment option, the report is rendered as an HTML fragment to the right of the application
- IFrame—By contrast, the IFrame option displays the report in the HTML Viewer by requesting the report by URL.

Creating a Silverlight project

Start by creating a Silverlight Application project in Visual Studio 2008. Visual Studio 2008 includes C# and Visual Basic project templates to create a solution with the basic settings and code files for a Silverlight-based managed application.

1. In Visual Studio 2008, click File ⇨ New ⇨ Project.
2. In the New Project dialog box, expand the Visual C# folder (or Visual Basic) and select one of the Silverlight project types.
3. In the Templates pane, select the Silverlight Application template.
4. Enter *SilverlightReporter* as a project name. Specify a project location and click OK.

   You can host your Silverlight application in an ASP.NET page or in an HTML page.
5. In the Add Silverlight Application dialog box, accept the default settings and click OK.

Visual Studio generates a solution with two projects. The Silverlight application project contains the configuration, assembly references, and code files that are required to build and run a minimal Silverlight application. The Page page (Page.xaml) represents the user interface of the Silverlight application. Use its code-behind class (Page.xaml.cs) to write code to manipulate the presentation layer. The App class defines the starting point of the application and instantiates the Page class.

The SilverlightReporter_Web ASP.NET project is provided to host and test the Silverlight application. It contains two test pages which are pre-wired to host the Silverlight application. The SilverlightReporterTestPage.aspx file is configured as a startup web page. When the Silverlight-based application project is built, the application package (.xap) is copied to the web site in order for the test page to be able to download and run it.

The SilverlightReporterTestPage.html page includes an <OBJECT> tag to configure and instantiate the Silverlight plug-in that downloads and runs the Silverlight-based application. The .aspx file uses the Silverlight ASP.NET server control, which generates similar HTML when the page is rendered.

Designing the user interface

You can use Visual Studio to implement the user interface but I found the pre-release functionality somewhat lacking. Instead, I used Expression Blend to design the user interface of the Page class. Discussing Expression Blend in detail is beyond the scope of this book. I found the samples and tutorials gallery on the Expression Blend team blog (see Resources) very useful for getting started with this tool. Next, I will highlight some the implementation steps for authoring the SilverlightReporter user interface.

Expression Blend and Visual Studio 2008 share the same project file format, so you can use them interchangeably. For example, you can create a Silverlight project in Visual Studio and open it in Expression Blend and vice versa.

1. Start Microsoft Expression Blend 2.5.
2. In the splash screen, select the Projects tab and click the Open Project link.
3. Navigate to the Visual Studio project (SilverlightReporter.csproj) that you created and click Open to load the project in Expression Blend.

   Expression Blend designer includes several panes. The right pane has Project, Properties, and Resources tabs. Similar to the Visual Studio Solution Explorer, the Project tab shows the structure of your project. The Properties tab lets you configure the user controls. You can optionally declare a style, such as a brush, as a resource so that it can be shared by multiple elements. The Resources tab shows you all resources defined in the project. To apply a particular style to a control, you can simply drag it from the Resources pane and drop it onto the control.
4. Click the Project tab and double-click the Page.xaml page.

   Similar to Report Designer, Expression Blend includes a graphical What You See Is What You Get (WYSIWYG) designer for laying out the user interface (see Figure 15.11). The rectangular area in the middle pane is called an artboard. You can design the page presentation by adding controls from the toolbox to the artboard.

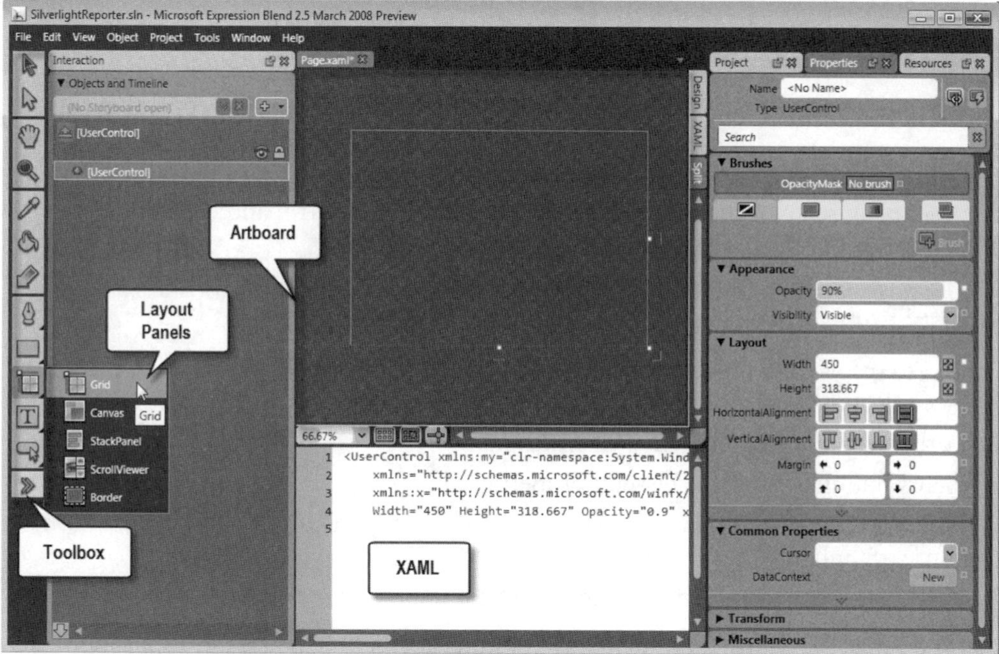

Figure 15.11 Expression Blend supports a graphical WYSIWYG designer.

The Toolbox provides access to various elements which you can use to assemble the presentation layer. The layout panels are containers that control the layout and positioning of the elements they contain. The Grid layout panel is the most flexible layout container because it lets you arrange elements in a freeform fashion. Just like desktop or web applications, Silverlight supports a set of common controls, such as TextBox, Button, RadioButton, CheckBox, and so on. The big difference is that these controls are rendered using vector graphics so you can shape, position, style these controls any way you want. Third-party vendors can provide additional controls.

5. Double-click the Grid layout panel to add it to the artboard.
6. Click the Split tab on the right of the artboard to see or edit the XAML definition that describes the page layout.
7. Click the Selection button in the toolbox and click the grid in the artboard to select the grid element.
8. In the Properties tab, change the background brush to White. Next, lay out the user interface, as shown in Figure 15.12.

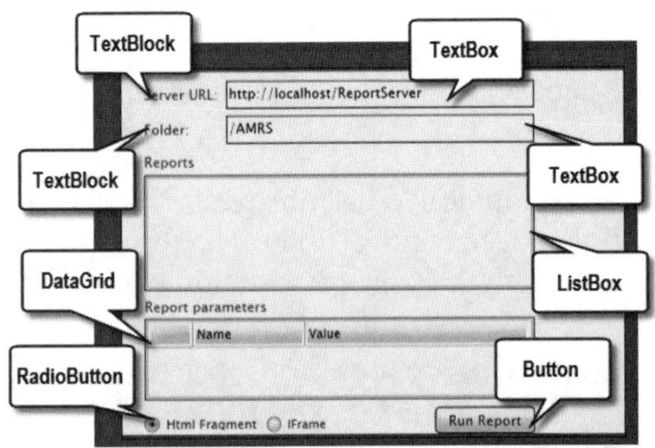

Figure 15.12 The Silver Reporter presentation layer includes several controls.

9. To add a TextBox control for the Server URL field, double-click the TextBox control in the toolbox.
10. To add a TextBlock control for implementing labels, click and hold the TextBox control in the toolbox. In the menu selector that follows, select the TextBlock control and then double-click the TextBlock control in the toolbox.

> **TIP** To see all controls, click the double arrow (last button) in the toolbox. In the Asset library that follows, click a control and drag it to the grid panel.

Since we need to display the report parameters when the user selects a report, we need to register a ListBox SelectionChanged event.

11. Select the ListBox control and click the Properties pane.
12. Click the Events button next to the ListBox properties.
13. Enter *lstReports_SelectionChanged* in the SelectionChanged property and double-click on it to create an empty event handler in the page code behind.
14. Repeat the last three steps to configure a click event for the button control.

You can let the DataGrid control auto-generate columns at run time when the application binds it to data or you can explicitly specify the columns and bindings at design time. This is not much different than configuring the Windows Forms DataGrid control that you may be already familiar with. Use the Columns property in the Miscellaneous section to configure the column properties. Alternatively, you can enter the required changes manually by changing the DataGrid XAML definition:

```
<my:DataGrid Margin="20,213,0,0" x:Name="grdParams" AutoGenerateColumns="False"
   HorizontalAlignment="Left" VerticalAlignment="Top" RowHeight="20" Widt h="350" Height="70"
      d:LayoutOverrides="GridBox" RowBackground="Cornsilk" AlternatingRowBackground="LemonChiffon">
         <my:DataGrid.Columns>
            <my:DataGridTextBoxColumn Header="Name" Width="100" IsReadOnly="True"
                        DisplayMemberBinding="{Binding Name}" FontSize="12" />
```

```
        <my:DataGridTextBoxColumn Header="Value" Width="200" FontSize="12"
                 DisplayMemberBinding="{Binding Value}" />
    </my:DataGrid.Columns>
</my:DataGrid>
```

This definition defines two columns for the parameter Name and Value properties. I use the DisplayMemberBinding property to define the column binding. For example, DisplayMemberBinding="{Binding Name}" binds the column to a Name field.

Configuring the hosting page

As noted, you can host the Silverlight application in an ASP.NET page or an HTML page. The ASP.NET page is more flexible because it can include ASP.NET controls and server-side code. This is why I decided to host the Silverlight Reporter application in the SilverlightReporterTestPage.aspx. I had to add a couple of HTML elements to display the report content:

1. In Visual Studio, double-click the SilverlightReporterTestPage.aspx to open it in the designer.
2. Click the Source tab to view the page source:

```
<form id="form1" runat="server">
   <asp:ScriptManager ID="ScriptManager1" runat="server"></asp:ScriptManager>
   <div style="height:350px">
      <asp:Silverlight ID="Xaml1" runat="server" Source="~/ClientBin/Silv erlightReporter.xap"
          Version="2.0" Width="380" Height="350" />
   </div>
   <div style="position:relative;top:-426px;left:386px;z- index:20" id="reportPlaceholder"></div>
</form>
<iframe id="iReport" style="position:relative;top: -87px;left:23px;z- index:10;margin- bottom:4px;"
   height="100%" width="820px" frameborder="0" />
```

I added the reportPlaceholder DIV element to display the report as a HTML fragment. I also added an IReport IFRAME element whose Src property I set programmatically to the report URL. The Silverlight server control generates the browser plug-in at run time that downloads the application package (SilverlightReporter.xap) and initializes the application. Visual Studio adds also a ScriptManager control to the page. This control is needed for ASP.NET pages that use Silverlight server control.

15.4.3 Report-enabling Silverlight Applications

Now that the user interface is defined, it's time to write some code that wires it up to your application. Similar to ASP.NET applications, Silverlight lets you use managed code to control UI elements. Unlike ASP.NET, the code is downloaded and executed on the client and not the server. This is important because it eliminates page refreshes and lets the application maintain state on the client.

Invoking Web services

SilverReporter calls down to the ReportService2005 management endpoint to load the report list and obtain the parameters of the selected report. This requires adding a service reference to the ReportService2005 management endpoint:

1. In Solution Explorer, right-click the SilverlightReporter project node and click Add Service Reference.
2. In the Add Service Reference dialog box, enter the address of the management endpoint. By default, this is http://localhost/ReportServer/ReportService2005.asmx?wsdl. Click Go to retrieve the service contract definition.

3. Enter *ReportService* as the service namespace and click OK.

   Let's take a closer look at the code that loads the reports:

```
private void LoadReports(){
   Binding binding = new BasicHttpBinding();
   EndpointAddress address = new EndpointAddress(this.ReportServiceAddress);
   ReportingService2005SoapClient rs = new ReportingService2005SoapClient(binding, address);
   rs.ListChildrenCompleted += new
            EventHandler<ListChildrenCompletedEventArgs>(ListChildrenCompleted);
   rs.ListChildrenAsync(txtFolder.Text, false);
}
void ListChildrenCompleted(object sender, ListChildrenCompletedEventArgs e) {
   CatalogItem[] items = e.CatalogItems;
   foreach (CatalogItem item in items)
   {
      if (item.Type == ReportService.ItemTypeEnum.Report && item.Name.Contains("Chart"))
                     lstReports.Items.Add(item.Name);
   }
   if (lstReports.Items.Count > 0)
   {
      lstReports.SelectedIndex = 0;
      btnRun.IsEnabled = true;
   }
}
private string ReportServiceAddress {
   get {return String.Format("{0}/ReportService2005.asmx", txtServerUrl.Text);}
}
```

As it stands, Silverlight supports only SOAP 1.1 and cannot use WS-* protocols, such as WS-Addressing. These requirements are met by configuring the proxy to use BasicHttpBinding. LoadReports configures the Web service proxy to use BasicHttpBinding and the user-specified report server URL. Notice that I don't set the proxy's credentials to DefaultCredentials. In fact, Silverlight doesn't let you overwrite the proxy's credentials. This is because the Silverlight communication stack is built on top of the browser networking stack. Consequently, the browser authenticates the user to the report server by using Windows integrated security.

NOTE Because the SilverlightReporter project is configured to use the ASP.NET developer server, which listens on a random port, Silverlight treats localhost (the Reporting Services host) and localhost:port (the host on which the ASP.NET application runs) as two different domains. Because Silverlight doesn't allow cross-domain calls for security reasons, the method call will fail. As a workaround, deploy the clientaccesspolicy.xml file found in the ch15\SilverlightReporter folder in the book source code to your local IIS default folder (usually C:\inetpub\wwwroot). In addition, configure the Default Web Site for Anonymous Access.

As noted, Silverlight supports only asynchronous out-of-band service calls to prevent blocking the user interface. This requires configuring a callback handler for each method invocation. The callback handler for the ListChildren method call is ListChildrenCompleted. Once LoadReports configures the callback handler, it calls ListChildrenAsync to invoke the method asynchronously.

When the method calls complete, .NET calls the ListChildrenCompleted method. ListChildrenCompleted obtains the results (CatalogItems). Then, it loops through the catalog items and adds the item to the lstReports ListBox control if the item is a report and its name contains "Chart". The decision to add only chart reports to the list was a personal preference to avoid wasting too much real estate with wider and taller reports. If the report list is not empty, ListChildrenCompleted selects the first report.

Handling report parameters

When the user selects a report, .NET triggers the lstReports_SelectionChanged event. This event calls the LoadReportParameters helper method. ListReportParameters invokes the Reporting Services GetReportParameters API asynchronously as discussed before. When the method returns, .NET calls the GetReportParametersCompleted event handler:

```
private void GetReportParametersCompleted(object sender, GetReportParametersCompletedEventArgs e) {
   _userParameters= new List<EntityParameter>();
   foreach (ReportParameter p in e.Parameters)
   {
      _userParameters.Add(new EntityParameter(p.Name,
         p.DefaultValues==null?String.Empty: String.Join(",", p.DefaultValues)));
   }
   grdParams.ItemsSource = _userParameters;
   btnRun.IsEnabled = true;
}
```

GetReportParameters returns an array of ReportParameter objects that we need to display in the Parameters grid. Although the SilverLight DataGrid control supports binding to a collection of objects, we cannot use it to populate the Parameters grid because the ReportParameter DefaultValues property returns a string array, which we cannot bind directly to a DataGrid column. We have at least two approaches to solve this predicament. We can implement a value converter to "flatten" the string and bind the converter to the Value column in the grid. Scott Morrison demonstrates this approach in his Defining Columns for a Silverlight DataGrid control (see Resources).

Another approach is to use an object that presents the report parameters in the desired format. This is the approach I took in the WinReporter and WebReporter samples. However, as it stands, Silverlight doesn't support ADO.NET datasets so I had to create a simple EntityParameter class with Name and Value properties.

The DataGrid control is a very flexible control that supports data edits. In our case, I configured the parameters grid to let the user change the Value column. For the sake of simplicity, I didn't implement data validation that would ensure that the parameter value or format is correct. Again, this is another example of a case where a data converter would be useful.

Generating reports

When the user clicks the Run Report button, .NET fires a click event that SilverReporter handles in the Button_Click event handler:

```
private void Button_Click(object sender, RoutedEventArgs e) {
   string url = this.ReportUrl;
   if (radHtmlFragment.IsChecked == true
   {
     WebRequest request = WebRequest.Create(new Uri(url));
     IAsyncResult arResp = request.BeginGetResponse(
        new AsyncCallback(this.ReportRenderResponseCompleted), new object[]
         { request, lstReports.SelectedItem.ToString()});
   }
   else _doc.GetElementById("iReport").SetProperty("src", this.ReportUrl);
   SaveUserSettings();
}
private void ReportRenderResponseCompleted(IAsyncResult ar){
   string reportPayload = null;
   object[] State = (object[])ar.AsyncState;
   WebRequest webReq = (WebRequest)State[0];
   WebResponse response = webReq.EndGetResponse(ar);
   using (StreamReader reader = new StreamReader(response.GetResponseStream()))
   {
      reportPayload = reader.ReadToEnd();
   }
   _doc.GetElementById("reportPlaceholder").SetProperty("innerHTML", reportPayload);
}
```

If the HTML Fragment radio button is checked, SilverReport generates the report by URL. To do so, Silverlight Reporter calls the WebRequest.GetResponse method asynchronously. This approach is similar to the URL Stream option which I demonstrated in the IntegrationOptions sample back in chapter 14. The report URL request uses device information settings to remove the toolbar (rc:Toolbar=False), export the report as an HTML fragment (rc:HtmlFragment=True), and zoom the report to 75 percent (rc:Zoom=75) to fit the report in the available space. Once the report stream is received, ReportRenderResponseCompleted converts the report payload to a string.

Similar to ASP.NET, Silverlight lets you manipulate the browser DOM object programmatically. To embed the report on the page, I call the DOM GetElementbyId method to get a reference to the reportPlaceholder DIV element and set its innerHTML property to the report HTML fragment. If the IFRAME option is selected, the Button_Click obtains a reference to the iReport IFRAME element and sets its SRC property to the report URL. This causes the IFRAME to request the report by URL.

Maintaining state

Maintaining user-specific state is an important requirement for most business applications. A Silverlight application can maintain application and user-specific state in the .NET isolated storage file system. In fact, a Silverlight application is sandboxed and cannot write only to its isolated storage. Silverlight Reporter demonstrates this by saving the user preferences (report server URL and folder path) so they are available between application restarts:

```
private void LoadUserSettings() {
   string data = null;
   IsolatedStorageFile iso = IsolatedStorageFile.GetUserStoreForApplic ation();
   using (IsolatedStorageFileStream isoStream = new IsolatedStorageFileStream("app.config", FileMode.Open, iso))
   {
      using (StreamReader reader = new StreamReader(isoStream))
      {
            data = reader.ReadToEnd();
      }
   }
   if (data != null)
   {
      string[] settings = data.Split(new char[] {'~'});
      txtServerUrl.Text  = settings[0];
      txtFolder.Text     = settings[1];
   }
}
private void SaveUserSettings() {
   string data = String.Format("{0}~{1}", txtServerUrl.Text, txtFolder.Text);
   IsolatedStorageFile iso = IsolatedStorageFile.GetUserStoreForApplication();
   using (IsolatedStorageFileStream isoStream = iso.CreateFile("app.config"))    {
      using (StreamWriter writer = new StreamWriter(isoStream))
      {
         writer.Write(data);
      }
   }
}
```

Because a Silverlight page doesn't have an Unload event, Silverlight Reporter saves the user preferences when the user clicks the Run Report button. SaveUserSettings calls IsolatedStorageFile.GetUserStoreForApplication to obtain user-scoped isolated storage corresponding for the application and writes the report server URL and folder path to an app.config file. When the application starts, the class constructor calls LoadUserSettings to retrieve the user preferences. LoadUserSettings reads the content of the app.config file and parses the report server URL and folder path.

15.5 Summary

Report-enabling a custom application doesn't have to be a tedious chore. If you are tasked to report-enable a .NET desktop or web application, definitely consider the Visual Studio ReportViewer controls to save yourself a considerable integration effort. Configure ReportViewer in remote processing mode when requesting server reports. Use local processing mode when you need to distribute reports with your application or bind reports to application datasets or business objects.

On the Web frontier, technology boundaries are blurring. Rich Internet applications are emerging to bring together the best of traditional desktop and web applications. Currently, the ReportViewer controls don't support natively RIA technologies like AJAX or Silverlight. However, thanks to the Reporting Services open architecture, you can report-enable RIAs by invoking the Report Services APIs and requesting reports by URL.

15.6 Resources

Browser Support for ReportViewer Web Server Controls
(http://tinyurl.com/2rg55o)—Explains the browser support for ReportViewer.

Microsoft Report Viewer Redistributable 2008
(http://tinyurl.com/2yyz5k)— The ReportViewer redistributable package. For ClickOnce deployment, use http://go.microsoft.com/fwlink/?LinkID=98185.

ReportViewer Controls Documentation
(http://tinyurl.com/ynvoam)—The ReportViewer documentation.

IReportViewerMessages Interfaces
(http://tinyurl.com/2v8vmy)—ReportViewer Windows Forms localization.
(http://tinyurl.com/3ap3bb)—ReportViewer Web server localization.

Web.config Settings for ReportViewer
(http://tinyurl.com/2k5uv7)—Explains how to customize ReportViewer operations.

machineKey Element (ASP.NET Settings Schema)
(http://tinyurl.com/3y762c)—Synchronize view state in a web farm environment.

ReportViewer Website
(http://www.gotreportviewer.com)—This ReportViewer website.

ReportViewer Discussion Forum
(http://tinyurl.com/2azpuq)—The ReportViewer discussion list.

Microsoft Silverlight Tools Beta 1 for Visual Studio 2008
(http://tinyurl.com/2spyr4)—A Visual Studio 2008 add-in for developing Silverlight applications.

Microsoft Expression Blend 2.5 March 2008 Preview
(http://tinyurl.com/2k8la2)—You can use Microsoft Expression Blend 2.5 to author the presentation layer of Silverlight applications.

Samples and Tutorials Gallery - Expression Blend
(http://tinyurl.com/35owal)—A set of resources for Expression Blend.

Defining Columns for a Silverlight DataGrid
(http://tinyurl.com/2sljeb)—Learn about the DataGrid control and Silverlight.

Chapter 16

Integrating with Analysis Services

To be frank, an organization that only occasionally reviews its data through spreadsheets or canned reports is probably missing the strategic value of its data. The data that you are already collecting and storing might very well be holding important answers to the next business decision you need to make. Once you've successfully mastered the basics of reporting, you may find that it is time to "graduate" to the next level—efficient, consistent, and rich data analytics. This is where Analysis Services comes in. I believe that every small to medium-size organization should tap into the power of Analysis Services to implement reporting solutions for historical and trend reporting, as well as predictive analysis.

Because this book is about Reporting Services, this chapter gives you just enough background to understand and use Analysis Services to build synergetic reporting solutions. It starts by introducing you to Analysis Services and laying out the fundamentals of this integration scenario. The bulk of this chapter covers building OLAP reports that draw data from Analysis Services cubes. You'll learn how to implement reports that leverage Analysis Services end-user features, including report actions and translations. I will also show you how to author data mining reports that display prediction results.

16.1 Understanding Analysis Services

As its name suggests, Microsoft SQL Server Analysis Services promotes better data analytics by giving information workers powerful ways to analyze data. To be more specific, we can describe Analysis Services as a server-based platform that provides two core services—On-Line Analytical Processing (OLAP) and Data Mining. Let's cover these two terms in more detail.

16.1.1 Understanding OLAP

There are two types of database-driven systems that serve very different requirements: On-Line Transactional Processing (OLTP) systems and OLAP systems. To understand Analysis Services, it is important to learn how these two system types compare.

About OLTP systems

OLTP systems are designed for fast transactional input to support transaction-oriented applications such as data entry applications. Typically, the schema of a database that stores OLTP data is highly normalized, which means that it both minimizes duplication of information and safeguards the database against certain types of logical or structural problems that can compromise data integrity.

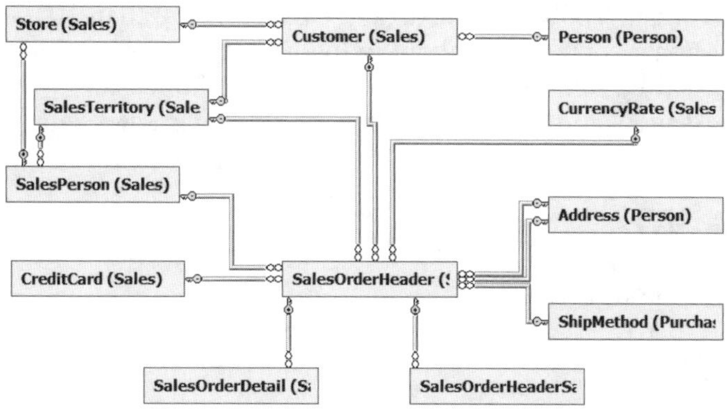

Figure 16.1 OLTP database schemas are highly normalized and optimized for data storage.

The AdventureWorks2008 sample database demonstrates a realistic OLTP schema. As it stands, its database schema contains more than 70 tables. Figure 16.1 contains a portion of the AdventureWorks2008 database schema that shows some of the tables that capture sales order data. Notice that the schema is highly normalized. For example, the order header information is captured in the SalesOrderHeader table while the order detail information is stored separately in the SalesOrderDetail table. Similarly, the Customer table stores customer identity information, while the customer address details are kept in a separate Address (Person) table.

OLTP systems have three key benefits:

- Efficient storage—Since the schema is normalized, there is no duplication of data.
- Fast data entry—Relational databases (RDBMS) are optimized to process data changes quickly (by that, I mean insert, delete, and update operations).
- Fast retrieval by primary keys or indexes—Relational databases can retrieve indexed records extremely fast. For example, assuming that the sales order number column is indexed, retrieving the details of a single order can appear to be instantaneous.

At the same time, OLTP databases have well-known disadvantages:

- Inefficient report processes—In general, the more data the report aggregates, the slower the query response time will be if the report gets its source data from an OLTP database. To make things worse, SELECT statements may lock the underlying data while the report is processing, which can negatively impact the performance of the OLTP applications that use the database.
- Not intuitive to end users—OLTP systems are designed with the system and not the user in mind. Consequently, business users may find it difficult to navigate the database schema and understand which tables need to be joined to author ad-hoc reports.

About OLAP systems

By contrast, OLAP systems are designed to support data analytics and reporting needs. This is achieved by reducing the number of tables available for reporting, de-normalizing data, and simplifying the database schema. OLAP is geared toward having the user online with the data, slicing and dicing the data to view it in different ways, drilling down into the data to see more detail.

The AdventureWorksDW2008 sample database demonstrates an OLAP database that has been designed in accordance with dimensional modeling methodology. This OLAP database runs in the SQL Server Database Engine alongside its OLTP counterpart. In comparison with its OLTP counterpart, the AdventureWorksDW2008 sample database contains less than 30 tables. Figure 16.2 shows just the tables that contain data about individual sales. The FactInternetSales table stores the numeric facts used to measure sales to consumers. Dimension tables, such as DimDate, DimCustomer, and so on, let the user slice the consumer sales data in the fact table by subject areas.

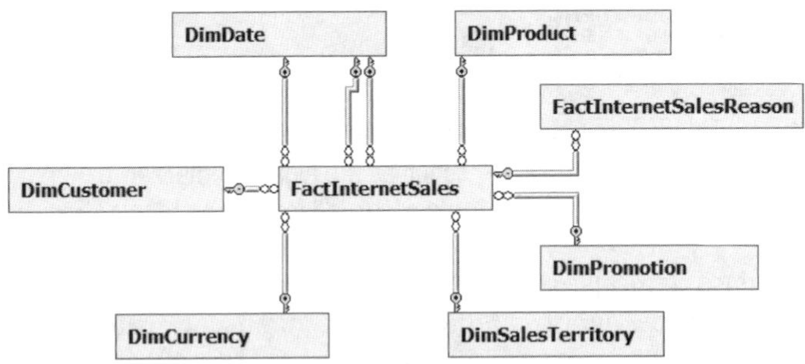

Figure 16.2 OLAP database schemas are optimized for data analytics and reporting.

As you might have immediately noticed, the fact table (FactInternetSales) and its related dimension tables form the star pattern that is typical of OLAP. With a star schema, the dimension data is contained within a single table. This requires denormalizing the dimension data, which is another common OLAP data modeling technique. For example, a Product dimension able may contain all product-related data, such as products, product category, model, color, and so on.

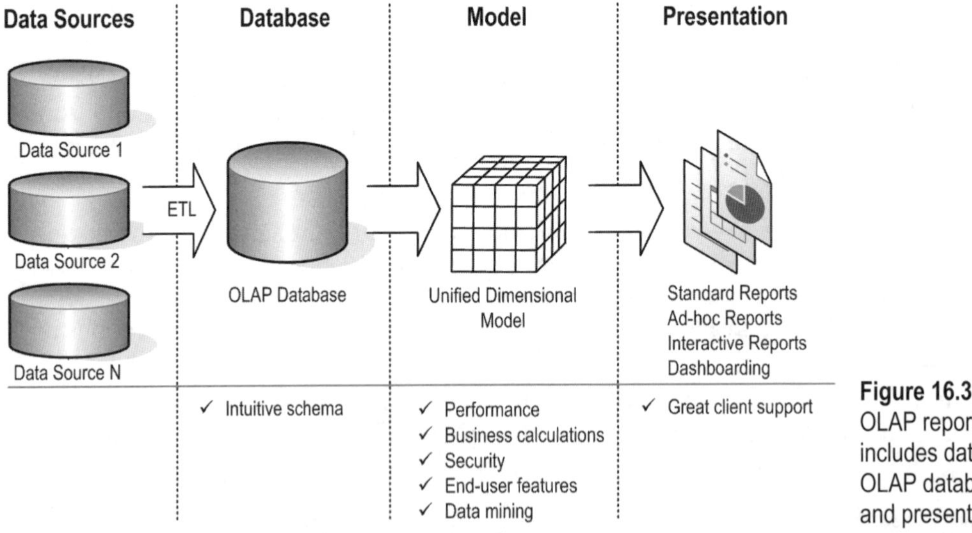

Figure 16.3 A typical OLAP reporting solution includes data sources, OLAP database, model, and presentation layers.

If the dimension hierarchy is left normalized, then the schema is of a *snowflake* type. For example, if for some reason product category data is located in a separate dimension table, the product dimension table would reference the product category dimension table. Analysis Services supports both star and snowflake schemas. However, star schemas usually work best with OLAP and you should gravitate toward them whenever possible. Ad-hoc reporting processes can also benefit from a star schema because it minimizes the number of tables that you work with.

On the downside, as you've probably guessed, OLAP requires more effort for designing the dimensional schema and implementing the data logistics processes that load the OLAP database. Figure 16.3 shows these processes in the context of a typical OLAP reporting solution. ETL (Extract, Transform, and Load) packages implemented as Microsoft SQL Server Integration Services packages periodically extract data from the operational data sources, such as OLTP databases or flat files. The data is scrubbed and loaded into a multidimensional OLAP database, such as a data mart or a data warehouse database.

Why use Analysis Services?

If we can design and use an OLAP database that is already optimized for reporting through the SQL Server Database Engine, why do we need Analysis Services? The answer to that question can be found in the rich metadata layer that Analysis Services provides. Analysis Services builds on an OLAP database by adding the Unified Dimensional Model (UDM), also known as an Analysis Services cube, between the database and presentation layer. UDM brings substantial benefits besides just slicing and dicing data.

DEFINITION The cube is a logical storage object that combines dimensions and measures to provide a multidimensional view of data. The term Unified Dimensional Model (UDM) promotes the idea that an Analysis Services cube is more than a traditional OLAP cube because it combines characteristics of relational (attributes, flexible relationships) and dimensional models (dimensions, measures, hierarchies). I will use the terms "UDM" and "cube" interchangeably.

Let's enumerate some of the most important Analysis Services benefits.

1. Performance—To start with, Analysis Services is designed to deliver exceptional performance with large data volumes. According to Microsoft, data can be expected to grow at the rate of 35% each year on average. Nowadays, it is not uncommon for organizations to accumulate hundreds of gigabytes, if not terabytes, of data. Historical and trend reports that directly query a relational data source and aggregate huge data loads are likely to present performance challenges. Moreover, ad-hoc reports aggravate this situation even further because the auto-generated queries they create are so variable that they can't use the database optimization techniques (such as indexing) that you provide.
2. Business calculations—Relational databases are not suitable for defining business calculations, such as year-to-date, percent of total, moving averages, year-to-year growth, and so on. This is because relational databases have no notion of the hierarchical relationships in data—for example, years that break down into semesters, which break down into quarters, and so on. By contrast, Analysis Services understands the semantics of data and lets you extend your cubes with business calculations in the form of (**M**ulti-**D**imensional E**X**pressions) MDX expressions.
3. Security—How do you secure your report data? If your current data security solution is either non-existent or hopelessly complex, you can benefit from the flexible role-based security model provided by Analysis Services. This security model is enforced when the user connects to the cube. If you want to learn more about Analysis Services security, you may find my Protect UDM with Dimension Data Security article (see Resources) helpful.
4. End-user features—Analysis Services supports additional features that provide an intuitive end-user experience. Actions can extend your cubes in versatile ways. For example, suppose that the user has drilled down to the lowest level of the Product dimension and wants to see

the individual sales orders that have been placed for that product. If the order information is not stored in the cube, you can implement a reporting action that lets the user request a report that displays the order data from another system. Key performance indicators (KPIs) measure the company's performance and can be displayed on the report. Translations let you localize the cube data and metadata for international users.

5. Good client support—There are many Microsoft-provided and third-party tools that support Analysis Services and its MDX query language. For example, executive managers can use Microsoft Excel for interactive historical and trend reporting and Reporting Services for standard and ad-hoc reporting.
6. Data mining—Data mining is one of my favorite Analysis Services features. It also happens to be one of the least understood features, so let's discuss it next in more detail.

16.1.2 Understanding Data Mining

The second main service that Analysis Services provides is data mining. Data mining is a science in itself. Generally speaking, data mining is concerned with the process used to predict the unknown based on known statistical facts. However, instead of asking us to look into a crystal ball, Analysis Services employs sophisticated mathematical models that can analyze large volumes of data, discover patterns and trends, and produce prediction results.

NOTE OLAP and data mining are two different technologies and shouldn't be used interchangeably. OLAP gives you slicing and dicing data with a click of a mouse. However, you can click all day long and still not be able to discern hidden data patterns, such as understanding your customer profiles or the factors that influence a customer's decision to purchase a given product. This is where data mining can help.

Why use data mining?

Typical examples of how data mining can help include forecasting, customer profiling, and basket analysis. For instance, by examining historical sales data, data mining can answer the following questions:

- What are the forecasted sales numbers for the next few months?
- What additional products is a customer likely to buy along with the product he or she already chose?
- What type of customer (described in terms of gender, age group, income, and so on) is likely to buy a given product?

Let's take a closer look at how data mining can help you with sales forecasting. Suppose that the Adventure Works management has asked you to forecast sales by territory for the next five months. Instead of dusting off your college math book, you prudently decide to use Analysis Services. Once you build the data mining model, you can produce a report similar to the one shown in Figure 16.4 with a few mouse clicks.

Using data mining for sales forecasting

This report uses the Adventure Works Forecasting data mining model, which is one of the sample mining models included in the Adventure Works Analysis Services project. It shows the Adventure Works historical sales on the left side of the vertical line. The dotted line represents the forecasted sales. You can change the Prediction Steps up-down field to tell the model how many periods of forecasted data you want to see. In this case, the report shows only European sales. Behind the scenes, the model uses the Microsoft Time Series algorithm to predict expected sales.

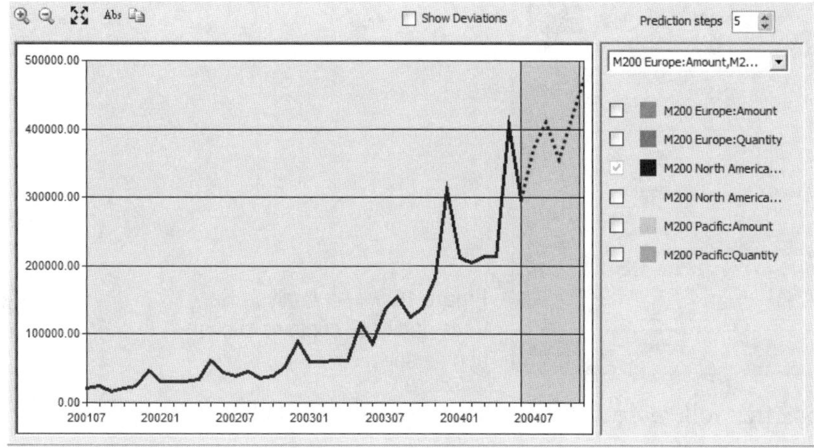

Figure 16.4 Use data mining to discover trends in data, such as forecasting future sales.

16.1.3 Historical and Trend Reporting

Analysis Services can be best understood when seen in action. Assuming that you have deployed the Adventure Works cube and have Microsoft Excel 2007, let's take a look at how a business user might leverage the OLAP capabilities of Analysis Services for historical and trend reporting. This demo will also help us clarify some Analysis Services terms. You can find the finished report (Reseller Sales.xlsx) in the Excel folder of the book source code.

Connecting to the cube

Start by setting up a connection to the Adventure Works cube.

1. Open Microsoft Excel 2007. Click the Data main menu.
2. Expand the From Other Source drop-down menu located in the Get External Data ribbon group and click From Analysis Services to start the Data Connection Wizard.
3. In the Connect to Database Server step, enter the server name that hosts the Adventure Works cube, such as *(local)* if the cube is deployed locally.
4. In the Select Database and Table step, shown in Figure 16.5, expand the drop-down and select Adventure Works DW 2008, which is an Analysis Services database that hosts the Adventure Works cube.

NOTE Don't confuse the Adventure Works DW 2008 OLAP database with the AdventureWorksDW2008 RDBMS database. The Adventure Works DW OLAP database runs under Analysis Services. The latter runs under SQL Server.

Observe that the Adventure Works DW 2008 Analysis Services database contains cubes and perspectives. An Analysis Services perspective is a logical subset of the cube. Its main purpose is to reduce the perceived complexity of a large cube by exposing only a subset of the cube objects. For example, the Channel Sales perspective includes only reseller-related objects.

5. Assuming that you are interested in analyzing reseller sales only, select the Channel Sales perspective and click Next.
6. Accept the defaults in the Save Data Connection and Finish step and click Finish.

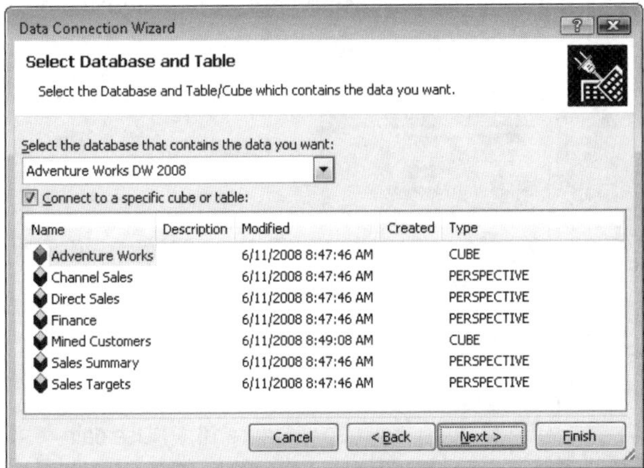

Figure 16.5 An Analysis Services database contains cubes and perspectives.

7. In the Import Data dialog box that follows, accept the default settings and click OK.

   Excel generates an empty PivotTable report and displays the cube metadata in the PivotTable Field List pane, as shown in Figure 16.6.

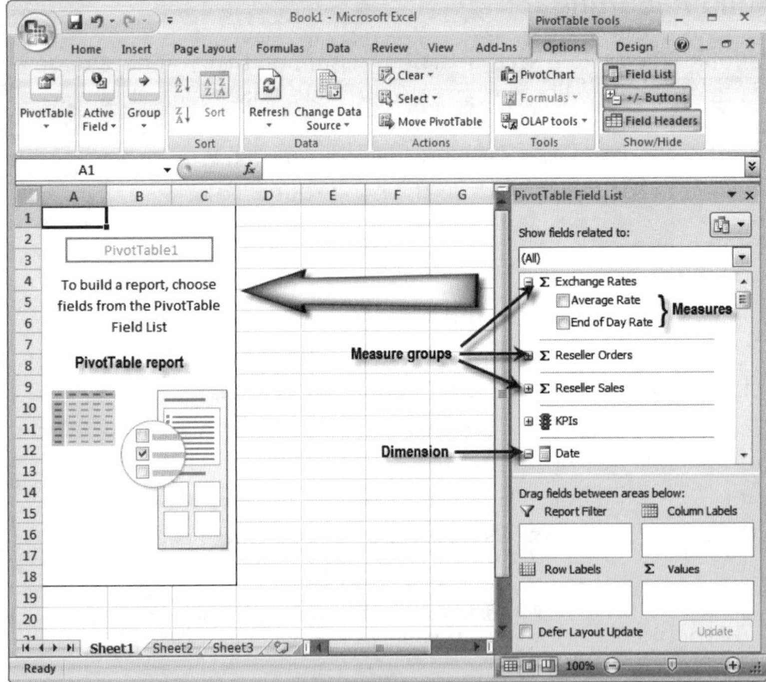

Figure 16.6 You can author an Excel PivotTable report by selecting dimensions and measures.

Understanding Analysis Services metadata

You can easily tell OLAP objects apart by glancing at the PivotTable Field List. Measure groups, which usually correspond to fact tables in the database, are prefixed with a special sum ∑ symbol. The Channel Sales perspective includes measure groups for Exchange Rates, Reseller Orders, and Resellers Sales. A measure group is a container of measures. For example, the Exchange Rates measure group contains Average Rate and End of Day Rate measures.

The main goal of Analysis Services and dimensional models is to let users slice and dice data along dimensions, such as time, geography, and product, so that you can isolate and view the factors that contribute to or detract from the value of a measure. Dimensions are containers of attributes (not shown in the screenshot) that map to columns in the underlying dimension table. For example, the Calendar Year attribute in the Date dimension may map to a CalendarYear column in a table in the data source.

Each dimension attribute can form its own hierarchy. This brings tremendous flexibility for analyzing data. For example, most attribute hierarchies include a special All member that returns an aggregated grand total value for a measure used on the report. Given an attribute hierarchy of Calendar year and a Reseller Sales Amount measure, the All member of Calendar year will show total reseller sales across all years.

Besides attribute hierarchies, the modeler may have defined useful navigational paths in UDM by combining attributes in user-defined hierarchies. For example, it is likely that a user might prefer to slice data by the date natural hierarchy, such as Year ⇨ Semester ⇨Quarter ⇨ Month ⇨ Date. Consequently, you can set up a Calendar hierarchy consisting of these levels, which are formed by the corresponding attributes.

Reseller Sales Amount	Column Labels				
Row Labels	CY 2001	CY 2002	CY 2003	CY 2004	Grand Total
Brakes and Gears	$88,003.66	$247,559.40	$361,627.85	$179,916.29	$877,107.19
Excellent Riding Supplies	$73,842.73	$317,507.39	$323,324.43	$139,174.63	$853,849.18
Vigorous Exercise Company	$162,738.91	$316,681.80	$252,613.29	$109,874.78	$841,908.77
Totes & Baskets Company	$56,811.47	$296,913.35	$328,615.66	$134,415.10	$816,755.58
Retail Mall	$79,747.30	$336,746.33	$291,364.58	$91,419.69	$799,277.90
Corner Bicycle Supply	$66,495.98	$288,884.07	$315,833.45	$116,559.55	$787,773.04
Outdoor Equipment Store		$246,607.15	$360,839.91	$138,870.46	$746,317.53
Thorough Parts and Repair Services	$67,451.77	$190,638.51	$294,930.72	$187,964.84	$740,985.83
Health Spa, Limited	$72,581.80	$267,647.07	$294,128.38	$96,441.46	$730,798.71
Fitness Toy Store	$76,086.19	$276,086.15	$297,219.90	$77,880.41	$727,272.65
Latest Sports Equipment	$102,220.61	$226,350.89	$272,497.87	$123,230.26	$724,299.64
First Bike Store	$38,099.42	$236,445.56	$308,893.80	$128,425.99	$711,864.76
Great Bikes	$55,186.21	$247,370.31	$249,537.33	$148,709.93	$700,803.79
Farthermost Bike Shop	$74,349.51	$328,362.94	$237,193.84	$53,596.20	$693,502.49
Field Trip Store		$116,789.48	$368,440.99	$186,387.56	$671,618.03
Metropolitan Equipment		$235,385.62	$307,274.84	$101,085.44	$643,745.90
Eastside Department Store		$208,261.62	$309,514.91	$118,449.94	$636,226.47
The Gear Store	$63,565.20	$264,313.10	$210,357.48	$80,380.35	$618,616.13
Sheet Metal Manufacturing		$200,016.03	$306,032.50	$111,291.92	$617,340.46
Top Sports Supply		$159,424.53	$308,875.49	$134,259.87	$602,559.89
Grand Total	**$1,077,180.75**	**$5,007,991.30**	**$5,999,117.21**	**$2,458,334.67**	**$14,542,623.93**

Figure 16.7 This report shows the top 20 resellers.

Authoring a report

Once a user becomes familiar with the cube metadata, authoring a trend report is a matter of selecting the desired measures and attributes. Let's author the report shown in Figure 16.7. This report shows the top 20 Adventure Works resellers sorted by their overall sales.

1. Expand the Reseller Sales measure group and select the Reseller Sales Amount measure.

As soon as you select the measure, Excel auto-generates an MDX query, sends it to the server, and displays the results in single cell. The result represents the grand total reseller sales amount across all dimensions.

TIP Excel doesn't let you view the auto-generated MDX query. You can use the SQL Server Profiler (in the Microsoft SQL Server 2008 ⇨ Performance Tools program group) to connect to the server and trace the calls to it.

2. To slice the Reseller Sales Amount measure by time, in the PivotTable Field List, expand the Date dimension and the Calendar display folder, and select the Date.Calendar user-defined hierarchy. It consists of Calendar Year, Calendar Semester, Calendar Quarter, Month, and Date levels.

   Excel updates the report to show reseller sales broken out by time. Because the Calendar.Year has multiple levels, you can drill down to the next level. For example, to drill down to the semester level of calendar year 2001, expand the plus sign of the CY 2001 member.

3. In the PivotTable Field List, scroll down to the Reseller dimension. Expand the More Fields folder which groups the attributes of the Reseller dimension. Select the Reseller attribute.

   The report now shows reseller sales data broken down by resellers on rows and time on columns. The lower area of the PivotTable Field List shows the objects used on the report. You can move the objects around to change the report layout. For example, if you want to see the report broken down by time and resellers on rows, drag the Date.Calendar field from the Column Labels list and drop it before the Reseller field in the Row Labels list. The Excel Undo (Ctrl-Z) command is your best friend if you need to cancel unwanted changes.

4. To define a top 20 filter, right-click any reseller on the report, and click Filter ⇨ Top 10.
5. In the Top 10 filter dialog box that follows, change the filter to top 20 and click OK. Excel updates the report to show the top 20 resellers by their grand total sales.
6. To sort the report by grand total in descending order (top-selling resellers on top), right-click any cell in the Grand Total column and choose Sort ⇨ Sort Largest to Smallest.

   As you can imagine, although we've only scratched the tip of the iceberg, this type of interactive reporting is a dream come true for data analysts and executive managers. With a click of the mouse, you can slice and dice data efficiently to analyze the company performance from different angles.

16.1.4 Introducing Analysis Services and Reporting Services Integration

While Excel is a great tool for interactive historical and trend analysis, its PivotTable component has a fairly rigid layout that does not lend itself to authoring standard reports. For example, Excel doesn't let you define report groups. In addition, Excel alone doesn't support enterprise reporting features, such as report catalog, subscriptions, security, and so on. This is where Reporting Services comes in.

Understanding integration options

You can integrate Reporting Services and Analysis Services to distribute and visualize cube data in new and interesting ways. As Figure 16.8 demonstrates, reports that you build in Reporting Services can draw data from an Analysis Services cube. When using a cube as a data source, Reporting Services can benefit from the Analysis Services breadth of features, which I discussed before.

At the same time, Reporting Services complements Analysis Services by providing a presentation layer for delivering reports. Developers and power users can use the graphical MDX Query Designer included in the BIDS Report Designer and Report Builder 2.0 to author full-featured standard and ad hoc reports. Non-technical users can consider using Report Builder 1.0 to author simple reports, as I demonstrated in chapter 9. In addition, you can author and deploy strategic reports, such as performance reports with KPIs, to SharePoint-based executive dashboards.

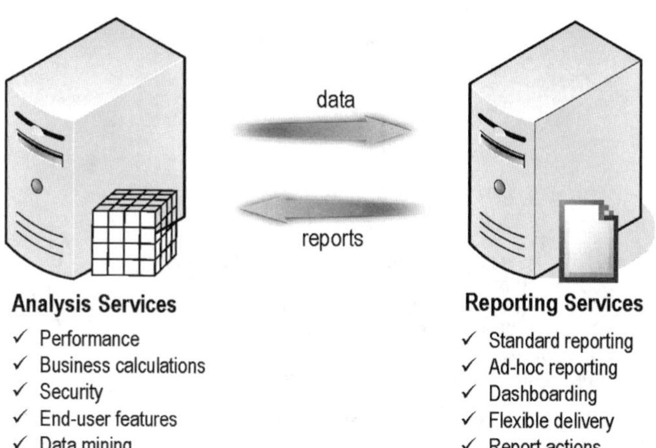

Figure 16.8 You can integrate Reporting Services and Analysis Services to get the best of both worlds.

From a Reporting Services standpoint, an OLAP or data-mining report is no different than any other report. This means that you can use Reporting Services' flexible delivery options to distribute reports on demand or via subscriptions.

Glancing back at the solution depicted in Figure 16.7, UDM is a focal point for data analysis and serves most of the reporting needs. But what if you want to extend UDM with reports that show data that is not stored in the cube? Fortunately, the integration between Analysis Services and Reporting Services is bi-directional. Not only can UDM be used as a report data source but also it can request reports. UDM reporting actions let you display Reporting Services detailed reports by querying directly the OLAP database or the operational data source. I will demonstrate this scenario in section 16.3.2.

Understanding the Analysis Services data provider

To facilitate integration with Analysis Services, Reporting Services installs an Analysis Services data provider which I will also refer to as the *built-in* Analysis Services data provider. This data provider remains unchanged from the previous release. It is implemented as a Microsoft .NET data processing extension that uses the ADOMD.NET programming library to communicate with Analysis Services. The Analysis Services data provider supports several features that would otherwise require significant development effort on your part, such as parameterized queries, server aggregates, and extended properties.

Analysis Services can return query results in two formats: cellset and rowset. The cellset format preserves the hierarchical nature of the multi-dimensional data, including row axes, column axes, and server (All member) aggregates. Most OLAP browsers, Microsoft Excel included, prefer the cellset format. By contrast, the rowset format "flattens" the results into a tabular dataset. The Analysis Services data provider uses the rowset format. As a result, the All member totals are excluded by default from the query results.

Another unfortunate limitation of the Analysis Services data provider is that it supports only static query schemas with fixed columns. Figure 16.9 shows how dynamic (left diagram) and static schemas (right diagram) differ. Most OLAP browsers have no restrictions on the MDX query schema. For example, the Excel PivotTable report I demonstrated earlier requests the Date dimension on columns and Reseller dimension on rows. If a new year is added to the

Date dimension, the report will pick it up and add a new column the next time you refresh the report data.

Category	2002	2003	2004
Bikes	200	300	400
Clothing	200	300	400
Components	200	300	400

```
SELECT [Date].[Calendar Year].ALLMEMBERS ON COLUMNS,
[Product].[Category].Members ON ROWS
FROM [Adventure Works]
WHERE [Measures].[Reseller Sales Amount]
```

Category	Year	Amount
Bikes	2002	200
Bikes	2003	300
Bikes	2004	400
Clothing	2002	200

```
SELECT [Measures].[Reseller Sales Amount] ON COLUMNS,
[Product].[Category].[Category] *
[Date].[Calendar Year].[Calendar Year] ON ROWS
FROM [Adventure Works]
```

Figure 16.9 Reporting Services supports static columns only, as the example on the right shows.

By contrast, unless you have a matrix report, the layout of a Reporting Services report is fixed at design time and cannot "expand" to accommodate new columns. What will happen the next time you request the report if the dimension has new members that are not included in the report layout? The new members simply won't show up, while deleted members will result in empty columns. This is why the built-in Analysis Services data provider doesn't let you place dimensions on columns.

To help you avoid a broken report layout at run time, Reporting Services requires that you place dimensions on rows and measures on columns, as demonstrated in the right diagram. In case you are curious, the asterisk (*) operator in the second query is used to cross-join the Category attribute hierarchy of the Product dimension with the Calendar Year attribute hierarchy of the Date dimension. You can use the SQL Server Management Studio to test the MDX query. To do so, connect to Analysis Services, click the Analysis Services MDX Query toolbar button, enter the query text, and click the exclamation button.

I personally think that this limitation is overly restrictive. A better approach could have been to support dynamic query schemas anyway, allowing the report author to assume the risk to report layout and then mitigate that risk using code or advanced features. In section 16.2.6, I will demonstrate two options for getting around the static schema limitation.

NOTE Does the static query schema get in the way? Chris Webb (SQL Server MVP) and Andrew Wiles have implemented a commercial Intelligencia Query product (see Resources) that supports arbitrary MDX queries. Behind the scenes, Intelligencia Query rewrites the query results by transforming columns to rows. This lets you use the Reporting Services matrix region to pivot the results back and recreate the original structure of the query.

Understanding the MDX Query Designer

The Report Designer includes a handy graphical MDX Query Designer, which you were introduced to briefly during the hands-on lab in chapter 1. Figure 16.10 shows the components of the MDX Query Designer.

The Cube Selection control lets you select a cube or perspective in the connected database. The Metadata pane displays the cube metadata. The MDX Query supports two modes that you can toggle by clicking the Design Mode toolbar button. In design mode, the MDX Query Designer auto-generates the MDX query as a result of dragging and dropping objects from the Metadata pane to the Data pane. This facilitates ad-hoc reporting since the user doesn't have to know MDX to prepare the report query. You can drag attribute and user-defined hierarchies, hierarchy levels, measures, calculated members, and KPI constituents (Value, Goal, Target, and Status).

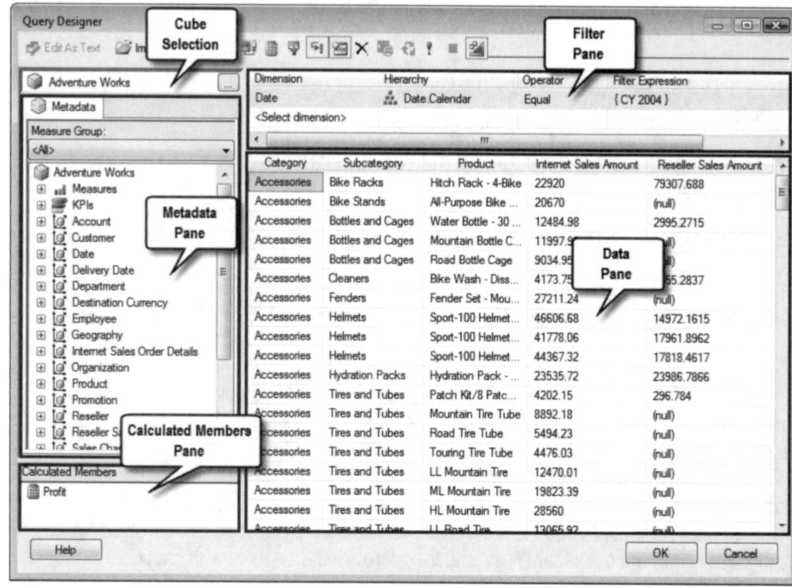

Figure 16.10 The MDX Query Designer auto-generates the MDX query as you drag and drop objects from the Metadata pane to the Data pane.

In some cases, you will need to change the MDX query to support more advanced scenarios, such as when you need more control over query parameters. The query mode lets you view the raw MDX query and make changes to it. However, be aware that your changes will be lost if you switch back to design mode. In other words, the MDX Query Designer cannot reverse-engineer changes made in the Query mode. Once you choose query mode and edit the query directly, you need to stay in that mode. Saving and reopening the query restores the ability to work in design mode.

You can filter the query results by dragging objects from the Metadata pane to the Filter pane. You can drag attribute and user-defined hierarchies, individual members, hierarchy levels, and named sets.

DEFINITION A named set is a pre-defined set of dimension members that is assigned an alias. For example, the Reseller dimension in the Adventure Works cube includes a Large Reseller set that selects that returns resellers with a number of employees between 81 and 100.

Finally, the Calculated Members pane lets you define expression-based members that can be used on the report. For example, you can define a Profit calculated member that uses the following MDX expression:

```
[Measures].[Sales Amount] - [Measures].[Total Product Cost]
```

Understanding security

Bear in mind that Analysis Services supports Windows authentication only. This means you need to be aware of the "double hop" issue with NTLM when Reporting Services and Analysis Services are installed on different machines (this issue was discussed in chapter 2). The best way to avoid double-hop connection errors is to configure Kerberos so Reporting Services can delegate the user identity to Analysis Services.

If configuring Kerberos is not possible, you have two options: use a single set of stored credentials that retrieves data for all users, or prompt the user for credentials. First, consider the trusted account approach that sends all report queries to Analysis Services under the same Windows account, as follows:

1. Open the data source properties page in Report Manager.
2. Select the Credentials Stored Securely in the Report Server option.
3. Enter the credentials of a Windows account that has minimum permissions to retrieve data from the cube.
4. Check the Use as Windows Credentials When Connecting to the Data Source option. Click Apply.

The trusted account approach is easy to set up. However, Analysis Services won't be able to differentiate users.

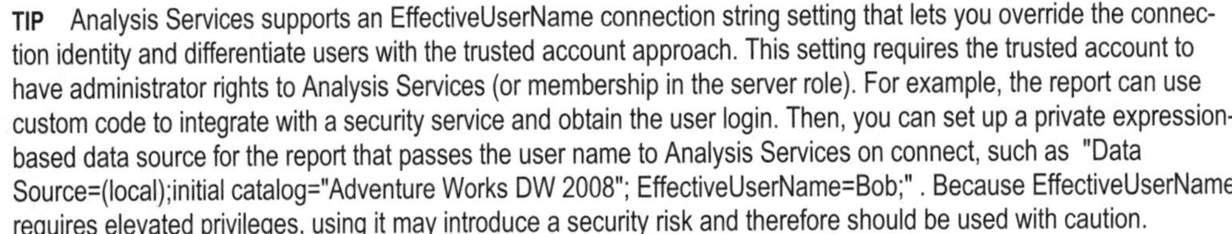

TIP Analysis Services supports an EffectiveUserName connection string setting that lets you override the connection identity and differentiate users with the trusted account approach. This setting requires the trusted account to have administrator rights to Analysis Services (or membership in the server role). For example, the report can use custom code to integrate with a security service and obtain the user login. Then, you can set up a private expression-based data source for the report that passes the user name to Analysis Services on connect, such as "Data Source=(local);initial catalog="Adventure Works DW 2008"; EffectiveUserName=Bob;" . Because EffectiveUserName requires elevated privileges, using it may introduce a security risk and therefore should be used with caution.

The second option is to prompt users for credentials, as follows:

5. In Report Manager, select the Credentials Supplied by the User Running the Report option on the data source properties page.
6. Check the Use as Windows Credentials Option When Connecting to the Data Source option.

In this case, the user must enter a user name and password each time he or she views the report. Because credentials are passed on the wire from the client to the server, you should only use prompted credentials if the connection is encrypted.

If direct access to Analysis Services is not an option, such as when you need to connect Report Designer to a cube located on a web server, you can configure Analysis Services for HTTP connectivity and use a HTTP-based connection string in the report data source. For more information about this deployment scenario, read the Configuring HTTP Access to SQL Server 2005 Analysis Services on Microsoft Windows Server 2003 paper (see Resources).

16.2 Authoring OLAP Reports

Now that you have a good grasp of Analysis Services and how it can integrate with Reporting Services, let's start by authoring a basic report that retrieves source data from the Adventure Works cube. We will extend this report later on to demonstrate more advanced features.

16.2.1 Authoring a Basic Report

Figure 16.11 shows the Product Sales Basic report, which uses the Adventure Works cube as a data source. The report shows Internet sales and resellers sales grouped by product category, subcategory, and product. The report demonstrates the following main features:

- Connecting to Analysis Services using the Analysis Services data provider
- The MDX Query Designer drag-and-drop support

Product Sales Basic

Category	Subcategory	Product	Internet Sales	Reseller Sales
Accessories	Bike Racks	Hitch Rack - 4-Bike	$39,360	$197,736
	Bike Stands	All-Purpose Bike Stand	$39,591	
	Bottles and Cages	Water Bottle - 30 oz.	$21,178	$7,477
		Mountain Bottle Cage	$20,230	
		Road Bottle Cage	$15,391	
		Total	**$56,798**	**$7,477**
	Cleaners	Bike Wash - Dissolver	$7,219	$11,188
	Fenders	Fender Set - Mountain	$46,620	
	Helmets	Sport-100 Helmet, Red		$11,385

Figure 16.11 The Product Sales Basic report sources data from the Adventure Works cube.

Setting up a data source

Begin authoring the report by setting up a data source for connecting to the Adventure Works cube.

1. In BIDS, create a new Report Server project.
2. In the Solution Explorer, right-click the Shared Data Sources folder and click Add New Data Source.
3. In the Shared Data Source Properties dialog, enter *AdventureWorksAS2008* in the Name field.
4. Expand the Type drop-down list and select the Microsoft SQL Server Analysis Services data provider, as shown in Figure 16.12.

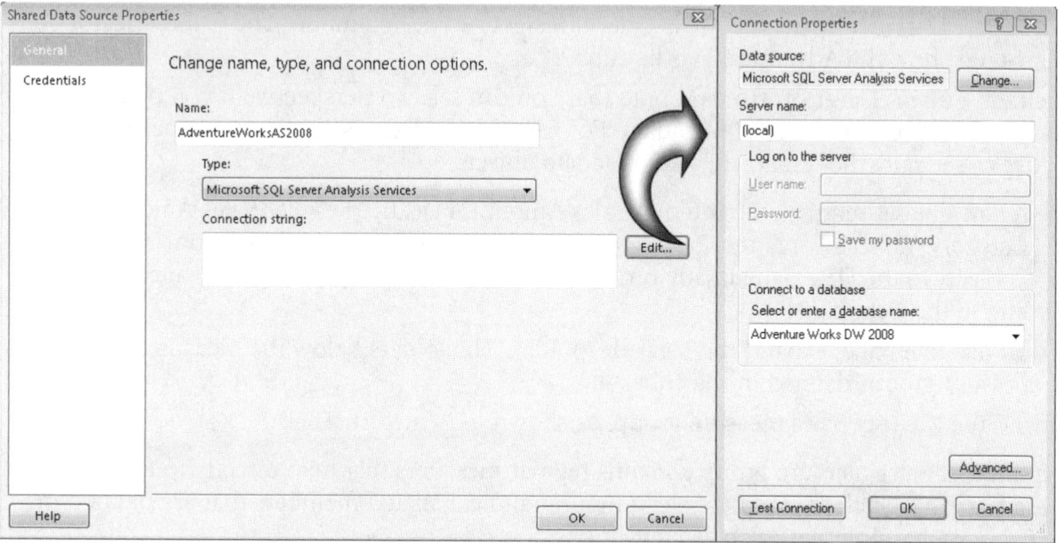

Figure 16.12 Choose the Microsoft SQL Server Analysis Services data provider.

5. Click the Edit button to open the Connection Properties dialog box.

6. In the Connection Properties dialog box, enter the name of the Analysis Services server, such as *(local)*.
7. Expand the Database Name drop-down list and select Adventure Works DW 2008.
8. Click Test Connection to test connectivity and click OK to return to the Shared Data Source Properties dialog box. BIDS generates the following connection string:

```
Data Source=(local);Initial Catalog="Adventure Works DW 2008"
```

9. Select the Credentials page and verify that the Use Windows Credentials option is selected. Click OK to create the AdventureWorksAS2008 data source.

Setting up the report dataset

Once the data source is in place, we are ready to create the report and define a dataset.

1. In the Solution Explorer, right-click the Reports folder and select Add ⇨ New Item.
2. In the Add New Item dialog box, select the Report template and name the new report *Product Sales Basic.rdl*. Click Add to create the report definition and open it in the Report Designer.
3. Next, you need to associate the report with the AdventureWorksAS2008 data source. In the Report Data window (press Ctrl-Alt-D if not shown), expand the New drop-down menu and click Data Source.
4. In the Data Source Properties dialog box that follows, name the data source *AdventureWorksAS2008*. Select the Use Shared Data Source Reference option and in the drop-down list and choose the AdventureWorksAS2008 data source that you've created. Click OK to set up the data source reference.
5. In the Report Data window, right-click the AdventureWorksAS2008 data source and click Add Dataset. This associates the new dataset with the AdventureWorksAS2008 data source.
6. In the Dataset Properties dialog box that follows, enter *Main* as a dataset name and click the Query Designer button.

   The Report Designer opens the MDX Query Designer in design mode. The Cube Selector control should show the Adventure Works cube.

7. Click the Cube Selector control and note that you can select a perspective if you prefer to work with a subset of the cube metadata. For example, you can select the Channel Sales perspective to see only the reseller-related metadata objects.

   The report dataset requires the Internet Sales Amount measure, Reseller Sales Amount measure, Category, Subcategory, and Product attributes from the Product dimension. You can add these objects to the Data pane in any order but you will see query results only after you add a measure to the Data pane.

8. In the Metadata pane, expand the Measures folder. The folders below the Measures node are the measure groups defined in the cube.
9. Expand the Internet Sales measure group, as shown in Figure 16.13.

   The Internet Sales measure group contains regular measures that map directly to fact columns in the fact table, such as Internet Sales Amount, and calculated members that are defined in the cube, such as Internet Average Unit Price.

10. Drag the Internet Sales Amount measure and drop it on the Data pane. As you hover the mouse pointer over the Data pane, a red vertical line shows the possible locations where you can drop the object.

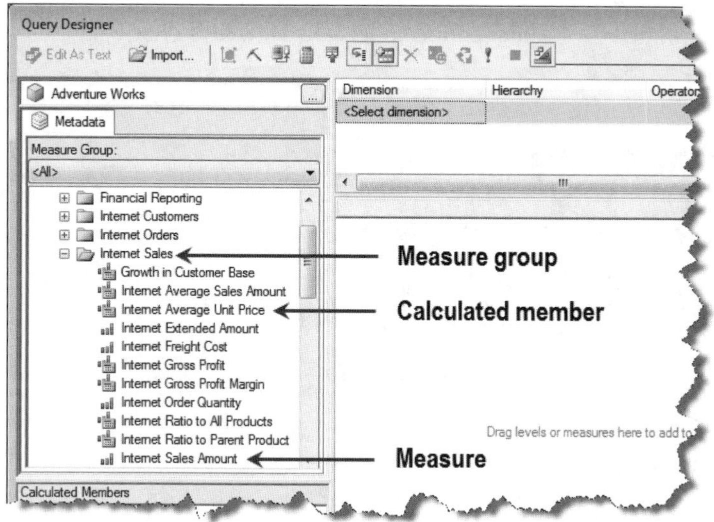

Figure 16.13 The Metadata pane organizes the cube metadata in dimension and measure group folders.

The MDX Query Designer auto-generates the query, executes it, and display the results. The query results in a single cell that represents the overall sales to customers across all subject areas.

TIP The MDX Query Designer is configured to execute the query automatically as soon as the Data pane changes. You can toggle the Auto Execute toolbar button to disable this behavior. To execute the query on demand, click the Run Query button.

11. In the Metadata pane, expand the Reseller Sales measure group and drag the Reseller Sales Amount measure to the Data pane.
12. The Product Sales Basic report slices the measures by the product category, subcategory, and product. In the Metadata pane, expand the Product dimension.

You can drag the Category, Subcategory and Product attributes, or you can drag the Product Categories' user-defined hierarchy which includes these attributes. While both approaches produce the same results, user-defined hierarchies may yield better performance with larger cubes so you should use them whenever possible.

NOTE User-defined hierarchies have certain performance advantages over attribute hierarchies. First, the navigation paths are optimized at processing time. Second, the navigation tree of a user-defined hierarchy is materialized on disk. Finally, cube aggregations (pre-calculated summaries of data) favor user-defined hierarchies.

Drag the Product Categories user-defined hierarchy to the Data pane. At this point, your query results should match Figure 16.14.

Category	Subcategory	Product	Internet Sales Amount	Reseller Sales Amount
Accessories	Bike Racks	Hitch Rack - 4-Bike	39360	197736.156
Accessories	Bike Stands	All-Purpose Bike Stand	39591	(null)
Accessories	Bottles and Cages	Water Bottle - 30 oz.	21177.56	7476.6036
Accessories	Bottles and Cages	Mountain Bottle Cage	20229.75	(null)
Accessories	Bottles and Cages	Road Bottle Cage	15390.88	(null)
Accessories	Cleaners	Bike Wash - Dissolver	14211.6	11188.3725

Figure 16.14 The dataset for the Product Sales Basic report.

Understanding Query Mode

As noted, the MDX Query Designer supports a query mode to let you view and change the auto-generated MDX query.

1. Click the Design Mode toolbar button to switch to query mode, as shown in Figure 16.15.

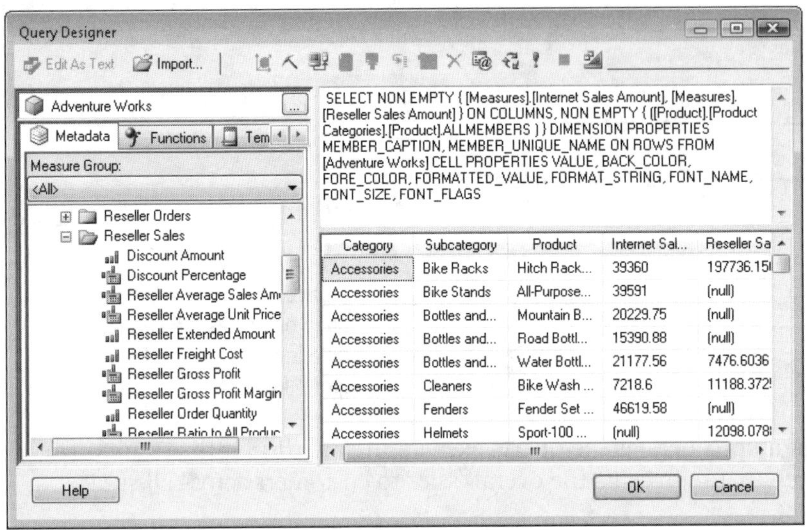

Figure 16.15 In query mode, the MDX Query Designer lets you view and change the MDX query.

In query mode, the MDX Query Designer displays the MDX query in a text window. In our case, the MDX Query Designer has generated the following SELECT statement.

```
SELECT NON EMPTY { [Measures].[Internet Sales Amount], [Measures].[Reseller Sales Amount] } ON COLUMNS, NON EMPTY
{ ([Product].[Product Categories].[Product].ALLMEMBERS ) } DIMENSION PROPERTIES MEMBER_CAPTION,
MEMBER_UNIQUE_NAME ON ROWS
FROM [Adventure Works] CELL PROPERTIES VALUE, BACK_COLOR, FORE_COLOR, FORMATTED_VALUE, FORMAT_STRING,
FONT_NAME, FONT_SIZE, FONT_FLAGS
```

Let's dissect this query and explain its parts. It requests the two measures on the COLUMNS axis (that is, on columns) and the All members of the Product Categories user-defined hierarchy on the ROWS axis. Cubes are usually rather sparse and have a huge number of empty cells. For example, customers are unlikely to purchase every product, so many members of the Product and Customer dimensions simply don't exist with respect to each other. The NON EMPTY keywords are used to exclude such empty cells from the query results. In design mode, you can click the Show Empty Cells button to see the effect of the NON EMPTY clause.

Besides selecting the data you want to use, the query also requests extended properties. The CELL PROPERTIES clause requests some common cell properties, such as color, background color, format string, and so on, which can be used on the report. Similarly, the DIMENSION PROPERTIES clause requests the MEMBER_CAPTION (the translated member name) and MEMBER_UNIQUE_NAME (a system name to reference a member) properties.

As noted, changes made in query mode are not carried back to design mode. If you click the Design Mode button within the same session (meaning you haven't closed the report), the MDX Query Designer will ignore the changes made in query mode and restore the original query. If you do this between sessions, the MDX Query Designer will remove the entire query and you have to start from scratch.

In query mode, the Metadata pane adds two new tabs that come in handy for constructing MDX queries. The Functions pane shows a list of the supported MDX functions. The Templates tab contains common templates of calculated members and named sets, such as a Top N Count template to select top dimension members based on a given numeric criteria.

In the process of authoring the MDX query you may need to validate that it is syntactically correct. The Prepare button executes the query and displays any error messages. The Query Parameters button lets you view and change the query parameters. As in design mode, use the Run Query button to execute the query and see the results.

2. Click the Design Mode toolbar button to switch to design mode again without making any changes.
3. Click OK to return to the Dataset Properties dialog box and click OK again to create the dataset.

The report dataset is added to the Report Data window. It has five fields (Category, Subcategory, Product, Internet_Sales_Amount, Reseller_Sales_Amount). To edit the query later on, right-click the dataset in the Report Data window and choose Query to open the MDX Query Designer.

TIP The auto-generated field names tend to become quite long. If you don't like the system-generated names, such as Reseller_Sales_Amount, you can rename the fields. To do so, right-click the dataset and click Edit. In the Dataset Properties dialog box, select the Fields tab and rename the fields as needed.

From here, laying out the report is nothing you haven't seen so far, so I won't discuss the remaining steps.

16.2.2 Working with Filters and Parameters

As it stands, the Product Sales Basic report reads from the entire cube space and doesn't let end users filter the report data. Adding parameters gives you a way to return a more manageable amount of data. To illustrate the use of parameters, the Product Sales Parameterized.rdl file (see Figure 16.16) builds upon the Product Sales Basic report by adding Product Categories and From Date parameters.

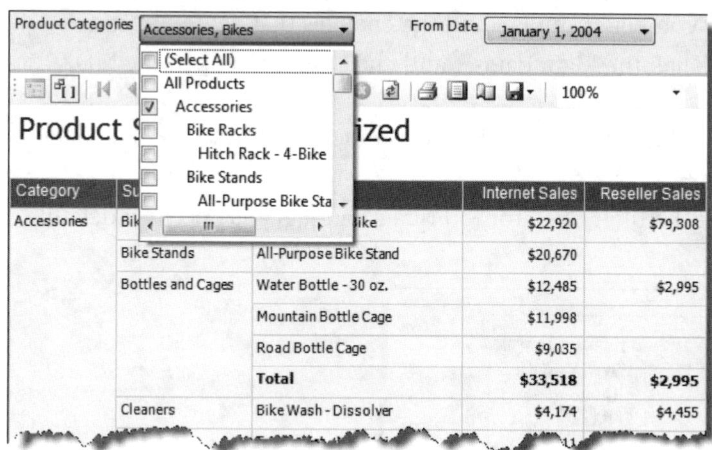

Figure 16.16 The Product Sales Parameterized report lets the user filter the report data by product category and specify a start date.

In the finished report, the user can select one or more members of the Product Categories user-defined hierarchy in the Product Categories parameter. In addition, the user can specify a start date to filter the report data from this date onward by using the From Date parameter. The report demonstrates the following main features:

- Working with Equal and InRange filters
- Promoting filters to report parameters

Understanding filters

The MDX Query Designer lets you apply filters to attributes in user-defined hierarchies to restrict the query results. Table 16.1 shows the supported filter operators.

Table 16.1 The filter operators supported by the MDX Query Designer

Operator	Description
Equal	Equal to one of a set of members.
Not Equal	Not equal to any of a set of members.
In	The members must be in a given named set.
Not In	The members are not in a given named set.
Contains	The name, key or caption of the member contains a given string. The comparison is case-insensitive.
Begins With	The name, key or caption of the member begins with a given string. The comparison is case-insensitive.
Range	In the range from one member/value to another member/value. The range can be based on key, name or caption, and can be inclusive or exclusive. Either From or To can be left null, providing LessThanOrEqualTo and GreaterThanOrEqualTo. The comparison is based on natural ordering of the members.
MDX	MDX expression is used to specify the set of members from the hierarchy of the filtered item.

You can specify a set of filters that use different filter operators if the report needs to filter on several hierarchies.

Implementing an Equal filter

Let's use the Equal filter operator for the Product Categories parameter. The steps marked with (Optional) are meant to help you better understand the changes that are taking place.

1. In the Report Data window, right-click the Main dataset and click Query to open the MDX Query Designer.
2. Drag the Product Categories user-defined hierarchy (Product dimension) from the Metadata pane and drop it on the Filter pane.

   The MDX Query Designer defaults the filter operator to Equals and lets you specify a default value for the filter.

Figure 16.17 Setting up a filter involves choosing a hierarchy, filter operator, and default value.

3. Expand the Filter Expression drop-down list, as shown in Figure 16.17.

   The Filter Expression drop-down list shows members of the Product Categories user-defined hierarchy. You can select a single member or multiple members from the list.

4. Select the Bikes product category to show Bike-related sales by default.
5. (Optional) Switch to query mode and inspect the generated MDX query. You will see the following filter expression:

```
FROM ( SELECT ( { [Product].[Product Categories].[Category].&[1] } ) ON COLUMNS
FROM [Adventure Works]
```

   This expression defines a subcube by applying the filter operator you specified. [Product].[Product Categories].[Category].&[1] is the unique name of the Bikes category.

6. Preview the report.

   Notice that now the report totals are lower because the report shows bike sales only. As it stands, the Product Categories filter is not very useful because it doesn't let the user change the filter value without modifying the query directly. Let's promote the filter to a report parameter so that users can pick a filter value at run time. This takes a mouse click.

7. In the Filter pane, check the Parameters checkbox and click OK to return to the Report Designer.

   Several things happen behind the scenes. First, the MDX Query Designer generates a new report-level parameter. Next, it creates a new dataset for the parameter available values. Finally, the designer changes the MDX query to use the new parameter.

8. In the Report Data window, right-click the AdventureWorksAS2008 node and click Show Hidden Datasets. Expand the AdventureWorksAS2008 node and note that there is a new ProductProductCategories dataset.
9. (Optional) Right-click the ProductProductCategories dataset and click Query. The MDX Query Designer switches to query mode (see Figure 16.18) because the parameter query is system-generated.

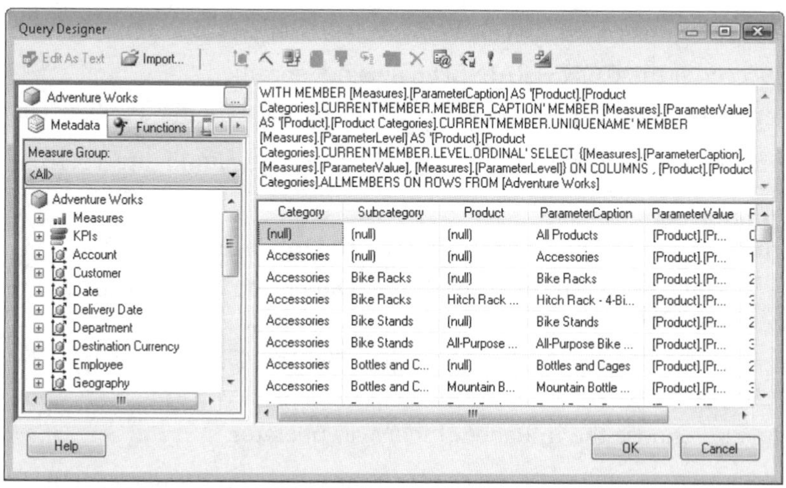

Figure 16.18 The MDX Query Designer generates a dataset for the parameter available values.

The ProductProductCategories query returns all members in the Product Categories hierarchy. In addition, it defines several calculated members to return the member caption (ParameterCaption), unique name, (ParameterValue) and hierarchy level (ParameterLevel). Although not shown, the Report Designer generates an additional calculated field ParameterCaptionIndented to indent the member values in the parameter prompt area.

```
<Field Name="ParameterCaptionIndented">
  <Value>=Space(3*Fields!ParameterLevel.Value) + Fields!ParameterCaption.Value</Value>
</Field>
```

10. Back to the Report Data window, expand the Parameters node and notice that the MDX Query Designer has generated a ProductProductCategories report-level parameter.
11. Double-click the ProductProductCategories parameter to open its properties.
12. Select the Available Values page and note that the ProductProductCategories available values are derived from the ProductProductCategories dataset. The ProductProductCategories is configured as a multivalued parameter and its default value is set to Bikes category ([Product].[Product Categories].[Category].&[1]). Click OK to close the Report Parameter Properties dialog box.
13. (Optional) In the Report Data window, right-click the Main dataset and select Query.
14. (Optional) In the MDX Query Designer, switch to query mode by clicking the Design Mode toolbar button.

    Notice that the MDX Query Designer has changed the query subselect filter as follows:

```
FROM ( SELECT ( STRTOSET(@ProductProductCategories, CONSTRAINED) ) ON COLUMNS
FROM [Adventure Works])
```

    At run time, the @ProductProductCategories parameter returns a comma-delimited string containing the unique names of the selected members, such as:

```
[Product].[Product Categories].[Product].&[1], [Product].[Product Categories].[Product].&[2], . . .
```

    In the next statement, the StrToSet function converts the strings into an MDX set. To reduce the risk of injection attacks, the CONSTRAINED flag forces the query to specify a set of specific members. For example, this query will return an error if the CONSTRAINED filter clause is specified:

```
STRTOSET([Product].[Product Categories].[Product].Members, CONSTRAINED)
```

    In contrast, the query will succeed if the CONSTRAINED flag is not specified.

15. Click OK to return to the Report Designer and preview the report by selecting the Preview tab.

    Notice that the report now includes a Product Categories parameter (see again Figure 16.16).

Implementing an InRange filter

Follow these steps to configure the From Date parameter to use the InRange filter operator.

1. In the Filter pane, click <Select Dimension> in the second row (Dimension column) and select the Date dimension from the dimension list.
2. In the Hierarchy column, expand the drop-down list, and select the Date.Date hierarchy, which represents the lowest level (day) of the Date dimension.
3. Expand the Operator column and choose the In Range (Inclusive) operator.

    The MDX Query Designer generates two Filter Expression columns and two Parameters columns to accommodate the lower and upper range values. If you leave the second (upper) filter expression empty, the last member in the hierarchy will be used. Let's use January 1, 2004, for the lower range of the time period. In section 16.2.6, we will replace this fixed value with a sliding time window that includes all dates within the past month.

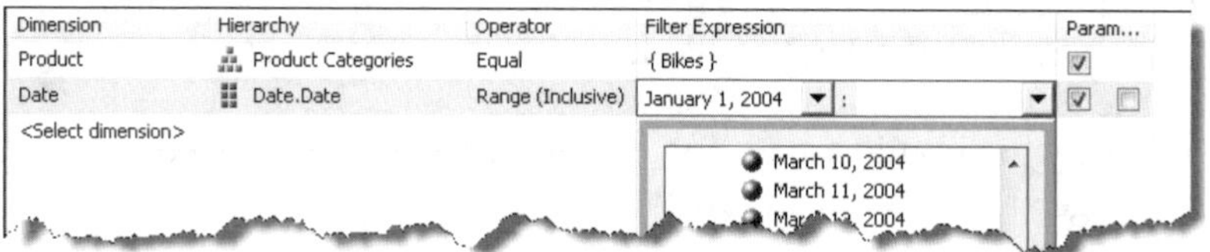

Figure 16.19 An InRange filter has lower and upper ranges.

4. Expand the drop-down list inside the first Filter Expression column, as shown in Figure 16.19.

   Since the Date attribute contains many members, the drop-down list displays the first 1,000 members only. However, at the end of the list, there is a Filter Members link that lets you find a specific member.

5. Click the Filter Member link to open the Filter Members dialog box.
6. Configure the Filter Members dialog box to search for January 1, 2004, as shown in Figure 16.20.

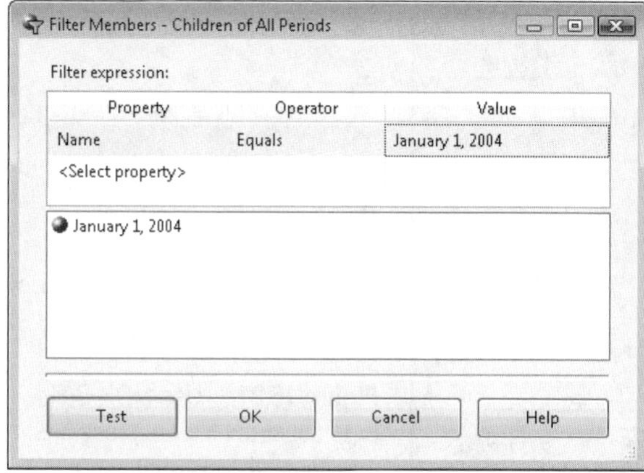

Figure 16.20 The Filter Members dialog lets you search for members by different filter conditions.

7. Click the Test button. The filter should return a single member.
8. Select the January 1, 2004 member and click OK to return to the MDX Query Designer.
9. The drop-down lists should display the January 1, 2004 member on top. Select this member and click OK.
10. Check the first Parameter checkbox to promote the filter to report parameter. Click OK to return to the Report Designer.
11. Double-click the FromDateDate parameter and change its prompt to *From Date*.
12. Preview the report.

    The report now should look like the one shown in Figure 16.16.

NOTE The MDX Query Designer configures each new parameter as a cascading parameter that depends on the parameters defined before it in the Filter pane. For example, changing the Product Categories parameter executes the From Date parameter query to retrieve only the dates that exist for the selected members of the Product dimension.

Implementing an MDX filter

Unfortunately, the Filter pane doesn't let you filter on measures, thereby preventing you from performing common queries like filtering the top ten selling products based on their resale sales. Fortunately, there is a workaround. The Filter pane includes an MDX filter operator that can get the job done. This is an open-ended operator that lets you use an MDX expression to return a set of members from the filtered hierarchy.

The Product Sales Top report, which builds upon the Product Sales Parameterized report, demonstrates how you can leverage an MDX expression to return the top ten products based on the Internet Sales Amount measure.

1. In the Filter pane, add a new filter that uses the Product hierarchy or the Product dimension and choose the MDX operator.
2. Use the handy MDX Builder to author the MDX expression. MDX Builder includes a Metadata pane that exposes the cube metadata and Functions pane that lists the MDX functions organized in logical categories. Click the button inside the Filter Expression column to launch MDX Builder, as shown in Figure 16.21.

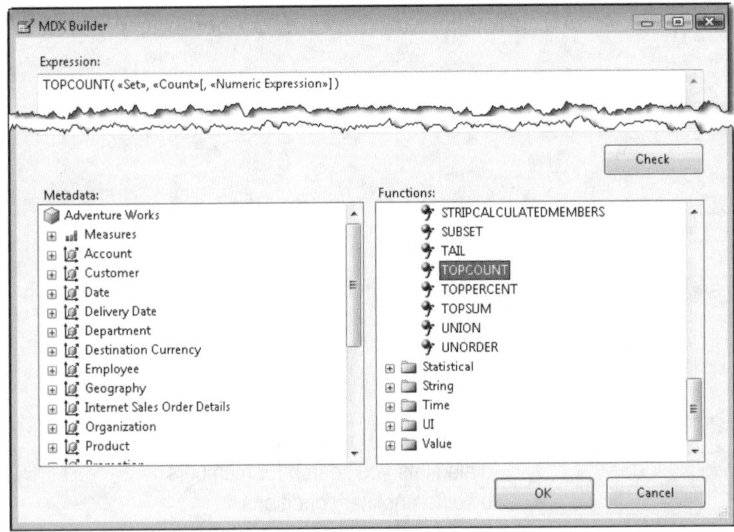

Figure 16.21 Use MDX Builder to construct filter expressions and check the syntax.

3. Expand the Set category and double-click the TOPCOUNT function. The MDX Builder generates the following expression text:

```
TOPCOUNT( «Set», «Count»[, «Numeric Expression»])
```

   The Set argument accepts a valid MDX set, such as members of the Product dimension. The Count argument specifies the top count. The Numeric Expression argument specifies a numeric expression that will be used for filtering, such as a measure or a calculated member. You can drag objects from the Metadata pane to replace the argument placeholders.

4. Change the MDX expression as shown below and click OK.

```
TOPCOUNT([Product].[Product].[Product].Members, 10, [Measures].[Internet Sales Amount])
```

   [Product].[Product].[Product].Members returns a set of all members of the Product attribute hierarchy inside the Product dimension excluding the All member. Consequently, the server will return the top ten members based on their Internet sales.

TIP The MDX Query Designer doesn't support auto-generating parameters with filters that use the MDX operator. If you need to parameterize the operator, such as to let the user specify an arbitrary measure or the top count, you need to use the OLE DB Provider for Analysis Services and an expression-based query, as I'll demonstrate in section 16.2.6.

16.2.3 Working with Calculated Members

A calculated member is an expression-based dimension member that you can define at the cube or report level. In general, useful business expressions should be defined as cube-level calculated members to make them available to all reporting clients. In contrast, the MDX Query Designer lets you define report-level calculated members that are available only in the containing report.

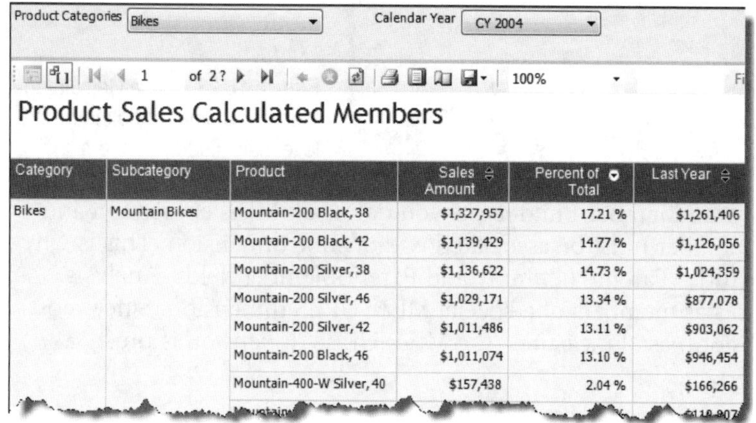

Figure 16.22 The Product Sales Calculated Members reports includes Percent of Total and Last Year calculated members.

The Product Sales Calculated Members report, shown in Figure 16.22, includes two report-level calculated members. The PercentOfParent calculated member (Percent of Total column) shows the percentage contribution of the product to its parent total. For example, the Mountain-200 Black, 38 bike has contributed 17.21% to the Mountain Bikes sales for year 2004. The LastYearSalesAmount calculated member (Last Year column) returns the product sales (Sales Amount measure) for the preceding year. For example, Mountain-200 Black, 38 bike has made $1,327,957 in 2004 and $1,261,406 in 2003. This report demonstrates the following features:

- Report-level calculated members
- Using query mode to change the parameter dataset query
- Interactive sorting to let the user sort the numeric columns on the report

This report builds upon the Product Sales Parameterized report with a few exceptions. I replaced the Date InRange filter with an Equal operator that uses the Date.Calendar Year hierarchy. I removed the Internet Sales Amount and Reseller Sales Amount measures and added the Sales Amount measure.

Implementing calculating members

Follow these steps to implement the PercentOfTotal calculated member:

1. Open the Main dataset in the MDX Query Designer.

2. Click the Add Calculated Member toolbar button to open the Calculated Member Builder dialog box, as shown in Figure 16.23.

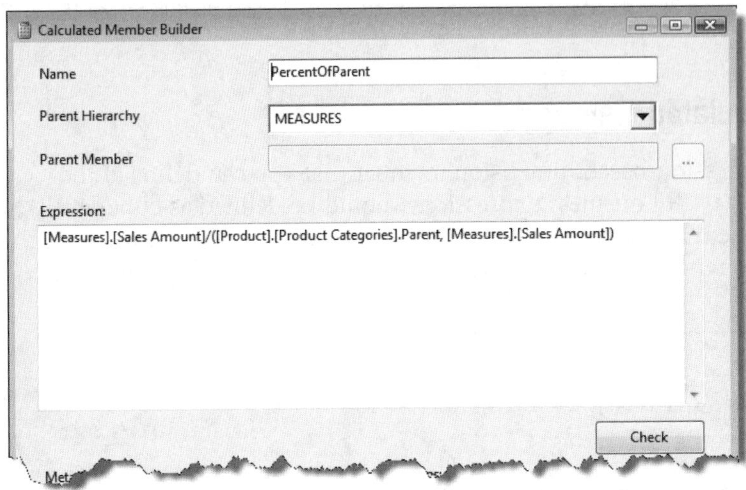

Figure 16.23 Use Calculated Member Builder to define report-level calculated members.

Similar to MDX Builder, Calculated Member Builder lets you define an MDX expression and check its syntax. A calculated member must be associated with a cube dimension. This is why Calculated Member Builder includes Parent Hierarchy and Parent Member fields. Analysis Services treats the cube measures as members of a special MEASURES dimension. Since most calculated members are expression-based measures, the MEASURES dimension is pre-selected.

3. Enter *PercentOfParent* in the Name field.
4. Enter the following expression in the Expression pane:

```
[Measures].[Sales Amount]/([Product].[Product Categories].Parent, [Measures].[Sales Amount])
```

MDX includes functions for hierarchy navigation. The Parent function returns the parent member of the current member. For example, the parent member of Mountain-200 Black, 38 in the Product Categories hierarchy, is its product subcategory Mountain Bikes. Consequently, the coordinate ([Product].[Product Categories].Parent, [Measures].[Sales Amount]) returns the total Sales Amount for the Mountain Bikes subcategory. Although very simple, this example demonstrates how easy it is to leverage Analysis Services and MDX to create business calculations that take into account the hierarchical relationships within data.

5. Click the Check button to verify the syntax and the OK button to create the member.
6. Repeat steps 1-4 to create a LastYearSalesAmount calculated member that uses the following expression:

```
(PARALLELPERIOD( [Date].[Calendar].[Calendar Year], 1, [Date].[Calendar].CurrentMember), [Measures].[Sales Amount])
```

The ParallelPeriod function returns a member from a prior period in the same relative position as a specified member given a hierarchy level. In this case, ParallelPeriod returns the previous year based on the current year specified in the report parameter.

7. Click OK to go back to the MDX Query Designer and click OK again to return to Report Designer. The Main dataset should now include two new fields.
8. Test the new fields on the report by binding them to columns in the tablix region.

Changing the Calendar Year parameter

The LastYearSalesAmount calculated member requires that the user selects a single year. This necessitates a small change to the DateCalendarYear dataset, which is used for the available values of the Calendar Year parameter. Specifically, I had to change the ROWS axis to return only the calendar years, excluding the All member, as follows:

```
[Date].[Calendar Year].[Calendar Year].ALLMEMBERS ON ROWS
```

I also unchecked the Multi-value property of the CalendarYear parameter.

16.2.4 Working with Server Aggregates

Server aggregates are query subtotals calculated by the data provider. All reports that we've discussed in this chapter have recreated the report subtotals in the table groups by using the Reporting Services built-in aggregate functions, such as Sum. That's fine with fully additive measures that can be summed across any dimension, such as Sales Amount, Internet Sales Amount, and so on.

In some cases, Reporting Services cannot produce the group subtotals. This will be the case when you deal with semi-additive measures calculated in the cube, such as averages, that cannot be summed across any dimension. Or, the cube may use custom rollup formulas and special semi-additive aggregate functions, such as LastNonEmpty and AverageOfChildren, which are not available in Reporting Services. In such cases, we can instruct the Analysis Services data provider to return server aggregates by using the Aggregate function in the group subtotals.

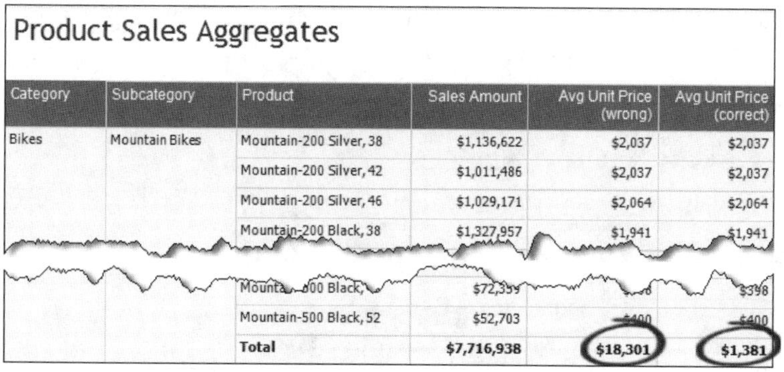

Product Sales Aggregates

Category	Subcategory	Product	Sales Amount	Avg Unit Price (wrong)	Avg Unit Price (correct)
Bikes	Mountain Bikes	Mountain-200 Silver, 38	$1,136,622	$2,037	$2,037
		Mountain-200 Silver, 42	$1,011,486	$2,037	$2,037
		Mountain-200 Silver, 46	$1,029,171	$2,064	$2,064
		Mountain-200 Black, 38	$1,327,957	$1,941	$1,941
		Mounta[illegible]00 Black,	$72,3[illegible]	[illegible]	$398
		Mountain-500 Black, 52	$52,703	$400	$400
		Total	**$7,716,938**	**$18,301**	**$1,381**

Figure 16.24 This report demonstrates how to use the Aggregate function to obtain the server aggregates.

Requesting server aggregates

The Product Sales Aggregates report, shown in Figure 16.24, which starts off by using Reporting Services built-in aggregate functions, can be used to demonstrate how to obtain the server aggregates from Analysis Services. As originally defined, it displays the Average Unit Price measure (Sales Summary measure group) broken down by Product Categories. Average Unit Price is defined in the cube as a calculated member that uses the formula [Measures].[Internet Unit Price]/[Measures].[Internet Transaction Count].

Notice that the report shows correct and incorrect group subtotals to help you understand why and when to use Analysis Services aggregates. The first Avg Unit Price column on the report uses the Sum function and produces wrong group subtotals because averages cannot be summed up. By contrast, the second Avg Unit Price column is correct. It uses the Aggregate function to obtain the aggregates from the server, as shown in Figure 16.25.

Category	Subcategory	Product	Sales Amount	Avg Unit Price (wrong)	Avg Unit Price (correct)
[Category]	[Subcategory]	[Product]	[Sales_Amount]	[Average_Unit_Price]	[Average_Unit_Price]
		Total	**[Sum (Sales_Amount)]**	**[Sum (Average_Unit_Price)]**	**[Aggregate (Average_Unit_Price)]**
	Total		**[Sum (Sales_Amount)]**	**[Sum (Average_Unit_Price)]**	**[Aggregate (Average_Unit_Price)]**
Total	Total		**[Sum (Sales_Amount)]**	**[Sum (Average_Unit_Price)]**	**[Aggregate (Average_Unit_Price)]**

Figure 16.25 Request server aggregates by using the Aggregate function.

Viewing server aggregates

The server aggregates are not automatically inferred and returned by the Analysis Services data provider. Instead, the report author must explicitly request them at design time by using the Aggregate function in report groups. When you add the function, the Report Designer appends a collection of Aggregate elements to the query specification (under the QueryDefinition element) in the report definition file.

```
<Aggregates<Aggregate><Levels><Level><DimensionName>Product</DimensionName><HierarchyName>Product
Categories</HierarchyName><HierarchyUniqueName>[Product].[Product
Categories]</HierarchyUniqueName><LevelName>Category</LevelName><UniqueName>[Product].[Product
Categories].[Category]</UniqueName></Level></Levels></Aggregate></Aggregates>
```

The Aggregate nodes specify the dimension name, hierarchy name, and hierarchy level name for which the server aggregates are requested. The Report Designer then calls to the Analysis Services data provider to obtain the modified MDX query statement, which now includes the All member on the ROWS axis, such as:

```
SELECT NON EMPTY { [Measures].[Sales Amount], [Measures].[Average Unit Price] } ON COLUMNS,
NON EMPTY {{[Product].[Product Categories].[All Products]}, [Product].[Product Categories].[Category].ALLMEMBERS, . . .
```

You can view the server aggregates in the MDX Query Designer (design mode) by toggling the Show Aggregates button on and executing the query, as shown in Figure 16.26.

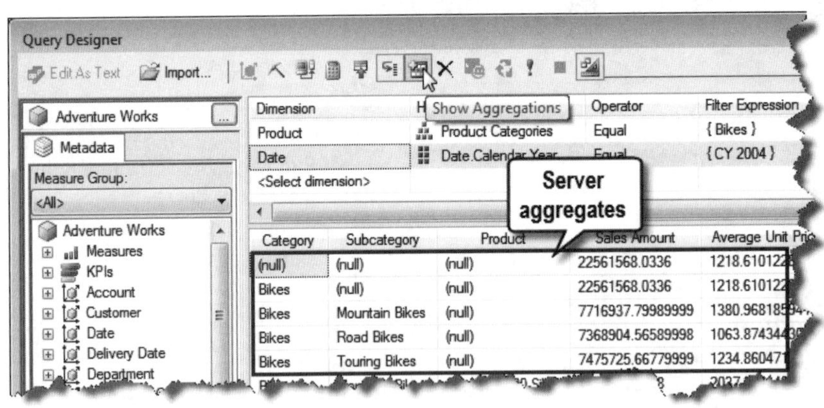

Figure 16.26 Toggle the Show Aggregations button to view the server aggregates in the query results.

The rows with (null) values in the dimension columns are the server aggregates. By default, Reporting Services displays the server aggregates only in the group total or grand total rows and not in the detail rows. If you want the server aggregates to be treated as details rows, set the Interpret Subtotals As Detail Rows option to True on the Option page in the dataset properties (Optons tab). This option should be used with caution because server aggregates on detail rows may skew the subtotals if standard aggregate functions are used, such as Sum.

16.2.5 Implementing Detailed Reports

If you are building detailed reports on large dimensions, you will undoubtedly encounter performance and usability issues when retrieving a dataset for the parameter available values list. Resolving these issues will require your best troubleshooting and design expertise. We will need to abandon the laissez-faire approach we've followed so far and explore two options for dealing with large dimensions: cascading parameters and lookup.

Using cascading parameters

The first option, demonstrated in the Customer Details Cascading report (see Figure 16.27), takes advantage of the Reporting Services cascading parameters feature. Suppose you need to author a report that displays the details of a given customer that the user picks from a large Customer dimension. Loading all customers in a huge drop-down list is definitely something you should avoid.

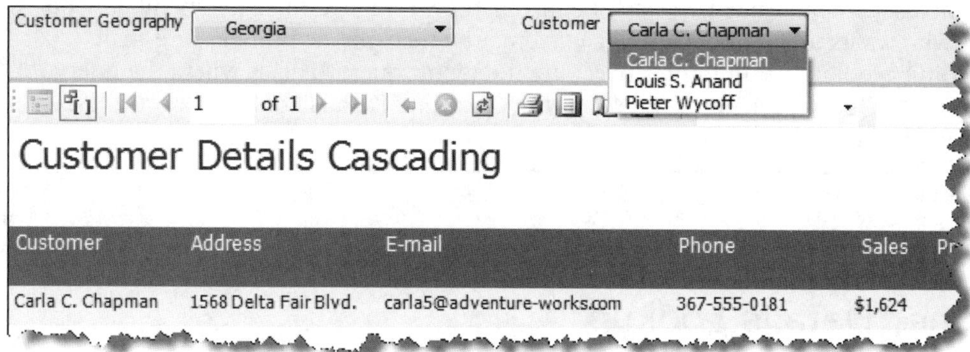

Figure 16.27 Cascading parameters lets you narrow the available values with large dimensions.

Instead, consider narrowing the customer list by using another attribute or user-defined hierarchy. For example, the Customer Details Cascading report uses the Customer Geography user-defined hierarchy to let the user select a city first. Because the Customer parameter depends on the Customer Geography parameter, the report refreshes to display only the customers that are located in that city. Implementing this report involves several steps.

1. Define two Equal filter conditions that use the Customer Geography and Customer hierarchies in this order. As a result, the Customer query will depend on the Customer Geography parameter.
2. Prune the Customer Geography hierarchy. In Adventure Works, the Customer Geography hierarchy consists of Country, State-Province, City, Postal Code, and Customer levels. To make the parameter drop-down list more manageable, I limited the query to return only the first three levels by using the following MDX expression:

```
Exists(
   DESCENDANTS([Customer].[Customer Geography].[All Customers],
   [Customer].[Customer Geography].[City], SELF_AND_BEFORE)
   ,, "Internet Sales")
```

The MDX Descendants function returns the members below a given member to a specified level. The Exists function limits the list further by returning only those cities that have data in the Internet Sales measure group. In other words, only customer cities with sales are returned.

3. Change the CustomerCustomer query that returns the customer available values to exclude the All member by using the triple hierarchy convention:

```
[Customer].[Customer].[Customer].ALLMEMBERS ON ROWS
```

4. Make both parameters single-valued parameters so the user can select a single value.

This report also demonstrates working with member properties. Address, EmailAddress, and Phone don't exist as attribute hierarchies in the Customer dimension. Instead, they are defined as member properties of the Customer attribute. To show them on the report, I defined corresponding calculated members. For example, to display the customer's address, I added an Address calculated member that uses the following expression:

```
[Customer].[Customer].Properties( "Address" )
```

Using lookup

A second approach for making large dimensions more manageable is to add a lookup capability that lets the user enter a value that must be matched by a single dimension member. Consider a user who wants to look up a specific customer by their phone number or e-mail address. Adding a lookup field requires tweaking the report query. This is where the query mode of the MDX Query Designer can help, as the Customer Details Lookup report (see Figure 16.28) demonstrates.

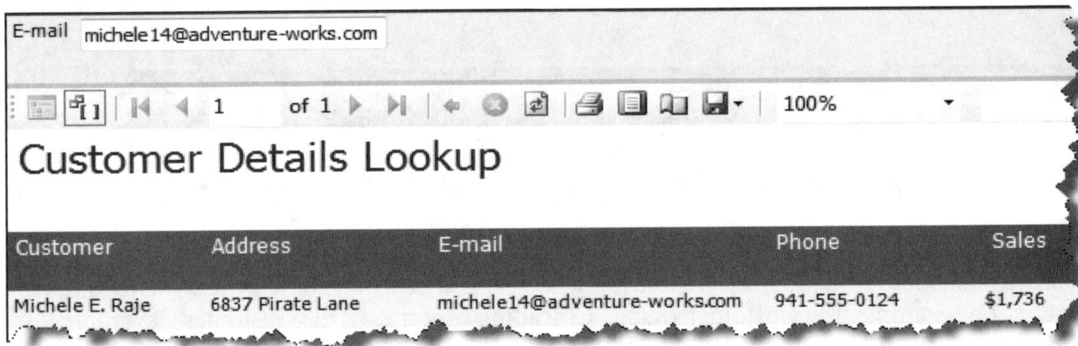

Figure 16.28 This report finds a customer by an e-mail address.

5. Start by defining a single filter parameter that uses the Customer.Customer hierarchy. This will generate a Customer parameter and configure the main dataset to use it.
6. Delete the CustomerCustomer dataset. You won't need it because the user will type in an e-mail address in the Customer parameter instead of selecting a customer from a drop-down list.
7. Change the prompt of the CustomerCustomer parameter to *E-mail* and specify a default value, such as *michele14@adventure-works.com*, so that you can easily test the report.
8. Switch the MDX Query Designer in query mode and open the Query Parameters dialog box by clicking the Query Parameters button. which is available only in query mode.

Recall that by switching to query mode, you've taken the red pill (see Matrix the movie). Once you've changed the query, there is no going back to design mode. Consequently, you will now need to configure query parameters manually in the Query Parameters dialog box.

9. Configure the Query Parameters dialog box, as shown in Figure 16.29. Assigning a default parameter value will help you test the query in the MDX Query Designer. Click OK.

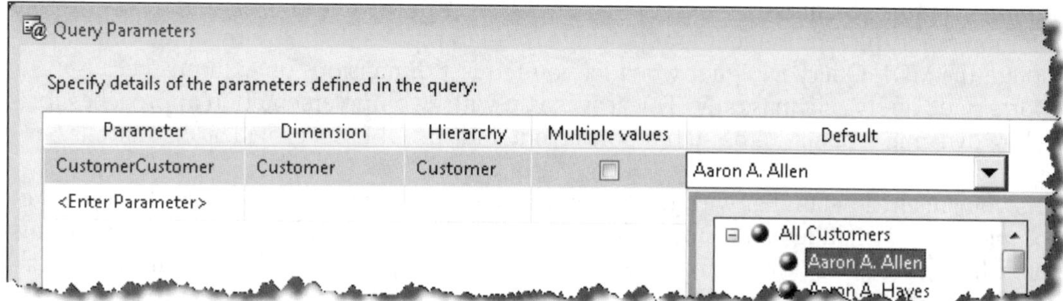

Figure 16.29 Use the Query Parameters dialog to define parameters in query mode.

10. Change the FROM clause in the query as follows:

```
FROM ( SELECT (
 Exists
     (
       [Customer].[Customer].[Customer].Members,

            Iif (
                         InStr(1, @CustomerCustomer, "[") <> 0, StrToMember(@CustomerCustomer),
                         Filter
                         (
                         [Customer].[Customer].[Customer].Members,
                         [Customer].[Customer].Properties( "Email Address" ) = @CustomerCustomer)
                         ) /*Filter*/
                 ) /*IIF*/
     ) /*Exists*/
))
```

Let's explain what's going on here. To find a customer by e-mail, the Exists function cross-joins the members of the Customer attribute hierarchy (all customers) with the given customer. This is where things get trickier. When you test the query in the MDX Query Designer, the default parameter value gives you the unique name of the customer member, such as [Customer].[Customer].&[20075]. However, when you run the report, you will get only the e-mail address from the report parameter.

I use the MDX IIF function to support both cases. This function checks if the @CustomerCustomer parameter includes a square bracket. If this is the case, we are in query mode and we will get the member unique name as a string, which we pass to the StrToMember function to convert it to the actual member. Otherwise, at run time, we use the Filter function to find a customer with a matching e-mail address.

16.2.6 Working with the OLE DB Provider for Analysis Services

For some scenarios, the Analysis Services data provider is simply not up to the task. For example, you may need to handle dynamic query schemas, which this provider doesn't support. In such cases, you can bypass this provider and use the OLE DB Provider for Analysis Services. The Microsoft OLE DB Provider for Analysis Services 10.0 (msolap100.dll) is an interface for applications interacting with Microsoft Analysis Services 2008. Client applications can use this provider to execute MDX queries and interact with multidimensional data. This provider is more flexible, but requires more coding on your part because you need to handle parameters, server aggregates, and other server features.

Handling dynamic schemas

A common reporting requirement is authoring cross-tab reports that have dynamic columns. As noted, the MDX Query Designer won't let you request dimensions on columns because it supports static query schemas only. This leaves you with two implementation approaches for handling dynamic schemas: cross-tab report layout and the OLE DB Provider for Analysis Services.

As you are already familiar with the first approach, I won't discuss its details. For the sake of completeness, I included a Product Sales by Year Matrix report with the source code for this chapter. It demonstrates how to implement a cross-tab report that uses the Adventure Works cube as a data source by rotating the members of the Date dimension from rows to columns.

Configuring the OLE DB Data Provider

If you need to execute an arbitrary MDX query, such as a query that you obtained from Microsoft Excel, consider the OLE DB Provider for Analysis Server. Readers who have experience with Reporting Services 2000 and Analysis Services will probably recall this provider, as this was the only option for integrating reports with Analysis Services cubes. To use the OLE DB data provider, do the following:

1. Configure the data source to use the OLE DB provider type, as shown in Figure 16.30.

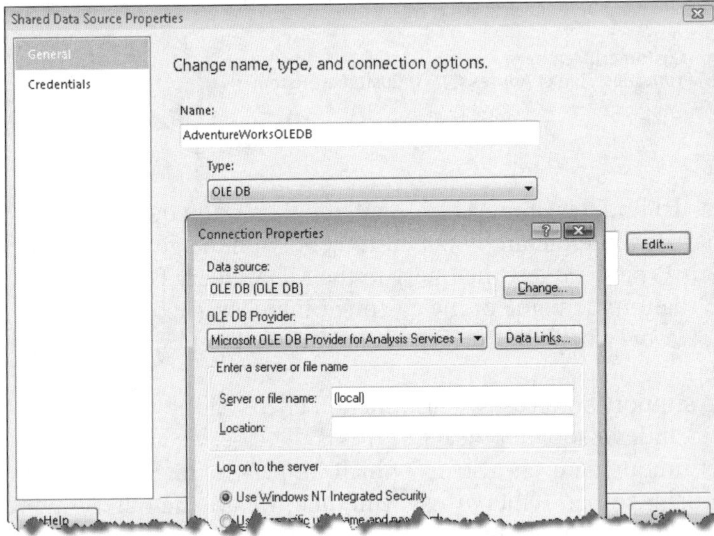

Figure 16.30 Consider the OLE DB Provider for Analysis Services 10.0 for direct access to Analysis Services 2008.

2. In the Connection Properties dialog box, select the Microsoft OLE DB Provider for Analysis Services 10.0 and specify the connection details, including the server name and cube name.

Working with the OLE DB Provider

The Product Sales by Year OLEDB report, shown in Figure 16.31, demonstrates the OLE DB provider in action. Similar to the Product Sales by Year Matrix report, it lets the user select one or more calendar years and displays a cross-tab report with years on columns. Unlike its counterpart, however, it has fixed columns because its query requests the Date dimension on the COLUMNS axis using this query.

```
= "SELECT NON EMPTY {" & JOIN(Parameters!DateCalendarYear.Value, ",") + "} ON COLUMNS,
NON EMPTY {[Product].[Category].[Category].Members} ON ROWS
FROM [Adventure Works]
WHERE [Measures].[Reseller Sales Amount]"
```

Year CY 2001, CY 2002, CY 2003, C

1 of 1 100%

Product Sales by Year OLEDB

Category	Y2001	Y2002	Y2003	Y2004
Accessories	$20,235.36	$92,735.35	$296,532.88	$161,794.33
Bikes	$7,395,348.63	$19,956,014.67	$25,551,775.07	$13,399,243.18
Clothing	$34,376.34	$485,587.15	$871,864.19	$386,013.16
Components	$615,474.98	$3,610,092.47	$5,482,497.29	$2,091,011.92

Figure 16.31 Consider the OLE DB Provider for Analysis Services to execute arbitrary MDX queries.

In this example, the Join function is used to turn a multivalued report parameter into an MDX set.

NOTE When working with Analysis Services, report parameter values need to return the UniqueName value of the dimension member because this is how Analysis Services identifies members. This is particularly important when passing parameters to subreports or drillthrough reports. A common mistake is attempting to the pass the member Caption value. While passing the caption might indeed match the parameter label, it won't match the parameter values.

If you need to parameterize the query, you must resort to expression-based query text because the OLE DB provider doesn't support parameters. The query obtains the selected years from the DataCalendarYear parameter (which in turn uses another query for the parameter available values) and concatenates them together. For example, it the user selects all years, the resulting query will be:

```
SELECT NON EMPTY {[Date].[Calendar Year].&[2001],[Date].[Calendar Year].&[2002],
[Date].[Calendar Year].&[2003],[Date].[Calendar Year].&[2004]} ON COLUMNS,
NON EMPTY {[Product].[Category].[Category].Members} ON ROWS
FROM [Adventure Works] WHERE [Measures].[Reseller Sales Amount]
```

When you request dimension members on columns, your report layout needs to account for new and deleted members. This is why the report includes four columns for the years 2001-2004. What do you think will happen if the user selects a subset of all members, such as 2003 and 2004 only? The report columns for the missing members will show up as empty. This is why I set a conditional Hidden property for each of the four columns to account for missing dataset fields. For example, the expression *=Fields!Y2001.IsMissing* hides the Y2001 column if the user has excluded this year from the parameter selection.

While the report accommodates missing dimension members, it doesn't handle new dimension members, such as year 2005, when they are added to UDM. New members require changing the report layout and redeploying the report. To avoid the overhead of having to manually update the report layout for new members, consider adding additional columns to the table to accommodate future members.

Handling advanced parameters

Another scenario that may require the OLE DB provider involves handling more advanced parameter requirements. For example, when we designed the Product Sales Top report, we used a fixed top count value to select the top products. What if we want to let the user specify the top count number? Unfortunately, the Analysis Services data provider configures parameters to use cube dimensions. However, what's really needed in this case is a regular text-based parameter. This requires using the OLE DB provider, which the Product Sales Top Advanced report (see Figure 16.32) demonstrates.

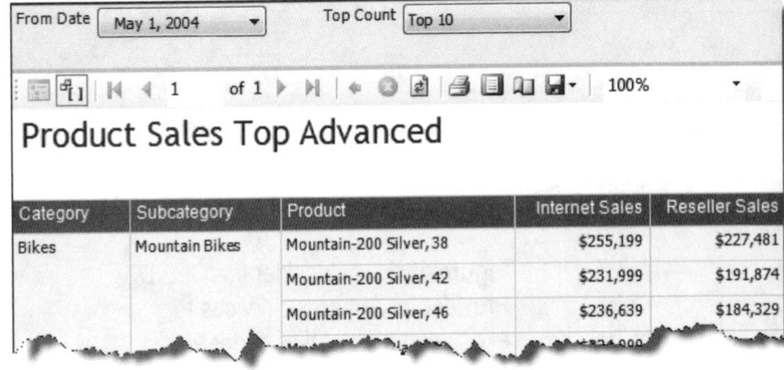

Figure 16.32 Consider the OLE DB Provider for Analysis Services to handle arbitrary parameters.

The user can select one of the pre-defined values in the Top Count parameter to filter the query results accordingly. The report uses an expression-based query to construct the MDX statement.

```
=String.Format ("SELECT NON EMPTY {{ [Measures].[Internet Sales Amount],
[Measures].[Reseller Sales Amount] }} ON COLUMNS,
NON EMPTY [Product].[Product Categories].[Product].ALLMEMBERS ON ROWS
FROM (SELECT ( TOPCOUNT( [Product].[Product].[Product].Members, {1},
[Measures].[Internet Sales Amount] ) ) ON COLUMNS
FROM ( SELECT ( STRTOMEMBER('{0}', CONSTRAINED) : null ) ON COLUMNS
FROM [Adventure Works]))", Parameters!FromDateDate.Value, Parameters!Top.Value)
```

This expression leverages the .NET string formatting support for replacing format items enclosed in curly brackets with positional values. Thus, the first argument {0} will be replaced with Parameters!FromDateDate.Value, while the second is replaced with Parameters!Top.Value.

TIP When using the OLE DB provider, start with a MDX query that is not expression-based and doesn't use any parameters. Make sure that the query works in the generic query designer. Then, convert the query to an expression-based statement. Make sure to double any curly braces in the query.

This report also demonstrates how to work with both Analysis Services data providers in the same report. The dataset for the available values of the From Date parameter uses the built-in Analysis Services data provider, while the main dataset uses the OLE DB provider. Another interesting feature of this report is that the From Date query implements a sliding time window to return the available dates within the last month by using the following filter:

```
{ParallelPeriod([Date].[Calendar].[Month], 1, Tail(EXISTS([Date].[Calendar].[Date].Members, ,
"Reseller Sales")).Item(0)):Tail(EXISTS([Date].[Calendar].[Date].Members, ,"Reseller Sales")).Item(0)}
```

The Tail function returns the last date for which there are reseller sales in the Reseller Sales measure group. The MDX ParallelPeriod function lags one month from that date. Consequently, the range operator (:) returns the members that fall within one month of the last date with reseller sales.

16.2.7 Working with Parent-Child Hierarchies

Parent-child hierarchies represent recursive relationships among dimension members. For example, the Adventure Works cube includes an Employees parent-child hierarchy (in the Employee dimension) that models an employee-manager relationship and an Accounts hierarchy (in the Account dimension) that defines a chart of accounts.

Unfortunately, the built-in Analysis Services data provider collapses the parent-child hierarchy into one column as a part of flattening the result set. This presents an issue if you want to work with the hierarchical relationships on the report. Next, I will present two options for reporting on parent-child hierarchies. The first option leverages the Reporting Services recursive hierarchy support, while the second uses the OLE DB provider.

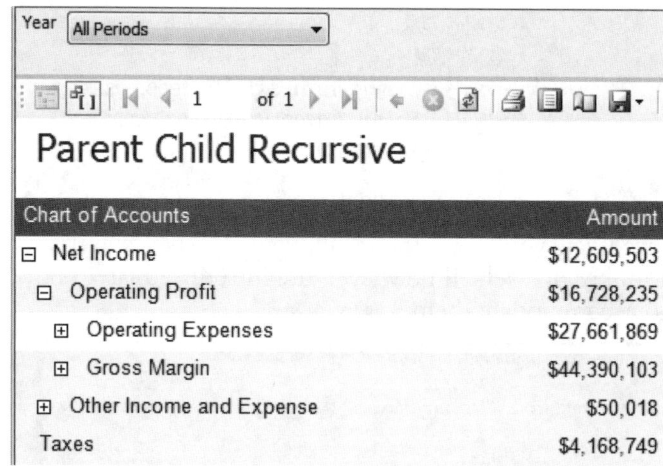

Figure 16.33 You can use the Reporting Services recursive hierarchy support to display parent-child hierarchies.

Using the Reporting Services recursive hierarchy support

The Parent Child Recursive report, shown in Figure 16.33, is an example of a financial report that shows the Adventure Works account categories and the amount for each category. It uses the built-in Analysis Services data provider to retrieve the members of the Accounts parent-child hierarchy and the Amount measure in the Financial Reports measure group. It also defines two calculated members, MemberName and ParentName, which returns the unique names of the current account and its parent category. Reporting Services provides a way to expand parent-child hierarchies by configuring the details grouping of the Tablix region, as follows:

1. In the Row Groups pane, double-click the Details group. In the General tab, notice that I group on the [MemberName] field.
2. Click the Advanced Tab. Notice that the Recursive Parent field groups on the [ParentName] field.

At run time, Reporting Services walks the hierarchy recursively and expands it on the report. I also set the left padding of the first column to indent its text, as follows:

```
=2 + Level() * 8 & "pt"
```

The Reporting Services Level function returns the current level of depth in a recursive hierarchy.

Using the OLE DB provider

The Reporting Services recursive hierarchy support is easy to set up but it doesn't let you define additional groups on the report, such as displaying the account category total in the group footer. The Parent Child OLEDB report (see Figure 16.34) uses the Analysis Services OLE DB provider and an MDX query to expand the hierarchy.

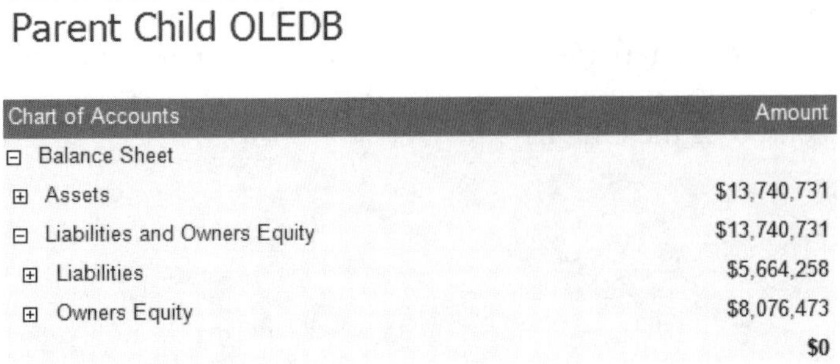

Parent Child OLEDB

Chart of Accounts	Amount
⊟ Balance Sheet	
⊞ Assets	$13,740,731
⊟ Liabilities and Owners Equity	$13,740,731
⊞ Liabilities	$5,664,258
⊞ Owners Equity	$8,076,473
	$0

Figure 16.34 This report uses an MDX query to expand the parent-child hierarchy.

The resulting dataset (see Figure 16.35) includes a column for each hierarchy level. This gives you more control over the layout because it lets you group the results for each level. On the downside, the report assumes a fixed number of levels. If new levels are introduced later on, you need to change the report layout to accommodate them.

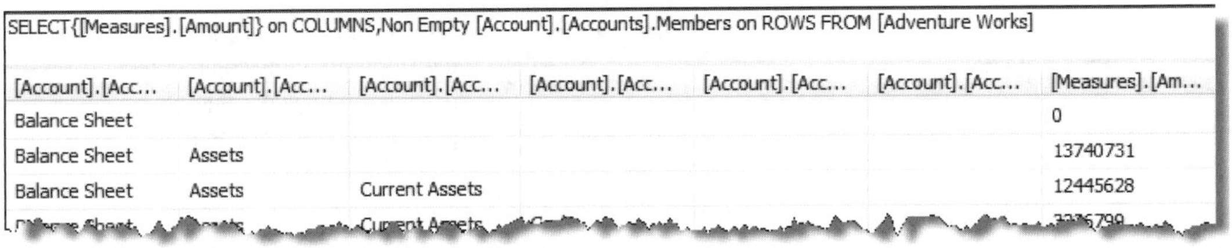

```
SELECT{[Measures].[Amount]} on COLUMNS,Non Empty [Account].[Accounts].Members on ROWS FROM [Adventure Works]
```

[Account].[Acc...	[Account].[Acc...	[Account].[Acc...	[Account].[Acc...	[Account].[Acc...	[Account].[Acc...	[Measures].[Am...
Balance Sheet						0
Balance Sheet	Assets					13740731
Balance Sheet	Assets	Current Assets				12445628

Figure 16.35 This query expands the parent-child hierarchy by generating a column for each hierarchy level.

16.3 Extending Reports with End-User Features

UDM is an end-user oriented model that is designed for interactive reporting and data analysis. You can extend UDM with additional features that enrich the reporting experience. Features that are of particular interest to report authors include key performance indicators (KPIs), extended properties, actions, and translations. I will cover KPIs in chapter 21, where I will show you how to build a custom report item for visualizing the KPI values. Next, I will show you how to leverage extended properties, actions, and translations on your reports.

16.3.1 Working with Extended Properties

Besides values, dimension members and cube cells have format properties (such as format string, color, background color) that determine a cell's appearance. As a report author, you can query these properties and set them in the report.

Understanding extended properties

As noted, when auto-generating the MDX query, the Analysis Services data provider appends additional statements to retrieve dimension (DIMENSION PROPERTIES clause) and cell (CELL PROPERTIES clause) properties. Extended properties are not automatically added to the report dataset but you can write expressions to extract and use these properties on the report.

In Reporting Services, extended properties include predefined and custom properties. Reporting Services extends the Field object to support predefined properties, which Table 16.2 shows alongside their UDM equivalents.

Table 16.2 Predefined extended properties

RDL Property	UDM Equivalent	Purpose	Example
Value	MEMBER_CAPTION (dimension members) unformatted value (cell)	Specifies the data value of the field.	Bikes (the localized name for the Bikes dimension member)
UniqueName	<Member>.UniqueName	Returns the member fully qualified name.	[Date].[Calendar Year].&[2001]
BackgroundColor	BACK_COLOR	Returns the cell background color in hex format.	#00FF40 /*green*/
Color	FORE_COLOR	Returns the cell foreground color in hex format.	#00FF40 /* red*/
FontFamily	FONT_NAME	Returns the font name.	Arial
FontSize	FONT_SIZE	Returns the font size in pixels.	10
FontStyle	FONT_FLAGS.	Returns the font style.	3 (Bold italic)
FontWeight	FONT_STYLE	Returns the font style.	3 (Bold italic)
FormattedValue	N/A	Returns the cell formatted value as text.	$14.56
LevelNumber	<HierarchyLevel>.Level.Ordinal	For parent-child hierarchies, returns the level ordinal number.	1
ParentUniqueName	<Member>.Parent.UniqueName	For parent-child hierarchies, returns a fully qualified name of the parent.	[Account].[Accounts].&[1]

The property style values of the BackgroundColor, FontFamily, and FontWeight properties don't match between RDL and UDM. For example, the RDL colors are RGB, while the UDM colors are defined as integers. However, when accessing extended properties, Reporting Services converts the values automatically into the RDL style values. The IntelliSense support in the Expression dialog box (right-click a field and choose Expression) shows the predefined extended properties, as shown in Figure 16.36.

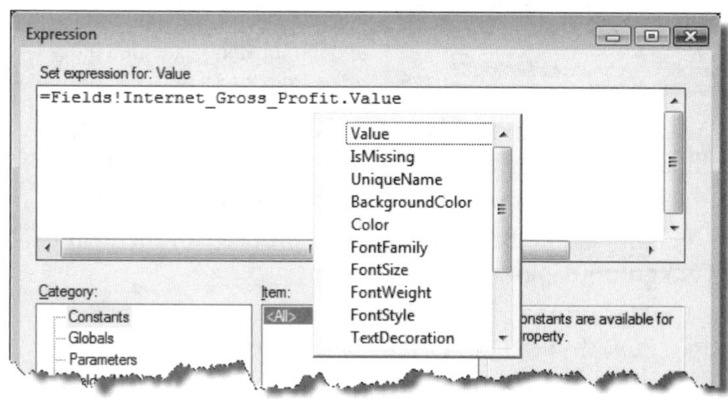

Figure 16.36 The predefined extended properties are exposed in the Expression dialog box.

You can retrieve these property values on the report by using either of the following syntaxes:

```
Fields!Field.Property or Fields!Field("Property")
```

In addition to pre-defined extended properties, UDM defines custom dimension member and cell properties, such FORMAT_STRING, that are not directly accessible from the field properties. However, once you add a custom property to the DIMENSION PROPERTIES or CELL PROPERTIES clause in the query, you can access it using the following syntax:

```
Fields!Field("Property")
```

This syntax is case-sensitive. The property name must exactly match the casing as it is returned by the ADO MD provider. SQL Server Books Online (see Resources) provides a full list of the supported custom properties. As noted, the built-in Analysis Services provider converts the integer value to a Reporting Services-compatible hex format. If you target the OLE DB provider, you can use the following function to convert the integer value:

```
Function ConvertColor (ByVal value as String) as String
      Dim isValid as Boolean
      Dim intValue As Integer = Convert.ToInt32(value, isValid)
      If isValid Then
        Return String.Format("#{0:x2}{1:x2}{2:x2}",(intValue And 255),(intValue >> 8) And 255,(intValue >> 16) And 255)
      Else
        Return String.Empty
      End If
End Function
```

NOTE By default, the Analysis Services OLE DB provider doesn't return extended properties. You must reconfigure the report data source by adding the ReturnCellProperties setting in the advanced data source properties, so that its connection string becomes Provider=MSOLAP.4;Data Source=(local);Initial Catalog="Adventure Works DW 2008";**Extended Properties="ReturnCellProperties=true"**.

Using extended properties

The Extended Properties report, shown in Figure 16.37, demonstrates how you can work with extended properties.

Extended Properties

Scenario	FY 2002	FY 2003	FY 2004	FY 2
Actual	$3,250,075.00	$4,606,605.00	$4,752,823.00	
Budget	$5,583,900.00			
Budget Variance	($2,333,825.00)	Not Budgeted	Not Budgeted	Not
Budget Variance %	-41.80 %			

FORMAT_STRING: Percent;BackgroundColor: #d16c61

Figure 16.37 This report obtains the cell background color and format string extended properties from the UDM.

The report cells obtain the field background color and format string from the UDM. When you point your mouse cursor to a cell, a tooltip pops up to show the values of the extended properties that were retrieved from the UDM. Follow these steps to implement the report:

1. To obtain the predefined background color, set the BackgroundColor property of the field to =Fields!Amount.BackgroundColor.BackgroundColor.
2. To obtain the format string from the UDM, set the Format property to =Code.ConvertFormat(Fields!Amount("FORMAT_STRING"))

The ConvertFormat helper function translates the UDM standard format strings to Reporting Services culture-independent equivalents. For example, "Currency" will be mapped to "C". If the modeler has specified a custom format string, such as #,#0.00 to format the cell values with a thousand separator and two decimal values, the custom format string will pass through to the report.

16.3.2 Working with Reporting Actions

A UDM action is a pre-defined MDX expression that targets a specific part of the cube. Actions can extend the UDM in versatile ways. For example, suppose that the user has drilled down to the lowest level of the Customer dimension and wants to see the individual sales orders that have been placed by this customer. If the order information is not stored in the cube, you can implement a reporting action that lets the user request a Reporting Services report that displays the order data from another data source.

Understanding actions

With the exception of a drilldown action, which is carried out by the server, UDM actions are interpreted and executed by the client application. UDM actions are user-initiated. What this means is that the user has to select a part of the cube to which the action applies and invoke the action. This, of course, assumes that the client application, whether a third-party OLAP browser or a custom application, supports the action.

NOTE Actions are defined in the cube but are interpreted and initiated by the client application. Not all clients support actions. For example, Excel 2007 supports actions, but the Reporting Services designers don't have built-in support for actions. Therefore, before implementing actions, consider what reporting tools your users will use to browse the cube.

UDM supports three types of actions:

- Regular actions—These are multi-purpose actions that can target different client applications. In this case, the action content type tells the client application what the action expression represents. For example, if the content type is set to URL, the expression should return a valid URL.
- Drillthrough actions—Let the client access the details behind a cube cell. This is the only action that is executed by Analysis Services.
- Reporting actions—This action type can be used to request a Microsoft Reporting Services report. The action command is the report path with optional report parameters.

A client application can request a list of actions defined for the cube by querying the cube metadata. As part of the action discovery stage, the client provides the cube scope in the form of coordinates to retrieve the actions defined for that scope. Upon receiving the request, the server evaluates the action condition to determine if any actions are defined for this scope. If a suitable action exists, UDM resolves the action command and returns it to the client. The client is responsible for presenting the action to the user and executing the action.

Implementing a reporting action

Suppose that the customer order data doesn't exist in the cube and is kept in the operational data source. Let's implement a reporting action that let the end user right-click a customer in a Microsoft Excel 2007 PivotTable report and launch a Reporting Services report. The Customer Orders report, which we will use for this practice, retrieves the customer orders from the AdventureWorks2008 database.

1. Assuming that you have installed the AdventureWorksDW2008 database from CodePlex (see the book front matter for instructions), open the Adventure Works Analysis Services project

from \Program Files\Microsoft SQL Server\100\Tools\Samples\AdventureWorks 2008 Analysis Services Project\enterprise\Adventure Works DW 2008.dwproj.

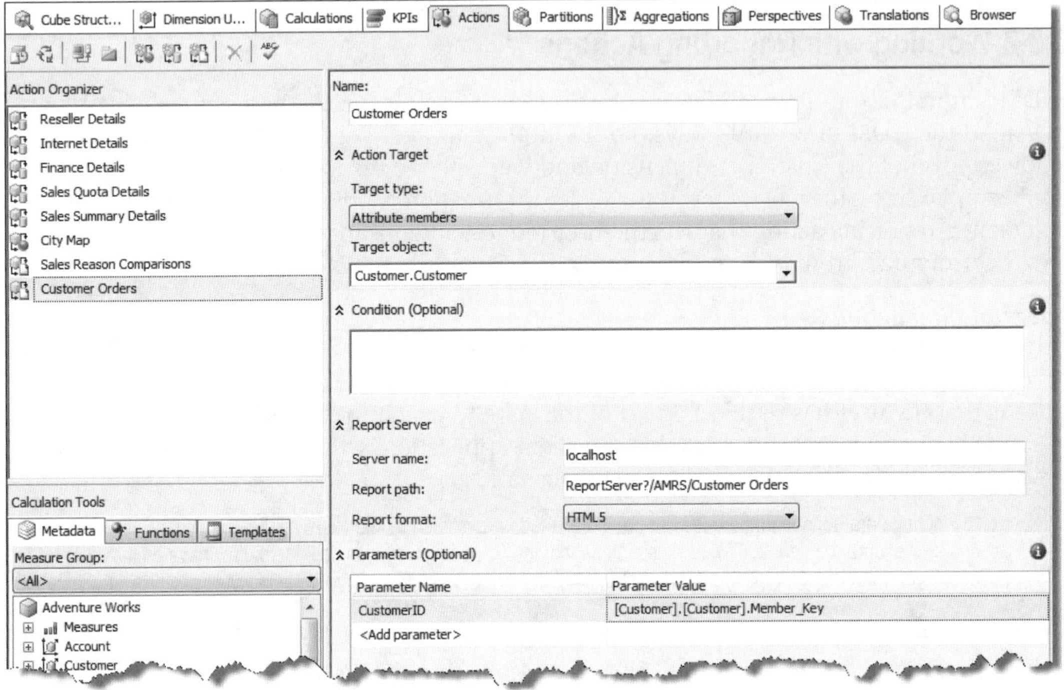

Figure 16.38 Implement a reporting action by specifying the report URL and parameters.

2. In the Solution Explorer, double-click the Adventure Works.cube file to open the cube definition in the Cube Designer.
3. Click the Actions tab, as shown in Figure 16.38.
4. Click the New Reporting Actions toolbar button.
5. Enter *Customer Orders* in the Name field.
6. Set the Target Type drop-down list to Attribute Members to target the members of the Customer attribute hierarchy.
7. Expand the Target Object drop-down list and select the Customer attribute hierarchy in the Customer dimension. Consequently, the Customer Orders action will be available for this hierarchy only.
8. Enter *localhost* in the Server Name field. This assumes that Reporting Services is installed on the same machine.
9. In the Report Path field, enter *ReportServer?/AMRS/Customer Orders*.

   The Customer Orders report takes the customer identifier as a parameter. The parameter corresponds to the CustomerID column in the Sales.SalesOrderHeader table in the AdventureWorks2008 database. The CustomerKey column (which the Customer attribute hierarchy uses as an attribute key) carries over the custom identifier to the AdventureWorksDW2008 database. The Member_Key property returns the value of the attribute key that we need to pass to the report.

10. In the Parameters section, create a *CustomerID* parameter and enter *[Customer].[Customer].Member_Key* as its value, as shown in Figure 16.39.

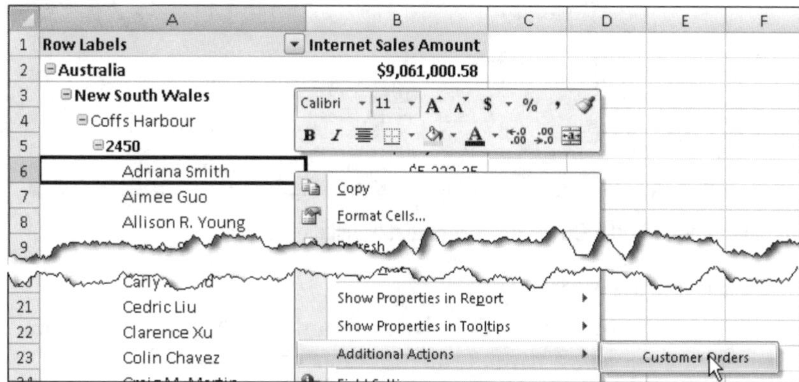

Figure 16.39 Use Microsoft Excel 2007 to test UDM actions.

11. Save and deploy the Analysis Services project.
12. Deploy the Customer Orders report to the report server.

Testing the reporting action

Let's use Excel 2007 as an OLAP browser to test the Customer Orders action.

1. Open Excel 2007 and connect to the Adventure Works cube.
2. Create a PivotTable report that requests the Customer Geography user-defined hierarchy, as shown in Figure 16.39. The report can be found in the Reporting Action.xlsx file.
3. Right-click a customer and hover on the Additional Actions context menu.

   Excel sends a discover command to Analysis Services and sends the coordinates of the user selection. Analysis Services evaluates the actions defined for the Customer attribute hierarchy and returns the Customer Orders action which Excel presents to the user.

4. Click Customer Actions.

   Excel requests the Customer Orders report by URL. You should see the Customer Orders report displayed in Internet Explorer. The report should show the orders placed by the selected customer.

16.3.3 Localizing Reports with Translations

Analysis Services makes it easy for you to target international users by defining translations in the cube. As its name suggests, a translation is a translated version of cube metadata, including captions of measures, dimensions, perspectives, and data (that is, members of attribute hierarchies).

Understanding translations

The Adventure Works cube includes sample French and Spanish metadata and data translations. By default, Analysis Services selects a translation based on the local culture of the current thread. At design time, the easiest way to test translations is to browse the cube in SQL Server Management Studio or BIDS and select the desired language from the Languages drop-down list.

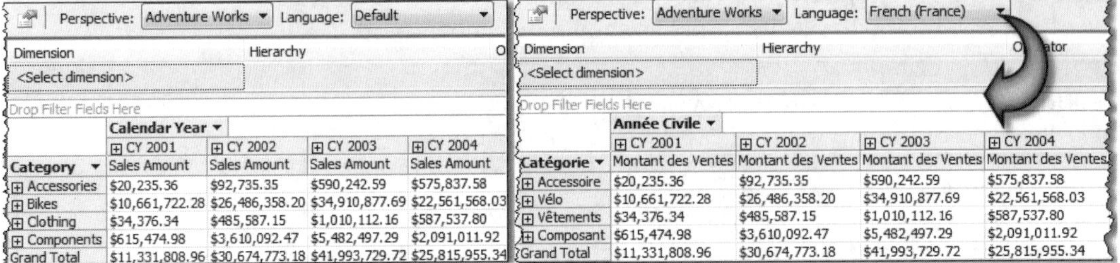

Calendar Year				
	CY 2001	CY 2002	CY 2003	CY 2004
Category	Sales Amount	Sales Amount	Sales Amount	Sales Amount
Accessories	$20,235.36	$92,735.35	$590,242.59	$575,837.58
Bikes	$10,661,722.28	$26,486,358.20	$34,910,877.69	$22,561,568.03
Clothing	$34,376.34	$485,587.15	$1,010,112.16	$587,537.80
Components	$615,474.98	$3,610,092.47	$5,482,497.29	$2,091,011.92
Grand Total	$11,331,808.96	$30,674,773.18	$41,993,729.72	$25,815,955.34

Année Civile				
	CY 2001	CY 2002	CY 2003	CY 2004
Catégorie	Montant des Ventes	Montant des Ventes	Montant des Ventes	Montant des Ventes
Accessoire	$20,235.36	$92,735.35	$590,242.59	$575,837.58
Vélo	$10,661,722.28	$26,486,358.20	$34,910,877.69	$22,561,568.03
Vêtements	$34,376.34	$485,587.15	$1,010,112.16	$587,537.80
Composant	$615,474.98	$3,610,092.47	$5,482,497.29	$2,091,011.92
Grand Total	$11,331,808.96	$30,674,773.18	$41,993,729.72	$25,815,955.34

Figure 16.40 Use SQL Server Management Studio Cube Browser to test translations.

1. Open SSMS and connect to the Adventure Works cube.
2. Create the report as the report on the left in Figure 16.40 by dropping the Product Categories user-defined hierarchy (Product dimension) on rows, Date.Calendar user-defined hierarchy (Date dimension) on columns, and Sales Amount (Sales Summary measure group) on data.

   Assuming that that your operating system culture is English, the report data and metadata should show up in English.
3. Expand the Language drop-down list and select French (France).

   The Cube Browser refreshes the report. The captions of the dimension members are now shown in French. The cube metadata (not shown) also shows the French translations.

Implementing localized reports

UDM translations definitely make it easier to localize reports. The Translations report, shown in Figure 16.41, demonstrates how you can leverage Analysis Services translations. To pass the user culture to the cube, configure the report to use a report-specific data source with an expression-based connection string.

```
="Data Source= (local);Initial Catalog=""Adventure Works DW 2008"";Locale Identifier=" &
New System.Globalization.CultureInfo(User.Language).LCID.ToString()
```

Translations

User language:en-US, Locale identifier: 1033

Category	Subcategory	Internet Sales Amount
Accessories	Bike Racks	22920
Accessories	Bike Stands	20670
Accessories	Bottles and Cages	33517.92
Accessories	Cleaners	11166.75
Accessories	Fenders	27211.24

Figure 16.41 The Translations report uses the Analysis Services translations feature to localize column captions and fields.

Analysis Services supports passing the locale identifier (LCID) in the connection string. I obtain the locale identifier from the .NET CultureInfo object by passing the user's language code (User.Language) and set the Locale Identifier connection string setting accordingly. Thus, when a user in the USA requests a report, the locale identifier will be 1033. The locale identifier for a French user in France will be 1252. See the Locale Identifier Constants and Strings topic in the Resources section for a complete list of locale identifiers.

Once the data source is set up, localizing the fields on the report is easy because the query results include the localized data, such as member names. However, localizing report metadata, such as column captions, requires more effort on your part.

Localizing the report metadata

If you open the report in layout mode, you will see that I use dynamic column captions by calling an external custom assembly:

```
Prologika.RS.Extensibility.Translator.GetTranslatedCaption("[Product].[Category]")
```

Specifically, it calls the GetTraslatedCaption method of the Translator class and it passes the name of the attribute hierarchy.

```
static Hashtable cache = new Hashtable();
[PermissionSet(SecurityAction.Assert, Unrestricted = true)] // grant callers FullTrust
public static string GetTranslatedCaption(string item) {
   string caption = null;
   try
   {
      // get language identifier, e.g. 1033 for En- US
      string lid = Thread.CurrentThread.CurrentUICulture.TextInfo.LCID.ToString();
      Trace.WriteLine(String.Format("Language ID: {0}", lid));
      // get cache identifier
      string cacheID = GetCacheIdentifier(item, lid);
      // attempt to get item from cache
      caption = (string)cache[GetCacheIdentifier(item, lid )];
      if (caption == null)
      {
         CacheMetadata(lid);
         caption = (string)cache[GetCacheIdentifier(item, lid)];
      }
   }
   catch (Exception ex)   { caption = ex.ToString();}
   return caption;
}
```

GetTranslatedCaption obtains the locale identifier from the calling thread and attempts to obtain the translated version of the item from an internal cache. Because the metadata isn't loaded yet, this action will result in a cache miss when the report is requested for the first time for each locale identifier. However, in the next step, GetTranslatedCaption calls the CacheMetadata method to obtain the translated metadata from Analysis Services.

```
private static void CacheMetadata(string lid){
   AdomdRestrictionCollection restrictions = new AdomdRestrictionCollection();
   DataSet ds = new DataSet();
   AdomdConnection conn = new AdomdConnection(String.Format(@"Data Source=(local);
       Initial Catalog=Adventure Works DW;Integrated Security=SSPI;Locale Identifier={0};", lid));
   conn.Open();
   lock (cache.SyncRoot)
   {
      // cache dimensions
      restrictions.Add("CUBE_SOURCE", 2);
      ds = conn.GetSchemaDataSet("MDSCHEMA_CUBES", restrictions);
      foreach (DataRow row in ds.Tables[0].Rows)
      {
         string cacheID = GetCacheIdentifier(row["CUBE_NAME"].ToString(), lid);
         if (cache[cacheID] == null) cache.Add(cacheID, row["CUBE_CAPTION"].ToString());
      }
      // cache all attributes
      restrictions.Clear();
      ds = conn.GetSchemaDataSet("MDSCHEMA_HIERARCHIES", restrictions);
      foreach (DataRow row in ds.Tables[0].Rows)
      {
         string cacheID = GetCacheIdentifier(row["HIERARCHY_UNIQUE_NAME"].ToString(), lid);
         if (cache[cacheID] == null) cache.Add(cacheID, row["HIERARCHY_CAPTION"].ToString());
      }
```

```
        // cache all measures
        restrictions.Clear();
        ds = conn.GetSchemaDataSet("MDSCHEMA_MEASURES", restrictions);
        foreach (DataRow row in ds.Tables[0].Rows)
        {
            string cacheID = GetCacheIdentifier(row["MEASURE_UNIQUE_NAME"].ToString(), lid);
            if (cache[cacheID] == null) cache.Add(cacheID, row["MEASURE_CAPTION"].ToString());
        }
    }
}
```

CacheMetadata opens an ADOMD.NET connection to the Analysis Services cube. ADOMD.NET is a built-in data provider that client applications can use to communicate with Analysis Services. It is important to note that the connection goes out under the Reporting Services service account even if you specify the credentials of a Windows account in the connection string. Consequently, you must grant the service account read permissions to the cube.

ADOMD.NET lets you retrieve the cube metadata definitions by calling the GetSchemaDataSet method. CacheMetadata uses this method to retrieve the cube schema (MDSCHEMA_CUBES). Since Analysis Services treats dimensions as cubes, MDSCHEMA_CUBES returns the localized versions of both cubes and dimensions.

Next, CacheMetadata obtains the name of the attribute hierarchies in all dimensions by using the MDSCHEMA_HIERARCHIES schema. Finally, CacheMetadata retrieves the captions of the cube measures by using the MDSCHEMA_MEASURES schema. For performance reasons, all translations are cached in the internal cache once for each locale identifier. When a cached report translation is subsequently requested a second time, GetTranslatedCaption returns the cached translation.

Deploying custom code

Before running the report, follow these steps to deploy the Prologika.RS.Extensibility assembly:

1. Open the Translations.sln solution file in Visual Studio and build the solution (Ctrl+Shift+B). I've defined post-build events in the Prologika.RS.Extensibility project properties that deploy the assembly to the Report Designer folder and report server bin folder.
2. Open the Report Designer RSPreviewPolicy.config file (located in \Program Files\Microsoft Visual Studio 9.0\Common7\IDE\PrivateAssemblies) and add the following after the last CodeGroup element:

```
<CodeGroup class="UnionCodeGroup" version="1" Na me="SecurityExtensionCodeGroup"
      Description="Code group for the RsViewer library" PermissionSetName="FullTrust">
   <IMembershipCondition class="UrlMembershipCondition" version="1" Url="C: \Program Files\Microsoft Visual Studio
9.0\Common7\IDE\PrivateAssemblies\Prologika.RS.Extensibility.dll" />
</CodeGroup>
```

   This element grants the Prologika.RS.Extensibility assembly FullTrust rights at design time.

3. Open the report server rssrvpolicy.config file (located in \Program Files\Microsoft SQL Server\MSRS10.MSSQLSERVER\Reporting Services\ReportServer) and add the following after the last CodeGroup element:

```
<CodeGroup class="UnionCodeGroup" version="1" Name="SecurityExtensionCodeGroup"
      Description="Code group for the RsViewer library" PermissionSetName="FullTrust">
   <IMembershipCondition class="UrlMembershipCondition" version="1" Url=" C:\Program Files\Microsoft SQL
Server\MSRS10.MSSQLSERVER\Reporting Services\ReportServer\bin\Prologika.RS.Extensibility.dll"/>
</CodeGroup>
```

   This element grants the Prologika.RS.Extensibility assembly FullTrust rights at run time.

16.4 Authoring Data Mining Reports

Business intelligence should help users analyze patterns from the past to plan for the future. Data mining presents ample opportunities to implement a new generation of reports with predictive analytics features. Such reports could process historical patterns to present views of opportunities and trends. The Targeted Campaign report included in this chapter demonstrates how you can leverage the data mining features of Analysis Services to author "smart" reports. The report presents a list of the top fifty customers that are most likely to purchase a given product.

16.4.1 Understanding the Targeted Mailing Data Mining Model

Adventure Works has already implemented a set of mining models to analyze the sales data and derive patterns. One of them is the Targeted Mailing mining structure that includes a series of mining models. Each of these models employs a different algorithm to identify the most important factors that may influence the customer decision to purchase a bike.

Understanding the Decision Tree results

Let's explore one of these models—the Decision Tree mining model.

1. Open SSMS and connect to Analysis Services.
2. Expand the Adventure Works DW 2008 database and the Mining Structures folder under it.
3. Expand the Targeted Mailing folder, select the TM Decision Tree algorithm, and click Browse.

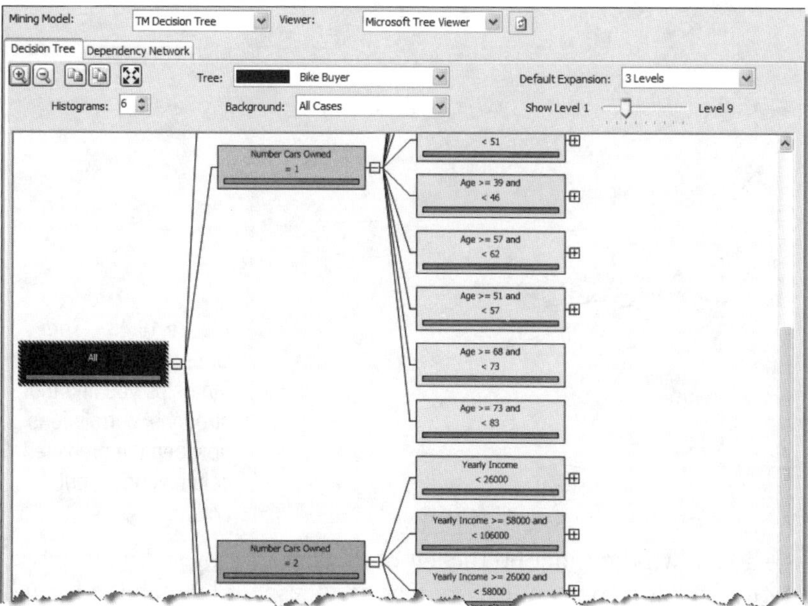

Figure 16.42 The Dependency Network tab helps you find the strongest correlations between the predicted columns and input criteria.

Microsoft provides viewers for each mining algorithm. The Decision Tree algorithm includes Decision Tree and Dependency Network viewers. The Decision Tree viewer is shown in Figure 16.42.

Let's see what conclusions we can make by inspecting the decision tree graph. When the Background drop-down is set to All Cases (default selection), you can use the Decision Trees Viewer to find which factors may influence the customer decision to purchase a bike. For example, the model has determined that the most significant factor is the number of cars owned. That's why the first split (after the root All node) is done on the Number Cars Owned factor.

The background color of each tree node is significant. The darker the color is, the larger the customer population. The root node of the tree is always the darkest. Pointing the mouse pointer to the root node, or examining the mining legend, reveals that we have 18,484 customers. Of those customers, almost 50% have purchased a bike (bike buyer is 1). The same information can be approximated by glancing at the color bar inside each node.

Moving to the second level of the tree graph, we discover that the second darkest node represents 6,457 customers who have two cars. Therefore, this group of customers is also likely to purchase a bike. By clicking on this node and looking at the mining legend (not shown in Figure 16.42), we discover that about 40% of these customers have purchased bikes.

Understanding the dependency network

In real life, your decision tree may have many splits and it may be difficult to find the most significant factors by using only the Decision Tree tab. The Dependency Network tab, shown in Figure 16.43, is designed to help you find these correlations quickly.

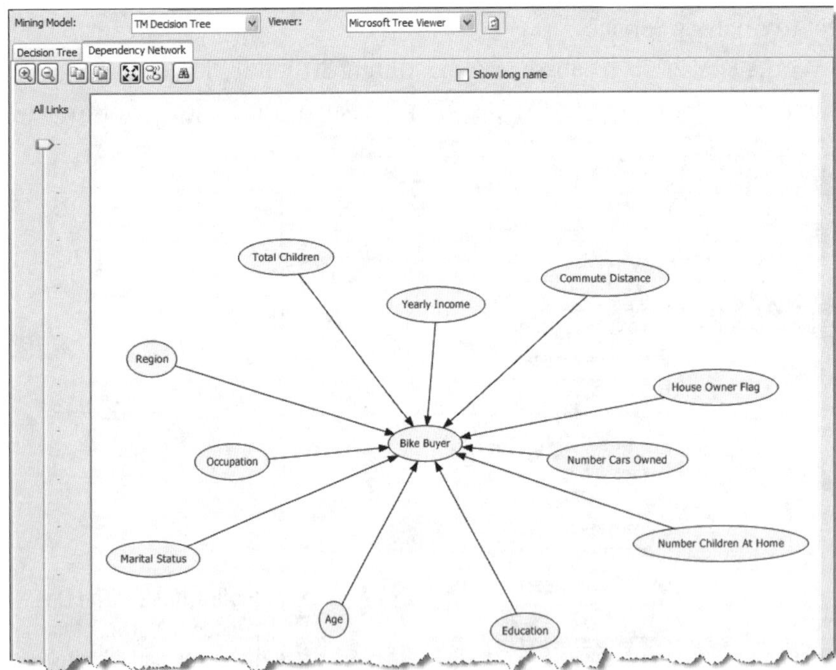

Figure 16.43 The Dependency Network tab helps you find the strongest correlations between the predicted columns and input criteria.

To find the strongest links, slide down the slider on the left of the diagram. By sliding it down, you are in essence filtering out the less significant factors. The results should match the Decision Tree viewer. For example, you will find that the most significant factor influencing customers to purchase a bike is the number of cars owned. Backing up to the previous node, we determine that the second important factor is customer's age.

16.4.2 Implementing "Smart" Reports

Given the Targeted Mailing mining mode, we can author a standard report that lists the most likely buyers, as the one shown in Figure 16.44. The end user can filter the report by sales region. The report shows the top fifty customers that may purchase a product from the selected region and the estimated probability.

Constructing the DMX query

To facilitate a wide spread adoption of data mining and minimize the learning curve, Microsoft adopted a SQL-like query language that is familiar to database developers and easy to use. Client applications can create and query data mining models and obtain predictions by sending DMX (**D**ata **M**ining E**X**tensions) statements. The MDX Query Designer supports a DMX command mode that lets you query data mining models.

1. Create a dataset that uses AdventureWorksAS2008 data source.
2. In the MDX Query Designer, select the pickaxe toolbar button to switch to the DMX command mode.
3. Click Select Model button in the Mining Model pane. In the Select Mining Model dialog box that follows, expand Targeted Mailing node and select the TM Decision Tree mining model that we've just discussed.

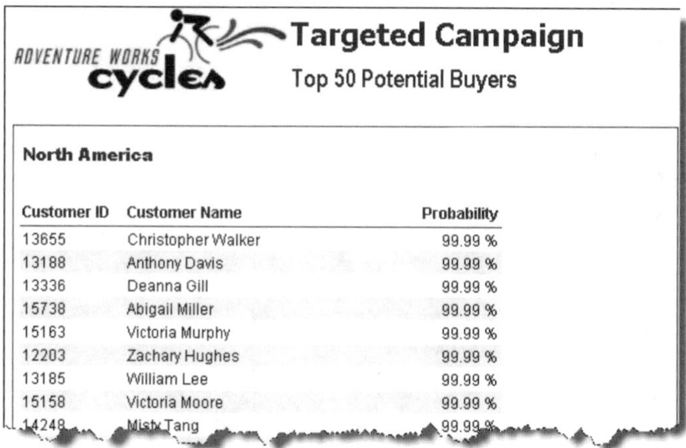

Customer ID	Customer Name	Probability
13655	Christopher Walker	99.99 %
13188	Anthony Davis	99.99 %
13336	Deanna Gill	99.99 %
15738	Abigail Miller	99.99 %
15163	Victoria Murphy	99.99 %
12203	Zachary Hughes	99.99 %
13185	William Lee	99.99 %
15158	Victoria Moore	99.99 %
14248	Misty Tang	99.99 %

Figure 16.44 The Targeted Campaign report uses a data mining model to display a list of potential buyers.

Suppose that the Adventure Works management has provided you with a list of potential customers to use as an input for the data mining algorithm. The vTargetMail view, which is included in the AdventureWorksDW2008 database, returns these customers from the database. We will pass this list to the TM Decision Tree model to identify the top most likely buyers.

4. In the Select Input Table(s) pane, click the Select Case Table button.
5. In the Select Table dialog box that follows, select the vTargetMail view and click OK.

The Data Mining Designer attempts to map the columns of the mining model with the vTargetMail view by naming convention. If the columns have different names, you can link them manually by dragging a column from the Mining Model pane and dropping it over the corresponding column in the Select Input Table(s) pane. Let's now specify the columns that we want the query to return.

6. Drag the CustomerKey column from the Mining Model pane and drop it in the grid. Enter Customer ID as a column alias.
7. Drag the FirstName and LastName columns from the Mining Model pane and drop them in the grid.

   DMX supports various prediction functions. The function that we need to return the probability of a bike purchase is PredictProbability. This function lets you predict a column from a mining model.
8. On the new row of the grid, expand the Source drop-down list and select the Prediction Function item. Expand the Field column and select the PredictProbability function. Drag the Bike Buyer column from the mining model to the Criteria/Argument column to replace the default criteria of the PredictProbability function.
9. To parameterize the query by sales region, drag the Region column from the Mining Model pane and drop it on the grid. Enter *=@Region* in the Criteria/Argument column, as shown in Figure 16.45.

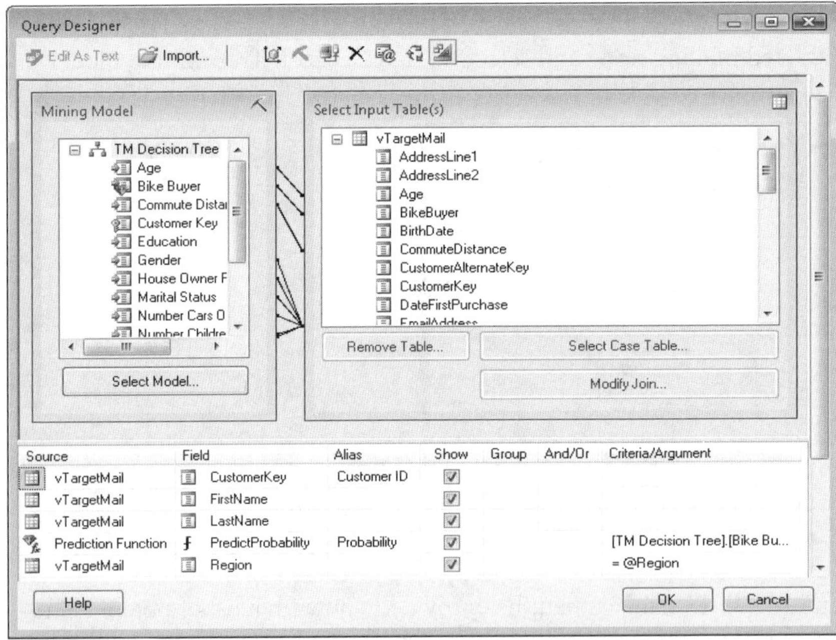

Figure 16.45 Use the Data Mining Designer to build and test DMX queries.

As with the MDX command mode, the moment you introduce a parameter placeholder in the DMX query, the Report Designer creates a report-level parameter. To make the parameter data-driven, I used a second dataset (dsRegion) that fetches the product categories from the AdventureWorksDW2008 database. I used this dataset to derive the parameter available values. You can view the finished report from the book source to see how the dataset is defined.

Working with query mode

Since the report needs a top N clause, which the graphical designer doesn't support, you need to finalize the query by switching to query mode.

1. Right-click on an empty space in the upper pane (outside the Mining Model and Select Input Table panes) and click Query.

2. Enter a TOP 50 clause and ORDER BY clause to sort the customers by probability in descending order. The finished query is shown below with changes highlighted in bold.

```
SELECT TOP 50
 (t.[CustomerKey]) as [Customer ID],
 t.[FirstName], t.[LastName], t.Region,
 PredictProbability([TM Decision Tree].[Bike Buyer]) As [Probability]
From
 [TM Decision Tree]
PREDICTION JOIN
 OPENQUERY([Adventure Works DW],
  'SELECT
    [CustomerKey],[FirstName],[LastName],[MaritalStatus],[Gender],[YearlyIncome],[TotalChildren],
    [NumberChildrenAtHome],[HouseOwnerFlag],[NumberCarsOwned],[CommuteDistance],[Region],[Age],
    [BikeBuyer]
  FROM
    [dbo].[vTargetMail]') AS t
ON
 [TM Decision Tree].[Marital Status] = t.[MaritalStatus] AND
 [TM Decision Tree].[Gender] = t.[Gender] AND
 [TM Decision Tree].[Yearly Income] = t.[YearlyIncome] AND
 [TM Decision Tree].[Total Children] = t.[TotalChildr en] AND
 [TM Decision Tree].[Number Children At Home] = t.[NumberChildrenAtHome] AND
 [TM Decision Tree].[House Owner Flag] = t.[HouseOwnerFlag] AND
 [TM Decision Tree].[Number Cars Owned] = t.[NumberCarsOwned] AND
 [TM Decision Tree].[Commute Distance] = t.[CommuteDistance] AND
 [TM Decision Tree].[Region] = t.[Region] AND
 [TM Decision Tree].[Age] = t.[Age] AND
 [TM Decision Tree].[Bike Buyer] = t.[BikeBuyer]
WHERE t.Region = @Region
ORDER BY PredictProbability([TM Decision Tree].[Bike Buyer]) DESC
```

As with the MDX Query Designer, once you've made changes in query mode, you cannot switch back to design mode without losing changes. The Data Mining Designer lets you execute the query and view results.

3. Click on the Query Parameters toolbar button. In the Query Parameters dialog box that follows, replace @Region with a value region name, such as North America.
4. Right-click on an empty space and select Result.

   The Data Mining Designer executes the query and displays the results.

5. Right-click an empty space in the Results pane and choose Query to return to query mode. Click on the Query Parameters toolbar button again and replace the region name with @Region to let the end user pass the selected region as a report parameter.

Once the report query and parameters have been taken care of, authoring the report layout is nothing you haven't seen so far. I used a tablix region that uses the Main dataset. Next, I dragged the Main fields from the Datasets pane and dropped them on the table region to bind the three columns. The report also demonstrates how expression-based conditional formatting can be used to alternate the background color of the table rows.

NOTE Need more "smart" report examples? Check my Implementing Smart Reports with the Microsoft Business Intelligence Platform article (see Resources). It demonstrates how you can leverage the SQL Server CLR stored procedures and data mining to create compelling and consistent sales forecast reports.

16.5 Summary

Reporting Services and Analysis Services are complementary technologies that you can use together to implement end-to-end business intelligence solutions. Analysis Services provides OLAP and data mining services. The MDX Query Designer uses the Analysis Services provider and supports drag-and-drop, auto-generating MDX queries, parameters, server aggregates, and calculated members. However, it is limited to static query schemas only. When the Analysis Services data provider is not enough, consider the OLE DB Provider for Analysis Services. It lets you send any MDX query but requires more programming effort.

You can leverage UDM end-user features on your reports. Extended field properties let you inherit the server-side formatting settings from UDM. You can implement reporting actions in a cube to allow users to launch Reporting Services reports. If your cube includes translations, you can localize the cube metadata and data on reports by obtaining the translations from UDM.

Leverage the Analysis Services data mining features to author "smart" reports for predictive analysis. Data mining reports fetch data by sending DMX queries to the mining model. Use the DMX mode of the MDX Query Designer to create and test DMX queries.

16.6 Resources

Protect UDM with Dimension Data Security
(http://tinyurl.com/yop6oj)—Discusses the fundamentals of Analysis Services dimension data security and two practical approaches for implementing it.

Intelligencia Query
(http://www.it-workplace.co.uk/IQ.aspx)—A custom data extension with a graphical MDX query designer that supports any MDX query schema.

Configuring HTTP Access to SQL Server 2005 Analysis Services on Microsoft Windows Server 2003 by Edward Melomed
(http://tinyurl.com/bgb5g)—This paper explains the steps required to set up HTTP access to Analysis Services.

Dimension Member and Cell Properties
(http://tinyurl.com/2m6p2q and http://tinyurl.com/2r9hl7)—Lists all dimension member and cell properties.

Locale Identifier Constants and Strings
(http://tinyurl.com/3dpq6a)—Describes predefined constants and strings for locale identifiers used in multilingual applications.

Implementing Smart Reports with the Microsoft Business Intelligence Platform
(http://tinyurl.com/232vb2)—This article demonstrates how you can use data mining and CLR stored procedures to implement reports with forecasting capabilities.

Chapter 17

Integrating with SharePoint

We all need to share information. If your organization has formalized its information sharing needs by adopting tools and business processes to support that effort, chances are your company is already using SharePoint to manage documents and collaborate online. As an IT professional who is also using Reporting Services, wouldn't it be nice if you could upload strategic reports to a SharePoint site to quickly disseminate insightful information across the enterprise? Or, quickly assemble a digital dashboard page to help a management team understand company business and make decisions?

To meet these needs, Reporting Services supports SharePoint integration features that let you view and manage reports from a SharePoint site. This chapter starts with an overview of the SharePoint technologies. Then, I will explain different options for integrating Reporting Services with SharePoint. I will walk you through the process of installing Windows SharePoint Services and configuring Reporting Services for SharePoint integration. Finally, I will conclude by showing you how to manage and view reports inside SharePoint and implement web part pages that display report content on a SharePoint site.

17.1 Understanding SharePoint Integration

Nowadays, many organizations leverage Microsoft SharePoint products and technologies for web-based document management and collaboration. To ensure that business reports are available within this collaborative environment, Reporting Services has included in the last several releases a set of features that allow you to run reports from a SharePoint site. This integration scenario presents numerous benefits, including centralized report management and viewing through SharePoint sites, and leveraging SharePoint collaboration capabilities to bring versioning and workflow support to your Reporting Services reports.

Before we dive into this integration scenario, let's take a moment to step back and understand the SharePoint technologies.

17.1.1 Understanding SharePoint Products and Technologies

SharePoint Products and Technologies is collective name for three applications: Windows SharePoint Services, Microsoft Office SharePoint Server and Microsoft Office SharePoint Designer, as shown in Figure 17.1.

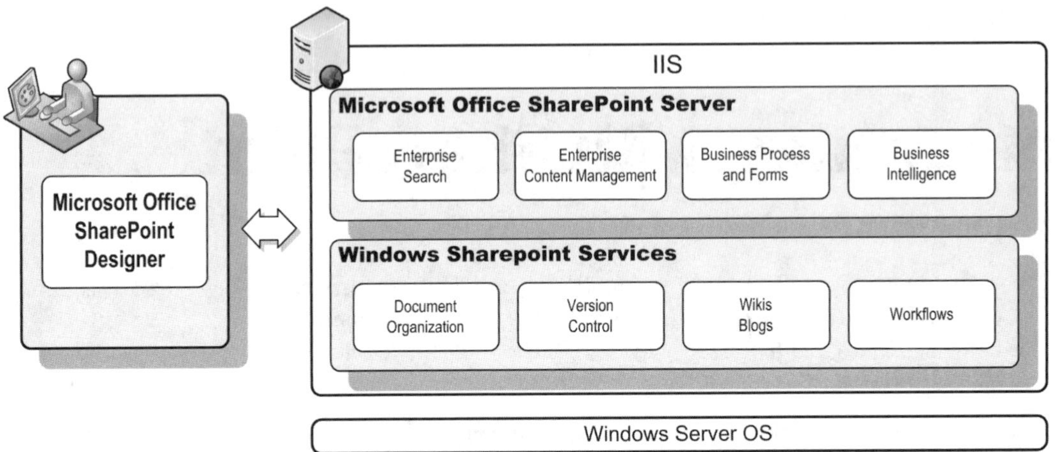

Figure 17.1 SharePoint Products and Technologies include Windows SharePoint Services, Microsoft Office SharePoint Server, and Microsoft Office SharePoint Designer

Let's briefly take a look at each of these components and their features.

Windows SharePoint Services

Windows SharePoint Services (WSS), previously known as SharePoint Team Services, is a free web technology download that runs on Windows Server operating systems (see Resources). WSS is a core technology upon which other Microsoft web-based applications are based, including Microsoft Office SharePoint Server and Microsoft Office Project Server.

WSS provides basic features that let you quickly build web pages for showing content. Typically, information workers leverage SharePoint to implement personalized web pages consisting of web parts. A SharePoint web part is an ASP.NET control that exposes content, such as a report. A SharePoint site includes a collection of SharePoint pages. A SharePoint web application hosts a collection of sites and runs under IIS. Similar to Reporting Services, WSS uses SQL Server databases to store documents, metadata, and configuration information, such as security policies. SharePoint requires a Windows Server operating system with IIS and ASP.NET enabled.

Now in its third major release, WSS provides essential services for document management and collaboration, including document editing, document organization and version control capabilities. It also includes other popular content features, such as wikis, blogs, to-do lists, alerts, discussion boards, and workflows. WSS integrates well with Microsoft Office to let you open and publish documents to and from WSS sites and libraries.

For more information about Windows SharePoint Services and its features, visit its official web page at http://office.microsoft.com/sharepointtechnology.

Microsoft Office SharePoint Server

Microsoft Office SharePoint Server (MOSS) is a product of the Microsoft Office system. MOSS is built on top of Windows SharePoint Services and adds more features, web parts, and infrastructure. Specifically, it offers enterprise search capabilities across multiple SharePoint sites and external resources. It extends the WSS content management features by consolidating content from multiple sources into a centrally managed and scalable repository. Microsoft InfoPath Forms Services, which is a component of MOSS, can streamline business processes by allowing information workers to fill in Web forms.

MOSS also offers several business intelligence features that you may find interesting. First, its Excel Services lets you execute Excel spreadsheets on the server. For example, you can author an Excel PivotTable report connected to an Analysis Services cube and publish the spreadsheet to MOSS. When the user requests the spreadsheet, Excel Services refreshes the spreadsheet on the server and streams it in HTML format. Consequently, end users don't need to have Microsoft Excel installed locally to view the results.

Another interesting BI-related feature is Business Data Catalog. Organizations can leverage the MOSS Business Data Catalog to present business data from back-end server applications, such as SAP or Siebel 2007, without writing any code.

MOSS also provides additional web parts that are not available in the WSS technology download. Reporting Services users may find the MOSS filter web parts particularly interesting. Suppose you have implemented a dashboard page that displays a Reporting Services report and an Excel chart side-by-side and both web parts accept a date parameter. You can use a Date Filter web part to collect the date from the end user and synchronize the web parts automatically, as opposed to entering the date parameter for each web part.

NOTE Reporting Services does not include any MOSS-specific features. This is why this chapter targets exclusively Windows SharePoint Services, with the exception of the Analysis Services filter web part that I cover its section 17.4.3. That said, you should evaluate the MOSS Business Intelligence capabilities, such as Excel Services and filter web parts, when planning to integrate Reporting Services with SharePoint and determine whether those features justify an upgrade to MOSS.

Microsoft Office SharePoint Designer

Microsoft Office SharePoint Designer is an HTML editor for creating and customizing Microsoft SharePoint Web sites. It is a successor to Microsoft FrontPage but it was redesigned to include SharePoint-specific features for opening SharePoint sites, working with web parts, and adding workflow support. Hence, the name changed to SharePoint Designer.

You can use Microsoft Office SharePoint Designer to create and edit basic SharePoint pages without writing any code. Should you need programming logic and more advanced functionality, such as implementing connectable web parts, you can use Visual Studio to build ASP.NET web parts that are fully supported by SharePoint.

17.1.2 Understanding Partial Integration

Reporting Services supports two SharePoint integration options. Partial integration is supported through a pair of web parts that you install on a SharePoint site and point to a report server configured for native mode. SharePoint full integration is achieved by configuring the report server for SharePoint integration mode. This section describes the features that provide partial integration support.

Understanding the Version 2.0 web parts

Reporting Services 2000 Service Pack 2 introduced two web parts: Report Explorer and Report Viewer, that provided a quick and easy way to integrate SharePoint with Reporting Services. These web parts continue to be available in Reporting Services 2008.

NOTE Because the Report Explorer and Report Viewer were originally designed for SharePoint version 2.0, the documentation refers to them as SharePoint 2.0 web parts. The Report Explorer and Report Viewer web parts continue to work with SharePoint 3.0.

The Report Explorer web part lets users browse the report catalog, subscribe to reports, and launch the Report Builder 1.0 client. The Report Viewer web part can be used to view reports. From an implementation standpoint, these web parts are very simple. They are implemented as HTML IFRAME elements that reference Report Manager pages with some part-to-part communication built in so that the Report Explorer drives the Report Viewer web part. Figure 17.2 shows the WebParts20.aspx page (included in the book source code) that demonstrates these web parts.

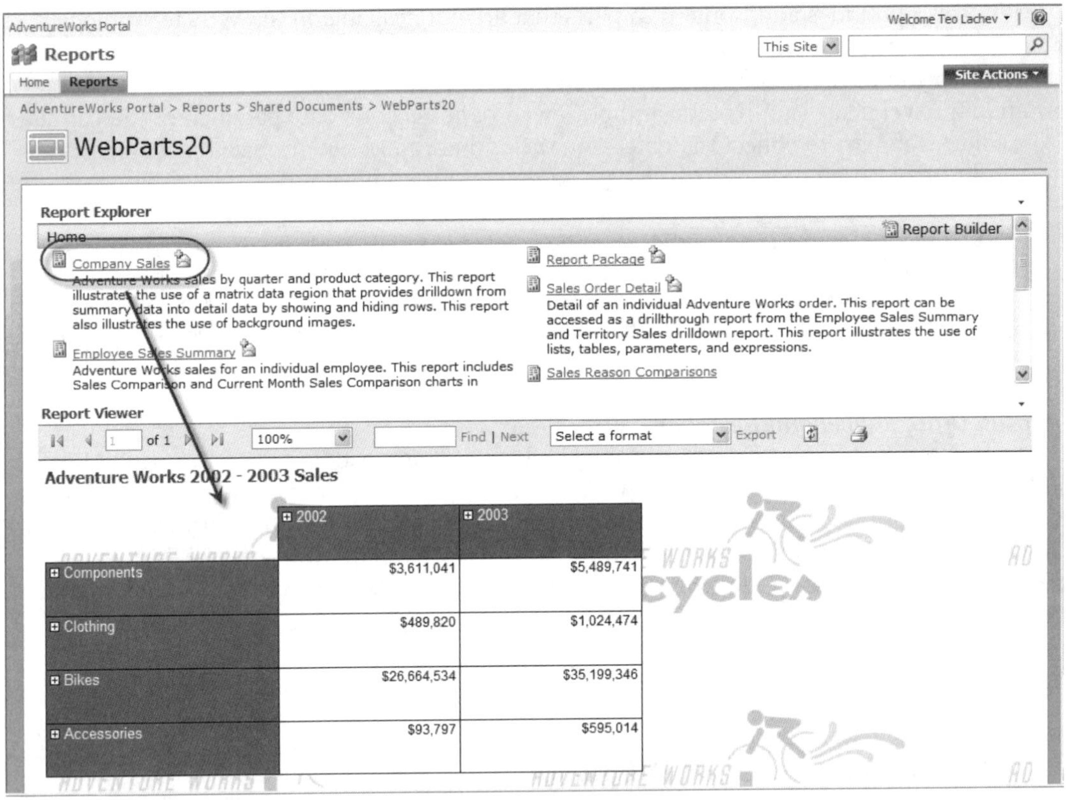

Figure 17.2 The Report Explorer web part passes the report path to the Report Viewer web part.

On the top half of the page, the Report Explorer web part lets you navigate the report server folder namespace. When you click a report link, the Report Explorer web part passes the report path to the Report Viewer web part that is embedded on the bottom half of the page. Report Viewer displays the report by sending a client-side URL request to the report server.

Installing the version 2.0 web parts

Follow these steps to install the Report Explorer and Report Viewer web parts on an existing SharePoint site.

1. Copy the web parts .cab file (\Program Files\Microsoft SQL Server\100\Tools\Reporting Services\SharePoint\RSWebParts.cab) to the SharePoint server.

2. Open the Windows Command Prompt and navigate to the folder that has the Stsadm.exe tool, such as \Program Files\Common Files\Microsoft Shared\web server extensions\12\bin.
3. Execute the following command:

```
STSADM.EXE - o addwppack - filename "<path> \RSWebParts.cab" - globalinstall
```

Replace the path placeholder with the path to the folder where you copied the RSWebParts.cab file.

Configuring the version 2.0 web parts

Follow these steps to configure the web parts on a new page.

1. Open the SharePoint site in the browser. Expand the Site Actions drop-down lis and click Create.
2. In the Create page, click the Web Part Page link in the Web Pages section.
3. In the New Web Part Page page, name the page *WebParts20*, accept the default Header, Footer, 3 Columns layout template and click Create.

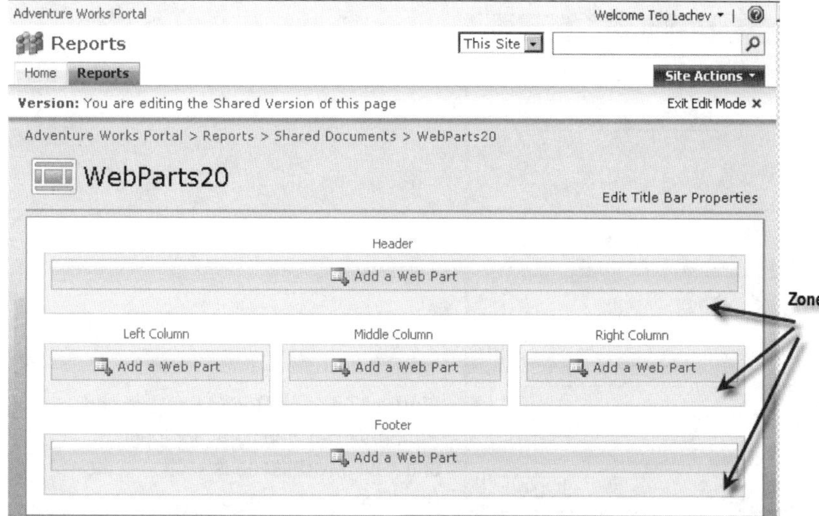

Figure 17.3 A web part page contains web part zones which can contain one or more web parts.

SharePoint creates a new page and opens it in Edit mode, as shown in Figure 17.3. The page contains Headers, Left Column, Middle Column, Right Column, and Footer web part zones. Each zone contains an Add a Web Part link which you can click to add a new web part to that zone.

4. Click the Add a Web Part link inside the Header zone.
5. In the Add Web Parts dialog box that follows, scroll down to the Miscellaneous section, as shown in Figure 17.4, select the Report Explorer web part, and click Add.

SharePoint adds the Report Explorer web part to the Header zone and opens its configuration pane to let you configure it.

6. Configure the Report Explorer web part as shown in Table 17.1. Click the Apply button.

Table 17.1 **Report Explorer configuration properties**

Category	Property	Setting	Description
Configuration	Report Manager URL	http://<servername>/reports	The URL address of a functional Report Manager.
	Start Path	AdventureWorks Sample Reports	The path to a folder that will be displayed by default. Leave it empty if you want to display the Home folder.
	View Mode	List	Corresponds to the Show Details mode of Report Manager.
Appearance	Height	150 pixels	The web part height.

SharePoint initializes and renders the Report Explorer web part. At this point, the Report Explorer web part should display the content of the AdventureWorks Sample Reports folder assuming you have deployed them to the target report server. Next, you configure the Report Viewer web part and connect it to the Report Explorer web part.

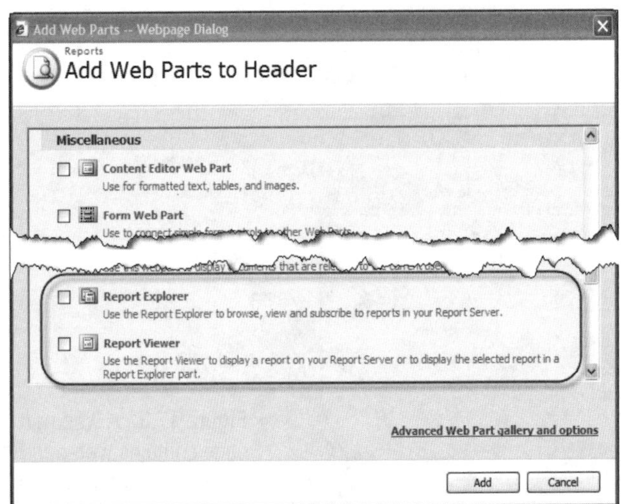

Figure 17.4 The Report Explorer and Report Viewer web parts are found under the Miscellaneous section in the Add Web Parts dialog box.

7. Click the Add a Web Part link in the Footer zone.
8. In the Add Web Parts dialog box, select the Report Explorer web part.
9. Size the Report Explorer as needed by changing the Height property. Leave the rest of the properties set to their default values.

   SharePoint supports connectable web parts to let web parts exchange information with each other. The Report Explorer is designed as a provider web part so it can pass the path of the selected report to the Report Viewer web part, which is implemented as a consumer web part. Connect the two web parts as follows.

10. Expand the Edit drop-down of the Report Explorer web part.
11. Select Connections ⇨ Show Report In ⇨ Report Viewer, as shown in Figure 17.5.

    SharePoint refreshes the page to apply the connection changes. At this point, you can click a report link in the Report Explorer web part and the report will appear in the Report Viewer web part. Repeat the last two steps if you decide to disconnect the web parts later on.

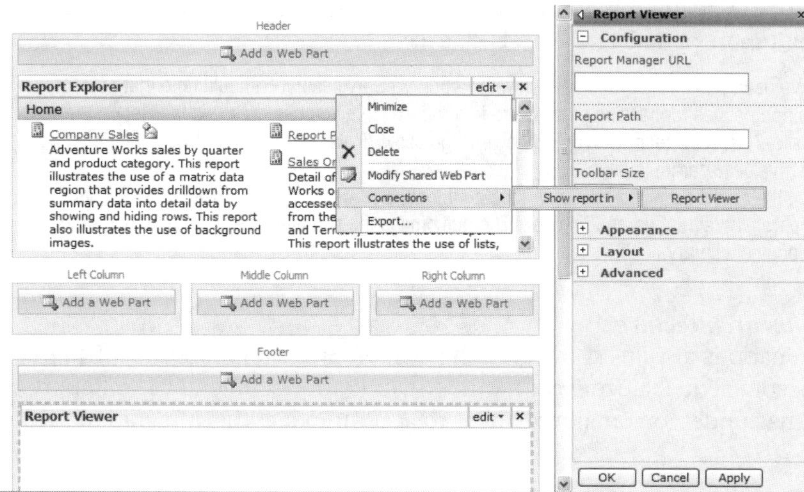

Figure 17.5 The Report Explorer and Report Viewer web parts are implemented as connectable web parts.

12. Click the Exit Edit Mode link in the upper right corner of the page to exit the edit mode and render the page as it will be shown to the end user.

Pros and Cons of partial integration

The partial SharePoint integration option has the following advantages:

- Easy setup—You don't have to reconfigure the report server to let end users navigate the report catalog and view reports inside SharePoint.
- Full-featured Reporting Services support—This integration option doesn't disable any Reporting Services features.
- No impact to existing applications—If you have an existing applications that integrate with Reporting Services, they will not be affected.

At the same time, the partial SharePoint integration option is just that. It provides a partial support for SharePoint and it has the following limitations:

- Separate management interfaces—The administrator must use the SharePoint environment to manage the SharePoint content and Report Manager to manage the report catalog.
- Different security models—The administrator must maintain separate security policies for document and report management and viewing. Access to a report depends equally on SharePoint permissions on the web part page and role assignments on the report server.
- Separate content stores—Because report definitions are kept outside SharePoint, you cannot leverage the SharePoint management features, such as version control and workflows. In addition, if you target Microsoft Office SharePoint Server, you won't be able to use its filter web parts to synchronize reports on the page.

17.1.3 Understanding Full Integration

Realizing the deficiencies of the partial integration option, Microsoft introduced full support for SharePoint in SQL Server 2005 Service Pack 2, which is discuss throughout the rest of this chapter. You can implement this deployment scenario by configuring Reporting Services for

SharePoint integration mode. Version 2008 of Reporting Services adds support for data-driven subscriptions and passing report parameters with URL access.

NOTE Readers who have used the full integration option with Reporting Services 2005 should note that now Reporting Services supports two approaches for passing parameters to a report. First, you can do so via the Report Viewer web part, such as http://<site>/_layouts/ReportServer/RSViewerPage.aspx?/RelativeReportUrl=/DocumentLibrary <ReportPath >.rdl?param1=value1¶m2=value2.
Second, you can reference the report definition directly in the document library, such as http://<site>/< DocumentLibrary>/<ReportPath>.rdl?param1=value1¶m2=value2. The outcome is the same—a full page rendering of the report in the SharePoint document library.

Understanding integration architecture

The major goal of this scenario is a *seamless* integration between SharePoint and Reporting Services where reports become equal citizens with other SharePoint documents. The Reporting Services architecture has undergone major changes to accommodate this integration scenario, as shown in Figure 17.6.

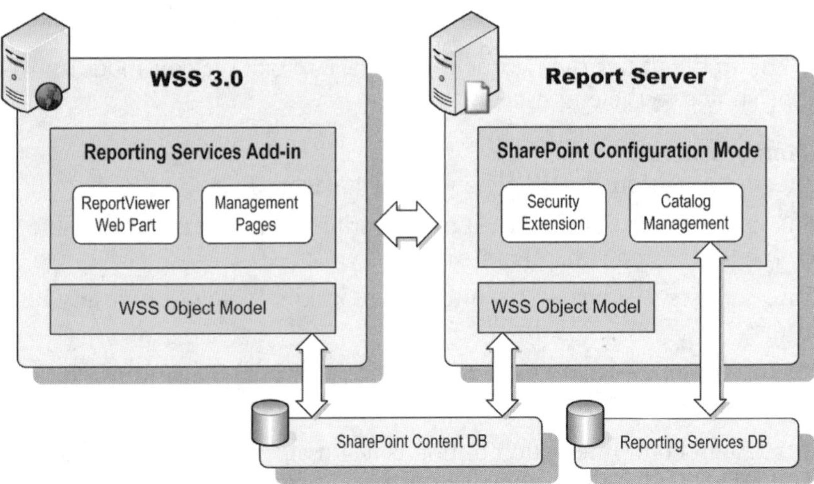

Figure 17.6 In SharePoint integration mode, file definitions and security configuration are stored in the SharePoint database.

In SharePoint integration mode, the SharePoint database hosts the report namespace, security policies, report definitions, data source definitions, Report Builder models, and resources. This lets you manage the report catalog inside the SharePoint environment just like you manage any other SharePoint document. Because SharePoint doesn't provide equivalent functionality, the report server database stores all non-file definitions, including schedules, caching, and subscriptions. As with native mode, the report server is responsible for report rendering and executing background tasks.

To let SharePoint "know" about Reporting Services, you need to download and install a Microsoft SQL Server 2008 Reporting Services Add-in for Microsoft SharePoint Technologies on the SharePoint server. This add-in installs a ReportViewer web part for report viewing, and management pages for managing the report catalog. I will be quick to point out that although having identical names, the ReportViewer web part in full integration mode has nothing to do with the version 2.0 ReportViewer web part. The former wraps the ReportViewer Web server control (discussed in chapter 15) and renders reports on the server side. As noted, the version 2.0 ReportViewer web part is just an IFRAME that request reports by URL on the client side.

On the report server side, a special security extension integrates with the SharePoint security model and inherits the SharePoint security policies. For example, the SharePoint standard Owners group will get unrestricted rights to the report catalog, while the Members group will have Contributor level permissions, including rights to create and view reports. The security extension is an internal component that you cannot configure or manage. A SharePoint-specific endpoint, ReportService2006.asmx, extends the catalog management APIs and lets SharePoint and custom applications communicate with a report server configured for SharePoint integration mode.

Although the diagram shows two separate servers, Reporting Services and SharePoint can be hosted on the same server. A single-server deployment is of course easier to set up and more cost-effective. Distributed deployment requires installing the WSS object model on the report server by performing a SharePoint Web Front End (server farm) install.

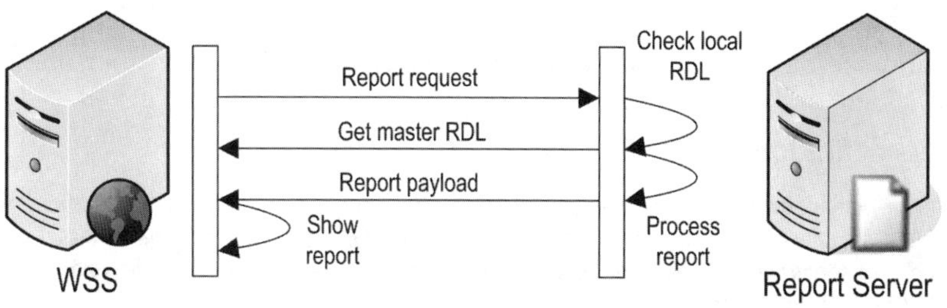

Figure 17.7 The report server synchronizes the report definition on-demand.

Understanding runtime interaction

Although totally transparent to the end user, on-demand report delivery involves a bi-directional communication between SharePoint and Reporting Services, as shown in Figure 17.7. SharePoint always keeps the most recent (master) copy of the report definition. When the user runs a report, SharePoint forwards the report request to the report server. The report server checks if the report definition exists in the report server database and if it is the same as the master copy.

The report server doesn't receive document management events from SharePoint. If the report definition doesn't exist (a new report) or is not up to date, the report server calls back to SharePoint to get the latest version. Next, the report server processes the report as usual and sends the report payload to SharePoint. SharePoint displays the report in the ReportViewer web part.

Understanding security

In SharePoint integration mode, the Reporting Services security model is superseded by the SharePoint security model. Consequently, Reporting Services operations map to SharePoint Web or List rights. For example, the Reporting Services CreateReport operation maps to the Add Items SharePoint right. Similarly, site permissions replace Reporting Service system operations. For example, the CreateSchedules operation is replaced with the Manage Web Site SharePoint site permission.

In SharePoint mode, the Reporting Services item-level roles are replaced by the standard SharePoint permissions levels. Table 17.2 shows the standard SharePoint permission levels and the permitted Reporting Services features.

Table 17.2 Security mapping

SharePoint Role	Reporting Services Features
Read	View/run reports, view data sources and models. Create and delete user-owned subscriptions, view report history and snapshots.
Contribute	Create, edit, and delete reports, data sources, and models. Create and delete snapshots.
Design	Create and delete folders.
Full Control	Create, edit, and delete shared schedules and any subscription.

To view the SharePoint permissions levels and the permitted tasks:

1. In SSMS connect to the report server using the SharePoint site URL, such as http://<servername>.
2. Expand the Security folder and the Roles folder under it. SSMS shows the SharePoint permission levels as roles.
3. Double-click a role to view its definition.

NOTE You can use SQL Server Management Studio to connect to a report server running in SharePoint integration mode to view its server properties, security policies, and schedules. You can connect using the server name or the SharePoint site URL, such as http://<servername>. The latter option is preferable because you will able to view and manage shared schedules and view role definitions.

You can only view and not modify the SharePoint permission levels in SSMS. You need to use SharePoint if you want to change them. SharePoint includes three predefined groups (Owners, Members, and Visitors) that have assigned permission levels. To simplify security management, I recommend you stick with the standard SharePoint groups whenever possible. For example, you can grant a user Full Control rights to the report catalog by assigning the user to the Owners group. The Members group has Contribute level permissions. Finally, the Visitors group has Read level permissions. In SharePoint integration mode, Report Services supports two mutually exclusive security modes, as shown in Figure 17.8.

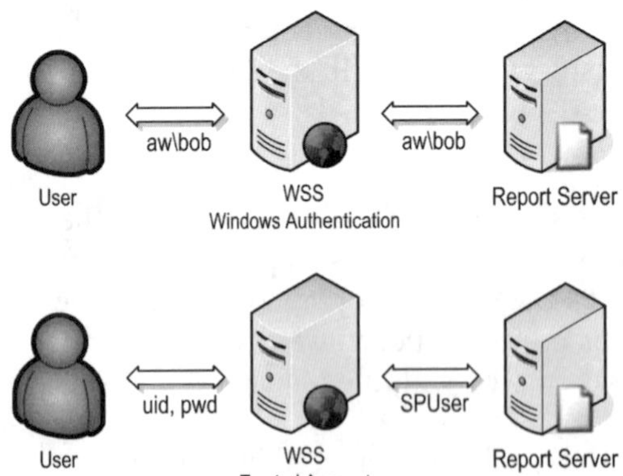

Figure 17.8 Reporting Services supports Windows Integrated and Trusted Account security modes.

Windows Authentication

Windows Authentication is the default security mode for a report server configured for SharePoint integration. This is preferred mode for intranet deployments with Active Directory where the user is authenticated based on the user's Windows identity. In this case, SharePoint impersonates the call to the report server.

For example, if Bob logs in to the Adventure Works domain as aw\bob, SharePoint forwards the call to the report server as aw\bob. The report server uses the internal security extension to call into the WSS object model and asks SharePoint to authorize the user to perform the requested action. If the report server and SharePoint are installed on separate servers, you will need to configure Kerberos delegation on the SharePoint server to avoid the "double hop" issue. For more information how this could be done, read the Configuring Kerberos for SharePoint 2007 blog by Martin Kearn (see Resources).

Trusted Account

Trusted account mode refers to a special "trusted" account that SharePoint uses to communicate with a report server. All requests that flow from SharePoint to a report server are made under this single account. Within the request, SharePoint prepares an encrypted token containing the user identity and sends this token to the report server. If SharePoint is configured for Forms Authentication, this token contains the user login name. If SharePoint is configured for Windows authentication, the token contains the Windows login.

Consider using trusted account mode when Windows authentication is not appropriate. For example, a SharePoint portal may be Internet-facing, using Forms Authentication to verify user identity. Or, you might need to use trusted account if your organization does not allow Kerberos within distributed server deployments.

As with Windows authentication mode, you can use the User!UserID property to retrieve the user identity and use it on the report. On the downside, in trusted account mode, you can't use Windows integrated security to connect to report data sources. Instead, you must use stored or prompted credentials for data source connections. With data sources that require Windows authentication, such as Analysis Services, you can store or prompt for Windows credentials.

Pros and Cons of full integration

The SharePoint full integration option offers the following benefits:

- Centralized report management—You can manage reports inside SharePoint.
- Centralized security—SharePoint security policies supersede the report server security model.
- SharePoint-specific features—Since reports are stored in the SharePoint databases, they are treated as any other document type. Consequently, you get features that are not available in native mode, such as decorating reports with additional metadata properties, applying version control, subscribing to alerts when a report is changed, attaching a business workflow to a report, and so on.

At the same time, the full integration option is subject to the following limitations:

- Impact on existing applications—Re-configuring a report server for SharePoint integration will break existing applications that integrate with Reporting Services as a result of changes to navigational paths and unsupported features. For example, a native report path of /AMRS/Company Sales becomes http://<Site >/<Document Library>/AMRS/Company Sales.rdl. Consequently, you need to rewrite your applications to use this format.
- No automatic upgrade path—Re-configuring a report server for SharePoint integration necessitates creating a new report catalog and redeploying the report content.

- Feature loss—The following Reporting Services features are not available in SharePoint integration mode: Report Manager, Report Scripting Host (rss.exe), linked reports, My Reports, custom security (SharePoint supports its own Forms Authentication model), and method batching.

TIP It's possible to implement custom applications that target both native and SharePoint integration modes by referencing the appropriate endpoint (ReportService2005.asmx for native mode and ReportService2006.asmx for SharePoint mode) and constructing correct navigational paths. You need to code to the lowest common denominator by avoiding features that SharePoint integration doesn't support.

17.2 Configuring SharePoint Integration

Unfortunately, configuring Reporting Services for SharePoint integration mode is not an automated process. In this section, I will walk you through the steps of installing SharePoint and configuring Reporting Services for SharePoint integration. When you complete this section, you will have implemented a Reports SharePoint site, similar to the one shown in Figure 17.9. Later on, you will use the predefined Shared Documents library in the Reports site to deploy report server content. The following steps assume clean installations of Windows SharePoint Services and SQL Server 2008 on a single server running Windows Server 2003.

17.2.1 Performing Initial Installation

During the initial setup process, you will install SQL Server 2008 and Windows SharePoint Services 3.0. I suggest you set up SQL Server 2008 first to let SharePoint use it for hosting its database. This will avoid the SQL Server 2005 Express Edition instance that the SharePoint basic setup would install.

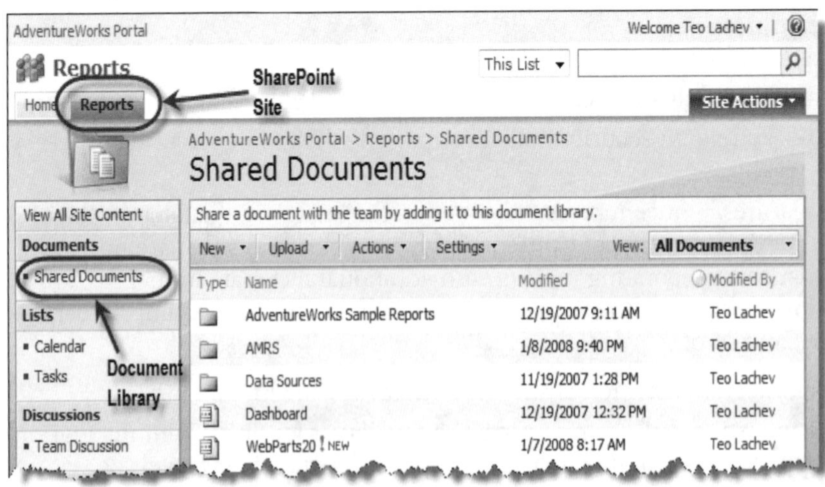

Figure 17.9 The Shared Documents document library in the Reports site hosts the report content.

Installing prerequisites

WSS requires Internet Information Services and .NET Framework 3.0, which you need to install prior to running the WSS setup.

1. Run the Manage Your Server tool found in the Administrative Tools program group of Windows Server 2003. Click the Add or Remove a Role button and configure the server as an Application Server with IIS and ASP.NET.
2. Install SQL Server 2008. SharePoint integration is supported with Standard, Developer, and Enterprise editions of SQL Server 2008. Choose the Install the SharePoint Mode Default Configuration setup option on the Report Services Configuration page. Step-by-step instructions for installing SQL Server 2008 are provided in chapter 2.

   The Install the SharePoint Mode Default Configuration option creates a report server database in SharePoint integration mode and disables Report Manager. However, the report server will not be operational after Setup completes. You still need to install WSS and the Reporting Services Add-in, and configure SharePoint integration before you can use the new installation. If you are reconfiguring an existing report server from native to SharePoint integration mode, use the Reporting Services Configuration Manager to create a new report server database in SharePoint integration mode.

Installing Windows SharePoint Services

I recommend you run the WSS setup in Advanced mode to avoid installing a SQL Server 2005 Express Edition instance to host the SharePoint database. Not only will this prevent you from scaling up and out SharePoint but it will compete for resources with the SQL Server 2008 instance.

1. Download Windows SharePoint Services 3.0 (see Resources) and run SharePoint.exe.
2. Choose the Advanced installation option.
3. On the Server Type step, select the Web Front End option. Do not choose the Stand-alone option because it performs the same setup steps as the Basic setup. Click Install Now to install the SharePoint components.
4. After the initial setup completes, the setup program gives you an option to run the SharePoint Products and Technologies Configuration Wizard to complete the configuration. Leave this option selected and click the Close button to run the wizard.

NOTE If you install Reporting Services on a separate server than SharePoint, you need to install the WSS object model on that server so Reporting Services can communicate with SharePoint. You can do so by running the SharePoint setup program and choosing the Web Front End option. After the setup is done, you need to run the SharePoint Products and Technologies Configuration Wizard to join the web front end to the appropriate SharePoint farm. However, you don't need to keep SharePoint running on the report server. You can disable the web Front end service via Central Admin ⇨ Operations ⇨ Services on Server (under Topology and Services section). Click Stop for the started Windows SharePoint Services Web Application service.

Running the Configuration Wizard

The Configuration Wizard has several steps that let you configure the SharePoint installation.

1. In the Connect to a Server Farm step, choose the No, I Want to Create a New Server Farm option.
2. In the Specify Configuration Database Settings step, specify the connection to the SQL Server that will host the SharePoint configuration database. For example, to host the SharePoint configuration database on the local SQL Server 2008 instance, enter *localhost* in the Database Server field.

The default name of the SharePoint configuration database is SharePoint_Config. You need to also specify the credentials of a Windows account, which WSS will use to connect to the database. Use a domain account (domain\login) or local Windows account (machinename\login) if the database is hosted on the same server.

3. Accept the default values in the remaining steps of the wizard.
4. If all is well, the Configuration Wizard will display a Configuration Successful summary page. Click Finish to close the wizard and open the SharePoint Central Administration application.

Creating a web application and site collection

At this point, you should have a working SharePoint Central Administration web application. Now, it's time to create a SharePoint web application that will host the SharePoint portal. You can create a new IIS web application or use an existing one, such as the Default Web Site.

DEFINITION A site collection is a set of SharePoint sites in the same web application that have the same owner and share administration settings. Each site collection contains a top-level site and can contain one or more subsites.

1. In the SharePoint Central Administration application, click the Application Management tab.
2. Click the Create or Extend Web Application link found under the SharePoint Web Application Management section.
3. In the Create or Extend Web Application page, click the Create a New Web Application link.
4. In the Create New Web Application page, you can create a new IIS web application or use an existing one, such as the Default Web Site. Assuming that you want to reuse the existing Default Web Site, choose the Use an Existing IIS Web Site option.
5. In the Application Pool section, choose Create New Application Pool. Select the Predefined option for Select a Security Account for This Application Pool. Make sure that the Network Service account is selected the drop-down list below. Click OK.

   SharePoint configures the Default Web Site but it doesn't create a SharePoint site it. SharePoint creates also a new SQL Server database (WSS_Content) to host the content, such as documents and reports. If all is well, the Application Created page will open automatically.
6. Click the Create Site Collection link on the Application Created page.
7. In the Create Site Collection page, enter *Adventure Works Portal* in the Title field.
8. In the Primary Site Collection Administrator section, enter a Windows account (domain\login), such as your domain account, in the Username field. Click the Check Names button to the right to verify the account. Click OK button.

   SharePoint creates a new site collection based on the Team Site template in the web application you've just created. In addition, SharePoint creates a top-level site in the site collection. The Top-Level Site Successfully Created page should open automatically. When it does, you will see a link to the top-level site (for example, http://<servername>). Before you click the link, reset IIS.
9. Click Start ⇨ Run ⇨ issreset to reset IIS.
10. On the SharePoint Central Administration page, click the top-level side link. You should see the Adventure Works Portal home page. There should be only one (Home) tab.

    You may get an Access Denied error when you navigate to the top-level site. One reason for this may be that Windows integrated security is not enabled on the IIS web site. Check the application security settings in IIS and make sure that Windows authentication is the only enabled option. If http://<servername>/default.aspx works but http://<servername>/ gives you Access Denied, the most likely reason is that the virtual folders of the web applications run in different IIS application pools. To fix this, start IIS Manager, open the properties of the site and each of the virtual folders under it one at the time. If any of the virtual folders is configured for a different application pool, click the Create button to create an application, change the application pool, and click the Remove button to remove the application.

Creating a Reports site

You can use the top-level site to host report content so this configuration step is optional. Let's create a Reports subsite so the user can access the reports by clicking on the Reports tab (see Figure 17.9 for an illustration of the end result).

1. In the Adventure Works Portal, expand the Site Actions drop-down menu on the top right corner and select Create.
2. In the Create page, click the Sites and Workspaces link found under the Web Pages section.
3. In the New SharePoint Site page, enter *Reports* as the site title and *reportsite* in the URL name field so the Reports site URL is http://<servername>/reportsite.

WARNING When choosing the site URL, make sure it doesn't conflict with the Reporting Services URLs. For example, a site URL of http://<servername>/reports will conflict with the Report Manager URL although Report Manager is not available in SharePoint integration mode. Consequently, you will get a Reporting Services error when navigating to the site. To avoid this, use different URLs or use the Reporting Services Configuration Manager to change (or unregister) the Reporting Services URLs.

4. In the Select a Template drop-down list (Template Selection section), make sure that the Team Site template is selected. Click the Create button to create the Reports site.

At this point, the Adventure Works portal should match Figure 17.9 with the exception that the Shared Documents library in the Reports site is empty.

17.2.2 Configuring Reporting Services Integration Settings

Welcome to part two of setting up SharePoint integration. Before we can deploy report content, we need to configure report server integration settings in SharePoint Central Administration and in the SharePoint portal. Steps include installing the Reporting Services Add-in, configuring the Reporting Services features in Central Administration, and registering the Reporting Services content types.

Installing the Reporting Services Add-in

Recall that the Reporting Services Add-in provides the management pages and the ReportViewer web part. You need to install the add-in on the SharePoint server. You must be a SharePoint Web farm administrator and Site Collection administrator to install the Reporting Services Add-in. Ideally, the person who installs SharePoint should install the add-in.

1. Download the Microsoft SQL Server 2008 Reporting Services Add-in for Microsoft SharePoint Technologies from the latest SQL Server 2008 Feature Pack page. Make sure to choose the appropriate version (32-bit or 64-bit) based on the server hardware.
2. Double-click SharePointRS.msi to begin the installation.

When you install the add-in, it enables Reporting Services integration on all site collections in the SharePoint application. However, if the user installing the add-in is not a Site Collection administrator on any of the site collections in the farm, then Reporting Services is installed in a deactivated state. In this case, the administrator needs to activate the feature to enable Reporting Services integration in that site.

3. To activate the feature, expand the Site Actions drop-down menu of the top-level site, and select Site Settings.
4. In the Site Settings page, click the Site Collection Features link under the Site Collection Administration section.
5. In the Site Collection Features page, if the Report Server Integration Feature is deactivated, click the Activate button.

TIP I recommend you examine the add-in log file after the add-in setup completes to verify its state. You'll find the log file (RS_SP_<N>.log) in your temp folder, such as \Documents and Settings\<login>\Local Settings\Temp. Specifically, check that all activation tasks have completed successfully and that there are no errors.

Configuring Reporting Services integration

Configuring Reporting Services integration in SharePoint involves specifying the report server URL, security mode, and server defaults.

1. Open the SharePoint 3.0 Central Administration web application and select the Application Management tab.

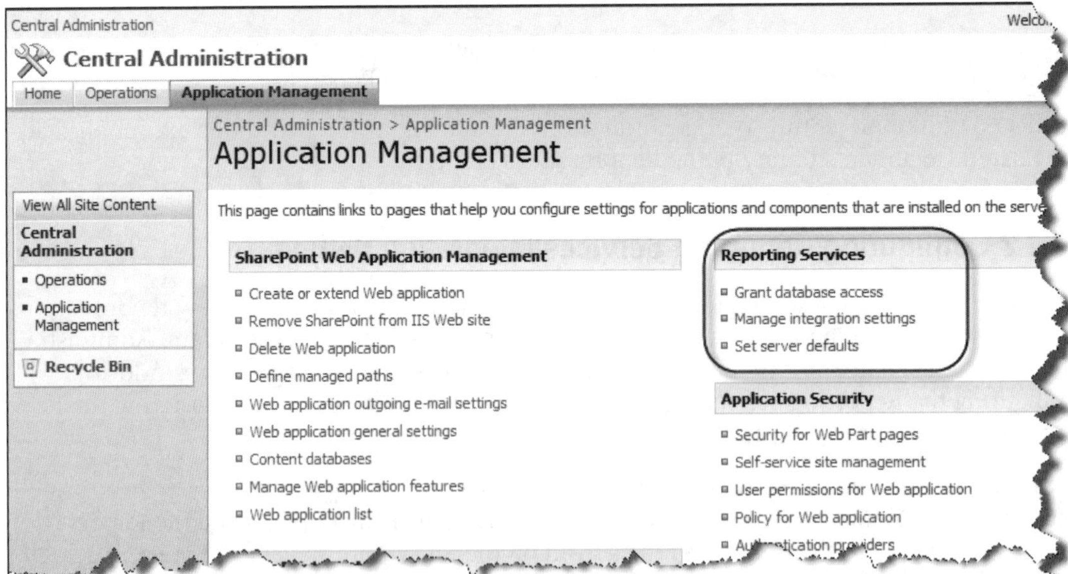

Figure 17.10 Use the Application Management page to configure the Reporting Services integration settings.

There should be a new Reporting Services section, as shown in Figure 17.10. If this section is missing, the Reporting Services Add-in is not installed. Configure the Reporting Services integration options in the order shown.

2. Click the Grant Database Access link to open the Grant Database Access page.

In the Grant Database Access page, SharePoint grants the report server service account access to the SharePoint databases. A database login and permissions are created for each Reporting Services service account.

3. Enter the name of the server that hosts Reporting Services. If Reporting Services is installed on a named instance, select the Named Instance option, and enter the instance name. Click OK.
4. In the Enter Credentials dialog box that follows, specify the credentials of a Windows account in the format domain\login to connect to the report server and retrieve the report server service account. Enter the credentials of an account that is a member of the local Administrators group on the report server. If you use a local account with a single-server deployment, use the servername\login format, such as millennia02\administrator. Click OK to close the dialog box and OK again to return to the Application Management page.
5. Click the Manage Integration Settings link.
6. In the Reporting Services Integration page, specify the Report Server Web service URL (for example, http://<servername>/ReportServer) and the security mode (such as Windows Authentication or Trusted Account). Since SharePoint communicates with the report server internally, specify the machine NetBIOS name even if SharePoint is Internet-facing. If you unsure what the Web service URL is, open the Reporting Services Configuration Manager and select the Web Service URL tab. Click OK.
7. Click the Set Server Defaults link and review the Reporting Services default configuration options, such as report history settings, execution timeout, and so on. Make changes if needed and click OK.

Adding Reporting Services content types

Now, we need to register the Reporting Services content types for report definitions (.rdl), data sources (.rsds) and Report Builder models (.smdl) files in the document library where the report content will be deployed. Only site administrators or users with Full Control rights can register content types.

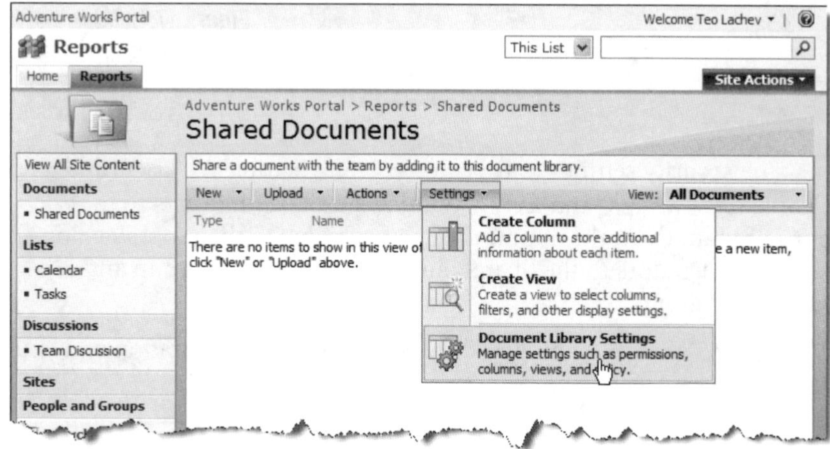

Figure 17.11 Register the Reporting Services content types from the Document Library Settings menu.

1. Open the Adventure Works portal by navigating to http://<servername>/default.aspx.
2. Select the Reports tab and click the Shared Documents menu link in the Quick Launch menu to access the Shared Documents document library.

3. Expand the Settings drop-down menu and select Document Library Settings menu, as shown in Figure 17.11.
4. Under General Settings on the Customize Shared Documents page, click Advanced settings to open the Document Library Advanced Settings page.
5. In the Content Types section, select Yes to allow management of content types, and click OK.
6. On the Customize Shared Documents page, click the Add From Existing Site Content Types link in the Content Types section.
7. In the Add Content Types page, select the Report Server Content Types item in the drop-down list.

TIP If you don't see the Reporting Services content types, it could be because the Report Server Integration Feature is deactivated. Follow the steps in the Installing the Reporting Services Add-in section to activate the Report Server Integration feature.

8. In the Available Site Content Types list, select all items, as shown in Figure 17.12, and click Add to add them to the Content Types to Add list on the right. Click OK.

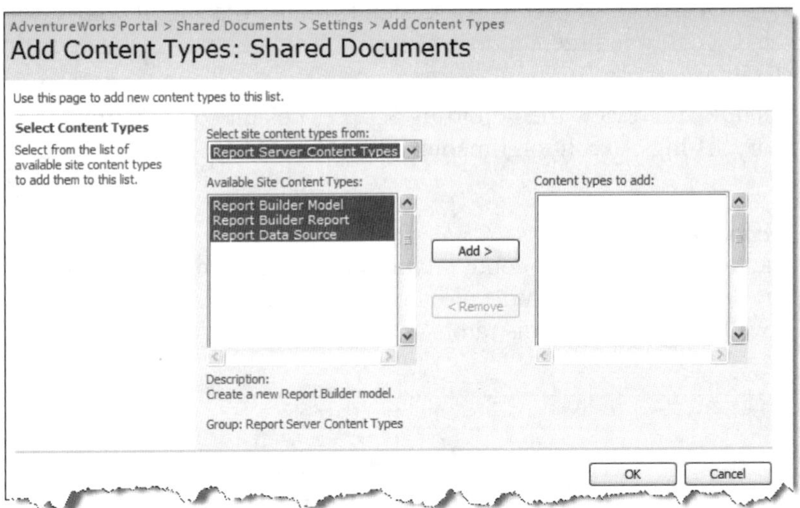

Figure 17.12 Use the Add Content Type page to register the Reporting Services content types.

9. On the Reports site, review the security settings (Site Actions ⇨ Site Settings ⇨ Users and Permissions section ⇨ People and Groups) and assign Windows users and groups to the SharePoint standard groups to grant them the appropriate access rights to the report catalog. For example, assign report administrators to the SharePoint standard Owners group and report contributors to the Members group.

That's it! At this point, Reporting Services is configured for SharePoint full integration and you are ready to perform reporting tasks.

17.3 Managing Report Content

The major advantage of configuring Reporting Services for SharePoint full integration is that you can perform all reporting tasks inside the SharePoint environment, including managing report content and viewing reports. Moreover, you can leverage additional document management tasks that native mode doesn't support, such as document approval and version control. Next, I'll walk you through the steps for carrying out some of these tasks.

17.3.1 Uploading Reports

As it stands, the Shared Documents document library in the Reports site is empty. In SharePoint integration mode, Reporting Services supports several ways for uploading report content, including using BIDS for automatic deployment, manually uploading report files, and automating deployment by writing code.

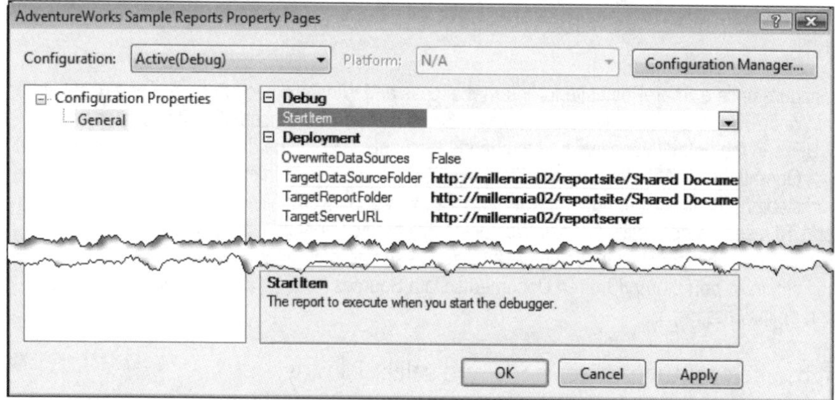

Figure 17.13 Use the Project Properties dialog box to configure deployment.

Uploading report content from BIDS

By far the easiest way to upload report content is to use the BIDS deployment features. Let's use BIDS to upload the Adventure Works sample reports to the Shared Documents library.

1. Open the AdventureWorks Sample Reports project, which is included with the book source code, in BIDS.
2. In Solution Explorer, right-click on the AdventureWorks Sample Reports project node and choose Properties.
3. In the Properties dialog box, configure the deployment properties, as shown in Figure 17.13 and click OK.

Table 17.3 lists the changes that you need to make to the deployment properties.

Table 17.3 Deployment properties for deploying the AdventureWorks report samples

Property	Value
TargetDataSources	http://<servername>/reportsite/Shared Documents/Data Sources
TargetReportFolder	http://<servername>/reportsite/Shared Documents/AdventureWorks Sample Reports
TargetServerURL	http://<servername>/

These properties specify the target folders for the data source and report definitions in the project. We will deploy the data source definitions to the Data Sources folder and report definitions to the AdventureWorks Sample Reports folder.

NOTE An unfortunate bug was introduced late in the SQL Server 2008 development cycle that prevents you deploying a folder whose name includes a space, such as Data Sources. When you attempt to do this, you'll get "Error rsInvalidItemName: The name of the item 'Data%20Sources' is not valid. The name must be less than 128 characters long. The name must not start with slash; other restrictions apply." However, if the folder already exists, deployment is successful. Unfortunately, due to time constraints this bug didn't get fixed in the final release. As a workaround, don't use spaces in the target folders, such as use DataSources instead of Data Sources.

Note that when you deploy to SharePoint, you need to specify full URLs as opposed to relative paths. On deploy, BIDS updates references to external resources, such as references to shared data sources and images, in the report definition to use absolute paths. In SharePoint integration mode, the TargetServerURL setting specifies the URL of the SharePoint site to which you'll deploy the reports.

REAL LIFE I had to configure once a SharePoint site for Internet access and Windows security where end users were authenticated using local Windows accounts created on the server. Since Reporting Services 2008 only supports access from SharePoint URLs in the default zone, we had to change the public URL of the default zone (SharePoint 3.0 Central Administration ⇨ Operations ⇨ Alternate Access Mappings) to the web server Internet URL, such as http://www.adventure-works.com/. This wasn't enough, however, because reports were failing with rsItemNotFound errors although the report URLs seemed perfectly normal. We solved this predicament by changing the <servername> in the TargetDataSources and TargetReportFolder settings to include the server Internet address, such as http://www.adventure-works.com/Report Library/Shared Documents/Data Sources for the TargetDataSource setting, and redeploying the report definitions.

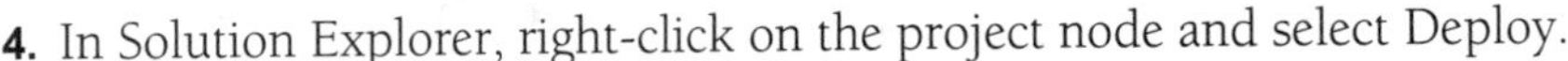

4. In Solution Explorer, right-click on the project node and select Deploy.
5. Open the Adventure Works Portal SharePoint site. Click the Reports tab and then the Shared Documents menu link.

   The Shared Documents library now includes the AdventureWorks Sample Reports and Data Sources folders.
6. Click the AdventureWorks Sample Reports folder link to verify that the report files have been uploaded successfully.

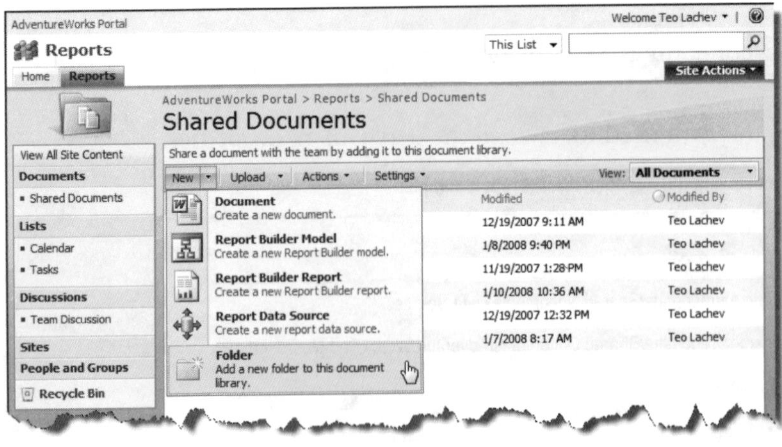

Figure 17.14 Use the New menu to create folders, Report Builder models and reports.

Uploading report content manually

You can also upload report content manually. Next, you will create a new folder and upload two reports that you'll use to create a dashboard page later on. Start by creating a new folder.

1. In Shared Documents library of the Reports site, expand the New drop-down menu, as shown in Figure 17.14.

   Observe that the New menu lets you initiate several reporting actions, including auto-generating a new Report Builder 1.0 model from a data source definition, creating a Report Builder 1.0 report, setting up a new data source, and creating a new folder.
2. Select the Folder submenu to create a new folder.
3. In the New Folder page, name the folder AMRS and click OK.
4. Click the AMRS folder link to navigate to the AMRS folder.
5. Expand the Upload drop-down menu and click Upload Multiple Documents.
6. In the Update Documents page, navigate to the source code for this chapter and select the Chart.rdl and Gauge.rdl files in the Reports folder and click OK. When prompted, confirm the upload process.

   The Chart and Gauge reports connect to the Adventure Works Analysis Services cube to retrieve data. Follow the instructions in the book front matter to install the AdventureWorks cube on the SharePoint server. Next, you'll create a data source that points to the cube.
7. Navigate to the Data Sources folder. Expand the New menu and click Report Data Source.
8. In the Data Source Properties page, name the data source *AdventureWorksAS2008*. Notice that the document extension for data sources in SharePoint integration mode is *.rsds as opposed to *.rds (native mode).
9. Expand the Data Source Type drop-down and select Microsoft SQL Server Analysis Services.
10. Enter the following connection string in the Connection String field and click OK.

```
Data Source=(local); Initial Catalog="Adventure Works DW 2008"
```

Managing report data sources

If you attempt to view the Chart and Gauge reports at this point, you will get an error because their data source properties do not contain valid SharePoint URLs to the AdventureWorksAS2008 shared data source that you've just created. Follow these steps to update these reports to reference the AdventureWorksAS2008 data source in the Data Sources folder.

1. In the AMRS folder, point the mouse to the Chart report and expand the report drop-down menu, as shown in Figure 17.15.

   Notice that that report drop-down menu lets you initiate report management tasks, such as managing the report subscriptions, parameters, and data sources.
2. In the drop-down menu, click Manage Data Sources.
3. Note that the Manage Data Sources page shows an exclamation point because the report data source is not configured. Click the AdventureWorksAS2008 data source link.
4. In the next page, enter *http://<servername>/reportsite/Shared Documents/Data Sources/Adventure WorksAS2008.rsds* and click OK. Alternatively, click the ... button next to the Data Source Link field. In the Select an Item page, navigate to the Data Sources folder and select the AdventureWorksAS2008 data source.
5. Click OK to return to the Manage Data Sources page and click Close to return to the AMRS folder.

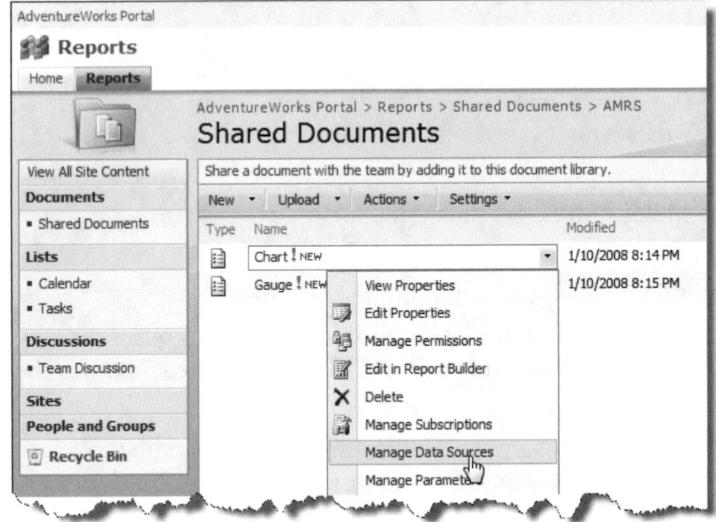

Figure 17.15 The report drop-down menu lets you manage the report settings.

6. Follow similar steps to configure the Gauge report to reference the AdventureWorksAS2008 shared data source.

Uploading report content programmatically

You may need to automate deploying report content to SharePoint. Unfortunately, Microsoft currently doesn't provide a utility that supports deployment to a server running in SharePoint integration mode. However, you can create a custom application that integrates with the Report Server Web service to automate management tasks. The ReportingSetup utility included in the book source code demonstrates how you upload report content to a SharePoint library. It creates a folder under the Shared Documents library and uploads the Company Sales and Product Catalog Adventure Works sample reports to this folder. Make the following changes before running the utility:

1. Open the app.config configuration file and update the ReportingSetup_WSS_ReportingService2006 and RootFolder settings to reflect your setup.
2. Open the report definitions (.rdl files) in the \bin\debug folder and update the data source reference to reflect the SharePoint path to the AdventureWorks data source. Again, you must enter the full URL address since SharePoint doesn't support relative paths. You don't need to update the DataSourceID node. This is what my report definition looks like after the change:

```
<DataSource Name="AdventureWorks">
  <rd:DataSourceID>25d3314c-0d4f- 49cc-9c22-10194e825490</rd:DataSour ceID>
   <DataSourceReference> http://millennia02/ReportSite/Shared Documents/Test/AdventureWorks.rsds
   </DataSourceReference>
</DataSource>
```

TIP If you need to automate updating the data source references in the report definitions, you can do so programmatically. For example, you can load the definitions in XmlDom or use the RDL Object Model, as I demonstrated in chapter 7.

ReportingSetup is implemented as a Windows Forms application. When you run it, it will ask you for the name of the target folder (Test by default) and will let you overwrite the Web service endpoint if needed. When you click the Create button, the application invokes the UploadContent method, whose abbreviated code is shown below.

```
private string[] _reports = Directory.GetFiles(Application.StartupPath, "*.rdl");
. . .
private void UploadContent() {

   // Folders
   CreateFolder(_folder, String.Format("{0}/", _rootFolder));

   //Datasource
   CreateSQLDataSource("AdventureWorks", String.Format("{0}/{1}/", _rootFolder, _folder));
   CreateASDataSource("AdventureWorksAS", String.Format("{0}/{1}/", _rootFolder, _folder));

   //Custom Reports
   if (_reports.Length > 0)
   {
      foreach (string customReport in _reports)
         CreateReport(customReport, String.Format("{0}/{1}/", _rootFolder, _folder));
   }
}
```

The code starts by creating a folder to host the report content. Then, the method calls the CreateSQLDataSource and CreateASDataSource helper methods to create the AdventureWorks and AdventureWorksAS data sources. Next, UploadContent checks if there are any report definitions in the application startup folder. For each report definition, UploadContent calls the CreateReport helper method. CreateReport (not shown) loads the report definition as a byte array and calls the CreateReport API to upload the report. The application also includes a CreateResource method for uploading resource files, such as images.

17.3.2 Viewing Reports

Similar to Report Manager, you can use SharePoint to view reports.

Requesting live reports

Follow these steps to view the Chart report:

1. Navigate to the AMRS folder.
2. Click the Chart report link.

SharePoint makes a call to the report server. The report server synchronizes the report definition, generates the report, and sends the report payload back to SharePoint. SharePoint displays the report on a web page that uses the Report Viewer web part, which I will discuss in more detail in section 17.4. Figure 17.16 shows the generated report.

The toolbar supports common reporting tasks, such as refreshing the report, page navigation, searching text on the report, and zooming. The Actions drop-down menu lets you initiate additional report actions, such as opening the report with the Report Builder 1.0 client (if this is a Report Builder 1.0 report), subscribing to the report, printing it, and exporting the report to one of the supported export formats.

Working with report parameters

Report parameters are exposed in the Parameters pane. The end user can collapse the pane by clicking its left bar (with the triangle symbol) to free more real estate for displaying the report. As with Report Manager, SharePoint doesn't let you customize the toolbar or Parameters pane.

1. The Chart report accepts a sales territory country as a parameter. Expand the Sales Territory Country drop-down list and select another country.
2. Click the Apply button to generate the report with the new parameter value.

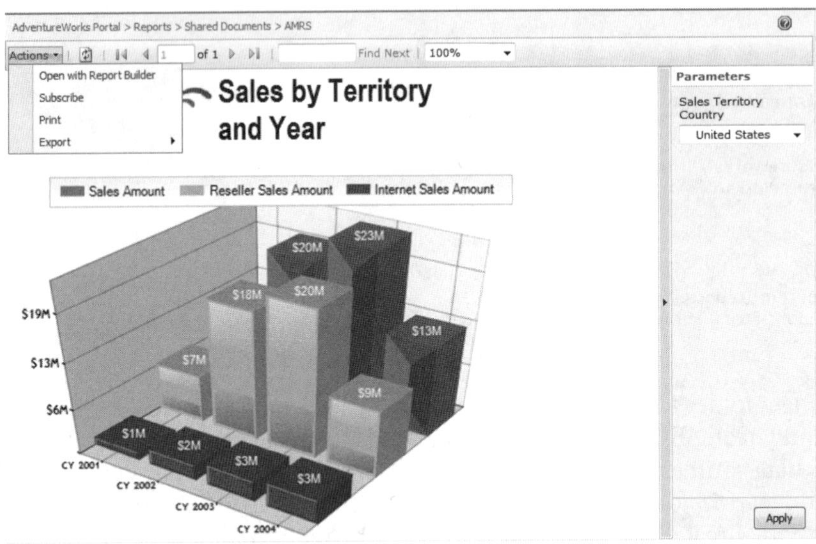

Figure 17.16 The ReportViewer web part displays reports and lets you perform common reporting actions, such as printing and exporting the report.

17.3.3 Working with SharePoint Document Management Features

SharePoint full integration lets you leverage SharePoint-specific features for document management, such as version control, document properties, alerts, and others. Two interesting features that I will demonstrate next are content approval and version control.

Suppose that new reports published to the Adventure Works Portal require management approval before they are available for public viewing. You can configure the site versioning settings to meet this requirement. When a new report definition is uploaded, it will be assigned a pending status, in which case it is visible only to its creator and to users who have permission to manage lists, such as members of the Owners group. Once the report is approved, it is assigned an Approved status, making it visible to anyone with permission to view the list or library.

NOTE You can address more complicated process requirements by using the SharePoint workflow support. For example, Microsoft Office SharePoint Server 2007 comes with a predefined workflow for document approval. Windows SharePoint Services includes only a simple three-state workflow that is designed to track the status of a document. You can author custom workflows using SharePoint Designer or Visual Studio. For more information about the SharePoint workflow features, read the whitepaper Understanding Workflow in Windows SharePoint Services and the 2007 Microsoft Office System (see Resources).

Configuring versioning settings

To enable content approval for the Shared Documents library in the Reports site:

1. If the Shared Documents library is not already open, open the Reports site and click the Shared Documents link in the Quick Launch menu.
2. Expand the Settings drop-down menu and click Document Library Settings.
3. In the Customize Shared Documents page, click the Versioning Settings link in the General Settings section.
4. In the Document Library Versioning Settings page, select Yes in the Content Approval section.

5. To keep track of report changes, in the Document Version History section, select the Create Major and Minor (Draft) Versions option.
6. In the Draft Item Security, make sure that the Only Users Who Can Approve Items (And The Author of The Item) option is turned on. Click OK.

Working with document control

Let's test the effect of the versioning control settings you've just made.

1. In the Shared Documents library, navigate to the AMRS folder.

   Notice that the Shared Documents view now includes a new Approval Status column and all existing documents have been assigned an Approved status.

2. Upload a report definition file. You can use one of the sample Adventure Works reports, such as Company Sales.

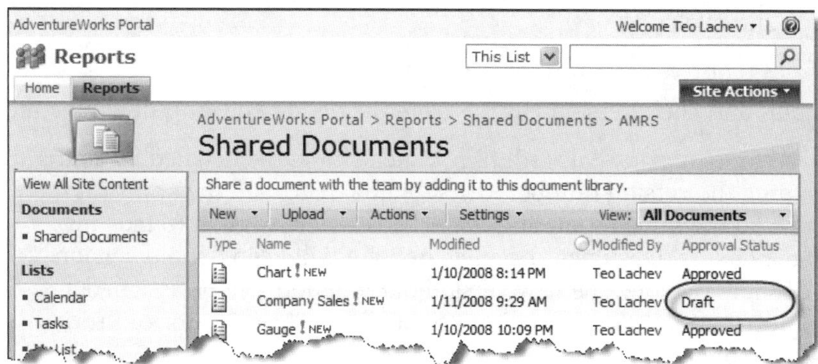

Figure 17.17 Once you enable content approval, new documents are submitted as drafts and are not immediately accessible.

   Observe that the new report is assigned a Draft status, as shown in Figure 17.17.

3. Optionally, log in as a user who belongs to the SharePoint Members group and notice that the user cannot see the Company Sales report. An authorized user needs to approve the report before making it available to other users.
4. Point the mouse to the Company Sales report, expand the document drop-down menu, and click View Properties.

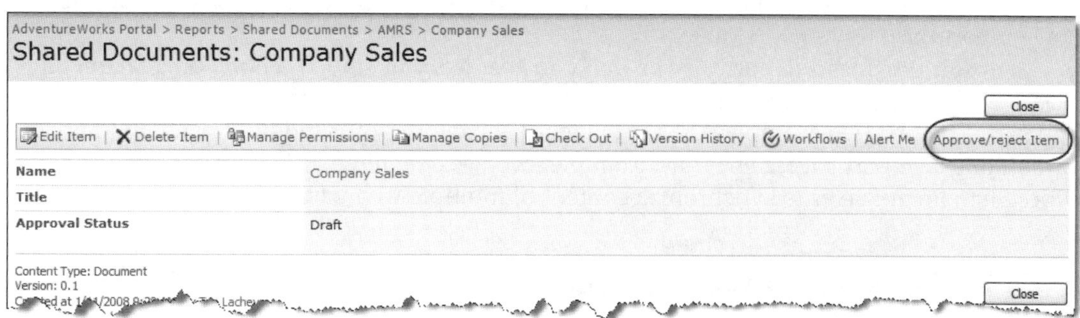

Figure 17.18 An authorized user needs to approve a draft document to make it publicly available.

The document properties page, which is shown in Figure 17.18, lets you perform various document management tasks, such as managing the document permissions, viewing the document versioning history, subscribing to alert notifications when the document is updated, and approving or rejecting a draft.

5. Click Approve/reject Item.
6. In the next page, select the Pending option in the Approval Status section, and click OK.

   In the Shared Documents view, note that the Company Sales report is now in Pending status. In the next step, a user with approval rights can review and approve or reject the document.
7. Point the mouse to the Company Sales report and expand the document drop-down menu. Note that there is a new Approve/reject submenu.
8. Click Approve/reject.

   You will see the approval page again when it opens automatically, but this time it includes an Approved option in the Approval Status section.
9. Select the Approved option and click OK.

   Note that the Company Sales report is now in Approved status.
10. Point the mouse to the report and click Version History from the document drop-down menu.

    You will see a Version Saved for Company Sales.rdl page which shows the detailed version history of the report, including the version number, the submittal date, and the approval status. If you subsequently upload the same report and the Add as a New Version to Existing Files option is enabled in the Upload Document page, SharePoint will keep the old version and add the new report as a new version. The new version of the report will be assigned a Draft status again until someone approves it. More importantly, the administrator can review the version history to restore a previous version if needed.

17.4 Implementing Web Part Pages

Your ability to design effective solutions for your organization's business intelligence needs will depend in part on how you leverage web parts in your SharePoint application. In this section, we will look at how to create a web part page that displays several report views side-by-side. Deploying reports side-by-side can help business users better understand their data. Consider a dashboard page that shows a chart report displaying the overall sales alongside a gauge report that shows a KPI value.

Microsoft provides a Report Viewer web part that lets you embed reports on a SharePoint page. This section includes three examples that demonstrate how to use the Report Viewer web part. The first two examples use the standard capabilities of Windows SharePoint Services for building web part pages. The third example leverages the filtering features of Microsoft Office SharePoint Server to synchronize content of multiple web parts.

17.4.1 Implementing Dashboard Pages

By now, you've learned how to author standard and ad hoc operational reports that help information workers gain insights about their business. In this first example, you'll see how effective it can be to combine these reports on a single dashboard page to better fulfill your business intelligence needs.

Understanding digital dashboards

Before we start, let's make sure we understand what a digital dashboard is. Here is how Wikipedia defines it: "A digital dashboard, also known as an enterprise dashboard or executive dashboard, is a business management tool used to visually ascertain the status (or "health") of a business enterprise via key business indicators. Digital dashboards use visual, at-a-glance displays of data pulled from disparate business systems to provide warnings, action notices, next steps, and summaries of business conditions."

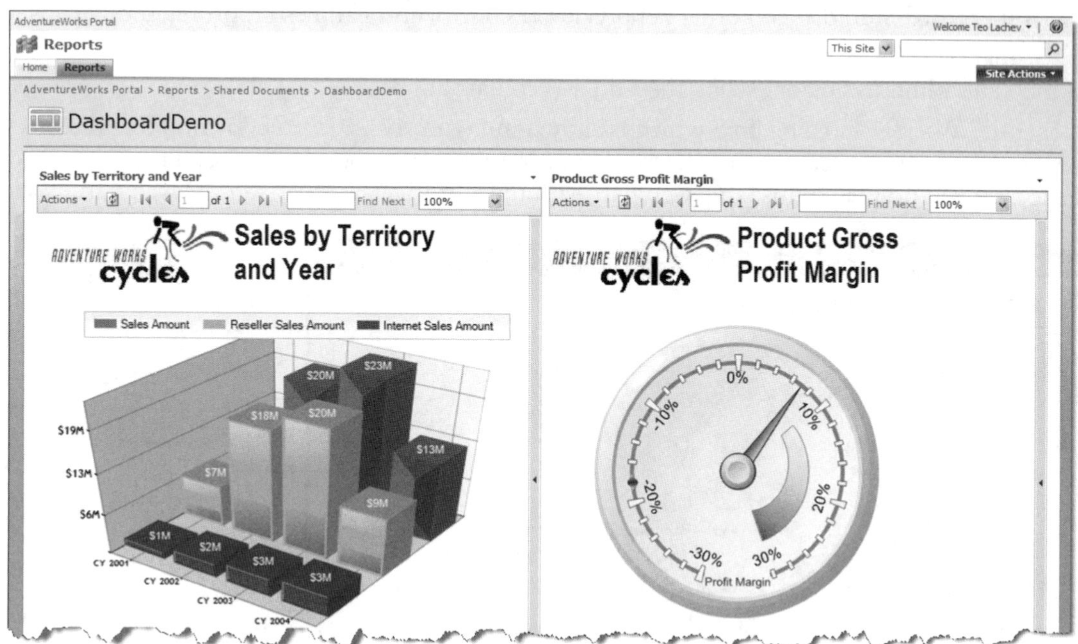

Figure 17.19 The Corporate Performance dashboard page displays two reports side by side.

The Corporate Performance page, which is shown in Figure 17.19, demonstrates an example of a dashboard page. The Sales by Territory and Year chart report shows the Adventure Works gross sales, reseller sales, and Internet sales. The Product Gross Profit Margin report displays the Product Gross Profit Margin KPI value and its goal. In this case, the KPI value is about 7% and it is slightly below the goal (the 10-30% range). As you can imagine, dashboard pages like this can be tremendously useful in helping Adventure Works managers identify trends in company business just by glancing at this page.

Creating the Corporate Performance page

The Corporate Performance dashboard page uses the chart.rdl and gauge.rdl reports that you've already deployed to your SharePoint site. These reports pull data from the Adventure Works Analysis Services cube. Constructing a dashboard page that uses these reports is straightforward. Start by creating a new web part page. You might recall how to do this from earlier steps where you used a page to test the Report Explorer and Report Viewer version 2.0 web parts.

1. In the Reports site, expand the Site Actions drop-down menu and click Create.
2. In the Create page, click Web Part Page under the Web Pages section.

3. In the Name section, enter *CorporatePerformance* as the page name.
4. Leave the rest of the settings at their default values and click Create.

SharePoint creates an empty web part page consisting of several zones and opens the page in Edit mode. Next, we will use the Report Viewer web part to embed the reports on the page.

Working with the Report Viewer web part

The Report Viewer web part is used for full-page report viewing and embedded reporting. It wraps the Visual Studio Web Forms ReportViewer control and handles report rendering calls to the report server.

1. In the Left Column web zone, click the Add a Web Part link.
2. In the Add Web Parts dialog box, which is shown in Figure 17.20, scroll down to the Miscellaneous section and select the SQL Server Reporting Services Report Viewer web part. Again, make sure you do not confuse this web part with the Report Viewer version 2.0 web part.

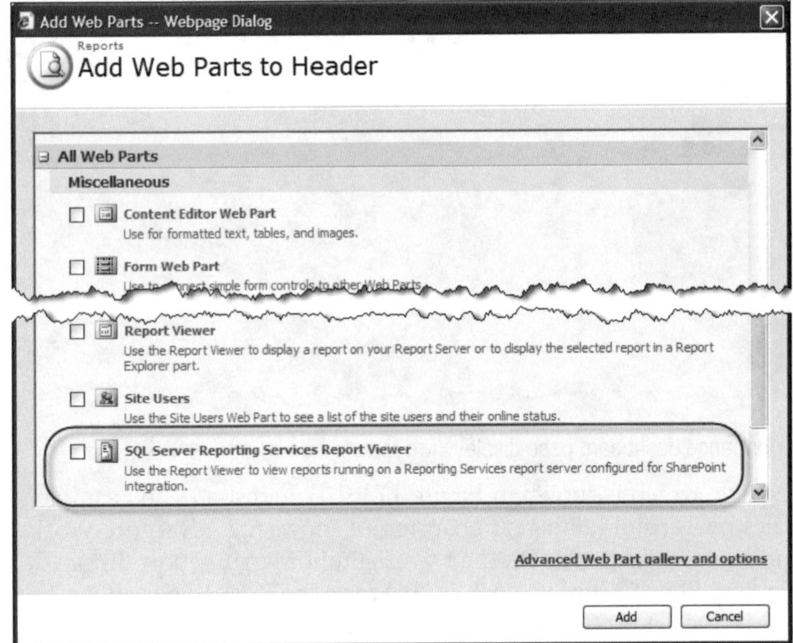

Figure 17.20 Use the Report Viewer web part for embedded reporting.

3. Click Add to add the Report Viewer web part to the page.
4. In the Report Viewer web part, click the Click Here to Open the Tool Pane link or expand the web part Edit drop-down menu in the top right corner and select Modify Shared Web Part.

NOTE Except for the properties exposed in the tool pane, the Report Viewer web part doesn't support further customization. For example, you cannot extend the report pane to validate the report parameters.

5. In the Tool pane, change the Report Viewer properties, as Table 17.4 shows.
6. Click Apply to save your changes. The Report Viewer web part displays the Sales by Territory and Year report.

Table 17.4 Report Viewer properties for the chart report

Category	Property	Setting	Description
Report	Report	http://<servername>/reportsite/Shared Documents/AMRS/chart.rdl	The report URL.
View	Auto-Generate Web Part Title	Unchecked	Auto-generates the web part title.
	Prompt Area	Collapsed	Controls the appearance of the parameter pane.
Parameters	Title	Sales by Territory and Year	The web part title.
	Height	600 pixels	The web part height.

7. Repeat steps 1-5 to add a another instance of the Report Viewer web part in the Right Column web zone and hook it to the gauge.rdl report. When configuring the web part, set the report URL to http://<servername>/reportsite/Shared Documents/AMRS/gauge.rdl and the title to Product Gross Profit Margin.

That's it! With a few clicks, you implemented a dashboard page that contains two Reporting Services reports that convey insightful information about company performance.

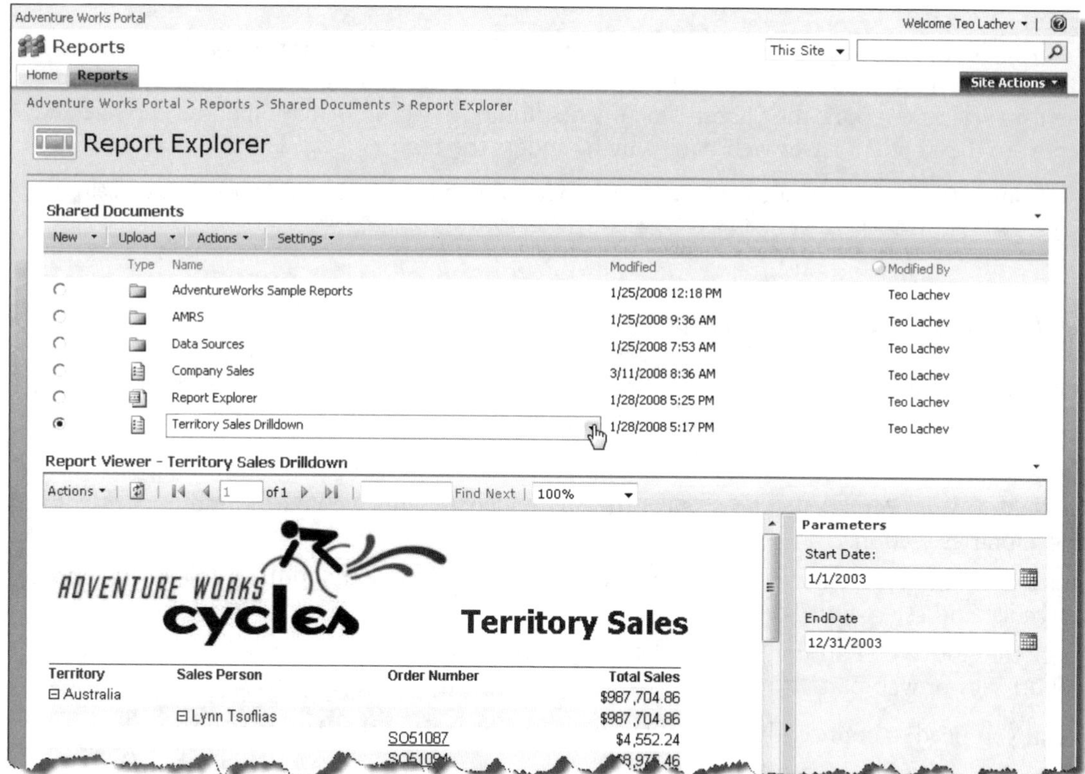

Figure 17.21 The Report Explorer page lets you navigate the report catalog and view reports.

17.4.2 Implementing Report Navigation

The Report Viewer web part implements IRowConsumer and IFilterValues interfaces to plug in the SharePoint connectable web parts infrastructure. The IRowConsumer interface allows the Report Viewer web part to receive information about the selected report from a web part that implements the IRowProvider interface, such as the Shared Documents web part. If you target MOSS, the IFilterValues interface lets you use the MOSS filter web parts to synchronize the content of all Report Viewer web parts on the page. In this next section, I will demonstrate how you can implement a Report Explorer page that lets the user navigate the report catalog and view reports.

Understanding the Report Explorer page

The Report Explorer page that you are about to create (see Figure 17.21) is similar to the WebParts20 page that you authored in section 17.1.2. It lets the end user navigate the report catalog and click a report to view it on a SharePoint site. It uses the default Shared Documents web part to list the reports that you will display in the Report Explorer page.

Because you configured SharePoint and Reporting Services integration, you automatically get all of the report-specific interactive features that are available for report definition (.rdl) files when you access the report in a document library on the Report Explorer page. For example, as shown in Figure 17.21, you can expand the report drop-down list to manage the report.

The Report Explorer page leverages the Report Viewer version 3.0 web part for report viewing. The Report Viewer web part is connected to the Shared Documents library. When the user selects a report, the Shared Documents library passes information about the selected report to the Report Viewer web part, which renders the report.

NOTE Due to an unfortunate bug with SharePoint, the connection between the Shared Documents library web part and Report Viewer doesn't work if the document library has folders and the user navigates to folders to view reports. The page refreshes but the report is not shown in the Report Viewer web part.

Implementing the Report Explorer page

Implementing the Report Explorer page is straightforward; all it takes is adding and connecting two web parts.

1. Create a new web part page and name it *Report Explorer*.
2. Click the Add Web Part link in the Header zone.
3. In the Add Web Parts dialog box, select the Shared Documents web part found under the Lists and Libraries section.
4. In the Configuration Pane of the Shared Documents web part, expand the Toolbar Type drop-down list and select Full Toolbar.
5. Click the Add Web Part link in the Footer zone and add the SQL Server Reporting Services Report Viewer web part.

Next, you need to connect the Shared Documents web part to the Report Viewer web part.

6. Expand the Edit drop-down list of the Shared Documents web part and click Connections ⇨ Provide Row To ⇨ Report Viewer.

Once the connection is established, the Shared Documents web part will show radio buttons next to each report item to let the user select the item.

17.4.3 Working with Filter Web Parts

As useful as it is, the Corporate Performance page, which you authored in section 17.4.1, has one shortcoming. Both reports take a sales territory country as a parameter. Consequently, the user has to change the parameter in each part to see the results for another country. The Enterprise Edition of Microsoft Office SharePoint Server includes filter web parts that let you filter the content of connected web parts simultaneously. You can set the filter on the page by selecting a value from a list of values that you obtained from an Analysis Services cube, a list of static values, or a date filter.

TIP When the MOSS filter web parts are not enough, you can implement custom filter web parts. For example, you may need to populate the filter list from a relational data source or validate the user selection before passing the value to a report parameter. The MOSS SDK (see Resources) includes a sample that demonstrates how you can implement a filter provider web part.

Let's improve the Corporate Performance page by leveraging the MOSS filtering capabilities. Figure 17.22 shows the new version of the page.

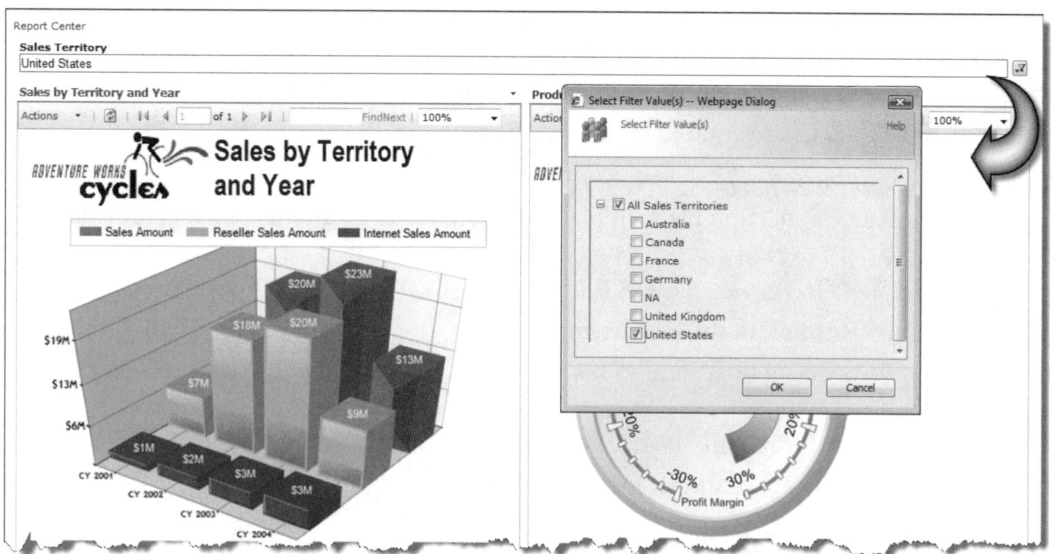

Figure 17.22 MOSS includes filter web parts to let you synchronize web part content.

The Sales Territory web part in the header zone of the page is a SQL Server Analysis Services Filter web part which is connected to the Adventure Works cube. I set its default value to United States. The user can click on the filter button to open the Sales Filter Value(s) dialog box, which displays the available territories. Once the end user makes a selection and clicks OK, the page will refresh and the web parts will show data for the selected country.

Creating an Office Data Connection file

Since our report draws data from an Analysis Services cube, we will use the SQL Server Analysis Services Filter web part to obtain the parameter values from the Adventure Works cube. As a prerequisite for using this filter part, we need to specify an Office Data Connection (.odc) file to connect to the Adventure Works cube. The easiest way to create an Office Data Connection file is through Microsoft Excel 2007.

1. In Microsoft Excel 2007, click the Data tab.
2. Click the From Other Source button in the Get External Data ribbon group and select From Analysis Services, as shown in Figure 17.23, to open the Data Connection Wizard.

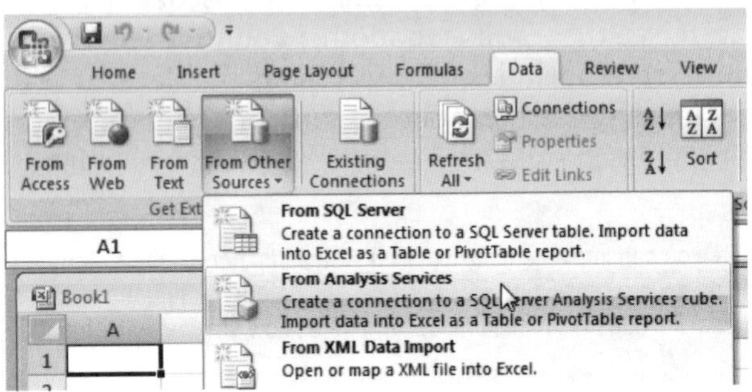

Figure 17.23 Use Microsoft Excel 2007 to create an Office Database Connection file.

3. Use the Data Connection Wizard to configure a connection to the Adventure Works cube.
4. By default, the wizard will save the .odc file in the My Documents\My Data Sources folder. You can change the location in the Save Data Connection File and Finish step.
5. In the Adventure Works MOSS portal, go to the Report Center (Reports tab), and click the Data Sources link found under the Resources section in the Quick Launch menu.
6. Upload the Office Data Connection file you've just created.

Configuring the Filter web part

Once the Office Data Connection file is in place, you are ready to use the SQL Server Analysis Services filter web part.

1. Open the Corporate Performance page in Edit mode.
2. Click the Add Web Part link in the Header zone.
3. In the Add Web Parts dialog box, scroll down to the Filters section and select the SQL Server Analysis Services filter web part.
4. Click the Open the Tool Pane link inside the filter web part.
5. Configure the filter web part as shown in Table 17.5.

Table 17.5 Report Viewer properties for the filter web part

Category	Property	Setting	Description
Filter	Filter Name	Sales Territory	The filter name to identify the filter.
	Office Data Connection File	/Reports/Data Connections/Adventure Works.odc	The path to the .odc file.
	Dimension	Sales Territory	The cube dimension.
	Hierarchy	Sales Territory Country	The web part title.
	Require User to Choose a Value	Checked	When checked, forces the user to select a value.
	Default Value	[Sales Territory].[Sales Territory Coun-try].&[United States]	The default filter value.
Appearance	Title	Sales Territory	The filter title to display on the page.

Once you specify the path to the Office Data Connection file, the filter part will connect to the cube and retrieve the cube metadata to help you set up the Dimension and Hierarchy properties. The Sales Territory filter should look like the one in Figure 17.24.

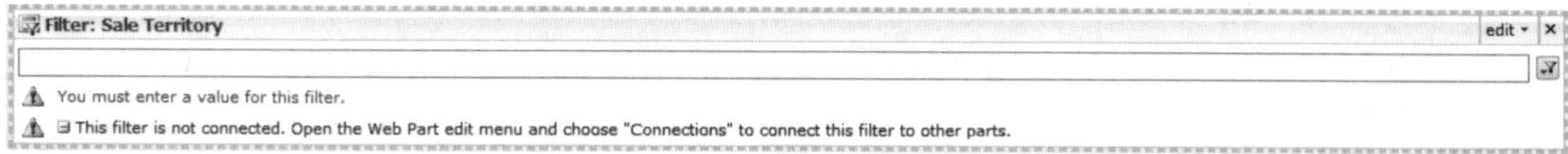

Figure 17.24 The Sales Territory filter before it is connected.

Connecting the web parts

The filter web part is not useful if it is not connected to another web part. Follow these steps to connect the Report Viewer web parts to the Sales Territory filter.

1. Expand the Edit drop-down menu of the Sales by Territory and Year web part.
2. Select Connections ⇨ Get Report Parameters From ⇨ Filter: Sales Territory menu, as shown in Figure 17.25. Alternatively, expand the Edit drop-down menu of the Sales Territory filter web part and choose Connections ⇨ Send Filter Values To ⇨ Sales by Territory and Year.

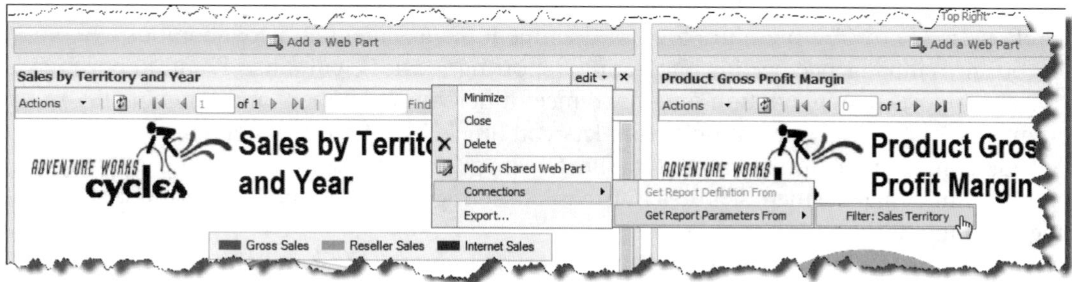

Figure 17.25 Connect the Report Viewer web part to the Sales Territory filter web part.

SharePoint displays the Configure Connections dialog box, as shown in Figure 17.26. Compatible web parts that support connections can discover each other at design time. This is why the Report Viewer web part, which is implemented as a filter consumer, discovers the filter web part, which is implemented as a filter provider.

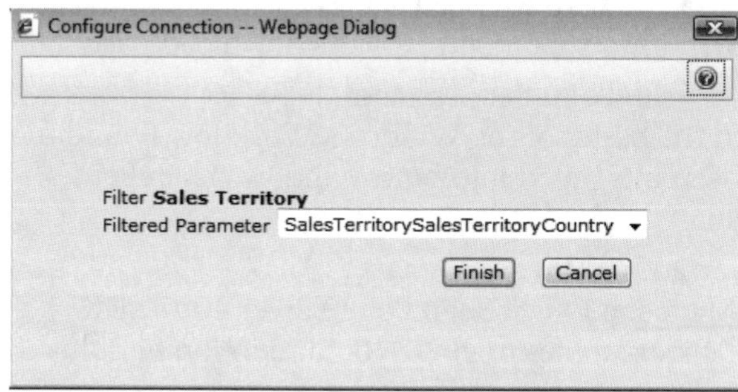

Figure 17.26 Compatible web parts discover each other at design time.

Because the Sales by Territory and Year report has a single parameter, the Configure Connection dialog box defaults to this parameter. If it includes multiple parameters, you can expand the Filter Parameter drop-down and select which parameter you want to connect to the filter web part.

3. Click Finish to finalize the connection.

   To let you know that it is connected, the Sales Territory filter displays the following text:

   Sending values to: Sales Territory and Year

   In addition, the Report Viewer web part hides the Prompt area because its parameter obtains its values from the filter.

4. Repeat steps 1-3 to connect the Product Gross Profit Margin web part to the Sales Territory filter web part.
5. Change the value of the Sales Territory filter web part.

   The Corporate Performance dashboard page refreshes and the reports detect and use the new parameter values. If you want to disconnect the filter, use Connections ⇨ Get Report Parameters From ⇨ Filter: Sales Territory menu again. In the Configure Connection dialog box, click Remove Connection button.

17.5 Summary

SharePoint is Microsoft's premium tool for document management and collaboration. A common business intelligence need is integrating Reporting Services with SharePoint. Reporting Services supports two integration options to meet different deployment and functionality requirements. The partial integration option lets you quickly configure SharePoint for report navigation and viewing, but is more difficult to manage. Full integration supports all SharePoint document management features but requires configuring the report server in SharePoint integration mode.

You can use the Report Viewer web part to embed reports on SharePoint pages. I showed you how to assemble dashboard pages from existing reports that display vital company performance metrics, such as KPIs. If you target Microsoft Office SharePoint Server, you can leverage its filtering capabilities to synchronize the content of multiple web parts.

17.6 Resources

Download Windows SharePoint Services 3.0 with Service Pack 1 (http://tinyurl.com/2bjvpr)—The Windows SharePoint Services download page.

Understanding Workflow in Windows SharePoint Services and MOSS (http://tinyurl.com/2qxvnv)—Learn the basics of the Windows Workflow Foundation and how this technology has been integrated into both Windows SharePoint Services and the 2007 Office System.

The Microsoft Office SharePoint Server 2007 SDK (http://tinyurl.com/36n8fc)—The Microsoft Office SharePoint Server 2007 SDK contains conceptual overviews and code samples to guide you in developing solutions based on Microsoft Office SharePoint Server 2007.

PART 6

Extensibility

With Reporting Services, you are not limited to a fixed set of features. Its modularized and extensible architecture lets developers plug in custom modules in the form of extensions to accommodate future growth. This part of the book discusses the implementation details of several custom extensions that enhance the report server capabilities

First, you'll learn how to implement custom data extensions to extend the Reporting Services data architecture. The sample custom dataset extension lets you bind an ADO.NET dataset to a server report—a scenario not natively supported by Reporting Services.

Out of the box, the report server is configured for Windows security. However, some reporting solutions, such as Internet-facing applications, may rule out Windows security and Active Directory. Fortunately, you can replace the Windows-based security model with a custom security extension. The sample security extension demonstrates how you authenticate users from a database profile store and authorize them using custom security rules.

Out of the box, Reporting Services can deliver subscribed reports to e-mail recipients, Windows folders, and SharePoint document libraries. However, you can write a custom delivery extension to send the report to other destinations if needed. To practice this extensibility scenario, you'll implement a Web service delivery extension that sends reports to a Web service.

You can also extend the data visualization capabilities of Reporting Services by implementing custom report items. The Progress Tracker sample demonstrates how you can convert a .NET Windows Forms control into a report item to render progress indicators on reports.

Finally, report definition customization extensions are a new extensibility mechanism with Reporting Services 2008. They let you change report definitions dynamically based on factors such as report parameters and the identity of the interactive user.

Chapter 18

Extending Data Access

Since its first release, Reporting Services has supported a plethora of data sources. Out of the box, its data modules (called data extensions) let you build reports from SQL Server relational databases, Analysis Services cubes, Oracle databases, and any other database that comes with an OLE DB or ODBC provider. But what if you want to build a report from a data source that isn't a database or doesn't have a provider? For example, suppose your business requirements include binding a server report to an ADO.NET dataset. Thanks to the Reporting Services extensible architecture, you can meet advanced data integration requirements by implementing a custom data processing extension.

This chapter shows you how to take advantage of the unique extensibility model of Reporting Services by building a custom data processing extension that uses an ADO.NET dataset as a report data source. To help users set up the dataset definition at design time, you will learn how to implement a custom query designer that runs in Report Designer. Finally, I will show you how to deploy and debug a custom data processing extension. You will need Visual Studio 2008 to work with the source code for this chapter.

18.1 Understanding Custom Data Processing Extensions

A data processing extension in Reporting Services is a module that the report server uses to retrieve report data at run time. It implements specific interfaces and returns a flattened rowset that is merged into the report layout before it is rendered in a visual format. Depending on the data source type you are using, the data processing extension might even optimize the query before sending it to the database server.

A custom data processing extension is a .NET module that pushes the report server data access capabilities in new directions. You might create a custom data processing extension to access additional data source types that are not supported off the shelf, or to build-in data conversion or manipulation functionality before passing the data back to the report.

A custom data processing extension must follow certain rules and implement a few programming interfaces. At design time, the report designer calls these interfaces to understand the data structure, such as what parameters it supports and what fields are provided in the dataset. At run time, the report server interacts with the data processing extension to retrieve the custom dataset and bind it to the report.

18.1.1 Choosing a Data Integration Approach

Implementing a custom data processing extension requires solid experience in .NET and interface programming. Before you decide to invest in creating a custom data processing extension, it's worth exploring other data integration options for accessing non-standard data sources that require less effort. Table 18.1 summarizes these options, the effort required for their implementation, and recommended usage scenarios.

Table 18.1 Data integration options for non-standard data sources

Approach	Effort	When to use
ReportViewer Controls (local mode)	Low	Generating a local report and binding it to an ADO.NET dataset or a collection-based object.
XML Data Provider	Low	Reporting from ADO.NET datasets or XML documents from URL-addressable resources, such as Web services.
CLR stored procedure	Medium	Preparing a dataset in a SQL Server 2005+ database.
Custom data processing extension	High	Reporting from custom data sources.

ReportViewer controls

The first option to consider is the ReportViewer controls that ship with Visual Studio. You can embed the ReportViewer controls in a Windows form or Web page. Both ReportViewer Windows Forms and Web server controls provide equivalent functionality; they host a rendered report directly in a custom application that you write. You can configure these controls for local report processing where the application is responsible for supplying the report data.

In local-processing mode, the application binds a local report to various collection-based objects, including ADO.NET regular or typed datasets. If you need to distribute your reports as a part of your application and you don't need to deploy them to the report server, the ReportViewer controls may be the way to go. I discussed the ReportViewer controls in chapter 15. You can refer to that chapter if you think this approach best fits your needs.

XML data provider

Reporting Services includes an XML data provider that supports using XML documents as a data source. Consider using the XML data provider if you need to integrate your report with URL-addressable providers that return XML documents. For example, your report might connect to a Web service that passes back an XML document or an ADO.NET dataset that is serialized to XML. I demonstrated this scenario in chapter 4 where I showed you how to use the XML data provider to invoke a Web service and use the returned ADO.NET dataset as a data source.

CLR stored procedures

A third possibility is to prepare the dataset in the database. For example, if your application targets SQL Server 2005 or later, you could implement a CLR stored procedure to build the dataset. Consider this option when you need to extract data from many table objects but want to avoid multiple roundtrips from the application to the database. Chapter 4 demonstrates this integration scenario as well.

Custom data processing extension
Finally, you can consider implementing a custom data processing extension. This approach gives you the most flexibility, but requires the most effort. The rest of this chapter is all about understanding and implementing this data integration option. As with the other Reporting Services extensibility features, custom data processing extensions are supported only with Standard and Enterprise editions. Report Builder 2.0 doesn't support custom data processing extensions with local mode processing.

18.1.2 Introducing the Dataset Custom Data Processing Extension

Why should you use a custom data processing extension? As I mentioned earlier, you might want to create a custom data processing extension to report on a data source that isn't supported out of the box or you require additional processing on the data before it is merged into the report layout. As shipped, Reporting Services doesn't support binding a server report to an ADO.NET dataset. Yet many integration scenarios require a custom application to pre-process the data before handing it off to a report. For example, you might need a custom application that retrieves a dataset from the middle tier, updates the data based on some business rules, and passes the dataset to a server report. This is exactly the scenario my Dataset data processing extension is designed to handle.

Building this data processing extension is useful on many levels. In addition to picking up the skills necessary for implementing, debugging, and deploying the extension, you will learn how to create and deploy a custom query builder that runs in Report Designer.

Understanding design goals and limitations
Custom data processing extensions can be complex. When I started on the Dataset data processing sample, I tried to strike a reasonable balance between features and simplicity. To that end, the Dataset sample has the following high-level design objectives:

- It supports both serialized and file-based ADO.NET datasets. In the first case, the application serializes the dataset to XML and passes it as a report parameter. In the latter case, the application passes the full path to the dataset file to the report. A file-based ADO.NET dataset is useful at design time when you need to work with the dataset definition.
- It includes a custom query designer to help the report author configure the data processing extension at design time.
- It lets the report author select an arbitrary table in a multi-table dataset. Having multiple tables could be useful when you need multiple report datasets from the same ADO.NET dataset.
- It maps the dataset XML schema to fields in the report dataset and preserves the dataset field types. This lets the report author use the familiar drag-and-drop technique to lay out the report.

The implementation of the Dataset extension is also subject to the following limitations:

- Uploading large datasets from the application to the report server may impact server performance.
- ADO.NET data relations and joining dataset tables are not supported. However, you can enhance the Dataset sample to support this scenario or tailor it to meet other data integration needs.

- Due to its query parameter size limitation, the URL access option for requesting dataset-bound reports is impractical for this sample. If you require URL access to a report, your application should integrate with the Report Server Web service to pass the serialized ADO.NET dataset via SOAP. That said, URL addressability is certainly possible in a data processing extension similar to the Datasets sample if you work with file-based datasets where the application passes the file path only.

Let's now see how the Dataset data processing extensions fits into the report server architecture.

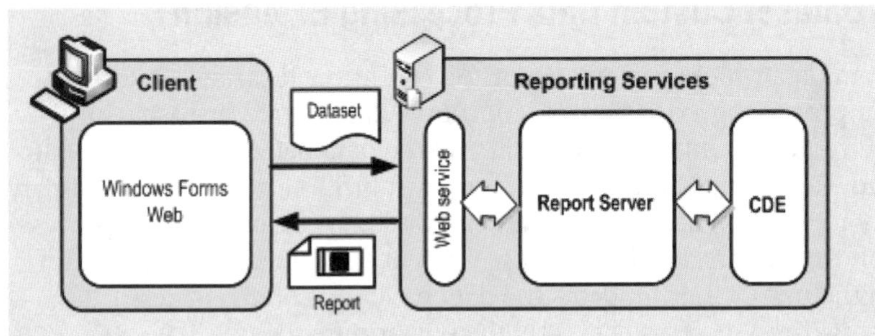

Figure 18.1 The figure shows the high-level integration view for using the Dataset custom data processing extension to bind an ADO.NET dataset to a report.

Understanding Data Processing Integration

Figure 18.1 shows a typical integration scenario that leverages the Dataset data processing extension. The client application, either Windows Forms or web-based, is responsible for preparing the ADO.NET dataset. The client serializes the dataset to XML and passes it as a parameter to a report that is configured to use the Dataset extension.

While processing the report, the report server discovers that the report uses the Dataset extension and sends to it the serialized dataset. The Dataset extension de-serializes the dataset back to an ADO.NET dataset and exposes it as an SSRS-compatible object that implements the required interfaces. Finally, the report server navigates the dataset in a forward-only fashion and populates the report with data.

18.2 Using Custom Dataset Extensions with Reports

Before delving into the implementation details, let's see the Dataset extension in action. First, I will show you how to use it at design time for report authoring. Next, you will see how client applications can bind application datasets to reports that use the Dataset extension.

If you want to skip the implementation steps, you will find in the book source code a Reports project that includes a TestDS report that you can use to test the Dataset extension. I also included WinTestHarness and WebTestHarness projects that demonstrate how Windows Forms and ASP.NET client applications can generate reports from ADO.NET datasets.

18.2.1 Using the Extension at Design Time

After installing and registering the Dataset extensions, the process of authoring a report that uses it is the same as using any of the standard data providers. This includes setting up a data source, a command statement, and a report dataset definition. Once the dataset definition is ready, you can drag and drop fields to lay out the report.

Preparing the ADO.NET dataset file

At run time, the application passes the ADO.NET dataset to a report parameter. At design time, however, you cannot pass an ADO.NET dataset to the Report Designer. Setting a default value of the report parameter is not practical either. Instead, save your dataset to a file and point the Dataset extension to the file location. You can save the schema of a regular or typed ADO.NET dataset programmatically, as follows:

```
System.Data.DataSet ds = GetData();                    // get ADO.NET dataset from somewhere
ds.WriteXmlSchema(@"c:\DatasetSalesOrder.xsd");  // saves only the schema to disk
```

First, you need to obtain an ADO.NET dataset that will have the same schema as the application dataset that supplies the report data. Then, you call the dataset's WriteXmlSchema method to save the dataset as a disk file. Having only the schema is sufficient to prepare the report dataset definition and lay out the report. However, the report won't show any data when you preview it. Therefore, I recommend you include both the dataset schema and data in the file, as follows:

```
System.Data.DataSet ds = GetData(); // get ADO.NET dataset from somewhere
ds.WriteXml(@"C:\DatasetSalesOrder.xml", System.Data.XmlWriteMode.WriteSchema); //saves schema and data
```

The WriteXml method with the WriteSchema option serializes both the data and the schema. In the book source, you will find a sample file (DatasetSalesOrder.xml), which you can use to test the TestDS report. It includes an extract from the Adventure Works sales order data.

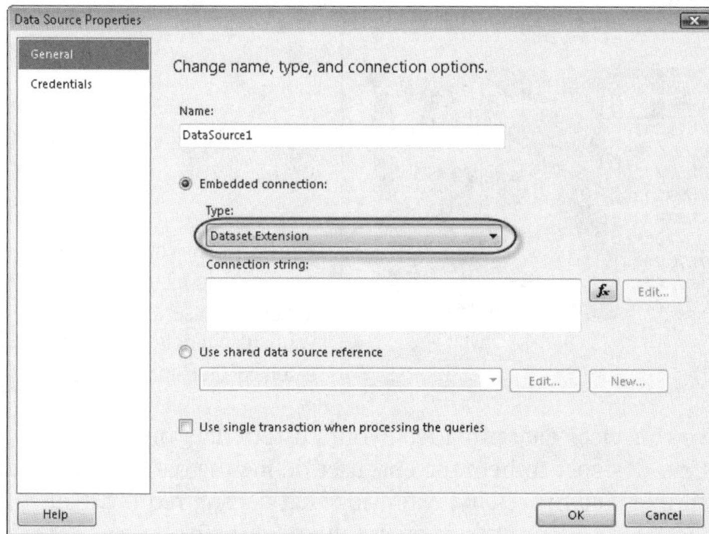

Figure 18.2 If the Dataset extension is deployed and registered properly, it will appear in the Type drop-down list.

Setting up the report dataset

Once you have a dataset file, you are ready to author a report that uses the Dataset extension. Start authoring the report by setting up a data source. The next steps assume that you will use the BIDS Report Designer.

1. Create a new report in Report Designer.
2. In the Report Data window, expand the New button and click New Data Source.
3. In the Data Source Properties step, expand the Type drop-down list and select the Dataset Extension, as shown in Figure 18.2. If you don't see the Dataset Extension in the list, it is not registered with the Report Designer. Go to section 18.4.1 and verify the deployment steps.

4. The Dataset extension doesn't connect to a data source because the application passes the data to the report at run time. This is why we leave the connection string field empty. Switch to the Credentials tab and verify that the Use Windows Authentication (Integrated Security) option is selected. Click OK to create the data source.

NOTE Since the Dataset extension doesn't establish a connection, the credential settings are irrelevant. However, if you select the No Credentials options, the report server will attempt to authenticate using the unattended execution account. If you haven't set up the unattended execution account, the server report will fail at run time. Therefore, if your extension uses the No Credentials option, remind yourself to set up the unattended execution account before you run the server report. You can use the Reporting Services Configuration Manager to configure the unattended execution account.

5. In the Report Data window, right-click DataSource1 and click Add Dataset. Click the Query Designer button.

   If you have registered the Dataset Query Designer that's included in the Dataset extension, you will see its user interface, as shown in Figure 18.3. Otherwise, the generic query designer will be shown.

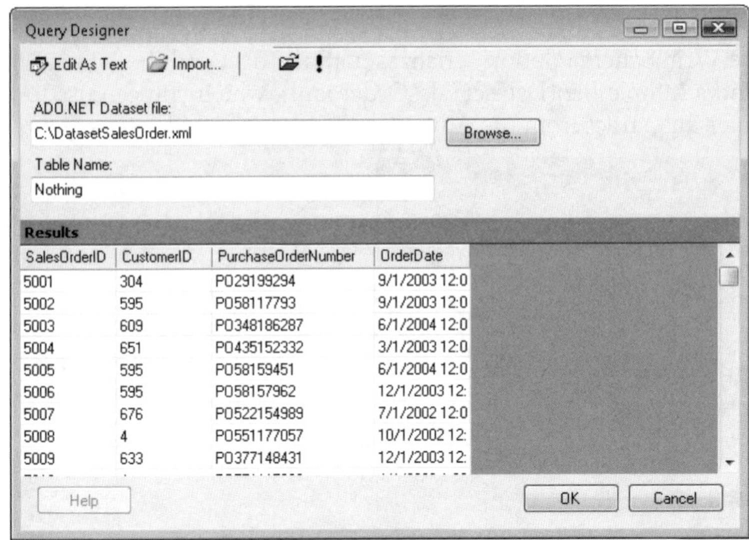

Figure 18.3 You can implement a custom query designer to help end users work with your custom data processing extension in Report Designer.

Just like the SQL Server and Analysis Services data providers, your custom data processing extension can include a custom query designer to help the end user define the dataset query at design time. If you are creating a simple data processing extension that doesn't require a custom query designer, you can use the Microsoft-provided generic query designer.

The Dataset extension includes a custom Dataset Query Designer that lets you specify the path to the dataset file and the name of the dataset table that will be used for reporting. As with the standard query designers, you can execute the query by pressing the Run (!) button on the query designer toolbar.

6. Click the Browse button or the Open toolbar button to specify the location of the DatasetSalesOrder.xml dataset file.

7. In the Table Name text box, enter the name of the dataset table. You can enter *Nothing* to let the Dataset extension use the first table. Or, you can enter *SalesOrderHeader* because the first table in the DatasetSalesOrder dataset is called SalesOrderHeader.

8. Click Run (!) on the toolbar to execute the query and retrieve data. The data processing extension de-serializes the DataSetOrder.xml file to an ADO.NET dataset object and shows its data in the Results grid.
9. Click the Edit As Text toolbar button to switch to the generic query designer and see the command text. Note that the Dataset Query Designer has generated the following command:

```
C:\DatasetSalesOrder.xml|Nothing
```

NOTE As noted, the Dataset sample supports both an instance of an ADO.NET dataset and a path to a dataset file. This complicates the command text somewhat because in the latter case the command must include both the file path and the table name. To make the things easier, I came up with the convention FilePath|TableName for the command text when a dataset file is used as a data source. The custom extension parses the command text to extract these two identifiers.

10. Click Run (!) to test the dataset again.
11. Click the Edit As Text toolbar button to switch back to the Dataset Query Designer. As long as the command text follows the FilePath|TableName format, you can make changes in both designers and your changes will be preserved when you toggle between them.
12. Click OK to return to the Dataset Properties dialog. Click OK to create the report dataset.
13. If the Report Data window is not visible, press Ctrl+Alt+D to open it.

The Report Data window should show the dataset. The dataset should have four fields: SalesOrderID, CustomerID, PurchaseOrderNumber, and OrderDate.

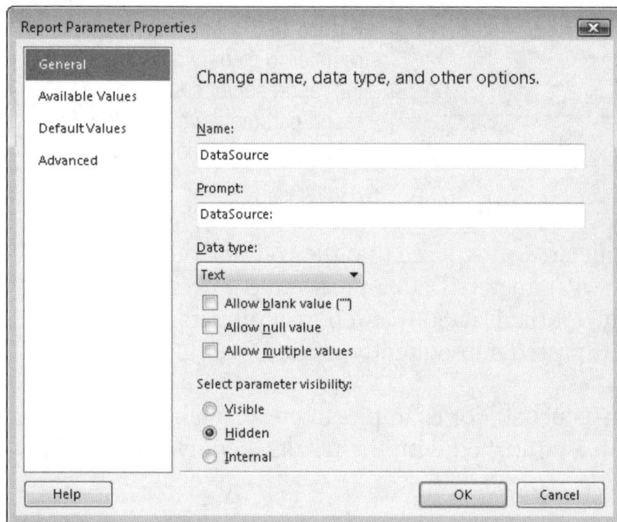

Figure 18.4 At run time, the client application passes the application dataset to the hidden DataSource parameter.

Setting up report parameters

As noted, at run time, the client application passes the ADO.NET dataset as a report parameter. The Dataset Extension notifies the query designer that it supports a DataSource parameter. Consequently, the Report Designer should have created a DataSource report-level parameter and linked it to the query DataSource parameter. If this is not the case, follow these steps to create a DataSource parameter that will accept the run-time dataset.

1. In the Report Data window, right-click on the Parameters node and choose Add Parameter.
2. Create a DataSource parameter, as shown in Figure 18.4.

3. Check the Hidden checkbox to hide the parameter from the end user.
4. Optionally, specify a default parameter value. Switch to the Default Values tab and select the Specify Values option. Click the Add button and enter the file path to the dataset file, such as C:\DatasetSalesOrder.xml|Nothing.

   Having a default parameter value is useful if you want to test the report in the Report Manager and use a dataset file as the report data source. The next step is very important. To pass the dataset to the data processing extension successfully, you must link the report-level DataSource parameter to a query parameter. This step is required because only query parameters can be passed to a custom data extension.
5. In the Report Data window, double-click DataSet1 to open the Dataset Properties dialog box.
6. Select the Parameters tab.
7. If there are no parameters defined, press the Add button and enter *@DataSource* as a parameter name, as shown in Figure 18.5.

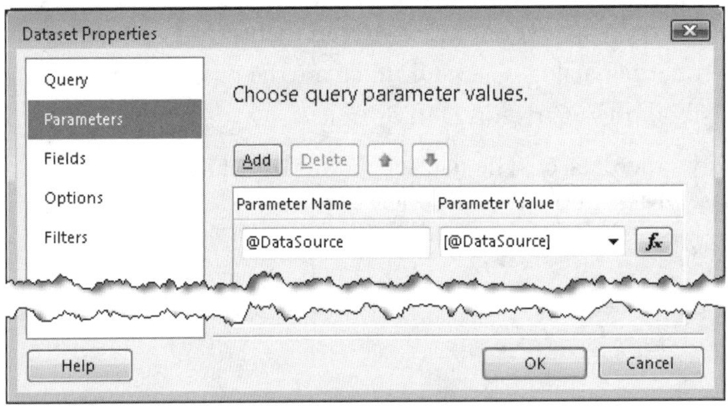

Figure 18.5 Link the report parameter to a query parameter so the report server can pass the report parameter value to the data processing extension at run time.

8. Expand the Parameter Value drop-down and select the [@DataSource] report-level parameter.

   If you press the *fx* button next to the parameter, you will see that the [@DataSource] expression placeholder represents the expression =Parameters!DataSource.Value. When the report is processed, the report server passes the value of the DataSource report-level parameter to the DataSource query-level parameter, which is passed subsequently to the Datasets data processing extension.

From here, proceed with report layout as usual. For example, to create a table report, you drag and drop dataset fields to it. Once you are satisfied with the results, deploy the report to the report server.

18.2.2 Understanding Runtime Interaction

Once the report is deployed to the server, a custom application can feed the report with an ADO.NET dataset. The source code that accompanies the book includes Windows Forms (WinTestHarness) and ASP.NET (WebTestHarness) projects that demonstrate how custom applications can use the Datasets sample. The test projects leverage the ReportViewer controls to generate the TestDS report. If, for some reason, you cannot use the ReportViewer controls in your application, you can call the ReportExecutionService.Render method (see Resources), which is what the controls do behind the scenes.

Rendering the report

Thanks to the fact that the ReportViewer controls simplify access to the Report Server Web service, generating the TestDS report is straightforward.

```
private void RunRemote() {
  reportViewer.ProcessingMode = Microsoft.Reporting.WinForms.ProcessingMode.Remote;
  reportViewer.ServerReport.ReportServerUrl = new Uri(txtReportServer.Text);
  reportViewer.ServerReport.ReportPath = "/AMRS/TestDS";
  // Bind the dataset
  SetParameters();
  reportViewer.RefreshReport();
}
```

The code configures the ReportViewer for remote mode since we will be requesting a server report. Then, the code sets the ReportServerUrl property, such as http://localhost/ReportServer, and the ReportPath property to the full path of the server report.

Binding the dataset

Next, the code calls SetParameters to pass the dataset as a report parameter.

```
private void SetParameters() {
  ReportParameter[] parameters = new ReportParameter[1];
  EntitySalesOrder entitySalesOrder = new EntitySalesOrder();
  sqlDataAdapter.Fill(entitySalesOrder);
  parameters[0] = new ReportParameter("DataSource", entitySalesOrder.GetXml());
  reportViewer.ServerReport.SetParameters(parameters);
}
```

For testing purposes, the code loads the ADO.NET dataset from a file. In real life, as long as it conforms to the dataset schema used by the report, the dataset can come from anywhere, including a business logic layer. Next, the code creates a new DataSource parameter. The code obtains the XML payload of the dataset by calling the GetXml method and passes it to the DataSource parameter. Finally, the code calls the RefreshReport method of ReportViewer to submit the report request and render the report.

18.3 Implementing Custom Data Processing Extensions

Now that you've seen the Dataset data processing extension in action, let's take a closer look at the implementation. First, I will walk you through the code of the data processing module. Then, I will discuss the internals of the custom query designer. You can find the Dataset source code in the CustomDataProcessingExtension project that comes with this book.

18.3.1 Understanding the Classes and Interfaces

Microsoft provides a sample data processing extension called FsiDataExtension (see Resources) that shows you how to use the data processing interfaces. After working with this sample, I found that creating my own custom extension to be straightforward. In a nutshell, the process involves coding several classes that implement standard interfaces provided by Reporting Services.

These interfaces are defined in the Microsoft.ReportingServices.Interfaces assembly located in the \Program Files\Microsoft SQL Server\100\SDK\Assemblies folder. Your custom data processing project needs to reference this assembly. You will also need to reference the Microsoft.ReportingServices.QueryDesigners assembly in the \Program Files\Microsoft SQL Server\100\Tools\Binn\VSShell\Common7\IDE folder. Table 18.2 lists the standard data processing extension classes and interfaces and shows whether the Dataset extension uses them.

Table 18.2 A custom dataset extension has several classes that implement standard interfaces

Class	Interfaces	Purpose	Used in the sample
DsConnectionWrapper	IDbConnection, IDbConnectionExtension, IExtension	Establishes a database connection.	
DsTransaction	IDbTransaction	Enlists the database commands in a the data source transaction.	
DsCommand	IDbCommand, IDbCommandAnalysis	Handles the report query statement.	✓
DsDataParameter	IDataParameter	Represents a query parameter.	✓
DsDataParameterCollection	IDataParameterCollection	Represents a collection of the query parameters.	✓
DsDataReader	IDataReader	Handles the access to the dataset data.	✓

If you have implemented a custom .NET data provider, you will find the Reporting Services and ADO.NET classes and interfaces very similar. Based on your data requirements, you may find that most of these classes require either minimal or no code. For example, because the sample Dataset extension doesn't establish a database connection, it doesn't use the DSConnectionWrapper class.

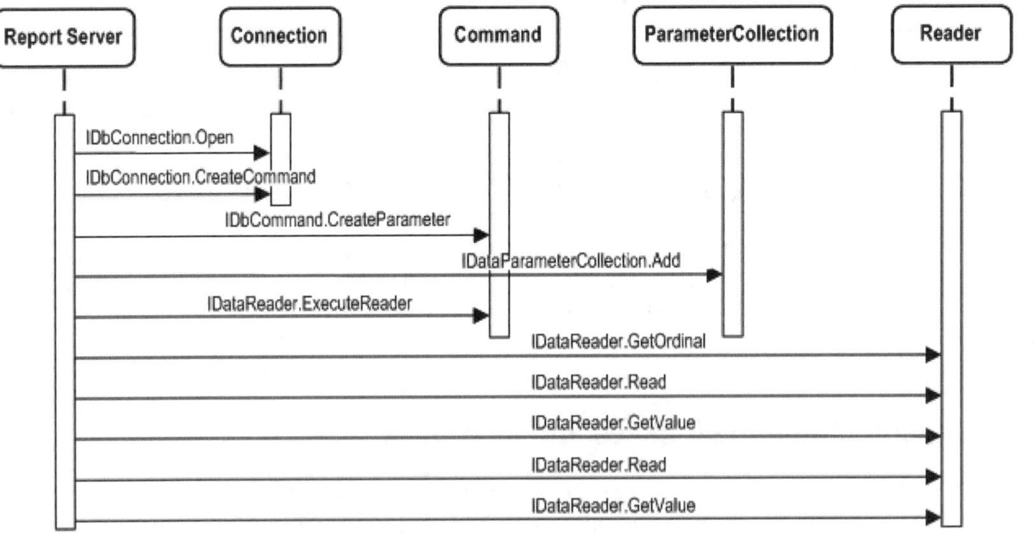

Figure 18.6 At run time, Reporting Services invokes the custom data processing extension interfaces to configure the extension and retrieve data.

Understanding runtime interaction

To understand the implementation details, you first need to understand how the report server interacts with the data processing extension at run time. As Figure 18.6 shows, the report server first asks the data processing extension to open a connection to the data source, passing the connection string. Next, the report server calls IDbConnection.CreateCommand to obtain a reference to a command object that it uses to send the query.

The report server then calls the IDbCommand.CreateParameter method as many times as needed to create all query parameters. The custom data processing extension class that represents a query parameter must implement the IDataParameter interface. This allows the report server to configure the parameter and add it to an object that implements IDataParameterCollection.

After populating the parameter collection, the report server calls the IDataReader.ExecuteReader method of the Command object, which is responsible for retrieving data from the data source and exposing the data as an object that implements IDataReader interface. For each field in the report dataset, the report server calls the IDataReader interface's GetOrdinal method to get the positional index of that field in the reader field collection. Later, the report server will ask for the value of the field by its positional index.

After matching the fields of the report dataset with the fields of the data processing extension DataReader, the report server begins retrieving data in a forward-only fashion by calling IDataReader.Read until it reaches the end of the rowset. The reader field values are retrieved via calls to the IDataReader.GetValue method.

Now that you know about the data processing sequence of events, let's drill down into the implementation details.

Handling connections

As noted, the Dataset extension doesn't connect to a data source because it gets everything it needs from the query parameter as a serialized dataset or a path to file. But if you build an extension that needs to connect to a data source, you must implement the IDbConnection interface. The most important method on this interface is IDbConnection.Open. Before calling this method, the report server will pass the data source properties that were set at design time to the IDbConnection properties, including the connection string, which you can get from ConnectionString property.

The IDbConnectionExtension interface defines methods for authenticating the user to the data source. For example, it passes the user name and password that the report author has entered in the data source properties. The IExtension interface specifies two methods: SetConfiguration and LocalizedName. The report server calls SetConfiguration to pass the extension configuration section as defined in the report server configuration file (rsreportserver.config). For example, the administrator can create a configuration section that specifies the default location of the dataset file. Before the report server gives control to the data processing extension, it gives the extension a chance to configure itself by passing the configuration section as an XML fragment. The Dataset extension doesn't need configuration settings.

The LocalizedName method should return the localized name of the extension based on the thread culture. The report server shows this name in Report Designer when you configure the report data source and in Report Manager.

Implementing a command object

If you have done any ADO.NET programming, you know that you need to create a command object to retrieve data. Similarly, the DsCommand class represents the data processing extension command object. It stores the actual command statement. Recall that the command statement of the Dataset extension must be in the format FilePath|TableName. At design time, the command statement includes everything the extension needs to retrieve the data from the dataset file. Therefore, the DsCommand object doesn't define any parameters.

If your custom data processing extension needs to support design-time parameters, consider implementing the IDbCommandAnalysis.GetParameters method. For example, if the parameters are defined as placeholders inside the query text, GetParameters would parse the query text and return a parameter collection. In our case, the GetParameters method simply verifies the syntax of the statement, and raises an error if it doesn't follow the FilePath|TableName format.

TIP You can help the Report Designer discover the query parameters at design time so it can prompt the user for their values. To support this feature, implement the IDbCommandAnalysis interface in the Command object. This interface exposes a single method called GetParameters. When you click on the Exclamation toolbar button to run the report query, the Report Designer probes the extension to find out if it implements this interface, and if so, calls the GetParameters method. This method is responsible for parsing the query string set at design time and returning a collection with the parameter placeholders.

The DsCommand object is responsible for preparing and returning a DataReader object that implements the IDataReader interface. The ExecuteReader method handles this.

```
public IDataReader ExecuteReader()
{
 if (m_parameters.Count == 0  ||
((DsDataParameter)m_parameters[0]).Value.ToString().IndexOf(Util.PARAM_DELIMITER) > -1)
  SetParametersFromCommandString();
 DsDataReader reader=new DsDataReader(m_connection,this.CommandTextWithoutParameter,m_parameters);
 reader.LoadDataset();
 return reader;
}
```

When the report server needs data, it calls the ExecuteReader method. First, the ExecuteReader method verifies the parameters. Depending on the context in which the method is called, this step will be addressed in one of these ways:

- No parameters—At design time, there will be no parameters because the command text provides everything the extension needs. The Dataset extension extracts the file path and table name from the command text.
- One parameter that contains the file path—At design time, the Dataset Query Designer passes this parameter when the user executes the query. The Dataset extension doesn't need to parse the command text.
- One parameter in the format FilePath|TableName—At run time, if you run the report in Report Manager, there will be one parameter in the format FilePath|TableName. The Dataset extension extracts the file path and table name from the command text.
- One parameter that contains an instance of the ADO.NET dataset. At run time, the custom application will pass the dataset instance to the DataSource parameter.

Next, ExecuteReader instantiates a new DsDataReader object and passes the connection string, command text, and parameters. Finally, ExecuteReader calls the LoadDataset of the reader object to prepare the dataset and returns the reader object to the report server.

Implementing DataReader

The DataReader object is the workhorse of the data processing extension. It is responsible for preparing the report dataset and providing forward record navigation. The most interesting method is LoadDataset.

```
internal void LoadDataset() {
  string dataSource = null;
  DsDataParameter parameter = m_parameters.GetByName(Util.DATA_SOURCE) as DsDataParameter;
  dataSource = parameter.Value.ToString();
  m_dataset = GetDataSet(dataSource);
  if (m_cmdText.Trim().ToLower()=="nothing")
    m_datatable = m_dataset.Tables[0];
  else
    m_datatable = m_dataset.Tables[m_cmdText];
  m_ie = m_datatable.Rows.GetEnumerator();
}
private DataSet GetDataSet(string dataSource) {
  DataSet dataset = new DataSet();
  if (dataSource.IndexOf("<") >=0 ) {
    StringReader reader = new StringReader(dataSource);
    dataset.ReadXml(reader);
  }
  else {
    FileIOPermission permission = new FileIOPermission(FileIOPermissionAccess.Read, dataSource);
    permission.Assert();
    dataset.ReadXml(dataSource);
  }
 return dataset;
}
```

First, LoadDataset gets the value of the DataSource parameter and passes it to the GetDataSet helper function. GetDataSet uses a simple algorithm to check what the parameter contains. If the value of the DataSource parameter starts with "<", GetDataSet assumes that DataSource contains a serialized ADO.NET dataset, in which case it deserializes the parameter value back to an ADO.NET dataset.

Otherwise, GetDataSet assumes that the parameter value specifies the path to the dataset file. Note that I am specifically demanding a read Code Access Security (CAS) permission to the physical file. Regardless of the fact that you will configure the extension assembly for full access, CAS is layered on top of operating system security and you need to demand the required permission in order for the call to succeed.

The rest of the DsDataReader code implements the IDataReader standard property and methods, such as methods for providing a forward-only enumerator (Read method), returning the field count (FieldCount property), getting a field value (GetValue method), and so on.

18.3.2 Implementing the Dataset Query Designer

Reporting Services lets you build in custom query designers to support any custom data processing extensions that you provide. Similar to a custom extension, a custom query designer is a .NET module that implements a standard interface. Unlike a custom extension, a custom query designer has a visible interface. At design time, the report author uses the user interface to define the data processing command statement.

Query designers can provide complex graphical interfaces that abstract the technicalities of the targeted data sources. Take for example the SQL Server and Analysis Services graphical query designers, which you are already familiar with. In short, consider implementing a custom query designer when the built-in generic query designer is not enough.

Understanding IQueryDesigner interface

A custom query designer must implement the IQueryDesigner interface, which is currently not documented. Table 18.3 lists the methods of the IQueryDesigner interface.

Table 18.3 The IQueryDesigner methods

Method	Purpose	Used in the sample
ServiceProvider property	Lets the custom query designer access the services provided by the Report Designer host.	
Connection property	Passes the connection string to the query designer.	
Command property	Passes and returns the command text.	✓
InitializeQueryDesigner method	Lets the query designer inform the Report Designer if it has initialized successfully.	
QueryDesigner property	Returns a reference to the UI control.	✓
Toolbar property	Returns a reference to the query designer toolbar.	✓
EnableAltDesignerChanged event	Provides a communication mechanism between the custom query designer and the generic query designer, such as enabling or disable the toolbar buttons.	
OnActivateView	Lets the query designer update its UI before activating it.	✓
OnDeactivateView	Gives the query designer a chance to perform tasks before the Report Designer deactivates it.	✓

Let's see how the Dataset Query Designer uses the IQueryDesigner interface.

Understanding design-time Interaction

A custom query designer is used only at design time. You access the custom query designer by right-clicking the dataset in the Report Data window and choosing Edit Query. The Report Designer determines which query designer to load. If a custom query designer is registered in the Report Designer configuration file and the rd:UseGenericDesigner property of the Query element in the report definition is False (or the rd:UseGenericDesigner property is not present), the Report Designer will attempt to load the custom query designer.

Next, the Report Designer calls the ServiceProvider property to pass a reference to the Report Designer host. The custom query designer can use the ServiceProvider property to get access to the services provided the Report Designer host. The Dataset Query Designer doesn't use any of the services. The Report Designer passes a reference to the DsConnection object that the Dataset extension implements. A custom query designer can use this object to obtain the connection string if it needs to connect to the data source. Next, the Report Designer calls the Command property and passes a reference to the DsCommand object. The Dataset Query Designer retrieves the command text, parses it to obtain the file path and the dataset table name, and passes this information to the user interface.

Then, the Report Designer asks the custom query designer if it has initialized itself successfully by calling the InitializeQueryDesigner property. As optimistic as it is, the Dataset Query Designer doesn't perform any internal checks and always confirms a successful initialization. The Report Designer follows by calling the QueryDesigner property to obtain a reference to the user interface. Your custom data processing extension can pass back a reference to any Windows Forms control. Since the user interface will be hosted inside the Report Designer, the Dataset Query Designer returns a reference to the panel control on the QueryDesignerUI form.

Implementing a custom toolbar

Next, the Report Designer invokes the Toolbar property to check if there are any items to add to the Report Designer toolbar. The standard toolbar of the Report Designer provides the Edit as Text and Import toolbar buttons. The Edit as Text toolbar button lets you switch to the generic query designer. The Import toolbar button lets you import query statements from external *.sql or *.rdl files.

Your custom query designer can add additional buttons if needed. The Dataset Query Designer prepares a custom toolbar with Open and Execute buttons (see again Figure 18.3) and hooks their ButtonClick events to event handlers inside the Dataset Query Designer. The user can press the Open button to select a dataset file and the Execute button to run the dataset query. When the user presses the Execute button, the QueryDesignerUI form calls the ExecuteCommand method.

```
public void ExecuteCommand(IDbCommand command) {
   IDataReader reader = null;
   command.CommandText = this.TableName;
   ((DsDataParameterCollection)command.Parameters).Clear();
   command.Parameters.Add(new DsDataParameter(Util.DATA_SOURCE, txtPath.Text));
   reader = command.ExecuteReader(CommandBehavior.SingleResult);
   System.Data.DataTable dataTable = new System.Data.DataTable();

   for (int i = 0; i < reader.FieldCount; i++) {
            string fieldName = reader.GetName(i);
      dataTable.Columns.Add(fieldName);
   }

   while (reader.Read()) {
      System.Data.DataRow dataRow = dataTable.NewRow();
      for (int i = 0; i < reader.FieldCount; i++) {
        dataRow[i] = reader.GetValue(i);
      }
        dataTable.Rows.Add(dataRow);
   }
   dataGrid1.DataSource = dataTable;
}
```

ExecuteCommand passes the table name to CommandText property of the DsCommand object. It also passes the dataset file path as a parameter to the DsCommand object. It calls its ExecuteReader method to obtain a reader to the report dataset. It navigates through the reader and populates the Results grid.

When the user closes the Dataset Query Designer or clicks the Refresh Fields or the Generic Query Designer buttons, the Report Designer calls the get accessor of the CommandText property to obtain the new command text. Subsequently, the Dataset Query Designer obtains the file path and table name values from the QueryDesignerUI form, prepares the command text in the format FilePath|TableName and passes it back to the Report Designer. You can switch to the generic query designer to see the command text that the Dataset Query Designer has generated.

18.4 Deploying and Debugging

Before using the Dataset extension, you need to deploy it. At design time, you need to register the Dataset extension with Report Designer. You also need to deploy the data processing extension binaries to the designer folder. Once you have tested the extension, you can deploy it to the report server for production use.

Configuring the extension involves modifying several configuration files. For your convenience, I included my version of the affected configuration files in the Config folder, but do not just replace your configuration files with mine. Instead, use them as reference to make changes in the files in your installation.

18.4.1 Design-time Deployment

At design time, the data processing extension is used by the Report Designer.

Registering the extension

Follow these steps to deploy and register the extension with the BIDS Report Designer.

1. Copy the extension binaries, Prologika.CustomDataProcessingExtension.dll and Prologika.CustomDataProcessingExtension.pdb to the Report Designer folder.

   The BIDS Report Designer default folder is \Program Files\Microsoft Visual Studio 9.0\Common7\IDE\PrivateAssemblies.

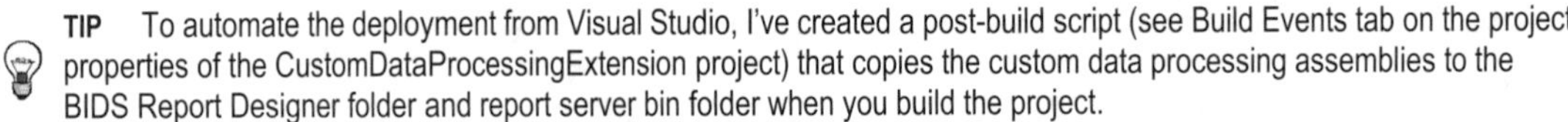

TIP To automate the deployment from Visual Studio, I've created a post-build script (see Build Events tab on the project properties of the CustomDataProcessingExtension project) that copies the custom data processing assemblies to the BIDS Report Designer folder and report server bin folder when you build the project.

2. In the same folder, open the RSReportDesigner.config file and locate the <Data> element.
3. Add the following line after the last <Extension> element in the <Data> section.

```
<Extension Name="DATASET" Type="Prologika.RS.Extensibility.CustomDataProcessingExtension.DsConnectionWrapper,
Prologika.CustomDataProcessingExtension"/>
```

4. To register the custom query designer, add the following line after the last <Extension> element in the <Designers> section.

```
<Ext ension Name="DATASET" Type="Prologika.RS.Extensibility.CustomDataProcessingExtension.DatasetQueryDesigner,
Prologika.CustomDataProcessingExtension"/>
```

Granting security rights

The next configuration step involves granting the custom dataset extension FullTrust rights.

1. Open the Report Designer preview policy configuration file (rspreviewpolicy.config). The default location of this file is C:\Program Files\Microsoft Visual Studio 9.0\Common7\IDE\-PrivateAssemblies.
2. Add the following CodeGroup element after the last CodeGroup element:

```
<CodeGroup class="UnionCodeGroup" version="1" Name="CustomDataExtensionCodeGroup"
      Description="Code group for the Custom Data Extension" PermissionSetName="FullTrust">
      <IMembershipCondition class="UrlMembershipCondition" versio n="1"
      Url="C:\ Program Files\Microsoft Visual Studio 9.0\Common7\IDE\PrivateAssemblies\
        Prologika.CustomDataProcessingExtension.dll"/>
</CodeGroup>
```

3. If you use the BIDS Report Designer and the Visual Studio IDE is open, restart it and reflect the configuration changes.

   At this point, the Report Designer configuration is complete. You should be able to create a data source using the Dataset extension.

18.4.2 Report Server Deployment

At run time, the report server interacts with the data processing extension. Here is how to configure the Dataset extension with the report server.

Registering the extension

As with Report Designer deployment, you need to deploy and register the extension in the report server configuration file.

1. Deploy the extension binaries, Prologika.CustomDataProcessingExtension.dll and Prologika.CustomDataProcessingExtension.pdb to the report server binary folder \Program Files\Microsoft SQL Server\MSRS10.MSSQLSERVER\Reporting Services\ReportServer\bin.
2. Open the rsreportserver.config file from the \Program Files\Microsoft SQL Server\MSRS10.-MSSQLSERVER\Reporting Services\ReportServer folder.
3. Locate the <Data> element and register the extension just like you did with the Report Designer configuration file.

Granting security rights

Next, you need elevate the Code Access Security rights so the extension can execute successfully.

1. To grant the code the necessary security permissions, open the rssrvpolicy.config in the same folder.
2. Add the following CodeGroup element after the last code group:

```
<CodeGroup class="UnionCodeGroup" version="1" Name="CustomDataExtensionCodeGroup"
  Description="Code group for the Dataset CDPE" PermissionSetName="FullTrust">
    <IMembershipCondition class="UrlMembershipCondition" version="1"
      Url="C:\Program Files\Microsoft SQL Server\MSRS10.MSSQLSERVER\Reporting
          Services\ReportServer\bin\Prologika.CustomDataProcessingExtension.dll "/>
</CodeGroup>
```

You don't need to restart the report server after making this change because it will automatically restart itself when it detects a change to its configuration files. After these steps, you should be able to successfully run a server report that uses the Dataset extension.

18.4.3 Debugging Custom Data Processing Extensions

You can debug the custom data processing extension code both at design time when you test the extension with the Report Designer report, and at run time when the extension is used by a server report.

Design-time debugging

Follow these steps to step through the custom code in Visual Studio at design time.

1. Open the CustomDataProcessingExtension project in Visual Studio. Open the project properties and set up the Debug tab, as shown in Figure 18.7.

Specifically, assuming that you want to use the BIDS Report Designer, select the Start External Program option and enter the path to the Report Designer executable, which is by default \Program Files\Microsoft Visual Studio 9.0\Common7\IDE\devenv.exe.

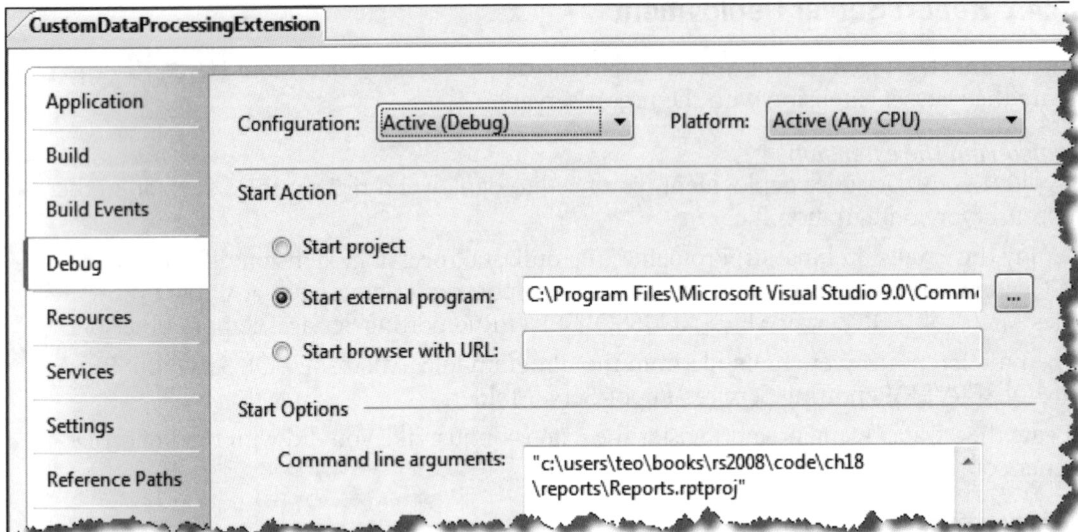

Figure 18.7 Use the Start External Program option to debug from a report that uses the Dataset extension.

2. In the Command Line Arguments field, enter the path to a report project that uses the extension, such as C:\Users\teo\Books\RS2008\Code\ch18\Reports\TestDS.rptproj.
3. In Visual Studio Solution Explorer, set the CustomDataProcessingExtension project as a startup project.
4. Place breakpoints in the code as needed and hit F5 to start debugging.

   Depending on how you configured the Debug properties, Visual Studio will launch Report Designer in a separate instance of Visual Studio.
5. Execute the dataset query.

   At this point, execution should hit your breakpoint and you should be able to step through the code of the Dataset extension.

Runtime debugging

You may need to debug your custom extension at run time. For example, you might want to determine what parameters a custom application passes to the report. Follow these steps to debug the extension at run time.

1. Deploy the latest binaries to the report server binary folder.
2. Open the CDPE project in Visual Studio and set breakpoints in the source code as needed.
3. Go to Debug ⇨ Attach to Process main menu.
4. In the Attach to Process dialog, check the Show Processes From All Users and Show Processes in All Sessions checkboxes found toward the bottom of the window.
5. In the Available Processes grid, locate the ReportingServicesService.exe process and select it.
6. Press the Attach button to attach to the Reporting Services Windows service.
7. Request the report from your custom application.

TIP By default, the Reporting Services service will time out the debugging session after 150 seconds. To prevent this from happening, add a new registry key "UnderDebugger" (DWORD) with the value 1 under HKLM\Software\Microsoft\-Microsoft SQL Server\100\Reporting Services parent key (create the Reporting Services key if it doesn't exist). Restart the Reporting Services service (ReportingServicesService.exe) and attach to it as described before. Now, your debugging session shouldn't time out. Please note that this setting disables the management thread that ensures the Windows service is up and running correctly. For this reason, while you can leave this setting permanently to 1 on your development machine, set it to 0 on your production server or delete it.

Once the report server starts processing the report, it will pass the control to your custom extension and you should be able to break into the Dataset extension code.

18.5 Summary

In this chapter, you've seen how to extend the Reporting Services data architecture by writing a custom data processing extension. You can use the Dataset extension to build reports that use data from ADO.NET datasets. Consider using this extension when your application requirements include binding an ADO.NET dataset to a server report – a scenario which is not currently supported by Reporting Services. You can provide a custom query designer with your custom extension to help the report author use the dataset to create the report layout.

To use a custom data processing extension in Report Designer, you must deploy it to the Report Designer folder before you can author reports that use it. Once you have tested the extension, you must deploy and register it with the report server. You can use Visual Studio to debug the extension both at design time and run time.

18.6 Resources

Microsoft File Share Data Processing Extension Sample
(http://tinyurl.com/2vs69p)— Microsoft has provided the File Share Data Processing Extension sample.

ReportExecutionService.Render API
(http://tinyurl.com/2zjp5x)—You can call the Render API to generate a report if your application cannot use the ReportViewer controls.

Chapter 19

Customizing Security

You can use Reporting Services to make data easily accessible both on your company intranet and on the Internet. Internet reporting brings additional challenges, the first and foremost being security. Out of the box, Reporting Services authenticates and authorizes end users with Windows security. However, Windows security is usually not practical when delivering reports to external users. Nor will it help you if you are trying to report-enable an Internet-facing application that uses a different, non-Windows security model.

In this chapter, I will show you how to customize report server security by replacing the Reporting Services Windows security model with a custom security extension. First, you'll learn the ropes of implementing a custom security extension. Then, you'll enhance it by adding role membership features to simplify maintenance. This chapter also demonstrates how to leverage custom security to report-enable Internet-facing web application. Finally, I will show you how to deploy, debug, and troubleshoot a custom security extension. You will need Visual Studio 2008 to work with the source code for this chapter.

19.1 Introducing Custom Security

By default, Reporting Services is configured to use Windows security, where the user is authenticated and authorized based on his or her Windows identity. For example, if Bob has logged in to the adventure-works domain as adventure-works\bob, the report server will authentication and authorize Bob based on the security policies the report administrator has set up in the report catalog for adventure-works\bob. Windows security is good because Bob doesn't need to explicitly log in to the report server because Windows transparently passes his credentials to the report server. In addition, Windows maintains Bob's password, not you.

19.1.1 When to Use Custom Security

Windows security works great for intranet applications where the report server and the end users are usually in the same or in a trusted domain, and you are using the Active Directory infrastructure that is already in place. However, sometimes Windows security may not be a practical option.

Scenarios for using custom security
Here some scenarios that may rule out Windows security:

- Internet reporting—Windows-based security almost never works for Internet-facing reporting solutions. Creating and maintaining thousands of Windows user accounts can overwhelm the network administrator.
- Integrating with custom security service—Your organization may have an existing security solution already in place. Operational requirements may dictate integrating Reporting Services with the custom security infrastructure.
- Anonymous access—Reporting Services 2008 doesn't natively support Anonymous access. For an added level of security and to discourage you from using it, Anonymous access has been intentionally made difficult to set up in this release. If you really need Anonymous access, you must implement custom security that does no authentication and authorization.

What should you do when you cannot use Windows security? The good news is that you can replace the default Windows security model with a custom security solution when Windows security gets in the way. On the downside, customizing Reporting Services security is a rather invasive procedure that requires a significant implementation effort, so consider it as a last resort.

How does custom security work

Recall that the report server has a modular architecture where custom modules, called extensions, can be plugged in to extend the report server functionality. Custom security extensions provide the practical means by which you authenticate and authorize non-Windows users. If the user requests a resource and has not been previously authenticated, the user is redirected to a logon form that the developer has created beforehand. This is why Reporting Services custom security is also known as Forms Authentication.

Custom security gives you complete control over the authentication and authorization process. Once the logon form collects the user credentials, you can authenticate and authorize the user anyway you want. For example, you can authenticate the user against a user profile table in a database. Upon successful user authentication, Reporting Services issues an authentication ticket to the user in a form of a session cookie. The report server verifies this authentication ticket with each subsequent request. Developers, familiar with the ASP.NET Forms Authentication model, will undoubtedly find the Reporting Services custom security very similar. In fact, they both share the same plumbing infrastructure.

NOTE The report server cannot be configured for a mixed authentication mode. In other words, you cannot set up Reporting Services to support both Windows and custom security modes. Once you re-configure the server for custom security, you can't use Windows-based security even for administrator-level access. Unlike the other extension types, such as data and delivery extensions, you can have only one custom security extension deployed to the server. Since changing the security mode is a rather invasive procedure, make sure you back up the report server configuration files in case you decide to switch back to Windows security.

Custom security is available with Workgroup, Standard, Enterprise, and Developer editions of SQL Server 2008. You cannot use custom security with a report server that is configured for SharePoint integration mode because SharePoint provides its own Forms Authentication mechanism.

19.1.2 Understanding Custom Security Extensions

To customize Reporting Services security, you need to implement a custom security extension. As it turns out, custom security extension is a collective name for two modules, also called extensions. Specifically, the custom security extension must include one authentication extension and one authorization extension.

Understanding authentication and authorization

The authentication extension handles user authentication (that is, verifying who the user is). During the authentication stage, the custom security extension determines the user's identity by obtaining it from a trusted authority, such as a user profile store. A successful outcome of this phase is an authentication ticket in the form of a session cookie that the report server sends to the client.

Authorization occurs after authentication. The authorization extension is responsible for authorizing the user (that is, determining what the user can do). For example, if the user has submitted a report request, during the authorization phase your custom security extension must verify whether the user has the rights to do so. The authorization policies that the report server uses to determine user rights are defined through role assignments that you create in Report Manager. When the user interacts with the report server, your authorization extension evaluates the role assignments and grants or revokes user access.

Understanding security interfaces

From an implementation standpoint, a custom security extension is a .NET module that implements two standard interfaces provided by Reporting Services. The authentication extension implements the IAuthenticationExtension interface, while the authorization extension implements the IAuthorizationExtension interface. These interfaces are defined in the Microsoft.ReportingServices.Interfaces assembly located in the \Program Files\Microsoft SQL Server\100\SDK\Assemblies\ folder. Table 19.1 shows the interface methods and their purpose.

Table 19.1 Reporting Services provides IAuthenticationExtension and IAuthorizationExtension interfaces

Interface	Methods	Description
IAuthenticationExtension	GetUserInfo	Returns the user identity.
	LogonUser	Authenticates the user as a result of calling LogonUser API.
	IsValidPrincipalName	Validates the user name.
IAuthorizationExtension	CheckAccess method overloads	Handles user authorization based on the attempted action by user.
	CreateSecurityDescriptor	Returns a security descriptor associated with a report catalog item.
	GetPermissions	Returns the user permissions for an item in the report catalog.

In addition, since both IAuthenticationExtension and IAuthorizationExtension interfaces inherit from the generic IExtension interface, you need to implement the IExtension methods so your custom security extension can be successfully registered with the report server. The IExtension interface defines only two methods: SetConfiguration and Localized Name. The report server calls SetConfiguration to pass the extension configuration section as defined in the report server configuration file (rsreportserver.config).

For example, the administrator can create a configuration section that includes the administrator credentials and the connection string to the user profile store. Specifying these settings in the configuration file makes this information available to the extension when the server starts up, before the report server calls the extension methods.

The LocalizedName method should return the localized name of a custom extension based on the thread culture of the interactive user. However, since the custom security extension name doesn't appear in either Report Designer or Report Manager, this method can simply return null.

19.1.3 Understanding Runtime Interaction

Figure 19.1 shows the sequence of events between the client and a report server that is configured to use a custom security extension. The client could be any application that can call Web services, such as Report Manager or a custom .NET application.

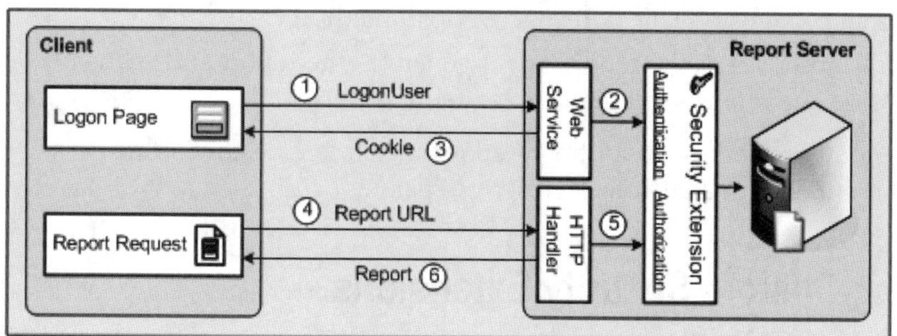

Figure 19.1 The custom security extension is responsible for authenticating and authorizing all requests to the report server.

Authentication phase

During the authentication phase, the client application is responsible for collecting user credentials and passing them to the custom security extension for authentication.

1. The client application displays a logon form to prompt the user for credentials. In the case of ASP.NET applications, ASP.NET Forms Authentication can be used to redirect the user to the login form automatically if the user has not yet been authenticated.

   What follows next is an exchange of information that either results in a successful authentication operation or an access denied error. Each step in the process is numbered in the diagram and explained below.

2. Once the user credentials are collected, the application invokes the Reporting Services LogonUser API to log the user to Reporting Services. This corresponds to step (1) in the diagram.
3. Next, the report server asks the custom security extension to authenticate the user by calling your implementation of IAuthenticationExtension.LogonUser. This is step (2). How the custom security extension authenticates the user is of no concern to the report server. Typically, with a large number of users, a database store will be used to store user profile data and credentials.
4. If the custom security extension authenticates the user successfully, the report server issues (3) a ticket in the form of a session cookie, which the report server expects to find in subsequent calls from the client. When a browser is used as a client, the session cookie will be automati-

cally passed back with all subsequent requests. When other types of clients are used, you will need to add an extra step to store and pass the cookie to the report server.

TIP If the client is a web application that uses ASP.NET Forms Authentication, it is possible to bypass the LogonUser call and reuse the authentication ticket by following the instructions in the Forms Authentication Across Applications article (see Resources). This is the approach I followed in the Adventure Works Web Reporter demo, which I discuss in section 19.4.

Authorization phase

Although Figure 19.1 assumes a request for viewing a report, any type of action against the report catalog must pass the authorization checks. For example, if the client is Report Manager, each time the user initiates a new management task, the report server will call down to the authorization extension to let it authorize the task.

1. The client submits a report request either by URL or SOAP.
2. The report server asks the custom security extension to authorize the user request by calling the appropriate IAuthorizationExtension.CheckAccess overload method.
3. If the request is successfully authorized, the report server generates the report and sends it back to the client. Otherwise, the report server rejects the request.

Now that you have a good understanding about how Reporting Services custom security works, let's look at how to implement a custom security extension.

19.2 Implementing Custom Security Extensions

Developers who are already familiar with interface-based programming should find creating a custom security extension to be fairly straightforward. My implementation is based on the Microsoft Security Extension sample (see Resources) that is included in the Reporting Services product samples. Although originally written for Reporting Services 2000, I highly recommend you also review the whitepaper Using Forms Authentication in Reporting Services (see Resources) by Microsoft for additional insights about Reporting Services custom security.

ADVENTURE WORKS cycles

Customer Orders for 11000

Product #	Product Name	Order Qty	Unit Price	Discount	Total
⊟ Order: SO43793	7/22/2001				**$3,399.99**
BK-M82S-38	Mountain-100 Silver, 38	1	$3,399.99	0.00 %	$3,399.99
⊟ Order: SO51522	7/22/2003				**$2,341.97**
BK-M68S-38	Mountain-200 Silver, 38	1	$2,319.99	0.00 %	$2,319.99
FE-6654	Fender Set - Mountain	1	$21.98	0.00 %	$21.98
⊟ Order: SO57418	11/4/2003				**$2,507.03**
BK-T79U-46	Touring-1000 Blue, 46	1	$2,384.07	0.00 %	$2,384.07
TI-T723	Touring Tire	1	$28.99	0.00 %	$28.99
TT-T092	Touring Tire Tube	1	$4.99	0.00 %	$4.99
HL-U509-R	Sport-100 Helmet, Red	1	$34.99	0.00 %	$34.99
SJ-0194-S	Short-Sleeve Classic Jersey, S	1	$53.99	0.00 %	$53.99

Figure 19.2 The Customer Orders report obtains the customer identify from User!UserID and shows the orders submitted by the customer.

The chapter source code includes three projects: CustomSecurity, Reports, and Web. The custom security extension is implemented in the CustomSecurity project. The Reports project contains a sample report, Customer Orders, which you can use to test the custom security extension. The Web project is a web application that demonstrates how a custom application can integrate with a report server configured for custom security. The custom security extension sample requires a few schema and data changes to the AdventureWorks2008 database. You will find the script files in the Database folder.

19.2.1 Introducing the Adventure Works Web Reporter

To add a realistic touch to the code sample, imagine that Adventure Works would like to enhance their Adventure Works Web Internet portal by letting its customers generate reports online. As typical with many popular online stores, one of the first reports requested is the Customer Orders report that shows the order history for a given customer, as shown in Figure 19.2.

Understanding security requirements

Before integrating custom security with the Adventure Works Web portal, we will use Report Manager to test the custom security extension for report management and delivery, as follows:

1. The administrator logs in to Report Manager and grants end users rights to browse reports. For the purpose of this demo, the administrator credentials are specified in the RSReportServer.config file. Alternatively, your real-life extension can authenticate the administrator by other means, such as by querying a database.
2. Once security is set up, we can use Report Manager to test report delivery on behalf of a customer. If the customer has not yet been authenticated, Report Manager displays a logon form to collect the customer credentials.
3. As it stands, the AdventureWorks2008 database doesn't associate a login identifier with a customer. As a workaround, we will use the BusinessEntityID column from the Person.Person table as a user name and the PasswordSalt column from the Person.Password table as a password.
4. Report Manager calls the LogonUser API to let the custom security extension authenticate the user.
5. The custom security extension authenticates the user by passing the login credentials to the AdventureWorks2008 database.
6. If the user authenticates successfully, the user can view the Customer Orders report.

Understanding the Customer Orders report

Let's take a moment to discuss the internals of the Customer Orders report. This report is ideally suited for security testing because it leverages the user identity and it uses interactive report features that call back to the report server. Recall from chapter X that User!UserID is the standard User collection provided by Reporting Services, and UserID is the user who requested the report. Because custom security extensions can return the identity of the interactive user, the Customer Orders report can use the User!UserID property, so you don't have to pass the user name as a report parameter.

In our case, the User!UserID property returns the customer identifier that the user enters in the login page to log in to the Report Manager. The Report Manager passes this identifier to the first argument of the LogonUser API. For testing purposes, the customer identifier is displayed on the top of the report (for example, Customer Orders for 11000). If you open the parameter properties of the report dataset, you will see the following expression for the @CustomerID query-level parameter:

```
=Iif(IsNumeric(User!UserID), User!UserID, -1)
```

This expression checks if the user identity is numeric. This will be the case if a customer is requesting the report. The report server passes the customer identifier to the WHERE clause of the report query to retrieve the orders for that customer only. In contrast, if either the administrator or a Windows domain user (such as when the report is tested in BIDS) requests the report, User!UserID would probably return a text value that specifies the user account. In cases where the expression detects a text value, the expression returns -1 as a customer identifier and the query brings back no rows.

The report also leverages some of the interactive features supported by Reporting Services. Specifically, the report lets the end user drill down a given order by clicking on the plus sign to expand it and see the order items.

Let's now drill into the implementation details to understand how custom security extensions handle user authentication and authorization.

19.2.2 Implementing the Authentication Extension

Recall that the authentication extension needs to implement the IAuthentication interface, which includes the GetUserInfo, LogonUser, and IsValidPrincipalName methods. In addition, you will probably need to implement IExtension.SetConfiguration to load some configuration settings from the report server configuration file, such as connection strings and administrator credentials.

Implementing SetConfiguration

When configuring the custom security extension, you need to specify a connection string to the Adventure Works database. Since our extension reads the administrator credentials from the configuration file, you need to specify also the administrator credentials. If the user credentials match the administrator credentials, the security extension grants the user full rights to the report server. The SetConfiguration method reads the configuration settings and stores them in class members:

```
public void SetConfiguration(String configuration) {
        XmlDocument doc = new XmlDocument();
        doc.LoadXml(configuration);
        if (doc.DocumentElement.Name == "AdminConfiguratio n")
        {
                foreach (XmlNode child in doc.DocumentElement.ChildNodes) {
                  switch (child.Name)
                {
                        case CONNECTION_STRING: m_connectionstring = child.InnerText; break;
                        case ADMIN_USER_NAME: m_adminUserName = child.InnerText; break;
                        case ADMIN_USER_PWD: m_adminPassword = child.InnerText; break;
                        default: throw new Exception("Unrecognized configuration element.");
                }
                  }
        }
        else
    throw new Exception("Loading config data.");
}
```

The report server passes the configuration settings verbatim as they are stored in the report server configuration file (that is, as an XML fragment). SetConfiguration loads the settings in an XmlDocument object. Next, SetConfiguration iterates through the settings and stores them in class members for future use.

Implementing LogonUser

The LogonUser method is responsible for verifying the user credentials. The report server calls the IAuthentication.LogonUser method after the client application calls the LogonUser API. The report server passes the user credentials to the first two arguments of LogonUser. You may wonder about the purpose of the third argument—authority. It is an open-ended argument that you can use to pass additional information that might be necessary for authenticating a user. For example, suppose the customer identifier is not unique across all customers and you have to use an additional identifier, such as the company name, to uniquely identify a customer. In this case, you can pass the company name to the third argument.

```
public bool LogonUser(string userName, string password, string authority)
{
   if ((0 == String.Compare(userName,m_adminUserName,true,CultureInfo.CurrentCulture)) &&
          (password == m_adminPassword))
      return true;
   else
      return AuthenticationUtilities.IsValidUser(userName, password, m_connectionstring);
}
```

First, LogonUser checks if the interactive user is an administrator by comparing the input credentials with the administrator's credentials specified in report server configuration file. If the user is an administrator, no further validation is necessary. Otherwise, LogonUser verifies the credentials by calling the IsValidUser helper method. In real life, you can authenticate the user against a database profile store, Active Directory, or whatever trusted authority makes sense. In our case, IsValidUser calls a stored procedure (uspValidateUser) that attempts to find a matching customer in the AdventureWorks2008 database. Returning true from LogonUser tells the report server that the user is authentic. The report server responds by issuing an authentication ticket to the user.

Implementing IsValidPrincipalName

The report server calls the IsValidPrincipalName method when the administrator defines a new role assignment in Report Manager, such as granting a customer Browser rights to a given folder. The report server passes the user name and asks the custom security extension to verify it.

```
public bool IsValidPrincipalName(string principalName)
{
  return AuthenticationUtilities.IsValidPrincipalName(principalName, m_connectionstring);
}
```

My implementation of IsValidPrincipalName executes the uspIsValidPrincipalName stored procedures. This stored procedure queries the table Person.Person in the AdventureWorks2008 database to find out if a record with that customer identifier exists. Please note that the purpose of the IsValidPrincipalName method is only to verify that a user with such an identifier exists; it doesn't authenticate the user. This is similar to verifying the user identity or group name when the Reporting Services Windows-based security is used. The actual user authentication is performed in the LogonUser method.

Implementing GetUserInfo

The purpose of this method is to return a human-readable user name that will be displayed in Report Manager. For example, you can use this method to translate a system-generated customer identifier to the customer name. The report server invokes GetUserInfo for each request. Therefore, I recommend you implement some sort of caching if you decide to translate the user identity.

```
public void GetUserInfo(out IIdentity userIdentity, out IntPtr userId){
  if (HttpContext.Current != null && HttpContext.Current.User != null)
      userIdentity = HttpContext.Current.User.Identity;
  else
     userIdentity = null;

  userId = IntPtr.Zero;
}
```

My implementation of GetUserInfo doesn't translate the user identity. As a result, Report Manager shows the customer identifier in the Security pages.

19.2.3 Implementing Authorization Extension

Once the user is authenticated successfully, the report server will call your custom authorization extension for each action performed by the user, where actions might consist of navigating the report catalog, viewing reports, creating new reports, and so on. The authorization extension is responsible for validating the necessary security rules and approving or denying the user action.

Implementing CheckAccess

Upon receiving an incoming request, the report server first validates the authentication cookie. Next, it proceeds by asking your custom security extension to authorize the user request by calling one or several CheckAccess method overloads. Which CheckAccess overload that is actually called will depend on the type of the action attempted. For example, if the user requests a report, the report server calls the following CheckAccess overload:

```
public bool CheckAccess(string userName, IntPtr userToken, byte[] secDesc, ReportOperation requiredOperation)
```

All CheckAccess overload methods have the same signature except for the last enumeration argument, which specifies the type of action that is being attempted. For this reason, I refactored the authorization logic in a helper function called CheckOperations. First, the code in this function determines whether the user name matches the administrator name. If it does, access is granted to the user regardless of the requested operation. If not, the CheckOperations proceeds by inspecting the security policy defined for this user.

Note that the report server doesn't pass the user password to CheckAccess because at this point authentication has already succeeded. As long as the authentication ticket is present and valid, the report server considers the user authentic. This eliminates the need for authenticating the user with each request.

The report server may decide to call a single CheckAccess overload several times. For example, when the user requests a report, the report server first calls a CheckAccess overload to determine whether the user has permission to the given report (requiredOperation is ReadProperties). The report server then calls the same overload to determine whether the user has rights to execute the report (requiredOperation is ExecuteAndView). The authorization extension tells the report server if the user is permitted to perform the requested action. If the user is not authorized, the report server denies access and throws a Not Authorized Error exception.

Unfortunately, the report server doesn't pass the report catalog item to CheckAccess, such as the report name, when the user views a report. Yet, you may need to know what item the user is trying to access in order to implement more granular security policies. Currently, the only way to "get" the item is to parse the request payload, as follows:

```
System.Web.HttpContext.Current.Request request = System.Web.HttpContext.Current.Request;
 if (request.Headers["SOAPAction"] == null)       {
    // GET request; request.Url contains the report path
 }
 else     {
   // POST request
   stream = request.InputStream;
   byte[] requestBody = new byte[stream.Length];
   stream.Read(requestBody, 0, requestBody.Length);
   request.InputStream.Position = 0L;
   string request = Encoding.ASCII.GetString(requestBody);
   // parse the request POST payload to get the item path
 }
```

The authorization extension determines if the user is authorized to perform a given action by inspecting the security policy set up for this user. When the report server calls CheckAccess, it also passes the security policy defined for the catalog item as a byte array under the secDesc argument. For example, suppose the user has requested the Customer Orders report and you have authorized four users to view the report.

After the authorization extension deserializes the security descriptor, the access control list collection contains four elements, one for each user. Each user element has additional collections that contain the permissions defined for all supported operations (for example, FolderOperation, ReportOperation, and so on). The report server simply tells you "Here is the item security policy that you have defined in Report Manager (or programmatically) for this user. Now tell me if I should let the user perform this action?"

Developers will probably appreciate the flexibility that the Reporting Services custom security framework provides. At its simplest implementation, authorization logic just needs to enumerate through the access control list in an attempt to find a match for the logged on user. At the same time, it supports more involved authorization scenarios. For example, section 19.3 demonstrates how to modify the authorization extension to support role membership.

Implementing GetPermissions

Another implementation detail that deserves more attention is the IAuthorizationExtension.GetPermissions method. The report server calls this method when the GetPermissions SOAP API is invoked. For example, if the user opens Report Manager and navigates through the folder structure, the Report Manager calls the GetPermissions SOAP API to determine whether the user has the required permissions to view or change catalog items. When custom security is used, the report server redirects the call to your implementation of IAuthorizationExtension.GetPermissions.

The report server passes the role-based security policy as defined in the report catalog. In its simplest form, the GetPermissions implementation filters out the permissions defined for the given user and returns them to the report server. More complicated authorization requirements may call for validating additional business rules to determine if the role-based security policy set up for this user should be honored or not.

19.2.4 Implementing Logon Pages

When the report server is configured for Windows security, the user doesn't need to log in explicitly because the application can obtain the user identity from Active Directory. However, with custom security, the user must enter login credentials. As a part of coding the custom security extension, you need to implement two ASP.NET logon pages to collect the login credentials in Report Manager and the report server.

NOTE The Microsoft-provided report designers support custom security and don't need custom logon forms. For example, when you deploy a report to the server, the report designers will discover that the server is configured for custom security and prompt the user to enter login credentials.

Implementing the Report Manager Logon page

The sample custom security extension includes a UILogon.aspx page to collect a user login before opening the Report Manager home page. If the user has not been authenticated or the authentication ticket has expired, Report Manager redirects the user to this page, which is shown in Figure 19.3.

Report Manager Login

User ID:

Password:

Logon

Figure 19.3 If the user has not logged on to the server, Report Manager redirects the user to the UILogon.aspx page.

The user enters login credentials and clicks the Logon button.

```
protected void BtnLogon_Click(object sender, System.EventArgs e)
{
    ReportServerProxy server = new ReportServerProxy();

    // Get the server name and instance from the report server web.config file
    string reportServer = ConfigurationManager.AppSettings["ReportServer"];
    string instanceName = ConfigurationManager.AppSettings["ReportServerInstance"];

    // Get the server URL from the report server using WMI
    server.Url = AuthenticationUtilities.GetReportServerUrl(reportServer, instanceName);
    server.LogonUser(TxtUser.Text, TxtPwd.Text, null);
}
```

Behind the scenes, the BtnLogon_Click event gets the server name of the machine where the report server is installed and the SQL Server 2008 instance name from the Report Manager web.config file. Then, the code calls the GetReportServerUrl to obtain the report server URL. GetReportServerUrl (code not shown) uses the Reporting Services Windows Management Instrumentation (WMI) provider to query the report server configuration file. Finally, the UILogon page calls the Reporting Services LogonUser API to log on the user to the report server. The report server delegates the call to the LogonUser method in the custom authentication extension.

When a client application invokes a Web service, the client cookie collection is not automatically sent with the call. To delegate the Report server authentication ticket to the report server, the client application (Report Manager in this case) must override the Web service proxy. Although not shown in code, the ReportServerProxy class inherits from the auto-generated proxy class and overrides its GetWebRequest and GetWebResponse methods. The GetWebRequest method forwards the cookie to the report server, while the GetWebResponse method delegates the cookie to the browser.

Implementing the Report Server Logon page

Recall that you can access the report catalog by navigating directly to the report server URL, such as http://localhost/reportserver. The Logon.aspx page collects the login credentials when this happens. Its implementation is very similar to the Report Manager logon page (UILogon.aspx) albeit much simpler.

```
private void ServerBtnLogon_Click(object sender, System.EventArgs e){
  bool passwordVerified = false;
  if ((0 == String.Compare(TxtUser.Text, "admin", true, CultureInfo.CurrentCulture)) &&  (TxtPwd.Text == "admin"))
        passwordVerified = true;

     if (passwordVerified)
     {
       FormsAuthentication.RedirectFromLoginPage(TxtUser.Text, false);
     }
     else
     {
       Response.Redirect("logon.aspx");
     }
}
```

My implementation of the Logon.aspx lets only administrators access the report server directly. For the sake of simplicity, I compare the user credentials with the administrator credentials. Note that the report server logon page doesn't need to call the LogonUser API. If the user authenticates successfully, the logon page lets the user continue by calling FormsAuthentication.RedirectFromLoginPage. As a result, the report server bypasses the authentication stage and proceeds with the authorization process.

WARNING If you change the assembly name if the web project or the namespace in the UILogon page code behind file , open the UILogon and Logon pages in design mode and update the @Page directive on the top of each page. If you don't, neither Report Manager nor the report server will be able to load the pages at run time.

19.2.5 Deploying Custom Security Extensions

Once you implement the custom security extension, you need to deploy it to the report server. Deploying a custom security extension requires many configuration steps. Missing a step will very likely result in a non-operational report server or Report Manager. To help you configure custom security, I provided copies of my configuration files in the Config folder of the book source code. However, do not just replace your files with mine! Instead, use them for reference only. Before you start, make sure to back up the report server configuration files (rsreportserver.config, web.config, and rssrvpolicy.config) and the Report Manager configuration files (web.config and rsmgrpolicy.config).

General deployment considerations

The most common scenario for using custom security is Internet report delivery. In general, Internet reporting requires installing the report server on an Internet-facing server. If you are planning to use Report Manager for report delivery, you need to make it accessible for Internet access as well. Plan to configure Report Manager and report server for Secure Sockets Layer (SSL) to secure data over the wire. Another deployment option is to make only the Report Manager accessible over Internet and install the report server on the private LAN and behind a firewall. However, the following features will not work with this deployment scenario:

- Report drillthrough in Web archive (MHTML), Excel, and HTML3.2 formats will fail to connect.
- Links in e-mail subscriptions will not work.
- Report Builder will not be available.

For more considerations about configuring the report server for Internet access, read chapter 2 and the Configuring a Report Server for Internet Access topic in SQL Server Books Online.

Deploying to the report server

Follow these steps to deploy the custom security extension to the report server.

1. Copy the Prologika.CustomSecurityExtension.dll and Prologika.CustomSecurityExtension.dll to the \Program Files\Microsoft SQL Server\MSRS10.MSSQLSERVER\Reporting Services\ReportServer\bin report server binary folder.
2. Copy the Logon.aspx page to the report server folder at \Program Files\Microsoft SQL Server\MSRS10.MSSQLSERVER\Reporting Services\ReportServer.
3. Open the report server configuration file, rsreportserver.config, in your favorite editor.
4. Locate the Extensions element and the Security and Authentication elements under it and replace them as follows:

```
<Security>
    <Extension Name="Forms"
    Type="Prologika.RS.Extensibility.CustomSecurityExtension.AuthorizationExtension,
          Prologika.CustomSecurityExtension">
                <Configuration>
                </Configuration>
    </Extension>
</Security>
    <Authentication>
        <Extension Name="Forms"  ype="Prologika.RS.Extensibility.CustomSecurityExtension.AuthenticationExtension,
                Prologika.CustomSecurityExtension">
            <Configuration>
              <AdminConfiguration>
                <ConnectionString>Data Source=.;Initial Catalog=AdventureWorks2008;
            Integrated Security=SSPI</ConnectionString>
                    <AdminLogin>Admin</AdminLogin>
                    <AdminPassword>admin</AdminPassword>
                    </AdminConfiguration>
                </Configuration>
        </Extension>
    </Authentication>
```

5. In the rsreportserver.config file, locate the AuthenticationTypes element and update it as follows:

```
<Authentication>
   <AuthenticationTypes>
         <Custom/>
      </AuthenticationTypes>
   <EnableAuthPersistence>true</EnableAuthPersistence>
</Authentication>
```

6. Open the rssrvpolicy.config file and add the following code group to grant full trust code access security rights to the extension assembly:

```
<CodeGroup class ="UnionCodeGroup"  version ="1" PermissionSetName ="FullTrust" Name="CustomSecurity"
         Description="Code group for the custom security extension">
         <IMembershipCondition class ="UrlMembershipCondition" version ="1"
      Url ="C:\ Program Files\Microsoft SQL Server\MSRS10.MSSQLSERVER\Reporting
         Services\ReportServer\bin\Prologika.CustomSecurityExtension.dll" />
</CodeGroup >
```

7. Open the report server web configuration file, web.config, and make the following changes:

```
<system.web> <!- for reference only-- >
    <authentication mode="Forms">
        <forms loginUrl="logon.aspx" name="sqlAuthCookie" timeout="60" slidingExpiration="true" path="/">
        </fo rms>
    </authentication>
    <authorization>
        <deny users="?" />
    </authorization>
```

Here, we change the report server authentication mode to Forms, specify the login page and the cookie details. Change the cookie timeout (in minutes) as needed.

8. Finally, set the identity setting to False as follows:

```
<identity impersonate="false"/>
```

Deploying to Report Manager

Follow these steps to deploy the custom security extension to Report Manager:

1. Copy Prologika.RS.Extensibility.CustomSecurityExtension.dll and Prologika.RS.Extensibility.CustomSecurityExtension.pdb to the Report Manager binary folder at \Program Files\Microsoft SQL Server\MSRS10.MSSQLSERVER\Reporting Services\ReportManager\Bin.
2. Copy the UILogon.aspx page to the \Program Files\Microsoft SQL Server\MSRS10.-MSSQLSERVER\Reporting Services\ReportManager\Pages folder.
3. Open the Report Manager web.config file and change the identity setting to False:

```
<identity impersonate="false"/>
```

4. Locate the appSettings element and add the following application settings to it.

```
<add key="ReportServer" value="<server>"/>
<add key="ReportServerInstance" value="<Instance Name>"/>
```

The UILogon.aspx passes these settings to the WMI provider to obtain the report server URL. Set the ReportServer setting to the machine name where the report server is installed. Set the ReportServerInstance setting to the name of the SQL Server instance, such as MSSQLSERVER if the SQL Server is installed on the default instance.

5. Open the Report Manager policy file, rsmgrpolicy.config, located in the \Program Files\Microsoft SQL Server\MSRS10.MSSQLSERVER\Reporting Services\ReportManager folder. Locate the MyComputer code group and change the PermissionSetName attribute from Execution to *FullTrust* as follows:

```
<CodeGroup class="FirstMatchCodeGroup" version="1" PermissionSetName=" FullTrust"
    Description="This code group grants MyComputer code Execution permission. ">
    <IMembershipCondition class="ZoneMembershipCondition" version="1" Zone="MyComputer" />
```

6. Open rsreportserver.config located in the \Program Files\Microsoft SQL Server\MSRS10.MSSQLSERVER\Reporting Services\ReportServer folder. Find the UI element and change it as follows:

```
<UI>
  <CustomAuthenticationUI>
    <loginUrl>/Pages/UILogon.aspx</loginUrl>
    <UseSSL>False</UseSSL>
  </CustomAuthenticationUI>
  <ReportServerUrl>http://<server>/ReportServer</ReportServerUrl>
  <PageCountMode>Estimate</PageCountMode>
</UI>
```

Set UseSSL to True if the report server is configured to use SSL. The server name in the ReportServerUrl setting is important because the authentication ticket will be bound to this name. Therefore, if you use localhost, you will only be able to access Report Manager by using localhost in the Report Manager URL, such as http://localhost/reports. I recommend you specify the machine name instead of localhost and always use the machine name in the Report Manager and report server URLs to avoid delegation issues with cookies.

7. Use the Windows Services applet or Reporting Services Configuration Manager and restart the SQL Server Reporting Services service.

Additional deployment steps

Based on your custom security extension requirements and implementation, you may need additional deployment steps to finalize the extension configuration and tighten security. The following list suggests extra steps that can be appropriate for some deployments:

1. Change the connection string in RSReportServer.config (ConnectionString setting) to point to your user profile database.
2. Change the administrator credentials, AdminLogin and AdminPassword to something less guessable.
3. Check the file permissions on the RSReportServer.config file to verify that only local administrators have permission to open it.
4. If end users won't use Report Manager for report delivery, consider moving Report Manager to an intranet server in a private LAN so it is not accessible by web users. This deployment scenario is discussed in more details in chapter 2.
5. Definitely consider using SSL to secure the connection to the report server. Once the server certificate is installed, change the SecureConnectionLevel setting in the rsreportserver.config to level 2.
6. This is a step specific for the custom security extension sample. Execute the ddl.sql script in the Database folder to the AdventureWorks2008 database to create the stored procedures.
7. This is a step specific for the custom security extension sample. Since the connection string uses Windows Integrated security to connect to the AdventureWorks2008 database, grant the login that the Reporting Services service runs under read permissions to the AdventureWorks2008 database. You can obtain the account from the Reporting Services Configuration Manager (Service Account tab).
8. This is a step specific for the custom security extension sample. Deploy the sample Reports project to the desired report server folder. By default, the project will be deployed to the AMRS folder.

Now that the custom security extension is deployed, let's take it for a ride.

19.2.6 Working with the Custom Security Extension

To quickly test that custom security is working, navigate to the report server URL, such as http://<server>/ReportServer. If all is well, the report server should redirect you to the Logon.aspx page. Enter *admin* as a user name and password. The report server should show the report catalog folders. If this is not the case or you confronted with an error message, don't panic. Go through the deployment steps in section 19.2.5 and make sure that you haven't skipped a step. In addition, review the troubleshooting and debugging tips in this section.

Setting up security policies

By default, only the administrator can log in to the report server. To let end users access the report catalog, you need to grant them the necessary rights in Report Manager. Follow these steps to grant Adventure Works customers rights to view the Customer Orders report.

1. Open the Report Manager application by navigating to the Report Manager URL, such as http://<server>/reports. To avoid delegation issues with the authentication ticket, make sure to use the same URL as the one you specified in the ReportServerUrl setting in the RSReportServer.config file.
2. Report Manager should show the UILogon.aspx page (see again Figure 19.3). Enter *admin* as a user name and password and click the Logon button.

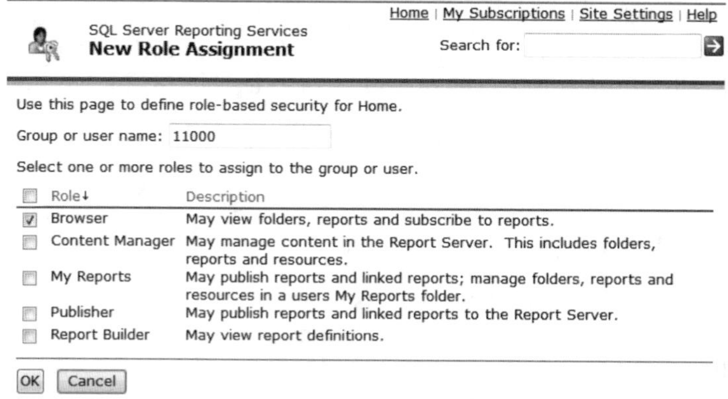

Figure 19.4 Use Report Manager to define for every user a role assignment that grants Browser rights to the Home folder.

To make things easier, we will grant users Browser rights to the root Home folder as they will propagate to all subfolders. In real life, consider more granular security policies.

3. Select the Properties tab to access the Security page for the Home folder.
4. Click the New Role Assignment button to open the New Role Assignment page, as shown in Figure 19.4.
5. In the Group or User Name field, enter the customer identifier, such as 11000. You can open the Sales.vIndividualCustomer view in the AdventureWorks2008 database to see the customer details. Use the CustomerID column for the user name.
6. Check the Browser role and click OK.
7. Repeat the last two steps to add a few more customers.

Each time you add a new customer, the report server calls your implementation of IAuthenticationExtension.IsValidPrincipalName to verify the user name.

Verifying user access

Once the Adventure Works customers have been granted access, they can request reports. Let's log in as one of the users you've just set up and verify that the user can run the Customer Orders report.

1. Open a new instance (not a new tab) of Internet Explorer and navigate to the Report Manager application.

2. In the UILogon.aspx page, enter the customer identifier for user name, such as 11000. Use the following query to obtain the customer password.

```
SELECT    P.BusinessEntityID as CustomerID, PW.PasswordSalt as Password
FROM      Person.Person AS P INNER JOIN
          Person.Password AS PW ON P.BusinessEntityID = PW.BusinessEntityID
WHERE     (P.BusinessEntityID = 11000)
```

3. Navigate to the AMRS folder and click the Customer Orders report. If all is well, you should see the report in Figure 19.4.

   If you don't see the Customer Orders report, open the Reports project in BIDS and deploy the project to the report server.

19.3 Implementing Role Membership

As useful as it is, our custom security implementation has one caveat. It requires you to set up individual security polices for each user, which isn't very practical for Web applications that support thousands of users. Thankfully, application roles provide a practical means for you to group users with identical permissions—in the same manner that Windows groups simplify maintaining Windows-based security.

19.3.1 Understanding Role Membership

In practice, your application may already support assigning users to application-defined roles. For example, if your organization is doing business with several companies, you might already have company-specific login for the employees of those companies that require access to your extranet site. If you have a set of existing login accounts, you can simplify security maintenance by assigning report server permissions on a per company basis using application roles. In this example, your application roles will be scoped at the company level.

To bring a touch of reality to this code sample, assume that Adventure Works has introduced several levels of customer membership based on the customer order volume, such as Platinum, Gold, and Silver. Please note that it is entirely up to the developer to determine the actual implementation and semantics of the application roles. The business rules behind the role membership are of no importance to the role-based implementation. Adding another level of flexibility, this role-based membership implementation supports assigning users to multiple roles. The granted permissions are additive as well, which means that the user receives a superset of the permissions assigned to all the roles the user belongs to, plus the individual permissions assigned explicitly to the user.

Here are the high-level implementation goals for this custom role-based authentication:

- Support for assigning users to multiple roles.
- Allow the report administrator set up both individual- and role-based security policies.
- Authorize the user by granting a superset of individual- and role-based permissions assigned to the user.
- Improve performance by caching the user role in the ASP.NET cache object.

Now, let's see what it will take to enhance the sample custom security extension to support role membership.

19.3.2 Implementing Database Schema

As it stands, the Adventure Works database schema doesn't include support for role membership. That is why you'll need to add two additional tables: Security.CustomerRole and Security.Role, as shown in Figure 19.5.

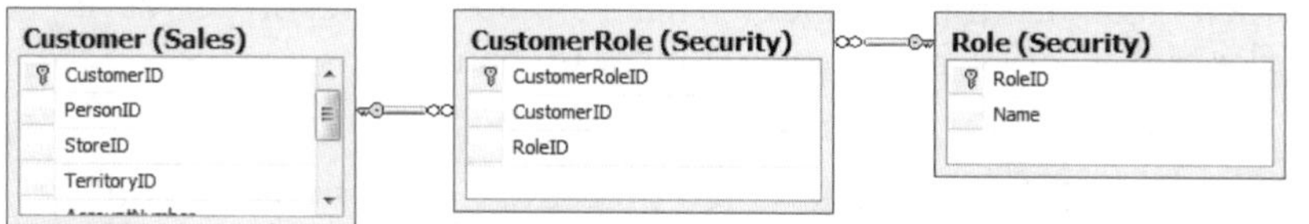

Figure 19.5 Add the CustomerRole and Role tables to support role membership.

The table Role stores the application roles, while the table CustomerRole defines the roles to which a given customer belongs. Remember, a customer may belong to more than one role. There are two scripts in the Database folder of the book source code. The ddl.sql script creates the new tables and stored procedures required for supporting role membership. The data.sql script populates the new tables with some sample data. The report server doesn't impose any restrictions on the role membership schema, so feel free to enhance the schema to meet your requirements, like supporting nested roles, subsets of permissions, and so on.

19.3.3 Implementing Role Authentication

Extending the custom security extension to support role authentication and authorization is easy. First, we need to enhance the authentication extension to support role names as valid principal names. Second, we need to change the authorization extension to evaluate not only the user permissions but the permissions assigned to the roles to which the user belongs.

Validating the principal name

Recall that the report server calls IsValidPrincipalName each time you change or add a security policy. Before the new security policy is created, the report server calls IsValidPrincipalName in your custom extension to validate the principal name. However, the report server doesn't validate the semantics of the principal name, such as whether it is for a role or an individual user. In fact, the report server itself has no built-in support for handling role assignments.

This custom security extension is responsible for enforcing the role membership authentication and authorization rules. Once the security extension acknowledges that the principal name is valid by returning true from the IsValidPrincipalName call, the report server simply proceeds by recording the changes to the security policy in the report catalog. Therefore, to validate the principal name, change the uspIsValidPrincipalName stored procedure to handle both possibilities: an individual user or an application-defined role.

```
ALTER PROCEDURE [Security].[uspIsValidPrincipalName]
(
  @PrincipalName nvarchar(50)
)
AS
IF ISNUMERIC(@principalName) = 1
       SELECT BusinessEntityID FROM Person.Person WHERE BusinessEntityID=CAST(@PrincipalName AS INT)
ELSE
      SELECT RoleID FROM Role WHERE Name = @PrincipalName
```

Since now the input principle name could be either a customer identifier or a role, you need to query the appropriate table. If a match is found, IAuthenticationExtension.IsValidPrincipalName returns true and the report server happily records the policy change.

Interestingly, even if you change a single policy, the report server validates all security policies assigned for this item. For example, suppose you create a new policy assignment to grant a user Browser rights to a given folder. The report server calls IsValidPrincipalName as many times as the number of policies assigned for this folder. That is because the report server rebuilds the entire security descriptor for every item each time it is changed.

Creating role assignments

Once you've changed the uspIsValidPrincipalName stored procedure, you can use Report Manager to define role-based security policies. Follow these steps to grant members of the Gold role rights to view all reports.

1. Open the Report Manager application by navigating to the Report Manager URL, such as http://<server>/reports.
2. Report Manager should show the UILogon.aspx page. Enter admin as a user name and password and click the Logon button.
3. Select the Properties tab to access the Security page for the Home folder.
4. Click the New Role Assignment button to open the New Role Assignment page.
5. In the Group or User Name field, enter *Gold* to grant members of the Gold role rights to view reports.
6. Check the Browser role and click OK.

The report server calls IAuthentication.IsValidPrincipalName for each role assignment to verify the principal name. If all is well, the Report Manager will create the Gold role assignment successfully and your Security page should match the one shown in Figure 19.6.

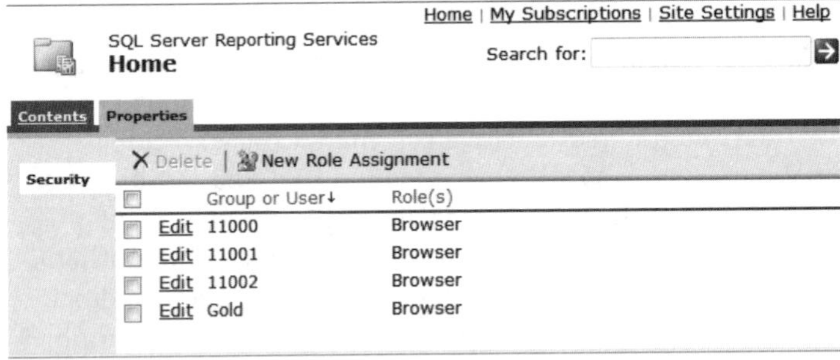

Figure 19.6 Use Report Manager to define both user and role security policies.

19.3.4 Implementing Role Authorization

When the report server receives a request for a given action against the report catalog, it asks the security extension to authorize the request by calling one or more CheckAccess methods in the custom authorization extension. The report server passes the principal name (the customer identifier in this case) and the security policy descriptor associated with the given report catalog item to IAuthorizationExtension.CheckAccess so the custom extension can evaluate the security policy and authorize or deny the operation. The report server doesn't know or care if the security policy is an individual- or role-based policy. Therefore, the security descriptor may contain both individual and role-based polices.

Enhancing CheckAccess

Implementing role-based authorization requires not only checking whether the user has been assigned explicit rights to the report catalog item, but also if the user belongs to roles that are permitted to perform the requested action. Fortunately, this enhancement to the CheckOperations helper function is easy.

```
private bool CheckOperations(string principalName, AceCollection acl, object requiredOperation)
{
    if (IsUserAuthorized(principalName, acl, requiredOperation)) return true;

   // No individual policy established. Check user role membership
   string[] roles = this.GetPrincipalRoles(principalName);

   if (roles != null)    {
      foreach (string role in roles)
      {
         if (IsUserAuthorized(role, acl, requiredOperation)) return true;
      }
   }
   return false;
}
```

First, the code checks whether the user has an individual security policy assigned. For example, glancing back to Figure 19.6, if customer 11000 requests a report, IsUserAuthorized returns true because this user has explicit rights to view reports. However, this wouldn't be the case for customer 11003 because this customer doesn't have an explicit security policy defined. However, 11003 may have been assigned to a role that has the required rights. To verify customer role membership permissions, the code retrieves the roles associated with the customer by calling the GetPrincipalRoles helper method. Next, the code iterates through the roles in an attempt to find a role permitted to perform the action.

Caching roles

You'll need to decide up front at what point your custom security extension retrieves the user roles. Of course, this has to happen before the user request is authorized. One approach is to retrieve the roles in each CheckAccess overload. However, this can generate excessive database traffic since a single action against the report catalog may result in several CheckAccess calls. Instead, consider retrieving the roles on demand for each user and caching them in the ASP.NET cache object. The GetPrincipalRoles method demonstrates this technique.

```
private string[] GetPrincipalRoles(string principalName) {
   // attempt to retrieve roles from cache
   string[] roles = HttpContext.Current.Cache[principalName] as string[];

   if (roles == null)
   {
      // get user roles
      DataSet dsRoles = Util.GetUserRoles(principalName);
      if (dsRoles.Tables[0].Rows.Count > 0)
      {
         roles = new string[dsRoles.Tables[0].Rows.Count];
         for (int i = 0; i < dsRoles.Tables[0].Rows.Count; i++)
         {
            roles[i] = dsRoles.Tables[0].Rows[i][0].ToString();
         }
         // cache the user roles
         HttpContext.Current.Cache.Insert(principalName, roles);
      }
   }
   return roles;
}
```

First, the code attempts to load the roles from the cache. If the user roles are not yet cached, the code retrieves them by calling the GetUserRoles helper function. Next, the code loads the roles in a string array and caches it in the ASP.NET cache object. Since the report server application domain is hosted by ASP.NET, I use HttpContext.Current to access the ASP.NET cache object.

NOTE Because this example does not specify explicit cache expiration, the cached roles will remain in the cache for the lifetime of the report server application domain. If your application serves many concurrent users and you are worried about excessive memory consumption, you may want to consider implementing a cache expiration policy.

You may wonder why I am not retrieving and caching the user roles in the LogonUser method. Recall that the LogonUser is called once for each user. In a web farm environment, this means that the LogonUser will be invoked only on the server that handles the authentication request. Consequently, the other servers will never be able to access and evaluate the role policies. Since the custom authorization extension is called with each request, it retrieves and caches roles on each server.

Enhancing GetPermissions

The report server also calls IAuthorizationExtension.GetPermissions when the GetPermission SOAP API is invoked. For example, Report Manager needs to know if the user has the rights to browse a given folder so it can hide or show that folder. Report Manager calls GetPermission in order to update the user interface based on the user's security policy. Use the following code to make IAuthorizationExtension.GetPermissions role-aware:

```
public StringCollection GetPermissions(string userName, IntPtr userToken, SecurityItemType itemType, byte[] secDesc)
{
   StringCollection permissions = new StringCollection();
   if (0 == String.Compare(userName, m_adminUserName, true,  CultureInfo.CurrentCulture))
   {
      foreach (CatalogOperation oper in m_CatOperNames.Keys)
      {
            if (!permissions.Contains((string)m_CatOperNames[oper])) permissions.Add((string)m_CatOperNames[oper]);
       }
   }
    // add the rest of the permissions to administrator. . .
   else
   {
      AceCollection acl = DeserializeAcl(secDesc);
      // get permission for the individual user
      GetPermissions (userName, acl, permissions);
      // add also the permissions assigned to the user roles
      string[] roles = HttpContext.Current.Cache[userName] as string[];
      if (roles != null)
      {
           foreach (string role in roles) GetPermissions(role, acl, permissions);
      }
   }
}
```

First, the code checks if the user is an administrator. If this is the case, the code grants the user unrestricted access by returning all permissions. Otherwise, the code calls the GetPermissions helper method twice to return the union of the individual permissions assigned to the user and the permissions assigned to the role. To test a role, start Report Manager, log in as customer 11003, and view the Customer Orders report. Although you haven't granted individual rights to 11003, the customer can view the report because the data.slq script assigns this customer to the Gold role.

19.4 Integrating Custom Security

Now that we've successfully tested custom security with Report Manager, let's integrate it with the Adventure Works Web portal. The web portal leverages the ASP.NET Forms Authentication infrastructure to authenticate and authorize the user. As part of this integration effort, let's also migrate the Customer Orders report to the Adventure Works portal integrate the report with the application security model.

19.4.1 Custom Security vs. Trusted Subsystem

Before showing you how to integrate custom security with client applications, I would like to remind you that custom security is not the only option. For example, another common approach for enforcing restricted access from the application to the report server is *trusted subsystem*.

Understanding trusted subsystem

With the trusted subsystem approach, the ReportViewer control submits all requests to the report server under a single "trusted" Windows account, as shown in Figure 19.7. Separately, the application authenticates and authorizes users using ASP.NET Forms Authentication or another authentication method. As such, the Report Viewer assumes that only authenticated, authorized users are able to request a report in the first place. When the user does request a report, the application submits the report request under a "trusted" account that is used for all requests sent to the report server.

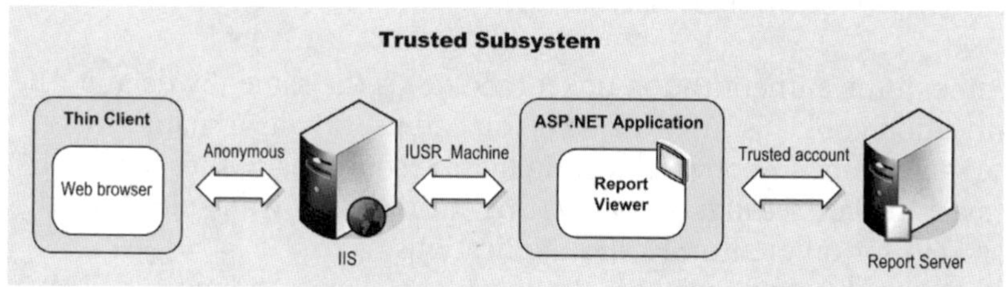

Figure 19.7 With the trusted subsystem, the calls to the report server go under a single trusted account.

By default, the application will pass the Windows identity it runs under as the trusted account. This will be the ASP.NET process identity (IIS 5.0) or the application pool identity (IIS 6.0). For example, if the application runs under IIS 6 or above (Vista or Windows 2003 and above), you can change the identity of the IIS application pool to which the application is assigned to a domain account. With IIS 5.0 (Windows XP or Windows 2000) you can change the ASP.NET process identity in the ASP.NET machine.config. Alternatively, with IIS 5.0, you can change the IIS application protection mode to High and use Component Services to set the identity of the COM+ Application.

Trusted Subsystem pros and cons

The advantage of the trusted subsystem approach is that it is fairly easy to set up. The application authenticates and authorizes access to the report server. If the user is authorized, the application runs the report under the trusted account on behalf of the user.

On the downside, when trusted subsystem is used, the report server sees all requests coming under the same account as though they came from the same user. In other words, the report server won't be able to differentiate among users. As a result, the users cannot use the My

Reports feature. In addition, the report author cannot configure data source connections to use Windows integrated security, or use the User!UserID expression to filter data based on the user's identity. If you need the user's identity in your reports, I recommend you use custom security. I purposely exclude passing the customer identifier as a parameter to the report since this approach has security risks.

19.4.2 Integrating Custom Security

Implementing custom security in web applications is not something you haven't seen already. That's because Report Manager is in itself a web application. Before the user can view a report, your web application needs to log in the user similar to what you've seen already with the Report Manager UILogon.aspx page. However, integrating custom security with a web application that uses ASP.NET Forms Authentication can be even easier. That's because with the proper configuration, the report server and the web application can share the same authentication ticket. The Web project that is included in the book source code demonstrates this scenario.

Configuring Forms Authentication

To share the authentication ticket, be sure to use the same Forms Authentication settings in the web.config files of the application and report server as follows:

```
<forms loginUrl="logon.aspx" name=".ASPXAUTH" timeout=  "600" slidingExpiration="true" path="/"></forms>
<machineKey
validationKey="36AB5B499984F8AA309BC02E4C00E7DBD4DBF575561F1846639016F80CE99D0DF4B597C7949C07BD89
559D319C843BC7C2006B438D1B125FF6DE7A686092D782"
decryptionKey="CD8BCADC2EF8DF8ACA256FE1DF681E7DB2254526DE94D9EB"
validation='SHA1'/>
```

First, make sure that the name of the authentication ticket (cookie) is the same. By default, the name of the Forms Authentication cookie is .ASPXAUTH. You can use whatever name you want as long as you use the same name in both web.config files. Second, make sure that both applications use the same machine key settings for encrypting the cookie. By default, ASP.NET generates different machine keys for different ASP.NET applications.

If you want all applications on the server to share the same key, change the machine key settings in the machine.config.comments file which is located in the \Windows\Microsoft.NET\Framework\<version>\CONFIG folder. Or, if you want only the report server and the web application to share the same machine key, add the machineKey setting to their web.config files. If you have a web farm of report servers, they need to have the same machine key in order for custom security to work. For more information about the machineKey setting, read the articles How to Configure MachineKey in ASP.NET 2.0 and Forms Authentication Across Applications (see Resources).

Configuring the ReportViewer Web Server control

If you use the ReportViewer control for report delivery, remember to set up its ReportServerCredentials property to support custom security. If you skip this step, you will get the following rather obscure error message when you attempt to view a report:

```
<title>Object moved</title></  head><body> <h2>Object moved to
<a href="/ReportServer/login.aspx?ReturnUrl=%2freportserver%2fReportExecution2005.asmx">here</a  >
```

The reason for this error is that, by default, ReportViewer doesn't pass the authentication ticket to the report server. As a result, the report server redirects to the Login page. To avoid this issue, configure the ReportServerCredentials property as follows:

```
reportViewer.ServerReport.ReportServerUrl = new Uri(ConfigurationManager.AppSettings["serverUrl"]);
reportViewer.ServerReport.ReportPath = "/AMRS/Customer Orders";
reportViewer.ServerReport.ReportServerCredentials = new MyReportServerCredentials();

public class MyReportServerCredentials : IReportServerCredentials {
   public MyReportServerCredentials() { }
   public WindowsIdentity ImpersonationUser    {
      get {return null;}
   }
   public ICredentials NetworkCredentials    {
      get { return null;}
   }
public bool GetFormsCredentials(out Cookie authCookie, out string user, out string password, out string authority)    {
      user = password = authority = null;
      HttpCookie cookie = HttpContext.Current.Request.Cookies[".ASPXAUTH"];
      if (cookie == null) HttpContext.Current.Re sponse.Redirect("login.aspx");

      Cookie netCookie = new Cookie(cookie.Name, cookie.Value);
      if (cookie.Domain == null)
         netCookie.Domain = ttpContext.Current.Request.ServerVariables["SERVER_NAME"].ToUpper();
      netCookie.Expires = cookie.Expires;
      netCookie.Path = cookie.Path;
      netCookie.Secure = cookie.Secure;
      authCookie = netCookie;
      return true;
   }
} // MyReportServerCredentials
```

You need to set the ReportServerCredentials property to an instance of a class that implements IReportServerCredentials. Since the report server is configured for custom security, you need to implement the GetFormsCredentials method only. Behind the scenes, the ReportViewer Web server control caches the IReportServerCredentials results. It invokes GetFormsCredentials when the control is initialized. Then, the control invokes the LogonUser API and caches the authentication ticket. Subsequent report requests, such as navigating a page or using the interactive features in a report, reuse the cached authentication ticket.

When the custom application uses ASP.NET Forms Authentication, the implementation of GetFormsCredentials is simple. First, the code sets the user, password, and authority output arguments to null because we will use the authentication ticket returned by the ASP.NET Forms Authentication infrastructure. Alternatively, if you prefer to work with user credentials, you could set the authCookie argument to null and use the user credentials for authentication. However, working with the user credentials may present a security risk so it should be avoided whenever possible.

Next, the code assumes that the user has already logged in to the application and the ASP.NET Forms authentication ticket has been generated. If this is not the case, the code redirects the user to the login page. If the cookie is present, the only task left is to translate the cookie to System.Net.Cookie and pass it back to the ReportViewer control.

19.5 Troubleshooting Custom Security

Getting a custom security extension to work as intended could be more challenging than implementing it. First, there could be bugs in the code, which you can eliminate by debugging the extension. External factors, such as browser security and cookie delegation issues, can cause some grief as well.

19.5.1 Debugging the Custom Security Extension

When testing your custom security extension, you may need to step through the code. Follow these steps to debug the security extension:

1. Open the Report Manager application in a browser.
2. In Visual Studio, go to the Debug ⇨ Attach to Process menu and check the Show Processes from All Users and Show Processes in All Sessions checkboxes.
3. In the Available Processes, locate the ReportingServicesService.exe process and click the Attach button.
4. Set breakpoints in the security extension as needed. For example to troubleshoot user authentication, set a breakpoint inside the LogonUser method.
5. Log on in to Report Manager using the credentials of the user you want to test.

As you navigate through the report catalog, the code breakpoints will be hit.

TIP Debugging the custom security extension from a web application is even easier. Add both the web application and security extension projects to the same VS.NET solution. Set the web application as a startup project. Press F5 to debug the solution.

19.5.2 Troubleshooting Tips

Here are some tips which may save you hours of debugging and head scratching when troubleshooting custom security. To start with, I can't emphasize this fact enough: just like ASP.NET Forms Authentication, Reporting Services custom security is cookie-based. If the browser doesn't pass the cookie back to the report server, the user will be redirected to the Logon page. What follows is a list of the most common reasons the browser fails to pass the cookie back and how to avoid or work around them.

Using localhost
Using localhost to launch the client tricks the browser into believing that the report server and your Web applications are on different domains. Instead, when testing custom security locally, specify the machine name , such as http://<mymachinename>/adventureworks/default.aspx) as opposed to http://localhost/adventureworks/default.aspx.

Restrictive browser policies
Sometimes, the authentication cookie is not transmitted back because the browser privacy settings are configured to block cookies. This may sound like a no-brainer, but you will be surprised how often folks forget to glance at the browser status bar to see if the authentication cookie simply can't get through. If this is the case, assign the report server Web site to the Trusted Sites zone.

Cross-domain security issues
Suppose you have installed the report server and the Web application on two different domains. For example, the report server machine belongs to the www.abc.com domain, while

the Web application is on the www.xyz.com domain. For security reasons, Internet Explorer doesn't permit cross-domain cookies, so the authentication cookie won't be sent to the report server.

The no-brainer workaround for this problem is to move the applications to the same domain. You'll also need to change the TranslateCookie method in the overloaded proxy class and set the cookie Domain property to your domain (.xyz.com in this example). Please note that both applications can be physically located on two separate servers as long as both machines belong to the same domain.

If adding both computers to the same domain is not an option, another workaround is to invoke the LogonUser API on the report server machine. For example, once the custom application authenticates the user, it can redirect to an ASP.NET page residing on the report server machine, which in turn calls LogonUser. As a result, the authentication cookie is scoped to the domain to which the report server belongs.

Of course, you still need decide how the Web application will pass the user credentials to the report server. This may present a security risk because a hacker may intercept the request to the report server, so take extra steps to ensure that security is not compromised. For example, you could use IP address filtering and restrict access to the ASP.NET page that contains IP address of the Web application server.

Cookie configuration

Reporting Services uses the same syntax to set the authentication cookie as ASP.NET Forms Authentication. For example, if you find out that the authentication cookie expires too soon and you get an Object Moved error, you may want to increase the cookie timeout. If the report server is deployed in a web farm environment, the cookie configuration settings of the cluster machines may not match. Check all instances of the report server web.config configuration files and make sure that you use identical cookie settings. Please see the Forms Authentication across Applications link in the Resources section.

If Report Manager integrates with a third-party or a custom authentication service that issues its own authentication cookie and you need to pass the cookie to the report server, you need to configure Report Manager to relay the cookie. By default, the Report Manager sends only the report server authentication cookie (the one that you specify in the Forms element). To configure Report Manager to relay additional cookies, open the rsreportserver.config file, locate the <UI> element and add a PassThroughCookies collection that specifies the name of the custom cookies, as follows:

```
<UI>
  <CustomAuthenticationUI>
      <CustomAuthenticationUI>
            <loginUrl>/Pages/UILogon.aspx</loginUrl>
            <Us eSSL>False</UseSSL>
      </CustomAuthenticationUI>
      <ReportServerUrl>http://nw8000/ReportServer</ReportServerUrl>
    <PassThroughCookies>
      <PassThroughCookie>cookiename1</PassThroughCookie>
      <PassThroughCookie>cookiename2</PassThroughCookie>
    </PassThroughCookies>
  </CustomAuthenticationUI>
   ...
</UI>
```

Issues with non-browser clients

While the browser automatically sends the cookie to the report server, you are on your own when integrating Windows Forms clients and other types of applications with a report server that is configured for Forms Authentication. Basically, you need to store the authentication cookie after the LogonUser call and send it back with each subsequent request. Although originally written for Reporting Services 2000, my Forms Authentication Tester sample (see Resources) can help you understand the implementation details.

In search for cookies

When you're through troubleshooting custom security, it's time to verify that the cookie is successfully sent by the client application. By now, it should be clear to you that the Holy Grail of custom security is successful cookie management. But suppose that after following the above troubleshooting tips, the browser still redirects to the login page. The most likely reason for this behavior is that the browser doesn't send the cookie to the report server.

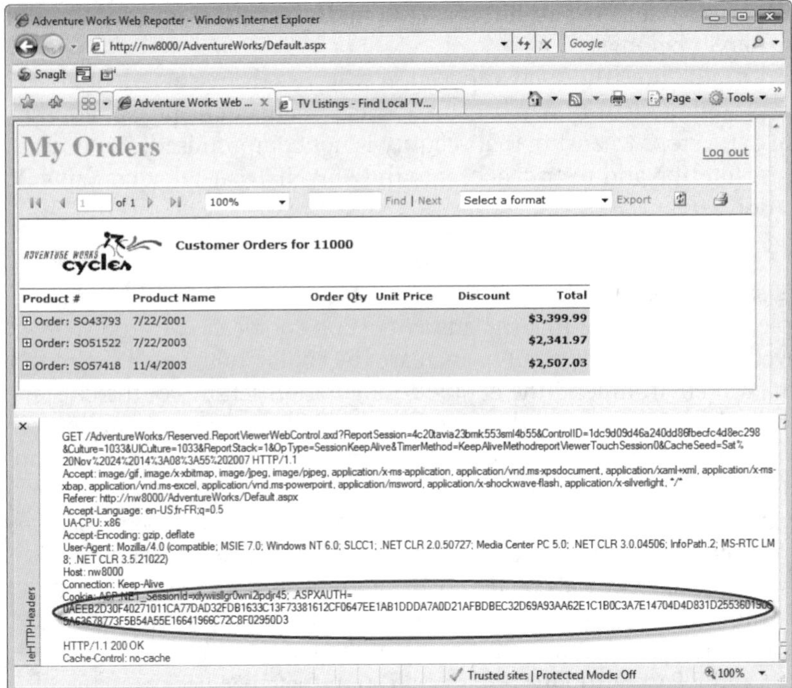

Figure 19.8 You can use the ieHTTPHeaders tool to verify that the browser sends the authentication ticket to the server.

Therefore, it is essential to verify that the authentication cookie has been sent back to the report server. You can do this using a tracing utility, such as ieHttpHeaders (see Resources). It intercepts the traffic between the browser and server and displays the HTTP headers on the screen. The steps below explain how to use ieHTTPHeaders to verify that the authentication cookie has been successfully transmitted.

1. Download and install ieHTTPHeaders.
2. Open Internet Explorer and enable ieHTTPHeaders by going to the Tools ⇨ Toolbars ⇨ Explorer Bar ⇨ ieHTTPHeaders.
3. Request the default.aspx page in the Web project. The ieHttpHeaders pane will show the HTTP headers sent to the server, including the cookies, as shown in Figure 19.8.

If the authentication cookie is not included in the client request, custom security will fail because the report server will not be able to find the authentication ticket.

Script synchronization issues

Another reason for authentication failure is when the request to the report server is submitted before the browser retrieves the authentication cookie. This one got me really bad when implementing custom security in one of my projects. It turned out that, for some reason, the developer didn't want to use the ReportViewer control to render the report. Instead, the developer had decided to use a client-side JavaScript function that sets the browser window.location property to the report URL.

Eventually, I traced this down to a synchronization issue. The browser would submit the request before the page was fully loaded. The resolution in such a case is to use ReportViewer or make sure that your client-side script is called from the browser window.onload event.

19.6 Summary

In this chapter, you've seen how to extend the Reporting Services security architecture by writing a custom security extension. Consider custom security when the default Windows security is not an option, such as when report-enabling an Internet-facing application and you want to pass the user identity to the report server.

A custom security extension includes a custom authentication extension and a custom authorization extension. The custom authentication extension is responsible for authenticating the user. The custom authorization extension grants access based on the security policies that the administrator has set up in Report Manager. To simplify the effort required to set up many individual polices, consider adding role membership features to your custom security extension.

19.7 Resources

Microsoft Security Extension Sample
(http://tinyurl.com/33lhoy)— The Microsoft Custom Security sample demonstrates how to implement a custom security extension.

Using Forms Authentication in Reporting Services
(http://tinyurl.com/3xvkvg)— Although written for Reporting Services 2000, this whitepaper is a great resource for learning the internals of custom security.

How To: Configure MachineKey in ASP.NET 2.0
(http://tinyurl.com/3coh67)— This How To explains the <machineKey> element in the Web.config file and shows how to configure the <machineKey> element.

Forms Authentication across Applications
(http://tinyurl.com/397ntu)— By using these instructions, you can use reuse the ASP.NET Forms Authentication ticket in the report server.

Forms Authentication Tester
(http://tinyurl.com/2wkkvs)— Shows how you can integrate a Windows Forms application with Reporting Services custom security.

IEHTTPHeaders
(http://tinyurl.com/yyg3eh)— ieHTTPHeaders is an explorer bar for Microsoft Internet Explorer that will display the HTTP Headers sent and received by Internet Explorer and can be used for debugging cookies.

Chapter 20

Extending Report Delivery

Recall that Reporting Services supports on-demand and subscription report delivery. The latter option lets users subscribe to reports to automate the report delivery process. Out of the box, Reporting Services supports subscription delivery to e-mail recipients, shared folders, and SharePoint libraries. However, you can extend Reporting Services subscriptions by plugging in custom delivery extensions that send reports to other destinations.

This chapter teaches you how to implement a custom delivery extension for delivering reports to a Web service. My Web Service delivery extension can send a report to an arbitrary web method that you specify when you configure the extension. First, I will give you an overview of custom delivery extensions so that you have better understanding of how they work. Then, I will walk you through the steps to implement, deploy, and debug the Web Service delivery extension. Finally, I'll show you how to configure and use the custom delivery extension to deliver a report to a Web service. You need Visual Studio 2008 to work with the source code for this chapter.

20.1 Understanding Custom Subscription Delivery

When a user requests a report on demand, the report server generates the report synchronously and sends the report to the user. By contrast, when the user subscribes to a report, the report server generates the report asynchronously at some later date and time in response to a notification event that is usually schedule-driven. Report subscriptions are paired with delivery extensions. As a part of setting up a report subscription, the user chooses one of the available delivery extensions. The extension is responsible for rendering the report and sending it to its final destination.

Recall that a report server can be configured in two different modes. Native mode describes a deployment where Reporting Services provides all functionality using only its components. SharePoint integration mode refers to a report server that uses the content management and collaboration features of a SharePoint product or technology deployment. The mode in which you configure the report server determines the delivery extensions you can use.

In native mode, Reporting Services provides e-mail and file share delivery extensions that address the two most common delivery scenarios: sending a report to a recipient via e-mail and saving a report as a file on a network share. In SharePoint integration mode, Reporting Services provides an extension that can deliver a report to a SharePoint library. As useful as the standard extensions are, they are unlikely to address all delivery scenarios. For example, an organization may want to send a report to its partner's Web service on a regular basis. If you have a Standard or Enterprise edition of SQL Server 2008, you can customize subscription-based report delivery to meet such integration needs.

20.1.1 Understanding Custom Delivery Extensions

You extend subscription-based report delivery by implementing a custom delivery extension. Similar to data and security extensions, a custom delivery extension is a .NET module that implements standard Reporting Services interfaces as defined in the \Program Files\Microsoft SQL Server\100\SDK\Assemblies\Microsoft.ReportingServices.Interfaces.dll assembly.

Understanding delivery interfaces

A custom delivery extension must implement the IDeliveryExtension interface. Optionally, a custom delivery extension can include a web control that implements the ISubscriptionBaseUIUserControl interface to let the user configure the extension in Report Manager. You can think of a custom delivery extension as a container of two extensions: a delivery extension that handles report delivery and an optional web control extension that plugs into the subscription definition pages in Report Manager. Table 20.1 shows the standard delivery interfaces, methods, and their purpose.

Table 20.1 The standard delivery interfaces

Interface	Methods	Description
IDeliveryExtension	ExtensionSettings property	The report server uses the value returned by the ExtensionSettings property to obtain the settings defined for the delivery extension.
	IsPrivilegedUser property	The report server sets this Boolean property to True if the user has Manage All Subscriptions rights.
	ReportServerInformation property	The report server passes a list of the available rendering extensions.
	Deliver method	Delivers the subscribed report.
	ValidateUserData method	Validates the extension settings specified by the user.
ISubscriptionBaseUIUserControl	Description property	Returns the description of the delivery extension.
	IsPrivilegedUser property	Same as IDeliveryExtension.IsPrivilegedUser.
	ReportServerInformation property	Same as IDeliveryExtension.ReportServerInformation.
	UserData property	Gets or sets the user-specified extension settings.

In addition, similar to other extension types, a custom delivery extension must implement the generic IExtension interface so it can be successfully registered with the report server. Recall from chapters 18 and 19 that the IExtension interface defines only two methods: SetConfiguration and Localized Name.

The SetConfiguration method is used to pass the extension configuration section as defined in the report server configuration file (rsreportserver.config). Before the report server calls the extension methods, it waits for the extension to read configuration settings that are passed to it as an XML fragment. Within the configuration file, an administrator might specify default settings for the delivery extension. For example, as a part of configuring the Web Service delivery extension, you will add a configuration section to the report server configuration file that specifies default settings for the Web service endpoint and the name of the web method that handles the report delivery.

The LocalizedName method should return the localized name of a custom extension based on the thread culture of the interactive user. Report Manager displays the localized name when it presents a list of the available delivery extensions to the user.

Understanding run time events

Once the report server has received a notification event, it interacts with the custom delivery extension as shown in the sequence diagram in Figure 20.1. First, the report server calls the IExtension.SetConfiguration method and passes the configuration section (if any) to the extension. Next, it calls IDeliveryExtension.IsPrivilegedUser to let the extension know if the user has Manage All Subscription rights. The report server then invokes IDeliveryExtension .ReportServerInformation to pass the list of the available rendering extensions.

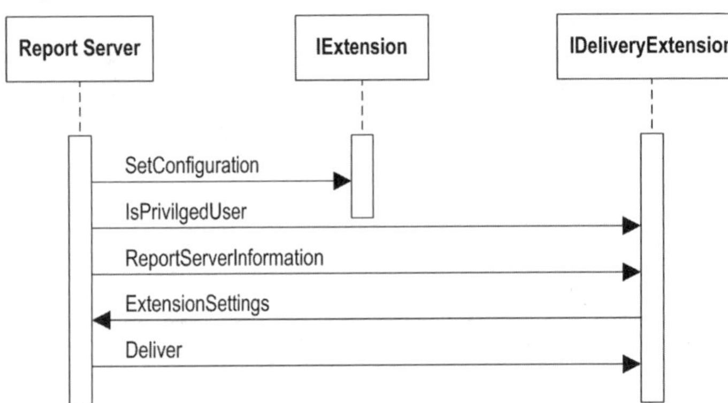

Figure 20.1 At run time, the report server interacts with the extension to pass configuration settings and delegate report delivery.

The report server proceeds next by calling the IDeliveryExtension.ExtensionSettings method to obtain the settings defined for the extension. Finally, the report server prepares a notification object that includes information about the report subscription and extension settings. The report server passes the notification object to the IDeliveryExtension.Deliver method and delegates the report delivery to the extension. If the subscription is a data-driven subscription, the report server invokes the Deliver method once for each recipient.

Understanding configuration events

A custom delivery extension can optionally provide a web control to help the end user specify the delivery settings for the subscription in Report Manager. The web control is an ASP.NET control that implements the ISubscriptionBaseUIUserControl and IExtension interfaces. Figure 20.2 displays a simplified sequence diagram showing the events that take place when you specify delivery settings in Report Manager.

When the user selects the delivery extension during the process of setting up a new subscription, Report Manager calls IExtension.SetConfiguration method to let the control retrieve any configuration settings specified for it in the report server configuration file. Next, Report Manager calls ISubscriptionBaseUIUserControl.ReportServerInfo and ISubscriptionBaseUI-UserControl.IsPrivilegedUser.

Then, Report Manager sites the web control. The web control is a container of child controls, such as ASP.NET TextBox controls, that collect and validate any user settings that you might require in your custom delivery extension. During the control rendering phase, the web control initializes and renders the child controls. Once the control is initialized, Report Manager calls the ISubscriptionBaseUIUserControl.UserData method so the control can display the default values that were retrieved from the configuration file.

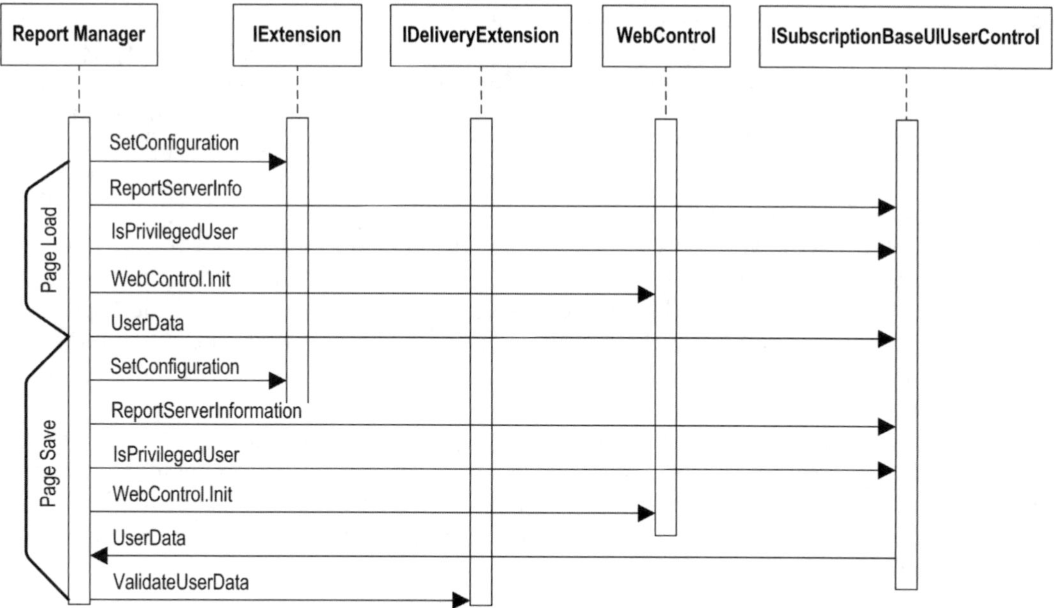

Figure 20.2 Report Manager interacts with the custom delivery extension as you configure it.

Once the control is rendered, the user can overwrite the default values by selecting other options or values that you provide. When the user saves the page, Report Manager initiates a page postback and calls IExtension.SetConfiguration, ISubscriptionBaseUIUserControl.ReportServerInfo, ISubscriptionBaseUIUserControl.IsPrivilegedUser as before. Then, Report Manager calls the get accessor of ISubscriptionBaseUIUserControl.UserData to obtain and read the new extension settings that the user has entered.

Next, Report Manager calls the IDeliveryExtension.ValidateUserData method to let your custom extension validate the user settings. If all is well, Report Manager calls down to the report server Web service API to store the subscription definition in the report server database and schedule the subscription with the SQL Server Agent service.

NOTE Reporting Services uses the SQL Server Agent service for scheduling subscribed report delivery. If the SQL Server Agent service is not running, you will get an error when saving the subscription settings in Report Manager.

20.1.2 Introducing the Web Service Delivery Extension

Now that you know how custom report delivery works at a high level, let me introduce you to the Web Service custom delivery extension sample. As noted, you can use the Web Service delivery extension to send any report to an arbitrary web method. The only requirement for the web method is that it must have a single argument that will receive the XML representation of the report.

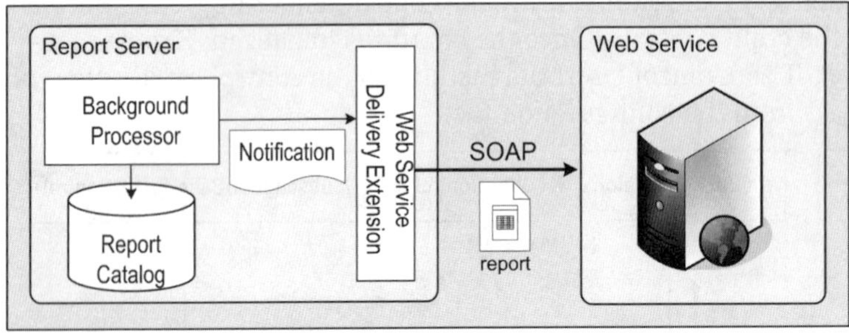

Figure 20.3 Configure the Web Service delivery extension by specifying the Web service endpoint and method name.

Understanding the solution architecture

Figure 20.3 shows how the Web Service delivery extension fits into the Reporting Services subscription delivery architecture. When the subscription schedule is triggered, the SQL Server Agent service inserts a record in the Notifications table in the report catalog. The Reporting Services Background Processor polls the Notifications table on a regular basis. When it discovers a new notification, the Background Processor prepares a notification object and forwards it to the Web Service delivery extension.

The Web Service delivery extension obtains the report details from the notification object and renders the report. Next, the extension gets the Web service invocation details from the notification object and generates a dynamic in-memory proxy to communicate with the Web service. Finally, the extension sends the exported report to the Web service and returns a delivery status to the report server.

Understanding design goals and limitations

The high-level design goals for our custom delivery extension are:

- Sends the report to an arbitrary Web service—The extension should let the user specify the target Web service. To accomplish this goal, the Web Service delivery extension generates the Web service proxy at run time.
- Provides a user interface for configuring the extension—The Web Service delivery extension provides a web control to let the end user configure and schedule the extension in the subscription definition pages in Report Manager.

To keep the implementation as simple as possible, the Web Service delivery extension has the following limitations.

- Exports the subscribed report to XML only—The Web service delivery extension doesn't let the user specify an export format although it could easily be enhanced to do so. For example, you could add a drop-down list to the web control and populate the list with the available export formats which you can obtain by calling the ListExtensions API.
- Requires a specific web method signature—The Web Service delivery extension passes the exported report to the first argument, which must be of a string data type. If you need to work with different method signatures, you can easily enhance the extension to enumerate the methods and invoke the method you require.

Configuring the Web service delivery extension

Once you install the Web Service delivery extension (which you will do later in section 20.3), you can use it to configure a subscription in Report Manager.

1. Open Report Manager and navigate to the report to which you want to subscribe. Recall from chapter 12 that the report data source must use stored credentials with subscription-based report delivery.
2. Open the report properties page and select the Subscriptions tab.
3. Click the New Subscription button to create a standard subscription or the New Data Subscription button for a data-driven subscription. For the sake of simplicity, the next steps assume a standard subscription.
4. Expand the Delivery By drop-down list and select Web Service, as shown in Figure 20.4. If the Web Service item doesn't show up, the Web Service delivery extension is not deployed properly. Review section 20.3 for deployment steps.

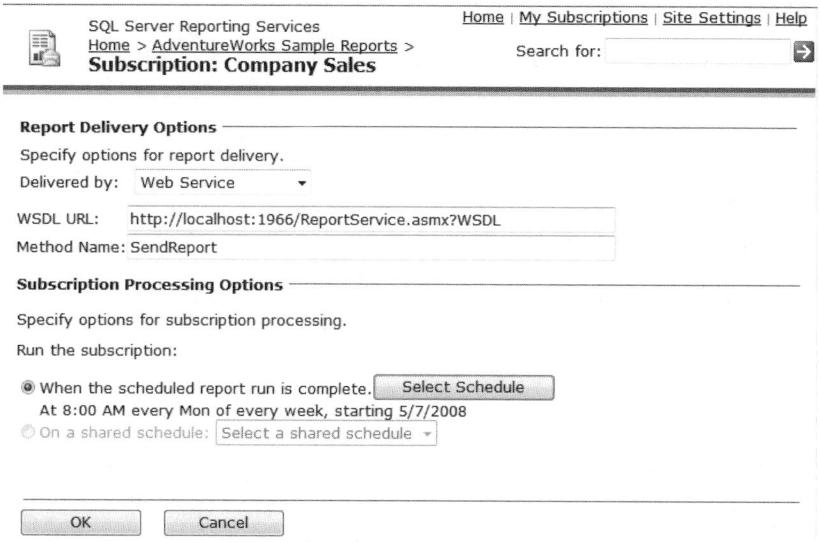

Figure 20.4 Configure the Web Service delivery extension by specifying the Web service endpoint and method name.

Report Manager pre-populates the WSDL URL and Method Name fields from the extension configuration section in the RSReportServer.config configuration file but these can be overwritten by the user.

5. Verify that the WSDL URL field is set to http://localhost:1966/ReportService.asmx?WDDL.

> **TIP** For testing purposes, use the ReportService Web service project that is included with the source code for this chapter. It uses the ASP.NET Development Server that is configured to listen on port 1966. To verify the WSDL URL, right-click on the ReportService.asmx file and select View in Browser. In the web page that follows, click the Service Description link to view the WSDL definition. Scroll all the way to the end of the definition. The Web service endpoint is found under the wsdl:service element.

6. Verify that the Method Name field is set to SendReport. If you use your own web method, enter the name of the web method. The web method must accept a single string argument.

Scheduling and running the subscription

To test the extension quickly, create a report-specific schedule that runs once, as follows.

1. Click the Select Schedule button.
2. In the Schedule Details section (see Figure 20.5), select the Once option.

SQL Server Reporting Services
Home > AdventureWorks Sample Reports >
Subscription: Company Sales

Home | My Subscriptions | Site Settings | Hel
Search for:

Use this schedule to determine how often this report is delivered.

Schedule details

Choose whether to run the report on an hourly, daily, weekly, monthly, or one time basis.

All times are expressed in (GMT -05:00) Eastern Standard Time.

Hour
Day
Week
Month
Once

One-time Schedule

Report runs only once.

Start time: 08 : 48 A.M. P.M.

Start and end dates

Specify the date to start and optionally end this schedule.

Begin running this schedule on: 6/28/2008

Stop this schedule on:

OK Cancel

Figure 20.5 Set up a report schedule to test the Web Service delivery extension.

3. Enter a start time that is a minute or two ahead of the current time.
4. In the Start and End Dates section, click the DatePicker button and select today's date.
5. Click OK to return to the subscription configuration page. Make sure that the description below the Before the Scheduled Report Run is Complete option (see Figure 20.4) says that the report is scheduled to run once, with a start time of a few minutes ahead of the current time. For example, if the current date is 6/28/2008 8:46 A.M. and you schedule the report for 6/28/2008 8:48 A.M., the schedule description should be "At 8:48 A.M. on 6/28/2008".
6. Click OK to schedule the subscription with the SQL Server Agent Service.

When the scheduled time arrives, the background processing application processes the report and forwards it to the extension. The extension exports the report to XML and sends it to the web method you specified.

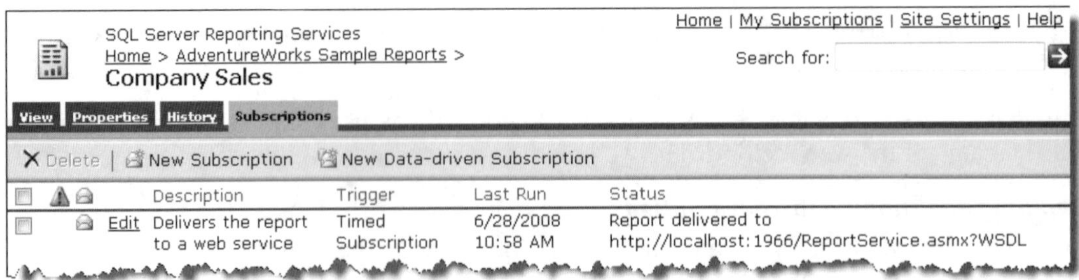

Figure 20.6 Use the Subscriptions page to view the status of the subscription and delivery.

7. On the Subscriptions tab, refresh the page in the browser to determine the subscription status.

If the subscription was successful, the Status column will show that the report is delivered to <WSDL URL>. The Last Run column should show the date of the last run (see Figure 20.6). Now that you know how to work with the extension, let's drill into its implementation details.

20.2 Implementing Custom Report Delivery

Microsoft has provided a Printer Delivery Extension sample (see Resources) to demonstrate how you can implement a custom delivery extension. The Printer delivery extension sends a report to a network printer. Once I familiarized myself with the Microsoft sample, implementing the Web Service delivery extension was very straightforward. In this section, we will dive into the code of both the Web Service delivery extension and the web control that provides the user interface for specifying delivery settings in Report Manager.

20.2.1 Implementing the Custom Delivery Extension

The WebServiceDeliveryProvider class in WebServiceDeliveryProvider.cs source file contains the source code of the custom delivery extension. It implements the IExtension and IDeliveryExtensions interfaces used to plug into the report server subscription delivery architecture. Let's discuss the most significant methods in the order in which they are executed by the report server at run time (see again Figure 20.2 for an overview).

Implementing SetConfiguration

As part of deploying the extension, the administrator can optionally specify default configuration settings in the report server configuration file (rsreportserver.config). The Web Service delivery extension supports two settings that can be specified in this file: the Web service URL and the name of the web method that receives the report.

```
public void SetConfiguration (string configuration) {
    XmlDocument doc = new XmlDocument();
    doc.LoadXml(configuration);

    if (doc.DocumentElement.Name == Constants.CONFIG_ROOT)        {
        foreach (XmlNode child in doc.DocumentElement.ChildNodes)
        {
                switch (child.Name)
                {
                    case Constants.CONFIG_WSDL: this._wsdl = child.InnerText; break;
                    case Constants.CONFIG_METHOD_NAME: this._methodName = child.InnerText; break;
                }
        }
    }
}
```

When the report server calls IExtension.SetConfiguration method, it passes the configuration settings verbatim as they appear in the configuration file. SetConfiguration loads the configuration section in an instance of the XmlDocument class, extracts the configuration values, and stores them in class-level members.

Implementing IsPrivilegedUser and ReportServerInformation

Although the Web Service delivery extension doesn't use IDeliveryExtension.IsPrivilegedUser, it must implement this property so that the report server can properly manage it. IsPrivilegedUser stores the Boolean value passed by the server in a class-level member and returns it when the report server asks for it.

Before delivering the report, the custom delivery extension is responsible for rendering the report in one of the supported formats. However, the report administrator could disable a renderer in the report server configuration file. This will cause a run time exception when the custom delivery extension tries to export the report. This is why the report server passes a list of the available rendering extensions to the ReportServerInformation property. ReportServerInformation stores the list in a class-level member. Before the custom delivery extension renders the report, it enumerates this list to make sure that the XML renderer is available.

Implementing ExtensionSettings

Recall that the report server calls IDeliveryExtension.ExtensionSettings to retrieve the settings that the delivery extension supports. Custom clients can call the GetExtensionSettings API of the Report Server Web service to obtain the settings too.

```
public Setting[] ExtensionSettings {
	get	{
		if (_settings == null)				{
				_settings = new Setting[2];
				_settings[0] = new Setting();
				_settings[0].Name = Constants.CONFIG_WSDL;
				_settings[0].ReadOnly = false;
				_settings[0].Required = true;
				_settings[0].Value = this._wsdl;
				_settings[0].AddValidValue(Constants.CONFIG_WSDL, this._wsdl);
				_settings[1] = new Setting();
				_settings[1].Name = Constants.CONFIG_METHOD_NAME;
				_settings[1].ReadOnly = false;
				_settings[1].Required = true;
				_settings[1].Value = this._methodName;
				_settings[1].AddValidValue(Constants.CONFIG_METHOD_NAME, this._methodName);
		}
		return _settings;
	}
}
```

The get accessor of the ExtensionSettings property constructs a two-dimensional array for the WSDL endpoint and web method name. It configures both settings as required and defaults their values to the configuration values specified in the extension configuration section.

Implementing ValidateUserData

The report server invokes IDeliveryExtension.ValidateUserData so that your extension can validate any user-defined extension settings that the user might have provided in the subscription definition.

```
public Setting[] ValidateUserData(Setting[] settings) {
	foreach (Setting setting in settings)	{
		if (setting.Field == null || setting.Field == "")			{
		  switch (setting.Name) {
		    case (Constants.CONFIG_WSDL):
		      if (setting.Value.Trim() == String.Empty)
			setting.Error = String.Format(String.Format("{0} is a required field.", setting.Name)); break;
		    case (Constants.CONFIG_METHOD_NAME):
			if(setting.Value.Trim() == String.Empty)
			setting.Error = String.Format("WSDL is a required field.");
			break;
		   default: setting.Error = String.Format("Unknown setting {0}", setting.Name); break;
		    }
		}
	}
	return settings;
}
```

ValidateUserData enumerates through the subscription settings and checks if the Field property is null. Next, ValidateUserData checks the WSDL endpoint and web method name settings. Since both settings are required, ValidateUserData indicates an error if the settings are empty.

Because the user specifies delivery extension settings in the subscription definition pages in Report Manager, the validation controls in the web control will catch empty fields. This may lead you to believe that the ValidateUserData checks are redundant. However, they are useful for client applications that call the Report Server Web service directly. In this case, building in programmatic validation of the delivery extension settings ensures that the settings are correct when the user interface component is unavailable.

Implementing report delivery

The IDeliveryExtension.Deliver method is the workhorse of the custom delivery extension. It is responsible for rendering the report in one of the supported export formats and delivering the report to its final destination. Let's discuss its implementation in detail.

```
public bool Deliver(Notification notification) {
	bool retry = false;
	if (!this.IsExtensionSupported("XML")) throw new Exception("The XML rendering extension is disabled.");
	notification.Status = "Processing web service delivery ...";
	Setting[] userSettings = notification.UserData;
	SubscriptionData subscriptionData = new SubscriptionData();
	subscriptionData.FromSettings(userSettings);
	DeliverReport(notification, subscriptionData);
	return retry;
}
private void DeliverReport(Notification notification, SubscriptionData data) {
	StringWriter stringWriter = null;
	_files = notification.Report.Render("XML", @"<DeviceInfo/>");

	if (_files[0].Data.Length > 0)
	{
		byte[] reportPayload = new byte[_files[0].Data.Length];
		_files[0].Data.Position = 0;
		_files[0].Data.Read(reportPayload, 0, reportPayload.Length);
		_files[0].Data.Flush();
		string payload = Convert.ToBase64String(reportPayload);
		StringBuilder stringBuilder = new StringBuilder();
		stringWriter = new StringWriter(stringBuilder);
		XmlTextWriter writer = new XmlTextWriter(stringWriter);
		writer.Formatting = Formatting.Indented;
		writer.WriteStartElement("Report");
		 writer.WriteElementString("ReportPayload", payload);
		 writer.WriteEndElement();
		string[] parameters = null;
		WebServiceProxyFactory factory = new WebServiceProxyFactory(data.WSDL);
		object proxy = factory.Build();
		Type type = proxy.GetType();
		MethodInfo method = type.GetMethod(data.methodName);
		if (method == null || (!CheckMethod(method)))
			throw new System.Exception(String.Format("Method {0} is not valid.", method));
		parameters = new string[1];
		parameters[0] = stringBuilder.ToString();
		string result = method.Invoke(proxy, parameters) as string;
		if (result.ToLower()!="success") throw   new Exception(String.Format("Delivering report {0} has
				resulted in an exception.", notification.Report.Name));
	}
	else throw new Exception(String.Format("Rendering report {0} has resulted in no data.", notification.Report));
	notification.Status = String.Format("Report delivered to {0}", data.WSDL);
}
```

When the schedule is triggered, the report server prepares a notification object and passes it to the Deliver method. The notification object contains information about the subscription, such as the identity of the user who owns the subscription, information about the report, and subscription settings. First, the Deliver method checks whether the XML renderer is available on the server by examining the list of rendering extensions that the report server has passed to the ReportServerInformation property. Next, the Deliver method prepares a SubscriptionData helper object that contains the subscription settings and calls the DeliverReport method.

The notification object contains a Report object that provides convenient access to the report for which the subscription is being created. For example, rendering a report is as simple as calling the Report.Render method. The Render method returns a RenderedOutputFile object that contains the report payload and other properties, such as the report name, the name of the rendering extension used to export the report, the encoding type, and the MIME type of the report stream.

The report payload is returned as one or more streams. If you request the report in the HTML multi-stream rendering formats, the first stream will include the report payload, while the subsequent streams contain the report images. Single-stream rendering formats, such as Web archive (MHTML), will always produce one stream with the images embedded in it. Since we are rendering the report in XML, we can get the entire report from the first stream. The DeliverReport method extracts the report payload as a byte array from the Data property of the RenderedOutputFile object and converts it to a Base64 string so it can be safely transmitted over the wire.

Delivering to a Web service

Next, the DeliverReport method sends the report payload to the target Web service specified by the user. However, this presents an implementation challenge because the Web service is not known at design time and we cannot generate a Web service proxy to communicate with it. What we need is a way to generate the proxy dynamically at run time. This "magic" happens in the WebServiceProxyFactory class, which is based on the Rodolfo Finochietti's Dynamic Proxy Factory sample. The Delivery method instantiates a WebServiceProxyFactory object and passes the Web service WSDL URL to its constructor. Without discussing WebServiceProxyFactory in detail, it uses the .NET Code Document Object Model (CodeDOM) to dynamically generate the proxy assembly.

I've made two changes to the Rodolfo's sample. First, I removed the contract dependence between the factory and the Web service so that the custom delivery extension can integrate with an arbitrary Web service. Second, instead of saving the proxy assembly to disk, WebServiceProxyFactory generates it in memory so you don't have to grant special Code Access Security permissions to the location where the proxy assembly is generated.

Once the DeliverReport method obtains a reference to the proxy assembly from the WebServiceProxyFactory.Build method, it uses the .NET reflection technology to obtain a reference to the proxy class by calling the GetType method. If you use the ReportService Web service, GetType returns the Reporter class. Next, DeliverReport calls GetMethod on the type to get a reference to the user-defined method by name, such as SendReport. Then, DeliverReport checks whether the method both exists and passes certain validation rules, such as whether it is a public instance-based method.

If the method passes validation, DeliverReport invokes it dynamically by calling its Invoke method. The Invoke method takes the reference to the object as a first argument and a string-based array of the values for the method arguments. If the ReportService receives the report payload successfully, it returns "success". DeliverReport checks the method return value, and if all is well, sends the notification status message to indicate that the report has been delivered successfully.

20.2.2 Implementing the Web Control

Recall that a custom delivery extension can provide a user interface in the form of a web control to facilitate configuring the extension in Report Manager. The source code of the web control for the Web Service delivery extension is located in the WebServiceDeliveryUIControl.cs source file.

The WebServiceDeliveryUIControl class inherits from the System.Web.UI.WebControls.-WebControl class and implements the ISubscriptionBaseUIUserControl interface. The Web-Control base class provides the required ASP.NET plumbing for initializing and rendering the control. The ISubscriptionBaseUIUserControl interface lets the control plug into the report server subscription delivery architecture. Let's discuss the control events in the order in which they are executed by Report Manager (see again Figure 20.2).

Initializing the Web control

As with the custom delivery extension, the report server calls the IExtension.SetConfiguration method so that the web control can initialize using default values specified in the optional configuration section. Because the WebServiceDeliveryUIControl doesn't support any configuration settings, the SetConfiguration does nothing. As with the custom delivery extension, the report server passes the list of the available rendering extensions to the ReportServerInformation property and calls the IsPrivilegedUser to indicate whether the user has Manage All Subscriptions rights.

Next, Report Manager sites the control. This invokes the control Init method. In our case, the Init method creates two text boxes and some ASP.NET validation controls to validate the user input values before the page is submitted. Each text box control gets its default value by calling the GetControlValue private member, which obtains the value from the ISubscriptionBaseUIUserControl.ReportServerInformation.ServerSettings property. Finally, the ReportServer calls the set accessor of ISubscriptionBaseUIUserControl.UserData to pass the saved control values.

```
public Setting[] UserData {
      get
      {
            SubscriptionData data = new SubscriptionData();
            data.WSDL = this._text_WSDL.Text;
            data.methodName = this._text_MethodName.Text;
            return data.ToSettingArray();
      }
      set
      {
            this._hasUserData = true;
            SubscriptionData data = new SubscriptionData();
            data.FromSettings(value);
            this._wsdl = data.WSDL;
            this._methodName = data.methodName;
            this._text_MethodName.Text = this._methodName;
      }
}
```

The set accessor overwrites the control values so the user sees the values that he or she saved.

Saving the subscription settings

At this point, the subscription page is rendered in Report Manager and the user can overwrite the extension settings or schedule the subscription. When the user clicks the Save button, the subscription page posts back. Subsequently, Report Manager calls the get accessor of the ISubscriptionBaseUIUserControl.UserData property to get the user-defined values. Finally, Report

Manager calls IDeliveryExtension.ValidateUserData to allow the extension to validate the new values.

If the validation succeeds, Report Manager calls the SetSubscriptionProperties API of the Report Server Web service to save the subscription settings in the report catalog. Next, Report Manager creates a SQL Server Agent job and schedules the job.

20.3 Deploying Custom Delivery Extensions

Before you can set up a subscription that uses the Web Service delivery extension, you need to deploy the custom delivery extension to the server. Specifically, you need to deploy and register the custom delivery extension with the report server so the report server can load the extension at run time. For your convenience, I have provided my versions of the modified configuration files in the Config folder inside the chapter source code.

20.3.1 Deploying to the Report Server

Deploying the delivery extension to the report server involves copying the extension binaries to the report server bin folder and configuring the extension security.

Deploying and registering the extension

Follow these steps to deploy the Web Service delivery extension to the report server.

1. Deploy the Prologika.CustomDeliveryExtension.dll and Prologika.CustomDelivery-Extension.pdb to the report server binary folder whose default location is \Program Files\Microsoft SQL Server\MSRS10.MSSQLSERVER\Reporting Services\ReportServer\bin.
2. Open the report server configuration file, rsreportserver.config, located in the report server folder whose default location is \Program Files\Microsoft SQL Server\MSRS10.MSSQLSERVER\Reporting Services\ReportServer. Locate the <Delivery> element and add a new extension section, as follows:

```
<Extension Name="Web Service Delivery Extension"
  Type="Prologika.RS.Extensibility.CustomDeliveryExtension.WebServiceDeliveryProvider,
        Prologika.CustomDeliveryExtension">
    <Configuration>
        <WebServiceConfiguration>
        <WSDL>http://localhost:1966/ReportService.asmx?WSDL</WSDL>
        <MethodName>SendReport</MethodName>
    </WebServiceConfiguration>
  </Configuration>
</Extension>
```

Change the WSDL and MethodName settings if needed.

Configuring security

As usual when deploying custom code, you need to elevate the code access security rights for the extension assembly.

1. Open the report server policy configuration file, rssrvpolicy.config, located in the report server folder whose default location is \Program Files\Microsoft SQL Server\MSRS10-.MSSQLSERVER\Reporting Services\ReportServer.

2. Add a new CodeGroup element, as follows:

```
<CodeGroup class="UnionCodeGroup" version="1" Name="CustomDelive ryExtensionCodeGroup"
  Description="Code group for the Web Service Delivery Extension" PermissionSetName="FullTrust">
    <IMembershipCondition class="UrlMembershipCondition" version="1"
          Url="C:\Program Files\Microsoft SQL Server\MSRS10.MSSQLSERVER\Reporting
         Services\ReportServer\bin\Prologika.CustomDeliveryExtension.dll"/>
</CodeGroup>
```

20.3.2 Deploying to Report Manager

If the extension provides a web control, you need to deploy and register the control with Report Manager. Since the Web Service delivery extension provides user interface, we need to register its web control so the user can configure the extension in Report Manager.

Deploying and registering the extension

Follow these steps to deploy the Web Service delivery extension to Report Manager.

1. Deploy the Prologika.CustomDeliveryExtension.dll and Prologika.CustomDeliveryExtension.pdb to the Report Manager binary folder whose default location is \Program Files\Microsoft SQL Server\MSRS10.MSSQLSERVER\Reporting Services\ReportManager\bin.
2. Open the report server configuration file, rsreportserver.config, located in the report server folder whose default location is \Program Files\Microsoft SQL Server\MSRS10.MSSQLSERVER\Reporting Services\ReportServer. Locate the <DeliveryUI> element and add a new extension section:

```
<Extension Name="Web Service Delivery Extension "
 Type="Prologika.RS.Extensibility.CustomDeliveryExtension.WebServiceDeliveryUIControl,
 Prologika.CustomDeliveryExtension"/>
```

Configuring security

Next, you need to configure code access security for the custom delivery extension.

1. Open the Report Manager policy configuration file (rsmgrpolicy.config) and add a new CodeGroup element:

```
<CodeGroup class="UnionCodeGroup" version="1" Name="CustomDeliveryExtensionCodeGroup"
  Description= "Code group for the Web Service Delivery Extension" PermissionSetName="FullTrust">
  <IMembershipCondition class="UrlMembershipCondition" version="1"
      Url="C:\ Program Files\Microsoft SQL Server\MSRS10.MSSQLSERVER\Reporting Services\
      ReportManager\Bin\Prologika.CustomDeliveryExtension.dll"/>
</CodeGroup>
```

At this point, the Web Service delivery extension is deployed and registered with the report server and Report Manager.

20.3.3 Debugging Custom Delivery Extensions

Thanks to the new hosting model in Reporting Services 2008, debugging a custom extension is easy. Because the Background Processor and Report Manager are both hosted in the ReportingServicesService.exe process, you only need to attach the debugger to a single process to debug the extension and the web control.

Debugging during the configuration stage

To debug the custom delivery extension during the configuration stage:

1. Deploy the latest version of the extension binaries to the Report Manager binary folder (\Program Files\Microsoft SQL Server\MSRS10.MSSQLSERVER\Reporting Services\ReportManager\Bin).
2. Open the Report Manager application in a browser.
3. Open the custom delivery extension project (CustomDeliveryExtension.csproj) in Visual Studio.
4. In Visual Studio, go to the Debug ⇨ Attach to Process menu and check the Show Processes from All Users and Show Processes in All Sessions checkboxes.
5. In the Available Processes, locate the ReportingServicesService.exe process and click the Attach button.
6. Set breakpoints in the custom delivery extension as needed. For example to troubleshoot the web control initialization, set a breakpoint inside the Control_Init method.
7. In Report Manager, create a new subscription or edit an existing subscription.

At this point, the breakpoints should get hit.

Run time debugging

To debug the extension at runtime when the report server initiates the subscribed report delivery:

1. Deploy the latest version of the extension binaries to the report server binary folder (\Program Files\Microsoft SQL Server\MSRS10.MSSQLSERVER\Reporting Services\ReportServer\Bin).
2. In Visual Studio, go to the Debug ⇨ Attach to Process menu and check the Show Processes from All Users and Show Processes in All Sessions checkboxes.
3. In the Available Processes, locate the ReportingServicesService.exe process and click the Attach button to attach the Visual Studio debugger to it.
4. Set breakpoints in the custom delivery extension as needed. For example to debug the report delivery, set a breakpoint inside the Deliver method.
5. Schedule the subscription to start a few minutes from the current time.

Once the schedule is triggered, the report server will start processing the subscription and you should be able to step through the code.

Understanding logging

Since most of the custom delivery extension activity takes place in the DeliverReport method, I implemented a simple logging function in this method to help you troubleshoot it without debugging. If a run time exception occurs in DeliverReport, it calls the WriteLog helper method to write the exception details to a disk file. The disk file is written to the system temp folder and its default path is \Windows\Temp\WSDeliveryLog.txt. If the extension fails on delivery, you can open the WSDeliveryLog.txt file and inspect the exception stack.

20.4 Summary

Out of the box, Reporting Services can deliver subscription-based reports to e-mail recipients, shared folders, and SharePoint libraries only. However, thanks to the Reporting Services extensible architecture, you can extend Reporting Services to deliver reports to any destination by implementing a custom delivery extension. To help you understand the nuts and bolts of this extension type, I walked you through the implementation details of the Web Service delivery extension sample that uses a subscription to send a report to an arbitrary web service.

A custom delivery extension can optionally include a user interface. Consider including an ASP.NET web control in your custom delivery extension to help the user specify delivery settings in Report Manager. You can step through the custom delivery extension code at design time and run time by attaching to the report server process. Before using the extension, you need to deploy and register it with the report server and Report Manager.

20.5 Resources

Microsoft Printer Delivery Extension Sample
(http://tinyurl.com/29jthp)— The Printer Delivery Extension sample demonstrates report delivery to a printer.

Rodolfo Finochietti's Dynamic Proxy Factory sample
(http://tinyurl.com/ywjqvo)— This sample demonstrates how to dynamically generate a web service proxy.

Chapter 21

Implementing Custom Report Items

The new Reporting Services charts and gauges can take you far when it comes to presenting data in a visually compelling way, but even with the latest enhancements there is still room for the occasional requirement that simply cannot be met with the built-in controls. For example, suppose a user needs to convey information graphically using a chart type that Reporting Services does not support? Fortunately, you can extend the Reporting Services data visualization capabilities by implementing your own custom controls in the form of custom report items.

In this chapter, I will introduce you to this exciting extensibility area of Reporting Services that lets you transcend the limitations of traditional text-based reporting. I will walk you through the steps of implementing a custom report item that displays a progress indicator. Finally, I will show you how to deploy and test the custom report item and use it on a report.

21.1 Understanding Custom Report Items

A custom report item is a Microsoft .NET component that extends Reporting Services presentation capabilities. Once implemented, a custom report item can be used just like any native report item. For example, you can drag a custom report item to the report layout and then bind it to a report dataset to display a field value graphically. As you can imagine, custom report items redefine the concept of a standard report and open a new world of possibilities for visualizing data on reports.

DEFINITION A custom report item is a Microsoft .NET component that extends Reporting Services presentation capabilities. A custom report item can render only static, image-based content.

21.1.1 What is a Custom Report Item?

As a developer, you have undoubtedly used Microsoft or third-party controls to spice up the presentation layer of your .NET applications. You can think of custom report items as the Reporting Services equivalent of .NET controls. Unlike .NET controls, however, Reporting Services custom report items have some limitations.

First, custom report items can only render static, image-based content. Second, custom report items support a subset of interaction features that provide simple navigation like clicking on an image area to jump to another report or a bookmark in the same report. As you have probably guessed, the time for fully interactive AJAX or Silverlight report widgets is yet to come.

Despite its limitations, custom report items can be very useful. Given that most reports are static, custom report items let you extend your reports to convey information in powerful ways. For example, you may have used or seen demos of the Dundas Reporting Services components, including the Dundas Chart, Gauge, Map, and Calendar. You will probably be surprised to learn that these feature-rich components were implemented as custom report items. And as you'll see, building a simple custom report item on your own is not all that difficult.

Report item types

To understand how a custom report item works, it helps to revisit a few fundamentals about Reporting Services report items. Recall that Reporting Services provides two types of report items. First, there are regular report items that include text box, image, line, and rectangle items. The most popular among these is the textbox report item, which can be used to display a fixed or expression-based value.

Second, there are data regions, such as table, matrix, list, and chart. A data region can be bound to a report dataset just like ASP.NET or Windows Forms data-bound controls can be bound to ADO.NET datasets. While each of the data regions presents the underlying data in different ways, they all act as repeaters of data. For example, a table region generates one table row for each row in the underlying dataset.

Custom report items let you implement both regular report items and full-blown data regions. The Progress Tracker sample included in this chapter walks you through the process of building a regular custom report item that you can bind to a dataset field inside a table, matrix, or list data region. Should your custom report item requirements call instead for the more complex data region structures, you will be able to devise an appropriate strategy once you grasp the concepts presented in the following sections.

About the custom report item lifecycle

If you have ever built a Windows Forms or Web Forms custom control, you will find that implementing a custom report item is not all that different. Similar to a control, a custom report item has a dual life. At design time, the report author configures the custom report item in the Report Designer. At run time, the report server passes properties to the control and requests that the control be rendered on the page.

To meet the needs of both environments, a custom report item must include a design-time component and a run-time component. These components are implemented as .NET Framework assemblies and can be written in any CLS-compliant language. Let's discuss each component in more detail.

21.1.2 Understanding the Design-Time Component

The design-time component enables the report author to create a custom report item in Report Designer by providing various services for specifying report properties, handling verbs and adornment features, using custom editors, and previewing the results. To provide these services, the design-time component must inherit from the Reporting Services CustomReportItemDesigner class.

Understanding design-time services

Deciding which design services you need to implement is a tradeoff between usability requirements and the time it takes to implement your design. The more sophisticated the custom report item is, the more complex its design-time component is likely to be. Take for example the Reporting Services chart data region, which features the full-blown design-time component shown in Figure 21.1.

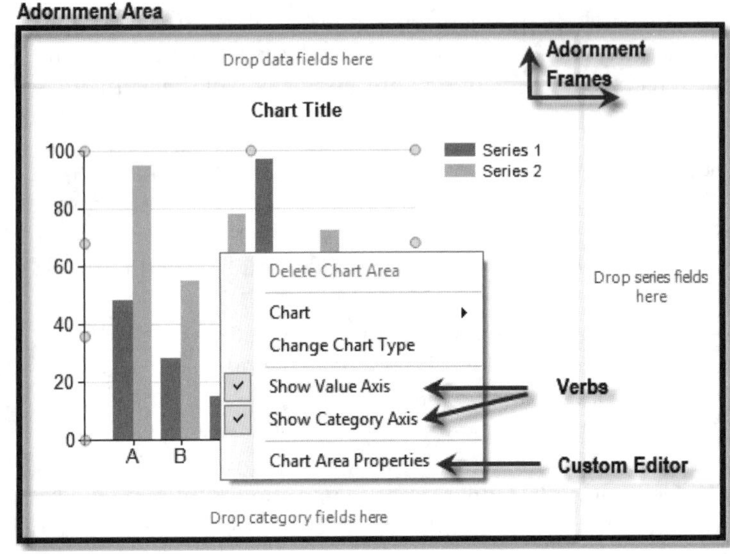

Figure 21.1 The design-time component can provide various services for configuring custom report items at design time.

As you select chart areas, the Properties window (not shown in the figure) shows the control properties. Some properties, such as Font and Color, are standard. Others are control-specific, such as CategoryAxes, ValueAxes, and so on. As you change the control properties, the chart region updates its design-time appearance so that you can see the effect of changing a specific value.

Simple custom report items are likely to support only the basics: control properties and design-time rendering. More complex custom report items might provide adornment services, verbs, and custom property editors.

Adornment

When you click on the chart region at design time, the control draws an adornment area outside the main control window. This area has three frames (data fields, category fields, and series fields) that act as drop containers for dataset fields. Microsoft has added the adornment services to the chart control to let the report author configure the chart grouping and data by simply dragging dataset fields and dropping them in the appropriate frame. If you are familiar with implementing Windows Forms controls, the Reporting Services adornment infrastructure is essentially a pass-through implementation of the Windows Forms Adorner class.

As you can imagine, rendering the adornment frame and responding to user events can get rather complex. The good news is that the adorner infrastructure is entirely optional. For the sake of simplicity, Progress Tracker doesn't implement adornment services. If you decide to adorn, the Microsoft Polygon sample, which is one of the Reporting Services extensibility samples, demonstrates how you can add adornment features to your custom report item.

Verbs

Another nice feature you may want to implement is verbs. Designer verbs let you implement custom actions that can be launched by right-clicking on the control design surface and choosing the action from the context menu. For example, when you right-click the chart area, the context menu shows various verbs, such as Show Value Axis, Show Category Axes, and Delete Chart Area, which allow the report author to carry out various actions.

You can implement verbs in custom report items by overriding the CustomReportItemDesigner Verbs property. Next, add a new verb to DesignerVerbCollection and specify the desired caption and the callback event handler. When the user selects the action from the context menu, CustomReportItemDesigner will invoke the callback event handler, where you can execute whatever code is needed.

Custom property editors

The Properties window can help the report author configure simple properties. More complex properties, however, may require custom editors. For example, when you select the Chart Area Properties context menu (see again Figure 21.1), the chart region opens a rather sophisticated custom editor that lets you configure the appearance of the chart area, including 3D options and visibility properties.

Custom editors can be associated with the design-time component as a whole or with individual properties that may require more complex configuration and validation rules. Progress Tracker demonstrates how you can implement property and component-based custom editors.

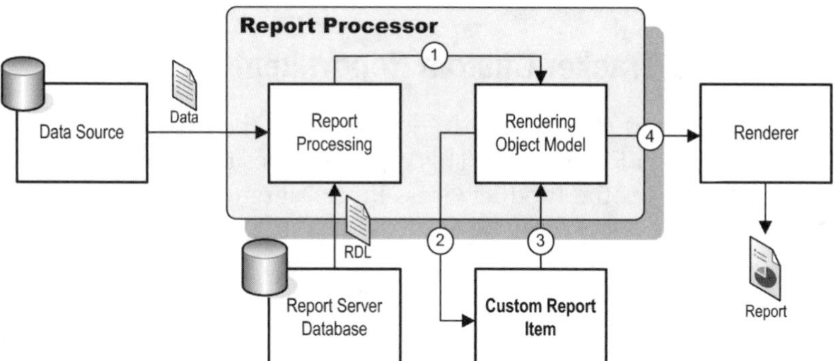

Figure 21.2 At run time, the Report Processor passes data and properties to the custom report item.

21.1.3 Understanding the Run-Time Component

Implementing the run-time component for a custom report item is much simpler than implementing its design-time counterpart. That's because you only need to worry about drawing the run-time image of the item—which after all is the main purpose of having a custom report item. The run-time component must implement the Reporting Services ICustomReportItem interface. Figure 21.2 shows the run-time interaction between the Report Processor and the custom report item.

Run-time interaction

When the report is requested, the Report Processor executes report queries and retrieves the data. The Report Processor obtains the report definition (RDL) from the report server database. Next, the report server creates (1) a rendering object model (ROM) by combining the report data and definition.

When the Report Processor encounters a custom report item, it instantiates the run-time component of the custom report item each time it needs to be rendered on the report. The

Report Processor passes (2) the ROM object to each instance. The custom report item run-time component traverses the object and generates an image and returns (3) the image back to the ROM. Finally, the Report Processor passes (4) the ROM to the rendering extension associated with the requested export format to render the final report.

Run-time properties

When the Report Processor instantiates a custom report item, it passes to it a set of static or expression-based properties that were defined at design time and saved in the report definition. Most property values are static. Common examples of static properties include values for Color and Font. Interestingly, if the property value is expression-based, the Report Processor evaluates and resolves the expression before passing the value to the custom report item.

For example, if the Value property is bound to a dataset field, the Report Processor resolves the property value from the underlying dataset field. Because the expression-based property value is resolved in advance, your custom report item can handle static and dynamic properties the same way (as name-value pairs), saving an enormous amount of plumbing work on your part.

Now that you have a solid foundation of what a custom report item is, let me introduce you to the Progress Tracker custom report item that I developed.

21.1.4 Introducing the Progress Tracker Custom Report Item

The Adventure Works Performance Report (KPIDemo.rdl) demonstrates the Progress Tracker custom report item in action, as shown in Figure 21.3. This report queries the Adventure Works Analysis Services cube and retrieves the Product Gross Profit Margin KPI that is defined in the cube.

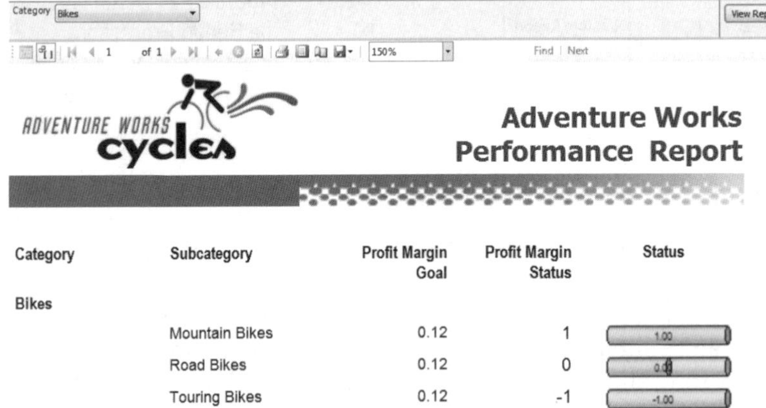

Figure 21.3 The Adventure Works Performance Report uses the Progress Tracker custom report item to show a KPI status graphically.

The Adventure Works Performance report

KPIs can be implemented easily with Microsoft SQL Server Analysis Services. You can use MDX expressions to derive the KPI value, goal, status, and trend properties. To facilitate querying the KPI objects, Analysis Services provides four functions: KPIValue, KPIGoal, KPIStatus, and KPITrend, which you can use in the report query to retrieve the KPI properties and display them on the report. As with regular measures, Analysis Services automatically calculates the KPI properties as the user slices the data. The abbreviated MDX query of the Adventure Works Performance Report follows:

```
SELECT NON EMPTY { KPITrend("Product Gross Profit Margin"),
KPIStatus("Product Gross Profit Margin"),
KPIGoal("Product Gross Profit Margin") } ON COLUMNS,
NON EMPTY { ([Product].[Product Categories].[Category].ALLMEMBERS *
[Product].[Subcategory].[Subcategory].ALLMEMBERS ) } ON ROWS
FROM ( SELECT ( STRTOSET(@ProductCategory, CONSTRAINED) ) ON COLUMNS FROM [Adventure Works])
WHERE ( IIF( STRTOSET(@ProductCategory, CONSTRAINED).Count = 1, STRTOSET(@ProductCategory, CONSTRAINED),
[Product].[Category].currentmember ) )
```

This query requests the Product Gross Profit Margin properties on columns and breaks them down by product category and subcategory on rows. The query takes the product category as a query parameter, which the user selects at run time.

The report shows both the actual KPI status value (Profit Margin Status column) and the graphical value (Status column). Progress Tracker renders the graphical image in the Status column. Progress Tracker is configured at design time for a minimum value of -1 and maximum value of 1. This range corresponds to the KPI range in Analysis Services, where -1 is underperformance, 0 is acceptable performance, and 1 is good performance.

Configuring the Progress Tracker

At design time, you can configure the Progress Tracker custom report item in the Report Designer, as shown in Figure 21.4.

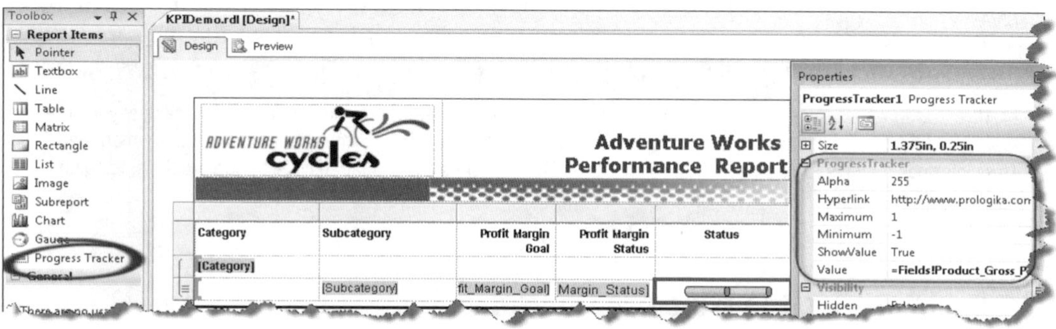

Figure 21.4 At design time, the report author can configure the Progress Tracker in the Report Designer.

You can drag Progress Tracker from the report toolbox and drop it inside a report region just as you would do with the standard report items. You can use the Properties window to set the Progress Tracker properties, which are listed under the ProgressTracker category. Notice that you can bind Progress Tracker to a dataset field by setting its Value property. Table 21.1 describes the Progress Tracker properties.

Besides the properties listed in Table 21.1, Progress Tracker re-uses some of the Reporting Services standard properties. For example, the Color property sets the bar color while the Font property defines the font of the bar text. The .NET designer host infrastructure provides these properties automatically for you. If you overwrite the default value of a standard property, Progress Tracker saves the new property value in the report definition.

Table 21.1 Progress Tracker properties

Property	Description	Default Value
Alpha	Specifies the value of the gradient alpha filter used to render the control.	255
Hyperlink	Lets the end user jump to a Web page.	http://www.prologika.com
Maximum	Defines the maximum value of the progress bar.	1
Minimum	Defines minimum value of the progress bar.	-1
ShowValue	When set to False, hides the numeric value inside the bar.	True
Value	Sets the progress value. This can be a static value or an expression, such as a field reference.	0

Now that you are familiar with the Progress Tracker sample, let's drill down to the implementation details.

21.2 Implementing Custom Report Items

The Progress Tracker sample started as a personal quest to find the answer to an interesting problem. I wanted to know what it would take to convert an existing .NET Windows Forms control to a custom report item. My hypothesis was that any .NET control that uses GDI+ to render an image could be converted to a custom report item. It turned out that not only was this true, it was even simpler than I anticipated.

NOTE Windows Graphics Device Interface (GDI+) is an application programming interface (API) that lets you create graphics, draw text, and manipulate graphical images as objects. The .NET Framework includes a GDI+ managed class interface that abstracts the GDI+ API and lets .NET developers use managed code to add graphics, imaging, and typography features to their applications.

21.2.1 Implementing the Windows Control

First, I had to find a suitable .NET control that comes with source code. Sieving through the plethora of control samples out there, I decided to narrow my search to a simple progress bar control that would graphically display a numeric value, such as a KPI value. Granted, the built-in Gauge report item is designed to do exactly that, but for the purpose of my investigation the Gauge report item was overkill for the type of progress bar I wanted to use.

TIP To minimize development and testing time, implement your custom report item as a Windows Forms control first. This will let you conveniently test and debug the control rendering code inside the Visual Studio IDE. Once the control is ready, converting it to a custom report item is easy.

About the CylinderTrackBar control

After some searching, I stumbled across an excellent CylinderTrackBar control by Mycos Technology (see Resources) that was ideal for the Progress Tracker custom report item. This control demonstrates advanced GDI+ capabilities, such as customizable gradient fill and animation. The original control supports interactive features. For example, a user can drag the fill of the cylinder up and down to set its value. However, as I mentioned at the start of the chapter, custom report items are limited to static content. For this reason, I wasn't able to migrate the control's interactive features to Progress Tracker.

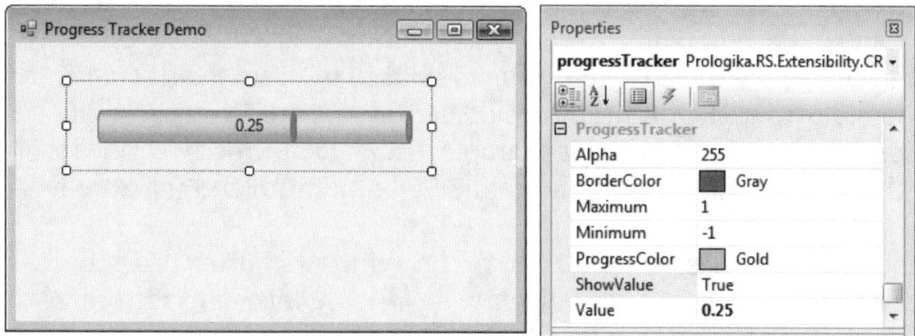

Figure 21.5 The Progress Tracker Windows control sited on a Windows Form.

Figure 21.5 shows the Progress Tracker Windows Forms control placed on a Windows Form. You can find the control implementation in the ProgressTracker class library project, which is included with the book source code. You can use the TestHarness Windows Forms project to test the control. My humble contribution to the original control was rendering the control horizontally to minimize the real estate when the control is placed inside a report region.

Implementing the control properties

The Progress Tracker control inherits from System.Windows.Forms.UserControl, which provides most of the plumbing required to implement a custom Windows Forms control. This includes control positioning, resizing, and support for standard properties. For example, because Progress Tracker extends UserControl, it inherits standard properties like ForeColor, BackColor, and so on. With so many of the basic properties already handled, all that's left to implement is custom properties and rendering the control image on the page.

In practice, it is not always possible to perfectly map a run-time control to the properties of a custom report item in Report Designer. As Figure 21.5 shows, the Progress Tracker run-time control supports the same properties as its custom report item counterpart, but with two exceptions. First, the custom report item provides a BorderColor property (the run-time control does not support such a property). Second, the Progress Tracker run-time control does not have a Hyperlink property. The Hyperlink property is a Reporting Services-specific implementation detail that anticipates a drill through action. There is no equivalent counterpart in the simple progress bar control that is the basis of Progress Tracker.

Setting control properties is straightforward. At design time, the developer can use the Visual Studio Properties Window to change the custom properties and configure the control. Alternatively, the properties can be set at run time through code. This is no different than interacting with any of the standard Windows Forms Controls, such as TextBox or ComboBox. Thanks to the Windows Forms hosting infrastructure, implementing the custom properties is remarkably simple. The following example shows code that sets the Value property.

```
[Category("ProgressTracker"), DefaultValue(0f)]
public float Value {
  get {return this._value ;}
  set {
          if (this._value != value)
          {
            if (value < this._min || value > this._max)
               throw new ApplicationException("The progress value must be between the minimum and maximum values.");
            this._value = value; this.Invalidate();
          }
      }
}
```

The Visual Studio Properties window will pick up any public custom property. You can decorate the property with additional attributes to fine-tune its appearance. For example, the Category attribute assigns the property to the ProgressTracker category and the DefaultValue attribute assigns a default value of 0 to the Value property. If the user overwrites the property value, the Properties window will show the changed value in bold to indicate that the new value is different from the default value. If you need to validate the property, you can write validation code inside the property set accessor. For example, the Value property verifies that the user input falls within the range of valid values (as defined by minimum and maximum values) and throws an exception if this rule is not met.

Each property stores the value in a class-level member. The Windows Forms designer infrastructure takes care of saving the property values when you close the form and restoring them when you open the form in the Forms Designer.

Understanding control rendering

When implementing a custom control, the bulk of the implementation effort goes into rendering the control. Progress Tracker overwrites the OnPaint event and renders the control image on the graphics canvas, which the Windows Forms designer passes as an input argument.

```
protected override void OnPaint(PaintEventArgs pe)
{
      base.OnPaint(pe);
      Graphics g = pe.Graphics;
      g.SmoothingMode = SmoothingMode.AntiAlias;
       this.DrawControl(g, this.ForeColor);
}
private void DrawControl(Graphics g, Color foreColor) {
      bool outLine = this._borderColor != Color.Transparent;
      Rectangle bar = this.ClientRectangle;

      bar.Inflate(-20, -20);
   DrawingUtils.DrawBar(g, bar, Color.FromArgb(this.Alpha, foreColor), this.BorderColor, outLine);

   if (this.Value >= this.Minimum && this.Value <= this.Maximum)
   {
      float value = bar.Width * ((this.Value - this.Minimum) / (this.Maximum - this.Minimum));
      Rectangle progress = Rec tangle.FromLTRB(bar.Left, bar.Top, bar.Left +
                        (int)value, bar.Bottom);
      DrawingUtils.DrawBar(g, progress, Color.FromArgb(this.Alpha, this.ProgressColor), this.BorderColor, outLine);
      // Draw the progress text inside the control
      if (this._showValue && progress.Height > 10)
      {
         StringFormat format = new StringFormat();
         format.Alignment = StringAlignment.Center;
         format.LineAlignment = StringAlignment.Center;
         g.DrawString(this._value.ToString("F2"), this.Font, Brushes.Black, bar, format);
         format.Dispose();
      }
   }
}
```

The OnPaint event delegates the control rendering to the DrawControl helper method. This method obtains the client area of the control from the base control's ClientRectangle property. Then, it calls the Inflate method to decrease the rectangle area by 20 pixels. Next, it calls the DrawBar helper method (not shown) in the DrawingUtilities class to render the control.

Without going into too much detail, the DrawBar method draws a cylinder on the GDI+ graphics canvas using the GDI+ primitives, starting with the left plane, right plane, and cylinder body. If you decide to experiment with the control, you might find it useful to place a return statement at different points of the FillCylinder logic to watch what has been drawn on the graphics canvas.

Once the cylinder is drawn you can move on to the next step, which is to render the progress bar as an inner cylinder. The DrawControl method uses the Value property to calculate a new rectangle. Then, it calls the DrawBar method again to paint the progress cylinder. Finally, if the ShowValue property is True, DrawBar renders the actual value as text inside the control by calling the DrawString GDI+ method.

21.2.2 Implementing the Design-Time Component

Once you are sure that the Windows Forms control is correctly handling property settings and render operations, you can promote it to a custom report item. The source code of the Progress Tracker custom report item can be found in the ProgressTrackerCRI class library project. In this section, we examine the design-time component that is used set properties on the Progress Tracker custom report item and preview the results. As I mentioned earlier, a custom report item consists of a design-time component and a run-time component that reads properties and renders the control on the page.

During design-time, the report author configures the custom report item by setting its properties. For the sake of convenience, the design-time component should also draw an image so that the report author can see the effect of setting properties and make any necessary adjustments without leaving the design environment. Although the Progress Tracker custom report item doesn't show it, your custom design-time component could also implement additional services, such as adornment, verbs, and custom editors.

In comparison to the code you will need to write for the run-time component, the design-time component is by far more difficult to implement. The Progress Tracker design-time component is implemented in the ProgressTrackerDesigner class (ProgressTrackerDesigner.cs source file).

About the CustomReportItemDesigner class

The design-time component must inherit from the Reporting Services CustomReportItemDesigner class. This class wraps the underlying Windows Forms host designer infrastructure and provides the basic services that the design time component needs. See the article Create and Host Custom Designers with The .NET Framework 2.0 in the Resources section if you want to learn more about the .NET designer host architecture.

```
[LocalizedName("Progress Tracker")]
[ToolboxBitmap(typeof(ProgressTrackerDesigner), "ProgressTracker.ico")]
[CustomReportItem("ProgressTracker")]
[Editor(typeof(CustomEditor), typeof(ComponentEditor))]
public class ProgressTrackerDesigner : CustomReportItemDesigner {. . .}
```

The LocalizedName attribute specifies the name of the custom report item that the report author will see in the Report Designer toolbox. The ToolboxBitmap attribute references an icon file that will be shown in the toolbox. The CustomReportItem attribute must correspond to the name of the custom report item as defined in the rsreportserver.config file. The Editor attribute associates the design-time component with a custom editor that the report author can use to configure the component. I will discuss custom editors in more detail later on in this section.

Initialization

When the user adds the custom report item to the report, the CustomReportItemDesigner class fires the InitializeNewComponent event. This event gives the developer a chance to initialize the design-time component for first use.

```
public override void InitializeNewComponent(){
   SetDefaults();
}
private void SetDefaults(){
   // custom properties
   this.Maximum = 1f;
   this.Minimum = -1f;
   this.Alpha = 255;
   this.Hyperlink = "http://www.prologika.com";
   this.ShowValue = true;

   // standard properties
   this.Style.Border.Color = new ReportExpression<ReportColor>(new ReportColor(Color.Black));
   this.Style.Border.Style = new ReportExpression<BorderStyles>(BorderStyles.Solid);
   this.Style.Color = new ReportExpression<ReportColor>(new ReportColor(Color.Gold));
   this.Style.FontSize = new ReportExpression<ReportSize>(new ReportSize(8.0, SizeTypes.Point));
   this.ChangeService().OnComponentChanged(this, null, null, null);
}
public IComponentChangeService ChangeService() {
   if (this._changeService == null)
   {
      this._changeService = (IComponentChangeService)Site.GetService(typeof(IComponentChangeService));
      _changeService.ComponentChanged += new ComponentChangedEventHandler(OnComponentChanged);
   }
   return this._changeService;
}
private void OnComponentChanged(object sender, ComponentChangedEventArgs ce)
{
   Invalidate();
}
```

The ProgressTrackerDesigner InitializeNewComponent event calls the SetDefaults helper method to initialize the properties of the design-time component. ProgressTrackerDesigner inherits standard properties from the CustomReportItemDesigner, such as Font-related properties, which you can then access using CustomReportItemDesigner.Style.<PropertyName> syntax. As it stands, the custom report item architecture provides no way of hiding the standard properties in case you don't need them or they are redundant. For this reason, before introducing a new custom property, check if you can reuse an existing standard property instead.

ProgressTrackerDesigner reuses several Reporting Services standard properties. For example, it uses the Color property for the color of the progress bar and the Font property for the text font. The SetDefaults method initializes both custom and standard properties to default values.

NOTE Due to an unfortunate bug, the changes you've made to standard properties in InitializeNewComponent, such as Style.Color, are not available in the Draw method. In other words, only the default values of the standard properties are available when you add a new instance of the custom report item. This issue will most likely be fixed in a first cumulative update package.

The .NET designer host infrastructure provides services for letting the host and the component exchange information. For example, the IComponentChangeService service supports bidirectional communication between the host and the design-time component. When the user changes a property in the Report Designer Properties grid, the Report Designer fires the OnComponentChanged event to let the component know about the change by passing both the old and new values in the ComponentChangedEventArgs argument. In our case, OnComponentChanged simply invalidates the design-time components to force it to repaint itself.

Similarly, the design-time component can call the OnComponentChanged event to inform the host that its internal state has changed. The SetDefaults method calls IComponentChange-Service.OnComponentChanged to inform Report Designer that its properties have changed. This causes a refresh of the Reporting Designer Properties window to synchronize the component properties with their new values. Finally, SetDefaults calls the Invalidate method, which triggers a call to its Draw event to redraw its image.

Properties

Similar to its Windows Forms control counterpart, any public property of the design-time component is automatically exposed in the Report Designer Properties window. Consequently, the implementation of the custom properties remains essentially the same with a few exceptions. The following code snippet demonstrates the changes to the Value property.

```
[Category("ProgressTracker"), DefaultValue("0"), Description("The actual value.")]
[Editor(typeof(CustomExpressionEditor), typeof(System.Drawing.Design.UITypeEditor))]
public string Value {
   get
   {
      string v = this.GetCustomProperty(Shared.PROP_VALUE);
      return string.IsNullOrEmpty(v) ? ((_progress.Maximum + _progress.Minimum)/2).ToString() : v;
   }
   set
   {
      float result;
      if (float.TryParse(value, out result))
      {
         if (result < _progress.Minimum || result > _progress.Maximum)
            throw new ArgumentException("The progress value must be between the minimum and maximum values.");
         else
         {
            _progress.Value = result;
         }
      }
      else
      {
         if (value.Trim() != String.Empty && !value.Trim().StartsWith("="))
            throw new ArgumentException("Expressions must start with an equal sign.");
      }
      SetCustomProperty(Shared.PROP_VALUE, value); // store in RDL
      this.ChangeService().OnComponentChanged(this, null, null, null);
      Invalidate();
   }
}
```

Unlike the Windows Forms control, whose designer manages property storage, the design-time component is responsible for saving and restoring the property values to and from the report definition. The set accessor calls the SetCustomProperty helper method to serialize the property value to the report definition. Here is what a serialized instance of ProgressTracker looks like:

```
<CustomReportItem Name="progressTracker1">
  <Type>ProgressTracker</Type>
  <Style>
    <Color>Gold</Color>
    <FontFamily>Arial Narrow</FontFamily>
    <FontSize>8pt</FontSize>
  </Style>
  <CustomProperties>
    <C ustomProperty>
      <Name>Value</Name>
      <Value>=Fields!Value.Value</Value>
    </CustomProperty>
    <CustomProperty>
      <Name>ShowValue</Name>
```

```
    <Value>True</Value>
  </CustomProperty>
  <CustomProperty>
    <Name>Hyperlink</Name>
    <Value>=Fields!Hyperlink.Value</Value>
  </CustomProperty>
 </CustomProperties>
</CustomReportItem>
```

When the value of a custom property is changed, the code calls the Invalidate method to force the design-time component to repaint itself. To read the property value from the report definition when the control is instantiated, the get accessor calls the GetCustomProperty method.

Design-time rendering

To help the user visualize the effect of setting the properties, ProgressTracker draws an image at design time. More sophisticated custom report items, such as the Reporting Services chart, may provide different visualization techniques to support design-time and run-time appearances. In our case, ProgressTracker uses the same code to draw its image in both modes. The Report Designer fires the Draw event each time the design-time component needs to be repainted.

```
public override void Draw(Graphics gr, ReportItemDrawParams dp)
{
   float value = 0f;
   _progress.Alpha = this.Alpha;
   _progress.ProgressColor = this.Style.Color.Value.Color;
   _progress.BorderColor = this.Style.Border.Color.Value.Color;
   _progress.ProgressColor = this.Style.Color.Value.Color;
   _progress.Maximum = this.Maximum;
   _progress.Minimum = this.Minimum;
   _progress.Value = float.TryParse(this.Value, out value) ? value :
            (_progress.Maximum + _progress.Minimum) / 2;
   _progress.ShowValue = this.ShowValue;
   _progress.Font = Shared.GetDrawingFontFromReportFont(this.Style.FontFamily.Value,
      this.Style.FontStyle.Value.ToString(), this.Style.FontWeight.Value.ToString(),
      (float) this.Style.FontSize.Value.Value);
   _progress.Height = (int) this.Height;
   _progress.Width = (int) this.Width;
   _progress.DrawControl(gr);
   this.ChangeService();
}
```

The Draw event configures the internal ProgressTracker class and calls its DrawControl method to draw the design-time image on the graphics canvas, which Windows passes as an input argument. Because the rendering code remains practically unchanged from the original Windows Forms control, no further discussion of it is necessary here.

Drag and drop support

Recall that the Value and Hyperlink properties of the Progress Tracker custom report item can be expression-based. For example, the expression =Fields!Value.Value binds the Value property to a dataset field called Value. While the user can type the expression text directly in the property grid, ProgressTrackerDesigner lets the user drop a dataset field onto the image, as shown in Figure 21.6, and constructs the expression text automatically

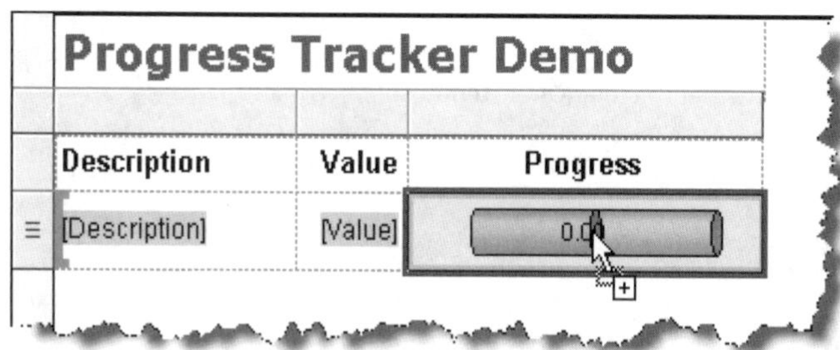

Figure 21.6 Progress Tracker lets the user drags a dataset field to bind the Value property to that field.

Behind the scenes, ProgressTrackerDesigner uses the CustomReportItemDesigner drag-and-drop support. The drag-and-drop implementation is essentially the same as in Windows Forms so I won't spend much time discussing it. The only behavior difference that is worth mentioning takes place in the OnDragEnter event handler, which causes the border area to be drawn.

```
public override void OnDragEnter(DragEventArgs e) {
   IFieldsDataObject fieldsDataObject = e.Data.GetData  (typeof(IReportItemDataObject)) as IFieldsDataObject;

   if (fieldsDataObject != null && fieldsDataObject.Fields != null && fieldsDataObject.Fields.Length > 0) BeginEdit();
}
```

In the absence of the adorner window, BeginEdit draws a selection border around the custom report item when the dragged item is placed in the custom report item area. The net effect is the same as when you drag a dataset field over a table cell of the standard table region. The OnDragDrop event (not shown) constructs the expression and sets the Value property.

Verbs

Another end-user feature that you might want to implement is verbs. Designer verbs let the report author perform custom actions that can be launched by right-clicking the control design surface. ProgressTrackerDesigner implements a Reset Defaults verb that resets the properties of the design-time component to their default values, as shown in Figure 21.7.

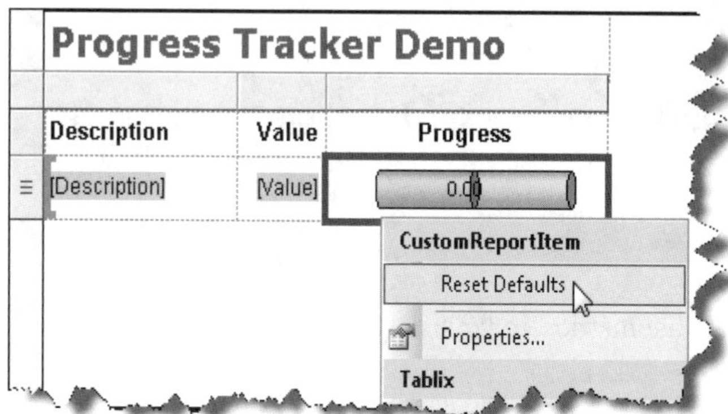

Figure 21.7 The Reset Defaults verb lets the report author reset the custom report item to its default property values.

You implement a verb by overriding the CustomReportItemDesigner Verbs property. Next, add a new verb to the DesignerVerbCollection collection and specify the desired caption and the callback event handler. When the user selects the action from the context menu, CustomReportItemDesigner will invoke the callback event handler where you can execute whatever code is needed.

```
public override DesignerVerbCollection Verbs {
   get {
      if (_verbs == null) {
         _verbs = new DesignerVerbCollection();
         _verbs.Add(new DesignerVerb("Reset Defaults", new EventHandler(OnCustomAction)));
      }
      return _verbs;
   }
}
private void OnCustomAction(object sender, EventArgs e) {
   switch (((System.ComponentModel.Design.DesignerVerb)sender).Text)
   {
      case "Reset Defaults": SetDefaults(); Invalidate(); break;
      default: MessageBox.Show("Not supported"); break;
   }
}
```

In our case, ProgressTrackerDesigner adds a Reset Defaults verb and specifies the OnCustomAction method as a callback event handler. When the report author selects the Reset Defaults context menu, the OnCustomAction fires and calls the SetDefaults method to reset the property values.

Custom editors

Some properties may have more advanced configuration requirements that are best addressed through a custom property editor. For example, suppose you want to apply validation rules to specific properties, or provide a property value from a drop-down list of choices. Or, how about letting the user configure expression-based properties using the standard Reporting Services expression editor? You can associate a property with a custom editor by decorating it with the Editor attribute:

```
[Category("ProgressTracker"), DefaultValue("0"), Description("The actual value.")]
[Editor(typeof(CustomExpressionEditor), typeof(System.Drawing.Design.UITypeEditor))]
public string Hyperlink {}
```

In this example, the Hyperlink property is associated with a custom editor that I implemented. Consequently, the PropertyGrid control will show a button when you click inside the property, as shown in Figure 21.8.

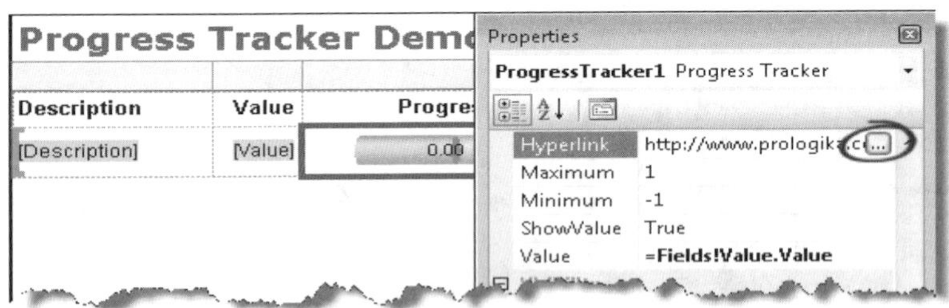

Figure 21.8 You can associate a custom property editor with a property to support more advanced configuration or evaluate business rules.

Clicking the button will invoke the EditValue method in your custom editor class.

```
internal sealed class CustomExpressionEditor : System.Drawing.Design.UITypeEditor {
 public override System.Drawing.Design.UITypeEditorEditStyle GetEditStyle(ITypeDescriptorContext t)
 {
   return System.Drawing.Design.UITypeEditorEditStyle.Modal;
 }
public override object EditValue(ITypeDescriptorContext t,System.IServiceProvider s, object oldValue)
{
   ExpressionEditor editor = new ExpressionEditor();
   object newValue = editor.EditValue(null, ((Microsoft.ReportDesigner.CustomReportItemHost)(t.Instance)).
              CustomReportItemDesigner.Site, new ReportExpression(oldValue.ToString()));
         return newValue != null?newValue:oldValue ;    }
}
```

This class both launches the standard expression editor and provides a way to validate the returned expression. The ExpressionEditor.EditValue method launches the standard expression editor, passing the old value. If the user cancels the expression editor, null will be returned, in which case the custom editor returns the original property value.

Since the WindowsForms Property Grid control uses the same custom editor mechanism as the design-time component, you may find the article Getting the Most Out of the .NET Framework PropertyGrid (see Resources) helpful if you want to learn more about working with custom property editors. Because the Progress Tracker custom report item does not require a custom editor, the ProgressTrackerDesigner class includes only stub code to show you how you might implement a custom editor.

```
[Editor(typeof(CustomEditor), typeof(ComponentEditor))]
class ProgressTrackerDesigner : CustomReportItemDesigner {...}

internal sealed class CustomEditor : ComponentEditor {
   public override bool EditComponent(ITypeDescriptorContext context, object component)
{
      MessageBox.Show("Implement CRI Properties Window here!");
      return true;
}
```

Although I do not provide sample code that implements a custom editor, building a custom editor is relatively easy if you follow these basic steps. First, implement a custom form that will represent the user interface of the editor. Then, decorate the design-time component with the Editor attribute, which references a class that inherits from ComponentEditor. When the report author right-clicks the custom report item, the context menu will show a Properties verb (see Figure 21.7). Selecting the Properties context menu will invoke the EditComponent method, which can instantiate the form, collect the new property values, and apply them to the design-time component. The Microsoft Polygons custom report item sample demonstrates a working custom editor.

21.2.3 Implementing the Run-Time Component

Once you have met and mastered the challenge of creating the design-time component, you will find implementing the run-time component to be simple by comparison. With the run-time component, you only need to worry about drawing the runtime image of the custom report item. To review the source code for the ProgressTracker run-time component, refer to the ProgressTrackerRenderer class in the ProgressTrackerRenderer.cs source file.

Table 21.2 The Reporting Services ICustomReportItem interface

Members	Type	Description
GenerateReportItemDefinition	Method	Generates the definition of the custom report item. Called once per report execution.
EvaluateReportItemInstance	Method	Generates the instance of the custom report. Called for each CRI instance.

About the ICustomReportItem interface

The run-time component of a custom report item must implement the ICustomReportItem Reporting Services interface whose definition is shown in Table 21.2. Implementing GenerateReportItemDefinition is a matter of plugging in a few lines of boilerplate code. The EvaluateReportItemInstance method is the workhorse of the run-time component. It is responsible for rendering the run-time appearance of the custom report item.

Initialization

When the report server executes the report and encounters a custom report item, it instantiates the run-time component (ProgressTrackerRenderer in our case) as many times as the custom report item needs to be rendered on the report. For example, if you have a tablix region bound to a dataset with three rows and place ProgressTracker in a detail cell, when the report is run, the report server will instantiate three instances of its run-time component.

```
public void GenerateReportItemDefinition(CustomReportItem cri)
{
   cri.CreateCriImageDefinition();
   Image progressImage = (Image)cri.Genera tedReportItem;
}
public void EvaluateReportItemInstance(CustomReportItem cri)
{
   // Get the Image definition
   Image progressImage = (Image)cri.GeneratedReportItem;
   // Render the image for the custom report item
   progressImage.ImageInstance.ImageData = DrawImage(cri);
}
private void Initialize(CustomReportItem cri) {
   if (null == _progress)
   {
      _progress = new ProgressTracker();
   }
   _progress.Alpha = Int32.Parse(LookupCustomProperty(cri.CustomProperties,
      Shared.PROP_ALPHA, 255).ToString());
   _progress.ProgressColor = cri.Style.Color.Value.ToColor();
   _progress.BorderColor = cri.Style.Border.Color.Value.ToColor();
   _progress.Font = Shared.GetDrawingFontFromReportFont(cri.Style.FontFamily.Value,
            cri.Style.FontStyle.Value.ToString(), cri.Style.FontWeight.Value.ToString(),
            (float)(cri.Style.FontSize.Value.ToPoints()));
   _progress.Maximum = float.Parse(LookupCustomProperty(cri.CustomProperties,
            Shared.PROP_MAXIMUM, 1f).ToString());
   _progress.Minimum = float.Parse(LookupCustomProperty(cri.CustomProperties,
            Shared.PROP_MINIMUM, -1f).ToString());
   _progress.Value = float.Parse(LookupCustomProperty(cri.CustomProperties,
            Shared.PROP_VALUE, 0).ToString());
   _progress.ShowValue = boo l.Parse(LookupCustomProperty(cri.CustomProperties,
            Shared.PROP_SHOW_VALUE, "true").ToString());
   _progress.Hyperlink = (string)LookupCustomProperty(cri.CustomProperties,
            Shared.PROP_HYPERLINK, String.Empty);
   // size the control
   _progress.Height = (int)(cri.Height.ToInches() * Shared.DPI);
   _progress.Width = (int)(cri.Width.ToInches() * Shared.DPI);
}
```

When the report is processed, the report server invokes the GenerateReportItemDefinition method only once per report execution. This method returns the definition (template) of the image that will be rendered in place of the custom report item. Then, for each CRI instance, the report server calls EvaluateReportItemInstance, passing the image definition. The EvaluateReportItemInstance method is responsible for generating the actual image and setting the ImageData property. If you think of GenerateReportItemDefinition producing a class then EvaluateReportItemInstance provides the instances of this class.

The Initialize method is called by the Draw method, which I will discuss next. The purpose of the Initialize method is to read the custom report item properties. The CustomReportItem object contains the standard and custom properties that were set at design time. Currently, it is not possible to reference other report items on the report or the report object itself. It is important to note that if the property value is expression-based, it is evaluated and resolved by the report processor before the CustomReportItem object is passed to the run-time component. For example, if the ProgressTracker component is bound to a dataset field (its Value property is set to a Fields!<FieldName>.Value expression), the actual field value is retrieved by the report processor and made available under the Value property.

Run-time rendering

The EvaluateReportItemInstance method calls the DrawImage helper method to obtain the run-time image of the custom report item.

```
private byte[] DrawImage(CustomReportItem cri)
{
   byte[] imageData;
   // initialize CRI from properies in RDL
   Initialize(cri);
   CreateAction(cri); // creates a hyperlink action

   Drawing.Bitmap image = new Drawing.Bitmap(_progress.Width,
      _progress.Height, PixelFormat.Format32bppArgb);
   System.Drawing.Graphics graphics = Drawing.Graphics.FromImage(image);
   Drawing.Color backgroundColor = cri.Style.BackgroundColor.Value.ToColor();
   if (backgroundColor.IsEmpty) backgroundColor = Drawing.Color.White;
   graphics.Clear(backgroundColor);

   _progress.DrawControl(graphics);
   // create a memory stream to save the image
   using (MemoryStream stream = new MemoryStream())
   {
      image.Save(stream, ImageFormat.Bmp);
      imageData = new byte[(int)stream.Length];
      stream.Seek(0, SeekOrigin.Begin);
      stream.Read(imageData, 0, (int)stream.Length);
   }
   return imageData;
}
```

The code starts by calling the Initialize method to initialize the custom report item using the properties that are configured for it. Next, DrawImage calls the CreateAction helper method to create a hyperlink action. After the hyperlink is created, the code creates a Graphics object from a bitmap image. Finally, it calls the same DrawControl method that is used by the design-time component to render the design-time image.

TIP As it stands, Reporting Services supports rendering custom report items as raster images only. Vector formats, such as EMF and SVG, are not supported. By default, the custom report item will be rendered with a resolution of 300 DPI. You can specify a custom resolution by calling the Drawing.Bitmap SetResolution method. You can also control the image size by setting the CustomReportItem.GeneratedReportItem.Sizing property to one of the pre-defined settings, such as FitProportional.

Once the image is drawn, it is saved in a memory stream so it can be converted to a byte array. DrawImage sets the image MIME type to image/bmp, but you can choose another standard image format if needed.

Report actions

A custom report item can support Reporting Services navigation actions, including bookmark, hyperlink, and drillthrough actions. A bookmark action lets the report user jump to another place on the report. A hyperlink action navigates the user to a Web page. A drillthrough action opens another report.

Implementing an action requires creating an image map that will be imposed on the run-time image. Progress Tracker implements a hyperlink action that uses the URL address from the Hyperlink property. As a result, once the report is rendered, the report user can click on the custom report item image to navigate to a web page, as shown in Figure 21.9.

Progress Tracker Demo

Description	Value	Progress
Positive Value	0.25	0.25

Figure 21.9 The report user can click on the custom report item image when the report is rendered to navigate to a Web page.

The CreateAction method implements the action.

```
private void CreateAction () {
      if (!string.IsNullOrEmpty(_progress.Hyperlink))
      {
      Image progressImage = (Image)cri.GeneratedReportItem;
      ActionInfoWithDynamicImageMap imageMap =
            progressImage.ImageInstance.CreateActionInfoWithDynamicImageMap();
      Action action = imageMap.CreateHyperlinkAction();
      action.Instance.HyperlinkText = _progress.Hyperlink;
      // top left and bottom right coordinates (last two are in percentage points!)
      float[] coordinates = new float[] { 20, 5, 90, 90 };
      imageMap.CreateImageMapAreaInstance(ImageMapArea.ImageMapAreaShape.Rectangle, coordinates);
      }
}
```

First, the CreateAction method checks if the user has set the Hyperlink property. If this is the case, CreateAction obtains the image map by calling CustomReportItem.ImageInstance.-CreateActionInfoWithDynamicImageMap and calls CreateHyperlinkAction to obtain a reference to the Action object of the image map. Next, CreateAction sets the action target to the value of the Hyperlink property.

CreateAction constructs the four map coordinates of a rectangle that will represent the clickable area. The first two values define the upper left coordinates of the image map in pixels. I am offsetting the x-coordinate by 20 pixels and the y-coordinate by 5 pixels because the custom report item doesn't occupy the entire containing cell. The last two coordinates specify the width and height of the map area as percentage values. I am setting them to 90 percent of the map area because there is a gap between the image and the right cell border when the custom report item is rendered inside a tablix cell. Finally, CreateAction calls CreateImageMapAreaInstance to create a rectangular image map area with these coordinates.

21.3 Working with Progress Tracker

Now that you've seen how the Progress Tracker custom report item is implemented, let's learn how to use it. First, I will walk you through the steps to deploy and register Progress Tracker. Next, I will show you how to use it on a report. Finally, I will demonstrate how you can debug Progress Tracker to step through its code for troubleshooting purposes.

21.3.1 Deploying Progress Tracker

Before using Progress Tracker you need to deploy its binaries to the BIDS Report Designer and report server binary folders. In addition, you need to make changes to the Reporting Services configuration files. For your convenience, I enclosed my versions of the configuration files in the Config folder. Use them for reference only! Do not overwrite your configuration files with mine.

Deploying to Report Designer

To use Progress Tracker in the BIDS Report Designer, you need to deploy and register it as follows:

1. Deploy the Prologika.ProgressTracker binaries (Prologika.ProgressTracker.dll and Prologika.ProgressTracker.pdb) to Visual Studio 2008 (\Program Files\Microsoft Visual Studio 9.0\Common7\IDE\PrivateAssemblies folder). For your convenience, I've created a post-build script (see the Build Events tab in the project properties) that copies the binaries after the project is built successfully.
2. To register Progress Tracker with Report Designer, add an entry for the Progress Tracker custom report item in the Report Designer configuration file (\Program Files\Microsoft Visual Studio 9.0\Common7\IDE\PrivateAssemblies\RSReportDesigner.config), as follows:

```
<ReportItemDesigner>
    <ReportItem Name="ProgressTracker"
    Type="Prologika.RS.Extensibility.ProgressTrackerCRI.ProgressTrackerDesigner, Prologika.ProgressTracker"/>
</ReportItemDesigner>
<ReportItems>
<ReportItem Name="ProgressTracker"
    Type="Prologika.RS.Extensibility.ProgressTrackerCRI.ProgressTrackerRenderer, Prologika.ProgressTracker"/>
</ReportItems>
```

To elevate the Progress Tracker CAS security rights:

3. Open the Report Designer preview policy file (RSPreviewPolicy.config), which is located by default in C:\Program Files\Microsoft Visual Studio 9.0\Common7\IDE\PrivateAssemblies, and add the following CodeGroup element:

```
<CodeGroup class="UnionCodeGroup" version="1" Name="CRICodeGroup"
        Description="Code group for the ProgressTracker CRI" PermissionSetName="FullTrust">
        <IMembershipCondition class="UrlMembershipCondition" version="1"
        Url="C:\ Program Files\Microsoft Visual Studio 9.0\Common7\IDE\PrivateAssemblies\
        Prologika.ProgressTracker.dll" />
</CodeGroup>
```

The next steps add the Progress Tracker custom report item to the Reporting Services toolbox.

4. Open Business Intelligence Development Studio and create a Report Server project or open an existing Report Server project.
5. Open a report in the Report Designer and switch to the Layout tab.
6. Right-click the Toolbox pane and select Choose Items.
7. In the Choose Toolbox Items dialog box that follows, leave the .Net Components tab selected. Click the Browse button and navigate to the ProgressTracker assembly (\Program Files\Microsoft Visual Studio 9.0\Common7\IDE\PrivateAssemblies\Prologika.ProgressTracker.dll).

If Progress Tracker doesn't show up in the Preview tab of the Report Designer and there are no errors, it is probably not registered properly. Double-check steps 1 and 2.

Deploying to Report Server

Follow these steps to deploy the Progress Tracker custom report item to the report server:

1. Deploy the Prologika.ProgressTracker assembly to the report server binary folder (\Program Files\Microsoft SQL Server\MSRS10.MSSQLSERVER\Reporting Services\ReportServer\bin).

Because the Report Processor interacts with the run-time component only, it is sufficient to just register the ReportItem element in the report server configuration file.

2. Add the ReportItem section to the report server configuration file (\Program Files\Microsoft SQL Server\MSRS10.MSSQLSERVER\Reporting Services\ReportServer\rsreportserver.config).

```
<ReportItem Name="ProgressTracker"
    Type="Prologika.RS.Extensibility.ProgressTrackerCRI.ProgressTrackerRenderer,
    Prologika.ProgressTracker"/>
</ReportItems>
```

3. Elevate the security permissions of the custom report item assembly for run-time execution by adding the following CodeGroup to the report server policy file (\Program Files\Microsoft SQL Server\ MSRS10.MSSQLSERVER \Reporting Services\ReportServer\rssrvpolicy.config).

```
<CodeGroup class="UnionCodeGroup" version="1" Name="CRICodeGroup"
  Description="Code group for the ProgressTracker CRI" PermissionSetName="FullTrust">
  <IMembershipCondition class="UrlMembershipCondition" version="1"
  Url="C:\Program Files\Microsoft SQL Server\MSRS10.MSSQLSERVER\Reporting Services\
    ReportServer\bin\Prologika.ProgressTracker.dll"/>
</CodeGroup>
```

NOTE If your custom report item references dependent assemblies, you have to deploy these assemblies to the Report Designer and report server as well.

Testing Progress Tracker

The KPIDemo and ProgressTrackerDemo reports included in the Report Server Reports project demonstrates the Progress Tracker custom report item. The ProgressTrackerDemo is simpler because it doesn't connect to a data source. I followed these steps to author the ProgressTrackerDemo report:

1. Create a report dataset that has the following query:

```
select 0.25 as Value, 'Positive Value' as Description, 'http://www.prologika.com' as Hyperlink
union
select -.25, 'Negative Value', 'http://www.contoso.com'
union
select 0, 'No Change',  'http://www.adventure-works.com'
order by 1 DESC
```

This query generates a static dataset without connecting to a data source.

2. While you can use Progress Tracker outside a report region and set its properties to static values, it is most useful when it is bound to a dataset field. Switch to the Layout tab and drop a table region into the report area.
3. Drag Progress Tracker from the Reporting Services Toolbox and drop it in a table detail field.
4. Drag a dataset field and drop it on Progress Tracker to bind it to the field. Alternatively, enter the field expression in the Progress Tracker Value property or use the expression editor.
5. Right-click on the design-time image and test the Reset Default and Properties verbs.
6. Optionally, bind the Hyperlink property to a dataset field that contains URL addresses, such as the Hyperlink field, if you used the above query.
7. Preview the report.

Test the hyperlink action by hovering on the Progress Tracker image. The mouse cursor should change to a hand. When you click on the image, the report should redirect you to the correct URL address.

21.3.2 Debugging Progress Tracker

There are several techniques to debug a custom report item. If you just want to step through the code, you'll probably find stand-alone preview most convenient, so let's start with it.

Standalone preview

Debugging with stand-alone preview is easy to setup.

1. Add the report project and the CRI project to the same Visual Studio solution.
2. In the report project properties, set the StartItem property to the report that hosts the custom report item, such as ProgressTrackerDemo.rdl.
3. In the Solution Explorer, right-click the report project and click Set as Startup Project.
4. Press F5.

The report will be loaded in the stand-alone preview window and you will be able to step through the run-time component. However, you won't be able to debug the design-component, nor you will be able to make code changes to the custom report item. This is because when custom code is loaded, the Report Designer locks the custom report item assembly in the process space of the Visual Studio IDE that hosts the report project. Unfortunately, the only way to re-deploy a new version of the assembly is to shut down the Visual Studio instance. As you can imagine, this can be quite irritating during the implementation stage.

Start external program

When stand-alone preview gets in the way, you can launch the report project in a separate instance of Visual Studio.

1. Exclude the report project from your Visual Studio solution that contains the code projects.
2. Right-click on the ProgressTrackerCRI project in the Solution Explorer and select Set as Startup Project.
3. Open the ProgressTrackerCRI project properties and switch to the Debug tab as shown in Figure 21.10.
4. In the Start External Program field, enter the full path to the Visual Studio 9.0 executable, such as C:\Program Files\Microsoft Visual Studio 9.0\Common7\IDE\devenv.exe.
5. In the Command Line Arguments field, enter the path to the Report Server project that contains a report that uses the custom report item.
6. Set breakpoints in your design-time and/or run-time components.
7. Press F5 to start debugging.

The Visual Studio debugger will load the Report Server project in another instance of Visual Studio. The debug breakpoints inside the design-time component should be hit when you work with the custom report item in the Design tab of the Report Designer. The debug breakpoints inside the run-time component should be hit when you preview the report by clicking the Preview tab.

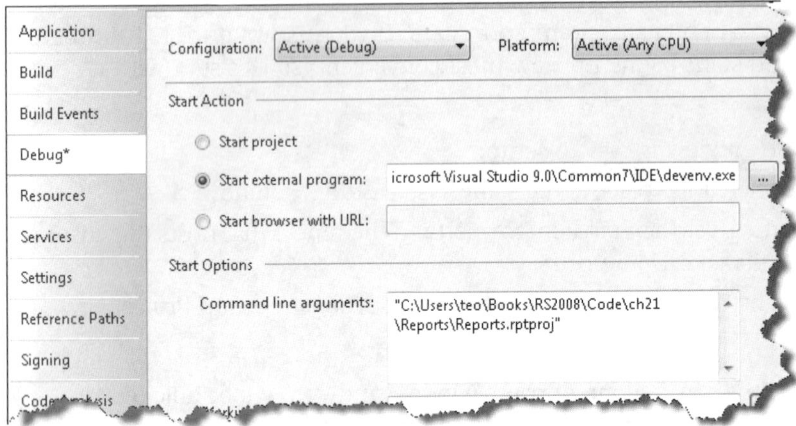

Figure 21.10 To facilitate debugging your custom report item, set up the project debug setting to load the external report project.

21.4 Understanding Custom Data Regions

Progress Tracker is implemented as a single-valued standard report item, not unlike a standard text box report item. But what if your requirements call for a full-blown report data region, such as a chart, that binds to a dataset and displays multiple values? The Microsoft Polygons sample demonstrates how this can be done. In this section, we will take brief detour from the Progress Tracker sample to discuss the changes that are required to develop a custom data region. To do this, I will walk you through relevant portions of the Polygons sample code.

21.4.1 Understanding the CustomData Object

The key to implementing a custom data region is in understanding how the Reporting Services CustomData object encapsulates the data region groupings and data. Table 21.3 lists the most interesting properties of the CustomData object.

Table 21.3 The CustomData object includes the following important properties

Members	Description
RowCollection	Contains the data values within each detail cell of the custom report item.
DataColumnHierarchy	Represents the column groupings of the data region.
DataRowHierarchy	Represents the row groupings of the data region.

21.4.2 Using CustomData at Design Time

The CustomData object is available both at design time and run time. At design time, the custom report item populates the CustomData object with the definitions of the data region column and row groupings. At run time, the CustomData object provides the actual data cell ues.

Using CustomData at design time

Just like a tablix region, your custom data region can contain groups. The following abbreviated code from the InitializeNewComponent method in Polygons design-time component (PolygonsDesigner) shows how the Polygons custom report item defines a row grouping.

```
public override void InitializeNewComponent(){
   CustomData = new CustomData();
   CustomData.DataRowHierarchy = new DataHierarchy();

   // Shape grouping
   CustomData.DataRowHierarchy.DataMembers.Add(new DataMember());
   CustomData.DataRowHierarchy.DataMembers[0].Group = new Group();
   CustomData.DataRowHierarchy.DataMembers[0].Group.Name = Name + "_Shape";
   CustomData.DataRowHierarchy.DataMembers[0].Group.GroupExpressions.Add(new ReportExpression());
```

Defining a new grouping involves specifying the group name, expression, and additional properties that are available in the grouping dialog box in Report Designer, such as filters, page breaks, and so on. Similarly, you can add column groupings to the CustomData.ColumnHierarchy, such as when you want to implement matrix-style regions.

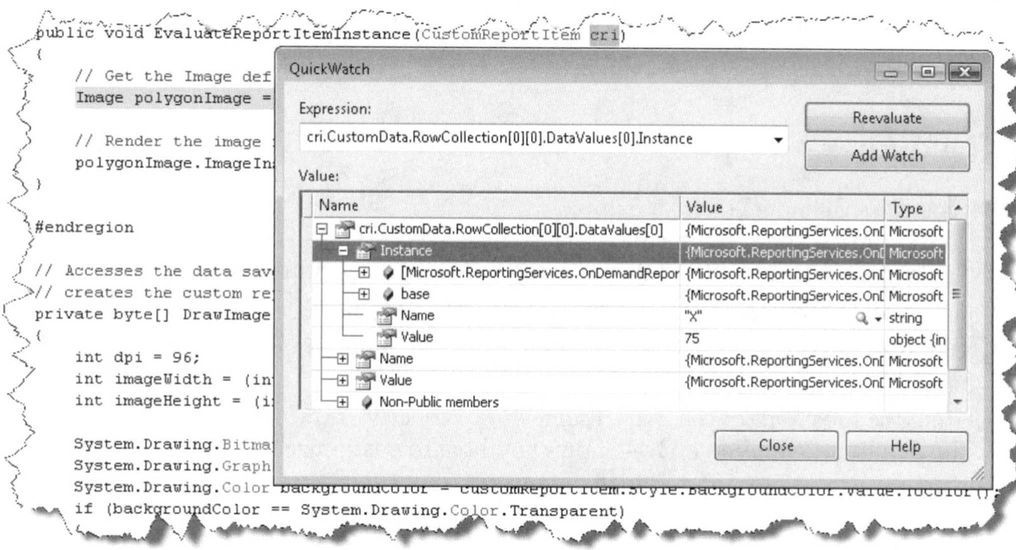

Figure 21.11 The CustomReportItem object includes a CustomData object that provides the data cell values.

Using CustomData at run time

At run time, you need more than the group definitions to render the data region. You need the actual data cell values. Fortunately, the Report Processor passes the data in the RowCollection object, as shown in Figure 21.11. To understand how this worked, I put a breakpoint in the EvaluateReportItemInstance method. I highlighted the cri argument that represents the CustomReportItem object and pressed Ctrl-Alt-Q to inspect it in the Visual Studio QuickWatch window.

Notice that the CustomData RowCollecton object gives you access to the data cell values. You can think of the RowCollecton object as a two-dimension array where the first argument specifies the row index, while the second specifies the column index. Thus, RowCollection[0,0].DataValues[0] returns the cell value in the first row and first column. Once you locate the value, you can use its IsExpression property to determine if it contains a static value or an expression. In the latter case, call the Instance.Value property to obtain the actual value. From here, your custom data region can loop through the data values to render the run-time image, such as plotting the values on a chart as the Polygons custom report item does.

21.5 Summary

Custom report items let you extend report server presentation capabilities. Consider implementing a custom report item when your reporting requirements go beyond what the standard report items can deliver. Custom report items help you convey information in the form of graphics elements and images. Anything that can be rendered as an image with GDI+ can be implemented as a custom report item and rendered on reports.

A custom report item has a design-time component and a run-time component. The design-time component provides a user interface for specifying custom properties, adornment, and verbs, as well as launching custom editors for advanced configuration scenarios. At ru time, the report server interacts with the run-time component to render the custom report item in the report.

21.6 Resources

Mycostech's CylinderTrackBar Sample
(http://tinyurl.com/35qpmc or http://tinyurl.com/2qlj2n)—The Mycostech's CylinderTrackBar sample on which the Progress Tracker was built.

Create And Host Custom Designers with The .NET Framework 2.0
(http://tinyurl.com/qfj5m)—Learn about the .NET designer host infrastructure and services.

Getting the Most Out of the .NET Framework PropertyGrid Control
(http://tinyurl.com/ymvep3)—Shows you how to customize the Windows Forms PropertyGrid control and implement custom property editors.

Chapter 22

Customizing Report Definitions

Recall from part 1 of this book that expressions let you customize the report presentation, such as hiding a column at run time based on a parameter value. Sometimes, however, your customization requirements may go beyond what expressions and conditional visibility can deliver. For example, you may need to add new columns to a tablix or generate an entirely new section based on certain conditions. This is where report definition customization extensions can help.

In this chapter, I will introduce you to this extensibility area. After laying down the fundamentals, I'll walk you through the steps of implementing a report definition customization extension that varies the report presentation per user. Finally, I will show you how to deploy and test the sample extension.

22.1 Understanding Report Definition Customization Extensions

Report definition customization extensions are an entirely new extensibility feature in Reporting Services 2008. They were introduced to meet the needs of Microsoft Dynamics, which required more flexible ways for customizing reports. The Reporting Services team addressed this requirement elegantly by introducing a new extension type and making its interface publicly available. Report definition customization extensions are supported in Standard and Enterprise editions of SQL Server 2008 only.

22.1.1 What is a Report Definition Customization Extension?

As its name suggests, a report definition customization extension lets you customize the report definition at run time. As a developer, it is up to you to decide what level of customization the extension would provide. This can range from changing a few report properties to replacing the entire report with a completely new report definition. Once the report is configured for customization, you have complete control over its definition and you can apply dynamically whatever modifications are needed to the original report.

When to use report definition customization extensions

Here are a few scenarios where report definition customization extensions could be useful:

- Personalizing the report content—You can modify the report definition at run time based on certain conditions. For example, you can add or remove report sections based on parameter values.

- Localizing reports—You can replace the original report definition with a localized (translated) report definition based on the user culture.
- Simplifying the report presentation for handheld devices—You could use a parameter to collect a user preference for viewing a full or partial report, and then swap out the full report when user specifies a preference for viewing the partial report.

I am sure you will find many other practical usage scenarios that may benefit from report definition customization extensions. As you can imagine, this extensibility mechanism brings a lot of flexibility. On the downside, it requires additional development and configuration effort.

NOTE Personally, instead of a new extensibility mechanism, I'd prefer server-side events, such as OnPrint, BeforeReportProcess, and so on, that would provide access to the report object model. Events would allow developers to change the report definition dynamically in expression or custom code. This will reduce development and management effort as you don't have to implement and configure an extension. However, as its stands, Reporting Services doesn't support events. While waiting for this enhancement, consider report definition customized extensions for addressing more advanced customization requirements.

Understanding run-time interaction

From a Reporting Services perspective, interacting with a report definition customization extension is simple. The report server hands the extension a stream containing the published report definition and expects a revised RDL stream in return. Figure 22.1 shows the run-time interaction between the report server and the extension.

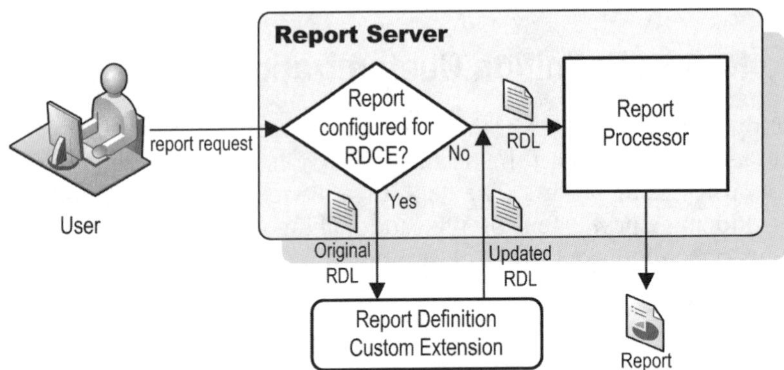

Figure 22.1 At run time, the report server gets the updated report RDL from the report definition customization extension.

When the end user submits a report request, the report server checks if the requested report is configured for customization. If it is, the report server calls the report definition customization extension for every incoming request to that report. The report server executes the extension code *before* it processes the report definition but *after* query and report parameters are already evaluated. This is important because it lets you evaluate the report execution context to decide how to customize the report definition.

Specifically, the report server invokes the ProcessReportDefinition method of the IReportDefinitionCustomizationExtension interface and passes the original (published) report definition, the report context, and user context. Next, it is up to you to decide how to customize the report definition. If needed, you can load an entirely new report definition from disk and return it to the report server. For example, if you have different presentation requirements for different groups of users, you could load an entirely new report definition from disk depending on the user's group membership. Or, you can make more granular changes by loading the report definition in the RDL Object Model (discussed in chapter 7), manipulating the model in an object-oriented way, including changing properties, adding columns, and so on.

Once the report server receives the customized report definition, it publishes it internally to replace the original report definition. However, the customized report definition doesn't permanently replace the original definition. Instead, its lifetime is bound to the user report execution session only. This lets you implement user-specific customization features. Once published, the customized report is processed and rendered just like any other report.

Report definition customization extensions are exclusive to live reports. Because report definition customizations are user-specific, you cannot configure a customized report for snapshot execution. Another important consideration to keep in mind is that the report definition customization extensions are a server-only feature. Consequently, you cannot test the extension in the report design tools. Once the extension is ready, you must configure it on the server. As a part of the configuration process, you must configure each customizable report to reference a report definition customization extension. You can implement one extension that customizes several reports or you can have report-specific extensions. A report can be associated with only one report definition customization extension.

22.1.2 Understanding Programming Interfaces

As with the other Reporting Services custom extensions, the report definition customization extension must implement standard interfaces. Specifically, it must implement the IReportDefinitionCustomizationExtension and IExtension interfaces.

Understanding the IReportDefinitionCustomizationExtension interface

The IReportDefinitionCustomizationExtension interface is included in the Microsoft.ReportingServices.Interfaces assembly. The default location of this assembly is C:\Program Files\Microsoft SQL Server\100\SDK\Assemblies. The IReportDefinitionCustomizationExtension interface defines a single ProcessReportDefinition method whose arguments are described in Table 22.1.

Table 22.1 The IReportDefinitionCustomizationExtension.ProcessReportDefinition method arguments

Argument	Type	Description
reportDefinition	byte[]	Contains the original report definition.
reportContext	IReportContext	Exposes the report context, such as parameter values.
userContext	IUserContext	Provides the user context, including the user login.
reportDefinitionProcessed	out byte[]	Contains the customized report definition.
customizedElementIds	out IEnumerable<RdceCustomizableElementId>	Describes which elements are customized.

The report server passes the published report definition to the report definition argument as a byte array. It also passes the report context to the reportContext argument. The report context includes configuration information about the requested report, including the report type (linked report or subreport), report parameters and their run-time values, the report name and path.

The userContext class contains the user name and authentication type. For example, if the report server is configured for Windows authentication and the report server belongs to an

Active Directory domain, the userContext.AuthenticationType property returns "Windows" and the userContext.UserName property returns the Windows identify of the interactive user in the format domain\login. Unfortunately, as it stands, the report server doesn't pass the security policies defined in the Report Manager for the user. If this is required, consider integrating the extension with the Report Server Web service. For example, the extension can call the GetPermissions API to obtain and evaluate the security policies associated with the user.

TIP The userContext argument doesn't include the user language (User!Language), which you will need if you want to provide a culture-specific report customization. However, you can set up a hidden report parameter with the default value of =User!Language. At run time, the report server will pass all report parameter values to your extension and you can obtain the user language from the hidden parameter.

Your report definition customization extension can examine the report context and user context to determine if report customization is necessary. If you decide to customize, you must return the new definition as a byte array by setting the reportDefinitionProcessed argument. You need to inform the server which elements have been customized by setting the customizedElementIds argument. For example, if you've made changes to the report body only, add RdceCustomizableElementId.Body to the customizedElementIds collection. If you set customizedElementIds to null, the report server will not change the report definition although the reportDefinitionProcessed argument may return a customized version. If customizedElementIds is not null, the report server will merge the original report definition with your changes as specified by the RdceCustomizableElementId argument and publish the merged definition.

The ProcessReportDefinition method returns a Boolean value that indicates if the report definition needs to be changed. If you decide to customize the report definition, set the return value to True to let the report server know about the change so it can publish the new report definition. If ProcessReportDefinition returns False, the report server will not merge the processed definition with the original report definition. Instead, it will use the original report definition.

Understanding the IExtension interface

The IReportDefinitionCustomizationExtension interface implements the IExtension interface, which you are already familiar with as you used it to implement the custom extensions discussed in the preceding chapters. Recall that the IExtension interface defines two methods: LocalizedName and SetConfiguration.

You can use the LocalizedName property to return a localized name of the extension based on the culture settings of the interactive user. However, since the report definition customization extensions are not displayed in Report Manager, our implementation of LocalizedName returns a static label.

You can use the SetConfiguration method to initialize the extension from a custom configuration section. For example, if you want to show content for specific users, you can enumerate the user logins in the configuration section. With each report request, even if it originates from the same user, the report server will call SetConfiguration before calling ProcessReportDefinition.

22.2 Working with the Extension Sample

Suppose that you want to vary the report content based on the interactive user. For example, you may want the report to show sensitive information only to privileged users. One implementation approach could be to hide report content conditionally using expressions. However, suppose that strict security or operational requirements dictate that the report cannot retrieve and process sensitive information if the user is not authorized. This scenario is ideal for considering a custom report definition extension.

My RDCE sample extension shows how you can leverage this new extensibility mechanism to implement such requirements. The source code is provided in the Visual Studio RCDE solution file. This solution includes the code of the report definition customization extension and a sample report to test it. You will need Visual Studio to work with the source code.

22.2.1 Implementing a Report Definition Customization Solution

Implementing a report definition customization extension involves several steps, including:

- Authoring the report(s) that users the customization extension
- Implementing the extension
- Deploying and testing the extension

Let's start by understanding the sample report that our extension will customize.

About the Sales Persons report

We will use the Sales Persons report, shown in Figure 22.2, to demonstrate customizing the report definition dynamically. This report shows a list of all Adventure Works sales people. By default, the report doesn't retrieve, process, or display the sales person's base rate. If you examine the report dataset, you would notice that its query requests only FirstName, LastName, HireDate, and LoginID columns from the DimEmployee table in the Adventure-WorksDW2008 database.

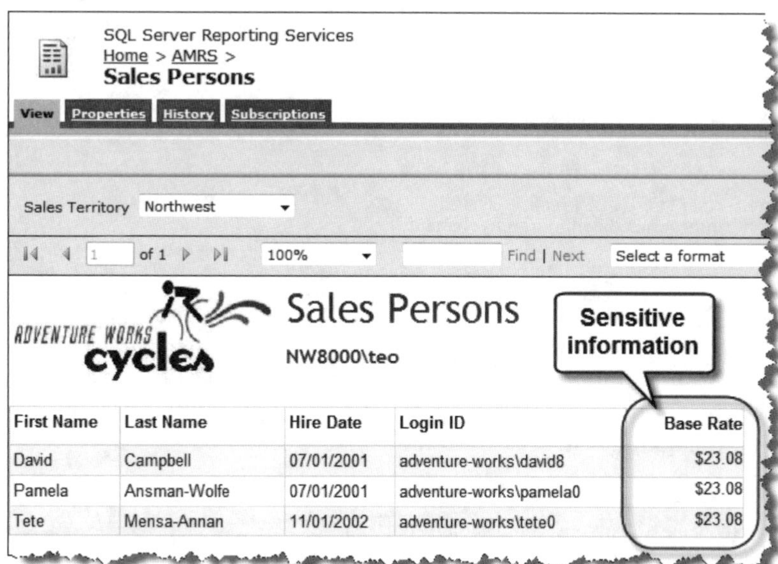

Figure 22.2 This report retrieves and displays the sales person rate only if the user is authorized to see it.

The dataset query doesn't request the BaseRate column. Consequently, the dataset doesn't include a BaseRate field and the table region doesn't define this column. So how does BaseRate get added to the report? Thanks to a report definition customization extension, the BaseRate column shows up at run time when the Sales Persons report is requested by a user who is authorized to view BaseRate information. The extension starts by examining the identity of the interactive user. If the user is privileged, the extension changes the report definition on the fly. Specifically, the extension customizes the report definition by dynamically adding the following elements:

- A new BaseRate column to the report query
- A new BaseRate dataset field that references the BaseRate query column
- A new Base Rate column to the table region

For the sake of simplicity, the extension supports only a single privileged user whose identity you can specify when you configure the extension. A real-life solution would probably require more involved authorization process, such as querying a database profile store or integrating with a custom security service.

Implementing IExtension

To implement a report definition customization extension, I wrote a ReportDefinitionCustomizationExtension class that implements the IReportDefinitionCustomizationExtension interface. Recall that IExtension is a common interface available to all custom extensions. You can use its methods to localize the extension name and perform initializing tasks. For our purposes, we will use IExtension to get the identity of the privileged user from the extension configuration section.

```
public string LocalizedName
{
   get { return "Prologika Report Definition Customization Extension Sample"; }
}

public void SetConfiguration(string configuration) {
   // Retrieve the identity of the privileged user who is authorized to see sensitive data
   XmlDocument doc = new XmlDocument();
   doc.LoadXml(configuration);
   if (doc.DocumentElement.Name == "RDCEConfiguration")
   {
      foreach (XmlNode child in doc.DocumentElement.ChildNodes)
      {
         switch (child.Name)
         {
            case PRIVILEGED_USER: _user = child.InnerText; break;
            default: throw new Exception("Unrecognized configuration element.");
         }
      }
   }
   else throw new Exception("Loading config data.");
}
```

The report server invokes the SetConfiguration method with each report request and passes the extension configuration section as specified in the report server configuration file (rsreportserver.config). Here is what the configuration section looks like:

```
<ReportDefinitionCustomization>
     <Extension Name="PrologikaRDCE"
          Type="Prologika.RS.Extensibility.ReportDefinitionCustomizationExtension,
          Prologika.ReportDefinitionCustomizationExtension">
          <Configuration>
                    <RDCEConfiguration>
                              <PrivilegedUser> nw8000\teo</PrivilegedUser>
                    </RDCEConfiguration>
          </Configuration>
     </Extension>
</ReportDefinitionCustomization>
```

SetConfiguration loads the configuration section in an XmlDocument object and navigates its elements in an attempt to find a PrivilegedUser element that specifies the Windows identity of the privileged user (nw8000\teo in my case). SetConfiguration stores the Windows logon in the _user class-level member.

Implementing ProcessReportDefinition

The ProcessReportDefinition method is the workhorse of the custom extension.

```
public class ReportDefinitionCustomizationExtension : IReportDefinitionCustomizationExtension {
   internal const string PRIVILEGED_USER = "PrivilegedUser";
   private string _user = null;
   Microsoft.ReportingServices.RdlObjectModel.Report _report = null;
   RdlSerializer _serializer = new RdlSerializer();

   public bool ProcessReportDefinition(
      byte[] reportDefinition,
      IReportContext reportContext,
      IUserContext userContext,
      out byte[] reportDefinitionProcessed,
      out IEnumerable<RdceCustomizableElementId> customizedElementIds) {

      MemoryStream mstream = null;
      if (String.Compare(_user, userContext.UserName, StringComparison.OrdinalIgnoreCase) != 0)
      {
         // not the right user so return the original RDL without any changes
         reportDefinitionProcessed = null;
         customizedElementIds = null;
         return false;
      }
      // use RDLOM to deserialize the original RDL as a report object
      using (mstream = new MemoryStream(reportDefinition))
      {
            mstream.Position = 0;
            _report = _serializer.Deserialize(mstream);
      }

      AddQueryFields();          // add query fields
      AddDatasetFields();        // add dataset fields
      AddColumns();              // add tablix columns

      // serialize the report payload to byte array
      using (mstream = new MemoryStream())
      {
            _serializer.Serialize(mstream, _report);
            reportDefinitionProcessed = mstream.ToArray();
      }
      // let RS know what's been changed
      List<RdceCustomizableElementId> ids = new List<RdceCustomizableElementId>();
      ids.Add(RdceCustomizableElementId.Body);
      ids.Add(RdceCustomizableElementId.DataSets);
      customizedElementIds = ids;

      return true; // RDL is customized
   }
```

ProcessReportDefinition starts by checking the identity of the interactive user. If it doesn't match the identity of the privileged user, ProcessReportDefinition exits and returns false to tell the report server that no changes have been made. Otherwise, ProcessReportDefinition proceeds with customizing the report definition.

As noted in chapter 7, Reporting Services now includes an unsupported RDL Object Model (RDLOM) that lets you access the report definition as an object. ProcessReportDefinition uses RDLOM to load the original report definition and make changes. ProcessReportDefinition instantiates a .NET MemoryStream object to load the original report definition in memory. Then, it uses the RDLOM Serializer object to deserialize the report definition. Next, it calls the

AddQueryFields, AddDatasetFields, and AddColumns helper methods to customize the report definition. These methods use RDLOM to perform similar changes as the ones described in the RDLOM sample in chapter 7, so discussing them here will be redundant.

Once the RDL changes have been made, we need to serialize the report definition back to a byte array because this is what the report server expects as an output from ProcessReportDefinition. ProcessReportDefinition uses a memory stream to deserialize the RDL object model to memory. Then, it calls the MemoryStream ToArray method to obtain the report payload as a byte array. Next, ProcessReportDefinition constructs a list of RdceCustomizableElementId elements to tell the report server what changes have been made. The RdceCustomizableElementId enumeration supports changes in five types of elements (Body, DataSets, Page, PageHeader, and PageFooter). Since the extension performs data and layout changes only, it adds only the Body and DataSets items to inform the server only these elements have changed. Finally, ProcessReportDefinition returns True to inform the report server that the report definition has been changed.

22.2.2 Deploying and Testing

Recall that the report definition customization extensions are a server only feature. Consequently, you cannot test the extension in Report Designer. Instead, you must deploy the extension to the report server first and use Report Manager to view the customized report. Deploying the custom extension requires that you change the report server configuration files. Included with the source code for this chapter, you will find my version of the affected files. Use these files for your reference only. Do not replace your configuration files with mine.

Deploying the extension binaries

Start by deploying the (Prologika.ReportDefinitionCustomizationExtension assembly to the report server.

1. Copy the Prologika.ReportDefinitionCustomizationExtension.dll and Prologika.ReportDefinitionCustomizationExtension.pdb binaries from the project output folder.
2. Paste them in the report server bin folder whose default location is C:\Program Files\Microsoft SQL Server\MSRS10.MSSQLSERVER\Reporting Services\ReportServer\bin.

For your convenience, I have defined a post-build script in the RDCE project properties that copies the binaries automatically to the report server bin folder after a successful build.

Registering the extension with the report server

By default, the report server doesn't allow executing report definition customization extensions for security reasons. Follow these steps to enable their execution:

1. Open the report server configuration file (rsreportserver.config) in your favorite text editor. The default location of this file is C:\Program Files\Microsoft SQL Server\MSRS10.MSSQLSERVER\Reporting Services\ReportServer.
2. Locate the <Service> element and add the IsRdceEnabled setting as follows:

```
    <IsRdceEnabled>True</IsRdceEnabled>
</Service> <!-- for reference only -- >
```

3. Scroll down to the end of the file and locate the </Extensions> element. Add a new Extension section just before the </Extensions> element as follows:

```
<Extension Name="PrologikaRDCE"
      Type="Prologika.RS.Extensibility.ReportDefinitionCustomizationExtension,
      Prologika.ReportDefinitionCustomizationExtension">
   <Configuration>
    <RDCEConfiguration>
      <PrivilegedUser><login></PrivilegedUser>
    </RDCEConfiguration>
   </Configuration>
  </Extension>
</ReportDefinitionCustomization>
</Extensions> <! —for reference only -- >
```

Replace the <login> token with the Windows identity of the privileged user in the format domain\login, such as adventure-works\bob. Only this user will be able to see the Base Rate column.

Configuring code access security

As with any external custom code, you need elevate the CAS security for the extension assembly. Failure to do so will result in the following error when the report is executed:

```
An error occurred during client rendering. An internal error occurred on the report server.
```

If you inspect the report server log files, you will see the following error:

```
System.Security.SecurityException: That assembly does not allow partially trusted callers.
```

To configure the code access security for the custom extension:

1. Open the report server security policy file (rssrvpolicy.config) whose default location is C:\Program Files\Microsoft SQL Server\MSRS10.MSSQLSERVER\Reporting Services\ReportServer.
2. Scroll to the end of the file and add a new CodeGroup element as follows:

```
      <CodeGroup class="UnionCodeGroup" version="1" Name="Prologika RDCE"
         Description="Code group for the Report Definition Customization Extension"
         PermissionSetName="FullTrust">
        <IMembershipCondition class="UrlMembershipCondition" version="1"
           Url="C:\Program Files\Microsoft SQL Server\MSRS10.MSSQLSERVER\Reporting
           Services\ReportServer\bin\Prologika.ReportDefinitionCustomizationExtension.dll"/>
      </CodeGroup>
  </CodeGroup> <! —for reference only -- >
</CodeGroup> <!— for reference only -- >
```

Make sure that the path to the extension assembly is correct.

Enabling the extension per report

Finally, you need to reconfigure each report that requires customization. This requires changing a special RDCE report property. The code that accompanies this chapter includes a sample script (EnableRDCE.rss) that automates this procedure.

1. Deploy the Sales Persons report to the ARMS report folder on the report server. Use Report Manager to run the report to make sure it's operational.
2. Open the Windows command prompt and navigate to the Script folder in the book source code.
3. Execute the following command:

```
"C:\Program Files\Microsoft SQL Server\100\Tools\Binn\rs.exe" - i enablerdce.rss - s http://localhost/reportserver
```

Alternatively, double-click the ExecuteScript.cmd file which includes the command. This command uses the Reporting Services rs.exe utility. The –i switch specifies the script file and the –s switch specifies the report server URL. The enablerdce.rss script includes the following Visual Basic code:

```
Public Sub Main()
      Dim props(0) As [Property]
      Dim SetProps As New [Property]
      SetProps.Name ="RDCE"
      SetProps.Value = "PrologikaRDCE"
      props(0) = SetProps
      rs.SetProperties("/AMRS/Sales Persons", props)
End Sub
```

The script creates a new property with a name of RDCE and a value of PrologikaRDCE. The property value must match the name of the extension as registered in rsreportserver.config. The script calls the SetProperties API to apply the property to the Sales Persons report. You need to execute this script only once. Subsequent redeployments of the report definition don't affect the property settings. However, if you delete the report definition and deploy it again, you need to rerun the script.

The RDCE property gets added to the custom properties of the report (Property column in the Catalog table in ReportServer database). If you want to find what reports are enabled for customization, call the GetChildren API to obtain the list of reports, followed by calling the GetProperties API for each report to retrieve the report properties.

Testing the Extension

Because report definition customization extensions are a server only feature, you can test the extension only after you publish an RDCE-enabled report to the report server. This complicates somewhat the testing process. Follow these steps to debug the extension:

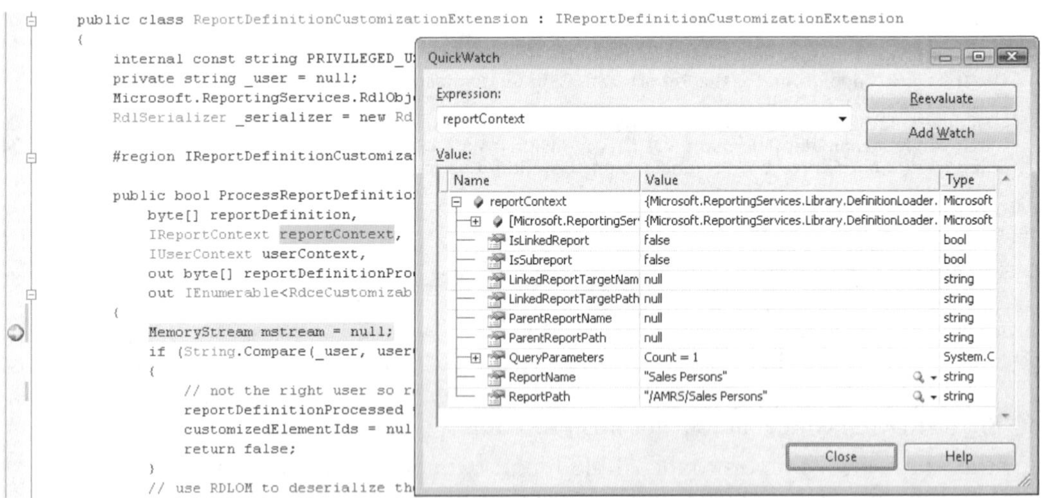

Figure 22.3 Attach to the ReportingServicesService.exe process to debug the extension code.

1. Make sure that you have deployed the latest code to the report server bin folder.
2. In Visual Studio, open the extension code and put breakpoints in the extension code as needed, such as at the beginning of the ProcessReportDefinition method.
3. Click Debug ➪ Attach to Process and attach to the ReportingServicesService.exe process.
4. Run the report in Report Manager.

The report server will discover that the report is enabled for customization and will invoke the extension. At this point, your breakpoints should be hit. For example, Figure 22.3 shows that use the Visual Studio Quick Watch window (Ctrl+Alt+Q) to inspect the reportContext argument.

You may need to obtain some performance statistics about your report definition customization extension, such as how long it took the server to invoke it. It turns out that the report server logs additional entries per report execution in the ExecutionLogStorage table in the ReportServer database. An example follows:

```
<AdditionalInfo>
  <RdcePreparationTime>184</RdcePreparationTime>
  <RdceInvocationTime>184</RdceInvocationTime> <! —- time spent in ProcessReportDefinition-- >
  <RdceSnapshotGenerationTime>7972</RdceSnapshotGenerationTime> <!—-   time spent updating RDL-- >
...
</AdditionalInfo>
```

22.3 Summary

Report definition customization extensions are a new extensibility feature in Reporting Services. A report definition customization extension can dynamically change a report definition before it is passed to the processing engine. This lets you customize a report before it is processed based on factors like report parameter values or user identity.

To implement a report definition customization extension, you write code that includes a class that implements the standard IReportDefinitionCustomizationExtension interface. At run time, the report server passes the report context and user context to the extension. Because report definition customization extensions are a server-side feature, testing them requires that you first deploy the extension to the server and debug the extension code by attaching to the report server process.

With this chapter we have reached the last stop of our Reporting Services journey. I sincerely hope that this book has helped you gain deep insight into how Reporting Services can be a powerful platform for delivering a rich reporting experience. If it has inspired you to use Reporting Services in your real-life projects, all the better. Got spinny?

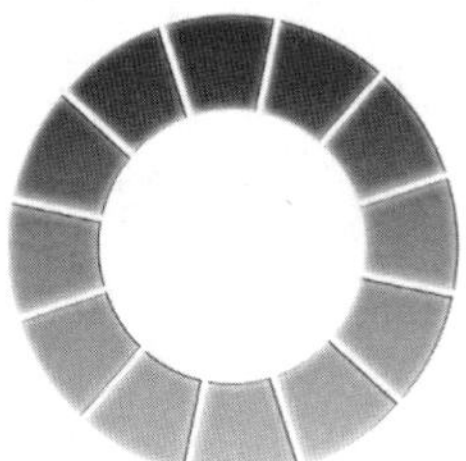

Report is being generated...

master resource list

This book is intended to serve as a comprehensive resource for building practical solutions with Reporting Services. Although I sincerely hope that this book is the only resource you need to master this technology, I know that this is an ambitious goal for the ever-changing and rapidly evolving world of the Microsoft business intelligence. Besides this book, you may find the following resources useful to take the most out of Reporting Services and stay up-to-date with the latest developments.

Books

Microsoft SQL Server 2008 Reporting Services by Brian Larson
http://tinyurl.com/4dvabr

Professional SQL Server 2008 Reporting Services by Paul Turley et al.
http://tinyurl.com/4jep8q

Pro SQL Server 2008 Reporting Services by Rodney Landrum et al.
http://tinyurl.com/4bjqnd

Microsoft SQL Server 2008 Reporting Services Unleashed by Michael Lisin et al.
http://tinyurl.com/59dn5b

Websites

Reporting Services Official Website
(http://www.microsoft.com/sqlserver/2008/en/us/reporting.aspx)—Product information, white papers, videos, and more.

SQL Server 2008 Books Online
(http://technet.microsoft.com/en-us/library/bb418491.aspx)—The SQL Server 2008 product documentation and articles.

Prologika website
(http://www.prologika.com)—My website includes a webpage with links to book resources and a web forum where you can post book-related questions.

Newsgroups

SQL Server Reporting Services MSDN Forum
(http://forums.microsoft.com/msdn/showforum.aspx?siteid=1&forumid=82)—Ask questions about Report Server, Report Designer, and Report Builder.

Reporting Services Public Newsgroup
(microsoft.public.sqlserver.reportingsvcs)—The Reporting Services Usenet newsgroup.

Blogs

Bob Meyers' Blog
(http://blogs.msdn.com/bobmeyers)—Bob M eyer is a Program Manager on the Reporting Services team who is responsible for Report Builder 1.0.

Brian Welcker's Blog
(http://blogs.msdn.com/bwelcker)—Brian Welcker is a former Group Program Manager on the Reporting Services team.

Chris Baldwin's Blog
(http://blogs.msdn.com/chrisbal)—Chris Baldwin is a Program Manager on the Reporting Services team who oversees the report rendering area.

Chris Hays's
(http://blogs.msdn.com/chrishays)—Chris Hays is an architect on the Reporting Services team and oversees the Report Definition Language.

John Gallardo's Blog
(http://blogs.msdn.com/jgalla)—John Gallardo is a Software Development Engineer on the Reporting Services team who is responsible for the report server.

Lukasz Pawlowski's Blog
(http://blogs.msdn.com/lukaszp)—Lukasz Pawlowski is a Program Manager on the Reporting Services team who is primarily responsible for the management feature of the product.

Russell Christopher's Blog
(http://blogs.msdn.com/bimusings)—Russell Christopher is a Business Intelligence consultant with Microsoft who posts great insights about working with Reporting Services.

Reporting Services Team Blog
(http://blogs.msdn.com/sqlrsteamblog/)—A collective blog of the Reporting Services team.

Reporting Services User Education Blog
(http://blogs.msdn.com/rosettaue)—From the user documentation team which is responsible for creating all the documentation that ships with the product.

Teo Lachev
(http://www.prologika.com/blog)—My blog which covers Reporting Services, Analysis Services, and Microsoft Business Intelligence news.

index

Symbols

A

B

C

D

E

F

N

O

P

Q

R

S

T

U

V

W

X

Y

Z

Also by Teo Lachev

Applied Microsoft Analysis Services 2005

and Microsoft Business Intelligence Platform

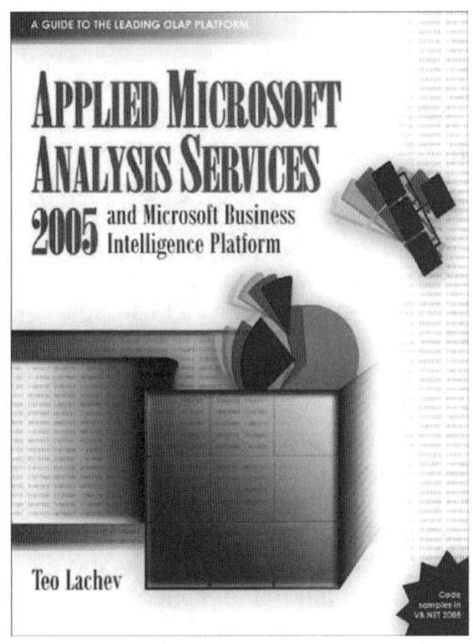

ISBN 978-0976635307
Publisher website: http://tinyurl.com/6q7xr
Amazon: http://tinyurl.com/6mtkyk
B&N: http://tinyurl.com/5rg8hp

Written for database administrators and developers, this book is a guide to leveraging the innovative Unified Dimensional Model (UDM) to design and manage sophisticated OLAP cubes that provide rich data analytics and data mining services. The necessary background to extend UDM with MDX expressions, scripts, and .NET code is provided. Also covered is how to implement a wide range of reporting applications that integrate with Analysis Services, Reporting Services, Microsoft Office, and third-party tools.

The book doesn't assume any prior experience with OLAP and Microsoft Analysis Services. It is designed as an easy-to-follow guide where each chapter builds upon the previous to implement the components of the innovative Unified Dimensional Model (UDM) in a chronological order. New concepts are introduced with step-by-step instructions and hands-on demos.

The book is available in bookstores worldwide.
Prices and availability may be subject to change.

Also by Teo Lachev

Microsoft SQL Server 2005

Business Intelligence Implementation and Maintenance

with Erik Veerman, Dejan Sarka, and Javier Loria

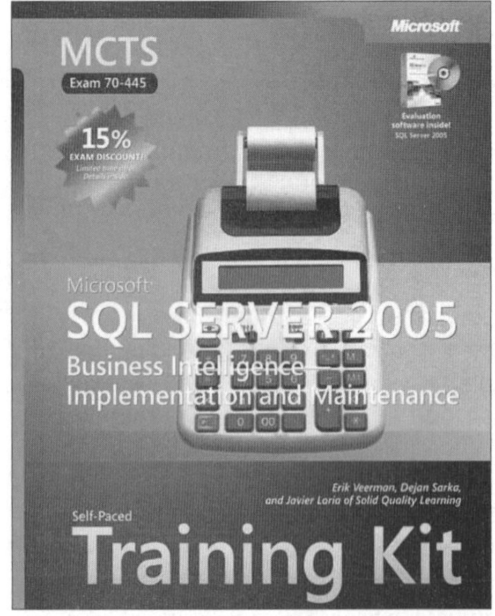

Ace your preparation for the skills measured by MCTS Exam 70-445—and on the job. Work at your own pace through a series of lessons and reviews that fully cover each exam objective. Then, reinforce what you've learned by applying your knowledge to real-world case scenarios and practice exercises. This official Microsoft study guide is designed to help you make the most of your study time.

Assess your skills with practice tests on CD. You can work through hundreds of questions using multiple testing modes to meet your specific learning needs. You get detailed explanations for right and wrong answers—including a customized learning path that describes how and where to focus your studies..

ISBN 978-0735623415
Publisher website: http://tinyurl.com/5ffm5k
Amazon: http://tinyurl.com/6b6vp3
B&N: http://tinyurl.com/5d8nwy

The book is available in bookstores worldwide. Prices and availability may be subject to change.